Macmillan Australian Student DICTIONARY

2ND EDITION

Published by Pan Macmillan Australia Pty Ltd
1 Market Street, Sydney, New South Wales, Australia, 2000

First edition published 2005 (revision 2010) by Macmillan Education Australia Pty Ltd
Second edition published 2015 by Pan Macmillan Australia Pty Ltd
Reprinted 2016, 2017 (twice), 2018, 2021, 2022 (twice), 2023 (twice), 2024, 2025

ISBN: 9781742619958

Cover design and illustration by Astred Hicks, Design Cherry
Typeset by MPS Limited, Bangalore, India
Printed in China

A Cataloguing-in-Publication entry is available from the National Library of Australia

A number of words entered in this dictionary are derived from trademarks. However, the presence or absence of indication of this derivation should not be regarded in any way as affecting the legal status of any trademark.

CONTENTS

EXAMPLE
OF DICTIONARY ENTRIES

Headword

bight *noun*
1. a bend or curve in the shore of the sea. **2.** a body of water bordered by such a bend or curve.

SIMILAR WORDS are **bay**, **gulf**, **inlet** and **cove**. **Bay** and **gulf** refer to fairly large areas of sea or ocean partly bounded by land, while an **inlet** or a **cove** is a small bay.

Extra information (similar words)

☑ SPELLING TIP Don't confuse the spelling of **bight** with **bite** or **byte** which sound the same. A **bite** is a wound made with the teeth or a mouthful of food. A **byte** is a unit of information stored by a computer.

Spelling guidance

Pronunciation

bigot /*say* **big**-uht/ *noun* someone who is convinced that their opinion is right and who is not fair-minded about other people's ideas.
☐ **bigoted**, *adjective* –**bigotry**, *noun*

bike *noun* a bicycle, tricycle or motorcycle.

Part of speech

bikini /*say* buh-**kee**-nee/ *noun* a two-piece swimming costume for women.

Extra information (word history)

WORD HISTORY named after *Bikini* Atoll in the northern Pacific Ocean, where the United States tested nuclear bombs from 1946 to 1958

☑ SPELLING TIP Notice that all the vowel sounds in this word are spelt with an *i*, and that there are no double letters.

Spelling guidance

bilateral *adjective* of or affecting two sides: *The two countries signed a bilateral agreement.*

Inflection

bilby *noun* (*plural* **bilbies**) a type of bandicoot. It is an animal currently rated as vulnerable rather than endangered.

WORD HISTORY from an Aboriginal language of New South Wales called Yuwaalaraay

Extra information (word history)

Pronunciation

bind /*rhymes with* find/ *verb* (**binds**, **binding**, **bound**, **has bound**)

Inflections

1. If you **bind** things together, you tie them up with something such as string or rope so that they are held tightly together: *Bind those papers together before you move them.* **2.** If you **bind** something, you tie it up firmly: *to bind up a sore arm.* **3.** If you **bind** substances together, you mix them so that they will stick together in a mass: *You need an egg to bind the ingredients.* **4.** If you **bind** a book, you fasten its pages together and put a cover around them: *This old book is falling apart – we'll have to get it bound again.*
☐ **binder**, *noun*: *Put all those loose papers in that cardboard binder.*

Definition

Example sentence

Word family

HOW TO USE

THE MACMILLAN AUSTRALIAN STUDENT DICTIONARY

The *Macmillan Australian Student Dictionary* gives you more than just the spellings and meanings of words. There is also a lot of other information – for example, pronunciation, part of speech, how to use a word in a sentence, word building, similar and opposite words, different spellings or forms of the word, help with difficult spellings and words that are often confused, word history, and so on. Here is some guidance on how all this information is set out. Also look at the examples of entries on the opposite page.

Finding the word you want to look up

The **headword** is the word you are looking up. You can find it easily because it is in large print and bold type.

The headwords are in alphabetical order. To help you find the word you are after, each page has a special guide word at the top of the page. You can use these to work out which words are on that page. The guide word matches the headword of the first entry on a left-hand page, and the headword of the last entry on a right-hand page.

If you are unsure of the spelling, get as close as you can to it by following the letters you are sure about, and then check several words until you find the one you're after. Check the *Spelling Guide* on page ix for help in finding words that might start with unusual spellings.

Pronunciation

Sometimes it can be quite hard to work out how to say a word. Each headword that might be difficult has a **pronunciation** after it. Usually a special system has been used which will allow you to sound out each part of the word. For details of this system, look at the *Pronunciation Guide* on page x. Sometimes, though, an easier word that rhymes with the headword will be given, or another word which has exactly the same sound. Here are some examples:

amphibian /*say* am-**fib**-ee-uhn/

cedar /*rhymes with* reader/

bass /*sounds like* base/

If a word has more than one acceptable pronunciation, these are shown with the one given first being that regarded as the most common. For example:

fault /*say* fawlt, folt/

Sometimes the pronunciation of a word changes according to what part of speech it is operating as. In this case, a new pronunciation is given for each part of speech. For example:

excuse /*say* uhks-**kyoohz**/ *noun*
1. an explanation or reason why something does not happen as it should: *He made some excuse for being late.*
–*verb* /*say* uhks-**kyoohz**/ **2.** If you **excuse** somebody, you find reasons for why they have done something, often when other people do not approve of it: *Please excuse my lateness – the train was not on time.*

Part of speech

The **part of speech** tells you how a word works in a sentence. A word might be a *noun*, *verb*, *adjective*, *adverb*, *preposition*, *conjunction*, *pronoun* or *interjection*. The dictionary also includes entries for *prefixes*. In addition, when a word is commonly used as part of a phrase, these are listed at the end of the entry with the label phrase. Look up these parts of speech in the *Grammar and Punctuation Guide* in the appendix for information on their functions.

The part of speech label comes after the headword or pronunciation. Then there are the meanings for that part of speech. Many words can work in different ways, so there may be another part of speech at the start of a new list of meanings.

Inflections

Many words change their ending according to the work they are doing in a sentence. These changes are called **inflections**. For example, most nouns can have an *-s* added at the end to show that there is more than one of them, most verbs can have *-ed* or *-ing* added and many adjectives and adverbs can have *-er* or *-est* added. When there is something unusual about the way the ending of the word changes (that is, it has an irregular inflection), this is shown in brackets after the part of speech.

For a noun, an irregular plural inflection is shown. For example:

> **fly** *noun* (*plural* **flies**)

For a verb, all of the following inflections are given if one or more of them are formed irregularly: third person singular present tense; present participle; past tense; past participle. For example:

> **fly** *verb* (**flies**, **flying**, **flew**, **has flown**)

For an adjective or adverb, irregular comparative and superlative inflections are shown. For example:

> **happy** *adjective* (**happier**, **happiest**)

If you do not understand any of the terms used above, look up the Grammar and Punctuation Guide in the appendix.

Definitions

The explanation of what the word means is called the **definition**. The definitions are written in simple language, using words that most people know so that they are easy to understand. If you do find a word that you don't know used in a definition, you will be able to look it up at its own headword in the dictionary.

Many words have more than one meaning. In this case, each definition is given a number. For example:

> **capacity**
> **1.** the quantity or amount which can be held or contained: *The fuel tank has a capacity of fifty litres.* **2.** mental ability: *Does he have the capacity to learn a foreign language?* **3.** the position or standing of someone: *In her capacity as magistrate, she sentenced him to a month's civic duty.*

If a word has meanings that are very different, each meaning is given under a new headword. When this happens, the headwords themselves are given numbers. For example:

> **alight**[1]
> *adjective* burning: *All the candles are alight.*

> **alight**[2]
> *verb* If you **alight** from a vehicle such as a train, you get out of or off it: *to alight from the bus at the next stop.*

Example sentences and phrases

Most definitions are followed by a helpful sentence or phrase which uses the word. This will help you understand more about the word's meaning and how it is used.

Labels

Labels are used to show if there is anything special about a word or any restriction on when a word is used. Sometimes a label applies to all the definitions in an entry, so the label or symbol is placed before all the definition numbers; sometimes it applies to only one definition, so it comes after that particular definition number. The following labels are used in this dictionary:

Informal

Informal words are used in everyday situations, such as when you are talking to your friends. For example, look up **broke**, **guy[1]**, **hassle**, **kid[1]** and **lousy**.

Old-fashioned

This label indicates that a word is not used very much nowadays. Some old-fashioned words are included in the dictionary because they are still sometimes found, particularly in writing from past times. For example, look up **abide**, **lass** and **rogue**.

Word families

Like people, words do not exist alone. Most of them have other words that are related to them because they have been built from one main word. At the end of many of the entries in this dictionary, you will find a list of such words, with their part of speech and sometimes with a definition and example phrase. The word family section of an entry begins with a small box symbol. For example, at the end of the entry for **accident**, you will find:

□ **accidental**, *adjective* –**accidentally**, *adverb*

Extra information about the word

The *Macmillan Australian Student Dictionary* gives a very wide range of extra information about words. This appears in a shaded box at the end of an entry, with a heading as follows:

- ANOTHER SPELLING/ OTHER SPELLINGS (more than one acceptable spelling)
- A SHORT FORM / SHORT FORMS (shortened forms of the headword that may be used in its place)
- ANOTHER WORD / SIMILAR WORDS (synonyms, often with additional information about shades of meaning)
- THE OPPOSITE (antonyms)
- COMPARE (a comparison between related terms such as **biannual** / **biennial**)
- DO NOT CONFUSE (an indication of the correct usage of words that are often confused, such as **alternate** / **alternative**)
- NOTE (extra information on the usage of a word, such as an indication that the use of the word can be offensive)
- WORD HISTORY (the origin of the word)

Spelling guidance

A special feature of this dictionary is the guidance given on the spelling of difficult words. These tips have been written with the advice of leading education academic Dr Donna Gibbs.

The spelling tips at the end of some entries are in the style of the notes described above. They cover a variety of spelling problems and are presented in several different styles, ranging from concise indication of a common problem, such as a silent letter, to more lengthy analysis of the structure of the word as an aid in remembering the spelling. Types of spelling tips include:

- double letters that have a single sound and so may be misspelt as a single letter; or single letters that may be misspelt as double. *Examples:* **dilemma**, **dispel**
- silent letters. *Examples:* **aghast**, **almond**
- reference to spelling rules. *Examples:* **believe**, **beige**
- homophones – clarification of spelling confusions caused by the same sound. *Example:* **eight** / **ate**
- sounds that can be represented by several different letters, or letter combinations – in some of these cases, reference is made to other words with the same pattern, to extend the range of the spelling advice. *Example:* **daughter**. Special emphasis is given to the schwa (or 'uh') sound which causes a problem in spelling because it can be represented by any of the vowels. *Examples:* **alligator**, **jubilant**
- word history – that is, breaking a word down into its root and word parts and linking this to its meaning, or referring to its derivation from another language. *Examples:* **agenda**, **lychee**, **dhal**
- 'rapping' – that is, mentally rehearsing a spelling pronunciation in a rhythmic way that accentuates all the syllables as an aid to remembering a spelling, particularly where unstressed vowels are involved. *Examples:* **hippopotamus**, **advertisement**

SPELLING GUIDE

This will help you find the word you are looking up if it starts with a letter that you don't hear when you say the word, or with a letter that is said in an unusual way.

Starting sound	Starting letters might be ...	Example
f	ph	**ph**one
g	gh	**gh**ost
g	gu	**gu**ess
h	wh	**wh**o
j	g	**g**entle
k	ch	**ch**emist
k	qu	**qu**ay
kw	qu	**qu**ite
n	gn	**gn**ome
n	kn	**kn**ife
r	rh	**rh**inoceros
r	wr	**wr**ap
s	c	**c**ertain
s	sc	**sc**ent
s	sw	**sw**ord
sh	s	**s**ugar
sk	sch	**sch**ool
t	tw	**tw**o
w	wh	**wh**eel
z	x	**x**ylophone

PRONUNCIATION GUIDE

This guide will help you understand the pronunciations that come after some headwords, following the word 'say'.

a sounds	***e*** sounds	***i*** sounds
a as in 'bat'	***e*** as in 'get'	***i*** as in 'bit'
ah as in 'cart'	***ee*** as in 'sleep'	***uy*** as in 'buy'
ay as in 'day'	***air*** as in 'hair'	***ear*** as in 'near'

o sounds	***u*** sounds	***er*** sounds
o as in 'dot'	***u*** as in 'but'	***er*** as in 'dirt'
oh as in 'coat'	***oo*** as in 'book'	***uh*** as in 'bett<u>er</u>'
aw as in 'saw'	***ooh*** as in 'boot'	
ow as in 'now'		
oy as in 'boy'		

th as in 'thin'	***zh*** as in 'treasure'	***g*** as in 'girl'
dh as in 'then'	***ch*** as in 'cheese'	***ng*** as in 'bang'
sh as in 'shed'	***j*** as in 'jam'	

Bold (thick) letters show the part of the word that is said with more stress than the other parts of the word.

a *indefinite article* You use the indefinite article before nouns: **1.** to mean one member of a class but not a particular one: *Jenny is a child*; *He was holding a book.* **2.** to mean one of something: *He bought a kilogram of rice*; *We drove a hundred kilometres.* **3.** to mean each or every one of something: *You must take the medicine twice a day.*

ANOTHER FORM is **an**, used when the following word begins with a vowel sound (usually words starting with *a, e, i, o* or *u*).

abacus /*say* **ab**-uh-kuhs/ *noun* a frame with rods through it which hold beads used for counting.

abalone /*say* ab-uh-**loh**-nee/ *noun* (*plural* **abalone** *or* **abalones**) a type of shellfish that is good to eat.

abandon[1] *verb*
1. When you **abandon** something, you leave it and do not mean to come back for it: *They abandoned the raft on the beach and continued their journey on foot.* **2.** To **abandon** is to give up: *We had to abandon the search*; *I've abandoned that idea.*
☐ **abandonment**, *noun*

abandon[2] *noun* freedom from constraint or what is normally expected: *The audience were dancing with wild abandon to the music.*

abattoir /*say* **ab**-uh-twah/ *noun* a building or place where animals are killed for food.

ANOTHER FORM is **abattoirs**. Note that this can be thought of as singular (*An abattoirs is being built*) or plural (*The abattoirs were closed down*).

☑ SPELLING TIP Remember that **abattoir** has one *b* and two *t*'s. Also don't forget the *oir* spelling at the end (which sounds like 'wah'). You find this spelling and sound in some words that have come from French. Another example is *reservoir*.

abbey *noun* a building or group of buildings where monks or nuns live.
☐ **abbess**, *noun* a nun in charge of an abbey. –**abbot**, *noun* a monk in charge of an abbey.

SIMILAR WORDS are **monastery** (for a place where monks live) and **convent** (for a place where nuns live).

abbreviate *verb* If you **abbreviate** something you make it shorter, as by leaving some letters out of a word: *You can abbreviate 'millilitre' to 'ml'.*
☐ **abbreviation**, *noun*

SEE the Grammar and Punctuation Guide appendix for information on how to write abbreviations.

abdicate *verb* When someone **abdicates**, they give up a position of power and responsibility, especially the right to be king or queen: *When King Edward abdicated, his brother became king.*
☐ **abdication**, *noun*

abdomen /*say* **ab**-duh-muhn, uhb-**doh**-muhn/ *noun*
1. the main part of the body that contains the stomach and other organs. **2.** the last part of the body of an insect or spider.
☐ **abdominal**, *adjective*

ANOTHER WORD for definition 1, used especially in informal language, is **belly**.

abduct *verb* To **abduct** someone is to kidnap them or carry them away by force.
☐ **abduction**, *noun* –**abductor**, *noun*

aberration /*say* ab-uh-**ray**-shuhn/ *noun* something that is not normal or usual: *Her illness is due to a genetic aberration*; *Luke does not usually behave like that – what he did was just an aberration.*

☑ SPELLING TIP *Single/double letter alert*: one *b* but double *r*.

abhor /*say* uhb-**haw**/ *verb* (**abhors**, **abhorring**, **abhorred**, **has abhorred**) If you **abhor** something, you think of it with disgust and hate: *She was a gentle soul and abhorred violence.*
☐ **abhorrence** /*say* uhb-**ho**-ruhns/, *noun* –**abhorrent** /*say* uhb-**ho**-ruhnt/, *adjective*

A SIMILAR WORD is **loathe**.

abide *verb* (**abides**, **abiding**, **abode** *or* **abided**, **has abode** *or* **has abided**)
1. If you cannot **abide** something, you do not like it and cannot to put up with it: *Our teacher can't abide rudeness.* **2.** *Old-fashioned* If you **abide** with someone, you stay with them: *At church, they sang a hymn called 'Abide with me'.*
–*phrase* **3. abide by**, **a.** to accept or act according to: *If you go in the contest, you have to abide by the rules.* **b.** to await or accept the consequences of: *I will abide by the decision.*

ability *noun* (*plural* **abilities**)
1. the power to do something or act in a certain way: *A newborn baby does not have the ability to walk.* **2.** skill: *Her ability in mathematics amazed us all.*

A SIMILAR WORD (for definition 2) is **talent**.

abiotic /*say* ay-buy-**ot**-ik/ *adjective* having to do with the non-living parts of an ecosystem.

ablaze *adjective*
1. on fire: *The house was ablaze.* **2.** shining brightly: *The desert sky was ablaze with stars.* **3.** filled with emotion: *They were ablaze with enthusiasm.*

able *adjective* You are **able** to do something if you have enough skill or knowledge to do it, or if you've got the time or freedom: *I'm free next Monday so I'll be able to stay and help*; *I am able to play the piano.*
□ **ably**, *adjective*

abnormal *adjective* unusual: *The weather has been abnormal for summer.*
□ **abnormality**, *noun* (*plural* **abnormalities**) –**abnormally**, *adverb*

THE OPPOSITE is **normal**.

aboard *adverb*
1. on or in a ship, train, bus, and so on: *All aboard!*
–*preposition* **2.** on: *We went aboard the boat.*

abode *noun Old-fashioned or humorous* the place where you live; your house.

abolish *verb* If someone **abolishes** something, they put an end to it: *The parliament passed a law to abolish capital punishment.*
□ **abolition**, *noun*

abominable *adjective* hateful or disgusting: *Selling children into slavery is an abominable thing.*
□ **abominate**, *verb* –**abomination**, *noun* –**abominably**, *adverb*

aboriginal /*say* ab-uh-**rij**-uh-nuhl/ *adjective* having to do with the earliest inhabitants of a country.

Aboriginal /*say* ab-uh-**rij**-uh-nuhl/ *adjective*
1. having to do with the people who have lived in Australia from the earliest known times, or with their culture.
–*noun* **2.** an Aboriginal person.

NOTE You can also use **Aborigine** for definition 2, although **Aboriginal** is the preferred term for the noun as well as the adjective. Other terms for Aboriginal people come from Aboriginal languages and usually depend on where the people are from. For example, **Koori** usually refers to people from southern NSW and Victoria, **Murri** to people from parts of Queensland and NSW, **Nunga** to those from southern South Australia, and **Nyungar** to people from south-western Western Australia. When both Aboriginal and Torres Strait Island people are being referred to, it is often best to say 'Indigenous Australian'.

aborigine /*say* ab-uh-**rij**-uh-nee/ *noun* one of the original people living in a country.

WORD HISTORY from a Latin word meaning 'from the beginning'

Aborigine /*say* ab-uh-**rij**-uh-nee/ *noun* one of the people whose ancestors lived in Australia from the earliest known times.

OTHER TERMS Most Indigenous people prefer you to use **Aboriginal** for this. See the note at **Aboriginal**.

aborted *adjective* failed: *an aborted attempt to reach Mars.*

abortion *noun* the removal or expelling of an unborn child from its mother's womb before it has grown enough to live on its own.
□ **abort**, *verb*

abound *verb* If something **abounds**, it exists in great numbers: *In the summer months, exotic fruits abound in the shops.*
□ **abounding**, *adjective*

about *preposition*
1. of or concerning: *She wrote an essay about our polluted beaches.* **2.** somewhere near or in: *There must be mice about the house – we can hear them at night.*
–*adverb* **3.** approximately: *It's about a kilometre from our house to the school.* **4.** almost: *Are you about finished?* **5.** around: *look about*; *move things about.*
–*phrase* **6. about to**, on the point of: *about to leave.*

above *adverb*
1. in a higher place: *Look above – there's a possum in the tree!*
–*preposition* **2.** over or higher than something or someone, in place, rank, or power: *I wanted to sleep in the top bunk above my brother*; *A general is above everybody else.* **3.** more than, in number or quantity: *The petrol gauge is showing just above empty.*

A SIMILAR WORD (for definition 1) is **overhead**.
THE OPPOSITE is **below**.

abrasion /*say* uh-**bray**-zhuhn/ *noun* a sore that is caused by a scrape: *He was covered with cuts and abrasions after the fall.*

abrasive *adjective* If something is **abrasive**, it is good for rubbing or scraping with: *Mum used a really abrasive sandpaper to get off the old paint.*
□ **abrasive**, *noun* –**abrasiveness**, *noun*

abreast *adverb* side by side: *They were walking three abreast – we couldn't pass them.*

abridged *adjective* If something written is **abridged**, it has been shortened: *The full novel is too long so we are going to study an abridged version of it.*
☐ **abridgement**, *noun*

abroad *adverb*
1. out of your own country: *to live abroad.* **2.** at large or around: *There are bad rumours abroad in the school.*

abrupt *adjective*
1. You say something is **abrupt** if it is sudden or unexpected: *I didn't like the story – the end was too abrupt.* **2.** An **abrupt** person is one who does not care about being pleasant or polite to others: *His manner is quite abrupt – it really makes people dislike him.*
☐ **abruptly**, *adverb* –**abruptness**, *noun*

A SIMILAR WORD (for definition 2) is **brusque**.
WORD HISTORY from a Latin word meaning 'broken off'

abscess /*say* **ab**-suhs/ *noun* an infected swelling in part of the body: *He had a nasty abscess on his leg.*

☑ SPELLING TIP *Silent letter alert*: don't forget the silent *c* following the first *s*. Also remember the *ess* ending.

abseil /*rhymes with* fail/ *verb* If you **abseil** down a cliff or wall, you go down it using ropes.

absent *adjective* If someone or something is **absent**, they are not present. They are away: *Because our teacher was absent for a week, a relief teacher was brought in.*
☐ **absence**, *noun*

absent-minded *adjective* Someone is **absent-minded** if they are forgetful.
☐ **absent-mindedly**, *adverb* –**absent-mindedness**, *noun*

absolute *adjective*
1. Absolute is used to emphasise what you are saying when you are expressing an opinion: *The house is in an absolute mess.* **2.** If something is **absolute**, it is complete or perfect: *absolute silence.*
☐ **absolutely**, *adverb*

absorb *verb* If something **absorbs** something else, it soaks it up or drinks it in: *We sat on the beach and absorbed the warmth of the sun*; *He can absorb a mass of new information with no trouble.*
☐ **absorbent**, *adjective* –**absorption**, *noun*

absorbed *adjective* If you are **absorbed** in an activity, your attention is totally given to it: *I didn't hear the laughter because I was totally absorbed in a book.*

abstain *verb* When you **abstain** from something, you keep yourself from doing it: *to abstain from eating sweets.*
☐ **abstention**, *noun* an act of abstaining. –**abstinence**, *noun* the habit of abstaining. –**abstinent**, *adjective*

abstract *adjective*
1. Something is **abstract** if it has to do with emotions and ideas rather than things: *abstract ideas like loyalty, love and duty.* **2.** Something is **abstract** if it has to do with general ideas rather than single points: *Her arguments are always so abstract – I'd be able to understand much better if she gave me some examples.* **3.** A work of art is **abstract** if it does not try to show things in a realistic way.
☐ **abstraction**, *noun*

THE OPPOSITE of definition 1 is **concrete**.

abstracted *adjective* lost in thought: *an abstracted look.*

A SIMILAR WORD is **preoccupied**.

abstract noun *noun* a word which refers to something that our five senses (touch, sight, hearing, smell and taste) can not pick up: *'Humour', 'fuss', 'length' and 'problem' are all abstract nouns.*

COMPARE this with **concrete noun**. Also see the Grammar and Punctuation Guide appendix.

abstruse *adjective* hard to understand: *abstruse instructions.*
☐ **abstrusely**, *adverb* –**abstruseness**, *noun*

WORD HISTORY from a Latin word meaning 'concealed'

absurd *adjective* Something is **absurd** if **1.** it is foolish or without common sense: *an absurd suggestion.* **2.** it is so ridiculous that it is funny: *Didn't he look absurd in that outfit!*
☐ **absurdity**, *noun* –**absurdly**, *adverb*

A SIMILAR WORD (for definition 1) is **ridiculous**; (for definition 2) **comical**.

abundant *adjective* plentiful or more than enough: *an abundant crop of lemons.*
☐ **abundance**, *noun* –**abundantly**, *adverb*

abuse *verb* /*say* uh-**byoohz**/
1. If someone **abuses** someone else they treat them badly, especially by forcing sexual activity on them when they are too young or too afraid to prevent it. **2.** Someone **abuses** a situation if they take unfair advantage of it, usually for their own gain: *She abused her position as treasurer by stealing money from the club.*
–*noun* /*say* uh-**byoohs**/ **3.** insults or hurtful language. **4.** wrong use: *abuse of library books by scribbling in them.* **5.** sexual activity forced upon someone who cannot prevent it, especially a child.
☐ **abusive**, *adjective*

abysmal /*say* uh-**biz**-muhl/ *adjective* so bad that it could not be worse: *an abysmal failure.*
☐ **abysmally**, *adverb*

☑ SPELLING TIP *Letter 'y' alert*: the first vowel sound is spelt *y* (not *i*). It might help if you remember that this word has been formed from *abyss* but with its last *s* dropped and the ending *mal* added.

abyss /*say* uh-**bis**/ *noun* a hole or space that is too deep to measure.

WORD HISTORY from a Greek word meaning 'without a bottom'

☑ SPELLING TIP *Letter 'y' alert*: the vowel sound is spelt *y* (not *i*). Many words that come from Greek have this kind of *y* spelling. For this word you might think of it as a letter with a tail that goes down into the deep hole that is an **abyss**. Also remember the double *s* at the end.

acacia /*say* uh-**kay**-shuh/ *noun* a wattle tree.

academic *adjective*
1. belonging to a college or university: *academic program.* **2.** full of theory instead of common sense: *Don't give me that academic rubbish – tell me the facts!*
☐ **academic**, *noun* –**academically**, *adverb*

academy *noun* (*plural* **academies**) a school or society for learning.

accede /*say* uhk-**seed**/ *verb* If you **accede** to something, you formally agree or consent to it: *I cannot accede to those conditions.*

accelerate /*say* uhk-**sel**-uh-rayt/ *verb* When something or someone **accelerates**, they move faster: *The bus accelerated so quickly that a couple of passengers fell over*; *He accelerated when he meant to brake.*
☐ **acceleration**, *noun*

accelerator /*say* uhk-**sel**-uh-ray-tuh/ *noun* a pedal in a car, which the driver presses to make the car go faster.

accent /*say* **ak**-sent/ *noun*
1. your own way of speaking: *She has been here for four years and still has a German accent.* **2.** a stress or stronger tone given to a part of a word or musical note, to make it different from the rest. **3.** a mark showing a stress or emphasis, or how a letter should be said.

☑ SPELLING TIP *Double letter alert*: there is a double *c* in **accent** but each *c* makes a different sound – the first has a 'k' sound and the second an 's' sound.

accentuate /*say* uhk-**sen**-chooh-ayt/ *verb* To **accentuate** something is to emphasise it: *She used a black pencil to accentuate her eyebrows.*
☐ **accentuation**, *noun*

accept /*say* uhk-**sept**/ *verb* When you **accept** something, you receive it willingly: *to accept a proposal.*
☐ **acceptance**, *noun* –**acceptable**, *adjective*

☑ SPELLING TIP *Double letter alert*: there is a double *c* in **accept** but each *c* makes a different sound – the first has a 'k' sound and the second an 's' sound.

access /*say* **ak**-ses/ *noun*
1. the right of coming to someone or something: *access to the boss*; *access to the library.* **2.** a way of getting to a place: *Where is the access to the property?*
–*verb* **3.** When you get in to a place, you **access** it: *You can access the classroom through this door.* **4.** When you find information in a computer, you **access** it.
☐ **accessible**, *adjective* –**accessibility**, *noun*

☑ SPELLING TIP *Double letter alert*: there is a double *c* in **access** but each *c* makes a different sound – the first has a 'k' sound and the second an 's' sound. Remember also that this word ends with a double *s*.

accessory /*say* uhk-**ses**-uh-ree/ *noun* (*plural* **accessories**)
1. something added for improvement or decoration but not necessary: *She wanted the accessories to match the apricot colour of the dress.* **2.** someone who helps carry out a crime: *Because she told lies to cover up his crime, she will be charged as an accessory.*

accident /*say* **ak**-suh-duhnt/ *noun*
1. an unwanted or unlucky happening: *He had an accident trying to jump over the fence.*
–*phrase* **2. by accident**, as a chance event: *I met him by accident in the street.*
☐ **accidental**, *adjective* –**accidentally**, *adverb*

☑ SPELLING TIP *Double letter alert*: there is a double *c* in **accident** but each *c* makes a different sound – the first has a 'k' sound and the second an 's' sound. If you remember this, you won't make a spelling error **accidentally**.

acclaim *verb* If you **acclaim** someone or something, you praise them enthusiastically: *Her win was acclaimed by the crowd who rose to their feet clapping and cheering.*
☐ **acclamation**, *noun*

A SIMILAR WORD is **applaud**.

acclimatise *verb* When someone or something **acclimatises**, they get used to new conditions: *You'll soon acclimatise to the hotter weather.*
☐ **acclimatisation**, *noun*

ANOTHER SPELLING is **acclimatize**.

accommodate *verb*
1. If a room or a place to stay **accommodates** a certain number of people, it has enough space and furniture for them all: *The caravan will*

accommodate four people. **2.** If you **accommodate** yourself to someone or something, you adapt and become used to them: *We will have to accommodate ourselves to the new arrangement.*

☑ SPELLING TIP *Double letter alert*: two *c*'s and two *m*'s. The double *m* is the hardest part to remember – you might try thinking that a place has room to **accommodate** two children (two *c*'s) and two men (two *m*'s). Also remember that the vowel sound after the double *m* is spelt *o*. Rap it out as *ac*+*com*+*mo*+*date*.

accommodation *noun* somewhere to stay, as at a hotel: *It was very hard to find accommodation during the holidays.*

accompany *verb* (**accompanies**, **accompanying**, **accompanied**, **has accompanied**)
1. If someone or something **accompanies** another person or thing, they go with them: *The child was accompanied by her father.* **2.** If you **accompany** a singer, you play a musical instrument while they sing or play another instrument.
□ **accompaniment**, *noun* –**accompanist**, *noun*

accomplice /*say* uh-**kum**-pluhs, uh-**kom**-pluhs/ *noun* someone who helps in a crime: *The thief's accomplice kept watch on the corner.*

accomplish /*say* uh-**kum**-plish, uh-**kom**-plish/ *verb* If you **accomplish** something, you carry it out successfully: *to accomplish a task.*
□ **accomplishment**, *noun*

SIMILAR WORDS are **perform** and **finish**.

accord *noun*
1. agreement: *The canteen mothers were in accord about getting rid of junk food.* **2.** a formal agreement or contract between two or more groups of people: *An accord was reached between the workers and the bosses.*
–*phrase* **3. of your own accord**, without being asked: *She put out the rubbish of her own accord.* **4. with one accord**, with complete agreement: *They all stood up to cheer with one accord.*
□ **accordance**, *noun*: *We did it in accordance with her wishes.*

according *phrase* **according to**, **1.** as set out in: *to work according to the rules.* **2.** in relation or proportion to: *to be paid according to the age you are and the amount of experience you've had.* **3.** as told by: *According to him, the shark was as big as a whale.*
□ **accordingly**, *adverb*

accordion *noun* a musical instrument that is squeezed to produce sound, and which you play by pressing buttons or keys.
□ **accordionist**, *noun* an accordion player.

accost *verb* If someone **accosts** you, they come up and speak to you, usually in an unpleasant way: *He was accosted by two men who demanded his wallet.*

WORD HISTORY from a Latin word meaning 'put side by side'

account *noun*
1. a sum of money belonging to a particular person or organisation which is held in a bank which the owner can add to or take away from. **2.** a record of money paid out and received by a person or business. **3.** a list of particular happenings: *We kept an account of each day of the rehearsals.* **4.** importance or value: *It was of no account to him that she was sick.*
–*phrase* **5. account for**, to explain: *Her measles accounts for the rash on her face.* **6. give a good account of yourself**, to do well. **7. take into account**, to give consideration to: *Take into account that they are only learners.* **8. on account of**, because of: *I can't go to the party on account of having a headache.*
□ **accountability**, *noun* –**accountable**, *adjective*

accountant *noun* someone whose job is to examine and record all the money that is earnt and spent in a business.
□ **accountancy**, *noun*

accumulate *verb* You **accumulate** something if you collect more and more of it: *He accumulates cans then recycles them.*
□ **accumulation**, *noun*

☑ SPELLING TIP *Double/single letter alert*: two *c*'s but only one *m*.

accurate /*say* **ak**-yuh-ruht/ *adjective*
1. Something is **accurate** if it is correct or exact: *an accurate account of the accident.* **2.** Someone is **accurate** if they are careful about small details: *an accurate typist.*
□ **accuracy**, *noun* –**accurately**, *adverb*

☑ SPELLING TIP *Tricky 'uh' sound*: the middle vowel is spelt *u*, giving a 'yuh' sound. Also remember that there is a double *c* in **accurate**. Notice that the last four letters make the word *rate*. If you get all of this right, your spelling will be rated **accurate**.

accuse *verb* If you **accuse** someone of something, you say they have done something wrong: *That boy accused me of stealing*; *She was accused of murder.*
□ **accusation**, *noun* –**the accused**, *noun*: *The judge asked the accused to stand up.*

accustomed *adjective* If you are **accustomed** to something, you are used to it, or in the habit of doing it: *They've become accustomed to working at night.*

☑ SPELLING TIP The spelling of **accustomed** will be easier if you see that is contains the word *custom*. The prefix *ac-* has been added at the beginning, giving it a double *c*, and the suffix *-ed* has been added at the end. Rap it out as *ac+cus+tomed*.

ace *noun*
1. a playing card with a single mark or spot: *Someone must have the fourth ace!* **2.** a serve in tennis which the other player cannot return at all. **3.** an expert: *an ace at gymnastics.*

ache /*rhymes with* cake/ *noun*
1. a continuous pain: *I had an ache in my shoulder for a week after the accident.*
–*verb* **2.** If you **ache**, or a part of your body **aches**, you feel a continuous pain: *I ache all over*; *My head aches.*

achieve /*say* uh-**cheev**/ *verb* If you **achieve** something, you obtain it or bring it about by trying hard: *He has achieved very good results this term.*
☐ **achievable**, *adjective* –**achievement**, *noun* –**achiever**, *noun*

☑ SPELLING TIP *Tricky vowel sound*: *ie* to spell the 'ee' sound. This follows the rule that *i* comes before *e*, except after *c*, when the sound is 'ee'.

acid *noun* a chemical substance which can eat away metals.
☐ **acid**, *adjective*: *an acid reaction.* –**acidic**, *adjective* –**acidity**, *noun*

acknowledge *verb*
1. If you **acknowledge** a fact, you admit or agree that it is true: *I acknowledge that I was wrong, but I wasn't the only culprit.* **2.** If you **acknowledge** a letter or message, you let the sender know that you have received it: *We acknowledge your email of 9 July and will reply in detail later.* **3.** If you **acknowledge** someone or something, you show that you recognise them or understand something important about them: *She saw him on the other side of the room and acknowledged him with a wave of her hand*; *The new law acknowledged the right of Indigenous people to live on their land.*
☐ **acknowledgement**, *noun*

acknowledgement of country *noun* a ceremony that takes place at the start of a public event in Australia officially recognising the Indigenous people who first lived in the area where the event is taking place.

ANOTHER FORM This can also be spelt with capital letters.
SEE the Welcome to Country and Acknowledgement of Country appendix for more information.

acne /*say* **ak**-nee/ *noun* a rash with a lot of pimples, especially on the face.

acorn *noun* a nut with a cup-shaped bottom part, which grows on an oak tree.

acoustics /*say* uh-**kooh**-stiks/ *noun*
1. the science or study of sound. **2.** the properties of a building which affect the quality of the sounds produced in it: *The theatre has good acoustics – we could hear their voices perfectly.*
☐ **acoustic**, *adjective* –**acoustically**, *adverb*

☑ SPELLING TIP *Single letter alert*: only one *c* after the opening *a*. There are several other tricky bits in the word. Remember that the ending is *ics* (although you might think that it sounds like 'icks'). Also, the sound in the middle is spelt *ou* (although the sound is 'ooh'). It might help if you think of a word you know well which has the same spelling for this sound, such as *group*.

acquaintance *noun* a person you know: *Dad met an old acquaintance at the conference.*

☑ SPELLING TIP Don't forget the *c* between the *a* and *q* at the start of this word. Also remember that the ending is *ance* (not *ence*).

acquainted *adjective*
1. familiar: *They held a workshop for the teachers to become acquainted with the new computer system.*
–*phrase* **2. get acquainted**, to get to know: *I'll leave you two to get acquainted.*

acquire *verb* If you **acquire** something, you get or obtain it: *to acquire knowledge by reading.*

acquit *verb* (**acquits**, **acquitting**, **acquitted**, **has acquitted**) If a jury **acquits** someone of a crime, the jury decides that they are not guilty of it: *Much to everyone's surprise, the defendant was acquitted.*
☐ **acquittal**, *noun*

THE OPPOSITE is **convict**.

acre /*rhymes with* baker/ *noun* a large area of land in the imperial system of measurement that is equal to almost half a hectare: *The cattle station covered thousands of acres.*

acrid *adjective* having a bitter or unpleasant taste or smell.

A SIMILAR WORD is **pungent**.

acrobat *noun* someone who performs daring gymnastic tricks: *The best act at the circus was the acrobat on the tightrope.*
☐ **acrobatic**, *adjective* –**acrobatics**, *noun*

WORD HISTORY from a Greek word meaning 'walking on tiptoe'

acronym /*say* **ak**-ruh-nim/ *noun* a word formed from the initial letters of a sequence of words, as *radar* (from *radio detection and ranging*) or *ANZAC* (from *Australian and New Zealand Army Corps*).

SEE the Grammar and Punctuation Guide appendix.

across *preposition*
1. from side to side of: *a plank across a drain.* **2.** on the other side of: *I live across the lake.*

–adverb **3.** from one side to another: *I rowed across in a boat.* **4.** on the other side: *We'll soon be across.*

acrostic */say* uh-**kros**-tik/ *noun* a series of words or lines, often of a poem, in which the first or last letters form a word or a phrase.

acrylic */say* uh-**kril**-ik/ *noun*
1. a synthetic material used for clothing. **2.** a type of synthetic paint that can be mixed with water.
□ **acrylic**, *adjective*: *an acrylic cardigan.*

ANOTHER FORM (of definition 2) is **acrylic colour.**

act *noun*
1. something done or performed: *It was an act of great kindness.* **2.** a law or order, especially one determined by a legislature: *The Act covering trade practices has been amended many times.* **3.** one of the main divisions of a stage play: *They hated the play and left at the end of the first act.*
–verb You **act** when you **4.** do something: *If you don't act soon you'll miss your chance!* **5.** do someone's duties when they are unable to: *They need someone to act in her place while she is away.* **6.** play the part of: *He wanted to act as the warrior king but the teacher put him in the crowd scene.* **7.** behave as: *to act the benefactor.*
–phrase **8. act on** (or **upon**), **a.** to follow: *Why don't you act on my suggestion?* **b.** to affect: *Alcohol acts on the brain.* **9. act out**, to express an idea, a feeling and so on, by acting. **10. act up**, *Informal* to cause trouble.

ANOTHER FORM Definition 2 is usually spelt with a capital letter.

action *noun*
1. an act: *a fearful action.* **2.** the state of being active: *The medical crew went into action straight away.* **3.** a way of moving: *The sick man's actions were slow and weary.*
–phrase **4. in action**, **a.** doing something in particular: *Have you ever seen a juggler in action?* **b.** in operation: *Keep right away from this machine when it's in action.* **5. out of action**, **a.** not working: *The washing machine has been out of action for a week.* **b.** not able to do what you usually do: *His accident put him out of action for a month.*

activate *verb* If you **activate** something, you make it active or set it in motion: *Turn the key to activate the engine*; *to activate a plan.*
□ **activation**, *noun*

active *adjective*
1. If you are **active**, you are always doing things: *On the camp, we were active the whole time – swimming, canoeing and bushwalking.* **2.** If you are **active** in a particular area, you do things in that area: *He took an active part in the election campaign.* **3.** A verb or sentence is said to be **active** or in the **active voice** if the one who does the action is also the subject of the verb or sentence. *The dog bit me* is active because 'the dog' is doing the biting and is also the subject. **4.** If a volcano is **active**, it still erupts from time to time.
□ **actively**, *adverb* –**activist**, *noun*: *an activist in the peace movement.*

COMPARE definition 3 with **passive** (definition 2). See also the Grammar and Punctuation Guide appendix.

activity *noun* (*plural* **activities**) a thing you do, often involving lots of energy: *Swimming is an enjoyable summer activity.*

actor *noun* someone who acts the part of a character in a play, film or on television: *She loved the stage and wanted to be an actor.*

NOTE An **actor** can be either male or female. The word **actress** for a female actor is not used as much now as in the past.

actress *noun* a girl or woman who acts the part of a character in a play, film or on television.

actual */say* **ak**-chooh-uhl/ *adjective* real or true: *This is the actual spot where Ned Kelly was captured.*

☑ SPELLING TIP Remember that **actual** starts with the word *act*. This will remind you that it includes the letter *t* although, with the *u* following, it has a 'ch' sound and you don't hear the *t*.

actually */say* **ak**-chooh-uh-lee/ *adverb* as a real or existing fact.

acupuncture */say* **ak**-yuh-punk-chuh, **ak**-uh-punk-chuh/ *noun* a practice in traditional Chinese medicine which treats illness or pain by sticking needles into certain parts of the body.
□ **acupuncturist**, *noun*

acute *adjective*
1. Something is **acute** if it is very severe: *The drought has caused acute water shortages*; *acute appendicitis.* **2.** Your mind and senses are **acute** if they are sharp and can notice small differences: *an acute sense of smell.*
□ **acutely**, *adverb*

WORD HISTORY from a Latin word meaning 'sharpened'

acute angle *noun* an angle of less than 90°.

AD *abbreviation* short for *anno domini*, Latin words meaning 'in the year of our Lord': *Mount Vesuvius erupted and destroyed the town of Pompeii in AD 79.*

NOTE The calendar widely used throughout the world dates events from the year of the birth of Jesus Christ. Years after this are called **AD** and years before this are **BC** (before Christ). **BC** always comes after the year (*526 BC*), while **AD** can be placed before or after the year (*AD 1813* or *1813 AD*). The abbreviation **CE** (as in *1813*

CE) is sometimes used instead of **AD**. It stands for (*of the*) *Common Era*.

adage /*say* **ad**-ij/ *noun* a wise saying: *'It's the thought that counts' is my father's favourite adage – especially when my birthday is getting near.*

A SIMILAR WORD is **proverb**.

adagio /*say* uh-**dah**-zhee-oh, uh-**dah**-jee-oh/ *adverb* played or sung slowly and calmly.

NOTE This is used as an instruction in music. Like most musical instructions, it comes from Italian which explains the ending *-gio*.

adamant /*say* **ad**-uh-muhnt/ *adjective* staying firm in what you decide: *Mum was adamant that the wall should stay red.*
☐ **adamantly**, *adverb*

☑ SPELLING TIP *Single letter alert*: only one *d* and one *m*.

adapt *verb*
1. If you **adapt** to something, you change so that you become suited to a new or different situation: *We quickly adapted to the different climate when we moved to Brisbane.* **2.** If you **adapt** something, you change it to make it suitable for a new or different situation: *The story for the film was adapted from a French novel.*
☐ **adaptable**, *adjective* –**adaptation**, *noun* –**adaptor**, *noun*

add *verb*
1. If you **add** something to something else, you put it with or in something else: *The library has added a lot of books to its collection this year.* **2.** If you **add** numbers or amounts, you find what their total is: *What do you get if you add 2+2?*
–*phrase* **3. add to**, If something **adds to** something else, it increases it: *Air conditioning will add to our costs*; *To add to his troubles, the car wouldn't start.* **4. add up**, **a.** If you **add up** numbers or amounts, you find what their total is: *Can you add all those prices up for me?* **b.** If something **adds up**, it makes sense. You can understand it: *It just doesn't add up – he's never done anything like that before.*

adder *noun* a small, venomous snake.

addict /*say* **ad**-ikt/ *noun* someone who cannot do without something, especially drugs: *a heroin addict.*
☐ **addicted** /*say* uh-**dik**-tuhd/, *adjective* –**addiction**, *noun* –**addictive**, *adjective*: *an addictive substance.*

WORD HISTORY from a Latin word meaning 'devoted'

addition *noun*
1. something added which increases the size or number of things: *A new puppy is the latest addition to our family.* **2.** the act of adding numbers together.
☐ **additional**, *adjective* –**additionally**, *adverb*

additive *noun* something which is added, especially a chemical added to food to keep it fresh.

address *noun* /*say* uh-**dres**, **ad**-res/
1. the details of the place where you live. **2.** a formal speech: *The first address at the conference introduced the major topics to be covered.* **3.** on a computer, a group of letters, numbers and symbols that you key in to send an email to someone, or which identifies a website on the internet.
–*verb* /*say* uh-**dres**/ **4.** When you **address** an envelope or parcel, you write the receiver's name and the details of the place where they live on it: *The letter was addressed to me.* **5.** When you **address** a group of people, you make a speech to them: *The mayor addressed the meeting.*
☐ **addressee**, *noun*

adenoids *plural noun* the mass of soft growths at the back of the nose which sometimes block it and have to be removed.

adept *adjective* skilful: *He is a reasonably adept tennis player.*
☐ **adeptness**, *noun*

adequate /*say* **ad**-uh-kwuht/ *adjective*
1. enough: *They can't afford adequate heating.* **2.** suitable: *We don't need a new car – this one is quite adequate.* **3.** If someone's performance is **adequate**, it is just good enough: *His work is adequate, but certainly not brilliant.*
☐ **adequacy**, *noun* –**adequately**, *adverb*

☑ SPELLING TIP *Tricky 'uh' sound*: the middle vowel is spelt *e* and the vowel after the *qu* is spelt *a*. It will help if you see that **adequate** includes the word *equate* (meaning 'to make equal'). The prefix *ad* (meaning 'towards') has been added.

adhere *verb* If something **adheres** to something else, it sticks firmly to it: *Mud adhered to our boots*; *You must adhere strictly to the rules.*
☐ **adherent**, *noun* someone who follows or supports a person or idea. –**adherence**, *noun*

adhesive *noun* a substance which sticks things together.
☐ **adhesion**, *noun* –**adhesive**, *adjective*: *an adhesive bandage.*

adjacent /*say* uh-**jay**-suhnt/ *adjective* If something is **adjacent** to something else, it is right next to it: *They work in adjacent offices.*

adjective *noun* a word which describes a noun, such as 'fat' in *a fat frog.*
☐ **adjectival**, *adjective*

SEE the Grammar and Punctuation Guide appendix.

adjourn /*say* uh-**jern**/ *verb*
1. If you **adjourn** something, you put it off until another time: *We had to adjourn the meeting because the room was locked.* **2.** If you **adjourn** to another place, you move there: *Let's adjourn to the verandah.*
☐ **adjournment**, *noun*

adjudicate /*say* uh-**jooh**-duh-kayt/ *verb* If someone **adjudicates** an argument or competition, they act as a judge in it.
☐ **adjudication**, *noun* –**adjudicator**, *noun*

adjust *verb* To **adjust** something is to cause it to fit or work properly: *I adjusted my dog's collar*; *We adjusted the temperature control on the freezer so the ice-cream wouldn't melt.*
☐ **adjustable**, *adjective* –**adjustment**, *noun*

administer *verb*
1. If you **administer** something, you run it or have charge of it: *An accountant was chosen to administer the business.* **2.** If you **administer** medicine, you give it to a sick person or animal: *The nurses administer the medicines after dinner.*

administration *noun* the people that run a business or government: *The Rugby League administration is keen to increase the popularity of the sport.*
☐ **administrative**, *adjective* –**administrator**, *noun*

admiral *noun* the highest ranking officer in a navy.

admire *verb*
1. If you **admire** someone, you think that the way they behave is very good. You respect them: *I really admire his honesty*; *I admire her for her generosity.* **2.** If you **admire** something or someone, you think they look good: *We admired Josh's birthday cake which was in the shape of a spaceship.*
☐ **admirable**, *adjective* –**admiration**, *noun* –**admirer**, *noun*

admission *noun*
1. the process of entering: *His admission into hospital took over two hours.* **2.** the price paid for entrance, such as to the theatre, etc. **3.** confession of a mistake, crime, etc.: *He made an admission of guilt.*

admit *verb* (**admits**, **admitting**, **admitted**, **has admitted**)
1. If you **admit** something about yourself, you agree that it is true: *They finally admitted that it was their fault*; *I must admit I was exhausted afterwards.* **2.** If someone is **admitted** to a place, they are allowed to go in: *Children are not admitted unless accompanied by an adult.*

A SIMILAR WORD (for definition 1) is **confess**.
NOTE You usually **admit** or **confess** to something bad, or something you are not proud of.

admonish *verb* If you **admonish** someone, you warn or caution them: *She admonished us for talking during the film.*
☐ **admonition**, *noun* –**admonitory**, *adjective*

adolescence /*say* ad-uh-**les**-uhns/ *noun* the time between reaching puberty and being an adult.
☐ **adolescent**, *noun*, *adjective*

☑ SPELLING TIP *Tricky 'uh' sound*: the second vowel sound is spelt with an *o*. Also, don't forget the silent *c* after the *s*.

adopt *verb*
1. If someone **adopts** a child, they legally take responsibility for that child and treat him or her as part of their own family: *The couple adopted a boy and a girl.* **2.** If you **adopt** an idea or a method, you choose it: *They've adopted a new way of teaching singing.*
☐ **adopted**, *adjective* –**adoption**, *noun*

COMPARE definition 1 with **foster** (definition 1).

adore *verb*
1. To **adore** someone is to feel very strong love for them: *She adored her grandfather.* **2.** To **adore** something is to like it very much: *I adore ice-cream.*
☐ **adorable**, *adjective* –**adoration**, *noun*

adorn *verb* To **adorn** someone or something is to make them more beautiful or pleasant: *Christmas lights adorned the tree.*
☐ **adorningly**, *adverb* –**adornment**, *noun*

SIMILAR WORDS are **decorate** and **embellish**.

adrenaline /*say* uh-**dren**-uh-luhn/ *noun* a chemical produced by the body, which is sent into the blood when the body is feeling stress or being active. It increases the heart rate, blood pressure and blood sugar levels.

ANOTHER SPELLING is **adrenalin**.
NOTE This word is related to the word **adrenal** which is based on the Latin word for the kidneys; the **adrenal glands,** which make adrenaline, are found near the top of the kidneys.

adult /*say* uh-**dult**, **ad**-ult/ *adjective*
1. To be **adult** is to be grown-up: *During the war all adult males were called up for national service.* –*noun* **2.** a fully grown person or animal. **3.** someone who has reached 18 years of age.
☐ **adulthood**, *noun*

adulterate *verb* If you **adulterate** something, you spoil it by adding something inferior or weaker to it: *to adulterate milk with water.*
☐ **adulteration**, *noun*

adultery *noun* a sexual relationship in which at least one of the two people is married to someone else.
☐ **adulterer**, *noun* –**adulterous**, *adjective*

advance *verb*
1. To **advance** is to move forward: *She advanced to the front of the class.* **2.** If you **advance** something, you move it or bring it forward: *They advanced the troops to the next town.* **3.** To **advance** is to improve or develop: *Now that we are training every week, our team is advancing fast.*
–*noun* **4.** progress or movement forward. **5.** money which is given ahead of the due date: *I need an advance to pay for my textbooks.*
–*phrase* **6. in advance, a.** in front or before: *We reached the summit in advance of the others.* **b.** ahead of time: *Mum paid for the trip in advance.*
☐ **advanced**, *adjective* –**advancement**, *noun* –**advancing**, *adjective*

SIMILAR WORDS (for definition 1) are **proceed** and **progress**.

advantage *noun*
1. something that gives you a benefit or puts you ahead of others: *A good education is always an advantage*; *Being tall is an advantage when you are playing basketball.* **2.** in tennis, the first point following the score of deuce (when both players have 40 points).
–*phrase* **3. take advantage of, a.** to make use of: *You should take advantage of this chance to go overseas.* **b.** to make too many demands on someone: *to take advantage of his kindness.*
☐ **advantageous** /*say* ad-van-**tay**-juhs/, *adjective*

☑ SPELLING TIP The word **advantage** is related to the word *advance*. This might help you to remember the *ad-* prefix at the start. Also remember that the last three letters are the same as in the word *age*. Some people think there is no **advantage** in age – some older people disagree!

adventure *noun* an exciting and sometimes hazardous experience.
☐ **adventurous**, *adjective*

adverb *noun* a word which tells you something extra about a verb, adjective or another adverb, such as 'bitterly' in *he complained bitterly* or 'terribly' in *she was terribly cold*.
☐ **adverbial**, *adjective*

SEE the Grammar and Punctuation Guide appendix.

adversary /*say* **ad**-vuhs-ree/ *noun* (*plural* **adversaries**) someone you compete against or fight with.
☐ **adverse**, *adjective* hostile. –**adversity**, *noun* misfortune.

☑ SPELLING TIP Remember the *ary* ending. You usually don't hear the *a* when the word is pronounced.

advertise /*say* **ad**-vuh-tuyz/ *verb* To **advertise** something is to draw attention to it, especially in order to sell it: *We advertised our garage sale by putting signs on the telegraph poles.*
☐ **advertising**, *noun*

advertisement /*say* uhd-**ver**-tuhs-muhnt/ *noun* a notice telling you about an event that is coming, or about something lost or for sale.

☑ SPELLING TIP The word **advertisement** comes from the word **advertise**, although there is a change in the sound. This should remind you not to leave out the *e* before the final *ment*. The spelling rule is that words ending in *e* keep their *e* when followed by a suffix that begins with a consonant. Rap it out as *ad+ver+tise+ment*.

NOTE This word is sometimes shortened to **ad**.

advice /*say* uhd-**vuys**/ *noun* an opinion someone gives you to help you decide what to do: *If you ask my advice, I think you should leave now.*

☑ SPELLING TIP See **advise** and remember that the noun **advice** ends with *ice* while the verb **advise** ends with *ise*. This is the pattern with other pairs of words with these endings, for example *practice* (noun) and *practise* (verb). Try thinking that *ice* is usually a noun as a way to remember that the noun forms end with *ice*.

advisable *adjective* sensible: *It's advisable to watch for snakes when walking in hot weather.*
☐ **advisability**, *noun*

advise /*say* uhd-**vuyz**/ *verb* If you **advise** someone to do something, you tell them what you think they should do: *The doctor advised him to go on a diet*; *We were advised against buying that type of car*; *Can you advise me on what to buy him as a present?*
☐ **adviser**, *noun*

ANOTHER SPELLING for **adviser** is **advisor**.

☑ SPELLING TIP See **advice**.

advocate *noun* /*say* **ad**-vuh-kuht/
1. someone who speaks in favour of a person or cause: *She was an advocate for peace.*
–*verb* /*say* **ad**-vuh-kayt/ **2.** If you **advocate** something, you speak in favour of it: *They advocated dropping the price so we would sell more.*

aeon /*say* **ee**-uhn/ *noun* a long period of time: *We found fossils in the rocks that were formed aeons ago.*

ANOTHER SPELLING is **eon**.
WORD HISTORY from a Greek word meaning 'a lifetime' or 'an age'

aerial *noun*
1. a wire or rod that you put up to receive radio or television signals.
–*adjective* **2.** living or reaching into the air: *The rainforest was full of aerial roots growing down*

from above. **3.** having to do with an aeroplane: *an aerial photo*; *an aerial attack.*

ANOTHER WORD (for definition 1) is **antenna**.

aero- *prefix* a word part meaning **1.** air, as in *aerobic*. **2.** gas, as in *aerosol*. **3.** aeroplane, as in *aerodrome*.

aerobics *plural noun* exercises done to improve your physical fitness by stimulating your heart and lungs.
☐ **aerobic**, *adjective*

aerodrome *noun* a landing field for aeroplanes which is smaller than an airport but which has hangars and other buildings.

aerodynamics /*say* air-roh-duy-**nam**-iks/ *noun* the scientific study of the way things move through the air.
☐ **aerodynamic**, *adjective*

aeronautics *noun* the science of flight.
☐ **aeronautical**, *adjective*

WORD HISTORY from a Latin word meaning 'sailing in the air'

aeroplane *noun* a winged machine which is driven by propellers or jet engines through the air.

THE SHORT FORM of this is **plane**, which is the more common word.

aerosol /*say* **air**-ruh-sol/ *noun* a container for keeping liquids, such as paint or household cleaner, under pressure so that you can spray them.

aesthetics /*say* uhs-**thet**-iks/ *noun* the study of beauty, especially in art.
☐ **aesthetic**, *adjective*

ANOTHER SPELLING is **esthetics**.

affable *adjective* friendly and approachable: *The guest speaker was both affable and entertaining.*
☐ **affability**, *noun* –**affably**, *adverb*

affair *noun*
1. an event or matter: *The affair that spoiled the school concert would eventually lead to a change in the rules.* **2. affairs**, events and activities relating to government, politics, etc.: *This section of the newspaper covers international affairs*; *He writes about economic affairs.* **3.** a sexual relationship between two people.

affect[1] *verb* If you **affect** someone or something, you cause a change in them: *The drought affected crops severely and profits were down.*

DO NOT CONFUSE **affect** with verb **effect**, which is to produce, or to bring about, or with the noun **effect**, which is something which is produced by some cause, as in *Wrinkles are an effect of age.*

affect[2] *verb* To **affect** is to pretend or make a show of a particular feeling, way of behaving or characteristic: *He affected not to care, but we knew he was really very upset.*
☐ **affected**, *adjective* artificial: *The actor's voice was very affected.*

affectation *noun* a deliberately exaggerated sort of behaviour: *We thought that his French accent was an affectation.*

affection *noun* warm feelings of love or liking.
☐ **affectionate**, *adjective*

affiliate *verb* When one organisation **affiliates** with another larger organisation, it joins or becomes connected with it: *Our club is affiliated with the national body.*
☐ **affiliation**, *noun*

WORD HISTORY from a Latin word meaning 'adopt as a son'

affinity *noun* (*plural* **affinities**) a natural liking or sense of closeness: *He had a great affinity with horses.*

affirm *verb* If you **affirm** something, you say that it is true: *I affirm that I will always do my duty.*
☐ **affirmation**, *noun*

THE OPPOSITE is **deny**.

affirmative *adjective* agreeing: *an affirmative response.*
☐ **affirmatively**, *adverb*

A SIMILAR WORD is **positive**.
THE OPPOSITE is **negative**.

afflict *verb* If something **afflicts** you, it troubles you greatly or causes you pain: *to be afflicted with a disease.*
☐ **affliction**, *noun* –**afflicted**, *adjective*

affluent /*say* **af**-looh-uhnt/ *adjective* wealthy or rich: *an affluent family.*
☐ **affluence**, *noun*

afford *verb*
1. If you can **afford** something, you have got enough money to pay for it: *We can't afford to go to that expensive restaurant.* **2.** If you can **afford** the time, energy, etc., to do something, then you have enough time or energy to be able to do it.
☐ **affordable**, *adjective* –**affordability**, *noun*

affront *noun*
1. something that hurts your pride or your feelings: *They took his late arrival as a personal affront.*
–*verb* **2.** If something **affronts** you, it hurts your pride or your feelings: *The main thing that affronted her was the fact that he didn't remember her name.*
☐ **affronted**, *adjective* offended.

☑ SPELLING TIP Remember that this word starts with an *a*. Don't confuse it with the spelling of **effrontery** which has a related meaning.

afraid *adjective*
1. frightened or feeling fear: *I'm afraid of spiders*; *He's afraid of flying.* 2. worried about: *I'm afraid of breaking this delicate cup.* 3. feeling sorry or regretful: *I'm afraid I'll be late.*

afresh *adverb* again: *to start afresh.*

after *preposition*
1. behind, or at the end of: *She always tags after me*; *You can play your piece after me.* 2. about: *I want to ask after his health.*
–*adverb* 3. behind or in the rear: *We all followed after.* 4. afterwards: *happy ever after.*
–*conjunction* 5. following the time that: *She was very tired after the baby was born.*
–*phrase* 6. **name after**, to give the name of: *The Egyptian port of Alexandria was named after Alexander the Great.*

aftermath *noun* conditions which follow a disaster: *the aftermath of the storm.*

afternoon *noun* the time from the middle of the day until evening.

after-school care *noun* a place where you can go in the afternoon when school finishes, where people look after you until you go home.

afterwards *adverb* at a later time: *We had dinner and afterwards went to a movie.*

ANOTHER FORM is **afterward**.

again *adverb* once more or another time: *He has to do it all over again.*

against *preposition*
1. towards or on: *The rain beat against the window.* 2. pressing on: *Prop the ladder up against the wall.* 3. opposed to: *twenty votes against ten.* 4. in resistance to: *Are you vaccinated against measles?*

agate /*rhymes with* maggot/ *noun* a type of hard stone which is often marked with lines or rings of colour.

age *noun*
1. the length of time that someone or something has existed: *The age of our dog is ten years.* 2. a period of historical time: *the age of dinosaurs*; *the Elizabethan age.* 3. a stage of human life: *middle age.*
–*verb* (**ages**, **ageing** *or* **aging**, **aged**, **has aged**) 4. When you **age**, you grow old or look older: *She has aged a lot since we saw her last.*
–*phrase* 5. **act** (or **be**) **your age**, *Rather informal* to behave in the way that people expect for someone your age. 6. **under age**, not legally old enough to do something, such as drink alcohol or drive a car.

agency *noun* (*plural* **agencies**) an organisation which acts on behalf of other people: *Monica set up an agency to find publishers for writers.*

agenda /*say* uh-**jen**-duh/ *noun* the list or plan of what has to be done or talked about, especially at a meeting: *They reserved the issue about junk food for the next meeting's agenda.*

☑ SPELLING TIP This word is quite easy to spell if you remember that there is a soft *g* giving the 'j' sound. Don't confuse it with **gender** which is the state of being male or female. **Agenda** ends with *a* because it comes from Latin where it is the plural of *agendum* (meaning 'something to be done') from the verb *agere* (meaning 'to do'). Think of other words that come from the same origin, such as *agency* and *agent*.

agent *noun*
1. someone who organises things for you: *a real estate agent.* 2. something used for a special purpose: *a cleaning agent.*

aggravate /*say* **ag**-ruh-vayt/ *verb*
1. To **aggravate** something is to make it worse: *The hot weather aggravated their discomfort.* 2. If you **aggravate** someone, you annoy them: *She aggravates people by complaining all the time.*

NOTE Some people think that definition 2 is informal, or should not be used at all. However, it is now accepted by most people, particularly in the adjective form *aggravating* (*the dog's whining is very aggravating*).

aggregate /*say* **ag**-ruh-guht/ *noun* the total or sum of single things: *The aggregate of all the marks was divided by the number of students to get the average mark for the class.*
☐ **aggregate**, *adjective*

☑ SPELLING TIP *Double/single letter alert*: the letter *g* turns up three times in **aggregate** – the first time as a double *g*, the second time as a single letter. Also note the *ate* spelling at the end (although the sound is 'uht').

aggressive *adjective* likely to attack: *an aggressive guard dog.*
☐ **aggression**, *noun* –**aggressively**, *adverb* –**aggressiveness**, *noun* –**aggressor**, *noun*

aggrieved /*say* uh-**greevd**/ *adjective* feeling hurt or wronged: *I was aggrieved that I had not been invited.*

aghast /*say* uh-**gahst**/ *adjective* shocked and frightened: *We were aghast to find that the water from the flood had reached the back door.*

☑ SPELLING TIP *Silent letter alert*: don't forget the silent *h* after the *g*. Try thinking that you would be **aghast** if you saw *a ghost*. Join these words together, change to the *o* to an *a*, and you have **aghast**.

agile /*say* **aj**-uyl/ *adjective* quick, lively and active: *an agile acrobat*; *an agile mind.*
☐ **agilely**, *adverb* –**agility**, *noun*

agitate *verb*
1. If something **agitates** you, it upsets you and makes you nervous: *I was so agitated by his letter that I couldn't think straight.* **2.** If you **agitate** for a certain change, you work to make it happen, especially by making the public aware of it: *Students are agitating for the library to be open more often.* **3.** If you **agitate** something, you shake it: *The machine agitates the clothes without damaging them.*
□ **agitation**, *noun*

agnostic /*say* ag-**nos**-tik/ *noun* someone who believes that you cannot know whether any god exists.
□ **agnostic**, *adjective* –**agnosticism** /*say* ag-**nos**-tuh-siz-uhm/, *noun*

COMPARE this with **atheist**.

ago *adverb* past: *some time ago*; *long ago.*

agog *adjective* excited and astonished: *Having never seen snow before, the children were all agog.*

WORD HISTORY from French words meaning 'in a merry mood'

agony *noun* (*plural* **agonies**) great pain or suffering.

agrarian /*say* uh-**grair**-ree-uhn/ *adjective* having to do with the land or farming: *an agrarian civilisation.*

agree *verb*
1. If you **agree** with someone, you have the same opinion as they do: *I agree with her on that point.* **2.** If you **agree** to do something, you say you will do it: *They have agreed to deliver the furniture tomorrow.* **3.** If people **agree** on a plan, they decide to follow it: *We need to agree on a date for the next meeting.* **4.** If two words **agree**, they are both singular or both plural, or both first person, second person or third person: *Check that the subject and the verb agree.* **5.** If some kind of food does not **agree** with you, it has a bad effect on you: *Cheese just doesn't agree with me – I always feel sick after I eat it.*
□ **agreed**, *adjective*

THE OPPOSITE (of definition 1) is **disagree**.
NOTE For definition 4, see **person** (definition 2).

agreeable *adjective* Someone who is **agreeable** is **1.** pleasant or likeable: *a very agreeable personality.* **2.** willing to agree: *They were agreeable to hosting the party at their place.*
□ **agreeableness**, *noun*

agreement *noun*
1. the same way of thinking: *There was general agreement on going to the beach first.* **2.** an arrangement: *Our family has an agreement about who does the washing up each night.*

agriculture *noun* farming: *The dry slopes were unsuitable for agriculture.*
□ **agricultural**, *adjective*

ahead *adverb*
1. in front or forward.
–*phrase* **2. be ahead**, to be better off or be winning: *I'm well ahead in the deal.* **3. get ahead of**, to pass or beat someone at something.

aid *noun*
1. help or support. **2.** a helper.
–*phrase* **3. in aid of**, for or intended to achieve: *What was all that shouting in aid of?*

ANOTHER SPELLING (for definition 2) is **aide**.

AIDS /*say* aydz/ *noun* a disease caused by a virus (HIV) which breaks down the body's natural way of protecting itself, resulting in severe infections and eventually death.

WORD HISTORY an acronym made by joining the first letters of *acquired immune deficiency syndrome*

ailing *adjective* sickly: *an ailing child.*
□ **ailment**, *noun* an illness.

aim *verb*
1. If you **aim** a gun or other weapon at someone or something, you point it towards them: *The soldier was aiming straight at the target.* **2.** If you **aim** what you say at someone, you especially mean them to notice it: *He aimed his outburst at the teacher*; *Was that question aimed at me?* **3.** If you **aim** to do something, you try to do it. You have it as a goal: *They're aiming to finish by the end of the year.*
–*noun* **4.** a purpose or target: *Our aim was to win the race.*
–*phrase* **5. take aim**, to point a weapon. **6. aim for**, **a.** to direct or point (something) in the direction of: *to aim for the target.* **b.** to direct one's action or energies towards: *to aim for perfection.*
□ **aimless**, *adjective* –**aimlessly**, *adverb*

air *noun*
1. the mixture of gases which surrounds the earth and which we breathe. **2.** appearance: *The house had an air of mystery about it.* **3.** in music, a tune or song.
–*verb* **4.** To **air** a room is to let air into it. **5.** To **air** an opinion or idea is to make it known to people: *The interview was an opportunity for him to air his views.* **6.** To **air** a program is to broadcast it on television or radio.
–*phrase* **7. give yourself airs** or **put on airs**, to pretend to be more important than you really are. **8. into** (or **in**) **thin air**, without a sign or completely out of sight. **9. on** (**the**) **air**, being broadcast on radio or television: *The presenter of the TV show did not realise he was on air when he scratched his head.* **10.** (**up**) **in the air**, not decided or uncertain: *Their plans for next year are still up in the air.*

air conditioning *noun* a way of keeping the air in a building or vehicle cool.
☐ **air conditioner**, *noun* –**air-conditioned**, *adjective*

ANOTHER FORM is **air-conditioning**.

aircraft *noun* any machine that can fly, such as an aeroplane or helicopter.

air force *noun* the part of a country's armed forces which uses aircraft for attack and defence.

COMPARE this with **army** (definition 1) and **navy** (definition 1).

airline *noun* a company which provides a regular aircraft service for passengers and goods.

airport *noun* a large area where aircraft land and take off, passengers get on and off, and goods are loaded and unloaded onto aircraft.

air pressure *noun*
1. the pressure caused by the weight of the atmosphere at a particular place on the earth. **2.** the pressure of air, usually inside a tyre.

OTHER TERMS (for definition 1) are **atmospheric pressure** and **barometric pressure**.
NOTE You measure the pressure in definition 1 with a **barometer**.

airtight *adjective* tightly closed so that air can't get in or out: *an airtight seal.*

airy *adjective* (**airier**, **airiest**)
1. A room is **airy** if it has air moving through it. **2.** If a movement is **airy**, it shows that the person making it is in a careless or happy mood: *She gave us an airy wave, then rode off.*
☐ **airiness**, *noun*

aisle /*say* uyl/ *noun* a clear path between seats in a hall, aircraft, and so on.

☑ SPELLING TIP *Silent letter alert*: don't forget the unusual spelling of *ais* (with a silent *s*) to give a 'uy' sound. **Aisle** is spelt and pronounced in this way because it comes from French.

ajar *adverb* partly open: *The door was ajar and we could see the light was on.*

akimbo *adverb* with your hands on your hips and your elbows pointing out: *He lounged against the shed, with his arms akimbo.*

akin *adjective* related or alike: *Painting is roughly akin to drawing, but sculpture is quite different.*

alacrity /*say* uh-**lak**-ruh-tee/ *noun* cheerful willingness: *She set about the job with alacrity.*

alarm *noun*
1. a warning sound or signal. **2.** sudden fear caused by discovering that you are in danger: *The huge cloud of bushfire smoke filled us with alarm.*
–*verb* **3.** If something **alarms** you, it frightens or worries you: *The light flashing outside my window alarmed me.*
☐ **alarmed**, *adjective* –**alarming**, *adjective*

WORD HISTORY from an Italian phrase meaning 'to arms'

albatross *noun* a very large seabird that can fly long distances.

albino /*say* al-**bee**-noh, al-**buy**-noh/ *noun* (*plural* **albinos**) a human or an animal with pale skin, white hair and pink eyes due to a lack of pigmentation in their skin.

album *noun*
1. a book with blank pages used for keeping things like photographs and stamps. **2.** a recording on which there is a collection of music or songs.

alcohol *noun* a colourless liquid which is found in some drinks and which makes you drunk if you have too much.

alcoholic *noun* someone who continually drinks too much alcohol.
☐ **alcoholic**, *adjective*

alcoholism *noun* a disease caused by drinking too much alcohol over a long time.

alcopop *noun* a sweet fizzy soft drink with alcohol added to it, sold already mixed: *She warned them that alcopops could be dangerous because you can't taste the alcohol in them.*

alcove *noun* a small space or recess set off from the main part, especially in a room.

alderman *noun* (*plural* **aldermen**) someone elected to a local council: *You should speak to your local alderman about getting more seats in the park.*

NOTE The more usual term for this is now **councillor**.

ale *noun* a type of beer.

alert *adjective*
1. watchful and quick to react: *After the thunderstorm, we were alert to every sound.*
–*noun* **2.** a warning or alarm: *The police put out an alert that the prisoner had escaped and was dangerous.*
–*phrase* **3. on the alert**, watchful or ready for danger.
☐ **alertness**, *noun* –**alertly**, *adverb*

alfalfa /*say* al-**fal**-fuh/ *plural noun* sprouts from the seeds of a particular plant, often used in salads.

ANOTHER TERM for this is **alfalfa sprouts**.

algae /*say* **al**-jee, **al**-gee/ *plural noun* (*singular* **alga** /*say* **al**-guh/) a type of green plant found in or near water: *Seaweed is a type of algae.*
☐ **algal** /*say* **al**-guhl/, *adjective*

algebra /*say* **al**-juh-bruh/ *noun* the part of mathematics which uses letters to stand for numbers.
☐ **algebraic** /*say* al-juh-**bray**-ik/, *adjective*

algorithm /*say* **al**-guh-ridh-uhm/ *noun* a step-by-step method for doing a sum.

alias /*say* **ay**-lee-uhs/ *noun* (*plural* **aliases**)
1. a false name: *The magazine writer produced a column under the alias of 'Lady Jane'.*
–*adverb* **2. Alias** means 'also known as': *A well-known bushranger was Francis Christie (alias Frank Gardiner).*

ANOTHER TERM (for definition 2) is **aka** (short for 'also known as').
WORD HISTORY from a Latin word meaning 'at another time or place'

alibi /*say* **al**-uh-buy/ *noun* (*plural* **alibis**) a defence by someone that they were somewhere else when a crime was committed: *The police let him go after they had checked his alibi.*

alien /*say* **ay**-lee-uhn/ *noun*
1. someone who is not a citizen of the country in which they are living. **2.** in science fiction, a being from outer space.
–*adjective* **3.** strange or foreign: *alien speech.*
–*phrase* **4. alien to**, opposed to: *ideas alien to our way of thinking.*

WORD HISTORY from a Latin word meaning 'belonging to another'

alienate /*say* **ay**-lee-uh-nayt/ *verb* If you **alienate** someone, you make them become unfriendly to you: *He has alienated most of his neighbours by refusing to turn down his loud music.*
☐ **alienation**, *noun*

alight[1] *adjective* burning: *All the candles are alight.*

alight[2] *verb* If you **alight** from a vehicle such as a train, you get out of or off it: *to alight from the bus at the next stop.*

align /*say* uh-**luyn**/ *verb* If you **align** things, you put them into line with each other: *Could you align the table with the window, please.*
☐ **alignment**, *noun*

☑ SPELLING TIP You need to be careful with the spelling of this word because the meaning does not help with the spelling. Don't forget that it has a silent *g* so that the last part is spelt *lign* (even though it sounds like 'line' and even though the word means 'to put things in a line'). This is because **align** comes from a French word, rather than being formed directly from the English word *line*.

alike *adjective*
1. similar: *The girls were so alike that we thought they were sisters.*
–*adverb* **2.** in the same way: *He treated all his students alike.*

alimentary canal /*say* al-uh-**ment**-ree/ *noun* the passage in a person's or animal's body which goes from the mouth to the anus and is used for digesting food.

ANOTHER TERM for this is **alimentary tract**.

alive *adjective* living and not dead: *All my grandparents are alive*; *Is that pot plant still alive?*

alkali /*say* **al**-kuh-luy/ *noun* (*plural* **alkalis**) a chemical that reduces the effect of acid.
☐ **alkaline**, *adjective*

WORD HISTORY from an Arabic word for the ashes of certain beach plants

all *adjective*
1. All is used to refer to the whole amount or total number of things: *Put all the vegetables in the refrigerator*; *all day long.*
–*pronoun* **2. All** of something is the whole of it: *all of the cake.* **3. All** can mean 'the only thing': *All I want is chocolate*; *Is that all she said?*

allay /*say* uh-**lay**/ *verb* To **allay** is to make less or relieve: *to allay fears*; *to allay thirst.*

allege /*say* uh-**lej**/ *verb* If someone **alleges** something, they say that something is true, but do not prove it: *It's been alleged that they're involved in stealing cars.*
☐ **allegation**, *noun* –**alleged**, *adjective*: *the alleged spy.*

allegiance /*say* uh-**lee**-juhns/ *noun* loyalty or faithfulness: *My dad was thanked for his allegiance to the company.*

☑ SPELLING TIP *Tricky vowel sound*: there is only a single *e* spelling for the 'ee' sound in the middle. Also remember that there is an *i* before the *ance* ending although you do not hear it when you say the word.

allegory /*say* **al**-uh-guh-ree/ *noun* (*plural* **allegories**) a story which seems simple but has an extra meaning.
☐ **allegorical** /*say* al-uh-**go**-rik-uhl/, *adjective*

allegro /*say* uh-**lay**-groh, uh-**leg**-roh/ *adverb* played or sung at a fast speed.

NOTE This is used as an instruction in music. Like most musical instructions, it comes from Italian.

allergy /*say* **al**-uh-jee/ *noun* (*plural* **allergies**) an unusual sensitivity to things that are normally harmless, like pollen, dust and certain foods: *Some people have an allergy to wattle.*
☐ **allergic** /*say* uh-**ler**-jik/, *adjective*

☑ SPELLING TIP *Tricky 'uh' sound*: the middle vowel sound is spelt *er*. This will be easier to remember if you think about the pronunciation of the adjective **allergic** where you can hear the 'er' sound.

alleviate /*say* uh-**lee**-vee-ayt/ *verb* If you **alleviate** pain or suffering, you make it easier to bear: *Flying doctors to remote areas of the country alleviated much hardship and suffering.*
☐ **alleviation**, *noun*

☑ SPELLING TIP *Tricky vowel sound*: there is only a single *e* spelling for the 'ee' sound in the middle. The *lev* spelling is there because **alleviate** comes from *levare*, the Latin word meaning 'to raise', as do some other words like *elevate*.

alley *noun* (*plural* **alleys**)
1. a narrow passage between buildings. **2.** a long, narrow enclosure with a smooth wooden floor for games like tenpin bowling.

alliance /*say* uh-**luy**-uhns/ *noun* an agreement to work together, especially an agreement between countries.

alligator /*say* **al**-uh-gay-tuh/ *noun* an animal like a crocodile, but with a broader snout, found mainly in America.

☑ SPELLING TIP *Tricky 'uh' sounds*: the vowel sound before the *g* is spelt *i* and the final sound is spelt *or*. Also remember the double *l*. **Alligator** comes from two Spanish words – *al* (a form of *el* meaning 'the') and *lagarto* (meaning 'lizard'). When you put them together, you get a double *l*.

alliteration *noun* the repeated use of the same letter or sound to start two or more words in a group, as in 'Around the rugged rocks the ragged rascal ran'.
☐ **alliterative**, *adjective*

COMPARE this with **assonance**.

allocate *verb* If someone **allocates** something for a certain purpose, they decide that it will be used for that purpose: *I allocated a lot of my Christmas money to buying presents for my friends.*
☐ **allocation**, *noun*

allot *verb* (**allots**, **allotting**, **allotted**, **has allotted**) To **allot** something is to divide it up among a number of people: *The government allotted forty acres to each man.*
☐ **allotment**, *noun* –**allotted**, *adjective*: *the allotted tasks of the class.*

A SIMILAR WORD is **allocate**.

allow *verb*
1. If someone **allows** you to do something, they say that you may do it: *You are allowed to talk in this part of the library.* **2.** If someone **allows** something to happen, they do not stop it from happening: *I allowed the discussion to go on.* **3.** If something **allows** someone or something to do something, it makes it possible for them to do it: *The automatic control allows you to open and close the garage door without having to get out of the car.* **4.** If a court of law or a referee of a game **allows** something, they say it is all right. They accept it: *The umpire allowed the serve.* **5.** If someone **allows** a certain amount of time and money for something, they make it available for that purpose: *We need to allow at least a month for planning.*
–*phrase* **6. allow for**, to provide for: *We should leave home earlier than that to allow for the traffic.*

A SIMILAR WORD (for definition 1) is **permit**.

allowance *noun*
1. money given for a special purpose: *She asked for a small allowance to cover her food costs.*
–*phrase* **2. make allowance for**, to take into account: *You have to make allowance for his headstrong behaviour.*

alloy *noun* a metal made by mixing different metals together: *Brass is an alloy of copper and zinc.*

all right *adjective*
1. safe: *'Is she all right?', they asked anxiously.* **2.** adequate or good enough to accept: *The meringues we made were all right but the brownies were much better.* **3.** acceptable: *Is it all right if I leave early?*
–*adverb* **4.** correctly or to an acceptable standard: *I did all right in the exam.*

ANOTHER SPELLING is **alright**. Some people don't think it is correct, but it is increasingly common.

allude *verb* If you **allude** to something, you refer to it briefly: *The guest speaker alluded to her interest in archaeology.*
☐ **allusion**, *noun* passing mention of something.

WORD HISTORY from a Latin word meaning 'play with'

allure *noun* temptation or attraction: *the allure of a morning at the beach.*
☐ **alluring**, *adjective*

alluvial *adjective* made of sand or mud which has been washed down by a river: *Alluvial soil is often good for growing rice.*

ally *noun* /*say* **al**-uy/ (*plural* **allies**)
1. a country which has signed an agreement to help another country: *Australia counts America as an ally.* **2.** a friend or supporter.
–*verb* /*say* uh-**luy**/ (**allies**, **allying**, **allied**, **has allied**) **3.** If you are **allied** with someone, you are joined with them or are on their side: *The families were allied by marriage.*
☐ **allied**, *adjective*

almanac /*say* **awl**-muh-nak, **al**-muh-nak/ *noun* a calendar which gives information about the sun, moon, tides, weather or other special information.

ANOTHER SPELLING is **almanack** but this is now old-fashioned.

almighty *adjective*
1. very powerful: *an almighty storm*; *an almighty monarch.* **2.** very great or extreme: *to be in almighty trouble.*
–*noun* **3. the Almighty**, God.

☑ SPELLING TIP *Single letter alert*: only one *l*. Although this word is made up of *all* and *mighty*, the second *l* in *all* has been dropped.

almond /*say* **ah**-muhnd/ *noun* an oval-shaped, cream-coloured nut with a sweet taste.

☑ SPELLING TIP *Silent letter alert*: don't forget the silent *l*. Remember that **almond** begins with *al* but all you hear is the sound 'ah'.

almost *adverb* very nearly: *She's almost an adult now.*

alms /*say* ahmz/ *plural noun* money and other gifts given to poor people.

A SIMILAR WORD is **charity**.

☑ SPELLING TIP *Tricky vowel sound*: don't forget the *l*. The *alm* spelling gives the 'ahm' sound. Don't confuse this word with **arms** which has the same sound.

alone *adjective*
1. on your own: *She was alone and afraid in the old house*; *I enjoy living alone.* **2.** only: *He alone knows what really happened that day.*

NOTE This word is used in the predicate or placed after the noun.

along *preposition*
1. from one end to the other of: *to walk along the path.*
–*adverb* **2.** in company or together with: *Can we come along?*
–*phrase* **3. all along**, all the time: *I've been here all along.* **4. get along**, **a.** to leave or go: *I must get along or I'll miss my bus.* **b.** to be friendly: *I get along with all of them.* **c.** to manage well: *I'm getting along okay with my studies now.* **5. go along with**, to agree with.

aloof /*rhymes with* roof/ *adjective*
1. withdrawn and proud: *Hannah seemed aloof but I think she was just shy.*
–*adverb* **2.** at a distance apart: *At the funeral, the stranger stood aloof from the family.*

aloud *adverb*
1. in a normal speaking voice: *Vijay read the sign aloud.* **2.** loudly: *He shouted aloud when he saw his friends waiting for him.*

alphabet *noun* all the letters of a language arranged in their usual order: *My little sister has just learned to say the alphabet.*
☐ **alphabetical**, *adjective*

alpine *adjective* having to do with high, mountainous country: *We stay at an alpine lodge when we go skiing*; *alpine daisies.*

alps *plural noun* a high mountain range, usually covered with snow, such as the Australian Alps or the Swiss Alps.

already *adverb* at an earlier time or sooner than expected: *I don't want to go to that movie because I've seen it already*; *Have you cleaned your room already?*

☑ SPELLING TIP *Single letter alert*: only one *l*. Although this word is made up of *all* and *ready*, the second *l* in *all* has been dropped.

alright *adjective*, *adverb* See **all right**.

Alsatian /*say* al-**say**-shuhn/ *noun* a large, strong, wolf-like dog, often trained as a guard dog and used by the police.

ANOTHER NAME for this is **German shepherd**.

also *adverb* too or in addition.

altar /*say* **awl**-tuh, **ol**-tuh/ *noun* a table which is used for religious ceremonies in a church or other place of worship.

☑ SPELLING TIP Don't confuse the spelling of **altar** with **alter** which sounds the same. To **alter** something is to change it.

alter /*say* **awl**-tuh, **ol**-tuh/ *verb* If you **alter** something, you change it: *This list is no longer the same – someone's altered some of the items.*
☐ **alteration**, *noun* –**altered**, *adjective*

☑ SPELLING TIP Don't confuse the spelling of **alter** with **altar** which sounds the same. An **altar** is a special table used in a church.

altercation /*say* awl-tuh-**kay**-shuhn, ol-tuh-**kay**-shuhn/ *noun* an angry disagreement or dispute.

alternate *verb* /*say* **awl**-tuh-nayt, **ol**-tuh-nayt/
1. If one thing **alternates** with another, the two things follow each other in turn: *My brother and I alternate doing the washing up.*
–*adjective* /*say* awl-**ter**-nuht, ol-**ter**-nuht/ **2.** You can say something happens on **alternate** days when it happens every second day: *He had to report to the hospital for treatment every alternate day for nearly a year.*
☐ **alternately**, *adverb*

DO NOT CONFUSE definition 2 with **alternative**.

alternative /*say* awl-**ter**-nuh-tiv, ol-**ter**-nuh-tiv/ *noun* one of two or more choices: *Going by public transport is a better alternative than taking a car.*
☐ **alternative**, *adjective*: *an alternative route.*

DO NOT CONFUSE **alternative** with **alternate**.

alternative energy *noun* electrical or other power that comes from sources such as the sun, wind, the tides, etc., not from fossil fuels such as oil.

although /*say* awl-**dhoh**/ *conjunction* even though: *It's winter, although you wouldn't think so, because it's so warm.*

☑ SPELLING TIP *Single letter alert*: only one *l*. **Although** has been formed from *all* (with one *l* dropped) and *though*. Notice that in both **although** and *though* there is the spelling *ough* for the 'oh' sound.

altimeter /*say* **al**-tuh-mee-tuh/ *noun* the instrument in a plane which measures altitude or height.

altitude *noun* height above sea level: *I watched the altimeter in the plane to see the altitude we were at.*

alto /*say* **al**-toh/ *noun*
1. the lowest range of musical notes which can be sung by a female singer. **2.** a woman who sings alto.

ANOTHER WORD for this is **contralto.**
NOTE An **alto** is higher than a **tenor, baritone** or **bass** but lower than a **soprano.**
WORD HISTORY from a Latin word for 'high'

altogether *adverb*
1. totally or completely: *I know you're sad but the news is not altogether bad*; *His money has run out altogether.* **2.** in total: *When the two families go out there are ten of us altogether.*

☑ SPELLING TIP *Single letter alert*: only one *l*. Although this word is made up of *all* and *together*, the second *l* in *all* has been dropped.

aluminium /*say* al-yuh-**min**-ee-uhm/ *noun* a light-weight, silver-grey metal which is used to make drink cans, cooking pots, aeroplane parts, etc., and can be rolled into thin sheets of foil.

always *adverb*
1. all the time or without interruption: *She is always happy.* **2.** every time: *She always sings in the shower.*

Alzheimer's disease /*say* **alts**-huy-muhz duh-zeez/ *noun* a brain disease which appears usually in older adults and which causes the person to become confused and have memory problems.

ANOTHER FORM is **Alzheimer's.**

am *verb* the first person singular present tense indicative of the verb **be**.

NOTE For an explanation of *indicative*, see **mood**[2]. Also see the Grammar and Punctuation Guide appendix.

a.m. *abbreviation* short for *ante meridiem*, Latin words meaning 'before noon', covering the period between 12 o'clock at night and 12 o'clock in the middle of the day: *The paper is delivered at 8 a.m.*

ANOTHER FORM is **am.**

amalgamate /*say* uh-**mal**-guh-mayt/ *verb* If two or more things **amalgamate**, they join together: *The two companies amalgamated and moved to a new location.*
☐ **amalgamation**, *noun*

amateur /*say* **am**-uh-tuh, **am**-uh-chuh/ *noun*
1. someone who does something for enjoyment and not to earn money from it. **2.** an athlete who does not earn money from playing sport. **3.** someone who does a job unskilfully: *I'm only an amateur so there are quite a few mistakes.*
☐ **amateur**, *adjective* –**amateurish**, *adjective*

THE OPPOSITE is **professional.**

☑ SPELLING TIP *Tricky 'uh' sound*: the middle vowel sound is spelt *a*. Also remember the *eur* ending. This ending occurs in several words that have come from French and means 'someone who does something', as in *entrepreneur* and *chauffeur.*

amaze *verb* If you **amaze** someone, you surprise them a lot: *I didn't know he could speak six languages – he never ceases to amaze me.*
☐ **amazement**, *noun* –**amazing**, *adjective* –**amazingly**, *adverb*

amazon /*say* **am**-uh-zuhn, **am**-uh-zon/ *noun* a tall powerful woman.
☐ **amazonian**, *adjective*

ambassador /*say* am-**bas**-uh-duh/ *noun*
1. the highest official who is sent by a government to represent it in a foreign country. **2.** someone, such as a famous singer or sports star, who brings honour to their own country while visiting another.
☐ **ambassadorial** /*say* am-bas-uh-**daw**-ree-uhl/, *adjective*

☑ SPELLING TIP *Double letter alert*: two *s*'s. Also remember that the ending is *or* (not *er*). Rap it out as *am* + *bas* + *sa* + *dor*.

amber *noun*
1. a hard, yellow-brown substance which can be polished as a semi-precious stone. **2.** the yellowish colour used as the warning light of a traffic signal.
☐ **amber**, *adjective*

ambi- *prefix* a word part meaning 'both' or 'on both sides', as in *ambivalent*.

WORD HISTORY this prefix comes from Latin

ambidextrous /*say* am-bee-**deks**-truhs/ *adjective* To be **ambidextrous** is to be able to use both hands equally well.
☐ **ambidexterity** /*say* am-bee-deks-**te**-ruh-tee/, *noun*

ambiguous /*say* am-**big**-yooh-uhs/ *adjective* unclear, due to having more than one meaning:

As the question was quite ambiguous, we had to ask the teacher what she meant.
☐ **ambiguity**, *noun* (*plural* **ambiguities**)

☑ SPELLING TIP Remember the *ous* spelling at the end of this word, and you should not have trouble sounding out its parts and spelling it.

ambition *noun*
1. strong desire for something in the future, especially money or fame: *Because of his ambition, he wanted to be first in everything he attempted.* **2.** the object that is desired: *Achieving peace was his ambition.*
☐ **ambitious**, *adjective*

ambivalent /*say* am-**biv**-uh-luhnt/ *adjective* having opposite and conflicting feelings towards someone or something: *I am ambivalent about plastic bags – they are very useful for lots of things, but they damage the environment.*
☐ **ambivalence**, *noun* –**ambivalently**, *adverb*

amble *verb* If you **amble**, you walk at a relaxed or comfortable pace.
☐ **ambling**, *adjective*

ambulance *noun* a vehicle which is specially equipped to carry sick or injured people and which is driven by experts in first aid.

ambush *verb*
1. If you **ambush** someone, you come out from a hiding place and attack them.
–*noun* **2.** a sudden attack from a hidden place.

amenable /*say* uh-**men**-uh-buhl, uh-**meen**-uh-buhl/ *adjective* in agreement with and cooperative: *We were amenable to the suggestion that we leave early.*
☐ **amenably**, *adverb*

amend *verb*
1. If you **amend** something that is written, such as a law or rule, you alter it. **2.** If you **amend** your behaviour, you improve or correct it.
☐ **amendment**, *noun*

amends *singular or plural noun in the phrase* **make amends**, to make up for something wrong or an injury done: *to make amends for forgetting your birthday.*

amenity *noun* (*plural* **amenities**) anything which makes a place more comfortable and pleasant: *The council provides amenities in the park like toilets, drinking water and ramps for wheelchairs.*

amethyst /*say* **am**-uh-thuhst/ *noun* a purple-coloured precious stone.

WORD HISTORY from a Greek word meaning 'without drunkenness'

amiable /*say* **ay**-mee-uh-buhl/ *adjective* friendly and cooperative: *They met and had an amiable discussion about how to proceed.*
☐ **amiability**, *noun*

ammonia *noun* a strong-smelling gas, often dissolved in water to make a liquid which may be used for cleaning.

ammunition *noun* the bullets and other objects used in firing guns or other weapons.

amnesia /*say* am-**nee**-zhuh, am-**nee**-zee-uh/ *noun* loss of memory: *Because of his amnesia, he no longer remembers where he lived.*

amnesty *noun* (*plural* **amnesties**) a pardon, usually given for crimes against a government.

amoeba /*say* uh-**mee**-buh/ *noun* (*plural* **amoebae** /*say* uh-**mee**-bee/ *or* **amoebas**) a one-celled animal which can be seen only with a microscope and which changes shape as it moves and absorbs food.
☐ **amoebic**, *adjective*

ANOTHER SPELLING is **ameba**.
WORD HISTORY from a Greek word meaning 'change'

among *preposition*
1. surrounded by: *She was among friends.* **2.** one included in a group of: *That's among the songs we'll sing.* **3.** between more than two people: *Distribute these pencils among you*; *They should settle the dispute among themselves.*

ANOTHER FORM is **amongst**.

amorous *adjective* feeling or showing love, especially of a sexual kind: *her amorous feelings for him*; *an amorous glance.*
☐ **amorously**, *adverb* –**amorousness**, *noun*

☑ SPELLING TIP This comes from *amor*, the Latin word for 'love'. Notice that there is no *u* in this part of the word, as you might think if you know *amour*, the French word for 'love'.

amount *noun*
1. how much there is of something: *What amount of sugar goes into the cake?*
–*verb in the phrase* **2. amount to**, to add up to or be equal to: *The casualties of the earthquake amounted to more than one thousand*; *Her advice didn't amount to much in the end.*

ampere /*say* **am**-pair/ *noun* a unit of electric current.

THE SYMBOL for this is **A**

ampersand *noun* the sign '&' which is used to mean 'and' as in *Cobb & Co.*

amphi- *prefix* a word part meaning **1.** of both kinds, as in *amphibious*. **2.** around, as in *amphitheatre*.

WORD HISTORY this prefix comes from Greek

amphibian /*say* am-**fib**-ee-uhn/ *noun* an animal that begins life in the water and lives on land as an adult, such as a frog.
☐ **amphibious**, *adjective*

amphitheatre /*say* **am**-fee-thear-tuh/ *noun* a round building with an open area in the centre and rows of seats rising around it: *Men fought with lions in the amphitheatres of ancient Rome.*

ample *adjective* enough or more than enough: *We have ample money for the trip.*

A SIMILAR WORD is **abundant**.

amplify /*say* **am**-pluh-fuy/ *verb* (**amplifies**, **amplifying**, **amplified**, **has amplified**) If you **amplify** something, especially sounds, you make it larger or greater than it was before.
☐ **amplification**, *noun* –**amplifier**, *noun*

amputate *verb* If someone **amputates** something, they cut it off, especially for medical reasons: *His hand was crushed in an accident and he had to have two fingers amputated.*
☐ **amputation**, *noun*

amulet /*say* **am**-yuh-luht/ *noun* a charm, especially one which is supposed to keep evil away.

amuse *verb*
1. If you **amuse** someone, you make them smile or laugh: *We were very amused by his jokes and we couldn't stop laughing.* **2.** If you **amuse** yourself doing something, you entertain yourself doing something that you enjoy: *I can amuse myself for hours, just playing computer games.*
☐ **amusing**, *adjective*

amusement *noun*
1. the feeling of being amused. **2.** something which amuses, such as a concert or a game.

an *indefinite article* the form of the article **a** used when the following word begins with a vowel sound (usually words starting with *a, e, i, o* or *u*): *She is eating an apple*; *What an unusual flower.*

anaemia /*say* uh-**nee**-mee-uh/ *noun* a lack of red blood cells in your blood. This makes you look pale, and feel weak and tired a lot of the time.
☐ **anaemic**, *adjective*

ANOTHER SPELLING is **anemia**.

anaesthetic /*say* an-uhs-**thet**-ik/ *noun* a drug that stops you feeling pain. A **local anaesthetic** can be used to numb a particular area of your body, while a **general anaesthetic** will make you unconscious.
☐ **anaesthetist** /*say* uh-**nees**-thuh-tuhst/, *noun* –**anaesthetise**, *verb*

ANOTHER SPELLING is **anesthetic**. Other spellings for **anaesthetise** are **anaesthetize**, **anesthetise** or **anesthetize**.

anagram *noun* a word made by changing the order of the letters in another word: *'Stare' is an anagram of 'rates'.*

analgesic /*say* an-uhl-**jee**-zik/ *noun* a medicine that removes or lessens pain.
☐ **analgesia**, *noun* the inability to feel pain. –**analgesic**, *adjective* removing pain.

analog *adjective* showing measurement by use of a pointer that keeps moving, such as the needle on a dial: *An analog watch is one that has hands to show the time.*

ANOTHER SPELLING is **analogue**.
COMPARE this with **digital** (definition 3).

analogy /*say* uh-**nal**-uh-jee/ *noun* (*plural* **analogies**) a likeness between two or more things which makes you compare them: *to draw an analogy between the brain and a computer.*
☐ **analogous** /*say* uh-**nal**-uh-guhs/, *adjective* similar. –**analogously**, *adverb*

analyse /*say* **an**-uh-luyz/ *verb*
1. If you analyse something, you examine it in detail in order to understand or explain it: *to analyse a poem*; *to analyse a method of doing a mathematical sum.* **2.** If someone **analyses** a chemical substance, they separate it into parts to find out what it consists of.
☐ **analyst** /*say* **an**-uh-luhst/, *noun* –**analytical** /*say* an-uh-**lit**-ik-uhl/, *adjective* –**analytically**, *adverb*

☑ SPELLING TIP *Letter 'y' alert*: remember the *y* spelling in the last syllable (*yse*, not *ise*, because **analyse** is from **analysis**).

analysis /*say* uh-**nal**-uh-suhs/ *noun* (*plural* **analyses** /*say* uh-**nal**-uh-seez/)
1. the act of examining something in detail to find out more about it: *to make an analysis of someone's behaviour*; *an analysis of a novel.* **2.** separation into parts.

COMPARE definition 2 with **synthesis**.

☑ SPELLING TIP *Letter 'y' alert*: the middle vowel sound is spelt *y*. As with many words that have a *y* spelling, **analysis** comes from Greek.

Anangu /*say* uh-**nang**-gooh/ *noun* an Aboriginal person from Central Australia.
☐ **Anangu**, *adjective*: *Anangu traditions*.

WORD HISTORY from the Pitjantjatjara language of Central Australia

anarchy /*say* **an**-uh-kee/ *noun*
1. a society where there is no government or law. **2.** any situation where there is no control or rules: *There was anarchy in the classroom while the teacher was away.*
☐ **anarchist**, *noun*

☑ SPELLING TIP The spelling will be easier if you see that **anarchy** is made up of the prefix *an-* (meaning 'not' or 'lacking') and the suffix *-archy* which means 'rule' or 'government'. This suffix comes from Greek and is found in several other words relating to government, such as *monarchy*.

anatomy /*say* uh-**nat**-uh-mee/ *noun*
1. the structure of the body of a human, animal or plant: *The anatomy of a human is very similar to that of an ape.* 2. the study or science of the structure of humans, animals and plants.
☐ **anatomical** /*say* an-uh-**tom**-ik-uhl/, *adjective*

ancestor /*say* **an**-ses-tuh/ *noun* someone related to you who lived long ago: *My ancestors came to Australia with the First Fleet.*
☐ **ancestral**, *adjective* –**ancestry**, *noun*

NOTE The study of who your ancestors were is called **genealogy**.

☑ SPELLING TIP Remember that there is a *c* (not an *s*), at the start of the second syllable of **ancestor**. Also note that the ending is *or* (not *er*). Think *o* for old, because that is what **ancestors** are!

anchor /*rhymes with* banker/ *noun*
1. a heavy object chained to a boat and dropped into the water to stop the boat from floating away.
–*verb* 2. When you **anchor** a boat, you drop the anchor into the water. 3. When you **anchor** an object, you stop it from moving: *We anchored the cloth with several heavy bowls to stop the wind catching it.*
☐ **anchorage**, *noun*

☑ SPELLING TIP Remember that **anchor** is spelt with *ch* (for the 'k' sound). Think of other words that you know that are like this, such as *chorus* and *Christmas*. Also note that the ending is *or*.

anchovy /*say* **an**-chuh-vee, an-**choh**-vee/ *noun* (*plural* **anchovies**) a small fish with a very salty taste.

ancient /*say* **ayn**-shuhnt/ *adjective*
1. happening or existing a long time ago: *The people of ancient Egypt worshipped many gods*; *The ancient Romans built very good roads.* 2. *Old-fashioned or humorous* If someone is **ancient**, they are very old: *The poem was about an ancient sea captain*; *I feel ancient!*

and *conjunction* 1. with: *pens and pencils.* 2. as a result: *Practise harder and your piano playing will improve.* 3. afterwards: *Go to the movie and come straight home.* 4. as well as: *nice and warm.*

NOTE This word is used for connecting words, phrases or clauses.

andante /*say* an-**dan**-tay/ *adverb* played or sung fairly slowly and evenly.

NOTE This is used as an instruction in music. Like most musical instructions, it comes from an Italian word (meaning 'walking').

anecdote /*say* **an**-uhk-doht/ *noun* a short story that tells about a funny or interesting person or event: *She kept us entertained with anecdotes about her family.*
☐ **anecdotal**, *adjective*

anemone /*say* uh-**nem**-uh-nee/ *noun*
1. a small flower, usually red, blue or white. 2. an animal that lives in the sea and catches food with its tentacles.

ANOTHER NAME (for definition 2) is **sea anemone**.

☑ SPELLING TIP The trickiest parts in this word are the *o* spelling for the 'uh' sound and the last syllable which is a simple *e* (although the sound is 'ee'). It has this ending because it comes from Greek (where it means 'windflower'). Rap it out as *a* + *nem* + *on* + *e*.

angel /*say* **ayn**-juhl/ *noun*
1. in Judaism, Christianity and Islam, one of God's messengers, usually pictured to look like a human with wings. 2. someone who is very kind, good or beautiful: *You are an angel to help me with the shopping.*
☐ **angelic** /*say* an-**jel**-ik/, *adjective*

☑ SPELLING TIP Don't confuse the spelling of **angel** with **angle** which looks similar. An **angle** is the pointed shape made when two lines meet.

anger *noun*
1. a strong feeling of displeasure or annoyance caused by thinking that something wrong has been done to you.
–*verb* 2. If you **anger** someone, you make them feel cross and upset: *The unions were angered that they had not been consulted.*

SIMILAR WORDS (for definition 1) are **fury**, **rage** and **wrath**. Note that **wrath** is more formal and less commonly used than **anger** – it has become rather old-fashioned. **Fury** and **rage** both refer to a very strong feeling of anger.

angle[1] *noun*
1. the pointed shape made when two straight lines or surfaces meet each other: *A road goes off to the left at a very sharp angle.* 2. point of view: *What is your angle on the problem?*
–*verb* 3. If you **angle** something in a particular direction, you move it so it faces or points in that direction: *Can you angle the light so it shines on the painting?*
–*phrase* 4. **at an angle**, sloping or not at a right angle to: *Straighten the picture because it's at an angle.*

☑ SPELLING TIP Don't confuse the spelling of **angle** with **angel** which looks similar. An **angel** is a messenger of God.

angle[2] *verb* To **angle** is to fish with a hook and line.
☐ **angler**, *noun*

☑ SPELLING TIP See **angle**[1].

angophora /*say* ang-**gof**-uh-ruh/ *noun* an Australian tree related to the eucalypt, with gnarled pinkish branches and creamy-white flowers.

angry *adjective* (**angrier**, **angriest**) To be **angry** is to feel or show anger: *an angry young man*; *an angry expression.*
☐ **angrily**, *adverb*

SIMILAR WORDS are **cross**, **annoyed**, **furious**, **incensed** and **irate**. Note that **furious**, **incensed** and **irate** all refer to a feeling of very strong anger, while **cross** and **annoyed** suggest a less strong feeling.

anguish /*say* **ang**-gwish/ *noun* very great pain, sorrow or worry: *The anguish of losing his family never went away.*
☐ **anguished**, *adjective*: *anguished cries*; *an anguished expression.*

angular *adjective* having a pointed or sharp shape like an angle: *Her sharp, angular features had softened as she aged.*
☐ **angularity**, *noun*

animal *noun*
1. a living thing that is not a plant and can feel and move about. **2.** any animal except a human being: *I like seeing the animals at the zoo.* **3.** someone who is rough and badly-behaved.

animate *verb* /*say* **an**-uh-mayt/
1. To **animate** someone or something is to make them lively and energetic: *Looking after her dogs was the only thing that seemed to animate her.* **2.** If you **animate** something, you make it move as if alive: *to animate puppets.*
–*adjective* /*say* **an**-uh-muht/ **3.** alive: *animate creatures.*
☐ **animated**, *adjective* –**animation**, *noun*

animosity *noun* a strong feeling of dislike or unfriendliness: *There was continuing animosity between the two families.*

aniseed *noun* a strong-smelling seed which is used in cooking and medicines.

ankle *noun* the part of the body which joins the foot to the leg.

anklet *noun* an ornament worn around the ankle.

annals /*say* **an**-uhlz/ *plural noun* historical records that are kept year by year.
☐ **annalist**, *noun*

annex *verb* /*say* **an**-eks, uh-**neks**/
1. To **annex** something is to join it to what is already owned: *The club annexed the neighbouring land for a sportsground.* **2.** If a country **annexes** a region, it invades and takes possession of that area.
–*noun* /*say* **an**-eks/ **3.** a new building joined to an existing one.
☐ **annexation**, *noun*

ANOTHER SPELLING (for definition 3) is **annexe**.

annihilate /*say* uh-**nuy**-uh-layt/ *verb* To **annihilate** something is to destroy or defeat it completely: *Bombs annihilated the enemy base.*
☐ **annihilation**, *noun*

☑ SPELLING TIP *Double letter alert*: two *n*'s. Also remember the *h* between the two *i*'s, which you don't hear when you say the word. It may be easier to remember this if you see that the stem of **annihilate** is *nihil* (the Latin word for 'nothing'). The prefix *an-* has been added, giving the double *n*, and also the suffix *-ate*. Rap it out as *an+ni+hil+ate*.

anniversary *noun* (*plural* **anniversaries**) a yearly celebration of something which took place in an earlier year: *It was the anniversary of the first time they had gone out together.*

announce *verb* If you **announce** something, you tell it or make it known in public: *We will announce the winner on Friday.*
☐ **announcement**, *noun* –**announcer**, *noun*

annoy *verb* If you **annoy** someone, you anger them or make them bad-tempered: *His constant complaining annoys me.*
☐ **annoyance**, *noun* –**annoying**, *adjective*

A SIMILAR WORD is **irritate**.

annual *adjective*
1. happening once a year: *It was the annual surfing competition.*
–*noun* **2.** a plant that lives for only one season or year.
☐ **annually**, *adverb*

COMPARE definition 2 with **perennial** (definition 3).

anoint *verb* If you **anoint** someone, you put ointment or oil on them: *In ancient Egypt they anointed the dead bodies with oils.*
☐ **anointment**, *noun*

☑ SPELLING TIP *Single letter alert*: only one *n*.

anonymous /*say* uh-**non**-uh-muhs/ *adjective* An **anonymous** person does not allow their name to be revealed publicly: *The club received some money from an anonymous supporter.*
☐ **anonymity** /*say* an-uh-**nim**-uh-tee/, *noun*

THE SHORT FORM of this is **anon**.

☑ SPELLING TIP *Letter 'y' alert*: the vowel sound in the middle is spelt *y*. This forms part of the stem of the word, *onym* which comes from the Greek word for 'name' or 'word'. The prefix *an-* (meaning 'without') and the adjective suffix *-ous* have been added. You may know other words relating to words or names which include *onym* such as *synonym* which is a word with the same meaning as another word.

anorexia /*say* an-uh-**rek**-see-uh/ *noun*
1. an extreme loss of appetite for food. 2. an illness in which the person has an obsessive desire to lose weight by refusing to eat.
□ **anorexic**, *adjective*

NOTE Definition 2 is a short way of saying **anorexia nervosa**.

another *adjective*
1. second or additional: *another piece of fruit.* 2. different: *another day*; *another book.*
–*pronoun* 3. one more: *Please take another.*

answer *noun*
1. a reply or response: *I will give you an answer in the morning.* 2. a solution to a problem.
–*verb* 3. If you **answer**, you say or do something as a reaction to a question: *If you can't answer the question, you haven't done your homework!*; *He answered with a nod of his head.* 4. If you **answer** a signal, such as a telephone ring, you respond to it: *I heard a knock on the door. Could you please go and answer it.*
–*phrase* 5. **answer back**, to speak rudely or cheekily to someone as a reaction to something they have said to you.

answerable *adjective* responsible: *answerable to one's superiors*; *answerable for watering the garden.*

ant *noun* a small insect that usually lives in a large family group or community called a colony.

antagonise /*say* an-**tag**-uh-nuyz/ *verb* If you **antagonise** someone, you make them dislike you or feel angry towards you: *Don't antagonise him – if we lose his support we won't have enough people on our team.*
□ **antagonistic**, *adjective* –**antagonism**, *noun* –**antagonist**, *noun*

ANOTHER SPELLING is **antagonize**.

antarctic /*say* an-**tahk**-tik/ *adjective*
1. having to do with the area near the South Pole.
–*noun* 2. **the Antarctic**, the area near the South Pole.

ANOTHER NAME (for definition 2) is **Antarctica**.
COMPARE this with **arctic**.
WORD HISTORY from a Greek word meaning 'opposite the north'

ante- *prefix* a word part meaning 'before in space or time', as in *antedate*.

WORD HISTORY this prefix comes from Latin

anteater *noun* an animal with a long, sticky tongue that feeds on ants.

NOTE Different varieties found in Australia are called **echidnas** or **numbats**.

antecedent /*say* an-tuh-**see**-dnt/ *noun* anything that goes before another.

☑ SPELLING TIP The spelling of this word will be easier if you remember that it begins with the prefix *ante*, meaning 'before' (not the prefix *anti-*, meaning 'against'). Also remember the *c* spelling for the 's' sound. The last part of the word comes from *cedere*, the Latin word meaning 'to go'.

antelope *noun* a slight, fast animal with horns, related to cattle, sheep and goats.

antenna /*say* an-**ten**-uh/ *noun* (*plural* **antennae** /*say* an-**ten**-ee/ *for definition 1*, **antennas** *for definition 2*)
1. a feeler found on the head of some animals.
2. a wire or rod that you put up to receive radio or television signals.

ANOTHER WORD (for definition 2) is **aerial**.

anthem *noun*
1. a ceremonial song for a country or organisation: *It was good hearing all of the national anthems at the Olympic Games.* 2. a hymn.

anthology *noun* (*plural* **anthologies**) a collection of poems, plays, short stories or songs, each by a different author or songwriter.
□ **anthologist**, *noun*

WORD HISTORY from a Greek word meaning 'a gathering of flowers'

anthropogenic *adjective* caused by human beings: *anthropogenic climate change.*

anthropology *noun* the systematic study of the beginnings and growth of humankind.
□ **anthropologist**, *noun*

anti- *prefix* a word part meaning 1. against, as in *antiseptic*. 2. opposed to, as in *anticlockwise*.

WORD HISTORY this prefix comes from Greek

antibiotic *noun* a drug able to kill bacteria.
□ **antibiotic**, *adjective*

anticipate *verb*
1. If you **anticipate** something, you expect it to happen or you think that it could happen: *We anticipate that progress will continue at the current rate.* 2. If you **anticipate** something, you see that it is about to happen and you act accordingly, often to stop it from happening: *We anticipated the storm and made sure we had our raincoats.* 3. If you **anticipate** something pleasant or exciting is going to happen, you look forward to it: *I can't wait for the holidays. I'm anticipating a good time.*
□ **anticipation**, *noun*

anticlimax *noun* a disappointing ending or outcome.
□ **anticlimactic**, *adjective*

anticlockwise *adjective* going around in the opposite direction to the way the hands of a clock move: *To unscrew the lid of the jar, turn it anticlockwise.*

THE OPPOSITE is **clockwise**.

antics *plural noun* odd or silly behaviour.

antidote *noun* something to stop the bad effects caused by a disease or a poison: *We are lucky that there is an antidote for a funnel-web spider bite.*

antipathy /*say* an-**tip**-uh-thee/ *noun* a feeling of strong dislike: *She had developed a strong antipathy to loud music.*
□ **antipathetic** /*say* an-tee-puh-**thet**-ik/, *adjective*

antipodes /*say* an-**tip**-uh-deez/ *plural noun* **1.** places directly opposite each other on the earth, such as the North Pole and the South Pole. **2. the Antipodes**, Australia as the antipodes of Britain.
□ **antipodean** /*say* an-tip-uh-**dee**-uhn/, *adjective*

antiquary /*say* **an**-tuh-kwuh-ree/ *noun* an expert on ancient things.
□ **antiquarian**, *adjective*

antiquated /*say* **an**-tuh-kway-tuhd/ *adjective* old-fashioned or out of date: *an antiquated washing machine.*

antique /*say* an-**teek**/ *noun* an object which was made a long time ago: *His collection of antiques had some pieces from the seventeenth century.*
□ **antique**, *adjective*

WORD HISTORY from a Latin word meaning 'old'

☑ SPELLING TIP Remember that the ending of **antique** is spelt *ique* (although it sounds like 'eek'). It might help if you think of some other words that have the same spelling for this sound, such as *technique* and *unique*.

antiquity /*say* an-**tik**-wuh-tee/ *noun* (*plural* **antiquities**)
1. ancient times or the early stages of history. **2.** great age: *paintings of great antiquity.*

antiseptic *noun* a chemical used to kill germs that produce disease.
□ **antiseptic**, *adjective*

anti-terrorism *noun* See **counterterrorism**.

antithesis /*say* an-**tith**-uh-suhs/ *noun* (*plural* **antitheses** /*say* an-**tith**-uh-seez/)
1. the direct opposite: *Her confident manner was the antithesis of her brother's shyness.* **2.** a contrast between two opposites: *the antithesis between rigidity and flexibility.*

☑ SPELLING TIP It is best to break this word into its two parts – *anti-* (a prefix meaning 'against') and *thesis* (an idea, argument or explanation). Although the pronunciation does not match this division into two parts, it will be easier to learn the spelling this way.

antivenene /*say* an-tee-vuh-**neen**/ *noun* an injection to fight the venom from a spider or snake bite.

ANOTHER SPELLING for this is **antivenin**.
ANOTHER WORD for this is **antivenom**.

antler *noun* a long, hard, branch-like horn on the head of a male deer and other similar animals.

antonym /*say* **ant**-uh-nim/ *noun* a word which has an opposite meaning to another word: *'Hot' is the antonym of 'cold'.*

THE OPPOSITE is **synonym**.
SEE the Grammar and Punctuation Guide appendix.

anus /*say* **ay**-nuhs/ *noun* the opening in the body where waste material from the bowel comes out.

anvil *noun* a heavy iron block with a smooth surface on which hot metals are hammered and shaped before they go cold and hard.

anxiety /*say* ang-**zuy**-uh-tee/ *noun* (*plural* **anxieties**)
1. feelings of worry or fear: *I had a feeling of anxiety before my music exam.* **2.** eagerness: *Her anxiety to help can sometimes be overwhelming.*

☑ SPELLING TIP The most difficult bit in spelling this word is remembering the *x*. Try thinking that if you are feeling **anxiety**, it can make you act as if you are cross – and there is a cross in the form of an *x* in the word.

anxious /*say* **ang**-shuhs/ *adjective*
1. nervous or worried that something bad might happen: *She was very anxious about her sick friend.* **2.** very eager: *She was most anxious to please her father.*
□ **anxiously**, *adverb* –**anxiousness**, *noun*

SIMILAR WORDS (for definition 1) are **nervous**, **worried**, **concerned**, **troubled** and **uneasy**.

☑ SPELLING TIP The spelling of this word will be easier if you see that it has been formed from *anxiety* with the noun ending changed to the adjective prefix *-ious* (a form of *-ous*, meaning 'full of').

any *adjective*
1. one or some: *Have you had any breakfast?*
–*pronoun* **2.** any person or thing: *He is more responsible than any before him.*
–*adverb* **3.** at all: *Do you feel any better?*

anyhow *adverb*
1. in any case: *We cancelled the picnic because Mum was sick, but it's going to rain anyhow.* **2.** in a careless way: *He threw down his clothes anyhow.*

anyone *pronoun* any person.

ANOTHER WORD for this is **anybody**.

anything *pronoun* any thing whatever.

anyway *adverb* in any case: *I know that no-one will see it, but I will tidy up anyway.*

anywhere *adverb* in, at or to any place: *I don't want to go anywhere at all.*

Anzac *noun*
1. a member of the Australian and New Zealand Army Corps during World War I: *There are no Anzacs still alive.* **2.** any soldier from Australia or New Zealand.

WORD HISTORY an acronym made by joining the first letters of the words *Australian (and) New Zealand Army Corps*

aorta /*say* ay-**aw**-tuh/ *noun* the main artery carrying blood from the left side of the heart to nearly all parts of the body.

apart *adverb*
1. to pieces: *My mobile phone fell apart.* **2.** separated or not together: *They were kept apart because of the mischief they created together.* –*phrase* **3. apart from**, aside from or leaving out: *Apart from my parents, I love you the best.*

apartheid /*say* uh-**pah**-tuyd, uh-**pah**-tayt/ *noun* a political system based on the separation of races according to their differences in colour: *Under apartheid, black and white children went to different schools.*

☑ SPELLING TIP *Silent letter alert*: don't forget the silent *h* after the *t*. Also remember the unusual spelling *heid* for the last part of the word. This spelling is because the word comes from Afrikaans, the language spoken in South Africa where **apartheid** used to be in practice. It might make it easier if you can see that it is made up of *apart* and a suffix *-heid* which has a meaning like *-hood* in English (in words such as *childhood*).

apartment *noun* a single room or set of rooms, among others in a building, which people live in.

OTHER WORDS for this are **flat** and **unit**. See the note at **flat**[2].

apathy /*say* **ap**-uh-thee/ *noun* no feeling for, or interest in things other people find interesting or exciting: *James's apathy in class was worrying his teacher.*
☐ **apathetic** /*say* ap-uh-**thet**-ik/, *adjective*

ape *noun*
1. a large monkey without a tail.
–*verb* **2.** To **ape** someone is to copy them.
☐ **apelike**, *adjective* –**apish**, *adjective*

aperture /*say* **ap**-uh-chuh/ *noun* a hole, crack or other opening, especially the opening in a camera that limits the amount of light it lets in.

apex /*say* **ay**-peks/ *noun* (*plural* **apexes** *or* **apices** /*say* **ay**-puh-seez/) the top of something, or its highest point: *At the apex of the tree was a little silver star.*

aphid /*say* **ay**-fuhd/ *noun* a small insect which sucks the juice from plants.

ANOTHER FORM is **aphis** (*plural* **aphides** /*say* **ay**-fuh-deez/).

☑ SPELLING TIP The first part of **aphid** is the tricky bit. Remember that the opening vowel sound is spelt by the letter *a* alone (although it sounds like 'ay') and that the next sound is spelt *ph*, as in many other words that have this spelling for a 'f' sound.

apiary *noun* (*plural* **apiaries**) a place where bees and their hives are kept.
☐ **apiarist**, *noun*

aplomb /*say* uh-**plom**/ *noun* the ability to handle difficult or unusual situations: *Our school captain introduced the guest speaker with aplomb.*

☑ SPELLING TIP *Silent letter alert*: don't forget the silent *b* at the end.

apocalypse /*say* uh-**pok**-uh-lips/ *noun* a great and terrifying event, such as the end of the world.
☐ **apocalyptic**, *adjective*

☑ SPELLING TIP *Letter 'y' alert*: the vowel sound in the last syllable is spelt *y*. Like many words with a *y* spelling, **apocalypse** comes from Greek.

apologise /*say* uh-**pol**-uh-juyz/ *verb* If you **apologise** to someone, you say you are sorry for upsetting them, or causing them some trouble or difficulty: *She apologised for standing on my foot.*
☐ **apology**, *noun* (*plural* **apologies**) –**apologetic**, *adjective*

ANOTHER SPELLING is **apologize**.

apostle /*say* uh-**pos**-uhl/ *noun*
1. one of the followers of Christ chosen by him to spread his teachings. **2.** someone who strongly supports a new idea: *She saw herself as an apostle of women's rights.*
☐ **apostolic** /*say* ap-uh-**stol**-ik/, *adjective* having to do with an apostle.

ANOTHER FORM Definition 1 is often spelt with a capital letter.
WORD HISTORY from a Greek word meaning 'someone sent away'

☑ SPELLING TIP *Silent letter alert*: don't forget the *st* (not double *s*) spelling. The *t* is silent.

apostrophe /*say* uh-**pos**-truh-fee/ *noun*
1. a sign (') used to show a letter has been left out, as in *They're here*. **2.** a sign (') used with *s* to show something is owned, as in *Tom's hat* and *the lions' manes*.

NOTE **Apostrophes** are punctuation marks. See the Grammar and Punctuation Guide appendix.

app *noun* a digital product which can be downloaded onto a smart phone, tablet, etc.: *Mum has an app which tells her what the traffic is like in different parts of the city.*

appal /*say* uh-**pawl**/ *verb* (**appals**, **appalling**, **appalled**, **has appalled**) If something **appals** you, it fills you with fear and shock: *The farmers were appalled by the prospect of yet another year of drought.*
☐ **appalled**, *adjective* –**appalling**, *adjective* shocking and unpleasant.

WORD HISTORY from a French word meaning 'make pale'

☑ SPELLING TIP *Double/single letter alert*: a double *p* in the middle and only one *l* at the end. Some people now accept the spelling with a double *l* at the end, which is used in American English, but it is best to learn the single *l* spelling. Also remember that the second vowel sound is spelt by an *a* alone (although it sounds like 'aw').

apparatus /*say* ap-uh-**rah**-tuhs, ap-uh-**ray**-tuhs/ *noun* a collection of tools or machines used for a particular purpose: *The science lab was filled with the apparatus for the experiment.*

A SIMILAR WORD is **equipment**.

☑ SPELLING TIP *Double letter alert*: double *p* but all the other letters are single. **Apparatus** ends with *us* because it comes straight from Latin where it means 'made ready'.

apparel *noun* your outer clothing: *That shop has a nice range of winter apparel.*

☑ SPELLING TIP *Double/single letter alert*: two *p*'s but only one *r* and only one *l*. Rap it out as *ap+pa+rel*.

apparent *adjective* If something is **apparent 1.** it is able to be seen or understood: *It was apparent that she was late.* **2.** it seems to be real, but you cannot be certain that it is: *Her apparent shyness disappeared once she felt comfortable with us.*
☐ **apparently**, *adverb*

apparition *noun* a ghostly appearance: *a scary apparition.*

SIMILAR WORDS are **ghost**, **phantom**, **spectre** and **spook**.

appeal *noun*
1. a call or request for something needed: *They put out an appeal for donations over the radio.* **2.** the ability to attract or interest: *Knitting socks has limited appeal for most people.*
–*verb* **3.** If you **appeal** for something, you make a call or request for it: *The boy appealed for his stolen bag to be returned to him*; *to appeal for fair play.* **4.** If something **appeals** to you, you find it attractive in some way: *Her honesty appealed to him*; *The thought of a long holiday really appeals to me.*

appear *verb*
1. If someone or something **appears**, they come into view so that they can be seen: *A car appeared over the hill.* **2.** If someone or something **appears** to have a particular quality or to be in a certain condition, they seem that way to you: *He appears happy to me.* **3.** When someone **appears** in a show or film, they take part in it: *She appears in the movie, but only at the end.*
☐ **appearance**, *noun*

appease *verb*
1. If you **appease** someone, you make them peaceful, quiet or happy: *He appeased the angry crowd.* **2.** To **appease** is to satisfy: *to appease your thirst.*
☐ **appeasement**, *noun* –**appeasing**, *adjective*

A SIMILAR WORD (for definition 1) is **placate**.

appendicitis /*say* uh-pen-duh-**suy**-tuhs/ *noun* an illness in which the appendix becomes infected and painful. You often need an operation to remove the appendix.

☑ SPELLING TIP The spelling of **appendicitis** will be easier if you see that it is made up of *appendix* (with the final *x* changed to a *c* which has an 's' sound) and the suffix *-itis* (meaning 'inflamed condition'). Think of a similar word such as *tonsillitis*. They both end with *-itis* (spelt with *is*, not *us*, at the end).

appendix /*say* uh-**pen**-diks/ *noun* (*plural* **appendixes** *or* **appendices** /*say* uh-**pen**-duh-seez/)
1. an extra part added to the main part of a book to give further information. **2.** a small tube-like piece of flesh joined to the bowel in the right side of the abdomen.

appetising *adjective* looking or smelling good to eat: *the appetising smell of a ripe peach.*
☐ **appetiser**, *noun* food or drink that makes you feel like eating more.

ANOTHER SPELLING is **appetizing**.

appetite /*say* **ap**-uh-tuyt/ *noun* the desire for food or drink: *Your appetite is always good when you go hiking in the bush.*

☑ SPELLING TIP *Double/single letter alert*: double *p* but a single *t* both times *t* appears. Also remember that the 'uh' sound in the middle is spelt *e*.

applaud /*say* uh-**plawd**/ *verb* To **applaud** is to express approval, especially by clapping your hands or calling out: *The crowd applauded her enthusiastically as she ran to the finish line.*
☐ **applause**, *noun*

apple *noun* a crisp, round fruit with thin red or green skin.

applet *noun* a small computer program which can be transferred over the internet and which runs on a person's own computer rather than the server.

appliance *noun* a tool which has a motor worked by electricity: *The best appliance in the kitchen is the dishwasher.*

applicable /*say* uh-**plik**-uh-buhl/ *adjective* suitable or able to be used: *The course is especially applicable to people interested in astronomy.*
☐ **applicability**, *noun* –**applicably**, *adverb*

applicant *noun* someone who applies for something: *She won the job ahead of ten other applicants.*

A SIMILAR WORD is **candidate.**

application *noun*
1. a request: *to make an application to build a garage.* **2.** something put or laid on: *an application of polish.* **3.** in computers, a program which is written to perform a specific task.

apply /*rhymes with* fly/ *verb* (**applies**, **applying**, **applied**, **has applied**)
1. If you **apply** a particular rule or piece of knowledge, you put it into use in a particular situation: *This maths is easy. Just apply the rule that the angles of a triangle add up to 180 degrees.* **2.** If you **apply** to have something or to do something, you fill in a form or write a formal letter saying that you would like to be considered for it: *He applied for ten jobs.* **3.** If you **apply** something to a surface, you put it onto the surface or rub it in: *She had to apply the ointment three times a day.* **4.** If you **apply** yourself or your mind to a certain job, you give all your attention to it: *He finds it hard to apply himself to his studies.*

appoint *verb* If you **appoint** someone to a job or position or for a special purpose, you choose them for it and offer it to them: *The education department has appointed a new principal for our school.*

appointment *noun*
1. the arrangement of a special time: *Mum made an appointment with the dentist.* **2.** the placing of someone in a special position: *Dad was pleased with his appointment to the position of manager.* **3.** the job or special position to which someone is appointed: *She has a teaching appointment in a country town.*

appraise *verb* If you **appraise** someone or something, you make a judgement about their value or character: *I sensed her appraising my appearance – looking me up and down very carefully.*
☐ **appraisal**, *noun*

appreciable /*say* uh-**preesh**-uh-buhl/ *adjective*
1. able to be seen or noticed: *There has been an appreciable increase in train passengers – it is harder to get a seat now.* **2.** fairly large: *He makes appreciable contributions to various charities.*
☐ **appreciably**, *adverb*

A SIMILAR WORD (for definition 1) is **noticeable.**

☑ SPELLING TIP If you see that **appreciable** has been formed from the more familiar word *appreciate*, it will be easier to remember the *c* spelling for the 'sh' sound, and that there is a silent *i* following the *c*.

appreciate /*say* uh-**pree**-shee-ayt, uh-**pree**-see-ayt/ *verb*
1. If you **appreciate** something, you think highly of it: *She appreciated his concern for her situation.* **2.** If something **appreciates**, it increases in value: *This painting will continue to appreciate over the years.*
☐ **appreciation**, *noun*

☑ SPELLING TIP *Tricky vowel sound*: a single *e* to spell the 'ee' sound. Also remember the *c* spelling for the 'sh' or 's' sound.

apprehend *verb* If a police officer **apprehends** someone, they catch or arrest them.

apprehension *noun* fear that something might happen: *I opened the envelope with apprehension.*
☐ **apprehensive**, *adjective*

apprentice *noun* someone who is learning a trade.
☐ **apprenticeship**, *noun*

approach *verb*
1. If someone or something **approaches**, they come closer or nearer: *At last we were approaching the township*; *The time is approaching when we will have to say goodbye.* **2.** If you **approach** someone about a request or an idea, you speak to them about it for the first time: *I'm going to approach him about buying his bike.*
☐ **approach**, *noun*

approachable *adjective* friendly and easy to talk to: *Because our netball coach is so approachable, we all enjoy training.*

appropriate /*say* uh-**proh**-pree-uht/ *adjective* If something is **appropriate**, it is suitable for a particular purpose: *A swimming costume is appropriate to wear at the beach.*

☑ SPELLING TIP *Double/single letter alert*: the first time *p* appears it is a double letter, the next time single. Note also that the final sound is spelt *ate* (though it sounds like 'uht').

approval *noun* agreement or permission: *I'll have to get approval to leave early to catch the train.*

approve *verb*
1. If someone officially **approves** a plan, they agree to it and say that it can happen or be put into effect: *The council approved the plans for the new library.*
–*phrase* **2. approve of**, **a.** to consider good or satisfactory: *I wasn't sure if my parents would approve of my going to the party.* **b.** If you **approve of** a person or a thing, you accept and like

them: *My parents approve of my new friends.*
☐ **approving**, *adjective*

approximate *adjective* fairly accurate but not completely exact: *The approximate time of arrival is 11 a.m.; the approximate value.*
☐ **approximately**, *adverb* –**approximation**, *noun*

apricot *noun* a small, round, orange-yellow fruit with soft juicy flesh and one large seed inside.

April *noun* the fourth month of the year, with 30 days.

THE ABBREVIATION is **Ap.** or **Apr.**

apron *noun* a piece of clothing worn in front to protect the clothes underneath it.

WORD HISTORY from a Latin word meaning 'napkin' or 'cloth'

apt *adjective*
1. likely or inclined: *People with fair skin are apt to get sunburnt.* **2.** suitable or appropriate: *The park was an apt choice for the party – there was much more room.*

aptitude *noun* the ability to learn quickly: *My mother has an aptitude for languages and has no trouble learning new ones.*

A SIMILAR WORD is **talent**.

aqualung *noun* a cylinder of air strapped to the back of a diver, with a tube that takes air to the mouth or nose.

A SIMILAR WORD is **scuba**.

aquamarine *noun* a greenish-blue stone used in jewellery.

WORD HISTORY from Latin words meaning 'sea water'

aquarium /*say* uh-**kwair**-ree-uhm/ *noun* (*plural* **aquariums** *or* **aquaria**) a glass container in which fish and water plants are kept.

aquatic /*say* uh-**kwot**-ik/ *adjective*
1. living or growing in water: *aquatic plants.* **2.** done in or on water: *He is good at all aquatic sports.*

☑ SPELLING TIP *Tricky vowel sound*: an *a* spelling for the 'o' sound in the middle. This will be easier to remember if you see that **aquatic** comes from *aqua*, the Latin word for 'water'.

aqueduct /*say* **ak**-wuh-dukt/ *noun* an artificial channel for carrying water in which the water usually flows by gravity.

☑ SPELLING TIP *Tricky 'uh' sound*: an *e* spelling for the middle vowel sound. The spelling of **aqueduct** will be easier if you see that it is made up of *aqua* (the Latin word for 'water'), with its final *a* changed to an *e*, and *duct* (something for carrying a liquid). You have *ducts* in your eyes which do just that – carry water in the form of tears.

aquiline /*say* **ak**-wuh-luyn/ *adjective* If a nose is **aquiline**, it is curved like the beak of an eagle.

☑ SPELLING TIP *Tricky 'uh' sound*: an *i* spelling for the middle vowel sound. As you can see from the meaning, this word is not related to the others that come from *aqua*, the Latin word for 'water'. **Aquiline** comes from *aquila*, the Latin word for 'eagle'.

arable *adjective* suitable for growing crops: *Only half of the property was arable – the rest was thick bush.*

WORD HISTORY from a Latin word meaning 'that can be ploughed'

☑ SPELLING TIP *Single letter alert*: only one *r*.

arachnid /*say* uh-**rak**-nid/ *noun* a spider, scorpion, mite, etc.

arbitrary /*say* **ah**-buh-truh-ree, **ah**-buh-tree/ *adjective* If someone does something in an **arbitrary** way, their action is not based on reason or a system but on how they feel at the time: *The team thought that the umpire's decisions were quite arbitrary so they were not happy.*
☐ **arbitrarily**, *adverb*

arbitration *noun* the settling of a disagreement by someone chosen to find a solution.
☐ **arbitrate**, *verb*

arboreal /*say* ah-**baw**-ree-uhl/ *adjective* having to do with, or living in trees: *Koalas are arboreal animals.*

arbour *noun* a shady place formed by trees and shrubs.

ANOTHER SPELLING is **arbor**.

arc *noun*
1. a curved line.
–*verb* **2.** To **arc** is to form a smooth curved line: *The beach arcs south to the headland.*
☐ **arced** /*say* ahkt/, *adjective*

WORD HISTORY from a Latin word meaning a 'bow'.

☑ SPELLING TIP Don't confuse the spelling of **arc** with **ark** which sounds the same. An **ark** is a large, covered boat.

arcade *noun*
1. in architecture, **a.** a series of arches supported on columns. **b.** a part of a building with an arched roof. **2.** a covered passage with shops on either side.

arch *noun* (*plural* **arches**)
1. a curved structure such as one which helps support a bridge or building, or forms the top of a doorway.

–*verb* **2.** When something **arches**, it curves or makes a curved shape: *The cat arched its back*; *The rainbow arched across the horizon.*

archaeology /*say* ah-kee-**ol**-uh-jee/ *noun* the study of the people and customs of ancient times, made by digging up and describing remains that are found.
☐ **archaeologist**, *noun* –**archaeological**, *adjective*

ANOTHER SPELLING is **archeology**.

archaic /*say* ah-**kay**-ik/ *adjective* Something is **archaic** if it is old-fashioned and out of date: *My grandfather's clothes are really archaic.*
☐ **archaism**, *noun*

archangel /*say* **ahk**-ayn-juhl/ *noun* one of the chief angels.

archbishop *noun* a head bishop.

archenemy /*say* ahch-**en**-uh-mee/ *noun* (*plural* **archenemies**) someone's greatest enemy.

archer *noun* someone who shoots with a bow and arrows.
☐ **archery**, *noun*

archipelago /*say* ah-kuh-**pel**-uh-goh/ *noun* (*plural* **archipelagos** *or* **archipelagoes**)
1. a large body of water with many islands. **2.** a group of islands in a sea.

WORD HISTORY from an Italian word meaning the 'chief sea'

architect /*say* **ah**-kuh-tekt/ *noun* someone whose job is to plan and design new buildings and be certain that they are built correctly.

WORD HISTORY from a Greek word meaning the 'chief builder'

architecture *noun* the art or science of drawing up plans for buildings.
☐ **architectural**, *adjective*

archives /*say* **ah**-kuyvz/ *plural noun* a collection of historical documents about a family, business or country: *It's fascinating reading through the old archives.*
☐ **archival**, *adjective* –**archivist** /*say* **ah**-kuh-vuhst/, *noun*

arctic /*say* **ahk**-tik/ *adjective*
1. having to do with the area near the North Pole. **2.** very cold.
–*noun* **3. the Arctic**, the area near the North Pole.

COMPARE this with **antarctic**.
WORD HISTORY from a Greek word meaning 'of the bear' (constellation of stars) or 'northern'

ardent *adjective* enthusiastic or full of feeling: *He was an ardent lover of nature*; *Ardent words have to be followed up with actions!*
☐ **ardently**, *adverb*

arduous *adjective* needing a lot of hard work: *an arduous walk across the dunes.*

A SIMILAR WORD is **strenuous**.

are *verb* the first, second and third person plural present tense indicative of the verb **be**.

NOTE For an explanation of *indicative*, see **mood**[2]. See also the Grammar and Punctuation Guide appendix.

area *noun*
1. a particular part: *a suburban area*; *an area of study.* **2.** the size of a flat or curved surface: *The national park has an area of 9500 hectares.*

arena /*say* uh-**ree**-nuh/ *noun*
1. an enclosed space for sports events. **2.** any activity that involves competition: *the arena of politics.*

WORD HISTORY from a Latin word meaning 'sand' or 'sandy place'

aren't a short form of *are not*.

arguable *adjective*
1. able to be proved by argument: *There is certainly an arguable case for wearing a crash helmet.* **2.** doubtful: *The value of the project is arguable.*
☐ **arguably**, *adverb*

☑ SPELLING TIP **Arguable** has been formed from the verb **argue**. Although some words keep their *e* when the suffix *-able* is added, **argue** doesn't. So remember that there is no *e* after the *u* in **arguable**.

argue *verb* (**argues**, **arguing**, **argued**, **has argued**)
1. If you **argue** with someone about something, you say things, often in an angry way, which show that you disagree with them: *The two brothers would argue for hours over who had first go.* **2.** If you **argue** something, you provide clear reasons for or against it: *She argued that school should finish earlier in winter because of the shorter days.*

A SIMILAR WORD (for definition 1) is **quarrel**.

argument *noun*
1. a disagreement: *They had an argument over who was the better cook.* **2.** a reason: *a good argument for postponing the meeting.* **3.** a discussion in which reasons for and against something are stated.
☐ **argumentative**, *adjective*: *an argumentative old man.*

☑ SPELLING TIP *Exception to rule*: **argument** is formed from the verb **argue**. Words formed from **argue** do not follow the rule which says that words that end with *e* keep the *e* before a suffix starting with a consonant. So in **argument** the *e* from **argue** has been left out. There's no **argument** about that!

aria /*say* **ah**-ree-uh/ *noun* a song sung by one person in an opera.

arid *adjective* dry and hot: *Some animals have evolved to cope with arid conditions.*
☐ **aridity**, *noun*

arise *verb* (**arises**, **arising**, **arose**, **has arisen**)
1. If a situation or problem **arises**, it appears and comes to your attention: *Each time we look at the question, different problems arise*; *A strong wind arose each night at about 5 p.m.* **2.** If something **arises** out of a particular situation, it is created or caused by that situation: *Strong resentment arose in the people as a result of the food shortages.*

aristocracy /*say* a-ruh-**stok**-ruh-see/ *noun* in some societies, the people of highest rank.
☐ **aristocrat** /*say* **a**-ruh-stuh-krat, uh-**ris**-tuh-krat/, *noun* –**aristocratic**, *adjective*

A SIMILAR WORD is **nobility**.

arithmetic *noun* /*say* uh-**rith**-muh-tik/
1. calculation with numbers.
–*adjective* /*say* a-ruhth-**met**-ik/ **2.** having to do with arithmetic: *an arithmetic problem.*
☐ **arithmetically**, *adverb* –**arithmetician** /*say* a-ruhth-muh-**tish**-uhn/, *noun*

ark *noun* a large, covered boat, like the one built by Noah to escape from the Flood, as the story is told in the Bible.

☑ SPELLING TIP Don't confuse the spelling of **ark** with **arc** which sounds the same. An **arc** is a curved line.

arm[1] *noun*
1. the part of the body from shoulder to hand. **2.** the part of a chair on which your arm rests.

arm[2] *verb* To **arm** someone is to supply weapons to them.
☐ **armed**, *adjective*: *the armed forces.*

armada /*say* ah-**mah**-duh/ *noun* (*plural* **armadas**) a large number of warships.

armadillo /*say* ah-muh-**dil**-oh/ *noun* (*plural* **armadillos**) a South American burrowing animal with a covering of bony plates.

WORD HISTORY from a Spanish word meaning 'armed man'

armament *noun* the weapons on a military aircraft or ship.

armistice /*say* **ah**-muh-stuhs/ *noun* a temporary agreement between countries at war to stop fighting so they can talk about peace.

A SIMILAR WORD is **truce**.

☑ SPELLING TIP *Tricky 'uh' sounds*: the vowel sounds in the middle and last syllables are both spelt *i*. Also remember the *e* at the end.

armour *noun* metal or leather covering that soldiers and knights used to wear when fighting.
☐ **armoured**, *adjective*: *an armoured truck.* –**armoury**, *noun* (*plural* **armouries**) a place for storing weapons.

ANOTHER SPELLING is **armor**.

armpit *noun* the hollow part under the arm at the shoulder.

arms *plural noun* **1.** weapons: *All arms had to be surrendered.*
–*phrase* **2. take** (**up**) **arms**, to prepare to fight. **3. up in arms at**, angry: *We're up in arms at the way she refuses to talk to us.*

army *noun* (*plural* **armies**)
1. the part of a country's armed forces which is trained to fight on land. **2.** a large number: *An army of helpers prepared the hall for the show.*

COMPARE this with **air force** and **navy** (definition 1).

aroma /*say* uh-**roh**-muh/ *noun* a pleasant smell: *the aroma of freshly baked bread.*

A SIMILAR WORD is **fragrance**. However, this is used mostly of flowers and perfumes.
WORD HISTORY from a Greek word meaning 'spice' or 'sweet herb'

around *adverb*
1. in a circle on every side: *to gather around.* **2.** about or here and there: *to travel around.* **3.** with a circular movement: *the wheels go around.* –*preposition* **4.** surrounding: *a scarf around her head.* **5.** on the other side of: *a house around the corner.* **6.** approximately: *to meet around ten o'clock.*

arouse /*say* uh-**rowz**/ *verb*
1. If someone or something **arouses** your interest, they cause you to become interested in them: *My interest in poetry was aroused by the enthusiasm of my teacher.* **2.** When someone or something **arouses** you from sleep, they wake you up: *I was aroused from a deep sleep by someone banging loudly on my bedroom window.*
☐ **arousal**, *noun*

ANOTHER WORD (for definition 2) is **rouse**[1].

arpeggio /*say* ah-**pej**-ee-oh/ *noun* (*plural* **arpeggios**) a musical chord played by sounding its notes one after the other.

WORD HISTORY from an Italian word meaning 'play on the harp'

arrange *verb*
1. If you **arrange** something, you make plans for it to happen. **2.** If you **arrange** something with

someone, you make plans with them: *I arranged to meet her at the cinema.* **3.** If you **arrange** flowers or books, etc., you make them look attractive or tidy.
☐ **arrangement**, *noun*

A SIMILAR WORD is **organise.**

array *noun*
1. a group of things on show: *an excellent array of children's art.*
–*verb* **2.** To **array** things is to arrange them where they can be seen: *The trophies were arrayed on the shelf.*

arrest *verb*
1. To **arrest** someone is to take them prisoner: *He was arrested by the police.* **2.** If you **arrest** something, you stop it: *The doctor arrested the flow of blood.*
–*noun* **3.** capture by police: *The policewoman placed him under arrest.*

arrive *verb*
1. If you **arrive** somewhere, you reach the place that you are going to: *He arrived at the hotel rather late.* **2.** To **arrive** is to come: *Your card arrived yesterday.* **3.** If you **arrive** at a certain decision, you reach it, usually after some thought: *It took the jury eight hours to arrive at their decision.*
☐ **arrival**, *noun*

WORD HISTORY from a Latin word meaning 'come to shore'

arrogant /*say* **a**-ruh-guhnt/ *adjective* acting in a proud, rude and unfriendly way because you think you are more important than others: *His arrogant behaviour turned everyone against him.*
☐ **arrogance**, *noun* –**arrogantly**, *adverb*

A SIMILAR WORD is **haughty.**

arrow *noun*
1. a thin, pointed piece of wood shot from a bow.
2. a sign used to point the way to go.

arrowroot *noun* a white, floury substance used in cooking.

arsenal *noun* a store of weapons and ammunition and often the building they are kept in.

arsenic *noun* a poisonous chemical substance.

arson *noun* the deliberate burning of a building or other valuable property.
☐ **arsonist**, *noun*

art *noun*
1. the expression, especially by painting, drawing or sculpture, of an idea, feeling, etc.: *the art of ancient Egypt.* **2.** such things that people make: *works of art.* **3.** a skill: *the art of public speaking; the performing arts.*

artefact /*say* **ah**-tuh-fakt/ *noun* a useful thing made by someone, such as a tool, cooking item, etc.: *We can find out a lot about ancient societies by studying the artefacts they left behind.*

ANOTHER SPELLING is **artifact.**

artery /*say* **ah**-tuh-ree/ *noun* (*plural* **arteries**) a vessel which takes blood from the heart to other parts of the body.
☐ **arterial** /*say* ah-**tear**-ree-uhl/, *adjective*

artesian bore /*say* ah-**tee**-zhuhn/ *noun* a well sunk through a layer of rock holding water, in which pressure keeps the water rising to the surface and pumping is not needed.

ANOTHER NAME for this is **artesian well.**

arthritis /*say* ah-**thruy**-tuhs/ *noun* a disease that causes swelling and pain in the joints of the body.
☐ **arthritic** /*say* ah-**thrit**-ik/, *adjective*

artichoke /*say* **ah**-tuh-chohk/ *noun* a thick, round flower which grows on a thistle-like plant and is used as a vegetable.

☑ SPELLING TIP *Tricky 'uh' sound*: the middle vowel sound is spelt *i*. You can think of this as joining together two familiar words, *art* and *choke*, even though these are not related to the meaning of **artichoke**.

article *noun*
1. a particular thing: *Every article in the exclusive dress shop was a famous brand.* **2.** a piece of writing about a particular subject in a newspaper or magazine. **3.** the words *a*, *an* and *the*. *The* is called the **definite article**, and the others are referred to as forms of the **indefinite article**.

A SIMILAR WORD (for definitions 1 and 2) is **item.**
SEE the Grammar and Punctuation Guide appendix (for definition 3).

articulate *verb* /*say* ah-**tik**-yuh-layt/
1. When you **articulate**, you speak clearly so that every syllable and word is distinct.
–*adjective* /*say* ah-**tik**-yuh-luht/ **2.** If you are **articulate**, you are able to put your ideas clearly into words.
☐ **articulately**, *adverb* –**articulation**, *noun*

A SIMILAR WORD (for definition 2) is **fluent.**

articulated *adjective* having joints or divisions: *A semitrailer is an articulated truck.*

artificial /*say* ah-tuh-**fish**-uhl/ *adjective*
1. not occurring naturally but made by humans: *The artificial flowers in the foyer are so good that they look real.* **2.** An **artificial** situation, emotion or state is awkward or unconvincing: *After our disagreement he gave me an artificial smile.*
☐ **artificiality**, *noun* –**artificially**, *adverb*

THE OPPOSITE is **natural.**

☑ SPELLING TIP *Tricky 'uh' sound*: the vowel sound after the *t* is spelt *i*. You should also notice the spelling of the last part of this word – *cial* (giving the sound 'shuhl'). Another word with this pattern is *official*.

artificial intelligence *noun* the ability of a computer to function as if it is working things out like a human being.

THE ABBREVIATION is **AI**.

artillery *noun*
1. large guns on wheels. **2.** the part of an army that uses these guns.

artisan */say* **ah**-tuh-zuhn/ *noun*
1. a skilled worker who makes useful things like tools, cooking items, etc.
–*adjective* **2.** having to do with food which is made by traditional methods, often taking a lot of time and effort: *artisan bread.*

☑ SPELLING TIP *Tricky 'uh' sound*: the vowel sound after the *t* is spelt *i*. The other tricky letter is the *s* which sounds like a 'z'.

artist *noun*
1. someone who creates works of art, such as a painter or sculptor. **2.** a performer or entertainer. **3.** someone who uses the skills of art in their work: *a commercial artist*; *an artist with words.*
☐ **artistic**, *adjective* able to create beautiful things. –**artistically**, *adverb* –**artistry**, *noun*

arvo *noun Informal* afternoon.

as *adverb*
1. to the same amount or degree (followed by the conjunction *as*): *as good as gold.*
–*conjunction* **2.** though: *Bad as it is, you can't blame him.* **3.** when or while: *As he came towards me, the clock began to chime.* **4.** since or because: *As I am here, I might as well stay for dinner.*
–*phrase* **5. as yet**, up to now: *As yet I haven't told anyone.*

asbestos */say* uhs-**bes**-tuhs, as-, -tos/ *noun* a grey substance which is mined and does not burn; it was once used as a building material, but is now banned in many countries as it can cause very serious diseases.

ascend */say* uh-**send**/ *verb* To **ascend** is to go upwards: *The procession ascended the cathedral stairs*; *Spray ascended from the waterfall.*
☐ **ascent**, *noun*

THE OPPOSITE is **descend**.

☑ SPELLING TIP *Silent letter alert*: remember that there is a silent *c* after the *s* in **ascend**. Don't confuse its noun form **ascent** with **assent** which means 'to agree'. The *c* in **ascend** is left over from the Latin origins of the word – *ad-* (meaning 'towards') and *scandere* (meaning 'to climb'). Notice that the silent *c* also appears in the opposite word, **descend**. Going up or coming down, don't forget the *c*!

ascertain */say* as-uh-**tayn**/ *verb* When you **ascertain** something, you find out or determine that it is the case: *The detectives ascertained that the suspect had not even been at the scene.*
☐ **ascertainable**, *adjective* –**ascertainment**, *noun*

☑ SPELLING TIP *Silent letter alert*: don't forget the silent *c* following the *s*. This word is related to *certain*. Think of the two words *as* and *certain* and put their spelling (but not their sound) together to make **ascertain**.

ascetic */say* uh-**set**-ik/ *noun* someone who, often for religious reasons, lives simply without many of the usual comforts of life.
☐ **ascetically**, *adverb*

WORD HISTORY from a Greek word meaning 'monk' or 'hermit'

☑ SPELLING TIP *Silent letter alert*: don't forget the silent *c* following the *s*.

ash[1] *noun*
1. the greyish or black dust left after a substance such as wood has burnt completely. **2. ashes**, what is left after a human body has been cremated.
☐ **ashen**, *adjective*: *a face ashen with shock.* –**ashy**, *adjective* (**ashier**, **ashiest**)

ash[2] *noun* a tree from which we get a valuable, hard timber.

ashamed *adjective*
1. If you are **ashamed**, you feel guilt or sorrow: *I'm ashamed that I didn't help them sooner.* **2.** If you are **ashamed** to do something, you are unwilling to do it because you think that others may laugh at you: *She was ashamed to be seen in her old clothes and decided not to go to the dance at all.* **3.** If you are **ashamed** of someone, you disapprove of something that they have done: *I'm ashamed of you for being so nasty.*

aside *adverb*
1. on or to one side: *to step aside.*
–*noun* **2.** words spoken quietly so that only some people present can hear: *an aside to the waiter.*

ask *verb*
1. If you **ask** someone something, you call on that person for an answer to your question: *The teacher asked the new boy his name.* **2.** If you **ask** someone to do something, you request them to do it: *The teacher asked him to leave his homework on the desk.* **3.** If you **ask** for something, you request it: *Just ask for help if you need it.* **4.** If you **ask** someone somewhere, you invite them somewhere: *I have asked ten people to my party.*

askance */say* uh-**skans**/ *adverb* showing distrust or disapproval: *The teacher looked askance at me and I realised that I had said something wrong.*

askew /*rhymes with* few/ *adverb* out of position: *His cap had slipped askew.*

A SIMILAR WORD is **awry**.

asleep *adjective*
1. sleeping. **2.** If a part of your body such as a foot or an arm is **asleep**, it has no feeling in it.

asp *noun* a small, venomous snake, especially one found in Egypt.

asparagus *noun* a plant with long green shoots, used as a vegetable.

☑ SPELLING TIP *Single letter alert*: only one *r* and one *g*. There are no double letters in **asparagus**.

aspect *noun*
1. the way a thing appears: *the bleak aspect of the land*; *We considered all aspects of his plan.* **2.** the direction a building faces: *an ocean aspect.* **3.** the form of a verb which indicates whether the action it refers to is complete or not. Verbs with **perfect aspect** usually refer to actions that are complete, as in *I have done my work*, and those with **continuous aspect** refer to actions that are still in progress, as in *I am doing my work*.

SEE the Grammar and Punctuation Guide appendix (for definition 3).

Asperger's syndrome /*say* **as**-per-guhz sin-drohm, **as**-per-juhz/ *noun* (formerly) a form of autism characterised by a tendency to social isolation and eccentric behaviour.

OTHER FORMS are **Asperger syndrome** and **Asperger's**.

asphalt /*say* **ash**-felt, **as**-felt/ *noun* a black, sticky substance, mixed with crushed rock and used for making roads.

☑ SPELLING TIP There is no ash used in the making or in the spelling of *asphalt* even though it often sounds as if there is. This word begins with *as* and then there is *ph* for the 'f' sound. After that, the *alt* ending seems easy, even though the *a* is pronounced as 'e'!

aspic *noun* a cold food in which jelly is used to set fish, meat or vegetables in a mould.

aspire *verb* If you **aspire** to do something, you aim to achieve it: *to aspire to be prime minister.*
☐ **aspirant**, *noun* –**aspiration**, *noun*

aspirin *noun* a drug used to stop pain.

ass *noun*
1. a long-eared, four-footed animal related to the horse. **2.** *Informal* a foolish person.

ANOTHER WORD for this is **donkey**.

assassinate *verb* To **assassinate** an important or well-known person is to kill them suddenly or secretly after careful planning, especially for political reasons: *They plotted to assassinate the prime minister.*
☐ **assassin**, *noun* someone who assassinates a person. –**assassination**, *noun*

☑ SPELLING TIP *Double letter alert*: a double *s* appears twice in this word.

assault /*say* uh-**solt**, uh-**sawlt**/ *noun*
1. an attack: *We begin the assault on the castle at dawn.* **2.** in law, an unlawful attack or threatened attack on someone, with or without a weapon.
–*verb* **3.** If someone **assaults** you, they make a physical attack on you.
☐ **assaulter**, *noun*

assemble *verb*
1. When people **assemble**, they gather together in a group: *All the children assembled in the playground to listen to the principal speak.* **2.** If you **assemble** something such as a machine, you put the parts of it together: *He spends hours assembling his model aeroplanes.*

assembly *noun* (*plural* **assemblies**)
1. a number of people gathered together for a special purpose. **2.** the putting together of something that is in parts: *All the ingredients were ready for the assembly of his sandwich.*

assent *verb* If you **assent** to something, you agree to it: *My parents finally assented to my having a mouse as a pet.*
☐ **assent**, *noun*

☑ SPELLING TIP *Double letter alert*: two *s*'s. Don't confuse this with **ascent** which sounds the same. **Ascent** is a movement upwards.

assert *verb* If you **assert** something, you state or declare it strongly: *She asserted that the jewels had definitely been in the safe that morning.*
☐ **assertion**, *noun* a strong, positive statement. –**assertiveness**, *noun* the quality of expressing yourself strongly. –**assertive**, *adjective*

assess /*say* uh-**ses**/ *verb* If you **assess** something, you work out its value: *We need an expert to assess the paintings.*
☐ **assessment**, *noun*

☑ SPELLING TIP *Double letter alert*: a double *s* appears twice in this word.

A SIMILAR WORD is **evaluate**.

asset *noun*
1. something you own: *My bike is my most valuable asset.* **2.** anything of value: *His knowledge of French is an asset.* **3. assets**, in commerce, property or possessions owned by a person or a business, such as machinery, buildings, cash and so on.

COMPARE definition 3 with **liability** (definition 3).

☑ SPELLING TIP *Double/single letter alert*: two *s*'s and only one *t* in **asset**.

assign /*say* uh-**suyn**/ *verb* If you **assign** a job or role to someone, you give it to them: *The teacher assigned the various classroom duties to some of the students.*

> ☑ SPELLING TIP *Silent letter alert*: don't forget the silent *g* before the *n*, just the same as in *sign* which forms the basis of this word. The prefix *ad* (meaning 'to') has been changed to *as-*, making a double *s*.

assignment *noun* a particular piece of work: *Your assignment is to measure the length of the field.*

assimilate /*say* uh-**sim**-uh-layt/ *verb*
1. If you **assimilate** something, you understand its meaning: *He waited for us to assimilate the news.* **2.** If someone is **assimilated** into a group, they become part of that group and feel that they belong there: *It didn't take long for the new students to become assimilated into the class.*
☐ **assimilation**, *noun*

> ☑ SPELLING TIP *Double/single letter alert*: two *s*'s but only one *m* and only one *l*. Note also the *i* spelling of the 'uh' sound before the final syllable. Rap it out as *as+sim+il+ate*.

assist *verb* If you **assist** someone, you help them: *I assisted them with the cleaning.*
☐ **assistance**, *noun* –**assistant**, *noun*

associate *verb* /*say* uh-**soh**-shee-ayt, uh-**soh**-see-ayt/
1. If you **associate** someone or something with a particular idea, feeling or memory, you connect the two in your mind: *In most cultures, the colour red is associated with danger.* **2.** If one thing is **associated** with another, the two are connected together: *Medicine is a career often associated with long working hours.* **3.** If you **associate** with a particular group of people, you spend a lot of time with them: *I wish she wouldn't associate with such a rough group.*
–*noun* /*say* uh-**soh**-shee-uht, uh-**soh**-see-uht/
4. a partner, colleague, or someone who shares your interests: *work associates.*

association *noun*
1. a group of people interested in the same thing: *a birdwatching association.* **2.** the connection of ideas in your mind: *Most people recognise the association between smoking and cancer.*

assonance /*say* **as**-uh-nuhns/ *noun* the repetition of the same vowel sound in words close together, as in 'fly high'.
☐ **assonant**, *adjective*

> COMPARE this with **alliteration.**

assortment *noun* a collection of things of various kinds: *an assortment of odd socks.*
☐ **assorted**, *adjective*

assume /*say* uh-**syoom**/ *verb*
1. If you **assume** something to be the case, you believe it to be true but you don't have proof of it: *Am I right in assuming that you have been here before?* **2.** If someone **assumes** control, power or responsibility, they take it: *After the revolution, the army assumed control of government.*
☐ **assumption** /*say* uh-**sum**-shuhn/, *noun*

assurance *noun*
1. a promise or guarantee: *The coach wanted an assurance that we would turn up for every training session.* **2.** confidence or faith in your own ability: *Her assurance in tackling the problem meant the rest of us could relax.*

> DO NOT CONFUSE **assurance** with **insurance** which is a system of paying money so that you will be paid back if something you own is lost or damaged.

assure /*say* uh-**shaw**/ *verb*
1. If you **assure** someone that something is true, you tell them that there is no doubt that it is true: *After he assured me that I would pass the exam I felt much happier.* **2.** If you **assure** yourself of something, you make yourself believe it: *She checked her homework again to assure herself that she hadn't left out anything important.*
☐ **assuredly**, *adverb*

asterisk /*say* **as**-tuh-risk/ *noun* a star shape (*) used in printing or writing to show that something has been written as a note at the bottom of the page, or been left out.

> WORD HISTORY from a Greek word meaning a 'star'

asteroid *noun* one of the hundreds of tiny planets lying between Mars and Jupiter.

> WORD HISTORY from a Greek word meaning 'like a star'

asthma /*say* **as**-muh/ *noun* a breathing disorder which causes difficulty in breathing, coughing and a feeling of tightness in the chest.
☐ **asthmatic**, *adjective* –**asthmatic**, *noun*

> ☑ SPELLING TIP *Silent letter alert*: don't forget the silent *th*. Think about how you get a thick feeling in your chest when you have **asthma** and remember to add in the *th* when you spell it.

astonish *verb* If something or someone **astonishes** you, they surprise you very much: *I was astonished to hear that you were going to live overseas.*
☐ **astonishing**, *adjective* –**astonishment**, *noun*

> A SIMILAR WORD is **astound**.

astound *verb* If something or someone **astounds** you, they surprise you very much: *His angry outburst completely astounded me.*
☐ **astounding**, *adjective*

A SIMILAR WORD is **astonish**.

astray *adverb* away from the proper path: *He was led astray by a group of rough kids.*

astride *adverb* with the legs on either side of: *He sat astride the horse.*

astringent /*say* uh-**strin**-juhnt/ *noun* **1.** a liquid put on the skin to tighten it and cause it to tingle. –*adjective* **2.** tightening and refreshing the skin: *an astringent lotion for the skin.* **3.** harsh or bitter: *She was hurt by her aunt's astringent criticism.*
☐ **astringency**, *noun*

astrology *noun* the study of the possible effects of the stars and planets on our lives.
☐ **astrologer**, *noun* –**astrological**, *adjective*

DO NOT CONFUSE **astrology** with **astronomy** which is the scientific study of the sun, moon, stars and planets.
NOTE An astrological forecast or chart is called a **horoscope**.

astronaut *noun* someone specially trained to travel in a spaceship.

ANOTHER WORD for this, especially when referring to a Russian space traveller, is **cosmonaut**.

☑ SPELLING TIP The spelling of **astronaut** will be easier if you see that it is made up of *astro-* (a prefix formed from the Latin word meaning 'star') and *naut* (a word part formed from the Latin word meaning 'sailor').

astronomical *adjective* **1.** having to do with astronomy. **2.** *Informal* very large: *an astronomical food bill.*

astronomy *noun* the scientific study of the sun, moon, stars and planets.
☐ **astronomer**, *noun*

DO NOT CONFUSE **astronomy** with **astrology** which is the study of the possible effects of the stars and planets on our lives.

astute *adjective* having clear and quick understanding: *an astute comprehension of the complexities involved.*
☐ **astuteness**, *noun*

A SIMILAR WORD is **shrewd,** which refers especially to being clever with money and practical matters.

asunder *adverb Rather old-fashioned* in or into pieces: *The huge rocks had been split asunder by the earthquake.*

asylum /*say* uh-**suy**-luhm/ *noun* **1.** protection or safety, given by the government of a country to people who have left their own country because of war or persecution: *The Afghan refugees applied for asylum in New Zealand.* **2.** *Old-fashioned* an institution caring for people who are mentally ill.

☑ SPELLING TIP *Letter 'y' alert*: the second vowel sound is spelt *y* (although it sounds like 'uy'). It might help if you think of another word that you know well that has the same spelling for this sound, such as *why*. Also remember that there is only one *s* sheltering in **asylum**.

at *preposition* a word used to show a place, time, order, experience, and so on: *at home*; *at noon*; *at zero*; *at work.*

atheist /*say* **ay**-thee-uhst/ *noun* someone who believes that there is no God.
☐ **atheism**, *noun* –**atheistic**, *adjective*

COMPARE this with **agnostic**.

☑ SPELLING TIP The basis of **atheist** is *theos*, the Greek word for 'god'. Forms of this word, with the *e* sounding as 'ee', appear in many English words having to do with 'god', such as *theology* (the study of religious truth). In **atheist**, *theos* has been shortened to *the*, with the addition of the prefix *a-* (meaning 'not' or 'without') and the suffix *-ist* (used in words referring to a person who does or believes something).

athlete *noun* someone who trains in various sports, especially running and jumping.
☐ **athletic**, *adjective* –**athletics**, *noun*

atlas *noun* a book of maps.

ATM *abbreviation* See **automatic teller machine**.

atmosphere /*say* **at**-muhs-fear/ *noun* **1.** the air that surrounds the earth. **2.** a feeling or mood: *an atmosphere of excitement.*
☐ **atmospheric** /*say* at-muhs-**fe**-rik/, *adjective*

atoll *noun* a coral island with a saltwater lagoon in the middle.

☑ SPELLING TIP *Single/double letter alert*: a single *t* and a double *l*. Think of having to pay *a toll* to land on the **atoll**.

atom *noun* the smallest part that an element can be divided into and still keep its special qualities or take part in a chemical reaction. An atom is made up of protons, neutrons and electrons.

WORD HISTORY from a Greek word meaning 'not able to be divided'

atomic *adjective* **1.** having to do with atoms. **2.** driven by atomic energy: *an atomic generator*; *an atomic missile.* **3.** using weapons like the atomic bomb: *an atomic attack*; *an atomic test.*

atomic bomb *noun* a bomb which explodes with great force when the energy that holds an atom together is released.

ANOTHER TERM for this is **atom bomb**.

atomic energy *noun* the energy or power which is obtained by causing changes within atoms.

ANOTHER TERM for this is **nuclear energy**.

atonal /*say* ay-**tohn**-uhl/ *adjective* not in any musical key: *The atonal music was not really popular with the audience.*

atone *verb* If you want to **atone** for something you have done wrong, you want to make up for it or show you are sorry: *I bought her a new book to atone for the one I lost.*
☐ **atonement**, *noun*

atrocious /*say* uh-**troh**-shuhs/ *adjective* very bad or unpleasant: *atrocious swearing*; *an atrocious movie*; *His treatment of his animals is atrocious.*

☑ SPELLING TIP *Tricky vowel sound*: remember that the middle 'oh' sound is spelt with a simple *o*. Also notice the *cious* spelling for the 'shuhs' sound at the end (as in many other words such as *precious*).

atrocity /*say* uh-**tros**-uh-tee/ *noun* (*plural* **atrocities**) a terribly wicked or cruel act.

atrophy /*say* **at**-ruh-fee/ *verb* (**atrophies**, **atrophying**, **atrophied**, **has atrophied**) If something **atrophies**, it loses strength or size: *Body tissue and organs atrophy with disuse or deficiency of blood supply.*

attach *verb*
1. If you **attach** one thing to something else, you add it or join it onto the main thing: *I've attached some pictures of a rainforest at the end of my essay*; *Attach the handle to the door using these screws.* **2.** If someone is **attached** to something such as an organisation or group, they work for them: *For part of the year my mother was attached to the United Nations.*
–*phrase* **3. attached to**, very affectionate towards: *He is very attached to his mother.*
☐ **attachment**, *noun*

☑ SPELLING TIP *Double letter alert*: Remember that there are two *t*'s side by side, **attached** to each other, in the first part of this word. However, there is is no 't' in the *ach* at the end (although it sounds as though it could be spelt *atch*). **Attach** has a partner word with the opposite meaning, **detach**, which means 'to separate'. Joining on or taking away, don't forget the *ach* spelling!

attack *verb*
1. If you **attack** someone or something, you use violence against them in order to hurt them: *Suddenly the shark attacked.* **2.** If you **attack** someone or something verbally or in writing, you strongly criticise them: *The film was attacked by the critics.* **3.** If you **attack** something such as a job or a problem, you deal with it with energy and enthusiasm.
–*noun* **4.** a military operation which aims to defeat an enemy and destroy its forces. **5.** a sudden onset of illness: *an asthma attack.*
☐ **attacker**, *noun*

attain *verb* If you **attain** something that you have been trying hard to do, you achieve your aim: *He attained a good mark in the exams.*
☐ **attainable**, *adjective* –**attainment**, *noun*

attempt *verb*
1. If you **attempt** to do something, you try to do it, even though it might not be possible: *He attempted the course but it was too hard.*
–*noun* **2.** an effort or try: *He made an attempt to climb the mountain.*

attend *verb*
1. If you **attend** an event, you are there. You are present at it. **2.** If you **attend** to someone or something, you deal with it, or take notice of it: *The sales assistant attended to the customer*; *I must attend to my work or it will not be done on time.* **3.** If you **attend** someone, you look after them: *The doctor is attending a patient at the moment.*
☐ **attendance**, *noun*

attendant *noun* someone who helps or looks after someone else: *a museum attendant.*

attention *noun*
1. the act of fixing your mind on something: *He turned his attention to his homework.* **2.** a military position in which you stand straight and still: *They had to stand at attention for hours.*
☐ **attentive**, *adjective* –**attentively**, *adverb*

☑ SPELLING TIP *Double/single letter alert*: there are three *t*'s in this word – two drawing **attention** to themselves together near the beginning and one by itself before the *ion* at the end. The final spelling *tion* makes a 'shuhn' sound, as in many other words.

attic *noun* a room or a space directly under the roof of a building: *We turned the attic into an extra bedroom.*

A SIMILAR WORD is **garret**.

attire *verb* To **attire** yourself is to to dress, particularly for a special occasion: *Aunty Dot was attired in a very stylish pink outfit with feathers.*
☐ **attire**, *noun*: *stylish attire.*

attitude *noun*
1. the way you think or behave: *an unfriendly attitude.* **2.** a way of holding your body: *Her shoulders dropped in an attitude of defeat.*

☑ SPELLING TIP *Double/single letter alert*: there are three *t*'s in this word – two together near the beginning and one by itself before the *ude* at the end.

attorney /*say* uh-**ter**-nee/ *noun* (*plural* **attorneys**)
1. a person, usually a solicitor, appointed by someone to do legal business for them. **2. power of attorney**, legal permission to make decisions or sign documents for another person.

> ☑ SPELLING TIP The difficult part in this word is the *or* spelling for the 'er' sound. Remind yourself that an **attorney** might be a lawyer *or* might not.

attract *verb*
1. If something **attracts** other things to it, it draws them to it: *The lure flashing in the water attracted the fish.* **2.** If someone or something **attracts** you, they have certain qualities which cause you to notice and admire them: *He was attracted by her friendly smile.*
☐ **attraction**, *noun*

attractive *adjective*
1. pleasing: *an attractive thought.* **2.** pleasing to look at: *an attractive face.*

attribute *verb* /*say* uh-**trib**-yooht/
1. If you **attribute** something to an event or situation, you think it was caused by that event: *I attribute my good marks to the amount of study I did.*
–*noun* /*say* **at**-ruh-byooht/ **2.** something which is thought of as belonging to something or someone: *The most exciting attribute of the new sports complex is the swimming pool.*
☐ **attribution**, *noun*

atypical /*say* ay-**tip**-ik-uhl/ *adjective* not typical, or different from usual: *His failure in the exam was atypical because he normally got good marks.*

aubergine /*say* **oh**-buh-zheen/ *noun* See **egg-plant**.

auburn *adjective* reddish-brown: *His hair had been auburn but was now turning grey.*

auction /*say* **ok**-shuhn/ *noun*
1. a public sale at which things are sold to the person who offers (or bids) the most money: *We bought the painting at an auction.*
–*verb* **2.** If you **auction** something, you sell it by auction: *The house will be auctioned this weekend.*
☐ **auctioneer**, *noun* someone whose job is to sell things by auction.

audacious /*say* aw-**day**-shuhs/ *adjective* bold or daring: *He made an audacious move in the chess game which won him the match.*
☐ **audacity** /*say* aw-**das**-uh-tee/, *noun*

audible *adjective* loud enough to be heard: *When you are using the telephone, it's important to have an audible clear voice.*
☐ **audibility**, *noun* –**audibly**, *adverb*

audience *noun*
1. a group of people listening or watching. **2.** a meeting with someone important: *an audience with the queen.*

audio *adjective* having to do with sound or hearing: *an audio book.*

audio- *prefix* a word part meaning 'hearing', as in *audiovisual*.

audit *noun*
1. an inspection and checking of business accounts, usually done once a year.
–*verb* (**audits**, **auditing**, **audited**, **has audited**) **2.** To **audit** someone's business accounts is to inspect them and check that they are in order.
☐ **auditor**, *noun*

audition *noun*
1. a test given to see how suitable an actor or performer is for a particular job: *She was so nervous about the audition for the show that she didn't sing well.*
–*verb* **2.** To **audition** someone is to test them by giving them an audition: *to audition singers for the lead role.* **3.** To **audition** is to do a trial performance: *They were auditioning in front of the director.*

> NOTE An audition for a part in a film is called a **screen test**.
> WORD HISTORY from a Latin word meaning 'a hearing'

auditorium *noun* a hall or other large space for meetings or concerts.

auditory *adjective* having to do with hearing or the ears: *the auditory nerve.*

augment *verb* If you **augment** something, you make it larger by adding to it: *My dad had to augment his income and has taken a second job.*
☐ **augmentation**, *noun*

august /*say* aw-**gust**/ *adjective* causing you to feel awe and respect: *The scientist was proud to join the august body of international researchers.*

August /*say* **aw**-guhst/ *noun* the eighth month of the year, with 31 days.

> THE ABBREVIATION is **Aug.**
> WORD HISTORY named after the first Roman emperor, *Augustus* Caesar

aunt *noun*
1. the sister of your father or mother. **2.** your uncle's wife.

> NOTE An informal term for **aunt** is **aunty** which can also be spelt **auntie**.

aura /*say* **aw**-ruh/ *noun* a special character or feel: *She has an aura of calm about her.*

> ☑ SPELLING TIP *Tricky vowel sound*: the first sound is spelt *au* but sounds like 'aw'. From the *a* ending you can guess that this word comes from Latin (where it means 'breath' or 'wind').

aural /*say* **aw**-ruhl/ *adjective* having to do with hearing or listening: *I failed the aural test in the music exam because I had a bad cold.*

DO NOT CONFUSE **aural** with **oral**, which has to do with the mouth or speaking.

auricle /*say* **aw**-rik-uhl, **o**-rik-uhl/ *noun* either of the two main cavities of the heart in which blood collects.

COMPARE this with **ventricle**.

aurora /*say* uh-**raw**-ruh/ *noun* a natural display of moving lights in the sky.

auspicious *adjective* favourable or showing signs of success: *We won our first game which was an auspicious start to the season.*

Aussie /*say* **oz**-ee/ *noun Informal* an Australian.
☐ **Aussie**, *adjective*

austere /*say* ost-**ear**, awst-**ear**/ *adjective*
1. very plain and simple: *an austere room*; *an austere life.* **2.** An **austere** person is one who is very strict and serious.
☐ **austerity**, *noun* (*plural* **austerities**)

☑ SPELLING TIP *Tricky vowel sound*: the first sound is spelt *au* but sounds like 'o' or 'aw'. The second problem is the *ere* spelling for the 'ear' sound.

Australian Rules *plural noun* a type of football requiring two teams of 18 players, which originated in Australia.

OTHER NAMES for this are **Australian National Football**, **Australian Football** and **Aussie Rules**.

authentic *adjective* real or genuine: *an authentic diamond.*; *Her tears were authentic.*
☐ **authenticity**, *noun*

author *noun* someone who writes a book, article or poem.
☐ **authorship**, *noun*

authorise /*say* **aw**-thuh-ruyz/ *verb* If someone **authorises** something, they give their official and legal permission for it to happen: *He authorised payment from the account.*
☐ **authorisation**, *noun* –**authorised**, *adjective*

ANOTHER SPELLING is **authorize**.

authoritarian /*say* aw-tho-ruh-**tair**-ree-uhn, uh-tho-ruh-**tair**-ree-uhn/ *adjective* An **authoritarian** government or ruler is one which controls a country strictly and does not allow people to have freedom and individual rights.
☐ **authoritarianism**, *noun*

authority /*say* aw-**tho**-ruh-tee, uh-**tho**-ruh-tee/ *noun* (*plural* **authorities**)
1. the right to decide or judge: *The council has authority over what trees can be planted in the local park.* **2.** a right that gives power: *The park rangers don't have the authority to make arrests.* **3.** a source of information that you can trust: *Mario is an authority on cricket.*

autism spectrum disorder *noun* a name for the condition of autism and its wide range of symptoms.

THE ABBREVIATION is **ASD**.

autistic *noun* If you are **autistic**, your mind works differently to other people's minds, so you might sometimes behave in a way that isn't ordinary and you might say some unexpected things.
☐ **autism**, *noun*

auto- *prefix* a word part meaning 'self', as in *autograph*.

WORD HISTORY this prefix comes from Greek

autobiography *noun* (*plural* **autobiographies**) your own life story written by yourself.
☐ **autobiographical**, *adjective*

COMPARE this with **biography**.

autocracy /*say* aw-**tok**-ruh-see/ *noun* (*plural* **autocracies**)
1. unlimited rule by one person over others. **2.** a country ruled by someone with unlimited power.
☐ **autocrat**, *noun* –**autocratic**, *adjective*

autograph *noun*
1. someone's own writing, especially their signature.
–*verb* **2.** If you **autograph** something, you write your name on or in it: *to autograph a book.*

☑ SPELLING TIP The spelling of **autograph** will be easier if you see that it is made up of *auto-* (a prefix meaning 'self') and *graph* (a word part meaning 'written', from the Greek word *graphos* meaning 'something drawn or written'). This word part turns up in several other words, such as *paragraph* and *photograph*.

automatic *adjective*
1. An **automatic** machine is one that has controls that allow it to go through a process by itself: *The dishwasher is fully automatic.* **2.** If something is **automatic**, you say it or do it without having to think, because you have done it so many times before: *Cleaning my teeth before I go to bed is automatic for me.*
–*noun* **3.** a car with a gear change that works by itself.
☐ **automatically**, *adverb*

☑ SPELLING TIP It will help if you recognise the prefix *auto-* (meaning 'self'). The other part of the word, *matic*, comes from a Greek word meaning 'acting' or 'moving'.

automatic teller machine *noun* a machine that you can get money from by using a special plastic card and a PIN.

THE ABBREVIATION is **ATM**.

automation /*say* aw-tuh-**may**-shuhn/ *noun* the use of machines instead of people to do jobs in factories.

automaton /*say* aw-**tom**-uh-tuhn/ *noun* (*plural* **automatons** *or* **automata** /*say* aw-**tom**-uh-tuh/) a robot or someone who acts like a robot.

automobile *noun* a car.

NOTE This term is used mainly in American English.

autonomous /*say* aw-**ton**-uh-muhs/ *adjective* self-governing: *East Timor is now an autonomous nation.*

A SIMILAR WORD is **independent**.

autopsy /*say* **aw**-top-see/ *noun* (*plural* **autopsies**) the examination of a dead body to discover the cause of death.

ANOTHER WORD for this is **post-mortem**.
WORD HISTORY from a Greek word meaning 'seeing with your own eyes'

autumn /*say* **aw**-tuhm/ *noun* the season of the year, following summer, when the leaves change colour and fall from some trees.
□ **autumnal** /*say* aw-**tum**-nuhl/, *adjective*

☑ SPELLING TIP *Silent letter alert*: don't forget the silent *n* at the end of **autumn**.

auxiliary /*say* og-**zil**-yuh-ree/ *adjective*
1. having to do with extra equipment or machinery that is kept in case it is needed, or in reserve: *an auxiliary power supply*; *auxiliary staff.*
–*noun* (*plural* **auxiliaries**) **2.** a person, group, or thing that is brought in to help: *a nursing auxiliary.*

☑ SPELLING TIP There are several difficult parts in the spelling of this word. The first is the *aux* opening which is quite different from the way it sounds ('ogz'). Then you need to remember that there is only one *l* and that it has an *i* following it.

auxiliary verb *noun* a verb that goes with main verbs to show person, tense, mood and so on. The most common auxiliary verbs are those that come from *be* and *have*, as in 'I am eating', 'they were eating' and 'I had eaten'.

SEE the Grammar and Punctuation Guide appendix.

available *adjective* ready, or able to be used: *Is the hall available for rehearsals?*; *She is available to help.*
□ **availability**, *noun*

avalanche /*say* **av**-uh-lansh, **av**-uh-lahnsh/ *noun* a large mass of snow sliding or falling suddenly down a mountain slope.

☑ SPELLING TIP *Silent letter alert*: don't forget the *e* at the end. **Avalanche** has this spelling because it comes from French.

avarice /*say* **av**-uh-ruhs/ *noun* greed, especially for money.
□ **avaricious** /*say* av-uh-**rish**-uhs/, *adjective*

☑ SPELLING TIP *Tricky 'uh' sound*: the middle vowel sound is spelt *i*. Also remember the *ice* ending which gives an 'uhs' sound. Other words that follow this pattern include *office*, *notice* and *practice*.

avenge *verb* If you **avenge** something bad that has been done, or **avenge** someone for a harmful act done to them, you hurt or punish the person responsible: *He was determined to avenge his father's death.*
□ **avenger**, *noun*

avenue *noun* a street or road, especially one lined with trees.

THE ABBREVIATION is **Ave** or **ave**.

average /*say* **av**-rij, **av**-uh-rij/ *noun*
1. the result of dividing the sum of two or more quantities by the number of quantities: *The average of 4, 5 and 6 is 5.* **2.** an ordinary amount, kind, quality or rate: *Her height was the average for her age*; *The apples we bought by the side of the road were much better than average.*
–*verb* **3.** To **average** a certain number is to get the average of the total sum: *to average an hour's homework most nights*; *to average about six cups of tea a day.*

☑ SPELLING TIP Remember that there is an *e* in the middle of **average**, making three syllables in its spelling, though you usually say it with two syllables only. Also note the *age* spelling at the end of the word (although it sounds like 'ij'). If you think of finding the **average** age of your class, it might help to remind you how to spell the ending.

averse *adjective* opposed or not willing: *Lazy people are averse to too much activity.*

aversion *noun* a strong dislike: *Chloe has an aversion to pink clothes.*

avert *verb*
1. If you **avert** your eyes, gaze or face, you turn it away: *They averted their eyes for all the scary parts of the film.* **2.** If you **avert** something, you prevent it from happening: *Warfare was averted because of a number of wise decisions.*

avian /*say* **ay**-vee-uhn/ *adjective* having to do with birds.

avian influenza *noun* any of a number of influenza viruses that are normally passed only between birds but which can sometimes be passed to humans.

SIMILAR WORDS are **avian flu** and **bird flu.**

aviary /*say* **ayv**-yuh-ree/ *noun* (*plural* **aviaries**) a large cage or enclosure where birds are kept.

WORD HISTORY from the Latin word for 'bird'

aviation *noun* the science or act of flying in an aircraft: *aviation fuel*; *aviation history.*

avid /*say* **av**-uhd/ *adjective* very enthusiastic or keen: *She is an avid reader.*
☐ **avidly**, *adverb*

avocado *noun* (*plural* **avocados**) a green, pear-shaped fruit with a large seed.

avoid *verb*
1. If you **avoid** something, you take action in order to prevent it happening or from affecting you: *Try to avoid stress.* **2.** If you **avoid** someone or something, you keep away from them: *I don't like her so I try to avoid her.*
☐ **avoidable**, *adjective* –**avoidance**, *noun*

WORD HISTORY from a French word meaning 'empty out'

await *verb*
1. If you **await** someone or something, you wait for them: *She was awaiting the night bus.* **2.** If something **awaits** you, it is ready for you: *The beach is awaiting us – let's go!*

awake *adjective*
1. If you are **awake**, you are not sleeping: *He was so worried, he lay awake all night.*
–*verb* (**awakes** *or* **awakens**, **awaking**, **awoke**, **has awoken**) **2.** When you **awake** or something **awakens** you, you wake up: *I awoke from a deep sleep*; *I was awakened by the sound of rain drumming on the roof.*

awakening *noun*
1. a waking up from sleep. **2.** a renewing of interest: *an awakening of public concern for the importance of saving water.*

award *noun*
1. something won for skill or excellence: *an award for frisbee throwing.*
–*verb* **2.** If you are **awarded** something, you are given it because of your skill or excellence: *James was awarded the frisbee trophy.*

aware *adjective* having a feeling or knowledge: *He was aware of someone walking behind him.*
☐ **awareness**, *noun*

away *adverb*
1. off: *to go away.* **2.** at a distance: *to stand away from the wall.* **3.** from your possession: *to give money away.* **4.** at once: *right away.*
–*adjective* **5.** absent: *away from home.* **6.** distant: *six kilometres away.*
–*phrase* **7. do away with**, to kill. **8. make away with**, to steal.

awe *noun* a feeling of great respect mixed with fear: *The huge openness of the outback scenery filled us with awe.*

awesome *adjective*
1. filling you with feelings of respect and fear: *the awesome power of a huge storm.* **2.** *Informal* very good or impressive: *Everyone agreed that the party was awesome.*

☑ SPELLING TIP The spelling of **awesome** will be easier if you see that it is made up of *awe* with the suffix *-some* (meaning 'tending towards' or 'involving'). Compare the spelling of **awesome** with **awful** and note that in **awesome**, *awe* keeps its *e*.

awful *adjective* very bad or unpleasant: *The flood left an awful mess*; *Her death was an awful shock*; *I have a headache – I feel awful.*

☑ SPELLING TIP The trick here is to remember that the original meaning of **awful** was 'full of awe'. Then you can see that **awful** is made up of *awe* (without its *e*) and the suffix *-ful* (meaning 'full of'). Remember that *full* always loses an *l* when it is changed into the suffix form *-ful*. Now it's not so **awful**!

awkward *adjective*
1. clumsy: *The baby took her first, awkward steps.* **2.** difficult to do or to use: *The machine was very awkward to operate.* **3.** embarrassed: *I felt awkward and out of place at the party.* **4.** causing embarrassment and difficult to deal with: *We were in a very awkward situation – we didn't know quite what to do.*
☐ **awkwardly**, *adverb* –**awkwardness**, *noun*

☑ SPELLING TIP The spelling of this word is **awkward** to remember, mainly because there are two *w*'s – one before the *k* and one after it. Remember that the last part of the word is the suffix *-ward*, the same as appears in words such as *forward* and *backward*.

awning *noun* a roof-like shelter over a window or door, and so on, to give protection from the weather: *We stopped under the shade of an awning.*

awry /*rhymes with* fly/ *adverb* **1.** turned to one side: *The fence posts were leaning awry.* **2.** wrong: *His business dealings went awry and he lost thousands.*

A SIMILAR WORD (for definition 1) is **askew.**

axe *noun*
1. a tool with a blade for chopping.
–*phrase* **2. get the axe**, *Informal* **a.** to be cut down or stopped: *Our project got the axe because it was costing too much.* **b.** to be dismissed from a job.

☑ SPELLING TIP *Silent letter alert*: don't forget the silent *e* at the end. The spelling **ax** is used in

American English but **axe** is the standard spelling in Australian English.

axiom *noun* something that is obviously true.
□ **axiomatic**, *adjective*

axis /*say* **ak**-suhs/ *noun* (*plural* **axes** /*say* **ak**-seez/)
1. an imaginary line which something turns around: *The earth turning on its axis gives us night and day.* **2.** a central line that divides something exactly in half: *an axis of symmetry.*

axle *noun* the rod in the middle of a wheel on which the wheel turns.

axolotl /*say* aks-uh-**lot**-l/ *noun* an amphibian with a long tail and short legs, found in Mexican lakes: *We kept our axolotl in a separate tank from our goldfish.*

☑ SPELLING TIP *Tricky 'uh' sound*: the second vowel sound is spelt with an *o*. Also remember the *tl* ending which is a combination that would not normally appear at the end of an English word. **Axolotl** comes from a Native American language.

ayatollah /*say* uy-uh-**tol**-uh/ *noun* a Muslim religious leader in Iran.

azalea /*say* uh-**zayl**-yuh/ *noun* a shrub which produces attractive flowers in spring.

☑ SPELLING TIP *Tricky vowel sound*: remember that the vowel before the final *a* is *e* (not *i*).

baba ganoush /*say* bub-uh guh-**noosh**/ *noun* a food made from cooked eggplant, herbs and garlic, made into a paste, originating in Middle Eastern cooking.

ANOTHER SPELLING is **baba ghanoush**.

babble *verb* To **babble** is to **1.** speak quickly and unclearly: *The excited girl babbled on and on.* **2.** make a soft, continuous sound the way a stream does.
□ **babble**, *noun*

baboon *noun* a large monkey with a mouth like a dog and a short tail, found in Africa and Arabia.

WORD HISTORY from a French word meaning a 'stupid person'

baby *noun* (*plural* **babies**)
1. a very young child or animal.
–*adjective* **2.** like or suitable for a baby: *a baby voice*; *baby clothes.*
–*verb* (**babies**, **babying**, **babied**, **has babied**) **3.** To **baby** someone is to treat them like a baby: *to baby a teenager.*

babysit *verb* (**babysits**, **babysitting**, **babysat**, **has babysat**) to look after a child while the parents are out.
□ **babysitter**, *noun*

bachelor *noun* a man who is not married.

☑ SPELLING TIP Remember that the first part of **bachelor** does not have a *t*. It is spelt *bach* (although it sounds like it could be spelt *batch*). Also remember that the ending is spelt *or*. Rap it out as *ba* + *chel* + *or*.

back[1] *noun*
1. the part of something that is farthest from the front: *the back of the cupboard.* **2.** the rear part of the body, from the neck to the bottom of the spine. **3.** a defending player in football and other games.
–*verb* **4.** To **back** something is to make it move backwards: *My brother backed his car into the parking spot.* **5.** To **back** someone is to support them: *I back the local hockey team.*
–*phrase* **6. back down**, to give up your point of view in an argument and so on. **7. back out of**, to avoid fulfilling or carrying out something: *to back out of a deal.* **8. back up**, **a.** to support or encourage someone: *This new evidence backs up my claim.* **b.** to make a copy of computer data in case the original data is lost or corrupted. **9. behind someone's back**, in secret or without someone knowing. **10. turn your back on**, to ignore or have nothing further to do with a person or thing.
□ **backer**, *noun* someone who gives money to support a business, film, play, and so on. –**back**, *adjective*: *back door.*

back[2] *adverb*
1. at or to the rear: *to hang back.* **2.** as an answer or in return: *to phone back*; *to pay back.* **3.** in or towards an earlier time or place: *to go back to your old school.*
–*phrase* **4. back and forth**, first in one direction and then the other.

backbone *noun*
1. the spine of a person's body or the similar set of bones in other animals. **2.** courage to stand up for what you believe.

backfire *verb*
1. When a car engine **backfires**, it makes a loud, explosive sound from the exhaust pipe because petrol was burnt too early: *My brother's car needs fixing – it keeps backfiring.* **2.** You say a plan **backfires** when it does not work out the way you wanted it to: *Her scheme backfired when her father found out about it.*

backgammon *noun* a board game in which two people take turns to move pieces after throwing dice.

background *noun*
1. the back part of a view or scene: *in the background of the painting.* **2.** the events and conditions that lead up to and explain something: *the background to the present crisis.* **3.** your social position, experience and education.
–*phrase* **4. in the background**, out of sight, or not noticed.

backhand *adjective* A **backhand** stroke in a game like tennis is one made to the left side of the body (when the player is right-handed).
□ **backhand**, *noun*

COMPARE this with **forehand**.

backing *noun*
1. support of any kind, such as a piece of material placed behind another to strengthen it, or money made available to help something, like the production of a film or a new business. **2.** musical background for a singer.

backlog *noun* a piling up of things that need to be done or looked at: *When we got back* *from our holidays there was a backlog of emails to read.*

backpack *noun* a light, strong bag designed to be carried on the back, especially by travellers, walkers, school students, etc.
☐ **backpacker**, *noun* someone who travels with their clothes, etc., in a backpack, usually staying in low-priced accommodation.

backstroke *noun* a stroke in swimming in which you lie on your back in the water and move your arms backwards in turn.

COMPARE this with **breaststroke**, **freestyle**, and **butterfly stroke**.

backup *noun*
1. support or help: *His plan received a lot of backup.* **2.** something kept for use when needed. **3.** a collection of something, especially of a liquid, that has built up: *the backup of floodwater.*

ANOTHER SPELLING is **back-up**.

backward *adjective*
1. turned or going towards the back: *a backward glance*; *a backward move.* **2.** behind others in growth, or ability to learn: *a backward reader.*
☐ **backward**, **backwards**, *adverb*: *to move backward.* –**backwardness**, *noun*

backwater *noun*
1. a pool of still water that is joined to a river but not reached by its current. **2.** a place where nothing seems to happen.

backyard *noun* the enclosed area behind a house.
☐ **backyard**, *adjective*: *backyard cricket.*

bacon *noun* meat from the back and sides of a pig, salted and either dried or smoked.

bacteria /*say* bak-**tear**-ree-uh/ *plural noun* (*singular* **bacterium**) tiny living bodies with one cell, which multiply by dividing themselves in two and which can cause disease and decay.
☐ **bacterial**, *adjective*

NOTE This is a plural word, so in general you should speak of *these bacteria* and *this bacterium*. However, **bacteria** is being increasingly used in the singular (as in *This bacteria is dangerous*), and many people think that this is acceptable.
WORD HISTORY from a Greek word meaning 'a little stick'

bad *adjective* (**worse**, **worst**)
1. not pleasing: *bad news*; *a bad smell*; *a bad mood.* **2.** poor in quality: *a bad film*; *a bad tennis shot.* **3.** not able to do something well: *I've always been bad at maths.* **4.** harmful to your health: *Smoking is bad for you.* **5.** severe or serious: *a bad headache.* **6.** not good in behaviour: *Bad girl, stop that!* **7.** decayed or rotten: *This meat's gone bad – it smells awful.*
–*phrase* **8. feel bad**, to feel sorry, sad or ashamed: *Don't feel bad about breaking that cup – it was an accident.* **9. go bad**, decay: *My apple has gone bad.* **10. not bad**, *Informal* quite good or fair in quality.
☐ **badness**, *noun* –**badly**, *adverb*

SIMILAR WORDS (for definitions 1 and 2) are **awful**, **horrible** and **terrible**; (for definition 6) **badly-behaved**, **disobedient**, **mischievous** and **naughty**. Note that all the similar words for definitions 1 and 2 describe something which is very bad. There are some other words which you use to describe something which is extremely bad or shocking, such as **abominable**, **atrocious**, and **abysmal**. Something that is **abominable** is very seriously bad.

badge *noun* a disc or sign that you wear on your clothes to show people what you are a member or supporter of, or what rank you hold.
☐ **badging**, *noun*

badger *noun* an animal found in Europe and America, which has a white mark on its head and which lives in a hole in the ground.

badminton *noun* a game in which two or four players use racquets to hit a feathered shuttlecock over a high net.

WORD HISTORY named after *Badminton*, a village in England, where the game was first played

baffle *verb* If you **baffle** someone, you confuse them: *I'm baffled by all these puzzling questions.*
☐ **bafflement**, *noun* –**baffling**, *adjective*

bag *noun*
1. a container for holding or carrying things: *a bag of sugar*; *a shopping bag.*
–*verb* (**bags**, **bagging**, **bagged**, **has bagged**)
2. If you **bag** something, you put it into a bag: *Bag these apples please.* **3.** To **bag** an animal is to kill or catch it while hunting.

bagel /*say* **bay**-guhl/ *noun* a small, hard roll, in the shape of a ring and made of dough.

WORD HISTORY this word comes from Yiddish

baggage *noun* the bags and other things which a traveller carries: *I managed to drag my baggage to the train.*

ANOTHER WORD for this is **luggage**.

☑ SPELLING TIP *Double letter alert*: double *g* in the middle. Also remember that the ending is spelt *age* (although it sounds like 'ij').

bagpipes *plural noun* a musical instrument you play by blowing into a bag with pipes attached.
☐ **bagpiper**, *noun*

bail[1] *noun*
1. money which must be paid so that someone who is charged with a crime can go free until they are tried in court.

–verb in the phrase **2. bail someone out, a.** to help someone get their freedom by giving them bail. **b.** to help someone out of trouble: *My uncle lent my brother some money to bail him out until he got paid.*

NOTE **Bail** and **bale** sound the same but have different meanings. **Bail** has several meanings (see above and also **bail**[2] and **bail**[3]). A **bale** is a large bundle of something such as *a bale of wool*. To make it more confusing, **bale** can also be another spelling for **bail**[2], that is, the action of someone removing water from a boat, or of someone jumping from an aeroplane (*We had to bail/bale out the water; He bailed/baled out of the plane when it caught on fire*).

bail[2] *verb*
1. To **bail** is to empty a boat with a bucket, can, or something similar: *They had to bail for an hour after the storm hit them.* **2. bail out**, to jump from a plane with a parachute: *He had to bail out when the engine failed.*

ANOTHER SPELLING is **bale**. See also the note at **bail**[1].

bail[3] *noun* one of the two small pieces of wood that rest on top of cricket stumps.

NOTE See the note at **bail**[1].

bait *noun*
1. food used on a hook, or in a trap, to catch fish or animals. **2.** food with poison in it, used to kill or drug animals.
–verb **3.** To **bait** something is to add bait to it: *He baited the trap.* **4.** To **bait** someone is to tease them in order to upset or annoy them: *He baits his sister by criticising her clothes.*

bake *verb*
1. You **bake** food by cooking it in an oven. **2.** When you heat something to make it hard, you **bake** it: *The bricks are baked in a large furnace.*
☐ **baker**, *noun*

baker's dozen *noun* thirteen.

bakery *noun* (*plural* **bakeries**) a place where bread is baked and, sometimes, sold.

ANOTHER WORD is **bakehouse**.

baklava /*say* **bak**-luh-vuh, **bahk**-luh-vuh/ *noun* a Middle Eastern dessert made from filo pastry layered with chopped walnuts, and soaked in a honey and sugar syrup.

☑ SPELLING TIP Notice the *k* spelling in this word, and the *a* ending. It is spelt like this because it comes from Turkish.

balaclava /*say* bal-uh-**klah**-vuh/ *noun* a knitted cap that pulls down over your head and under your chin: *My balaclava looks like a helmet.*

WORD HISTORY named after *Balaclava*, a seaport on the Black Sea, where soldiers first wore these caps in the Crimean War (1853–1856)

balance *verb*
1. If you **balance** something, you keep it in a steady position so that it doesn't fall or tip over: *I can't balance on my new skates; He balanced a plate on his head.*
–noun **2.** steadiness: *balance of judgement; The cat kept its balance as it walked along the narrow fence.* **3.** the difference between the total of the money paid into, and the money taken out of, a bank account. **4.** an instrument for weighing, often a bar which rests at the centre and which has containers hanging at the ends with the weights on one side and the goods to be weighed on the other. **5.** in a work of art, an arrangement of the shapes, colour and so on, that is pleasing to the viewer.

ANOTHER WORD (for definition 4) is **scales**.

balcony *noun* (*plural* **balconies**) a verandah, usually above ground level, that often has a roof and a kind of fence around it.

bald /*say* bawld/ *adjective*
1. without hair: *a bald head; a bald man.* **2.** plain and to the point: *a bald question.*
☐ **balding**, *adjective* –**baldness**, *noun*

bale[1] *noun* a large amount of goods to be stored or transported, such as wool or hay, tied up tightly with cords or wire.

NOTE **Bale** and **bail** sound the same but have different meanings, as well as one meaning for which either word can be used. As well as the meaning given here, to **bale** can also mean 'to scoop water out of a boat', or 'to jump out of an aeroplane'. When it has this meaning, it is more usually spelt **bail** (see **bail**[2]). **Bail** also refers to the money left with a court to ensure that an accused person will come back for trial. If you **bail** someone out you help them out of a difficult situation. A **bail** is also part of a wicket in cricket.

bale[2] *verb* See **bail**[2].

NOTE See the note at **bale**[1].

baleful *adjective* full of hate: *The snarling dog watched through the fence with a baleful expression.*
☐ **balefully**, *adverb* –**balefulness**, *noun*

ball[1] *noun*
1. a round or egg-shaped object which you can bounce, kick, catch, or hit in games. **2.** something which is shaped like a ball: *a ball of string.* **3.** a rounded part of your body: *the ball of your thumb.*
–phrase **4. ball of muscle** (or **strength**), *Informal* a person who is very healthy and strong. **5. on the ball**, quick to learn, understand or take action. **6. start** (or **keep**) **the ball rolling**, to start or keep something going.

ball[2] *noun* a large formal dance: *The president wore a jewelled gown to the ball.*

ballad *noun* a simple poem with short verses, which tells a story and is often turned into a song.

ballast *noun*
1. heavy material carried by a ship to keep it steady. **2.** something heavy like bags of sand carried by a balloon (definition 2) to control its height.

ballerina *noun* a female ballet dancer.

ballet /*say* **bal**-ay/ *noun* a formal type of dancing, performed by a group, who act out a story, using graceful and controlled movements.
☐ **ballet**, *adjective*: *ballet dancers.*

> ☑ SPELLING TIP *Silent letter alert*: don't forget the silent *t* at the end – the *et* spelling makes an 'ay' sound. Other words with this ending are *bouquet* and *beret*. They all come from French. (Although **ballet** came into English from French, it comes from an earlier Italian word meaning a 'little dance'. Compare **ball**[2].)

ballistics *noun* the study of the movement of missiles, bullets, or other objects fired from a gun.
☐ **ballistic**, *adjective*

> ☑ SPELLING TIP *Double letter alert*: double *l* in the middle.

ballkid *noun* in tennis, a young person whose job is to retrieve balls and supply them to the server.

balloon *noun*
1. a small rubber bag which is filled with air or gas and used as a toy. **2.** a large bag filled with hot air or other light gas, which may have a basket for passengers and can rise and float in the air.
–*verb* **3.** To **balloon** is to swell out: *Her skirt ballooned in the wind.*

> ANOTHER TERM (for definition 2) is **hot air balloon.**
> WORD HISTORY from an Italian word meaning 'ball'

ballot *noun*
1. a ticket or paper you must fill in to record your vote: *Please mark your ballots and put them in the box.* **2.** a secret way of voting.
–*verb* (**ballots**, **balloting**, **balloted**, **has balloted**) To **ballot** is to **3.** vote by ballot. **4.** draw lots: *to ballot for duties in the classroom.*

> ANOTHER TERM (for definition 1) is **ballot paper**; (for definition 2) **secret ballot**.

> ☑ SPELLING TIP *Double/single letter alert*: double *l* in the middle and only one *t* at the end. Remember that the *t* remains single when you add *-ed* or *-ing*, following the rule that the consonant remains single if the final syllable is not stressed.

ballpoint pen *noun* a pen whose point is a small ball which rolls around.

balm /*rhymes with* farm/ *noun*
1. a sweet-smelling ointment or oil which heals or makes something less painful. **2.** something soothing: *Arriving home to food and rest was balm to the exhausted firefighters.*
☐ **balmy**, *adjective*: *a balmy summer evening.*

> ☑ SPELLING TIP *Tricky vowel sound*: don't forget the *l*. The *alm* spelling gives the 'ahm' sound. It might help if you think that 'a balm makes you feel calm' – *calm* is spelt in a similar way.

balsa /*say* **bawl**-suh/ *noun* a very light wood, often used in making models of boats, planes, etc.

balsam /*say* **bawl**-suhm/ *noun*
1. a sweet-smelling gum that comes from some trees. **2.** a kind of garden plant with red, pink or white flowers.

balustrade /*say* **bal**-uh-strayd/ *noun* a rail with a row of short pillars holding it up which is usually part of a balcony or staircase.
☐ **baluster**, *noun* one of the short pillars in the row.

bamboo *noun* a woody, tree-like plant whose hollow stem is used for building, for making furniture, and so on.

bamboozle *verb* If you **bamboozle** someone, you confuse or deceive them: *The magician bamboozled us with his conjuring tricks.*

> A SIMILAR WORD is **baffle**.

ban *verb* (**bans**, **banning**, **banned**, **has banned**) To **ban** something is to forbid people to see, read, use or do it: *The principal banned mobile phones from the school.*

> A SIMILAR WORD is **prohibit**.

banal /*say* buh-**nahl**, **bay**-nuhl/ *adjective* ordinary and unoriginal: *The show was so banal that I couldn't be bothered watching it.*
☐ **banality**, *noun*

> ☑ SPELLING TIP *Single letter alert*: Remember that this word has a single *n* in the middle, with an *a* on either side of it.

banana *noun* a long, curved fruit with a yellow skin.

band[1] *noun*
1. a group of people acting together for a common purpose: *a band of thieves.* **2.** a group of musicians: *a jazz band.*
–*verb* **3.** To **band** together is to join in a group: *to band together to protect the environment.*

band[2] *noun*
1. a strip of material for tying, binding or decorating: *an arm band*; *an elastic band.* **2.** a narrow

strip that is different from its surroundings: *a band of blue around the top.* **3.** in mining, a layer of stone containing valuable material, such as gold. **4.** in radio, a limited or specified range of frequencies: *Truck drivers talk to each other over the radio using a particular frequency band.*

A SIMILAR WORD (for definition 2) is **stripe**.

bandage *noun*
1. a strip of cotton or elastic material used to bind up a cut or injured part of the body.
–verb **2.** If you **bandage** a part of someone's body, you tie a bandage around it: *Her leg was heavily bandaged.*

bandaid *noun* a cover that you stick over an abrasion or sore to protect it.

bandana /*say* ban-**dan**-uh/ *noun* a large, bright handkerchief or scarf: *She tied a blue bandana around her head.*

ANOTHER SPELLING is **bandanna**.
WORD HISTORY from a Hindustani word for a form of dyeing in which the cloth is tied to stop some parts from receiving the dye

bandicoot *noun* a rat-like Australian marsupial which feeds at night on insects, worms and plant roots. Some species are vulnerable or endangered.

WORD HISTORY from a Telugu word (a language spoken in south-eastern India) for the pig-rat of India and Sri Lanka

bandit *noun* an armed robber.

bandy *verb* (**bandies**, **bandying**, **bandied**, **has bandied**)
1. If you **bandy** words or insults with someone, you exchange them back and forth, as in an argument: *We bandied insults with the supporters of the rival team.*
–adjective **2.** If someone's legs are **bandy**, they bend outwards at the knees: *The old drover had bandy legs from so many years spent in the saddle.*
□ **bandy-legged**, *adjective*

bane *noun* someone or something that ruins or destroys: *I hate washing up! It's the bane of my life.*
□ **baneful**, *adjective* –**banefully**, *adverb* –**banefulness**, *noun*

bang *noun*
1. a sudden loud noise.
–verb **2.** If you **bang** something, you hit it or close it, making a loud noise: *I banged the drum*; *She banged the lid.* **3.** If something **bangs**, it hits something or closes, with a loud noise: *The door banged because of the wind.*

bangle *noun* a ring-shaped band worn to look pretty round your wrist or ankle.

banish *verb* To **banish** someone is to send them away as a punishment: *The evil magician was banished from the palace forever.*
□ **banishment**, *noun*

banister *noun* the rail that runs along a stairway: *She held onto the banister for support while going up the stairs.*

ANOTHER SPELLING is **bannister**.

banjo *noun* (*plural* **banjos**) a musical instrument with a round body and strings which you play by plucking the strings or running your fingers across them.
□ **banjoist**, *noun*

bank[1] *noun*
1. a pile or mass: *a bank of earth*; *a huge cloud bank.* **2.** the land beside a river or stream: *We moored our boat close to the left bank.*
–verb **3.** If something **banks**, it tips or slopes to one side: *The plane banked steeply as it turned to come in for a landing.*
–phrase **4. bank up**, *Colloquial* **a.** to gather or build up: *Our mail banked up while we were away.* **b.** to gather something into a pile or mass: *to bank up dead leaves.*

bank[2] *noun*
1. a place where you can keep your money and take it out again when you wish.
–verb **2.** To **bank** something like money or a cheque is to place it in a bank.
–phrase **3. bank on**, to depend on: *I'm banking on you to feed my fish while I am away.*

A SIMILAR WORD (for definition 2) is **deposit**.

banknote *noun* See **note** (definition 3).

bankrupt *adjective*
1. unable to pay your debts: *The company is bankrupt.*
–noun **2.** someone who is unable to pay their debts.
□ **bankruptcy**, *noun*

banksia *noun* an Australian shrub or tree with leathery, notched leaves and tiny yellow flowers massed together in spikes.

WORD HISTORY named after the English naturalist Joseph *Banks* (1743–1820) who accompanied Captain Cook on the *Endeavour*

banner *noun*
1. a flag which sometimes has a message or slogan on it: *A big banner told everyone about the fete.* **2.** a large rectangular section on a web page, often used to display the website's brand or for advertising.

ANOTHER TERM (for definition 2) is **web banner**.

banquet /*say* **bang**-kwuht/ *noun* a large formal dinner for many guests, usually held in honour of someone or for a special occasion.

A SIMILAR WORD is **feast**.

☑ SPELLING TIP Remember that the sound in the middle of **banquet** is spelt *qu*. There are many words in which *qu* sounds like 'kw', such as *quiet* and *queen*. Think of 'a queen attending a banquet'. Remember also that there is only one *t* at the end.

bantam *noun* a small breed of domestic fowl.

WORD HISTORY named after *Bantam*, a village in Indonesia, where these fowls are said to have come from

banter *noun*
1. playful teasing: *friendly banter.*
–*verb* **2.** If you **banter** with someone, you joke with them or tease them in a friendly way.

baptism *noun* a Christian ceremony in which someone is sprinkled with, or put under, water to show that they are accepted as a member of the church.
☐ **baptise**, *verb* –**baptismal**, *adjective*

ANOTHER SPELLING for **baptise** is **baptize**.
ANOTHER WORD for this is **christening**.

bar[1] *noun*
1. a long plank, piece of metal or other hard material, often used as a barrier: *the bottom bar of the gate.* **2.** the counter in a hotel where drinks are served. **3. a.** one of the upright lines drawn across the stave in written music, to separate the groups of beats. **b.** the part between two of these lines.
–*verb* (**bars**, **barring**, **barred**, **has barred**) **4.** If something or someone **bars** you from a place or from doing something, they stop or prevent you from going there or doing it: *Rocks barred our way forward*; *Security officers barred the gang from entering.*

ANOTHER TERM (for definition 3a) is **bar line**.
A SIMILAR WORD (for definition 4) is **ban**.

bar[2] *noun* a metric unit for measuring pressure, equal to 10 units a square metre.

barb *noun*
1. the sharp point that sticks out backwards, as on a hook for fishing or fence wire. **2.** a hurtful remark.
☐ **barbed**, *adjective*: *barbed wire.*

barbarian /*say* bah-**bair**-ree-uhn/ *noun* someone with bad manners and not much education.
☐ **barbarian**, *adjective*: *barbarian behaviour.* –**barbarism** /*say* **bah**-buh-riz-uhm/, *noun* –**barbarity**, *noun*

WORD HISTORY first used by the ancient Greeks and Romans to describe a person belonging to an uncivilised country

barbaric /*say* bah-**ba**-rik/ *adjective* wild or cruel: *War produces barbaric acts.*
☐ **barbarically**, *adverb*

barbecue /*say* **bah**-buh-kyooh/ *noun*
1. a metal frame for cooking meat over an open fire. **2.** an outdoor meal or party where the food is cooked on a barbecue.
–*verb* **3.** If you **barbecue** food, you cook it on a barbecue.

ANOTHER SPELLING is **barbeque**, much more common in Australia than in America or England. The short forms **bar-b-q** and **BBQ** are sometimes also used, but many people say these should not be used in formal writing.

☑ SPELLING TIP *Tricky 'uh' sound*: the vowel sound in the middle is spelt *e*. The ending can be spelt *cue* (like the stick you use in playing pool or billiards) or *que*.

barber *noun* someone whose job it is to cut men's hair.

barbiturate /*say* bah-**bich**-uh-ruht/ *noun* a drug used to ease pain or to calm and soothe someone, which can be addictive.

barcode *noun* a printed code with a series of vertical bars that identify all goods being sold in a shop, which a computerised cash register can scan.
☐ **barcoding**, *noun*

ANOTHER FORM is bar code.

bard *noun Old-fashioned* a poet or singer.
☐ **bardic**, *adjective*

bare *adjective*
1. uncovered or naked: *bare floor*; *bare legs.* **2.** empty: *Our refrigerator is usually bare by Friday.* **3.** plain or simple: *the bare facts.*
–*verb* **4.** To **bare** something is to uncover it: *The fierce dog began to bare its teeth.*
☐ **bareness**, *noun*

☑ SPELLING TIP Don't confuse the spelling of **bare** with **bear** which sounds the same. A **bear** is a large animal with short fur. To **bear** something is to hold or carry it.

barely *adverb* You use **barely** to mean that something is only just so: *We had barely begun*; *He's earning barely enough to live on.*

bargain *noun*
1. something bought cheaply: *The bike was a bargain at nearly half price.* **2.** an agreement or arrangement to buy or sell something.
–*verb* **3.** To **bargain** is to argue for a better price.
–*phrase* **4. bargain for**, to expect or be prepared for: *to get more than you bargain for.* **5. bargain on**, to depend or count on.
☐ **bargainer**, *noun*

barge *noun*
1. a flat-bottomed boat that carries cargo.
–*verb* 2. If you **barge** into or through something, you push into it quickly in a rude and rough way: *The police barged through the crowd.* 3. If you **barge** in, you interrupt someone while they are talking or doing something: *He barged in without knocking.*

baritone /*say* **ba**-ruh-tohn/ *noun* a man with a fairly deep singing voice.
☐ **baritone**, *adjective*

NOTE The range of a **baritone** is higher than that of a **bass**, but lower than that of a **tenor**, **alto** or **soprano**.

☑ SPELLING TIP *Tricky 'uh' sound*: the vowel sound in the middle is spelt *i*. Remember also that **baritone** has only one *r*. Rap it out as *ba + ri + tone*.

barium /*say* **bair**-ree-uhm/ *noun* a substance which, when it is swallowed, shows up on X-rays.

bark[1] *verb* To **bark** is to **1.** make the noise of a dog. **2.** speak sharply and harshly: *to bark an order.*
–*noun* **3.** the harsh cry of a dog or other similar animal.

bark[2] *noun* the outer covering of a tree.

barley *noun* a grain used as food, and in making beer and whisky.

bar mitzvah /*say* bah **mits**-vuh/ *noun* the Jewish ceremony and feast held when a boy reaches his thirteenth birthday and is old enough to take on religious responsibilities as an adult member of the Jewish community.

WORD HISTORY from a Hebrew word meaning 'son of the commandment'

barn *noun* a building to store hay or shelter animals.

barnacle *noun* a shellfish which sticks to the bottoms of ships and to other objects beneath the sea.

barometer /*say* buh-**rom**-uh-tuh/ *noun* an instrument that measures air pressure, used to help work out what height you are at and what changes in the weather can be expected: *The barometer is falling which means we are in for bad weather.*
☐ **barometric** /*say* ba-ruh-**met**-rik/, *adjective*

NOTE When you use a barometer to see what height you're at, it is called an **altimeter**.

baron *noun* in Britain and some European countries, a nobleman of a certain rank. In Britain, a baron is of the lowest rank of nobility.
☐ **baronial**, *adjective*

NOTE A woman with this rank is called a **baroness**.

baroque /*say* buh-**rok**, buh-**rohk**/ *adjective*
1. in a style of art and architecture that developed in Italy during the 16th century, noted for its dramatic style and ornate detail. **2.** having to do with a later style of music which is similarly ornate.

barrack *verb* When you **barrack** for someone, you shout encouragement for them: *We barracked for the Australian runner.*
☐ **barracker**, *noun*

A SIMILAR WORD is **cheer**.

barracks *plural noun* the buildings where soldiers live.

barrage /*say* **ba**-rahzh/ *noun*
1. a heavy attack from a set of guns. **2.** a long, continuous verbal attack: *a barrage of questions.*

barramundi /*say* ba-ruh-**mun**-dee/ *noun* (*plural* **barramundi** *or* **barramundis**) a large silver-grey fish which is good to eat.

WORD HISTORY This word comes from an Aboriginal language of Queensland.

☑ SPELLING TIP *Double letter alert*: double *r*. Also remember the *i* ending.

barrel *noun*
1. a large container made of vertical strips of wood held together with metal bands, usually used to store beer or wine. **2.** the metal tube of a gun.

barren *adjective*
1. unable to produce crops: *barren soil*; *barren land.* **2.** *Old-fashioned* unable to have children.

barricade *noun*
1. a barrier or wall, especially one built in a hurry: *a barricade to stop pedestrians*; *The soldiers blocked the road with a barricade of rubble.*
–*verb* **2.** To **barricade** something is to block or defend it with a barricade.

barrier *noun* anything which bars or blocks the way: *a road barrier*; *a trade barrier*; *a barrier to communication.*

barrister *noun* a lawyer whose main work is to argue cases in court.

COMPARE this with **solicitor**.

barrow *noun*
1. a street seller's cart. **2.** a wheelbarrow.

barter *verb* To **barter** is to trade by giving goods for the things you want, instead of using money.
☐ **barter**, *noun*

base[1] *noun*
1. the bottom part of anything, giving support: *the base of a jug.* **2.** the centre of operations: *The space station lost contact with the base.* **3.** the starting point for a counting system in maths, such as ten in the decimal system. **4.** one of the four fixed positions on a baseball or softball

field to which the players try to run. **5.** a primary place of living, employment, etc.: *His base is Hong Kong but he travels widely.*
–*verb* **6.** To **base** something on something else is to use the first thing as a support for the second: *to base an argument on facts.*

base[2] *adjective* mean or selfish: *a base trick.*
☐ **basely**, *adverb* –**baseness**, *noun*

baseball *noun*
1. a game played by two teams with a bat and a ball, on a field with four bases which the batter must pass to score a run. **2.** the ball used in this game.
☐ **baseballer**, *noun* Someone who plays baseball is a **baseballer**.

basement *noun* a room or area of a building below the ground floor.

bash *verb*
1. If you **bash** someone or something, you hit them very hard: *The boys bashed each other*; *He bashed the ball.*
–*noun* **2.** *Informal* a try or attempt: *I'll have a bash.*

bashful *adjective* very modest or shy: *Don't be bashful – tell them about your award.*
☐ **bashfully**, *adverb* –**bashfulness**, *noun*

basic *adjective*
1. simple, with no unnecessary things added: *Our motel room was very basic, but clean and cheap.*
2. You say something is **basic** if it is the main or most important thing on which other things depend, rest or are built: *The basic ingredient of an omelette is eggs.*
☐ **basically**, *adverb*

basil *noun* a herb used in cooking and salads.

> WORD HISTORY from a Greek word meaning 'royal'

basin *noun*
1. a sink or container that holds water for washing. **2.** a bowl for mixing or cooking. **3.** an area of water surrounded by land: *a river basin.*

basis /*say* **bay**-suhs/ *noun* (*plural* **bases** /*say* **bay**-seez/)
1. a solid support that forms the base of something: *These bricks will be the basis of our bookshelf.* **2.** the main or necessary part: *The basis of her novel was an incident that happened to her parents.*

bask /*rhymes with* ask/ *verb* If you **bask** in something, you let yourself enjoy the pleasant feeling it gives you, especially a feeling of warmth: *Cats love to bask in the sun*; *I basked in the compliments I received after my performance.*

basket *noun* a container woven out of materials, such as cane or plastic, for storing or carrying things: *a washing basket*; *a shopping basket.*

basketball *noun*
1. a game played by two teams of five players, who try to score points by shooting a ball through a metal hoop at the top of the other team's goal post. **2.** the ball used in this game.
☐ **basketballer**, *noun*

basmati rice /*say* baz-**mah**-tee ruys/ *noun* a kind of rice which has long grains which separate easily when cooked, especially used with meals originating in Indian cooking.

> WORD HISTORY from a Hindi word meaning 'fragrant'

bass /*sounds like* base/ *noun*
1. a man with a deep singing voice. **2.** the lowest tone in a musical chord, or the lowest part in a composition.
–*adjective* **3.** A **bass** guitar, drum or other musical instrument is one which makes a deep sound.
☐ **bass**, *adjective*

> NOTE The range of a **bass** is lower than that of a **baritone**, **tenor**, **alto** or **soprano**.

> ☑ SPELLING TIP Remember the double *s* spelling of this word. Don't confuse it with **base** which has the same sound. The **base** of something is its bottom. **Base** also has several other meanings.

basset *noun* a long-bodied dog with short legs and long ears, originally used for hunting foxes and badgers.

> ANOTHER TERM for this is **basset hound**.

bassinet *noun* the basket in which a very young baby sleeps.

> ANOTHER SPELLING is **bassinette**.

bassoon /*say* buh-**soohn**/ *noun* a low-sounding woodwind instrument.

bastard *noun*
1. *Old-fashioned* someone whose parents were not married when he or she was born. **2.** *Informal* someone you think is unpleasant or bad-tempered, usually a man.

> NOTE The use of this word may offend people.

bastion *noun* a fortified place.

> WORD HISTORY from an Italian word meaning 'build'

bat[1] *noun*
1. the stick used to hit the ball in games like cricket and baseball.
–*verb* (**bats**, **batting**, **batted**, **has batted**)
2. When you **bat** something, you hit it with a bat or with another object: *to bat the ball in cricket*; *to bat flies away with your hand.*
☐ **batsman**, *noun* –**batter**, *noun*

bat[2] *noun* a mouse-like winged animal which is active at night.

batch *noun* (*plural* **batches**) a number of things or people which have something in common and are seen as a set: *a batch of invitations*; *last year's batch of students.*

bath *noun*
1. a container for washing yourself in, which is large enough for you to sit or lie in. **2.** the water used in the bath: *The bath is too hot.* **3.** the act of washing yourself in a bath: *to have a bath.*
–*verb* **4.** If you **bath** someone, you put or wash them in a bath: *to bath the baby.*

ANOTHER WORD (for definition 1) is **bathtub**.

bathe /*say* baydh/ *verb*
1. If you **bathe** something, you wash it clean: *Bathe the cut with warm water.* **2.** If you **bathe**, you have a swim: *We bathed in the sea.*
☐ **bather**, *noun* a swimmer. –**bathers**, *plural noun* a swimming costume.

bathroom *noun* a room where you wash yourself, usually containing a bath or shower, a basin, and a toilet.

batik /*say* **bah**-tik, **bat**-ik/ *noun*
1. a way of dyeing cloth in which the parts not to be coloured are covered with wax. **2.** cloth dyed in this way.

WORD HISTORY from a Malay word meaning 'painted'

bat mitzvah /*say* baht **mits**-vuh/ *noun* the Jewish ceremony and feast held when a girl turns twelve, and becomes an adult member of the Jewish community.

WORD HISTORY from a Hebrew word meaning 'daughter of the commandment'

baton /*say* **bat**-n, buh-**ton**/ *noun*
1. a thin stick used to beat time by the person directing an orchestra. **2.** a short stick, especially one handed by one runner to the next in a relay race.

☑ SPELLING TIP *Single letter alert*: only one *t*. Also notice the following *o*. Don't confuse **baton** with **batten**, which is a piece of wood supporting something.

battalion *noun* an army unit of three or more smaller groups of soldiers known as companies.

☑ SPELLING TIP *Double/single letter alert*: double *t*, and only one *l* (which is also true of the related word *battle*).

batten *noun* a light strip of wood, used to strengthen or support something.

☑ SPELLING TIP Don't confuse the spelling of **batten** with **baton** which is a short stick, as one used by the conductor of an orchestra.

batter[1] *verb* To **batter** is to beat or hit hard or often: *to batter on the door.*
☐ **battering**, *noun*

batter[2] *noun* a mixture of flour, eggs and milk or water, beaten together for use in cooking.

battery *noun* (*plural* **batteries**)
1. a group of electric cells connected together to make or store electricity: *a torch battery*; *a car battery.* **2.** a group of guns or machines to be used together. **3.** a large number of cages in which chickens and other animals are kept.

battle *noun*
1. a fight between two large groups: *a battle between armies*; *a battle to win the election.*
–*verb* **2.** If you **battle** something or with something, you struggle with it or find it difficult to do: *to battle the weeds*; *to battle with maths.*

battlement *noun* a wall with openings for shooting through, as on a castle: *The historical film shows how archers on the battlement shot arrows down at the enemy.*

battleship *noun* a heavily armed warship.

bauble /*say* **baw**-buhl/ *noun* a cheap, bright ornament: *We hung baubles on the Christmas tree.*

WORD HISTORY from a Latin word meaning 'pretty'

baulk /*rhymes with* fork/ *verb* If someone **baulks** at something, they refuse to do it or are very reluctant to do it: *She baulked at making a speech before such a large crowd.*

☑ SPELLING TIP Remember that there is an *l* in this word. The *aulk* combination gives an 'ork' sound.

bauxite /*say* **bawk**-suyt/ *noun* the rock that you crush to get aluminium.

bawdy *adjective* (**bawdier**, **bawdiest**) containing rough talk and jokes about sex: *a bawdy song.*
☐ **bawdily**, *adverb* –**bawdiness**, *noun*

bawl *verb*
1. If you **bawl** something, you shout it in a very loud, rough way: *The sergeant bawled a quick order.* **2.** A child **bawls** when it cries noisily.
–*phrase* **3. bawl out**, to scold harshly: *to bawl someone out for stealing.*
☐ **bawl**, *noun*

bay[1] *noun* a sheltered part of a sea or lake, formed by a curve in its shore.

SIMILAR WORDS are **bight**, **gulf**, **inlet** and **cove**. **Bight** and **gulf** refer to fairly large areas of sea or ocean partly bounded by land, while an **inlet** or a **cove** is a small bay.

bay[2] *verb*
1. To **bay** is to make a long, sad sound like a dog: *to bay at the moon.*

–*noun* **2.** a deep, long sound, like that made by a hunting dog.
–*phrase* **3. at bay, a.** forced to stand and face an enemy: *The wolf stood at bay.* **b.** away or at a distance: *We kept boredom at bay by working hard.*

bay[3] *noun* a space or area: *a parking bay.*

bay[4] *adjective* reddish-brown: *a bay horse.*

bayonet /*say* **bay**-uh-nuht/ *noun*
1. a blade designed to be joined to the end of a rifle.
–*verb* (**bayonets**, **bayoneting**, **bayoneted**, **has bayoneted**) **2.** If someone **bayonets** someone else, they push the point of a bayonet into them.

WORD HISTORY named after *Bayonne* in France, where these weapons were first made

bazaar /*say* buh-**zah**/ *noun* a market with stalls selling many different kinds of goods.

☑ SPELLING TIP Don't confuse the spelling of **bazaar** with **bizarre** (describing something odd or unusual) which sounds the same. Remember that there are three *a*'s in **bazaar**, two of which are sitting side by side between the *z* and the *r*. The spelling is unusual because this word comes from Persian.

BC *abbreviation* before Christ: *The Great Pyramids of Egypt date back to 3000 BC.*

NOTE The calendar widely used throughout the world dates events from the year of the birth of Jesus Christ. Years before this are called **BC**, and those after are called **AD** (see **AD**). The abbreviation **BCE** (as in *44 BCE*) is sometimes used if the speaker or writer wants to avoid the reference to Christ. It stands for *Before* (*the*) *Common Era*.

be *verb* (I **am**; we, you, they **are**; he, she, it **is**; **being**; I, he, she, it **was**; we, you, they **were**; **has been**)
1. The verb **to be** connects a subject either with a predicate or with adjectives, in statements, questions, and commands: *You are late*; *Tomorrow is Thursday*; *Is he here?*; *Be good at school today.* **2.** To **be** is to exist or have reality: *He is no more.* **3.** To **be** can mean to take place or happen: *The wedding was last week.* **4. Be** is used as an auxiliary verb **a.** with a present participle of another verb, to form the continuous tenses: *I am waiting*; *She was running.* **b.** with a past participle, in passive forms of transitive verbs: *The date was fixed.*

SEE the Grammar and Punctuation Guide appendix.

beach *noun* (*plural* **beaches**)
1. the sandy or pebbly land at the edge of a sea, lake or river.
–*verb* **2.** If you **beach** a boat, you force it to go up onto the beach from the water: *They quickly beached the boat before the storm arrived.* **3.** If a whale **beaches** itself, it swims in to the shore and remains stranded on the beach.

☑ SPELLING TIP Don't confuse the spelling of **beach** with **beech** which sounds the same. A **beech** is a kind of tree.

beachcomber /*say* **beech**-koh-muh/ *noun* someone who lives on or near a beach and collects things washed up by the sea.

☑ SPELLING TIP *Silent letter alert*: don't forget the *b* in the *comber* part of the word, which comes from the word *comb* (to search thoroughly).

beacon *noun*
1. a signal which shows the way or warns of danger: *We'll leave the outside light on as a beacon for you if it's dark.* **2.** a lighthouse.

bead *noun*
1. a small ball with a hole through the middle, that can be threaded on a string. **2.** a drop of liquid: *beads of sweat.* **3. beads**, a necklace.

beagle *noun* a small hunting dog with short legs and long ears.

beak *noun* the hard, horny part of a bird's mouth.
☐ **beaked**, *adjective*

ANOTHER WORD for this is **bill**[1].

beaker *noun*
1. a large cup or mug. **2.** a glass container with a pouring lip shaped like a beak, used in laboratories.

beam *noun*
1. a long, strong piece of wood, concrete or metal, often used as a support: *beams supporting the balcony*; *a balancing beam for gymnastics.* **2.** the widest part of a ship: *twelve metres across the beam.* **3.** a ray of light: *the beam of headlights*; *a sunbeam.* **4.** a radio or other similar signal, used to direct pilots through the darkness or in bad weather.
–*verb* To **beam** is to **5.** send out rays of light. **6.** smile happily: *He beamed when he saw her waiting for him.*
–*phrase* **7. off beam**, wrong: *The answer was completely off beam.*

bean *noun*
1. a plant with smooth seeds growing in a long pod. **2.** the seed or pod of a bean plant which can be eaten raw or cooked.
–*phrase Informal* **3. full of beans**, full of energy: *We were full of beans after our long sleep.* **4. spill the beans**, to let out a secret.

☑ SPELLING TIP Don't confuse the spelling of **bean** with **been** which sounds the same but is spelt with a double *e*. **Been** is the past participle of the verb **be**, as in *Have you been well lately?*

beanbag *noun*
1. a large cushion that you can sit on, filled with pellets. **2.** a small cloth bag filled with beans and thrown in catching games.

bean sprout *noun* a small shoot from a bean plant, used for food.

bear[1] *verb* (**bears**, **bearing**, **bore**, **has borne** *or* **has born**)
1. To **bear** is to hold up or carry: *I don't think the branch is strong enough to bear our weight*; *The swimmer was borne along with the current.* **2.** If you cannot **bear** something, you cannot put up with it: *I can't bear pain*; *I can't bear people who tell lies.* **3.** If a woman **bears** a child, she gives birth to it: *She bore three children.* **4.** If a plant **bears** something, it produces it: *This tree bears delicious mangoes.* **5.** If someone **bears** a particular sign or quality, they have or show that sign or quality: *The children bear a strong resemblance to their father*; *to bear signs of age.*
□ **bearable**, *adjective*: *bearable pain.*

NOTE The word **born** as in *She was born in 1980* came from this verb.

☑ SPELLING TIP Don't confuse the spelling of **bear** with **bare** which sounds the same. **Bare** describes something or someone without any covering.

bear[2] *noun* a large, heavy animal with short rough fur and a very short tail.

☑ SPELLING TIP See **bear**[1].

beard *noun*
1. the hair that grows on a man's face. **2.** a beard-like growth of hair, such as that on a goat's jaw, below a bird's beak and growing on wheat.
□ **bearded**, *adjective*

bearing *noun*
1. the way you stand or behave: *a woman of proud bearing.* **2.** a supporting part of a machine. **3.** connection or relevance: *This news will have no bearing on my decision to leave.* **4. bearings**, direction or position: *We couldn't find our bearings in the mist.*

A SIMILAR WORD (for definition 1) is **carriage**.

beast *noun*
1. a four-footed animal. **2.** a rough, cruel person, especially someone you dislike.
□ **beastly**, *adjective*

beat *verb* (**beats**, **beating**, **beat**, **has beaten**)
1. If you **beat** someone or something, you hit them hard over and over again: *to beat someone severely*; *to beat a drum*; *The hail beat on the roof.* **2.** If you **beat** someone in a race, contest or game, you defeat them: *I could never beat my brother at chess.* **3.** If you **beat** someone to a place, you get there before them: *He always beats me to the bus stop and grabs the best seat.* **4.** If you try to **beat** a difficulty, you do everything you can to deal with it: *My sister tried everything to beat her illness.* **5.** If something **beats**, it makes movements in a regular rhythm: *Your heart should beat about 70 times a minute.* **6.** If you **beat** eggs or cream, you mix them with regular, quick movements using a fork or whisk: *Beat the eggs until they are thick, then fold in the sugar.*
–*noun* **7.** a sound made over and over again: *the beat of your heart.* **8.** regular rhythm in music: *The conductor kept the beat while the orchestra played.* **9.** a path or route which someone usually takes: *a police officer on his beat.*
□ **beating**, *noun*

☑ SPELLING TIP Don't confuse the spelling of **beat** with **beet** which sounds the same but is spelt with a double *e*. **Beet** is a kind of vegetable.

beaut *adjective Informal* very good and enjoyable: *a beaut party.*

beautician /*say* byooh-**tish**-uhn/ *noun* someone who works in a beauty salon.

beautiful *adjective*
1. attractive and enjoyable to look at, hear, taste, smell or feel: *a beautiful baby*; *beautiful weather*; *a beautiful song.* **2.** You can say something is **beautiful** if it is done or carried out extremely well: *They scored a beautiful goal just two minutes before full time.*
□ **beautifully**, *adverb*

SIMILAR WORDS (for definition 1) are **pretty**, **exquisite**, **gorgeous**, **lovely**, and **stunning**. Note that **pretty** usually refers to appearance only (*a pretty woman*, *a pretty garden*). It is not such a strong word as **beautiful**. **Exquisite** suggests a fine or delicate quality and **gorgeous** describes someone or something that is richly beautiful: *She appeared in a gorgeous red satin dress.* Someone or something that is **stunning** is very beautiful in a way that captures your attention or surprises you.

beauty *noun* (*plural* **beauties**)
1. the quality of being beautiful: *a harbour famous for its beauty.* **2.** advantage: *The beauty of this job is that I get to take home any unsold food.*
□ **beautify**, *verb* (**beautifies**, **beautifying**, **beautified**, **has beautified**)

beaver *noun* a brown, furry animal of North America, with sharp teeth and a wide, flat tail, which builds dams in rivers.

because *conjunction*
1. for the reason that: *We went shopping because we needed new shoes.*
–*phrase* **2. because of**, by reason or on account: *The game was abandoned because of rain.*

beckon *verb* If you **beckon** to someone, you signal or wave to them to come over to you: *The teacher beckoned to her group to follow her.*

become *verb* (**becomes**, **becoming**, **became**, **has become**)
1. When someone or something **becomes** something else, they come to be that thing: *It*

takes many years to become a doctor; *The dog became angry and started to growl.*
–*phrase* **2. become of**, happen to: *What will become of her garden?*

becoming *adjective*
1. proper or suitable: *language which is becoming for the classroom.* **2.** flattering or making you look attractive: *a becoming outfit.*
☐ **becomingly**, *adverb*

bed *noun*
1. a place to sleep, especially a piece of furniture with soft coverings to make sleeping comfortable. **2.** a small area of earth in a garden: *a rose bed.* **3.** the ground under a sea or river: *on the sea bed.*

bedlam *noun* a scene of great noise and confusion: *There was bedlam on sale day as eager shoppers rushed into the store.*

bedraggled /*say* buh-**drag**-uhld/ *adjective* wet, dirty and hanging limply: *His clothes were muddy and bedraggled.*

bedridden *adjective* forced to stay in bed: *She is bedridden with a heart condition.*

bedrock *noun*
1. the solid, unbroken rock under the top layers of soil. **2.** the bottom level of anything: *We were already wet and cold, but our spirits really hit bedrock when the tent began to leak.*

bedroom *noun* a room in a home where people sleep: *Our house has three bedrooms.*

bee[1] *noun* a stinging insect with four wings, which collects nectar and pollen from flowers to make into honey.

> NOTE The place where bees live is called a **beehive** or **hive**, and a group of bees together is called a **swarm**.

bee[2] *noun*
1. a small group of people gathered together for some type of work: *a working bee.* **2.** a contest: *a spelling bee.*

beech *noun* (*plural* **beeches**) a tree with smooth, grey bark and triangular nuts, whose hard wood is often used for making furniture.

> ☑ SPELLING TIP Don't confuse the spelling of **beech** with **beach** which sounds the same. A **beach** is the sandy or pebbly land at the edge of a sea, lake or river.

beef *noun* the meat from a cow or bull: *a roast beef sandwich.*

beeline *noun* a direct line, like the course bees take when returning to their hive: *We made a beeline for the exit as soon as the show was over.*

beer *noun* an alcoholic drink made from malt and flavoured with hops.

beet *noun* a plant with a dark red root that you can eat and from which sugar can be made.

> ☑ SPELLING TIP Don't confuse the spelling of **beet** with **beat** which sounds the same. To **beat** is to hit over and over again or to defeat. It can also refer to a regular rhythm, such as your heart makes or in music.

beetle *noun* an insect with two pairs of wings, one of which is hard and protects the delicate flying wings underneath.

> WORD HISTORY from an Old English word meaning 'biter'

beetroot *noun* the dark red root of the beet plant which is eaten as a vegetable.

befall *verb* (**befalls**, **befalling**, **befell**, **has befallen**) If something, usually bad, **befalls** you, it happens to you: *She worries that harm will befall her children when she's not with them.*

befit *verb* (**befits**, **befitting**, **befitted**, **has befitted**) If something **befits** someone or something, it is suitable or appropriate for them: *Wear clothes that befit this special occasion.*

before *adverb*
1. ahead or in front: *She went before to prepare the way.* **2.** earlier, or at an earlier time: *Have you been here before?*; *Begin writing when I tell you, not before.*
–*preposition* **3.** in front or ahead of: *I was before you in the queue.* **4.** earlier than: *before the earthquake.* **5.** in the presence or sight of: *before an audience.* **6.** under consideration of: *The case is before the judge.*
–*conjunction* **7.** rather than: *I'll scrap the whole project before I give in to your demands.*

beforehand *adverb* in advance: *Let me know beforehand.*

before-school care *noun* a place where you can go in the mornings, where people look after you before school starts.

befriend *verb* If you **befriend** someone, you make friends with them and help them: *She befriended the new girl in the class.*

beg *verb* (**begs**, **begging**, **begged**, **has begged**)
1. If you **beg** someone to do something, you ask them strongly to do it as a favour: *She kept begging her mother to buy her a new CD.* **2.** If someone **begs**, they ask people to give them food or money to live on.
–*phrase* **3. go begging**, to be unwanted or unclaimed: *That last chocolate biscuit is going begging.*

beggar *noun* someone who lives by asking people for food or money.

begin *verb* (**begins**, **beginning**, **began**, **has begun**) To **begin** is to start an action or event:

You can begin writing now; *When do the holidays begin?*
□ **beginning**, *noun*

beginner *noun* someone who has just started learning something.

begrudge *verb*
1. If you **begrudge** someone something, you envy them for it: *She begrudges me my happiness.* **2.** If you **begrudge** doing something, you are unwilling to do it: *We begrudged paying for such a bad meal.*

beguile /*say* buh-**guyl**/ *verb* If something or someone **beguiles** you, they charm or enchant you: *The kitten's bright eyes and playful tricks beguiled us into buying her.*
□ **beguiling**, *adjective* –**beguilingly**, *adverb* charming.

☑ SPELLING TIP Don't forget the silent *u* before the *i* in **beguile**. There are many words where *gu* sounds like a hard 'g'. It might help if you think of some of them, such as *guide* and *guard*.

behalf /*say* buh-**hahf**/ *phrase* **on behalf of**, on the side of or for: *I speak on behalf of the whole class.*

☑ SPELLING TIP *Tricky vowel sound*: don't forget the *l*. The *alf* spelling gives the 'ahf' sound.

behave *verb*
1. If you **behave** in a certain way, you act in that way: *Even though he's only ten, he behaves like an adult*; *Our cat has been behaving strangely these last few days.*
–*phrase* **2. behave yourself**, to act properly or in an acceptable way: *The children behaved themselves in the restaurant.*

THE OPPOSITE of definition 2 is **misbehave**.

behaviour /*say* buh-**hay**-vyuh/ *noun* the way someone behaves: *good behaviour*; *bad behaviour*; *strange behaviour.*
□ **behavioural**, *adjective* –**behaviourally**, *adverb*

ANOTHER SPELLING is **behavior**.

behead *verb* To **behead** someone is to cut off their head: *The count was beheaded during the French Revolution.*

ANOTHER WORD for this is **decapitate**.

behind *preposition*
1. at the back of: *behind the garden shed.* **2.** after or later than: *I'm behind schedule with my homework.* **3.** less advanced than: *behind the rest of his class in reading.*
–*adverb* **4.** at or towards the back: *She lagged behind.* **5.** late: *She's behind with her essay.*
–*noun* **6.** *Informal* your buttocks.

beige /*say* bayzh/ *adjective* very light brown: *beige curtains.*
□ **beige**, *noun*

☑ SPELLING TIP *Exception to rule*: this word does not fit in with the rule that says *i* comes before *e* except after *c* rule. This is because that rule only works when the sound is 'ee' as in *believe*. Notice that in **beige** the sound is 'ay' so the rule does not apply. Remember also the *ge* at the end which gives a soft 'zh' sound. All this is because **beige** comes from French.

being *noun*
1. something which lives: *beings from another planet*; *a human being.*
–*phrase* **2. come into being**, to be born or start to exist: *The world came into being many millions of years ago.*

belated *adjective* late: *My birthday was in the middle of the exams, so I had a belated party.*
□ **belatedly**, *adverb* –**belatedness**, *noun*

NOTE This word is never used of people, only of things.

belch *verb*
1. If you **belch**, you pass wind noisily from your stomach through your mouth. **2.** To **belch** smoke, fire or steam, is to push or throw it out violently: *The burning building belched out black smoke.*
□ **belch**, *noun* (*plural* **belches**)

A SIMILAR WORD (for definition 1) is **burp**.

beleaguer /*say* buh-**lee**-guh/ *verb* If someone or something **beleaguers** you, they surround you: *The army planned to beleaguer the city*; *He was beleaguered with doubts.*
□ **beleaguered**, *adjective* –**beleaguerer**, *noun*

belfry /*say* **bel**-free/ *noun* (*plural* **belfries**) a tower with a bell hanging in it: *the belfry of the old church.*

belief *noun*
1. something that you believe and accept as true: *It is my belief that children should not watch too much television*; *a religious belief.* **2.** trust: *She has a strong belief in her own abilities.*

believe *verb*
1. If you **believe** something, you think it is true and correct: *Do you believe his story?* **2.** If you **believe** someone, you think they are telling the truth: *Please believe me when I say I'm sorry.* **3.** You can say you **believe** something when you think something but do not know for certain it is right: *I believe he's gone to live in London, but you'd better check to make sure.*
–*phrase* **4. believe in**, to accept as real or true: *Do you believe in ghosts?* **5. make believe**, to pretend: *He made believe that he hadn't seen us*; *Let's make believe we are pirates.*
□ **believable**, *adjective* –**believer**, *noun*

☑ SPELLING TIP Remember that **believe** has *ie* (to spell the 'ee' sound) following the *l*. This follows the rule that *i* comes before *e* except after *c*.

belittle *verb* If you **belittle** someone or something, you make them seem unimportant: *I was upset when she belittled my poem.*

bell *noun*
1. a hollow, cup-shaped object, usually made of metal, which makes a ringing sound when the hanging piece in the middle hits the side. **2.** the ringing sound of a bell. **3.** something which makes the sound of a bell.
–*phrase* **4. ring a bell**, to sound familiar: *Her name rings a bell.*

bellbird *noun* a small bird that has a clear, ringing call like the sound of a bell and lives in bushy areas along the east coast of Australia.

belligerent /*say* be-**lij**-uh-ruhnt/ *adjective*
1. angry and aggressive: *She was shocked by her neighbour's belligerent behaviour.* **2.** involved in a war: *They tried to get the belligerent countries to discuss a peace agreement.*
☐ **belligerence**, *noun* –**belligerently**, *adverb*

☑ SPELLING TIP *Double letter alert*: double *l* (because it comes from the Latin word *bellum* meaning 'war'). Remember also that the ending is spelt *ent* (not *ant*). Rap it out as *bel+ lig+ er+ ent*.

bellow /*rhymes with* yellow/ *verb* To **bellow** is to cry loudly and deeply: *to bellow across the river; The elephant bellowed with pain.*
☐ **bellowing**, *noun*

bellows *plural noun* an instrument for pumping air: *I pumped the bellows to get the fire started.*

belly *noun* (*plural* **bellies**)
1. the front part of the body that contains the stomach: *He punched him in the belly.* **2.** the inside of anything: *the belly of the aircraft.*

ANOTHER WORD for (definition 1) is **abdomen**.

belong *verb*
1. If someone or something **belongs** in a certain place, that is the place where they are usually found or live, or where they should be: *Put your toys back in the box where they belong.*
–*phrase* **2. belong to, a.** to be the property of: *The book belongs to him.* **b.** to be part of: *That cover belongs to this jar.*

belongings *plural noun* things that you own: *She put her belongings in a locker when she went for a swim.*

A SIMILAR WORD is **possessions**.

beloved /*say* buh-**luv**-uhd, buh-**luvd**/ *adjective*
1. much loved: *a beloved pet.*
–*noun* **2.** *Rather old-fashioned* someone you love very much: *She misses her beloved.*

below *adverb*
1. beneath: *The rain fell onto the parched earth below.* **2.** downstairs: *the floor below.* **3.** at a later point on a page or in your writing: *See below for further examples.* **4.** in a lower rank or level: *the year below.*
–*preposition* **5.** lower than: *below the eye; below the normal temperature.*

THE OPPOSITE is **above**.

belt *noun*
1. a strip of strong material, often worn around your waist or hips to hold up your clothes. **2.** a large strip of land where a particular thing is grown: *the wheat belt; a belt of trees.*
–*verb* **3.** If someone **belts** someone else, they hit them very hard.
–*phrase* **4. below the belt**, unfair or against the rules: *That comment was below the belt!* **5. belt out**, to sing very loudly. **6. belt up, a.** *Informal* to be quiet: *Just belt up and let me have some peace!* **b.** to fasten a seatbelt.

bemused *adjective* muddled or confused: *He was bemused by all the different stories they told.*

bench *noun* (*plural* **benches**)
1. a seat long enough for several people to sit on: *a garden bench.* **2.** a strong table for working at: *a carpenter's bench.* **3.** a seat for members of parliament or judges in court. **4.** the group of judges sitting together to hear a case: *The accused man was brought before the bench.*

bend *verb* (**bends**, **bending**, **bent**, **has bent**)
1. If you **bend** something, you change its shape or position from straight to round or angular: *She bent the coathanger to form a hook; He bent his head in sorrow.* **2.** If something **bends**, it changes its shape from straight to curved or it changes its direction: *The creek bends sharply left at the big rock.* **3.** If you **bend**, you move the upper part of your body downwards or to the side so that it is rounded or at an angle: *Bend down and try to pick up the parcel.*
–*noun* **4.** a curve or change in direction: *a bend in the track.*
–*phrase* **5. bend over backwards**, to try as hard as you can: *I bent over backwards to get you a ticket to the concert.* **6. round the bend**, *Informal* mad.
☐ **bendable**, *adjective*

SIMILAR WORDS (for definition 2) are **curve**, **loop** and **wind**.

bene- *prefix* a word part meaning 'well', as in *benediction*.

WORD HISTORY this prefix comes from Latin

beneath *adverb*
1. below, or underneath: *Snow fell onto the freezing ground beneath; the sky above and the earth beneath.*
–*preposition* **2.** under, or underneath: *beneath the same roof; He sat on the branch beneath me.* **3.** not worthy of: *That comment is beneath my notice.*

benediction /*say* ben-uh-**dik**-shuhn/ *noun* a blessing.

benefactor /*say* **ben**-uh-fak-tuh/ *noun* someone who gives help or money to those who need it: *The hospital was able to open a new ward because of a gift from a benefactor.*

beneficial /*say* ben-uh-**fish**-uhl/ *adjective* helpful: *beneficial information*; *the beneficial effect of a long holiday.*

☑ SPELLING TIP You can remember the *bene* spelling of the first part of this word by reminding yourself that it comes from *benefit*. Also notice the spelling of the last part – *cial* (giving the sound 'shuhl'). Other words with this pattern are *artificial* and *official*.

beneficiary /*say* ben-uh-**fish**-uh-ree/ *noun* (*plural* **beneficiaries**) someone who receives assistance, especially money left in a will.

benefit /*say* **ben**-uh-fuht/ *noun*
1. anything that is good for you: *the benefits of a good diet.* **2.** a concert to raise money for charity.
–*verb* (**benefits**, **benefiting**, **benefited**, **has benefited**) **3.** If something **benefits** you, it helps you or is good for you: *Medical advances benefit us all.*

☑ SPELLING TIP *Single letter alert*: only one *n* and one *t*. It might help if you know that its meaning comes from the idea of something being done well or being a good thing, and you can see that it is made up of *bene* (a word part meaning 'well' from the Latin word with the same meaning) and *fit* (which in this instance comes from a Latin word meaning 'thing done'). Notice that the *t* at the end remains single when you add *-ed* or *-ing*, following the rule that the consonant remains single if the final syllable is not stressed.

benevolent /*say* buh-**nev**-uh-luhnt/ *adjective* wanting to help other people: *a benevolent organisation for homeless children.*
□ **benevolence**, *noun* –**benevolently**, *adverb*

benign /*say* buh-**nuyn**/ *adjective*
1. Someone or something is **benign** if they are kind and gentle: *She gave the children a benign smile.* **2.** A tumour or lump in the body is **benign** when it does not grow or spread to cause serious illness and death.

THE OPPOSITE (especially of definition 2) is **malignant**.

☑ SPELLING TIP Don't forget the *g* in this word. The letter combination *ign* gives the 'uyn' sound.

bent *adjective*
1. curved or not straight: *a bent stick.*
–*noun* **2.** a liking or preference: *a bent for poetry.*
–*phrase* **3. bent on**, determined or set on: *bent on going to the concert.*

bequeath /*say* buh-**kweedh**, buh-**kweeth**/ *verb* If you **bequeath** something, you hand it down or pass it on to someone who comes after you: *My grandmother bequeathed us money in her will*; *What a mess we are bequeathing the next generation.*
□ **bequest**, *noun* money left by someone in a will.

☑ SPELLING TIP Remember that the sound in the middle of **bequeath** is spelt *qu*. There are many words in which *qu* sounds like 'kw', such as *quiet* and *queen*. Notice also that the second vowel sound is spelt *ea* (although it sounds like 'ee').

bereaved *adjective* If someone is **bereaved**, someone dear to them, such as someone in their family or a close friend, has died recently.
□ **bereavement**, *noun*

beret /*say* **be**-ray/ *noun* a soft, round cap.

☑ SPELLING TIP *Silent letter alert*: don't forget the silent *t* at the end – the *et* spelling makes an 'ay' sound. Other words with this ending are *ballet* and *bouquet*. They all come from French.

berry *noun* (*plural* **berries**) a small fruit with tiny seeds, often brightly coloured.

☑ SPELLING TIP Don't confuse the spelling of **berry** with **bury** which sounds the same. To **bury** is to put something in the ground and cover it with earth.

berserk /*say* buh-**zerk**/ *adjective* uncontrollably crazy and wild: *The crowd went berserk when he kicked the winning goal.*

☑ SPELLING TIP Don't forget that the first syllable is spelt *ber* though you do not hear the *r*. It is spelt like this because *ber* comes from an Icelandic word meaning 'bear-like'. A *berserker* was a Norse warrior of great courage and strength who fought with frenzied fury in battle.

berth *noun*
1. a place to sleep on a boat or train: *Our compartment has two berths.* **2.** a place where a ship can tie up.
–*verb* **3.** When a ship **berths**, it sails into a place where it can tie up: *The ocean liner berthed at 10 o'clock.*
–*phrase* **4. give a wide berth to**, to avoid or keep away from.

☑ SPELLING TIP Don't confuse the spelling of **berth** with **birth** which sounds the same. **Birth** is the act of being born, as in *the birth of the baby.*

beseech *verb* (**beseeches**, **beseeching**, **besought** *or* **beseeched**, **has besought** *or* **has beseeched**) If you **beseech** someone to do something, you ask them in a anxious and desperate way to do it: *I beseech you to believe me!*

NOTE This is used more in literature than in ordinary language.

beside *preposition*
1. near or at the side of: *Sit down beside me.* **2.** compared with: *Beside her, he is tall.* **3.** nothing to do with: *That excuse is beside the point.*
–*phrase* **4. beside yourself**, too upset to think clearly or act reasonably: *He's beside himself with grief.*

besides *preposition*
1. in addition to: *Did anyone go besides you?*; *It was pouring with rain besides being terribly cold.* **2.** other than: *I have no-one to talk to besides you.*
–*adverb* **3.** in addition to what has already been said: *Besides, you are too sick to go.*

besiege /*say* buh-**seej**/ *verb*
1. If a group of people, especially soldiers, **besiege** a place, they crowd round and surround it: *Enemy troops besieged the castle.* **2.** If you **besiege** someone, you surround them closely: *The pop singer was besieged by fans wanting autographs.*

☑ SPELLING TIP Remember that **besiege** has *ie* (to spell the 'ee' sound) following the *s*. This follows the rule that *i* comes before *e* except after *c*.

best *adjective*
1. of highest quality. **2.** favourite: *my best friend.*
–*adverb* **3.** most successfully: *She sings best.* **4.** most: *I like hockey best.*
–*noun* **5.** your good clothes: *to put on your best for the concert.*
–*phrase* **6. all the best**, something you say when you want to wish someone well. **7. make the best of**, to manage as well as you can in difficult conditions.

NOTE For other forms of the adjective, see **good**. For other forms of the adverb, see **well**[1].

best man *noun* the chief attendant or helper of the bridegroom at a wedding.

bestow /*rhymes with* show/ *verb* If you **bestow** an honour or award, you give it as a gift or reward: *The president bestowed a medal on the brave soldier.*
☐ **bestowal**, *noun*

bet *noun*
1. a promise that you will give money or something similar to someone who differs from you, if that person is right and you are wrong: *My sister made a bet that she was taller than me.* **2.** the money or thing that you promised: *She lost her bet.*
–*verb* (**bets**, **betting**, **bet** *or* **betted**, **has bet**) **3.** If you **bet** on something, you risk money or something valuable on the result of a future event: *to bet on a horserace.* **4.** If you say that you **bet** something is true or will happen, you mean that you feel certain about it: *I bet I can jump higher than you.*

betray *verb*
1. If someone **betrays** someone or a country, they are unfaithful to that person or country: *He betrayed us by telling our secrets to our enemies.* **2.** If you **betray** something, you show or reveal it when you do not want to or should not: *His face betrayed his anger.*
☐ **betrayal**, *noun*: *She was deeply hurt by her friend's betrayal.* –**betrayer**, *noun*

NOTE You can call someone who betrays you a **betrayer** but the most common word for this is **traitor**.

betrothed /*rhymes with* clothed/ *adjective* engaged to be married.
☐ **betrothal**, *noun* –**betrothed**, *noun* –**betroth**, *verb*

better *adjective*
1. of higher quality: *The view is better from this window.* **2.** larger, or greater: *It took him the better part of a week to paint the room.* **3.** improved in health: *I hope he is feeling better today.*
–*adverb* **4.** in an improved or more suitable manner: *She behaved better today.*
–*verb* **5.** If you **better** something, you improve it: *He bettered his score in the first round by ten points.*
–*phrase* **6. better off**, in better conditions: *I'm better off living near the school.* **7. had better**, would be wiser or safer to: *You had better stay at home in such bad weather.* **8. think better of**, to think again and decide more wisely: *to think better of walking on the hot sand with bare feet.*

NOTE For other forms of the adjective, see **good**. For other forms of the adverb, see **well**[1].

bettong /*say* **bet**-ong/ *noun* a very small kangaroo that looks like a small wallaby with a short nose.

WORD HISTORY from an Aboriginal language of New South Wales called Dharug

between *preposition*
1. in the space, time or amount separating two or more things: *a path between the buildings*; *a break between exams*; *a difference between prices.* **2.** connecting: *a bridge between the island and the mainland.* **3.** concerning or involving: *an economic agreement between Canada and the United States.* **4.** by sharing an effort or action: *to carry the bags between them.*
–*phrase* **5. between you and me** or **between ourselves**, in secret.

beverage *noun* a drink of any kind.

beware *verb* If a sign or person tells you to **beware**, or to **beware of** something, they are telling you to be very careful and to watch out for danger: *If you go to the shops, beware of the traffic!*

bewilder *verb* If something **bewilders** you, it confuses or puzzles you: *Her explanation completely bewildered him.*
☐ **bewilderment**, *noun*

A SIMILAR WORD is **perplex**.

bewitch *verb*
1. If someone or something **bewitches** you, you are charmed by what they do or how they look: *The singer bewitched thousands with her performance.* **2.** In a fairytale, if someone has been **bewitched**, they have had a magic spell put on them.
☐ **bewitching**, *adjective*: *She looked bewitching in her new dress.*

beyond *preposition*
1. further on or more distant than: *beyond the horizon*; *beyond the house.* **2.** past: *beyond human understanding.* **3.** more than: *They spend beyond their income.*

bi- *prefix* a word part meaning 'two', as in *bicycle, bigamy, binoculars*.

WORD HISTORY this prefix comes from Latin

biannual *adjective* happening twice a year: *a biannual publication.*
☐ **biannually**, *adverb*

COMPARE this with **biennial** (definition 1).

bias /*say* **buy**-uhs/ *noun*
1. a strong opinion which often stops you from seeing the other side of an argument: *The teacher's bias towards sport was obvious.* **2.** a sloping line or direction.
–*verb* (**biases**, **biasing**, **biased**, **has biased**) **3.** If someone or something **biases** you, they influence you and form your opinion for you, often in a bad way: *Don't let his arguments bias you against the real facts.*
☐ **biased**, *adjective*: *The report was heavily biased.*

☑ SPELLING TIP The prefix *bi* means twice or double. It is thought that **bias** comes from the Latin word *biaxius* meaning 'having two axes'.

bib *noun* a small cloth tied to protect a baby's clothes at mealtime.

WORD HISTORY from a Latin word meaning 'drink'

Bible *noun* the sacred book of the Christian religion, consisting of the Old and New Testaments.
☐ **Biblical**, *adjective*

WORD HISTORY from a Greek word meaning 'book'

biblio- *prefix* a word part meaning 'book', as in *bibliography*.

WORD HISTORY this prefix comes from Greek

bibliography /*say* bib-lee-**og**-ruh-fee/ *noun* (*plural* **bibliographies**) a list of books, as those used by a writer and mentioned in their own writing.
☐ **bibliographer**, *noun* –**bibliographic**, *adjective* –**bibliographical**, *adjective*

bicentenary /*say* buy-suhn-**teen**-uh-ree, buy-suhn-**ten**-uh-ree/ *noun* (*plural* **bicentenaries**) a 200th anniversary: *Australia had its bicentenary in 1988.*
☐ **bicentennial**, *adjective*

☑ SPELLING TIP The spelling of **bicentenary** will be easier if you see that it contains two important word parts – the prefix *bi-* (meaning 'two') and *cent* (which comes from Latin and appears in many words whose meaning relates to 100, such as *cent* and *century*). Then you can concentrate on remembering the single *e* in the next part of the word (though it is usually pronounced with an 'ee' sound), followed by a single *n*.

biceps /*say* **buy**-seps/ *noun* a large muscle at the top of the arm or the back of the leg that helps you to bend them.

☑ SPELLING TIP Remember that the first part of **biceps** is spelt *bi* (although it sounds like 'buy'). The prefix *bi-* means 'two', as in *bicycle*. A *bicycle* has two wheels and the **biceps** muscle has two 'heads' (meaning that it is joined at both ends).

bicker *verb* If people **bicker**, they argue about small, unimportant things: *The boys were bickering over who should clean up.*
☐ **bickering**, *noun*

bicycle *noun* a two-wheeled machine for riding on, which you steer by a bar shaped for the rider to hold on to and drive by pushing pedals.
☐ **bicyclist**, *noun*

THE SHORT FORM of this is **bike**.

bid *verb* (**bids**, **bidding**, **bade** /*say* bad/ *for definition 1*, **bid** *for definition 2*, **has bidden**, **bid**)
1. If you **bid** someone to do something, you ask or command them to do it: *The judge bade the jury to leave the courtroom.* **2.** If you **bid** for something that is being sold at an auction, you offer to pay a particular price for it: *They did not get the house they wanted because someone else bid more for it.*
–*noun* **3.** the amount offered for something, especially at an auction. **4.** an attempt to achieve a goal or purpose.
☐ **bidder**, *noun* –**bidding**, *noun*

biennial /*say* buy-**en**-ee-uhl/ *adjective*
1. If something is **biennial**, it happens once every two years: *a biennial festival.* **2.** If a plant is **biennial** it lives for two years, or produces seeds in its second year.
☐ **biennial**, *noun*

COMPARE definition 1 with **biannual**.

bier /*sounds like* beer/ *noun* a stand on which a dead body, or the coffin holding it, rests before it is buried.

☑ SPELLING TIP Don't confuse the spelling of **bier** with **beer** which sounds the same but is spelt with a double *e*. **Beer** is an alcoholic drink.

bifocals *plural noun* a pair of glasses with lenses which have two parts, one for seeing things far away and one for seeing things close to you.
☐ **bifocal**, *adjective*

big *adjective* (**bigger**, **biggest**)
1. large in size or amount: *a big car*; *a big score.* **2.** older: *her big brother.* **3.** important: *big business.*
–*phrase* **4. big on**, knowing a lot and eager about: *She's big on computers.* **5. talk big**, to talk in a way that is meant to make people think you are important.

SIMILAR WORDS (for definition 1) are **colossal**, **giant**, **huge**, **immense**, and **massive**. Note that all these words describe something which is extremely big.

bigamy /*say* **big**-uh-mee/ *noun* the crime of marrying someone while you are still married to someone else.
☐ **bigamist**, *noun*

☑ SPELLING TIP *Single letter alert*: only one *g*. Think of the word *big* although this is not related to its meaning. In fact, **bigamy** is made up of the prefix *bi-* (meaning 'two') and *gamy* (a word part coming from the Greek word for 'marriage'). See also **monogamy** and **polygamy** which contain this same word part.

big bang *noun* the first explosion of matter believed to be the beginning of the universe.

bight *noun*
1. a bend or curve in the shore of the sea. **2.** a body of water bordered by such a bend or curve.

SIMILAR WORDS are **bay**, **gulf**, **inlet** and **cove**. **Bay** and **gulf** refer to fairly large areas of sea or ocean partly bounded by land, while an **inlet** or a **cove** is a small bay.

☑ SPELLING TIP Don't confuse the spelling of **bight** with **bite** or **byte** which sound the same. A **bite** is a wound made with the teeth or a mouthful of food. A **byte** is a unit of information stored by a computer.

bigot /*say* **big**-uht/ *noun* someone who is convinced that their opinion is right and who is not fair-minded about other people's ideas.
☐ **bigoted**, *adjective* –**bigotry**, *noun*

bike *noun* a bicycle, tricycle or motorcycle.

bikini /*say* buh-**kee**-nee/ *noun* a two-piece swimming costume for women.

WORD HISTORY named after *Bikini* Atoll in the northern Pacific Ocean, where the United States tested nuclear bombs from 1946 to 1958

☑ SPELLING TIP Notice that all the vowel sounds in this word are spelt with an *i*, and that there are no double letters.

bilateral *adjective* of or affecting two sides: *The two countries signed a bilateral agreement.*

bilby *noun* (*plural* **bilbies**) a type of bandicoot. It is an animal currently rated as vulnerable rather than endangered.

WORD HISTORY from an Aboriginal language of New South Wales called Yuwaalaraay

bile *noun* a bitter, yellowish liquid which is produced by the liver and which helps you digest food.

bilingual /*say* buy-**ling**-gwuhl/ *adjective* able to speak two languages.
☐ **bilingualism**, *noun* –**bilingually**, *adverb*

bilious /*say* **bil**-yuhs/ *adjective* feeling sick in the stomach.
☐ **biliousness**, *noun*

NOTE **Bilious** is the adjective from **bile**.

bill[1] *noun*
1. a written statement telling you how much money you owe for something. **2.** a notice or advertisement on display. **3.** a plan for a new law to be presented to Parliament.
–*verb* **4.** To **bill** something is to advertise it by notice or advertisement: *The new show was billed for next week.* **5.** To **bill** someone is to send them an account for the goods they have bought.

A SIMILAR WORD (for definitions 1 and 5) is **invoice**.

bill[2] *noun* a bird's beak.

billabong *noun* a waterhole which used to be part of a river.

WORD HISTORY from an Aboriginal language of New South Wales called Wiradjuri

billet *noun*
1. a place for someone to live for a while, usually in someone else's home: *The exchange student was given a billet in the teacher's own home.*
–*verb* (**billets**, **billeting**, **billeted**, **has billeted**) **2.** To **billet** someone is to provide a place for them to stay: *We billeted a student from Japan in our home.*

☑ SPELLING TIP *Double/single letter alert*: double *l* in the middle, and only one *t* at the end. Think of the word *bill* with *et* added at the end. Notice that the *t* remains single when you add

-ed or *-ing*, following the rule that the consonant remains single if the final syllable is not stressed.

billiards /*say* **bil**-yuhdz/ *noun* a game played by two or more people on a long table, with hard balls hit by a long stick called a cue.

billion *noun*
1. a. a thousand times a million, or 10^9. **b.** a million times a million, or 10^{12}. **2.** *Informal* a large amount.
☐ **billion**, *adjective* –**billionth**, *adjective*, *noun*

NOTE The meaning in definition 1b is becoming rare because there is a worldwide tendency to standardise **billion** as meaning 'a thousand millions'. However, it is usually safer to write the number in figures.

billow *noun*
1. a large wave: *the billows of the ocean.*
–*verb* **2.** If something **billows**, it swirls slowly upwards: *Smoke billowed from the chimney.*
☐ **billowy**, *adjective*

billy *noun* (*plural* **billies**) a tin container with a lid, used for boiling water.

billycart *noun* a four-wheeled cart which has a box for a seat and which you steer by ropes attached to its front axle.

ANOTHER WORD for this is **go-cart**.

billy goat *noun* a male goat.

ANOTHER FORM is a **billygoat**.
NOTE The female is a **nanny goat**.

bin *noun* a box or container used to store things: *Put the rubbish in the bin.*

binary /*say* **buy**-nuh-ree/ *adjective*
1. If something is **binary**, it is made up of two parts or things: *a binary star.* **2.** If a system is **binary**, it uses the numbers 0 and 1: *binary code.*

bind /*rhymes with* find/ *verb* (**binds**, **binding**, **bound**, **has bound**)
1. If you **bind** things together, you tie them up with something such as string or rope so that they are held tightly together: *Bind those papers together before you move them.* **2.** If you **bind** something, you tie it up firmly: *to bind up a sore arm.* **3.** If you **bind** substances together, you mix them so that they will stick together in a mass: *You need an egg to bind the ingredients.* **4.** If you **bind** a book, you fasten its pages together and put a cover around them: *This old book is falling apart – we'll have to get it bound again.*
☐ **binder**, *noun*: *Put all those loose papers in that cardboard binder.*

bindi-eye *noun* a small plant with tiny, sharp thorns, sometimes found in grass.

NOTE You can call this plant a **bindy** or **bindi** for short. The plant also has other names in some parts of Australia, such as **joey** and **jo-jo**.

WORD HISTORY from Aboriginal languages of New South Wales called Kamilaroi and Yuwaalaraay

binge *noun Informal* a period of too much eating, drinking or spending money.

bingo *noun* a gambling game in which you cross numbers, called in any order, off a card, the winner having all the numbers called.

binoculars /*say* buh-**nok**-yuh-luhz/ *plural noun* a piece of equipment with magnifying glasses for both eyes, used for making distant objects seem nearer.

ANOTHER TERM for this is **field glasses.**

☑ SPELLING TIP Remember that the first part of **binoculars** is spelt *bi*. This is a prefix meaning 'two'. The next part of the word comes from the Latin *oculus* meaning 'eye'.

bio- *prefix* a word part meaning 'life' or 'living things', as in *biology.*

WORD HISTORY this prefix comes from Greek

biodegradable *adjective* A **biodegradable** chemical or substance is one that can be broken down by the sun or bacteria into products which are not harmful to the environment: *biodegradable soap powder.*

biodiversity *noun* the number and variety of different plant and animal life forms that live in an area: *There is far greater biodiversity in a tropical rainforest than in a desert.*

biofuel *noun* a fuel made from recently living material such as vegetable oil, plants with a high sugar content, and waste from food crops: *Biofuel can be used to runs cars and to make power for factories.*

COMPARE this with **fossil fuel**.

biography *noun* (*plural* **biographies**) the story of a person's life, written by someone else.
☐ **biographer**, *noun* –**biographical**, *adjective*

COMPARE this with **autobiography**.

biology *noun* the science or study of all living things.
☐ **biological**, *adjective* –**biologist**, *noun*

bionic /*say* buy-**on**-ik/ *adjective* A **bionic** person has had parts of their body replaced by electronic equipment so as to give them supernatural strength: *The film was about a bionic man.*

biopsy *noun* (*plural* **biopsies**) the removal of a small section of someone's body to check if it is diseased.

biosystem *noun* a group of living things that interact with each other as part of their life cycle.

birch *noun* (*plural* **birches**) a tree of cold countries, with slender branches and smooth bark.

bird *noun* a two-legged creature which lays eggs and has wings and feathers.

bird flu *noun* See **avian influenza**.

birth *noun*
1. the act of being born. **2.** any beginning: *the birth of television*; *the birth of an idea.*

☑ SPELLING TIP Don't confuse the spelling of **birth** with **berth** which sounds the same. A **berth** is a place to sleep on a boat or train or a place where a ship can tie up.

birthday *noun*
1. the day on which someone is born. **2.** the annual celebration of the day of someone's birth: *It is my brother's seventh birthday tomorrow.*

biscuit /*say* **bis**-kuht/ *noun* a small, thin cake which has been baked until it is crisp.

WORD HISTORY from Latin words meaning 'cooked twice'

☑ SPELLING TIP Don't forget the *ui* spelling for the 'uh' sound.

bisect *verb* To **bisect** something is to cut or divide it into two parts or two equal parts: *Use a pair of compasses to bisect the line.*
☐ **bisection**, *noun*

COMPARE this with **dissect**.

bisexual *noun*
1. an animal, human or plant which has both male and female sex organs. **2.** someone who is sexually attracted to both males and females.

bishop *noun*
1. a Christian priest of high rank, in charge of a whole area. **2.** a chess piece which can only move diagonally.

NOTE **Episcopal** is a word meaning 'having to do with a bishop' (as in definition 1).

bison /*say* **buy**-suhn/ *noun* (*plural* **bison**) a large American animal with high shoulders and shaggy hair.

bistro *noun* (*plural* **bistros**) a small, casual restaurant or wine bar.

bit[1] *noun*
1. a metal bar placed in a horse's mouth and attached to the reins, used to help control it. **2.** the part of some tools which is used for cutting and making holes.

bit[2] *noun* a small piece or amount of something.

bit[3] *noun* a single, basic unit of information stored by a computer, having one of only two possible values, 0 or 1.

bitch *noun* (*plural* **bitches**)
1. a female dog. **2.** *Informal* a woman you think is unpleasant or bad-tempered.
–*verb* **3.** *Informal* If someone **bitches** all the time, they complain continually: *He was bitching about having to do homework every night.*
☐ **bitchy**, *adjective* –**bitchiness**, *noun*

NOTE The use of this word as in definition 2 may offend people.

bite *verb* (**bites**, **biting**, **bit**, **has bitten**)
1. When a person or animal **bites** something, they use their teeth to cut it, hold on to it or take a piece out of it: *The dog bit me on the leg.* **2.** When a mosquito, snake, ant, etc., **bites** you, it pierces your skin and puts something in you that stings or itches or is harmful in some way: *She was bitten on the toe by an ant.* **3.** If you are fishing and the fish are **biting**, they are eating the bait on your hook: *The fish are really biting tonight.*
–*noun* **4.** a cut or sore made by something that bites. **5.** a snack or small amount of food: *I'll just have a bite to eat and then go.* **6.** the act of biting: *He took a bite of the apple.*
–*phrase* **7. bite the dust**, *Informal* **a.** to be killed, especially in fighting. **b.** to fail: *Another good plan bites the dust.*

☑ SPELLING TIP Don't confuse the spelling of **bite** with **bight** or **byte** which sound the same. A **bight** is a curve in a shore forming a large bay. A **byte** is a unit of information stored by a computer.

bitmap *noun* a computer graphics image consisting of rows and columns of dots stored as bits (**bit**[3]).

bitter *adjective*
1. having a sharp, unpleasant, sour taste: *Lemons are bitter.* **2.** very cold: *a bitter wind blowing.* **3.** hard to accept or bear: *He felt a bitter sorrow when his mother died.* **4.** fierce and full of anger and hate: *The war has been very bitter*; *They've been bitter enemies for years.*
☐ **bitterness**, *noun*

bitumen /*say* **bich**-uh-muhn/ *noun*
1. a sticky, black mixture, like tar or asphalt, used to make roads. **2. the bitumen**, a tarred road: *We turned off the bitumen and followed a sandy track down to the creek.*

☑ SPELLING TIP There is a *bit* of a problem with **bitumen** – that is, the letter *t* spells the *ch* sound so that the word starts with *bit* (not *bitch*).

bivouac /*say* **biv**-ooh-ak/ *noun*
1. a camp set up for a short time: *The scouts went on a bivouac in the bush over the long weekend.*
–*verb* (**bivouacs**, **bivouacking**, **bivouacked**, **has bivouacked**) **2.** When you **bivouac**, you camp out: *The soldiers bivouacked in the jungle.*

☑ SPELLING TIP The last two syllables of **bivouac** are the difficult parts. Remember the *ou* spelling for the 'ooh' sound and the *ac* ending – not a *k* in sight until you add *-ed* or *-ing* when you must put a *k* after the *c*.

bizarre */say* buh-**zah**/ *adjective* very strange or unusual: *The doctors were very worried by his bizarre behaviour*; *That's one of the most bizarre films I've ever seen!*

☑ SPELLING TIP Don't confuse the spelling of **bizarre** with **bazaar** (a kind of market) which sounds the same. The word **bizarre** means 'unusual' and its spelling certainly is! Remember especially the *arre* ending. It comes from Basque, a language spoken in parts of Spain and France.

blab *verb* (**blabs**, **blabbing**, **blabbed**, **has blabbed**) *Informal* **1.** If someone **blabs**, they talk too much: *She blabbed on the phone for hours.* **2.** If you **blab**, you tell or reveal something without thinking.
☐ **blabbermouth**, *noun* someone who blabs.

black *adjective*
1. completely dark, or without colour and brightness: *a black night*; *a black shoe.* **2.** having dark-coloured skin. **3.** sad or connected with unhappiness: *It was a black day for the family when their house burnt down.* **4.** angry: *She gave us a black look.* **5.** of tea or coffee, without milk or cream. **6.** *Old-fashioned* evil or morally bad: *Murder is a black deed.*
–*noun* **7.** a black colour. **8.** someone who has dark-coloured skin.
–*verb* **9.** If you **black** something, you make it black or put black on it: *to black your shoes.*
–*phrase* **10. be in someone's black books**, to be out of favour with someone. **11. black out**, to lose consciousness.
☐ **blacken**, *verb*

blackberry *noun* (*plural* **blackberries**) the small, sweet, purple-black fruit of a prickly bush.

blackboard *noun* a smooth, dark board, used for writing or drawing on with chalk.

blackcurrant *noun* a small, black fruit which grows on a garden shrub.

blackguard */say* **blag**-ahd/ *noun Old-fashioned* someone who is dishonourable.

☑ SPELLING TIP To spell this word, you have to think of it as being made up of the two words *black* and *guard*, rather than thinking about the unusual way in which it is pronounced.

blackhead *noun* a small, black-tipped pimple, usually on the face.

black hole *noun* a region in outer space thought to be created by the collapse of a star under its own gravitational forces, from which no light or matter can escape.

blackmail *noun*
1. the act of demanding money from someone by threatening to reveal secrets about them.
–*verb* **2.** If someone **blackmails** someone else, they threaten to reveal secrets or to cause some other harm unless that person pays them money, or does what they want.
☐ **blackmailer**, *noun*

blackout *noun*
1. an electrical power failure. **2.** a loss of memory or consciousness which lasts for a short time.

blacksmith *noun* someone who works in or with iron or, in the modern era, steel.

bladder *noun*
1. the part inside the body that is like a bag and which stores urine. **2.** a bag that gets bigger if you fill it with air or liquid, like the rubber bag inside a football.

blade *noun*
1. the flat, cutting part of a knife, sword or dagger. **2.** the leaf of a plant: *a blade of grass.* **3.** the thin, flat part of an oar, bone or something similar: *The blade of the oar skimmed the surface of the water.*

blame *noun*
1. the responsibility for a mistake: *She took the blame for the accident.*
–*verb* **2.** If you **blame** a person or thing for something bad that happens, you say it is their fault: *He blamed the traffic for making him late.*
☐ **blameless**, *adjective* –**blameworthy**, *adjective*

blanch *verb*
1. If you **blanch**, you become white or pale because you are shocked or ill: *The boy's face blanched with fear.* **2.** If you **blanch** food, you put it in boiling water for a short time, and then in cold, in order to remove the skins or to kill germs before freezing: *to blanch nuts, vegetables, or fruit.*

bland *adjective*
1. If food is **bland**, it is mild, with little flavour or spice: *bland food.* **2.** If what someone says or does is **bland**, it is polite and reasonable, but often without real feeling or excitement: *He gave a bland smile.*
☐ **blandness**, *noun*

blank *adjective*
1. If a paper or space is **blank**, it has nothing written or printed on it: *The computer screen went blank*; *a blank piece of paper.* **2.** If someone's face is **blank**, it shows no understanding, feeling or interest: *After the accident, he just stood there with a blank expression on his face.* **3.** If your mind is **blank** or goes **blank**, you cannot remember something, especially the answer to a question: *I tried to think of his name but my mind went blank.*
–*noun* **4.** an empty space left for someone to fill in: *to fill in the blanks on a form.* **5.** a gun cartridge

which has powder inside it but no bullet: *to use blanks for practice shooting.*

WORD HISTORY from a French word meaning 'white'

blanket *noun*
1. a large piece of soft woollen or cotton material, used as a bed covering. **2.** any layer or covering that hides something: *A blanket of dust covered everything in the room.*
–*verb* (**blankets**, **blanketing**, **blanketed**, **has blanketed**) **3.** If something **blankets** something else, it covers it in a layer, like a blanket: *Fog blanketed the town.*

blare *verb* If something **blares**, it makes a loud, harsh sound: *The radio blared.*
☐ **blare**, *noun*: *the blare of traffic.*

blasé /*say* blah-**zay**/ *adjective* not caring about and bored by the enjoyments and pleasures of life: *It was exciting at first to live by the sea but now I have become blasé about it.*

☑ SPELLING TIP Remember that this word ends with an *e*, and is usually spelt with an accent over it which gives it an 'ay' sound. This is because the word was originally French.

blaspheme /*say* blas-**feem**/ *verb* If someone **blasphemes**, they speak without respect about God or sacred things.
☐ **blasphemer**, *noun* –**blasphemy**, *noun* (*plural* **blasphemies**)

☑ SPELLING TIP The difficult part with this word is the second syllable. Remember the *ph* spelling for the 'f' sound, and the *eme* spelling for the 'eem' sound.

blast *noun*
1. a sudden, strong burst of wind or air. **2.** the sudden sound of a whistle or horn. **3.** an explosion.
–*verb* **4.** If someone **blasts** something, they destroy or break it up with bombs or explosives: *The construction team blasted the mountain to make the road.* **5.** *Informal* If someone **blasts** you, they criticise you severely: *Our mum blasted us for being disobedient.*

blatant /*say* **blay**-tuhnt/ *adjective* very obvious: *a blatant lie.*
☐ **blatancy**, *noun* –**blatantly**, *adverb*

WORD HISTORY made up by the 16th-century English poet Edmund Spenser and based on a Latin word meaning 'babble'

blaze[1] *noun*
1. a bright flame or fire. **2.** a sudden flash of light: *a blaze of sunshine.* **3.** a bright and colourful display: *The autumn trees are a blaze of colour.* **4.** sudden fury: *a blaze of temper.*
–*verb* To **blaze** is to **5.** burn brightly: *The fire blazed.* **6.** shine like a flame: *The house blazed with lights.*

blaze[2] *noun*
1. a white patch on the face of a horse or cow. **2.** a mark made on a tree to point out a path.
–*verb* **3.** To **blaze** a path is to mark it with blazes: *The workers blazed a trail through the forest.*

blazer *noun* a jacket, sometimes with a special design sewn on the pocket.

bleach *verb*
1. If you **bleach** something, you make it paler or remove a stain, either by using a chemical or by leaving it in the sun: *My brother bleached the ink stains out of his shirt.*
–*noun* **2.** a chemical used for bleaching.

bleak *adjective*
1. cold and harsh: *a bleak winter day.* **2.** empty and dreary: *A prisoner in a cell has a bleak life.*
☐ **bleakly**, *adverb* –**bleakness**, *noun*

bleary *adjective* (**blearier**, **bleariest**) dimmed from tears or tiredness: *bleary eyes.*
☐ **blearily**, *adverb* –**bleariness**, *noun*

bleat *verb*
1. To **bleat** is to make the cry of a sheep or goat. **2.** If someone **bleats**, they complain: *I'm sick of hearing you bleat about your problems.*
☐ **bleat**, *noun*

bleed *verb* (**bleeds**, **bleeding**, **bled**, **has bled**) If you **bleed**, you lose blood from your body because of an injury or illness: *Her arm's bleeding badly so we'll have to bandage it.*
☐ **bleeding**, *noun*

blemish *verb*
1. To **blemish** something is to spoil its perfection: *That one mistake blemished his career.*
–*noun* **2.** a spot, stain or other fault: *a blemish on his face*; *a blemish on the skin of the mango.*

A SIMILAR WORD (for definition 1) is **mar**.

blend *verb*
1. To **blend** things is to mix or combine them: *Blend the butter and sugar.* **2.** If things **blend**, they mix together: *The butter and sugar blended well.*
☐ **blend**, *noun*: *a delicious blend of fruit juices.*

blender *noun* an electric appliance which chops and mixes food.

bless *verb* (**blesses**, **blessing**, **blessed** *or* **blest**, **has blessed** *or* **has blest**) To **bless** someone or something is to ask for heavenly protection or help for them: *The priest blessed the fleet of fishing boats.*

blight *noun*
1. a plant disease: *tomato blight.* **2.** a damaging effect: *The bad weather put a blight on their holiday.*
–*verb* **3.** If something **blights** another thing, it damages or destroys it: *The long drought blighted our hopes of a good harvest.*

blind *adjective* If someone is **blind**, they are **1.** unable to see. **2.** unwilling to understand or be fair: *She was blind with jealousy.*
–*noun* **3.** a window cover which keeps out light.
–*verb* **4.** If something **blinds** you, you are unable to see: *The fierce light of the sun blinded him for a few minutes.*
☐ **blindly**, *adverb* –**blindness**, *noun*

blindfold *verb*
1. If you **blindfold** someone, you tie a piece of cloth over their eyes so that they cannot see: *The kidnappers blindfolded him.*
–*noun* **2.** a cover for the eyes: *We wear a blindfold for this game.*

blink *verb*
1. If you **blink**, you quickly close your eyes and open them again: *The camera flash made us blink.* **2.** When a light **blinks**, it flashes on and off: *We could see the lights of the ship blinking out at sea.*
–*noun* **3.** a blinking of the eye.
–*phrase* **4. on the blink**, *Informal* not working properly.
☐ **blinker**, *noun*

bliss *noun* a feeling of great happiness and pleasure.
☐ **blissful**, *adjective* –**blissfully**, *adverb* –**blissfulness**, *noun*

blister *noun*
1. a small watery swelling on the skin.
–*verb* **2.** If something **blisters** part of your body, it causes blisters there: *The boiling water blistered my finger.* **3.** If part of your body **blisters**, you get blisters there: *My bare shoulders blistered in the hot sun.*
☐ **blistering**, *adjective* –**blistery**, *adjective*

> WORD HISTORY from a French word meaning 'clod' or 'lump'

blitz *noun* a sudden attack: *a blitz on a city in wartime*; *a police blitz on drivers who speed.*

blizzard *noun* a violent storm with strong winds and driving snow.

bloat *verb* To **bloat** is to make bigger or cause to swell, especially with air or water.

bloc *noun* a group of countries sharing the same political ideas: *the former communist bloc.*

> ☑ SPELLING TIP Don't forget that this is *block* without the *k*. It is spelt like this when it has this particular meaning because it originally came from French.

block *noun*
1. a solid piece of hard material: *a child's building block.* **2.** a large building divided into flats or offices: *We live in a block of flats.* **3.** a group of buildings or houses surrounded by streets: *We drove around the block three times looking for a parking space.* **4.** an amount or part thought of or dealt with at one time: *to deal with the week's orders as a block.*
–*verb* **5.** To **block** is to be in the way of: *The accident blocked the traffic.*
☐ **blockage**, *noun*

> A SIMILAR WORD (for definition 5) is **obstruct**.

blockade *noun*
1. the closing of a port by enemy ships or soldiers to stop supplies from going in or out.
–*verb* **2.** If enemy ships **blockade** a port, they close it in order to stop supplies from going in or out.

> A SIMILAR WORD is **siege**.

blockbuster *noun* anything large and exciting, such as a grand theatrical production, successful film, best-selling book, and so on.

blog *noun* a type of website that has articles and information about a particular subject that people can comment on, often with links to other sites on the same subject: *Joe and Ben set up a blog so that they could record their trip across America and get comments from their friends.*
☐ **blog**, *verb* (**blogs**, **blogging**, **blogged**, **has blogged**): *She blogs about the environment.* –**blogger**, *noun*

bloke *noun Informal* a man.

blond *adjective*
1. light-coloured: *blond hair.*
–*noun* **2.** a blond person.

> ANOTHER SPELLING (for a girl or woman with fair hair) is **blonde**. Note that a **blond** can be a male or female with fair hair.
> WORD HISTORY from a Latin word meaning 'yellow'

blood *noun*
1. the red liquid that flows through the body.
–*phrase* **2. in cold blood**, calmly and without feeling: *They were murdered in cold blood.*

bloodbath *noun* the cruel killing of a large number of people.

> A SIMILAR WORD is **massacre**.

bloodcurdling *adjective* very frightening and horrible: *He jumped out with a bloodcurdling roar.*

bloodhound *noun* a large dog with a good sense of smell, used for hunting animals or finding lost people.

bloodshot *adjective* Eyes are said to be **bloodshot** when the white parts are red and sore: *His eyes were bloodshot – he hadn't slept for nearly three days.*

bloodthirsty *adjective*
1. taking pleasure in killing or violence: *Bloodthirsty bandits roamed the woods, robbing and killing travellers.* **2.** having to do with violence and killing: *a bloodthirsty film.*

A SIMILAR WORD (for definition 1) is **murderous**.

bloody *adjective* (**bloodier**, **bloodiest**)
1. stained or covered with blood: *a bloody knee.* 2. causing the loss of many lives: *a bloody battle.* 3. *Informal* very great: *a bloody nuisance*; *bloody good news.*

NOTE The use of this word as in definition 3 might offend people.

bloom *verb*
1. If a plant or tree **blooms**, it produces flowers. 2. If someone or something **blooms**, they are in a healthy or growing state: *The children bloomed in the wonderful climate*; *When they were put in the same class their friendship bloomed.*
–*noun* 3. a flower.

bloomers *plural noun* loose underpants, formerly worn by women.

WORD HISTORY named after a Mrs Amelia *Bloomer*, a magazine publisher of New York, who helped make these pants popular in about 1850

blossom *noun*
1. the flower of a plant, especially of a fruit tree.
–*verb* 2. If a plant or tree **blossoms**, it produces flowers. 3. If someone or something **blossoms**, they develop and grow in a pleasing way: *She blossomed into a wonderful musician.*

☑ SPELLING TIP *Double/single letter alert*: double *s* in the middle and only one *m* at the end. Think of the related word *bloom* and put a double *s* between the two *o*'s.

blot *noun*
1. a spot of ink on paper. 2. a stain: *a blot on your good record.*
–*verb* (**blots**, **blotting**, **blotted**, **has blotted**) 3. To **blot** or **blot up** something liquid is to soak it up: *She blotted up the spilt milk with a thick cloth.* 4. To **blot** something is to stain it: *The lie he told blotted his reputation.*
–*phrase* 5. **blot out**, to hide from view, as if you were hiding something on a page with a blot of ink: *The clouds blotted out the mountains.*

blotch *noun* (*plural* **blotches**) a large, unevenly shaped mark.
☐ **blotchy**, *adjective*

blouse /*say* blowz/ *noun* a woman's shirt.

blow[1] *noun*
1. a hard knock with the hand or something held in it. 2. a sudden shock: *a blow to your confidence.*

blow[2] *verb* (**blows**, **blowing**, **blew**, **has blown**)
1. When the wind **blows**, the air moves: *Can you hear the wind blowing through the trees?* 2. If the wind or a machine **blows** something somewhere, the thing is moved there by the force of the air: *The fan blew his papers onto the floor.* 3. When you **blow**, you push out air from your mouth: *I blew onto my fingers to keep them warm.* 4. If you **blow** a whistle, horn or other musical instrument, you make a sound come out of it by blowing into it. 5. When you **blow** your nose, you clear it by breathing hard through it and into a handkerchief, etc. 6. When an electrical fuse **blows**, it stops working because a part of it has burnt or melted.
–*noun* 7. a storm with strong wind: *a fierce blow.*
–*phrase* 8. **blow out**, to put out (something burning) with your breath: *Blow out the candle.* 9. **blow over**, **a.** to stop raging: *The storm has blown over now.* **b.** to cease to be a concern: *I'll tell him when the row has blown over.* 10. **blow up**, **a.** to force air into: *to blow up a balloon.* **b.** to destroy with explosives: *to blow up a bridge.* **c.** to come into being: *The storm blew up suddenly.*

blowfly *noun* (*plural* **blowflies**) a fly which lays eggs, especially on meat.

NOTE The eggs hatch into **maggots**.

blubber *noun*
1. the fat of a whale or similar sea animal.
–*verb* 2. To **blubber** is to cry noisily.

bludge *verb Informal* Someone who **bludges** avoids doing what they should: *While the others put up the tent, he bludged at the beach.*
☐ **bludger**, *noun*

bludgeon /*say* **bluj**-uhn/ *noun*
1. a short, heavy piece of wood used as a weapon.
–*verb* 2. If someone **bludgeons** someone or something, they hit them with a heavy object.

☑ SPELLING TIP The middle part of this word is spelt *udge* (as in many familiar words such as *judge*). Remember that you keep the *e* before the *on* ending, although you do not hear it in the pronunciation.

blue *adjective* (**bluer**, **bluest**)
1. having the same colour as the sky and the sea on a sunny day. 2. *Informal* sad and unhappy.
–*noun* 3. a blue colour. 4. *Informal* a mistake. 5. *Informal* a fight or argument.
–*phrase* 6. **out of the blue**, nowhere or the unknown: *It arrived one afternoon from out of the blue.* 7. **true blue**, loyal.

bluebottle *noun* a small, blue sea animal with long tentacles which can sting you.

blueprint *noun*
1. a copy of a building plan printed in white on blue paper. 2. any detailed plan which can be copied at a later time.

blues *plural noun* 1. *Informal* feelings of sadness: *to have the blues.* 2. a type of modern music, originating in the early 20th century among African Americans, usually songs about sadness or troubles, accompanied by a guitar.

blue screen *noun* a large blue background for a film or video shot which is then filled in with an image of the desired background.

blue-tongue *noun* a large Australian lizard with a broad blue tongue.

bluetooth wireless technology *noun* radio technology that allows computers and telecommunication devices such as mobile phones to connect with each other.

> WORD HISTORY named after the Viking king, Harald Bluetooth, who joined Denmark and Norway under one rule

bluff[1] *noun* a wide, steep cliff.

bluff[2] *verb*
1. To **bluff** is to do or say something to give someone a wrong idea, usually because you want to get an advantage for yourself, or to cover up fear: *He bluffed his way past the security guards by pretending to be a policeman*; *I'm not worried about her threats – I think she's only bluffing.*
–*noun* **2.** something you do or say when you are bluffing: *He said he could get more than $50 for his bike but we knew it was just a bluff*; *I wasn't really going to dive – it was just a big bluff.*
–*phrase* **3. call someone's bluff**, to encourage someone to go ahead and do something they have been threatening to do when you know that they probably will not do it.

blunder *noun*
1. a silly mistake.
–*verb* To **blunder** is to **2.** make a silly mistake. **3.** move or act clumsily: *I blundered into the bookshelves.*

blunt *adjective*
1. If something is **blunt**, it does not have a sharp edge or point: *blunt scissors.* **2.** If someone is **blunt**, they are plain and direct in what they say: *He was very blunt in his criticism.*
□ **bluntly**, *adverb* –**bluntness**, *noun*

> A SIMILAR WORD (for definition 2) is **straightforward**.

blur *verb* (**blurs**, **blurring**, **blurred**, **has blurred**)
1. To **blur** something is to make it unclear or confused: *Rain blurred the view from the window.*
–*noun* **2.** something that is unclear or confused: *The car was just a blur as it sped past.*
□ **blurry**, *adjective* (**blurrier**, **blurriest**)

blurb *noun* information about a book or a recording, often printed on its cover.

> WORD HISTORY made up by the American humorist and illustrator, Gelett Burgess (1866–1951)

blush *verb* If you **blush**, you become red in the face because you are embarrassed or ashamed.
□ **blush**, *noun*

bluster *verb* If you **bluster**, you speak or act in a noisy or violent way: *He tried to bluster his way out of it when we accused him of lying.*
□ **bluster**, *noun*

blustery *adjective* If wind is **blustery**, it is blowing strongly: *They had to cancel the yacht race because of the blustery conditions.*

BMX bike *noun* a strongly built bicycle, good for riding in rough areas.

> WORD HISTORY short for *Bicycle Motocross*, with the *cross* changed to *X* and pronounced as the letter 'x'

boa constrictor *noun* a snake of Central and South America, up to four metres long.

boar *noun* a male pig.

> ☑ SPELLING TIP Don't confuse the spelling of **boar** with **boor** or **bore** which sound the same. A **boor** is a rude person, and a **bore** is a hole made by drilling, or a dull person.

> NOTE The female is a **sow**.

board *noun*
1. a flat piece of wood, cut into long, thin pieces: *a timber board.* **2.** a thin, flat piece of wood or other material made for a special purpose: *a chess board*; *an ironing-board*; *a noticeboard.* **3.** a group of people who are in charge of a business or organisation: *the board of the club.*
–*verb* **4.** If you **board** a ship, train, bus or aircraft, you get on it in order to go somewhere. **5.** If you **board** at someone's house or at a hotel, you pay for a room and meals: *My sister has gone to university in another city and is boarding with our uncle.* **6.** If you **board** at your school, you live there.
–*phrase* **7. across the board**, affecting everything or everyone concerned: *The new regulations apply across the board.* **8. on board**, on or in a ship, aeroplane, or vehicle.

> ☑ SPELLING TIP Don't confuse the spelling of **board** with **bored** which sounds the same. **Bored** describes someone who is tired of something.

boarder *noun*
1. a pupil who lives at a boarding school during term. **2.** someone who pays for meals and a room to sleep in: *My aunt takes in boarders to earn extra money.*

> ☑ SPELLING TIP Don't confuse the spelling of **boarder** with **border** which sounds the same. A **border** is the edge of something.

boast *verb* When someone **boasts** about something they own or have done, they talk about it with too much pride: *She's always boasting about how good she is at tennis.*

□ **boast**, *noun*: *My father's boast was that he could fix anything.* –**boastful**, *adjective* –**boastfully**, *adverb* –**boastfulness**, *noun*

boat *noun*
1. a vessel for carrying people or things over water.
–*phrase* **2. in the same boat**, in the same situation, usually a bad one: *It wasn't only our family who had their house damaged in the storm. All our neighbours are in the same boat.*

NOTE In general, a **boat** is smaller than a **ship**. An old rule says that a boat can fit onto a ship but a ship cannot fit onto a boat. However, there are exceptions. For example, submarines, fishing boats, and patrol boats are always **boats** whatever their size.

boater *noun* a straw hat with a hard, flat brim.

boat people *plural noun* refugees who leave their own country and arrive in another country by sea, usually in small boats.

bob[1] *noun*
1. a short, quick movement: *a bob of the head.*
–*verb* (**bobs**, **bobbing**, **bobbed**, **has bobbed**) **2.** To **bob** is to make short, quick movements up and down: *The boat bobbed beside the jetty.*
–*phrase* **3. bob up**, to come into sight suddenly: *She bobbed up from behind a pile of books.*

bob[2] *noun* a woman's haircut in which the hair is cut short in a straight line evenly around the head.

bobbin *noun* a small reel on which thread is wound for use in a sewing machine or in spinning.

bocconcini /*say* bok-uhn-**chee**-nee/ *noun* a soft white cheese which is about the shape and size of a golf ball.

☑ SPELLING TIP *Double/single letter alert*: the letter *c* appears three times in this word, firstly as a double *c* (giving a 'k' sound) and then alone (giving a 'ch' sound). Also remember the *ini* ending. The *i* ending is common in plural words that have come from Italian. In Italian, **bocconcini** is a plural word meaning literally 'little mouthfuls'. Rap it out as *boc+con+ci+ni*.

bodice /*say* **bod**-uhs/ *noun* the part of a woman's dress above the waist.

body *noun* (*plural* **bodies**)
1. the whole physical structure of a person or animal. **2.** the physical part of a person or animal without the head, arms or legs. **3.** a dead person or animal. **4.** the main part: *the body of the plane*; *the body of the story.* **5.** a group of people or things: *a body of friends.*

A SIMILAR WORD (for definition 2) is **trunk**; (for definition 3) **corpse**.

body image *noun* the picture a person has in their mind of the way their own body looks: *He had a body image of himself as a fat person, even though he was really quite thin.*

bog *noun*
1. an area of soft, wet earth.
–*verb* (**bogs**, **bogging**, **bogged**, **has bogged**) **2.** If a vehicle is **bogged**, it has become stuck in something soft or wet: *The truck was bogged in the sand.*
□ **boggy**, *adjective* (**boggier**, **boggiest**)

bogey /*say* **boh**-gee/ *noun*
1. a swimming hole. **2.** a bath or shower. **3.** See **bogy**.

ANOTHER SPELLING is **bogie**.
WORD HISTORY from an Aboriginal language of New South Wales called Dharug

boggle *verb* (**boggles**, **boggling**, **boggled**, **has boggled**) to show alarm or surprise: *He boggled at the sight of the huge guard dogs prowling outside.* .

bogie /*say* **boh**-gee/ *noun*
1. a small trolley used by workmen on a railway line. **2.** a set of wheels supporting a railway engine or carriage. **3.** See **bogey** and **bogy**.

bogong *noun* a large Australian moth sometimes used as food.

ANOTHER SPELLING is **bugong**.
WORD HISTORY from an Aboriginal language of New South Wales and Victoria called Ngarigo

bogus /*say* **boh**-guhs/ *adjective* not real or true: *He used a bogus name to conceal his real identity.*

A SIMILAR WORD is **sham**.

bogy /*say* **boh**-gee/ *noun* (*plural* **bogies**) anything that frightens or worries you: *The dark is a real bogy for some small children.*

OTHER SPELLINGS are **bogey** and **bogie**.

boil[1] *verb*
1. When you **boil** a liquid, you heat it until it becomes so hot that bubbles form and steam comes off: *to boil water for tea.* **2.** If a liquid **boils**, it becomes as hot as that: *The soup is boiling.* **3.** If something **boils**, it holds, or is in, a boiling liquid: *The pot is boiling*; *The vegetables are boiling.* **4.** If you **boil** something, you cook it by boiling: *I boiled the rice.*
–*phrase* **5. boil down to**, to have as the most important part: *The situation boils down to the fact that I don't really like her.*

boil[2] *noun* an infected, swollen sore under the skin.

boiler *noun*
1. a container with a lid used for boiling things. **2.** a closed container in which steam is produced to drive engines.

boisterous *adjective* rough and noisy: *a boisterous welcome*; *a boisterous crowd of friends.*
☐ **boisterously**, *adverb* –**boisterousness**, *noun*

bok choy *noun* a vegetable with long green leaves and thick, pale stems.

ANOTHER SPELLING is **buck choy**.

bold *adjective*
1. not afraid to do things: *She was bold enough to stand up for her friends in the argument.* **2.** rude or insulting: *Don't speak to me in that bold voice.* **3.** easily noticed: *She always wears dresses with bold colours*; *bold handwriting.*
☐ **boldly**, *adverb* –**boldness**, *noun* –**embolden**, *verb*: *Her encouragement emboldened him to try again.*

bolognaise /*say* bol-uh-**nayz**/ *adjective* having to do with a sauce for pasta made with minced meat, onions, garlic, tomato paste and seasonings.

ANOTHER SPELLING is **bolognese**.
WORD HISTORY from the French name for the Italian city of Bologna

bolster *noun*
1. a long, round pillow. **2.** a support: *a bolster to your courage.*
–*verb* **3.** When something **bolsters** you, it makes you feel stronger or more confident: *The teacher's encouraging words bolstered Yusef's self-confidence.*

☑ SPELLING TIP *Single letter alert*: only one *l*.

bolt *noun*
1. a sliding bar which fastens a door or gate. **2.** a thick metal pin which screws into a nut (definition 3) and holds pieces of wood or metal together.
–*verb* **3.** If you **bolt** something, you fasten it with a bolt. **4.** If you **bolt**, you run away because you are afraid: *We bolted when we saw the snake.*
–*phrase* **5. a bolt of lightning**, a flash in the sky, with thunder. **6. bolt out of** (or **from**) **the blue**, something that happens suddenly and when you least expect it. **7. bolt upright**, in a stiff, vertical position: *She sat bolt upright when she heard the frightening noise.*

ANOTHER WORD (for definition 5) is **thunderbolt**.

bomb *noun*
1. a container filled with an explosive and used as a weapon.
–*verb* **2.** To **bomb** a place is to attack it with bombs: *Darwin was bombed during World War II.*
☐ **bomber**, *noun*

bombard /*say* bom-**bahd**/ *verb*
1. To **bombard** a place or building is to attack it with heavy guns or bombs: *The city was bombarded for weeks but did not give in.* **2.** To **bombard** something or someone is to hit or attack them with something many times: *The reporters bombarded the prime minister with questions.*
☐ **bombardment**, *noun*

bombast *noun* words or remarks that sound important but are often not sincere: *His answer was full of bombast.*
☐ **bombastic**, *adjective* –**bombastically**, *adverb*

WORD HISTORY from a Latin word meaning 'cotton' (as used for packing)

bombshell *noun*
1. a bomb. **2.** something which causes surprise and shock: *Her announcement came as a bombshell to us.*

bond *noun*
1. something which joins or unites people: *a bond of friendship.* **2.** a written promise or agreement, often to do a job or to pay money. **3.** a certificate that the government or a bank gives you when you lend them money, promising to pay the money back to you, with interest, after a fixed time.
–*verb* **4.** To **bond** things is to join or hold them together with glue or something similar: *He bonded the broken pieces together with strong glue.* **5.** If people **bond** or something **bonds** them, they develop feelings of love or friendship for each other: *The new girl quickly bonded with the rest of the class*; *The troubles they shared bonded them together for life.*

bondage *noun* the state of being controlled by someone or something.

A SIMILAR WORD is **slavery**.

bone *noun*
1. one of the separate hard pieces of the body that together with the rest form a skeleton: *a hip bone.*
–*verb* **2.** If you **bone** something, you take the bones out of it: *to bone a fish.*
–*phrase* **3. bare bones**, the most important parts or facts presented in their simplest form: *the bare bones of an argument.* **4. feel in your bones**, to have a strong feeling about something without knowing why. **5. have a bone to pick**, to have something to argue about.
☐ **bony**, *adjective* (**bonier**, **boniest**)

bonfire *noun* a large outdoor fire.

bongo *noun* (*plural* **bongos** *or* **bongoes**) one of a pair of small drums, which you play by beating with your fingers.

bonnet *noun*
1. a close-fitting hat, tied under the chin: *a baby's bonnet.* **2.** any other protective covering, such as the metal cover over the engine of a car.

bonsai /*say* **bon**-suy/ *noun*
1. the art of keeping trees and shrubs very small and shaping them in particular ways by cutting

their roots and branches. **2.** a tree or shrub grown this way.

☑ SPELLING TIP Remember that the last part of **bonsai** is spelt *ai* (although it sounds like 'uy'). This is because the word comes from Japanese (where it was formed from two words meaning 'pot' and 'to plant'). You might know some other words from Japanese that have this ending, such as *samurai*.

bonus /*say* **boh**-nuhs/ *noun* extra money paid to a worker as a reward for good work.

bonzer *Informal*, *Rather old-fashioned*
–*adjective* **1.** excellent or pleasing: *a bonzer result.*
–*interjection* **2.** an exclamation used to show pleasure or to show that you agree with something.

ANOTHER SPELLING is **bonza**.

boo *interjection* **1.** an exclamation you use to show that you do not think that something or someone is any good, or to frighten someone.
–*verb* (**boos**, **booing**, **booed**, **has booed**) **2.** If you **boo** something or someone, you call out 'boo', to show that you do not approve of them: *His performance was terrible and he was booed off the stage.*

boobook *noun* a small, brownish owl with a white-spotted back and wings, found in Australia and New Zealand.

boogie board *noun* a small, light and slightly curved board that you take into the surf so that you can lie on it and let the waves take you back to the shore.

book *noun*
1. a written or printed work of some length, especially on consecutive sheets bound or fastened together.
–*verb* **2.** If you **book** something, you ask someone to keep it for you to use later: *I booked a cabin on the ferry*; *to book theatre tickets.* **3.** If a police officer **books** someone, they officially record their name and the offence they have committed: *He was booked for speeding.*
☐ **booking**, *noun*: *We have made a booking at the new Vietnamese restaurant.*

bookish *adjective* eager to read or study: *Jim's sporty sisters were proud of the success of their bookish brother.*

bookkeeping *noun* the job of keeping records of all the money earned and spent in a business.
☐ **bookkeeper**, *noun*

bookmaker *noun* someone who takes the bets of other people, especially at a racecourse.
☐ **bookmaking**, *noun*

bookmark *noun*
1. a strip of cardboard, ribbon, or something similar, placed between the pages of a book to mark a place. **2.** the address of a website you might want to visit again, kept in a list on your browser.

bookworm *noun* someone who loves reading.

boom[1] *verb* To **boom** is to **1.** make a deep, echoing noise: *His voice boomed in the empty hall.* **2.** suddenly do very well: *During the holidays business was booming.*
–*noun* **3.** a loud, deep sound, like that made by waves or distant guns. **4.** a rapid increase in the amount of business done.

boom[2] *noun*
1. a long pole, used to keep the bottom of a sail straight. **2.** a movable arm that holds a microphone or floodlight above the actors in a television or film studio.

boomer *noun* a large male kangaroo.

boomerang *noun* a curved, flat piece of wood that returns to you if you throw it in the right way. Boomerangs were first used by Aboriginal people as hunting weapons.

WORD HISTORY from an Aboriginal language of New South Wales called Dharug

boon *noun* a help or advantage: *The rain will be a boon to the farmers.*

boor /*say* baw, boouh/ *noun* someone who is rude or not considerate.
☐ **boorish**, *adjective* –**boorishly**, *adverb*

WORD HISTORY from the Dutch word meaning 'peasant'

☑ SPELLING TIP Don't confuse the spelling of **boor** with **boar** or **bore** which sound the same. A **boar** is a male pig, and a **bore** is a hole made by drilling, or a dull person.

boost *verb*
1. To **boost** is to lift or increase: *He boosted the boy onto the back of the pony*; *Their praise boosted the nervous girl's confidence.*
–*noun* **2.** an upward push.
☐ **booster**, *noun*

boot[1] *noun*
1. a shoe which covers part of the leg. **2.** a separate space in a car for storing items, usually in the back.

boot[2] *verb* If you **boot** or **boot up** a computer, you switch it on and make it ready to work.

booth *noun* a small, closed-in place, usually made just big enough for one person to fit in: *a ticket booth.*

bootleg *adjective* made illegally: *We were warned about buying bootleg CDs.*

booty *noun* anything taken or won, especially in times of war: *The bank robbers shared their booty.*

booze *Informal*
–*noun* **1.** alcoholic drink: *to buy some booze for a party.*
–*verb* **2.** To **booze** is to drink a lot of alcoholic drink: *They are at the pub boozing.*
☐ **boozer**, *noun* –**boozy**, *adjective*

border *noun*
1. the edge or side of anything: *to plant pansies around the border.* **2.** the line where one country or state meets another.
–*verb* **3.** If something **borders** something else, it forms a border along the edge of it: *Their land borders a large forest.*

☑ SPELLING TIP Don't confuse the spelling of **border** with **boarder** which sounds the same. A **boarder** is someone who pays for meals and somewhere to sleep, or a student who lives at a school.

borderline *adjective* near the edge or boundary: *a borderline pass in the exam.*

bore[1] *verb*
1. To **bore** is to make a round hole: *to bore through rock.*
–*noun* **2.** a deep hole made in the earth to reach an underground water supply.

☑ SPELLING TIP Don't confuse **bore** with **boar** or **boor** which sound the same. A **boar** is a male pig, and a **boor** is a rude person.

bore[2] *verb*
1. If something or someone **bores** you, they make you feel tired or weary because they are not very interesting: *She bores me with her complaints.*
–*noun* **2.** a person who bores other people.
☐ **bored**, *adjective* –**boredom**, *noun*

☑ SPELLING TIP See **bore**[1].

bore[3] *verb* the past tense of **bear**[1].

☑ SPELLING TIP See **bore**[1].

borer *noun* an insect that bores into wood.

boring *adjective* not interesting: *a boring film.*

SIMILAR WORDS are **dull**, **tedious** and **monotonous**. Something that is **tedious** is long and boring (*a tedious meeting*) and something that is **monotonous** is boring because of being ordinary and repetitive, with no change (*a monotonous job*).

born *verb*
1. When someone is **born**, their mother gives birth to them: *My brother was born on 27 October 1998.* **2.** You say something is **born** when it comes into existence: *The game of cricket was born in the 18th century.*
–*adjective* **3.** having a particular talent or characteristic from the time they were born: *a born athlete*; *a born mimic.*

NOTE This word comes from the verb **bear**[1].

boronia /*say* buh-**roh**-nee-uh/ *noun* an Australian shrub with small pink or brown flowers.

WORD HISTORY named after the Italian botanist, Francesco *Borone* (1769–1794)

borrow *verb* If you **borrow** something from someone, you are allowed to have it for a while with the understanding that you will give it back to them later: *You can borrow up to five books at a time from the library.*
☐ **borrower**, *noun*

COMPARE this with **lend**.

bosom /*say* **booz**-uhm/ *noun* someone's chest or breast, especially a woman's.

☑ SPELLING TIP *Tricky vowel sounds*: remember that there are two single *o*'s in **bosom**, even though each *o* has a different sound. Put a single *s* in between them and you will have got over the difficulty in spelling this word.

boss *noun*
1. someone who employs and directs people, or controls a business.
–*verb* **2.** If you **boss** someone, you order them around.
☐ **bossy**, *adjective* (**bossier**, **bossiest**)

botany *noun* the study of plants.
☐ **botanical**, *adjective* –**botanist**, *noun*

botch *verb* If you **botch** something, you spoil or bungle it: *I botched the biscuits by leaving them in the oven too long.*

both *adjective*
1. two together: *Both shoes need cleaning.*
–*pronoun* **2.** the one and the other: *Both had been there.*
–*adverb* **3.** equally: *He is both ready and willing.*

bother *verb* To **bother** someone is to **1.** annoy them: *The heat bothered them so much they couldn't sleep.* **2.** worry or confuse them: *The exam really bothered her.*
☐ **bothersome**, *adjective*

bottle *noun*
1. a glass or plastic container used for holding liquids: *a bottle of fruit juice.*
–*verb* **2.** If you **bottle** something, you put it in a bottle: *to bottle fruit to make preserves.*
–*phrase* **3. bottle up**, to shut in or keep in check: *to bottle up your feelings.*

bottlebrush *noun* an Australian plant with red or pink, brush-like flowers.

bottleneck *noun* a place where progress becomes slow, especially the narrow part of a road where traffic cannot flow freely.

bottom *noun*
1. the lowest or deepest part of anything, opposite to the top: *the bottom of a hill*; *the bottom of the sea.* **2.** the place of least honour or achievement: *the bottom of the class.* **3.** the lowest or first gear of a motor. **4.** the underneath part: *the bottom of an iron.* **5.** the buttocks; the part of the body that you sit on.
–*adjective* **6.** lowest: *the bottom stair.*

bougainvillea /*say* boh-guhn-**vil**-ee-uh/ *noun* a tropical climbing plant with special brightly coloured leaves.

☑ SPELLING TIP This plant received its tricky name from Louis de *Bougainville*, a French scientist and explorer of the Pacific region. There are three pairs of vowels to remember – *ou*, *ai* and the final *ea*. You should also notice that the only double letter is *l*.

bough /*rhymes with* cow/ *noun* one of the larger main branches of a tree.

☑ SPELLING TIP Don't confuse the spelling of **bough** with **bow**, which is pronounced in the same way. The **bow** of a boat is its front end, and to **bow** is to bend towards someone as a sign of respect. When **bow** is pronounced to rhyme with 'so', it refers to a type of knot or to the bent piece of wood you use when shooting an arrow.

boulder /*rhymes with* colder/ *noun* a very large rock.

boulevard /*say* **booh**-luh-vahd/ *noun* a wide avenue or city street lined with trees.

☑ SPELLING TIP *Tricky 'uh' sound*: the middle vowel is spelt *e*. Also remember that the *ou* spelling for the 'ooh' sound in the first syllable. This word is spelt like this because it comes from French. You can also use the spelling **boulevarde** which is not the French spelling but is often used in English.

bounce *verb*
1. When a ball **bounces**, it immediately springs back after it hits the ground or a wall: *The ball bounced once before disappearing into the trees.* **2.** If you **bounce** a ball, you throw it against a surface to make it spring back towards you: *Tran bounced the ball against the wall.* **3.** If a cheque **bounces**, the bank does not accept it because the person who wrote it doesn't have enough money in their bank account to pay for it. **4.** If an email **bounces**, it returns to the sender because it was not received at the intended address.
–*phrase* **5. bounce back**, to return to a previous level of health or happiness: *It was good to see our friend bounce back after she'd been so ill.*
□ **bounce**, *noun* –**bouncy**, *adjective* –**bouncily**, *adverb*

bound[1] *adjective*
1. tied up: *The prisoner held out his bound hands.* **2.** fastened within a cover: *I had my assignment properly bound with a plastic cover.* **3.** certain to happen: *If you get there early, you are bound to get a good seat.* **4.** having a duty, or being under an obligation: *Having signed the contract, they were bound to sell.*

NOTE This word comes from the verb **bind**.

bound[2] *verb*
1. To **bound** is to move with big steps or leaps: *to bound over a gate*; *to bound after a ball.*
–*noun* **2.** a jump.

boundary *noun* (*plural* **boundaries**) a dividing line or limit: *the boundary between states*; *She drove around the boundary of her property.*

bountiful *adjective* plentiful or generous: *The fishing boats brought back a bountiful catch.*
□ **bountifully**, *adverb*

bounty *noun* (*plural* **bounties**)
1. generosity. **2.** a reward given for a special purpose: *There's a bounty for information about the hiding place of the outlaws.*

bouquet /*say* booh-**kay**, boh-**kay**/ *noun*
1. a bunch of flowers. **2.** a characteristic smell of something, especially wine.

☑ SPELLING TIP *Silent letter alert*: don't forget the silent *t* at the end – the *et* spelling makes an 'ay' sound. Other words with this ending are *ballet* and *beret*. They all come from French. Also remember the *qu* spelling for the 'k' sound in **bouquet**. The first vowel sound is spelt *ou* (although it can be pronounced as 'ooh' or as 'oh').

bout *noun*
1. a contest: *a wrestling bout.* **2.** a period or spell: *a bout of writing*; *a bout of the flu.*

boutique /*say* booh-**teek**/ *noun* a small shop, especially one that sells expensive or fashionable clothes.

☑ SPELLING TIP Remember that the end of **boutique** is spelt *ique* (although it sounds like 'eek'). It might help if you think of other words which have the same spelling for this sound, such as *antique* and *technique*. These are all spelt like this because they come from French. The beginning of **boutique** can also be tricky. Remember that the vowel sound is spelt *ou* (although it sound like 'ooh').

bovine /*say* **boh**-vuyn/ *adjective* having to do with the family of cud-chewing animals that includes cows, bulls and oxen.

bow[1] /*rhymes with* cow/ *verb*
1. If you **bow**, you bend the top part of your body forward to show respect or to accept applause.

–*phrase* **2. bow out**, to stop taking part in something: *She bowed out last month after twenty years as president of the society.*
☐ **bow**, *noun*: *He made a low bow.*

☑ SPELLING TIP Don't confuse the spelling of this or **bow**[3] with **bough** which sounds the same. A **bough** is a branch of a tree.

bow[2] /*rhymes with* so/ *noun*
1. a piece of wood bent by a string stretched between its ends, which is used to shoot arrows. **2.** a knot, made up of two loops and two ends. **3.** the special stick used to play stringed instruments like the violin.

bow[3] /*rhymes with* cow/ *noun* the front end of a boat.

☑ SPELLING TIP See **bow**[1].

bowel *noun* the long tube in the body which carries food from the stomach as waste matter out of the body.

A SIMILAR TERM is **large intestine**.
NOTE People often use the plural and speak of this as the **bowels**.
WORD HISTORY from a Latin word meaning 'sausage'

bower /*say* **bow**-uh/ *noun* a leafy shelter.

bowerbird *noun* an Australian bird which makes a bower-like shelter where it keeps special objects and courts its mate.

bowl[1] *noun*
1. a deep, round dish used for holding food or liquid. **2.** something shaped like a bowl: *the bowl of a pipe.*

bowl[2] *verb*
1. To **bowl** a ball is to throw or roll it.
–*noun* **2.** a heavy ball used in the game of bowls.
☐ **bowling**, *noun*

bowler[1] *noun* a hard felt hat with a rounded top and a narrow brim.

bowler[2] *noun*
1. a player who bowls the ball in a game like cricket. **2.** someone who plays bowls or tenpin bowling.

bowls *noun*
1. a game in which heavy balls are rolled across grass towards a target. **2.** a similar game, but one which is played inside.

ANOTHER TERM (for definition 1) is **lawn bowls**; (for definition 2) **carpet bowls**.

box[1] *noun*
1. a wooden or cardboard container with a lid. **2.** a small room or raised stand: *a box at the football*; *a witness box.*
–*verb in the phrase* **3. box in, a.** to build a box around. **b.** to surround or imprison: *to be boxed in by the traffic.*

box[2] *verb*
1. To **box** is to fight with your fists.
–*phrase* **2. box someone's ears**, to hit someone on the side of the head with your hand or fist.
☐ **boxer**, *noun* –**boxing**, *noun*

box office *noun* the place in a theatre where tickets are sold.

boy *noun* a male child.
☐ **boyhood**, *noun* –**boyish**, *adjective*: *At thirty, he still seemed awkward and boyish.*

boycott *verb* If you **boycott** something, you **1.** refuse to go to it: *to boycott a meeting.* **2.** stop buying or using it: *to boycott plastic shopping bags.*

WORD HISTORY named after Captain Charles C *Boycott* (1832–1897), an Irish land agent who was ignored by his tenants when he refused to lower rents in hard times

☑ SPELLING TIP *Double letter alert*: double *t* at the end. It is an unusual word because it comes from a surname.

boyfriend *noun* a man or boy with whom someone has a steady romantic relationship: *My sister has a new boyfriend.*

bra *noun* a piece of underwear worn by women which supports the breasts.

NOTE This is short for **brassiere**. It is more usual now to say **bra** than **brassiere**.

brace *noun*
1. something which holds parts together or in place. **2. braces, a.** wires placed on your teeth to help straighten them. **b.** straps worn over your shoulders for holding up your trousers.
–*verb* **3.** If you **brace** something, you physically support or strengthen it: *We'd better brace that shelf to keep it steady.* **4.** If you **brace** yourself for something difficult or unpleasant, you prepare yourself for it: *We braced ourselves for the bad news.*

bracelet *noun* an ornamental chain or band for wearing around your wrist.

WORD HISTORY from a Latin word meaning 'arm'

bracken *noun* a fern which is often found in the wetter parts of Australia.

bracket *noun* either of a set of signs, such as ( ) or [ ] or { }, used to enclose words which interrupt a sentence but add information to it, as in *John* (*my brother's friend*) *brought meat for our barbecue.*

SEE the Grammar and Punctuation Guide appendix.

brackish *adjective* slightly salty: *We couldn't drink the brackish water; Mangroves can grow in brackish water.*

brag *verb* (**brags**, **bragging**, **bragged**, **has bragged**) To **brag** is to talk openly about how clever or good you think you are.

braid *verb*
1. If you **braid** something, you weave or plait it: *to braid hair.*
–*noun* **2.** a plait: *She wore her hair in two braids.* **3.** a woven trimming: *The major's uniform was trimmed with braid.*

braille /*say* brayl/ *noun* a system of printing using raised dots which blind people can read by touch.

WORD HISTORY named after its inventor, Louis *Braille* (1809–1852)

☑ SPELLING TIP *Silent letter alert*: remember that **braille** has two *l*'s and a silent *e* at the end. Also remember the *ai* spelling for the 'ay' sound. The spelling is unusual because it comes from a French name.

brain *noun*
1. the soft, greyish mass of nerve cells inside the skull, which controls feeling, thinking and movement. **2.** understanding or intelligence: *a good brain.* **3.** *Informal* a very clever or well-informed person: *My sister is a real brain.*
–*phrase* **4. pick someone's brains**, to use another person's work or ideas to do yourself good.
☐ **brainy**, *adjective*: *He is very brainy and always does well in exams.*

NOTE You will often see definition 2 in the plural, as in *He has brains.*
NOTE **Cerebral** is a medical word meaning 'having to do with the brain'.

brainiac *noun Informal* a very intelligent person.

brainwave *noun* a sudden bright idea.

braise *verb* To **braise** food is to fry it quickly in a pan, then stew it gently in a covered pot.

brake *noun*
1. something which slows or stops a machine.
–*verb* **2.** To **brake** is to slow or stop a car or other vehicle: *Mum had to brake sharply when the dog ran onto the road.*

☑ SPELLING TIP Don't confuse the spelling of **brake** with **break** which sounds the same. **Break** has many meanings. For example, if you **break** a plate, it smashes. If you have a **break** from work, you have a rest.

bramble *noun* any thorny bush growing wild.
☐ **brambly**, *adjective*

bran *noun* the outer shell of wheat or rye, sometimes used in breakfast cereal.

branch *noun* (*plural* **branches**)
1. the limb of a tree or shrub. **2.** a part which divides from the main part: *our branch of the family; the branch of a river.* **3.** part of a large organisation: *the local branch of my bank.*
–*verb* **4.** To **branch** is to divide or separate: *The river branched in three directions.*
–*phrase* **5. branch out**, to develop in a new direction: *My father's business started off making garden furniture but now it has branched out into all kinds of other furniture.*

brand *noun*
1. the mark or sign on something which shows where it comes from or who makes it. **2.** the particular kind or make of something: *my favourite brand of jeans.*
–*verb* **3.** To **brand** something is to mark it with a brand: *to brand the cattle.*

brandish *verb* When you **brandish** something, you shake or wave it: *The warriors brandished their spears.*

brandy *noun* a strong alcoholic drink made from wine.

brash *adjective* over-confident: *I hoped I could keep my brash promise.*
☐ **brashly**, *adverb* –**brashness**, *noun*

brass *noun*
1. a yellowish metal mixed from copper and zinc. **2.** the trumpet and horn family of musical instruments: *I play in the strings, and my brother plays in the brass.*
–*adjective* **3.** made of brass: *brass instruments.*
☐ **brassy**, *adjective*

brassiere /*say* **braz**-ee-uh/ *noun* See **bra**.

brat *noun Informal* a child, especially one who is annoying: *Some little brat left chocolate stains all over our new white sofa.*

NOTE This word is usually used in an unfriendly way.

bravado /*say* bruh-**vah**-doh/ *noun* bravery and confidence which is often pretended: *She was full of bravado until the time came for her to sing.*

☑ SPELLING TIP Remember that **bravado** has *ado* at the end. You could think of the sentence: 'She ate an avocado with bravado!' Like *avocado*, **bravado** has this spelling because it comes from Spanish.

brave *adjective*
1. willing to do something that is dangerous, or to suffer pain without complaining.
–*verb* **2.** If you **brave** something unpleasant or dangerous, you endure it instead of avoiding it: *We braved the cold and went swimming anyway.*
☐ **bravely**, *adverb* –**braveness**, *noun* –**bravery**, *noun*

WORD HISTORY from a Spanish word meaning 'vicious' (first used about bulls)

brawl *noun*
1. a noisy fight.
–*verb* **2.** If you **brawl** with someone, you quarrel noisily with them.

brawn *noun* well-developed muscles or muscular strength: *With his brawn, he should have no trouble lifting it.*
□ **brawny**, *adjective* (**brawnier**, **brawniest**)

bray *verb*
1. When a donkey **brays** it makes a loud, harsh noise. **2.** If someone **brays**, they make a loud and harsh sound when speaking or laughing.
□ **bray**, *noun*

brazen *adjective*
1. If something is **brazen**, it is made of brass. **2.** If someone is **brazen**, they are cheeky or rude: *brazen behaviour.*

A SIMILAR WORD (for definition 2) is **insolent**.

brazier /*say* **bray**-zee-uh/ *noun* a metal container for holding burning fuel and used for heating or cooking.

breach *noun* (*plural* **breaches**)
1. a failure to keep or observe: *a breach of trust*; *a breach of the rules.* **2.** a gap or opening: *a breach in the castle wall.*
–*verb* **3.** If you **breach** a promise or a law, you break it. **4.** When a whale **breaches** it thrusts itself above the water.

☑ SPELLING TIP Don't confuse the spelling of **breach** with **breech** which sounds the same. The **breech** of a gun is its barrel.

bread *noun*
1. a food made by baking flour and water, usually with yeast to make it rise: *a loaf of bread.* **2.** food in general: *to earn our daily bread.*

breadth /*say* bredth/ *noun*
1. the distance from one side of something to the other. **2.** the range or reach of something: *breadth of knowledge.*

A SIMILAR WORD (particularly for definition 1) is **width**.

☑ SPELLING TIP Don't forget the *ea* spelling (although it sounds like it would be spelt with just an *e*). The *bread* part of this word is not related to what you eat but is a form of the word *broad*. Then there is the suffix *-th* (used to make words referring to quality or condition).

breadwinner *noun* someone who earns the money to keep a family.

break *verb* (**breaks**, **breaking**, **broke**, **has broken**)
1. If something **breaks**, it separates into pieces, usually because it has been dropped or hit: *The cup broke when it fell onto the floor.* **2.** If you **break** a bone in your body, it cracks or separates into two or more pieces: *to break an arm.* **3.** If you **break** a piece of equipment, you damage it in some way so that it doesn't work any more: *He borrowed our video recorder and broke it.* **4.** If someone **breaks** a rule or law, they do not obey it. **5.** If someone **breaks** a promise or agreement, they do not do what they promised or agreed to do. **6.** If you **break** a record, for example in sport, you do better than the best performance so far: *She broke the record for the 100 metres backstroke.* **7.** If you **break** the news to someone, you tell them what has happened: *He gently broke the news to her that her father was sick.* **8.** If you **break** a habit, you stop doing a particular thing that you usually do. **9.** If something **breaks** an activity or some state, it ends or interrupts it: *A loud bang broke the silence.* **10.** If something **breaks** someone's heart, it makes them extremely unhappy. **11.** If someone's voice **breaks** when they are speaking, they sound as if they are going to cry: *Her voice broke during the speech and she reached for a glass of water.* **12.** When a boy's voice **breaks**, it gets deeper because he is becoming a man: *My brother's voice broke when he was thirteen.*
–*noun* **13.** a place where there is a way through: *a break in the wall.* **14.** an attempt to escape: *a break for freedom.* **15.** a short rest: *They took a break from studying.*
–*phrase* **16. break down**, **a.** to destroy by breaking. **b.** to become upset: *She broke down when she heard the bad news.* **c.** to stop working properly. **17. break in**, **a.** to interrupt. **b.** to get a horse used to being handled by people. **c.** to enter a house using force. **18. break into**, **a.** to interrupt. **b.** to enter using force. **19. break off**, **a.** to separate by breaking: *to break off some bread.* **b.** to put a stop to: *to break off an engagement.* **c.** to stop suddenly: *to break off a conversation.* **20. break out**, to escape: *Two prisoners broke out of prison last night.* **21. break out in**, to suffer from a sudden appearance of (a skin condition): *to break out in a rash.* **22. break up**, **a.** to separate or finish: *to break up a marriage.* **b.** to finish a school term for the holidays. **c.** *Informal* to burst into laughter.
□ **breakable**, *adjective* –**breakage**, *noun*

☑ SPELLING TIP Don't confuse the spelling of **break** with **brake** which sounds the same. A **brake** is a device used to slow down or stop a machine such as a car.

breakdown *noun*
1. a failure to work properly: *a car breakdown*; *a nervous breakdown.* **2.** separation into simple parts: *the breakdown of figures for analysis.*

breakfast /*say* **brek**-fuhst/ *noun* the first meal of the day.

> ☑ SPELLING TIP Remember that the first part of **breakfast** is actually the word *break*, although you say it as 'brek'. The basic idea behind the word is that you are breaking a *fast* (a time of not eating).

breakneck *adjective* dangerous: *to ride at a breakneck speed.*

breakthrough *noun* an important discovery or advance which is made after a lot of hard work and usually a number of failures: *This discovery gave police their first real breakthrough in the investigation.*

bream /*sounds like* brim/ *noun* an Australian saltwater fish which is good for eating.

> ☑ SPELLING TIP *Tricky vowel sound*: *ea* to spell the 'i' sound. Don't confuse the spelling of **bream** with **brim** which sounds the same. A **brim** is the top edge of something hollow or the outer edge of a hat.

breast *noun*
1. one of the two round, fleshy parts on a woman's chest that can produce milk to feed a baby. **2.** *Old-fashioned* the chest.

breaststroke *noun* a way of swimming in which your arms move in a circle in front of your chest and your legs kick in a frog-like manner.

> COMPARE this with **backstroke**, **freestyle**, and **butterfly stroke**.

breath /*say* breth/ *noun*
1. the air taken into your lungs and let out again: *short of breath.* **2.** an act of breathing once: *He took a deep breath.* **3.** a light current: *A breath of wind rustled the leaves.*
–*phrase* **4. below** (or **under**) **your breath**, very softly. **5. out of breath**, finding it difficult to breathe, the way you do after hard exercise. **6. take your breath away**, to surprise.
☐ **breathy**, *adjective* –**breathless**, *adjective*

breathalyser *noun* a machine used to measure the amount of alcohol in someone's breath.

> ☑ SPELLING TIP The spelling of **breathalyser** will be easier if you see that it is made up of **breath** and **analyser** (which has lost the *an* at the start). *Analyser* comes from *analyse* (to examine something scientifically by looking at each of its parts). If you remember that this word is spelt with a *y*, the main difficulty is over.

breathe /*say* breedh/ *verb* To **breathe** is to **1.** draw in and give out air: *We breathe without thinking.* **2.** speak softly: *He breathed a word of warning.*
–*phrase* **3. breathe freely**, to relax or be freed from worry or fear.
☐ **breathing**, *noun*

breathtaking *adjective* If something is **breathtaking**, it causes excitement or pleasure: *a breathtaking ride*; *breathtaking scenery.*

breech *noun* (*plural* **breeches**) the barrel of a gun.

> ☑ SPELLING TIP Don't confuse the spelling of **breech** with **breach** which sounds the same. A **breach** is a failure to keep a promise, or an opening in something.

breeches /*rhymes with* stitches/ *plural noun* trousers covering the hips and thighs: *riding breeches.*

breed *verb* (**breeds**, **breeding**, **bred**, **has bred**)
1. If animals **breed**, they mate and produce young: *Rabbits breed extremely rapidly.* **2.** If you **breed** animals or plants, you keep them so that they will produce more of their kind for you: *They've bred a new variety of flower.* **3.** If you say that something **breeds** something unpleasant or unwanted, you mean that it causes it to develop: *Garbage breeds disease.*
–*noun* **4.** a type or kind: *a breed of cat.*
☐ **breeder**, *noun*

breeding *noun*
1. the mating and rearing of animals. **2.** good manners which are the result of training.

breeze *noun*
1. a light wind or movement of air. **2.** *Informal* an easy job: *It's a breeze.*
–*phrase* **3. breeze along** (or **in**), to move in a relaxed way. **4. breeze through**, to do something easily: *to breeze through exams.*
☐ **breezy**, *adjective* (**breezier**, **breeziest**) –**breezily**, *adverb*

brethren /*say* **bredh**-ruhn/ *plural noun Old-fashioned* brothers.

brevity /*say* **brev**-uh-tee/ *noun* shortness or briefness: *The brevity of the lecture surprised us.*

brew *verb*
1. If you **brew** tea, you make it by pouring boiling water over tea leaves, then leaving the hot liquid to become flavoured by the tea leaves. **2.** If you say that something is **brewing**, you mean it is starting to develop: *We could see a storm brewing on the horizon.*
☐ **brew**, *noun* –**brewer**, *noun*

briar /*rhymes with* fire/ *noun* a prickly bush.

bribe *noun*
1. money or a gift you give to someone if they promise to do something for you that they really shouldn't.
–*verb* **2.** To **bribe** someone is to give or promise them a bribe: *He tried to bribe the policeman to let him go.*
☐ **bribery**, *noun*

brick *noun* a small, hard block of baked clay, used for building.

NOTE Someone who builds with bricks is called a **bricklayer**.

bride *noun* a woman who is going to be married or who has just been married.
□ **bridal**, *adjective*

bridegroom *noun* a man who is going to be married or who has just been married.

THE SHORT FORM of this is **groom**.

bridesmaid *noun* a woman who helps a bride on the day she is married.

bridge[1] *noun*
1. a structure built over a river, road or railway line, to provide a way of getting from one side to the other. **2.** a raised part of the deck of a ship for the captain or other officers. **3.** the upper part of the nose.
–*verb* **4.** To **bridge** a river or valley is to build a bridge across it.

bridge[2] *noun* a card game for two pairs of players.

bridle *noun*
1. the leather straps, bit and reins fitted around the head of a horse and used to control it.
–*verb* **2.** To **bridle** a horse is to put a bridle on it.

brief *adjective*
1. short: *a brief holiday*; *a brief talk*; *a brief skirt.*
–*noun* **2.** information or instructions given very quickly on a subject, especially for use by a barrister looking after a legal case.
–*verb* **3.** To **brief** someone is to give them information and instructions to prepare them for a particular job: *I will need you to brief me about this job before I start work.*
–*phrase* **4. in brief**, in as few words as possible, or in a shortened form: *In brief, here is an outline of the problem*; *the news in brief.*
□ **briefness**, *noun* –**briefly**, *adverb*

☑ SPELLING TIP Remember that **brief** is spelt with *ie* (to spell the 'ee' sound). This follows the rule that *i* comes before *e* except after *c*. Think of similar words such as *thief* and *chief.*

briefcase *noun* a flat case for carrying books and papers.

briefs *plural noun* close-fitting underpants without legs.

brigade *noun*
1. a large group of soldiers. **2.** a group of people trained for a special purpose: *a fire brigade.*

brigalow *noun* a type of acacia that grows in Queensland and northern New South Wales, and which has strong, heavy wood traditionally used by Aboriginal people for carving.

WORD HISTORY from an Aboriginal language of New South Wales called Kamilaroi

brigand /*say* **brig**-uhnd/ *noun* one of a band of robbers who live in mountain or forest areas.

bright *adjective*
1. having a strong, noticeable colour: *I like to wear bright clothes.* **2.** shining strongly: *The moon is very bright tonight.* **3.** clever: *a bright pupil.* **4.** happy and cheerful: *I am always glad to see her bright face.*
□ **brighten**, *verb*: *to brighten your life.* –**brightly**, *adverb* –**brightness**, *noun*

brilliant *adjective*
1. shining brightly: *The sun was a brilliant orange.* **2.** extremely clever: *a brilliant idea*; *a brilliant scientist.*
□ **brilliance**, *noun* –**brilliantly**, *adverb*

brim *noun*
1. the top edge of something hollow: *I filled my cup to the brim.* **2.** the outer edge of a hat.

WORD HISTORY from an Old English word meaning 'sea'

brindled *adjective* grey or brownish-yellow with darker streaks or spots.

brine *noun* strongly salted water, often used in preserving some foods.

bring *verb* (**brings**, **bringing**, **brought** /*say* brawt/, **has brought**)
1. If you **bring** something or someone when you come to a place, you carry the object with you or get the person to come with you: *Those black clouds will bring rain*; *Can I bring my friend to your party?* **2.** If something **brings** someone or something to a place or a condition, it causes them to be in that place or state: *The floods brought suffering to everyone.*
–*phrase* **3. bring about**, to cause: *to bring about change.* **4. bring back**, to make you remember: *to bring back memories.* **5. bring down**, **a.** to cause something to fall: *The hard tackle brought down the footballer*; *The plane was brought down by enemy fire.* **b.** to reduce: *to bring down prices.* **6. bring in**, to introduce: *to bring in new ideas.* **7. bring round**, **a.** to persuade someone to have the same opinion as you about something. **b.** to bring back to consciousness. **8. bring up**, **a.** to care for during childhood. **b.** to mention or introduce in a conversation or at a meeting. **c.** to get rid of food in your stomach by vomiting: *We knew she was not well when she brought up her dinner.*

☑ SPELLING TIP Remember that the vowel sound in the past form **brought** is spelt *ough* (although it sounds like 'aw'). Other words like this are *bought* and *thought*.

brink *noun*
1. the edge of a steep or dangerous place: *the brink of a cliff.*
–*phrase* **2. on the brink of**, about to begin: *countries on the brink of war.*

brisk *adjective* fast and energetic: *a brisk walk*; *a brisk breeze.*
☐ **briskly**, *adverb* –**briskness**, *noun*

bristle /*say* **bris**-uhl/ *noun*
1. a short, stiff hair or hair-like material: *pigs' bristles*; *the bristles of a brush.*
–*verb* **2.** If the hair on an animal's body **bristles**, it stands up from the skin because they are angry, frightened or cold: *The hair on the dog's back bristled and it began to growl.* **3.** If something makes you **bristle**, you show that you are annoyed about it by the way you behave when someone mentions it: *She bristled at the remark.*
–*phrase* **4. bristle with**, to be full of: *The streets were bristling with police after the bank robbery.*
☐ **bristly**, *adjective*: *a bristly beard.*

> ☑ SPELLING TIP *Silent letter alert*: don't forget the *st* (not double *s*) spelling. The *t* is silent.

brittle *adjective* hard, but easily broken: *brittle glass.*
☐ **brittleness**, *noun*

broach *verb* When you **broach** a subject, you ask about it for the first time: *It's been five weeks since I broached the subject of getting a new bike.*

broad *adjective*
1. wide: *a broad river*; *Swimmers develop very broad shoulders.* **2.** stretching out for a long way in all directions: *broad plains.* **3.** covering many different types of things: *a broad range of interests*; *broad knowledge.* **4.** not detailed: *the broad outline of the story.*
☐ **broaden**, *verb* –**broadly**, *adverb*

> ☑ SPELLING TIP *Tricky vowel sound*: remember the *oa* spelling. Think of a 'broad board'. *Board* also has an *oa* spelling – in fact, it has all the same letters as **broad**, but with the *r* in a different position.

broadband *noun* high-speed access to the internet on a cable that can carry a number of different kinds of information at the same time, such as voice and data: *With broadband you can use several telephones and computers at the same time.*

broadcast *verb* (**broadcasts**, **broadcasting**, **broadcast** *or* **broadcasted**, **has broadcast** *or* **has broadcasted**)
1. To **broadcast** a program or message is to send it by radio or television: *The news is broadcast at 7 p.m. each evening.* **2.** To **broadcast** information is to tell it to people so that it becomes widely known: *I want to keep this quiet, so don't go broadcasting it around.*
–*noun* **3.** a radio or television program.
☐ **broadcaster**, *noun* –**broadcasting**, *noun*

broad-minded *adjective* able to accept other people's behaviour and opinions.

> A SIMILAR WORD is **tolerant**.
> THE OPPOSITE is **narrow-minded**.

brocade /*say* bruh-**kayd**/ *noun* cloth woven with a raised pattern on it.
☐ **brocaded**, *adjective*

broccoli /*say* **brok**-uh-lee, **brok**-uh-luy/ *noun* a vegetable with thick stems and many small, green flower-like heads.

> ☑ SPELLING TIP *Double/single letter alert*: double *c* and only one *l*. Also remember the *i* spelling for the 'ee' or 'uy' sound at the end. All of this is because **broccoli** comes from Italian.

brochure /*say* **broh**-shuh, bruh-**shoouh**/ *noun* a small book with a paper cover, containing information or advertisements.

> A SIMILAR WORD is **pamphlet**.

> ☑ SPELLING TIP *Tricky vowel sound*: just an *o* spelling for the 'oh' sound in the first syllable. This word comes from the French *brocher* meaning 'to stitch (a book)'. The suffix *ure* is added to the stem *broch* to form **brochure**.

broke *adjective Informal* having no money.

> NOTE This word comes from the verb **break**.

broken *adjective*
1. If something is **broken**, it has separated into pieces, usually because it has been dropped or hit: *a broken plate.* **2.** If a piece of equipment is **broken**, it does not work any more because it has been damaged in some way: *a broken dishwasher.* **3.** A **broken** promise is one that has not been kept. **4.** A **broken** home is a family where the parents are separated or divorced.

> NOTE This word comes from the verb **break**.

broker *noun* someone who buys or sells things for someone else: *a stockbroker*; *a wool broker.*
☐ **brokerage**, *noun*

brolga *noun* a large silvery-grey bird with long legs, which dances.

> NOTE This used to be better known as **native companion**.
> WORD HISTORY from an Aboriginal language of New South Wales called Kamilaroi

bronchitis /*say* brong-**kuy**-tuhs/ *noun* an illness in which the lining of the air passages in the chest becomes red and sore.

> ☑ SPELLING TIP Remember the *ch* spelling for the 'k' sound. The spelling of **bronchitis** will be easier if you see that it contains a shortened form of *bronchus* (one of the passages in your lungs) and the suffix *-itis* (meaning 'inflamed condition'). Think of a similar word such as *appendicitis*. They both end with *-itis* (spelt with *is*, not *us*, at the end).

brontosaurus /*say* bron-tuh-**saw**-ruhs/ *noun* a large plant-eating dinosaur with a long neck and tail, that died out millions of years ago.

WORD HISTORY from a Greek word for 'thunder' added to a Greek word for 'lizard'

bronze *noun*
1. a dark reddish-brown metal mixed from copper and tin. **2.** a dark reddish-brown colour.
□ **bronze**, *adjective*

brooch /*rhymes with* coach/ *noun* (*plural* **brooches**) a piece of jewellery made to be fastened to clothes with a pin.

☑ SPELLING TIP *Tricky vowel sound*: double *o* spelling for the 'oh' sound. If you think of the two *o*'s as being like two little round pearls in a **brooch** you will remember this tricky part.

brood *noun*
1. a number of young animals, especially birds, born at the same time.
–*verb* **2.** If a bird **broods**, it sits on eggs until the baby birds are born.
–*phrase* **3. brood on**, to worry about: *She brooded on her failure.*
□ **broody**, *adjective*: *a broody hen.*

brook *noun* a small stream.

NOTE In Australian English this is usually called a **creek**.

broom *noun* a brush with a long handle, used for sweeping.

broth *noun* a thin soup of fish, meat or vegetables.

brothel *noun* a house where prostitutes work.

brother *noun*
1. a male relative who has the same parents as you. **2.** a person who works with you: *They are brothers in the battle to protect the natural environment.* **3.** a male member of certain religious organisations.
□ **brotherhood**, *noun* –**brotherly**, *adjective*

brother-in-law *noun* (*plural* **brothers-in-law**)
1. the brother of someone's husband or wife. **2.** the husband of someone's sister. **3.** the husband of the sister of someone's wife or husband.

brow *noun*
1. See **forehead**. **2.** See **eyebrow**. **3.** the edge or top of a steep place: *the brow of a hill.*

browbeat *verb* (**browbeats**, **browbeating**, **browbeat**, **has browbeaten**) If you **browbeat** someone, you bully them and try to make them do what you want.

brown *adjective*
1. of the colour of earth, a mixture of red, yellow and black. **2.** having skin darkened from being in the sun: *She was very brown by the end of summer.*
–*verb* **3.** When something **browns** or if you **brown** something, it becomes browner in colour: *Drought browned the land*; *Brown the onions.*
□ **brown**, *noun*

brownie *noun*
1. a thick, brown biscuit. **2.** in the past, a junior guide (definition 4).

ANOTHER FORM Definition 2 was sometimes spelt with a capital letter.

brown sugar *noun* unrefined or partially refined sugar.

browse *verb*
1. If you **browse** through a book or a shop, you look through it to see what it contains. **2.** If you **browse** the internet, you look for information on it by visiting different websites. **3.** If animals **browse**, they feed, especially on growing grass: *The horses browsed in the grass.*
□ **browse**, *noun*

A SIMILAR WORD (for definition 3) is **graze**.

browser *noun*
1. a computer program that allows you to visit and display web pages. **2.** someone who like browsing through books.

bruise /*say* broohz/ *verb* To **bruise** is to **1.** cause a blue-black mark on the body: *The fall bruised my leg.* **2.** develop such a mark on the body: *to bruise easily.*
–*noun* **3.** the blue-black mark or injury caused.

brumby *noun* (*plural* **brumbies**) a wild horse living freely in the bush.

WORD HISTORY perhaps from an Aboriginal language, or perhaps named after Lieutenant *Brumby*, a horse-breeder who let some horses run wild in the early 1800s

brunch *noun* (*plural* **brunches**) a meal in midmorning instead of breakfast and lunch.

WORD HISTORY made by joining the first two letters of *br*(*eakfast*) to the last four letters of (*l*)*unch*

brunette *noun* a woman or girl with dark hair.

brunt *noun* the main shock or force: *The town bore the brunt of the storm.*

bruschetta /*say* broos-**ket**-uh, broo-**shet**-uh/ *noun* grilled slices of bread brushed with olive oil and fresh garlic, often served with a topping such as chopped tomato.

☑ SPELLING TIP Remember the *u* spelling for the 'oo' sound and the *ch* spelling which you can say as 'k' or 'sh'. This word comes from Italian where a *c* followed by an *h* is pronounced 'k', but in English you can say **bruschetta** in either way.

brush[1] *noun*
1. an instrument made of hair or bristles set in a handle: *a scrubbing brush*; *a hair brush.* 2. an act of brushing: *I gave my hair a brush.* 3. a short meeting or experience that is unpleasant or dangerous: *She's had brushes with the police but has never been charged*; *We had a brush with death when the plane almost crashed.*
–*verb* To **brush** something is to 4. use a brush on it: *Brush your teeth after eating.* 5. touch it lightly: *Leaves brushed my face as I walked through the garden.*
–*phrase* 6. **brush aside** (or **off**), to ignore: *He brushed my arguments aside.* 7. **brush up on**, to improve your skill in: *to brush up on your mathematics.*

brush[2] *noun* a thick growth of bushes.

brusque /*say* brusk, broosk/ *adjective* quick to say something and not very polite: *His brusque manner sometimes upsets people.*
☐ **brusquely**, *adverb* –**brusqueness**, *noun*

☑ SPELLING TIP Remember that the end of **brusque** is spelt *que* (although it sounds like 'k'). This is like some other words that come from French, such as *picturesque*.

brussels sprout *noun* a green vegetable like a tiny cabbage.

brutal *adjective* very cruel: *a brutal blow.*
☐ **brutality**, *noun* –**brutally**, *adverb*

brute *noun*
1. an animal. 2. a cruel person.

bubble *noun*
1. a small ball of air or gas rising through liquid. 2. a small ball of air in a fine coating of liquid: *to blow bubbles.*
–*verb* 3. If a liquid **bubbles**, it has bubbles rising through it. 4. If someone **bubbles**, they are very happy and energetic: *The children bubbled with excitement.*
☐ **bubbly**, *adjective*

bubblegum *noun* chewing gum which can be blown into bubbles.

bubbler *noun* a small fountain which sends up a short stream of drinking water.

buccaneer *noun* in the past, a pirate.

☑ SPELLING TIP *Double/single letter alert*: double *c* in the middle and only one *n*. Also note that it ends with the suffix *-eer* which is used in many words that refer to a person who does something, such as *engineer* and *pioneer*. Rap it out as *buc*+*can*+*eer*.

buck[1] *noun* a male deer, rabbit or hare.

NOTE The female is called a **doe**.

buck[2] *verb* To **buck** is to 1. jump with an arched back and stiff legs: *The young horse bucked.* 2. throw by bucking: *The mare bucked off her rider.*

bucket *noun* a round, open container with a flat bottom and a handle.
☐ **bucketful**, *noun*

buckle *noun*
1. a fastening for a belt or strap.
–*verb* 2. If you **buckle** a belt, you do it up: *Buckle your seatbelt before you drive.* 3. To **buckle** is to bend or twist, or cause something to bend or twist: *The metal buckled in the heat*; *The heat buckled the metal.*
–*phrase* 4. **buckle down**, to start working hard. 5. **buckle under**, to give way.

bucktooth *noun* (*plural* **buckteeth**) a tooth in the upper jaw that sticks out.
☐ **bucktoothed**, *adjective*

bud *noun* a flower or leaf before it has fully developed.

Buddhism /*say* **bood**-iz-uhm/ *noun* a world religion, founded by the teacher Buddha who lived in India about the sixth century BC, which teaches that we can achieve happiness by ridding ourselves of greed and hatred. Followers of Buddhism are called Buddhists and worship in a temple.
☐ **Buddhist**, *adjective*: *a Buddhist temple.*

WORD HISTORY named after *Buddha*, a Sanskrit name meaning 'wise' or 'enlightened'

buddy *noun* (*plural* **buddies**) *Informal* a friend or mate: *my best buddy.*

budge *verb* To **budge** is to move: *Don't budge until I return*; *I can't budge that heavy cupboard.*

NOTE This is usually used with the word *not*.

budgerigar /*say* **buj**-uh-ree-gah/ *noun* a small yellow and green parakeet found in inland parts of Australia, but also kept in cages and bred in other colours.

THE SHORT FORM of this is **budgie**, which is used mainly in informal language.
WORD HISTORY from an Aboriginal language of New South Wales called Kamilaroi

budget *noun*
1. a plan showing what money you will earn and how you will spend it.
–*verb* (**budgets**, **budgeting**, **budgeted**, **has budgeted**) 2. To **budget** is to make such a plan.
–*adjective* 3. cheap: *budget furniture.*

☑ SPELLING TIP *Single letter alert*: only one *t* at the end. Remember that the *t* remains single when you add *-ed* or *-ing*, following the rule that the consonant remains single if the final syllable is not stressed.

buff *verb*
1. If you **buff** something, you polish it by rubbing.
–*noun* 2. an expert: *a film buff.*
–*adjective* 3. light yellowish-brown.

buffalo *noun* (*plural* **buffalos** *or* **buffaloes**) a kind of ox sometimes used for pulling heavy loads.

☑ SPELLING TIP *Double/single letter alert*: double *f*'s (a bit like this animal's two curly horns), but only one *l*. Also note the *o* ending, which occurs in many words which come from Italian, as **buffalo** does.

buffer *noun* something that softens a blow, especially one of the two springs at each end of a railway carriage to take the shock of a collision.

buffet[1] /*say* **buf**-uht/ *verb* (**buffets**, **buffeting**, **buffeted**, **has buffeted**) When something **buffets** another thing, it strikes, shakes or knocks it about: *Gale force winds buffeted the town.*
☐ **buffet**, *noun* a blow or a slap.

buffet[2] /*say* **buf**-ay/ *noun*
1. a table or counter holding food. 2. a low cupboard for holding cups and plates.
–*adjective* 3. set out on a table from which you serve yourself: *a buffet dinner.*

☑ SPELLING TIP *Silent letter alert*: don't forget the silent *t* at the end – the *et* spelling makes an 'ay' sound. Other words with this ending are *ballet* and *bouquet*. They all come from French.

buffoon *noun* someone who acts the fool.
☐ **buffoonery**, *noun* –**buffoonish**, *adjective*

bug *noun*
1. any tiny insect. 2. an illness caused by an infection. 3. something that is going wrong: *There's a bug in my system.* 4. a hidden microphone. 5. a mistake in a computer program.
–*verb* (**bugs**, **bugging**, **bugged**, **has bugged**) 6. To **bug** something is to hide a microphone in it: *The detectives bugged the room.* 7. *Informal* If someone or something **bugs** you, they annoy you: *His stupid jokes bug me.*

bugbear *noun* something that worries or annoys you: *People who are always complaining are my bugbear.*

buggy *noun* (*plural* **buggies**) a light carriage with two wheels, pulled by one horse, used in the past for carrying people.

bugle /*say* **byooh**-guhl/ *noun* a wind instrument, used in the army to sound signals.
☐ **bugler**, *noun*

WORD HISTORY from a Latin word meaning 'ox' (because it was originally made from the horn of an ox)

build *verb* (**builds**, **building**, **built**, **has built**) If you **build** something, you 1. make it by joining parts together: *to build a bridge*; *to build a computer.* 2. form or develop it over a long time: *to build a friendship.*
–*noun* 3. the shape of someone's body: *a heavy build.*
–*phrase* 4. **build up**, **a.** to increase gradually in numbers or amount: *The papers on my desk are building up into a huge pile*; *You should talk about it rather than letting your anger build up.* **b.** to construct or develop: *They have built up a very successful business.* **c.** to make strong or healthy again: *Eating lots of good food will build you up after your illness.* 5. **build up to**, to prepare or get ready for: *The music is building up to a climax.*
☐ **builder**, *noun*

A SIMILAR WORD (for definition 1) is **construct**.

building *noun* something built for people to live or work in, such as a house, block of flats or office block.

bulb *noun*
1. the rounded root-like stem of certain plants, such as the onion. 2. anything with a shape like that: *an electric light bulb.*
☐ **bulbous**, *adjective*

bulge *noun*
1. a round part that swells out.
–*verb* 2. If something **bulges**, it swells outwards: *Her bag was bulging with books.*

bulk *noun*
1. the size of something including its length, width and depth: *a ship's bulk.* 2. the main part: *The bulk of the money has already been spent.*
☐ **bulky**, *adjective* (**bulkier**, **bulkiest**): *a bulky coat.*

bull *noun*
1. a male of the cattle family. 2. a male elephant, whale or seal.

NOTE The female is a **cow**.

bull ant *noun* a large ant which can give a painful bite.

bulldog *noun* a type of dog with a large head and a small, strong body.

bulldozer *noun* a powerful tractor with a blade in front, used to move trees and rocks, and to level land.
☐ **bulldoze**, *verb*

bullet *noun* a small piece of metal shot from a small gun.

bulletin *noun* a short written or spoken news report: *the latest bulletin on the weather.*

bullion /*say* **bool**-yuhn/ *noun* bars of gold or silver.

☑ SPELLING TIP Think that 'the bank has **bullion** that is worth a *million*'. This sentence might help you to remember the spelling of the end of

bullion, because it has the same sound and spelling as *million*.

bullock *noun* a bull, which has been castrated, used to pull loads.

bullroarer *noun* a thin piece of wood on a string, which is whirled in the air to make a roaring noise, and used in Aboriginal religious ceremonies.

NOTE The Aboriginal name for this is **churinga**.

bullseye *noun* the central spot on a target.

bully *noun* (*plural* **bullies**)
1. someone who hurts, frightens or orders about smaller or weaker people.
–*verb* (**bullies**, **bullying**, **bullied**, **has bullied**) **2.** To **bully** someone is to behave as a bully towards them.

bulrush *noun* a kind of tall rush which grows in wet places, such as on the banks of rivers, and which is used to make mats, and so on.

ANOTHER SPELLING is **bull-rush**.

bumblebee *noun* a kind of large bee.

bump *verb*
1. If you **bump** something, you knock against it or hit it accidentally: *I bumped the table and the glass of water spilt*; *I bumped my knee on the chair.* **2.** If a vehicle **bumps** while being driven, it bounces about because the surface of the road is uneven: *The car bumped along the rough track.*
–*noun* **3.** a light hit or knock. **4.** a small, raised area: *a bump on the nose*; *a bump on the road.*
–*phrase* **5. bump into**, to meet by chance. **6. bump off**, *Informal* to kill. **7. bump up**, *Informal* to increase: *to bump up prices.*
☐ **bumpy**, *adjective* (**bumpier**, **bumpiest**) –**bumpily**, *adverb*

bumper *noun* the bar across the front or back of a car which protects it in a collision.

ANOTHER TERM for this is **bumper bar**.

bumpkin *noun* someone who is socially awkward and clumsy: *a country bumpkin.*

WORD HISTORY from a Dutch word meaning 'little barrel'

bumptious /*say* **bump**-shuhs/ *adjective* showing your importance in a way that offends people: *a bumptious young man.*
☐ **bumptiously**, *adverb* –**bumptiousness**, *noun*

bun *noun*
1. a kind of round bread roll which can be plain or sweetened. **2.** hair arranged at the back of a woman's head in the shape of a bun.

bunch *noun* (*plural* **bunches**)
1. a group of things joined or gathered together: *a bunch of grapes*; *a bunch of flowers.*
–*verb* **2.** To **bunch** is to gather together.

bundle *noun*
1. a group of things loosely held together: *a bundle of sticks.*
–*verb* **2.** To **bundle** things is to tie or wrap them together: *She bundled the papers and put them in her desk.* **3.** If you **bundle** things or people somewhere, you push them there carelessly or you hurry them there: *I bundled my clothes into the washing machine*; *She bundled us into her office.*
–*phrase* **4. drop your bundle**, *Informal* to give up and lose hope, especially after something bad happening.

bung *noun*
1. a stopper for the hole in a wine cask.
–*verb* **2.** *Informal* If you **bung** something somewhere, you throw or toss it there, especially in a rough way: *Bung that stuff over here!*
–*phrase* **3. bung up**, to block with an obstruction: *Don't put that down the sink, it could bung up the drain*; *My nose is bunged up.*

bungalow *noun* a house with only one storey.

bungee jumping /*say* **bun**-jee/ *noun* a sport in which someone jumps from a high place to which they are attached by a long, thick elastic cord around their feet.

bungle *verb*
1. If you **bungle** something, you do it badly: *She bungled the exam.*
–*noun* **2.** something badly done.

bunion /*say* **bun**-yuhn/ *noun* a swelling of a joint on the foot, especially on the big toe.

☑ SPELLING TIP You could think of a **bunion** as being shaped like a little bun on your toe. That would give you the first three letters and then you add the suffix *ion* to make **bunion**. Notice that there is no *y* – the letter *i* makes the 'y' sound.

bunk *noun*
1. a bed built like a shelf, in a boat. **2.** one of a pair of beds built one above the other.

bunker *noun*
1. a large container for fuel. **2.** an underground shelter, such as one used during an air attack. **3.** a sandy hollow on a golf course.

bunkum *noun* talk that is foolish or not sincere.

bunting *noun* brightly coloured cloth used to make flags for decoration.

bunyip *noun* an imaginary creature of Aboriginal legend, said to live in swamps and billabongs.

WORD HISTORY from an Aboriginal language of Victoria called Wembawemba

buoy /*sounds like* boy/ *noun*
1. a float or one of a set of floats anchored in the water, which marks deep parts in the water, hidden rocks, and so on. **2.** a ring used to help people float in an emergency at sea.
–*verb in the phrase* **3. buoy up**, to encourage someone or lift their spirits: *The thought of a hot dinner buoyed them up.*

ANOTHER WORD (for definition 2) is **lifebuoy**.

☑ SPELLING TIP Don't confuse the spelling of **buoy** with **boy** which has the same sound. Remember the extra letter *u* in **buoy**.

buoyant /*say* **boy**-uhnt/ *adjective*
1. If something is **buoyant**, it is able to float: *Cork is an extremely buoyant material.* **2.** If someone is **buoyant**, they are cheerful and energetic: *She encouraged us all with her buoyant good humour.*
☐ **buoyancy**, *noun*

burden *noun*
1. a load: *to carry a heavy burden.* **2.** a difficult job that you don't really want to do: *We found looking after the huge garden a burden.*
–*verb* **3.** To **burden** someone or something is to give them a load: *I won't burden you with my problems.*
☐ **burdensome**, *adjective*

bureau /*say* **byooh**-roh/ *noun* (*plural* **bureaus** *or* **bureaux** /*say* **byooh**-rohz/)
1. a writing desk with drawers. **2.** a government office where people can get information: *a tourist bureau.*

ANOTHER FORM This word (as in definition 2) is often spelt with a capital letter, especially if you are writing about the title of a particular organisation: *the Weather Bureau*.

☑ SPELLING TIP *Tricky vowel sound: eau* spelling for the 'oh' sound at the end. **Bureau** has this spelling because it comes from French. Another word like this is *plateau*.

bureaucracy /*say* byooh-**rok**-ruh-see/ *noun* (*plural* **bureaucracies**)
1. the rules and procedures, some of which may be very complicated or seem unnecessary, for the way things must be done in large organisations or government offices. **2. the bureaucracy**, the people who make these rules or run such a system of administration.
☐ **bureaucrat**, *noun* –**bureaucratic**, *adjective*

☑ SPELLING TIP The spelling of **bureaucracy** will be easier if you see that it is made up of the word *bureau* (meaning 'a government office where people can get information') and the suffix *-cracy* (meaning 'rule' or 'authority'). Think of other words that have this ending, such as *democracy* and *aristocracy*.

burglary *noun* (*plural* **burglaries**) the crime of breaking into a building to steal things.
☐ **burglar**, *noun* –**burgle**, *verb*: *Our house has been burgled three times.*

burial *noun* the act of putting a dead person into the ground: *After the service we went to the cemetery for the burial.*

burlesque /*say* ber-**lesk**/ *noun* a play or a book which makes people laugh by making fun of serious matters.

☑ SPELLING TIP Remember that the end of **burlesque** is spelt *esque* (although it sounds like 'esk'). It is spelt like this because it comes from French. Other words like this which also come from French are *grotesque* and *picturesque*.

burly *adjective* (**burlier**, **burliest**) big and solidly built: *a burly farmer.*

burn *verb* (**burns**, **burning**, **burnt** *or* **burned**, **has burnt** *or* **has burned**)
1. If something is **burning**, it is on fire: *The roof is burning!* **2.** If you **burn** something, you set it on fire and allow it to be destroyed: *to burn your garbage.* **3.** If you **burn** something you are cooking, you spoil it by using too much heat or cooking it for too long: *The dinner is completely burnt.* **4.** If you **burn** part of your body, you injure it by fire or something very hot, or by a chemical: *I burnt my fingers on the stove.* **5.** If you **burn** with some emotion, you feel it very strongly: *Her remark made him burn with anger.*
–*noun* **6.** a sore made by something hot: *I have a burn on my hand from where I touched the iron.*
☐ **burnt**, *adjective* –**burning**, *adjective*: *a burning building.*

burner *noun* the part of a stove or lamp where the flame comes out.

burnish *verb* When you **burnish** metal, you polish it until it is bright and shiny.
☐ **burnished**, *adjective*: *Her hair shone like burnished copper.*

burp *verb*
1. If someone **burps**, they make a noise because air comes up from their stomach out through their throat and mouth: *Fizzy drinks make you burp.* **2.** If you **burp** a baby, you pat it gently on the back to make it burp up any air it has swallowed.
☐ **burp**, *noun*

A SIMILAR WORD (for definition 1) is **belch**.

burqa /*say* **ber**-kuh/ *noun* a traditional garment for Muslim women, giving full body covering with a narrow opening for the eyes.

ANOTHER SPELLING is **burka**.

burr *noun* the prickly case around some seeds.

burrow *noun*
1. a hole in the ground dug by an animal, to live and shelter in: *Wombats sleep in burrows during the day.*

–*verb* **2.** To **burrow** is to dig a burrow. **3.** If you **burrow** through something, you use a digging movement in looking for something: *I burrowed in my pockets for some coins.*
☐ **burrowing**, *adjective*: *a burrowing animal.*

bursary *noun* (*plural* **bursaries**) money given to a student to help pay for school fees, textbooks, uniforms and other expenses.
☐ **bursar**, *noun* the person in charge of money at a school or college.

burst *verb* (**bursts**, **bursting**, **burst**, **has burst**) **1.** If something **bursts**, it suddenly cracks or breaks open, often with an explosive noise: *The balloon burst with a loud bang.* **2.** If you **burst** something, you make it break open with a bang: *Try not to burst the balloons.* **3.** If you say something is **bursting** with something, you mean it is very full of it: *The room was bursting with people.* **4.** If you **burst** into a room, you enter it suddenly with a lot of energy: *The crowd burst into the stadium as the gates were opened.*
–*noun* **5.** a sudden effort or action: *a burst of speed*; *a burst of clapping.*
–*phrase* **6. burst out**, **a.** to express your feelings suddenly: *to burst out laughing*; *to burst out crying.* **b.** to say suddenly with a lot of feeling: *'You're a liar!', he burst out angrily.*

bury /*rhymes with* very/ *verb* (**buries**, **burying**, **buried**, **has buried**)
1. To **bury** a dead person or animal, or a thing you want to hide, is to put it in the ground and cover it with earth: *Grandfather is buried in the cemetery by the sea*; *The pirates buried their treasure at the bottom of the cliff.* **2.** To **bury** something is to cover it over completely: *Your note was buried under a pile of books.*

> ☑ SPELLING TIP Don't confuse the spelling of **bury** with **berry** which sounds the same. A **berry** is a small fruit.

bus *noun* (*plural* **buses** *or* **busses**)
1. a long vehicle with many seats, for carrying passengers: *to catch the bus to the movies.*
–*verb* (**busses** *or* **buses**, **bussing** *or* **busing**, **bussed** *or* **bused**, **has bussed** *or* **has bused**) **2.** To **bus** is to travel by bus. **3.** To **bus** people is to transport them by bus.

> WORD HISTORY a shortened form of *omnibus*, which was the original word for a 'bus', and came from the Latin word meaning 'for all'

bush *noun*
1. a plant like a small tree with many branches coming out from the trunk near the ground: *a rose bush.* **2.** an area of land covered with native trees and bushes.
–*phrase* **3. the bush**, the Australian country as opposed to the city: *Dad went to school in the bush but Mum grew up in the city.* **4. beat about the bush**, to take a long time coming to the point in a conversation.

bush band *noun* a group of musicians who perform Australian folk music, using instruments such as the accordion and guitar.

bushcraft *noun* knowledge of how to live in and travel through rough bush country.

bushed *adjective Informal* **1.** very tired: *He was bushed after a long day's ride.* **2.** lost or confused: *I lost my map and ended up completely bushed.*

bushel *noun* an old-fashioned measure of large quantities of goods such as grain or fruit.

> ☑ SPELLING TIP *Single letter alert*: only one *l* at the end.

bushfire *noun* an unplanned fire in forest, scrub or grassland, often caused by lightning.

bushman *noun* someone who lives in the bush and knows how to survive there.
☐ **bushmanship**, *noun*

bushranger *noun* someone who hid in the Australian bush and lived by robbing travellers at gunpoint: *Ned Kelly was a famous bushranger.*
☐ **bushranging**, *noun*

bushwalking *noun* walking through the bush for exercise or pleasure.
☐ **bushwalk**, *noun*: *a long, tiring bushwalk.*
–**bushwalker**, *noun*

bushwhacker *noun Informal* someone who lives in the bush and is not used to city life.

bushy[1] *adjective* (**bushier**, **bushiest**) thick or dense like a bush: *a bushy tail.*

bushy[2] *noun* (*plural* **bushies**) *Informal* someone living in the country.

> ANOTHER SPELLING is **bushie**.
> NOTE The **bushy** is often compared with the *city slicker*, who is thought to be more trendy and talkative, but not perhaps as genuine.

business /*say* **biz**-nuhs/ *noun*
1. the work someone does to earn a living. **2.** buying and selling goods to make a profit: *to be in business.* **3.** an organisation involved in the buying and selling of goods or providing a service: *They own a small printing business.* **4.** a matter which someone has a right to know about: *I'm not telling you the person I voted for – it's none of your business.*
–*phrase* **5. mean business**, to be serious in intent: *The teacher told us we had to improve and she meant business.*
☐ **businessperson**, **businessman**, **businesswoman**, *noun*

> ☑ SPELLING TIP *Silent letter alert*: don't forget the *i* in the middle of **business**. This will be easier to remember if you see that it is made up of *busy* (with the *y* changed to an *i*) and the

suffix *-ness* (used in words referring to a certain state or condition).

busker *noun* a musician who performs in the street hoping to get donations of money from people passing by.
☐ **busk**, *verb*

bust[1] *noun*
1. a woman's breasts or chest. **2.** a sculpture of someone's head and shoulders.

bust[2] *Informal*
–*verb* **1.** To **bust** something is to break or burst it: *to bust a bubble.* **2.** If the police **bust** someone, they find them doing something wrong and arrest them: *He was busted for stealing.*
–*phrase* **3. bust up**, to argue and separate: *She has just busted up with her boyfriend.* **4. go bust**, to lose all your money: *His business has gone bust.*
☐ **busted**, *adjective*: *a busted pipe.*

bustard /*sounds like* busted/ *noun* a large, heavy bird which lives in the grassy plains of Australia.

WORD HISTORY from a Latin word meaning 'slow bird'

bustle /*say* **bus**-uhl/ *verb* If you **bustle**, you move or act in a busy way: *He bustled in and out of the room.*

☑ SPELLING TIP *Silent letter alert*: don't forget the *st* (not double *s*) spelling. The *t* is silent.

busy *adjective* (**busier**, **busiest**)
1. If someone is **busy**, they are working hard or have a lot of work to do: *If you're busy now, I'll come back later.* **2.** If a place is **busy**, it is full of activity: *The town centre is always very busy on Saturday mornings.* **3.** If a telephone line or a toilet is **busy**, it is already being used by someone else.
–*verb* (**busies**, **busying**, **busied**, **has busied**) **4.** To **busy** yourself is to keep yourself active doing something: *He busied himself in the garden until it was time for lunch.*
☐ **busily**, *adverb* –**busyness**, *noun*

ANOTHER WORD (for definition 3) is **engaged**.

busybody *noun* (*plural* **busybodies**) someone who is too interested in other people's business.

but *conjunction*
1. and on the other hand: *All my friends went, but I didn't.*
–*preposition* **2.** except or save: *No-one answered but me.*
–*adverb* **3.** despite this: *But this isn't the end of the story.*
–*phrase* **4. all but**, almost: *The year has all but finished.* **5. but for**, were it not for: *We would have gone but for the rain.*

butcher *noun*
1. someone who prepares and cuts up meat to sell. **2.** a cruel and violent murderer.
–*verb* **3.** To **butcher** an animal is to kill it and cut it up into pieces ready to cook and eat. **4.** To **butcher** another person is to kill them in a very cruel and violent way.
☐ **butchery**, *noun*

butcherbird *noun* a black and grey Australian bird which hangs its dead prey on branches.

butler *noun* the head servant, usually a man, in a rich person's house.

WORD HISTORY from a French word meaning 'bottle'

butt[1] *noun*
1. the thick end of a weapon or tool: *the butt of a rifle.* **2.** an end which is not used up: *a cigarette butt.*

☑ SPELLING TIP *Double letter alert*: double *t* at the end. Don't confuse this word with the conjunction **but**.

butt[2] *noun* someone at whom jokes or mean remarks are aimed: *She is often the butt of their jokes.*

☑ SPELLING TIP See **butt**[1].

butt[3] *verb* To **butt** is to push with the head or horns: *The lamb butted me.*
☐ **butt**, *noun*

☑ SPELLING TIP See **butt**[1].

butter *noun*
1. a soft, yellow spread made from cream.
–*verb* **2.** If you **butter** something, you spread butter on it: *to butter bread.*
☐ **buttery**, *adjective*

butterfly *noun* (*plural* **butterflies**) an insect with large wings which are often brightly coloured.

butterfly stroke *noun* a stroke in swimming in which both your arms are lifted together from the water and thrown forward.

COMPARE this with **breaststroke**, **freestyle**, and **backstroke**.

buttermilk *noun* a sour liquid left after butter has been made from cream.

butterscotch *noun* a kind of toffee or flavouring.

buttock *noun* either of the two rounded, fleshy parts of the body on which you sit.

button *noun*
1. a small, usually round, object sewn onto clothing to join two parts together. **2.** anything shaped like a button, such as a small switch you press to ring a bell. **3.** a small icon on a computer screen that you can click on with the mouse in order to select it so that it will perform a function.
–*verb* (**buttons**, **buttoning**, **buttoned**, **has buttoned**) **4.** To **button** something is to fasten it with a button: *I buttoned my shirt.*

buttonhole *noun* a small, thin opening in clothing through which buttons are passed to fasten parts of it together.

buttress *noun*
1. a support for a wall or building.
–*verb* 2. To **buttress** a wall or building is to support it with a buttress.

buxom /*say* **buks**-uhm/ *adjective* If a woman is **buxom**, she is plump in an attractive way.

buy *verb* (**buys**, **buying**, **bought** /*say* bawt/, **has bought**)
1. If you **buy** something, you get it by paying money for it: *I need to buy some new shoes.* 2. *Informal* If you **buy** someone's story or explanation, you accept it or believe it: *The police won't buy that story.*
–*noun* 3. something bought: *a good buy.*
☐ **buyer**, *noun*

A SIMILAR WORD (for definition 1) is **purchase**, although this is a bit more formal.

☑ SPELLING TIP Don't confuse the spelling of **buy** with **by** or **bye** which sound the same. If something is **by** something else, it is near it. A **bye** is when your sporting team does not have to play in a certain round. **Bye** can also mean 'goodbye'. Also remember the *ough* spelling for the 'aw' sound in the past form **bought**. Other words like this are *brought* and *thought*.

buzz *noun*
1. a low, unchanging sound: *the buzz of bees*; *the buzz of a distant plane.*
–*verb* 2. To **buzz** is to make a buzzing noise: *The fly buzzed around my head*; *The room was buzzing with conversation.*
–*phrase* 3. **buzz off**, *Informal* to go or leave.
☐ **buzzer**, *noun*: *If you need the nurse, just press the buzzer.*

WORD HISTORY this imitates the sound that bees make

buzzard *noun* a large bird belonging to the hawk family.

by *preposition*
1. near to: *I left my bag by my desk.* 2. using as a way: *to come in by the back door*; *to travel by road.* 3. past (something nearby): *to go by the swimming pool.* 4. during: *by night*; *by day.* 5. not later than: *Be home by midnight.*
–*adverb* 6. near: *The bird's nest must be close by.* 7. past something nearby: *The train sped by.*

by- *prefix* a word part meaning 1. secondary, as in *by-product*. 2. out of the way, as in *byway*. 3. near, as in *bystander*.

ANOTHER SPELLING is **bye-**.

bye[1] *noun* in a sporting competition, a game which a team or competitor does not have to play in a particular round of the contest.

bye[2] *interjection* goodbye.

by-election *noun* an extra election held to fill the seat of a member of parliament who has died or retired.

bypass *noun*
1. a road built to take traffic around the edge rather than through a town or a busy traffic area. 2. an operation on the heart in which artificial tubes are put in to make the flow of blood go around a blocked or diseased part.
–*verb* 3. To **bypass** someone or something is to try to avoid them in order to make something happen more easily or quickly: *It's no good trying to bypass the committee*; *The expressway bypasses the town.*

by-product *noun* something produced in addition to the main product: *Molasses is a by-product of making sugar*; *The increase in traffic in the area was a by-product of the building of the new flats.*

bystander *noun* someone who is present when something happens, but does not take part in it: *Police are anxious to interview bystanders who witnessed the incident.*

byte /*say* buyt/ *noun* a unit of information stored by a computer.

☑ SPELLING TIP Remember the *y* in **byte**. Don't confuse it with **bight** or **bite** which sound the same. A **bight** is a curve in a shore forming a large bay. A **bite** is a wound made with the teeth, or a mouthful of food.

byway *noun* a road not used very often.

cab *noun*
1. See **taxi**. **2.** the covered part of a truck where the driver sits.

cabanossi /*say* kab-uh-**nos**-ee/ *noun* a thin beef sausage with seasoning, which you buy already cooked.

☑ SPELLING TIP *Single/double letter alert*: only one *b* and one *n*, but a double *s*. Also remember the *i* ending. **Cabanossi** has this spelling because it comes from Italian. Rap it out as *ca*+*ba*+*nos*+*si*.

cabaret /*say* **kab**-uh-ray/ *noun* a musical or comedy show performed at a restaurant or club.

☑ SPELLING TIP *Silent letter alert*: don't forget the silent *t* at the end – the *et* spelling makes an 'ay' sound. Other words with this ending are *ballet* and *beret*. They all come from French.

cabbage *noun* a kind of vegetable with large green leaves wrapped tightly around a short stem.

cabbage tree *noun* a tall palm with large leaves and with buds that you can eat, found growing along the coast of eastern Australia.

ANOTHER NAME for this is **cabbage tree palm**.
NOTE In the early days of European settlement in Australia, people made wide-brimmed hats from the leaves of this palm.

cabin *noun*
1. a small house. **2.** a room in a ship where passengers sleep. **3.** the space inside a aircraft where the people sit.

cabinet *noun*
1. a piece of furniture with shelves and drawers. **2.** the group of leading people in a government: *the prime minister and his cabinet.*

ANOTHER FORM This word (as in definition 2) is often spelt with a capital letter.

cable *noun*
1. thick, strong rope or chain, made from several wires twisted together. **2.** a bundle of insulated wires that carry electricity.

cache *noun* /*say* kash/
1. a hiding place for storing things. **2.** the things that are hidden in a cache. **3.** /*say* kaysh/ a section of computer memory where information is stored and can be accessed or retrieved quickly. –*verb* /*say* kash/ (**caches**, **caching**, **cached**, **has cached**) **4.** If you **cache** something, you hide it. **5.** /*say* kaysh/ If you **cache** information on your computer, you store it so you can access it quickly at a later time.

☑ SPELLING TIP Remember the *ache* spelling for the 'ash' sound at the end. **Cache** is spelt in this way because it comes from French.

cackle *verb* To **cackle** is to laugh or talk with the kind of noisy sound that a hen makes after laying an egg.
☐ **cackle**, *noun*

cacophony /*say* kuh-**kof**-uh-nee/ *noun* a loud, unmusical sound: *a cacophony of car horns.*
☐ **cacophonous**, *adjective*

☑ SPELLING TIP This word will be easier to spell if you see that it is made up of *caco-* (a word part formed from the Greek word for 'bad' or 'unpleasant') and *phony* (from the Greek word for 'sound').

cactus /*say* **kak**-tuhs/ *noun* (*plural* **cacti** /*say* **kak**-tuy/ *or* **cactuses**) a spiky plant which stores water in its thick skin and grows in hot dry places.

cadaver /*say* kuh-**dav**-uh, kuh-**dahv**-uh/ *noun* a dead body, particularly of a human being.

A SIMILAR WORD is **corpse**.

☑ SPELLING TIP *Tricky 'uh' sounds*: the first vowel sound is spelt *a* and the one at the end of the word is spelt *er*.

caddie *noun* someone who is paid to carry a golfer's playing clubs and find the ball.

ANOTHER SPELLING is **caddy**.

caddy *noun* (*plural* **caddies**)
1. a small box or tin: *a tea caddy*; *a nail caddy.* **2.** a rack or holder: *a shower caddy.*

cadence /*say* **kay**-duhns/ *noun*
1. the rising and falling of sounds, especially in the sound of your voice when reading poetry. **2.** a group of musical notes or chords which mark the end of a section or piece of music.

cadet *noun* someone who is being trained in a job or an organisation, like the army or a school military group.
☐ **cadetship**, *noun*

cafe /*say* **kaf**-ay/ *noun* a kind of restaurant where coffee, tea and small meals are served.

NOTE The 'e' is pronounced because this comes from the French word *café* which means 'coffee'. ANOTHER TERM for this is **coffee shop**.

cafeteria *noun* a cheap self-service restaurant.

WORD HISTORY from an American Spanish word for a coffee shop

caffeine /*say* **kaf**-een/ *noun* a stimulating drug found in coffee and tea which stops you falling asleep.

☑ SPELLING TIP *Double letter alert*: double *f*. Also don't forget that it has *ei* (to spell the 'ee' sound) in the second part of the word. This follows the rule that *i* comes before *e* except after *c*. Finally, don't forget the silent *e* at the end. It is spelt in this way because it comes from French.

caftan *noun*
1. a full-length piece of clothing with long, wide sleeves and tied at the waist, worn by Middle Eastern people. **2.** a similar long, loose piece of clothing.

ANOTHER SPELLING is **kaftan**.

cage *noun*
1. an enclosure made of wires or bars, in which animals or birds can be kept. **2.** anything that is like a prison.
–*verb* **3.** To **cage** someone or something is to put them in a cage or in a situation like a cage: *The hens were caged in the morning and let out on the grass in the afternoon.*

cagey *adjective* (**cagier**, **cagiest**) careful not to tell very much: *She got quite cagey when I asked about the party.*
☐ **cagily**, *adverb* –**caginess**, *noun*

A SIMILAR WORD is **secretive**.

cajole /*say* kuh-**johl**/ *verb* When you **cajole** someone, you persuade them by praising them or making promises.
☐ **cajolery**, *noun*

A SIMILAR WORD is **coax**.

cake *noun*
1. a sweet food, usually made with butter, flour, sugar, eggs, and a flavouring, which is baked in an oven: *a chocolate cake*; *a birthday cake.* **2.** a small mass of something with a particular shape: *a fish cake*; *a cake of soap.*
–*verb* **3.** If you **cake** something, you cover it with a thick coating of something: *She caked her face with make-up.*
–*phrase Informal* **4. piece of cake**, something which is done or obtained easily: *The maths exam was a piece of cake.* **5. take the cake**, to be the best: *He certainly takes the cake for rudeness.*

calamari /*say* kal-uh-**mah**-ree/ *noun* squid, especially when eaten as a food, for example, cut into rings, covered with batter or breadcrumbs and fried.

WORD HISTORY from the Italian word for 'squid'

calamity *noun* (*plural* **calamities**) a terrible happening or disaster: *The floods last month were a terrible calamity.*
☐ **calamitous**, *adjective*

calcium /*say* **kal**-see-uhm/ *noun* a soft, silver-white metal which is found in limestone and chalk, and in teeth and bones.

☑ SPELLING TIP There are two *c*'s in **calcium** – one at the beginning and one in the middle – but they have two different sounds. The second *c* sounds like an *s*. Rap it out as *cal*+*ci*+*um*.

calculate *verb* To **calculate** something is to **1.** work it out by using numbers: *He got out his ruler and calculated the area of the square.* **2.** work it out by thinking: *She had to calculate the effect on her family.*
☐ **calculated**, *adjective* done deliberately or with careful planning: *a calculated risk*; *a calculated manoeuvre.* –**calculation**, *noun* –**calculating**, *adjective* shrewd: *a calculating mind.*

calculator *noun* a small electronic machine that can be used to do mathematical operations.

calendar *noun* a chart that shows the days and weeks of each month of the year.

WORD HISTORY from a Latin word meaning 'account book'

calf[1] /*say* kahf/ *noun* (*plural* **calves**) the young of a cow, and some other animals.

☑ SPELLING TIP *Tricky vowel sound*: don't forget the *l*. The *alf* spelling gives the 'ahf' sound.

calf[2] /*say* kahf/ *noun* (*plural* **calves**) the back part of the leg, below the knee: *You should stretch out your calves before going for a run.*

☑ SPELLING TIP See **calf**[1].

calibre /*say* **kal**-uh-buh/ *noun*
1. the measurement across something round, like the barrel of a gun. **2.** the ability or character of a person: *A person of such high calibre is not easy to find.*

☑ SPELLING TIP There are two difficult spelling parts in this word that will test your **calibre**. Remember that the vowel sound in the middle is spelt *i*, and that the vowel sound at the end is spelt *re*, even though it sounds like 'uh'. It might help if you think of other words which you know well with the same spelling for this sound, such as *centre* and *theatre*.

calico *noun* a rough, cotton cloth, usually whitish in colour.

WORD HISTORY named after *Calicut* (now Kozhikode), a city on the coast of India where this cloth was first made

caliper *noun* a metal splint used as a support for an injured leg or arm.

ANOTHER SPELLING is **calliper**.

call *verb*
1. To **call** is to cry out in a loud voice: *She called for help but nobody heard.* **2.** If you **call** someone something, you give them a name: *We called our fish Goldie*; *Her new book's called 'Dinosaurs'.* **3.** If you **call** someone something, you are describing them as that thing: *Are you calling me a liar?*; *He's been called the greatest composer of the twentieth century.* **4.** If you **call** someone on the telephone, you ring them: *Call me when you get there.* **5.** If you **call** something such as a meeting or an election, you arrange that it will take place: *The prime minister has called an election for next month*; *The class captain called a meeting.* **6.** If you **call** someone, you send for them or ask them to come to see you for a particular purpose: *The taps aren't working – we'd better call a plumber.* **7.** If someone **calls** or **calls in**, they make a short visit: *He called at the library*; *She called in, but we were out.*
–*noun* **8.** a shout or cry. **9.** a short visit. **10.** a telephone conversation: *an international call.* **11.** a request to go somewhere for a particular purpose: *The fire brigade had many calls last night.*
–*phrase* **12. call back**, to ring someone again, or in answer to their call to you: *I'll call you back tonight.* **13. call for**, **a.** to pick someone up, so that you can go somewhere together: *I'll call for you at 2 o'clock.* **b.** to need or be suitable for: *This good news calls for a celebration.* **c.** to request something strongly and publicly: *The students are calling for safer equipment.* **14. call off**, to give up totally or put off to a later date: *They called off the sports competition because of rain.* **15. call out**, to say out loud or shout: *We called out to the others to join our game.* **16. on call**, available for duty at short notice: *My mother's a doctor – she's often on call on Sundays.*
☐ **caller**, *noun*: *callers at our house*; *callers on the phone.* –**calling**, *noun* someone's job or profession: *Writing is his calling.*

call centre *noun* a business which conducts telephone services for organisations.

calligraphy /*say* kuh-**lig**-ruh-fee/ *noun* the art of doing beautiful writing, often with a special pen or brush.
☐ **calligrapher**, *noun*

callous /*say* **kal**-uhs/ *adjective* showing no concern for another person's feelings: *Ignoring his cry for help was both callous and cruel.*
☐ **callousness**, *noun*

A SIMILAR WORD is **insensitive**.

☑ SPELLING TIP Don't confuse the spelling of **callous** with **callus** which has the same sound but is spelt with *us* at the end. A **callus** is a hard, thick growth on the skin.

callus /*say* **kal**-uhs/ *noun* a hard, thick part of the skin caused by something rubbing against it: *I've got a callus on my finger from my pen.*

☑ SPELLING TIP Notice the *us* ending of **callus**. Don't confuse it **callous** which has the same sound. Someone who is **callous** has no concern for how other people feel. **Callus** comes directly from Latin where *us* is a common ending for nouns

calm /*say* kahm/ *adjective*
1. remaining quiet and steady, and not getting excited or upset about things that happen: *He always stays calm when there's trouble.* **2.** very still, with no rough movements: *We can't surf today, it's too calm.*
–*verb* **3.** If you **calm** someone, you do or say something to quieten them or to make them feel less worried: *He gently calmed the nervous foal.*
–*phrase* **4. calm down**, to begin to feel less excited and upset: *Calm down and tell me what happened.*
☐ **calm**, *noun* –**calmness**, *noun* –**calmly**, *adverb*

☑ SPELLING TIP *Tricky vowel sound*: don't forget the *l*. The *alm* spelling gives the 'ahm' sound.

calorie /*say* **kal**-uh-ree/ *noun* a measurement of heat or the energy value of food: *All humans require a certain number of calories in food to provide energy to do things.*

NOTE This is now being replaced by **kilojoule** which is the unit of measurement in the metric system.

camel *noun* an animal with one or two humps on its back, used to carry people and loads across the desert.

cameo /*say* **kam**-ee-oh/ *noun*
1. a piece of jewellery made from a stone or shell which has been carved so that the design stands out from its background. **2. cameo part**, a small but interesting part in a film or play.

camera *noun*
1. a machine with which you take photographs. **2.** a machine for filming live action: *a television camera*; *a video camera.*

camouflage /*say* **kam**-uh-flahzh/ *noun*
1. a kind of disguise, either natural or artificial, that makes something hard to see against its surroundings: *The stick insect has the best camouflage – it looks just like a stick.*
–*verb* **2.** If you **camouflage** something, you disguise it so it is hard to see against its

surroundings: *The soldiers were camouflaged in green and brown clothes.*

☑ SPELLING TIP *Tricky 'uh' sound*: the middle vowel sound is spelt *ou*. Also remember the *age* spelling for the 'ahzh' sound at the end. This is because **camouflage** comes from French.

camp[1] *noun*
1. a group of tents, caravans or shelters for outdoor living. **2.** a place for these kinds of shelters. –*verb* **3.** When you **camp**, you live for a while in a tent: *They camped beside the beach for a week.*
☐ **camper**, *noun* –**camping**, *noun*

camp[2] *adjective*
1. (of a male) homosexual. **2.** in an exaggerated or amusing style: *a camp style of dressing.*

campaign /*say* kam-**payn**/ *noun*
1. a series of planned attacks by an army, in a particular area or for a particular purpose: *Two companies would be involved in the campaign.* **2.** any planned series of actions with a particular purpose: *She started the campaign to save the dolphins.*
–*verb* **3.** If you **campaign** for something, you take part in planned actions to try to make it happen: *We campaigned for more buses on the weekend.*
☐ **campaigner**, *noun*

☑ SPELLING TIP This word comes from French which is why the end part is spelt *aign* (although it sounds like 'ayn'). In particular, don't forget the silent *g* before the *n*.

campervan *noun* a vehicle with a cabin for the driver at the front and a kitchen, beds, and so on, at the back.

THE SHORT FORM of this is **camper**.
COMPARE this with **caravan**.

campus *noun* the grounds of a university or college.

WORD HISTORY from a Latin word meaning 'field'

can[1] *verb* When **can** is used with another verb, it means **1.** that it is possible for someone to do something or for something to happen: *Can you reach the top shelf?* **2.** that someone knows how to do something: *He can play the piano.* **3.** that someone is allowed to do something: *You can cross the street now – the light is green.*

NOTE This is always used with another verb in the form *I can* or *I could*. See *modal verbs* in the Grammar and Punctuation Guide appendix.
NOTE Some people say you should always use **may**, not **can**, for definition 3.

can[2] *noun* a tin container for food and drink: *a can of soup*; *a can of juice.*
☐ **canned**, *adjective*

canal /*say* kuh-**nal**/ *noun* an artificial river made for ships or barges to travel along.

canary *noun* (*plural* **canaries**) a small, yellow bird that sings sweetly and is often kept as a pet.

WORD HISTORY named after the *Canary* Islands where these birds were first seen

cancel *verb* (**cancels**, **cancelling**, **cancelled**, **has cancelled**)
1. If you **cancel** an event, you stop it from happening although it's already been arranged: *We'll have to cancel the match if it rains really hard.* **2.** If you **cancel** something such as a name on a list, you cross it out by drawing a line through it. –*phrase* **3. cancel out**, If something **cancels out** something else, the two things are equal but opposite, so that together they add up to zero effect: *You've just paid for the ice-creams, so that cancels out the bus fare you owe me.*
☐ **cancellation**, *noun*

cancer *noun* the harmful growth of a group of cells in someone's body, which destroys the nearby cells and can spread through the whole body, often causing death.
☐ **cancerous**, *adjective*

candelabrum /*say* kan-duh-**lah**-bruhm/ *noun* (*plural* **candelabra**) an ornamental holder for a number of candles.

candid *adjective* honest and sincere: *He was quite candid and told me I had very little chance of winning.*

candidate /*say* **kan**-duh-duht, **kan**-duh-dayt/ *noun*
1. someone sitting for an examination. **2.** someone who is applying for a job or an award, or is standing in an election.
☐ **candidacy**, *noun* –**candidature**, *noun*

WORD HISTORY from a Latin word meaning 'dressed in white', after the white togas that Roman candidates wore when they were standing for office

candle *noun* a wick coated in wax, which is burnt to give light.

candour /*rhymes with* panda/ *noun* honesty and sincerity: *Her candour surprised some people – she always said exactly what she thought.*

ANOTHER SPELLING is **candor**.

candy *noun* (*plural* **candies**) a sweet made of boiled sugar.

cane *noun*
1. the thin, woody stem of bamboo, sugar cane and other similar plants. **2.** a stick you can lean on to help with walking.
–*verb* **3.** To **cane** someone is to hit them with a cane as a punishment.

ANOTHER TERM (for definition 2) is **walking stick**.

cane toad *noun* a toad brought into Queensland to get rid of cane beetles and which is now a pest.

canine /*say* **kay**-nuyn/ *adjective*
1. having to do with dogs.
–*noun* **2.** the pointed tooth on each side of your upper and lower jaws.

canister *noun* a small container, often made of metal: *canisters for tea, flour and rice.*

> ☑ SPELLING TIP *Single letter alert*: only one *n*. Think of the word *can* (though in fact **canister** comes from the word *cane*, rather than *can*).

cannabis /*say* **kan**-uh-buhs/ *noun* See **marijuana**.

cannibal /*say* **kan**-uh-buhl/ *noun* someone who eats human flesh.
☐ **cannibalism**, *noun*

> ☑ SPELLING TIP *Tricky 'uh' sound*: the middle vowel sound is spelt *i*. Also remember the *al* (not *le*) ending.

cannon *noun* a large gun on wheels.

cannot *verb* a form of *can not*.

canoe /*say* kuh-**nooh**/ *noun*
1. a light, narrow boat that you move by using paddles.
–*verb* (**canoes**, **canoeing**, **canoed**, **has canoed**) **2.** If you **canoe**, you paddle or travel in a canoe.
☐ **canoeist**, *noun*

> ☑ SPELLING TIP *Tricky vowel sound*: the final vowel sound is spelt *oe* (not *oo*). It might help if you think of a word you know well which has the same spelling for this sound, such as *shoe*.

canopy /*say* **kan**-uh-pee/ *noun* (*plural* **canopies**) a pretty or protective covering: *a canvas canopy*; *a canopy of jungle foliage.*

> WORD HISTORY from a Greek word meaning 'mosquito net'

can't a short form of **cannot**.

cantaloupe /*say* **kan**-tuh-lohp, **kan**-tuh-loohp/ *noun* a sweet-flavoured, round melon with orange flesh and a hard, rough skin.

> ANOTHER WORD for this is **rockmelon**.

cantankerous *adjective* bad-tempered and quarrelsome: *a cantankerous old man.*
☐ **cantankerously**, *adverb* –**cantankerousness**, *noun*

canteen *noun*
1. a small shop or counter where food is sold in a factory, office, or school. **2.** a small container for carrying drinking water.

canter *noun*
1. the movement of a horse which is a little slower than a gallop.
–*verb* **2.** When a horse **canters**, it moves in a canter.

cantor *noun* a Jewish church leader who sings during the religious service.

canvas *noun*
1. heavy cotton cloth used for sails, tents, etc. **2.** a piece of this used for painting on: *He smeared the paint thickly onto the canvas.*

> ☑ SPELLING TIP Don't confuse the spelling of this word (only one *s*) with **canvass** which is to ask people for their votes or support.

canvass *verb* If you **canvass** people, you ask for their votes or support: *The new candidate was canvassing supporters at all of the local clubs.*
☐ **canvasser**, *noun*

> ☑ SPELLING TIP *Double letter alert*: double *s* at the end. Don't confuse this word with **canvas**, which is a thick, strong material.

canyon *noun* a deep valley with steep sides.

cap *noun*
1. a soft, close-fitting hat with a part to keep the sun off the face. **2.** a lid or top.
–*verb* (**caps**, **capping**, **capped**, **has capped**) **3.** If you **cap** something such as a story or achievement, you improve on what you or someone else has previously said: *She capped his joke with an even funnier one.*

capable *adjective*
1. having ability or skill at a particular thing, or able to do most things well: *We need a capable captain for the soccer team.*
–*phrase* **2. capable of**, **a.** able to do: *She is capable of great things.* **b.** likely to do: *Do you think he is capable of treachery?*

capacity /*say* kuh-**pas**-uh-tee/ *noun* (*plural* **capacities**)
1. the quantity or amount which can be held or contained: *The fuel tank has a capacity of fifty litres.* **2.** mental ability: *Does he have the capacity to learn a foreign language?* **3.** the position or standing of someone: *In her capacity as magistrate, she sentenced him to a month's civic duty.*
☐ **capacious**, *adjective* able to hold a lot: *a capacious bag.*

cape[1] *noun* a loose cloak which is fastened at your neck and hangs over your shoulders.

cape[2] *noun* a piece of land sticking out into the sea: *The cape was the best place to build the lighthouse.*

caper *verb* If you **caper**, you jump or dance about.
☐ **caper**, *noun* a prank: *Climbing on the roof was a foolish caper.*

capillary /*say* kuh-**pil**-uh-ree/ *noun* (*plural* **capillaries**) one of the smallest vessels for taking blood around the body.

☑ SPELLING TIP *Single/double letter alert*: one *p* and a double *l*. It should help if you think of the word *pill* being hidden inside the word **capillary**.

capital *noun*
1. the city which is the official seat of government of a state or country: *Paris is the capital of France.* **2.** a large letter, such as *A, B, C* and so on: *They say if you use capitals in emails it's like shouting.* **3.** the amount of money owned by a business or person. **4.** any form of wealth used to produce more wealth.
–*adjective* **5.** A **capital** city is the chief or main one in a country or state. **6.** A **capital** letter is one in the large style.

ANOTHER TERM for a **capital** letter is an **upper case** letter.
SEE the Grammar and Punctuation Guide appendix for information on the use of capital letters.

☑ SPELLING TIP Remember that the end of **capital** is spelt *al* (not *le*). It might help if you think of other words which have the same spelling for this sound, such as *metal* and *total*.

capitalism *noun* the economic system under which industries are owned privately, not by the government.
☐ **capitalist**, *noun*

COMPARE this with **communism**.

capital punishment *noun* punishment by death.

capitulate /*say* kuh-**pich**-uh-layt/ *verb* If you **capitulate**, you give in or surrender: *He stayed firm and refused to capitulate.*
☐ **capitulation**, *noun*

cappuccino /*say* kap-uh-**chee**-noh/ *noun* coffee with frothy milk added, made in a special machine.

☑ SPELLING TIP *Double letter alert*: a double *p* and double *c* (giving a 'ch' sound). Also note the *o* ending, which occurs in many words which come from Italian, as **cappuccino** does.

caprice /*say* kuh-**prees**/ *noun* a sudden change of mind without an apparent reason.
☐ **capricious**, *adjective* –**capriciousness**, *noun*

A SIMILAR WORD is **whim**.

☑ SPELLING TIP Remember that this word ends with *ice* (although it sounds like 'ees'). **Caprice** is spelt in this way because it comes from French (from the original Italian).

capsicum /*say* **kap**-suh-kuhm/ *noun* a type of vegetable, usually green or red, which is often used in salads.

ANOTHER NAME for this is **pepper**.

☑ SPELLING TIP *Tricky 'uh' sound*: the middle vowel sound spelt with an *i*. Also notice that the ending is spelt *um*. It might help if you think of other words which have the same spelling for this sound, such as *album* and *maximum*. Words with this ending usually come from Latin. **Capsicum** comes from the Latin word for 'box'. Rap it out as *cap+si+cum*.

capsize *verb* If a boat **capsizes**, it turns over in the water: *Their yacht capsized during the race.*

capsule *noun*
1. a small case or covering, like the one that holds a dose of medicine. **2.** the part of a spaceship which holds the people or instruments.

captain /*say* **kap**-tuhn/ *noun*
1. someone who is in charge of a ship or aeroplane. **2.** someone who commands a group of soldiers. **3.** a leader: *In his position as a captain of industry, he held a respected position in society.*
☐ **captaincy**, *noun*

☑ SPELLING TIP Remember that the final part of this word is spelt *ain*. Other words with this spelling for an 'uhn' sound are *certain*, *curtain*, *fountain* and *mountain*.

captcha /*say* **kap**-chuh/ *noun* a test used on a website to make sure the user is a person rather than a computer program, where the user has to do a task such as reading distorted letters that a human could recognise but a computer could not.

caption *noun* the words written underneath a picture to describe or explain it: *The people in the photo are named in the caption.*

captivate *verb* If something **captivates** you, it charms and delights you: *The audience was captivated by her beautiful singing.*
☐ **captivation**, *noun*

captive *noun* someone who has been taken prisoner.
☐ **captive**, *adjective*: *captive animals.* –**captivity**, *noun*

capture *verb*
1. To **capture** someone or something is to take them by force: *The soldiers captured ten rebels*; *The army captured the city after a long battle.* **2.** If you **capture** a special mood or moment, you record it on film, in a picture or in words: *The artist has captured the character of the place.*
☐ **capture**, *noun*

car *noun*
1. a vehicle with wheels driven by its own engine, for carrying a small number of passengers along roads. **2.** a railway carriage or wagon.

NOTE This word (as in definition 1) was originally short for **motor car**.

carafe /*say* kuh-**rahf**, kuh-**raf**/ *noun* a glass bottle used for serving water, wine or fruit juice at a meal table.

☑ SPELLING TIP *Single letter alert*: only one *f* in the *afe* ending (unlike the ending of the word *giraffe* which has the same sound).

caramel *noun*
1. a type of sweet, or a colouring or flavouring made from burnt sugar. **2.** a light brown colour.
☐ **caramel**, *adjective*

☑ SPELLING TIP *Single letter alert*: there are no double letters – the *r*, *m* and *l* are all single letters.

carat *noun*
1. a unit of weight for measuring precious stones, equal to 200 milligrams. **2.** a measure of the purity of gold: *The colour specialist told Anna she should wear 9 carat gold rather than silver.*

caravan *noun*
1. a vehicle that can be pulled by a car, and in which people can live, especially when they are on holidays. **2.** a group of people travelling together, especially across a desert.

COMPARE definition 1 with **campervan**.

caraway *noun* a herb with small seeds which are used in cooking.

carbine *noun* a rifle with a short barrel.

carbohydrate *noun* a substance, such as sugar, which contains oxygen, hydrogen, and carbon, and which is present in all living things.

carbon *noun*
1. a common element found in all living things but particularly coal. **2.** this element existing in the form of carbon dioxide or methane, as in *carbon footprint*.

carbon capture *noun* a process that traps and removes carbon dioxide that is given out from places like factories and power stations, thus preventing it from entering the atmosphere and adding to the greenhouse effect.

carbon dioxide *noun* a colourless gas which has no smell and does not burn, present in the atmosphere, and in the air humans and animals breath out, used in industry as dry ice and in fizzy drinks, fire extinguishers, etc. Release of carbon dioxide into the atmosphere, as a result of the burning of fossil fuels, etc., is thought to be involved in the increase in greenhouse gases in the atmosphere and therefore in global warming.

carbon emission *noun* an amount of carbon dioxide released into the atmosphere when coal is used as fuel for transport or to generate electricity, or during forest burning or some processes used in agriculture.

carbon footprint *noun* a measure of the amount of carbon dioxide that an individual or organisation produces by activities that involve the burning of fossil fuels, such as travelling by cars or planes and using electricity: *Dad said we could reduce our carbon footprint by riding our bicycles a lot, instead of being driven everywhere.*

carbon gas *noun* carbon dioxide, the principal greenhouse gas.

carbon monoxide *noun* a colourless poisonous gas which has no smell.

carbon paper *noun* paper that is coated with carbon, used between sheets of writing or typing paper to make copies.

carbon price *noun* a price on carbon as a fuel which takes into account the damage that it does to the environment.

carbon sink *noun* a large area covered with trees or bushes which absorbs carbon dioxide from the atmosphere, thus reducing the level of greenhouse gases.

carbuncle *noun* a painful, pus-filled swelling, like a large boil.

carburettor /*say* kah-byuh-**ret**-uh/ *noun* the part of an engine in which fuel and air are mixed together to form an explosive gas.

carcass /*say* **kah**-kuhs/ *noun* the dead body of an animal.

ANOTHER SPELLING is **carcase**.

card *noun*
1. a small piece of stiff paper or cardboard: *a thankyou card*; *a place card.* **2.** one of a set of cards used for playing card games.
–*phrase* **3. on the cards**, likely to happen.

cardboard *noun* a thick, stiff type of paper.

cardiac *adjective* having to do with the heart: *a cardiac surgeon.*

cardigan *noun* a knitted jacket with buttons down the front.

WORD HISTORY named after an English lord, the 7th Earl of *Cardigan* (1797–1868)

cardinal *adjective*
1. chief or of first importance: *a cardinal rule.*
–*noun* **2.** a priest with a senior position in the Roman Catholic Church.

A SIMILAR WORD (for definition 1) is **fundamental**.

cardinal number *noun* in mathematics, a number such as '1', '2', '3' and so on, which tells you how many things are in a given set but not the order in which they appear.

COMPARE this with **ordinal number**.

cardiovascular /*say* kah-dee-oh-**vas**-kyuh-luh/ *adjective* having to do with the heart and blood vessels.

care *noun*
1. worry or anxiety: *She was worn out by care*; *to leave all your cares behind.* **2.** thoughtful attention: *Drive with care.* **3.** protection or charge: *She was in the care of her grandmother while her parents were away.*
–*verb* **4.** If you **care** about something, you are interested in it because you think it is important: *We should all care more about the environment.*
–*phrase* **5. care for**, **a.** to like or love. **b.** to look after: *We must help care for the sick.* **6. care of**, at the address of: *You can write to him care of his mother.* **7. take care**, to pay thoughtful attention in order to do something well or in order not to damage something. **8. take care of**, **a.** to look after someone or something: *Take care of your pets.* **b.** to deal with something: *to take care of the arrangements.*
☐ **carefree**, *adjective*

career *noun*
1. the job or profession in which you earn your living: *a career in publishing*; *a career in law.*
–*verb* **2.** If someone or something **careers** somewhere, they move fast and dangerously because they are not under proper control: *The truck careered down the slope and crashed into a tree.*

careful *adjective*
1. taking care not to make a mistake that could cause harm or damage: *Be careful with the vase – it's very fragile.* **2.** If you are **careful** when you do something, you put a lot of time and effort into it to make certain it's all correct: *He's very careful about his homework.*
☐ **carefully**, *adverb* –**carefulness**, *noun*

A SIMILAR WORD (for definition 1) is **cautious**; (for definition 2) **thorough**.

careless *adjective*
1. not paying enough attention to what you are doing: *My brother's very careless. He's always losing things.* **2.** done or said without thought: *I was hurt by her careless remark.*
☐ **carelessly**, *adverb* –**carelessness**, *noun*

caress /*say* kuh-**res**/ *noun*
1. an action which shows affection, such as a gentle touch, a hug or a kiss.
–*verb* **2.** If you **caress** someone or something, you touch them with affection.

WORD HISTORY from a Latin word meaning 'dear'

☑ SPELLING TIP *Single/double letter alert*: only one *r* in the middle and a double *s* at the end.

caret /*say* **ka**-ruht/ *noun* a mark (‸) you make in writing or printing to show where something has to be added.

☑ SPELLING TIP Don't confuse the spelling of **caret** with **carat** or **carrot** which have the same sound. A **carat** is a unit of weight used for measuring precious stones and a **carrot** is an orange-coloured vegetable.

caretaker *noun* someone who looks after a thing or a place, especially a building.

cargo *noun* (*plural* **cargoes**) the goods carried on a ship, aircraft, truck, etc.: *The ship was carrying a live cargo of sheep.*

caricature /*say* **ka**-rik-uh-choo-uh/ *noun* a picture or description of someone or something which makes fun of their unusual or characteristic features.
☐ **caricaturist**, *noun* someone who creates these pictures.

carillon /*say* kuh-**ril**-yuhn/ *noun* a set of bells hung in a tower and used to play tunes.
☐ **carillonist**, *noun* someone who plays these bells.

carnage *noun* the killing of many people: *The carnage on the roads has led to more regulation of speed limits.*

A SIMILAR WORD is **slaughter**.

carnal *adjective* having to do with the body: *carnal appetites.*

carnation *noun* a garden plant with red, pink, or white flowers.

carnival *noun*
1. a period of time during which sporting events are held: *a surf carnival*; *a racing carnival.* **2.** a time of processions and public celebrations, usually for a special occasion: *The town holds a spring carnival every year.*

ANOTHER WORD (for definition 2) is **festival**.

carnivore /*say* **kah**-nuh-vaw/ *noun* an animal that mostly eats meat.
☐ **carnivorous** /*say* kah-**niv**-uh-ruhs/, *adjective*

COMPARE this with **herbivore**, **insectivore** and **omnivore**.

carob /*say* **ka**-ruhb/ *noun* a substitute for chocolate which comes from the seed pods of a Mediterranean tree.

carol *noun* a joyful song, especially a Christmas song or hymn.

carousel /*say* ka-ruh-**sel**/ *noun*
1. See **merry-go-round**. **2.** the continuously moving belt from which travellers get their bags at the end of a journey by ship, aeroplane or bus.

☑ SPELLING TIP *Tricky 'uh' sound*: the middle vowel is spelt *ou*. Also notice the *el* ending. It has this spelling because it comes from French.

carp *noun* (*plural* **carp**) a large freshwater fish.

car park *noun* a place where it is permitted to park your car, as an area of land or a specially designed building.

carpenter *noun* someone who makes things out of wood and puts up wooden parts of a building.
□ **carpentry**, *noun*

carpet *noun*
1. a thick, woven floor covering.
–*verb* (**carpets**, **carpeting**, **carpeted**, **has carpeted**) **2.** If you **carpet** a room, you lay carpet on it. **3.** If something **carpets** a surface, it covers it thickly: *Leaves carpeted the path.*

carriage /*say* **ka**-rij/ *noun*
1. one of the passenger-carrying cars on a train. **2.** a vehicle on wheels, pulled by a horse or horses, used in the past for carrying people. **3.** the way you hold your head and body when you walk or stand: *He had the carriage of a soldier.*

SIMILAR WORDS (for definition 3) are **bearing** and **deportment**.

carrion *noun* the rotting flesh of dead animals in the wild: *Hyenas eat carrion.*

carrot *noun* an orange-coloured root vegetable.

carry *verb* (**carries**, **carrying**, **carried**, **has carried**)
1. When you **carry** something, you take it with you from one place to another, usually in your hands: *Could you carry this chair over there?* **2.** When a vehicle **carries** people, they travel inside it and it takes them to the place they want to go to: *This bus can carry sixty passengers.* **3.** When something such as a river or wind **carries** something somewhere, it takes it along with it as it moves: *The current carried us out to sea.* **4.** If a sound **carries**, it can be heard a long way away: *The sound of the explosion carried as far as the next town.*
–*phrase* **5. carry away**, to excite: *We were carried away by the enthusiasm of the crowd.* **6. carry off**, **a.** to win: *to carry off the prize.* **b.** to handle confidently and successfully: *The band was nervous playing in front of so many people, but they carried it off!* **7. carry on**, **a.** to behave in an excited way, more than is reasonable: *You're always carrying on about your pets.* **b.** to continue: *Carry on with what you were doing.* **8. carry out**, to complete: *to carry out a plan.*
□ **carrier**, *noun*: *The carrier has arrived to pick up the furniture*; *a disease carrier.*

cart *noun*
1. a small vehicle, sometimes pulled by a horse, used for carrying a load.
–*verb* **2.** If you **cart** something somewhere, you carry or transport it: *She carted the baby around all day.*
□ **carter**, *noun*

cartilage /*say* **kah**-tuh-lij/ *noun* a firm elastic substance forming part of your bone structure.

☑ SPELLING TIP *Tricky 'uh' sound*: the middle vowel sound is spelt with an *i*. Also remember that the ending of **cartilage** is spelt *age* (although it sounds like 'ij'). It might help if you think of some other words which have the same spelling for this sound, such as *average* and *sausage*.

carton *noun* a cardboard box often used for packaging food: *a drink carton*; *a carton of biscuits.*

cartoon *noun*
1. a funny drawing. **2.** a film made of many slightly different drawings which give the effect of movement when put through a projector.
□ **cartoonist**, *noun*

WORD HISTORY from a Latin word meaning 'paper'

cartridge *noun*
1. a case which holds the explosive powder and often also the bullet, for a gun. **2.** a container, especially for the recording tape for a computer or tape recorder, or for the ink for some types of pen.

cartwheel *noun*
1. the large wooden wheel of a cart, having many spokes. **2.** a sideways somersault with legs and arms outstretched.

carve *verb*
1. If you **carve** something, you cut pieces away from a block of stone or wood to make a particular shape or design: *My father carves wooden animals as a hobby.* **2.** If you **carve** a piece of meat, you cut slices from it.
□ **carved**, *adjective* –**carver**, *noun* –**carving**, *noun*

cascade *noun*
1. a flow of water over steep rocks.
–*verb* **2.** When water **cascades**, it flows fast down a hillside or over steep rocks.

case[1] *noun*
1. an example of the existence or occurrence of something: *a case of carelessness*; *a case of the flu.* **2.** a list of facts or reasons: *He made a strong case for an extra bus service.* **3.** an action against someone in a court of law. **4.** the form of a noun or pronoun which shows its relation to other words in a sentence.
–*phrase* **5. in any case**, under any circumstances: *I don't want to go, and in any case I don't have anything to wear.*

NOTE The three cases (definition 4) are **subjective**, **objective** and **possessive**. See the Grammar and Punctuation Guide appendix.

case[2] *noun* a container: *a CD case*; *a case of pineapples.*

cash *noun*
1. money in notes or coins: *I left some cash on the table and now it's gone.* 2. money available straight away: *They won't take credit cards – you have to have cash.*

cash card *noun* a card which allows you to perform banking activities via an automatic teller machine, or for EFTPOS payments.

OTHER NAMES for this are **ATM card** and **key card**.

cashew *noun* a small, kidney-shaped nut that you can eat.

cashier /*say* kash-**ear**/ *noun* someone who is in charge of the money in a shop or bank.

☑ SPELLING TIP Remember that the ending of **cashier** is spelt *ier* (although it sounds like 'ear'). It might help if you think of some other words which have the same spelling for this sound, such as *frontier* and *pier*.

cashmere *noun* fine wool obtained from the Kashmir goats of India, often used to make clothes.

casino /*say* kuh-**see**-noh/ *noun* (*plural* **casinos**) a building or large room where gambling games are played.

WORD HISTORY from a Latin word meaning 'cottage'

cask *noun* a barrel for holding wine and other liquids.

casket *noun*
1. a small chest or box. 2. a coffin.

cassata /*say* kuh-**sah**-tuh/ *noun* an Italian iced dessert, like gelato, made with chopped nuts or mixed dried fruit, and so on.

casserole *noun*
1. a covered baking dish. 2. the food, usually a mixture of meat and vegetables, cooked in it.

cassette *noun* the plastic container holding the recording tape used in videos and tape recorders.
□ **cassette**, *adjective*: *a cassette tape.*

☑ SPELLING TIP *Double letter alert*: double *s* and double *t*. Remember that the final syllable is spelt *ette* (although it sounds like 'et'). It is spelt like this because it comes from French (meaning 'little box'). Another word with this ending is *serviette*.

cassette recorder *noun* a machine that plays or records cassettes.

cassowary /*say* **kas**-uh-wuh-ree/ *noun* (*plural* **cassowaries**) a large, three-toed bird found in Australasia, which is almost as large as an ostrich and cannot fly.

cast *verb* (**casts**, **casting**, **cast**, **has cast**)
1. If you **cast** something, you throw it: *He cast the line out beyond the rocks.* 2. If something **casts** a shadow, it creates a shadow. 3. If a snake **casts** its skin, it sheds it. 4. If you are **cast** as a particular character in a play or film, you are chosen to act in that role: *I was cast as a doctor in the school play.* 5. If you **cast** an object, you make it by pouring hot metal into a specially shaped mould and leaving it there until it sets hard: *This statue was cast in bronze.*
–*noun* 6. all the actors in a play. 7. a mould of plaster around a broken limb.
–*phrase* 8. **cast about**, to search with your mind: *to cast about for a reason.*

castanets /*say* kas-tuh-**nets**/ *plural noun* a pair of shell-shaped pieces of wood which you hold in your hand and click together in time to music and dancing.

WORD HISTORY from Spanish, from a Latin word meaning 'chestnut'

☑ SPELLING TIP *Tricky 'uh' sound*: the middle vowel sound is spelt with an *a*. Remember that it has a complete word either side of it – *cast* and *nets* – though these don't have anything to do with the meaning of **castanets**.

castaway *noun* someone whose ship has sunk and who has been left somewhere by themselves, such as on an island.

caste *noun*
1. one of the social groups or divisions into which Hindus are born. 2. any strictly followed system of social divisions.

castigate *verb* If you **castigate** someone, you criticise or punish them severely.
□ **castigation**, *noun* –**castigator**, *noun*

castle /*say* **kah**-suhl/ *noun*
1. a large, strong fort, built especially in Europe in past times. 2. a piece in chess, shaped like a castle.

ANOTHER WORD (for definition 2) is **rook**[2].

☑ SPELLING TIP *Silent letter alert*: don't forget the *st* (not double *s*) spelling. The *t* is silent.

castor *noun* a small wheel attached to the bottom of a bed or under the legs of some tables and chairs to make them easier to move.

castor oil *noun* a sticky oil pressed from the seeds of a plant and used as a medicine.

castrate *verb* When a male animal is **castrated**, its testicles are removed so that it cannot have young.
□ **castration**, *noun*

casual /*say* **kazh**-yooh-uhl/ *adjective*
1. informal and relaxed: *It's a casual function – nothing to get dressed up for; Luckily we only have to wear casual clothes.* **2.** without thinking: *a casual comment.* **3.** happening by chance: *a casual meeting.* **4.** employed occasionally: *casual workers.*
□ **casually**, *adverb* –**casualness**, *noun*

casualty /*say* **kazh**-yooh-uhl-tee/ *noun* (*plural* **casualties**) someone hurt or killed in an accident or war.

> ☑ SPELLING TIP Remember that there are two vowels in the middle of **casualty** – *u* and *a*. People often say this word as if there were only three syllables (**kazh**-yuhl-tee), which is why you have to especially remember the *u* and the *a*.

casuarina /*say* kazh-yuh-**ree**-nuh/ *noun* a type of Australian tree or shrub with leaves which are like the needles of a pine tree, but jointed.

> ANOTHER NAME for this tree is **she-oak**.
> WORD HISTORY from the Malay word for the cassowary, because of the resemblance of the drooping leaves to the bird's feathers

cat *noun*
1. a small, furry animal, often kept as a pet. **2.** a member of the cat family, which includes lions, tigers and other similar animals. **3.** a spiteful girl or woman.
–*phrase* **4. let the cat out of the bag**, to give out information, often without meaning to. **5. rain cats and dogs**, to rain heavily.

> ANOTHER WORD (for definition 2) is **feline**.

catacomb /*say* **kat**-uh-kohm, **kat**-uh-koohm/ *noun* a series of underground tunnels and caves or rooms, once used as burial places.

> ☑ SPELLING TIP *Silent letter alert*: don't forget the *b* at the end. Also remember that there is only one *t*. Try thinking that **catacomb** contains both a *cat* and a *comb* (although this has nothing to do with the meaning).

catalogue /*say* **kat**-uh-log/ *noun*
1. a list, usually in alphabetical order, of names, books or items on sale or display and some information about them: *a catalogue of exhibits*; *a catalogue of agricultural machinery*; *an auction catalogue.*
–*verb* **2.** If you **catalogue** a collection of items, you sort them for listing in a catalogue.
□ **cataloguer**, *noun*

> ☑ SPELLING TIP *Silent letter alert*: don't forget the silent *ue* at the end. It is spelt in this way because it comes from French. Another word with this *logue* spelling for a 'log' sound is *dialogue*.

catalyst /*say* **kat**-uh-luhst/ *noun*
1. in chemistry, a substance which is added to speed up a chemical change but which is not really part of the reaction. **2.** someone or something that causes a change or a reaction.
□ **catalyse**, *verb* –**catalysis** /*say* kuh-**tal**-uh-suhs/, *noun* –**catalytic** /*say* kat-uh-**lit**-ik/, *adjective*

> ☑ SPELLING TIP *Letter 'y' alert*: the last syllable is spelt with a *y* (not *i*) because it comes from Greek. It might help if you think of some other words which have an *yst* ending, such as *amethyst* and *cyst*.

catamaran *noun* a boat with two hulls.

> THE SHORT FORM of this is **cat**.
> WORD HISTORY from a Tamil word meaning 'tied tree' or 'wood'

catapult *noun*
1. a Y-shaped stick with a length of elastic joined to the prongs, used for shooting stones at things.
–*verb* **2.** If something **catapults** or is **catapulted** somewhere, it moves very suddenly and quickly, as if fired from a catapult.

> OTHER WORDS (for definition 1) are **shanghai** and **slingshot**. See also **sling** (definition 2).

cataract *noun*
1. a large waterfall. **2.** a disease of the eye causing loss of sight.

catastrophe /*say* kuh-**tas**-truh-fee/ *noun* a sudden disaster: *Thousands of lives were lost in the catastrophe.*
□ **catastrophic** /*say* kat-uh-**strof**-ik/, *adjective*

> ☑ SPELLING TIP Remember that the ending of **catastrophe** is spelt *phe* (although it sounds like 'fee'). It is spelt in this way because it comes from Greek.

catch *verb* (**catches**, **catching**, **caught** /*say* kawt/, **has caught**)
1. If you **catch** an animal, you find and capture it: *I went fishing, but I didn't catch anything.* **2.** When the police **catch** criminals, they arrest them: *The police caught the car thieves last night.* **3.** If you **catch** a ball or something similar, you take hold of it as it moves through the air. **4.** If you **catch** a bus, train or aircraft, you get on it and travel from one place to another: *I slept in this morning and only just caught the bus.* **5.** If you **catch** someone doing something, you find them doing something that they should not be doing: *I'm sure he's cheating, but I can't catch him at it.* **6.** If you **catch** a disease, you become infected with it: *I don't want you to catch my cold.*
–*noun* (*plural* **catches**) **7.** the act of catching something, such as a ball: *Good catch!* **8.** something that's been caught, such as a

quantity of fish. **9.** a difficulty, usually one that you don't see: *What's the catch?*
–*phrase* **10. catch on**, **a.** to become popular: *That new song is really catching on.* **b.** to understand: *You keep explaining, but I can't seem to catch on.* **11. catch up**, to reach or become level: *Helen studied over the holidays and caught up with everybody else.*
☐ **catcher**, *noun*

☑ SPELLING TIP *Tricky vowel sound*: the vowel sound in the past form **caught** is spelt *augh* (although it sounds like 'aw'). It might help if you think of some other words which have the same spelling for this sound, such as *daughter* and *naughty*.

catechism /*say* **kat**-uh-kiz-uhm/ *noun* a book of questions and answers meant to help you learn about your religion.

☑ SPELLING TIP This word can appear difficult to spell. However, if you remember that the vowel sound in the middle is spelt *e* and that this is followed by *ch* (making a 'k' sound), the main difficulties are over. **Catechism** is spelt in this way because it comes from Greek.

category *noun* (*plural* **categories**) a group or division of people or things.
☐ **categorise**, *verb*

ANOTHER SPELLING for **categorise** is **categorize**.

cater *verb* If someone **caters** for a party or a special meal, they provide the food and drink that is needed, usually as a commercial service: *My mother's catering for a big wedding next week.*
☐ **caterer**, *noun*: *They decided to hire a caterer for the party.*

caterpillar *noun* the worm-like larva of a moth or butterfly.

☑ SPELLING TIP Some **caterpillars** will sting you if you step on them, and there are certainly several prickly bits in its spelling. Try thinking of the words *cat* and *pill*. Put *er* in between them and *ar* at the end.

caterwaul /*say* **kat**-uh-wawl/ *verb* If someone **caterwauls**, they cry or howl loudly, like quarrelling cats.

☑ SPELLING TIP *Tricky vowel sounds*: there are two tricky bits in this word – the *er* in the middle for the 'uh' sound and the *au* in the last syllable for the 'aw' sound.

catfish *noun* (*plural* **catfish** *or* **catfishes**) any of a number of freshwater and sea fishes with long feelers near the mouth that look like the whiskers of a cat.

cathedral *noun* a large church which is where a bishop presides.

cattle *plural noun* cows, especially when in a group: *He will take some cattle to market next week.*

cattle dog *noun* a dog bred to work at rounding up cattle.

catwalk *noun* a long, narrow platform on which models walk to display clothes.

caucus /*say* **kaw**-kuhs/ *noun* a meeting of the members of parliament belonging to a particular political party.

WORD HISTORY from a Native American word meaning 'adviser'

cauldron /*say* **kawl**-druhn/ *noun* a large, rounded container with a lid and handles, used to boil things.

cauliflower /*say* **kol**-ee-flow-uh/ *noun* a vegetable with a large round head of white flowers.

☑ SPELLING TIP A **cauliflower** is actually the flower of a particular plant, which makes the spelling of the last part of the word easy. The main thing to remember is the first part is spelt *caul* (although it sounds like 'kol').

cause *verb*
1. If something **causes** something else to happen, it makes it happen: *The rain caused him to be late for school.*
–*noun* **2.** someone or something which brings about an effect or result: *His joke was the cause of all the laughter.* **3.** something that you believe in: *They are raising money for a worthy cause.*
☐ **causal**, *adjective*

causeway *noun* a raised road or path across low or wet ground.

caustic /*say* **kos**-tik/ *adjective*
1. capable of burning or eating away living cells: *a caustic solution.* **2.** critical or sarcastic: *a caustic retort.*
☐ **caustically**, *adverb*

cauterise /*say* **kaw**-tuh-ruyz/ *verb* To **cauterise** something is to burn it with a hot instrument, especially to kill germs: *It took time to cauterise his wounds.*
☐ **cauterisation**, *noun*

ANOTHER SPELLING is **cauterize**.

caution /*say* **kaw**-shuhn/ *noun*
1. great care when there is danger: *People are advised to use caution when near fire.* **2.** a warning: *The teacher gave the students a caution about being late.*
–*verb* **3.** If you **caution** someone, you warn them of possible problems or danger: *She cautioned us to lock the door at night.*
☐ **cautionary**, *adjective* –**cautious** /*say* **kaw**-shuhs/, *adjective*

☑ SPELLING TIP *Tricky vowel sound*: the first vowel sound is spelt *au* (although it sounds like 'aw'). It might help if you think of some other words which have the same spelling for this sound, such as *audience*. Then, as in many other words, the ending *tion* is the spelling for a 'shuhn' sound at the end.

cavalcade *noun* a procession, especially of people in vehicles, or on horses, or so on.

cavalier /*say* kav-uh-**lear**/ *noun*
1. a soldier or knight on horseback.
–*adjective* **2.** not caring about important things: *Some people thought he had a cavalier attitude towards the national flag.*

cavalry *noun* (*plural* **cavalries**) a part of an army, which once rode on horseback, and is now often equipped with armoured vehicles.

cave *noun*
1. a hollow place in a hillside.
–*verb in the phrase* **2. cave in**, to fall or sink: *The tent caved in under the weight of the snow.*
☐ **caving**, *noun*: *to go caving in the holidays.*

cavern *noun* a large cave.
☐ **cavernous**, *adjective*

caviar /*say* **kav**-ee-ah, kav-ee-**ah**/ *noun* the salted eggs of sturgeon or other large fish.

cavity *noun* (*plural* **cavities**) an empty space or hollow: *a cavity in the ceiling*; *I can feel the cavity in my tooth with my tongue.*

CD *noun* a shortened form of **compact disc**.

CD-ROM /*say* see-dee-**rom**/ *noun* in computers, a compact disc which is used to store large amounts of data such as writing, sound and pictures, which you can access from the CD-ROM drive.

cease *verb* To **cease** doing something is to stop doing it: *Cease pestering me at once!*; *Finally, the rain ceased.*

cedar /*rhymes with* reader/ *noun* a type of tree, whose wood is often used to make furniture.

cede /*sounds like* seed/ *verb* When someone **cedes** something, they give it away by making a solemn written promise: *Under the treaty, the country that lost the war had to cede some of its territory to its neighbours.*

☑ SPELLING TIP Don't confuse the spelling of **cede** with **seed** which has the same sound. A **seed** is the small part of a plant from which a new plant grows.

ceiling /*say* **see**-ling/ *noun*
1. the inside lining that covers the top of a room. **2.** the top limit that something can reach: *Mum and Dad set a ceiling on the amount they would pay for the house.*

☑ SPELLING TIP Remember that **ceiling** begins with a *c* (with an *s* sound). Also remember the *ei* spelling of the 'ee' vowel sound. This follows the rule that *i* comes before *e* except after *c*.

celebrant /*say* **sel**-uh-bruhnt/ *noun* a special person who leads a religious ceremony.

celebrate *verb*
1. If you **celebrate** a special occasion, or some good news, you do something special and enjoyable, such as going out or having a party. **2.** If a country, organisation or business **celebrates** an event or occasion, they mark it by doing something special: *This year, our school will celebrate its centenary.*
☐ **celebration**, *noun* –**celebrated**, *adjective* famous.

celebrity /*say* suh-**leb**-ruh-tee/ *noun* (*plural* **celebrities**) a famous or well-known person.

A SIMILAR WORD is **personality**.

celery /*say* **sel**-uh-ree/ *noun* a vegetable with long, pale green stems.

☑ SPELLING TIP Remember that **celery** begins with a *c* (although it sounds like an *s*). Don't confuse it with **salary** (money that someone earns). Also notice that both the vowels in **celery** are *e*'s. Remind yourself that *e* is for *eat* which is what you do with **celery**.

celestial *adjective* heavenly: *the celestial gods*; *the celestial stars.*

celibacy /*say* **sel**-uh-buh-see/ *noun* the condition of being unmarried and not having sexual intercourse: *Priests in the Roman Catholic Church take a vow of celibacy.*
☐ **celibate** /*say* **sel**-uh-buht/, *adjective*

cell *noun*
1. a small room in a prison. **2.** the tiny, basic part of all living matter: *We looked at the cells under the microscope.* **3.** part of an electric battery.
☐ **cellular**, *adjective*

☑ SPELLING TIP Don't confuse the spelling of **cell** with **sell** which sounds the same. If you **sell** something you exchange it for money.

cellar *noun*
1. an underground room or store. **2.** a supply of wines.

cello /*say* **chel**-oh/ *noun* an instrument shaped like a large violin, which has four strings and is held upright on the floor between the knees of the player.
☐ **cellist**, *noun*

NOTE The **cello** sounds lower than the **violin** and **viola** and higher than the **double bass**.
WORD HISTORY short for *violoncello*

cellulose /*say* **sel**-yuh-lohs/ *noun* important material that forms the cell walls of plants and is found in wood, cotton, hemp and paper.

☑ SPELLING TIP The spelling of **cellulose** will be easier if you see that it is made up of a form of the word *cellula* (which is Latin for 'little cell') and the suffix *-ose* (meaning 'full of').

Celsius /*say* **sel**-see-uhs/ *adjective* The **Celsius** scale of temperature is that in which 0° is the melting point of ice and 100° is the boiling point of water.

ANOTHER WORD for this is **Centigrade**. This is rather old-fashioned now.
THE SYMBOL for this is **C**, as in *100°C*.
WORD HISTORY named after A *Celsius* (1701–1744), a Swedish astronomer

cement *noun*
1. a mixture of clay and limestone, used for making concrete. **2.** a type of glue.
–*verb* To **cement** something is to **3.** cover or fill it with concrete. **4.** stick or glue it to something else.
☐ **cementation**, *noun*

cemetery /*say* **sem**-uh-tree/ *noun* (*plural* **cemeteries**) a burial ground.

☑ SPELLING TIP Remember that **cemetery** begins with a *c* (with an *s* sound). Also remember that there are three *e*'s buried in **cemetery**.

cenotaph /*say* **sen**-uh-tahf/ *noun* a public memorial to those killed in war.

censor /*say* **sen**-suh/ *noun*
1. someone who is specially chosen to decide what books, films or news reports are to be made available to the public.
–*verb* **2.** If someone **censors** a book, film or news report, they cut out parts of it or ban it altogether.
☐ **censorial**, *adjective* –**censorship**, *noun* the act or practice of censoring.

☑ SPELLING TIP Remember that the beginning of **censor** is spelt with a *c* (although it sounds like an *s*). Also remember that the ending is spelt *or* (not *er*). It might help if you think of some other words which have the same spelling for this sound, such as *doctor* and *tractor*.

censure /*say* **sen**-shuh/ *verb* If you **censure** someone, you find fault with them, or condemn them: *The teacher censured us for giggling in assembly.*
☐ **censure**, *noun*

census /*say* **sen**-suhs/ *noun* an official recording of all the people who live in a place or country to gather information about them.

☑ SPELLING TIP There are three *s* sounds in **census** – but remember that the first one, at the start of the word, is spelt *c*. Also remember that the ending is *us* which is a common ending in words that come from Latin as this one does.

cent *noun* a unit of money, one hundredth of a dollar.

WORD HISTORY from the Latin word for 'a hundred'

☑ SPELLING TIP Don't confuse the spelling of **cent** with **sent** or **scent** which sound the same. **Sent** is the past form of the verb **send** (*I sent the letter yesterday*). A **scent** is a pleasant smell.

centaur /*say* **sen**-taw/ *noun* a creature of Greek legend, said to be half man and half horse.

centenary /*say* sen-**teen**-uh-ree, sen-**ten**-uh-ree/ *noun* (*plural* **centenaries**) a 100th anniversary.
☐ **centennial**, *adjective*

☑ SPELLING TIP You can see that **centenary** begins with the word *cent* (from the Latin word for 'a hundred'). Then you have to remember the single *e* in the middle and the *ary* ending. Notice also the single *n* changes to a double *n* when the adjective **centennial** is formed. This appears in other words, such as *bicentennial*.

centi- *prefix* a word part expressing a hundredth part of a given unit, as in *centimetre*.

WORD HISTORY this prefix comes from Latin

Centigrade *adjective* See **Celsius**.

centimetre *noun* a measure of length in the metric system equal to a hundredth of a metre.

THE SYMBOL for this is **cm**.

centipede *noun* a small creature with a long, thin body and many pairs of legs.

☑ SPELLING TIP The spelling of **centipede** will be easier if you see that it is made up of the prefix *centi-* (which comes from the Latin word for 'hundred', just like *cent* does) and the word ending *-pede* (from the Latin word for 'foot'). So the idea is that a **centipede** has a hundred feet – more or less!

central processing unit *noun* the main part of the computer which handles the data, considered separately from things like the keyboard or the printer.

THE ABBREVIATION is **CPU**.

centre *noun*
1. the middle point of an area: *There was a show in the centre of the plaza.* **2.** a place for a particular activity: *a health centre.*
–*verb* **3.** If something is **centred** on something, it is strongly directed towards it: *All attention was now centred on the champion to see if she could defend her title.*
☐ **central**, *adjective*

centrefold *noun* the double page in the middle of a magazine, usually a large photograph for pinning up on a wall.

centri- *prefix* a word part meaning 'centre', as in *centrifugal*.

> WORD HISTORY this prefix comes from Latin and Greek

centrifugal /*say* sen-**trif**-yuh-guhl, sen-truh-**fyooh**-guhl/ *adjective* moving out from the centre: *There was a carnival ride where centrifugal force throws people out to the walls as they spin around.*

centurion *noun* the leader of one hundred men in the ancient Roman army.

century *noun*
1. a period of 100 years. **2.** any group of 100: *Everyone was hoping Steve would score a century in his last cricket match.*

ceramic /*say* suh-**ram**-ik/ *adjective*
1. made of clay: *a ceramic tile.*
–*noun* **2. ceramics**, the skill of making things out of clay: *Eleni studies ceramics at the art school.* **3.** the things made: *There is a display of ceramics in the shopping mall.*

cereal *noun*
1. a grain plant, such as wheat, maize or rice. **2.** a food made from grain, especially a breakfast food.

> ☑ SPELLING TIP Don't confuse the spelling of **cereal** with **serial** which sounds the same. A **serial** is a story that is published or broadcast in parts.

cerebral /*say* **se**-ruh-bruhl, suh-**ree**-bruhl/ *adjective* having to do with the brain.

cerebral palsy /*say* se-ruh-bruhl **pawl**-zee/ *noun* a condition caused by injury to someone's brain, usually at birth. It can result in reduced control over their movement and speech.

ceremony *noun* (*plural* **ceremonies**) the solemn actions performed on an important occasion: *a baptismal ceremony*; *There was a ceremony to welcome the new students.*
☐ **ceremonial**, *adjective* –**ceremonially**, *adverb* –**ceremonious**, *adjective*

> ☑ SPELLING TIP Remember that the beginning of **ceremony** is spelt with a *c* (although it sounds like an 's'). It may help to rap it out as *ce+re+mon+y*. Another word with similar spelling is *harmony*.

cerise /*say* suh-**rees**/ *adjective* cherry red.

certain *adjective*
1. having no doubt that something is so: *I'm certain it's here somewhere.* **2.** sure to happen: *It's certain to be a big event.* **3.** definite or particular, but not named: *My mother only goes into the office on certain days each week.*
–*phrase* **4. make certain**, to be completely sure: *Before you cross the road, make certain there's nothing coming.*
☐ **certainly**, *adverb* –**certainty**, *noun*

> ☑ SPELLING TIP Remember that **certain** begins with a *c* (with an *s* sound) and that the final part is spelt *ain*. Think of other words with this spelling for an 'uhn' sound, such as *captain* and *curtain*. But be sure not to confuse **certain** with **curtain** (something you hang over a window).

certificate *noun* a written paper stating certain facts: *a wedding certificate*; *a doctor's certificate.*

certify *verb* (**certifies**, **certifying**, **certified**, **has certified**) If you **certify** something, you say officially that it is true: *I asked my teacher to certify the facts in my scholarship application.*
☐ **certification**, *noun*

cervix /*say* **ser**-viks/ *noun* (*plural* **cervixes** *or* **cervices** /*say* suh-**vuy**-seez/) the entrance to the womb.
☐ **cervical** /*say* **ser**-vik-uhl, suh-**vuy**-kuhl/, *adjective*

chador /*say* **chah**-duh/ *noun* an outer piece of clothing, consisting of a loose, dark cloak which covers the whole body and hides the face below the eyes, worn by some Muslim women.

chafe *verb*
1. If something such as a piece of clothing **chafes** your skin, it rubs against it repeatedly so that your skin becomes sore: *The handcuffs had chafed the prisoner's wrists.* **2.** If you **chafe** at something, you are annoyed about it: *They chafed against the non-stop rain.*

chaff *noun*
1. the husks or dry outer coverings of grain: *They slept in the shed on top of some bags of chaff.* **2.** straw cut up small and used for animal feed.

chagrin /*say* shuh-**grin**, **shag**-ruhn/ *noun* a feeling of anger and disappointment: *I realised, to my chagrin, that my foolishness had cost our team the honour of winning the competition.*

chain *noun*
1. a series of metal rings joined together. **2.** a series of connected things: *a daisy chain*; *a chain of coincidences.* **3.** a number of shops, hotels or theatres that belong to one owner.
–*verb* **4.** If you **chain** someone or something, you fasten them with a chain: *He chained the dog to the tree*; *Chain the gate when you leave.*

chain mail *noun* the special clothing made of joined metal rings, which was worn by people fighting in medieval times.

chainsaw *noun* a portable saw which has metal teeth on a revolving chain driven by a motor.

chair *noun*
1. a seat with a back and often with arms.
–*verb* **2.** If someone **chairs** a meeting or debate, they are in charge of it.

chairperson *noun* (*plural* **chairpersons**) someone who controls a meeting.
☐ **chairman**, **chairwoman**, *noun*

chalet /*say* **shal**-ay/ *noun* a small house in the mountains, sometimes used as a holiday house.

☑ SPELLING TIP *Silent letter alert*: don't forget the silent *t* at the end. **Chalet** is spelt like this because it comes from French.

chalk *noun*
1. soft, white limestone. **2.** a stick of this for drawing or writing on blackboards.
–*verb in the phrase* **3. chalk up**, to score: *to chalk up 20 points in basketball.*
☐ **chalky**, *adjective*

challenge *verb*
1. If you **challenge** someone, you invite them to compete against you in a test of skill or strength: *She challenged me to a game of tennis.* **2.** If something **challenges** you, you need your full interest and effort to deal with it: *The advanced exercises challenge even the best students.*
☐ **challenge**, *noun* –**challenger**, *noun* –**challenging**, *adjective*

chamber *noun*
1. *Old-fashioned* a room, often a private room: *an upper chamber*; *a guest chamber.* **2. chambers**, a judge's rooms.

chamber music *noun* music for a small group of players, suitable for playing in a room rather than in a large concert hall.

chameleon /*say* kuh-**mee**-lee-uhn, shuh-**mee**-lee-uhn/ *noun* a lizard that can change its skin colour to blend into into its surroundings.

☑ SPELLING TIP Remember that the first part of **chameleon** is spelt *ch* (not *c* or *k* or *sh*). This is because it comes from Greek (from a word meaning a 'ground lion'). To help with this difficult word, you might think of a *camel*, add in the *h* after the *c* and then add *eon* at the end.

chamois /*say* **sham**-ee/ *noun* a soft cloth for polishing.

OTHER SPELLINGS are **chammy** and **shammy**.

champagne /*say* sham-**payn**/ *noun* a bubbly white wine.

WORD HISTORY named after *Champagne*, the region in France where this wine is made

☑ SPELLING TIP Remember that **champagne** begins with a *ch* (although it sounds like a 'sh'). However, the most difficult part is the ending which is spelt *agne* (for the sound that is usually spelt 'ain' or 'ane'). This is because the word, like the drink itself, comes from France.

champion *noun*
1. someone or something that holds first place in a sport or contest. **2.** someone who fights for a cause: *He is a champion for the rights of political prisoners.*
–*verb* **3.** If you **champion** a person or a cause, you strongly support them: *They championed the rights of refugees.*
☐ **championship**, *noun*

chance *noun*
1. the absence of any known reason for something happening: *Chance is an element in everything we do*; *Sally and Sarah met by chance.* **2.** risk: *There is a chance that they won't make it.* **3.** opportunity: *If you get a chance, join our team.*
☐ **chance**, *adjective*: *a chance meeting.*

chandelier /*say* shan-duh-**lear**/ *noun* a branched holder for a number of lights, hanging from the ceiling.

change *verb*
1. If something **changes**, it becomes different in some way: *A caterpillar changes into a butterfly*; *Things are changing for the better.* **2.** If you **change** something, you make it different in some way: *You've changed your hair – I like it like that*; *I've had to change my plans.* **3.** If you **change** something, you replace it with something else: *I changed seats with my brother.* **4.** If you **change** or **get changed**, you take off what you are wearing and put on different clothes. **5.** If you **change** a banknote, you give someone notes or coins of smaller value to make up the same total value.
–*noun* **6.** an alteration: *The coach made a few changes to the team.* **7.** something that is different from normal, and usually pleasant: *It will be a change to have our holidays in the snow.* **8.** the money you get back from a shop when the amount you give is greater than the price of the goods. **9.** money in coins, and sometimes also notes of low value: *loose change.*
–*phrase* **10. change your mind**, to change your opinions or plans: *I've changed my mind about going to the pictures.*
☐ **changeable**, *adjective*: *The weather's been very changeable lately.* –**changeless**, *adjective*

channel *noun*
1. a passage for water to flow through. **2.** a passage which ships use to travel between two seas. **3.** a frequency band for radio or television. **4.** a way of communicating: *Mum had to go through a number of channels to make the complaint.*
–*verb* (**channels**, **channelling**, **channelled**, **has channelled**) **5.** If you **channel** something somewhere, you direct it in a certain way: *They channelled the water into the drain*; *My big sister is channelling her interests into hockey instead of netball.*

☑ SPELLING TIP *Double/single letter alert*: double *n* in the middle and only one *l* at the end. However, you double the *l* when you add *-ed* or *-ing*.

chant *noun*
1. a simple tune, often repeating one note, especially sung in religious ceremonies. **2.** words repeated in an unchanging way.
–verb **3.** If you **chant**, or you **chant** something, you repeat a group of words over and over again: *The crowd chanted the name of their team*.

chaos */say* **kay**-os/ *noun* total confusion: *When the alarm rang there was chaos – nobody knew what to do.*
□ **chaotic**, *adjective*

☑ SPELLING TIP This word looks unusual because it comes from Greek. Remember that it starts with *ch* (with a 'k' sound as in other words like *character*). Also remember that the first vowel is spelt by an *a* alone (although the sound is 'ay').

chap *noun Informal*, *Rather old-fashioned* a man or boy.

chapel *noun* a small church, or part of a church: *The hospital has a small chapel*.

chaperone */say* **shap**-uh-rohn/ *noun*
1. an older person who is responsible for younger, less experienced people.
–verb **2.** If someone **chaperones** you, they go with you to make sure you behave in a respectable manner: *My parents will be here to chaperone the guests at the party.*

ANOTHER SPELLING is **chaperon**.

chaplain *noun* a member of the clergy who works in a school, hospital or the armed forces.
□ **chaplaincy**, *noun* the office or job of a chaplain.

☑ SPELLING TIP See the note at **captain** about words ending in *ain*.

chapped *adjective* cracked and made rough: *I have chapped lips from the wind.*

chapter *noun* one of the main divisions of a book, usually with a number and a title.

char *verb* (**chars**, **charring**, **charred**, **has charred**) To **char** is to **1.** burn or reduce to charcoal. **2.** scorch or burn slightly: *to char the chops on the barbecue.*

character */say* **ka**-ruhk-tuh/ *noun*
1. someone in a story or play. **2.** the special things about you that make you different from someone else. **3.** a strange or interesting person: *She's a local character who sells papers on the corner.* **4.** honesty, or high moral standards: *You can tell he's a person of character.* **5.** a mark, letter or other symbol, used in writing and printing.

characteristic */say* ka-ruhk-tuh-**ris**-tik/ *adjective*
1. typical or showing the special qualities of someone or something: *That generosity is characteristic of him.*
–noun **2.** a special feature: *Unfortunately, frequent barking is a characteristic of that breed of dog.*
□ **characterise**, *verb*: *Her painting style is characterised by very bright colours.* –**characteristically**, *adverb*

ANOTHER SPELLING for **characterise** is **characterize**.

☑ SPELLING TIP This is a long word but it is not really difficult to spell if you remember that it is made up the word *character* with the suffix *-istic*.

charade */say* shuh-**rahd**, shuh-**rayd**/ *noun*
1. any silly pretence which obviously isn't working: *Why don't you stop this charade and admit the truth?* **2.** **charades**, a game in which a player can not speak but has to act out a word or phrase which the other players have to guess.

charcoal *noun* partly burnt wood, used as a fuel or in sticks for drawing.

charge *verb*
1. If you **charge** someone a certain amount of money, you make them pay that amount for a certain item or service: *How much do you charge for delivery?* **2.** If something is **charged** to an account, its cost is added to the total that will have to be paid on that account later: *Mum charged a lot of the Christmas presents to her account so she could pay for them in January.* **3.** If the police **charge** someone with a crime, they formally accuse them of doing it: *He was charged with speeding.* **4.** If you **charge** somewhere, you rush there, often in an attack: *The soldiers charged into the enemy camp.* **5.** If you **charge** a battery, you pass an electric current through it to build up its store of electricity.
–noun **6.** an accusation or blame: *a charge of assault.* **7.** cost or price: *the charge for postage.* **8.** an amount of stored electricity: *This device lets you check the charge left in your batteries.*
–phrase **9.** **in charge**, having the power to control or give orders: *the teacher left me in charge.*
□ **charger**, *noun*: *I'll need to put my mobile phone on the charger – it has a flat battery.*

chariot *noun* a two-wheeled carriage used in ancient times.

charisma */say* kuh-**riz**-muh/ *noun* the power to attract and influence people: *He had such charisma that everybody voted for him.*
□ **charismatic**, *adjective*

☑ SPELLING TIP Remember that the first part of **charisma** is spelt *ch* (not *c* or *k*). This is because it comes from Greek (from a word meaning 'gift'). Also remember that the 'z' sound in the middle is spelt with an *s*. Another word with the same spelling for this sound is *prism*.

charity *noun* (*plural* **charities**)
1. the giving of help or money to people who need it. 2. an organisation for providing help: *They were so poor they had to go to a charity for food.* 3. kindness and understanding towards others.
☐ **charitable**, *adjective*

charlatan /*say* **shah**-luh-tuhn/ *noun* someone who claims to have knowledge or skill that they do not really have: *That charlatan promised these pills would cure my allergy, but it is as bad as ever.*

A SIMILAR WORD is **quack**.

☑ SPELLING TIP *Tricky 'uh' sounds*: the middle and last vowel sounds are both spelt *a*. This word has nothing to do with the name 'Charles'. It looks unusual because it is the French form of an original Italian word meaning 'to chatter'.

charm *noun*
1. the power of pleasing and attracting: *old buildings full of charm and history.* 2. a magic spell. 3. something you wear which is thought to bring good luck.
–*verb* 4. If you **charm** someone, you use your charm to please or attract them: *She charmed us with a smile.*
–*phrase* 5. **like a charm**, perfectly or successfully: *It worked like a charm.*
☐ **charmer**, *noun*: *The new baby is a real charmer.* –**charming**, *adjective*

chart *noun*
1. a printed sheet giving information, often as a table or with pictures. 2. a map, especially of the sea and rivers. 3. **the charts**, an up-to-date list of the best-selling popular recordings.
–*verb* 4. If you **chart** a route or course, you work out where to go by looking at a map.

charter *noun*
1. a document giving certain legal rights: *the charter of the United Nations.*
–*verb* 2. to hire: *We chartered a boat for the weekend.*

chase *verb* If you **chase** someone, you run after them in order to catch them: *We chased the thief, but she got away.*
☐ **chase**, *noun*: *a long and tiring chase.* –**chasings**, *noun*

chasm /*say* **kaz**-uhm/ *noun* a deep hole or opening in the ground.

☑ SPELLING TIP Remember that the beginning of **chasm** is spelt *ch* (giving a 'k' sound because it comes from Greek). Also remember that there is no vowel between the *s* and *m* at the end of the word.

chassis /*say* **shaz**-ee/ *noun* (*plural* **chassis** /*say* **shaz**-eez/) the frame, wheels and sometimes the machinery of a car or truck, designed to support its body.

☑ SPELLING TIP *Double letter and silent letter alert*: there is a double *s* in the middle and then another *s* which is silent at the end. This is because **chassis** comes from French.

chaste *adjective*
1. pure and without sexual experience. 2. decent and clean: *She has a chaste mind and would never dream of using that sort of language.*
☐ **chastity**, *noun*: *A monk takes a vow of chastity.* –**chastely**, *adverb*

chastise *verb* If you **chastise** someone, you punish or scold them: *The teacher chastised me for not doing my homework.*
☐ **chastisement**, *noun*

chat *verb* (**chats**, **chatting**, **chatted**, **has chatted**)
If you **chat**, you speak with someone in a friendly way, often about things which are not very important: *We chatted about last night's game while we waited for the bus.*
☐ **chat**, *noun* –**chatty**, *adjective* (**chattier**, **chattiest**)

chat room *noun* a site on the internet where many people can join in a discussion or conversation by typing text.

chatter *verb*
1. If people **chatter**, they talk quickly and continuously about unimportant things: *The teacher told us to stop chattering and pay attention.* 2. When your teeth **chatter**, they make a rapid clicking noise because they are knocking together from fear or cold.
☐ **chatter**, *noun*: *I could hardly hear the music above all the chatter.*

chauffeur /*say* **shoh**-fuh, shoh-**fer**/ *noun*
1. someone whose job is to drive you in a car: *For the wedding, they are hiring cars and chauffeurs to drive them.*
–*verb* 2. To **chauffeur** someone is to drive them to places in a car: *When we visited Sydney, our friends chauffeured us around to all the sights.*

☑ SPELLING TIP The word **chauffeur** is of French origin and so it has a *ch* spelling for the 'sh' sound at the start. Then the vowels which follow (*au*) are also typical of French, as is the *-eur* suffix which is used in words describing a person with a certain job or certain qualities.

chauvinism /*say* **shoh**-vuh-niz-uhm/ *noun* the belief that your own country, sex or other group is better than any others, especially a belief by a man that men are naturally better than women and should have more privileges: *'Male chauvinism is ridiculous', says my dad – but he still thinks that women can't drive!*
☐ **chauvinist**, *noun* –**chauvinistic**, *adjective* –**chauvinistically**, *adverb*

☑ SPELLING TIP *Tricky vowel sound*: *au* to spell the 'oh' sound. This spelling is unusual because **chauvinism** comes from a French surname – from Nicolas *Chauvin*, who was a very enthusiastic admirer of the emperor Napoleon. The suffix *-ism* (used in words meaning a certain state or condition) has been added.

cheap *adjective*
1. of low price: *The shop near the railway station sells cheap flowers.* **2.** of poor quality: *The bag was made of cheap material and didn't last long.*
□ **cheapen**, *verb* –**cheaply**, *adverb*: *I bought it cheaply at the market.* –**cheapness**, *noun*

☑ SPELLING TIP Don't confuse the spelling of **cheap** with **cheep** which sounds the same but is spelt with a double *e*. To **cheep** is to make a high, weak sound like a chicken does.

cheat *verb*
1. If someone **cheats**, they behave dishonestly: *As a boy he cheated in school, and as a man he cheated in business.* **2.** If someone **cheats** you, they take something from you in a dishonest, unfair way, usually by tricking you: *They cheated their cousins out of their inheritance.*
□ **cheat**, *noun*: *He's a cheat – he has copied his answers*; *the cheats for a computer game.*

check *verb*
1. If you **check** something, you make certain that it is correct or in order: *You can check your answers in the back of the book.* **2.** If you **check** something, you control it and prevent it from getting worse: *These drugs will check the spread of the disease.*
–*noun* **3.** something that stops or holds back something else: *The sudden change in the weather was a check to any idea they had of scaling the mountain.* **4.** a test to make sure that something is correct. **5.** a pattern of squares. **6.** in chess, the position of the king when it is threatened with a direct attack.
–*phrase* **7. check in**, to record your arrival at a hotel or airport. **8. check out**, **a.** to leave a hotel or something similar. **b.** *Informal* to have a look at: *Check out that weird guy!* **9. check up**, to investigate or ask questions about something.
□ **checked**, *adjective*

checkmate *verb* In chess, if you **checkmate** your opponent, you defeat them by trapping their king.
□ **checkmate**, *noun*

check-up *noun* a test to make sure that all is in order, especially your health: *Dad took my grandfather to the doctor for a complete check-up.*

cheddar *noun* a fairly hard, yellow cheese.

WORD HISTORY named after *Cheddar*, a town in Somerset in England, famous for its cheese

cheek *noun*
1. either side of the face, below the eyes. **2.** lack of respect: *The boy showed so much cheek that the teacher sent him out of the room.*
–*phrase* **3. tongue in cheek**, in a way that is not really meant but makes fun of someone: *Her praise was tongue in cheek.*

cheeky *adjective* (**cheekier**, **cheekiest**) lacking respect: *Because he was cheeky, he was sent out of the room.*
□ **cheekily**, *adverb* –**cheekiness**, *noun*

cheep *verb* A chicken **cheeps** when it makes weak, high sounds.
□ **cheep**, *noun*

☑ SPELLING TIP Don't confuse the spelling of **cheep** with **cheap** which sounds the same. **Cheap** describes something which does not cost very much.

cheer *noun*
1. a shout of encouragement or approval.
–*verb* **2.** If you **cheer**, you shout out in order to show your approval or to encourage someone: *We cheered for our team.*
–*phrase* **3. cheer up**, to make or become happier: *His kind words cheered us up*; *She cheered up when her father arrived.*
□ **cheerful**, *adjective* –**cheerfulness**, *noun* –**cheery**, *adjective* (**cheerier**, **cheeriest**)

cheer squad *noun* a small group of people who cheer a competitor or team, usually a sports team.

cheese *noun* a food made from milk.
□ **cheesy**, *adjective* (**cheesier**, **cheesiest**)

cheetah *noun* a leopard-like animal that belongs to the cat family and is the fastest animal on earth.

chef /*say* shef/ *noun* a cook, especially the head cook in a restaurant.

☑ SPELLING TIP *Single letter alert*: only one *f* at the end. Also remember that the beginning of **chef** is spelt *ch* (not *sh*). It might help if you think of some other words which have the same spelling for this sound, such as *chalet* and *champagne*. These words are all spelt in this way because they come from French.

chemical /*say* **kem**-i-kuhl/ *adjective*
1. having to do with chemistry.
–*noun* **2.** a substance obtained by or used in chemistry.
□ **chemically**, *adverb*

chemist /*say* **kem**-uhst/ *noun*
1. a scientist who studies and does research in chemistry. **2.** someone who has studied drugs and medicines and keeps a shop selling them.

ANOTHER WORD (for definition 2) is **pharmacist**.

chemistry /*say* **kem**-uhs-tree/ *noun* the science of what substances are made of and the ways they react with each other.

cheongsam /*say* chong-**sam**/ *noun* a Chinese-style dress, which is cut very straight and has a high collar and often a slit up one side of the skirt.

☑ SPELLING TIP *Tricky vowel sound*: remember the *eo* spelling for the 'o' sound in the first part of this word.

cheque /*say* chek/ *noun* a written order asking a bank to pay a certain amount of money to a particular person.

☑ SPELLING TIP Note that **cheque** sounds the same as the word *check* (which is the spelling used for this word in American English). The spelling we use comes from French, which is why the letters *que* make the sounds of 'k'.

chequered *adjective*
1. marked with squares. **2.** marked by changes in good or bad luck: *He had a chequered background, which made him apprehensive about trusting people.*
☐ **chequer**, *noun* a pattern of squares.

cherish *verb* If you **cherish** someone or something, they are very dear to you and you look after them well: *Children are cherished by their parents*; *She cherishes the jewellery which her grandmother left her.*

☑ SPELLING TIP The spelling of **cherish** will be easier if you know that it comes from French and starts with the French word for 'dear' – *cher*. Then you only need to add *ish* at the end.

cherry *noun* (*plural* **cherries**) a small, juicy fruit with a stone in the middle, varying in colour from pink to black.

cherub /*say* **che**-ruhb/ *noun* (*plural* **cherubim**)
1. an angel, pictured as a child with wings. **2.** a child with a chubby face.
☐ **cherubic** /*say* chuh-**rooh**-bik/, *adjective* round and innocent-looking: *a cherubic child.*

chess *noun* a game played by two people, each with sixteen pieces, on a board marked with squares.

chest *noun*
1. the front part of the body from the neck to the waist. **2.** a box, usually large and strong with a hinged lid.
–*phrase* **3. get** (**something**) **off your chest**, to talk about something that is worrying you.

chestnut *noun*
1. a hard brown nut from a European tree. **2.** a reddish-brown colour.
☐ **chestnut**, *adjective*

chew *verb* If you **chew** something, you bite it in your mouth several times to make it easier to swallow.
☐ **chewy**, *adjective* (**chewier**, **chewiest**)

chewing gum *noun* a lolly that you only chew and do not swallow.

chic /*say* sheek/ *adjective* attractive and stylish: *a chic new haircut.*

WORD HISTORY from a French word, which is why it sounds like this

chick *noun* a young chicken or other bird.

chicken *noun*
1. a young hen or rooster, or its meat. **2.** *Informal* a coward: *I was too much of a chicken to jump off the high diving board.*
–*adjective* **3.** *Informal* cowardly.
–*phrase* **4. chicken out**, *Informal* to back out because you are frightened.

chickenpox *noun* a contagious disease, common in children, causing fever and itchy blisters.

chickpea *noun* a small, round, yellow vegetable.

chide *verb* (**chides**, **chiding**, **chided**, **chid**, **has chid** *or* **has chidden**) If you **chide** someone, you scold or find fault with them: *He chided me for forgetting to pass on the message.*
☐ **chidingly**, *adverb*

chief *noun*
1. the head person or boss in a group.
–*adjective* **2.** most important or main: *The farmer's chief worry was lack of rain.*
☐ **chiefly**, *adverb*

☑ SPELLING TIP *Tricky vowel sound*: *ie* for the 'ee' sound. This follows the rule that *i* comes before *e* except after *c*.

chieftain *noun* the leader of a tribe.

☑ SPELLING TIP See the note at **captain** about words ending in *ain*.

chiffon /*say* shuh-**fon**, **shif**-on/ *noun* light, transparent material made of silk or nylon.

chilblain *noun* a red swelling on the fingers or toes caused by the cold.

child *noun* (*plural* **children**)
1. a boy or girl. **2.** a son or daughter.
☐ **childhood**, *noun*

childish *adjective*
1. silly or stupid: *childish screaming.* **2.** of, or like a child: *childish questions.*

chill *noun*
1. coldness: *The winds from the south are bringing a chill with them.* **2.** a cold, shivery feeling that is often the first stage of a cold: *I caught a chill after getting wet in the rain.*
–*verb* **3.** If you **chill** something, you cool it: *We chilled the orange juice in the refrigerator.*
–*phrase* **4. chill out**, *Informal* to relax.
☐ **chilly**, *adjective* (**chillier**, **chilliest**)

chilli *noun* (*plural* **chillies**) a type of small capsicum which tastes hot.

chime *verb*
1. When a bell or a clock **chimes**, it makes a musical ringing sound: *I could hear the clock chiming in the distance.*
–*noun* **2. chimes**, a set of metal tubes or bells which make musical sounds when rung.
☐ **chime**, *noun*: *the chime of the bells.*

WORD HISTORY from a Latin word meaning 'cymbal'

chimney *noun* (*plural* **chimneys**) a long opening from the fire to the roof of a building, which draws smoke away from the fire.

chimpanzee *noun* a small African ape.

THE SHORT FORM of this is **chimp**.

chin *noun*
1. the part of the face below the mouth.
–*phrase* **2. keep your chin up**, to remain cheerful and not be discouraged: *Keep your chin up – things will get better soon.*

china *noun* plates, cups and bowls made from a special kind of clay: *Mum set the table with her best china.*
☐ **china**, *adjective*: *china plates.*

ANOTHER WORD for this is **crockery**.
WORD HISTORY named after the country of *China* where delicate crockery was first made

chintz *noun* (*plural* **chintzes**) shiny, brightly patterned cotton material, used to make curtains and furniture coverings.
☐ **chintzy**, *adjective* shiny and cheap-looking.

chip *noun*
1. a small piece chopped or cut off something larger: *wood chips for the fire*; *chocolate chips.* **2.** a place where a small piece has broken off: *Does Mum know there is a chip in this good dinner plate?* **3.** a long, thin piece of fried potato, eaten hot. **4.** a thin slice of fried potato eaten cold. **5.** a tiny square which contains electronic circuits, used in a computer, watch or electronic game: *a silicon chip.*
–*verb* (**chips**, **chipping**, **chipped**, **has chipped**) **6.** If you **chip** something, you break it off in small pieces: *We chipped off some ice to suck.* **7.** If you **chip** something, or it **chips**, you damage it by breaking off a small piece: *Joe chipped his tooth playing hockey*; *The plate chipped when I dropped it.*
–*phrase Informal* **8. a chip on the shoulder**, a long-lasting feeling of bitterness: *She has a chip on her shoulder about being left out of the debating team.* **9. chip in**, to give money or help: *Let's all chip in to buy her some flowers.*

ANOTHER TERM for **chips** (definition 3) is **French fries**.
ANOTHER WORD (for definition 4) is **crisp**.

chipmunk *noun* a type of small, striped squirrel that lives in the forests of North America and Asia.

chiropractor /*say* **kuy**-ruh-prak-tuh/ *noun* someone trained to treat back pain and other types of illness by massaging and adjusting the spine.
☐ **chiropractic**, *adjective*

chirp *verb* When a bird **chirps**, it makes short, high sounds.
☐ **chirp**, *noun* –**chirpy**, *adjective* –**chirpily**, *adverb*

ANOTHER WORD for this is **chirrup**.

chisel /*say* **chiz**-uhl/ *noun*
1. a cutting tool with a sharp end, used to cut or shape wood and stone.
–*verb* (**chisels**, **chiselling**, **chiselled**, **has chiselled**) **2.** When you **chisel** wood or stone, you cut and shape it with a chisel.

☑ SPELLING TIP *Single letter alert*: a single *s* in the middle (giving a 'z' sound) and a single *l* at the end. However, you double the *l* when you add *ed* or *-ing*.

chivalry /*say* **shiv**-uhl-ree/ *noun* polite behaviour, especially old-fashioned good manners of a man towards a woman.
☐ **chivalrous**, *adjective*

chives *plural noun* a small, grass-like plant which tastes like onion, the leaves of which are used in cooking.

chlorine /*say* **klaw**-reen/ *noun* a poisonous, greenish-yellow gas with a strong, unpleasant smell, which is dissolved in water and used to whiten clothes or to clean swimming pools.

chlorophyll /*say* **klo**-ruh-fil/ *noun* the green colouring in leaves and plants, which traps the energy of sunlight and is sometimes used as a dye.

☑ SPELLING TIP The spelling of **chlorophyll** will be easier if you see that it contains *chloro* (the Greek word for 'green') and the suffix *-phyll* (meaning 'leaf'). If you remember that this word is spelt with a double *l* at the end, the main difficulty is over.

chock *noun* a block of wood put firmly under something to stop it moving: *We put a chock under the wheels of the trailer so it wouldn't roll down the hill.*

chocolate *noun*
1. a sweet food or drink made from the seeds of a small, tropical American tree. **2.** a small sweet made of this.
☐ **chocolate**, *adjective*: *a chocolate cake.*

WORD HISTORY from a word in a Native American language meaning 'bitter water'

☑ SPELLING TIP The main thing to remember about **chocolate** is that it has an *o* in the middle, even though this sound is often not pronounced. The last three letters make the word *ate* which is what happens to **chocolate** – it gets eaten all too quickly.

choice *noun*
1. the act of choosing: *I made a quick choice.* **2.** the thing chosen: *Ice-cream is my choice.* **3.** a number of things from which you can choose: *a wide choice of flavours.*
–*adjective* **4.** Something **choice** is of high quality: *a choice piece of fruit.*

choir /*say* **kwuy**-uh/ *noun* an organised group of people who sing together.

☑ SPELLING TIP Remember that **choir** starts with *ch* (with a 'k' sound as in other related words like *chorus* and *choral*). The unusual thing about the word *choir* is its *oir* ending.

choke *verb*
1. If you **choke**, you have trouble breathing because you can't get enough air into your lungs: *They emerged choking and gasping from the smoke-filled room.* **2.** If something **chokes** you, it makes it difficult for you to breathe: *The smoke from the fire was choking me.* **3.** To **choke** someone is to strangle them. **4.** If something is **choked** with something, it is blocked so that it is difficult for things to get through: *The drains are choked with leaves.*
–*noun* **5.** a device used when starting an engine, which controls the amount of air that is mixed with the petrol.

choko *noun* (*plural* **chokos** *or* **chokoes**) a green, pear-shaped vegetable with a prickly skin, which grows on a vine.

cholera /*say* **kol**-uh-ruh/ *noun* an infectious tropical disease of the digestive system which can cause death.

cholesterol /*say* kuh-**les**-tuh-rol/ *noun* a substance found in the body and some foods. It is thought that a high level of cholesterol in the blood increases the risk of heart disease.

chook *noun Informal* a chicken.

choose *verb* (**chooses**, **choosing**, **chose**, **has chosen**)
1. If you **choose** something, you pick out which one you want from a range: *She chose some earrings which matched her dress exactly.* **2.** If you **choose** to do something, you decide to do it: *I chose to go to the beach instead of the pictures.*
☐ **choosy**, *adjective* hard to please.

chop *verb* (**chops**, **chopping**, **chopped**, **has chopped**)
1. If you **chop** something such as wood, you hit into it with quick, strong blows using an axe: *Dad chopped some wood for the fire*; *They chopped the tree down.* **2.** If you **chop** food, you cut it into smaller pieces: *Chop the celery into very small bits.*
–*noun* **3.** a quick, cutting stroke. **4.** a slice of meat with bone in it: *lamb chops.*

chopper *noun*
1. someone or something that chops, especially a butcher's cleaver. **2.** *Informal* a helicopter.

choppy *adjective* (**choppier**, **choppiest**) forming short broken waves: *Spray from the choppy waves bounced against the boat.*

chopsticks *plural noun* a pair of thin, smooth sticks, used to pick up food, especially Asian food, when you are eating.

chord /*say* kawd/ *noun* three or more musical notes played together: *Alan only knew three chords but they were enough to sing a song to.*

☑ SPELLING TIP Remember the *h* in **chord**. Don't confuse it with **cord** which sounds the same. A **cord** is a strong string.

chore *noun* a boring or unpleasant job: *My worst chore is washing the dishes after dinner.*

choreography /*say* ko-ree-**og**-ruh-fee/ *noun* the art of designing ballets and dances.
☐ **choreograph**, *verb* –**choreographer**, *noun*

☑ SPELLING TIP You will be able to spell this word if you remember that it starts with *ch* for the 'k' sound, and there is an *e* (not an *i*) after the *r*. It might help also if you know that it contains *choreo-* (a suffix formed from the Greek word for 'dance') and the suffix *-graphy* (used in words meaning a kind of art).

chorister /*say* **ko**-ruhs-tuh/ *noun* someone who sings in a choir.

☑ SPELLING TIP The word **chorister** has been formed from the word *chorus* which is why it has only one *r*. There are two tricky 'uh' sounds in *chorister*: the middle vowel sound is spelt *i* and the one at the end of the word is spelt *er* (similar to the vowels in the word *sister*).

chortle *verb* If you **chortle**, you chuckle loudly with amusement.

WORD HISTORY made up by Lewis Carroll in *Through the Looking-Glass* in 1871; a blend of *chuckle* and *snort*

chorus /*say* **kaw**-ruhs/ *noun*
1. the part of a song that is repeated after each verse. **2.** a piece of music for several people to sing together. **3.** a group of people singing together.
☐ **choral**, *adjective* sung by a choir or chorus: *a choral composition.*

A SIMILAR WORD (for definition 1) is **refrain**; (for definition 3) **choir**.

christen /*say* **kris**-uhn/ *verb*
1. When a baby is **christened** by a priest or minister, the baby is given a name and made a member of a Christian church: *She was christened last Sunday.* **2.** If you **christen** someone, you give them a name: *We christened him*

'Sleepyhead' because he was always tired. **3.** *Informal* If you **christen** a new possession, you use it for the first time: *We'll christen the new barbecue tonight.*
☐ **christening**, *noun*

☑ SPELLING TIP *Silent letter alert*: don't forget the silent *t* after the *s*. Remember that this word comes from *Christian* where you can hear the *t*.

Christianity *noun* a world religion which is based on belief in Jesus Christ as the Son of God who lived on earth as a man, died and came back to life on earth before going to heaven. It is also based on Jesus's teachings as written in the New Testament of the Bible, which emphasised kind, good and unselfish behaviour as a response to God's love for the world. Followers of Christianity are called Christians, and worship in a church.
☐ **Christian**, *adjective*: *the Christian faith.*

WORD HISTORY named after Jesus *Christ*, from a Hebrew name meaning 'anointed'

Christian name *noun* See **given name**.

chromatic *adjective*
1. having to do with a musical scale that moves by small steps, using all of the twelve semitones. **2.** having to do with colour: *chromatic patterns.*
☐ **chromatically**, *adverb*

chrome /*say* krohm/ *noun* a hard, shiny, silver-coloured metal used to cover other metals to protect them and to stop rust.

WORD HISTORY short for *chromium*

chromosome /*say* **kroh**-muh-sohm/ *noun* a tiny, threadlike body found in the central part of all living cells, which carries the characteristics of the organism: *Human cells have 23 pairs of chromosomes.*

chronic /*say* **kron**-ik/ *adjective*
1. constant or continuing for a long time: *She has chronic back pain.* **2.** very bad: *a chronic shortage of food.*
☐ **chronically**, *adverb*

☑ SPELLING TIP Remember that the beginning of **chronic** is spelt *ch* (giving a 'k' sound). The same sound at the end of the word is spelt with just a *c*.

chronicle *noun*
1. a record or history of events: *He was interested in reading any chronicles of ancient times.*
–*verb* **2.** When you **chronicle** a series of events, you record them in the order in which they happened: *He chronicled the grim days following the outbreak of war.*
☐ **chronicler**, *noun*

chronological /*say* kron-uh-**loj**-ik-uhl/ *adjective* arranged in order according to the date when it happened.

☑ SPELLING TIP Remember that the beginning of **chronological** is spelt *ch* (giving a 'k' sound). The spelling of this long word will be easier if you can see that it is made up of *chrono* (a word part meaning 'time') and *-logical* (the adjective form of the word part *-logy* which is used in the name of many types of knowledge or science).

chrysalis /*say* **kris**-uh-luhs/ *noun* (*plural* **chrysalises** *or* **chrysalids**) the form that a butterfly or moth takes when changing from a grub to its adult form inside a hard-shelled cocoon.

ANOTHER WORD for this is **pupa**.

☑ SPELLING TIP Remember that the first part of **chrysalis** is spelt *ch* (not *c* or *k*). Also remember that the 'i' sound in the middle is spelt with a *y* (not an *i*). This word comes from Greek.

chrysanthemum /*say* kruh-**san**-thuh-muhm/ *noun* a tall plant with big white or brightly coloured flowers, often given as a present on Mother's Day.

☑ SPELLING TIP Think of **chrysanthemums** being given to 'the mum' on Mother's Day (*the-mum* is how you spell the last two syllables of this word). The opening syllable *chrys* has a *y* for the 'uh' sound because it is from the Greek word *chrysos* meaning 'gold'.

chubby *adjective* (**chubbier**, **chubbiest**) plump and round: *chubby cheeks.*
☐ **chubbiness**, *noun*

chuck *verb* If you **chuck** something somewhere, you throw it, or put it there in a rather careless way: *He just chucked the books into a corner.*

chuckle *verb* If you **chuckle**, you laugh quietly: *He just sat there chuckling to himself.*
☐ **chuckle**, *noun*: *He let out a delighted chuckle.*

chunk *noun* a thick piece or lump: *a chunk of cake.*
☐ **chunky**, *adjective* (**chunkier**, **chunkiest**)

church *noun* (*plural* **churches**)
1. a building where Christians gather to worship. **2.** the whole body of Christian believers. **3.** an organisation of Christians who share the same religious beliefs: *the Roman Catholic church*; *the Uniting church.*

ANOTHER FORM This word (as in definitions 2 and 3) is often spelt with a capital letter.

churinga /*say* chuh-**ring**-guh/ *noun* a sacred wooden object important in Aboriginal culture.

WORD HISTORY from an Aboriginal language of the Northern Territory called Arrernte

churn *noun*
1. a large metal container for milk. **2.** a machine for making butter from cream or milk.
–*verb* **3.** If you **churn** cream, you shake or stir it in order to make it into butter. **4.** When your

stomach **churns**, you feel it moving: *When I came off the ride, my stomach churned and I felt sick.*

chute */sounds like* shoot*/ noun* a sloping way through or passage for sending or carrying things to a lower level: *The goats moved directly from the truck onto the ship through a chute.*

chutney *noun* a spicy, jam-like food made from fruit, sugar, spices and vinegar.

cicada */say* suh-**kah**-duh, suh-**kay**-duh*/ noun* a large flying insect which is found in trees and which makes a loud noise in hot weather.

cider */say* **suy**-duh*/ noun* a drink, sometimes containing alcohol, made from apples.

> WORD HISTORY from a Hebrew word meaning 'strong drink'

cigar */say* suh-**gah***/ noun* a tight roll of tobacco leaves which can be smoked.

cigarette *noun* a roll of dried tobacco inside very thin paper, which is lit at one end and smoked.

> ☑ SPELLING TIP The spelling of **cigarette** will be easier if you see that it is made up of the word *cigar* and the suffix *-ette* (which comes from French and is used to indicate a small version of something). Another word with this ending is *serviette*.

cinder *noun* a burnt and partly blackened piece of wood or coal.

cinema *noun* a theatre where films are shown.

> WORD HISTORY a shortened form of *cinematography*

> ☑ SPELLING TIP The 's' sound at the start is spelt with a *c*. This is because *cine* is a word part which comes from Greek and means 'motion'.

cinnamon */say* **sin**-uh-muhn*/ noun* a yellowish or reddish-brown spice made from the inner bark of certain trees and used in cooking.

> ☑ SPELLING TIP Remember that **cinnamon** begins with a *c* (although it sounds like an *s*). Also remember that there are three *n*'s in **cinnamon** (two together near the beginning and one at the end) and only one of each of the other letters. The last vowel sound is spelt with an *o*. Rap it out as *cin + na + mon*.

cipher */say* **suy**-fuh*/ noun* secret writing or a code: *We rewrote the message in a cipher so the enemy couldn't understand it.*

> ☑ SPELLING TIP You can also use the spelling **cypher**. In either case, you have to remember the *c* at the start for the 's' sound, the *ph* for the 'f' sound, and the *er* ending. You might know the word *decipher* (to decipher something is to work out its meaning), which you can see includes the word **cipher**.

circle *noun*
1. a perfectly round shape. **2.** anything that has the shape of a circle or part of a circle: *The dog jumped around in circles.* **3.** a group of people who do things together: *a sewing circle.*
–*verb* **4.** If something **circles**, it moves in the shape of a circle: *Our plane had to circle until the other plane landed.*
☐ **circular**, *adjective*: *a circular mark.* –**circular**, *noun* a letter or notice sent to a number of people. –**encircle**, *verb*

circuit */say* **ser**-kuht*/ noun*
1. a circular path or journey all around something: *We made a circuit of the town.* **2.** a circular racing track. **3.** an arrangement of wires joined so as to carry an electric current: *a closed circuit.*
☐ **circuitous** */say* suh-**kyooh**-uh-tuhs*/, adjective*: *a circuitous journey.*

circulate *verb*
1. If something **circulates**, it moves around so that finally it comes back to where it started from: *Your blood circulates faster when you are walking and running.* **2.** If you **circulate** something, you send or pass it from place to place or from person to person: *Rumours circulate very quickly in a small town.*

circulation *noun*
1. continuous circular movement: *blood circulation.* **2.** the number of copies of a newspaper or magazine sent out: *Circulation dropped with the new style of magazine cover.*

circum- *prefix* a word part referring to movement all around or on all sides, as in *circumference*.

> WORD HISTORY this prefix comes from Latin

circumcise *verb* To **circumcise** a male is to cut away the loose skin around the end of the penis: *The religion of Jewish people says that boys should be circumcised.*
☐ **circumcision**, *noun*

circumference *noun* the distance around something, especially around a circle or circular object: *The good thing about knowing the circumference of a circle is that you can then work out its diameter!*

> A SIMILAR WORD is **perimeter**.

circumnavigate *verb* When you **circumnavigate** a place, you sail round it: *The first person to circumnavigate Australia was Matthew Flinders.*
☐ **circumnavigation**, *noun*

circumspect *adjective* cautious and watchful.
☐ **circumspection**, *noun*

circumstance *noun*
1. a condition which influences a person or an event. **2. circumstances**, the conditions

someone is experiencing, especially of a financial nature: *Changed circumstances forced them to cancel their overseas holiday.*
□ **circumstantial**, *adjective*

circus *noun* a travelling show with performers, and sometimes animals, who do all types of clever and funny things.

WORD HISTORY from a Greek word meaning 'ring'

cirrus /*say* **si**-ruhs/ *noun* (*plural* **cirri** /*say* **si**-ree/) a high, feathery cloud.

COMPARE this with **cumulus** and **nimbus**.
WORD HISTORY from a Latin word meaning 'tuft'

cistern /*say* **sis**-tuhn/ *noun* a tank for holding water, such as the one above a toilet.

citadel *noun* a fort or strongly defended place, built to protect or control a city.

cite /*say* suyt/ *verb* If you **cite** something, you mention or refer to it: *The police officer was cited for bravery in the honours list*; *I cited three examples of water transport in my answer.*
□ **citation**, *noun* a mention.

☑ SPELLING TIP Remember that **cite** starts with a *c*. Don't confuse it with **site** or **sight** which sound the same. A **site** is a piece of land where something is built. **Sight** is the ability to see.

citizen *noun*
1. a member of a nation who has certain rights and duties: *Babies born to Australian parents are automatically Australian citizens.* **2.** someone who lives in a particular place: *a citizen of Paris.*
□ **citizenship**, *noun*

citrus *noun* a small evergreen tree such as the lemon, orange, lime, grapefruit or mandarin.
□ **citrus**, *adjective*: *citrus flavour.*

city *noun* (*plural* **cities**)
1. a large or important town. **2.** the people who live in a city: *The whole city celebrated the great news.*

civic *adjective* of or concerning a city or citizens: *They held a civic reception to welcome the players back to their home town*; *She's a very civic-minded person.*

civil *adjective*
1. having to do with the government or citizens: *the civil administration*; *civil rights.* **2.** polite or courteous, although perhaps not particularly friendly: *She's always been perfectly civil to me.*
□ **civility**, *noun* (*plural* **civilities**) –**civilly**, *adverb*

civilian /*say* suh-**vil**-yuhn/ *noun* someone who is not a member of the armed forces.
□ **civilian**, *adjective*: *He found it hard to adjust to civilian life after being in the army for so long.*

☑ SPELLING TIP Remember that **civilian** begins with a *c* (although it sounds like an *s*). It is made up of the word *civil* (meaning 'having to do with citizens or the public') and the common suffix *-ian* (meaning 'relating to'). You see this suffix in many other words, such as *magician* and *musician*.

civilisation *noun* the highly developed way of life of a particular people, including their science, art and writing: *the civilisation of ancient China.*

ANOTHER SPELLING is **civilization**.

civilised *adjective*
1. having a highly developed social organisation and control: *Who would believe that such terrible acts could occur in a civilised country?* **2.** polite and controlled: *I expect you to behave in a civilised manner when we visit – no putting your feet on the chairs.*

ANOTHER SPELLING is **civilized**.

civil war *noun* a war between people living in the same country.

claim *verb*
1. If you **claim** something, you ask for it on the grounds that it legally belongs to you: *You can claim your hat at the lost property office.* **2.** If you **claim** that something is true, you say that it is, although other people may not believe you: *He claims he's sick, but I have my doubts.*
–*noun* **3.** a demand: *She made a claim for extra money.* **4.** a statement that something is true, without necessarily having any proof to support it. **5.** the right to something: *an Aboriginal land claim.* **6.** something claimed, such as a piece of land for mining: *He struck gold on the second day of working his claim.*

clairvoyant /*say* klair-**voy**-uhnt/ *adjective* claiming to be able to see into the future.
□ **clairvoyance**, *noun* –**clairvoyant**, *noun*

☑ SPELLING TIP The spelling of **clairvoyant** will be easier if you see that it contains *clair* (the French word for 'clear') and *voyant* (meaning 'seeing'). If you remember that the ending is spelt *ant* (not *ent*), the main difficulty is over.

clam *noun*
1. a large shellfish whose two shells are hinged and can be tightly closed.
–*verb in the phrase* (**clams**, **clamming**, **clammed**, **has clammed**) **2. clam up**, *Informal* to refuse to give information about something.

clamber *verb* If you **clamber** somewhere, you climb there with difficulty: *Tapan clambered up the rocky headland.*

clammy *adjective* (**clammier**, **clammiest**) damp and sticky: *Her hands and feet are clammy and she has a temperature.*
□ **clamminess**, *noun*

clamour /*say* **klam**-uh/ *noun*
1. the loud noise of many voices: *We could hear a clamour from inside the packed hall.*

–*verb* **2.** To **clamour** is to make a loud noise or ask noisily: *At the end of each song, the audience clamoured for more.*
☐ **clamorous**, *adjective*

ANOTHER SPELLING is **clamor.**

clamp *noun*
1. a device which holds things tightly together.
–*verb* **2.** If you **clamp** two things together, you hold them together with a clamp. **3.** If you **clamp** your teeth together, you press them together very tightly.
–*phrase* **4. clamp down**, to become more strict.

clan *noun* a group of related families who share a common ancestor.

clandestine /*say* klan-**des**-tuhn/ *adjective* secret and unlawful: *the clandestine activities of the rebels.*
☐ **clandestinely**, *adverb*

clang *verb* If something **clangs**, it makes a loud, deep, ringing noise: *I could hear the bells clanging.*
☐ **clang**, *noun* a loud, metallic sound.

clap *verb* (**claps**, **clapping**, **clapped**, **has clapped**)
1. If you **clap**, you make a noise by hitting your hands together repeatedly to show that you are pleased with a performance: *The audience clapped loudly.* **2.** If you **clap** your hands, you make a noise by hitting your hands together, often as a signal: *Stop when I clap my hands.* **3.** If you **clap** someone on the back, you give them a friendly hit with your open hand: *He clapped me on the back on his way past.*
☐ **clap**, *noun*: *Let's give him a clap for his hard work*; *She gave me a clap on the back.* –**clapper**, *noun*

clarify *verb* (**clarifies**, **clarifying**, **clarified**, **has clarified**) If you **clarify** something, you make it clear: *You'll need to clarify your answer, as I'm not sure what you mean.*
☐ **clarification**, **clarinettist** *noun*

clarinet *noun* a musical instrument belonging to the woodwind family which makes a deeper sound than the flute.
☐ **clarinetist**, **clarinettist** *noun*

WORD HISTORY from a French word meaning 'little clarion' (an old-fashioned high trumpet)

clarity *noun* the quality of being clear: *The mountains were reflected in the waters of the lake with incredible clarity*; *The clarity of Pui's argument convinced the class that she was right.*

clash *verb*
1. If objects **clash** together, they hit each other with force. **2.** If you **clash** with someone, you argue heatedly with them: *The two governments clashed over the question of nuclear weapons.* **3.** If two colours or patterns **clash**, they go together badly and create an unpleasant appearance: *Don't you think the pink carpet will clash with the green furniture?* **4.** If two appointments or events **clash**, they both happen at the same time so that people cannot go to both of them: *I couldn't go to the party because it clashed with my exams.*
☐ **clash**, *noun*

clasp *noun*
1. something which fastens things together. **2.** a firm hold.
–*verb* **3.** If you **clasp** something or someone, you hold them tightly: *She clasped my hand in hers.*

class *noun*
1. a group of people or things which are like each other in some way. **2.** a group of students who are taught together: *the geography class.* **3.** the group in society to which someone belongs, judged by their possessions or their family: *working class*; *middle class*; *upper class.* **4.** a level of comfort in travel: *In first class on the plane, you can stretch out and sleep.*
–*verb* **5.** When you **class** someone or something, you consider them as belonging to a particular group or grade: *Do you class yourself as a strong swimmer?*

classic *adjective*
1. typical: *The patient had a classic case of measles.* **2.** simple and stylish, without decoration: *She was wearing a plain black dress of classic design.*
–*noun* **3.** a book, film or song which is famous and popular for a long time. **4. the classics**, the writings of ancient Greece and Rome.

ANOTHER WORD (for definitions 1 and 2) is **classical**.

classical music *noun* music composed according to the conventional European models that have existed for a long time, usually for traditional instruments, as opposed to forms such as jazz, folk, rock or pop music.

classify *verb* (**classifies**, **classifying**, **classified**, **has classified**) If you **classify** things, you put them into groups or classes which have similar characteristics: *Would you classify soup as a food or a drink?*
☐ **classifiable**, *adjective* –**classification**, *noun* –**classified**, *adjective*

classroom *noun* a room in a school where students have lessons.

clatter *verb* If something **clatters**, it makes a series of short knocking or banging sounds: *The stones clattered down the slope.*
☐ **clatter**, *noun*

clause /*say* klawz/ *noun* a group of words containing a subject and a verb, which may be a part of a sentence, such as *after the boy arrived*, or a whole sentence, such as *She heard the news*.

SEE the Grammar and Punctuation Guide appendix.

claustrophobia /*say* klos-truh-**foh**-bee-uh/ *noun* an extreme fear of being shut in a small place.
☐ **claustrophobic**, *adjective*

☑ SPELLING TIP *Tricky vowel sound*: the first vowel sound is spelt *au* (although it sounds like 'o'). The spelling of this difficult word may be easier if you see that it is made up of *claustro* (a form of the Latin word *claustrum*, meaning 'enclosure') and the suffix *-phobia* (meaning 'fear' or 'dread').

claves *plural noun* a simple musical instrument which consists of two wooden sticks which are hit together: *Claves belong in the percussion section of an orchestra.*

claw *noun*
1. the sharp, curved nail on the foot of an animal or bird. **2.** the sharp pincers of crabs and lobsters.
–*verb* **3.** If an animal **claws** something, it scratches or seizes it with its claws or nails: *The lion clawed at the ground.*

clay *noun* a thick, sticky earth which is used in making pottery and bricks.
☐ **clayey**, *adjective*

clean /*say* kleen/ *adjective*
1. free from dirt and stains: *The house was clean but a bit untidy.* **2.** without marks or writing: *I put a clean sheet of paper in the printer.* **3.** smooth and simple: *The boat has a good clean line to it.*
–*verb* **4.** If you **clean** something, you make it free from dirt and stains: *Have you cleaned your teeth?*
–*phrase* **5. clean up**, to tidy up or put in order.
☐ **clean**, *noun* –**cleaner**, *noun* –**cleanliness** /*say* **klen**-lee-nuhs/, *noun* –**cleanly**, *adverb*

cleanse /*say* klenz/ *verb* When you **cleanse** something, you make it clean or pure: *The nurse cleansed the wound with a mild antiseptic.*
☐ **cleanser**, *noun*

☑ SPELLING TIP Notice that **cleanse** includes the word *clean*. This will help you to remember the *ea* spelling (though the sound has changed to 'e').

clear *adjective*
1. easily understood: *It was clear to us that he was not feeling well.* **2.** certain, without doubt: *One point was clear – there was no television before homework.* **3.** transparent: *the clear water of the lake.* **4.** bright and sunny: *a clear day.* **5.** not blocked by anything: *a clear view*; *a clear road.*
–*verb* **6.** If you **clear** something, you move things away from it so that it is empty or unblocked: *I cleared the table after tea*; *to clear a drain.* **7.** If you **clear** something with someone, you get their permission: *I had to clear leaving early with my teacher.* **8.** If someone is **cleared** after an official investigation, they are freed from blame or suspicion: *He was cleared of all the charges against him.*
–*phrase* **9. clear up, a.** to settle a problem or disagreement so that it does not cause difficulties any more: *I'm glad we've cleared up that misunderstanding.* **b.** to tidy things away, putting everything back in its correct place: *We were too tired to clear up after dinner.*
☐ **clearly**, *adverb*: *This one is clearly better.*

clearance *noun*
1. the space between two things: *The boat had a clearance of ten centimetres under the bridge.* **2.** permission to go ahead with something: *They needed clearance from the council to build their balcony.*

clearing *noun* a piece of cleared land in the middle of bush or forest.

clearway *noun* a busy street or highway on which cars may park only at certain times or in case of emergency.

cleat *noun* a wedge-shaped piece of wood or metal which a climber drives into a steep mountain side to make a ledge for their foot.

cleavage *noun* a division or split.

cleaver *noun* a chopper with a long blade, used for cutting meat.

clef *noun* a symbol placed on a line of music that shows the height or pitch of the notes: *treble clef*; *bass clef.*

WORD HISTORY from a Latin word meaning 'key'

cleft *noun* a narrow opening or split.

clench *verb* To **clench** something is to close or press it tightly: *She clenched her mouth tightly trying not to cry*; *He clenched his fists in frustration.*

clergy *noun* the priests and ministers of the Christian church.
☐ **clergyman**, *noun* a man who belongs to the clergy. –**clerical**, *adjective*: *The clergyman was wearing his clerical vest and collar.* –**cleric**, *noun*: *a kindly cleric.*

clerk /*rhymes with* bark/ *noun* someone who works in an office, keeping records and accounts and taking care of letters and papers.
☐ **clerical**, *adjective*

☑ SPELLING TIP *Tricky vowel sound*: remember that this word is spelt with an *er* although the way it is usually pronounced in Australian English suggests an *ar* spelling. Some people do now pronounce the ending as 'erk' which is the way it is said in American English.

clever *adjective*
1. good at thinking or learning quickly. **2.** skilled: *She is clever with her hands.* **3.** sensible and

practical: *That's a clever idea!*; *a clever device.*
☐ **cleverly**, *adverb* –**cleverness**, *noun*

SIMILAR WORDS (for definition 1) are **intelligent**, **brainy**, **bright**, **smart** and **brilliant**. Note that you use **brilliant** to describe someone who is extremely clever.

cliché /*say* **klee**-shay/ *noun* a saying which has become stale or dull because it has been used too often, such as *from the bottom of my heart*, *at the end of the day.*
☐ **clichéd**, *adjective*

NOTE There is an accent over the *e* because this was originally a French word.

click *verb*
1. If something **clicks**, it makes a short, sharp sound: *The door clicked shut.* **2.** *Rather informal* If something **clicks**, it falls into place, or is understood: *After I studied the maths problem for a long time, it finally clicked.* **3.** If you **click** on an icon on a computer screen, you press the mouse button when the pointer is on the icon.
☐ **click**, *noun*: *Did you hear the click of the door?*

client *noun* someone who uses the services that someone else provides professionally: *an architect's client.*

cliff *noun* a steep, rocky slope.

climate *noun* the usual weather of a particular place.
☐ **climatic**, *adjective*

climate change *noun* a major change in the usual climatic conditions of the world which lasts for a long time, especially a change thought to be caused by global warming: *Climate change is thought to be the reason for the increased number of icebergs breaking off Greenland's glaciers.*

climax *noun* the highest, or most important and exciting point of anything: *The climax of the book took place in a fierce storm.*
☐ **climactic**, *adjective*: *the climactic moment.* –**climactically**, *adverb*

climb *verb*
1. To **climb** is to move or rise upwards: *He climbed the stairs*; *The moon climbs slowly into the sky.* **2.** If something **climbs**, it increases in value or amount: *Food prices have climbed sharply in the past year.*
☐ **climb**, *noun* –**climber**, *noun*

clinch *verb*
1. If you **clinch** something, you settle it once and for all: *To clinch the sale, my parents have to sign papers by this afternoon.*
–*noun* (*plural* **clinches**) **2.** a close hold in boxing, which makes it difficult for your opponent to hit you.
☐ **clincher**, *noun* something decisive: *That chess move was the clincher.*

cling *verb* (**clings**, **clinging**, **clung**, **has clung**)
1. If you **cling** to someone or something, you hold on to them tightly: *The baby koala clung to its mother's back.* **2.** If someone or something **clings** to you, they stay with you and will not go away: *The smell of the bushfire clung to the house for days.*
☐ **clingy**, *adjective* (**clingier**, **clingiest**): *a clingy child.*

clinic *noun* a medical centre where you can go to see a doctor or have special tests or treatment, such as an X-ray.
☐ **clinical**, *adjective* –**clinically**, *adverb*

clip[1] *verb* (**clips**, **clipping**, **clipped**, **has clipped**)
1. If you **clip** something, you cut small pieces from it: *to clip a hedge.* **2.** If you **clip** something out of a magazine or newspaper, you cut it out. **3.** To **clip** someone or something is to give them a sharp hit: *My elbow clipped the edge of the table as I fell.*
–*noun* **4.** a trimming: *His moustache needs a clip.* **5.** a short part of a film.
☐ **clipped**, *adjective* –**clipping**, *noun*

clip[2] *noun*
1. something which holds things in place: *My purse won't stay shut because the clip is broken.*
–*verb* (**clips**, **clipping**, **clipped**, **has clipped**) **2.** When you **clip** something to something else, you fasten them together with a clip: *Please clip these papers together.*

clipper *noun*
1. a cutting tool, especially for your hair or nails.
2. a fast sailing ship of the past.

ANOTHER FORM This word (as in definition 1) is often used in the plural form, **clippers**.

clique /*rhymes with* meek/ *noun* a small group of people who keep themselves apart from others.
☐ **cliquey**, *adjective* –**cliquish**, *adjective* –**cliquishly**, *adverb*

☑ SPELLING TIP This word comes from a French word meaning 'people hired to applaud in a theatre', which is why the spelling *ique* gives an 'eek' sound. Think of other words with the same spelling for this sound, such as *antique* and *technique*.

clitoris /*say* **klit**-uh-ruhs/ *noun* the part of a female's genitals at the upper end of the vulva.

cloak *noun*
1. a sleeveless coat or cape which does up at your neck.
–*verb* **2.** To **cloak** something is to hide it or keep it hidden: *Her smile cloaked her real feelings*; *The valley is cloaked by mist.*

clock *noun* something which measures and tells you the time.

clockwise *adjective* going around in the same direction as the hands on a clock face.

THE OPPOSITE is **anticlockwise**.

clockwork *noun*
1. the inner parts that make a clock or a wind-up toy work.
–*phrase* **2. like clockwork**, smoothly and without interruption: *Our move into the new house went like clockwork.*

clod *noun*
1. a lump, especially of earth. **2.** a stupid person.

clog *verb* (**clogs**, **clogging**, **clogged**, **has clogged**)
1. If something is **clogged** or **clogged up**, it is blocked: *Rubbish clogged the drain.*
–*noun* **2.** a heavy wooden shoe made from one piece of wood.

cloister /*say* **kloy**-stuh/ *noun*
1. a covered path by the side of a building such as a church. **2.** a place where nuns or priests live quietly, away from the rest of the world.

clone *noun*
1. a plant or animal which is exactly the same as its parent and has been formed, not by the joining of male and female cells, but from one of its parent's own cells.
–*verb* **2.** To **clone** an animal or plant is to produce it as a clone: *Scientists have cloned a sheep.*

WORD HISTORY from a Greek word meaning 'slip' or 'twig'

close *verb* /*say* klohz/ **1.** If you **close** something, you shut it: *Close the door, please.* **2.** If you **close** something such as a meeting or a discussion, you end it: *The subject is closed – I don't want to discuss it any more.* **3.** If a road is **closed**, it is blocked off so it cannot be used: *On the day of the parade, many roads in the city were closed.*
–*adjective* /*say* klohs/ **4.** nearby: *I live close to the local shops*; *The photographer got us to stand closer together.* **5.** similar: *We're very close in age.* **6.** careful and thorough: *This book needs close study.* **7.** narrow or tight: *These shoes are a close fit.*
–*noun* /*say* klohz/ **8.** conclusion.
☐ **closed**, *adjective* –**closely**, *adverb* –**closeness**, *noun* –**closure**, *noun*

closet /*say* **kloz**-uht/ *noun* a cupboard or small room where things are stored.

clot *noun*
1. a solid lump: *a clot of blood*; *a clot of ash.* **2.** *Informal* a fool.
–*verb* (**clots**, **clotting**, **clotted**, **has clotted**) **3.** When a liquid **clots**, it forms into clot.

cloth *noun* material made by weaving fibres together: *She wore a sari of beautiful silk cloth*; *We wiped the wet table down with a cloth.*

☑ DO NOT CONFUSE the noun **cloth** with the verb **clothe**.

clothe /*say* klohdh/ *verb* When you **clothe** someone, you provide them with clothes: *to feed and clothe a family.*
☐ **clothing**, *noun* –**clothes**, *plural noun*

cloud *noun*
1. a white or grey mass of water vapour, ice, smoke or dust that floats in the air. **2.** anything which looks or acts like a cloud: *a cloud of green gas*; *a dense cloud of grasshoppers.*
–*phrase* **3. the cloud**, in computers, the software resources and the services, particularly storage, made available through the internet.
☐ **cloudy**, *adjective* (**cloudier**, **cloudiest**) –**cloudiness**, *noun*

clout *noun*
1. a hard hit with the hand. **2.** power or influence: *What we need is someone with a bit of clout!*
–*verb* **3.** If you **clout** someone, you hit them: *I was so angry that I felt like clouting them.*

clove *noun* the dried flower bud of a tropical tree, used as a spice.

clover *noun* a plant with leaves divided into three parts and a white flower, often used as food for cattle.

clown *noun*
1. someone in a circus, often dressed up with a white face, a red nose and silly clothes, who makes people laugh.
–*verb* **2.** If someone **clowns**, they act foolishly, usually to make people laugh.
☐ **clowning**, *noun* –**clownish**, *adjective*

A SIMILAR WORD (for definition 1) is **jester**. This was used more often in the past.

club *noun*
1. a heavy stick, used as a weapon. **2.** a stick used to hit the ball in games like golf. **3.** a group of people who have joined together because they share a particular interest or hobby: *We started a chess club at school.* **4.** a place run by a group, which offers entertainment and cheap food and drink to those who belong. **5.** the black three-leaved shape on some playing cards.
–*verb* (**clubs**, **clubbing**, **clubbed**, **has clubbed**) **6.** If you **club** someone or something, you beat them with a club.

cluck *verb* A hen **clucks** when it is calling its chicks.
☐ **clucky**, *adjective* feeling a strong desire to have children. –**cluck**, *noun*

clue *noun* something which helps to explain a puzzle or mystery: *The vital clue was the hat found under the stairs.*

clump *noun*
1. a group of things growing together, such as trees or grasses.

–*verb* **2.** If a group of things **clump** together, they gather together or are found together in a clump: *Bamboo tends to clump.*

clumsy *adjective* (**clumsier**, **clumsiest**) awkward in movement and tending to bump into things and drop things: *I can't dance at all – I'm very clumsy on my feet.*
☐ **clumsily**, *adverb* –**clumsiness**, *noun*

cluster *noun*
1. a number of things growing or placed close together: *a cluster of lights*; *a cluster of palms.*
–*verb* **2.** If people or things **cluster**, they gather together in close groups: *All the kids clustered around him asking for his autograph.*

clutch *verb*
1. If you **clutch** something, you hold it tightly: *The little girl clutched her doll.*
–*noun* (*plural* **clutches**) **2.** the part of a machine, especially a car, which is used in changing gears.
–*phrase* **3. clutch at**, to try to take hold of: *She clutched at the rope as it swung towards her.*

clutter *verb* To **clutter** something is to make it untidy: *The floor of his room was cluttered with clothes.*
☐ **clutter**, *noun*: *Please get rid of this clutter.*

co- *prefix* a word part meaning **1.** with, as in *cohesion*. **2.** at the same time, as in *coincidence*.

WORD HISTORY this prefix comes from Latin

coach *noun* (*plural* **coaches**)
1. a large comfortable bus, usually for long trips. **2.** a railway carriage. **3.** a closed carriage pulled by horses, used in the past to transport people. **4.** someone who trains athletes.
–*verb* **5.** If you **coach** someone, you train them in a sport or give them special teaching: *He coaches swimming*; *I need someone to coach me in maths.*

coagulate /*say* koh-**ag**-yuh-layt/ *verb* When a liquid **coagulates**, it changes into a thick lump, such as a clot.
☐ **coagulation**, *noun*

coal *noun* a black or dark brown rock, formed from the remains of ancient trees, used as fuel.

coalesce /*say* koh-uh-**les**/ *verb* When two or more things **coalesce**, they grow or join together: *The two groups coalesced to make a united team.*
☐ **coalescence**, *noun* –**coalescent**, *adjective*

☑ SPELLING TIP *Silent letter alert*: don't forget the silent *c* following the *s*. So the ending of the word is spelt *lesce* (not *less*).

coalition /*say* koh-uh-**lish**-uhn/ *noun* the joining together of two or more groups, at least for a while: *Alone, the two political parties were weak so they formed a coalition.*

coal seam gas *noun* gas that is released from fractures in seams of coal and mined to be used for energy.

THE ABBREVIATION is **CSG**.

coarse /*say* kaws/ *adjective*
1. thick or rough: *coarse hair*; *coarse fabric.* **2.** rude or offensive: *coarse manners*; *a coarse remark.*
☐ **coarsely**, *adverb* –**coarsen**, *verb* –**coarseness**, *noun*

☑ SPELLING TIP Don't confuse the spelling of **coarse** with **course** which sounds the same. **Course** has several meanings. It can be a part of a meal, a series of classes, or the way along which something progresses.

coast *noun*
1. the seashore or the land beside the sea.
–*verb* **2.** To **coast** is to travel down a sloping road in a car or on a bicycle, without using power. **3.** If someone **coasts** along or through something, they get by without making much effort.
–*phrase* **4. the coast is clear**, the danger has gone.
☐ **coastal**, *adjective* –**coastline**, *noun*

WORD HISTORY from a Latin word meaning 'rib' or 'side'

coastguard *noun* someone whose job is to patrol the coast of a country, helping ships in danger and looking out for smugglers or illegal fishing boats.

coat *noun*
1. a piece of clothing with sleeves, which you wear over other clothes. **2.** the fur or wool of an animal. **3.** a layer: *Mum was scraping off all the old coats of paint.*
–*verb* **4.** If you **coat** something with something else, you cover it with a thin layer of it: *We coated the cake with chocolate icing.*
☐ **coating**, *noun*: *a coating of chocolate.*

coathanger *noun* a curved piece of wood, plastic, etc., with a hook attached, on which clothes are hung.

coat of arms *noun* the special design, often with a motto, belonging to a noble family or nation: *The Australian coat of arms has a kangaroo and an emu on it.*

coax /*say* kohks/ *verb* If you **coax** someone, you persuade them gently and patiently: *We had to coax the baby to swallow the medicine.*
☐ **coaxer**, *noun*

cob *noun*
1. the head on which corn seeds grow: *We like eating the cobs with salt sprinkled over them.* **2.** a male swan.

NOTE The female (of definition 2) is a **pen**.

cobalt /*say* **koh**-bawlt, **koh**-bolt/ *noun* a silver-white metal which gives a blue colouring to pottery.

WORD HISTORY from a German word for 'goblin'

cobble *noun* a rounded paving stone: *The streets in the old village were made of cobbles.*

ANOTHER WORD for this is **cobblestone**.

cobbler *noun Old-fashioned* someone who mends shoes.

cobra /*say* **kob**-ruh, **koh**-bruh/ *noun* a venomous snake which can spread out the skin of its neck so it looks like a hood.

cobweb *noun*
1. the fine thread spun by a spider to catch insects. **2.** something very light or fine.
☐ **cobwebby**, *adjective*

cocaine /*say* koh-**kayn**/ *noun* a bitter drug which is made from the leaves of a South American shrub.

cock *noun* a rooster or male bird.

NOTE The female is a **hen**.

cockatiel /*say* kok-uh-**teel**/ *noun* a small parrot with a long tail and a crest on top of its head like a cockatoo.

cockatoo *noun* a crested parrot.

cockeyed /*say* **kok**-uyd/ *adjective*
1. crooked: *Your hat is cockeyed.* **2.** foolish or absurd: *a cockeyed scheme.*

cockle *noun* an edible shellfish which is enclosed in two shells that fit together.

cockpit *noun*
1. the front end of an aeroplane where the pilot sits. **2.** the driver's seat in a racing car.

cockroach *noun* (*plural* **cockroaches**) an insect, usually active at night, with a flattened body and long feelers, which is a common household pest.

cocktail *noun*
1. an alcoholic drink made of a spirit mixed with wine, fruit juice, and so on, often chilled and sweetened. **2.** fruit or tomato juice drunk before a meal to stimulate the appetite.
☐ **cocktail**, *adjective* small enough to be eaten in your fingers: *cocktail frankfurt.*

cocky[1] *adjective* (**cockier**, **cockiest**) *Informal* too confident or smart: *He is a bit too cocky and is headed for disaster.*
☐ **cockily**, *adverb* –**cockiness**, *noun*

A SIMILAR WORD is **cocksure**. This is more formal.

cocky[2] *noun* (*plural* **cockies**) *Informal* **1.** a cockatoo. **2.** a farmer, especially of a small farm.

cocoa /*say* **koh**-koh/ *noun*
1. the crushed and powdered seeds of a tropical tree. **2.** a drink made from the brown powder which is also used to make chocolate.

☑ SPELLING TIP *Tricky vowel sounds*: the two vowel sounds in **cocoa** sound the same, but remember that the first one is spelt just *o* and the second one is spelt *oa* (as in many other words such as *boat*).

coconut *noun* the large, hard nut of a kind of palm tree, which is lined with white flesh and contains a clear milk.

☑ SPELLING TIP The *coco* in **coconut** has nothing to do with *cocoa* (the drink that is like chocolate) which is why it is spelt differently (with no *a*). The *coco* is a kind of palm tree, on which **coconuts** grow.

cocoon /*say* kuh-**koohn**/ *noun*
1. the covering which grubs such as the silkworm spin around themselves for their chrysalis stage before their next stage of growth.
–*verb* **2.** To **cocoon** something or someone is to cover or protect them.

WORD HISTORY from a French word meaning 'shell'

cod *noun* any of a number of freshwater and saltwater fishes valued as a food.

coda /*say* **koh**-duh/ *noun* the part which finishes a piece of music.

WORD HISTORY from an Italian word meaning 'tail'

coddle *verb*
1. When you **coddle** someone, you look after them in a way that gives them too much protection: *His grandmother coddles him as if he was a little baby.* **2.** When you **coddle** an egg, you cook it very slowly in almost boiling water.

code *noun*
1. a set of rules or laws: *traffic code*; *codes of conduct.* **2.** a system for giving a secret message: *We worked out a code for warning each other*; *morse code.*
☐ **encode**, *verb* –**encoded**, *adjective*

coeducation *noun* the joint teaching of boys and girls, in the same school or classroom.
☐ **coeducational**, *adjective*

THE SHORT FORM of this is **co-ed**.

coerce /*say* koh-**ers**/ *verb* If you **coerce** someone to do something, you force them to do it: *We tried to coerce him into telling us the secret code.*
☐ **coercion** /*say* koh-**er**-shuhn/, *noun* –**coercive** /*say* koh-**er**-siv/, *adjective*

☑ SPELLING TIP The prefix *co-* begins **coerce**. The final syllable ends with *ce* in which the *c* is softened and pronounced as 's'.

coffee *noun*
1. a drink made from the cooked and ground beans of a tropical shrub. **2.** the brown powder you use to make this drink.

coffin *noun* the box in which a dead body is placed.

cog *noun*
1. one of the tooth-like parts sticking out of a wheel which connects it with another wheel. **2.** one of many unimportant people in an organisation.

cogitate /*say* **koj**-uh-tayt/ *verb* To **cogitate** is to think long and hard.
☐ **cogitation**, *noun* –**cogitative**, *adjective*

cognac /*say* **kon**-yak/ *noun* a high quality brandy.

WORD HISTORY named after the French town called *Cognac* where this drink was first made

☑ SPELLING TIP *Silent letter alert*: don't forget the silent *g* before the *n*. Also remember that there is no *y* in this word although you hear a 'y' sound when you say it. This is because it comes from French.

coherent /*say* koh-**hear**-ruhnt/ *adjective* clear and well thought out: *She presented a coherent argument for taking immediate action.*
☐ **cohere**, *verb* –**coherence**, *noun* –**coherently**, *adverb*

THE OPPOSITE is **incoherent**.

cohesion /*say* koh-**hee**-zhuhn/ *noun* the state of sticking together or being connected.
☐ **cohesive**, *adjective*: *a cohesive group of students, all of the same age.*

coil *noun*
1. a loop or spiral.
–*verb* **2.** If you **coil** something, or it coils, it is wound around so that its whole length is in the shape of rings, usually one on top of or beside the other: *The snake had coiled itself around the branch of the tree*; *Coil the rope and store it in the garage.*

coin *noun*
1. a metal piece of money.
–*verb* **2.** If someone **coins** a word, they invent it.
☐ **coinage**, *noun*

WORD HISTORY from a Latin word meaning 'wedge'

coincidence /*say* koh-**in**-suh-duhns/ *noun* the surprising fact of things happening together by chance: *By coincidence, our class had an excursion on the same day as another class in the school.*
☐ **coincidental**, *adjective* –**coincide**, *verb*: *The holidays coincided with the fine weather.*

☑ SPELLING TIP Remember that **coincidence** is made up of the prefix *co-* meaning 'with' and *incid-* from the Latin word meaning 'happen', with an *ence* noun ending.

coke *noun* a solid fuel made from heating coal which contains mostly carbon.

colander /*say* **kul**-uhn-duh, **kol**-uhn-duh/ *noun* a bowl with many small holes, which is used in the kitchen for draining off liquid.

ANOTHER SPELLING is **cullender**.

☑ SPELLING TIP *Single/double letter alert*: notice that if you use the spelling starting with *co* there is only one *l* following. However, if you use the other spelling starting with *cu*, the following *l* is doubled. There is also a difference in the spelling of the next vowel. Finally, don't confuse this word with **calendar** which is a chart showing the days of each month of the year.

cold *adjective*
1. having a very low temperature: *It's cold in here*; *Put the heater on if you feel cold*; *a cold drink.* **2.** unfriendly: *The people next door were quite cold after we accidentally broke their window.*
–*noun* **3.** the absence of heat. **4.** an illness which usually comes with a blocked or runny nose, sore throat, coughing, and so on.
–*phrase* **5. get cold feet**, to have no courage or confidence about doing something. **6. leave someone cold**, to fail to make someone feel good or positive: *Brussels sprouts leave me cold.*
☐ **coldly**, *adverb* –**coldness**, *noun*

THE OPPOSITE (of definitions 1 and 3) is **hot**.

cold-blooded *adjective*
1. showing no pity or sympathy: *cold-blooded killers.* **2.** A **cold-blooded** animal has a body temperature that alters depending on the environment they are in. Reptiles and fish are examples of cold-blooded animals.
☐ **cold-bloodedly**, *adverb* –**cold-bloodedness**, *noun*

COMPARE definition 2 with **warm-blooded**.

coleslaw *noun* a salad made with sliced raw cabbage.

colic /*say* **kol**-ik/ *noun* a sharp pain in the stomach.
☐ **colicky**, *adjective*

☑ SPELLING TIP *Single letter alert*: only one *l*. Also remember that **colic** ends with a single *c* (not *ck*) but this changes and a *k* is added when you make the adjective **colicky**.

collaborate *verb*
1. If people **collaborate**, they work together in order to achieve something: *If we collaborate on the project, we should finish by the end of the day.*

2. If someone **collaborates** with the enemy during a war, they deceive their own country by helping its enemy.
☐ **collaboration**, *noun* –**collaborative**, *adjective* –**collaborator**, *noun*

☑ SPELLING TIP *Double/single letter alert*: double *l*, and only one *b*. Also remember its meaning and note that it has the word *labor* (a form of *labour*, meaning 'to work') inside it.

collage /*say* kuh-**lahzh**, **kol**-ahzh/ *noun* a picture made from various materials, such as pieces of paper, cloth or other materials, fixed onto paper or board.

COMPARE this with **montage**.

collapse *verb*
1. To **collapse** is to fall down or fall apart suddenly: *Halfway through the hike, he collapsed*; *The grandstand collapsed in the storm.* **2.** Something **collapses** if it is made so that its parts can be folded flat together: *We want a camping table that collapses so it can be packed into the car.*
☐ **collapse**, *noun* –**collapsible**, *adjective*

collar *noun*
1. the part of a piece of clothing that is worn around your neck. **2.** a leather band put around an animal's neck.
–*verb* **3.** *Informal* If someone **collars** you, they catch you when you are trying to avoid them: *Archie tried to get out of the room but they collared him at the door.*

☑ SPELLING TIP Remember that the ending is spelt *ar* (not *er*).

collarbone *noun* one of two long bones that go from the base of the neck to the shoulder: *He broke his collarbone playing football.*

ANOTHER WORD for this is **clavicle**. This a more formal, scientific word.

collate /*say* kuh-**layt**/ *verb* When you **collate** pieces of information or pages of a document, you gather them together in the proper order.
☐ **collation**, *noun* –**collator**, *noun*

colleague /*say* **kol**-eeg/ *noun* someone you work with, usually in the same workplace.

☑ SPELLING TIP Remember that **colleague** has a double *l* in the middle, and that it ends with the spelling *eague* (for the 'eeg' sound). The ending is spelt like this because the word comes from French (like the word *league* that has the same sound).

collect *verb*
1. To **collect** is to gather together: *We collected all the mushrooms we saw growing in the grass*; *Hundreds collected at the airport to see the film star arrive*; *We collected money for charity.* **2.** If you **collect** things, you own as many of them as possible as a hobby: *My grandfather collects old clocks.* **3.** If you **collect** something from a place, you pick it up from there: *We collected the meat from the butcher.*
☐ **collection**, *noun* –**collectively**, *adverb* –**collector**, *noun*

collective *adjective*
1. belonging to or shared by a number of people: *The audience turned its collective gaze to the apparition coming onto the stage.*
–*noun* **2.** a group of people who share what they own and who work together for the good of them all: *My parents belong to a collective that buys fruit together.*

collective noun *noun* a noun that is singular in its form but expresses a grouping of single objects or people: *Words like 'bouquet', 'choir' and 'herd' are all collective nouns.*

SEE the Grammar and Punctuation Guide appendix.

college *noun*
1. a place for learning, rather like a university, that you can go to after you finish high school. **2.** a place within a university where students live.

collide *verb* To **collide** is to hit together: *The boats collided because of the storm.*
☐ **collision**, *noun*

collie *noun* a kind of sheepdog with long, thick hair and a bushy tail.

colliery *noun* (*plural* **collieries**) a coalmine with all its buildings and equipment.
☐ **collier**, *noun* a coalminer.

colloquial /*say* kuh-**loh**-kwee-uhl/ *adjective* suitable for relaxed or informal language: *'Kid' is a colloquial word for 'child'.*

☑ SPELLING TIP The spelling of **colloquial** will be easier if you see that it is based on the Latin word *loqui* meaning 'to talk'. Add *col*, meaning 'with', at the start and *al* at the end.

cologne /*say* kuh-**lohn**/ *noun* a liquid you put on your skin to make you smell good.

OTHER TERMS for this are **eau de Cologne** or **Cologne water**.
WORD HISTORY named after the German city of *Cologne* where the perfume has been made since 1709

colon /*say* **koh**-luhn/ *noun* a mark of punctuation (:) which is used to separate the main part of a sentence from a list of examples, as in *I want you to bring the following things: a pencil, a rubber, and a piece of paper.*

SEE the Grammar and Punctuation Guide appendix.

colonel /*say* **ker**-nuhl/ *noun* an important officer in the army.

☑ SPELLING TIP **Colonel** is a difficult word because the spelling does not match the way you say it. Don't confuse it with the spelling of **kernel** (the inner part of a nut) which has the same sound. Remember that, although **colonel** looks like it has three syllables, it only has two, and learn the *colo* spelling (for the 'ker' sound).

colonise *verb* To **colonise** an area is to start a colony there: *France colonised a number of Pacific islands.*
☐ **colonisation**, *noun* –**colonist**, *noun*

ANOTHER SPELLING is **colonize**.

colony /*say* **kol**-uh-nee/ *noun* (*plural* **colonies**)
1. a group of people who have left their home and formed a settlement in a new land ruled by the parent country. **2.** a group of animals or plants of the same kind that live close together.

☐ **colonial**, *adjective*

colossal *adjective* very great in size.
☐ **colossally**, *adverb*

☑ SPELLING TIP *Double/single letter alert*: a double *s* and a single *l* (appearing twice, in the middle and at the end). Rap it out as *co+los+sal*.

colour *noun*
1. the look that something has which is caused by the way light is reflected by it: *The colours of the rainbow are violet, indigo, blue, green, yellow, orange and red.* **2.** something used to give colour, such as paint or dye. **3.** details that make something interesting: *You need to put some colour into the story – it's very ordinary at the moment.*
–*verb* **4.** If you **colour** something, you use dye or paint to make it a different colour. **5.** If something **colours** your judgement or opinion, it has an effect on it even though it is not strictly related: *The stereotype they had of anybody from another country coloured their attitude to their new neighbours.*
–*phrase* **6. off colour**, ill or not well. **7. show your true colours**, to show what type of person you really are. **8. with flying colours**, very successfully.
☐ **colourful**, *adjective* –**colouring**, *noun* –**colourless**, *adjective*

ANOTHER SPELLING is **color**.

colour blindness *noun* a fault in someone's eyesight that stops them from being able to tell the difference between some colours, such as red and green.
☐ **colourblind**, *adjective*

ANOTHER SPELLING is **color blindness**.

coloured *adjective*
1. having colour. **2.** belonging to a group of people that do not have white skin.

ANOTHER SPELLING is **colored**.

colt *noun* a male horse that is younger than four years old.

column /*say* **kol**-uhm/ *noun*
1. a long, upright support: *a row of columns along the front of the building.* **2.** anything with a similar shape to a column: *The column of traffic stretched back beyond the bridge.* **3.** an upright row of numbers or of print going down a page. **4.** a piece of writing on a particular subject that appears regularly in a newspaper or magazine: *My neighbour writes a magazine column on cooking tips.*

☑ SPELLING TIP *Silent letter alert*: don't forget the silent *n* at the end.

coma *noun* a very long, deep unconsciousness, which may be caused by disease, injury, poison, and so on.
☐ **comatose**, *adjective*

comb *noun*
1. a piece of plastic or metal with a set of thin pointed teeth, which is used to tidy or hold back hair. **2.** a comb-shaped part on the head of a hen, rooster or turkey.
–*verb* **3.** If you **comb** your hair, you tidy it using a comb. **4.** If you **comb** a place, you search it thoroughly because you are looking for something or someone: *I combed my room for my left shoe.*

☑ SPELLING TIP *Silent letter alert*: don't forget the silent *b* at the end.

combat *noun* /*say* **kom**-bat/
1. the fighting that takes place between opposing armies: *The soldiers were locked in combat.* **2.** a competition between two people, which is not necessarily violent: *The chess players were in combat for days.*
–*verb* /*say* kuhm-**bat**/ **3.** If you **combat** something, you try to stop it happening: *He is always trying to combat his craving for sweet things.*
☐ **combatant**, *noun*, *adjective*

☑ SPELLING TIP *Single letter alert*: a single *t* at the end. Remember that the *t* remains single when you add a verb ending such as *-ed* or *-ing* or make the word *combatant*.

combine *verb* If you **combine** two or more things or if they **combine**, they become joined together to form a single thing: *If you combine red and blue, you get purple*; *All the school choirs combined for the concert.*
☐ **combination**, *noun*

combustion *noun* the process of burning.
☐ **combustible**, *adjective*

come *verb* (**comes**, **coming**, **came**, **has come**)
1. If someone **comes** somewhere, they move towards where you are: *Come over here, please.* **2.** If a date or event **comes**, it happens in the course of time: *At last my birthday came.* **3.** If someone or something **comes** into view or into sight, they appear: *At last she came into sight at the top of the hill.* **4.** If something **comes** to a certain point, it reaches that far: *Her hair comes to just below her shoulders.*
–*phrase* **5. come about**, to occur or happen in due course. **6. come across**, to meet or find: *I came across an echidna in the bush.* **7. come round**, **a.** to regain consciousness. **b.** to change your mind to agree with someone else. **8. come by**, **a.** to get or obtain: *Where did you come by that great hat?* **b.** to stop for a visit: *We'll come by at about noon.* **9. come down with**, to become ill with: *to come down with measles.* **10. come into**, to receive from someone who has died: *They came into a lot of money when their father died.* **11. come out with**, to tell or make known.

comedy *noun* (*plural* **comedies**)
1. a play, film, story or other entertainment that is funny or makes you feel happy. **2.** any funny event or series of events.
☐ **comedian**, *noun*

WORD HISTORY from a Greek word for 'amusement' added to a Greek word for 'singer'

comet *noun* an object in space that moves around the sun and has a bright central part surrounded by a smoky part that finishes in the shape of a tail.

WORD HISTORY from a Greek word meaning 'long-haired'

comfort /*say* **kum**-fuht/ *verb*
1. If you **comfort** someone, you cheer them up or make them feel less sad or worried: *I comforted my little brother after he hurt his foot.*
–*noun* **2.** a feeling of being less sad or worried. **3.** someone or something that comforts: *My mum said it was a comfort to have someone to help.* **4.** pleasant enjoyment with what you need provided and with no troubles: *The hotel promises absolute comfort.*
☐ **comforter**, *noun* –**comforting**, *adjective*

THE OPPOSITE is **discomfort**.

☑ SPELLING TIP *Tricky vowel sounds*: the vowel sound in the first syllable is spelt *o*, although it gives a 'u' sound, and the sound in the second syllable is spelt *or*, although it gives an 'uh' sound.

comfortable /*say* **kumf**-tuh-buhl, **kumf**-uh-tuh-buhl/ *adjective*
1. Something is **comfortable** if it gives you comfort: *a comfortable bed*; *a comfortable income.* **2.** If you are **comfortable**, you are feeling relaxed in your body or mind: *The cat looked comfortable fast asleep in the lounge chair*; *I'm not comfortable about singing in front of an audience.*

☑ SPELLING TIP The spelling of **comfortable** is really quite easy, as long as you remember that it is made up of the word *comfort* and *-able*, even though you pronounce the *comfort* part in a short way as if there was nothing between the *f* and *t*.

comic *adjective*
1. funny or amusing: *It was a comic situation where everybody thought they were the only one who knew the secret.*
–*noun* **2.** a magazine containing a series of drawings that tell a funny story or an adventure story.
☐ **comical**, *adjective*

comma *noun* a mark of punctuation (,) that is used to show small breaks in a sentence.

SEE the Grammar and Punctuation Guide appendix.

command *verb*
1. If you **command** someone to do something, you order them to do it: *He commanded us to stop immediately.* **2.** If you **command** something, you control it totally and you are responsible for it: *The head chef commanded the operations in the kitchen.* **3.** To **command** something, such as respect, is to deserve and receive it.
–*noun* **4.** an order: *She issued a command for everybody to cease talking.* **5.** power to give orders or be in charge: *You always need to know who has command.* **6.** an instruction to a computer which is carried out by means of a program.
–*phrase* **7. in command**, having the power to control or give orders: *The deputy was in command while the principal was away.*
☐ **commander**, *noun* –**commandment**, *noun*

commando *noun* (*plural* **commandos** *or* **commandoes**) someone who belongs to a small fighting force that is specially trained to make quick attacks inside enemy areas.

commemorate *verb* When we **commemorate** someone or something, we keep alive their memory: *Australia Day commemorates the settling of Europeans in Australia*; *They discussed ideas about how to commemorate those killed on 11 September 2001.*
☐ **commemoration**, *noun* –**commemorative**, *adjective*

☑ SPELLING TIP *Double/single letter alert*: there are three *m*'s – first a double *m* and then a single *m*. It might help if you see that **commemorate** has most of the word *memory* included (except for the last letter), with the prefix *com-* (meaning 'with') coming before it, which gives the double *m*. Rap it out as *com+mem+or+ate*.

commence *verb* To **commence** is to begin or start: *The school year commences at the end of January; The performance will commence in five minutes.*
☐ **commencement**, *noun*

commend *verb* If you **commend** someone or something, you **1.** suggest them as being suitable for trust, a reward, or a job: *I commended Sali as a babysitter; Karl was commended for a bravery medal.* **2.** praise them: *The teacher commended us for our good work.*
☐ **commendable**, *adjective* deserving praise. –**commendation**, *noun* –**commendatory**, *adjective*

A SIMILAR WORD (for definition 1) is **recommend**.

comment *noun*
1. a short note or remark that gives an opinion or explanation.
–*verb* **2.** If you **comment** on something, you remark or write a short note that gives an opinion or explanation: *She made a comment about my new haircut.*

commentary *noun* (*plural* **commentaries**) a series of written or spoken comments: *The commentary in the swimming races was exciting to listen to.*
☐ **commentate**, *verb* –**commentator**, *noun*

commerce *noun* the buying and selling of goods, especially as carried on between different countries or between different parts of the same country.

A SIMILAR WORD is **trade**.

commercial /*say* kuh-**mer**-shuhl/ *adjective*
1. having to do with commerce: *The commercial part of town is down by the port.* **2.** intended to or able to make a profit: *The company will only get involved if they think the project is commercial.*
–*noun* **3.** an advertisement on radio or television.
☐ **commercialism**, *noun* –**commercialise**, *verb*

ANOTHER SPELLING for **commercialise** is **commercialize**.

commiserate *verb* When you **commiserate** with someone, you share their sorrow or disappointment: *I commiserated with Julie when her pet dog died.*
☐ **commiseration**, *noun*

A SIMILAR WORD is **sympathise**.

☑ SPELLING TIP *Double/single letter alert*: double *m* and only one *s*. It might help if you see that **commiserate** has most of the word *misery* included (except for the last letter), with the prefix *com-* (meaning 'with') coming before it, which gives the double *m*. Rap it out as *com+mis+er+ate*.

commission *noun*
1. an order, direction or particular duty, given by someone who is in charge. **2.** an order for a particular piece of creative work. **3.** a group of people who have been given particular official duties: *The commission was set up to regulate fishing permits.* **4.** use or service: *My phone has been out of commission all day.* **5.** a sum of money given to an employee, such as a salesperson for each successful effort: *He gets a commission for each mobile phone that he sells.*
–*verb* **6.** If someone **commissions** a piece of work, they arrange for it to be done according to their instructions in return for payment: *His friends commissioned a portrait to mark his 80th birthday.*

ANOTHER FORM This word (as in definition 3) is often spelt with a capital letter, as in *Health Insurance Commission*.

☑ SPELLING TIP *Double letter alert*: a double *m* and a double *s*.

commissioner *noun*
1. someone who is a member of an official commission. **2.** someone who is in charge of a government department.

ANOTHER FORM This word (as in definition 2) is often spelt with a capital letter, as in *the Taxation Commissioner*.

commit *verb* (**commits**, **committing**, **committed**, **has committed**) To **commit** something is to **1.** give it into someone's charge or trust: *The department committed the care of the children to the orphanage.* **2.** put it into a particular form in order to keep: *She committed his instructions to memory and hoped she wouldn't forget anything.* **3.** do or perform it: *They committed a wonderful act of generosity when they raised money for the appeal.*
–*phrase* **4. commit yourself**, to bind yourself by making a promise: *She committed herself to staying until the end of the year.*
☐ **committed**, *adjective* –**commitment**, *noun*: *He made a commitment to play with the team for the whole season.* –**committal**, *noun*

committee *noun* a group of people chosen from a larger group to discuss or make decisions about a particular subject: *There is a separate committee set up for each stall at the fete.*

commodity *noun* (*plural* **commodities**) something useful, especially something that is bought and sold: *We can stock up on basic commodities such as rice, coffee and eggs when we go to the supermarket.*

commodore *noun*
1. a senior captain in the navy. **2.** the president of a boat club.

common *adjective*
1. shared by two or more people: *The land at the back of the houses is shared as common property.* 2. general or shared by all: *It's common knowledge that the factory is closing next month.* 3. found or happening often: *The eucalypt is a common tree in Australia.*
–*phrase* 4. **in common**, shared by people: *As we chatted, it became clear that we had many interests in common.*
□ **commonly**, *adverb*

common noun *noun* a noun which can be used of any one of a class of things and which does not have a capital letter: *'Vietnam' is not a common noun, but 'country' is.*

COMPARE this with **proper noun**. See also the Grammar and Punctuation Guide appendix.

commonplace *adjective* Something that is **commonplace** is ordinary because it occurs or is said often: *a commonplace garden plant*; *a commonplace saying.*

common sense *noun* the ability to behave sensibly and make sensible decisions: *She showed a great deal of common sense by taking a large bottle of water on her bushwalk.*

ANOTHER FORM is **commonsense**.

commonwealth *noun*
1. all the people of a country or state. 2. a country that is made up of several states, in which there is one government for the whole country as well as a government for each of the states. 3. a group of people or countries united by a common interest.

ANOTHER FORM This word (as in definition 2) is often spelt with a capital letter, especially in the name of a country: *the Commonwealth of Australia.*
A SIMILAR WORD (for definition 2) is **federation**.

commotion *noun* a wild or noisy disturbance: *There was a great commotion when the dog got into the chicken shed.*

communal *adjective* shared or used by several people: *The hostel has a communal kitchen where anybody can make meals at any time.*

commune /*say* **kom**-yoohn/ *noun* a group of people who live together, sharing their property and work, and following their own rules and standards.

A SIMILAR WORD is **collective**.

communicate *verb*
1. If you **communicate** with someone, you get in touch with them, either by writing, telephoning or speaking to them directly: *We will communicate with the committee about this matter.* 2. If people **communicate** with each other, they understand each other: *Somehow I feel we're just not communicating.*
□ **communicator**, *noun*

communication *noun*
1. the passing on or sharing of thoughts, ideas or information. 2. something that is communicated, such as a piece of news. 3. **communications**, ways of passing on information, such as computers, telephone, radio, and television: *With modern communications such as the internet, many people can work from home.*

communion *noun* the sharing of thoughts, feelings or interests: *a communion of spirits.*

communiqué /*say* kuh-**myooh**-nuh-kay/ *noun* an official news report.

☑ SPELLING TIP Remember that the ending is spelt *qué*, giving a 'kay' sound. This is because this word comes from French.

communism *noun*
1. a way of living in which all property is owned equally by all the people in a society. 2. a way of organising a country, in which there is only one political party and all trade and business is run by the government.
□ **communist**, *adjective* –**communist**, *noun*

COMPARE this with **capitalism**.

community *noun* (*plural* **communities**)
1. a group of people who live in one area, have the same government, and often share a common history or culture. 2. a group of people within a society with a shared ethnic or cultural background.

community centre *noun* a building in which members of a community meet for various social activities relating to health, entertainment and relaxation.

commute *verb* If you **commute**, you travel a long distance to work from your home and back again each day: *Now that we live close to the city, Dad doesn't have to commute.*

WORD HISTORY from a Latin word meaning 'change wholly'

compact *adjective* /*say* kom-**pakt**, **kom**-pakt/
1. not taking up much space: *The cubbyhouse is compact but we can fit everything we want in there.* 2. packed closely and tightly beside each other.
–*verb* /*say* kom-**pakt**/ 3. To **compact** things is to crush them closely together: *A huge machine compacts all the rubbish.*
–*noun* /*say* **kom**-pakt/ 4. a small flat case which holds face powder and a mirror.

compact disc *noun* a small disc for storing information which can be read by the beam of a laser and then sent to a sound system, a computer, or a television set.

THE ABBREVIATION is **CD**.

companion *noun* someone who goes out with or spends time with another: *We all wondered who her mysterious companion was.*
☐ **companionship**, *noun*

company /*say* **kum**-puh-nee/ *noun* (*plural* **companies**)
1. an organisation involved in the buying and selling of goods or providing a service: *Dad works for a car manufacturing company.* **2.** a group of people brought together for a particular purpose: *an amateur theatrical company.* **3.** a group of soldiers forming part of an army.

SIMILAR WORDS (for definition 1) are **business**, **firm**, **enterprise** and **operation**.

comparative *adjective*
1. studying the similarities and differences between things: *a comparative look at customs from different countries.* **2.** judged by comparison: *After his early struggles he lived a life of comparative luxury.* **3.** having to do with the form of an adjective or adverb which expresses a greater degree: *'Harder' is the comparative form of 'hard' and 'more exactly' is the comparative form of 'exactly'.*

A SIMILAR WORD (for definition 2) is **relative**.
COMPARE definition 3 with **superlative** (definition 2). See also the Grammar and Punctuation Guide appendix.

☑ SPELLING TIP Remember that the last part of **comparative** is spelt *ative* (not *itive*).

compare /*say* kuhm-**pair**/ *verb*
1. If you **compare** two or more things or **compare** one thing with another, you examine them to see how much they are alike: *I compared the samples of handwriting.* **2.** If something **compares** with something else, it is as good as the other thing: *These paintings compare with any in the world.*
☐ **comparison** /*say* kuhm-**pa**-ruh-suhn/, *noun*

compartment *noun* a separate room or part: *We got into the railway compartment nearest the guard.*

compass /*say* **kum**-puhs/ *noun*
1. an instrument with a magnetic needle pointing to north which is used to find directions. **2.** range: *The compass of her voice is very wide – from a low alto to the top C of a soprano.* **3.** an instrument for measuring and drawing circles, which has two legs hinged together.

ANOTHER TERM (for definition 3) is a **pair of compasses**.
WORD HISTORY from a Latin word meaning 'step'

compassion *noun* a feeling of sorrow or pity for someone.
☐ **compassionate**, *adjective*

A SIMILAR WORD is **sympathy**.

compatible *adjective*
1. able to agree or exist side by side: *The various fire services have worked out a compatible system for fighting fires across the state.* **2.** able to be used together: *The two computers are compatible with each other*; *a compatible blood donor.*
☐ **compatibility**, *noun* –**compatibly**, *adverb*

☑ SPELLING TIP *Single letter alert*: only one *t*. Also remember the *-ible* ending (not *-able*).

compel *verb* (**compels**, **compelling**, **compelled**, **has compelled**) To **compel** is to force or pressure someone to do something: *Their dishonesty compelled me to speak out*; *The government compelled all young men to register for national service.*

☑ SPELLING TIP *Single letter alert*: only one *l* at the end. However, the *l* is doubled when you add *-ed* or *-ing*.

compensate *verb*
1. If you **compensate** someone for something, you pay them money or do something to make good a loss or wrong that they have suffered: *The insurance company compensated them for the losses in the fire.* **2.** If you **compensate** for treating someone badly, you do something to make up for it: *We offered to help with the cleaning up to compensate for arriving late.*
☐ **compensation**, *noun*

A SIMILAR WORD (for definition 1) is **recompense**.

compere /*say* **kom**-pair/ *noun*
1. someone who introduces the acts in a show: *a television compere.*
–*verb* **2.** When someone **comperes** a show, they introduce the acts.

☑ SPELLING TIP Remember the *ere* ending (which comes from French and gives an 'air' sound). Don't confuse **compere** with **compare** which is to see how similar things are.

compete *verb* To **compete** is to set yourself against at least one other person to gain or win something: *The commercial television stations compete with each other for advertising*; *to compete in a race.*
☐ **competitor**, *noun*

competent *adjective* able or skilful: *She is a competent driver.*
☐ **competence**, *noun* –**competency**, *noun*

competition *noun*
1. a test or situation in which people compete against each other. **2.** the people against whom someone competes: *The competition is not very strong this week – I bet we'll win!*

competitive *adjective*
1. very eager to do better than other people: *I don't like playing chess with my brother – he's so*

competitive and has to win every time. **2.** having to do with or decided by competition: *a competitive market.*

compile *verb* When you **compile** information, you collect it and put it together into one list, account or book.
☐ **compilation**, *noun* –**compiler**, *noun*

complacent *adjective* pleased or satisfied with yourself.
☐ **complacency**, *noun* –**complacently**, *adverb*

complain *verb*
1. If you **complain**, you say that you are not happy or pleased about something: *The neighbours complained about the noise.* **2.** If you **complain** of a certain symptom, you tell a doctor about what you are experiencing: *The patient complained of intense itching in the big toe of her right foot.*

complaint *noun*
1. an expression of dissatisfaction, blame or pain: *We made a complaint about the long delay*; *She worked all day in the canteen without complaint.* **2.** a sickness or illness.

complement *noun* /*say* **kom**-pluh-muhnt/
1. something which completes or makes perfect: *The music was a beautiful complement to the words of the song.* **2.** the number that is needed: *We need another two speakers to reach the full complement for the debating teams.* **3.** in geometry, the angle needed to bring a given angle to a right angle.
–*verb* /*say* **kom**-pluh-ment/ **4.** If something **complements** something else, it goes with it or completes it: *Pale blue clothes complement her fair skin.*
☐ **complementary**, *adjective*

☑ SPELLING TIP Remember the *e* in the middle of **complement**. Don't confuse it with **compliment** (with an *i*), which is something you say or do to praise someone. Take care also with **complementary** and **complimentary**. **Complementary** describes something which completes or brings the best out of something else (*complementary accessories*), and **complimentary** means 'free' (*complimentary tickets*) or 'relating to a compliment' (*complimentary remarks*).

complete *adjective*
1. having all its parts: *I have a complete set of cards.* **2.** finished and ready: *Can you have the report complete by Friday?* **3.** total or absolute: *Your bedroom is a complete mess.*
–*verb* **4.** If you **complete** something, you finish it: *He hopes to complete his studies next year.* **5.** If you **complete** something, you supply what is missing: *You'll need to add a verb to complete the sentence.*
☐ **completely**, *adverb* –**completion**, *noun*

complex *adjective*
1. made up of many different parts that are connected to each other: *The complex pattern in this weaving makes it a work of art.* **2.** difficult to understand: *This is a complex matter and it is not obvious who is in the right.*
–*noun* **3.** a group of buildings or shops: *a shopping complex.* **4.** *Rather informal* a fixed idea, often of concern: *He has a complex about his height.*
☐ **complexity**, *noun*

complexion *noun* the colour and appearance of your skin, especially of your face.

compliant /*say* kuhm-**pluy**-uhnt/ *adjective* agreeable or willing to do what is asked or needed.
☐ **compliance**, *noun*

complicate *verb* If you **complicate** something, you make it harder to understand or deal with: *She complicated the story by including every tiny detail.*
☐ **complicated**, *adjective* –**complication**, *noun*

WORD HISTORY from a Latin word meaning 'folded together'

complicity *noun* the state of being a partner or taking part in doing something which is wrong: *He was accused of complicity in the bank robbery because he drove the getaway car.*

compliment *noun* /*say* **kom**-pluh-muhnt/
1. words or actions expressing praise and admiration: *She paid me a compliment about the poem I wrote.*
–*verb* /*say* **kom**-pluh-ment/ **2.** If you **compliment** someone, you praise them.

☑ SPELLING TIP Remember the *i* in the middle of **compliment**. See the note at **complement**.

complimentary *adjective*
1. expressing praise or admiration: *a complimentary review.* **2.** free: *a complimentary drink.*

comply *verb* (**complies**, **complying**, **complied**, **has complied**) If you **comply** with a request, wish, command or rule, you act in agreement with it.

component *noun* a part of a whole: *Fruit is an important component of our diet.*
☐ **component**, *adjective*

compose *verb*
1. If you **compose** music or poetry, you make it up and write it: *Beethoven composed nine symphonies.*
–*phrase* **2. be composed of**, to be made up of or formed from: *Toffee is composed of sugar and water.* **3. compose yourself**, to make your mind and body quiet and calm.
☐ **composer**, *noun*

composite /*say* **kom**-puh-zuht/ *noun* something made up of different parts.
☐ **composite**, *adjective*: *The hero of the film is a composite character of many who fought for the revolution.*

composition *noun*
1. the putting together of parts to make a whole. **2.** the way in which parts are combined: *What is the composition of toffee?* **3.** something that has been composed, such as a piece of music.

compost *noun* a mixture of rotting materials, like old vegetables, leaves and animal waste, used to enrich the soil.

composure /*say* kuhm-**poh**-zhuh/ *noun* calmness of mind.

compound[1] *adjective* /*say* **kom**-pownd/
1. A **compound** word is made up of two or more parts: *'Seatbelt' is a compound word.*
–*noun* /*say* **kom**-pownd/ **2.** a chemical substance made by joining two or more chemicals: *Salt is a compound of sodium and chlorine.* **3.** a mixture: *Their decision to leave was a compound of a few anxieties – the place was too small, it was near a busy road and the landlord had put up the rent.*
–*verb* /*say* kuhm-**pownd**/ **4.** To **compound** something is to add to it or increase it: *This has just compounded their problems.*

compound[2] /*say* **kom**-pownd/ *noun* a closed-off area containing a building or a group of buildings.

compound verb *noun* a verb made up of more than one verb as *am running* or *might have been killed*.

SEE ALSO **participle** and **auxiliary verb**, as well as the Grammar and Punctuation Guide appendix.

comprehend *verb* If you **comprehend** something, you understand its meaning: *I can't comprehend this question.*
□ **comprehensible**, *adjective*

WORD HISTORY from a Latin word meaning 'seize'

comprehension *noun*
1. the ability to understand or the act of understanding: *My grandfather has no comprehension of how computers work.* **2.** a school exercise in reading and understanding, usually tested by a set of short questions.

compress *verb*
1. If you **compress** something, you press it or squeeze it so that it takes up less space: *The gas in the cylinder is compressed.* **2.** If you **compress** something such as a piece of writing, you make it shorter while still keeping the same structure: *I originally wrote six pages but I compressed it into three.*
□ **compression**, *noun*

comprise *verb* To **comprise** is to include or be made up of: *The library comprises several rooms.*

compromise /*say* **kom**-pruh-muyz/ *noun*
1. the settlement of an argument by both sides agreeing to give way a bit: *The compromise was that he could go to the party if he finished his homework first.*
–*verb* **2.** If you **compromise**, you agree to accept less than you originally wanted: *You have to be willing to compromise in your dealings with other people.* **3.** If someone **compromises** something, they do something which puts it in doubt or danger: *We mustn't compromise quality for the sake of saving time.*

compulsion *noun*
1. the use of force or pressure: *to act under compulsion.* **2.** a strong feeling that you have to do something, even though you know it may be harmful.

compulsory *adjective* If something is **compulsory**, you have to do it whether you want to or not: *In some countries voting is compulsory for all citizens.*

THE OPPOSITE is **optional** or **voluntary**.

compute *verb* To **compute** something mathematical is to calculate it: *Use the calculator to compute the answer to the question.*
□ **computation**, *noun*

computer *noun* an electronic machine which stores and gives out information, and does calculations very quickly, according to a set of instructions called a program.

computer game *noun* a game that is played on a computer.

computerise *verb*
1. To **computerise** data is to put it into a binary format and store it on a computer. **2.** To **computerise** a place, such as an office, is to bring in computers to be used for the work done there.

ANOTHER SPELLING is **computerize**.

computer terminal *noun* a keyboard and screen connected to a computer.

THE SHORT FORM of this is **terminal**.

comrade *noun Rather old-fashioned* a close friend.
□ **comradeship**, *noun*

WORD HISTORY from a Latin word meaning 'chamber' or 'room'

con *verb* (**cons**, **conning**, **conned**, **has conned**) *Informal* If you **con** someone, you trick or cheat them.
□ **con**, *noun*: *just a big con.*

WORD HISTORY a shortened form of *confidence trick*

concave *adjective* hollow and curved like the inside of a circle: *The concave mirrors in the sideshow made us look short and fat.*

THE OPPOSITE is **convex**.

conceal *verb*
1. If you **conceal** something, you hide it: *She concealed the book in her bag.* **2.** If you **conceal** something such as facts or emotions, you keep them secret from other people: *We promised to conceal what he had told us*; *She tried to conceal her delight at the news.*
☐ **concealment**, *noun*

☑ SPELLING TIP Remember that there is no seal **concealed** in this word. The last syllable of **conceal** is spelt *ceal*.

concede *verb*
1. If you **concede** something, you admit that it is true: *In the end I had to concede that I was mistaken.* **2.** If you **concede** to someone, you allow them to have or do something: *Eventually Mum conceded me the right to choose the program on TV.*
☐ **concession**, *noun* something given or conceded.

conceit *noun* pride in yourself and your own importance or ability.
☐ **conceited**, *adjective*

☑ SPELLING TIP Remember that **conceit** has two *c*'s – one at the start of the word (giving a 'k' sound) and one in the middle (giving an *s* sound). Also don't forget that it has *ei* (to spell the 'ee' sound) following the *c*. This follows the rule that *i* comes before *e* except after *c*.

conceive *verb*
1. If someone **conceives** a plan or idea, they think of it or invent it: *He conceived a brilliant way to solve the design problems of the building.* **2.** If a woman **conceives**, she becomes pregnant.
☐ **conceivable**, *adjective*

☑ SPELLING TIP Remember that **conceive** has two *c*'s – one at the start of the word (giving a 'k' sound) and one in the middle (giving an *s* sound). Also don't forget that it has *ei* (to spell the 'ee' sound) following the *c*. This follows the rule that *i* comes before *e* except after *c*.

concentrate *verb*
1. If you **concentrate**, you give all your attention to a particular matter: *Be quiet, I'm trying to concentrate on my homework.* **2.** To **concentrate** something is to direct it towards one point: *We concentrated the light from our torches to where we could hear the noise.* **3.** To **concentrate** a substance is to make it stronger or purer, usually by removing liquid: *concentrated detergent.*
–*noun* **4.** a substance that has been made stronger by removing liquid from it.
☐ **concentration**, *noun*

concentration camp *noun* a prison camp for prisoners of war or enemies of a country.

concentric *adjective* If two or more circles are **concentric**, they have the same centre: *The teacher told us to draw three concentric circles with our compasses by leaving the point in the same spot but moving the other end out.*

concept *noun* a general idea or understanding of something: *The concept of digging half a hole is nonsense.*
☐ **conceptual**, *adjective*

conception *noun*
1. an idea or thought: *His conception of how the room should be arranged is quite different from mine.* **2.** the beginning of pregnancy, or the act of conceiving a child.

concern *verb*
1. If something **concerns** you, it relates to you or involves you: *This announcement concerns the whole school.*
–*noun* **2.** a matter of interest or importance: *The environment has always been a concern of mine.* **3.** worry or anxiety: *The father's concern for his child's safety was obvious.*
☐ **concerned**, *adjective*: *I am very concerned about your health.*

concert *noun* a public musical performance by one or more musicians or other performers.

concertina *noun* a small musical instrument like an accordion.

concerto /*say* kuhn-**cher**-toh/ *noun* (*plural* **concertos** *or* **concerti** /*say* kuhn-**cher**-tee/) a piece of music for one or more solo instruments, such as a piano or violin, and an orchestra.

☑ SPELLING TIP In spite of the different sound, you could think of this word as being spelt *concert* with an *o* added at the end. In fact, **concerto** is an Italian word which explains the 'ch' sound for the *c* spelling in the middle.

conciliate *verb* To **conciliate** is to try in a calm and friendly way to end a disagreement between two people or groups.
☐ **conciliation**, *noun* a way of working out arguments, especially between employees and employers. –**conciliator**, *noun* –**conciliatory**, *adjective*

A SIMILAR WORD is **reconcile**.

concise *adjective* If something is expressed in a **concise** way, it is expressed clearly without using any unnecessary words: *We had to write a concise report on our weekend in half a page.*
☐ **concisely**, *adverb* –**conciseness**, *noun*

WORD HISTORY from a Latin word meaning 'cut up' or 'cut off'

conclude *verb*
1. If you **conclude**, you finish something or bring it to an end: *After a song by the school choir, the concert concluded*; *She concluded her talk by thanking us all for coming.* **2.** If you **conclude** that something is the case, you decide or deduce

from the facts that it is so: *She concluded that the butler was the murderer.*
☐ **conclusion**, *noun* –**conclusive**, *adjective*

concoct *verb* If you **concoct** a story, account or excuse, you make it up or invent it.
☐ **concoction**, *noun*

WORD HISTORY from a Latin word meaning 'cooked together'

concrete *noun*
1. a mixture of cement, sand, water, and small stones, that hardens as it dries and is used in building.
–*adjective* **2.** based on actual facts or information, rather than ideas or feelings: *He offered sympathy, but no concrete suggestions about what I could do.*
–*verb* **3.** When you **concrete** something, you cover it with concrete: *Dad concreted a path through the garden.*

THE OPPOSITE (of definition 2) is **abstract**.

☑ SPELLING TIP Remember that the final part of **concrete** is spelt *ete* (although it sounds as though it could be spelt *eet* or *eat*). It might help if you think of some other familiar words that have the same spelling for this sound, such as *complete* and *compete*.

concrete noun *noun* a word which refers to something that our five senses (touch, sight, hearing, smell and taste) can pick up: *'disk', 'fork' and 'boa constrictor' are all concrete nouns.*

COMPARE this with **abstract noun**. See also the Grammar and Punctuation Guide appendix.

concubine /*say* **kong**-kyooh-buyn/ *noun* a wife after the first wife (in a society where a man can have more than one wife at the same time).

concur *verb* (**concurs**, **concurring**, **concurred**, **has concurred**) When you **concur**, you agree: *I concur with your view.*
☐ **concurrent**, *adjective* occurring together.: *concurrent events.* –**concurrence**, *noun* –**concurrently**, *adverb*

concussion *noun*
1. a shock, or violent shaking caused by a blow or collision. **2.** an injury of the brain or spine caused by a blow or fall.
☐ **concussed**, *adjective*

condemn /*say* kuhn-**dem**/ *verb*
1. If you **condemn** someone or something, you strongly express your disapproval of them: *The government condemned the actions of the terrorists.* **2.** If a local authority **condemns** a building, they state officially that it is no longer allowed to be used. **3.** If a judge **condemns** someone who has been found guilty of a crime, the judge says what the punishment is to be: *The prisoner was condemned to death.*
☐ **condemnation** /*say* kon-dem-**nay**-shuhn/, *noun*

☑ SPELLING TIP *Silent letter alert*: don't forget the silent *n* at the end.

condensation *noun*
1. the changing of a gas to a liquid or solid: *The condensation of steam from the shower covered the mirror.* **2.** a short version of a book, report, etc.: *This summary is a condensation of a much longer chapter.*

condense *verb*
1. If you **condense** a liquid, you make it thicker or reduce its volume: *The recipe used a tin of condensed milk.* **2.** If a gas **condenses**, it changes to a liquid or solid: *The mist condensed into large drops.* **3.** To **condense** something is to say or write it in fewer words: *The television show condensed the town's history into just a few minutes.*
☐ **condenser**, *noun*

condescend *verb* If someone **condescends** to do something, they do it even though they think that they are really too important for it: *It's not often that the boss condescends to have lunch with the workers.*
☐ **condescending**, *adjective*

☑ SPELLING TIP *Silent letter alert*: don't forget the silent *c* after the *s*. This is the same as in the word *descend* (meaning 'to go down') which is included in **condescend**.

condition *noun*
1. the state of someone or something: *He was in superb condition after training for months*; *The house was in such bad condition it was better to pull it down.* **2.** anything that has to be done before another thing can be done: *A condition of going into the bowling club is that men have to be wearing a shirt and shoes – and pants.*
–*verb* **3.** To **condition** someone is to put them in a fit state for something they are about to do or experience: *Living in the outback conditioned us to put up with hot weather.*
–*phrase* **4. on condition that**, if, or provided that.

conditional *adjective* depending on something else: *Going on the canoe trip was conditional on the weather being good.*

condolences *plural noun* the expressions of sympathy you make to someone when a relative or friend of theirs has just died: *We sent her our condolences on the death of her father.*
☐ **condolence**, *noun*: *letters of condolence.*

condone /*say* kuhn-**dohn**/ *verb* If you **condone** something, you pardon, excuse or overlook it: *I will never condone cruelty to animals.*

conduct *noun* /*say* **kon**-dukt/
1. someone's behaviour or way of acting: *polite conduct.*
–*verb* /*say* kuhn-**dukt**/ **2.** To **conduct** something is to manage it or carry it out: *The company*

conducted a well-planned campaign to launch their new shampoo. **3.** If you **conduct** an orchestra, you direct or lead it. **4.** If you **conduct** someone, you lead them or show the way: *She conducted the visitor to the principal's office*; *The guide conducted us on a tour of the museum.* **5.** If something **conducts** heat or electricity, it acts as a pathway for it: *Metals conduct heat efficiently.*
–*phrase* **6. conduct yourself**, to behave: *He conducted himself well today.*
☐ **conductibility**, *noun*

conductor *noun*
1. a leader or someone who shows the way. **2.** someone who sells tickets on a tram, train or bus. **3.** a person who directs the playing of an orchestra or chorus. **4.** something that easily conducts heat, electricity or sound: *Metal is a good conductor of heat.*

☑ SPELLING TIP Remember that the last part of **conductor** is spelt *or* (not *er*). If you think of the *o* being the shape of the coins a bus conductor collects that might help.

cone *noun*
1. a solid shape with a flat round bottom, whose sides meet at the top in a point. **2.** anything shaped like this: *Mum bought ice-cream cones at the shop.* **3.** the cone-like fruit of pine and fir trees.

confectionery *noun* sweets.
☐ **confectioner**, *noun*

confederacy *noun* (*plural* **confederacies**) a group of people or countries joined together for a common purpose.
☐ **confederate**, *noun* an ally. –**confederate**, *adjective* –**confederation**, *noun*

confer *verb* (**confers**, **conferring**, **conferred**, **has conferred**)
1. To **confer** something is to give it as a gift, favour or honour: *The governor conferred a medal for bravery on the firefighter.* **2.** To **confer** is to consult together: *They conferred for some time about where to plant the tree.*

conference *noun* a meeting arranged to discuss something important.

☑ SPELLING TIP Remember that there are three syllables in **conference**, although the middle one is sometimes not pronounced. It might help if you see that it is made up of *confer* (meaning 'to consult together') and the suffix *-ence* (used in some nouns to indicate a certain action).

confess *verb* If you **confess**, you admit that you did something: *I confess that I ate the last piece of cake.*
☐ **confession**, *noun*

confetti *noun* small bits of coloured paper, thrown at weddings or carnivals.

☑ SPELLING TIP Remember that **confetti** has only one *f* and two *t*'s. This word comes from Italian where, as the *i* ending shows, it is a plural noun. However, in English it is usually considered singular and therefore is used with a singular verb: *This confetti is made of tiny coloured paper hearts.* Several other words that come from Italian end in this way, such as *spaghetti*.

confide *verb*
1. If you **confide** information to someone, you tell them something that you do not want other people to know: *He confided details of his business dealings to his lawyer.*
–*phrase* **2. confide in**, to tell someone about your problems or secrets: *She seemed upset and asked if she could confide in me.*

confidence *noun*
1. trust in someone. **2.** a belief in yourself and what you can do: *She spoke before the audience with confidence.* **3.** a secret: *It was not wise to reveal those confidences to a stranger.*
–*phrase* **4. in confidence**, as a secret or private matter: *I told him that in confidence.*

confident *adjective* If you are **confident**, you are sure: *I am confident that the weather will improve soon.*

confidential *adjective* secret or private: *Her confidential records were lost in the fire.*
☐ **confidentially**, *adverb*

confine *verb*
1. If you **confine** something, you keep it within certain limits: *You need to confine your eating of sweet food to only a small amount each day.* **2.** If someone is **confined** in a certain place, they are kept or detained there: *She was confined to bed for three days.*
☐ **confinement**, *noun*

confirm *verb*
1. If you **confirm** arrangements, you state that you will certainly go ahead with them: *Mum sent a deposit to confirm our booking of the holiday house.* **2.** If something **confirms** what you already thought or suspected, it proves that you were right: *His performance confirmed my opinion that he was a good batsman.*
☐ **confirmation**, *noun*

confiscate *verb* If someone in authority **confiscates** something, they take it and keep it: *The teacher confiscated my whistle till the end of term.*
☐ **confiscation**, *noun*

WORD HISTORY from a Latin word meaning 'put away in a chest'

conflict *noun* /*say* **kon**-flikt/
1. a fight or disagreement: *a conflict between nations.*
–*verb* /*say* kuhn-**flikt**/ **2.** If one thing **conflicts** with another, it disagrees with it: *What you've told us conflicts with your brother's story of what happened.*

conform *verb* If you **conform**, you behave in the way that people expect you to: *He refused to conform to the rules.*
☐ **conformist**, *noun* –**conformity**, *noun*

confront *verb*
1. If you **confront** someone about something, you speak to them openly about something you are in disagreement about: *He tried to lie, until his mother confronted him with the evidence.* **2.** If something **confronts** you, you are faced with a difficult or unpleasant situation and you have to deal with it: *A hard decision confronted her.*
☐ **confrontation**, *noun*: *an angry confrontation.*

confuse *verb*
1. If you **confuse** people or things, you mistake one for the other: *I often confuse him with his brother – they look so much alike.* **2.** If someone or something **confuses** you, they make you feel puzzled or mixed up: *The more she tried to explain, the more she confused me.*
☐ **confused**, *adjective*: *a confused account of events.* –**confusion**, *noun*

A SIMILAR WORD (for definition 2) is **perplex**.

congeal *verb* When a liquid **congeals**, it thickens or becomes solid: *There was a layer of congealed fat on the bottom of the frying pan.*

☑ SPELLING TIP Remember that **congeal** has a *g* in the middle (giving a *j* sound). Also remember that the ending is spelt *eal* (not *eel*). It might help if you think of some other familiar words which have the same spelling for this sound, such as *meal*, *seal* and *appeal*.

congenial *adjective* pleasant or agreeable: *congenial surroundings*; *congenial friends.*
☐ **congeniality**, *noun* –**congenially**, *adverb*

congenital *adjective* If a medical condition is **congenital**, it has been there since the person was born.
☐ **congenitally**, *adverb*

congest *verb*
1. To **congest** something it to overfill it or overcrowd it: *Thousands of eager shoppers congested the shops during the sales.* **2.** To **congest** something is to block it up: *She had the flu and her chest was congested.*
☐ **congestion**, *noun*

congratulate *verb* If you **congratulate** someone, you tell them how pleased you are that they have done well or that something good has happened to them: *We congratulated him on his exam results.*
☐ **congratulation**, *noun*

congregate *verb* If people **congregate** somewhere, they gather there in large numbers: *Fans began congregating at the entrance to the sportsground in the early hours of the morning.*
☐ **congregation**, *noun*: *the congregation in the church.*

conifer /*say* **kon**-uh-fuh, **koh**-nuh-fuh/ *noun* an evergreen tree which produces cones, like the pine or fir.
☐ **coniferous** /*say* kuh-**nif**-uh-ruhs/, *adjective*

conjunction *noun* a word, such as 'and' or 'because', used for joining parts of a sentence.

WORD HISTORY from Latin words meaning 'with' and 'joining'
SEE the Grammar and Punctuation Guide appendix.

conjure /*say* **kun**-juh, **kon**juh/ *verb*
1. To **conjure** is to do magic tricks.
–*phrase* **2. conjure up**, **a.** to call or bring into existence by magic. **b.** to remember or bring to mind.
☐ **conjurer**, *noun*

ANOTHER SPELLING for **conjurer** is **conjuror**.

connect *verb*
1. If you **connect** two things, you join them together: *Connect this hose to the tap.*
–*phrase* **2. be connected with**, to have to do or be associated with: *James is connected with a birdwatching group.*
☐ **connection**, *noun* –**connective**, *adjective*

connoisseur /*say* kon-uh-**ser**/ *noun* someone who has a special interest in or knowledge of a particular subject: *a connoisseur of Japanese art*; *a connoisseur of exotic wines.*

☑ SPELLING TIP This word came into English from French (from a Latin word meaning 'come to know') and there are several difficult parts to remember. Concentrate on the double *n* and double *s* with the *oi* vowel combination (giving an 'uh' sound) coming in between. Then there is the *-eur* suffix, found in other words from French, such as *amateur* and *chauffeur*, which refers to a person who does something or has certain qualities.

conquer *verb*
1. If one country **conquers** another, it defeats it in a war. **2.** If you **conquer** something, you manage to control it, usually with an effort: *She seems to have conquered her fear of heights.*
☐ **conqueror**, *noun* –**conquest**, *noun*

☑ SPELLING TIP Remember the *qu* spelling for the 'k' sound in the middle and the *er* ending, and you will have **conquered** this word. Also don't forget that *-or* (not *-er*) is added to make **conqueror**.

conscience /*say* **kon**-shuhns/ *noun* the ability to see the difference between right and wrong in what you do.

☑ SPELLING TIP Remember that there is an *sc* in this word, spelling the 'sh' sound. It will help if you can see that it contains the word *science* although it is said in a different way. *Science* comes from the Latin word for 'knowledge' and the essential meaning of **conscience** is 'having the ability to know or judge'.

conscientious /*say* kon-shee-**en**-shuhs/ *adjective* If you are **conscientious**, you are always very careful to do good work: *She is too conscientious to leave a job unfinished.*
☐ **conscientiousness**, *noun*

☑ SPELLING TIP The adjective **conscientious** is formed from the noun *conscience*, with the addition of the suffix *-ious*. It therefore has a *sc* spelling for the 'sh' sound. See the note at **conscience**. Also remember the silent *i* in the suffix.

conscious /*say* **kon**-shuhs/ *adjective*
1. If you are **conscious** of something, you are aware of it: *I was conscious of a ringing in my ears.* **2.** To be **conscious** is to be aware of what is happening around you: *He was conscious during the medical procedure.*
☐ **consciousness**, *noun*

☑ SPELLING TIP Remember the *sci* spelling in this word, giving the 'sh' sound. Like the word *science*, **conscious** comes from the Latin word for 'knowledge'. If you think about the *sc* spelling in *science*, it will help you to spell **conscious**. Remember also the silent *i* before the *ous* ending.

conscript *verb* /*say* kuhn-**skript**/
1. If a government **conscripts** someone, they are forced to join the army, navy or air force.
–*noun* /*say* **kon**-skript/ **2.** someone who has been conscripted.
☐ **conscription**, *noun*

conscription *noun* the compulsory enrolment of people in the armed forces.

consecrate *verb* When a place, building or object is **consecrated**, it is officially declared to be holy: *The new building was consecrated by the bishop.*
☐ **consecration**, *noun*

consecutive /*say* kuhn-**sek**-yuh-tiv/ *adjective* following one after the other: *This is the third consecutive year of drought.*
☐ **consecutively**, *adverb*

consensus *noun* general agreement.

☑ SPELLING TIP Remember that the middle part of **consensus** is spelt *sen* (not *cen* as in the word *census*). Think about the spelling of *consent*. **Consensus** has much more to do with *consent* than with a *census*.

consent *verb* If you **consent** to something, you allow it or give your permission for it to happen: *Shona consented to be bridesmaid.*
☐ **consent**, *noun*: *I gave my consent to her request.*

consequence /*say* **kon**-suh-kwuhns/ *noun*
1. a result: *A consequence of their forgetfulness is that they are now in the rain without a tent.* **2.** importance or value: *a matter of no consequence.*

conservation *noun* the protection of natural areas, plants and animals, as well as buildings and objects of historical interest.
☐ **conservationist**, *noun*

☑ DO NOT CONFUSE **conservation** with **conversation**.

conservative *adjective* If someone is **conservative**, they are conventional in behaviour, dress and views and do not like new ideas or sudden change of any kind.
☐ **conservatism**, *noun* –**conservative**, *noun*

conservatorium *noun* a school where you learn music.

conservatory *noun* (*plural* **conservatories**) a room or building made of glass, where plants are displayed.

conserve *verb* /*say* kuhn-**serv**/
1. When you **conserve** something, you keep it from being lost or wasted: *to conserve water.*
–*noun* /*say* **kon**-serv/ **2.** a type of jam.

consider *verb*
1. If you **consider** something, you think carefully about it: *After considering all the suggestions, I think this is the best solution.* **2.** If you **consider** someone or something in a certain way, that is what you think or believe about them: *I consider Ann to be the best tennis player.*

considerable *adjective* large or important enough to think about: *a considerable sum of money.*
☐ **considerably**, *adverb*

considerate *adjective* thoughtful of other people's needs and feelings.

consideration *noun*
1. careful thought: *They gave a lot of consideration to the financial plight of the school.* **2.** something taken, or that should be taken, into account: *The cost of the car is a consideration.* **3.** thoughtfulness for others: *Her consideration for her old parents is a comfort to them.*

consist *verb* If something **consists** of various other things, it is made up of them: *The garden consists of several sections, each planted with flowers of a different colour.*

consistency *noun*
1. agreement or evenness between all the parts of something: *The teacher said that some of her work was good but it lacked consistency.* **2.** the

density, or degree of thickness: *The sauce had the consistency of honey.*
□ **consistent**, *adjective*: *a consistent effort.*

console[1] /*say* kuhn-**sohl**/ *verb* If you **console** someone, you comfort them or cheer them up: *He was very upset when his dog died and we could do nothing to console him.*
□ **consolation**, *noun*

console[2] /*say* **kon**-sohl/ *noun* a control panel, especially for a computer.

consonant *noun*
1. a speech sound made by blocking the flow of your breath with the tongue or lips. **2.** any letter of the alphabet, other than *a*, *e*, *i*, *o* or *u*.

COMPARE this with **vowel**. See also the Grammar and Punctuation Guide appendix.
WORD HISTORY from a Latin word meaning 'sounding together'

consort /*say* **kon**-sawt/ *noun* the husband or wife of a ruling queen or king.

conspicuous *adjective* noticeable or standing out: *She was conspicuous in the group because she was so tall.*

☑ SPELLING TIP Remember that there is no *k* in the word. The letter *c* alone gives the 'k' sound. Rap it out as *con+spic+u+ous*.

conspire *verb* If people **conspire**, they plan secretly together, especially to do something wrong or illegal: *The men conspired to bring down the king.*
□ **conspiracy**, *noun* (*plural* **conspiracies**) –**conspirator**, *noun* –**conspiratorial**, *adjective*

constable /*say* **kun**-stuh-buhl/ *noun* a police officer of the lowest rank.

WORD HISTORY from Latin words meaning 'count of the stable' or 'master of the horse'

constant *adjective*
1. continuing without stopping: *The rain has been constant for three days now.* **2.** *Rather old-fashioned* loyal and faithful: *She has been a constant friend.*
□ **constancy**, *noun* –**constantly**, *adverb*

WORD HISTORY from a Latin word meaning 'standing firm'

constellation *noun* a group of stars.

consternation *noun* shock and fear causing you to feel confused: *His face filled with consternation when he opened his credit card bill.*

constipation *noun* the unpleasant condition of not being able to empty the bowels regularly or easily.

constituency *noun* (*plural* **constituencies**) See **electorate**.
□ **constituent**, *noun*

constitute *verb* To **constitute** something is to make up or form it: *Her rudeness constitutes quite a problem.*

constitution *noun*
1. the health or condition of your body: *a racehorse with a strong constitution.* **2.** a set of basic rules for governing a state, society, or other organisation: *the Australian Constitution*; *the constitution of the basketball club.*
□ **constitutional**, *adjective*

constitutional monarchy *noun* (*plural* **constitutional monarchies**) a system of government where a king or queen is the head of state, but where the amount of power they have is limited by a constitution, and where power to govern is usually held by a parliament: *Australia, Canada and the United Kingdom are constitutional monarchies.*

constraint *noun*
1. something that restricts or controls the way you behave or what you can do at certain times: *If it were not for the constraint of needing to earn a living, I would spend my days travelling the world.* **2.** control or the keeping back of your natural feelings and impulses: *to act with constraint.*
□ **constrain**, *verb* to compel, or restrain. –**constrained**, *adjective*

constrict *verb* To **constrict** something is to make it tighter or narrower: *Sudden bright light constricts the pupils of the eyes.*
□ **constriction**, *noun*

THE OPPOSITE is **dilate**.

construct *verb* If you **construct** something, you build it or you make it by putting it together: *They constructed their house to withstand cyclones*; *The theory was constructed to explain all the available facts.*
□ **construction**, *noun*

constructive *adjective* helpful or useful: *If you haven't got anything constructive to say, don't say anything!*

consul *noun* an official sent by a government to represent it in a foreign country.
□ **consular**, *adjective* –**consulate**, *noun*

consult *verb* When you **consult** someone or something, you try to get advice from them: *to consult a lawyer*; *to consult the index of a book.*
□ **consultant**, *noun* –**consultation**, *noun*

consume *verb*
1. If you **consume** something, you eat or drink it: *to consume a huge meal.* **2.** To **consume** something is to use it up or destroy it: *The project consumed a lot of our time*; *The theatre was consumed by fire.*

consumer *noun* someone who buys and uses goods and services: *Some laws have been set up to protect consumers.*

THE OPPOSITE is a **producer**.

consumption *noun* the act of eating or using up: *consumption of meat*; *consumption of petrol.*

contact *noun* /*say* **kon**-takt/
1. a meeting or touching: *to come into contact*; *to make contact with an old friend.* **2.** the moving part of a switch that completes and breaks an electrical circuit. **3.** a useful person to meet: *a medical contact.*
–*verb* /*say* **kon**-takt, kuhn-**takt**/ **4.** When you **contact** someone, you telephone, email or write to them to tell or ask them something: *I'll contact you about the next meeting.*

contact lenses *plural noun* lenses to improve your sight, which fit closely over the iris or coloured part of your eye.

contagious /*say* kuhn-**tay**-juhs/ *adjective* easily spread from one person to another: *Measles is contagious and the whole class caught it*; *contagious laughter.*

contain *verb* If something **contains** something else, it has that thing inside it: *This jar contains jam*; *The film contains quite a bit of violence.*
☐ **containment**, *noun*

container *noun*
1. anything that can hold something: *Why don't you pour some of it into another container?* **2.** a very large box for carrying goods on ships or trucks.

container ship *noun* a ship that carries cargo in large containers.

contaminate *verb* To **contaminate** something is to make it dirty or impure: *The lake has been contaminated by chemicals from the factory.*
☐ **contamination**, *noun*

contemplate /*say* **kon**-tuhm-playt/ *verb*
1. If you **contemplate** something, you look at it or think about it carefully for a long time: *She contemplated the painting for several minutes.* **2.** If you **contemplate** doing something, you think that you may do it: *They are contemplating a trip to Europe next year.*
☐ **contemplation**, *noun* –**contemplative** /*say* **kon**-tuhm-play-tiv, kuhn-**tem**-pluh-tiv/, *adjective*

contemporary /*say* kuhn-**tem**-puh-ree, kuhn-**tem**-pree/ *adjective*
1. existing at the same time: *Contrary to what science fiction says, the dinosaurs were not contemporary with human beings.* **2.** modern or existing now: *My aunt knows everything about contemporary film-making techniques.*
☐ **contemporary**, *noun* (*plural* **contemporaries**) someone of about the same age as you.

contempt *noun* the feeling that someone or something is mean and disgraceful: *We had nothing but contempt for the kids who had vandalised our cubbyhouse.*

A SIMILAR WORD is **scorn**.

contemptible *adjective* deserving people's disgust: *Accusing your brother of stealing when you took the money yourself was a contemptible action.*

contemptuous /*say* kuhn-**temp**-chooh-uhs/ *adjective* showing dislike or disgust: *She was contemptuous of his untidy appearance and poor manners.*

SIMILAR WORDS are **scornful** and **supercilious**.

☑ SPELLING TIP Remember that **contemptuous** is formed from *contempt* with the adjective suffix *-uous* added. This will help you to remember the *tu* spelling (which gives a 'chooh' sound).

contend *verb*
1. If you have to **contend** with something such as a problem or difficulty, you have to deal with it: *The school has had to contend with vandals for a year now.* **2.** If you **contend** that something is the case, you state firmly that it is true, although other people argue that it is not: *He contends that he was not speeding.*
☐ **contender**, *noun* –**contention**, *noun*

content[1] /*say* **kon**-tent/ *noun*
1. the volume, capacity, or amount contained. **2. contents**, whatever is inside or contained in: *the contents of a bottle*; *The contents of a book are often listed at the front.*

content[2] /*say* kuhn-**tent**/ *adjective*
1. pleased or satisfied: *He is quite content to spend the afternoon at home.*
–*verb* **2.** If you **content** yourself with something, you are happy with or satisfied by that thing: *The principal contented himself with giving us a lecture rather than punishing us.*
☐ **contented**, *adjective* –**contentedly**, *adverb* –**contentment**, *noun*

contest *noun* /*say* **kon**-test/
1. a competition.
–*verb* /*say* kuhn-**test**/ To **contest** something is to **2.** try to get or win it: *She contested the seat in her electorate.* **3.** argue against or object to it: *The family contested the will.*
☐ **contestant**, *noun*

context *noun* the surrounding circumstances or words: *It is misleading to take my remark about the photograph out of context.*

continent *noun* one of the main land masses of the world: *You can think of Australia as either the smallest continent or the largest island.*
☐ **continental**, *adjective*

WORD HISTORY from a Latin word meaning 'holding together'

continental quilt *noun* See **doona**.

continual *adjective* happening over and over again: *We were annoyed by his continual lateness.*
□ **continually**, *adverb*

☑ DO NOT CONFUSE **continual** with **continuous** which means 'happening without interruption or break'.

continue *verb* To **continue** is to **1.** keep on: *They continued to talk late into the night.* **2.** go on after being interrupted: *They continued their conversation despite being told to go to sleep.* **3.** go on with: *Their continued their search for the missing papers for years.*
□ **continuation**, *noun*

continuous *adjective*
1. keeping on without stopping: *the continuous roar of the surf.* **2.** having to do with the form of a verb which shows that something is continuing, such as 'are searching' in *They are searching*.
□ **continuously**, *adverb*

☑ DO NOT CONFUSE **continuous** with **continual**.

SEE the Grammar and Punctuation Guide appendix (for definition 2).

WORD HISTORY from a Latin word meaning 'hanging together'

contort *verb*
1. To **contort** something is to twist it out of shape: *An expression of rage contorted her face.* **2.** If something **contorts**, it becomes twisted and no longer has its natural shape: *Her face contorted with pain.*
□ **contortion**, *noun* –**contortionist**, *noun*

A SIMILAR WORD is **distort**.

contour /*say* **kon**-taw, **kon**-too-uh/ *noun*
1. the outer shape or form: *the contours of the mountain range.* **2.** a line on a map joining points of equal height.

contra- *prefix* a word part meaning 'against', 'opposite', or 'opposing', as in *contradict*.

WORD HISTORY this prefix comes from Latin

contraband *noun* goods imported or exported illegally.

contraception *noun* the prevention of pregnancy.
□ **contraceptive**, *adjective* –**contraceptive**, *noun*

ANOTHER TERM for this is **birth control**.

contract *noun* /*say* **kon**-trakt/
1. an agreement, especially a legal one: *They signed the contract for buying the land.*
–*verb* /*say* kuhn-**trakt**/ **2.** If something **contracts**, it becomes smaller: *The metal of her ring had contracted in the cold and she couldn't get it off.* **3.** If you **contract** to do something, you sign a formal legal agreement stating that you will do it: *A catering company has contracted to supply the food for my grandfather's eightieth birthday dinner.*

contraction *noun*
1. a shortened form of a word, such as *can't* for *cannot*. **2.** one of the movements of a woman's womb during the birth of a baby.

SEE the Grammar and Punctuation Guide appendix (for definition 1).

contradict /*say* kon-truh-**dikt**/ *verb*
1. If you **contradict** someone, you say the opposite to what they have just said: *Whatever he says, you contradict him.* **2.** If two things **contradict** each other, they give opposite or different accounts of something: *My experience contradicts what you say.*
□ **contradiction**, *noun* –**contradictory**, *adjective*

☑ SPELLING TIP *Tricky 'uh' sound*: the middle vowel sound is spelt as an *a*. It might help if you see that **contradict** is made up of *contra* (the Latin word for 'against' which is used in English as a prefix) and *dict* (which is a form of the Latin word for 'speak' or 'say').

contralto *noun*
1. the lowest range of musical notes which can be sung by a female singer. **2.** a woman who sings contralto.

ANOTHER WORD for this is **alto**.
NOTE The **contralto** range is higher than a **tenor, baritone** or **bass** but lower than a **soprano**.

contraption *noun* a complicated device or piece of machinery: *Where's that spinning contraption for drying the salad?*

A SIMILAR WORD is **device**.

contrary *adjective*
1. /*say* **kon**-truh-ree/ opposed or different: *Your version of what happened is contrary to mine.*
2. /*say* kuhn-**trair**-ree, **kon**-truh-ree/ awkward and difficult to get on with: *a contrary child.*
–*noun* /*say* **kon**-truh-ree/ **3.** the opposite: *You say she is innocent, but I can prove the contrary.*
–*phrase* /*say* **kon**-truh-ree/ **4. on the contrary**, in opposition to what has been said: *'A good pet has to be a large animal, like a cat or dog.' 'On the contrary, I think that an axolotl is a very good pet.'*.

contrast *verb* /*say* kuhn-**trahst**/
1. If two things **contrast**, they show a difference in comparison: *The warmth of the cottage contrasted with the wintry weather outside.*
–*noun* /*say* **kon**-trahst/ **2.** a marked difference: *a contrast in styles*; *a contrast in attitudes.*

contribute /*say* kuhn-**trib**-yooht/ *verb*
1. If you **contribute** to something, you give or pay a share towards it: *They contributed to the school building fund.* **2.** If you **contribute** something you have written to a a magazine or newspaper, you write it and give it to them to be published: *Bruno contributed a poem to the school magazine.*
☐ **contribution**, *noun* –**contributor**, *noun*

contrite /*say* kuhn-**truyt**/ *adjective* feeling sorry or sad that you have done something wrong: *He was very contrite about leaving the gate open and letting the chickens escape.*
☐ **contritely**, *adverb* –**contrition** /*say* kuhn-**trish**-uhn/, *noun*

contrive *verb* If you **contrive** to do something, you cleverly plan for it to happen: *We contrived to be waiting at the station when his train arrived.*
☐ **contrivance**, *noun*

control *verb* (**controls**, **controlling**, **controlled**, **has controlled**)
1. If you **control** someone or something, you have power or influence over them and make decisions about what is to happen to them: *He controls how much food the fish get each day.* **2.** To **control** something is to change it as necessary: *This knob controls the volume.*
–*noun* **3.** command or check: *You have to show your dog that you have control.* **4.** a device that allows you to change something such as temperature or speed.
–*phrase* **5. control yourself**, to force yourself to act calmly even though you are angry or upset. **6. in control**, **a.** in charge: *Who's in control here?* **b.** successfully managed: *She was able to keep her feelings in control.* **7. out of control**, no longer able to be controlled or stopped: *The bushfires are completely out of control.* **8. under control**, **a.** able to be controlled: *You must keep your dog under control in the park.* **b.** being dealt with in a suitable way: *Are the arrangements for the wedding under control?*
☐ **controllable**, *adjective* –**controller**, *noun*

> ☑ SPELLING TIP *Single letter alert*: one *l* at the end. However, when you add *-ed* or *-ing*, the *l* is doubled.

controversy /*say* **kon**-truh-ver-see, kuhn-**trov**-uh-see/ *noun* (*plural* **controversies**) an argument or difference of opinion: *The art gallery's purchase of the abstract painting was a matter of controversy.*
☐ **controversial**, *adjective*

conundrum /*say* kuh-**nun**-druhm/ *noun* a riddle or puzzle.

convalesce /*say* kon-vuh-**les**/ *verb* If someone is **convalescing**, they are growing stronger after an illness: *They took her to the mountains so she could convalesce in the cool, clean air.*
☐ **convalescence**, *noun* –**convalescent**, *adjective* –**convalescent**, *noun*

> ☑ SPELLING TIP *Silent letter alert*: don't forget the *c* in the *esce* ending. **Convalesce** comes from the Latin *convalescere* meaning 'to grow strong'. If you think to yourself that 'Con and Val are getting well', you will remember the spelling of the first two syllables!

convection *noun* the spreading of heat by the movement of heated air or water.
☐ **convector**, *noun*

convene *verb* If you **convene** a meeting, you arrange it.
☐ **convener**, *noun*

> ☑ SPELLING TIP Remember that the ending is *ene* (not *een*). Some other words with the same spelling for this sound are *serene* and *gangrene*.

convenient *adjective* suited to your needs: *Let's choose a training time that is convenient for everybody.*
☐ **convenience**, *noun*

> ☑ SPELLING TIP *Tricky vowel sounds*: the second vowel sound is spelt with a single *e* (although it gives an 'ee' sound).

convent *noun*
1. a group of buildings where nuns live. **2.** a school run by nuns.

convention *noun*
1. a large meeting: *This year the annual convention will be held in Perth.* **2.** a rule, often unwritten, which everyone accepts: *There is a convention that where cars are going from two lanes to one, they take turns to move into the one lane.*
☐ **conventional**, *adjective*

converge *verb* If things **converge**, they move towards each other, or towards a common point: *A number of roads converge at the intersection.*

conversation *noun* talk among people: *During the cricket, we had a conversation about the best players.*
☐ **conversational**, *adjective* –**conversationalist**, *noun*

> ☑ DO NOT CONFUSE **conversation** with **conservation**.

converse[1] /*say* kuhn-**vers**/ *verb* When you **converse** with someone, you talk with them: *They conversed happily about their dogs.*

converse[2] /*say* **kon**-vers/ *noun* the opposite: *There can be no winners unless there are losers and the converse is also true.*
☐ **conversely**, *adverb*

convert *verb* /*say* kuhn-**vert**/
1. If you **convert** something, you change it completely: *Jack converted the garage into a pottery studio.* **2.** If someone **converts** you, they change your belief in or support of something: *We converted her from Rugby to Aussie Rules.*

–*noun* /*say* **kon**-vert/ **3.** someone who has changed their religion or other beliefs.
□ **convertible**, *adjective* able to be changed. –**conversion**, *noun*

convex *adjective* curved or bulging outwards: *The convex mirror at the show made us look long and gangly.*
□ **convexity**, *noun*

THE OPPOSITE is **concave.**

convey /*say* kuhn-**vay**/ *verb* To **convey** something is to carry it: *A small ferry conveyed our group across the river*; *Her speech conveyed a message of hope.*
□ **conveyable**, *adjective*

WORD HISTORY from a Latin word meaning 'way' or 'journey'

convict *verb* /*say* kuhn-**vikt**/
1. If a judge or jury **convicts** someone of a crime, they find that person to be guilty of it: *He was convicted of murder and sent to jail.*
–*noun* /*say* **kon**-vikt/ **2.** someone who has been found guilty of a crime: *Convicts used to be sent from England to Australia to serve their sentence.*

THE OPPOSITE of definition 1 is **acquit**

conviction *noun*
1. the occasion of being found guilty: *She has a conviction for speeding.* **2.** strong belief: *My firm conviction is that we should stay and help.*

convince *verb*
1. If someone **convinces** you that something is so, they make you believe that it is true: *She convinced me that she was telling the truth.* **2.** If someone **convinces** you to do something, they persuade you to do it: *I convinced them to change the day for the picnic to Saturday.*
□ **convincing**, *adjective* –**convincingly**, *adverb*

convoy *noun* a number of ships or vehicles travelling together, sometimes for protection: *a convoy of trucks.*

cooee /*say* **koo**-ee, koo-**ee**/ *noun* a long, loud call used to signal someone, especially when you are in the bush.

WORD HISTORY from an Aboriginal language of New South Wales called Dharug

cook *verb*
1. If you **cook** food, you prepare it by boiling, baking, and so on.
–*noun* **2.** someone who cooks or prepares food.
□ **cookery**, **cooking**, *noun*

cookie *noun*
1. a sweet biscuit. **2.** *Informal* a person: *a smart cookie.* **3.** in computers, a small file sent by a website to a user's own computer so that the website will recognise the user when they log on to that site again.

NOTE This word (as in definition 1) is used mainly in American English.

cool *adjective*
1. If something is **cool**, it has a fairly low temperature: *a cool drink.* **2.** If someone is **cool**, they are **a.** calm or unexcited: *Rata remained cool as she was announced as the winner.* **b.** unfriendly: *to be cool towards someone you dislike.* **3.** You can describe something as **cool** when it is attractive or fashionable: *I'm saving up for a pair of cool new jeans.*
–*phrase* **4. cool down**, **a.** to become or make cool. **b.** to become less angry.
□ **cool**, *noun* –**coolly**, *adverb* –**cooling**, *adjective*

coolamon /*say* **kooh**-luh-mon/ *noun* a wooden dish traditionally used by Aboriginal people.

WORD HISTORY from an Aboriginal language of New South Wales called Kamilaroi

coolibah /*say* **kooh**-luh-bah/ *noun* a gum tree found in inland Australia which has short, twisted branches.

ANOTHER SPELLING is **coolabah.**
WORD HISTORY from an Aboriginal language of New South Wales called Yuwaalaraay

coop *noun*
1. a small cage for hens.
–*verb in the phrase* **2. coop up**, to keep in a small place: *They were cooped up in the hut until it stopped raining.*

cooperate /*say* koh-**op**-uh-rayt/ *verb*
1. If you **cooperate** with someone, you work together with them to achieve something: *The three of us cooperated on the school project.* **2.** If you **cooperate**, you are helpful: *We cooperated by helping with the cleaning up after the fete.*
□ **cooperation**, *noun* –**cooperative**, *adjective*

ANOTHER FORM is **co-operate.**

coordinate *verb* /*say* koh-**aw**-duh-nayt/
1. If you **coordinate** things, you combine them or put them together: *It can be hard to coordinate all the different things the people in my family want to do.* **2.** Things **coordinate** if they match or go well together: *Aunt Dot always makes sure that her shoes and handbag coordinate.* **3.** To **coordinate** things is to move them together smoothly: *He has a major problem coordinating his feet.*
–*noun* /*say* koh-**aw**-duh-nuht/ **4.** in mathematics, any of the numbers which limit the position of a point, line, and so on, by reference to a fixed figure, system of lines, and so on.
□ **coordination**, *noun* –**coordinator**, *noun*

ANOTHER FORM is **co-ordinate.**

cop *Informal*
–*noun* **1.** a member of the police force.
–*verb* (**cops**, **copping**, **copped**, **has copped**) **2.** To **cop** something is to get it: *I copped a lecture for cheating.*
–*phrase* **3. cop it**, to get into trouble.

cope *verb* If you **cope** with something, you manage to deal with it successfully although it might be rather difficult: *She coped well with the increased amount of work.*

copper *noun*
1. a fairly soft, reddish-brown metal. **2.** a reddish-brown colour.
☐ **copper**, *adjective*

copulate *verb* To **copulate** is to have sexual intercourse.
☐ **copulation**, *noun*

copy *noun* (*plural* **copies**)
1. something which is made the same as something else: *I made two copies of my letter.* **2.** a single example of the same book or magazine.
–*verb* (**copies**, **copying**, **copied**, **has copied**) **3.** If you **copy** someone, you do the same thing as them: *He copied his brother and became a physicist.* **4.** If you **copy** something, you make another thing that is exactly like it: *to copy a painting.*

copyright *noun* the legal right you have to protect work that you write or compose, and to control who can copy it.

coral *noun* the hard, colourful shapes formed from the skeletons of small sea animals.

coral bleaching *noun* the whitening of coral that occurs when the algae which gives the coral its colour is expelled from the coral, usually because of an increase in ocean temperature that causes the algae to become toxic.

cord *noun*
1. a strong string, not as thick as rope. **2.** wire, which is protected by cloth or plastic, used to connect electrical goods to a power point.

> ANOTHER WORD (for definition 2) is **flex** (definition 2).
> WORD HISTORY from a Greek word meaning 'gut'

> ☑ SPELLING TIP Don't confuse the spelling of **cord** with **chord** which sounds the same. A **chord** is a group of musical notes.

cordial *adjective*
1. If someone is **cordial**, they are warmly friendly: *They were very cordial and came out to the car to greet us.*
–*noun* **2.** a fruit-flavoured syrup that you mix with water to make a drink.
☐ **cordiality**, *noun* –**cordially**, *adverb*

corduroy /*say* **kaw**-duh-roy, **kaw**-juh-roy/ *noun* a cotton material with a pattern of ridges.

core *noun*
1. the inner or middle part, especially of fruit. **2.** the central or innermost, or essential part of anything.
☐ **core**, *adjective* central: *Every student must take three core subjects.*

corgi /*say* **kaw**-gee/ *noun* (*plural* **corgis**) a dog with short legs and a thick body.

coriander /*say* ko-ree-**an**-duh/ *noun* a small plant with strong-smelling, seedlike fruit, used in cooking and medicine.

cork *noun*
1. the outer bark of a type of tree, used for making stoppers of bottles. **2.** a piece of cork, or other material (such as rubber), used as a stopper for a bottle.

corkscrew *noun* a sharp metal spiral with a handle, for pulling corks out of bottles.

corn[1] *noun* a grain plant that you can eat as a vegetable or use to make flour.

corn[2] *noun* a hard, painful lump on a toe or other part of the feet.

corner *noun*
1. a place where two lines or surfaces meet and form an angle: *a street corner*; *the corner of a box*; *the corners of a page.* **2.** a place or region: *His fame spread to every corner of the world.*
–*verb* **3.** If you **corner** someone, you trap them so that they cannot get away: *The police finally cornered the thief at the end of a closed alley.*
–*phrase* **4. cut corners**, to do something with as little time, effort, or money as possible.

cornet *noun* a wind instrument like the trumpet, but smaller.

cornflour *noun* the fine flour made from maize which is used in cooking, especially to thicken sauces.

coronation *noun* the ceremony at which a person becomes king or queen.

coroner *noun* an official who is in charge of trying to discover the cause of sudden or unexplained deaths.

coronet *noun* a small crown.

corporal[1] *adjective* having to do with the body: *Corporal punishment is no longer used in schools.*

corporal[2] *noun* an army or air force officer ranking below a sergeant.

corporation *noun* a business or other united group of people: *My sister works for an international corporation.*

corps /*say* kaw/ *noun* (*plural* **corps** /*say* kawz/) a unit of soldiers: *an army corps.*

☑ SPELLING TIP *Silent letter alert*: don't forget the *ps* at the end. **Corps** has this spelling and sound because it comes from French where it means 'body'. But remember that a **corps** is a group or body of people. Don't confuse it with **corpse**, which is a dead body.

corpse *noun* a dead body, especially of a human being.

A SIMILAR WORD is **cadaver**.

corpuscle /*say* **kaw**-pus-uhl/ *noun* a minute body in the blood.

SEE ALSO **red blood cell** and **white blood cell**.

correct *verb*
1. If you **correct** something, you do what is necessary to make it right: *I read through the letter to correct the spelling.* **2.** If you **correct** someone, you point out to them that they have made a mistake.
–*adjective* **3.** If something is **correct**, it is right: *No, I'm afraid the correct answer is Venezuela.* **4.** If something is **correct**, it is socially acceptable and right: *correct behaviour.*
☐ **correction**, *noun* –**corrective**, *adjective* –**correctly**, *adverb*

correspond *verb*
1. If something **corresponds** with something else, it agrees with it or matches it: *His version of what happened corresponds closely with mine.* **2.** If two people **correspond**, they write to each other: *We correspond by email.*
☐ **corresponding**, *adjective*

correspondence *noun*
1. letters between people. **2.** similarity: *There is a strong correspondence between the two stories.*

☑ SPELLING TIP *Double letter alert*: double *r*. Think of the word *respond* which appears in **correspondence** with *cor* before it, giving the double *r*. Also remember that the ending is spelt *ence* (not *ance*). It might help if you think of a *sentence* which has the same ending. You use a lot of sentences when writing **correspondence**.

correspondent *noun*
1. someone who writes letters. **2.** a reporter paid to send in articles and news reports from a distant place.

corridor /*say* **ko**-ruh-daw/ *noun*
1. a connecting passage in a building. **2.** a passage into which several rooms, flats, or railway compartments open.

☑ SPELLING TIP *Tricky 'uh' sound*: the middle vowel sound is spelt as an *i*. Also, don't forget the *or* ending (not *ore*).

corroboree /*say* kuh-**rob**-uh-ree/ *noun* an Aboriginal dance ceremony which includes singing and rhythmic music. Many people come together for the ceremony in which the dancers are decorated with clay in traditional designs.

WORD HISTORY from an Aboriginal language of New South Wales called Dharug

☑ SPELLING TIP *Double/single letter alert*: a double *r*, a single *b*; then a single *r*, and a double *e*.

corrode /*say* kuh-**rohd**/ *verb* When a metal **corrodes**, it is gradually eaten away: *The old car was corroded by rust.*
☐ **corrosion**, *noun* –**corrosive**, *adjective*

corrugated /*say* **ko**-ruh-gay-tuhd/ *adjective* having ridges or bumps: *Rain ran down the channels of the corrugated iron roof.*
☐ **corrugate**, *verb* to wrinkle. –**corrugation**, *noun*

☑ SPELLING TIP *Tricky 'uh' sound*: the middle vowel sound is spelt as a *u*. Also remember that **corrugated** has two *r*'s, but only one *g*. Rap it out as *cor*+*ru*+*ga*+*ted*.

corrupt *adjective*
1. If someone is **corrupt**, they do dishonest things, especially in order to get money: *The corrupt policeman accepted payment from the drug dealers and agreed not to arrest them.*
–*verb* **2.** If someone **corrupts** you, they influence you to do dishonest or immoral things. **3.** If a computer program or computer data is **corrupted**, it is damaged so that it contains errors and cannot be read properly any more: *My computer got a virus and all my files were corrupted.*
☐ **corruptible**, *adjective* –**corruption**, *noun*

corset *noun* underwear worn by women which gives shape or firm support to the body.
☐ **corsetry**, *noun*

cosmetic *noun* a product which is intended to improve the look of your face and hair.
☐ **cosmetic**, *adjective* –**cosmetically**, *adverb*

cosmic *adjective* having to do with the universe: *The film was about aliens fighting with cosmic rays.*
☐ **cosmically**, *adverb*

WORD HISTORY from a Greek word meaning 'of the world'

cosmonaut *noun* See **astronaut**.

cosmopolitan /*say* koz-muh-**pol**-uh-tuhn/ *adjective*
1. having people or customs from many parts of the world: *The conference attracted a cosmopolitan audience.* **2.** feeling at home in many parts of the world: *Growing up in a diplomat's house gave him a cosmopolitan outlook.*

☑ SPELLING TIP *Tricky 'uh' sound*: the middle vowel sound is spelt as an *o*. This will be easier to remember if you think of the word *cosmos* (meaning 'the world' or 'the universe') and can see that **cosmopolitan** begins with a shortened form of this word. Also remember that the last part is spelt *an* (not *en*).

cosmos /*say* **koz**-mos/ *noun* the universe.

cost *noun*
1. the price to be paid for something. **2.** a loss or expense: *They finally stopped the bushfire, but at the cost of five houses.*
–*verb* **3.** If something **costs** a certain amount of money, that is how much you have to pay to buy it: *I really like that chair – how much did it cost?* **4.** If something **costs** you something, it causes you to lose that thing: *It was a terrible mistake that cost them their lives.*
–*phrase* **5. at all costs**, regardless of difficulty: *We must have it ready tomorrow at all costs.*
☐ **costly**, *adjective*: *We can't afford such a costly car.*

costume *noun* a set of clothes, especially to make you look like someone else or for a particular purpose: *The dancers wore costumes of silvery feathers*; *a one-piece swimming costume.*

cosy *adjective* (**cosier**, **cosiest**) close and friendly: *The room was warm and cosy.*
☐ **cosily**, *adverb* –**cosiness**, *noun*

cot *noun* a small bed with raised sides that a baby sleeps in.

cottage *noun* a small one-storey house.

cottage cheese *noun* a cheese made from curdled, skim milk.

cotton *noun*
1. a light material made from the soft, white hairs covering the seeds of the cotton plant. **2.** a thread used for sewing.

cottonwool *noun* soft cotton in a mass, used especially for cleaning cuts or sores, putting on and removing beauty products, etc.

couch *noun* (*plural* **couches**) a long, padded seat for two or more people, with a back and two sides.

OTHER WORDS for this are **lounge**, **sofa** and **settee**.

cough /*rhymes with* off/ *noun*
1. the noisy outgoing air from your lungs which you get in some illnesses, or when something is stuck in your throat.
–*verb* **2.** When you **cough**, you force air out through your throat with a sudden noise: *The smoke made me cough.*

☑ SPELLING TIP Remember that there is no *f* in **cough** – the spelling *ough* gives the 'off' sound.

could /*rhymes with* wood/ *verb*
1. the past tense of the verb **can**: *He could play the piano from the age of four.* **2. Could** is used to refer to **a.** a possible situation: *You could do it if you tried.* **b.** an uncertain situation: *They could still be alive, but I doubt it.* **3.** When **could** is used to make a request, it sounds more polite than **can**: *Could you pass the sauce, please?*

NOTE This is always used with another verb. See *modal verbs* in the Grammar and Punctuation Guide appendix.

couldn't a short form of *could not*.

council /*say* **kown**-suhl/ *noun*
1. a group of people that meets regularly to discuss or decide certain things. **2.** the government of a small area such as a city or its suburbs: *It is the job of the council to clean the streets.*
☐ **councillor**, *noun* a member of a council.

☑ SPELLING TIP Remember the *cil* ending, giving the 'suhl' sound. Don't confuse **council** with **counsel** which has the same sound, but means 'advice'.

counsel /*say* **kown**-suhl/ *noun*
1. advice. **2.** a lawyer who is paid to give advice to someone in a court case.
–*verb* (**counsels**, **counselling**, **counselled**, **has counselled**) **3.** If you **counsel** someone, you advise them: *to counsel against the trip.*
☐ **counsellor**, *noun* an adviser, especially a psychologist.

☑ SPELLING TIP Remember the *sel* ending. Don't confuse **counsel** with **council** which has the same sound. A **council** is a group of people who meet to discuss something.

count[1] *verb*
1. If you **count**, you **a.** add up: *Yann counted the eggs as he put them in the basket.* **b.** name the numbers: *She can count up to five.* **2.** You can use **count** to mean 'include': *That makes eight of us, counting you.* **3.** If something **counts**, it matters or is important: *Playing the game counts more than winning.*
–*phrase* **4. count on**, to depend on: *The teacher is counting on us being on time.*
☐ **count**, *noun* –**countless**, *adjective* very many: *the countless stars.*

count[2] *noun* in some European countries, a nobleman of a certain rank.

NOTE A woman with this rank is called a **countess**.
WORD HISTORY from a Latin word meaning 'companion'

countenance *noun* your face or its expression: *Her puzzled countenance revealed her uncertainty.*

counter[1] *noun*
1. a long shelf or bar where goods are sold or food is prepared or eaten. **2.** something used for keeping count, especially in a game.

counter[2] *adverb*
1. in the opposite direction: *Her argument ran counter to the opinions of her friends.*

–*verb* **2.** If you **counter** something, you make it less effective: *She countered their unkind comments with a friendly smile.*
–*adjective* **3.** opposite or opposed: *a counter attack.*

counterfeit /*say* **kown**-tuh-fuht, **kown**-tuh-feet/ *adjective*
1. made to look exactly like something else in an attempt to deceive people: *a counterfeit coin.*
–*verb* **2.** If someone **counterfeits** something, they make it so it looks like something else: *His business was illegal – counterfeiting passports.*
☐ **counterfeit**, *noun*

☑ SPELLING TIP In spite of one of its pronunciations, **counterfeit** has absolutely nothing to do with your feet. Remember that the last part is spelt *feit*.

counterpart *noun* one of two people or things which matches or looks like the other.

counterterrorism *noun* the actions taken by a government to prevent or control terrorist activities, such as gathering information about possible attacks, making sure that places that might be attacked are secure, etc.

ANOTHER WORD for this is **anti-terrorism**.

country *noun* (*plural* **countries**)
1. an area of land separated from other areas by having its own government: *The country closest to Australia is Papua New Guinea.* **2.** the land where someone is born or the land of which someone is a citizen. **3.** (as used by Aboriginal people) traditional land with its embedded cultural values relating to the Dreamtime: *The elders told the younger people about the importance of country.* **4. the country**, the land outside towns and cities.

A SIMILAR WORD (for definition 1) is **nation**; (for definition 4) **countryside**.

country and western *noun* a type of music which consists of songs about country life, accompanied by a stringed instrument such as a guitar or fiddle.

ANOTHER TERM for this is **country music**.

county *noun* (*plural* **counties**) a large area within a state, bigger than a shire.

coup /*say* kooh/ *noun* (*plural* **coups** /*say* koohz/) a sudden, forceful move: *The army took control of the government in a coup.*

☑ SPELLING TIP *Silent letter alert*: don't forget the silent *p* at the end, which is there because **coup** is a French word.

couple /*rhymes with* supple/ *noun*
1. two people, especially if married: *the couple at the next table.* **2.** any two things: *a couple of hours.*
☐ **coupling**, *noun*

couplet /*say* **kup**-luht/ *noun* a pair of lines of poetry which rhyme.

coupon /*say* **kooh**-pon/ *noun*
1. a ticket or card which you can exchange for goods or money. **2.** a form which must be filled in to order goods, or enter a competition.

courage /*say* **ku**-rij/ *noun* the strength to do or face something you find frightening: *She hasn't the courage to own up to breaking the vase.*
☐ **courageous** /*say* kuh-**ray**-juhs/, *adjective* –**courageously**, *adverb*

courier /*say* **koo**-ree-uh/ *noun*
1. someone who carries messages or parcels for others. **2.** someone who looks after a group of tourists and their travel arrangements.

WORD HISTORY from a Latin word meaning 'run'

course /*rhymes with* horse/ *noun*
1. one stage of a meal: *For the first course, we had garlic prawns.* **2.** a series, especially of lessons: *I'm doing a French course.* **3.** the ground or water on which a race takes place. **4.** movement or progress: *During the course of the journey, they saw many different countries.*
–*phrase* **5. in due course**, at the right time: *The committee will deal with your question in due course.* **6. of course**, certainly: *Of course it will stop raining.*

☑ SPELLING TIP Don't confuse the spelling of **course** with **coarse** which sounds the same. **Coarse** describes something thick or rough (*coarse fabric*). It can also describe something which is rude or offensive (*coarse jokes*).

court /*rhymes with* short/ *noun*
1. the hard ground where games such as tennis and basketball are played. **2.** the home of a king or queen and the people who live or work there. **3.** the place where legal cases and trials are heard. **4.** a courtyard or space enclosed by walls.
–*verb* **5.** *Old-fashioned* If someone **courts** someone else, they try to win their love or favour: *He courted her with exquisite gifts.*
☐ **courtier**, *noun* someone who serves the king or queen at court. –**courtly**, *adjective* polite: *courtly manners.* –**courtship**, *noun*

courteous /*say* **ker**-tee-uhs/ *adjective* well-mannered or polite: *a courteous answer*; *a courteous child.*
☐ **courteously**, *adverb*

☑ SPELLING TIP Don't forget that the first part of **courteous** is spelt *court* (although it sounds like *curt*). In fact, the meaning of this word is related to a *court* in the sense of the manners used at the court of a king or queen in the past.

courtesy /*say* **ker**-tuh-see/ *noun*
1. politeness and good manners. **2.** permission: *The photograph is used by courtesy of the photographer.*

court martial *noun* (*plural* **courts martial** *or* **court martials**)
1. a court of officers which tries anyone in the armed forces who breaks the military law.
–*verb* (**court-martials**, **court-martialling**, **court-martialled**, **has court-martialled**) **2.** If a member of the armed forces is **court-martialled**, they are tried in a court martial.

courtroom *noun* a room in which a law court is held.

courtyard *noun* an area enclosed by walls or buildings.

couscous /*say* **koos**-koos/ *noun* a type of grain, originating in North Africa, often cooked with spices and meat or vegetables.

> ☑ SPELLING TIP Don't confuse the spelling of **couscous** with **cuscus** (pronounced '**kus**-kus') which is a small Australian animal like a possum.

cousin /*say* **kuz**-uhn/ *noun* a son or daughter of your uncle or aunt.

cove *noun* a small bay or inlet.

covenant *noun* a solemn promise: *They made a covenant to be faithful to each other.*

cover *verb*
1. If you **cover** something, you put something over it, often to protect it or to hide it: *She covered her books with plastic*; *We covered the stain on the carpet with a rug.* **2.** If something **covers** something else, it is spread all over it: *Snow covered the hills.* **3.** If something such as insurance **covers** you, you know that it will pay your costs if your property is damaged or stolen. **4.** If you **cover** a certain topic when you are speaking or writing, you deal with it or include it: *We've already covered what to do in an emergency.* **5.** If you are able to **cover** your expenses, you have enough money to pay for them: *Will this cover the cost of the ticket?* **6.** If you **cover** a certain distance when you are travelling, you move forward by that amount: *We covered 900 km in two days.*
–*noun* **7.** something which covers: *a food cover.* **8.** shelter: *The children ran for cover from the storm.*
–*phrase* **9. take cover**, to hide or shelter yourself. **10. under cover**, secretly: *to go on a mission under cover.*
☐ **coverage**, *noun*: *The TV news gave a good coverage of the event.* –**covering**, *noun*

covet /*say* **kuv**-uht/ *verb* (**covets**, **coveting**, **coveted**, **has coveted**) If you **covet** something, you very much want to have it: *He coveted the poster which she had got the rock star to sign.*
☐ **covetous**, *adjective* greedy. –**covetously**, *adverb* –**covetousness**, *noun*

cow *noun* the female of cattle and of some other large animals, such as the whale.

> NOTE The male is a **bull**. The young is a **calf**.

coward *noun* someone who acts badly or weakly out of fear.
☐ **cowardice**, *noun* –**cowardly**, *adverb*

cower *verb* If you **cower**, you draw away in fear: *The frightened child cowered in the corner.*

> A SIMILAR WORD is **cringe**.

coxswain /*say* **kok**-suhn, **kok**-swayn/ *noun* the person who steers a boat, especially in rowing.

> THE SHORT FORM of this is **cox**.

> ☑ SPELLING TIP The first pronunciation of this word makes its spelling difficult. You just have to memorise the *swain* spelling for the 'suhn' sound.

coy *adjective* shy, or pretending to be shy.
☐ **coyly**, *adverb* –**coyness**, *noun*

coyote /*say* koy-**oh**-tee/ *noun* a North American wild dog which makes a long, sad sound at night.

CPR *noun* an emergency procedure to save someone's life, in which you breathe into their lungs to try and start them breathing again, and massage their chest near the heart.

> WORD HISTORY short for *cardiopulmonary resuscitation*

crab *noun* a hard-shelled sea animal with five pairs of legs, the last two with pincers, around a flattish body.

crack *verb*
1. If you **crack** something or it **cracks**, it divides so that there is a long, narrow break in it, although often it doesn't actually fall apart: *You'll crack the glass if you pour boiling water into it*; *The glass cracked.* **2.** If something **cracks**, it makes a sudden, sharp sound: *I heard the plate crack when it hit the ground.* **3.** If you **crack** something or someone, you suddenly hit it hard: *I cracked my elbow on the table as I fell.* **4.** If you **crack** something such as a problem, you work out how to solve it: *I stared at the puzzle for ages before I finally cracked it.* **5.** If you **crack** a joke, you say something funny.
–*noun* **6.** a sudden, sharp noise. **7.** the line that appears when something cracks: *Cracks appeared but the bowl didn't break.* **8.** a hard blow: *He gave his thumb a crack with the hammer.*
–*adjective* **9.** very skilled: *a crack shot.*
–*phrase* **10. crack down on**, to become strict with: *to crack down on people who break school rules.*
☐ **cracked**, *adjective*

cracker *noun*
1. a thin, crisp, unsweetened biscuit. **2.** a firework. **3.** a twisted roll of paper with a surprise inside, which explodes when you pull it at both ends.

> ANOTHER WORD (for definition 3) is **bonbon**.

crackle *verb* If something **crackles**, it makes short, sharp sounds: *The stiff paper crackled as I turned the pages.*
☐ **crackle**, *noun*

cradle *noun*
1. a baby's small bed, usually built so it can be rocked. **2.** a frame which supports or protects: *The window cleaners worked from a cradle outside the building.* **3.** a box on rockers used to separate gold dust from sand and dirt.
–*verb* **4.** If you **cradle** someone, you hold or rock them, as if in a cradle.

craft *noun* (*plural* **crafts**)
1. skilfulness: *a writer's craft.* **2.** a job or trade needing special skill with your hands. **3.** a boat or an aircraft.

crafty *adjective* (**craftier**, **craftiest**) clever in a tricky or deceitful way.
☐ **craftily**, *adverb* –**craftiness**, *noun*

crag *noun* a steep rock sticking up from a cliff or mountain.
☐ **craggy**, *adjective* (**craggier**, **craggiest**)

cram *verb* (**crams**, **cramming**, **crammed**, **has crammed**) If you **cram** something into a space, you push it in there although there is not a lot of room: *She crammed her clothes into a suitcase.*

cramp *noun*
1. a sudden, painful stiffening of the muscles: *She had to pull out of the race because of a cramp in her leg.*
–*verb* **2.** If a part of your body **cramps**, it gets a cramp.

crane *noun*
1. a large bird with long legs, neck and bill, which feeds in shallow water. **2.** a machine with a long moving arm, which can lift and move heavy weights around.
–*verb* **3.** If you **crane** your neck, you stretch it out as far as you can in order to see something: *She craned her neck out of the window to see the procession.*

crank *noun* a bar for winding or levering: *He used a crank to start his old car.*

cranky *adjective* (**crankier**, **crankiest**) bad-tempered or irritable.
☐ **crankily**, *adverb* –**crankiness**, *noun*

cranny *noun* (*plural* **crannies**) a narrow opening, especially in rock.

crash *verb*
1. If something **crashes**, it falls suddenly and breaks: *The plate crashed to the ground.* **2.** If a vehicle **crashes**, or if you crash it, it hits into something, usually with a loud noise.
–*noun* **3.** the noise of breaking or hitting. **4.** an accident or collision.

crate *noun* a large wooden box.

crater *noun*
1. the cup-shaped opening at the top of a volcano. **2.** a round hole in the ground, like one made by a meteorite or a bomb.

WORD HISTORY from the Greek word for a bowl for mixing wine and water

cravat /*say* kruh-**vat**/ *noun* a man's scarf, loosely tied at the throat.

crave *verb* If you **crave** something, you want it very badly: *The hungry boy craved food; She craved the company of people her own age.*
☐ **craving**, *noun*

crawl *verb*
1. If you **crawl**, you move forward on your hands and knees: *Babies begin to crawl at about seven months.* **2.** If something such as a car **crawls**, it moves very slowly. **3.** *Informal* If someone **crawls**, they act very humbly towards someone and say nice things about them, often because they want something from them: *We didn't like him because he was always crawling to the teacher.*
☐ **crawl**, *noun*: *moving at a crawl.* –**crawler**, *noun*

crayfish *noun* (*plural* **crayfish** *or* **crayfishes**) a hard-shelled freshwater animal which looks like a small lobster.

ANOTHER NAME for this is **yabby**.

crayon *noun* a stick of coloured wax, chalk, and so on, used for drawing and colouring.

craze *noun* a short-lived fashion: *the latest craze.*

crazy *adjective* (**crazier**, **craziest**)
1. mad or insane. **2.** strange or foolish: *a crazy idea.*
☐ **crazily**, *adverb* –**craziness**, *noun*

creak *verb* If something **creaks**, it makes a sound when it moves: *The rusty gate creaked when I opened it; The floor boards creaked as we tiptoed across them.*
☐ **creaky**, *adjective* (**creakier**, **creakiest**)

☑ SPELLING TIP Don't confuse the spelling of **creak** with **creek** which sounds the same but is spelt with a double *e*. A **creek** is a small stream.

cream *noun*
1. the fatty part of milk, which rises to the surface. **2.** anything which is thick and smooth: *hand cream.* **3.** the top or best part: *The cream of our soccer players want to play in Europe.* **4.** a yellowish white colour.
–*verb* **5.** To **cream** something is to beat it or stir it until it forms a thick, smooth liquid: *to cream the butter and sugar.*
☐ **cream**, *adjective*: *a cream dress.* –**creamy**, *adjective* (**creamier**, **creamiest**)

crease *noun*
1. a sharp line or fold, especially in material or paper.

–*verb* **2.** If you **crease** something such as cloth or paper, or if it **creases**, it gets folds and wrinkles in it: *Don't sit on my coat – you'll crease it*; *This material creases easily.*
☐ **creased**, *adjective*

create /*say* kree-**ayt**/ *verb* If you **create** something, you make it or bring it into existence: *I love the characters that she has created in her new play*; *He created a magnificent meal from the most humble ingredients.*
☐ **creation**, *noun* –**creative**, *adjective* –**creativity**, *noun* –**creator**, *noun*

creature *noun* any animal: *Elephants are huge creatures.*

creche /*say* kraysh, kresh/ *noun* a nursery for babies and young children.

☑ SPELLING TIP This word comes from French (from an original German word meaning 'crib'). This is why there is an *e* at the end and a *ch* spelling for the 'sh' sound. This is probably also the reason for the two ways of saying **creche** in English. Whichever way you say the vowel sound in the middle, remember that it is spelt with just an *e*.

credit *noun*
1. trust or belief: *I don't put too much credit in what she says.* **2.** praise or approval: *He should get some of the credit for the team's success.* **3.** the amount someone is allowed to spend or borrow: *My mother said she had reached the limit of her credit over Christmas.* **4.** an amount of money added to an account. **5.** the amount of money in your favour in an account: *My bank account is ten dollars in credit.*
–*verb* (**credits**, **crediting**, **credited**, **has credited**) **6.** To **credit** something is to believe it: *Can you credit how expensive food is here?*; *You wouldn't credit the trouble I had finding you.*
–*phrase* **7. on credit**, with agreement to pay later.
☐ **credible**, *adjective*: *That new science fiction film is just not credible.*

COMPARE definition 4 with **debit** (definition 2).
NOTE Someone you owe money to is your **creditor** and someone who owes you money is your **debtor**.

credit card *noun* a plastic card which is used to make a record of what someone owes when they buy something but don't pay cash.

creed *noun* a statement of belief: *a social creed developed by the church.*

creek *noun* a small river.

☑ SPELLING TIP Don't confuse the spelling of **creek** with **creak** which sounds the same. To **creak** is to make a squeaking sound.

creep *verb* (**creeps**, **creeping**, **crept**, **has crept**)
1. If you **creep** somewhere, you move along slowly, trying hard not to make a noise: *I caught him creeping along the corridor.*
–*noun Informal* **2.** a person you think is unpleasant. **3. the creeps**, a feeling of fear or disgust: *He gives me the creeps.*

creeper *noun* a plant which climbs walls or grows along the ground.

cremate *verb* If someone is **cremated**, their body is burnt to ashes after they die.
☐ **cremation**, *noun*

crepe /*rhymes with* grape/ *noun*
1. a light, crinkled material made of cotton or silk. **2.** a finely wrinkled paper. **3.** a thin pancake.

☑ SPELLING TIP *Tricky vowel sound*: remember that the vowel in the middle is spelt *e* (not *a*). **Crepe** has this spelling and sound because it comes from French. This is why you sometimes see it spelt **crêpe** (with an accent over the *e*).

crescendo /*say* kruh-**shen**-doh/ *adverb* increasingly loud or forceful.

NOTE This is used as an instruction in music.

☑ SPELLING TIP Remember the *sc* spelling in the middle, giving the 'sh' sound. This is because **crescendo** is an Italian word, like most musical instructions.

crescent /*say* **krez**-uhnt/ *noun*
1. the shape of the moon in its first or last quarter. **2.** anything of a similar shape, especially a street.

ANOTHER FORM When definition 2 is the name of a street, you spell it with a capital letter and its abbreviation is **Cres**.

☑ SPELLING TIP *Silent letter alert*: don't forget the silent *c* following the *s*.

cress *noun* a fast-growing herb whose leaves are used in salads.

crest *noun*
1. the feathers or growth on the top of the heads of some birds. **2.** the very top of anything: *They were on the crest of achieving their dream.* **3.** part of a coat of arms which is used as a badge: *We had to sew the school crest onto our pockets.*
☐ **crested**, *adjective*

crestfallen *adjective* disappointed or sad: *We were quite crestfallen when our team was defeated in the grand final.*

crevasse /*say* kruh-**vas**/ *noun* a deep crack in a glacier or river of ice.

☑ SPELLING TIP *Double letter alert*: two *s*'s. Also don't forget the following *e*. **Crevasse** is spelt in this way because it comes from French.

crevice /*say* **krev**-uhs/ *noun* a crack forming an opening: *The water had wedged the branch into a crevice between two enormous boulders.*

☑ SPELLING TIP Remember that **crevice** ends with three letters that make the word *ice*. It might help if you picture a **crevice**, or crack, in a wall of ice. However, a **crevice** is a small crack or opening in anything. Don't confuse it with **crevasse** which is a huge crack or opening in ice.

crew *noun* the group of people who work together, especially on a ship or aeroplane.

crib *noun*
1. a baby's bed. **2.** a box or rack used to hold food for cattle and horses.

cricket[1] *noun* a jumping insect, similar to a grasshopper, which makes a loud noise by rubbing its wings on its abdomen.

WORD HISTORY from a French word that imitates the sound these insects make

cricket[2] *noun* a team game played with ball, bat and wickets.

WORD HISTORY from a French word meaning 'stick'

crime *noun*
1. an act which breaks the law. **2.** the breaking of laws: *It is hoped that an increase in police will stop the rising rate of crime.*

criminal *adjective*
1. having to do with crime: *Stealing that money was a criminal act.*
–*noun* **2.** someone who is guilty of a crime: *The police warned people that the criminals might have guns.*
☐ **criminally**, *adverb*

crimp *verb* If you **crimp** your hair, you style it into waves.

crimson *adjective* deep, purplish-red.
☐ **crimson**, *noun*

cringe *verb*
1. If a person or animal **cringes**, they bend down low or shy away because they are afraid. **2.** If you **cringe**, you feel very embarrassed about something, often because you feel for someone else: *We all cringed when he insisted on singing at the party.*

A SIMILAR WORD (for definition 1) is **cower**.

crinkle *verb* When something **crinkles**, or if you **crinkle** it, it becomes wrinkled or creased: *Her face crinkled with laughter*; *She has crinkled her clean blouse by dropping it on the floor.*
☐ **crinkle**, *noun* –**crinkly**, *adjective*

cripple *noun*
1. someone who has lost the use of one or more limbs.
–*verb* **2.** To **cripple** someone is to damage them, especially their legs: *She was crippled in a car accident.*

crisis /*say* **kruy**-suhs/ *noun* (*plural* **crises** /*say* **kruy**-seez/)
1. a time of danger or trouble. **2.** a turning point, especially in the course of an illness.

crisp *adjective*
1. hard, dry and easily broken: *crisp pastry.* **2.** cool, dry and fresh: *a crisp morning.*
–*noun* **3.** a thin slice of fried potato eaten cold.
☐ **crisply**, *adverb* –**crispness**, *noun*

criterion /*say* kruyt-**ear**-ree-uhn/ *noun* (*plural* **criteria**) a standard or rule for testing something.

☑ SPELLING TIP Remember that this word does not start with *cry* although the first part sounds like this. It might help if you see that **criterion** is related to the word *critic* – they both begin with the same four letters *crit*.

critic *noun*
1. someone who is a judge of quality or excellence: *The magazine's music critic praised the group's latest CD.* **2.** someone who finds fault.

critical *adjective*
1. Someone is **critical** if they find fault a lot: *She's always critical of what I wear.* **2.** Something is **critical** if it has to do with a time of danger: *She's in a critical condition in hospital.*

criticise /*say* **krit**-uh-suyz/ *verb* To **criticise** is to find fault with someone or something: *to criticise someone's friends.*
☐ **criticism** /*say* **krit**-uh-siz-uhm/, *noun*: *harsh criticism.*

ANOTHER SPELLING is **criticize**.

croak *verb* To **croak** is to make a low, rough sound: *'Don't worry about me – I've just got a bad cold', he croaked.*
☐ **croak**, *noun* –**croaky**, *adjective* (**croakier**, **croakiest**)

crockery *noun* cups, plates, dishes and similar articles made of china or pottery.

crocodile /*say* **krok**-uh-duyl/ *noun* a large, lizard-like reptile found living in the waters of tropical countries.

WORD HISTORY from a Greek word meaning 'lizard'

☑ SPELLING TIP *Tricky 'uh' sound*: the middle sound is spelt *o* (not *a*). Also remember that there is no *k* in **crocodile**. After that, you won't have any problems with this beast.

crook *noun*
1. a bent or curved part: *She tucked her hand into the crook of his arm.* **2.** a stick with a bend or curve at one end: *a shepherd's crook.* **3.** *Informal* a dishonest person.
–*adjective Informal* **4.** sick: *I feel crook.* **5.** unpleasant: *It's pretty crook when you have to wait an hour in the rain for a bus.*

–*verb* **6.** If you **crook** a part of your body, you bend or curve it: *He crooked his finger around the trigger.*

crooked /*say* **krook**-uhd/ *adjective*
1. bent: *a crooked fence.* **2.** dishonest: *crooked dealings.*

croon *verb* If you **croon**, you sing quietly in a low voice: *She was crooning to the baby to try to get it to sleep.*
□ **crooner**, *noun*

crop *noun*
1. products grown in the ground: *a good barley crop.* **2.** a short whip used by horse riders.
–*verb* (**crops**, **cropping**, **cropped**, **has cropped**) **3.** To **crop** something is to cut it short: *to crop a picture on the computer.*
–*phrase* **4. crop up**, to come as a surprise: *Suddenly news of a long-lost cousin cropped up.*

croquet /*say* **kroh**-kay/ *noun* a game played by hitting wooden balls with mallets through metal arches set in a lawn.

☑ SPELLING TIP *Silent letter alert*: don't forget the silent *t* at the end – the *et* spelling makes an 'ay' sound. Other words with this ending are *ballet* and *beret*. They all come from French. Also remember the *qu* spelling for the 'k' sound in **croquet**.

cross *noun*
1. anything in the shape made by two lines going through each other such as '+' or '×'. **2.** the result of mixing breeds of animals or plants.
–*verb* **3.** If you **cross** an area, you move from one side of it to the other: *She crossed the room to meet him.* **4.** If something **crosses** a space, it reaches from one side of it to the other: *The bridge crosses the river.* **5.** If two things **cross**, they meet and go across each other at an angle: *The two roads cross at an intersection some distance away.* **6.** If you **cross** two things, you place them across each other at an angle: *I crossed the sticks in the fireplace and piled up newspaper on top of them.*
–*adjective* **7.** annoyed: *They'll be cross when they see the mess.*
–*phrase* **8. cross out**, to draw a line through. **9. cross your mind**, to come as an idea, or occur to you.
□ **crossly**, *adverb*: *to speak crossly.*

cross-country *adjective*
1. having to do with a running race which is not run on a prepared track but across fields, parks and so on. **2.** having to do with skiing which involves long distances and gradual slopes.
–*noun* **3.** a cross-country race.

cross-examine *verb* If someone **cross-examines** you, they question you in order to check the truth of something already stated: *The lawyer cross-examined the witness to the murder.*
□ **cross-examination**, *noun* –**cross-examiner**, *noun*

crossing *noun*
1. a moving across: *We'll begin the crossing of the mountains in the morning.* **2.** a place where a road, river or railway line can be crossed.

crotch *noun* (*plural* **crotches**) a forked piece or part, such as of the human body or a pair of trousers where the two legs join.

crotchet /*say* **kroch**-uht/ *noun* a musical note equal to the time of one beat.

crotchety *adjective* bad-tempered or irritable.

crouch *verb* To **crouch** is to bend your knees and lean forward: *I crouched down to pat the kitten.*
□ **crouch**, *noun* (*plural* **crouches**)

croupier /*say* **krooh**-pee-uh/ *noun* someone who takes and pays out the money at a gambling table.

☑ SPELLING TIP *Tricky vowel sound*: the first vowel sound is spelt *ou* (although the sound is 'ooh'). It might help if you think of some other words which you know well which have the same spelling for this sound, such as *group* and *soup*. The ending *-ier* is there because this word comes from French.

crow[1] *noun* a bird with shiny, black feathers and a harsh-sounding call.

crow[2] *verb* If someone **crows** about something, they show off about it.

crowbar *noun* an iron bar used as a lever or to break hard ground.

crowd *noun*
1. a large number of people or things gathered closely together.
–*verb* **2.** When people **crowd**, they gather closely together: *All the journalists crowded around the prime minister.*
□ **crowded**, *adjective*: *a crowded room.*

crown *noun*
1. a round ornament, usually made of gold or silver and jewels, worn on the head of a king or queen. **2.** the top or highest part: *The crown of his head was completely bald.*
–*verb* **3.** To **crown** someone is to give them the position of a king or queen by placing a crown on their head: *The queen was crowned in 1953.*

crucial /*say* **krooh**-shuhl/ *adjective* extremely important: *The game was at a crucial point and the fans were tense with excitement.*

crucifix /*say* **krooh**-suh-fiks/ *noun* a cross with the figure of Jesus on it.

WORD HISTORY from a Latin word meaning 'fixed to a cross'

crucify /*say* **krooh**-suh-fuy/ *verb* To **crucify** someone is to put them to death by nailing them to an upright wooden cross.
☐ **crucifixion** /*say* krooh-suh-**fik**-shuhn/, *noun*

☑ SPELLING TIP The main difficulty in spelling *crucify* is the *c* spelling for the 's' sound in the middle. This word comes from *crux*, the Latin word for 'cross' (where the *x* changed to a *c* when endings were added to it). This may also help you to remember the spelling of the noun form **crucifixion** which is spelt with an *x* (a cross-shaped letter).

crude *adjective*
1. very basic and simple: *I made several crude attempts at drawing a tree.* **2.** rude and not in good taste: *a crude remark.* **3.** in a raw or natural state.
☐ **crudely**, *adverb* –**crudeness**, *noun* –**crudity**, *noun*

crude oil *noun* oil as it comes out of the ground, usually brown or black, often together with natural gas which forms a cap above it and salty water which collects underneath.

cruel *adjective* A **cruel** person enjoys hurting or upsetting people or animals.
☐ **cruelly**, *adverb* –**cruelty**, *noun*

cruise /*say* kroohz/ *verb* To **cruise** is to **1.** sail from place to place. **2.** travel at an average speed: *The ship cruised through the night.*
–*noun* **3.** a journey by sea: *a cruise around the islands.*
☐ **cruise**, *adjective*: *a cruise ship.* –**cruiser**, *noun*

☑ SPELLING TIP *Tricky vowel sound*: the vowel sound is spelt *ui* (although the sound is 'ooh'). Also remember that that there is an *s* giving the 'z' sound. Then you'll be really **cruising**!

cruisy /*say* **krooh**-zee/ *adjective Informal* not needing much effort: *Our team had a cruisy win today, but I think the game next week will be much harder.*

crumb *noun* a small piece of bread, cake or other dry food.

☑ SPELLING TIP Don't forget the silent *b* at the end (think of *b* for *breadcrumb*).

crumble *verb* If something **crumbles**, it falls apart into small pieces or powder: *The building was a century old and starting to crumble.*
☐ **crumbly**, *adjective* (**crumblier**, **crumbliest**)

crumpet *noun* a kind of light, soft bread, eaten toasted and buttered.

crumple *verb*
1. If you **crumple** something, you cause it to become folded, so it is not smooth: *I crumpled his note into a ball and threw it away.* **2.** If something **crumples**, it falls down or folds in on itself: *The wall crumpled in the earthquake.*

crunch *verb*
1. If an animal **crunches** its food, it crushes it with its teeth: *The horse crunched the apple noisily.*
–*noun* (*plural* **crunches**) **2.** the sound made in crunching. **3. the crunch**, *Informal* the moment of crisis.

crusade *noun*
1. a strong movement of support: *a crusade to restore the old inn.*
–*verb* **2.** If you **crusade** for something, you work for a particular cause that you feel strongly about: *She is out crusading against the war.*
☐ **crusader**, *noun*

crush *verb*
1. If you **crush** something, you squeeze or press it, usually so that it is broken: *He crushed the can and threw it away*; *The rock is crushed to extract the gold.* **2.** If someone is **crushed**, they suffer severely: *She was crushed by the news of her father's death.* **3.** If someone is **crushed**, they feel ashamed or disappointed: *I was crushed by his lack of interest.*
–*noun* **4.** a strong liking which often does not last long: *She had a crush on the lead singer.*

crust *noun*
1. the outside surface of bread, or a piece of it. **2.** any hard outer surface.
☐ **crusty**, *adjective* (**crustier**, **crustiest**)

crustacean /*say* krus-**tay**-shuhn/ *noun* a type of animal with a hard shell instead of a skeleton, such as a crab, usually living in water.

crutch *noun* (*plural* **crutches**)
1. a specially designed stick which you use for support if you have injured your leg: *She limped into the room on crutches.* **2.** something that you use as a help or support, especially mentally or emotionally: *It is time she lived independently, without the crutch of living with her parents.*

cry *verb* (**cries**, **crying**, **cried**, **has cried**)
1. If you **cry**, tears form in your eyes and run down your face, usually because you are sad. **2.** To **cry** or **cry out** is to shout or call out loudly: *They cried for help*; *He was crying out in pain.*
–*noun* (*plural* **cries**) **3.** a fit of crying. **4.** a shout: *She let out a cry of relief at the news.*
–*phrase* **5. a far cry**, **a.** a long distance. **b.** very different: *That colour paint is a far cry from the one I chose.*

SIMILAR WORDS (for definition 1) are **bawl**, **blubber**, **sob**, **wail** and **weep**; (for definition 2) **call**, **yell** and **scream**. For definition 1, note that **weep** is a more formal word for **cry**. All the other words refer to a particular kind of crying: to **bawl** is to cry loudly; to **blubber** is to cry loudly and in a childish way with a lot of tears; to **sob** is to cry, making a gulping noise as you breathe; to **wail** is to give a long, sad, high-pitched cry.

crypt /*say* kript/ *noun* an underground room under a church, often used as a burial place.

☑ SPELLING TIP *Letter 'y' alert*: the vowel sound is spelt *y* (not *i*), as in many words that come from Greek. **Crypt** comes from a Greek word meaning 'hidden'.

cryptic /*say* **krip**-tik/ *adjective* mysterious, or difficult to understand: *I was baffled by the cryptic email from her.*

☑ SPELLING TIP *Letter 'y' alert*: the first vowel sound is spelt with a *y* (not an *i*).

crystal *noun*
1. a clear mineral which looks like ice. **2.** a single grain or piece of this. **3.** a substance with a special and regular form due to the arrangement of atoms, ions, or molecules it has. **4.** very clear glass used to make jewellery and fine glass objects.
☐ **crystal**, *adjective* –**crystalline**, *adjective*

crystallise *verb*
1. When a substance **crystallises**, it forms into crystals. **2.** When fruit is **crystallised**, it is coated with sugar.
☐ **crystallisation**, *noun*

ANOTHER SPELLING is **crystallize.**

cub *noun* the young of certain animals such as the lion and bear.

cubbyhouse *noun* a small structure built for a child to play in.

cube *noun*
1. a solid shape with six equal square sides. **2.** the result of multiplying a number by itself twice: *The cube of 4 is 4 × 4 × 4, or 64.*
☐ **cubic**, **cubical**, *adjective*

cube root *noun* the number which, when multiplied by itself twice, gives the cube: *The cube root of 64 is 4.*

cubicle *noun* a partly enclosed, small space: *a shower cubicle.*

☑ SPELLING TIP Don't confuse the spelling of **cubicle** with **cubical** which is a form of the adjective *cubic*, formed from the noun *cube*.

cuckoo /*say* **kook**-ooh/ *noun* a bird which is known for its habit of laying its eggs in the nests of other birds.

cucumber *noun* a long, thin vegetable which is used in salads.

cud *noun* food which cattle and some other animals return from their first stomach to chew a second time.

cuddle *verb* If you **cuddle** someone, you hold them tightly in your arms to comfort them or show them affection: *He sat his daughter on his knee and cuddled her.*
☐ **cuddle**, *noun* –**cuddly**, *adjective* (**cuddlier**, **cuddliest**)

cudgel *noun*
1. a short, thick stick used as a weapon.
–*verb* (**cudgels**, **cudgelling**, **cudgelled**, **has cudgelled**) **2.** If a person **cudgels** someone, they beat them with a cudgel.

cue[1] *noun* anything said or done as a signal for what follows, especially in a play: *His falling on the stage was the cue for the actor playing the king to enter.*

cue[2] *noun* a long stick used to hit the ball in billiards and other similar games.

cuff[1] *noun*
1. a band or fold at the wrist of a sleeve. **2.** a part turned up at the end of a trouser leg.
–*phrase* **3. off the cuff**, without preparation: *to speak off the cuff.*

cuff[2] *verb* If you **cuff** someone, you hit them with your open hand.

cul-de-sac *noun* a short street which is closed at one end.

WORD HISTORY from French words meaning 'the bottom of a sack'

cull *verb*
1. To **cull** something is to pick out the best things from it: *We looked through the boxes of apples, culling the ripe ones.* **2.** To **cull** animals is to reduce the number of them by killing them: *The plan to cull large numbers of feral camels was to be voted on.*
☐ **cull**, *noun*: *She made a cull of the stories to put the best ones in the magazine.*

culminate *verb* When a situation or action **culminates** in something, it reaches its highest point after a period of gradual development: *The project culminated in a film.*
☐ **culmination**, *noun*

culottes *plural noun* trousers which are cut wide to look like a skirt.

culprit *noun* someone who has done something wrong: *When we find the culprits, they will be punished.*

cult *noun*
1. a religion. **2.** a strong belief and involvement in something: *the cult of physical fitness.*

cultivate *verb*
1. To **cultivate** the soil is to dig it for planting and growing. **2.** If you **cultivate** something, you make an effort to develop or improve it: *She tried hard to cultivate a love of reading in her children.*
☐ **cultivation**, *noun*

A SIMILAR WORD (for definition 1) is **till**.

culture *noun*
1. the way of life, especially skills, arts, beliefs and customs, regarded as being typical of a particular society or nation at a certain time: *Japanese culture*; *The cultures of the ancient Romans and the ancient Chinese were very different.* **2.** activities relating to the arts, literature, music, and so on, regarded as indicating a high level of civilisation: *He's not interested in culture, only in sport.* **3.** in biology, the growth of cells, such as bacteria, for scientific studies, medical use, and so on.
☐ **cultural**, *adjective*

cumbersome *adjective* awkward to handle: *a cumbersome bag.*

cumquat /*say* **kum**-kwot/ *noun* a fruit like a small mandarin, but not as sweet.

ANOTHER SPELLING is **kumquat**.
WORD HISTORY from a Chinese word meaning 'gold orange'

cumulus /*say* **kyooh**-myuh-luhs/ *noun* (*plural* **cumuli** /*say* **kyooh**-myuh-lee/) a cloud, usually white, which is flat at the bottom and has rounded shapes at the top.

COMPARE this with **cirrus** and **nimbus**.

cuneiform /*say* **kyooh**-nuh-fawm/ *adjective* identifying a style of writing, used in ancient Persia.

WORD HISTORY from a Latin word meaning 'wedge-shaped'

cunning *noun* skill used in a clever plan, or in tricking other people: *He used his cunning to outwit the enemy.*
☐ **cunning**, *adjective*: *a cunning design.*

cup *noun*
1. a small, round, open container, often with a handle on the side, used mainly to drink from. **2.** a pretty bowl, usually of silver or gold, given as a prize. **3.** a unit of volume, measuring 250 ml.
–*verb* (**cups**, **cupping**, **cupped**, **has cupped**) **4.** When you **cup** your hands, you form them into the shape of a cup: *She cupped her hands and scooped up some water to drink.* **5.** When you **cup** something in your hands, you hold it with your hands touching all around it: *He cupped the tiny bird in his hands.*

cupboard /*say* **kub**-uhd/ *noun* a piece of furniture, often attached to a wall, with doors and shelves, used for storing things.

☑ SPELLING TIP *Silent letter alert*: don't forget the silent *p*. You will remember this if you think of the two words that make up **cupboard** – *cup* and *board*.

curator /*say* kyooh-**ray**-tuh/ *noun* someone who looks after a museum, art gallery or similar kind of collection.

curb *verb* If you **curb** something, you keep it under control or within fixed limits: *to curb your TV watching.*

curd *noun* a jelly-like substance formed in milk which has been treated with an acid, eaten fresh or used for making cheese.

curdle *verb* When milk **curdles**, it becomes sour.

cure *verb*
1. If someone **cures** you of something, they make you better, usually by giving you medical treatment: *The doctor gave me antibiotics to cure my infected foot.* **2.** If someone **cures** something, they treat it in some way in order to preserve it: *You can cure fish by salting or smoking it.*
☐ **curable**, *adjective*: *a curable disease.* –**curative**, *adjective*: *a curative medicine.* –**cure**, *noun*: *a cure for the flu.*

curfew *noun* an order which says people are not allowed to be out on the streets after a certain time at night.

curious *adjective*
1. If someone is **curious**, they are anxious or eager to learn: *to be curious about dinosaurs.* **2.** If something is **curious**, it is unusual or strange: *a curious shape.*
☐ **curiosity**, *noun*

curl *noun*
1. a small ring of hair. **2.** a curved or twisted shape: *The carpenter left curls of wood on the ground.*
–*verb* **3.** If you **curl** something, you make it curved or rounded in shape: *to curl your toes.* **4.** If your hair **curls**, it naturally forms itself into curls.
☐ **curly**, *adjective* (**curlier**, **curliest**)

currant *noun* a small, dried, seedless grape.

☑ SPELLING TIP Remember that this word is spelt with an *a* (think of eating a **currant**). Don't confuse it with **current**, which describes something happening in the present. A **current** is also a flow.

currawong *noun* a large, black-and-white or greyish Australian bird with a large pointed bill and a loud ringing call.

WORD HISTORY probably from an Aboriginal language of Queensland called Yagara

currency *noun* (*plural* **currencies**) the type of money in current use in a country: *He changed his American dollars into Australian currency.*

current *adjective*
1. If something is **current**, it is happening at the present moment: *current temperature*; *the current month.*

–*noun* **2.** a flow or movement: *a current of cold air*; *a current of electricity*; *caught in the river currents.*

☑ SPELLING TIP Remember that this word is spelt with an *e*. Don't confuse it with **currant** which is a dried grape.

curriculum /*say* kuh-**rik**-yuh-luhm/ *noun* (*plural* **curriculums** *or* **curricula**) a set of courses of study: *The curriculum at the photography school includes a segment on black and white photography.*

☑ SPELLING TIP *Double/single letter alert*: double *r*'s and only one *l*. The word **curriculum** comes from Latin which explains the *um* ending and the *a* for one form of the plural.

curry *noun* (*plural* **curries**) a food made of meat and vegetables cooked in a hot-tasting, spicy sauce, originating in Indian cooking.

curse *noun*
1. a wish that evil will happen to someone: *In the story, the wicked witch put a curse on the prince.* **2.** an offensive expression or swear word: *He uttered a curse when he realised they had left him alone.*
–*verb* **3.** To **curse** is to swear: *He cursed under his breath when he banged his toe.*

cursive *adjective* describing writing or print with the letters joined together: *a cursive script.*

cursor /*say* **ker**-suh/ *noun* a moving dot or line on a computer video screen showing where the next letter or other character will appear.

curt *adjective* If someone is **curt**, they are rudely brief in speech or manner: *I was surprised by her curt reply.*

curtain *noun* a piece of material hanging from a rod over a window or across the front of a stage.

☑ SPELLING TIP Remember that the final part of **curtain** is spelt *ain*. Think of other words with this spelling for an 'uhn' sound, such as *captain* and *certain*. But be careful not to confuse **curtain** with **certain** (meaning 'sure').

curtsey *noun* (*plural* **curtseys**)
1. a respectful bow, usually made by a woman bending her knees with one foot in front of the other.
–*verb* (**curtseyed**, **curtseying**) **2.** When a woman or girl **curtseys**, she makes a curtsy.

ANOTHER SPELLING is **curtsy**.

curve *noun*
1. a bending line or shape with no angles: *the curves in the river.*
–*verb* **2.** When something **curves**, it has the shape of a curve: *The road curves ahead.*
☐ **curvature**, *noun* –**curvy**, *adjective* (**curvier**, **curviest**)

cuscus /*say* **kus**-kus/ *noun* a small, furry animal like a possum, which has a long tail and lives in New Guinea and northern Queensland.

☑ SPELLING TIP Don't confuse the spelling of **cuscus** with **couscous** (pronounced '**koos**-koos') which is a type of grain used in cooking.

cushion *noun*
1. a soft pad used to sit on, or lean against, especially on a chair.
–*verb* **2.** To **cushion** something is to lessen its force or effect: *A pile of leaves cushioned her fall.*

custard *noun* a food made of milk, eggs and sugar and eaten as a dessert.

custodian /*say* kus-**toh**-dee-uhn/ *noun*
1. someone who looks after or guards something: *She works at the museum as the custodian of rare books.* **2. traditional custodian**, an Aboriginal person who is entitled, by Aboriginal tradition, to have certain cultural knowledge.

custody *noun*
1. keeping or care: *The rare books are in the custody of the museum.* **2.** imprisonment: *He was terrified of being held in custody.*
☐ **custodial**, *adjective*: *a custodial sentence of the court.*

custom *noun*
1. habit or usual practice. **2. customs**, a tax paid on goods brought into the country.

customary /*say* **kus**-tuhm-ree/ *adjective* usual: *I left home at my customary time.*

☑ SPELLING TIP Remember that **customary** ends with *ary* (as in the name *Mary*), although the *a* is sometimes not pronounced.

custom-built *adjective* made in the way you ordered.

customer *noun* someone who buys goods or services from other people.

cut *verb* (**cuts**, **cutting**, **cut**, **has cut**)
1. If you **cut** something, you use a knife or similar object to divide it or to take a piece off it, sometimes accidentally: *She cut the cake and handed us each a slice*; *I cut my finger.* **2.** If you **cut** something, you reduce it: *All the stores will be cutting their prices in the sales.* **3.** If something such as a line or a road **cuts** something else, it crosses it.
–*noun* **4.** the result of cutting or a piece cut off: *a cut on her forehead*; *a cut of ham.*
–*phrase* **5. cut back**, to reduce or shorten. **6. cut off**, to stop: *Joe cut me off before I could answer.* **7. cut out**, **a.** to omit or leave out. **b.** to stop: *Cut out that rudeness!* **c.** to form or make by cutting: *to cut out a dress.*

cute *adjective* pretty: *What a cute baby!*
☐ **cuteness**, *noun*

cuticle *noun* the skin around the edges of a fingernail or toenail.

cutlass *noun* a short, heavy, slightly curved sword.

cutlery *noun* the knives, forks and spoons used for eating.

cutlet *noun* a small cut of meat, usually lamb or veal, that contains a rib.

cyanide /*say* **suy**-uh-nuyd/ *noun* a strong poison.

cyber /*say* **suy**-buh/ *adjective* having to do with the internet.

WORD HISTORY This word is used in many terms relating to computers, such as the following words. It comes from the word *cybernetics* which is based on the Greek word for 'helmsman' or 'steerer' and is the name for the scientific analysis of the operations of machines such as computers.

☑ SPELLING TIP *Letter 'y' alert*: the first vowel sound is spelt *y*. Many words that come from Greek have a 'y' spelling.

cyber attack *noun* an attack on a computer or a telecommunications network: *A cyber attack prevented customers from checking their online accounts.*

cyberbully /*say* **suy**-buh-bool-ee/ *noun* (*plural* **cyberbullies**) someone who bullies other people using email, chat rooms and other online methods.

cyber safety *noun* safety on the internet, involving things such as not sharing your personal information with anyone and avoiding situations where you are bullied, harassed, or sent inappropriate information, pictures, or messages.

cybersecurity /*say* suy-buh-suh-**kyooh**-ruh-tee/ *noun* protection put in place to prevent unauthorised access to an online information system such as a computer or a telecommunications network.

cyberspace /*say* **suy**-buh-spays/ *noun* the internet.

cyberstalking /*say* **suy**-buh-staw-king/ *noun* harassment of, or threats to, someone through the use of the internet, email, chat rooms, or other digital communications devices.

ANOTHER TERM for this is **internet stalking**.

cycle *noun*
1. a series of events happening in a regular, repeating order: *the cycle of the school year.* **2.** a bicycle.
–*verb* **3.** When you **cycle**, you ride a bicycle: *Sometimes we cycle to school.*
☐ **cyclic**, *adjective*: *a cyclic pattern of events.* –**cyclist**, *noun*

WORD HISTORY from a Greek word meaning 'ring' or 'circle'

cyclone /*say* **suy**-klohn/ *noun* a tropical storm with strong winds.

WORD HISTORY from a Greek word meaning 'moving in a circle'

cygnet /*say* **sig**-nuht/ *noun* a young swan.

☑ SPELLING TIP *Letter 'y' alert*: the first syllable is spelt *cyg* (not *sig*). When you think of this word, remember it has nothing to do with *signal*. It comes from the Greek word for 'swan'.

cylinder /*say* **sil**-uhn-duh/ *noun*
1. a tube-shaped object, either hollow or solid, with perfectly circular ends. **2.** the part of an engine in which the piston moves.
☐ **cylindrical**, *adjective*

☑ SPELLING TIP *Letter 'y' alert*: the first syllable is spelt *cyl* (not *sil*). As with many words that start *cy*, **cylinder** comes from Greek.

cymbal /*say* **sim**-buhl/ *noun* one of a pair of curved brass plates which are hit together to make a sharp, musical, ringing sound.
☐ **cymbalist**, *noun*

☑ SPELLING TIP Don't confuse the spelling of **cymbal** with **symbol** which has the same sound, but is a sign or representation. Remember that **cymbal** starts with *cy* (not *sy*) and has an *al* ending.

cynic /*say* **sin**-ik/ *noun* someone who does not believe in the goodness of people or events and is often scornful of them.
☐ **cynical**, *adjective* –**cynicism** /*say* **sin**-uh-siz-uhm/, *noun*

☑ SPELLING TIP *Letter 'y' alert*: the first vowel sound is spelt with a *y* (not an *i*) because the word comes from Greek. Also remember that **cynic** begins with a *c* (although it sounds like an 's').

cypress *noun* an evergreen cone-bearing tree with dark, overlapping leaves.

☑ SPELLING TIP *Letter 'y' alert*: this word starts with *cy* for the 'suy' sound. As with many words that start *cy*, **cypress** comes from Greek. Also remember that the ending is spelt *ess* (not *us* or *ous*).

cyst /*say* sist/ *noun* a small growth that appears in the body or under the skin, often containing liquid.
☐ **cystic**, *adjective*

☑ SPELLING TIP *Letter 'y' alert*: the vowel sound is spelt with a *y* (not an *i*) because it comes from Greek. Also remember that **cyst** begins with a *c* (although it sounds like an *s*).

dab *verb* (**dabs**, **dabbing**, **dabbed**, **has dabbed**)
1. To **dab** something on is to put it on in small amounts: *She dabbed a little perfume behind her ears.*
–*noun* **2.** a small amount: *a dab of paint.*

dabble *verb*
1. If you **dabble**, you splash in water: *She dabbled her feet in the creek.*
–*phrase* **2. dabble in**, to do as a hobby: *to dabble in photography.*
☐ **dabbler**, *noun*

dachshund /*say* **daks**-uhnd, **dash**-uhnd/ *noun* a small dog with a long body and very short legs.

☑ SPELLING TIP The spelling of this word is difficult because the word comes from German. It will be easier if you think about the two German words of which it is made up – *dachs* meaning 'a badger and *hund* meaning 'a dog'. So a **dachshund** was originally a dog (or hound – remember the *h*) used for hunting badgers.

dad *noun Informal* father.

ANOTHER FORM is **daddy**, especially among children.
NOTE You use these words when you are you are talking about your father in a rather informal way, or when you are addressing your father: *My dad has been very busy lately*; *When are we leaving, Daddy?*

daddy-long-legs *noun* (*plural* **daddy-long-legs**) a small spider with long, very thin legs.

daffodil /*say* **daf**-uh-dil/ *noun* a plant which has yellow, bell-shaped flowers in spring.

☑ SPELLING TIP *Double/single letter alert*: only one *l* at the end, but a double *f* in the middle. So don't be a dill! Remember that **daffodil** ends with *dil* with one *l*.

dagger *noun* a short hand-held weapon with a pointed blade.

daily *adverb* When something happens **daily**, it happens every day: *The park is open daily during school holidays.*
☐ **daily**, *adjective*: *daily newspaper*; *daily walk.*

dainty *adjective* (**daintier**, **daintiest**) If something is **dainty**, it is small and delicate: *dainty ornaments*; *dainty fingers.*
☐ **daintily**, *adverb* –**daintiness**, *noun*

dairy *noun* (*plural* **dairies**)
1. the place on a farm where cows are milked.
2. a cool place where milk and cream are stored and made into butter and cheese.
☐ **dairy**, *adjective*: *dairy products.*

☑ DO NOT CONFUSE **dairy** with **diary**, which is a book in which you write what happens each day.

dais /*say* **day**-uhs/ *noun* a raised place at the end of a hall for a speaker's desk, and for the seats of the guests of honour and so on.

☑ SPELLING TIP This word can be difficult to spell. Try thinking of the word *daisy* with the final *y* missing. This has nothing to do with the meaning of **dais** but will help you remember the spelling.

daisy *noun* (*plural* **daisies**) a common plant which has brightly coloured flowers with many petals surrounding a yellow centre.

WORD HISTORY from an Old English word meaning 'day's eye'

dal /*say* dahl/ *noun* a food made from cooked lentils, herbs and spices, originating in Indian cooking.

ANOTHER SPELLING is **dhal**.

dam *noun*
1. a strong wall built across a river to stop the flow of water and create a reservoir. **2.** the area of water created by this wall.
–*verb* (**dams**, **damming**, **dammed**, **has dammed**) **3.** To **dam** something is to hold it back: *My parents dammed the creek to make a swimming hole.*

damage *verb*
1. If you **damage** something, you harm or spoil it so that its condition or quality is no longer as good as it was: *The hail damaged the crops.*
–*noun* **2.** harm or injury: *The damage from the wild storm was going to take years to fix.*
3. damages, money that a court says you should get to make up for an injury or loss: *He was awarded damages of a million dollars.*
☐ **damaged**, *adjective* –**damageable**, *adjective*

☑ SPELLING TIP The tricky bit is remembering how to spell the last part of this word. You might remember that things sometimes get damaged because of their age – the spelling of *age* gives you the last three letters of the word **damage**.

Dame *noun* the title of a woman who has been awarded a particular kind of high honour: *She has been made a Dame of the Order of Australia*; *Dame Joan Sutherland.*

damn /*rhymes with* ham/ *interjection Informal* an expression of anger or annoyance, as in *'Damn! Where are my keys?'*.

NOTE The use of this expression may offend some people.

☑ SPELLING TIP *Silent letter alert*: don't forget the silent *n* at the end.

damned /*say* damd/ *adjective*
1. *Informal* annoying: *I wish these damned flies would go away.*
–*noun* **2. the damned**, in some religions, the people who have been condemned to punishment in hell.

NOTE Some people would think that the use of this word as in definition 1 is impolite.

☑ SPELLING TIP Like *damn*, **damned** has a silent *n*. Remember that the sound of a double *m* in the middle of the word is really spelt *mn*.

damp *adjective*
1. If something is **damp**, it is slightly wet or moist: *Take off those damp clothes.*
–*noun* **2.** wetness in the air or in clothes, or other objects like this.
☐ **dampen**, *verb*: *to dampen the cloth with warm water.* –**dampness**, *noun*

damper *noun* bread made from flour and water mixed to make a dough and baked in the coals of an open fire.

dance *verb*
1. When you **dance**, you move about to the rhythm of music, often using special steps or movements: *Everyone danced at the wedding.*
–*noun* **2.** a series of steps or movements for dancing. **3.** a party for dancing: *Are you going to the school dance?*
☐ **dancer**, *noun*

dance music *noun* a type of modern electronic music written for dancing to, with long repetitive tracks emphasising the bass guitar and drum beat.

dandelion /*say* **dan**-duh-luy-uhn/ *noun* a wild plant with bright yellow flowers which form fluffy balls when they go to seed.

☑ SPELLING TIP *Tricky 'uh' sound*: the middle vowel sound is spelt *e*. Otherwise, this word is not difficult to spell, especially as the last part is spelt as for *lion*, the animal. This is because **dandelion** comes from the French words *dent de lion* meaning 'tooth of a lion' (because the edge of the leaves look like teeth).

dandruff *noun* small white flakes of dead skin from your scalp.

danger *noun*
1. a possible cause of harm or injury: *Smoking is a danger to your health*; *That broken glass is a danger to people walking with bare feet.*
2. a situation in which harm or injury may happen: *The flooded river has put several houses in danger.*

dangerous *adjective* likely to harm or injure someone or cause someone to be harmed or injured: *Toys with small parts are dangerous for very young children*; *It is dangerous to run across the road.*
☐ **dangerously**, *adverb*

☑ SPELLING TIP The **dangerous** part in spelling this word is to remember that there is an *e* in it, although you sometimes do not pronounce it. This will be easier if you think about the meaning of the word and can see that it is made up of *danger* and the suffix *-ous* (meaning 'full of').

dangle *verb* To **dangle** is to hang down loosely: *She cut off the loose threads that were dangling from her jacket.*

dank *adjective* If a place is **dank**, it is a little wet in an unpleasant way: *a dank cellar.*
☐ **dankness**, *noun*

dappled *adjective* marked with spots or patches: *dappled leaves*; *dappled shade.*

dare *verb*
1. If you **dare** to do something, you are brave enough to do it: *Nobody dared to go into the yard where the snake was.* **2.** If you **dare** someone to do something, you make them prove they can do it: *I dare you to call him a liar.*
–*noun* **3.** something you do to prove that you are brave enough or clever enough to do it: *I rang the radio show for a dare.*
–*phrase* **4. dare say**, to think something is likely: *I dare say you'll go to university when you finish school.*
☐ **daring**, *adjective*: *a daring leap.*

daredevil *noun* someone who is very daring and takes lots of risks.

dark *adjective*
1. When it is **dark**, there is very little or no light: *It's getting dark.* **2.** A **dark** colour is one that is closer to black than white: *She has dark hair.* **3. Dark** can also mean that something is thought of as causing or connected with unhappiness: *He always looks on the dark side of things.* **4. Dark** can also mean that someone is angry or threatening: *She gave me a dark look.*
–*noun* **5.** absence of light: *My little brother is afraid of the dark.* **6.** night: *Please come home before dark.*

–phrase **7. in the dark**, knowing nothing: *We're in the dark about the arrangements.*
☐ **darken**, *verb*: *the sky darkened.* –**darkness**, *noun*

darkroom *noun* a room which is sealed so that no light can get in, used for developing and printing film.

darling *noun*
1. someone who is loved very much: *My baby sister is a darling.*
–adjective **2.** You use **darling** to describe a person you love very much: *my darling mother.* **3.** You can also use **darling** to describe an attractive animal or thing: *a darling kitten.*

darn *verb*
1. When you **darn** a hole in a piece of clothing, you fix it by sewing stitches through and across the hole.
–noun **2.** a darned part of a piece of clothing.

dart *noun*
1. a small metal arrow which is thrown by hand, usually as part of a game or sport.
–verb **2.** To **dart** is to move suddenly or quickly.

dash *verb*
1. If someone **dashes** somewhere, they rush or move there quickly: *Everyone dashed under cover when it started to rain.* **2.** If you **dash** someone's hopes or chances, you ruin or spoil them: *I hate to dash your hopes, but they've already sold the puppy.*
–noun **3.** a sudden or speedy rush. **4.** a small amount: *a dash of milk.* **5.** a horizontal line (–) used as punctuation to show a break in a sentence.
–phrase **6. dash off**, to write or make quickly: *to dash off an email.*

NOTE **Dashes** (definition 5) are punctuation marks. See the Grammar and Punctuation Guide appendix.

dashboard *noun* the panel in a car or plane which is in front of the driver's seat and has instruments for measuring things like speed, the distance you have travelled and the temperature of the engine.

THE SHORT FORM of this is **dash**.

data /*say* **day**-tuh, **dah**-tuh/ *plural noun* (*singular* **datum**)
1. facts or information: *We gathered data for our project on plants and animals that live near the creek.* **2.** information stored on a computer.

NOTE You can use either a singular or plural verb with **data**: *Your data is incorrect. Your data are incorrect.* If you are using it as a plural, note that the singular is **datum**, but this term is now mainly used in scientific writing.

database *noun* a collection of information stored in a computer and organised in categories so that it can be accessed easily.

datacast *verb* (**datacasts**, **datacasting**, **datacast** *or* **datacasted**, **has datacast** *or* **has datacasted**) To **datacast** is to broadcast digital information.
☐ **datacaster**, *noun* –**datacasting**, *noun*

date[1] *noun*
1. the day or year of something happening, or a statement of it in numbers: *What's the date of the meeting next month?*; *Today's date is the 12th.* **2.** the period of time to which something belongs: *This vase is valuable because of its early date.* **3.** an appointment made for a particular time or someone with whom you have an appointment: *a date with the hairdresser*; *Do you have a date for the school dance?*
–verb **4.** If you **date** something, you mark it with a date: *The letter was dated May 1904.* **5.** If you **date** someone, you go out with them as a girlfriend or boyfriend: *We have been dating for two months.*
–phrase **6. out of date**, old-fashioned: *The dress I bought last year is already out of date.* **7. to date**, to the present time.

WORD HISTORY from Latin words meaning 'things given'

date[2] *noun* the small brown fruit that grows on the **date palm**, which tastes very sweet and is often dried for eating.

daub /*say* dawb/ *verb* If you **daub** something or someone, you cover or coat them, especially with something soft or sticky like paint or mud: *to daub the children with sunscreen.*
☐ **daub**, *noun* sticky clay or mud: *a hut made of wattle and daub.*

daughter /*say* **daw**-tuh/ *noun* someone's female child: *My aunt has one daughter and two sons.*

☑ SPELLING TIP *Tricky vowel sound*: the first vowel sound is spelt *augh* (although it sounds like 'aw'). It might help if you think of other words with the same spelling for this sound, such as *naughty* and *caught*.

daughter-in-law *noun* (*plural* **daughters-in-law**) the wife of your son.

daunt /*say* dawnt/ *verb* If something **daunts** you, it makes you feel discouraged or frightened: *We were not daunted by the rain.*
☐ **daunting**, *adjective*: *What a daunting challenge!*

WORD HISTORY from a Latin word meaning 'tame' or 'subdue'

dawdle *verb* To **dawdle** is to waste time by being slow: *Don't dawdle on your way home.*
☐ **dawdler**, *noun*

dawn *noun*
1. the time of day when it begins to get light. **2.** the beginning of anything: *the dawn of the space age.*

–*verb* **3.** When something **dawns**, it begins: *A new day has dawned*; *A new era is dawning.*
–*phrase* **4. dawn on**, to begin to be understood by: *It finally dawned on him that he needed to study for the test.*

day *noun*
1. the time between sunrise and sunset when the sky is light. **2.** the 24-hour period between midnight of one day and the following midnight: *There are seven days in a week.* **3.** the time when you are actively doing things: *How did you spend your day?* **4.** a particular time or period: *There was no internet in my grandfather's day.*
–*phrase* **5. call it a day**, to finish doing something for the time being. **6. day by day**, daily, or each day. **7. day in, day out**, all day, every day for a period of time.
☐ **daytime**, *noun*

ANOTHER FORM This word (as in definition 4) can also be used in the plural form, as in *the olden days*.

daydream *verb* If you **daydream**, you do not give all your attention to what you're doing, but allow yourself to imagine pleasant things: *I often daydream about holidays.*
☐ **daydream**, *noun* –**daydreamer**, *noun*

daylight saving *noun* a system of putting the clock forward by one or more hours during the summer months so as to add more hours of daylight to the time that most people are awake: *10 o'clock in standard time becomes 11 o'clock in daylight saving.*

daze *verb*
1. If something such as a blow or sudden shock **dazes** you, it makes you feel uncertain about your surroundings: *He was dazed by a knock on the head*; *The suddenness of his success dazed him.*
–*noun* **2.** a confused state or condition: *to be in a daze.*
☐ **dazed**, *adjective*: *a dazed expression.*

dazzle *verb*
1. If a light **dazzles** you, it stops you seeing properly because of the way it shines into your eyes: *I was dazzled by the car's headlights.* **2.** If you **dazzle** someone, you surprise and interest them with your skill or beauty: *Her brilliant performance dazzled the audience.*
☐ **dazzling**, *adjective* –**dazzlingly**, *adverb*: *dazzlingly beautiful.*

de- *prefix* a word part showing that something is to be **1.** removed, as in *defoliate*. **2.** reversed, as in *deflate*.

dead *adjective*
1. When someone or something is **dead**, they are no longer alive: *dead flowers*; *a dead body.* **2.** If a part of your body goes **dead**, you have no feeling in it: *The dentist gave me an injection to make my gum go dead.* **3.** If a telephone, battery or piece of electrical equipment is **dead**, it isn't working: *The battery was dead so we couldn't start the car.* **4.** *Informal* If you feel **dead** after working or exercising, you are very tired: *I'm usually dead after a day of travelling.* **5.** *Informal* If you say that a place is **dead**, you mean that it is very boring and there is not much activity there. **6.** You can also use **dead** with certain nouns to emphasise that something is complete or absolute: *dead silence*; *a dead stop.*
–*phrase* **7. dead to the world**, very deeply asleep. **8. the dead**, the people who have died.
☐ **dead**, *adverb*: *to stop dead.*

A SIMILAR WORD (for definition 2) is **numb**.

deaden *verb* If something **deadens** a sound or feeling, it makes it weaker or less noticeable: *The vet gave my dog an injection to deaden the pain from her operation.*

deadline *noun* the latest time for finishing something: *The deadline for my project is next Monday.*

deadlock *noun* the point which people reach in an argument when neither side will give way.

deadly *adjective* (**deadlier**, **deadliest**)
1. Something that is **deadly** is likely or able to kill you: *a deadly weapon.* **2.** *Informal* very good: *That outfit is deadly.*
–*adverb* **3.** in a way that is like death or suggests death: *She turned deadly pale.* **4.** extremely: *The film was deadly boring*; *Listen to what I say – I am deadly serious.*

deaf *adjective*
1. If someone is **deaf**, they are unable to hear anything or they cannot hear very well. **2.** If you say that someone is **deaf** to something, you mean that they do not listen or pay attention to it: *She continued on her way, deaf to his advice.*
–*phrase* **3. the deaf**, people who are deaf. **4. turn a deaf ear**, to refuse to listen: *She turned a deaf ear to my request.*
☐ **deafen**, *verb*: *deafened by noise.* –**deafening**, *adjective* –**deafness**, *noun*

deal *verb* (**deals**, **dealing**, **dealt** /*say* delt/, **has dealt**)
1. To **deal** the cards is to give them out to each player: *I was dealt three aces.* **2.** To **deal** is to do business or trade: *We deal with clients around the world*; *My uncle deals in rare books.*
–*noun* **3.** quantity or amount: *a great deal of noise.* **4.** an arrangement or agreement: *We made a deal not to fight any more.*
–*phrase* **5. deal with**, **a.** to be about: *This book deals with the history of China.* **b.** to take action against: *The teacher will deal with the children who broke the window.* **c.** to treat or behave towards: *Our teacher always deals fairly with us.*
☐ **dealings**, *plural noun* business or connections between people.

dealer *noun*
1. someone who buys and sells things: *a car dealer.* **2.** the player who gives out the cards in a card game.

dean *noun*
1. the head of a section of a university. **2.** the head priest in charge of a cathedral.

WORD HISTORY from a Latin word meaning 'chief of ten'

dear *adjective*
1. If someone or something is **dear** to someone, they are loved by that person: *a dear aunt.* **2.** If something is **dear**, it costs a lot. **3. Dear**, (at the beginning of a letter) a word put before the name or title of the person you are writing to, as the usual polite way of starting a letter: *Dear Mr Matthews*; *Dear Madam.*
–*noun* **4.** someone you love: *How are you, my dear?*; *My little cousin is a dear.*
☐ **dearly**, *adverb*: *to pay dearly for a mistake.* –**dearness**, *noun*

A SIMILAR WORD (for definition 2) is **expensive**.

☑ SPELLING TIP Don't confuse the spelling of **dear** with **deer** which sounds the same. A **deer** is a type of animal.

death *noun*
1. the end of life: *He had been ill for several weeks before his death.* **2.** the end or destruction of anything: *The invention of the motor car was the death of the age of horses and carriages.*
–*phrase* **3. do to death**, **a.** to kill. **b.** to repeat until all meaning seems to be lost: *That joke has been done to death.* **4. put to death**, to kill, especially as a punishment for a crime. **5. sick to death of**, *Informal* bored and annoyed with.
☐ **deathly**, *adverb* like or as in death: *deathly pale.*

debate *noun*
1. an organised discussion: *a debate in parliament.* **2.** an organised contest in which two teams of speakers put forward opposite views on a chosen subject.
–*verb* **3.** If you **debate** something, you argue about it or discuss it: *We debated whether the book was a suitable gift.*
☐ **debater**, *noun*

debit *noun*
1. the recording of a debt in an account. **2.** an amount of money withdrawn from an account.
–*verb* (**debits**, **debiting**, **debited**, **has debited**) **3.** To **debit** someone is to charge them with a debt: *The shop will debit her for the purchase.*

COMPARE definition 2 with **credit** (definition 4).

debonair /*say* deb-uh-**nair**/ *adjective Rather old-fashioned* cheerful and with pleasant manners: *He had a debonair charm.*

debris /*say* **deb**-ree, **day**-bree, duh-**bree**/ *noun* the rubbish left when something is broken or destroyed.

☑ SPELLING TIP *Silent letter alert*: don't forget the silent *s* at the end. It is spelt in this way because it comes from French.

debt /*rhymes with* met/ *noun*
1. anything that you owe someone else.
–*phrase* **2. in debt**, owing money.
☐ **debtor**, *noun* Someone who owes you money is your **debtor**.

☑ SPELLING TIP *Silent letter alert*: don't forget the silent *b*.

deca- *prefix* a word part expressing ten times a given unit, as in *decade*, *decagon*, *decahedron*.

WORD HISTORY this prefix comes from Greek

decade /*say* **dek**-ayd/ *noun* a period of ten years.

WORD HISTORY from a Greek word meaning 'a group of ten'

decadent /*say* **dek**-uh-duhnt/ *adjective* If someone or something is **decadent**, they have low moral standards: *He claimed that vandalism was a sign of a decadent society.*
☐ **decadence**, *noun*

decaffeinated /*say* dee-**kaf**-uh-nay-tuhd/ *adjective* with the drug caffeine taken out: *decaffeinated coffee.*

decagon /*say* **dek**-uh-gon/ *noun* a flat shape with ten straight sides.
☐ **decagonal** /*say* duh-**kag**-uh-nuhl/, *adjective*

decahedron /*say* dek-uh-**heed**-ruhn/ *noun* a solid shape with ten flat faces.

decanter *noun* a container, often with a spout, for serving wine, water or juice at the table.
☐ **decant**, *verb* to pour gently from one container into another.

decapitate *verb* If someone or something **decapitates** a person or animal, they cut off the head of that person or animal.
☐ **decapitation**, *noun*

decathlon /*say* duh-**kath**-lon/ *noun* a contest in which athletes compete for the highest score in ten different events.

decay *verb* When something **decays**, it rots or goes bad.
☐ **decay**, *noun*: *tooth decay.*

deceased /*say* duh-**seest**/ *adjective*
1. You say someone is **deceased** if they have died: *She planted a tree in memory of her deceased husband.*
–*noun* **2. the deceased**, someone who has died: *He wore black out of respect for the deceased.*
☐ **decease**, *noun*: *We were saddened by his decease.*

☑ SPELLING TIP The spelling of **deceased** will be easier if you see that it contains the word *ceased* which means 'having come to an end'.

Remember the *c* spelling for the 's' sound and the *ea* spelling for the 'ee' sound.

deceive *verb* To **deceive** someone is to trick them or hide the truth from them: *He deceived his parents by pretending he was sick when really he just didn't want to go to school.*
☐ **deceit**, *noun* –**deceitful**, *adjective*

☑ SPELLING TIP *Tricky vowel sound*: *ei* to spell the 'ee' sound. This follows the rule that *i* comes before *e* except after *c* (when spelling an 'ee' sound).

December *noun* the twelfth month of the year, with 31 days.

THE ABBREVIATION is **Dec.**
WORD HISTORY the Latin name for the tenth month of the early Roman year

decent /*say* **dee**-suhnt/ *adjective*
1. Someone who is **decent** behaves in a proper way that is acceptable to society: *That sort of violent behaviour is an outrage to ordinary decent people.* **2.** Something that is **decent** is reasonable or enough: *a decent sleep*; *a decent wage.* **3.** You can also say someone is **decent** when they have done something kind or helpful: *It was decent of you to lend me a jumper.*
☐ **decency**, *noun* –**decently**, *adverb*

deception *noun* a trick or something that deceives.
☐ **deceptive**, *adjective* –**deceptively**, *adverb*

deci- *prefix* a word part expressing a tenth part of a given unit, as in *decimal*.

decibel /*say* **des**-uh-bel/ *noun* a measure of loudness used to show how much louder one sound is than another.

decide *verb*
1. If you **decide** to do something, you choose to do it after thinking about it for a time: *My parents have finally decided on a colour for the living room.* **2.** To **decide** something is to judge or settle what will happen: *We will ask our grandfather to decide which is the best drawing.*

decided *adjective*
1. definite and obvious: *a decided difference between my writing and yours.* **2.** having firmly made up your mind: *I tried to persuade him but he was quite decided.*
☐ **decidedly**, *adverb* definitely.

deciduous /*say* duh-**sid**-yooh-uhs/ *adjective* Trees which are **deciduous** lose their leaves every year.

COMPARE this with **evergreen**.

WORD HISTORY from a Latin word meaning 'falling down'

☑ SPELLING TIP Remember that there is a soft *c* making the 's' sound in **deciduous**. Remind yourself that this is like the soft sound that leaves make when they fall from **deciduous** trees.

decimal *adjective*
1. based on tenths or on the number ten: *decimal currency.*
–*noun* **2.** a decimal fraction or decimal number.

decimal fraction *noun* a fraction in which the bottom number is 10, 100, 1000, 10000, and so on, usually written with just the top number and a dot in front of it, as $0.4 = \frac{4}{10}$ and $0.04 = \frac{4}{100}$

decimal number *noun* a number consisting of a whole number and a decimal fraction, separated by a dot, such as 4.23.

decimal point *noun* the dot in a decimal fraction.

decipher /*say* duh-**suy**-fuh/ *verb* When you **decipher** something, you solve or find the meaning of it: *to decipher a code.*
☐ **decipherable**, *adjective* able to be understood or read.

☑ SPELLING TIP The spelling of **decipher** will be easier if you understand that a *cipher* (in which *ph* spells the 'f' sound) is a secret method of writing, or a code. Then you add the prefix *de-* (meaning 'separation' or 'taking away'). So when you **decipher** something, you take away the code and find out the hidden meaning.

decision *noun*
1. the act of deciding or making up your mind: *a hard decision.* **2.** an opinion or judgement: *The decision of the judges is final.* **3.** firmness and certainty in all you think and do: *a young man of decision.*
☐ **decisive**, *adjective*: *a decisive victory.* –**decisively**, *adverb*: *to act decisively.*

deck *noun*
1. the floor of a ship or bus. **2.** an open, raised platform or verandah, usually made of wood. **3.** the flat platform of a skateboard. **4.** a pack of playing cards.
–*phrase* **5. on deck**, on duty or ready for action. **6. hit the deck**, *Informal* to fall on the ground or the floor.

WORD HISTORY from a Dutch word meaning 'cover'

declare /*say* duh-**klair**/ *verb*
1. If you **declare** something, you announce it or make it publicly known: *He declared that he would return some day*; *The government declared war.* **2.** To **declare** can also be to close a cricket innings before all ten wickets have fallen.
☐ **declaration** /*say* dek-luh-**ray**-shuhn/, *noun*

decline *verb* /*say* duh-**kluyn**/
1. If something **declines**, it becomes worse, weaker or smaller: *After the accident, his health began to decline*; *The number of fatal car accidents has declined.* **2.** If someone **declines** a request, they politely refuse it: *I had to decline her invitation to dinner.*

–*noun* /*say* duh-**kluyn**, **dee**-kluyn/ **3.** a slope going down. **4.** a slow loss in health, strength, value, or something like this.

decode *verb* When you **decode** a message that is written in code, you change it back into the original language or form: *We managed to decode the enemy's signals.*
☐ **decoder**, *noun*

decompose *verb* When something **decomposes**, it rots or breaks up into smaller and simpler parts: *Leaves slowly decompose after they fall from trees.*
☐ **decomposition**, *noun*

decor /*say* **day**-kaw, **dek**-aw/ *noun* the way a building, such as a house or office, is decorated or furnished.

decorate *verb*
1. When you **decorate** something, you make it look attractive by adding things like flowers, balloons or lights: *We decorated the hall for the wedding.* **2.** When you **decorate** a room or house, you make it look good, as by painting it, or buying new carpets, curtains and furniture. **3.** If someone is **decorated** for bravery, they are given a special badge.
☐ **decoration**, *noun*: *party decorations.* –**decorative**, *adjective*: *a decorative frill.* –**decorator**, *noun*: *an interior decorator.*

decorum /*say* duh-**kaw**-ruhm/ *noun* proper behaviour, speech or dress: *She carried out her duties as school captain with grace and decorum.*
☐ **decorous** /*say* **dek**-uh-ruhs/, *adjective*

decoy /*say* **dee**-koy/ *noun* something or someone that tricks you, especially into danger or into a trap: *The police used a sports car as a decoy to catch the car thieves.*

decrease *verb* /*say* duh-**krees**/
1. If something **decreases**, it becomes smaller or weaker: *I have decreased the amount of chocolate I eat*; *Cinema audiences have decreased.*
–*noun* /*say* **dee**-krees, duh-**krees**/ **2.** A **decrease** is a weakening or reduction in something: *There has been a decrease in vandalism in our suburb.*

SIMILAR WORDS (for definition 1) are **reduce** and **diminish**.
THE OPPOSITE is **increase**.

decree *noun*
1. an official order or command: *a government decree.*
–*verb* (**decrees**, **decreeing**, **decreed**, **has decreed**) **2.** When someone **decrees** something, they give an official order or command: *The government decreed a new holiday.*

decrepit *adjective* made weak or broken down by old age: *a decrepit old dog*; *a decrepit car.*
☐ **decrepitly**, *adverb* –**decrepitude**, *noun*

dedicate *verb*
1. If you **dedicate** yourself to something, you give all your time and effort to it: *My grandfather dedicated his life to medicine.* **2.** If you **dedicate** a book, film or piece of music to someone, you honour them by putting their name on it as a sign of respect or thanks: *The composer dedicated the symphony to his daughter.*
☐ **dedicated**, *adjective*: *a dedicated teacher.* –**dedication**, *noun*

deduce *verb* If you **deduce** something, you reach that decision by reasoning and considering all the facts known to you: *From these figures we deduced that there was no significant difference between the two groups of animals.*
☐ **deducible**, *adjective*

deduct *verb* If you **deduct** an amount from a total, you reduce the total by that amount: *The judges will deduct points if your entry is late.*
☐ **deductible**, *adjective*

deduction *noun*
1. an amount taken away: *a $10 deduction*; *a tax deduction.* **2.** a conclusion or answer worked out from the facts.

deed *noun*
1. something done: *a good deed.* **2.** a signed agreement, usually about ownership of land.

deep *adjective*
1. If something is **deep**, it goes a long way down, in or back: *The cupboard isn't deep enough to fit all the books in.* **2. Deep** is used to describe the distance something goes down, in or back: *The pool is two metres deep here.* **3.** If something is **deep**, it is intense and serious: *deep respect*; *deep sleep.* **4.** If a sound is **deep**, it has a low pitch: *a deep voice.* **5.** If a colour is **deep**, it is dark and rich: *The ocean is a deep blue.* **6.** If someone is **deep**, they are thoughtful and clever, and sometimes difficult to understand: *My brother is the deep one in our family.*
–*phrase Informal* **7. go off the deep end**, to become very angry or excited. **8. in deep water**, in trouble or great difficulty.
☐ **deepen**, *verb*: *to deepen your voice.* –**deeply**, *adverb*

deep-fry *verb* (**deep-fries**, **deep-frying**, **deep-fried**, **has deep-fried**) To **deep-fry** food is to fry it in enough fat or oil to completely cover it while it is being cooked.

deer *noun* (*plural* **deer**) a large grass-eating animal with hooves, the male of which has branching horns or antlers.

NOTE The male is a **buck**; the female is a **doe**; the young is a **fawn**.

☑ SPELLING TIP Don't confuse the spelling of **deer** with **dear** which sounds the same. **Dear** describes someone who is loved: *a dear friend.*

deface *verb* To **deface** something is to damage its appearance: *Vandals defaced the room by spraying paint on the walls.*
☐ **defacement**, *noun*

de facto *adjective*
1. actually existing although not official or legal: *a de facto marriage*; *The rebels set up a de facto government.*
–*noun* **2.** a person who lives with someone as their husband or wife, without actually being married to them.

WORD HISTORY from Latin words meaning 'from the fact'

defame *verb* To **defame** someone is to damage their reputation: *The government minister said that she had been defamed by the newspaper article.*
☐ **defamation**, *noun* –**defamatory**, *adjective*

SEE ALSO **libel** and **slander**.

defeat *verb* If you **defeat** someone in a game, contest or war, you win a victory over them: *We easily defeated the visiting team.*
☐ **defeat**, *noun*: *to suffer a defeat.*

defect *noun* /*say* **dee**-fekt/
1. a fault or weakness: *a defect in the wood*; *a defect of character.*
–*verb* /*say* duh-**fekt**/ **2.** To **defect** is to leave your country without permission, not intending to return.
☐ **defection**, *noun* –**defective**, *adjective* –**defectively**, *adverb* –**defectiveness**, *noun* –**defector**, *noun*

defence *noun*
1. a protection against attack: *The high walls were part of the palace's defence.* **2.** an argument in support of something or in answer to a charge in court: *Her defence was that she was at home and asleep at the time of the attack.*
☐ **defensible**, *adjective* –**defensive**, *adjective*

defend *verb*
1. If you **defend** someone or something, you protect them from attack: *The soldiers defended the fort*; *The team defended their title.* **2.** If you **defend** someone or something, you support them by arguing in their favour: *My sister defended me against their lies.* **3.** If a lawyer **defends** someone in a court case, they try to prove that the person is not guilty of the crime they have been accused of.
☐ **defendant**, *noun* –**defender**, *noun*

defer *verb* (**defers**, **deferring**, **deferred**, **has deferred**) If you **defer** something, you put it off until another time: *The exam has been deferred until next week.*
☐ **deferment**, *noun*

SIMILAR WORDS are **delay**, **postpone** and **adjourn**. **Adjourn** is usually used in relation to court proceedings, parliamentary debates, or other formal meetings.

defiance *noun* brave disobedience to authority or any opposing force: *They showed their defiance by refusing to wear the uniform.*
☐ **defiant**, *adjective*: *a defiant stare.* –**defiantly**, *adverb*

deficient /*say* duh-**fish**-uhnt/ *adjective* lacking: *This soil is deficient in minerals.*
☐ **deficiency**, *noun* (*plural* **deficiencies**) –**deficiently**, *adverb*

deficit /*say* **def**-uh-suht/ *noun* an amount of money lacking: *There is a small deficit in the club's accounts.*

☑ SPELLING TIP Remember that there is a soft *c*, not an *s*, in **deficit**.

define *verb*
1. When you **define** a word, you explain what it means. **2.** When you **define** something, you establish its exact features or limits: *A constitution is used to define the rights and duties of every citizen.*
☐ **defined**, *adjective*: *a clearly defined figure.* –**definition**, *noun*

definite /*say* **def**-uh-nuht/ *adjective* Something **definite** is clear and certain: *When travelling overseas, it's a definite advantage to be able to speak at least one other language.*
☐ **definitely**, *adverb*

☑ SPELLING TIP *Tricky 'uh' sounds*: the middle and last vowel sounds are both spelt *i*. Many people get this wrong, especially by putting 'ate' at the end – but this word definitely has nothing to do with eating. Instead **definite** includes the word *finite* which means 'having limits or boundaries'.

deflate *verb*
1. If you **deflate** something, you let the air out of it: *I deflated the balloon.* **2.** If something **deflates** something, it lowers or reduces it: *Competition from other manufacturers has deflated the price of new cars.* **3.** If something **deflates** you, it makes you feel less important: *The criticism of their performance deflated the players.*
☐ **deflation**, *noun*

deflect *verb* If something **deflects** a moving object, it turns it away from its course: *His helmet deflected the arrow.*
☐ **deflection**, *noun*

defoliate *verb* If someone or something **defoliates** a plant, it takes off all its leaves: *A plague of big hairy caterpillars have almost completely defoliated the gum trees in the back yard.*
☐ **defoliant**, *noun* a chemical used to cause the leaves to fall from a tree. –**defoliation**, *noun*

deformed *adjective* Something is **deformed** if it is not its proper shape: *a deformed toe.*
☐ **deformity**, *noun* (*plural* **deformities**)

defrag /*say* dee-**frag**/ *verb* (**defrags**, **defragging**, **defragged**, **has defragged**) If you **defrag** data stored on a computer disk, you put in place a process that reorganises the data by collecting whole files together and storing them in the same place: *My computer is very slow, so I think I need to defrag it.*

WORD HISTORY short for **defragment** which has the same meaning and is the opposite of *fragment*

defraud *verb* To **defraud** someone is to cheat them, especially of money.

defrost *verb*
1. If you **defrost** something, you to remove ice from it: *to defrost a refrigerator.* **2.** If you **defrost** something, you thaw it out so that it is not frozen any more: *Defrost the steak so we can cook it tonight.*

deft *adjective* quick and neat: *deft movements.*
☐ **deftly**, *adverb* –**deftness**, *noun*

defuse *verb*
1. If someone **defuses** something, they remove the fuse from it: *to defuse a bomb.* **2.** If you **defuse** a tense or dangerous situation, you calm it by taking away the cause of the trouble: *to defuse mounting anger.*

☑ SPELLING TIP The spelling of **defuse** will be easier if you see that it is made up of *fuse* and the prefix *de-* (meaning 'separation' or 'taking away').

defy *verb* (**defies**, **defying**, **defied**, **has defied**)
1. If you **defy** a law or a person, you refuse to obey them: *The demonstrators openly defied the police.* **2.** If you **defy** someone to do something, you make them prove they can do it: *He defied him to do his worst.*

degenerate *verb* /*say* duh-**jen**-uh-rayt/
1. If someone or something **degenerates**, they become bad or worse than before.
–*adjective* /*say* duh-**jen**-uh-ruht/ **2.** If someone or something is **degenerate**, they have declined to a lower physical or moral level: *a degenerate society.*
☐ **degeneracy**, *noun* –**degeneration**, *noun*

degrade /*say* duh-**grayd**/ *verb* To **degrade** someone or something is to lower then or make them worse in character or nature: *She degraded herself by her terrible behaviour*; *The environment is being degraded by pollution.*
☐ **degradation** /*say* deg-ruh-**day**-shuhn/, *noun*

degree *noun*
1. a step or stage in a series: *Each new exercise advances a degree in difficulty.* **2.** a level: *Tapan is allowed a greater degree of freedom than his younger brothers.* **3.** in geometry, a unit of measurement of angles, one degree equalling $\frac{1}{360}$ of the circumference of a circle. **4.** a unit of measurement for temperature and for latitude or longitude. **5.** an award given by a university.
–*phrase* **6. by degrees**, slowly or gradually: *She is getting better by degrees.* **7. to a degree**, partly: *I think you're right, to a degree.*

THE SYMBOL for definitions 3 and 4 is ° as in *20° south*.

dehydrate *verb* To **dehydrate** something is to cause it to lose water or other fluids: *to dehydrate vegetables to preserve them*; *Drink lots of water to make sure you don't dehydrate in the hot sun.*
☐ **dehydration**, *noun*

deign /*say* dayn/ *verb* If you **deign** to do something, you stoop or lower yourself to do something you think is below you: *The queen deigned to answer her servant.*

A SIMILAR WORD is **condescend**.

☑ SPELLING TIP *Tricky vowel sound*: remember that the end of **deign** is spelt *eign* (although it sounds like 'ayn'). It might help if you think of a word you know well which has the same spelling for this sound, such as *reign* meaning 'to rule'. The *g* is left behind from their Latin origins.

deity /*say* **day**-uh-tee, **dee**-uh-tee/ *noun* (*plural* **deities**) a god or goddess.

☑ SPELLING TIP Remember that **deity** starts with *de* (though the most usual sound is 'day'). This is because it comes from *deus* (pronounced '**day**-uhs'), the Latin word for 'god'.

dejected *adjective* unhappy or depressed.
☐ **dejectedly**, *adverb* –**dejection**, *noun*

delay *verb*
1. If you **delay** doing something, you put it off until a later time: *We had to delay our holiday.* **2.** If something **delays** you, it makes you late for something or someone: *The traffic delayed us and we missed our flight.*
–*noun* **3.** a hold-up or stoppage: *The delay was due to a traffic accident.*

A SIMILAR WORD (for definition 1) is **postpone**.
WORD HISTORY from a Latin word meaning 'loosen'

delectable *adjective* delicious: *delectable food.*
☐ **delectably**, *adverb* –**delectation**, *noun*

delegate *noun* /*say* **del**-uh-guht/
1. a representative: *There were delegates from all over the world.*
–*verb* /*say* **del**-uh-gayt/ **2.** When you **delegate** a power or duty, you pass it on to someone else: *The job of keeping the kitchen clean was delegated to the boys.*
☐ **delegation**, *noun*

delete *verb* To **delete** something is to remove it in some way. If you **delete** something you have written, you take it out of your writing, for example, by crossing it out: *I think you should delete the last sentence from that email before you send it.*
☐ **deletion**, *noun*

☑ SPELLING TIP Remember that the end of **delete** is spelt *ete* (although it sounds like it could be spelt *eet* or *eat*). It might help if you think of a word you know well which has the same spelling for this sound, such as *compete*.

deliberate *adjective* /*say* duh-**lib**-uh-ruht/
1. A **deliberate** act is an intentional or carefully considered one.
–*verb* /*say* duh-**lib**-uh-rayt/ **2.** When you **deliberate**, you consider, or think carefully: *The meeting deliberated whether or not to accept the offer.*
☐ **deliberately**, *adverb* –**deliberation**, *noun*

delicacy /*say* **del**-uh-kuh-see/ *noun* (*plural* **delicacies**)
1. fineness: *the delicacy of the lace cloth.* **2.** a tasty or expensive food: *Lobster is a delicacy.*

delicate *adjective* If something is **delicate**, it is **1.** finely made or sensitive: *delicate lettering*; *a delicate measuring instrument.* **2.** easily damaged or weakened: *delicate glassware*; *delicate health.* **3.** pale or soft: *delicate skin*; *a delicate shade of pink.*
☐ **delicately**, *adverb*

delicatessen /*say* del-uh-kuh-**tes**-uhn/ *noun* a shop which sells a variety of foods, including cheeses, cold meats, and other prepared goods.

THE SHORT FORM of this, used in informal language, is **deli**.

☑ SPELLING TIP A **delicatessen** sells delicious foods and delicacies for you to eat. Inside this long word you can see two shorter words – *delicate* and *essen* (a German word meaning 'eat'). When they are put together, *essen* eats up the letter *e* at the end of *delicate*, making **delicatessen**.

delicious /*say* duh-**lish**-uhs/ *adjective* Something **delicious** is very pleasing to smell or taste: *a delicious lunch.*
☐ **deliciously**, *adverb*

delight *noun* great enjoyment or pleasure: *She squealed with delight when they announced she was the winner.*
☐ **delighted**, *adjective* –**delightful**, *adjective* –**delightfully**, *adverb*

☑ SPELLING TIP Remember that the end of **delight** is spelt *ight* (although it sounds like 'uyt'). It might help if you think of a word you know well which has the same spelling for this sound, such as *light*, *bright* and *sight*.

delinquent /*say* duh-**ling**-kwuhnt/ *noun* a young person who is in trouble with the law.
☐ **delinquent**, *adjective*: *delinquent behaviour.* –**delinquency**, *noun*

ANOTHER TERM for this is **juvenile delinquent**.

delirious /*say* duh-**lear**-ree-uhs/ *adjective* If someone is **delirious**, they are confused, unable to speak clearly, and sometimes see things that are not there, often because they have a fever.
☐ **deliriously**, *adverb* –**delirium** /*say* duh-**lear**-ree-uhm/, *noun*

☑ SPELLING TIP Remember that the spelling of the middle sound is *lir* (although it sounds like 'lear'). This comes from the Latin word *lira* meaning a 'furrow' (a straight ridge made in ploughing). The meaning of **delirious** comes from the idea of leaving what is straight or correct – in other words, going out of your mind.

deliver *verb*
1. When you **deliver** something, you take it somewhere or to someone and leave it or hand it over to them: *I had a large bunch of flowers delivered to my mother for her birthday.* **2.** When a doctor or midwife **delivers** a baby, they help the woman in giving birth: *Our doctor delivered two babies last night.* **3.** When a judge or jury **delivers** a verdict, they pronounce or say it publicly: *The jury delivered a verdict of 'not guilty'.* **4.** To **deliver** someone is to save them and set them free: *The police delivered the hostages from their captivity.*
☐ **delivery**, *noun*: *the delivery of a letter.* –**deliverance**, *noun*: *They were thankful for their deliverance from captivity.*

delta *noun* the flat rich land between outspreading river branches at the mouth of a river.

delude *verb* If someone **deludes** you, they trick you into thinking something that is not true: *He has deluded them into thinking that he is an honest man.*
☐ **delusion**, *noun* –**delusive**, *adjective*

deluge /*say* **del**-yoohj/ *noun*
1. a great flood or very heavy fall of rain. **2.** anything that pours out like a flood: *a deluge of words.*
–*verb* **3.** If you **deluge** someone with something, you give them a large amount of it, almost like a flood: *We put an advertisement in the paper and have been deluged with replies.*

deluxe /*say* duh-**luks**/ *adjective* of expensive high quality: *a deluxe car with leather seats.*

☑ SPELLING TIP *Silent letter alert*: don't forget the final *e*. **Deluxe** is made up of two French words: *de* meaning 'of' and *luxe* meaning 'luxury'.

delve *verb* When you **delve**, you search deeply: *She delved into her bag for the papers.*

demand *verb*
1. To **demand** something is to ask for it, as if it is your right: *He demands an apology.* **2.** If a job or situation **demands** something, that thing is needed for it to be successful: *This job demands a lot of patience.*

–*noun* **3.** a request or need: *The prime minister took notice of the public's demand for information about the war*; *There is a big demand for sandals in summer.*

demean *verb* If you **demean** yourself, you do something that lowers other people's opinion of you: *Don't demean yourself by lying.*

demeanour /*say* duh-**mee**-nuh/ *noun* the way you behave, and how this makes people think of you: *Everyone was upset by his sad demeanour.*

ANOTHER SPELLING is **demeanor.**

demented /*say* duh-**men**-tuhd/ *adjective* mad: *He was almost demented with fear*; *a demented laugh.*
☐ **dementedly**, *adverb*

dementia /*say* duh-**men**-shuh/ *noun* A person with **dementia** has impairment or loss of their mental powers, often as the result of a mental disease or other disease.

WORD HISTORY from a Latin word meaning 'madness'

democracy /*say* duh-**mok**-ruh-see/ *noun*
1. a way of governing a country, in which the people elect representatives to govern the country for them. **2.** a country with such a government. **3.** the idea that everyone in a country has equal rights: *The right of free speech for all is essential in a democracy.*
☐ **democrat** /*say* **dem**-uh-krat/, *noun* someone who supports democracy. –**democratic**, *adjective* –**democratically**, *adverb*

WORD HISTORY from the Greek word for 'people' added to the Greek word for 'rule' or 'authority'

demolish *verb* To **demolish** something is to knock it down or destroy it: *Dad demolished the old shed*; *She demolished my argument with a few relevant facts.*
☐ **demolition**, *noun*

demon /*say* **dee**-muhn/ *noun*
1. an evil spirit. **2.** *Informal* someone who does something with great energy: *He's a demon for punctuality.*
☐ **demonic** /*say* duh-**mon**-ik/, *adjective*

demonstrate /*say* **dem**-uhn-strayt/ *verb* To **demonstrate** something is to show it clearly: *The teacher demonstrated how to use the computer*; *He demonstrated how he felt by giving his mother a beaming smile.*
☐ **demonstrative** /*say* duh-**mon**-struh-tiv/, *adjective*: *She has a demonstrative nature and always shows her affection for her friends openly.*

demonstration *noun*
1. a march or other act to protest or to show support: *a demonstration against the war*; *a demonstration for lower university fees.* **2.** a public showing in order to advertise: *There is a demonstration of the new software in the computer store.*
☐ **demonstrator**, *noun*: *The demonstrators sang anti-war songs*; *A demonstrator showed me how to use the machine.*

demoralise *verb* If something **demoralises** you, it destroys your confidence: *She became demoralised when she found she couldn't keep up with the other swimmers.*
☐ **demoralisation**, *noun*

ANOTHER SPELLING is **demoralize.**

demote *verb* To **demote** someone is to make them lower in importance or rank: *She was demoted from team captain.*
☐ **demotion**, *noun*

demure *adjective* To be **demure** is to be shyly well-behaved: *a demure child.*
☐ **demurely**, *adverb*

den *noun*
1. an animal's burrow or shelter. **2.** a quiet room or place separate from other rooms: *He's reading in his den.*

denim *noun* a heavy cotton material used to make jeans and other clothes.

WORD HISTORY from French words meaning cloth 'of Nîmes' (a town in France)

denomination *noun* a religious group, especially in the Christian church.
☐ **denominational**, *adjective*

denominator *noun* the number under the line in a fraction which shows how many equal parts it may be divided into: *In the fraction ¾ 4 is the denominator.*

COMPARE this with **numerator.**

denote *verb* If something **denotes** something else, it means or shows it: *The first aid room is denoted by a red cross*; *His quiet way of talking denotes shyness.*

denounce /*say* duh-**nowns**/ *verb* To **denounce** someone is to speak out against them: *She denounced him as a liar and a cheat.*
☐ **denunciation** /*say* duh-nun-see-**ay**-shuhn/, *noun*

dense *adjective*
1. closely packed or thick: *dense bush*; *a dense fog.* **2.** *Rather informal* foolish or stupid.
☐ **densely**, *adverb* –**density**, *noun*

dent *noun*
1. a small hollow marking a surface: *My head made a dent in the pillow.*
–*verb* **2.** To **dent** something is to make a small hollow in it: *Hail dented the car roof.*

dental *adjective* having to do with teeth or dentists: *dental treatment*; *a dental nurse.*

dentist *noun* someone who is trained to treat your teeth.
☐ **dentistry**, *noun*

denture *noun* a plate with a false tooth or teeth attached, which fits into the mouth.

deny /*say* duh-**nuy**/ *verb* (**denies**, **denying**, **denied**, **has denied**)
1. When you **deny** something, you say that it is untrue: *She denied having stolen the money.* **2.** If you **deny** someone something, you refuse to give it to them: *He was denied permission to use the computer for a week.*
☐ **denial**, *noun*

deodorant /*say* dee-**oh**-duh-ruhnt/ *noun* something which prevents or removes bad smells.
☐ **deodorise**, *verb*

ANOTHER SPELLING for **deodorise** is **deodorize**.

☑ SPELLING TIP The spelling of **deodorant** will be easier if you see that it is made up of the prefix *de-* (meaning 'not' or 'without'), *odor* (a form of the word *odour*, meaning 'a smell'), and the suffix *-ant* (not *-ent*). You might remind yourself that **deodorant** stops you smelling like an ant!

depart *verb* To **depart** is to go away or leave.
☐ **departure**, *noun*

department *noun* a division in a large organisation such as a government, college, or store: *The electronics department is on the first floor.*
☐ **departmental**, *adjective*

department store *noun* a large shop selling a range of goods in different departments.

depend *verb*
1. If you can **depend** on someone, you know that you can trust them: *I can depend on you to keep my secret.* **2.** If something **depends** on something else, it is determined by it: *I should be able to get there in time, depending on the traffic.*
☐ **dependable**, *adjective*: *She is a dependable person who can always be relied on.*

NOTE **Depend** is usually followed by *on*.

dependant *noun* someone who needs the support of another.

☑ SPELLING TIP Remember that the last part of this noun is spelt with *ant*. Compare the related adjective **dependent**. It might help if you remind yourself that *ant* is a noun and so is **dependant**.

dependent *adjective* A **dependent** person is one needing support: *a dependent child.*
☐ **dependence**, *noun* –**dependency**, *noun*

☑ SPELLING TIP Remember that the final part of this adjective is spelt *ent*. Compare the related noun **dependant**.

depict *verb* If you **depict** someone or something, you describe or show them in words or pictures: *The painting depicts the story of King Arthur pulling the sword from the stone.*
☐ **depiction**, *noun*

deplete *verb* If you **deplete** something, you reduce it or make it less: *The drought has greatly depleted the wheat harvest.*
☐ **depletion**, *noun*

deplore *verb* If you **deplore** something, you feel deep regret or are very sorry about it: *We deplore the terrible way you were treated.*
☐ **deplorable**, *adjective* very bad: *deplorable behaviour.* –**deplorably**, *adverb*

deport *verb* When a country **deports** someone, it sends them away because they have broken the law or have no legal right to be there: *The illegal immigrants were deported.*
☐ **deportation**, *noun* –**deportee**, *noun*

deportment *noun* the way you stand.

SIMILAR WORDS are **carriage** and **bearing**.

depose *verb* To **depose** a ruler is to remove them from their position by force: *The army deposed the king.*

deposit *verb* (**deposits**, **depositing**, **deposited**, **has deposited**)
1. If you **deposit** something, you put it down somewhere: *I deposited my heavy bag before climbing the stairs.* **2.** When you **deposit** money in a bank, you put it there to be kept safe for you. –*noun* **3.** an amount given as the first part of a payment, or as a promise to pay. **4.** money placed in a bank. **5.** a layer which collects on a surface: *The floor was covered with a deposit of sand.*

depot /*say* **dep**-oh/ *noun*
1. a place where goods are stored or unloaded. **2.** a place where buses, trams, or trucks are kept.

☑ SPELLING TIP *Silent letter alert*: don't forget the silent *t* at the end. It is spelt in this way because it comes from French.

depraved /*say* duh-**prayvd**/ *adjective* If someone is **depraved**, they have become immoral in character: *Someone who commits a terrible crime like that must be depraved.*
☐ **depravity** /*say* duh-**prav**-uh-tee/, *noun*

depress *verb*
1. If something **depresses** you, it makes you feel sad and hopeless: *The death of her father depressed her terribly.* **2.** If something **depresses** prices or the economy, it makes them lower or less active: *A rise in interest rates has depressed the price of houses.*
☐ **depressed**, *adjective* –**depression**, *noun* –**depressing**, *adjective* –**depressive**, *adjective*

deprive *verb* If you **deprive** someone of something, you stop them from having it or using it: *The noisy party upstairs deprived us of sleep.*
☐ **deprivation**, *noun* –**deprived**, *adjective*

depth *noun*
1. deepness or distance downward: *You should check the depth of the water before you dive in.* **2.** strength, especially of colour or feeling: *No-one knew the depth of his hatred.*
–*phrase* **3. in depth**, without missing anything: *to study a subject in depth.* **4. out of your depth**, **a.** in water so deep that you cannot stand up. **b.** outside what you can do or understand. **5. the depths**, the deepest part, especially of the sea.

deputation *noun* people chosen to speak on behalf of the group to which they belong.

A SIMILAR WORD is **delegation**.

deputy /*say* **dep**-yuh-tee/ *noun* (*plural* **deputies**) someone who helps or acts for another person: *While the principal was sick, her deputy took over her duties.*
☐ **deputise**, *verb* –**deputy**, *adjective*: *the deputy principal.*

ANOTHER SPELLING for **deputise** is **deputize**.

derail *verb* If something **derails** a train, it makes it run off the tracks or rails on which it is travelling: *A rock on the track derailed the train and several people were injured*; *The train was derailed just before it came to the station.*
☐ **derailment**, *noun* an accident in which a train comes off its tracks.

deranged *adjective* wild and uncontrolled in the way you behave, especially because you are crazy or insane: *The deranged man had overturned all the garbage bins in the street.*
☐ **derange**, *verb* to throw into disorder. –**derangement**, *noun*

derelict /*say* **de**-ruh-likt/ *adjective*
1. If a building is **derelict**, it has not been used for a long while and has fallen into ruin: *A derelict shed stood in the yard of the old house.*
–*noun* **2.** a poor, homeless person.
☐ **dereliction**, *noun*

WORD HISTORY from a Latin word meaning 'forsaken utterly'

deride /*say* duh-**ruyd**/ *verb* If you **deride** someone or something, you make fun of them: *It is not nice to deride the way someone looks.*
☐ **derision** /*say* duh-**rizh**-uhn/, *noun*: *He tried to apologise but was greeted with cries of derision.* –**derisive** /*say* duh-**ruy**-siv, duh-**riz**-iv/, *adjective*

derive /*say* duh-**ruyv**/ *verb*
1. If you **derive** something from somewhere, you take or receive it from there: *Yusef derives his income from two jobs.* **2.** If you **derive** an answer to something, you work it out by reasoning: *Add all the figures together to derive the total.*
☐ **derivation** /*say* de-ruh-**vay**-shuhn/, *noun* origin. –**derivative** /*say* duh-**riv**-uh-tiv/, *adjective* coming from something else.

dermatitis /*say* der-muh-**tuy**-tuhs/ *noun* dryness and redness of the skin which is itchy or painful.

☑ SPELLING TIP The spelling of **dermatitis** will be easier if you see that it contains *derma* (the Greek word for 'skin') with the letter *t* added to join it to the suffix *-itis* (meaning 'inflamed condition'). Think of other similar words such as *tonsillitis* and *appendicitis*. They all end with *-itis* (spelt with *is*, not *us*).

derogatory /*say* duh-**rog**-uh-tree/ *adjective* unfairly critical: *Steve was hurt by their derogatory comments about his singing.*

☑ SPELLING TIP *Single letter alert*: only one *r* both times it appears, and only one *g*. Rap it out as *de+ rog+ a+ tor+ y*.

desalination /*say* dee-sal-uh-**nay**-shuhn/ *noun* the process of removing dissolved salts from sea water so that it becomes suitable for drinking by humans or animals or for use in agriculture.

descant /*say* **des**-kant/ *noun* a tune played or sung above the main tune.

descend *verb*
1. To **descend** is to go or come down: *The path descends steeply here*; *She began to descend from the tree.* **2.** If you are **descended** from someone who lived before you, you can track a relationship back through your family to them.
☐ **descendant**, *noun*: *She is a descendant of one of our early prime ministers.*

☑ SPELLING TIP *Silent letter alert*: don't forget the silent *c* after the *s*. This is left over from its Latin beginnings – *de-* (meaning 'down') and *scandere* (meaning 'to climb'). Notice that the silent *c* also appears in the opposite word **ascend**. Going up or coming down, don't forget the *c*!

descent /*say* duh-**sent**/ *noun*
1. the act of coming or going down: *He made a quick descent down the ladder.* **2.** the downward slope of a mountain or stairway. **3.** ancestry: *of Chinese descent.*

☑ SPELLING TIP See **descend**.

describe *verb* To **describe** someone or something is to give a picture of them using written or spoken words: *She described the man clearly*; *Conrad described what happened before we arrived.*
☐ **description**, *noun* –**descriptive**, *adjective*

☑ SPELLING TIP The spelling of **describe** will be easier if you see that it is made up of *scribe* (someone in the past whose job was to write or copy things in words) and the prefix *de-* (meaning 'down').

deselect *verb* If you **deselect** something selected on a computer screen (such as highlighted text), you click the mouse to cancel the selected item.

desert[1] /*say* **dez**-uht/ *noun* a sandy or stony place without enough rainfall to grow many plants.

☑ SPELLING TIP Don't confuse the spelling of **desert** with **dessert** (with a double *s*). A **dessert**, pronounced as 'duh-**zert**', is a sweet dish served at the end of a meal.

WORD HISTORY from a Latin word meaning 'abandoned'.

desert² /*say* duh-**zert**/ *verb* To **desert** is to leave or run away without intending to return.
□ **deserted**, *adjective* abandoned or lonely. –**deserter**, *noun* –**desertion**, *noun*

☑ SPELLING TIP Don't confuse the spelling of **desert** with **dessert**, which sounds the same but has a double *s*.

deserts /*say* duh-**zerts**/ *plural noun* something which is deserved, either as a reward or a punishment: *Everyone thought she got her just deserts.*

☑ SPELLING TIP Don't confuse the spelling of **deserts** with **desserts**, which sounds the same. **Desserts** is the plural of **dessert**, a sweet dish served at the end of a meal. **Deserts** are the things you *deserve*.

deserve /*say* duh-**zerv**/ *verb* If you **deserve** something, you are worthy of it or you have earned it: *He's been a good boy all day – I think he deserves a reward.*
□ **deserved**, *adjective* –**deservedly** /*say* duh-**zerv**-uhd-lee/, *adverb* –**deserving**, *adjective*

desiccated /*say* **des**-uh-kay-tuhd/ *adjective* dried, often so as to be in a powdery form: *desiccated coconut.*

☑ SPELLING TIP *Single/double letter alert*: one *s* but double *c*.

design /*say* duh-**zuyn**/ *verb*
1. If you **design** something, you work out how it should look and work, and present your ideas in drawings. **2.** If you **design** something for a particular purpose, you make it so that it is suitable for that purpose: *I designed the seams to lie flat.*
–*noun* **3.** a drawing or plan: *Here is my design for a long skirt.* **4.** a pattern: *There is a design of roses on the plates.* **5.** in art, the ability to combine the parts of a picture or other work of art into a pleasing whole.
–*phrase* **6. by design**, on purpose: *He met me here by design.*
□ **designer**, *noun*

☑ SPELLING TIP Remember the *g* in this word. The letter combination *ign* gives the 'uyn' sound, as in the word *sign*.

designate /*say* **dez**-ig-nayt/ *verb*
1. If something **designates** something else, it marks or shows it: *She used stickers to designate which pages she wanted to read to the class.* **2.** If you **designate** someone for a particular job, you choose them to have that job: *They designated Mary to be the one to carry the flag.*
□ **designated**, *adjective*

designated driver *noun* a person at a social occasion who agrees to drink no or very little alcohol in order to drive his or her companions home safely.

desirable *adjective* Something **desirable** is good or beautiful enough to be wanted: *The house is fairly small, but it's in a desirable location right on the beach.*
□ **desirably**, *adverb*

desire *verb* To **desire** something is to **1.** want it very much. **2.** ask for it in a formal way: *The president desired their presence at his country home.*
–*noun* **3.** need or want: *They had a strong desire to laugh*; *She has a desire for chocolate.* **4.** request: *Tell us your desires and we shall try to grant them.*

desist /*say* duh-**zist**/ *verb* If you **desist** from doing something, you stop doing it: *The lady sitting in front asked us to desist from talking during the movie.*

desk *noun*
1. a writing table, often with drawers or small spaces for papers. **2.** the place, usually at the front of an office or hotel, where information is given: *Ask at the desk about buses to the airport.*

desktop *noun*
1. the background image displayed on a computer screen, which includes signs representing programs, documents, etc.
–*adjective* **2.** having to do with a computer or other equipment which is small enough to be used at a desk.

desolate *adjective*
1. If a place is **desolate**, there is no-one there: *the desolate streets of the deserted town.* **2.** If someone is **desolate**, they feel sad and hopeless: *They felt desolate after losing all their possessions.*
□ **desolation**, *noun*

despair *noun*
1. a feeling of hopelessness: *She looked with despair at the still smouldering remains of her home.*
–*verb* **2.** If you **despair**, you lose or give up hope: *Following the latest disaster, we really despair of ever finishing this job.*

☑ SPELLING TIP The difficulty in spelling **despair** is remembering that the last part is spelt *air*. Try thinking that if you had no air to breathe, you would be sure to be full of **despair**.

desperate *adjective*
1. If you are **desperate**, you are in such a bad situation that you will risk anything to get out of it: *Do not approach this man – he is armed and desperate.* **2.** If you are **desperate** for something, you need it badly: *desperate for money*;

desperate for sleep. **3.** If a situation is **desperate**, it is very serious: *The plight of the lost walkers was becoming desperate.* **4.** A **desperate** action is one you take as a last resort: *a desperate plan.*
□ **desperately**, *adverb* –**desperation**, *noun*

despise *verb* To **despise** someone is to look down on them, especially with hatred: *They despised him for being so cowardly.*

despite *preposition* If something happens **despite** something else, it still happens, even though you might think that the second thing would prevent it: *Despite their different natures, the two boys are good friends.*

despondent *adjective* depressed or sad: *The bad news put him in a despondent mood.*
□ **despondency**, *noun* –**despondently**, *adverb*

despot *noun* a cruel and unjust ruler.
□ **despotic**, *adjective* –**despotically**, *adverb*

WORD HISTORY from a Greek word meaning 'master'

dessert /*say* duh-**zert**/ *noun* the fruit or sweets eaten at the end of a meal.

☑ SPELLING TIP *Double letter alert*: two *s*'s. You could try thinking that they stand for 'second serving' and that is why they turn up in **dessert** which is something sweet to eat, but not in **desert** which is a dry, sandy place.

destination *noun* the place you are travelling to, or to which something is sent.

destined /*say* **des**-tuhnd/ *adjective* If someone says that something is **destined** to happen, they believe it will happen in the future because of fate or because there is strong reason to believe that it will: *They were destined to marry*; *The song is destined to be a hit.*

destiny /*say* **des**-tuh-nee/ *noun* (*plural* **destinies**) fate, or something that had to happen: *It was her destiny to spend her life helping others.*

destitute *adjective* without money or the means of getting any: *The theft of his wallet and belongings left the traveller destitute.*
□ **destitution**, *noun*

destroy *verb*
1. If you **destroy** something, you put an end to its existence: *She destroyed the manuscript before she died.* **2.** If something or someone **destroys** something, they damage it so severely that it's completely useless: *The earthquake destroyed the city centre.* **3.** If someone **destroys** an animal, they kill it because it is dangerous or too ill or badly injured to be cured.
□ **destroyer**, *noun* –**destruction**, *noun* –**destructive**, *adjective* –**destructively**, *adverb*

detach *verb* If you **detach** one thing from another thing, you separate or unfasten it: *She detached herself from the group and came over to say hello*; *The inspector detached the top part of my ticket.*
□ **detachable**, *adjective*

WORD HISTORY from a French word meaning 'to remove a nail'

detached *adjective*
1. separate or standing apart: *detached houses.* **2.** not emotionally involved or concerned with the events and people around you: *He seemed detached and didn't talk to many people at the party.*

detachment *noun*
1. the ability to stand aside and not let your judgement be affected by your feelings. **2.** a force of soldiers or naval ships set aside for a special task.

detail *noun*
1. one of the single or small parts which go to make up a whole: *Try to remember every detail.* **2.** fine, delicate work: *The amount of detail in her paintings is astonishing.*
–*verb* **3.** If you **detail** something, you give full information about it: *She detailed her plans.*
□ **detailed**, *adjective*

detain *verb* To **detain** someone is to **1.** delay or hold them up: *Sorry, I didn't mean to detain you.* **2.** keep them under control or in prison: *The police detained him while they checked the truth of what he said.*
□ **detainee**, *noun*

detect *verb* If you **detect** something, you notice or discover it: *They detected him stealing from the shop.*
□ **detectable**, *adjective* –**detection**, *noun* –**detector**, *noun*

detective *noun* a person, usually a police officer, who is trained to discover who committed a crime.
□ **detective**, *adjective*: *a detective story.*

detention *noun*
1. imprisonment or confinement to a particular place: *They argued about whether illegal immigrants should be kept in detention.* **2.** the keeping in of a pupil after school hours as a punishment.

deter /*say* duh-**ter**/ *verb* (**deters**, **deterring**, **deterred**, **has deterred**) If you **deter** someone from doing something, you prevent or stop them: *a fine to deter drivers from speeding.*
□ **deterrent** /*say* duh-**te**-ruhnt, duh-**ter**-ruhnt/, *noun*

detergent *noun* powder or liquid used for cleaning.

deteriorate /*say* duh-**tear**-ree-uh-rayt/ *verb* If something **deteriorates**, it becomes worse: *If the weather keeps deteriorating, we will have to postpone our canoe trip.*
□ **deterioration**, *noun*

determination *noun* firmness of purpose: *a determination to succeed.*

determine *verb*
1. If one thing **determines** another, it decides it. It is responsible for the result: *Your score in the exam will determine which school you will go to.* **2.** If you **determine** something, you find it out or decide it for certain: *It was hard to determine the cause of death.* **3.** If you **determine** to do something, you decide firmly that you will do it: *I have determined to do better in mathematics.*
□ **determined**, *adjective*: *Their determined campaign saved the historic building.*

detest *verb* If you **detest** someone or something, you dislike them very much.
□ **detestable**, *adjective* –**detestation**, *noun*

detonate *verb*
1. If something **detonates**, it explodes: *The bomb detonated.* **2.** If something or someone **detonates** something, they cause it to explode: *They detonated the dynamite and immediately the building began to crumble.*
□ **detonation**, *noun* –**detonator**, *noun*

detour *noun*
1. a different way round, used when a road is closed.
–*verb* **2.** If you **detour**, you go by way of a detour or you make a detour: *We had to detour around the flooded creek*; *I made a detour to the post office on my way to soccer.*

detract *verb in the phrase* **detract from**, to take away some of, or reduce the value of: *Lying will detract from the respect people have for you.*
□ **detraction**, *noun* –**detractor**, *noun*

deuce /*say* dyoohs/ *noun* a stage in a game of tennis when both players have a score of 40 and one player must gain a lead of two points to win the game.

☑ SPELLING TIP The word **deuce** comes from the Latin word *duo* meaning 'two'. It has come into English from French, and on the way has changed its spelling. Concentrate on remembering the *eu* spelling of the vowel sound, as well as the soft *c* for the 's' sound.

devalue *verb* If someone or something **devalues** something, they lower its worth or its value: *to devalue someone's efforts*; *to devalue a currency.*
□ **devaluation**, *noun*

devastate *verb*
1. If something **devastates** a place, it ruins or destroys the place completely: *The fire devastated several buildings.* **2.** If something **devastates** someone, it upsets or depresses them greatly: *The news of her husband's death devastated her.*
□ **devastated**, *adjective* –**devastating**, *adjective* –**devastation**, *noun*

develop *verb*
1. When someone or something **develops**, they change or become more complete over a period of time: *As children grow and develop, they become more aware of others.* **2.** If something **develops**, it comes into existence: *If these growths are left untreated, cancer can develop.* **3.** If you **develop** something, you gradually build it up: *We encourage our students to develop their own interests.* **4.** If you **develop** something, you begin to have or experience it: *I think I'm developing a cold.* **5.** If someone **develops** something, they experiment with various possibilities to create or improve it, and gradually become more successful: *We're developing a new type of washing machine.* **6.** If someone **develops** an area of land, they build houses or other buildings on it so that it increases in value. **7.** When you **develop** a photographic film, you use chemicals to make negatives from it.
□ **developed**, *adjective* –**developer**, *noun* –**developing**, *adjective* –**development**, *noun*

deviate *verb* To **deviate** is to turn aside or away from something: *Because of the exam tomorrow, we will deviate from the normal lesson*; *to deviate from normal behaviour.*
□ **deviant**, *adjective*, *noun* –**deviation**, *noun*

device /*say* duh-**vuys**/ *noun* something which has been invented for a particular purpose: *This device counts each step you take.*

A SIMILAR WORD is **contraption**.

☑ SPELLING TIP Don't confuse the noun **device** with the verb **devise** which is to think out, invent or plan. It might help if you remind yourself that **device** contains the word *ice* which is a noun, just like **device** itself.

devil *noun*
1. in some religions, an evil spirit. **2. the Devil**, in religions such Judaism, Christianity and Islam, the most powerful evil spirit and enemy of God. **3.** *Informal* a naughty person, especially a child.
□ **devilish**, *adjective* –**devilment**, *noun* –**devilry**, *noun*

devious *adjective* A **devious** person is tricky or deceitful: *His devious ways made him a lot of enemies.*
□ **deviously**, *adverb* –**deviousness**, *noun*

devise /*say* duh-**vuyz**/ *verb* If you **devise** something, you invent or plan it: *to devise a new system of collecting taxes.*

☑ SPELLING TIP Don't confuse the spelling of the verb **devise** with the noun **device**, which is something which has been invented for a particular purpose. See the note at **device**.

devoid *adjective in the phrase* **devoid of**, free from or without: *The street was devoid of shade.*

devote *verb*
1. If you **devote** your time to doing something, you keep it for that purpose only: *My father devotes all his spare time to building his boat.* **2.** If you **devote** yourself to something, you give all

your attention to it: *This year I'm really going to devote myself to my studies.*
☐ **devoted**, *adjective* –**devotee**, *noun* –**devotion**, *noun*

devour *verb* If you **devour** food, you eat it hungrily and quickly, rather like wild animals do: *She devoured her dinner in a few minutes.*

devout *adjective* sincerely religious.
☐ **devoutly**, *adverb* –**devoutness**, *noun*

dew *noun* small drops of water that form during the night on any cool surfaces out of doors.
☐ **dewy**, *adjective*

☑ SPELLING TIP Don't confuse the spelling of **dew** with **due** which sounds the same. **Due** means 'expected': *The train is due at 10 o'clock.*

dexterity /*say* deks-**te**-ruh-tee/ *noun* skill or cleverness, especially in using your hands.
☐ **dexterous** /*say* **deks**-truhs/, *adjective*

☑ SPELLING TIP To spell **dexterity** you need to see that it contains *dexter* (which comes from the Latin word for 'right' or 'right-handed') with the addition of the suffix *-ity* (which means 'having the characteristics of'). This is a useful suffix to remember because it turns up on many other words such as *activity*, *possibility*, and *prosperity*.

dhoti /*say* **doh**-tee/ *noun* (*plural* **dhotis**) a piece of clothing worn by some Hindu men, consisting of a long cloth wrapped around the waist and between the legs.

☑ SPELLING TIP *Silent letter alert*: don't forget the silent *h* following the *d* at the beginning. This is a common spelling in words that come from Hindi, as **dhoti** does.

diabesity /*say* duy-uh-**bee**-suh-tee/ *noun* obesity accompanied by diabetes.

☑ SPELLING TIP The spelling of **diabesity** will be easier if you see that it is a combination of the words *dia*(*betes*) and (*o*)*besity*.

diabetes /*say* duy-uh-**bee**-teez/ *noun* a disease in which the body finds it difficult to use sugar and passes it out in your urine.
☐ **diabetic** /*say* duy-uh-**bet**-ik/, *noun*, *adjective*

☑ SPELLING TIP This word has an unusual spelling because it comes from Greek where it means 'a passing through'. The most difficult part to spell is the final part, *betes*. Remember that a single *e* turns up twice in this word part (each time giving the sound 'ee').

diabolical *adjective*
1. devilish or wicked. **2.** very difficult or unpleasant.

ANOTHER WORD for this is **diabolic**.
SIMILAR WORDS (for definition 1) are **fiendish** and **satanic**.

diagnosis /*say* duy-uhg-**noh**-suhs/ *noun* (*plural* **diagnoses** /*say* duy-uhg-**noh**-seez/) the working out of what disease a patient has.
☐ **diagnose**, *verb* –**diagnostic**, *adjective*

☑ SPELLING TIP **Diagnosis** looks difficult, but if you rap it out as *di+ag+no+sis*, it is not really very hard. You could also try remembering that it comes from Greek and is made up of *dia-* (meaning 'through') and *gnosis* (meaning 'knowing').

diagonal *noun* a sloping line joining the opposite corners of a rectangle or square.
☐ **diagonal**, *adjective* –**diagonally**, *adverb*

diagram *noun* a drawing which explains how something works or is laid out: *a diagram of the engine*; *a diagram of the hospital.*
☐ **diagrammatic**, *adjective* –**diagrammatically**, *adverb*

dial *noun*
1. the face of a clock, radio, or measuring instrument. **2.** a circular instrument, marked with measurements or other divisions, which you turn to change the setting of something: *The dial on the radio was broken.*
–*verb* (**dials**, **dialling**, **dialled**, **has dialled**)
3. When you **dial** a telephone number, you enter the separate numbers of it on the telephone so as to make a call: *A stranger answered – I must have dialled the wrong number.*

WORD HISTORY from a Latin word meaning 'day'

dialect *noun* a variety of a language spoken in a particular area or by a particular group of people.

dialogue *noun* a conversation between two or more people, especially in a play or story.

☑ SPELLING TIP *Silent letter alert*: don't forget the silent *ue* at the end. It is spelt in this way because it comes from French. The ending *logue* with the same sound turns up in several words that have to do with speaking, including **dialogue**'s partner word, *monologue*, which is a talk by one person.

dial-up *adjective* A **dial-up** service or system is one which you can use from your computer if you have a telephone line linked to it.

ANOTHER SPELLING is **dialup**.

diameter /*say* duy-**am**-uh-tuh/ *noun*
1. the straight line which goes through the centre of a circle from one side to the other. **2.** the length of such a line.
☐ **diametrical**, *adjective* –**diametrically**, *adverb*

diamond /*say* **duy**-muhnd/ *noun*
1. a very hard, clear, shining, precious stone which is used in jewellery. **2.** the red four-sided shape on some playing cards.

☑ SPELLING TIP *Silent letter alert*: don't forget the silent *a*.

diaphragm /*say* **duy**-uh-fram/ *noun*
1. the sheet of muscle inside the body between the chest and abdomen. **2.** a thin sheet or membrane.

☑ SPELLING TIP *Silent letter alert*: don't forget the silent *g*. Also remember that the 'f' sound is spelt *ph*. **Diaphragm** is spelt like this because it comes from Greek.

diarrhoea /*say* duy-uh-**ree**-uh/ *noun* a sickness in which there are stomach pains and watery matter passes frequently from the bowels.

☑ SPELLING TIP This word comes from Greek and there is no way you could guess the spelling, so you have to make sure you remember some special things about it. There is a double *r* in the middle, followed by a silent *h*. Worst of all, the 'ee-uh' sound at the end is spelt by the letters *oea*. **Diarrhoea** is not nice to have, and it is certainly not nice to spell!

diary *noun* (*plural* **diaries**) a book in which you write down daily events or thoughts.

☑ DO NOT CONFUSE **diary** with **dairy** which is a place where cows are milked.

dibbler *noun* a small native mouse with spots that lives in Western Australia. It is almost extinct.

WORD HISTORY from an Aboriginal language of Western Australia called Nyungar

dice *plural noun* (*singular* **die**)
1. small cubes marked on each side with a different number of spots, from one to six, used in games.
–*verb* **2.** To **dice** something is to cut it into small pieces: *to dice carrots.*
☐ **diced**, *adjective*: *diced vegetables.*

NOTE Although this is strictly a plural noun (with the singular **die**), many people use **dice** as the singular, and it is quite acceptable: *Please bring me that dice from the box.*

dictate *verb*
1. To **dictate** something is to say or read it aloud for someone else to write down: *The manager dictated a letter to his personal assistant.* **2.** To **dictate** that something be done is to order that it should be done.
☐ **dictation**, *noun*

dictator *noun* someone who has total power, especially in governing a country.
☐ **dictatorial**, *adjective* –**dictatorship**, *noun*

dictionary /*say* **dik**-shuhn-ree, **dik**-shuh-ne-ree/ *noun* (*plural* **dictionaries**) a reference work with an alphabetical list of words, their meanings, and sometimes other information such as their pronunciations and history.

☑ SPELLING TIP The spelling of **dictionary** will be easier if you see that it begins with *dictio*, which is Latin for 'word'.

did *verb* the past tense of **do**.

didjeridu /*say* dij-uh-ree-**dooh**/ *noun* a long, pipe-shaped, Aboriginal wind instrument made of wood.

ANOTHER SPELLING is **didgeridoo**.
WORD HISTORY from an imitation of the sound it makes

didn't a short form of *did not*.

die[1] *verb* (**dies**, **dying**, **died**, **has died**)
1. To **die** is to stop living.
–*phrase* **2. die down**, to pass slowly away: *The fire died down.* **3. die off**, to die one after the other until there are very few left. **4. die out**, to no longer live on earth: *Dinosaurs died out millions of years ago.*

☑ SPELLING TIP Don't confuse the spelling of **die** with **dye** which sounds the same. **Dye** is a substance you use to colour things.

die[2] *noun*
1. a tool for cutting, stamping, or shaping coins or other metal objects. **2.** See **dice**.

☑ SPELLING TIP See **die**[1].

diesel engine /*say* **dee**-zuhl/ *noun* a type of engine which burns heavy oil, not petrol, especially used in large vehicles such as goods trains and trucks.

☑ SPELLING TIP *Tricky vowel sound*: *ie* to spell the 'ee' sound. Although the spelling of **diesel** comes from the name of the German engineer who invented it, it also fits in with the English spelling rule that *i* comes before *e* except after *c* (when giving an 'ee' sound).

diesel oil *noun* a type of fuel for vehicles such as trucks.

diet /*say* **duy**-uht/ *noun*
1. the food you usually eat: *She is trying to reduce the amount of salt in her diet.* **2.** a plan for eating only certain foods to lose weight or improve your health: *a slimming diet*; *a low-fat diet.*
–*verb* (**diets**, **dieting**, **dieted**, **has dieted**) **3.** If you **diet**, you choose what you eat in order to lose weight or improve your health.
☐ **dietician** /*say* duy-uh-**tish**-uhn/, *noun* someone trained to give advice about the food you eat.
–**dietary**, *adjective* –**dieter**, *noun*

differ *verb*
1. If one thing or person **differs from** another, it is unlike it: *Sally's jeans differ from mine in that hers have pockets at the back*; *The twins differ in their personalities.* **2.** If you **differ with** someone else, you disagree with them: *I'm afraid I differ with you on that point.*

difference *noun*
1. a way of being unlike: *One big difference between Darwin and Hobart is the climate.* 2. a disagreement: *We've had a few differences over the years but we always stay friends.* 3. the amount by which two things differ: *The difference between 8 and 3 is 5.*

different *adjective*
1. not the same or similar: *Although they are brothers they have very different natures.* 2. separate or distinct: *a different country.* 3. various or several: *It comes in different colours.* 4. striking or not ordinary: *Wearing a suit to a barbecue is certainly different!*
□ **differently**, *adverb*

NOTE You will hear **different** followed by *from*, *to* and *than*. **Different from** is traditionally considered the most correct (*These two plates are different from the others*), but **different to** is also acceptable (*Your bag is different to mine*). **Different than** is used quite a lot in speech, but many people still regard it as incorrect (*He is different than the rest of his family*).

☑ SPELLING TIP *Double letter alert*: two *f*'s.

differentiate *verb* To **differentiate** is to see that one thing is different from another: *People who are colourblind find it difficult to differentiate between red and green.*
□ **differentiation**, *noun*

difficult *adjective*
1. If something is **difficult**, it is hard to do, understand or deal with: *Learning Japanese is very difficult for most English speakers.* 2. If someone is **difficult**, they are awkward and hard to please.
□ **difficulty**, *noun* (*plural* **difficulties**)

diffident *adjective* not confident or sure of yourself: *At first she felt diffident about singing in public.*
□ **diffidence**, *noun* –**diffidently**, *adverb*

diffuse /*say* duh-**fyoohs**/ *adjective*
1. scattered or spread out thinly: *a diffuse glow.* 2. using too many words: *a diffuse speech.*
□ **diffused** /*say* duh-**fyoohzd**/, *adjective*: *diffused light.* –**diffusion**, *noun*

dig *verb* (**digs**, **digging**, **dug**, **has dug**)
1. To **dig** is to break up or turn over soil. 2. If you **dig** something, you make it by digging: *to dig a tunnel*; *to dig a hole*; *to dig a garden.* 3. If you **dig** someone in the ribs, you push them there.
–*phrase* 4. **dig in**, a. to dig trenches for protection against the enemy in a war. b. to hold your position or opinion firmly. 5. **dig into**, *Informal* to begin with enthusiasm: *to dig into your dinner.* 6. **dig up** (or **out**), a. to free from being buried or stuck: *to dig out the survivors.* b. to discover by effort or searching: *to dig out some new information.*

digest *verb*
1. If you **digest** food, you break it down in your stomach and intestines for use by your body. 2. If you **digest** information, you think it over and take it in mentally.
□ **digestible**, *adjective* –**digestion**, *noun* –**digestive**, *adjective*

digger *noun*
1. a miner: *a digger on an old gold site.* 2. an Australian soldier, especially one from World War I.

diggings *plural noun* a place where miners dig.

digit /*say* **dij**-uht/ *noun*
1. any of the numerals from 0 to 9. 2. a finger or toe.

digital *adjective*
1. having fingers or toes. 2. having to do with a device that works by storing information in a similar way to a computer: *digital TV*; *a digital radio.* 3. using digits or numbers but no pointers to show time, amount, and so on: *a digital watch.*
□ **digitalise**, *verb* –**digitally**, *adverb*

ANOTHER SPELLING for **digitalise** is **digitalize**.
COMPARE definition 3 with **analog**.

digital camera *noun* a camera which takes and stores video and still pictures as digital files which can then be transferred onto a computer.

digitise *verb* To **digitise** information is to put it into a form that can be processed on a digital device.

ANOTHER SPELLING is **digitize**.

dignitary *noun* (*plural* **dignitaries**) someone who is in a high position in government or a religion.

dignity *noun*
1. If someone has **dignity**, they are controlled and quite formal in their manner, and others usually respect them for this: *He responded to their impudent questions with great dignity.* 2. a position or quality that is worthy of respect: *an official of high rank and dignity*; *We should recognise the dignity of all human life.*
□ **dignified**, *adjective*

digress *verb* If you **digress**, you wander away from the main subject you are writing or speaking about.
□ **digression**, *noun* –**digressive**, *adjective*

dilapidated /*say* duh-**lap**-uh-day-tuhd/ *adjective* If something is **dilapidated**, it is old and in need of repair: *a dilapidated house.*
□ **dilapidation**, *noun*

☑ SPELLING TIP *Tricky 'uh' sounds*: the first and third vowel sounds are spelt *i*. Also, did you notice that each of the five vowels in **dilapidated** has a single consonant either side of it? Rap it out as *di*+*lap*+*i*+*da*+*ted*.

dilate /*say* duy-**layt**/ *verb* When the pupils of your eyes **dilate**, they become larger.
☐ **dilation**, *noun* –**dilator**, *noun*

THE OPPOSITE is **constrict**.

☑ DO NOT CONFUSE **dilate** with **dilute** which is to make thinner or weaker by adding water.

dilemma *noun* a difficult situation in which you have to choose between two different things: *His dilemma was that if he went to the football game he would miss the party.*

☑ SPELLING TIP *Single letter alert*: only one *l*, but two *m*'s.

diligent /*say* **dil**-uh-juhnt/ *adjective* If someone is **diligent**, they pay careful attention to their work: *a diligent student.*

A SIMILAR WORD is **conscientious**.

dill[1] *noun* a strong-smelling plant that is used in cooking.

dill[2] *noun Rather informal* a fool.

dillybag *noun*
1. a small bag used for carrying food or your belongings. **2.** an Aboriginal bag made of twisted grass or fibre.

WORD HISTORY 'dilly' comes from an Aboriginal language of Queensland called Yagara and the English word 'bag' is added to it

dilute *verb* If you **dilute** a liquid, you make it thinner or weaker by adding water or some other liquid to it.
☐ **dilution**, *noun*

WORD HISTORY from a Latin word meaning 'washed to pieces' or 'dissolved'

dim *adjective* Something that is **dim** is **1.** not bright: *a dim light*; *a dim room.* **2.** not clear to the mind: *a dim memory.*
–*verb* (**dims**, **dimming**, **dimmed**, **has dimmed**) **3.** To **dim** is to make make less bright: *to dim the lights.*
☐ **dimly**, *adverb* –**dimness**, *noun*

dimension *noun* size measured in a particular direction: *We measured the dimensions of the room.*

NOTE The main dimensions are **height**, **width** (or **breadth**) and **depth**.

diminish *verb* If something **diminishes**, it becomes less: *The light diminished rapidly as the storm clouds gathered.*

diminuendo /*say* duh-min-yooh-**en**-doh/ *adverb* gradually reducing in force or loudness.

NOTE This is used as an instruction in music. Like most musical instructions, it comes from Italian.

diminutive *adjective*
1. very small.
–*noun* **2.** in grammar, a word which tells you something is small: *'Piglet' is the diminutive of 'pig'.*

dimple *noun* a small hollow in your cheek or chin.

dim sim *noun* a food made of seasoned meat wrapped in thin dough and steamed or fried, originating in Chinese cooking.

ANOTHER NAME for this is **dim sum**.

dim sum *noun*
1. individual servings of Chinese food, as offered during yum cha. **2.** See **dim sim**.

WORD HISTORY from Cantonese (a Chinese language) meaning literally 'little heart'

din *noun* a loud noise that goes on and on.

dine *verb* To **dine** is to have your evening meal: *We usually dine at eight.*
☐ **diner**, *noun*

dinghy /*say* **ding**-gee/ *noun* (*plural* **dinghies**) a small rowing boat, especially one that belongs to a launch or ship.

☑ SPELLING TIP *Silent letter alert*: don't forget the silent *h*. **Dinghy** comes from Hindi, in which the spelling with *h* makes the *g* sound hard, like the sound at the start of the word *go*. Don't confuse **dinghy** with **dingy** which is pronounced with a soft *g* and describes something which is shabby.

dingo *noun* (*plural* **dingoes** *or* **dingos**) an Australian wild dog which is brownish-yellow, has pointed ears and a bushy tail, and makes a yelping noise.

ANOTHER WORD for this is **warrigal**.
WORD HISTORY from an Aboriginal language of New South Wales called Dharug

dingy /*say* **din**-jee/ *adjective* (**dingier**, **dingiest**) having a dull dirty colour and looking shabby: *a dingy room.*
☐ **dinginess**, *noun*

dinkum *adjective Informal* honest and sincere: *a dinkum friend.*
☐ **dinkum**, *adverb* truly.

ANOTHER TERM for this is **dinky-di**.

dinner *noun*
1. the main meal of the day, usually eaten in the evening. **2.** a formal evening meal, often held for a special occasion or in honour of someone: *Over a hundred people attended the principal's retirement dinner.*

dinosaur /*say* **duyn**-uh-saw/ *noun* any of a number of very large lizard-like animals which died out millions of years ago.

☑ SPELLING TIP *Tricky 'uh' sound*: the middle vowel sound is spelt *o*. Remember also that the last part of **dinosaur** is spelt *saur* (although it sounds like 'saw'). This comes from the Latin word *saurus* meaning 'lizard'. The word parts *saur* or *saurus* appear in the names of many kinds of **dinosaur**, such as *brontosaurus*.

diorama /*say* duy-uh-**rah**-muh/ *noun* a miniature scene using coloured backgrounds and models and sometimes lights.

dip *verb* (**dips**, **dipping**, **dipped**, **has dipped**)
1. To **dip** something is to put it into a liquid for a short time: *I dipped my brush into the paint.* **2.** If the ground **dips**, it slopes down.
–*noun* **3.** a soft, tasty mixture that you dip biscuits into before you eat them. **4.** a downward slope or hollow: *a dip in the road.* **5.** a short swim.
–*phrase* **6. dip into**, **a.** to study or read for a short time: *to dip into a book.* **b.** to spend: *to dip into your savings.*
☐ **dipper**, *noun*

diphtheria /*say* dif-**thear**-ree-uh, dip-**thear**-ree-uh/ *noun* a serious infectious disease affecting the throat which makes it hard to breathe and which causes a high fever.

☑ SPELLING TIP Note that there are two ways of pronouncing **diphtheria**. In the first one, the *ph* makes an 'f' sound, as it often does, so the spelling is not too difficult although the word looks unusual. But if you use the second pronunciation and start the word with a 'dip' sound, as many people do, you have to remember that there is a silent *h* following.

diphthong /*say* **dif**-thong, **dip**-thong/ *noun* a speech sound made by the tongue moving smoothly from one vowel to another in the same syllable, such as *ei* in *vein*.

☑ SPELLING TIP Note that there are two ways of pronouncing **diphthong**. In the first one, the *ph* makes an 'f' sound, as it often does, so the spelling is not too difficult although the word looks unusual. But if you use the second pronunciation and start the word with a 'dip' sound, as many people do, you have to remember that there is a silent *h* following. **Diphthong** comes from a Greek word meaning 'having two sounds'. The *di-* prefix means 'two', and *phthong* means 'sound'.

diploma /*say* duh-**ploh**-muh/ *noun* an official document proving that you are qualified in a particular field of study: *a diploma in education.*

diplomacy /*say* duh-**ploh**-muh-see/ *noun* skill in managing relations between nations or people and keeping them friendly.
☐ **diplomat** /*say* **dip**-luh-mat/, *noun* –**diplomatic**, *adjective*

direct *adjective*
1. If something is **direct**, it goes in a straight line or by the shortest possible route: *Which is the most direct route to the city?* **2.** If something is **direct**, it is clear and cannot be taken to mean anything else: *a direct request.* **3.** If someone or something is **direct**, they are open and honest. **4.** If someone is a **direct** descendant of someone in the past, they are descended in an unbroken line from parent to child rather than by a route involving brothers or sisters: *He had no children and so no direct descendants.*
–*verb* **5.** If you **direct** something at someone, you point or aim it towards them: *He directed the ball at me*; *This question is directed at the treasurer.* **6.** If you **direct** someone to a place, you show or tell them how to get there: *Could you direct me to the library, please?* **7.** If you **direct** an activity, you control it: *A police officer was directing the traffic.* **8.** If someone **directs** you to do something, they tell you to do it. **9.** If someone **directs** a film or play, they instruct the actors and everyone else involved to get the results they want.
☐ **directly**, *adverb* –**directness**, *noun*: *his directness of manner.* –**director**, *noun*

direction *noun*
1. the line towards a certain point or area: *a southerly direction*; *He cycled off in the direction of the shops.* **2.** instruction on how to get to somewhere or how to do something: *Can you give me directions to the station, please?*; *Read the directions before you start putting it together.*
☐ **directional**, *adjective*

directory *noun* (*plural* **directories**) a book containing an alphabetical list of names and addresses, maps, or other types of information: *a telephone directory*; *a street directory.*

dirt *noun*
1. loose earth or soil: *He sat down in the dirt.* **2.** something unclean on floors, surfaces, clothing, etc.: *He swept away the dirt.*
☐ **dirt**, *adjective*: *a dirt road.*

dirty *adjective* (**dirtier**, **dirtiest**)
1. covered with dirt. **2.** unfair or mean: *a dirty fight.*
☐ **dirtily**, *adverb* –**dirtiness**, *noun*

SIMILAR WORDS (for definition 1) are **filthy**, **grimy**, **grubby** and **soiled**. Note that **filthy** describes something which is extremely dirty; **grimy** usually describes something with a covering of dirt on its surface (*grimy walls*); **soiled** is usually used in relation to clothes, bed linen, etc. There are also many words meaning covered with a particular kind of dirt, for example, **greasy**, **dusty** and **muddy**.

dis- *prefix* a word part meaning 'apart', 'away', often expressing the opposite, as in *disagree*, *discount*, *discredit*.

WORD HISTORY this prefix comes from Latin

disability *noun* (*plural* **disabilities**) a lack of strength or power in part of someone's body which makes it hard for them to do some things: *He has one leg shorter than the other, but he doesn't regard it as a disability.*

NOTE See the note at **disabled**.

disabled *adjective* If someone is **disabled**, they do not have their full physical or mental power or strength, usually due to injury or disease.

NOTE Although **disabled** is very commonly used, there are some people who don't like the negative nature of the word (*dis-* means *not*) and prefer something like **differently abled**, which is more positive, stressing the possession of different abilities, rather than the fact that some are missing.

disadvantage *noun*
1. something that makes what you do more difficult: *The distance she had to travel each day was a disadvantage.*
–*verb* **2.** If something **disadvantages** you, it makes what you are doing more difficult: *Playing away from home disadvantaged the other team.*
☐ **disadvantageous**, *adjective*: *a disadvantageous position.*

disagree *verb*
1. If you **disagree** with someone, you have a different opinion from them. **2.** If two reports or sets of figures **disagree**, they do not match up with each other: *Newspaper reports disagree on the number of casualties.* **3.** If something that you eat or drink **disagrees** with you, it causes you to feel ill.
☐ **disagreement**, *noun*

disagreeable *adjective*
1. not to your liking: *a disagreeable task.* **2.** unpleasant or unfriendly in manner: *a disagreeable person.*
☐ **disagreeably**, *adverb*

disappear *verb*
1. When someone or something **disappears**, you can no longer see them because they are not where they were before: *Joe disappeared into the crowd.* **2.** When something **disappears**, it stops existing: *Dinosaurs disappeared millions of years ago.*
☐ **disappearance**, *noun*

disappoint *verb* To **disappoint** someone is to fail to satisfy their hopes: *He disappointed his fans when he did not appear.*
☐ **disappointing**, *adjective* –**disappointingly**, *adverb* –**disappointment**, *noun*

☑ SPELLING TIP The spelling of **disappoint** will be easier if you remember that it starts with the prefix *dis-* (which means 'not' or 'without', and is often used at the beginning of words whose meaning have to do with things not happening). Also, don't forget the two *p*'s in the middle – or you'll be doubly disappointed.

disapprove *verb*
1. If you **disapprove** of someone, you have a bad opinion of them. **2.** If you **disapprove** of something, you think that it shouldn't happen: *My sister disapproves of the way I dress.*
☐ **disapproval**, *noun* –**disapproving**, *adjective* –**disapprovingly**, *adverb*

disarm *verb* To **disarm** someone is to **1.** take weapons from them. **2.** charm them so that they do not feel angry any more: *He had been going to criticise her, but Maria's smile disarmed him.*
☐ **disarmament**, *noun* –**disarming**, *adjective* –**disarmingly**, *adverb*

disarray *noun in the phrase* **in disarray**, very untidy: *Her clothes were in a state of disarray.*

disaster /*say* duh-**zah**-stuh/ *noun* any sudden happening which causes great suffering and damage.
☐ **disastrous**, *adjective*

☑ SPELLING TIP The spelling of **disaster** will be easier if you remember that it comes from the idea of not having a lucky star, and can see that it is made up of *aster* (which comes from the Italian word for 'star') and the prefix *dis-* (meaning 'not' or 'without').

disbelieve *verb* If you **disbelieve** something, you refuse to believe it.
☐ **disbelief**, *noun*

disc *noun*
1. any thin, flat, circular object. **2.** See **disk**.

☑ SPELLING TIP When you are talking about computers, you usually use the spelling **disk**, except for **compact disc**.

discard *verb* /*say* dis-**kahd**/
1. To **discard** something is to throw it away: *to discard old newspapers*; *to discard an ace in a card game.*
–*noun* /*say* **dis**-kahd/ **2.** something that is thrown away.

discern /*say* duh-**sern**/ *verb* To **discern** something is to **1.** see, recognise, or understand it clearly: *I discerned a slight accent when she spoke.* **2.** recognise it as separate or different: *to discern light from dark.*
☐ **discernible**, *adjective* –**discerning**, *adjective* –**discerningly**, *adverb* –**discernment**, *noun*

☑ SPELLING TIP *Silent letter alert*: don't forget the silent *c*. The *c* is left over from the Latin origin of the word: *dis-* (meaning 'apart') and *cernere* (meaning 'to separate').

discharge *verb* /*say* dis-**chahj**/
1. If something **discharges** a substance, it gives out or gives off the substance: *The pipe discharged water and steam*; *The factory discharges a lot of smoke.* **2.** If someone **discharges** a gun, they fire it. If a gun **discharges**, it fires: *He discharged the gun at the robber*; *The gun discharged.* **3.** If someone is **discharged** from

hospital, they are sent away or allowed to leave: *He will be discharged from hospital tomorrow.* **4.** If someone **discharges** an employee from a job, they tell them that they do not have that job any more: *I'm afraid we will have to discharge some of our workers.* **5.** If you **discharge** a duty or something that you must do, you perform it or carry it out: *He discharged his responsibilities well.*
–*noun* /*say* **dis**-chahj/ **6.** a substance, especially a liquid, which comes out of something: *There is no more discharge from the wound so it must be better.*

disciple /*say* duh-**suy**-puhl/ *noun* a follower of any set of ideas or of the person who puts them forward: *a disciple of the peace movement.*
☐ **discipleship**, *noun*

☑ SPELLING TIP *Silent letter alert*: don't forget the silent *c*. Also note the spelling *iple* for the 'uy-puhl' sound at the end.

discipline /*say* **dis**-uh-pluhn/ *noun*
1. training given to teach good behaviour: *I took my dog to a training school to improve her discipline.* **2.** orderliness resulting from this training: *Our pets display good discipline around the house.* **3.** punishment.
–*verb* If you **discipline** a person or animal, you **4.** train or control them: *She cannot discipline her class.* **5.** punish them: *The children were disciplined for their bad behaviour.*
☐ **disciplinarian**, *noun* –**disciplinary**, *adjective* –**discipline**, *verb* –**disciplined**, *adjective*

☑ SPELLING TIP *Silent letter alert*: don't forget the silent *c*. There is also a tricky 'uh' sound at the end. Remember that the end is spelt *ine*. You might think of the word *line* – after all, **discipline** is meant to keep you in line!

disclose *verb* To **disclose** something is to allow it to be seen or known: *Please don't disclose my secret.*
☐ **disclosure**, *noun*

A SIMILAR WORD is **reveal**.

disco /*say* **dis**-koh/ *noun* (*plural* **discos**)
1. a place or club in which people dance to recorded music. **2.** a type of music of the 1970s with singing and a quick, steady beat, designed for people in discos to dance to.

ANOTHER WORD for this is **discotheque** /*say* **dis**-kuh-tek). **Disco** is the short form of this word. You can also say **disco music** for definition 2.

discolour *verb*
1. To **discolour** something is to change its colour: *My jeans ran in the wash and discoloured my socks.* **2.** If something **discolours**, it changes colour or fades: *This wood discolours with age.*
☐ **discolouration**, *noun*

ANOTHER SPELLING is **discolor**.

discomfort *noun*
1. lack of comfort or pleasure: *Much to his discomfort, he discovered his trousers had shrunk in the wash and were too tight.* **2.** pain or uneasiness: *This injection should not cause you too much discomfort.*

disconcert /*say* dis-kuhn-**sert**/ *verb* If something **disconcerts** you, it disturbs or upsets you: *His sulky silence disconcerted me.*
☐ **disconcerting**, *adjective* –**disconcertingly**, *adverb*

discord *noun*
1. lack of agreement: *discord between the two groups.* **2.** a combination of musical notes which is unpleasant to listen to.
☐ **discordance**, *noun* –**discordant**, *adjective*

discount *verb*
1. /*say* **dis**-kownt/ When you **discount** something you are selling, you take an amount off the set price: *Everything in the sale has been discounted by at least 20 per cent.* **2.** /*say* dis-**kownt**/ When you **discount** an idea or theory, you disregard or take no notice of it: *Investigators have discounted arson as the cause of the fire.*
–*noun* /*say* **dis**-kownt/ **3.** an amount taken off a price: *She offered me a $10 discount.*

discourage *verb*
1. If something **discourages** you, it causes you to lose spirit or courage: *He was discouraged by never receiving any praise for his work.* **2.** If you **discourage** someone from doing something, you try to prevent them doing it: *We try to discourage the dog from sitting in muddy puddles.*
☐ **discouragement**, *noun* –**discouraging**, *adjective*

discover *verb* To **discover** something is to find it or find it out, especially for the first time: *I discovered my book under a pile of papers*; *to discover a family secret*; *He discovered that he could easily balance on one leg.*
☐ **discoverer**, *noun* –**discovery**, *noun*

discredit *verb* (**discredits**, **discrediting**, **discredited**, **has discredited**)
1. If something **discredits** someone, it makes people stop believing in them or having respect for them: *His cowardly action discredited him in her eyes.* **2.** If you **discredit** an idea or theory, you show that it is not worth believing in: *The new discovery discredited the idea that the world was flat.*
☐ **discredit**, *noun*: *to bring discredit on the school.*

discreet *adjective* If you are **discreet**, you are **1.** careful not to upset people: *discreet behaviour.* **2.** able to keep secrets: *You can tell her everything, she is very discreet.*
☐ **discreetly**, *adverb*

☑ SPELLING TIP Don't confuse the spelling of **discreet** with **discrete** which sounds the same. **Discrete** describes something which is separate from other things.

discrepancy /*say* dis-**krep**-uhn-see/ *noun* (*plural* **discrepancies**) a difference or an unlikeness: *There is a discrepancy between the two accounts.*

discrete *adjective* If something is **discrete**, it is clearly separate from other things: *Let's look at this poem as a discrete piece of work rather than as part of the series.*

☑ SPELLING TIP Don't confuse the spelling of **discrete** with **discreet** which sounds the same. **Discreet** describes someone who is careful in their behaviour and about what they say.

discretion /*say* dis-**kresh**-uhn/ *noun*
1. the ability to be discreet: *Can I rely on your discretion?* **2.** the ability or right to do what should be done: *I'll use my own discretion.*
☐ **discretionary**, *adjective*

NOTE **Discretion** is the noun formed from **discreet**.

discriminate *verb*
1. If you can **discriminate** between two things, you are able to tell the difference between them: *Can you discriminate between the two singers' voices?* **2.** If you **discriminate** against someone, you treat them unfairly because of some characteristic such as their gender or ethnic origin.
☐ **discrimination**, *noun* –**discriminatory**, *adjective*

discus /*say* **dis**-kuhs/ *noun* (*plural* **discuses** *or* **disci** /*say* **dis**-kuy/) a circular plate for throwing in athletic contests.

☑ SPELLING TIP Remember that **discus** contains the word *disc* (spelt with a *c*) and ends with *us* (not the suffix *-ous*). This is because it comes directly from Latin in which *us* is a common ending for nouns.

discuss *verb* To **discuss** something is to talk about it with other people.

A SIMILAR WORD is **debate**.
WORD HISTORY from a Latin word meaning 'struck apart'

discussion *noun*
1. a talk between people to share opinions. **2.** writing or speaking which gives more than one opinion on something.

☑ SPELLING TIP Remember that the letter *s* really wants to be heard in a **discussion**. It turns up three times – the first time by itself, the second time in company with another *s*.

disdain *noun* a feeling that someone or something is not worthy of your respect: *She treated what he said with disdain.*
☐ **disdainful**, *adjective*

disease *noun* a sickness which can affect a part or all of any living thing: *a skin disease*; *a bone disease*; *a plant disease.*
☐ **diseased**, *adjective*

☑ SPELLING TIP The spelling of **disease** will be easier if you see that it is made up the word *ease* and the prefix *dis-* (meaning 'not' or 'without'). This adds up to **disease** – something that always makes you feel uneasy.

disembark *verb* When you **disembark** from a ship or plane, you leave it.
☐ **disembarkation**, *noun*

disfigure *verb* To **disfigure** something is to spoil its appearance or beauty: *A scar disfigured his face*; *Someone has disfigured the poster with graffiti.*
☐ **disfigurement**, *noun*

disgrace *noun*
1. dishonour or loss of respect. **2.** a cause of dishonour: *She was ashamed of her stealing and the disgrace it brought on her family.*
–*verb* **3.** If you **disgrace** someone or something, you bring shame or dishonour on them: *to disgrace your school.*
–*phrase* **4. in disgrace**, looked at with disapproval: *He is in disgrace because of his lying.*
☐ **disgraceful**, *adjective* –**disgracefully**, *adverb*

disgruntled *adjective* annoyed and sulky: *They were very disgruntled to discover that tickets to the concert had already sold out.*
☐ **disgruntlement**, *noun*

disguise *verb* To **disguise** yourself is to change your appearance: *He grew a beard and dyed his hair to disguise himself.*
☐ **disguise**, *noun*: *He went to the party in disguise.*

disgust *verb*
1. If something **disgusts** you, you find it extremely unpleasant in a way that can make you feel sick: *The cruel way some people treat animals really disgusts me.*
–*noun* **2.** strong dislike.
☐ **disgusted**, *adjective* –**disgusting**, *adjective*

dish *noun*
1. an open, shallow container for serving food. **2.** a particular kind of food prepared for eating: *a meat dish.*
–*phrase* **3. dish up** (or **out**), to serve food: *to dish out the soup.*

dishevelled /*say* dish-**ev**-uhld/ *adjective* untidy or in disorder: *His hair was dishevelled*; *a dishevelled appearance.*

☑ SPELLING TIP This word looks messy, like its meaning. However, if you remember the double *l* before the *-ed* ending and rap it out as *di+ shev+ el+ led*, it is not really very difficult.

dishonest *adjective* If someone is **dishonest**, they are deceitful and cannot be trusted. They do things such as lie, cheat and steal.
☐ **dishonestly**, *adverb* –**dishonesty**, *noun*

dishonour /*say* dis-**on**-uh/ *noun*
1. a lack of respect: *His actions show dishonour to his school.* **2.** loss of respect from others because of some bad action: *Her actions brought dishonour on her country.*
–*verb* **3.** If you **dishonour** someone or something, you bring them shame or disgrace: *You have dishonoured your school by your behaviour.*
☐ **dishonourable**, *adjective*

ANOTHER SPELLING is **dishonor**.

dishwasher *noun* a machine that washes dishes automatically.

disinfectant *noun* any chemical substance which kills germs.
☐ **disinfect**, *verb*

☑ SPELLING TIP The spelling of **disinfectant** will be easier if you see that it is made up of the word *infect* and the prefix *dis-* (meaning 'not' or 'without'), as well as the suffix *-ant* (not *-ent*).

disintegrate *verb* To **disintegrate** is to break up into small parts: *The meteor disintegrated when it hit the ground.*
☐ **disintegration**, *noun*

disinterested *adjective* If you are **disinterested**, you are not directly involved in a situation. You are able to be fair because the result does not affect you: *We need a disinterested observer to settle this dispute.*

A SIMILAR WORD is **impartial**.

☑ DO NOT CONFUSE **disinterested** with **uninterested** which means 'not interested'.

disjointed *adjective* not fitting together: *The story was disjointed and very difficult to follow.*
☐ **disjointedly**, *adverb* –**disjointedness**, *noun*

disk *noun* a round flat piece of metal with a magnetic coating, used in computers for storing data.

ANOTHER SPELLING is **disc**. A **disc** is something that is flat and round in shape. However, you usually use the spelling **disk** when you are talking about computers, except for **compact disc**.

disk drive *noun* in computers, a device for rotating disks so that data can be accessed.

dislike *noun*
1. the feeling of not liking someone or something: *I have taken a strong dislike to him.*
–*verb* **2.** To **dislike** something or someone is to not like them: *I dislike vegetables.*

dislocate *verb* If you **dislocate** a joint in your body, you put it out of its normal place: *He dislocated his shoulder when he fell on it.*
☐ **dislocation**, *noun* –**dislocated**, *adjective*: *a dislocated finger.*

dismal *adjective*
1. If you are **dismal**, you feel sad or depressed: *He was quite dismal about his failure.* **2.** Something that is **dismal** makes you feel sad: *dismal news.*
☐ **dismally**, *adverb*

A SIMILAR WORD is **gloomy**.

dismantle *verb* If you **dismantle** something, you take it apart: *The mechanic dismantled the engine to see what was wrong.*
☐ **dismantlement**, *noun*

dismay *noun*
1. disappointment or fear.
–*verb* **2.** To **dismay** someone is to fill them with disappointment, sadness or fear: *We were dismayed to hear that Sara was so ill.*
☐ **dismayed**, *adjective*

dismiss *verb*
1. To **dismiss** someone is to order or allow them to leave: *He dismissed his dishonest employee*; *to dismiss the class.* **2.** In cricket, when the batter or batting side are **dismissed**, they are out: *Vijay was dismissed for 84*; *Tasmania was dismissed before tea.*
☐ **dismissal**, *noun* –**dismissive**, *adjective*

disobedient *adjective* A **disobedient** person refuses to obey: *a disobedient boy.*
☐ **disobedience**, *noun*

disobey *verb* To **disobey** is to refuse to obey: *to disobey an order*; *Do not disobey your parents.*

disorder *noun*
1. confusion or lack of order: *He never knows where anything is because his room is always in terrible disorder.* **2.** violence and noise in public: *Extra police were needed to deal with the disorder in the streets.* **3.** something wrong with your body: *a breathing disorder*; *a heart disorder.*
☐ **disordered**, *adjective* –**disorderly**, *adjective*

disorganised *adjective*
1. If you are **disorganised**, you do not plan or arrange things very well: *She is so disorganised – she's always late.* **2.** If something is **disorganised**, it is confused and badly planned: *a disorganised office.*

ANOTHER SPELLING is **disorganized**.

dispatch *verb* If you **dispatch** someone or something, you send them off: *to dispatch a police car*; *to dispatch a message.*
☐ **dispatch**, *noun* (*plural* **dispatches**)

WORD HISTORY from a French word meaning 'set free'

dispel *verb* (**dispels**, **dispelling**, **dispelled**, **has dispelled**) If you **dispel** something, you drive it off or scatter it: *She dispelled my doubts.*

☑ SPELLING TIP *Single letter alert*: only one *l* at the end. However, when you add *-ed* or *-ing*, the *l* is doubled.

dispensary *noun* (*plural* **dispensaries**) the part of a chemist's shop or hospital where medicines are made up and given out.

dispense *verb* To **dispense** something is to **1.** deal it out: *She moved along the row of desks dispensing pens and paper*; *to dispense justice.* **2.** to make it up from a prescription and give out: *The pharmacy will dispense that medicine for you.* –*phrase* **3. dispense with**, **a.** to do without. **b.** to get rid of: *We can dispense with this silly frill for a start.*
☐ **dispensable**, *adjective* able to be done without. –**dispensation**, *noun* –**dispenser**, *noun*

disperse *verb*
1. To **disperse** things is to scatter them around: *He dispersed seeds over the newly dug ground.* **2.** When a group of people **disperse**, or if something **disperses** them, they separate and move in different directions: *The crowd dispersed*; *The police dispersed the demonstrators.*
☐ **dispersal**, *noun* –**dispersion**, *noun*

☑ SPELLING TIP Remember that the meaning of **disperse** has nothing to do with a purse. The sound in the second part of the word is spelt with an *er*, as in the word *verse*.

displace *verb*
1. If something **displaces** people or things, it moves them out of their usual place: *The family was displaced by war.* **2.** If someone or something **displaces** another, it takes their place: *A new housing estate has displaced the orchards and paddocks of last century.*
☐ **displacement**, *noun*

display *verb*
1. If you **display** something, you arrange or place it in a position where people can see it: *I built some bigger shelves so I could display all my books.* **2.** If you **display** a quality or an emotion, you show it: *She displayed an early talent for drawing.*
–*noun* **3.** a show: *a display of goods in a shop window*; *a display of temper.* **4.** a showing of information on a computer screen.

displease *verb* To **displease** someone is to cause them to be unhappy or angry: *Her bad manners displeased her parents.*
☐ **displeasing**, *adjective* –**displeasure**, *noun*

dispose *verb* If you **dispose** of something, you get rid of it: *We disposed of all our old clothes when we moved.*
☐ **disposable**, *adjective* –**disposal**, *noun* –**disposed**, *adjective*

disposition *noun*
1. your personality or particular character: *a cheerful disposition.* **2.** arrangement in an order: *the disposition of troops.*

dispute *noun*
1. an argument.
–*verb* **2.** When people **dispute** about something, they argue about it for a long time: *They disputed about the arrangements all afternoon.* **3.** When someone **disputes** something, they argue about it or against it: *to dispute what to do*; *to dispute a claim.*
☐ **disputable**, *adjective*

disqualify *verb* (**disqualifies**, **disqualifying**, **disqualified**, **has disqualified**)
1. If you are **disqualified** from something, you are not allowed to do it, often because you have broken some rule. **2.** If someone is **disqualified** from a game or sport, they are ruled out of the competition: *He was disqualified for making a second false start.*
☐ **disqualification**, *noun*

disregard *verb* If you **disregard** someone or something, you **1.** pay no attention to them. **2.** treat them as unnecessary or unworthy of respect.

disrespect *noun* rudeness or lack of respect.
☐ **disrespectful**, *adjective* –**disrespectfully**, *adverb*

disrupt *verb* To **disrupt** something is to interrupt it or throw it into confusion: *Rain disrupted the match*; *The accident disrupted the traffic.*
☐ **disruption**, *noun* –**disruptive**, *adjective*

dissect *verb*
1. If someone, such as doctor or scientist, **dissects** a dead body or organ, they cut it up carefully to examine how it is formed: *The medical students dissected the sheep's heart.* **2.** If you **dissect** an argument, you examine it closely.
☐ **dissector**, *noun* –**dissection**, *noun*

COMPARE this with **bisect**.

☑ SPELLING TIP *Double letter alert*: two *s*'s in the middle. This is because **dissect** is made up of the prefix *dis-* (meaning 'separation') and the word part *sect* (from a Latin word meaning 'to cut') and so it has both the *s* from *dis-* and the *s* from *sect*.

dissension *noun* a disagreement or quarrel, especially one that goes on for a long time: *He was upset about the dissension in his family.*

dissent *verb*
1. To **dissent** is to disagree or have a different opinion: *to dissent from the chairperson's ruling.*
–*noun* **2.** difference of opinion: *There was only one voice of dissent.*
☐ **dissenter**, *noun* –**dissenting**, *adjective*

☑ SPELLING TIP *Double letter alert*: two *s*'s in the middle. This is because **dissent** is made up of the prefix *dis-* (meaning 'separation') and the word part *sent* (from the Latin *sentire* meaning 'to feel') and so it has the *s* from both these word parts. It might help you to remember this if you think of the basic idea of **dissent** as being 'to feel separately or differently'.

dissident *noun* someone who has a different opinion or belief, especially about a particular political system.
☐ **dissident**, *adjective*: *dissident beliefs.*

dissipate *verb*
1. To **dissipate** is to scatter or disappear in different directions: *The mist dissipated in the sun*; *Her reassuring smile dissipated my worries.* **2.** If you **dissipate** something, you scatter or use it wastefully: *He dissipated his inheritance by gambling.*
☐ **dissipation**, *noun*

dissolute /*say* **dis**-uh-looht/ *adjective* having a wasteful and immoral way of life.
☐ **dissolutely**, *adverb* –**dissoluteness**, *noun*

☑ SPELLING TIP *Double/single letter alert*: double *s* but only one *l*. It might help if you think of *dissolve*, a related word, which follows a similar pattern. Rap it out as *dis + sol + ute*.

dissolve *verb*
1. When you **dissolve** a solid substance in a liquid, you mix it in the liquid until it disappears: *I dissolved two spoonfuls of sugar in her tea*; *These tablets dissolve easily.* **2.** When a partnership or parliament is **dissolved**, it officially comes to an end: *The court dissolved their marriage*; *Parliament was dissolved at the end of the government's term.*
☐ **dissolution**, *noun*

dissonance *noun*
1. sound that is harsh and unpleasant. **2.** a combination of musical notes that does not sound pleasant.
☐ **dissonant**, *adjective* –**dissonantly**, *adverb*

distance *noun*
1. the length of a space: *the distance between Paris and London.* **2.** a part of the landscape which is far away: *We could see mountains in the distance.*
–*phrase* **3. go the distance**, to finish or complete something. **4. keep your distance**, to keep yourself apart from others.

distant *adjective* far off: *a distant city*; *the distant past.*
☐ **distantly**, *adverb*

distaste *noun* a dislike: *He has a distaste for showing his feelings in public.*
☐ **distasteful**, *adjective*

distemper *noun* a disease in young dogs which is easily spread.

distend *verb* If something **distends**, it swells or stretches: *The horse's nostrils distended with fear.*
☐ **distension**, *noun* –**distensible**, *adjective*

distil *verb* (**distils**, **distilling**, **distilled**, **has distilled**) If you **distil** a liquid, you heat it until it becomes a gas, and then cool the gas so that it becomes a liquid again. By doing this you can remove impurities or separate out different substances.
☐ **distillery**, *noun* –**distilled**, *adjective*: *distilled water.*

☑ SPELLING TIP *Single letter alert*: only one *l* at the end, even though the last part sounds like *still*. However, when you add *-ed*, *-ing* or *-ery*, the *l* is doubled.

WORD HISTORY from a Latin word meaning 'drip down'

distinct *adjective*
1. If one thing is **distinct** from another, they are clearly different or separate: *The word has several distinct meanings*; *We each had our own distinct reason for being there.* **2.** If something is **distinct**, it is able to be clearly seen, heard, smelt, etc.: *There was a distinct smell of bushfire smoke in the air.*
☐ **distinctive**, *adjective*: *He was wearing the distinctive colours of his team.* –**distinctly**, *adverb* –**distinctness**, *noun*

distinction *noun*
1. difference, or a marking of something as different: *The distinction between the two sets of sports clothes is obvious because they are different colours.* **2.** a mark of special favour: *I considered it a distinction to shake hands with the president.* **3.** greatness or superior quality: *a writer of distinction.*

distinguish /*say* duh-**sting**-gwish/ *verb*
1. If you can **distinguish** one thing from another, or **distinguish** between two things, you can tell the difference between them: *Sometimes I can't distinguish between my sister's and my mother's voice on the telephone.* **2.** If you can **distinguish** something, you can see or hear it with some difficulty. You can make it out: *I could just distinguish three figures in the mist.* **3.** If you **distinguish** yourself in a certain way, you do something so well that you become well-known: *My cousin distinguished herself as an athlete.*
☐ **distinguishable**, *adjective* –**distinguished**, *adjective* well-known and respected: *a distinguished artist.*

☑ SPELLING TIP Remember that the spelling of the last syllable of this word is *guish* (with a *u*, although it sounds like 'gwish'). Other words with the same spelling for this sound are *anguish* and *extinguish*.

distort *verb* To **distort** something is to **1.** twist it out of shape: *Anger distorted his face.* **2.** change it and make it incorrect: *to distort the truth.*
☐ **distorted**, *adjective* –**distortion**, *noun*

distract *verb* If someone or something **distracts** you, they take your attention away from what you are doing: *The loud music distracted me from my work.*
☐ **distraction**, *noun*

distress *noun*
1. great pain, worry or sorrow. **2.** danger or difficulty: *The lifesavers paddled out to the surfer in distress.*
–*verb* **3.** If something **distresses** you, it makes you feel great pain, worry or sorrow: *We were all distressed by the news of his accident.*

WORD HISTORY from a Latin word meaning 'drawn tight'

distribute *verb*
1. To **distribute** things is to give or share them out: *She distributed gifts to the children.* **2.** To **distribute** something is to scatter or spread it: *Distribute the seeds evenly over the garden.*
☐ **distribution**, *noun*

district *noun*
1. a particular area, region or local area: *a farming district.* **2.** an area marked out for some official purpose: *a postal district.*

disturb *verb* If you **disturb** someone, you **1.** interrupt their rest, quiet or peace: *Keep the noise low, or you'll disturb the baby's sleep.* **2.** interrupt them and direct their thoughts from what they are doing: *Cats don't like to be disturbed when they're eating.* **3.** If something **disturbs** you, it worries and upsets you. **4.** If you **disturb** something, you upset its position or its natural condition: *Who disturbed the papers on my desk?*
☐ **disturbance**, *noun* –**disturbed**, *adjective* –**disturbing**, *adjective*: *a disturbing development.*

disuse /*say* dis-**yoohs**/ *noun* a stopping of use: *The mine fell into disuse when the gold ran out.*
☐ **disused** /*say* dis-**yoohzd**/, *adjective*

☑ SPELLING TIP The spelling of **disuse** will be easier if you remember its meaning and can see that it is made up of *use* joined with the prefix *dis-* (meaning 'not' or 'without').

ditch *noun* (*plural* **ditches**)
1. a long narrow hollow dug in the earth, used as a passage for water.
–*verb* **2.** *Informal* When you **ditch** something or someone, you get rid of them.

dither *verb* If you **dither**, you cannot make a decision because you are confused or nervous: *Stop dithering and make up your mind!*
☐ **dither**, *noun* –**dithering**, *adjective*

ditto marks *plural noun* two small marks (") used in writing or printing to show that what is above is repeated.

ditzy *adjective Informal* silly or foolish: *Fortunately, no-one noticed my ditzy mistake.*

divan /*say* duh-**van**/ *noun* a low bed or couch without a back or arms.

dive *verb*
1. When you **dive** into water, you jump in head first with your arms held straight out in front of you: *He dived off the top diving board.* **2.** If a bird or aeroplane **dives**, it suddenly heads downward through the air.
☐ **dive**, *noun* –**diver**, *noun* –**diving**, *adjective*

NOTE In Australian and British English the past tense and past participle is **dived**. In American English it is **dived** or **dove**.

diverge *verb* If something **diverges**, it branches off: *Our track diverged to the right.*
☐ **divergence**, *noun* –**divergent**, *adjective*

diverse *adjective* of many different kinds or forms: *the diverse wildlife of the region.*
☐ **diversity**, *noun*

divert *verb*
1. To **divert** something or someone is make them move or travel in a different direction: *Police diverted the traffic around the overturned truck.* **2.** If you **divert** someone's attention, you take it away from something that you do not want them to notice: *He diverted the police while his friend escaped.*
☐ **diversion**, *noun*

divide /*say* duh-**vuyd**/ *verb*
1. If you **divide** something, you split it up or separate it into parts: *The developers divided the land into 67 building blocks.* **2.** If you **divide** something among a number of people, you give each person a part of it: *The birthday cake was divided among the children at the party.* **3. Divide** can also mean to separate into equal parts, using maths: *99 divided by 11 equals 9.* **4.** If something **divides** people, it is the cause of disagreement between them.
☐ **divisive** /*say* duh-**viz**-iv, duh-**vuy**-siv/, *adjective*: *a divisive argument.*

dividend *noun*
1. the number which is divided by another number: *In the sum 20 ÷ 5, 20 is the dividend.* **2.** your share of some money which is being given out, especially from the profits of a business.

COMPARE definition 1 with **divisor**.
SEE ALSO **quotient**.

divine *adjective*
1. Something **divine** is connected with a god: *divine intervention.* **2.** *Rather informal* If something is **divine**, it is extremely good: *This chocolate is divine.*
–*verb* **3.** If someone **divines** something, they discover it from omens or by magical means, or by clever guessing: *He managed to divine where his presents were hidden.*
☐ **divination**, *noun* –**divinely**, *adverb*

divining rod *noun* a forked stick which is said to tremble when it is held over a place where there is water or metal underground by a person supposed to have a special power.

divinity *noun* (*plural* **divinities**)
1. a god. **2.** the study of religion: *a student of divinity.*

ANOTHER WORD (for definition 2) is **theology**.

division *noun*
1. the act of dividing one number by another number in mathematics. **2.** a separation or dividing up: *division of the school into classes.* **3.** a part of a group: *an army division*; *She plays netball in the under-12 division.*
□ **divisional**, *adjective*

divisor /*say* duh-**vuy**-zuh/ *noun* a number by which you divide another number: *In the sum 20 ÷ 5, 5 is the divisor.*

COMPARE this with **dividend** (definition 1).
SEE ALSO **quotient**.

divorce /*say* duh-**vaws**/ *noun*
1. the official ending of a marriage: *They decided to get a divorce.*
–*verb* **2.** If one person **divorces** another, or if two people get **divorced**, their marriage is officially ended: *Her parents divorced last year.*
□ **divorcee** /*say* duh-vaw-**see**/, *noun* someone who is divorced. –**divorced**, *adjective*

divulge *verb* If you **divulge** something, you tell or reveal it: *She refused to divulge the secret code.*
□ **divulgence**, *noun*

WORD HISTORY from a Latin word meaning 'make common'

dizzy *adjective* (**dizzier**, **dizziest**) When you feel **dizzy**, you feel as though your head is spinning around and you will lose your balance.
□ **dizziness**, *noun* –**dizzily**, *adverb*

A SIMILAR WORD is **giddy**.
WORD HISTORY from an Old English word meaning 'foolish'

DNA *noun* a chemical substance found in each of the cells of a living thing, which is responsible for the passing on of genetic characteristics from parents to offspring.

WORD HISTORY short for *deoxyribonucleic acid*

do *verb* (**does**, **doing**, **did**, **has done**)
1. If you **do** something, you perform it or finish it: *I've done my homework already.* **2.** If you **do** something, you deal with it in whatever way is needed: *Could you do the dishes after dinner?*
–*phrase* **3. do away with**, **a.** to put an end to: *to do away with school uniforms.* **b.** to kill. **4. do in**, *Informal* **a.** to kill or murder. **b.** to tire out. **5. do or die**, to make a last great effort. **6. do up**, to repair or make like new again: *to do up the house.* **7. make do**, to manage with what you've got.

dob *verb* (**dobs**, **dobbing**, **dobbed**, **has dobbed**) *Informal* **1. dob in**, to name or suggest, especially for an unpleasant job: *We dobbed James in to do the washing up.* **2. dob on** (or **in**), to report or tell on, especially for doing something wrong: *He dobbed on them for wagging school*; *He dobbed them in for cheating in the test.*

docile /*say* **doh**-suyl/ *adjective* quiet and easily handled: *a docile horse.*
□ **docility** /*say* doh-**sil**-uh-tee/, *noun* –**docilely**, *adverb*

☑ SPELLING TIP Remember that there is a *c*, not an *s*, in the middle of **docile**. This is because it comes from a Latin word meaning 'able to be taught' which was formed from *docere* meaning 'to teach'.

dock[1] *noun*
1. a place where a ship ties up when it is in port. **2.** the part of a large building where trucks can enter to load or unload goods.
–*verb* **3.** When a ship **docks**, it comes or is brought into a dock for loading, unloading or repair: *The ship docks at 10 o'clock tonight.* **4.** When spaceships **dock**, they join together while in orbit.

dock[2] *noun* the part of a courtroom where the person on trial is put.

docket *noun*
1. a ticket or sign on a package stating what is inside. **2.** a receipt proving that you have paid for goods.

☑ SPELLING TIP Put your **docket** in your *pocket* with your *locket* – these three words have the same spelling, except for the first letter. Remember that there is only one *t* at the end.

doctor *noun*
1. someone who has learned about diseases and is allowed by law to look after sick people and give them medicine. **2.** someone who has received the highest degree given by a university: *After many years of research she was made a Doctor of Philosophy.*

WORD HISTORY from a Latin word meaning 'teacher'

doctrine /*say* **dok**-truhn/ *noun* something that is believed or taught: *a religious doctrine.*

document *noun* /*say* **dok**-yuh-muhnt/
1. a paper giving information or proof of something: *historical documents*; *Birth certificates and wills are important personal documents.* **2.** a computer file, especially one containing text.
–*verb* /*say* **dok**-yuh-ment/ **3.** To **document** something is to support it or back it up with documents: *You must document your case well if you hope to convince the judge.*
□ **documentary**, *adjective*: *documentary evidence.* –**documentation**, *noun* the documents provided to support a case.

documentary /*say* dok-yooh-**men**-tuh-ree, dok-yooh-**men**-tree/ *noun* (*plural* **documentaries**) a film, television or radio program about a real event or someone's life.

dodge *verb* To **dodge** something is to move downward or aside quickly, so as to avoid it: *He dodged the tackle*; *She dodged and the pillow flew past without hitting her.*

doe *noun* the female of animals such as a deer, rabbit or kangaroo.

NOTE The male animal is usually called a **buck**.

☑ SPELLING TIP Don't confuse the spelling of **doe** with **dough** which sounds the same. **Dough** is a mixture of flour and water or milk which is baked to make bread or pastry. It is also an informal word for money.

does *verb* the third person singular present indicative of **do**.

doesn't a short form of *does not*.

doff *verb* To **doff** clothing is to take it off: *He doffed his hat as he greeted the old lady.*

THE OPPOSITE is **don**.

dog *noun*
1. a four-legged animal which eats meat and may live in the wild, like a dingo or wolf, or may be kept as a pet, like a terrier or poodle. **2.** the male of this type of animal.
–*verb* (**dogs**, **dogging**, **dogged**, **has dogged**) **3.** To **dog** someone is pursue or follow them closely: *Bad luck dogged Olas all his life.*
–*phrase* **4. go to the dogs**, *Informal* to go to ruin. **5. lead a dog's life**, to have an unhappy existence. **6. let sleeping dogs lie**, to leave things alone that may cause trouble.

NOTE The female is called a **bitch**. A young dog is called a **pup**.

dogmatic *adjective* Someone who is **dogmatic** says what they think very forcefully and expects others to accept it as true.
□ **dogmatically**, *adverb* –**dogmatism**, *noun*

dole *noun*
1. the dole, *Informal* money paid by the government to help people who are out of work.
–*verb in the phrase* **2. dole out**, to give in small amounts: *She pulled the mandarin apart and doled out the segments.*

doleful *adjective* sad or gloomy: *a puppy with doleful eyes.*
□ **dolefully**, *adverb* –**dolefulness**, *noun*

doll *noun*
1. a child's toy which is made to look like a person.
–*phrase* **2. doll up**, to dress in your best clothes.

ANOTHER FORM Children often say **dolly** for definition 1.

WORD HISTORY from 'Doll' and 'Dolly', short forms of the woman's name 'Dorothy'

dollar *noun* a unit of money, either a coin or a banknote, which is equal to 100 cents, used in Australia and many other countries around the world.

THE SYMBOL for the dollar is $.

dolphin *noun* an intelligent, playful sea animal with a long sharp nose.

ANOTHER WORD (for some types of dolphin) is **porpoise**.

domain /*say* duh-**mayn**/ *noun*
1. a territory or realm that is owned or controlled: *France was once the domain of the Roman emperor.* **2.** an area of interest or knowledge: *Physics is not my domain.*

domain name *noun* the name of an internet site that includes the name of the organisation, followed by the type of organisation (the 'domain'), such as commercial, academic, news, etc., followed by the country of origin.

NOTE The United States is the only country that does not give a country of origin. That is because the internet started there.

dome *noun* a roof shaped like the top half of a hollow sphere or ball: *the dome of the cathedral.*
□ **domed**, *adjective*

domestic /*say* duh-**mes**-tik/ *adjective*
1. Activities and duties which are **domestic** have to do with the home or family: *Domestic chores such as cleaning and cooking should be shared.* **2.** Animals which are **domestic** live with people and are not wild.
□ **domesticate**, *verb* –**domesticated**, *adjective* –**domesticity** /*say* dom-es-**tis**-uh-tee/, *noun*

dominate *verb* To **dominate** someone or something is to **1.** rule over or control them: *He completely dominates his family.* **2.** tower above or throw a shadow over them: *The huge silo dominates the township.*
□ **dominance**, *noun* –**dominant**, *adjective* –**domination**, *noun*

domineering *adjective* bossy and overbearing.
□ **domineer**, *verb* –**domineeringly**, *adverb*

dominion /*say* duh-**min**-yuhn/ *noun*
1. power to rule or govern: *Japan has dominion over these islands.* **2.** the land ruled by one person or government: *Britain had many dominions.*

domino *noun* (*plural* **dominoes**) a flat piece of wood or plastic marked with a number of dots used to play a game.

don *verb* (**dons**, **donning**, **donned**, **has donned**) To **don** clothing is to put it on: *He donned his coat and left.*

THE OPPOSITE is **doff**.

donate *verb* To **donate** something is to give it as a gift: *to donate a computer to the school.*
□ **donation**, *noun*

doner kebab /*say* **doh**-nuh kuh-bab, **don**-uh kuh-bab/ *noun* a food made of cooked meat and salad rolled up in a piece of flat bread, originating in Middle Eastern cooking.

THE SHORT FORM of this is **kebab**.

donkey *noun*
1. a long-eared animal related to the horse. **2.** *Rather informal* someone who is stupid or stubborn.
–*phrase* **3. donkey's years**, *Informal* a long time.

ANOTHER WORD for this is **ass** (definition 1).
NOTE The male is a **jackass**; the female is a **jennet** or **jenny**; the young is a **foal**.

donor *noun* someone who gives something: *The charity needs more donors*; *a blood donor.*

don't a short form of *do not*.

doodle *verb* When you **doodle**, you draw patterns or pictures while you are thinking about something else, or because you are bored.
□ **doodle**, *noun* –**doodler**, *noun*

doom *noun* a dreadful outcome, fate or death: *The bus crashed off the cliff taking all its passengers to their doom.*
□ **doomed**, *adjective*: *With his food and water gone, the doomed explorer knew his death was near.*

doona *noun* a large bag stuffed with feathers or other material and used as a quilt on a bed.

ANOTHER TERM for this is **continental quilt**.
WORD HISTORY trademark

door *noun*
1. a large piece of wood which can be moved to open or close the entrance to a house, room or cupboard. **2.** the entrance to a room or house. **3.** a house or building: *The bank is three doors down from the coffee shop.*
–*phrase* **4. next door to, a.** in the next house to. **b.** very near. **5. out of doors**, outside.

ANOTHER WORD (for definition 2) is **doorway**.

dope *noun Informal* **1.** a stupid person. **2.** an illegal drug. **3.** the actual facts or information: *What's the latest dope on their plans?*
–*verb* **4.** If someone **dopes** a person or animal, they illegally give them a drug to alter their performance in a competition.
□ **dopey**, *adjective*

WORD HISTORY from a Dutch word meaning 'a dipping' or 'sauce'

dormant *adjective* Something is **dormant** when it is not active, as if asleep or resting: *Polar bears are dormant during winter*; *This volcano has been dormant for eight hundred years.*
□ **dormancy**, *noun*

dormitory *noun* (*plural* **dormitories**) a big room with many beds, especially in a boarding school or hostel.

dose *noun*
1. the amount of medicine taken at one time. **2.** an amount of something unpleasant: *a dose of the flu.*
–*verb* **3.** To **dose** someone is to give them a certain amount of medicine at one time: *to dose a patient.*
□ **dosage**, *noun*

dossier /*say* **dos**-ee-uh/ *noun* a bundle of documents containing information about a person or subject: *a dossier on his service in the navy*; *He kept a dossier on the number of times the train was late.*

A SIMILAR WORD is **file**.

dot *noun*
1. a very small spot or mark: *The pattern was composed of dots*; *The car soon became a dot on the horizon.*
–*phrase* **2. on the dot**, *Rather informal* exactly on time.
□ **dotted**, *adjective*: *a dotted line.*

dotcom *noun*
1. a company trading over the internet. **2.** a company involved in the information technology industry.

OTHER SPELLINGS are **dot com**, **dot-com** and **dot.com**.
WORD HISTORY from the suffix *.com* which appears at the end of the domain names of commercial businesses on the internet

dote *verb in the phrase* **dote on**, to love so much that you may appear to be silly: *He dotes on his dogs and talks about them all the time.*
□ **doting**, *adjective*: *doting parents.* –**dotingly**, *adverb*

dot painting *noun* a style of Aboriginal art in which colour is applied as a series of dots to build up a picture.

dotty *adjective* (**dottier**, **dottiest**) *Informal* mad or crazy.

double *adjective*
1. If something is **double** something else, it is twice that thing in some quantity: *This building is double the height of that one.* **2. Double** is used to describe something that is twice the normal size: *to use double quantities.* **3. Double** is used to describe something that consists of two parts: *double doors*; *a double pack.*
–*verb* **4.** If you **double** something, you bend or fold it in two: *I doubled the piece of paper.* **5.** If

you **double** something, or if it **doubles**, it is twice as big as it used to be. **6.** If something **doubles** as something else, it can be used in two ways: *The seats in my van unfold and double as a bed when we go camping.*
–*noun* **7.** anything that is doubled: *Four is the double of two.* **8.** someone who looks almost the same as someone else: *You look so much like my sister you could be her double.*
–*phrase* **9. double back**, to turn back the way you came. **10. on the double**, very quickly: *Get in here on the double.*
☐ **doubly**, *adverb*

double bass *noun* the largest instrument of the violin family, with a very deep sound, played resting upright on the floor.

double-click *verb* If you **double-click** on an icon on a computer screen, you select it so that it will perform a function.

doublecross *verb* To **doublecross** someone is to deceive them by promising one thing and doing another.
☐ **doublecross**, *noun*

doubt /*rhymes with* out/ *noun*
1. a feeling of uncertainty or suspicion: *There is some doubt about his reliability.*
–*verb* **2.** If you **doubt** something or someone, you have a feeling of uncertainty or suspicion about them: *I doubt that tomorrow will be warm enough for the beach*; *Do you doubt what I have told you?*
☐ **doubtful**, *adjective* –**doubtless**, *adjective*

> ☑ SPELLING TIP *Silent letter alert*: don't forget the silent *b*. The *b* is left behind from the Latin word it originally came from – *dubitare*.

dough /*rhymes with* slow/ *noun*
1. a mixture of flour and water or milk which is baked to make bread or pastry. **2.** *Informal* money.

> ☑ SPELLING TIP Don't confuse the spelling of **dough** with **doe** which sounds the same. A **doe** is the female of animals such as deer, rabbits and kangaroos.

doughnut *noun* a ring-shaped cake which is deep-fried and covered in sugar or icing.

> ANOTHER SPELLING is **donut**.

douse /*rhymes with* house/ *verb* If you **douse** a fire, you throw water on it to put it out.

dove /*say* duv/ *noun* a bird like a pigeon.

dowdy *adjective* (**dowdier**, **dowdiest**) shabby and unfashionable: *dowdy old clothes.*
☐ **dowdily**, *adverb* –**dowdiness**, *noun*

down[1] *adverb*
1. from higher to lower: *Climb down quickly!* **2.** on or to the ground: *He fell down.*
–*preposition* **3.** to or at a lower place on or in: *down the stairs*; *down the ladder.*
–*adjective* **4.** downwards: *From here the path is down for about 3 km.* **5.** in bed because you are sick: *He's down with a cold.* **6.** *Rather informal* unhappy: *See if you can cheer him up, he's a bit down at the moment.*
–*noun* **7.** a time of bad luck or depression: *Life is full of ups and downs.* **8.** *Informal* a grudge or feeling of dislike: *She invited everyone else, perhaps she's got a down on us.*
–*phrase* **9. down in the mouth**, feeling that life is too much for you. **10. down to earth**, with a practical or realistic approach to life.

down[2] *noun* fine soft hair or feathers: *down on his face*; *the down of a duckling.*
☐ **downy**, *adjective* (**downier**, **downiest**)

downfall *noun*
1. dishonour or ruin: *Laziness was the cause of his downfall.* **2.** a heavy fall of rain or snow.

download *verb* If you **download** data, you transfer or copy it from one computer to another, or from a computer to a disk: *It took me almost an hour to download all the information I found on the internet.*
☐ **download**, *noun*

> COMPARE this with **upload**.

downpour *noun* a heavy fall of rain.

downs *plural noun* open hilly country, usually covered with grass.

downstairs *adverb*
1. down the stairs.
–*noun* **2.** a lower storey or storeys.

Down syndrome *noun* a condition that some people are born with that makes them look a bit different from other people and means that they sometimes cannot do all the same things in school.

downtime *noun*
1. the time when a machine, computer, or factory is not operating. **2.** a time of relaxation: *By the end of the school year, we were looking forward to some downtime on the beach.*

downwards *adverb* towards a lower place, position, level, or degree.

> ANOTHER FORM is **downward**.

dowry *noun* (*plural* **dowries**) in some cultures, money or property that a woman brings to her husband when she marries.

doze *verb* To **doze** is to fall into a light sleep.
☐ **doze**, *noun*

dozen *noun* (*plural* **dozen** *or* **dozens**) a group of twelve things: *We usually sell them by the dozen*; *I've finished the first dozen.*

drab *adjective* (**drabber**, **drabbest**) Something that is **drab** is **1.** uninteresting because lacking in colour: *drab feathers.* **2.** uninteresting because lacking in excitement: *drab life.*
☐ **drabness**, *noun*

draft *noun*
1. a rough drawing or piece of writing. **2.** a letter instructing a bank to pay money: *a bank draft.* **3. the draft**, the selection of people to be enrolled in the armed forces under a system of compulsory service. See **conscription**.
–*verb* **4.** When you **draft** a piece of writing, you compose the first version of it: *to draft a letter.*
–*adjective* **5.** prepared as a draft or first version: *a draft document.*

NOTE **Draft** is another spelling for **draught**, especially in American English.

drag *verb* (**drags**, **dragging**, **dragged**, **has dragged**)
1. When you **drag** something, you pull it slowly and heavily along the ground: *We dragged the fallen tree off the track.* **2.** If someone **drags** you somewhere, they get you to go there even though you do not really want to. **3.** If you **drag** yourself somewhere, you force yourself to go there even though you are feeling tired or ill. **4.** If time or an event **drags**, it seems to pass very slowly because it is boring: *The talk dragged on for two hours.*
–*noun Rather informal* **5.** someone or something very boring: *The party was a drag so we left early.* **6.** women's clothes when worn by men: *to be dressed in drag.*

dragon *noun*
1. an imaginary fire-breathing monster, in European tradition a huge lizard with wings and fierce claws, and in Chinese tradition a magical creature with a long body and large head. **2.** *Informal* a very strict and bossy woman.

WORD HISTORY from a Greek word meaning 'serpent'

dragonfly *noun* (*plural* **dragonflies**) a large harmless insect with a long thin body and two pairs of long delicate wings of the same length.

drain *verb*
1. To **drain** something is to draw liquid away from it gradually: *to drain the pond of water.* **2.** To **drain** liquid is to draw it away from somewhere: *to drain water from the pond.* **3.** When a liquid **drains** somewhere, it flows there: *The water from the roof drains into these tanks.* **4.** If you **drain** a cup or glass, you drink all of its contents: *He was so thirsty he drained the glass of water in one go.*
–*noun* **5.** a pipe or passage which carries liquid away. **6.** a gradual outgoing, as of time, money, etc.: *The long trip to school is a drain on my time.*
–*phrase* **7. go down the drain**, *Informal* **a.** to be wasted: *all the lives that go down the drain in war.* **b.** to become worthless: *years of hard work going down the drain.*
☐ **drainage**, *noun*

drake *noun* a male duck.

NOTE The female is a **duck**; the young is a **duckling**.

drama *noun*
1. an exciting, sad or serious play acted on stage, film, television or radio. **2.** writing or speaking that is meant to be acted out, as in a play. **3.** any exciting series of events: *the drama surrounding the election.*
☐ **dramatic**, *adjective* –**dramatically**, *adverb*

dramatise *verb*
1. If you **dramatise** a book or a story, you make it into a play. **2.** If you **dramatise** a happening or situation, you express or show it in an exaggerated way: *Don't dramatise your sadness.*
☐ **dramatisation**, *noun* –**dramatist**, *noun* someone who writes plays.

ANOTHER SPELLING is **dramatize**.

drape *verb*
1. To **drape** a material is to hang it in loose folds: *He draped a shawl around her shoulders*; *A banner draped from the balcony.* **2.** To **drape** yourself over something is to put yourself on it in a relaxed manner: *She draped her arm over the back of the chair.*
–*noun* **3. drapes**, curtains.

WORD HISTORY from a French word meaning 'cloth'

drastic *adjective* Something **drastic** is violent, harsh or extreme: *Drastic action was needed to reach the injured man in time*; *Expelling her from school seems a little drastic.*
☐ **drastically**, *adverb*

draught /*say* drahft/ *noun*
1. a current of air or wind. **2.** *Old-fashioned* a drink: *a refreshing draught of water.* **3.** the depth of water which a ship needs so that it can float: *The yacht has a draught of five metres.* **4. draughts**, a game played by two people, each with twelve pieces which they move diagonally across a board with black and white squares.

☑ SPELLING TIP Remember that the central sound in **draught** is spelt *augh* (although it sounds like 'ahf'). It might help if you think of a word you know well which has the same spelling for this sound, such as *laugh*. The spelling of **draught** can be confusing because it is sometimes spelt **draft**, especially in American English. However, in Australian English, the spelling **draft** is used where the meaning is an outline of a story, and so on (see **draft**). **Draught** continues to be the main spelling in Australian English for the meanings above.

draught horse *noun* a big strong horse, used for pulling heavy loads in the days before tractors and trucks.

ANOTHER FORM is **draughthorse**.

draughtsman *noun*
1. someone who makes drawings of the plans or designs of things such as bridges, roads and

buildings. **2.** one of the pieces used in the game of draughts.

draw *verb* (**draws**, **drawing**, **drew**, **has drawn**) **1.** When you **draw**, you make a picture of something with a pen, pencil, crayon, etc. **2.** To **draw** is to pull, move or take something in a particular direction: *She could not draw her eyes away from his face*; *The train drew into the platform*; *Darkness draws near.* **3.** If something **draws** people, it attracts them: *The concert drew a record crowd.*
–*noun* **4.** the act of drawing or picking: *a lottery draw.* **5.** something that is picked or drawn: *a lucky draw.* **6.** a contest where neither side wins: *The game ended in a draw.*
–*phrase* **7. draw out**, **a.** to make longer: *to draw out a conversation.* **b.** to encourage someone to talk: *Try and draw that shy new girl out.* **8. draw up**, **a.** to come to a stop: *The car drew up outside the bank.* **b.** to prepare or set out, such things as documents or plans: *to draw up an agreement for peace.*
□ **drawing**, *noun* a picture that has been drawn. –**drawer**, *noun* –**drawn**, *adjective*

drawback *noun* a disadvantage or inconvenience: *It's a good idea, apart from one drawback.*

drawbridge *noun* in past times, a bridge which could be raised or lowered, as around a castle.

drawer /*sounds like* draw/ *noun* a container shaped like a box that slides in and out of furniture such as cupboards or desks: *I keep my pens in the top drawer.*

☑ SPELLING TIP *Silent letter alert*: **drawer** sounds the same as *draw*, but remember that it has a silent *er* added at the end.

drawl *verb* To **drawl** is to speak very slowly so that the sounds are long and drawn out.
□ **drawl**, *noun*

dray *noun* a low cart without sides, pulled by horses, used for carrying heavy loads.

WORD HISTORY from a Middle English word meaning 'sledge without wheels'

dread *noun* **1.** great fear.
–*verb* **2.** If you **dread** something, you are very much afraid of it: *to dread exams.*

dreadful *adjective* **1.** causing great fear: *a dreadful storm.* **2.** extremely bad or unpleasant: *They left the room in a dreadful mess.*
□ **dreadfully**, *adverb*

dream *noun* **1.** the thoughts and pictures that pass through your mind when you are sleeping. **2.** a hope or aim: *His dream is to become a famous actor.*
–*verb* (**dreams**, **dreaming**, **dreamed** *or* **dreamt**, **has dreamed** *or* **has dreamt**) **3.** To **dream** is to imagine or have a dream.
–*phrase* **4. dream up**, to invent or plan in your imagination.
□ **dreamer**, *noun* –**dreamy**, *adjective*

WORD HISTORY from an Old English word meaning 'gaiety' or 'noise'

dreaming *noun* **1.** an Aboriginal person's awareness and knowledge of the Dreamtime. **2. the Dreaming**, See **Dreamtime**.

Dreamtime *noun* the time in which Aboriginal people believe the earth came to have the form it has now and in which life and nature began.

ANOTHER NAME for this is the **Dreaming**.

dreary *adjective* (**drearier**, **dreariest**) dull or depressing: *a dreary job*; *dreary weather.*
□ **drearily**, *adverb* –**dreariness**, *noun*

A SIMILAR WORD is **gloomy**.

dredge *noun* **1.** a machine for drawing up sand or dirt from the bottom of a river, lake, harbour or dam.
–*verb* **2.** To **dredge** is to clear or search the bottom of a river, lake, harbour or dam using a machine which draws up sand or dirt.

dregs *plural noun* **1.** the solid part that settles at the bottom of a drink: *She emptied the dregs from the coffee pot.* **2.** a useless or worthless part of something: *the dregs of society.*

A SIMILAR WORD (for definition 1) is **sediment**, but remember that **sediment** is a singular noun while **dregs** is plural.

drench *verb* To **drench** something is to soak it or make it very wet: *The spilt water drenched the carpet.*

WORD HISTORY from an Old English word meaning 'make drink'

dress *noun* **1.** a piece of clothing worn by a woman, which covers her body from her shoulders to her legs. **2.** clothing in general: *The dancers are in traditional dress.*
–*verb* **3.** To **dress** is to put on your clothes: *I like to dress before breakfast.*
–*phrase* **4. dress up**, **a.** to put on your best clothes. **b.** to put on clothes that make you look like you are someone or something else, especially for a party.

A SIMILAR WORD (for definition 2) is **apparel**. This is a more formal word.

dress circle *noun* a curved section of seats upstairs in a theatre or cinema.

dresser *noun* a piece of furniture with shelves and drawers for dishes, cups and the like.

dressing *noun*
1. an act of getting dressed: *Dressing for school takes me ten minutes.* 2. a sauce for foods: *salad dressing.* 3. a bandage for a cut or sore.

dressing-gown *noun* a coat that is worn over your nightclothes.

dressing table *noun* a piece of furniture for your bedroom, usually with drawers and a mirror.

dribble *verb*
1. If liquid **dribbles**, it flows in small drops: *Water dribbled from the leak in the pipe.* 2. If someone **dribbles**, they let liquid flow out from their mouth: *The baby dribbled on my shirt.* 3. If you **dribble** the ball in a game such as soccer or hockey, you move it along by a series of little kicks or small blows with a stick.
□ **dribble**, *noun*

A SIMILAR WORD (for definition 1) is **trickle**.

drift *verb* To **drift** is to 1. be carried along by the movement of water or air. 2. travel without any particular aim or direction: *She has spent the last six months just drifting about.*
–*noun* 3. a general movement: *The drift of public opinion is towards more recycling.* 4. the general meaning: *Did you get the drift of his argument?*
□ **drifter**, *noun*

driftwood *noun* wood that is floating on water or has been washed onto the shore.

drill *noun*
1. a tool, usually electric, for making or boring holes. 2. a strict way of training or exercise that is repeated regularly: *a marching drill*; *We do a fire drill every month.*
–*verb* 3. If you **drill** something, you make a hole in it with a drill. 4. To **drill** someone is to train them by giving repeated exercises: *to drill the troops*; *He drilled the class in their 7 times tables.*

drink *verb* (**drinks**, **drinking**, **drank**, **has drunk**)
1. If you **drink** a liquid, you swallow it. You take it into your body as food. 2. You can use **drink** to mean to drink alcohol: *Don't drink and drive.*
–*noun* 3. any liquid that can be drunk. 4. an alcoholic drink: *They had a drink to celebrate.*
–*phrase* 5. **drink in**, to take in by paying attention: *We drank in his words.*
□ **drinker**, *noun*

drip *verb* (**drips**, **dripping**, **dripped**, **has dripped**)
1. If a liquid **drips**, it falls in small drops: *Water was dripping from the tap.* 2. If something **drips**, it lets a liquid fall in small drops: *The tap in the bathroom is dripping.*
–*noun* 3. a falling drop of liquid or the sound it makes. 4. a slow injection of liquid into the veins of a sick person. 5. *Informal* a dull or boring person.

dripping *noun* fat that has dripped from meat during cooking and which can be kept to be used again for frying.

drive *verb* (**drives**, **driving**, **drove**, **has driven**)
1. If you **drive** a vehicle, you control it so that the engine makes it go where you want: *He drove the car up the hill.* 2. If you **drive**, you travel in a vehicle: *We drove to Broken Hill last year.*
–*noun* 3. a journey in a car or other vehicle. 4. a road up to a private house: *She left the car in the drive.* 5. energy: *He has a lot of drive.* 6. an effort by many people to get something done: *There is a drive by environmentalists to persuade people to use fewer plastic bags.*
–*phrase* 7. **drive away**, to force to go away: *to drive away the mosquitoes with repellent.* 8. **drive someone up the wall**, *Informal* to annoy someone.
□ **driver**, *noun*

drive-in *noun*
1. an outdoor cinema where people watch films from their cars.
–*adjective* 2. A **drive-in** shop or service is one which serves customers in their cars.

drizzle *verb* If it **drizzles**, it rains lightly.
□ **drizzle**, *noun* –**drizzly**, *adjective*

drone[1] *noun*
1. a male bee which does not make honey and has no sting. 2. someone who does not want to work.

drone[2] *noun*
1. a low unchanging sound.
–*verb* 2. If something or someone **drones**, they make a dull unchanging sound: *A plane droned overhead*; *The teacher's voice droned on and on.*

drool *verb*
1. To **drool** is to let saliva fall from your mouth: *The dogs were drooling with hunger as they waited for their food.*
–*phrase* 2. **drool over**, to have a greedy interest in: *They drooled over the photos of tropical beaches in the holiday magazine.*

droop *verb*
1. If something **droops**, it bends, so that it is hanging down: *His head drooped with tiredness.* 2. If your spirits **droop**, you become discouraged: *Their spirits drooped when the boat's engine cut out and would not start again.*
□ **droop**, *noun* –**drooping**, *adjective* –**droopy**, *adjective*

drop *noun*
1. a small rounded amount of liquid which falls. 2. a small amount of anything, especially liquid: *a drop of blood.* 3. the distance or length by which anything falls: *That waterfall has the highest drop in the national park*; *These curtains have a drop of two metres.* 4. a fall in amount or value: *a drop in prices.*
–*verb* (**drops**, **dropping**, **dropped**, **has dropped**) 5. To **drop** is to fall or let fall: *She dropped onto the sofa*; *He dropped the ball.* 6. To **drop** someone is to set them down from a car or other vehicle: *Bruno dropped me off at the station.* 7. If you **drop** something, you make it lower: *She*

dropped her voice; *to drop the hem of a dress.*
–*phrase* **8. drop in** (or **by**), to visit for a short time. **9. drop off**, **a.** to get smaller or less: *Sales have dropped off.* **b.** to fall asleep.
☐ **droplet**, *noun* –**drop-out**, *noun* –**dropper**, *noun* –**droppings**, *noun*

drop-down menu *noun* See **pull-down menu**.

drought /*say* drowt/ *noun* a long period of dry weather.

☑ SPELLING TIP Remember that the vowel sound in **drought** is spelt *ough* (although it sounds like 'ow'). Other words like this are *plough* and *bough*.

drove[1] *verb* the past tense of **drive**: *We drove home.*

drove[2] *noun*
1. a herd of animals, such as cattle. **2. droves**, large numbers of people or things: *Droves of people were trying to buy tickets to the concert*; *They arrived at the beach in droves.*
–*verb* **3.** To **drove** is to move cattle or sheep over long distances: *He is droving cattle from the Northern Territory.*
☐ **drover**, *noun* someone who droves cattle.

drown *verb* To **drown** is to die from being under water for too long: *He drowned when the boat sank.*

drowse *verb* To **drowse** is to be almost asleep: *The old man drowsed in the afternoon sun.*
☐ **drowsy**, *adjective* (**drowsier**, **drowsiest**) –**drowsiness**, *noun* –**drowsily**, *adverb*

WORD HISTORY from an Old English word meaning 'droop' or 'become slow'

drudge *noun* someone who does boring or hard work.
☐ **drudgery**, *noun*

drug *noun*
1. a chemical substance given to someone to prevent or cure a disease. **2.** a substance that is habit-forming, many of which are illegal.
–*verb* (**drugs**, **drugging**, **drugged**, **has drugged**) **3.** To **drug** food or drink is to mix a drug with it. **4.** If someone **drugs** a person or animal, they poison or make them unconscious with a drug.

WORD HISTORY from a Dutch word meaning 'dry thing'

drum *noun*
1. a musical instrument with a round hollow body covered with a tightly stretched skin, which makes a deep sound when it is hit. **2.** a container for petrol or other liquid, in the shape of a drum.
–*verb* (**drums**, **drumming**, **drummed**, **has drummed**) **3.** When you **drum**, you beat or play a drum. **4.** If someone or something **drums**, they beat on anything continuously: *He drummed on the table with his fingers*; *Rain drummed on the tin roof.*
☐ **drummer**, *noun*

drunk *verb*
1. Drunk is the past participle of **drink**: *We'll leave after I've drunk this cup of coffee.*
–*adjective* **2.** If someone is **drunk**, they have had too much alcoholic drink.
–*noun* **3.** someone who has had too much alcohol.
☐ **drunkard**, *noun* –**drunken**, *adjective*

dry *adjective* (**drier**, **driest**)
1. If something is **dry**, it is not wet or damp. **2.** If the weather is **dry**, there is no rain: *It has been dry all week.* **3.** Wine that is **dry** does not taste sweet. **4.** If something that you read, watch or listen to is **dry**, it is boring: *It was a very dry speech, full of facts and figures.* **5.** If someone has a **dry** humour, their humour is funny while being expressed in a few words.
–*noun* **6. the dry**, the season without much rain in central and northern Australia, from April to November.
–*verb* (**dries**, **drying**, **dried**, **has dried**) **7.** When something **dries** or when you **dry** something, it becomes dry: *to dry the washing on the line*; *Makiko dried her hair with a towel.*
☐ **dryer**, *noun* a machine for drying something, such as clothes. –**dryly**, *adverb* –**dryness**, *noun*

ANOTHER FORM This word (as in definition 6) is sometimes spelt with a capital letter: **the Dry**.
ANOTHER SPELLING for **dryly** is **drily**.

dry-clean *verb* When clothes or other things made of fabric are **dry-cleaned**, they are cleaned with chemicals rather than water.
☐ **dry-cleaning**, *noun* –**dry-cleaner**, *noun*

dry dock *noun* a dock from which water can be emptied so that the underneath of ships can be repaired or cleaned.

dry ice *noun* solid frozen carbon dioxide which is used to keep things cold.

dual /*say* **dyooh**-uhl/ *adjective* **Dual** is used to describe something that has two parts: *Driving instructors teach in cars with dual controls*; *The twins held a dual birthday party.*
☐ **duality**, *noun*

☑ SPELLING TIP Don't confuse the spelling of **dual** with **duel** which sounds the same. A **duel** is a kind of fight.

dub[1] *verb* (**dubs**, **dubbing**, **dubbed**, **has dubbed**)
1. To **dub** someone is to tap them lightly with a sword when making them a knight: *The king dubbed him Sir William.* **2.** If you **dub** someone or something, you give a particular name to them: *The Sydney Harbour Bridge has been dubbed 'The Coathanger' because of its shape.*

dub[2] *verb* (**dubs**, **dubbing**, **dubbed**, **has dubbed**)
To **dub** a film is to give it a new soundtrack in a

different language: *a Japanese film dubbed into English.*

WORD HISTORY a shortened form of *double*

dubious /*say* **dyooh**-bee-uhs/ *adjective*
1. Someone is **dubious** if they are uncertain or doubtful: *I am dubious about my chances of winning the race.* **2.** Something is **dubious** if it is open to suspicion or question: *That explanation sounds dubious to me.*
☐ **dubiously**, *adverb* –**dubiousness**, *noun*

A SIMILAR WORD (for definition 2) is **questionable**.

☑ SPELLING TIP **Dubious** literally means 'full of doubt'. This might help you to remember that it ends with the common suffix *-ious* (meaning 'full of'). Remember that there are three vowels in this suffix and that they appear in the alphabetical order *i-o-u* – then there will be nothing at all **dubious** about your spelling.

duchess *noun* in Britain, **1.** the wife or widow of a duke. **2.** a woman who holds the same position as a duke.

duck[1] *noun*
1. a waterbird with a flat bill, short legs and webbed feet. **2.** a female duck.

NOTE The male is a **drake**; the female is a **duck**; the young is a **duckling**.
WORD HISTORY from an Old English word meaning 'diver'

duck[2] *verb*
1. To **duck** is to lower your head suddenly: *He ducked just in time to avoid the low branch.* **2.** To **duck** someone is to push them under water for a moment: *You're not allowed to duck people at the pool.*
–*phrase* **3. duck out** (or **off**), *Rather informal* to go away for a short time: *She has just ducked next door.*

duck[3] *noun* in cricket, a batting score of zero.

duct *noun*
1. any tube by which liquids are carried. **2.** a tube in the body that carries liquid: *a tear duct.*

dud *noun Informal* someone or something which turns out to be a failure: *This plan is a real dud – it's not going to work.*
☐ **dud**, *adjective*

due *adjective*
1. If something is **due**, it has to be paid by a certain date. **2.** If something is **due**, it is expected to arrive or happen at a certain time: *The bus is due at 7 o'clock.* **3.** If something is **due** to something else, it is caused by it: *His poor examination results are partly due to family problems.* **4.** If something is **due**, it is right or suitable in a particular situation: *due consideration.*
–*noun* **5.** something that is owed or deserved, especially praise or approval: *We must give him his due.* **6. dues**, payment or fees: *Members must pay their dues next meeting.*
–*adverb* **7.** directly or straight: *He sailed due east.*

duel /*say* **dyooh**-uhl/ *noun*
1. in past times, an arranged fight between two people with weapons such as guns and swords. **2.** any fight or contest between two sides.
–*verb* (**duels**, **duelling**, **duelled**, **has duelled**) **3.** To **duel** is to fight a duel.
☐ **duellist**, *noun*

☑ SPELLING TIP Don't confuse the spelling of **duel** with **dual** which sounds the same. **Dual** describes something with two parts.

duet /*say* dyooh-**et**/ *noun* a musical piece for two voices or two performers.

duffer *noun Informal* a stupid person.

duke *noun*
1. in Britain, a nobleman of the next highest rank to a prince. **2.** in Europe in the past, a prince who ruled a small country or a region.
☐ **dukedom**, *noun*

NOTE A woman with this rank is called a **duchess**.

dulcimer /*say* **dul**-suh-muh/ *noun* an old-fashioned musical instrument with metal strings that you strike with light hammers.

dull *adjective*
1. Something **dull** is **a.** boring or uninteresting: *a dull lesson*; *a dull film.* **b.** not bright or clear: *cloudy and dull.* **c.** not sharply felt: *a dull ache.* **2.** Someone **dull** is stupid or unintelligent.
–*verb* **3.** If something **dulls** a pain or feeling, it causes it to be less sharply felt: *a medicine that dulls the pain.*
☐ **dullness**, *noun* –**dully**, *adverb*

duly /*say* **dyooh**-lee/ *adverb* **1.** properly or as deserved: *He got the most points and was duly declared the winner.* **2.** at the proper time: *The letter duly arrived.*

dumb /*say* dum/ *adjective* If someone is **dumb**, they are **1.** completely unable to speak because of a medical condition. **2.** silent: *He was dumb with shock.* **3.** *Informal* stupid or unintelligent: *That was a dumb thing to do.*

NOTE This word (as in definition 1) is not used very much these days and may offend people. It is better to use another term such as **speech-impaired**.

☑ SPELLING TIP *Silent letter alert*: don't forget the silent *b* at the end.

dumbfound *verb* If you **dumbfound** someone, you cause them to be so surprised that they are unable to speak.
☐ **dumbfounded**, *adjective*: *dumbfounded horror.*

☑ SPELLING TIP The spelling of **dumbfound** will be easier if you see that it is made up two words joined together – *dumb* (remember the silent *b*) and *found* which is short for *confound* (meaning 'to surprise').

dummy *noun* (*plural* **dummies**)
1. a copy or model of something used for display or to show off clothes: *The only coat left in my size was the one on the dummy in the window.* **2.** a rubber teat given to a baby to suck.

dump *verb* To **dump** something is to **1.** throw it down or put it down heavily. **2.** hand it over or get rid of it: *He dumped the cleaning up on me*; *She dumped the old papers into the recycling bin.*
–*noun* **3.** a place where something is dumped or stored: *a rubbish dump*; *an ammunition dump.* **4.** *Informal* a place or house that is untidy and in bad condition.
–*phrase* **5. in the dumps**, *Rather informal* feeling very unhappy or discouraged: *down in the dumps.*

dumpling *noun* a small ball of dough, often cooked with vegetables and meat.

dumpy *adjective* (**dumpier**, **dumpiest**) A **dumpy** person is short and fat: *a dumpy old woman.*

dunce *noun* a stupid or unintelligent person.

WORD HISTORY from John *Duns* Scotus, who lived from about 1265 to about 1308, and whose writing about religion was attacked as being foolish

dune *noun* a sandhill formed by wind, near the beach or in deserts.

dung *noun* matter from the bowels of animals.

A SIMILAR WORD for this is **manure**.

dungarees /*say* dung-guh-**reez**/ *plural noun* work clothing, usually overalls, made from a rough cotton cloth.

☑ SPELLING TIP *Tricky 'uh' sound*: the vowel sound in the middle is spelt *a*. Apart from that, **dungarees** is quite easy to spell, although it looks unusual. Rap it out as *dun+ga+rees*.

dungeon /*say* **dun**-juhn/ *noun* a dark, small prison or cell, usually underground: *The soldiers were held captive in the cold, dark dungeons of the castle.*

☑ SPELLING TIP The first part of this word is spelt like *plunge* and *lunge* (and also sounds like them). If you remember this, you only need to add *on* to spell **dungeon**.

dunk *verb*
1. To **dunk** something is to dip it quickly into a liquid: *I like to dunk bread in my soup.* **2.** If you **dunk** a ball in basketball, you jump so high that your hand is above the hoop and you push the ball down through it.
☐ **dunk**, *noun*

dunnart *noun* a type of native mouse found only in Australia. It is endangered.

WORD HISTORY from an Aboriginal language of Western Australia called Nyungar

dunny *noun* (*plural* **dunnies**) *Informal* a toilet, especially an outside one.

duo *noun* a pair, especially of musicians: *a new singing duo.*

dupe *verb* To **dupe** someone is to trick or deceive them: *The burglars duped her into believing that they were police officers.*
☐ **dupe**, *noun* someone who has been tricked or deceived.

duple *adjective* having two beats to the bar: *That piece of music is in duple time.*

duplex *noun* a building consisting of two separate dwellings.

duplicate *verb* /*say* **dyooh**-pluh-kayt/
1. If you **duplicate** something, you make an exact copy of it: *to duplicate a document*; *to duplicate a meal.*
–*adjective* /*say* **dyooh**-pluh-kuht/ **2.** A **duplicate** item is exactly like the first: *I would like a duplicate copy of this map.*
–*noun* /*say* **dyooh**-pluh-kuht/ **3.** something which is exactly the same as something else, usually a copy.
☐ **duplication**, *noun*

durable *adjective* lasting for a long time: *durable leather shoes.*
☐ **durability**, *noun* –**durably**, *adverb*

duration *noun* the length of time that anything continues for: *He read for the duration of the train trip*; *I will play hockey for the duration of the term.*

duress /*say* dyooh-**res**/ *noun* the use of threats or force.

NOTE This word is usually used in the phrase **under duress**: *She only agreed to go under duress.*

☑ SPELLING TIP *Single/double letter alert*: two *s*'s at the end, but a single *r* in the middle. The fact that the stress is on the last syllable should help you with the *ess* sound having a double *s*. Also remember that the word part *dur* or *dure* turns up in several words which have to do with hardness or strength, such as *endure*, *endurance* and *durable*.

during *preposition*
1. through the whole course of: *It is hot during the day.* **2.** at some time in the course of: *He visited me during the day.*

dusk *noun* the time of the evening when it is half light and half dark.

ANOTHER WORD for this is **twilight**.
WORD HISTORY from a Latin word meaning 'dark brown'

dust *noun*
1. a fine, dry powder of earth or other matter.
–*verb* To **dust** something is to **2.** wipe dust away from it. **3.** cover it lightly with fine particles: *She dusted the cake with sugar.*
–*phrase* **4. bite the dust**, *Informal* **a.** to be killed, especially in fighting. **b.** to fail: *Another good plan bites the dust.*
☐ **duster**, *noun* –**dusty**, *adjective* (**dustier**, **dustiest**)

duty *noun* (*plural* **duties**)
1. what someone feels is the right thing to do: *He felt it was his duty to report the shoplifters.* **2.** what someone has to do because of their position: *What are the duties of the school captain?* **3.** a tax charged by the government: *customs duty.*
–*phrase* **4. on duty**, at work. **5. off duty**, not at work.
☐ **dutiful**, *adjective* –**dutifully**, *adverb*

dux *noun* the top student at a school.

WORD HISTORY from a Latin word meaning 'leader'

DVD *noun*
1. a special kind of disc which stores information such as film, music and computer games. **2.** a film or other entertainment on this kind of disc.

WORD HISTORY short for *Digital Video Disc*

dwarf /*say* dwawf/ *noun*
1. a person, animal or plant much below the ordinary height or size. **2.** a small man-like creature in fairytales: *Snow White and the Seven Dwarfs.*
–*verb* **3.** To **dwarf** something is to make it seem small: *The huge ocean liner dwarfed the sailing boats that bobbed in its wake.*
☐ **dwarfish**, *adjective*

☑ SPELLING TIP *Tricky vowel sound*: *ar* spelling for the 'aw' sound. Another word with this sound and spelling pattern is *wharf.*

dwell *verb* (**dwells**, **dwelling**, **dwelt**, **has dwelt**)
1. To **dwell** somewhere or in a certain way is to live there or like that: *She dwelt in the country all her life; I hope we can all dwell in peace and harmony.*
–*phrase* **2. dwell on**, to continue thinking, speaking, or writing about: *She doesn't like to dwell on her troubles.*
☐ **dwelling**, *noun*

NOTE This word (as in definition 1) is used more in literature or formal language than in ordinary language.

dwindle *verb* When something **dwindles**, it becomes smaller or less: *The creek has dwindled to a trickle.*

dye *noun*
1. a liquid that is used to colour cloth, hair, and other things.
–*verb* (**dyes**, **dyeing**, **dyed**, **has dyed**) **2.** If you **dye** something, such as cloth or your hair, you colour it with a dye.

☑ SPELLING TIP Don't confuse the spelling of **dye** with **die** which sounds the same. To **die** is to stop living.

dyke *noun* a bank built to hold back the water of a sea or river.

dyna- *prefix* a word part meaning 'power', as in *dynamite*, *dynamo.*

WORD HISTORY this prefix comes from Greek

dynamic /*say* duy-**nam**-ik/ *adjective* If someone is **dynamic**, they are energetic and forceful: *a dynamic leader.*

dynamics *plural noun* **1.** the science that studies the forces that make things move. **2.** the forces that are at work in any situation: *the dynamics of government.*

dynamite /*say* **duy**-nuh-muyt/ *noun*
1. a substance that makes a powerful explosion when set off. **2.** *Rather informal* anyone or anything likely to be dangerous or cause trouble.
–*verb* **3.** To **dynamite** something is to blow it up with dynamite: *to dynamite the bridge.*

☑ SPELLING TIP Remember that the beginning of **dynamite** is spelt *dyn* (although it sounds as though it could be spelt *dine*). This is the same in *dynamic* (meaning 'relating to force'), which is where the word **dynamite** comes from. *Dynamic* and many other words with a *dy* spelling come from Greek.

dynamo /*say* **duy**-nuh-moh/ *noun* (*plural* **dynamos**) a machine which produces electrical energy.

dynasty /*say* **din**-uh-stee/ *noun* (*plural* **dynasties**) a series of rulers who are members of the same family: *The Ming dynasty ruled in China for hundreds of years.*
☐ **dynastic**, *adjective* –**dynastical**, *adjective*

☑ SPELLING TIP Remember that the beginning of **dynasty** is spelt *dyn* (although it sounds like 'din'). **Dynasty**, like many other words with a *dy* spelling, comes from Greek (from a word meaning 'lord' or 'chief').

dys- *prefix* a word part often used in medicine meaning 'difficulty' or 'poor condition', as in *dyslexia.*

dyslexia /*say* dis-**lek**-see-uh/ *noun* a medical condition that makes it difficult to learn to read.
☐ **dyslectic**, *adjective* –**dyslexic**, *adjective*

☑ SPELLING TIP The spelling of **dyslexia** will be easier if you see that it is made up of *lexia* (coming from *lexis*, the Greek word for 'speech' or 'word') and the prefix *dys-* (which also comes from Greek and is used in many medical words to mean 'without' or 'in poor condition').

each *adjective*
1. every, when you consider two or more things one by one: *each hair on my head.*
–*adverb* **2.** for every piece or person: *The tickets cost five dollars each.*

eager *adjective*
1. enthusiastic: *an eager learner*; *the eager faces of the children arriving at the zoo.* **2.** wanting to do something very much: *They are eager to get to the beach as soon as possible.*
□ **eagerly**, *adverb* –**eagerness**, *noun*

WORD HISTORY from a Latin word meaning 'sharp'

eagle *noun* a large hunting bird with a strong curved beak and claws and very good eyesight.

ear[1] *noun*
1. the part of the body used for hearing. **2.** the ability to notice differences of sound: *an ear for music.*
–*phrase* **3. be all ears**, to listen very carefully. **4. play by ear**, to perform without looking at written music. **5. play it by ear**, to work out what to do as events happen. **6. turn a deaf ear**, to refuse to help: *He turned a deaf ear to their cries.*

ear[2] *noun* the top part of a plant such as corn, on which the grain grows.

earl /*rhymes with* girl/ *noun* a British nobleman.
□ **earldom**, *noun*

early *adverb* (**earlier**, **earliest**)
1. before the set time. **2.** at or near the beginning: *Early in the hike, they saw a snake.*
□ **early**, *adjective* –**earliness**, *noun*

earn *verb* (**earns**, **earning**, **earnt** *or* **earned**, **has earnt** *or* **has earned**)
1. If you **earn** money, you receive it as payment for a job you have done. **2.** If someone or something **earns** something, they get it and they deserve it: *They earned their reputation for being such willing workers.*
□ **earner**, *noun* –**earnings**, *noun*

☑ SPELLING TIP Remember the *ea* spelling of this word. Don't confuse it with **urn** which sounds the same. An **urn** is a kind of container.

earnest /*say* **er**-nuhst/ *adjective* serious or sincere: *Is she earnest about wanting to study?*
□ **earnestly**, *adverb* –**earnestness**, *noun*

THE OPPOSITE is **frivolous**.

☑ SPELLING TIP *Tricky vowel sound*: this word sounds like the man's name *Ernest* but you have to remember that, like the word *earn* itself, it has earned itself an *a* and is spelt **earnest**.

earphone *noun* a small listening device placed in or over the ear.

earring *noun* a ring or other ornament that you wear through or on the lobe of your ear.

earth *noun*
1. the planet we live on. **2.** dry land: *On the map, the earth is marked in green and the oceans in blue.* **3.** soil, rather than rocks or sand. **4.** a wire connecting an electrical appliance to the ground, for added safety.
–*phrase* **5. down to earth**, practical in your approach to things. **6. the earth**, a great deal: *to cost the earth*; *to want the earth.*
□ **earthly**, *adjective* –**earthy**, *adjective*

ANOTHER FORM This word (as in definition 1) is often spelt with a capital letter.

earthenware *noun* goods, such as pots, made of baked clay.

earthquake *noun* a shaking of the ground caused by movement of rock under the earth's surface.

THE SHORT FORM of this is **quake**.

earthworm *noun* a worm that lives in the soil.

ease *noun*
1. freedom from any problem or discomfort: *Vijay passed his exams with ease.* **2.** a free and relaxed manner: *His ease in new situations was a great asset.*
–*verb* **3.** If something **eases**, it becomes less intense: *At last the rain eased.*
–*phrase* **4. at ease**, **a.** in the armed forces, a standing position in which soldiers may relax but may not talk or move. **b.** in a relaxed state of mind.

easel *noun* a stand for holding an artist's canvas or a blackboard.

east *noun* the direction from which the sun rises.
□ **east**, *adjective*, *adverb* –**easterly**, *adjective*: *easterly winds.* –**eastern**, *adjective*

NOTE The opposite direction is **west**.

easy *adjective* (**easier**, **easiest**) able to be done or understood without a lot of trouble: *That was an easy job*; *Do you think maths is easy to learn?*

☐ **easily**, *adverb* –**easiness**, *noun*

THE OPPOSITE is **difficult** or **hard**.

eat *verb* (**eats**, **eating**, **ate**, **has eaten**)
1. If you **eat** something, you put it in your mouth, chew it and swallow it. **2.** If you **eat** at a certain time, you have a meal then: *They always ate at seven.*
–*phrase* **3. eat away**, to destroy slowly: *The sea had eaten away the cliff.* **4. eat out**, to eat in a restaurant. **5. eat up**, to use up in large quantities: *to eat up the power.*
☐ **eater**, *noun*

eating disorder *noun* abnormal eating behaviour that involves eating too much or too little, to such an extent that a person's physical and mental health is affected.

eaves *plural noun* the lower edges of a roof which stick out beyond the walls: *She had the eaves painted dark brown.*

eavesdrop *verb* (**eavesdrops**, **eavesdropping**, **eavesdropped**, **has eavesdropped**) To **eavesdrop** is to listen secretly.
☐ **eavesdropper**, *noun*

ebb *verb*
1. When the tide **ebbs**, the level of the sea becomes lower on the shore. **2.** If something **ebbs** or **ebbs away**, it goes away gradually, or becomes weaker: *His strength is ebbing.*
☐ **ebb**, *noun*: *at a low ebb.*

Ebola /*say* uh-**boh**-luh/ *noun* a serious disease caused by a virus that gives the person with it a high fever and internal bleeding.

WORD HISTORY named after the *Ebola* River in Africa where it first occurred

ebony /*say* **eb**-uh-nee/ *noun* a hard, black, shiny wood which is valuable for carving: *a handle made of ebony.*

ebook *noun* a book that can be read using a computer or other electronic device.

ANOTHER FORM is **e-book**.
WORD HISTORY short for *electronic book*

eccentric /*say* uhk-**sen**-trik/ *adjective*
1. behaving in a different way to most other people; rather strange: *eccentric behaviour.*
–*noun* **2.** an eccentric person: *He's a real eccentric.*
☐ **eccentrically**, *adverb* –**eccentricity**, *noun*

THE OPPOSITE (of definition 1 is **conventional**).

☑ SPELLING TIP *Double letter alert*: double *c* after the opening *e*. But remember that each of these *c*'s makes a different sound – the first has a 'k' sound and the second an 's' sound. It might help if you can see that the word is made up of the prefix *ec-* (meaning 'out of') and *centric* (a form of the word *central*, meaning 'relating to or situated at the centre'). So the basic meaning of the word is 'away from the centre'.

ecclesiastical /*say* uh-kleez-ee-**as**-tuh-kuhl/ *adjective* having to do with the church: *ecclesiastical authority.*

☑ SPELLING TIP This long word is not really difficult to spell if you remember that it begins with *e* and then has another single *e* in the second syllable making the 'ee' sound. Also remember the double *c*. Try rapping it out as *ec+cle+si+as+ti+cal*.

echidna /*say* uh-**kid**-nuh/ *noun* a spiny, ant-eating animal found only in Australia, which lays eggs and feeds its young with its own milk.

ANOTHER NAME for this is **spiny anteater**.

☑ SPELLING TIP The word **echidna** comes from Greek (meaning 'viper') which is why it has the spelling *ch* to make the 'k' sound.

echo /*say* **ek**-oh/ *noun* (*plural* **echoes**)
1. a repeating sound, when sound waves bounce off something hard.
–*verb* (**echoes**, **echoing**, **echoed**, **has echoed**)
2. If something **echoes**, it makes a repeating sound: *We could hear the sound of his shout echoing around the valley.*

eclipse /*say* uh-**klips**/ *noun*
1. the darkness caused when the sun's light is blocked by the moon, or when the moon's light is blocked by earth's shadow.
–*verb* **2.** If you **eclipse** someone, you do something much better than them: *Her tennis playing completely eclipsed her sister's.*

eco /*say* **ee**-koh/ *adjective* having to do with environmentally friendly practices, materials, technology, etc.: *eco baby products*; *eco shoes.*

ecological footprint *noun* a measure of the demands that an individual or group of humans makes on the environment which takes into account such factors as the amount of land and water needed to produce their food, the energy needed to build, heat, and cool their homes, and the making and use of their cars.

ecology /*say* uh-**kol**-uh-jee/ *noun* the study of the relationship between living things and their environment.
☐ **ecological**, *adjective* –**ecologically**, *adverb* –**ecologist**, *noun*

economical /*say* ek-uh-**nom**-i-kuhl, ee-kuh-**nom**-i-kuhl/ *adjective* not wasteful: *There is not a lot of money – we will have to be economical.*
☐ **economically**, *adverb*

economy /*say* uh-**kon**-uh-mee/ *noun* (*plural* **economies**)
1. the finances of a country. **2.** carefulness with money or supplies so as not to waste them: *to rearrange finances with economy.*
☐ **economic**, *adjective* –**economise**, *verb*

ANOTHER SPELLING for **economise** is **economize**.
A SIMILAR WORD (for definition 2) is **thrift**.

ecstasy /*say* **eks**-tuh-see/ *noun* a sudden feeling of great happiness.
□ **ecstatic**, *adjective* –**ecstatically**, *adverb*

☑ SPELLING TIP This word seems difficult because it has a lot of consonants coming together. But if you remember that the first part is spelt *ecs* (not *ex* or *eks*), and that the ending is *asy*, it is not too hard. Rap it out as *ec+sta+sy*.

eczema /*say* **ek**-suh-muh/ *noun* an itchy or painful rash in which the skin becomes red and flaky.

☑ SPELLING TIP There are not many words in English in which a *z* follows a *c*. If you remember this unusual combination, you will know that **eczema** starts with *ecz* (not *ecs* or *ex*). Also remember the *e* in the middle of the word, giving the word three syllables (although some people leave out this middle syllable when they say it).

eddy *noun* (*plural* **eddies**) a current moving in a circle, especially in a river.

edge *noun*
1. a border or line where two parts or surfaces meet: *the edge of the table.* **2.** the thin cutting part of something sharp, such as a knife.
–*verb* **3.** If you **edge**, you move gradually: *He edged carefully towards the bird.*
–*phrase* **4. have the edge**, *Rather informal* to have the advantage. **5. on edge**, **a.** excited and nervous: *She was on edge about the results of the test.* **b.** cross and annoyed: *The noise of the trucks put him on edge.*
□ **edgy**, *adjective*

edible *adjective* Food that is **edible** is able or fit to be eaten: *an edible mushroom.*

edict /*say* **ee**-dikt/ *noun* an order given by a ruler or someone else in authority: *The president issued a new edict.*

edifice /*say* **ed**-uh-fuhs/ *noun* a building, especially a large or impressive one.

edit *verb* (**edits, editing, edited, has edited**) If you **edit** a book, newspaper, or magazine, you prepare its contents so that it can be printed and published. You make corrections and organise the material: *I volunteered to edit the class magazine.*
□ **editor**, *noun*

edition *noun* a particular version of a book, newspaper, or magazine, that is printed at one time: *the morning edition*; *a new revised edition.*

editorial *noun* a newspaper article written by an editor, which expresses the editor's or the paper's views.
□ **editorial**, *adjective*

ANOTHER WORD for this is **leader** (definition 2).

educate *verb* To **educate** someone is to instruct or give knowledge to them: *He also educates the boys in skills such as fencing.*
□ **educated**, *adjective* –**education**, *noun* –**educator**, *noun*

eel *noun* an edible snake-like fish.

eerie /*rhymes with* cheery/ *adjective* (**eerier**, **eeriest**) strange and frightening: *The old deserted house had an eerie air about it.*
□ **eerily**, *adverb* –**eeriness**, *noun*

WORD HISTORY from an Old English word meaning 'cowardly'

☑ SPELLING TIP Remember that there are three *e*'s in **eerie** – the first two come together and the last one is part of the *ie* spelling which gives the 'y' sound at the end.

effect *noun*
1. something which is produced by some cause: *The shape of the mountain is the effect of centuries of erosion.* **2.** the power to produce results: *Talking to her has no effect.*
–*verb* **3.** To **effect** something is to make it happen: *to effect a change.*
–*phrase* **4. for effect**, for the sake of an appearance you wish to create: *I dress like this for effect.* **5. in effect**, **a.** in fact or reality: *What will happen in effect is that I will be acting principal.* **b.** working or in operation: *The new law will be in effect from tomorrow.*

☑ DO NOT CONFUSE **effect** with the verb **affect**, which is to cause a change in something.

effective *adjective* producing the desired result: *an effective medicine.*
□ **effectively**, *adverb* –**effectiveness**, *noun*

effeminate /*say* uh-**fem**-uh-nuht/ *adjective* If someone says that a man is **effeminate**, they mean that he behaves in a way that they think is too much like a woman.

effervescent /*say* ef-uh-**ves**-uhnt/ *adjective*
1. If a drink is **effervescent**, it is fizzy. **2.** If someone is **effervescent**, they are lively and exuberant: *Her effervescent personality kept us in good spirits.*
□ **effervesce**, *verb* –**effervescence**, *noun*

☑ SPELLING TIP Remember the double *f* and the *er* spelling for the second vowel sound. Finally, don't forget the silent *c* following the *s* just like in the word *scent*.

efficient /*say* uh-**fish**-uhnt/ *adjective*
1. If someone is **efficient**, they do things well without wasting time. **2.** If something is **efficient**, it works well and is practical: *This pump is very efficient – it gives a strong flow of water.*
□ **efficiency**, *noun* –**efficiently**, *adverb*

SIMILAR WORDS (for definition 1) are **competent** and **capable**.

effigy /*say* **ef**-uh-jee/ *noun* (*plural* **effigies**) a picture or statue of a person: *a bronze effigy.*

effluent /*say* **ef**-looh-uhnt/ *noun* something flowing out, such as the liquid waste from places like industrial sites and sewage works.
□ **effluent**, *adjective* flowing out. –**effluence**, *noun*

effort *noun*
1. the use of physical strength: *It took the effort of four men to move the piano.* **2.** a serious attempt: *He has made an effort to improve his homework.*
□ **effortless**, *adjective*

effrontery /*say* uh-**frun**-tuh-ree/ *noun* cheeky rudeness or impudence: *She had the effrontery to mock him.*

☑ SPELLING TIP Remember that this word starts with an *e*. Don't confuse it with the spelling of **affront** which has a related meaning.

EFTPOS /*say* **eft**-pos/ *noun* a system used in supermarkets and shops that allows you to pay using a plastic card with a special code and a PIN: *'Cash or EFTPOS?', the cashier asked.*

WORD HISTORY an acronym made by joining the first letters of *electronic funds transfer* (*at*) *point of sale*

e.g. *abbreviation* short for *exempli gratia*, Latin words meaning 'for example': *We have lots of team sports at our school, e.g. netball, soccer and cricket.*

egg *noun*
1. a roundish object produced by a female animal, bird or fish, which contains the organism that grows into its young: *We found some lizard eggs under the rock.* **2.** a bird's egg, especially a hen's: *eggs and bacon.*
–*verb in the phrase* **3. egg on**, to encourage someone to do something: *We egged her on to finish the course.*

eggplant *noun* a large, dark purple, more or less egg-shaped fruit, used as a vegetable.

ANOTHER WORD for this is **aubergine** /*say* **oh**-buh-zheen).

ego /*say* **ee**-goh/ *noun* (*plural* **egos**)
1. the 'I' or self of someone: *She has a good sense of her own ego – she knows exactly where she stands on things.* **2.** pride or belief in your own importance: *His ego is too big for her own good.*
□ **egoism**, *noun* –**egoist**, *noun* –**egoistic**, *adjective*

egotism *noun* the habit of thinking and talking about yourself all the time: *His egotism has lost him all his friends.*
□ **egotist**, *noun* –**egotistical**, **egotistic**, *adjective*

eiderdown /*say* **uy**-duh-down/ *noun* a quilt filled with duck feathers.

☑ SPELLING TIP The spelling of **eiderdown** will be easier if you know that it means 'the down of an eider' (*down* meaning 'feathers' and *eider* being a kind of duck). Concentrate on remembering the spelling of *eider*, especially the *ei* beginning.

eight *noun*
1. a cardinal number, seven plus one (7+1). **2.** the symbol for this number, as 8 or VIII. **3.** a set of eight people or things, especially a rowing crew.
□ **eight**, *adjective* –**eighth**, *adjective*, *noun*

☑ SPELLING TIP *Tricky vowel sound*: *eigh* spelling for the 'ay' sound. Remember that the number **eight** has nothing to do with eating, although it sounds like *ate*. Some other words which have an *eigh* spelling for the same sound are *neigh* and *weigh*. Also remember that when you add *th* to make **eighth**, you drop the *t* so that **eighth** has only one *t*.

eighteen *noun*
1. a cardinal number, ten plus eight (10+8). **2.** the symbol for this number, as 18 or XVIII.
□ **eighteen**, *adjective* –**eighteenth**, *adjective*, *noun*

eighty *noun* (*plural* **eighties**)
1. a cardinal number, ten times eight (10×8). **2.** the symbol for this number, as 80 or LXXX. **3. eighties**, the numbers from 80 to 89 of a series, especially someone's age, or the years of a century: *a man in his eighties.*
□ **eightieth**, *adjective*, *noun* –**eighty**, *adjective*

eisteddfod /*say* uh-**sted**-fuhd/ *noun* (*plural* **eisteddfods** *or* **eisteddfodau** /*say* uh-**sted**-fuh-duy/) a competition in which people sing, play music or recite poetry.

☑ SPELLING TIP The word **eisteddfod** comes from a Welsh word (meaning 'session') and the spelling contains combinations of letters that are common in Welsh but unusual in English. This also explains the unusual second plural form. The main spelling points to remember are that the sound at the beginning is spelt *ei* though it is pronounced 'uh', there is a double *d* in the middle, and the last syllable is *fod* although it sounds like 'fuhd'.

either /*say* **uy**-dhuh, **ee**-dhuh/ *adjective*
1. If you are talking about two things, you use **either** to refer to one or the other of them: *You can have either chocolate or strawberry flavouring – but not both!* **2.** You can also use **either** to refer to both of two things: *You can sit on either side of the hall; it doesn't matter which.*
–*pronoun* **3.** one or the other but not both: *Take either.*

–*conjunction* **4.** used together with **or** to show one of two equal things: *Either write to them or send an email.*

☑ SPELLING TIP There are two ways of saying **either**, but only one way of spelling it. The sound at the beginning is spelt *ei* whether you pronounce it as 'uy' or 'ee'.

ejaculate /*say* uh-**jak**-yuh-layt/ *verb* If a man or boy **ejaculates**, they send out semen from their penis.
☐ **ejaculation**, *noun*

eject *verb* To **eject** something or someone is to send them out with some force: *He was ejected from the room because he was causing a commotion.*
☐ **ejection**, *noun*

elaborate *adjective* /*say* uh-**lab**-uh-ruht/
1. worked out in great detail: *an elaborate quilt*; *an elaborate plan.*
–*verb* /*say* uh-**lab**-uh-rayt/ **2.** If you **elaborate on** something, you give fuller details about it.
☐ **elaboration**, *noun*

elapse *verb* Time **elapses** as it passes: *Years elapsed before they saw her again.*

elastic *adjective* If something is **elastic**, you can stretch it but it returns to its original size or shape when you let go: *an elastic band.*
☐ **elasticity**, *noun*

elated /*say* uh-**lay**-tuhd/ *adjective* in high spirits: *They were elated when they finally won a game.*
☐ **elation**, *noun*

elbow *noun* the joint between the upper and lower arm.

elder *adjective*
1. having been born first in a family: *The elder twin was a bit taller.*
–*noun* **2.** an older or more important person: *Dad said I should listen to my elders.* **3.** a senior person of status in an Aboriginal community, especially one who holds knowledge of traditional language and culture. **4.** an older person of high standing and influence in another traditional community, clan, tribe, etc., often a chief or ruler.

NOTE **Elder** as an adjective is the comparative form of **old**.

elderly *adjective* An **elderly** person is old or aged: *Elderly people sometimes can't hear as well as they used to.*

elect *verb* To **elect** someone is to choose by vote: *to elect the school captain.*
☐ **election**, *noun* –**elector**, *noun* –**electoral**, *adjective*

elective *adjective*
1. If a position in a group like a council or a government is **elective**, it is filled by somebody who is voted on in an election: *an elective position.* **2.** not required but optional: *Photography is an elective subject at school*; *elective surgery.*
☐ **elective**, *noun* an elective subject: *You can take two electives.*

electorate /*say* uh-**lek**-tuh-ruht, uh-**lek**-truht/ *noun* the area of a country, or the people in the area, which a member of parliament represents.

ANOTHER WORD for this is **constituency**.

electrician /*say* uh-lek-**trish**-uhn, e-lek-**trish**-uhn, ee-lek-**trish**-uhn/ *noun* someone who looks after the electrical wiring in buildings.

☑ SPELLING TIP Remember that the ending of **electrician** is spelt *ician*. Many other words have this spelling for an 'ishuhn' sound, such as *magician* and *musician*. Rap it out as *el+ec+tri+cian*.

electricity *noun* a form of energy from electrons, which can be used for heating, lighting, driving a motor, and other things.
☐ **electric**, *adjective* –**electrical**, *adjective*

electrify *verb* (**electrifies**, **electrifying**, **electrified**, **has electrified**)
1. To **electrify** something is to equip it for use with electricity: *The whole railway system was electrified.* **2.** To **electrify** someone is to excite them: *The news that the star would be visiting electrified the whole community.*
☐ **electrification**, *noun*

electrocute *verb* To **electrocute** someone is to kill them by electricity: *She was electrocuted when she put a knife into the toaster.*
☐ **electrocution**, *noun*

electrode *noun* a metal conductor through which electric current enters or leaves a battery.

electromagnet *noun* a magnet made from wire coiled around an iron or steel core, through which an electric current is passed.
☐ **electromagnetic**, *adjective* –**electromagnetically**, *adverb* –**electromagnetism**, *noun*

electron *noun* a very tiny particle which moves around the nucleus in all atoms and which has a type of energy that balances the energy of a proton.

NOTE The energy of an electron is called **negative**.
SEE ALSO **proton** and **neutron**.

electronic /*say* el-uhk-**tron**-ik, ee-lek-**tron**-ik/ *adjective* Something **electronic** is worked or produced by small changes in the flow of electricity: *an electronic security system.*
☐ **electronically**, *adverb* –**electronics**, *noun*

☑ DO NOT CONFUSE **electronic** with **electric**, which describes something which is run by electricity (*an electric stove*) or produced by it (*an electric shock*).

elegant *adjective* graceful or stylish: *elegant woman*; *an elegant style of furniture.*
☐ **elegance**, *noun* –**elegantly**, *adverb*

elegy /*say* **el**-uh-jee/ *noun* (*plural* **elegies**) a poem expressing sorrow over someone's death.

element *noun*
1. a substance that cannot be broken down into anything else: *Hydrogen and oxygen are both elements.* **2.** a wire that is the heating unit of an electric heater or similar electrical appliance. **3.** the natural or perfect surroundings for any person or thing: *I'm in my element in a hot bath with a good book.* **4. the elements**, the weather or atmospheric forces: *damaged by the elements.*
☐ **elemental**, *adjective*

elementary *adjective* simple or basic.

elephant *noun* a very large animal of Africa or India, with a thick grey skin, a long trunk which can grasp and carry things, and long curved tusks.

NOTE The male is a **bull;** the female is a **cow;** the young is a **calf**.

elevate *verb* To **elevate** is to lift or raise: *The head ends of hospital beds can be elevated.*
☐ **elevation**, *noun*

elevator *noun* See **lift** (definition 2).

eleven *noun*
1. a cardinal number, ten plus one (10 + 1). **2.** the symbol for this number, for example 11 or XI. **3.** a set of eleven people or things, especially a team of eleven players, as in soccer, cricket, hockey, and so on.
☐ **eleven**, *adjective* –**eleventh**, *adjective*, *noun*

elf *noun* (*plural* **elves**) a small being in fairytales who often plays tricks on people.

eligible /*say* **el**-uh-juh-buhl/ *adjective* If someone is **eligible** they are accepted as suitable.
☐ **eligibility**, *noun*

WORD HISTORY from a Latin word meaning 'pick out'

eliminate *verb* To **eliminate** something or some-one is to get rid of or remove them: *Our team was eliminated in the first round of the competition.*
☐ **elimination**, *noun*

elite /*say* uh-**leet**, ay-**leet**, ee-**leet**/ *noun* the group of people with the most money, power, and other advantages.
☐ **elite**, *adjective*

elixir /*say* uh-**liks**-uh, e-**liks**-uh, ee-**liks**-uh/ *noun* a sweet liquid medicine: *an elixir of wattle bark steeped in water.*

WORD HISTORY from a Greek word for 'a drying powder for wounds'

elk *noun* a large deer found in Europe and Asia.

ellipse *noun* an oval shape.
☐ **elliptical**, *adjective*

ellipsoid *noun* a solid oval, the shape of an egg.
☐ **ellipsoidal**, *adjective* like an ellipsoid.

elm *noun* a European tree which loses its leaves in winter and is often planted for shade.

elocution *noun* the study of how to make your speech sound pleasing.
☐ **elocutionary**, *adjective* –**elecutionist**, *noun*

elope *verb* To **elope** is to run away with a lover, usually to get married without the permission of parents.
☐ **elopement**, *noun*

eloquent /*say* **el**-uh-kwuhnt/ *adjective* able to speak in a flowing, expressive manner.
☐ **eloquence**, *noun* –**eloquently**, *adverb*

else *adverb*
1. a. instead of, or other than, the person or the thing mentioned: *somebody else*; *who else?* **b.** in addition: *What else can I do?*; *Who else is going?* **2.** other than yours: *somebody else's child*; *nobody else's business.* **3.** otherwise: *Eat your beans or else you can't have any ice-cream.*

elsewhere *adverb* somewhere else: *I can't see them – they must be elsewhere.*

elusive *adjective* hard to find or get hold of: *the elusive treasure*; *an elusive recollection.*
☐ **elusiveness**, *noun*

email /*say* **ee**-mayl/ *noun*
1. the sending of messages from one person to another by computer, especially by the internet. **2.** a message sent in this way.
–*verb* **3.** If you **email** a message to someone, you send it by email: *He emailed a reply*; *I will email you tomorrow.*

ANOTHER FORM is **e-mail**.
WORD HISTORY short for *electronic mail*

emancipate /*say* uh-**man**-suh-payt/ *verb* If you **emancipate** someone, you set them free: *At last the slaves were emancipated.*
☐ **emancipist**, *noun* a convict pardoned by the governor in early colonial times in Australia. –**emancipation**, *noun*

embalm /*say* em-**bahm**/ *verb* To **embalm** a corpse is to treat it in order to preserve it, now with chemicals but in the past with spices and substances from plants.

☑ SPELLING TIP *Tricky vowel sound*: don't forget the *l*. The *alm* spelling gives the 'ahm' sound.

embankment *noun* a pile of earth and stones to keep back water or to be the base for a road or railway.

embargo *noun* (*plural* **embargoes**) an order, usually made by a government against trade of some kind: *an embargo on the export of guns.*

embark *verb*
1. If you **embark**, you board a ship before the start of a cruise or journey: *They embarked early in the morning.*
–*phrase* **2. embark on**, to start: *They embarked on a new project.*
☐ **embarkation**, *noun*

THE OPPOSITE is **disembark**.

embarrass *verb* To **embarrass** someone is to cause them to feel uncomfortable: *My mother's old-fashioned ideas embarrassed me in front of my friends.*
☐ **embarrassing**, *adjective* –**embarrassment**, *noun*

☑ SPELLING TIP *Double letter alert*: remember that when you are embarrassed you feel doubly uncomfortable and there are two double letters in **embarrass** – a double *r* and a double *s*.

embassy *noun* (*plural* **embassies**) the office and house of an ambassador.

embellish *verb*
1. To **embellish** something is to make it beautiful by decorating it: *Precious jewels embellished the golden crown.* **2.** To **embellish** a story is to add details to it, usually ones that are not true: *I think he had embellished his description of the huge cat that attacked him.*
☐ **embellishment**, *noun*

ember *noun* a small piece of burning coal or wood remaining from a fire: *The embers of the fire were still glowing.*

embezzle *verb* If someone **embezzles** money, they steal it, usually by making false entries in account books: *The accountant embezzled thousands of dollars.*
☐ **embezzlement**, *noun* –**embezzler**, *noun*

emblem *noun* a badge or something that serves as a sign or symbol: *Our school emblem is an oak tree.*
☐ **emblematic**, *adjective*

emboss *verb* If you **emboss** something, you press a letter or design into it so that the letter or design stands out from its background: *The book's title was embossed in gold so it stood out on the shelf.*

embrace *verb*
1. To **embrace** someone is to hug them or hold them close.
–*noun* **2.** a hug.

embroider *verb* If you **embroider** a piece of cloth, you decorate it with decorative sewing.
☐ **embroidery**, *noun*

embryo /*say* **em**-bree-oh/ *noun* (*plural* **embryos**) a young animal or human in the very early stages of growing in the womb.
☐ **embryonic**, *adjective*

COMPARE this with **foetus**.

emerald *noun* a green precious stone.
☐ **emerald**, *adjective*

emerge *verb* To **emerge** is to come out from behind something: *They suddenly emerged from behind the house.*
☐ **emergence**, *noun*

emergency *noun* (*plural* **emergencies**) an unexpected serious happening that needs action at once: *This is an emergency – everybody should be helping!*

emergency exit *noun* an exit marked in a building to be used as a way out in an emergency like a fire or accident.

emigrate *verb* If you **emigrate**, you leave your own country to go and live in another country.
☐ **emigrant**, *noun* –**emigration**, *noun*

COMPARE this with **immigrate**.

eminent *adjective* important or high in rank.
☐ **eminently**, *adverb* –**eminence**, *noun*

☑ DO NOT CONFUSE **eminent** with **imminent**, which describes something which is likely to happen at any moment.

emission *noun* something that is emitted, especially a gas that is released into the atmosphere: *emissions of greenhouse gases.*

emit /*say* uh-**mit**/ *verb* (**emits**, **emitting**, **emitted**, **has emitted**) To **emit** is to **1.** discharge or send out: *to emit liquid, light, heat, sound, and so on.* **2.** issue: *to emit an order or decree.* **3.** express or utter: *birds that emit harsh sounds.*

emotion *noun* a feeling, such as love, hate, happiness, sadness or anger.
☐ **emotional**, *adjective* –**emotionally**, *adverb*

WORD HISTORY from a French word meaning 'excite'

emperor *noun* a man who rules over a group of countries or peoples: *Augustus was the first Roman emperor.*

NOTE A woman who rules an empire is called an **empress**.

emphasis /*say* **em**-fuh-suhs/ *noun* (*plural* **emphases** /*say* **em**-fuh-seez/) stress or importance: *The teacher placed great emphasis on punctuality.*
☐ **emphasise**, *verb* –**emphatic**, *adjective*

ANOTHER SPELLING for **emphasise** is **emphasize**.

☑ SPELLING TIP *Tricky 'uh' sound*: the middle vowel sound is spelt *a*. Also remember the *ph* spelling for the 'f' sound.

empire *noun*
1. a group of countries or peoples that are governed by one ruler: *Many of the former colonies of the British Empire now belong to the Commonwealth of Nations.* 2. a group of businesses or organisations under the control of one person or family: *The family's newspaper empire was gradually sold off.*

NOTE **Imperial** is a word meaning 'having to do with an empire'.

employ *verb*
1. To **employ** someone is to provide work for them: *The hospital employs hundreds of staff.* 2. To **employ** something is to use it: *to employ bright, happy images to sell the message.*
☐ **employee**, *noun* –**employer**, *noun* –**employment**, *noun*

empty *adjective* (**emptier**, **emptiest**)
1. If something is **empty**, it doesn't contain anything. There is nothing in it: *The room was completely empty of furniture.* 2. You can also say that a place like a room or a house is **empty** if there are no people there: *an empty house.* 3. If you say that words are **empty**, you mean that the person who spoke or wrote them does not really mean what they say: *an empty threat.*
–*verb* (**empties**, **emptying**, **emptied**, **has emptied**) 4. If you **empty** something, you take out what was inside. You remove the contents.
☐ **emptily**, *adverb* –**emptiness**, *noun*

emu *noun* a large Australian bird which cannot fly and is related to the cassowary.

WORD HISTORY from a Portuguese word for an ostrich or a cassowary

emulate *verb* If you **emulate** someone or something, you try to imitate them: *He tried to emulate his mother's cooking.*
☐ **emulation**, *noun* –**emulative**, *adjective* –**emulator**, *noun*

emulsion /*say* uh-**mul**-shuhn/ *noun* a milk-like mixture, often rather oily.
☐ **emulsify**, *verb* (**emulsifies**, **emulsifying**, **emulsified**, **has emulsified**)

WORD HISTORY from a Latin word meaning 'milked out'

en- *prefix* a word part meaning 'in' or 'into': *enchant, enclose.*

ANOTHER SPELLING is **em-,** as in *embrace.*
WORD HISTORY this prefix comes from Latin

enable *verb* If something **enables** you to do something, it makes it possible for you to do it: *These boots are tough and enable you to walk on very rough tracks.*

enamel *noun*
1. a very hard coating applied to metal. 2. a paint which is shiny when it dries.

☑ SPELLING TIP *Single letter alert*: remember that there are no double consonants in **enamel** – there is a single *n*, a single *m* and a single *l* at the end.

enchant *verb*
1. In fairytales, if someone **enchants** someone or something, they put a magic spell on them. 2. To **enchant** someone is to make them very happy: *The school concert enchanted all the parents.*
☐ **enchantment**, *noun*

enclose *verb*
1. If you **enclose** something, you surround it with something or shut it in on all sides. 2. If you **enclose** something with a letter or with goods, you put it in the same envelope or package.
☐ **enclosure**, *noun*

encore /*say* **on**-kaw/ *noun* an extra piece of music performed in answer to continued clapping by the audience: *I hope he doesn't play an encore – I want to go home!*

WORD HISTORY from a French word meaning 'again' shouted by an audience

encounter *verb*
1. If you **encounter** someone, you meet them: *to encounter an old friend a long way from home.* 2. If you **encounter** a problem or difficulty, you are faced with it unexpectedly: *to encounter a tree across the road.*
☐ **encounter**, *noun*

encourage *verb*
1. If you **encourage** someone, you support them in what they want to do. 2. If you **encourage** something, you support it and try to help it become bigger or better. 3. If you **encourage** someone to do something, you suggest that they should do it: *We encourage all our students to study a language.*
☐ **encouragement**, *noun* –**encouraging**, *adjective* –**encouragingly**, *adverb*

encroach *verb* If someone or something **encroaches** on an area, they go beyond their own area and onto some other area that is not theirs: *The outer areas of the town are encroaching on the bush*; *She is encroaching on my area of authority.*
☐ **encroachment**, *noun*

encyclopedia /*say* en-suy-kluh-**pee**-dee-uh/ *noun* a book or set of books that contains information on many different subjects. The articles are usually in alphabetical order.

ANOTHER SPELLING is **encyclopaedia** but this is not used very much these days.

☑ SPELLING TIP The main difficulty is the *cyc* spelling. Think of the word *cycle* to remind yourself of this. **Encyclopedia** is based on a Greek word meaning 'a cycle (or course) of learning'.

end *noun*
1. the finishing point.
–*verb* 2. If something **ends**, it finishes.
–*phrase* 3. **at a loose end**, not busy enough or having nothing to do. 4. **make both ends meet**, to spend no more than you earn. 5. **on end**, a. upright: *Her hair stood on end.* b. without stopping: *It has rained for days on end.*
☐ **ending**, *noun* –**endless**, *adjective*

endanger /*say* en-**dayn**-juh/ *verb* To **endanger** someone is to put them in danger or at risk: *They will endanger their lives if they go to sea in that leaky boat.*
☐ **endangered**, *adjective*

NOTE A group of animals which are in danger of all being killed is called an **endangered species**.

endeavour /*say* en-**dev**-uh/ *verb*
1. To **endeavour** to do something is to try or attempt to do it: *They were endeavouring to reach the summit without ropes.*
–*noun* 2. a strenuous effort or attempt: *a brave endeavour.*

ANOTHER SPELLING is **endeavor**.

endorse *verb*
1. If you **endorse** something written, you sign your name on it: *to endorse a petition.* 2. If you **endorse** a person or a plan, you give your approval and support to them: *to endorse someone for school captain*; *to endorse an idea.*
☐ **endorsable**, *adjective* –**endorsement**, *noun* –**endorser**, *noun*

endow /*rhymes with* cow/ *verb*
1. If you **endow** an institution like a school or a hospital, you give it money: *He made millions and endowed much of it to charity.* 2. If someone or something is **endowed** with something, they have been given it: *She has been endowed with many wonderful skills.*
☐ **endowment**, *noun*

endure *verb*
1. If you **endure** something difficult or painful, you suffer it or put up with it: *I can't endure the pain for much longer!* 2. If something **endures**, it lasts for a long time.
☐ **endurance**, *noun* –**enduring**, *adjective*

enemy *noun* (*plural* **enemies**)
1. someone who hates someone else, or wishes to harm them. 2. an unfriendly armed force which is prepared to fight: *a country in continuing fear of its enemy.*

energetic /*say* en-uh-**jet**-ik/ *adjective* strong and active: *Mum says that my little brother is too energetic.*
☐ **energetically**, *adverb*

energy /*say* **en**-uh-jee/ *noun*
1. the ability to be active: *enough energy to run up the stairs.* 2. electrical or other power: *increasing demands on available energy.* 3. in physics, the capacity for doing work, existing in various forms: *kinetic energy*; *nuclear energy.*

NOTE The metric unit used for measuring energy is the **joule**.

enforce *verb* To **enforce** something is to 1. make certain of obedience to it: *to enforce laws*; *to enforce rules.* 2. obtain it by force: *to enforce payment of a debt.*
☐ **enforceable**, *adjective* –**enforcedly**, *adverb* –**enforcer**, *noun* –**enforcement**, *noun*

☑ SPELLING TIP Remember that **enforce** begins with *en*, not *in*.

engage *verb*
1. If you **engage** someone, you employ them to do a job: *They engaged a woman to look after the baby.* 2. To **engage** parts of a machine is to make them to fit into each other and move together: *to engage gears.* 3. Armies **engage** in war when they begin to fight.

engaged *adjective*
1. If a telephone is **engaged**, you cannot speak to the person you have rung because their telephone is being used for another call: *the engaged tone.* 2. If you are **engaged** in something, you are in the process of doing it: *engaged in looking for insects.* 3. If two people get **engaged**, they decide (and usually tell everyone) that they are going to marry each other: *an engaged couple.*
☐ **engagement**, *noun*: *They celebrated their engagement with a party.*

engine /*say* **en**-juhn/ *noun*
1. a machine which changes energy from sources like petrol or steam into movement: *steam engine*; *diesel engine.* 2. a railway locomotive.

WORD HISTORY from a Latin word meaning 'invention'

engineer /*say* en-juh-**near**/ *noun* someone who is trained to design and build things and to use machinery: *His father was an engineer who built roads and bridges*; *an electrical engineer*; *a chemical engineer.*
☐ **engineering**, *noun*

☑ SPELLING TIP If you know the spelling of *engine* (with a soft *g*, not a *j*), you will be all right with **engineer** which literally means 'someone who constructs engines'.

engrave *verb*
1. If you **engrave** something such as stone or metal, you cut into it with a sharp tool, to leave words or a design on the surface. 2. If something is **engraved** in your memory, you remember it very clearly.
☐ **engraver**, *noun* –**engraving**, *noun*

engulf *verb*
1. To **engulf** something or someone is to swallow them up: *A tidal wave entirely engulfed the town*

on the coast. **2.** If something engulfs you it overwhelms you: *She was engulfed with remorse.*

enhance *verb* To **enhance** something is to improve it.
☐ **enhancement**, *noun*

enigma /*say* uh-**nig**-muh/ *noun* someone or something difficult or impossible to understand: *It was an enigma how they managed to escape.*
☐ **enigmatic**, *adjective* puzzling. –**enigmatically**, *adverb*

WORD HISTORY from a Greek word meaning 'riddle'

enjoy *verb*
1. If you **enjoy** something, you get pleasure from it: *I enjoy science fiction films.* **2.** If you **enjoy** something good or desirable, you have it: *I'm lucky enough to enjoy good health.*
☐ **enjoyable**, *adjective* –**enjoyment**, *noun*

enlarge *verb*
1. To **enlarge** something is to increase its size: *enlarge the playing area.*
–*phrase* **2. enlarge on**, to give more details about: *She gave a quick summary and then enlarged on the more important points.*
☐ **enlargement**, *noun*

enlighten *verb* To **enlighten** someone is to make something clear to them: *I will try to enlighten you on the basic principles of algebra.*

enlist *verb*
1. If you **enlist** someone or their service, you get them to help you do something. **2.** To **enlist** is to join the army, navy, or air force.
☐ **enlistment**, *noun*

enmity *noun* strong dislike or hatred: *The two families felt enmity for each other.*

enormous *adjective* of an unusually large size: *an enormous appetite.*
☐ **enormously**, *adverb*

enough /*say* uh-**nuf**/ *adjective*
1. If something is **enough**, it is all you need: *I've had enough food*; *Is there enough milk for breakfast?*
–*pronoun* **2.** the amount or quantity wanted or needed: *Yes, we have enough.*
–*adverb* **3.** in a quantity or degree that fulfils a need or desire. **4.** fairly or tolerably: *He sings well enough.*

☑ SPELLING TIP Remember that there is no *f* in **enough** – the spelling *ough* gives the 'uf' sound, as it does in some other words like *rough* and *tough*.

enquire *verb* See **inquire**.
☐ **enquirer**, *noun* –**enquiring**, *adjective* –**enquiringly**, *adverb*

enquiry *noun* (*plural* **enquiries**) See **inquiry**.

enrage *verb* If you **enrage** someone, you make them very angry: *His rudeness enraged us all.*

A SIMILAR WORD is **infuriate**.

enrich *verb*
1. If you **enrich** someone, you supply with them with money: *The family was enriched by the success of their business.* **2.** If you **enrich** the quality of something, you improve it: *They enriched the soil with fertiliser before they planted the seeds.*
☐ **enrichment**, *noun*

enrol *verb* (**enrols**, **enrolling**, **enrolled**, **has enrolled**)
1. If you **enrol** in a course or class, you put your name on an official list to become a member of it: *We have enrolled in an extra maths class.* **2.** To **enrol** someone is to record their name: *The office was enrolling the new kids yesterday.*
☐ **enrolment**, *noun*

☑ SPELLING TIP *Single letter alert*: only one *l* at the end, even though **enrol** is based on the word *roll*. However, when you add *-ed* or *-ing*, the *l* is doubled.

ensign /*say* **en**-suhn, **en**-suyn/ *noun* a flag or banner: *The boat raised its ensign as it sailed into the harbour.*

☑ SPELLING TIP Remember the *g* in this word. The letter combination *ign* gives the 'uhn' or 'uyn' sound.

ensuite /*say* on-**sweet**, **on**-sweet/ *noun* a small bathroom joined to a bedroom.

☑ SPELLING TIP Remember that you do not eat *sweet* food – or any other food – in an **ensuite**! The 'sweet' sound in this word is spelt *suite* and the 'on' sound is spelt *en*. This is because it comes from French words (meaning 'in a series or set').

ensure /*say* en-**shaw**/ *verb* To **ensure** something is to make certain it happens: *We bought the tickets early to ensure that we had good seats.*

☑ DO NOT CONFUSE **ensure** with **insure** which is to pay money so that the cost of something will be made up if it is stolen or damaged.

entangle *verb* If something is **entangled**, it is twisted around or caught in something: *My hair got entangled in the fence wire.*
☐ **entanglement**, *noun*

enter *verb* To **enter** is to **1.** come or go in: *They entered the room quietly*; *Sam entered after we did.* **2.** take part in as a competitor: *Samantha entered the 50 metres race.* **3.** put in or write, as on a list: *The hotel entered the guests' names in the register.* **4.** key data into a computer: *When we had entered the new information, we could see a pattern.*
–*phrase* **5. enter into**, to take an interest or part in: *to enter into the party spirit.*

enterprise /*say* **en**-tuh-pruyz/ *noun*
1. something to be done, especially something which involves effort or courage: *Running the science competition was quite an enterprise.* **2.** the energy and skill you need to do something like that: *a group of people full of enterprise.*
☐ **enterprising**, *adjective*

☑ SPELLING TIP Remember that the meaning of **enterprise** has nothing to do with entering a competition for a prize. The ending is spelt *prise* with an *s* (not a 'z'). (*Prise* is from the French word meaning 'seized' or 'taken'.)

entertain *verb* To **entertain** someone is to interest and amuse them.
☐ **entertainer**, *noun* –**entertaining**, *adjective* –**entertainment**, *noun*

enthusiasm /*say* en-**thooh**-zee-az-uhm/, *noun* great interest and excitement about something.
☐ **enthuse**, *verb* –**enthusiastic**, *adjective* –**enthusiastically**, *adverb*

A SIMILAR WORD is **zeal**.

☑ SPELLING TIP Remember that the letter *s* turns up twice in **enthusiasm** – both times it has the sound of a 'z'.

entice *verb* To **entice** someone is to persuade them with promises of good things to be gained.
☐ **enticement**, *noun* –**enticing**, *adjective*

entire *adjective* Something **entire** is whole or unbroken: *She bought one plate every week until she had the the entire set.*
☐ **entirely**, *adverb*: *entirely happy.* –**entirety**, *noun*

entitled *adjective* If you are **entitled** to something, then you have a right to have it.

entrails *plural noun* the intestines.

WORD HISTORY from a Latin word meaning 'within'

entrance[1] /*say* **en**-truhns/ *noun*
1. the act of entering: *His entrance was greeted with boos and jeers.* **2.** the way in: *The entrance is at the side of the house.*

entrance[2] /*say* en-**trans**, en-**trahns**/ *verb* To **entrance** someone is to fill them with delight: *The puppet show entranced everybody.*

entrant *noun* someone who takes part in a competition: *an entrant in the swimming competition.*

entreaty *noun* (*plural* **entreaties**) a serious request: *Her earnest entreaty was that we should come straight away.*
☐ **entreat**, *verb* to beg.

entree /*say* **on**-tray/ *noun* the small serving of food you eat at dinner before the main course.

☑ SPELLING TIP You might sometimes serve an **entree** on a tray – but remember that this has nothing to do with the meaning or spelling of the word. The 'on' sound is spelt *en* and the 'ay' sound at the end is *ee*. This is because it was originally a French word. This also explains why it is sometimes spelt with an accent on the second last *e*: **entrée**.

entrepreneur /*say* on-truh-pruh-**ner**/ *noun* a person who organises a business enterprise, especially a risky one: *The entrepreneur set up a wind farm.*
☐ **entrepreneurial**, *adjective*

☑ SPELLING TIP *Tricky vowel sounds*: think of the letter *e* when you spell this word. **Entrepreneur** comes from a French word (meaning 'undertake') which is why the 'o' sound at the beginning is spelt *e*. Then there are another three *e*'s, spelling the two 'uh' sounds in the middle and finally as part of the *-eur* ending. This ending occurs in several words that have come from French and means 'someone who does something', as in *amateur* and *chauffeur*.

entry *noun* (*plural* **entries**)
1. the act of coming or going in: *her entry into the room.* **2.** the way in: *There was a bus parked right across the entry.* **3.** a written record: *She made an entry in her diary.* **4.** someone or something entered in a competition: *We need more entries before we can hold the race.*

envelop /*say* en-**vel**-uhp/ *verb* To **envelop** someone or something is to wrap or cover them completely: *enveloped in plastic.*
☐ **enveloping**, *adjective* –**envelopment**, *noun*

envelope /*say* **en**-vuh-lohp, **on**-vuh-lohp/ *noun* a folded paper cover for a letter.

environment /*say* en-**vuy**-ruhn-muhnt/ *noun*
1. the whole surroundings of your life: *He grew up in a happy environment.* **2.** all the geographical features of an area, such as trees, land, water, and so on, and the system connecting these.
☐ **environmental**, *adjective* –**environmentalism**, *noun* –**environmentalist**, *noun*

environs /*say* en-**vuy**-ruhnz/ *plural noun* the surrounding districts: *the environs of Perth.*

envisage /*say* en-**viz**-uhj, en-**viz**-ij/ *verb* If you **envisage** something, you see it happening in the future: *I envisage a wonderful holiday for us all.*

envoy *noun* someone sent as a representative: *The envoy from America wanted to discuss sugar imports.*

envy *noun*
1. the desire for someone else's possessions or success: *Envy consumed him.*
–*verb* (**envies**, **envying**, **envied**, **has envied**)
2. If you desire someone else's possessions or success, you **envy** them: *Allie envied everything about Sally – especially her new bike.*

☐ **enviable**, *adjective* –**envious**, *adjective* –**enviously**, *adverb*

enzyme /*say* **en**-zuym/ *noun* a protein in the body which produces a chemical change: *Enzymes help food get digested in our stomachs.*

eon *noun* See **aeon**.

epaulet /*say* **ep**-uh-let/ *noun* an ornamental shoulder piece worn on uniforms.

ephemeral /*say* uh-**fem**-uh-ruhl/ *adjective* not lasting long: *Fame is an ephemeral thing – here today and gone tomorrow!*
☐ **ephemerally**, *adverb*

A SIMILAR WORD is **transitory**.

epi- *prefix* a word part meaning **1.** in addition to, as in *epilogue*. **2.** near, as in *epidemic*. **3.** on, as in *epitaph*. **4.** against, as in *epigram*.

WORD HISTORY this prefix comes from Greek

epic *noun* a very long poem, book or film, often about things that happened in the past.
☐ **epic**, *adjective*: *an epic journey.*

epidemic *noun* a lot of cases of an illness in a short period of time: *an epidemic of chickenpox.*
☐ **epidemic**, *adjective*

epigram *noun* a short and witty saying: *She came up with a clever epigram which made everybody laugh.*
☐ **epigrammatic**, *adjective* –**epigrammatically**, *adverb*

epilepsy *noun* an illness which produces fits of unconsciousness and uncontrollable movements of the body.
☐ **epileptic**, *adjective* –**epileptic**, *noun*

epilogue /*say* **ep**-ee-log, **ep**-uh-log/ *noun* a short part at the end of a play or written work which acts as an ending: *The epilogue gave the information that the story was based on real events.*

☑ SPELLING TIP *Silent letter alert*: don't forget the silent *ue* at the end. It is spelt in this way because it comes from French. Other words with a *logue* spelling for a 'log' sound are *catalogue* and *dialogue*.

episode *noun*
1. an event in your life: *a very happy episode in his life.* **2.** one part of a play, show, story, etc.: *We missed the last episode – did you watch it?*
☐ **episodic**, *adjective*

WORD HISTORY from a Greek word meaning 'coming in besides'

epitaph /*say* **ep**-ee-tahf, **ep**-uh-tahf/ *noun* the words, sometimes in verse, written on the stone above a grave.

epitome /*say* uh-**pit**-uh-mee/ *noun* the most typical example of something: *With her long fair hair, Kylie is the epitome of a pop star.*
☐ **epitomise**, *verb*

ANOTHER SPELLING for **epitomise** is **epitomize**.

☑ SPELLING TIP Try remembering that **epitome** ends with the common word *me*, even though this has no connection with its meaning. **Epitome** actually comes from a Greek word meaning 'to shorten'. Rap it out as *e + pit + o + me*.

epoch /*say* **ee**-pok, **ep**-ok/ *noun* (*plural* **epochs**) a period of time in history or geology: *the epoch of the dinosaurs.*

equal *adjective*
1. Things which are **equal** are of the same number, value, or other quality: *Give everyone an equal share of the cake.*
–*verb* (**equals**, **equalling**, **equalled**, **has equalled**) **2.** To **equal** is to add up to the same number as: *My eight dollars plus your two dollars equals ten dollars all together.*
–*noun* **3.** someone or something that equals another person or thing in some way: *Ken is the equal of Jim in computer games.*
☐ **equalise**, *verb* –**equality**, *noun* –**equally**, *adverb*

ANOTHER SPELLING for **equalise** is **equalize**.

equation *noun* a mathematical expression in which two quantities are said to be equal, such as $40 \div 2 = 20$.
☐ **equate**, *verb*: *to equate one thing with another.*

equator /*say* uh-**kway**-tuh/ *noun* the imaginary circle around the earth, halfway between the North Pole and the South Pole. The climate around the equator is mostly hot and wet.
☐ **equatorial**, *adjective*

equestrian /*say* uh-**kwes**-tree-uhn/ *adjective* having to do with horses or horseriding.

equi- *prefix* a word part meaning 'equal', as in *equilibrium*, *equivalent*.

WORD HISTORY this prefix comes from Latin

equilateral /*say* eek-wuh-**lat**-ruhl/ *adjective* having equal sides: *an equilateral triangle.*

equilibrium /*say* eek-wuh-**lib**-ree-uhm/ *noun*
1. equal balance: *With a child of equal weight on each end, the seesaw is in equilibrium.* **2.** steadiness of feelings: *She was shocked at what she saw but quickly recovered her equilibrium.*

equip *verb* (**equips**, **equipping**, **equipped**, **has equipped**) If you **equip** someone or something, you supply them with whatever they need for a particular job or situation: *to equip the ship with fresh water for a month.*

equipment *noun* anything used to equip for a job, especially a collection of tools, machines, materials, skills, and so on: *We have all the equipment we need for the job.*

equivalent /*say* uh-**kwiv**-uh-luhnt/ *adjective* equal or matching: *She moved from one company to an equivalent position in another.*
☐ **equivalence**, *noun*

☑ SPELLING TIP Remember that **equivalent** has a similar meaning to *equal*. If you know that *equal* is spelt with *qu* for the 'kw' sound, you should also be able to spell **equivalent**.

era /*rhymes with* nearer/ *noun* any long period of time with a special characteristic: *It was the era of the industrial revolution.*

eradicate *verb* To **eradicate** something is to remove or destroy it: *to eradicate rats from the warehouse.*
☐ **eradication**, *noun*

erase *verb* If you **erase** something, you rub it out or wipe it off: *We had to erase all our mistakes before we handed our work in*; *Unfortunately, important material was erased from the tape.*
☐ **eraser**, *noun* –**erasure**, *noun*

erect *adjective*
1. upright: *an erect seat.*
–*verb* **2.** To **erect** something is to build it: *They have erected a fence around the park.*
☐ **erection**, *noun*

ermine /*say* **er**-muhn/ *noun* a type of weasel which has a white coat of fur in winter.

erosion *noun* the wearing away by the weather, especially by the flow of water.
☐ **erode**, *verb*: *Rain has eroded the stone of the old building.*

erotic *adjective* having to do with sexual love and sexual desire.

err /*say* er/ *verb* To **err** is to **1.** make a mistake: *You erred when you took the left turn instead of the right.* **2.** do wrong: *He admitted that he had erred by stealing the car.*
☐ **erring**, *adjective*

errand *noun* a small job you are sent to do: *Would you mind doing an errand for me?*

erratic /*say* uh-**rat**-ik/ *adjective* irregular in behaviour or movement: *He walked at an erratic pace – it was hard to walk with him.*
☐ **erratically**, *adverb*

error *noun* a mistake: *Michelle lost a mark on her maths test because she made an error.*

erupt *verb* If a volcano **erupts**, it sends out molten rocks and ash into the air.
☐ **eruption**, *noun* –**eruptive**, *adjective*

escalate *verb* If something **escalates** it becomes larger or more intense: *Conflict escalated between the two gangs and eventually there was a fight.*
☐ **escalation**, *noun*

escalator /*say* **es**-kuh-lay-tuh/ *noun* a continuously moving stairway that carries people upwards or downwards.

☑ SPELLING TIP *Tricky 'uh' sounds*: both the vowel sounds in the middle of the word are spelt *a*. This is because **escalator** is based on *scala*, the Italian word for 'steps'. Also remember that the ending is *lator* (not *later*). Remember, if you go on the **escalator**, you get there sooner, not later.

escapade /*say* **es**-kuh-payd, es-kuh-**payd**/ *noun* a reckless adventure: *Luckily, nobody ever found out about our escapade.*

escape *verb* To **escape** is to **1.** get away: *to escape from jail.* **2.** avoid: *She ran home quickly and escaped the worst of the storm.*
☐ **escape**, *noun* –**escapee**, *noun* –**escaper**, *noun*

escort *noun* /*say* **es**-kawt/
1. someone who goes along with someone else as a guard or guide: *A large escort of security people accompanied the prime minister.*
2. someone who goes with you to a dance or party: *She asked him to be her escort to the school formal.*
–*verb* /*say* uhs-**kawt**, es-**kawt**/ **3.** If you **escort** someone somewhere, you go along with them to protect or guide them or just to accompany them: *The police escorted her home.*

especially /*say* uh-**spesh**-uh-lee/ *adverb* particularly: *especially good.*

espionage /*say* **es**-pee-uh-nahzh/ *noun* the practice of spying.

☑ SPELLING TIP See if you can spy a form of the word *spy* in this word. The meaning is about spying but note that the *y* has been changed to an *i*. Also remember the *age* spelling at the end, even though it is pronounced in a different way from usual. This is because the word has come straight from French.

espresso *noun* coffee made in a machine which forces steam through crushed coffee beans.

WORD HISTORY from the Italian word for this kind of coffee, meaning 'sent out under pressure'

☑ SPELLING TIP Although you can spell this as **expresso**, note that the usual spelling is with *es* at the beginning (because it comes from Italian). So, with the double *s* towards the end, you have three *s*'s in the word.

essay *noun* a short piece of writing on a particular subject: *The teacher hasn't marked our history essays.*

WORD HISTORY from a Latin word meaning 'a weighing'

essence *noun*
1. the basic nature: *The poem captures the essence of the horror of war.* **2.** the concentrated

liquid from a substance: *vanilla essence*; *essence of roses*.

essential /*say* uh-**sen**-shuhl/ *adjective* completely necessary: *If you want to pass your exam, it is essential that you work.*
☐ **essentially**, *adverb*

☑ SPELLING TIP *Double letter alert*: two *s*'s. Also remember the *tial* spelling for the 'shuhl' sound at the end. Another word with this spelling for the same sound is *initial*.

establish *verb*
1. To **establish** something, you set it up: *She established a new shop.* **2.** If people **establish** themselves, they settle in a place: *They established themselves in a completely new area.* **3.** To **establish** something is to prove it: *Can you establish the truth of that statement?*
☐ **established**, *adjective* –**establishment**, *noun*

estate *noun*
1. an area of land in the country, especially a large and valuable one: *There were many horses on the estate.* **2.** an area of land set aside for particular kinds of building: *housing estate*; *industrial estate.* **3.** the possessions and property of a person who has died: *He left his estate to charity.*

esteem *verb*
1. To **esteem** someone is to respect or think highly of them: *The whole country esteemed his wisdom and leadership.*
–*phrase* **2. hold in high** (**low**) **esteem**, to consider of great (little) worth: *We all hold our teacher in high esteem*; *The bully was held in low esteem.*

estimate /*say* **es**-tuh-mayt/ *verb* To **estimate** something is to work out its approximate value, size, or other qualities: *to estimate the cost of replacing the stolen items.*
☐ **estimate** /*say* **es**-tuh-muht/, *noun* –**estimation**, *noun*

estuary /*say* **es**-chooh-uh-ree, **es**-chuh-ree/ *noun* (*plural* **estuaries**) the mouth or lower part of a river which is affected by high tides.
☐ **estuarine** /*say* **es**-chuh-ruyn/, *adjective*

e-tag *noun* a device attached to a vehicle which sends information to an electronic reader, causing an amount for the road or bridge toll to be taken from the customer's bank account.

ANOTHER FORM is **etag**. The full name is **electronic tag**.

etc. /*say* et-**set**-ruh/ *abbreviation* short for *et cetera*, Latin words meaning 'and other things': *The stall was selling the usual things: cakes, toffees, etc.*

etch *verb*
1. If you **etch** something onto a material such as metal or glass, you cut it into the material with acid to leave a clear, lasting mark: *a silver tray etched with a floral design.* **2.** If you say that something is **etched** in your memory, you mean that you remember it clearly.
☐ **etching**, *noun*

eternal *adjective* lasting forever, or for as long as you can imagine: *He claimed he had invented a medicine that could give eternal life*; *You have my eternal thanks.*
☐ **eternally**, *adverb*

eternity *noun*
1. time without end: *Many religions believe that the spirit exists for eternity.* **2.** *Informal and humorous* a very long time: *James takes an eternity to have a shower.*

ether /*say* **ee**-thuh/ *noun* a chemical which used to be used to put a patient to sleep during an operation, but is now used as a solvent to dissolve other substances.

WORD HISTORY from a Greek word meaning 'upper air' or 'sky'

ethics *plural noun* the system of beliefs and rules used to judge human action: *The members follow a strict code of ethics.*
☐ **ethical**, *adjective*

ethnic *adjective* **Ethnic** refers to the different races or tribes that people belong to: *There are several different ethnic groups in India*; *ethnic dancing.*
☐ **ethnicity**, *noun*

etiquette /*say* **et**-ee-kuht/ *noun* behaviour which is thought of as polite and correct: *What would be correct etiquette in this situation?*

☑ SPELLING TIP *Single/double letter alert*: the *t* is single the first time it appears, then double towards the end of this word. Also remember the *qu* spelling for the 'k' sound. It is spelt in this way because it comes from French. Some other words with an *ette* ending are *cassette* and *serviette*.

etymology /*say* et-uh-**mol**-uh-jee/ *noun* (*plural* **etymologies**)
1. the study of the changes in words over a long period of time. **2.** an explanation of the history of a word, showing all the changes it has gone through: *The etymology of 'bus' is from a Latin word 'omnibus' meaning 'for all'.*
☐ **etymological**, *adjective* –**etymologist**, *noun*

☑ SPELLING TIP *Letter 'y' alert*: the vowel sound after the *t* is spelt *y* (not *i*). This part of the word comes from *etymon*, a Greek word meaning 'original form of a word'. The *n* has been dropped and the suffix *-logy* (meaning 'the study of') added.

eucalyptus /*say* yooh-kuh-**lip**-tuhs/ *noun* (*plural* **eucalyptuses** *or* **eucalypti** /*say* yooh-kuh-**lip**-tuy/ *or* **eucalyptus**) a type of tree found in Australia, with many different varieties, used for its wood and its strong oil.
☐ **eucalyptus**, *adjective*: *eucalyptus oil.*

OTHER TERMS for this are **eucalypt** and **gum tree**.

WORD HISTORY from a Greek word meaning 'well covered' (referring to the cap covering the buds)

euro[1] /*say* **yooh**-roh/ *noun* (*plural* **euros**) a type of wallaroo with short, red-coloured hair.

WORD HISTORY from an Aboriginal language of South Australia called Adnyamathanha

euro[2] /*say* **yooh**-roh/ *noun* (*plural* **euros**) the monetary unit of the European Union, introduced as legal tender in most of the member nations in 2002.

euthanasia /*say* yooh-thuh-**nay**-zhuh/ *noun* the act of letting someone die, or helping them to do it when they want to, because their pain or suffering has become too great.

☑ SPELLING TIP *Tricky vowel sound*: *eu* for the opening 'yooh' sound. This word part comes from Greek and means 'well'. The other part of the word comes from *thanatos*, the Greek word for 'death'. Its ending has been changed to *-asia* which is a suffix that appears in many medical words. So the basic meaning of **euthanasia** is 'a good death'.

evacuate /*say* uh-**vak**-yooh-ayt/ *verb* If people **evacuate** a place, they move out of it for a period of time because it would be dangerous to stay, often because of war or a natural disaster.
□ **evacuation**, *noun*

evade *verb* If you **evade** something, you avoid or escape it, often by a trick: *They evaded detection by creeping around the back.*
□ **evasion**, *noun* –**evasive**, *adjective* –**evasively**, *adverb*

evaluate *verb* If you **evaluate** something, you consider it carefully to decide how good, useful or valuable it is.
□ **evaluation**, *noun*

☑ SPELLING TIP Remember that **evaluate** starts with an *e* (not an *i*). Rap it out as *e+ val+u+ate*.

evangelist /*say* uh-**van**-juh-luhst/ *noun* someone who travels from place to place teaching from the Bible.
□ **evangelistic**, *adjective*

evaporate *verb* To **evaporate** is to **1.** turn to vapour: *When water boils, it evaporates into steam.* **2.** dry up: *In dry seasons, the lake evaporates.*
□ **evaporation**, *noun* –**evaporator**, *noun*

eve *noun*
1. the evening or the day before: *Many people are still shopping for Christmas presents on Christmas Eve.* **2.** the time just before an event takes place: *the eve of the battle*; *on the eve of their departure.*

even *adjective*
1. A number which is **even** is able to be divided by two: *Two, four, six and eight are even numbers.* **2.** A contest is **even** if the contestants are fairly matched. **3.** A voice is **even** if it is calm and steady. **4.** The ground is **even** if it is smooth or level: *The track is even and good for rollerblading.*
–*adverb* **5.** still or yet: *The canteen has even better food now.* **6.** although it may seem unlikely: *Even my dad likes hearing me play the trumpet.*
–*phrase* **7. break even**, to have your gains and losses equal: *Once the wages are paid, the restaurant will just break even.* **8. get even**, to get revenge for something bad someone has done to you: *Claude wanted to get even with Sam for putting the frog in his bag.*
□ **evenly**, *adverb*: *divided evenly.* –**evenness**, *noun*

THE OPPOSITE (of definition 1) is **odd**.

evening *noun* the late afternoon and early night.
□ **evening**, *adjective*: *evening meal.*

event *noun*
1. something which happens, especially something important: *The wedding was the biggest event in the town all year.* **2.** one of the items in a sports competition: *The next event is the 200 metres race.*
–*phrase* **3. at all events** or **in any event**, in any case or whatever happens.
□ **eventful**, *adjective* –**eventfully**, *adverb*

eventual /*say* uh-**ven**-chooh-uhl/ *adjective* final or last: *The eventual outcome will not be known until next week.*
□ **eventuality**, *noun*

☑ SPELLING TIP Remember that **eventual** starts with the word *event*. This will remind you that it includes the letter *t* although with the *u* following it has a 'ch' sound and you don't hear the *t*.

eventually *adverb* at long last; finally: *Eventually the driver arrived.*

☑ SPELLING TIP See **eventual**.

ever *adverb*
1. at all times: *He is ever ready to help.* **2.** continuously or without stopping: *ever since then.* **3.** at any time: *Did you ever see anything like this?* **4.** at all: *How did he ever manage it?*

evergreen *adjective* Trees which are **evergreen** have green leaves all year long.
□ **evergreen**, *noun*

COMPARE this with **deciduous**.

every *adjective*
1. Every refers to each single person or thing without any exceptions: *Everyone's hearing will be tested.* **2. Every** is also used for emphasis, to show that you are certain about something: *I have every confidence in his ability.*
–*phrase* **3. every bit**, *Rather informal* in all respects: *every bit as good.* **4. every now and**

then (or **again**) or **every once in a while**, from time to time. **5. every other**, every second, or alternate person or thing: *I catch the bus home every other day.*

everyday *adjective* Something is described as **everyday** if it has to do with ordinary or relaxed situations, rather than formal ones: *everyday language.*

everyone *pronoun* every person.

ANOTHER WORD for this is **everybody**.

everything *pronoun* every thing or detail of a group or total.

THE OPPOSITE is **nothing**.

everywhere *adverb* in all places or to all places: *I've looked everywhere, but I still can't find my keys*; *He goes everywhere by car.*

THE OPPOSITE is **nowhere**.

evict *verb* To **evict** someone is to turn them out or remove them, usually from their home: *The contract says you will be evicted if you do not pay the rent.*
☐ **eviction**, *noun*

evidence *noun*
1. something seen or heard that shows something to be true or false: *There was evidence in the caves that people had lived there.* **2.** a clear sign of something: *The first evidence that summer had come was a couple of blowflies.* **3.** in law, the information or objects recognised by witnesses, and presented to the court or jury to help prove the facts being argued.
–*phrase* **4. in evidence**, able to be easily seen: *Signs of the their presence were in evidence everywhere.*

evident *adjective* clear, or easily seen or understood: *It was evident that they did not have a clue!*
☐ **evidently**, *adverb*

evil *adjective*
1. Something or someone **evil** is morally bad and harmful.
–*noun* **2.** anything morally bad or harmful: *The evil they did destroyed many lives.*
☐ **evilly**, *adverb*

evolution /*say* ev-uh-**looh**-shuhn, eev-uh-**looh**-shuhn/ *noun*
1. in biology, the gradual continuous change of plants and animals to suit the environment. **2.** any process in which something grows or develops over time: *The book recorded the evolution of her ideas over a couple of decades.*
☐ **evolve**, *verb*

ewe /*say* yooh/ *noun* a female sheep.

NOTE The male is a **ram**.

☑ SPELLING TIP The spelling of **ewe** is unusual and you have to learn it. Don't confuse it with **you** which sounds the same.

ex- *prefix* a word part meaning **1.** out or from, as in *exclude*. **2.** former, as in *ex-husband*.

WORD HISTORY this prefix comes from Latin

exact *adjective*
1. If something is **exact**, it is correct or accurate in every detail. **2.** If you give an **exact** figure or repeat someone's **exact** words, you state the figure or words without changing them at all.
–*verb* **3.** If you **exact** something from someone, you get it from them, sometimes by force, although they do not want to give it to you: *She exacted a promise from her friends not to say where she had been.*
☐ **exactly**, *adverb*: *This is exactly what I want.*
–**exactness**, *noun*

exaggerate /*say* uhg-**zaj**-uh-rayt/ *verb* To **exaggerate** is to make something out to be greater than it is: *She exaggerates her wealth.*
☐ **exaggerated**, *adjective* –**exaggeration**, *noun*

☑ SPELLING TIP *Double letter alert*: two *g*'s.

exalt /*say* uhg-**zawlt**/ *verb*
1. If you **exalt** someone, you raise them in importance or power: *She was exalted to the leadership of the school.* **2.** If you **exalt** someone or something, you praise them: *Teachers always exalt the benefits of hard work and lots of study.*
☐ **exaltation**, *noun* –**exalted**, *adjective*

examination *noun*
1. an act of careful looking and testing: *a thorough examination of the building discovered termite damage.* **2.** a test of knowledge or skill which often has to be passed before the next stage of learning begins.
☐ **examine**, *verb*: *to examine the situation carefully.* –**examiner**, *noun*

THE SHORT FORM of definition 2 is **exam**.

example *noun*
1. a part of a whole thing which makes clear what it is like: *He showed us an example of volcanic rock.* **2.** a model or pattern to be followed: *You aren't setting a very good example to the others!*

exasperate /*say* uhg-**zas**-puh-rayt/ *verb* To **exasperate** someone is to annoy them very much.
☐ **exasperated**, *adjective* –**exasperation**, *noun*

WORD HISTORY from a Latin word meaning 'roughened'

☑ SPELLING TIP *Tricky 'uh' sound*: the vowel sound between the *p* and the *r* is spelt with an *e*. Remembering this is the most **exasperating** thing about this word. Rap it out as *ex+as+per+ate*.

excavate /*say* **eks**-kuh-vayt/ *verb* To **excavate** an area is to dig a hole in it or uncover it by digging: *Builders are still excavating the site to lay the foundation*; *Archaeologists have excavated many ancient cities that were buried under the earth.*
☐ **excavation**, *noun* –**excavator**, *noun*

exceed /*say* uhk-**seed**/ *verb* To **exceed** is to go outside a limit of some kind: *She exceeded our best expectations.*
☐ **exceedingly**, *adverb*: *exceedingly good.*

☑ SPELLING TIP Remember that **exceed** is spelt with a *c* for the 's' sound, and that the ending is spelt just as it sounds – *eed* (not *ede*).

excel /*say* uhk-**sel**/ *verb* (**excels**, **excelling**, **excelled**, **has excelled**) To **excel** is to be very good at doing something, better than anyone else: *He excels at all ball games.*

☑ SPELLING TIP *Single letter alert*: only one *l* at the end. However, don't forget that you double the *l* when you add *-ed* or *-ing* or make the word *excellent*. Also remember that **excel** is spelt with a *c* for the 's' sound.

excellent /*say* **ek**-suh-luhnt/ *adjective* very good or of a very high quality: *an excellent performance.*
☐ **excellence**, *noun* –**excellently**, *adverb*

SIMILAR WORDS are **wonderful**, **outstanding**, **marvellous**, **fantastic**, **fabulous**, **terrific**, **extraordinary**, **exceptional** and **phenomenal**. Note that **fantastic**, **fabulous** and **terrific** are more informal than the other words. Also note that something that is **extraordinary**, **exceptional** or **phenomenal** is so good as to be completely out of the ordinary.

except /*say* uhk-**sept**/ *preposition*
1. leaving or taking out: *They all went except me.*
–*conjunction* **2.** but not: *The room was all red except in the corner.*
–*phrase* **3. except that**, but for the fact that: *All the songs sounded the same, except that the last track on the album was much slower than the rest.*

☑ DO NOT CONFUSE **except** with **accept**, which is to take or receive something willingly.

exception /*say* uhk-**sep**-shuhn/ *noun* someone or something which doesn't follow the general rule or pattern: *There is generally an exception to every rule.*

exceptional /*say* uhk-**sep**-shuhn-uhl/ *adjective* unusually good: *an exceptional painting.*
☐ **exceptionally**, *adverb*

excerpt /*say* **ek**-serpt/ *noun* a short section of a book or a film or the like: *The excerpts they showed were so good that we want to see the whole film.*

excess /*say* uhk-**ses**, **ek**-ses/ *noun* an amount that is more than what is necessary or usual.
☐ **excess**, *adjective*: *excess baggage.* –**excessive**, *adjective* –**excessively**, *adverb*

exchange *verb*
1. If you **exchange** something, you replace it with something else. **2.** If you **exchange** things of the same type with someone else, you give them to each other: *We exchanged seats after the interval.*
–*noun* **3.** the act of exchanging: *a swift exchange.* **4.** a central office where letters and calls are received: *a mail exchange.*

excite /*say* uhk-**suyt**/ *verb* To **excite** someone is to cause eager feelings in them: *The concert really excited them.*
☐ **excitable**, *adjective*: *an excitable nature.* –**excitedly**, *adverb* –**excitement**, *noun* –**exciting**, *adjective*

WORD HISTORY from a Latin word meaning 'call forth' or 'rouse'

exclaim *verb* To **exclaim** is to cry out suddenly in fright, protest, or pleasure.

exclamation *noun* something you say or cry out suddenly to express an emotion you feel: *The news was greeted with exclamations of surprise.*

☑ SPELLING TIP The noun **exclamation** has been formed from the verb *exclaim*, but remember that the *i* has been dropped, so it begins *exclam*.

exclamation mark *noun* a mark of punctuation (!) used after an exclamation.

SEE the Grammar and Punctuation Guide appendix.

exclude *verb* If you **exclude** someone or something, you shut them out: *The curtains excluded the harsh light*; *They were excluded from voting.*
☐ **exclusion**, *noun*

exclusive *adjective* Something **exclusive** is **1.** not available to everyone, usually because it is too expensive: *exclusive fashions*; *an exclusive address.* **2.** not shared with others: *an exclusive interview.*
☐ **exclusively**, *adverb* –**exclusiveness**, *noun*: *the exclusiveness of Paris clothes.* –**exclusivity**, *noun*

excommunicate *verb* To **excommunicate** someone is to cut them off from receiving communion or being a member of a church: *The church in Rome decided to excommunicate the priest.*
☐ **excommunication**, *noun*

excrete *verb* Animals and humans **excrete** or pass out waste matter from their bodies.
☐ **excrement**, *noun* –**excretion**, *noun*

excruciating /*say* uhks-**krooh**-shee-ay-ting/ *adjective* very painful or causing great suffering: *The pain from her burns was excruciating.*
☐ **excruciatingly**, *adverb*

☑ SPELLING TIP Remember you don't have to be quiet if you are feeling **excruciating** pain. This will remind you there is no *sh* spelling in this word – the 'sh' sound is spelt with a *c*. Remember also that the vowel sound before the *c* is *u*, although it sounds like 'ooh'.

excursion *noun* a short journey usually taken for a special reason: *The best part of the museum excursion was the skeleton gallery.*

excuse *noun* /*say* uhks-**kyoohs**/
1. an explanation or reason why something does not happen as it should: *He made some excuse for being late.*
–*verb* /*say* uhks-**kyoohz**/ **2.** If you **excuse** somebody, you find reasons for why they have done something, often when other people do not approve of it: *Please excuse my lateness – the train was not on time.*

execute *verb*
1. To **execute** someone is to kill them, usually as a punishment for committing a serious crime. **2.** To **execute** an action or task is to do it or perform it: *She executed a perfect dive and received a mark of 10 out of 10 for it.*
☐ **execution**, *noun* –**executor**, *noun*

executive /*say* uhg-**zek**-yuh-tiv/ *noun* someone responsible for carrying out plans, especially in a business.

exempt *verb* If you **exempt** someone, you free them from a duty or rule: *Because of the accident, she was exempted from doing the exam.*
☐ **exempt**, *adjective* –**exemption**, *noun*

exercise *noun*
1. an activity of the body or mind to train or improve it. **2.** a putting into practice: *Voting in elections is an exercise of your right to have a say.*
–*verb* **3.** If you **exercise**, you move your body energetically to get fit: *You can't just diet – you have to exercise as well.*

exert /*say* uhg-**zert**/ *verb* If you **exert** your ability or influence, you use it or put it into action: *She had to exert all her energy to finish the race*; *Could you exert your influence and get me a free ticket?*

exertion *noun* effort: *The exertion of dragging the heavy sack made her hot and bothered.*

exhale *verb* To **exhale** is to breathe out.
☐ **exhalation**, *noun*

THE OPPOSITE is **inhale**.

exhaust /*say* uhg-**zawst**/ *verb*
1. If you **exhaust** yourself, you wear yourself out: *They exhausted themselves doing a long hike.* **2.** To **exhaust** something is to use it up completely: *to exhaust the remaining food supplies.*
–*noun* **3.** the used gases given off by an engine.
☐ **exhausted**, *adjective* –**exhausting**, *adjective* –**exhaustion**, *noun* –**exhaustive**, *adjective*

exhibit /*say* uhg-**zib**-uht/ *verb* (**exhibits**, **exhibiting**, **exhibited**, **has exhibited**)
1. To **exhibit** something is to put it on show.
–*noun* **2.** something shown or displayed to the public.
☐ **exhibiter**, *noun* –**exhibition**, *noun*

exhilarate /*say* uhg-**zil**-uh-rayt/ *verb* To **exhilarate** someone is to fill them with energy or excitement: *Surfing always exhilarates us.*
☐ **exhilarating**, *adjective* –**exhilaration**, *noun*

☑ SPELLING TIP *Single letter alert*: only one *l*. Also remember the *h* in **exhilarate** which is not pronounced.

exile *noun*
1. a long separation from your country or home: *Her exile lasted thirty years.* **2.** someone who has been forced to leave their country or home: *He was an exile from Iraq.*
–*verb* **3.** If somebody **exiles** a person, they force them to leave their country or home.

exist *verb*
1. If something **exists**, it is alive or present as a real thing: *When did the dinosaurs exist?* **2.** If someone **exists**, they only just manage to stay alive in very difficult conditions: *They exist on a single bowl of rice each day.*
☐ **existence**, *noun* –**existent**, *adjective* –**existing**, *adjective*

exit *noun*
1. a way out: *The other exit is at the back of the building.* **2.** a going away or a leaving: *She made an exit as quickly as possible.*
–*verb* (**exits**, **exiting**, **exited**, **has exited**) **3.** If you **exit**, you leave: *They were asked to exit the building straight away.*

exit strategy *noun* a plan for getting out of a situation if it turns out to be not favourable: *If we go to the party, we'll need to have an exit strategy in case we find that we are not enjoying ourselves.*

exodus *noun* a going out or departure, usually of a large number of people: *an exodus of refugees.*

exorcise /*say* **ek**-saw-suyz/ *verb* If somebody **exorcises** a person or place, they free them from evil spirits by prayers or a religious ceremony: *to exorcise the old house of its ghosts.*
☐ **exorcism**, *noun* –**exorcist**, *noun*

ANOTHER SPELLING is **exorcize**.

exotic *adjective* Something **exotic** is **1.** foreign or not belonging to your own country: *My mother likes exotic orchids but Dad likes Australian ones.* **2.** strange, or unusually colourful or beautiful: *exotic food*; *exotic places.*
☐ **exotic**, *noun*

expand *verb* If something **expands**, it becomes larger or spreads out: *The tyre expands as you pump air into it.*
☐ **expansion**, *noun*

THE OPPOSITE is **retract**.

expanse *noun* a large open space or widespread area: *There are large expanses of Australia where the view doesn't change for ages.*

expatriate /*say* eks-**pat**-ree-uht/ *noun* someone who has left their own country to live in another.

THE SHORT FORM of this is **expat**.

expect *verb*
1. If you **expect** that something will happen, you think it is likely that it will happen: *I expect it'll rain later.* **2.** If you **expect** someone or something, you think that they will arrive soon. **3.** If you **expect** someone to do something, you want them to do it. You have authority over them, and you think that they will do what you want: *I expect you to behave properly this afternoon.* **4.** If you say that a woman is **expecting**, you mean that she is pregnant. She is going to have a baby.
☐ **expectancy**, *noun* –**expectant**, *adjective* –**expectation**, *noun*

expedient *adjective* useful or suitable for a particular purpose: *It was expedient to do what he said if you didn't want an argument to start.*
☐ **expediency**, *noun* –**expediently**, *adverb*

expedite /*say* **eks**-puh-duyt/ *verb* If you **expedite** something you are doing, you hurry it up or do it quickly: *Parliament expedited the passing of several laws before the Christmas break.*
☐ **expeditious**, *adjective* quick. –**expeditiously**, *adverb*

expedition *noun*
1. a journey made for a special purpose: *a military expedition*; *an expedition to explore the centre of Australia*; *a shopping expedition.* **2.** the group of people and the transport used to go on such a journey: *Once they'd bought the horses, the expedition was ready to start.*

expel *verb* (**expels**, **expelling**, **expelled**, **has expelled**)
1. To **expel** someone from somewhere is to order them to leave: *The principal expelled two students for stealing.* **2.** To **expel** something from somewhere is to push it out by force: *The jet of air expelled the obstruction from the pipe.*
☐ **expulsion**, *noun*

☑ SPELLING TIP *Single letter alert*: only one *l* at the end. However, don't forget that you double the *l* when you add *-ed* or *-ing*.

expend *verb* To **expend** is to **1.** use up: *I expended all my patience listening to their complaints.* **2.** pay out or spend: *to expend my entire allowance in one day.*
☐ **expendable**, *adjective* –**expenditure**, *noun*

expense *noun*
1. cost or charge: *The biggest expense will be accommodation*; *Having termites in the house put us to a lot of expense.* **2. expenses**, the money used to pay for the costs of a job or undertaking: *Her travelling expenses are paid in addition to her salary.*
–*phrase* **3. at the expense of**, involving the loss or injury of: *They chose quantity at the expense of quality.*
☐ **expensive**, *adjective*

experience /*say* uhks-**pear**-ree-uhns/ *noun*
1. something that happens to you: *My worst experience was finding a cockroach in my soup.* **2.** the knowledge or practice you get from doing or seeing things: *a wealth of experience.*
–*verb* **3.** If you **experience** a feeling or a situation, it happens to you or you are affected by it: *to experience a sense of happiness.*
☐ **experienced**, *adjective*

experiment *noun*
1. a test or a trial carried out to discover something.
–*verb* **2.** If you **experiment**, you carry out a test or a trial to discover something.
☐ **experimental**, *adjective* –**experimentation**, *noun*

expert *noun* someone who has a lot of skill or knowledge about a special thing.
☐ **expert**, *adjective* –**expertise**, *noun*

expire *verb*
1. If something **expires**, it comes to an end: *My passport is due to expire.* **2.** If someone **expires**, they die: *Before the ambulance reached the scene, she had expired.*
☐ **expiration**, *noun* –**expiry**, *noun*

explain *verb* If you **explain** something, **1.** you talk about it to make someone understand what it is or how it works: *The official explained the rules to us.* **2.** you give reasons for it: *Let me explain why the computer isn't working.*

WORD HISTORY from a Latin word meaning 'make plain' or 'flatten out'

explanation *noun*
1. a reason why something happens or has happened. **2.** a written or verbal statement which tells how or why something happens.

☑ SPELLING TIP The noun **explanation** has been formed from the verb *explain*, but the *i* has been dropped. So remember the *explan* beginning for this word.

explicit /*say* uhks-**plis**-uht/ *adjective* clearly and fully set out: *Make the instructions explicit so we can understand them.*
☐ **explicitly**, *adverb*

☑ SPELLING TIP Remember the *c* spelling for the 's' sound.

explode *verb* If something **explodes**, it blows up or bursts into pieces with a loud noise: *The bomb exploded in the air.*

WORD HISTORY from a Latin word meaning 'drive out by clapping'

exploit[1] /*say* **eks**-ployt/ *noun* a notable or daring action: *He was known for his brave exploits.*

exploit[2] /*say* uhks-**ployt**/ *verb*
1. To **exploit** someone is to use them unfairly: *Employers can exploit workers who are not in any position to argue.* **2.** To **exploit** something is to put it to good use: *Recycled water can be exploited for use in agriculture.*
☐ **exploitation**, *noun*

explore *verb* To **explore** an area is to travel over it to discover things or places: *We explored the underground caves and found several bat colonies.*
☐ **exploration**, *noun* –**exploratory**, *adjective* –**explorer**, *noun*

explosion *noun*
1. a blowing up or exploding: *The explosion completely destroyed the front of the building.* **2.** a sudden burst of noise: *There was a sudden explosion of cheering from the crowd when he came onto the field.*
☐ **explosive**, *noun* a substance that can explode, such as dynamite. –**explosive**, *adjective* –**explosively**, *adverb*

export *verb* /*say* uhks-**pawt**, **eks**-pawt/
1. To **export** a product is to send it to other countries for sale: *to export oil.*
–*noun* /*say* **eks**-pawt/ **2.** something which is exported.
☐ **exportation**, *noun* –**exporter**, *noun*

COMPARE this with **import** (definitions 1 and 2).

expose *verb*
1. If you **expose** something, you uncover or reveal it. You allow something that was hidden to be seen or known: *Mum stripped the paint off the door to expose the natural wood.* **2.** If you **expose** someone to something, you allow them to have contact with it: *exposed to the elements*; *Going to that part of the world will expose you to all sorts of illnesses!*
☐ **exposed**, *adjective* –**exposure**, *noun*

exposition /*say* eks-puh-**zish**-uhn/ *noun*
1. a show or display that everyone can come and see. **2.** a written or verbal opinion on a topic.

ANOTHER FORM Definition 1 is sometimes shortened to **expo**.

express *verb*
1. If you **express** an idea, opinion or feeling, you put it into words: *He finds it hard to express his emotions.* **2.** You can also **express** a feeling or thought by your behaviour or the look on your face: *He expressed his disapproval by walking out of the room.*
–*adjective* **3. Express** services are performed faster or sooner than regular services, often for a higher price. **4.** Something **express** is clear, certain and exact. There can be no misunderstanding or mistake: *My express orders were to stay inside.*
☐ **expressive**, *adjective*: *an expressive face.* –**expressively**, *adverb*

expression *noun*
1. the act of putting into words: *The poem was an expression of her love for her country.* **2.** the look on someone's face: *a grim expression.* **3.** feeling or emotion: *Put some expression into the music.* **4.** in mathematics, a combination of numbers and symbols with no equals sign, which represents a number or something like this: $2x+4y$ *is a mathematical expression.*

expressway *noun* a road on which traffic can travel fast.

OTHER WORDS for this are **freeway** and **motorway**.

exquisite /*say* uhk-**skwiz**-uht, **ek**-skwuh-zuht/ *adjective* extremely delicate and beautiful: *an exquisite watercolour painting.*

extend *verb*
1. If something **extends** over a certain distance, it reaches or goes that far: *The park extends right down to the river.* **2.** If you **extend** something, you stretch it out: *Extend the rope between these two posts.*
☐ **extent**, *noun*

extension *noun*
1. a stretching out or lengthening. **2.** something added on: *an extension to our house.* **3.** an extra telephone connected to the one you already have.
☐ **extension**, *adjective*: *an extension ladder.*

extensive *adjective*
1. large in amount or size: *extensive land*; *an extensive group of friends.* **2.** covering a wide area: *an extensive search.*

exterior *adjective*
1. out of doors, or on the outside of something: *the exterior wall.*
–*noun* **2.** the outside: *the exterior of the building.*

THE OPPOSITE is **interior**.

exterminate *verb* If you **exterminate** pests, you kill them and get rid of them completely: *We put down some powder to exterminate the ants.*
☐ **extermination**, *noun* –**exterminator**, *noun*

WORD HISTORY from a Latin word meaning 'driven beyond the boundaries'

external *adjective*
1. on the outside: *Her external injuries weren't very serious.* **2.** coming from outside: *An external noise woke her up.*

THE OPPOSITE is **internal**.

extinct *adjective*
1. An **extinct** animal no longer exists: *Some animals living in Australia two hundred years ago*

are now extinct. **2.** An **extinct** volcano is no longer active.
☐ **extinction**, *noun*

extinguish /*say* uhk-**sting**-gwish/ *verb* To **extinguish** a fire is to put it out.
☐ **extinguisher**, *noun*

☑ SPELLING TIP Remember the *gu* spelling for the 'gw' sound.

extra *adjective*
1. more than usual: *extra staff.*
–*noun* **2.** something added: *This dish needs something extra – maybe some lemon.* **3.** someone playing a not very important part in a film, usually as part of a crowd.

extra- *prefix* a word part meaning 'outside' or 'beyond', as in *extraordinary.*

WORD HISTORY this prefix comes from Latin meaning 'outside (of)' or 'without'

extract *verb* /*say* uhk-**strakt**/
1. To **extract** a tooth is to pull or take it out. **2.** To **extract** something is to separate it from everything else around it: *to extract specks of gold from the dirt.*
–*noun* /*say* **ek**-strakt/ **3.** something taken out or separated: *an extract from the book*; *a herbal extract used in medicine.*
☐ **extraction**, *noun*

extraordinary /*say* uhk-**straw**-duhn-ree/ *adjective* To be **extraordinary** is to be **1.** more than ordinary: *She showed extraordinary courage.* **2.** unusual or remarkable: *extraordinary animals*; *extraordinary appearance.*
☐ **extraordinarily**, *adverb*

☑ SPELLING TIP *Silent letter alert*: don't forget the silent *a* in this word. Remind yourself that **extraordinary** is made up of two words you know well – *extra* and *ordinary.* When they are put together, the *a* at the end of *extra* remains in the spelling but not in the pronunciation. The prefix *extra-* in this sense means 'outside' or 'beyond', so the basic meaning of **extraordinary** is 'beyond what is ordinary'.

extravagant /*say* uhk-**strav**-uh-guhnt/ *adjective* If someone is **extravagant**, they spend too much money or they are wasteful: *Don't be too extravagant with paper – think of the environment.*

A SIMILAR WORD is **wasteful**.

extreme *adjective* Something **extreme** is **1.** very great: *extreme bravery*; *extreme effort.* **2.** outermost: *at the extreme borders of the rainforest.*
–*noun* **3.** an opinion, feeling, or way of behaving that is the opposite of another: *to experience the extremes of great happiness and deep sadness.*
–*phrase* **4. go to extremes**, to do something to an extent that is much more than is usual or sensible: *It's good to do some regular exercise, but you don't need to go to extremes.*
☐ **extremely**, *adverb* –**extremism**, *noun*

extreme sport *noun* a sport in which people do things that are daring and sometimes risky, like parachuting.

exuberant /*say* uhg-**zyooh**-buh-ruhnt/ *adjective* full of energy or high spirits: *The exuberant puppy jumped all over her and licked her face*; *an exuberant welcome.*
☐ **exuberance**, *noun* –**exuberantly**, *adverb*

exult /*say* uhg-**zult**/ *verb* If you **exult**, you show that you are happy because you have achieved or won something: *They exulted that their team had got into the finals.*
☐ **exultant**, *adjective* –**exultantly**, *adverb* –**exultation**, *noun* –**exultingly**, *adverb*

eye *noun*
1. the organ or part of the body with which we see. **2.** an ability to use your eyes well: *You have a good eye – can you see where the ship is now?*
–*phrase* **3. an eye for an eye**, the paying back of an injury or injustice in the same form that you received it. **4. catch someone's eye**, to attract someone's attention. **5. keep an eye on**, to watch carefully. **6. keep an eye out for**, to be looking out for. **7. the eye of the storm**, the centre of a cyclone where there is no wind or cloud. **8. turn a blind eye to**, to ignore or pretend not to see.

eyeball *noun* the round, ball-shaped object that forms the whole of the eye.

eyebrow *noun* the arch of hair on the bony part of the face above the eye.

THE SHORT FORM of this is **brow**.

eyelash *noun* one of the short curved hairs growing on the edge of the eyelid.

THE SHORT FORM of this is **lash**.

eyelid *noun* the lid of skin which moves up and down over the eye.

THE SHORT FORM of this is **lid**.

eyesight *noun* the power of seeing: *to have good eyesight.*

eyesore *noun* something unpleasant to look at: *Mum said my room was an eyesore and I must clean it up.*

eyewitness *noun*
1. someone who actually sees a particular action or happening.
–*adjective* **2.** given by an eyewitness: *an eyewitness account.*

fable *noun* a short, made-up story, often about animals, that teaches a lesson about how to behave: *the fable of the boy who cried wolf.*

fabric *noun* cloth made by weaving, knitting or pressing fibres together: *silk fabric*; *woollen fabric.*

fabulous /*say* **fab**-yooh-luhs/ *adjective* Something **fabulous** is **1.** *Informal* very good or wonderful: *It was a fabulous trip.* **2.** told about in stories or myths: *the fabulous exploits of Hercules.*
☐ **fabulously**, *adverb* –**fabulousness**, *noun*

☑ SPELLING TIP Don't forget that **fabulous** ends with *ous*.

facade /*say* fuh-**sahd**/ *noun* the front of a building.

☑ SPELLING TIP The meaning of **facade** is connected to the word *face* (something at the front). This will help with the spelling – drop the *e* from *face*, add *ade*, and you have **facade**.

face *noun*
1. the front of the head from the forehead to the chin: *Twins often have faces that look the same.* **2.** a look or expression: *She had a happy face.* **3.** a surface of something: *the face of the cliff*; *the face of a watch.*
–*verb* **4.** If something **faces** in a certain way, the front of it is towards that direction: *The building faces north and gets sun most of the day.*
–*phrase* **5. face to face**, meeting with: *face to face with death.* **6. face up to**, to meet or acknowledge: *Face up to the facts – the dog is gone!* **7. lose** (or **save**) **face**, to have your position or standing among your friends damaged (or made good again): *Joe lost face when he was caught telling a lie.*
☐ **facial**, *adjective*

facet /*say* **fas**-uht/ *noun*
1. one of the small, flat, polished surfaces of a gem: *The facets of the emerald shone brightly.* **2.** a side or part of something complicated like a personality, argument or a structure: *He has many facets to his character.*

WORD HISTORY from a French word meaning 'little face'

facetious /*say* fuh-**see**-shuhs/ *adjective* meant to be or trying to be amusing, at the wrong time or in an unsuitable way: *I was annoyed at his facetious remark about my sunburnt red nose.*
☐ **facetiously**, *adverb* –**facetiousness**, *noun*

face washer *noun* a small piece of soft cloth for washing your face or body.

OTHER TERMS are **washer**, **face cloth** and **flannel**.

facility /*say* fuh-**sil**-uh-tee/ *noun* (*plural* **facilities**)
1. something that makes doing a job easier: *The conference centre has every facility that visitors would need including a fax and photocopier.* **2.** skill or cleverness: *His facility with a soccer ball was something to see!* **3. facilities**, bathroom and toilet.
☐ **facilitate**, *verb*

ANOTHER WORD (for definition 3) is **amenities**.

fact *noun*
1. something that is true or real: *It is a fact that water boils at 100°C.*
–*phrase* **2. in fact**, really: *In fact, the girls beat the boys, not the other way around.*
☐ **factual**, *adjective*

faction *noun* a small group of people within a larger group, who hold a different opinion to the larger group.
☐ **factional**, *adjective* –**factionalism**, *noun*

factor *noun*
1. one of the things that brings about a result: *Her excellent defence was a factor in getting her a place on the team.* **2.** one of two or more numbers which, when multiplied together, give the product: *Factors of 21 are 3 and 7.*

WORD HISTORY from a Latin word meaning 'doer' or 'maker'

factory *noun* (*plural* **factories**) a building or group of buildings where goods are made.

faculty *noun* (*plural* **faculties**) one of the powers that you are born with: *Hearing and sight are very important faculties*; *Do you think he still has all his faculties?*

fad *noun* something that is popular for a short time: *Samantha always knows what the latest fad is.*
☐ **faddish**, *adjective* –**faddy**, *adjective*

fade *verb*
1. If a material **fades**, it loses colour: *My jeans faded very quickly.* **2.** If something **fades**, it disappears slowly: *The light faded as the sun went down.*

faeces /*say* **fee**-seez/ *plural noun* waste matter discharged from the intestines.

ANOTHER SPELLING is **feces**. This is the usual spelling in American English.
ANOTHER WORD for this is **excrement**. An informal word is **poo**.

☑ SPELLING TIP As well as the *ae/e* variation in the spelling of this word, the thing to notice is the *es* ending, giving an 'eez' sound. This ending happens in plural words that have come from Latin. The word **faeces** comes from the plural of the Latin word *faex*, meaning 'dregs'.

Fahrenheit /*say* **fa**-ruhn-huyt/ *adjective* The **Fahrenheit** scale of temperature is that in which the melting point of ice is 32° above zero and the boiling point is 212° above zero.

THE SYMBOL for this is **F**.
WORD HISTORY named after a German scientist, Gabriel *Fahrenheit*, who thought up this scale and was the first to put mercury into thermometers

fail *verb*
1. To **fail** something is to be unsuccessful in it: *I failed the spelling test.* **2.** If something **fails**, it does not work properly or turn out as expected: *The brakes failed*; *The corn crop failed.*
☐ **failed**, *adjective*: *a failed crop.* –**failing**, *noun* –**failure**, *noun*

faint *adjective*
1. If something is **faint**, it lacks strength in some way: *a faint sound in the distance*; *a faint colour.* **2.** Is you feel **faint**, you feel weak and as though you are going to lose consciousness.
–*verb* **3.** If you **faint**, you lose consciousness for a short time: *She fainted when she heard the news.*
☐ **faint**, *noun* –**faintly**, *adverb*

fair[1] *adjective*
1. A person who is **fair** does not show favouritism: *a fair referee.* **2.** A **fair** contest is one fought according to the rules: *a fair fight.* **3. Fair** weather is sunny and not cloudy. **4.** To be **fair** is to be of light colour: *fair skin colour.*
–*adverb* **5.** in a way that keeps to the rules: *to play fair.*
–*phrase* **6. fair and square, a.** directly: *to hit the target fair and square on the bullseye.* **b.** honestly or in a just way: *I trust him – he always deals fair and square.*
☐ **fairly**, *adverb* –**fairness**, *noun*

SIMILAR WORDS (for definition 1) are **just**, **even-handed** and **impartial**; (for definition 3) **clear** and **fine**.

☑ SPELLING TIP Don't confuse **fair** with **fare** which sounds the same. A **fare** is the money you pay for a ticket on a bus or train.

fair[2] *noun*
1. a group of sideshows and similar entertainments set up for a short time in one place. **2.** a regular gathering of buyers and sellers of a particular type of goods: *an antiques fair*; *an exotic foods fair.*

☑ SPELLING TIP See **fair**[1].

fair dinkum *adjective Informal* true or genuine: *He's a fair dinkum Aussie.*

fairway *noun* the part of a golf course between a tee and the green, where the grass is kept short.

fairy *noun* (*plural* **fairies**) a tiny imaginary creature with magical powers.
☐ **fairy**, *adjective*: *a fairy story.*

fairytale *noun*
1. a traditional story involving magical happenings or imaginary creatures.
–*adjective* **2.** so good, beautiful or unlikely that it seems to have been part of a fairytale: *a fairytale ending*; *a fairytale romance.*

ANOTHER TERM (for definition 1) is **fairy story**.

faith *noun*
1. trust in someone or something. **2.** the collection of beliefs of a religion: *the Hindu faith*; *the Islamic faith*; *the Christian faith.*

faithful *adjective* loyal and trustworthy: *a faithful dog*; *a faithful employee.*
☐ **faithfully**, *adverb* –**faithfulness**, *noun*

fake *verb*
1. If you **fake** something, you pretend that something is the case although, in fact, it is not: *She faked her mother's signature on the report card.*
–*noun* **2.** something that is designed to make you think that it is something else, usually something more expensive or valuable: *Those paintings, supposedly by a famous artist, turned out to be fakes.*
☐ **fake**, *adjective*

falafel /*say* fuh-**laf**-uhl, fuh-**lahf**-uhl/ *noun* fried balls of spiced chickpeas and hot peppers, which have been soaked in relish and chilli sauce.

ANOTHER SPELLING is **felafel**.

falcon /*say* **fal**-kuhn, **fawl**-kuhn/ *noun* a kind of hunting bird which captures its prey in flight.

WORD HISTORY from a Latin word meaning 'sickle'

fall *verb* (**falls**, **falling**, **fell**, **has fallen**)
1. If something **falls**, it moves through the air, from a higher to a lower point: *The book fell off the shelf.* **2.** If someone **falls**, they move from an upright position to the ground, often accidentally: *He tripped and fell.* **3.** If you say that things such as prices, standards or levels **fall**, you mean that they have dropped or become lower. **4.** You also

use **fall** in certain phrases to say that you pass into a different condition or state: *to fall ill*; *to fall asleep*; *to fall in love.* **5.** If something that is long **falls**, it hangs down from a higher level: *She has black hair falling to her waist.* **6.** If something **falls** on a particular day, it happens on that day: *My birthday falls on Easter Sunday this year.* **7.** If the government of a country **falls**, it loses its political power and control.
–*phrase* **8. fall apart**, to break into pieces or be destroyed in some way: *This house is falling apart around me.* **9. fall for**, **a.** to believe (a trick or deception of some kind): *We completely fell for his lies.* **b.** to fall in love with: *My dad fell for my mum the first time he saw her.* **10. fall out with**, to have an argument or disagreement with: *She fell out with her brother and they didn't speak for 2 years.* **11. fall short**, to not have enough for a particular purpose: *There should be enough bread for everyone, but we just may fall short.*
☐ **fall**, *noun*

fallible /*say* **fal**-uh-buhl/ *adjective* able to make a mistake: *We're all fallible!*
☐ **fallibility**, *noun*

fallout *noun* dangerous radioactive dust that falls from the air after a nuclear explosion.

fallow *adjective* **Fallow** ground is ploughed but left without anything planted in it to improve its quality: *The fields were ploughed and lay fallow, ready for next year's crops.*

false *adjective*
1. not true or correct: *a false statement.* **2.** intended to look like something else but actually only a copy of it: *false diamonds.*
☐ **falseness**, *noun* –**falsify**, *verb* (**falsifies**, **falsifying**, **falsified**, **has falsified**) –**falsity**, *noun* (*plural* **falsities**)

falsehood *noun* a statement that is not true.

ANOTHER WORD for this is **lie**[1] (definition 1), which is the more usual term.

falsetto /*say* fawl-**set**-oh/ *noun* (*plural* **falsettos**) a voice that men can produce which is above their normal range.
☐ **falsetto**, *adjective*: *a falsetto voice.*

falter *verb* To **falter** is to move or speak hesitatingly or unsteadily: *His legs faltered as he got tired.*
☐ **faltering**, *adjective* –**falteringly**, *adverb*

fame *noun* the state of being widely known: *He said that coping with the fame would be more difficult than winning the race.*

familiar /*say* fuh-**mil**-yuh/ *adjective*
1. well-known: *a familiar face.*
–*phrase* **2. familiar with**, having knowledge of: *We are familiar with his films.*
☐ **familiarise**, *verb* –**familiarity**, *noun*

ANOTHER SPELLING for **familiarise** is **familiarize**.

☑ SPELLING TIP Remember that the ending of *familiar* is spelt *iar* (not *ier*).

family *noun* (*plural* **families**)
1. parents and their children. **2.** a wider group of related people including grandparents, uncles, aunts and cousins. **3.** a group of related things: *the cat family*; *a tree of the palm family.*
☐ **family**, *adjective*: *a family home.*

family tree *noun* the branching plan of your family, which shows all your relations and ancestors.

famine /*say* **fam**-uhn/ *noun* a serious shortage of food, usually caused by drought.

famished *adjective Informal* very hungry.

famous *adjective* well-known.
☐ **famously**, *adverb*

SIMILAR WORDS are **renowned**, **celebrated**, **noted** and **notorious**. Note that someone who is **notorious** is famous for something bad (*a notorious criminal*).

fan[1] *noun*
1. something designed to move the air and make you feel cooler.
–*verb* (**fans**, **fanning**, **fanned**, **has fanned**) **2.** If you **fan** something, you make the air around it move, so as to cool it: *She fanned her face with a piece of folded paper.*

fan[2] *noun* someone who is an eager supporter: *a soccer fan.*

WORD HISTORY this word is a shortened form of *fanatic*

fanatic /*say* fuh-**nat**-ik/ *noun* someone who is extremely enthusiastic, often in an unthinking way, about something they believe in: *a fanatic about exercise.*
☐ **fanatical**, *adjective* –**fanaticism** /*say* fuh-**nat**-uh-siz-uhm/, *noun*

WORD HISTORY from a Latin word meaning 'having to do with a temple', 'inspired by a god', or 'frantic'

fanbelt *noun* the belt which drives the cooling fan of a motor.

fancy *noun* (*plural* **fancies**)
1. a liking: *We took a fancy to the dog with the spots on its nose.* **2.** something imagined: *She had a fancy that one day she would marry a prince.*
–*verb* (**fancies**, **fancying**, **fancied**, **has fancied**) **3.** If you **fancy** something, you think about it as a possibility: *Fancy winning the Melbourne Cup – how exciting would that be!* **4.** If you **fancy** something, you like it: *He particularly fancied dark chocolate.*
☐ **fanciful**, *adjective* –**fancy**, *adjective* (**fancier**, **fanciest**): *fancy clothes.*

fanfare *noun* a short, loud piece of music usually played on trumpets, used to mark the beginning of an event or the arrival of someone important.

fan fiction *noun* fiction written by fans of a popular television show or other work, involving characters and settings from that work, and often published on the internet or in a fan magazine.

THE SHORT FORM of this is **fanfic**.

fang *noun*
1. one of the long, sharp, hollow teeth of a snake, by which it injects venom. **2.** *Informal* a canine tooth.

fantastic *adjective*
1. strange or unusual: *fantastic carvings.* **2.** imaginary: *fantastic animals that spoke like humans.* **3.** very good: *a fantastic friend.*
□ **fantastically**, *adverb*

ANOTHER WORD (for definition 2) is **fantastical**.

fantasy *noun* (*plural* **fantasies**)
1. imagination: *creatures of fantasy.* **2.** the making of pleasant mental pictures: *Her fantasy was one day to travel the world.*
□ **fantasise**, *verb*

ANOTHER SPELLING for **fantasise** is **fantasize**.
A SIMILAR WORD (for definition 2) is **daydream**.

far *adverb* (**farther** *or* **further**, **farthest** *or* **furthest**)
1. at or to a great distance or point: *They travelled far in that year.*
–*phrase* **2. as far as**, to the distance or degree that: *I wouldn't trust him as far as I could throw him.* **3. by far**, very much: *By far the best thing you can do is to go home.* **4. far and away**, very much: *She is far and away the best player.* **5. far gone**, in an advanced or extreme state, usually of something bad, such as an illness. **6. so far**, up to now.
□ **far**, *adjective*: *a far city*; *the far side.*

faraway *adjective*
1. distant or a long way off: *a faraway planet like Pluto.* **2.** dreamy: *She had a faraway look on her face.*

farce *noun* a comedy in which the humour depends on a ridiculous and unlikely situation.
□ **farcical**, *adjective*

fare *noun* the money paid for a ticket on transport like a bus, train or aeroplane: *I just had enough money for the taxi fare.*

☑ SPELLING TIP Don't confuse the spelling of **fare** with **fair** which sounds the same. To be **fair** is to be just.

farewell *noun*
1. a saying of goodbye: *We wished her farewell.*
–*verb* **2.** If you **farewell** someone, you say goodbye to them: *We farewelled them at the airport.*

farm *noun*
1. an area of land used for growing crops or raising animals.
–*verb* **2.** To **farm** is to cultivate the soil, or run a farm.
□ **farmer**, *noun* –**farming**, *noun*

WORD HISTORY from a French word meaning 'fix'

fascinate /*say* **fas**-uh-nayt/ *verb* To **fascinate** someone is to attract them and hold their interest completely: *The film about the blue whales fascinated us.*
□ **fascinating**, *adjective* –**fascination**, *noun*

WORD HISTORY from a Latin word meaning 'enchanted'

☑ SPELLING TIP *Silent letter alert*: don't forget the silent *c* after the *s*.

fashion *noun*
1. a style of dress: *Fashion today is very relaxed.* **2.** a custom or way of doing things: *The current fashion at birthday parties is to have clowns performing.* **3.** manner or way: *Her reply was given in an abrupt fashion.*
–*verb* **4.** If you **fashion** something, you make it into a particular shape: *She fashioned the clay into the form of a tiger.*
□ **fashionable**, *adjective* –**fashionably**, *adverb*

fast[1] *adjective*
1. able to move quickly: *a fast runner.* **2.** finished in a short time: *a fast game.* **3.** ahead of the correct time: *My watch is fast.* **4.** fixed firmly in place: *He tied the rope fast to the tree.*
–*adverb* **5.** quickly: *They ran fast.* **6.** deeply: *The baby was fast asleep.* **7.** tightly: *Grip fast on the chain.*

SIMILAR WORDS (for definition 1) are **quick**, **rapid** and **speedy**.

fast[2] *noun*
1. a period of time when little or no food is eaten, usually for religious or health reasons.
–*verb* **2.** If somebody **fasts**, they eat little or no food: *They were fasting to raise money for children in other countries.*

fasten *verb* To **fasten** something is to fix it firmly in place.
□ **fastener**, *noun*

☑ SPELLING TIP *Silent letter alert*: don't forget the silent *t* after the *s*. Remember that this word comes from *fast* where you can hear the *t*.

fastidious /*say* fas-**tid**-ee-uhs/ *adjective* fussy or hard to please: *If you are too fastidious, people find it annoying.*
□ **fastidiously**, *adverb* –**fastidiousness**, *noun*

fat *noun*
1. the white or yellowish substance found in or around the flesh of animals and in some plants,

used in solid or liquid form in cooking: *First melt the fat in the pan.*
–*adjective* (**fatter**, **fattest**) **2.** having too much flesh: *I am too fat to fit into this dress.* **3.** having much edible flesh: *a fat lamb.*
☐ **fatten**, *verb* –**fatty**, *adjective*

SIMILAR WORDS (for definition 2) are **overweight**, **plump**, **stout** and **obese**. Note that **plump** describes someone who is rather fat and has a pleasant round shape. A **stout** person has a thick, heavy body. This word is used particularly in relation to older people: *He became stout in his middle age.* **Obese** is a formal, medical word which means that someone is extremely fat or too fat to be healthy.

fatal *adjective*
1. causing death: *a fatal car accident.* **2.** likely to have very important results: *a fatal move.*
☐ **fatalism**, *noun* –**fatality**, *noun* –**fatally**, *adverb*

fate *noun*
1. a force outside your control that seems to control the things that happen to you: *We will just have to leave the situation to fate.* **2.** the end or final result: *The fate of the ship was sealed when she was frozen in the ice.*
☐ **fateful**, *adjective*: *the fateful day when they met.*

☑ SPELLING TIP Don't confuse the spelling of **fate** with **fete** which sounds the same. A **fete** is a kind of fair to raise money for a school or charity.

father *noun*
1. a male parent. **2.** someone who shows the interest of a father: *He was a father to all.* **3.** someone who invents or begins something: *the founding fathers of the city.* **4. Father**, a respectful title and form of address for priests in some religions.
–*verb* **5.** If a man **fathers** a child, he is the man who, together with the mother, has produced it.
☐ **fatherhood**, *noun* –**fatherly**, *adjective*

father-in-law *noun* (*plural* **fathers-in-law**) the father of someone's husband or wife.

fathom /*say* **fadh**-uhm/ *noun*
1. an old-fashioned measure of the depth of water equal to 6 feet, or nearly 2 metres in the metric system.
–*verb* **2.** If you **fathom** something, you understand it completely: *We really couldn't fathom what the teacher was saying.*

THE ABBREVIATION (for definition 1) is **fm**.

fatigue /*say* fuh-**teeg**/ *noun*
1. severe mental or physical tiredness. **2.** weakening of material, especially metal, as a result of stress put on it through long use.
–*verb* (**fatigues**, **fatiguing**, **fatigued**, **has fatigued**) **3.** If someone or something **fatigues** a person, they make them tired: *Carrying the baby all day fatigued her.*
☐ **fatigued**, *adjective*

☑ SPELLING TIP Don't forget the *ue* at the end. The spelling *igue* gives an 'eeg' sound. Another word with the same sound and spelling at the end is *intrigue*.

fatuous /*say* **fach**-ooh-uhs/ *adjective* If something that someone says is **fatuous**, it is foolish because they have not thought properly about it.
☐ **fatuously**, *adverb* –**fatuousness**, *noun*

☑ SPELLING TIP Remember the *tu* spelling in this word (which gives a 'chooh' sound).

fault /*say* fawlt, folt/ *noun*
1. responsibility or cause for blame: *It was her own fault that she missed the bus.* **2.** a mistake or something that is not correct: *The judges could find no fault in her performance.* **3.** a failure to serve a ball according to the rules in tennis and similar games. **4.** in geology, a break or fracture in the surface of the earth, along which movement has occurred. **5.** in sport, a breach of the rules which results in a warning or a penalty.
–*verb* **6.** If you say you cannot **fault** somebody's performance, you mean that there is nothing wrong with it: *The teacher said she couldn't fault our singing of the national anthem.*
–*phrase* **7. at fault**, open to blame: *Who's at fault for the water all over the bathroom floor?* **8. find fault**, to find something wrong: *He's already found fault with the new car.* **9. to a fault**, to a great degree: *He was generous to a fault.*
☐ **faulty**, *adjective*

WORD HISTORY from a Latin word meaning 'deceive'

☑ SPELLING TIP *Tricky vowel sound*: the vowel sound is spelt *au* (although you say it as either 'aw' or 'o'). Some other words with the same spelling for this sound are *assault* and *vault*.

fauna /*say* **faw**-nuh/ *noun* the animals of a particular area or period of time: *Australia's fauna is unusual because of the continent's isolation.*

COMPARE this with **flora**.

☑ SPELLING TIP *Tricky vowel sounds*: the first vowel sound is spelt *au* (although you say it as 'aw') and the final vowel sound is spelt *a*. This word comes from Latin, from the name of the Roman goddess *Fauna*, the sister of *Faunus*, god of the woods.

favour *noun*
1. a kind act: *She did me a favour by taking my place.* **2.** a state of being thought well of: *Are you in favour at the moment?* **3.** If you **favour** one person or thing over another, you prefer them: *I favour the idea of stopping now instead of later.*

–*phrase* **4. in favour of, a.** on the side of: *I am in favour of stopping for lunch.* **b.** payable to: *a cheque in favour of the hospital.*
☐ **favoured**, *adjective*

ANOTHER SPELLING is **favor**.

favourable *adjective* If something is **favourable**, it is good, helpful and supports you and your plans: *Given favourable weather, we should be able to sail there in three days.*
☐ **favourably**, *adverb*

ANOTHER SPELLING is **favorable**.

favourite *noun*
1. someone or something most highly thought of: *Out of everything on this menu, my favourite is marinated chops.* **2.** a competitor who is expected to win. **3.** someone who is treated as being better than others without really deserving it: *the teacher's favourite.*
☐ **favourite**, *adjective*: *a favourite hat.* –**favouritism**, *noun*: *We all thought the ballet teacher showed favouritism when she said that Ann's dance was the best.*

ANOTHER SPELLING is **favorite**.

fawn[1] *noun*
1. a young deer.
–*adjective* **2.** pale yellowish-brown.

fawn[2] *verb* If you say that a person **fawns** over somebody, especially someone rich or famous, you mean that you think they are flattering that person just to get special treatment for themselves: *Of course, the whole family is fawning over him now that he has inherited the estate!*

fax *noun*
1. a way of sending written information and pictures by electronic means over the telephone system. **2.** a piece of writing or a picture sent this way.
–*verb* **3.** If you **fax** words or pictures, you send them electronically to another person: *I faxed James a timetable giving all the details.*

WORD HISTORY a changed spelling of the first part of *facs(imile)* /*say* fak-**sim**-uh-lee/, which means 'an exact copy'

fear *noun*
1. a feeling that danger or something unpleasant is near.
–*verb* **2.** If you **fear** something, you are worried that it might happen or you are scared of it.
–*phrase* **3. for fear of**, in order to avoid or stop: *We decided to stay here for fear of a storm.*
☐ **fearful**, *adjective* –**fearless**, *adjective* –**fearlessness**, *noun* –**fearsome**, *adjective*: *a fearsome storm.*

feasible /*say* **fee**-zuh-buhl/ *adjective* able to be done or achieved: *Your plan might be feasible if we can get enough people together.*
☐ **feasibility**, *noun*

feast *noun*
1. a large meal set out for many guests. **2.** a large quantity of something pleasing: *a feast of cheeses; a feast for the senses.*
–*verb* **3.** If you **feast** on something, you eat large quantities of it and enjoy it immensely: *We feasted on fresh seafood caught that day in the bay.*

A SIMILAR WORD (for definition 1) is **banquet**.

feat *noun* an action requiring great skill, courage or strength.

☑ SPELLING TIP Don't confuse the spelling of **feat** with **feet** which sounds the same but is spelt with a double *e*. Your **feet** are at the end of your legs.

feather /*say* **fedh**-uh/ *noun*
1. one of the growths that make up the covering of a bird's body.
–*phrase* **2. a feather in your cap**, an honour or mark of excellence you have earned. **3. feather your nest**, to provide well for yourself or make yourself rich.
☐ **feathered**, *adjective* –**feathery**, *adjective*

feature /*say* **fee**-chuh/ *noun*
1. any part of your face: *His nose is his best feature.* **2.** a special part or quality: *Seeing the bats as they flew out of their cave was a feature of our trip.*
–*verb* **3.** If a publication or a production **features** something, it gives it special importance or attention: *The play featured a story on the famous trumpet player; The trip to Central Australia features a twilight visit to Uluru.*
☐ **featured**, *adjective* –**featureless**, *adjective*

☑ SPELLING TIP *Tricky vowel sound*: the first vowel sound is spelt *ea* (although it sounds like 'ee'). Also remember that the ending is spelt *ture* (although it sounds like 'chuh'). Another word with the same spelling for these sounds is *creature* – think of 'a feature of a funny creature'!

February /*say* **feb**-rooh-uh-ree, **feb**-yooh-uh-ree/ *noun* the second month of the year, with 28 days, but 29 days in leap years.

THE ABBREVIATION is **Feb.**
WORD HISTORY from the Latin name for the Roman festival of purification, held on 15 February

☑ SPELLING TIP Remember the *r* after the *b* in **February**. Many people don't pronounce the sound of the *r*, but it should always be there when you spell it. Rap it out as *Feb + ru + ar + y*.

federal *adjective* having to do with a central government rather than state governments: *federal issues like immigration and defence.*
☐ **federally**, *adverb* –**federalism**, *noun* –**federalist**, *adjective*

federation *noun*
1. the forming of a nation by a number of states who give some of their powers and responsibilities to a central government. **2.** a nation formed in this way: *Australia is a federation.*

fee *noun* the money that is paid to a doctor, lawyer, school, and so on, for their services.

feeble *adjective*
1. weak in body or mind. **2.** lacking strength or brightness: *a feeble cry*; *feeble attempts.*
☐ **feebleness**, *noun* –**feebly**, *adverb*

feed *verb* (**feeds**, **feeding**, **fed**, **has fed**)
1. If you **feed** a person or animal, you give them something to eat. Sometimes to **feed** someone is to help them to eat their food. **2.** If a person or animal **feeds** on something, they eat it: *Frogs feed mainly on insects.* **3.** If you **feed** something, you provide it with whatever it needs to work properly or function smoothly: *We need to feed the fire with wood.* **4.** If you **feed** something into a machine, you put it in so that it will work as required: *I can't get the results until I've finished feeding the data into the computer.*
–*noun* **5.** food, especially for animals: *horses' feed.* **6.** *Informal* a meal.

feedback *noun*
1. information passed back about something that has been done or said: *Mum filled in a form giving feedback about the new shopping centre.* **2.** the return of part of the sound put out by a loudspeaker into the microphone so that a high-pitched noise is made.

feel *verb* (**feels**, **feeling**, **felt**, **has felt**)
1. If you **feel** something, you touch it with your hands to find out about it: *Feel this cloth – you can tell it's silk.* **2.** If you **feel** for something, you reach for it with your hands without looking or being able to see: *to feel for a torch in the dark.* **3.** If something **feels** a particular way to you, it makes you experience it in that way: *The water felt nice and cool on my feet.* **4.** If you **feel** a particular way, you experience that state or emotion: *to feel sick*; *to feel hungry*; *to feel a sharp pain.* **5.** If you **feel** something, it is your opinion: *I feel that we should give up on this plan.*
–*phrase* **6. feel for**, to have sympathy for: *I feel for her in her distress.* **7. feel like**, to want or wish for: *to feel like a walk.* **8. feel up to**, *Informal* to be able to deal with or manage: *to feel up to a jog.*
☐ **feel**, *noun*: *the feel of silk.*

feeler *noun* a thin, arm-like growth on some animals, like an antenna or tentacle, which is used for touching or grasping.

feeling *noun*
1. a particular sensation or emotion: *a feeling of nausea*; *a feeling of safety.* **2.** a belief or idea: *My feeling is that someone has stolen it.*

feet *plural noun* See **foot**.

☑ SPELLING TIP Don't confuse the spelling of **feet** with **feat** which sounds the same but is spelt with *ea*. A **feat** is an action requiring skill or strength.

feign /*say* fayn/ *verb* If you **feign** something, you pretend to have it: *She feigned chickenpox by drawing red spots on herself*; *to feign sympathy*; *to feign ignorance.*

☑ SPELLING TIP *Tricky vowel sound*: the ending of **feign** is spelt *eign* (although it sounds like 'ayn'). It might help if you think of a word you know well which has the same spelling for this sound, such as *reign* meaning 'to rule'. The *g* is left behind from their Latin origins.

feline /*say* **fee**-luyn/ *adjective* associated with cats or the cat family.
☐ **feline**, *noun*

fell[1] *verb* the past tense of **fall**.

fell[2] *verb* To **fell** something or someone is to cut them down or cause them to fall: *The men felled many of the tallest trees*; *Did the boxer manage to fell his opponent?*

fellow *noun*
1. a man or a boy. **2. Fellow**, a member of a professional society: *a Fellow of the Royal College of Physicians.*
–*adjective* **3.** having the same position or occupation: *his fellow train drivers.*
☐ **fellowship**, *noun*

felony /*say* **fel**-uh-nee/ *noun* a serious crime such as murder or burglary.
☐ **felon**, *noun* a criminal. –**felonious**, *adjective*

felt *noun* cloth made of wool, fur or hair which is not woven but pressed firmly together: *an old hat made of felt.*
☐ **felt**, *adjective*

felt pen *noun* a pen with a thick nib made of felt, usually available in a range of bright colours, used for colouring in, etc.

NOTE This is sometimes called a **texta** or a **felt-tip pen**.

female *noun* an animal, plant or person of the gender that can produce young ones.
☐ **female**, *adjective*

THE OPPOSITE is **male**.

feminine /*say* **fem**-uh-nuhn/ *adjective* If someone or something is **feminine**, they have qualities or characteristics which are thought to be typical of women.
☐ **femininity**, *noun*

THE OPPOSITE is **masculine**.

feminism *noun* the principle that women deserve the same rights and opportunities as men:

Feminism has had many influential supporters over the years.

fence *noun*
1. a wall or barrier put up around something to separate it from its surroundings. **2.** *Informal* someone who earns a living by buying and selling stolen goods.
–*verb* **3.** If you enclose or separate an area from its surrounds, you **fence** it: *We had to fence the vegetable garden to stop the chickens eating the lettuce.*
–*phrase* **4. sit on the fence**, to avoid taking sides in an argument.
☐ **fencer**, *noun*

fencing *noun*
1. the sport of sword fighting. **2.** material, such as wood or wire, used to build fences.
☐ **fencer**, *noun*

fend *verb in the phrases* **1. fend off**, to fight off or resist: *He fended off his attackers.* **2. fend for**, to look after or protect: *They fended for themselves for many years.*

feng shui /*say* feng **shway**, fung **shway**, feng **shwee**, fung **shwee**/ *noun* a practice in Chinese culture of placing yourself in a good relationship with the surrounding physical world so as to increase good luck. In particular it relates to the design of houses.

WORD HISTORY from Chinese words meaning 'wind and water'

feral /*say* **fe**-ruhl/ *adjective* wild or untamed: *Feral cats can grow extremely large.*

WORD HISTORY from a Latin word meaning 'wild beast'

ferment /*say* fuh-**ment**/ *verb* To **ferment** something is to change it in taste and appearance, because yeast or bacteria has turned sugar into alcohol and gas: *Bacteria in the air make grape juice ferment.*
☐ **fermentation** /*say* fer-men-**tay**-shuhn/, *noun*

fern *noun* a green, leafy plant that does not have flowers and grows in slightly wet places sheltered from the sun.

ferocious /*say* fuh-**roh**-shuhs/ *adjective* savagely fierce and violently cruel: *ferocious animals.*
☐ **ferociously**, *adverb* –**ferocity**, *noun*

☑ SPELLING TIP Remember that the ending of **ferocious** is spelt *cious* (although it sounds like *shuhs*). It might help if you think of some other words you know well which have the same spelling for this sound, such as *delicious* and *precious*.

ferret *noun*
1. an animal with a long thin body used on farms to go down rabbit holes and chase out rabbits.
–*phrase* **2. ferret out**, to search for and find: *We ferreted out the lost library book eventually.*

ferry *noun* (*plural* **ferries**)
1. a boat that carries people or cars across a river, lake, etc., for a fee.
–*verb* (**ferries**, **ferrying**, **ferried**, **has ferried**) **2.** When a boat carries people or cars across water, it **ferries** them.

fertile *adjective*
1. very productive: *The land is fertile because of the rich volcanic soil*; *You have such a fertile imagination you should write a book.* **2.** able to have babies.
☐ **fertility**, *noun*

WORD HISTORY from a Latin word meaning 'fruitful'

fertilise *verb*
1. If somebody **fertilises** land, they make it fertile or enrich it: *Mum fertilises the garden with manure from the hens.* **2.** When a male part **fertilises** a female part, it combines with it in order to create new life: *Pollen fertilises the reproductive part of the plant.*
☐ **fertilisation**, *noun* –**fertiliser**, *noun*

ANOTHER SPELLING is **fertilize**.

fervour /*say* **fer**-vuh/ *noun* great enthusiasm: *They pleaded their case with great fervour*; *religious fervour.*
☐ **fervent**, *adjective* –**fervently**, *adverb*

ANOTHER SPELLING is **fervor**.

festival *noun*
1. a celebration with marches, shows, and performances of music, dance and plays. **2.** a time of religious celebration: *the harvest festival.*

A SIMILAR WORD (for definition 1) is **carnival**.

festive *adjective* merry and joyful: *a festive mood.*
☐ **festivity**, *noun* (*plural* **festivities**)

festoon *noun* If somebody **festoons** a place, they hang things such as streamers or ribbons on it for decoration.
☐ **festoon**, *noun*: *a festoon of red and yellow and blue and green.*

WORD HISTORY from an Italian word meaning 'festival' or 'feast'

fetch *verb*
1. If you **fetch** something, you go to where it is, collect it and bring it back: *Fetch the ball, Fido!*; *They sent a courier to fetch the documents.* **2.** If something **fetches** a certain price, it is sold for that price: *Houses near water will always fetch good prices.*

fetching *adjective Old-fashioned* charming and attractive: *She had a fetching way about her.*
☐ **fetchingly**, *adverb*

fete /*rhymes with* gate/ *noun*
1. a small fair held to raise money for a school or charity.
–*verb* **2.** to treat as special and important: *The pop group was feted wherever it went.*

☑ SPELLING TIP Don't confuse the spelling of **fete** with **fate** which sounds the same. **Fate** is the force beyond your control that seems to control the things that happen to you. **Fete** comes from French. This is why it has the *ete* spelling for the 'ate' sound and why it is sometimes spelt with an accent on the first *e*: **fête**.

fetlock *noun* the part of a horse's leg with a tuft of hair just above the hoof.

fetta *noun* a soft white cheese from Greece, which has been preserved by being soaked in salted water.

ANOTHER SPELLING is **feta**.
WORD HISTORY from a Latin word meaning 'mouthful' or 'bite'

fetter *noun*
1. a chain or shackle tied around the ankles. **2.** anything that restricts or stops you from doing what you want.
–*verb* **3.** If something **fetters** a person, it restricts them.

ANOTHER FORM This word (as in definition 2) is often used in the plural form, as in *to shake off your fetters*.

fettuccine /*say* fet-uh-**chee**-nee/ *noun* a kind of pasta that has been cut into wide flat strips.

☑ SPELLING TIP *Double letter alert*: double *t* and double *c* (giving a 'ch' sound) – rather like two long strands of **fettuccine**, and then two curled strands that you might wrap around your fork. **Fettuccine** comes straight from the Italian word for this kind of pasta, which makes the spelling unusual. Another difficulty is the *e* spelling at the end (which gives an 'ee' sound).

feud /*say* fyoohd/ *noun*
1. a bitter, long-lasting disagreement, especially between two families: *The feud between my two uncles was very nasty and lasted for years.*
–*verb* **2.** People who **feud** fight bitterly, sometimes for years: *They feuded with their neighbours about what sort of fence they should erect.*

☑ SPELLING TIP *Tricky vowel sound*: the vowel sound is spelt *eu* (although it sounds like 'yooh'). The adjective form *feudal* also has an *eu* for this sound.

feudal /*say* **fyooh**-duhl/ *adjective* A **feudal** way of life was one in which ordinary people lived on and used the land of a nobleman, giving him military and other services in return.
☐ **feudalism**, *noun*

NOTE We usually talk about the **feudal system** which was in force in medieval Europe.

fever *noun*
1. an unusually high body temperature caused by illness. **2.** great excitement: *Eleni was in a fever of anticipation waiting for the plane.*
–*phrase* **3. fever pitch**, the height of excitement: *It didn't take the crowd long to reach fever pitch.*
☐ **feverish**, *adjective* –**feverishly**, *adverb* –**feverishness**, *noun*

few *adjective*
1. **Few** means 'not many': *Few kids wanted to be in the choir.*
–*phrase* **2. the few**, a small number: *This sport is only for the few who have superb fitness.* **3. a good few** or **quite a few**, a fairly large number.

fiancé /*say* fee-**on**-say/ *noun* the man that a woman is going to marry.

☑ SPELLING TIP See **fiancée**.

fiancée /*say* fee-**on**-say/ *noun* the woman that a man is going to marry.

☑ SPELLING TIP *Tricky vowel sounds*: *i* for the 'ee' sound in the first syllable, *an* for the 'on' sound and *ée* for the 'ay' sound at the end. Some other words with this sound for the *ee* ending are *entree* and *matinee*. They have all come from French which also explains the accent over the first *e* in **fiancée**. The other words are now mostly spelt without the accent in English, and you sometimes also see **fiancee** without the accent.

fiasco /*say* fee-**as**-koh/ *noun* an embarrassing or ridiculous failure.

☑ SPELLING TIP You spell **fiasco** in very much the same way as it sounds. You mainly should remember the *fi* beginning (which sounds like 'fee') and the *o* ending. It is spelt like this because it comes from Italian where many words end in *o*.

fib *Informal*
–*noun* **1.** a lie.
–*verb* (**fibs**, **fibbing**, **fibbed**, **has fibbed**) **2.** If you **fib**, you tell a lie.
☐ **fibber**, *noun*

fibre /*say* **fuy**-buh/ *noun*
1. a fine thread of wool, cotton or other material. **2.** the part of food that cannot be digested: *Baked beans are full of fibre.*

☑ SPELLING TIP *Tricky vowel sound*: the first vowel sound is spelt with just an *i*, and the vowel sound at the end is spelt *re* (even though it sounds like 'uh'). It might help if you think of other words which you know well with the same spelling for this sound, such as *centre* and *theatre*.

fibreglass *noun* material made of fine glass fibres. It is used to insulate buildings against heat and cold or mixed with plastic and used to make surfboards and boats.

fibro *noun* strong building material made of asbestos and cement.

fickle *adjective* changeable or likely to have changes of mind: *She was a fickle friend and couldn't be depended on*; *The weather in the mountains was often fickle.*
☐ **fickleness**, *noun*

fiction *noun* a story which is not true but is made up from the imagination.
☐ **fictional**, *adjective* –**fictitious**, *adjective*: *a fictitious name.*

THE OPPOSITE is **nonfiction** or **fact**.

fiddle *verb*
1. If you **fiddle** with something, you keep handling or touching it.
–*noun* **2.** *Informal* a violin.
–*phrase* **3. fit as a fiddle**, in very good health. **4. play second fiddle**, to take a less important part.
☐ **fiddler**, *noun*

fidelity /*say* fuh-**del**-uh-tee/ *noun*
1. faithfulness or loyalty: *The king rewarded his followers for their fidelity.* **2.** the ability to reproduce something as it should be: *the fidelity of a radio or amplifier*; *the fidelity of their report of the incident.*

fidget *verb* (**fidgets**, **fidgeting**, **fidgeted**, **has fidgeted**) If you **fidget**, you keep moving your body in a restless way because you are nervous or bored.
☐ **fidgety**, *adjective*

field /*say* feeld/ *noun*
1. a piece of open ground or space: *a field of corn*; *sporting fields.* **2.** an area of interest or activity: *She works in the field of computers.* **3.** in science, an area or space influenced by some force or thing: *an electric field*; *a magnetic field*; *a gravitational field.* **4.** in computers, an area on a record that has been specified in some way.
☐ **field**, *adjective*: *field sports.* –**fielder**, *noun*

☑ SPELLING TIP Remember the *ie* spelling for the 'ee' sound. This follows the rule that *i* comes before *e* except after *c*.

field glasses *plural noun* See **binoculars**.

fiend /*say* feend/ *noun*
1. a devil or an evil spirit. **2.** someone who is annoying or who causes trouble. **3.** *Informal* someone who spends a lot of time or energy in playing a game or sport: *a soccer fiend.*

☑ SPELLING TIP *Tricky vowel sound*: the vowel pair *ie* has the sound 'ee'. This follows the rule that *i* comes before *e* except after *c*.

fierce *adjective*
1. wild or violent: *fierce storm*; *fierce expression.* **2.** very strong or intense: *fierce bidding at the auction.*
☐ **fiercely**, *adverb* –**fierceness**, *noun*

☑ SPELLING TIP *Tricky vowel sound*: the vowel sound is spelt *ier* (for the 'ear' sound). This follows the rule that *i* comes before *e* except after *c*. Also don't forget the *ce* ending.

fiery /*say* **fuy**-uh-ree/ *adjective* (**fierier**, **fieriest**) If something is **fiery**, it is **1.** like fire: *fiery temperatures.* **2.** showing strong feelings: *He gave a fiery speech*; *She has a fiery temper.*

fiesta /*say* fee-**es**-tuh/ *noun* a holiday or festival, especially for a religious occasion.

WORD HISTORY from Spanish

fifteen *noun*
1. a cardinal number, ten plus five (10+5). **2.** a symbol for this number, as 15 or XV.
☐ **fifteen**, *adjective* –**fifteenth**, *adjective*, *noun*

fifty *noun* (*plural* **fifties**)
1. a cardinal number, ten times five (10×5). **2.** a symbol for this number, as 50 or L. **3. fifties**, the numbers from 50 to 59 of a series, especially the years of someone's age or the years of a century.
☐ **fiftieth**, *adjective*, *noun* –**fifty**, *adjective*

fig *noun* a small, soft, pear-shaped fruit containing many tiny seeds which is eaten fresh or dried.

fight *noun*
1. a violent struggle between two or more people involving hitting, kicking, etc.: *Eventually the argument turned into a physical fight.* **2.** a struggle between two or more armed forces. **3.** a quarrel: *It's not worth having a fight over the last biscuit.* **4.** a struggle or determined effort to stop something or to get something: *the fight for higher wages.*
–*verb* (**fights**, **fighting**, **fought**, **has fought**) **5.** If someone **fights** someone, they take part in a violent physical struggle with them: *The two robbers fought over who would carry the money*; *The two countries have been fighting for years.* **6.** If a person in the armed services **fights**, they take part in an armed conflict: *He fought in Vietnam.* **7.** If people **fight**, they quarrel: *They are always fighting about something.* **8.** If you **fight** a need or a desire, you try to defeat it: *to fight feelings of desperation.*
☐ **fighter**, *noun*

SIMILAR WORDS (for definition 1) are **brawl**, **skirmish**, **scuffle** and **punch-up** (*Informal*). Note that a **skirmish** or a **scuffle** is a small fight; (for definition 2) **battle**; (for definition 3) **disagreement**, **row** and **squabble**; (for definition 4) **come to blows**, **grapple**, **scuffle** and **tussle**.

figment *noun* something that is imaginary: *The box of chocolates in the letterbox instead of mail was just a figment of her imagination.*

NOTE You now only find this word used in the phrase *figment of (someone's) imagination*.

figure *noun*
1. a symbol that stands for a number: *the figure 7.* **2.** an amount or sum of money: *People pay big figures for some cars.* **3.** a shape, form, or pattern: *She is aiming to have the perfect figure!*; *All over the curtains were figures of boats and planes.* **4.** a person or character: *Some important figures will attend the opening.*
–*verb* **5.** If somebody or something **figures** in a situation, they appear: *Our class figured prominently in the school concert.*
–*phrase* **6. figure out**, to understand or decide: *Can you figure out the answer to this problem?*

figurehead *noun*
1. someone who has an important position in an organisation but has no real power. **2.** a carved figure which decorates the bow of a sailing ship.

figure of speech *noun* an expression in which words are used out of their usual meaning for special effect, like a metaphor or simile.

figurine *noun* a small statue or model.

WORD HISTORY from an Italian word meaning 'little figure'

filament *noun* a very thin thread: *a filament of wool*; *a wire filament.*
☐ **filamentous**, *adjective*

file[1] *noun*
1. an orderly collection of papers or the folder they are kept in. **2.** an ordered collection of data stored on a computer. **3.** a line of people or things one behind the other: *We had to stand in single file as soon as we reached the museum.*
–*verb* **4.** If you **file** papers, you place them in collections where they belong.
–*phrase* **5. on file**, tidily arranged for easy use.

file[2] *noun*
1. a metal tool with a rough edge for smoothing or cutting metal and other materials.
–*verb* **2.** If you **file** something, you smooth or grind it down with a file.

filigree /*say* **fil**-uh-gree/ *noun* a delicate lace-like design made out of metal thread, especially used in jewellery: *ornate silver filigree.*
☐ **filigree**, *adjective* –**filigreed**, *adjective*

☑ SPELLING TIP *Single letter alert*: only one *l*. Also remember that the middle vowel sound in **filigree** is spelt with an *i*.

fill *verb*
1. If something **fills** or you **fill** something, it becomes full. The space inside it is taken up by something: *We turned on the hose and the pool soon filled up*; *The room filled with people.* **2.** If something **fills** you with an emotion, it makes you feel that way: *Seeing so many homeless people on the streets filled them with sadness.*
–*phrase* **3. fill in**, **a.** to complete by writing in the blank spaces: *to fill in a competition form.* **b.** to stand in for, or replace: *We need someone to fill in for our goal keeper.* **4. fill out**, **a.** to stretch: *The wind filled out the sails.* **b.** to become larger or grow fat: *Her figure has filled out lately.* **c.** to finish the details of: *to fill out a design.*
☐ **filling**, *noun*: *a filling in a tooth*; *a pie with a sweet filling.*

fillet *noun* a slice of fish, meat or chicken without the bone.

WORD HISTORY from a French word meaning 'little thread'

filly *noun* (*plural* **fillies**) a female horse less than four years old.

NOTE A young male horse is a **colt**.

film *noun*
1. a thin sheet or layer of something: *sheets of plastic film*; *A film of dust covered everything.* **2.** material which is sensitive to light and is used in a camera for taking photographs. **3.** a moving picture which is shown on a screen: *My favourite film is on tonight.*
–*verb* **4.** If you **film** something, you photograph it with a camera: *They were filming the people in the village.*

ANOTHER WORD (for definition 3) is **movie**.

filmy *adjective* (**filmier**, **filmiest**) light and transparent: *filmy curtains.*
☐ **filminess**, *noun*

filo pastry /*say* **fee**-loh, **fuy**-loh/ *noun* a paper-thin pastry made from flour and water, originating in Greek cooking.

filter *noun*
1. a device for straining liquids or air to remove unwanted material: *They use a filter for their drinking water.*
–*verb* **2.** If you **filter** a liquid or something similar, you remove unwanted material from it by passing it through a filter: *They filtered the honey through a cloth.*

filth *noun* something that is disgustingly dirty or offensive.
☐ **filthy**, *adjective* (**filthier**, **filthiest**)

fin *noun*
1. one of the flat thin bits on the body of a fish, used for moving through the water. **2.** a small triangular part on an aircraft or boat, used to help with steering or balancing.

final *adjective*
1. Something **final** is last or coming at the end: *The final performance is tonight so this is your last chance to see it.*
–*noun* **2.** the one at the end of a series, especially of races or competitions: *We are hoping to get to the final.*
☐ **finalise**, *verb* –**finalist**, *noun* –**finally**, *adverb* –**finality**, *noun*

ANOTHER SPELLING for **finalise** is **finalize**.

finale /*say* fuh-**nah**-lee/ *noun* the last part of a concert, opera or ballet.

finance *noun*
1. the management of money: *She wants to get into finance.* **2. finances**, money supplies or revenue: *Finances are a bit tight at the moment.*
–*verb* **3.** If somebody **finances** a project or an undertaking, they provide money for it: *The bank is financing the building.*
☐ **financial**, *adjective*

financial institution /*say* fuy-nan-shuhl ins-tuh-**tyooh**-shuhn/ *noun* an organisation, such as a bank, which manages money.

finch *noun* (*plural* **finches**) a type of small, often brightly coloured bird.

find *verb* (**finds**, **finding**, **found**, **has found**) To **find** something is to **1.** come upon it by chance or after a search: *to find my other red sock*; *to find a lost child.* **2.** discover or learn it: *She found why her money had been disappearing.*
–*phrase* **3. find out**, to discover by asking, searching or experiencing: *He wanted to find out everything about echidnas.* **4. find your feet**, to be able to act without help from other people.
☐ **find**, *noun*: *What a find!* –**finder**, *noun*

fine[1] *adjective*
1. Something **fine** is excellent or of high quality: *a fine horse.* **2.** If the weather is **fine**, it is sunny, or without rain. **3.** A **fine** object is very thin or delicate: *fabric so fine you can see through it.* **4.** If you feel **fine**, you feel well or healthy.
☐ **finely**, *adverb* –**fineness**, *noun*

fine[2] *noun*
1. a sum of money paid as a punishment for doing something wrong.
–*verb* **2.** If somebody **fines** you, they force you to pay money for something you have done wrong: *Dad was fined when he parked the car at a bus stop.*

finesse /*say* fuh-**nes**/ *noun* fine skill or clever management: *She handled the awkward situation with great finesse*; *the finesse of a champion gymnast.*

☑ SPELLING TIP *Single/double letter alert*: only one *n*, but two *s*'s. Also don't forget the silent *e* at the end. **Finesse** has an *-esse* ending because it comes from French.

finger *noun*
1. any one of the five, long, end parts of the hand, especially one that is not the thumb. **2.** something shaped like a finger: *fish fingers*; *a hole in the finger of a rubber glove.*
–*phrase* **3. burn your fingers**, to get hurt or suffer from something you have done. **4. not lift a finger**, to do nothing.

fingerprint *noun* the pattern made by the curved lines on the skin of the tips of your fingers.

finicky *adjective*
1. very fussy or choosy: *If you are too finicky, you will never finish the job!* **2.** full of small, unimportant detail: *Dad said that painting the lattice fence would be a very finicky job.*

finish *verb*
1. When something **finishes**, it comes to an end: *The performance will finish at about 10 o'clock.* **2.** When you **finish** something, you bring it to an end, or you complete it: *I'll stop working when I've finished this page.* **3.** When you **finish** food or drink, you consume all of it. **4.** *Informal* If something **finishes** you, it uses up all your energy or money: *That race has finished me for the day.*
–*noun* **5.** the end. **6.** the surface layer of wood or metal or the substance put on it: *She polished the furniture to a sparkling finish.*

SIMILAR WORDS (for definition 1) are **conclude**, **stop**, **cease** and **terminate**.

finite /*say* **fuy**-nuyt/ *adjective* A **finite** quantity has limits which can be measured or counted: *I only have a finite amount of patience.*
☐ **finitely**, *adverb* –**finiteness**, *noun*

THE OPPOSITE is **infinite**.

fiord /*say* **fee**-awd/ *noun* See **fjord**.

fir *noun* a tree, like a traditional European Christmas tree, which has needle-like leaves and produces cones.

☑ SPELLING TIP Don't confuse the spelling of **fir** with **fur** which sounds the same. **Fur** is the hair on an animal.

fire *noun*
1. the heat, light and flames produced by burning: *The fire was raging out of control.* **2.** a mass of burning material: *We started a fire to cook our sausages.* **3.** the shooting of guns: *to open fire.*
–*verb* **4.** To **fire** is to shoot: *Stop or I'll fire!* **5.** If someone is **fired**, they are dismissed from their job: *Be careful or you'll be fired.* **6.** If something **fires** you, it excites you: *fired with optimism.*
–*phrase* **7. catch fire**, to start burning. **8. on fire**, burning: *The house is on fire!* **9. play with fire**, to play with something dangerous in a careless way. **10. under fire**, **a.** open to or in the line of enemy fire. **b.** under attack or suffering criticism from someone.

firearm *noun* any type of gun.

firebreak *noun* a strip of land which has been cleared of grass and trees to stop a fire from spreading.

firecracker *noun* a particular kind of firework, especially one which makes a loud noise.

firefighter *noun* a person whose job is to put out or prevent fires.

fireplace *noun* an open place, built of brick or stone, for lighting fires in.

fireproof *adjective* not able to be burnt or set on fire.

fireworks *plural noun* **1.** containers filled with a powder that burns or explodes, giving out brightly coloured sparks. **2.** *Informal* a fit of anger or bad temper: *There were fireworks when they saw what had happened to the car.*

firm[1] *adjective*
1. solid, hard, or stiff. **2.** not moving or shaking: *firm foundations.* **3.** strong, clear, and unchanging: *firm beliefs*; *a firm conviction.*
☐ **firm**, *adverb*: *to stand firm.* –**firmness**, *noun* –**firmly**, *adverb*

firm[2] *noun* a business company.

first *adjective*
1. coming before all others in time, order or importance: *The first pup was born a few minutes ago.*
–*adverb* **2.** before anyone or anything else in time, order or importance: *This parcel will be delivered first.* **3.** for the first time: *We first saw her at the oval.*
–*phrase* **4. first up**, at the first attempt.
☐ **first**, *noun* –**firstly**, *adverb*

THE OPPOSITE is **last**[1].

first aid *noun* emergency treatment given to someone hurt in an accident or someone who suddenly becomes sick.

first-class *adjective*
1. of the best quality, best equipped or most expensive: *a first-class location for a holiday*; *the first-class section of a plane.*
–*adverb* **2.** in a seat in the most expensive and comfortable section in a vehicle or plane: *She insists on travelling first-class.*

firsthand *adverb* directly from the source: *Come along and learn about the different boats firsthand.*
☐ **firsthand**, *adjective*: *firsthand experience.*

fish *noun* (*plural* **fish** *or* **fishes**)
1. a cold-blooded animal which lives in water, breathes through gills, swims by means of fins and has scales on its body.
–*verb* **2.** If somebody **fishes**, they try to catch fish by using a line or a net.
☐ **fishing**, *noun*

fisherman *noun* (*plural* **fishermen**) someone who fishes, either as a job or for pleasure.

OTHER WORDS for someone who fishes for pleasure are **fisher** or **angler**.

fishy *adjective* (**fishier**, **fishiest**)
1. A **fishy** smell or taste is like the smell or taste of fish. **2.** *Informal* A **fishy** story or situation is unreliable and not likely to have happened.

fissure /*say* **fish**-uh/ *noun* a crack or split: *a fissure in the cliff.*

fist *noun* the hand when the fingers are closed tightly into the palm.
☐ **fistful**, *noun*

fit[1] *adjective* (**fitter**, **fittest**)
1. If something is **fit**, it is suitable or good enough: *Is this suit fit for the ceremony?* **2.** Something **fit** is right or proper: *The teacher said it was fit that Emma should apologise to Sam for her rudeness.* **3.** A **fit** person is healthy and in good physical condition.
–*verb* (**fits**, **fitting**, **fitted**, **has fitted**) **4.** If something **fits**, it is suitable or the right size or shape. **5.** To **fit** something is to make or have space for: *We can fit a few more chairs in.*
–*phrase* **6. fit in**, to be or become suited: *Do you think this colour fits in with the room?* **7. fit out**, to provide with clothing or equipment.
–*noun* **8.** the way in which something fits: *It's not a very good fit – the waist is too loose.*
☐ **fitter**, *noun* –**fitness**, *noun*

fit[2] *noun*
1. a short, sudden experience of some emotion or slight illness: *a fit of temper*; *a fit of sneezing.* **2.** a sudden sickness in which someone's body twists uncontrollably and they sometimes become unconscious.

fitting *adjective* suitable or right: *The celebration was a fitting acknowledgement of all their hard work.*
☐ **fittingly**, *adverb*

five *noun*
1. a cardinal number, four plus one (4 + 1). **2.** the symbol for this number, as 5 or V.
☐ **fifth**, *adjective*, *noun* –**five**, *adjective*

fix *verb*
1. If you **fix** something, you make it so that it cannot move, often by fastening it to something else. **2.** If you **fix** your eyes, attention or mind on something, you look at it or think about it steadily: *You have to fix your mind on what you want to achieve.* **3.** If you **fix** something, you decide on it or settle it: *Let's fix a date for the next meeting now.* **4.** If you **fix** something that is broken, you make it work properly again.
–*noun* **5.** *Informal* a difficult situation: *Now you've really got yourself into a fix.*
–*phrase* **6. fix on**, to decide on. **7. fix up**, **a.** to arrange properly: *Please fix up the books on your*

desk. **b.** to put right: *This medicine will soon fix you up.*
☐ **fixed**, *adjective* –**fixedly**, *adverb* –**fixer**, *noun*

fixture *noun*
1. something fixed in place, especially in a house or other building. **2.** a sporting event that is to be held on a particular date.

fizz *verb* If a liquid **fizzes**, it releases a lot of tiny bubbles of gas: *If you put ice-cream in lemonade, it fizzes a lot.*
☐ **fizz**, *noun* –**fizzy**, *adjective* (**fizzier**, **fizziest**)

fizzle *verb*
1. If something like a fire **fizzles**, it goes out. –*phrase* **2. fizzle out**, *Informal* to fail after a good start: *Their enthusiasm just fizzled out.*
☐ **fizzle**, *noun*: *The party was a bit of a fizzle.*

fjord /*say* **fee**-awd/ *noun* a deep, narrow inlet of the sea with steep cliffs on each side: *I would love to see the fjords of Norway.*

ANOTHER SPELLING is **fiord.**

flabbergasted *adjective* very surprised: *She was flabbergasted by how high she could jump when she tried.*

A SIMILAR WORD is **astounded.**

flabby *adjective* (**flabbier**, **flabbiest**) having soft fatty flesh: *a flabby stomach.*
☐ **flabbily**, *adverb* –**flabbiness**, *noun*

flag[1] *noun* a piece of cloth with a particular design used as a symbol of a country or an organisation, or as a signal.

flag[2] *verb* (**flags**, **flagging**, **flagged**, **has flagged**) If people **flag**, they grow weak or tired: *The shop assistant was flagging at the end of the big sale day.*

flagon *noun* a large bottle, usually for wine.

flagrant /*say* **flay**-gruhnt/ *adjective* obvious in a shameless way: *a flagrant insult*; *a flagrant breach of the law.*
☐ **flagrancy**, *noun* –**flagrantly**, *adverb*

WORD HISTORY from a Latin word meaning 'blazing' or 'burning'

flair *noun*
1. natural talent: *He has a flair for playing the guitar.* **2.** stylish appearance: *The new model car has plenty of flair.*

☑ SPELLING TIP Don't confuse the spelling of **flair** with **flare** which sounds the same. A **flare** is a kind of bright light.

flake[1] *noun*
1. a small, flat, thin piece of anything: *a flake of paint*; *a flake of plaster.*
–*verb* **2.** If something **flakes**, small flat pieces of it peel off: *The paint is flaking off the wall.* **3.** *Informal* If you **flake**, you lie down or fall asleep from tiredness: *They flaked at the end of the hike.*
☐ **flaky**, *adjective* (**flakier**, **flakiest**) –**flakiness**, *noun* –**flakily**, *adverb*

flake[2] *noun* shark meat sold as food.

flamboyant *adjective* dazzlingly bright and showy.
☐ **flamboyance**, *noun* –**flamboyantly**, *adverb*

WORD HISTORY from a French word meaning 'small flame'

☑ SPELLING TIP If you rap this word out as *flam+boy+ant*, you should not have trouble with the spelling – especially if you also remember that it contains both a *boy* and an *ant*.

flame *noun*
1. a tongue of fire: *The parchment was devoured by the flames.*
–*verb* **2.** If something **flames**, it glows or burns like the flames of a fire: *Her face flamed with embarrassment.*

flameproof *adjective*
1. not easily burnt: *flameproof baby clothing.*
2. safe for use over flames: *a flameproof glass casserole dish.*

flamingo *noun* (*plural* **flamingos** *or* **flamingoes**) a water bird with a very long neck, long legs and dark pink feathers.

flammable *adjective* easily set on fire.

NOTE Another word for this is **inflammable**, but it is not used very much nowadays. Many people took it to mean *not* easily set on fire because *in-* at the beginning of a word often does mean 'not', as in *inactive*. This confusion could be dangerous, so it was decided to use **flammable** to mean easily set on fire and **nonflammable** as its opposite, to mean not likely to burn easily.

☑ SPELLING TIP The basic meaning of this word is 'able to be flamed'. When you think of this, you have to remember that *flame* has doubled its *m* and lost its *e* before adding the *-able* suffix.

flan *noun* a large shallow pie without a top which can have different kinds of filling: *a fruit flan.*

flank *noun*
1. the side of an animal between the ribs and hip.
2. the side of anything.
–*verb* **3.** If something is **flanked** by people or things, those things are to the side of it: *The road was flanked by trees*; *The prime minister was flanked by security guards.*

flannel *noun*
1. a warm soft cloth, usually made of wool: *trousers of grey flannel.* **2.** a small piece of soft cloth for washing your face or body.

OTHER TERMS (for definition 2) are **washer**, **face washer**, and **face cloth**.

flannelette *noun* a cotton cloth treated on one side to look and feel like flannel.

> ☑ SPELLING TIP *Double/single letter alert*: double *n* and double *t*, but only one *l*. **Flannelette** is made up of *flannel* and the suffix *-ette* which comes from French and means 'small' or 'feminine' or, as in this case, is used in the name of products that imitate this material. Think of other words with this ending such as *serviette*.

flannel flower *noun* an Australian plant with light-cream flowers and leaves that feel like flannel.

flap *verb* (**flaps**, **flapping**, **flapped**, **has flapped**)
1. If something **flaps**, it moves loosely up and down or from side to side: *The canvas kept flapping in the wind.*
–*noun* **2.** something flat and thin that is joined to something else on one side only and hangs loose: *The tent had a flap over the window to block the sun out.*

flare *verb*
1. If something **flares**, it suddenly burns more fiercely: *The candle flared as we held the paper to the flame.* **2.** If something **flares**, it is wider in one part than another: *Skirts which flare at the bottom are fashionable this year.*
–*noun* **3.** a bright light used as a signal.
–*phrase* **4. flare up**, **a.** to become more intense. **b.** to lose your temper.

> ☑ SPELLING TIP Don't confuse the spelling of **flare** with **flair** which sounds the same. **Flair** is natural talent.

flash *noun*
1. a sudden short burst of flame or light: *a sudden flash of light.* **2.** a short moment: *The answer came back in a flash.* **3.** a short, important piece of news on radio or television.
–*verb* **4.** If a light **flashes** or you **flash** a light, it shines brightly and suddenly: *They flashed their torches up into the trees.* **5.** If somebody or something **flashes**, they move quickly: *He flashed in and out before we had time to talk to him.*

flashback *noun* a part of a film or story that shows an event that happened at an earlier time.

flashforward *noun* a part of a film or story that is set in a time further in the future than the rest of the action: *In the flashforward she was a rich old woman, so I was curious to discover how she escaped the poverty of her childhood.*

flashlight *noun*
1. a bulb that gives a flash of very bright light, used when taking photographs inside or at night. **2.** a torch.

flask *noun* a small, often flat bottle.

flat[1] *adjective*
1. even or smooth: *We put the trampoline up on a flat area of our yard.* **2.** lying spread out: *The boxer was flat on the canvas.* **3.** not high: *Do you want flat heels or high heels?* **4.** emptied of air: *My bike tyre is flat – where's the pump?* **5.** clear and absolute: *a flat denial.* **6.** boring: *The evening was very flat – we couldn't wait for it to end.* **7.** no longer bubbly or fizzy: *flat lemonade.* **8.** not shiny: *a flat finish.*
–*adverb* **9.** in a flat position: *Lay the picnic cloth flat on the grass.*
–*noun* **10.** in music, **a.** a note played one semitone below the given note. **b.** the music sign '♭' which lowers a note by a semitone when it is placed before it. **c.** produced lower than it should be: *Her singing was flat.*
–*phrase* **11. fall flat**, to fail: *The party fell flat.* **12. flat out**, *Informal* **a.** as fast or hard as possible. **b.** very busy.
☐ **flat**, *noun* –**flatly**, *adverb* –**flatness**, *noun* –**flatten**, *verb*

> THE OPPOSITE (of definition 10) is **sharp** (definition 10).

flat[2] *noun* a group of rooms for living in, usually part of a larger building.

> SIMILAR WORDS are **unit**, **home unit**, **apartment** and **town house**. Note that sometimes the use of the word **apartment** can suggest a flat that is expensive or in a fashionable area. A **town house** is one of a block of houses, all similar, usually joined together and usually on two levels.

flat screen *noun* a very thin, flat screen for a television set.

flatter *verb* If you **flatter** someone, you say good things about them. Sometimes what you say may not be sincere. You may be doing this to get the person to do something you want.
☐ **flattered**, *adjective* –**flatterer**, *noun* –**flattering**, *adjective* –**flattery**, *noun*

flaunt /*say* flawnt/ *verb* If you **flaunt** something, you show it off boldly: *He annoyed them by flaunting his ability to beat them in any test.*

flautist /*say* **flaw**-tuhst/ *noun* someone who plays the flute.

> WORD HISTORY from an Italian word meaning 'flute'

flavour *noun*
1. taste, especially the special taste that something has: *aniseed flavour*; *caramel flavour.* **2.** the nature or quality of something: *The music had an Asian flavour.*
–*verb* **3.** If you **flavour** food or drink, you add something to make it taste a particular way: *We flavour our milk drinks with chocolate or strawberry.*
☐ **flavoured**, *adjective* –**flavouring**, *noun*

> ANOTHER SPELLING is **flavor**.

flaw *noun*
1. a fault: *Our club's major flaw is that it is disorganised*; *There is a flaw in the material of this dress*; *a flaw in his reasoning.*
–*verb* 2. If a thing **flaws** something that it is part of, it spoils it: *It's a good film but it's flawed by being too long.*
☐ **flawed**, *adjective* –**flawless**, *adjective*

flax *noun* a plant with narrow leaves and blue flowers, grown for its fibre which is made into linen, and for its seeds which contain oil.

flea *noun* a small wingless insect which moves by jumping and which sucks blood from animals.

fleck *noun* a spot or small patch of something.
☐ **flecked**, *adjective*

fledgling *noun*
1. a young bird that has just become able to fly. 2. someone who is young or new to something.

ANOTHER SPELLING is **fledgeling**.

flee *verb* (**flees**, **fleeing**, **fled**, **has fled**) To **flee** is to run away or escape.

fleece *noun* the coat of wool that covers a sheep or similar animal.
☐ **fleecy**, *adjective* (**fleecier**, **fleeciest**) –**fleeciness**, *noun*

fleet[1] *noun*
1. a large group of naval ships, usually under the command of one officer. 2. a group of boats, aeroplanes or vehicles: *a fleet of buses.*

COMPARE definition 1 with **flotilla**.

fleet[2] *adjective* very fast or swift.

NOTE This word is now mainly used in the phrase *fleet of foot* and as part of the adjective *fleet-footed.*

fleeting *adjective* very brief: *I caught only a fleeting glimpse of him as he rushed past.*
☐ **fleetingly**, *adverb*

flesh *noun*
1. the soft part of an animal body, which is made up of fat and muscle. 2. the human body when you think of it as separate from the mind or the spirit: *Humans are more than just flesh and bones.* 3. the soft part of a fruit or vegetable.
–*phrase* 4. **in the flesh**, **a.** alive. **b.** in person: *I saw my favourite TV star in the flesh.*
☐ **fleshy**, *adjective*

flex *verb*
1. If you **flex** your muscles, you bend or stretch them for exercise.
–*noun* 2. a cord containing an electric wire.

flexible *adjective*
1. easily bent or stretched: *a flexible twig.* 2. able to be changed easily: *The date for the party is flexible.*
☐ **flexibility**, *noun* –**flexibly**, *adverb*

SIMILAR WORDS (for definition 1) are **pliable** and **supple**.

flexitime *noun* an arrangement in which workers can choose their starting and finishing times, as long as they work the right number of hours altogether.

flick *noun*
1. a sudden light blow: *a flick of the whip*; *She brushed it off with a flick of her wrist.*
–*verb* 2. If something **flicks** in a particular direction, it moves in a sudden, quick movement: *The lizard's tongue flicked at the fly*; *She flicked the bit of dust off her sleeve.* 3. If someone **flicks** something like a switch, they turn it on or off.

flicker *verb*
1. If a flame **flickers**, it burns unsteadily. 2. If a light or image **flickers**, it is unsteady. It moves about slightly or varies in intensity: *Our shadows flickered on the cave walls.*

flight[1] *noun*
1. an act of flying or the way in which something flies: *supersonic flight.* 2. a number of things flying together: *a flight of wild geese.* 3. a journey by aeroplane: *The flight took four hours.* 4. a series of steps or stairs: *He fell down four flights.*

flight[2] *noun*
1. a running away.
–*phrase* 2. **put to flight**, to force to run away: *to put an invading army to flight.* 3. **take flight**, to run away.

flight attendant *noun* a person who works on a plane looking after the passengers.

flighty *adjective* (**flightier**, **flightiest**) often changing attitudes, opinions or feelings: *You can't rely on her – she's too flighty!*
☐ **flightiness**, *noun*

A SIMILAR WORD is **frivolous**.

flimsy *adjective* (**flimsier**, **flimsiest**)
1. Something **flimsy** is not strongly made: *a flimsy structure.* 2. A **flimsy** argument or excuse is weak or not carefully thought out: *The dog ate your homework? That's a flimsy excuse!*
☐ **flimsiness**, *noun*

flinch *verb* To **flinch** is to draw back from something dangerous, difficult, or unpleasant: *We flinched when we saw the raging river we had to cross.*

fling *verb* (**flings**, **flinging**, **flung**, **has flung**)
1. To **fling** something is to throw it, usually forcefully or angrily: *The baby flung his food on the floor.*
–*noun* 2. a time of pleasure or fun: *Let's have a last fling before the exams.* 3. an attempt or try: *I will have one more fling at jumping that height.*

flint *noun* a hard kind of stone which gives off sparks when hit with something hard.
☐ **flinty**, *adjective*

flip *verb* (**flips**, **flipping**, **flipped**, **has flipped**)
1. If you **flip** something, you move or throw it with a quick sudden movement of your hand: *Can you flip the pancake over?*; *Flip the coin to see who goes first.* **2.** If you **flip through** something like a book, you turn the pages over quickly: *She flipped through the magazine while she was waiting.*

flippant *adjective* not suitably serious: *Please do not make flippant remarks about my singing.*
☐ **flippancy**, *noun* –**flippantly**, *adverb*

> ☑ SPELLING TIP *Double letter alert*: double *p*. Also remember that the ending is spelt *ant* (not *ent*).

flipper *noun*
1. the broad flat limb of an animal such as a seal or whale that is used for swimming. **2.** a piece of rubber shaped like a flipper and worn on your foot to help in swimming.

flirt *verb* To **flirt** is to show romantic interest in someone, but not in a serious way.
☐ **flirt**, *noun* –**flirtation**, *noun* –**flirtatious**, *adjective*

flit *verb* (**flits**, **flitting**, **flitted**, **has flitted**) When something small and light **flits**, it moves quickly: *The butterflies were flitting from flower to flower.*

float *verb* To **float** is to **1.** rest or move gently on the top of a liquid: *He swam and then floated on his back.* **2.** move freely and easily: *We just floated through the day.*
–*noun* **3.** something that floats. **4.** a base on wheels that carries a display in a procession. **5.** a covered van for carrying horses.

flock *noun* a number of animals of the same kind that live and feed together, especially sheep and birds.

floe *noun* a large piece of ice floating on the sea.

flog *verb* (**flogs**, **flogging**, **flogged**, **has flogged**) To **flog** someone is to beat them hard with a whip or stick.

flood /*say* flud/ *noun*
1. a great amount of water, especially over land which is usually dry: *The flood has caused the river to rise.* **2.** any great pouring out: *a flood of angry words*; *a flood of good wishes.*
–*verb* **3.** If something **floods**, it overflows or covers with a flood: *The river flooded and covered the land beside it*; *The rains flooded the crops*; *The bath flooded because we left the taps on.*

> ☑ SPELLING TIP *Tricky vowel sound*: remember the *oo* spelling. Even though **flood** rhymes with *mud* (and there is a lot of mud after a flood), the spelling is different. Another familiar word with the *oo* spelling for the same sound is *blood*.

floodlight *noun*
1. an artificial light that gives out a strong beam.
–*verb* (**floodlights**, **floodlighting**, **floodlit**, **has floodlit**) **2.** If you **floodlight** an area or a building, you light it up with a floodlight: *We will floodlight the backyard for the party.*

flood-proof *verb*
1. If you **flood-proof** something, you protect it from flooding, as by building levees, walls, etc.
–*adjective* **2.** having to do with a place protected in such a way: *a flood-proof building.*

floor *noun*
1. the lowest flat part of a room or other place: *They fell to the floor*; *There were papers all over the floor of the car.* **2.** one of the different levels of a building: *Vanda's office is on the 42nd floor.*
–*verb* **3.** *Informal* If somebody **floors** an opponent, they beat or defeat them: *The man floored his attacker with a well-aimed punch.*

> ANOTHER WORD (for definition 2) is **storey**.

flop *verb* (**flops**, **flopping**, **flopped**, **has flopped**)
1. To **flop** onto or into something is to fall or drop down onto it suddenly, especially with a noise: *He flopped into a chair.*
–*noun* **2.** *Rather informal* something that is a failure: *The film was a complete flop.*
☐ **floppy**, *adjective*: *a floppy hat.* –**floppiness**, *noun* –**floppily**, *adverb*

floppy disk *noun* a flat plastic disk with a magnetic coating, used for storing data and moving it from one computer to another, now less popular than storage devices with more capacity, such as USB drives, external hard drives, etc.

> COMPARE this with **hard disk**.

flora *noun* the plants of a particular area or period of time.

> COMPARE this with **fauna**.
> WORD HISTORY named after *Flora*, the Roman goddess of flowers

floral /*say* **flo**-ruhl, **flaw**-ruhl/ *adjective* having to do with or made of flowers.

florid *adjective*
1. red-coloured: *a florid face under a battered canvas hat.* **2.** overly showy or flowery: *He showered her with florid praise*; *florid poetry.*

> A SIMILAR WORD (for definition 1) is **ruddy**; (for definition 2) **ornate**.
> WORD HISTORY from a Latin word meaning 'flowery'

florist *noun* someone who arranges and sells flowers.

floss *noun* a fine thread: *dental floss.*

flotilla *noun*
1. in the navy, a small fleet or group of smaller ships, sometimes part of a larger fleet and usually

of the same type, for instance, frigates, submarines, etc. **2.** a small fleet of any vessels.

COMPARE this with **fleet**[1].

☑ SPELLING TIP *Single/double letter alert*: only one *t* but a double *l*.

flounce[1] *verb* to move with an impatient or angry jerk of your body: *Belinda flounced from the room.*
☐ **flounce**, *noun*

flounce[2] *noun* a strip of material gathered together and used to decorate the bottom of a skirt or other clothing.
☐ **flouncing**, *noun* –**flouncy**, *adjective*

flounder[1] *verb*
1. If someone or something **flounders**, they struggle along with stumbling movements: *They floundered across the slippery rocks trying to get away from the waves.* **2.** If someone is **floundering**, they struggle helplessly because of embarrassment or confusion: *It was clear she was floundering and did not know what to say.*

☑ DO NOT CONFUSE the meaning of this word with **founder**[2]. When a ship **founders**, it sinks. When a horse **founders**, it goes lame.

flounder[2] *noun* (*plural* **flounder**) a kind of fish, eaten as food.

flour *noun* a fine powder made from rice, wheat, or other grain and used in cooking.
☐ **floury**, *adjective* (**flourier**, **flouriest**)

☑ SPELLING TIP Don't confuse the spelling of **flour** with **flower** which sounds the same. A **flower** is part of a plant.

flourish /*say* **flu**-rish/ *verb*
1. If a plant or animal **flourishes**, it grows well because the conditions it lives in are favourable: *That palm is really flourishing.* **2.** If something **flourishes**, it is active and successful: *Business is flourishing.* **3.** To **flourish** something is to wave it about in a showy way.
–*noun* **4.** a waving movement: *He gave a flourish of his sword.* **5.** anything used for show, such as a curve used to decorate writing.
☐ **flourishing**, *adjective*

A SIMILAR WORD (for definitions 1 and 2) is **thrive**; (for definition 3) **brandish**.
WORD HISTORY from a Latin word meaning 'bloom'

flout /*say* flowt/ *verb* If you **flout** rules or traditional ways, you do not obey or show respect for them: *She is the kind of person who likes to flout rules, just to show she is different.*
☐ **flouter**, *noun*

flow *verb*
1. If something like a fluid or a gas **flows**, it moves along in a stream: *The water was flowing quickly over the rocks.* **2.** If words or thoughts **flow**, they move along continuously and smoothly like a stream: *Words flowed easily for her.* **3.** If something like clothes or hair **flow**, they fall or hang loosely: *The long veil flowed behind her.*
☐ **flow**, *noun* –**flowing**, *adjective*

flow chart *noun* a diagram showing how something works or develops, stage by stage.

flower *noun*
1. the blossom of a plant, or that part which produces the seed.
–*verb* **2.** When a plant **flowers**, it produces flowers: *Daffodils flower in the winter.*

☑ SPELLING TIP Don't confuse **flower** with **flour** which sounds the same. **Flour** is the powder made from wheat for use in cooking.

flowerbed *noun* a small plot of ground in a garden where we plant and grow flowers.

flowery *adjective* (**flowerier**, **floweriest**)
1. covered with flowers. **2.** using a lot of fancy words: *We could have done without the flowery introduction!*
☐ **floweriness**, *noun*

flu *noun* See **influenza**.

fluctuate /*say* **fluk**-chooh-ayt/ *verb* If something **fluctuates**, it changes all the time: *The number of people at the beach fluctuates depending on the weather.*
☐ **fluctuation**, *noun*

flue /*say* flooh/ *noun* a tube, pipe or any space for air, gas or smoke to pass through.

fluent /*say* **flooh**-uhnt/ *adjective*
1. flowing smoothly and easily: *She speaks fluent French.* **2.** able to speak easily: *I wish I was fluent in German.*

☑ SPELLING TIP Remember that the beginning of **fluent** is spelt *flu* (giving the sound of 'flooh') – although you probably are not able to speak **fluently** when you have the flu! In fact, there is a connection because both **fluent** and *flu* come from *fluens*, a Latin word meaning 'flowing'.

fluff *noun* light, soft, tiny pieces from materials like cotton or wool: *Brush the fluff off your jacket.*
☐ **fluffy**, *adjective* (**fluffier**, **fluffiest**)

fluid *noun*
1. a substance that can flow, either a liquid or a gas.
–*adjective* **2.** changing easily or not fixed: *Our plans are quite fluid at the moment.*
☐ **fluidity**, *noun*

fluke *Informal*
–*noun* **1.** any accidental advantage or piece of good luck: *No, I'm not smart – it was a fluke!*

–*verb* **2.** If you **fluke** something, you are accidentally successful: *We fluked really good seats at the stadium.*
☐ **fluky**, *adjective* (**flukier**, **flukiest**)

fluorescent /*say* floo-uh-**res**-uhnt, fluh-**res**-uhnt/ *adjective* If something is **fluorescent**, it gives off a bright light when energy passes through it or light hits it: *fluorescent paint*; *a fluorescent sign.*
☐ **fluorescence**, *noun*

☑ SPELLING TIP *Silent letter alert*: don't forget the *fluo* spelling at the start of **fluorescent** (even though some people say it just as 'fluh' so you cannot hear that there are really two vowels – a *u* and an *o*). Also remember the silent *c* after the *s*, just like in the word *scent*.

fluoride /*say* **floo**-uh-ruyd, **flooh**-ruyd/ *noun* a chemical which protects your teeth from decay.
☐ **fluoridate**, *verb* –**fluoride**, *adjective*

☑ SPELLING TIP *Silent letter alert*: don't forget the *fluo* spelling at the start of **fluoride** (even though some people say it just as 'flooh' so you cannot hear that there are really two vowels – a *u* and an *o*).

fluoro /*say* **flooh**-roh/ *adjective* a very bright colour: *Maria's determined to get people's attention – look at those fluoro pants!*

NOTE This word is a short way of saying **fluorescent**.

flurry *noun* sudden excitement or confused movement: *a flurry of wind*; *a flurry of activity.*

flush[1] *verb*
1. If someone **flushes**, they become red in the face. **2.** To **flush** something is to flood it with water, especially for cleaning: *to flush the area with sterile water.*
☐ **flush**, *noun*

flush[2] *adjective* To be **flush** is to be even or level: *The lines of bricks aren't flush – that line sticks out.*
☐ **flush**, *adverb*: *Can you make them flush?*

fluster *verb* To **fluster** someone is to make them nervous or confused.
☐ **fluster**, *noun*

flute *noun* a musical wind instrument played by blowing across a hole near one of its ends.

WORD HISTORY from a Latin word meaning 'blown'

flutter *verb*
1. If something **flutters** or you **flutter** something, it makes small, quick movements from side to side or up and down: *The wings of the baby birds fluttered in their first attempt to leave the nest*; *She fluttered her scarf to attract their attention.* **2.** If your heart **flutters**, it does not beat in a regular way. You can use this phrase to describe how you feel when you are nervous: *His heart fluttered as his turn to perform came closer.*
☐ **flutter**, *noun*

fly[1] *verb* (**flies**, **flying**, **flew**, **has flown**)
1. If an aircraft or a bird **flies**, it moves through the air. **2.** If you **fly** somewhere, you go there in an aircraft: *They flew to Tasmania.* **3.** If someone **flies** an aircraft, they control its movement through the air: *She was the first woman to fly across the Pacific.* **4.** You can say that a loose object **flies** if it moves about freely in the air: *Her hair was flying about in the breeze.* **5.** You can say that someone or something **flies** in a particular direction if they move there very quickly or with force: *The runner flew down the track.*
–*noun* (*plural* **flies**) **6.** a flat thin bit of material hiding a zipper in clothing, especially in trousers. **7.** a piece of material that forms the door or outer roof of a tent.
–*phrase* **8. fly at**, to attack. **9. let fly**, **a.** to throw. **b.** *Informal* to allow to flow out, especially an attack of words: *He lost his temper and really let fly.*

fly[2] *noun* (*plural* **flies**)
1. an insect with two wings. **2.** a hook for fishing that is made to look like an insect.

flying fox *noun*
1. a large bat which has a foxlike head and feeds on fruit and blossoms. **2.** a machine which is worked by an overhead cable and is used to carry you over water or rough land.

flying saucer *noun* a disc-shaped flying object said to be a spaceship from outer space.

ANOTHER TERM for this is **UFO** which is short for *unidentified flying object*.

flyleaf *noun* (*plural* **flyleaves**) a blank page at the beginning or end of a book.

foal *noun* a young horse or donkey under one year of age, either male or female.

foam *noun*
1. a collection of very small bubbles. **2.** a spongy material made from plastic or rubber with tiny air holes all through it.
–*verb* **3.** If something **foams**, it produces foam or froth: *The drink foamed and became fizzy when I shook the bottle.*
☐ **foamy**, *adjective*

focus /*say* **foh**-kuhs/ *noun* (*plural* **focuses** *or* **foci** /*say* **foh**-kuy/)
1. a point at which rays of light meet after they have been reflected or bent. **2.** the point at which a lens gets a clear, sharp picture: *Let me know when we are in focus and then I'll start smiling!* **3.** the main point of interest or attraction: *The focus of everybody's attention was on the bright red front door.*
–*verb* (**focuses** *or* **focusses**, **focusing** *or* **focussing**, **focused** *or* **focussed**, **has focused** *or* **has focussed**) **4.** If you **focus** a camera, you change the lens so that the image is made clear. **5.** If you **focus** rays of light, you bring them together to a point: *If you focus the rays of the sun*

to a point on the paper, it will burn. **6.** If you **focus on** something, you give it all your attention.

fodder *noun* plants that cattle and horses eat.

foe *noun* an enemy.

foetus */say* **fee**-tuhs/ *noun* an unborn child or animal in the later months of pregnancy.
□ **foetal**, *adjective*

ANOTHER SPELLING is **fetus**.
COMPARE this with **embryo**.

fog *noun*
1. a cloud-like layer that forms close to the earth's surface and is made up of drops of water.
–*verb* (**fogs**, **fogging**, **fogged**, **has fogged**) **2.** If something **fogs up**, it becomes covered or obscured by fog: *The windows of the car fogged up and we couldn't see through them.*
□ **foggy**, *adjective*

fogey */say* **foh**-gee/ *noun* (*plural* **fogies**) an old-fashioned person.

ANOTHER SPELLING is **fogy**.

foghorn *noun* a loud horn or siren used for warning ships in foggy weather.

foible */say* **foy**-buhl/ *noun* a slight weakness in someone's character: *Her major foible is spending too much time thinking about how she looks.*

foil[1] *verb* To **foil** someone or something is to stop them from being successful: *She foiled their plans by accessing the computer files.*

foil[2] *noun*
1. metal which has been beaten, hammered or rolled out into very thin sheets: *gold foil*; *silver foil.* **2.** anything that shows up the qualities of something else in comparison with it: *His serious nature is a perfect foil to her high spirits.*

foil[3] *noun* a light thin sword with a button on the point which prevents injury in fencing.

foist *verb* If someone **foists** things onto another person, they try to make that person take it or do it, although he or she does not want to: *She tried to foist her old clothes onto me*; *He foisted the most boring part of the work on to me.*

fold[2] *noun* a closed-off pen for keeping animals like sheep.

fold[1] *verb*
1. If you **fold** something, you bend it over on itself: *They folded the sheets off the line.* **2.** To **fold** your arms is to cross them. **3.** If something **folds** or you can **fold** it, it is able to be bent over on itself: *Does this chair fold flat?*; *Fold the ironing board away.*
–*noun* **4.** a part that is folded or a layer of something folded. **5.** a line made by folding.

folder *noun*
1. a holder or cover for papers, usually made of a folded sheet of cardboard. **2.** on a computer, a group of files stored together.

foliage */say* **foh**-lee-ij/ *noun* the leaves of a plant.

☑ SPELLING TIP *Single letter alert*: only one *l*. Also remember that it ends with *age* (although it sounds like 'ij')

folk */rhymes with* coke/ *noun*
1. people in general. **2.** the people of a particular group: *City folk and country folk should be friends.* **3.** See **folk music** (definition 2). **4. folks**, *Rather informal* someone's own family, especially their parents: *Come home and meet my folks.*
□ **folk**, *adjective*: *folk music.*

☑ SPELLING TIP Remember the *olk* spelling for the 'ohk' sound. You cannot hear the *l* when you say this word.

folklore */say* **fohk**-law/ *noun* the beliefs, stories and customs of a people or a tribe passed down from each age group to the next.

folk music *noun*
1. a traditional style of music, originating and handed down among a people. **2.** music originating in America in the 1940s and 1950s, with traditional instruments and songs that concentrate on social issues.

ANOTHER FORM You can also call definition 2 **folk**: *They sing mainly folk.*

follow *verb*
1. If something **follows** something else, it comes after it: *Sunday follows Saturday.* **2.** If you **follow** someone, you go along behind them: *You go ahead and we'll follow you.* **3.** If you **follow** a road or a path, you drive or walk along it. **4.** If you **follow** what someone is saying, you understand it: *We were too tired to follow her instructions and got it all wrong.* **5.** If you **follow** someone on an internet social network site you can view the information they post on the site.
–*phrase* **6. follow through**, to carry through an action until it is completed. **7. follow up**, **a.** to investigate or examine closely: *to follow up a lead in a murder case.* **b.** to do something more at a later stage, especially to increase the effect of what has already been done: *We have to follow up our Monday training sessions with extra ones at the weekend.*
□ **follower**, *noun* –**following**, *adjective*

folly *noun* (*plural* **follies**)
1. foolishness. **2.** a foolish or silly act.

fond *adjective*
1. If you are **fond** of someone or something, you like them very much. **2.** A **fond** look or movement shows affection for someone or something.
□ **fondly**, *adverb* –**fondness**, *noun*

fondle *verb* If you **fondle** something or someone, you stroke or caress them lovingly.

fondue /*say* **fon**-dooh, **fond**-yooh/ *noun* a meal cooked at the table in which pieces of food are speared on the end of long forks and cooked in melted cheese, hot oil or melted chocolate.

WORD HISTORY from a French word meaning 'melt'

font[1] *noun* a large stone bowl in a church which holds the water used in baptism ceremonies.

font[2] *noun* a style of printing type: *The title on the cover was in a very ornate font.*

food *noun*
1. anything that can be eaten to keep a person's or animal's body alive and help it grow.
–*phrase* **2. food for thought**, something that might make you think up some new ideas.

fool *noun*
1. someone who is silly or without common sense.
–*verb* **2.** To **fool** someone is to trick or deceive them: *He fooled them into believing that he had plenty of money.*
–*phrase* **3. fool around**, to play around or waste time.

WORD HISTORY from a Latin word meaning 'bellows'

foolhardy *adjective* reckless and foolishly adventurous.
☐ **foolhardily**, *adverb* –**foolhardiness**, *noun*

foolish *adjective* silly or without common sense: *a foolish thing to say*; *a foolish driver.*
☐ **foolishly**, *adverb* –**foolishness**, *noun*

foolproof *adjective* designed not to fail or break, even when wrongly used.

foot *noun* (*plural* **feet**)
1. the part of the body at the end of the leg, which is used for standing and walking. **2.** the end or bottom part, rather than the top or head part: *the foot of a mountain.* **3.** a measure of length in the imperial system equal to about 30 centimetres.
–*phrase* **4. on foot**, walking: *Are you coming by car or on foot?* **5. put your foot down**, to be strict or firm. **6. put your foot in your mouth** (or **in it**), to say or do something embarrassing.
☐ **footing**, *noun*: *a firm footing.*

☑ SPELLING TIP Don't confuse the spelling of the plural form **feet** with **feat** which sounds the same but is spelt with *ea*. A **feat** is an action requiring skill or strength.

footage *noun* material recorded on a film or video camera.

football *noun*
1. any field game in which players are allowed to kick the ball. **2.** the ball used in these games.
☐ **footballer**, *noun*

footlights *plural noun* the row of lights at the front of the stage in a theatre.

footnote *noun* a note at the bottom of a page, usually in small printing, which tells you more about something in the main body of writing.

footpath *noun* a strip, often laid with concrete slabs, for walking on next to a road or street.

footprint *noun* a mark left by someone's foot: *We found where they were by following the footprints in the sand.*

footstep *noun*
1. the sound made by a step of the foot.
–*phrase* **2. follow in someone's footsteps**, to copy or follow someone in their work or way of life.

for *preposition*
1. with the purpose of: *to go for a swim.* **2.** intended to be used by or in connection with: *plates for a picnic*; *a box for tools.* **3.** in order to obtain: *a request for help.* **4.** in return for: *Thank you for your efforts.* **5.** suitable for: *a dress for the occasion.* **6.** in place of: *a substitute for butter.*
–*conjunction* **7.** because or since: *She laughed, for she suddenly felt happy.*

forage /*say* **fo**-rij/ *verb* If a person or animal **forages**, they search around for food or other supplies: *They foraged near their camp for water and wood for the fire.*
☐ **forage**, *noun* food or fodder for animals.

foray *noun*
1. a raid or attack in order to steal: *a daring foray into enemy territory.* **2.** a first attempt: *It was an early foray into oil painting for them.*

forbid *verb* (**forbids**, **forbidding**, **forbade**, **has forbidden**) If you **forbid** someone to do something, you do not allow them to do it: *The teacher forbade us to play near the road.*

force *noun*
1. strength or power: *the force of the entire army*; *to use force to push open the door.* **2.** an organised group of people working together: *the police force.* **3. a.** something which produces a motion or a change of motion. **b.** the strength of this thing.
–*verb* **4.** If someone or something **forces** you to do something, they make you do it even if you do not want to: *The crazy driver forced them off the road*; *The storm forced us to go home early.*
–*phrase* **5. in force, a.** operating: *The requirement to wear the new uniforms is in force from next week.* **b.** all together: *Her friends all voted for her in force.*
☐ **forceful**, *adjective* –**forcible**, *adjective*

forceps /*say* **faw**-suhps/ *noun* (*plural* **forceps**) a pair of tongs or tweezers used for grasping and holding objects, especially in operations.

ford *noun*
1. a shallow part of a river where you can walk or drive across.

–*verb* **2.** If you **ford** a river, you cross it where it is the shallowest and safest.

fore *adjective*
1. The **fore** parts of something are its front parts: *The fore limbs of the kangaroo are quite small.*
–*phrase* **2. to the fore**, at the front or in the best position.

fore- *prefix* a word part meaning **1.** front, as in *forehead*. **2.** ahead of time, as in *forecast*. **3.** superior, as in *foreman*.

WORD HISTORY this prefix comes from Middle English and Old English

forearm *noun* the part of the arm between the elbow and the wrist.

forecast *noun*
1. a prediction, especially about the weather.
–*verb* (**forecasts**, **forecasting**, **forecast**, **has forecast**) **2.** If somebody **forecasts**, they make a prediction about something in the future, especially the weather: *They've forecast rain for the big game.*
□ **forecaster**, *noun*

forefinger *noun* the finger next to the thumb.

ANOTHER TERM for this is **index finger**.

foreground *noun* the part of a view or picture nearest the front: *a bridge in the foreground and the mountains beyond.*

THE OPPOSITE is **background**.

forehand *adjective* A **forehand** stroke in a game like tennis is one made to the right side of the body (when the player is right-handed).
□ **forehand**, *noun*

COMPARE this with **backhand**.

forehead /*rhymes with* horrid/ *noun* the part of the face above the eyes and below where the hair starts growing.

A SIMILAR WORD is **brow**.

foreign /*say* **fo**-ruhn/ *adjective*
1. Someone or something **foreign** is from a country other than your own: *a foreign flavour.* **2.** If something is **foreign**, it does not belong in the place where it is found: *a plant foreign to that region.*
□ **foreigner**, *noun*

☑ SPELLING TIP *Tricky vowel sound*: the ending is spelt *eign* (not *in* or *en*). The *g* is silent.

foreman *noun* (*plural* **foremen**)
1. a worker who is placed in charge of other workers in a factory. **2.** the member of a jury who is chosen to chair its discussions and act as its representative.
□ **foreperson**, **forewoman**, *noun*

foremost *adjective* first or top: *The country's foremost cooks will compete in the competition.*
□ **foremost**, *adverb*

foresee *verb* (**foresees**, **foreseeing**, **foresaw**, **has foreseen**) If you **foresee** something happening, you think that it is going to happen: *I can foresee several difficulties with this plan.*

forest *noun* land thickly covered with trees.

☑ SPELLING TIP *Single letter alert*: only one *r*.

forever *adverb*
1. If something continues or lasts **forever**, it will never end or wear out. **2.** If someone is **forever** doing something, they do it continually: *He's forever complaining.*

A SIMILAR WORD (for definition 1) is **eternally**; (for definition 2) **incessantly**.

forfeit /*say* **faw**-fuht/ *noun*
1. something paid or lost because of carelessness, disobedience or crime: *In the game, if you say 'yes' or 'no' you have to pay a forfeit.*
–*verb* **2.** If you **forfeit** something like a chance, a right or a possession, you have to give it up, usually because you have broken a rule or made a mistake: *We arrived late for the game and forfeited our chance of winning.*

☑ SPELLING TIP *Exception to rule*: the ending is spelt *feit* (although the sound is 'fuht'). The *ei* spelling breaks the rule that *i* comes before *e* except after *c*.

forge[1] *verb* To **forge** something is to **1.** copy it in order to trick or deceive: *to forge a signature.* **2.** shape or form it: *Over the years we've forged a firm friendship.*
–*noun* **3.** a furnace for softening metal before shaping it to make tools and other things.
□ **forger**, *noun* –**forgery**, *noun*

forge[2] *phrase* **forge ahead**, to move forward with great effort: *She took the lead and forged ahead despite the difficulties.*

forget *verb* (**forgets**, **forgetting**, **forgot**, **has forgotten**)
1. If you **forget** something, it passes out of your mind. You do not remember it: *I'm sorry I forgot your birthday.* **2.** If you **forget** something, you accidentally leave it behind or do not bring it with you: *I forgot my umbrella on the bus.* **3.** If you **forget** yourself, you let your emotions control you and do something which you would not normally do: *She entirely forgot herself and gave him a big kiss in front of everybody!*
□ **forgetful**, *adjective* –**forgetfulness**, *noun* –**forgotten**, *adjective*

forgive *verb* (**forgives**, **forgiving**, **forgave**, **has forgiven**) To **forgive** someone is to excuse them without holding any bad feelings: *The old man*

forgave them despite the paint they had spilt all over his fence.
□ **forgiveness**, *noun* –**forgiving**, *adjective*

fork *noun*
1. an instrument with prongs for lifting food, digging the garden, and other things. **2.** a place in a tree, road, or river where it divides into several parts: *There's a sign at the fork in the road.* **3.** a divided part like the prongs of a fork.
–*verb* **4.** If you **fork** something, you use a fork to move it from one place to another: *to fork the grass out of the barrow onto the garden.* **5.** If a road **forks**, it divides into two or more branches: *The road forks after about ten kilometres – take the road to the left.*
□ **forked**, *adjective*

forklift *noun* a small truck with two horizontal arms or prongs for lifting and carrying heavy loads.

forlorn /*say* fuh-**lawn**/ *adjective* To be **forlorn** is to be left all alone and often sad: *She looked very forlorn waiting by herself at the bus stop.*

WORD HISTORY from an Old English word meaning 'lose' or 'destroy'

form *noun*
1. shape or appearance: *She can move her hand so that it makes a shadow on the wall in the form of a bird.* **2.** condition or fitness: *They were in fine form and ready to meet the opposing team.* **3.** a printed paper with blank spaces to fill in: *Fill in this form and send it back to us.* **4.** behaviour: *It is not good form to splutter while someone is giving a serious talk.* **5.** the set of classes in high school for students of about the same age: *in fifth form.* **6.** a long plain seat. **7.** in art, the organisation and relationship of lines, colours, shapes, and so on, in order to create a well-balanced image.
–*verb* **8.** To **form** something is to make, build or produce it: *to form a team*; *The aim was to form two triangles with eight sticks.*

OTHER WORDS (for definition 5) are **class**, **grade** and **year**.

formal *adjective*
1. If something such as a dinner or party is **formal**, it involves fairly strict rules of polite behaviour. **2. Formal** language is the type of language that is right for written communication on serious topics, and for speaking to people on special occasions. **3.** Something is described as **formal** if it is done in order to satisfy rules or regulations.
–*noun* **4.** a dance or other entertainment, at which formal evening clothes are worn: *Who are you inviting to the school formal?*
□ **formally**, *adjective*

formality *noun* (*plural* **formalities**)
1. a way of thinking and behaving that is formal and not relaxed. **2.** something done only because it fits in with formal or polite behaviour: *We heard by phone that we had won, so the letter was just a formality.*

format *noun* shape, plan or style: *You can now get the book in a soft cover format*; *a new television series following a different format.*

formation *noun*
1. the process of making or producing: *The formation of limestone structures takes millions of years.* **2.** something which has formed: *a weird rock formation.* **3.** a planned arrangement or pattern: *geese flying in formation.*
□ **formative**, *adjective*

former *adjective*
1. A **former** friend, job, possession, and so on, is one that you had or that existed some time in the past, but not any more. **2.** You can use **former** to refer to the first of two things mentioned: *He suggested that we could either go to the beach or the pool – I preferred the former idea.*
–*noun* **3. the former**, the first of two people or things that you mention: *We could draw either our favourite pet or a tree, so I chose the former.*
□ **formerly**, *adverb*

THE OPPOSITE (of definition 2) is **latter**; the opposite (of definition 3) is **the latter**.

formidable /*say* **faw**-muh-duh-buhl, faw-**mid**-uh-buhl/ *adjective*
1. very difficult and needing much hard work: *The teacher said we had some formidable challenges ahead in improving our spelling.* **2.** frightening: *Mum's visitor was a formidable woman and Dad said he would stay out in the shed.* **3.** inspiring respect: *The professor has a formidable intellect.*
□ **formidably**, *adverb*

formula /*say* **faw**-myuh-luh/ *noun* (*plural* **formulas** *or* **formulae** /*say* **faw**-myuh-lee/)
1. a set of rules or steps to be followed: *The formula we always follow at Christmas is to eat first and then open the presents.* **2.** in chemistry, the representation of the atoms in a molecule by symbols: *The formula for ordinary salt is NaCl.*

forsake *verb* (**forsakes**, **forsaking**, **forsook**, **has forsaken**) If you **forsake** someone or something, you give them up or abandon them.
□ **forsaken**, *adjective* –**forsakenly**, *adverb*

fort *noun*
1. a place like a castle, which is strongly built and armed against enemy attack.
–*phrase* **2. hold the fort**, to look after things for someone while they are away.

ANOTHER WORD (for definition 1) is **fortress**.
WORD HISTORY from a Latin word meaning 'strong'

forte[1] /*say* **faw**-tay/ *noun* something that you do particularly well: *Music is her forte.*

☑ SPELLING TIP *Tricky vowel sound*: notice the *e* spelling for the 'ay' sound at the end. **Forte** has this spelling because it comes from French, although it is not actually pronounced this way in

French. The pronunciation has possibly come about because of the Italian word *forte* which is pronounced this way. See **forte**[2].

forte[2] /*say* **faw**-tay/ *adverb* loudly: *The trumpets had to play forte.*
☐ **fortissimo**, *adverb* very loudly.

NOTE This is used as an instruction in music and is written as **f** (or **ff** for *fortissimo*). Like most musical instructions, it comes from Italian.

THE OPPOSITE is **piano**[2] (written as **p**).

☑ SPELLING TIP See **forte**[1].

forth *adverb*
1. forward: *to set forth into battle*; *from that day forth.*
–*phrase* **2. and so forth**, and so on.

forthcoming *adjective* happening or coming soon: *Who will win the forthcoming election?*

forthright *adjective* speaking your mind openly and honestly.
☐ **forthrightly**, *adverb* –**forthrightness**, *noun*

fortify /*say* **faw**-tuh-fuy/ *verb* (**fortifies**, **fortifying**, **fortified**, **has fortified**) To **fortify** someone or something is to make them strong so as to resist attack, damage and other harmful things: *houses built of materials to fortify them against the force of cyclones*; *Eat healthily to fortify yourself against disease.*
☐ **fortification**, *noun* –**fortified**, *adjective*

fortnight *noun* a period of two weeks, or fourteen days and nights.
☐ **fortnightly**, *adjective* –**fortnightly**, *adverb*

fortress *noun* a large building which is strongly defended against an enemy.

ANOTHER WORD for this is **fort** (definition 1).

fortunate *adjective* unexpectedly lucky: *We were fortunate to get there just when they served the food.*
☐ **fortunately**, *adverb*

fortune *noun*
1. a great amount of money or property: *He must be worth a fortune.* **2.** good luck: *We wished her good fortune as she set out.* **3.** fate or luck: *A lady wearing a large purple scarf was telling people their fortunes.*

THE OPPOSITE (of definition 2) is **misfortune**.

forty *noun* (*plural* **forties**)
1. a cardinal number, ten times four (10 × 4). **2.** a symbol for this number, as 40 or XL or XXXX. **3. forties**, the numbers from 40 to 49 of a series, especially years of a person's age, or the years of a century.
☐ **fortieth**, *adjective*, *noun* –**forty**, *adjective*

forum *noun*
1. an organised event where there is public discussion of a topic or topics of concern to people in general. **2.** a place, internet site, television program, section of a newspaper, etc., that provides the opportunity for public discussion: *This site is designed to act as a forum for debate on public transport issues.*

WORD HISTORY from the Latin word for the main square of a city where the people gathered in the time of the Romans

forward *adjective*
1. ahead or towards the front: *in the forward part of the plane.* **2.** behaving in a way that attracts the attention of others: *Don't be so forward – it is embarrassing!*
–*noun* **3.** someone who plays in an attacking position in sports such as football and hockey.
–*verb* **4.** If you **forward** an email or letter on to someone, you send on an email or letter which you have received to someone else.
☐ **forward**, **forwards**, *adverb* –**forwarding**, *adjective*: *a forwarding address.*

fossick *verb* If you **fossick**, you **1.** try to find gold or precious stones in ground that has already been worked over by others: *We spent some time fossicking around the old diggings.* **2.** search or hunt: *I fossicked through my drawers looking for my favourite shirt.*
☐ **fossicker**, *noun*

fossil *noun* the remains of an animal or plant from long ago, preserved as rock.
☐ **fossilise**, *verb* –**fossilisation**, *noun* –**fossilised**, *adjective*

ANOTHER SPELLING for **fossilise** is **fossilize**.
WORD HISTORY from a Latin word meaning 'dug up'

☑ SPELLING TIP Remember that the ending is *il*. Also notice that the *l* remains single when related words, such as *fossilise*, are formed.

fossil fuel *noun* coal and oil formed underground from the remains of plants and animals that lived long ago and now used as fuel.

COMPARE this with **biofuel**.

foster *verb*
1. If someone **fosters** a child, they care for the child as part of their own family but do not legally adopt them. **2.** If someone **fosters** an activity or an idea, they help or encourage it to grow: *He fostered his grandson's interest in painting.*
☐ **foster**, *adjective*: *a foster child*; *a foster home.*

COMPARE definition 1 with **adopt** (definition 1).

foul *adjective*
1. If something is **foul**, it is extremely unpleasant: *There was a foul smell of rotting fish.* **2. Foul** language consists of words which are offensive.

–*noun* **3.** an unfair action in sport.
–*phrase* **4. fall foul of**, to have or be in trouble with.
☐ **foul**, *noun* –**foulness**, *noun*

☑ SPELLING TIP Don't confuse **foul** with **fowl** which sounds the same. A **fowl** is a bird kept for eating or for its eggs, such as a hen, duck or turkey.

found *verb*
1. the past tense and past participle of **find**: *He found both his socks at last.* **2.** To **found** something is to set it up or start it: *They founded the town on the banks of the river.*
☐ **founder**, *noun* –**founding**, *adjective*

foundation *noun*
1. the founding or setting up of something. **2.** a base on which something rests or stands: *The foundations had to be set on rock*; *the foundations of our civilisation.*

NOTE This word (as in definition 2) is often used in the plural.

founder[1] *noun* someone who begins or starts up something: *He was one of the founders of the local cricket club.*

founder[2] *verb*
1. If a ship **founders**, it fills with water and sinks: *The ship foundered in treacherous waters and the crew had to take to the lifeboats.* **2.** If a horse **founders**, it goes lame, trips, or breaks down: *The horse had been galloped so hard that it foundered.*

☑ DO NOT CONFUSE the meaning of this word with **flounder**[1]. When someone **flounders**, they struggle in a clumsy or helpless way.

fountain *noun*
1. a decorated structure with flowing water, often situated in a public place. **2.** the origin or source: *the fountain of all wisdom.*

☑ SPELLING TIP See the note at **captain** about words ending in *ain*.

fountain pen *noun* a pen which has a small container inside for supplying ink to the nib.

four *noun*
1. a cardinal number, three plus one (3 + 1). **2.** a symbol of this number, as 4 or IV or IIII. **3.** a set of this many persons or things, especially in rowing: *a rowing four.*
–*phrase* **4. on all fours**, on your hands and feet (or knees).
☐ **four**, *adjective* –**fourth**, *adjective*, *noun*

fourteen *noun*
1. a cardinal number, ten plus four (10 + 4). **2.** a symbol for this number, as 14 or XIV or XIIII.
☐ **fourteen**, *adjective* –**fourteenth**, *adjective*, *noun*

four-wheel drive *noun* a car or truck which can travel over rough country or soft ground because all four wheels (rather than the usual two) are driven by the engine.

fowl *noun* (*plural* **fowl** *or* **fowls**) a bird kept for eating or for its eggs, such as a hen, duck, or turkey.

☑ SPELLING TIP Don't confuse **fowl** with **foul** which sounds the same. Something is **foul** if it is very nasty, dirty or unpleasant.

fox *noun*
1. a small wild dog with red-brown fur, a long bushy tail and pointed ears. **2.** someone who is clever but tricky.

NOTE The male is a **dog**; the female is a **vixen**; the young is a **cub**.

foyer *noun* the large entrance hall of a theatre or hotel.

fracas /*say* **frak**-ah, **frak**-uhs/ *noun* a noisy disturbance or fight: *The police were called to break up the fracas outside parliament.*

☑ SPELLING TIP *Silent letter alert*: if you say this word as in the first pronunciation, don't forget the silent *s* at the end. This pronunciation is used because **fracas** comes from French (from an earlier Italian word meaning 'make an uproar').

fracking *noun* See **hydraulic fracturing**.

OTHER SPELLINGS are **fracing** and **fraccing**.

fraction *noun*
1. a part of a whole number: *½ is a fraction.* **2.** a small piece or amount: *Open the window a fraction.*
☐ **fractional**, *adjective* –**fractionally**, *adverb*

WORD HISTORY from a Latin word meaning 'break'

fractious /*say* **frak**-shuhs/ *adjective* bad-tempered and uncooperative: *Everybody objected to his fractious manner.*
☐ **fractiously**, *adverb*

fracture *verb* To **fracture** is to crack or break: *He fractured his skull in the fall*; *The rock fractured when we hit it.*
☐ **fracture**, *noun*

fragile *adjective* delicate and easily damaged or broken: *a fragile piece of china.*
☐ **fragility**, *noun*

fragment *noun* /*say* **frag**-muhnt/
1. a part that has been broken off or left unfinished: *Broken glass fragments covered the road*; *We only heard a fragment of her story.*
–*verb* /*say* frag-**ment**/ **2.** If something **fragments** or if another thing **fragments** it, it breaks into small pieces: *The mirror fragmented with the force of the fall.*
☐ **fragmentary**, *adjective*

fragrant *adjective* sweet-smelling: *a fragrant flower.*
☐ **fragrance**, *noun*

frail *adjective* If a person is **frail**, they are weak or delicate: *She looked very frail lying in the hospital bed.*
☐ **frailness**, *noun* –**frailty**, *noun*

frame *noun*
1. the structure which fits around or supports something and gives it shape: *the frame of a mirror*; *The frame of the dog kennel was made of wood*; *the human frame.* **2.** one of the small pictures that make up a strip of film.
–*verb* **3.** To **frame** something, such as picture, is to put it in a frame (definition 1). **4.** *Informal* To **frame** someone is to make them seem guilty when they are innocent.
–*phrase* **5. frame of mind**, mood: *to be in a good frame of mind.*

franchise /*say* **fran**-chuyz/ *noun*
1. a citizen's right to vote. **2.** permission given by a manufacturer to a shopkeeper to sell the manufacturer's products.

WORD HISTORY from a French word meaning 'free'

frangipani /*say* fran-juh-**pan**-ee/ *noun* a small tree with thick, fleshy branches and sweet-smelling yellow, white or pink flowers.

ANOTHER SPELLING is **frangipanni**.

frank *adjective*
1. To be **frank** is to be completely open and honest in what you say: *I was frank and told her I didn't like the painting.*
–*noun* **2.** a mark put on a letter in place of a postage stamp to show that the postage has already been paid.
☐ **frankly**, *adverb* –**frankness**, *noun*

A SIMILAR WORD (for definition 1) is **sincere**.

frankfurt *noun* a red-coloured sausage, sometimes eaten in a bread roll and called a hot dog.

WORD HISTORY named after *Frankfurt*, a town in Germany

frantic *adjective* wild with excitement, fear, worry or pain.
☐ **frantically**, *adverb*

ANOTHER WORD for this is **frenetic**.

fraternal /*say* fruh-**ter**-nuhl/ *adjective* of or like a brother.
☐ **fraternity**, *noun* a group of people with the same interests or goals: *the medical fraternity.* –**fraternise**, *verb* to be friendly. –**fraternally**, *adverb*

ANOTHER SPELLING for **fraternise** is **fraternize**.

☑ SPELLING TIP *Tricky 'uh' sound*: the first vowel sound is spelt *a*. It might help if you remember that **fraternal** comes from *frater*, the Latin word for 'brother'.

fraud /*say* frawd/ *noun*
1. deliberate cheating or trickery: *to practise fraud.* **2.** someone or something that is not what they pretend to be: *He must be a fraud*; *the painting turned out to be a fraud.*
☐ **fraudulent**, *adjective* –**fraudulently**, *adverb*

☑ SPELLING TIP *Tricky vowel sound*: the trick in **fraud** is remembering that the vowel sound is spelt *au* (although it sounds like 'aw'). Think of some other words you know well which have the same spelling for this sound, such as *cause* and *sauce*.

fray[1] *noun* a noisy fight or quarrel: *Eventually the older kids joined the fray and then there really was trouble!*

fray[2] *verb* If something **frays**, it wears out: *Her dress was so old it was fraying at the hem*; *It frayed our tempers listening to him complaining all the time.*

frazzle *noun in the phrase* **1. burnt to a frazzle**, burnt, especially in the cooking process: *The toast was burnt to a frazzle.* **2. worn to a frazzle**, exhausted: *worn to a frazzle after running around all day.*

frazzled *adjective* weary or tired out: *At the end of the hot day we were all frazzled.*

freak *noun*
1. someone or something that is extremely strange or unusual.
–*verb in the phrase* **2. freak out**, *Informal* to become very upset or excited.
☐ **freak**, *adjective* –**freakish**, *adjective* –**freakishly**, *adverb* –**freakishness**, *noun*

freckle *noun* a small brown spot on the skin caused by the sun: *She put on a lot of make-up because she wanted to cover the freckles on her nose.*
☐ **freckled**, *adjective*

free *adjective*
1. If something is **free**, you do not have to pay for it: *Call for our free brochure.* **2.** If a person or animal is **free**, they can move about without being stopped or held back. **3.** If someone is **free** at a particular time, they are not busy doing anything. **4.** If something like a phone or a room is **free** at a particular time, it is not being used: *You can ring now – the phone is free*; *The bathroom is free.* **5.** If someone tells you that you are **free** to do something, they mean that you may do it: *You are free to add any comments you wish.*
–*verb* (**frees**, **freeing**, **freed**, **has freed**) **6.** If you **free** someone or something, you release them so that they are not in a prison, cage, etc., any more: *They freed the prisoners.*

☐ **free**, *adverb*: *to go free.* –**freely**, *adverb*: *to give freely.*

freedom *noun* the right to act or speak out as you wish.

A SIMILAR WORD is **liberty**.

☑ SPELLING TIP The spelling of **freedom** will be easier if you see that it contains *free* and the suffix *-dom* (meaning 'general condition'). Think of other words with this ending such as *kingdom* and *wisdom*.

freefall *noun*
1. the movement of something as it falls downwards with nothing to stop it or slow it. **2.** the part of a parachute jump before the parachute opens. *verb* (**freefalls**, **freefalling**, **freefell**, **has freefallen**) **3.** When something **freefalls** it falls quickly, with nothing to stop it or slow it.

ANOTHER FORM is **free-fall**.

freehand *adverb* If you draw something **freehand**, you draw it by hand, without the help of anything such as a ruler or a compass.
☐ **freehand**, *adjective*: *a freehand painting.*

freelance *noun*
1. someone, especially a writer, who does not work for a wage but who sells work to more than one employer.
–*verb* **2.** If somebody **freelances**, they work for various employers but are not employed full-time by any one of them: *Now that he is freelancing, he decides his own hours.*
☐ **freelance**, *adjective*

free-range *adjective*
1. of animals, able to walk around and feed freely, rather than being kept in a cage: *We only buy eggs from free-range chickens.* **2.** of food, produced by free-range animals: *free-range eggs*

freestyle *noun* a style of swimming in which the head and the front of the body are kept flat in the water, while the legs kick and the arms are used in turn to come up and over the head.

COMPARE this with **backstroke**, **breaststroke** and **butterfly stroke**.

free verse *noun* poetry with lines of different lengths so that it doesn't have a regular beat or rhyme pattern.

freeware *noun* computer software which is available online for free.

freeway *noun* a road on which traffic can travel fast.

OTHER WORDS for this are **expressway** and **motorway**.

freeze *verb* (**freezes**, **freezing**, **froze**, **has frozen**)
1. When something liquid **freezes**, it turns to ice: *The puddles froze*; *We froze our drinks.* **2.** If someone **freezes**, they feel very cold: *We froze last winter without any heating.* **3.** If you **freeze** food, you keep it fresh by putting it in a freezer: *She froze the meat.* **4.** You can say that someone **freezes** when they keep very still, as with fear: *There was a banging on the window and they froze.* **5.** When a computer **freezes**, it stops responding to commands because of a fault.
–*noun* **6.** a period of very cold weather: *the big freeze.* **7.** a period in which no change is allowed in something, such as prices or pay.
☐ **freezer**, *noun* –**freezing**, *adjective*

freight /*say* frayt/ *noun*
1. goods sent by air, sea or land. **2.** the charge for sending goods.
–*verb* **3.** If you **freight** goods, you send them to a particular destination.

☑ SPELLING TIP *Tricky vowel sound*: the vowel sound is spelt *eigh*, although it sounds like 'ay'. Remember that **freight** has nothing to do with eating, although it has the sound 'ate' in it. Some other words which have an *eigh* spelling for an 'ay' sound are *eight* and *weigh*.

French horn *noun* a brass wind instrument with a mellow tone.

frenetic /*say* fruh-**net**-ik/ *adjective* over-active or frantic: *His frenetic behaviour makes me tired.*
☐ **frenetically**, *adverb*

frenzy *noun* (*plural* **frenzies**) a wildly excited or angry state: *The crowd was in a frenzy when the rock group came onto the stage.*
☐ **frenzied**, *adjective* –**frenziedly**, *adverb*

frequency /*say* **free**-kwuhn-see/ *noun* (*plural* **frequencies**)
1. the fact of happening often: *Accidents occur here with great frequency.* **2.** the rate at which something happens: *the frequency of a pulse.* **3.** the rate of movements in a sound wave: *What is the frequency of your favourite radio station?*

frequent *adjective* /*say* **free**-kwuhnt/
1. happening often: *They make frequent appeals for help.*
–*verb* /*say* fruh-**kwent**/ **2.** To **frequent** a place is to visit it often: *We frequent that part of the town because the cinema is there.*
☐ **frequently**, *adverb*

☑ SPELLING TIP Notice that the pronunciation of **frequent** changes according to whether it is an adjective or a verb, but the spelling is the same. So the beginning letters *fre* spell two different sounds ('free' and 'fruh'). The *qu* spelling in the middle gives the same 'kw' sound in both cases, as it does in many other words, such as *queen*.

fresco *noun* (*plural* **frescoes** *or* **frescos**) a painting done on a freshly plastered wall or ceiling before it has dried, so that the colours sink in.

WORD HISTORY from an Italian word meaning 'cool'

fresh *adjective* To be **fresh** is to be **1.** in a natural state: *For breakfast there was fresh fruit or stewed fruit.* **2.** new: *a fresh approach to teaching spelling*; *fresh tracks in the sand.* **3.** cool: *The air was quite fresh this morning.* **4.** not salt: *fresh water.* **5.** bright, strong and not tired: *fresh colour*; *She looks fresh after her holiday.* **6.** just arrived: *fresh from overseas.*
☐ **freshly**, *adverb* –**freshness**, *noun* –**freshwater**, *adjective*: *a freshwater fish.*

fret[1] *verb* (**frets**, **fretting**, **fretted**, **has fretted**) To **fret** is to be worried or upset: *She is fretting about her sick cat.*

fret[2] *noun* one of the bars across the neck of a stringed instrument, such as a guitar, which shows the player where to press their fingers to make the correct notes.

friar *noun* a member of a religious order, such as the Dominicans or the Franciscans, who lives a simple life of prayer.
☐ **friary**, *noun* a place where friars live.

WORD HISTORY from a Latin word meaning 'brother'

friction *noun*
1. the rubbing of one thing against another: *You can start a fire with the friction of one twig rubbing against another.* **2.** an argument or tense situation between people: *The friction between the two groups got worse every day.*

Friday *noun* a day of the week, often the last day of the school or working week.

THE ABBREVIATION is **Fri.**

fridge *noun* See **refrigerator**.

friend *noun* someone you like and who likes you.
☐ **friendly**, *adjective* –**friendship**, *noun*

frieze /*rhymes with* breeze/ *noun* a band around the top of a wall which is often decorated with a painted or sculpted pattern.

☑ SPELLING TIP Don't confuse the spelling of **frieze** with **freeze** which has the same sound but is spelt with *ee*. To **freeze** is to turn to ice.

frigate /*say* **frig**-uht/ *noun* a small military ship, often used to sail with and protect other ships.

fright *noun*
1. a sudden feeling of fear or shock: *The sudden noise gave us a fright.* **2.** someone or something of a shocking or silly appearance: *She looked a fright in a hat adorned with passionfruits.*
☐ **frighten**, *verb* –**frightening**, *adjective* –**frighteningly**, *adverb*

☑ SPELLING TIP *Tricky vowel sound*: **fright** is spelt with an *ight* ending (although it sounds like 'uyt'). Think of other words that you know well which have the same spelling for this sound, such as *light*, *bright* and *sight*.

frightful *adjective* Something is **frightful** if it is **1.** frightening or unpleasant: *It was a frightful trip in a leaky boat across a wild ocean.* **2.** very bad: *The teacher said the way we sang the national anthem was frightful.*
☐ **frightfully**, *adverb*: *frightfully late.*

frigid /*say* **frij**-uhd/ *adjective* very cold: *frigid temperatures*; *a frigid expression on her face.*

frill *noun* a gathered edge, used to decorate something like the hem or neck of a dress.
☐ **frilly**, *adjective*

fringe *noun*
1. a border of loose or bunched threads on something like a rug. **2.** hair which has been cut across the forehead. **3.** the edge or outer part: *on the fringe of civilisation.*
–*verb* **4.** If something **fringes** an area, it appears around the edges of it: *Thick bush fringes the city.*
☐ **fringe**, *adjective*: *a fringe benefit.* –**fringed**, *adjective*: *a fringed umbrella.*

frisbee *noun* a saucer-shaped plastic disc which is thrown with a horizontal spin.

☑ SPELLING TIP The ending is spelt *ee* (not *y* or *ie*). Remember that a **frisbee** flies through the air, just like a *bee*.

frisk *verb*
1. To **frisk** is to jump around playfully. **2.** *Informal* If someone **frisks** you, they search you for hidden weapons: *The police frisked the suspect at the airport.*
☐ **frisky**, *adjective*

frittata /*say* fri-**tah**-tuh/ *noun* a thick omelette containing vegetables, cheese, seasonings, etc.

☑ SPELLING TIP *Double/single letter alert*: the letter *t* appears three times in this word, firstly as a double *t* and then alone. **Frittata** comes from Italian where it means 'fried'.

fritter[1] *noun* a piece of meat or fruit, covered in batter and fried: *a pineapple fritter.*

fritter[2] *verb in the phrase* **fritter away**, to waste gradually: *They frittered their money away until there was none left.*

frivolous /*say* **friv**-uh-luhs/ *adjective* not serious: *She was dressed in a frivolous outfit for the party*; *a frivolous remark.*
☐ **frivolity** /*say* fruh-**vol**-uh-tee/, *noun* –**frivolously**, *adverb*

fro *adverb in the phrase* **to and fro**, See **to** (definition 6).

frock *noun* a dress: *a summer frock.*

frog *noun* a tailless creature with webbed feet and long back legs for jumping, which lives in water or on land.

frogman *noun* (*plural* **frogmen**) a diver equipped with a wetsuit, flippers, mask and snorkel or air tank.

frolic *noun*
1. happy play: *The puppies were having a frolic on the grass.*
–*verb* (**frolics**, **frolicking**, **frolicked**, **has frolicked**) **2.** If you **frolic**, you run around and play in a happy way.
☐ **frolicsome**, *adjective*

WORD HISTORY from a Dutch word meaning 'joyful'

☑ SPELLING TIP Remember that this word ends in *ic* (not *ick*). However, when you add *-ed* or *-ing*, the *k* is added.

from *preposition* a word that marks a starting point, used to express **1.** distance in regard to space, time, order, and so on: *the bus from the city*; *from that moment on*; *to stop yourself from laughing.* **2.** difference or distinction: *to tell black from white.* **3.** source or origin: *to get an idea from your friend*; *to draw sketches from real life.* **4.** cause or reason: *to die from starvation.*

frond *noun* the divided leaf of plants such as ferns and palm trees.

front *noun*
1. the part or surface facing forward or most often seen: *the tree at the front of the house.* **2.** the line where fighting takes place in a war: *Letters from the front were read eagerly.* **3.** land facing a road or shore: *On the lake front, you can hire canoes.* **4.** in weather, a surface where two air masses with different temperatures meet: *A cold front is coming through.* **5.** manner, especially when it is concealing your real feelings: *a cool front.*
–*phrase* **6. front up**, *Informal* to arrive or turn up.
☐ **front**, *adjective*: *the front porch.*

frontier /*say* frun-**tear**/ *noun*
1. the border of a country or state. **2.** the edge of a known area: *the frontiers of knowledge.*

frost *noun*
1. the covering of ice formed when dew freezes.
–*verb* **2.** If something **frosts** a surface, it covers it: *Ice and snow frosted the windows*; *to frost a cake with icing.*
☐ **frosted**, *adjective* –**frosty**, *adjective* (**frostier**, **frostiest**)

frostbite *noun* damage to the body, especially the fingers, toes or ears, caused by exposure to extreme cold.
☐ **frostbitten**, *adjective*

frosting *noun*
1. a fluffy icing used to decorate cakes. **2.** a frostlike coating on glass, metal or other surfaces.

froth *noun*
1. the mass of tiny bubbles that rise to the top of some liquids.
–*verb* **2.** If a liquid **froths**, it gives out froth or foam.
☐ **frothy**, *adjective* (**frothier**, **frothiest**)

A SIMILAR WORD is **foam**.

frown *verb*
1. To **frown** is to wrinkle your forehead in a look of worry or annoyance.
–*phrase* **2. frown on** (or **upon**), to disapprove of.
☐ **frown**, *noun*

frugal /*say* **frooh**-guhl/ *adjective*
1. very careful not to waste anything: *She was very frugal with her money.* **2.** poor or cheap: *We existed on a frugal diet of rice and potatoes.*
☐ **frugality**, *noun* –**frugally**, *adverb*

fruit *noun*
1. the edible part which grows from the flowers of trees and plants, such as apples, oranges, pineapples, and many others. **2.** the result: *the fruit of years of labour.*
☐ **fruitful**, *adjective* –**fruity**, *adjective*

frustrate *verb* If something **frustrates** you, it prevents you from doing something and makes you feel annoyed or angry.
☐ **frustrated**, *adjective* –**frustrating**, *adjective* –**frustration**, *noun*

fry *verb* (**fries**, **frying**, **fried**, **has fried**) To **fry** food is to cook it in a pan, using fat or oil.
☐ **fried**, *adjective*

fudge *noun* a soft sweet made from sugar, butter and milk.

fuel *noun*
1. anything, such as wood, petrol or kerosene, which is burnt to give heat or to make an engine work.
–*verb* (**fuels**, **fuelling**, **fuelled**, **has fuelled**) **2.** If somebody **fuels** something, they add to it in the same way as adding fuel to a fire: *Her outburst fuelled their argument.*

WORD HISTORY from a Latin word meaning 'hearth' or 'fireplace'

fugitive /*say* **fyooh**-juh-tiv/ *noun* someone who is running away.
☐ **fugitive**, *adjective*

fugue /*say* fyoohg/ *noun* a piece of music in which a short melody is played or sung and then repeated by other instruments or voices.

WORD HISTORY from a Latin word meaning 'flight'

☑ SPELLING TIP Don't forget the *ue* at the end.

fulcrum /*say* **fool**-kruhm/ *noun* (*plural* **fulcrums** *or* **fulcra**) the point on which something balances or turns: *To make a seesaw we put a plank of wood on a barrel which acted as the fulcrum.*

☑ SPELLING TIP *Single letter alert*: only one *l*.

fulfil *verb* (**fulfils**, **fulfilling**, **fulfilled**, **has fulfilled**) To **fulfil** something is to **1.** carry it out: *He fulfilled his promise to get his homework done before dinner.* **2.** satisfy it: *The harvest that year fulfilled their hopes entirely.*
□ **fulfilled**, *adjective* –**fulfilling**, *adjective* –**fulfilment**, *noun*

☑ SPELLING TIP *Single letter alert*: both the syllables of this word end with a single *l* (which can be confusing because of the spelling of *full* and *fill*). Note that the final *l* is doubled when you add *-ed* or *-ing* but the middle *l* remains single. Some people now accept the spelling with a double *l* at the end, which is used in American English, but it is best to learn the single *l* spelling.

full *adjective*
1. If something is **full**, it contains as many things or as much of something as can fit into it: *a box full of oranges*; *a jug full of milk.* **2.** You can say that something is **full** of things or people if it contains a large number of them: *His teeth are full of fillings.* **3.** You can say something or someone is **full** of a particular feeling or feature if they have a lot of it: *Her trip had been full of excitement.* **4. Full** can also indicate the greatest amount or degree that something can reach: *The cars were racing at full speed.* **5.** A **full** name, address, number, and so on, is the whole of it. It is complete. **6.** If someone is **full**, they have had enough or too much to eat or drink.
–*phrase* **7. full of yourself**, conceited and vain. **8. in full**, **a.** to or for the full amount: *You must pay in full.* **b.** not shortened or reduced: *to read a book in full.* **9. on the full**, of a ball, as it is flying through the air before bouncing: *Catch it on the full.*
□ **fully**, *adverb*

SIMILAR WORDS (for definition 1) are **bulging**, **crammed**, **bursting**, **overflowing** and **packed**. These words all mean that something is completely full, or too full.

full stop *noun* a mark of punctuation (.) which is used at the end of a sentence, as in *She held the dog.* or to show that a word has been shortened, as in *adj.* (adjective).

SEE the Grammar and Punctuation Guide appendix.

full-time /*say* **fool**-tuym/ *adjective* working most of the week at any job: *a full-time teacher.*
□ **full-time** /*say* fool-**tuym**/, *adverb*: *She works full-time.*

COMPARE this with **part-time**.

fumble *verb* To **fumble** is to handle something clumsily: *Ella almost caught the ball, but then she fumbled and dropped it.*
□ **fumbler**, *noun* –**fumbling**, *adjective*

fume *noun*
1. fumes, smoke or gas which can be easily seen or smelt.
–*verb* **2.** If something **fumes**, it gives out smoke or gas. **3.** If someone **fumes**, they show that they are very angry or annoyed: *Dad really fumed when he saw the hole in the wall.*
□ **fuming**, *adjective*: *a fuming chimney*; *He was fuming with anger.*

fumigate /*say* **fyooh**-muh-gayt/ *verb* To **fumigate** an area is to treat it with chemical fumes to get rid of insect pests.
□ **fumigation**, *noun* –**fumigator**, *noun*

☑ SPELLING TIP *Tricky 'uh' sound*: the middle vowel sound is spelt *i*.

fun *noun*
1. enjoyment. **2.** playfulness: *She was always full of fun.*
–*phrase* **3. make fun of**, to tease.

function *noun*
1. what someone or something is meant to do: *A function of the referee is to make sure that the game is played fairly*; *Do you know what the function of this key is?* **2.** a social or official occasion, such as a dinner to raise money.
–*verb* **3.** If something **functions**, it works or goes: *The television is functioning again.*
□ **functional**, *adjective* –**functionally**, *adverb*

☑ SPELLING TIP Remember that there is a *c* in the middle of **function** and that the ending is *tion* which gives a 'shuhn' sound as in many other words. Another word with a similar pattern is *junction*.

function key *noun* a key on a computer keyboard which can be programmed to perform special actions.

fund *noun*
1. a supply of money: *They have set up a fund to help the people in the floods.* **2.** a supply: *What a wonderful fund of knowledge he has!*
–*verb* **3.** If somebody **funds** something, they provide it with money: *The education department is funding our new school library.*
□ **funding**, *noun*

fundamental *adjective*
1. most important or basic: *There are a few fundamental road rules you must understand before you take your bike onto the road.*
–*noun* **2. fundamentals**, the basic rules or principles that form the basis for any system: *We have started to learn the fundamentals of geometry.*
□ **fundamentally**, *adverb*

WORD HISTORY from a Latin word meaning 'foundation'

funeral /*say* **fyoohn**-ruhl, **fyooh**-nuh-ruhl/ *noun* a service held to honour someone who has died, which usually is followed by the burial or cremation of the body.

fungus
/*say* **fung**-guhs/ *noun* (*plural* **fungi** /*say* **fung**-gee, **fung**-guy, **fun**-juy/ *or* **funguses**) a simple plant, such as the mushroom, mould or yeast, which grows in dark or slightly wet places.

☑ SPELLING TIP *Tricky 'uh' sound*: the ending is spelt *us* (not *ous*). **Fungus** comes from Latin (meaning 'mushroom'). The *us* ending is mainly found in words like this that have come straight from Latin.

funk *noun* a type of modern music, played mostly by African Americans, with a strongly emphasised bass part, complex rhythms, and often the use of horn instruments.

funnel *noun*
1. an open-ended cone used for pouring liquid or dry goods into a container with a narrow opening. **2.** the wide tube which forms the chimney of a ship or steam engine.
–*verb* (**funnels**, **funnelling**, **funnelled**, **has funnelled**) **3.** If you **funnel** something, you direct it through a narrow space: *We funnelled the honey into jars.*

☑ SPELLING TIP *Double/single letter alert*: double *n* in the middle and only one *l* at the end. However, when you add *-ed* or *-ing*, the *l* is doubled.

funnel-web spider *noun* a large, black venomous spider of eastern Australia, which builds a funnel-shaped web.

ANOTHER FORM is **funnel-web**.

funny *adjective* (**funnier**, **funniest**)
1. amusing: *a funny drawing.* **2.** strange: *We knew something funny was going on when we saw the sign.*

SIMILAR WORDS (for definition 1) are **comical**, **humorous** and **hilarious**. Note that **hilarious** means 'extremely funny'.

funny bone *noun* the point of the elbow which tingles when it is hit.

fun run *noun* a long running race, usually used to raise money.

fur *noun* the hairy coat of some animals, such as dogs, cats and monkeys.
□ **furry**, *adjective* (**furrier**, **furriest**)

☑ SPELLING TIP Don't confuse **fur** with **fir** which sounds the same. A **fir** is a kind of tree.

furious *adjective*
1. extremely angry. **2.** strong or violent: *Furious waves pounded the coast.*
□ **furiously**, *adverb*

furl *verb* To **furl** something is to roll it up: *The captain commanded them to furl the sail.*

furnace *noun* a structure with a big fire inside it for making heat, as in industry or for heating buildings.

furnish *verb*
1. If you **furnish** a room, you put things such as furniture, lights and curtains in it. **2.** To **furnish** someone with something is to provide or supply them with it: *They furnished the walkers with enough food until the next day.*
□ **furnished**, *adjective* –**furnisher**, *noun* –**furnishings**, *plural noun*: *I don't like the furnishings in the house – too dark and heavy!*

furniture *noun* the chairs, beds, tables and other large, movable objects of a room or house.

☑ SPELLING TIP *Tricky vowel sound*: remember that **furniture** has nothing to do with ferns, and so the first vowel sound is spelt with *ur* (not *er*). Other things to remember are the *i* spelling for the middle vowel sound and the *ture* ending (although it sounds like 'chuh'). Many other words end with this spelling and sound, such as *creature* and *picture*.

furore /*say* **fyooh**-raw/ *noun* a public reaction of anger, disapproval, etc.: *The scandal caused a furore.*

furphy /*say* **fer**-fee/ *noun* a false story: *Ann reckoned she hadn't eaten all day but that was probably a furphy.*

WORD HISTORY named after a Victorian man, John *Furphy*, who, during World War I, made carts for carrying water, which used to be centres of gossip for the soldiers

furrow *noun*
1. a groove, especially one made by a plough.
–*verb* **2.** If someone **furrows** their forehead or something is **furrowed**, deep grooves appear there: *He furrowed his brow while he concentrated*; *His brow furrowed – we could see he was very worried.*

further *adverb*
1. at or to a greater distance: *You can see further than me – what's that sign in the distance say?* **2.** in addition: *Scientists need to work further to get an answer.*
–*adjective* **3.** A **further** thing is an additional one: *a further offer of help.*
–*verb* **4.** If you **further** something, you help it develop: *to further a good cause.*

ANOTHER FORM (for definition 1) is **farther**.
NOTE **Further** (or **farther**) is part of the set **far, further, furthest**.

☑ SPELLING TIP Remember that the first vowel sound is spelt with *ur* (not *er*) – you can remind yourself that *u* is **further** along in the alphabet than *e*. However, *er* is used for the vowel sound at the end of the word.

furtive *adjective* stealthy or sly: *After a furtive look around, he produced the money.*
☐ **furtively**, *adverb*

fury *noun* extreme or violent anger: *He smashed the door in his fury.*

fuse[1] *noun*
1. the wick which sets off an explosive when it is lit. **2.** the safety wire in an electrical circuit which cuts off the power if there is a fault.

fuse[2] *verb* To **fuse** is to melt into one: *The burnt wires fused.*

fuselage /*say* **fyooh**-zuh-lahzh/ *noun* the body of an aircraft.

☑ SPELLING TIP *Tricky 'uh' sound*: the middle vowel sound is spelt *e*. Also remember that the ending is spelt *age* (although it sounds like 'ahzh'). Other words with this spelling and sound at the end are *collage* and *massage*. They are all spelt and pronounced in this way because they come from French. (In French, **fuselage** means 'shaped like a spindle'.)

fuss *noun*
1. unnecessary trouble: *He asked for a party with no fuss.* **2.** a noise or disturbance: *The people at the back were making such a fuss we couldn't hear what he was saying.*
–*verb* **3.** If someone **fusses**, they get unnecessarily busy or worried about something: *She fusses so much that we don't tell her lots of things.*
☐ **fussy**, *adjective* (**fussier**, **fussiest**)

futile *adjective* useless and not effective: *James made a few futile attempts to reach the frisbee, but unfortunately it was carried out to sea.*
☐ **futility**, *noun* uselessness. –**futilely**, *adverb*

future *noun* the time which has not yet come: *You shouldn't worry about the future.*
☐ **future**, *adjective* –**futuristic**, *adjective*

SEE ALSO **future tense**.

future tense *noun* the form of a verb, using 'will' or 'shall', which shows that something is going to happen, such as 'will run' in *I will run in the race tomorrow*.

SEE the Grammar and Punctuation Guide appendix.

fuzz *noun*
1. something fine and soft which is on the surface: *a fuzz of hair on his chin.* **2.** *Informal* the police.
☐ **fuzzy**, *adjective* (**fuzzier**, **fuzziest**)

gaberdine /*say* gab-uh-**deen**, **gab**-uh-deen/ *noun* closely woven cloth made of wool, cotton, or spun rayon.

ANOTHER SPELLING is **gabardine**.

gable *noun* the triangular part of a wall between the two slopes of a roof.

gadget *noun* a useful piece of machinery which performs a particular job: *Have you got a gadget for opening up oyster shells?*

gag[1] *verb* (**gags**, **gagging**, **gagged**, **has gagged**) **1.** To **gag** someone is to cover their mouth to stop them from speaking or making a sound: *The intruders gagged him so he couldn't call for help.* **2.** To **gag** on food is to be unable to swallow, and make sounds as though you are vomiting: *My little brother always gags on cabbage.*
–*noun* **3.** something pushed into or tied round your mouth to prevent you from speaking.

gag[2] *noun* a joke or trick.
☐ **gagger**, *noun*

gaggle *noun* a flock (of geese).

WORD HISTORY the word imitates the noise that geese make

gaiety /*say* **gay**-uh-tee/ *noun* cheerfulness or high spirits: *There was a feeling of gaiety and happiness around.*
☐ **gaily**, *adverb*: *They set out gaily knowing they would easily get to their destination.*

gain *verb*
1. To **gain** something is to get or win it: *She did so well she gained first prize.*
–*phrase* **2. gain ground**, to advance or get an advantage: *At long last, the troops are gaining ground in the battle for the town.* **3. gain on**, to catch up with: *As the other runners began to fall behind, he had a chance to gain on them.*
☐ **gain**, *noun* –**gainful**, *adjective*

gait /*say* gayt/ *noun* a way of walking or moving: *an awkward gait*; *a rolling gait.*

☑ SPELLING TIP Remember the *ai* spelling in **gait**. Don't confuse it with **gate** which sounds the same. A **gate** is a part of a fence that opens and shuts.

gala /*say* **gah**-luh/ *adjective* festive or showy: *It was to be a gala occasion and everybody wanted to be there.*

WORD HISTORY from a Dutch word meaning 'riches'

galah /*say* guh-**lah**/ *noun*
1. an Australian cockatoo with pink and grey feathers. **2.** *Informal* a foolish person.

WORD HISTORY from an Aboriginal language of New South Wales called Yuwaalaraay

galaxy *noun* (*plural* **galaxies**) any large group of stars held together by its own gravity and separated from any other system by large areas of space.
☐ **galactic**, *adjective*

NOTE The galaxy of which the Earth is a part is sometimes called the **Milky Way**.
WORD HISTORY The word 'galaxy' comes from a Greek word meaning 'milk'

gale *noun* a very strong wind.

gallant /*say* **gal**-uhnt, guh-**lant**/ *adjective*
1. brave and noble: *a gallant band of men.* **2.** very polite and courteous: *In his typically gallant way, he opened the door for her.*

WORD HISTORY from a French word meaning 'magnificent'

gall bladder /*say* gawl/ *noun* a part of the body attached to the liver, which stores bile.

galleon /*say* **gal**-ee-uhn, **gal**-yuhn/ *noun* a kind of large Spanish sailing ship.

gallery *noun* (*plural* **galleries**)
1. a room or building where paintings and sculptures are exhibited. **2.** an upper floor or balcony where you can sit, especially in a theatre.

☑ SPELLING TIP *Double letter alert*: double *l* in the middle. Also remember that the ending is spelt *ery* (not *ary*).

galley *noun* (*plural* **galleys**)
1. a long, low ship moved along by oars. **2.** the kitchen in a ship or aeroplane.

gallon *noun* a measure of liquid in the imperial system equal to about 4.5 litres.

gallop *noun*
1. the fastest pace a horse can run at.
–*verb* **2.** When a horse **gallops**, it runs very fast. **3.** When a person **gallops**, they ride a horse

that is galloping: *We galloped as fast as we could to the closest house.*

WORD HISTORY from a German word meaning 'run well'

gallows *noun* a wooden frame for hanging criminals.

galore /*say* guh-**law**/ *adverb* in great numbers: *There were ants galore under the bed where I had hidden my lunch.*

NOTE This word can be used only following a noun.

galvanise *verb*
1. If something **galvanises** you, it makes you act immediately: *The shock galvanised him into action.* **2.** If a metal is **galvanised**, it is coated with zinc to prevent rust: *galvanised iron.*
☐ **galvanisation**, *noun*

ANOTHER SPELLING is **galvanize**.

gamble *verb* To **gamble** is to **1.** play a game in which you risk losing something, especially money. **2.** take a chance: *We gambled on Mum not noticing the broken window.*
☐ **gambler**, *noun* –**gambling**, *noun*

gambol /*say* **gam**-buhl/ *verb* (**gambols**, **gambolling**, **gambolled**, **has gambolled**) If a person or animal **gambols**, they jump about in play: *The seals gambolled and frolicked in the waves.*

game *noun*
1. something you can play, usually with set rules: *a game of tennis*; *a board game.* **2.** wild animals, including birds and fish, hunted for food or sport: *to kill game with a spear.*
–*adjective* **3.** If you are **game** to do something, you are ready to do it despite the danger involved.
–*phrase* **4. play the game**, to act fairly, or according to the rules.

gameplay *noun* the amount of time that it takes to complete a computer game.

gamut /*say* **gam**-uht/ *noun* the whole scale or range: *Holiday movies cover the full gamut from thrillers to romance.*

gander *noun* a male goose.

gang *noun*
1. a band or group: *a gang of small boys*; *a gang of thieves.* **2.** a group of people working together: *a railway gang.*
–*verb in the phrase* **3. gang up on**, to combine against: *To get their way, they ganged up on the others.*

gangly /*say* **gang**-glee/ *adjective* awkwardly tall and thin: *He was a long, gangly fellow with arms that seemed to reach to his knees.*

ANOTHER WORD for this is **gangling**.

gangplank *noun* a movable board used as a bridge for getting on and off a ship.

ANOTHER WORD for this is **gangway**.

gangrene /*say* **gang**-green/ *noun* the rotting of flesh on the body caused by the blood supply being cut off.
☐ **gangrenous** /*say* **gang**-gruh-nuhs/, *adjective*

☑ SPELLING TIP *Tricky vowel sound*: the end is spelt *ene* (not *een*). Remember that **gangrene** has nothing to do with the colour green.

gangster *noun* a member of a group of criminals.

gangway *noun*
1. a passageway, especially on a ship: *We squeezed along the gangway with our suitcases.*
2. See **gangplank**.

gaol /*say* jayl/ *noun* See **jail**.

gap *noun*
1. a break or opening: *We could hear the wind whistling through gaps in the door.* **2.** a blank or unfilled space or time: *There was a gap in his account of what happened which made the police suspicious.*

gape *verb* To **gape** is to **1.** look with your eyes and mouth wide open when something unusual happens: *We all gaped at our grandmother's newest hat.* **2.** to be wide open: *The explosion left a huge hole gaping in the wall of the house.*
☐ **gaping**, *adjective*

garage /*say* **ga**-razh, guh-**rahzh**/ *noun*
1. a building for keeping a car, bus or truck. **2.** a place where cars are repaired and petrol is sold.

OTHER TERMS (for definition 2) are **petrol station** and **service station**.
WORD HISTORY from a French word meaning 'put in shelter'

garbage *noun* rubbish or waste material.

garbled *adjective* If something you hear or read is **garbled**, it is mixed up so that it is hard to understand: *There was a garbled message left on the answering machine.*

garden *noun*
1. an area, usually with trees and plants, used for pleasure and as a place to relax: *They were sent outside to play in the garden.* **2.** an area set aside for growing flowers or vegetables: *They planted a herb garden beside the path.*
☐ **gardener**, *noun* –**gardening**, *noun*

☑ SPELLING TIP Remember that the word **gardener** is made up of *garden* with the suffix *-er* added. This will help you to remember the *e* in the middle.

gargle *verb* To **gargle** is to move a liquid around inside your throat without swallowing, usually as a way of rinsing your mouth or applying medicine: *I annoy my sister by gargling very loudly.*

gargoyle /*say* **gah**-goyl/ *noun* a spout, often carved in the shape of an ugly head with an open mouth, which carries rainwater off a roof.

garish /*say* **gair**-rish, **gah**-rish/ *adjective* bright and attracting attention: *garish lipstick.*
□ **garishly**, *adverb* –**garishness**, *noun*

A SIMILAR WORD is **gaudy**.

garland *noun* a string of flowers or leaves you wear on your head or around your neck.

garlic *noun* a plant whose strong-smelling bulb is used in cooking and sometimes as a medicine.

garment *noun* a piece of clothing, such as a dress, shirt or coat.

garnish *verb* If you **garnish** food, you make it more pleasing to look at or taste: *Mum garnished the dish with parsley.*
□ **garnish**, *noun*

garret *noun* a room just under the roof of a house.

ANOTHER WORD for this is **attic**.

garrison *noun*
1. a group of soldiers who are ready to defend a fort or town. **2.** a place that has been strengthened against attack.

☑ SPELLING TIP *Double/single letter alert*: a double *r* and only one *s*. Do you know the actor Harrison Ford? Think of his first name, change the *h* to a *g* and you will remember how to spell **garrison**.

garrulous /*say* **ga**-ruh-luhs/ *adjective* very talkative.
□ **garrulity** /*say* guh-**rooh**-luh-tee/, *noun* talkativeness. –**garrulously**, *adverb* –**garrulousness**, *noun*

☑ SPELLING TIP *Double/single letter alert*: double *r* and only one *s*. Also remember that the middle vowel sound is spelt *u* and that the ending is *ous*.

gas[1] *noun* (*plural* **gases**)
1. any air-like substance that will take up the whole of the space that contains it. **2.** coal gas or natural gas used as a fuel: *Most people who have gas in their homes have natural gas.*
–*verb* (**gases**, **gassing**, **gassed**, **has gassed**) **3.** If a person is **gassed**, they are made sick or can even die if the gas is poisonous.
□ **gaseous**, *adjective* like gas. –**gassy**, *adjective* full of gas.

COMPARE definition 1 with **solid** and **liquid**.
WORD HISTORY made up by a Flemish chemist in the early 1600s who based it on a Greek word meaning 'chaos'

gas[2] *noun* petrol.

NOTE This term is used mainly in American English.
WORD HISTORY short for *gasoline*

gash *noun*
1. a long, deep cut: *a gash in my foot from walking on coral.*
–*verb* **2.** If you **gash** yourself, you get a long deep cut in some part of your body: *Dad accidentally gashed himself with pruning shears.*
□ **gash**, *verb*

gasket *noun* a metal or rubber fitting used to seal a joint, especially one in a car engine.

gasp *noun*
1. a sudden short taking in of breath: *She gave a gasp when she saw what we had done.*
–*verb* **2.** If you **gasp**, you take a sudden short breath in surprise: *The teacher gasped when we told her we had finished the work.*

gastric *adjective* having to do with the stomach: *a gastric ulcer.*

gastro- *prefix* a word part meaning 'stomach', as in *gastroenteritis*.

WORD HISTORY this prefix comes from Greek

gastroenteritis /*say* gas-troh-en-tuh-**ruy**-tuhs/ *noun* an illness in which the intestines become inflamed.

THE SHORT FORM of this is **gastro** which is used mainly in informal language.

gate *noun*
1. a movable frame for closing an entrance or blocking a passageway. **2.** an opening through which you can enter an enclosed area.

gatecrash *verb* To **gatecrash** an event is to enter or be present at it without paying or being invited: *The people who caused all the trouble had gatecrashed the party.*
□ **gatecrasher**, *noun*

gather *verb* To **gather** is to **1.** collect or pick: *Gather some sticks for a fire.* **2.** understand: *We gathered we still had about an hour to walk.* **3.** draw fabric into small folds on a thread: *Now pull the thread gently through the material and it will gather it evenly.* **4.** come together: *We all gathered around the fire for warmth.*
□ **gathering**, *noun*

gauche /*say* gohsh/ *adjective* clumsy and awkward: *His gauche manners embarrassed everybody.*
□ **gaucherie**, *noun* clumsiness. –**gaucheness**, *noun*

☑ SPELLING TIP *Tricky vowel sound*: *au* spelling for the 'oh' sound. Also notice that the ending is *che* giving a soft 'sh' sound. This is because **gauche** comes from French where it means 'left-handed' as well as meaning 'awkward'.

gaudy /*say* **gaw**-dee/ *adjective* (**gaudier**, **gaudiest**) bright and attracting attention: *Her gaudy outfit stood out in the crowd.*
☐ **gaudily**, *adverb* –**gaudiness**, *noun*

gauge /*say* gayj/ *noun*
1. thickness, especially of thin objects: *The wire was ten gauge.* **2.** an instrument for measuring: *a temperature gauge.* **3.** the distance between the two lines of a railway track: *The line was narrow gauge.*
–*verb* **4.** If you **gauge** something, you judge the measurement of it. **5.** If you **gauge** a person or situation, you consider them carefully and make a judgement about them: *They went along to gauge how much damage there was.*

> ☑ SPELLING TIP *Tricky vowel sound*: *au* for the 'ay' sound. Also remember that there are two *g*'s in this word – one at the beginning and one near the end – though they each make a different sound.

gaunt /*say* gawnt/ *adjective* Someone is **gaunt** if they are very thin and tired-looking in appearance.

> WORD HISTORY from a French word meaning 'rather yellow'

gauze /*say* gawz/ *noun*
1. thin, transparent cloth. **2.** similar material, such as one made of wire.
☐ **gauzy**, *adjective* (**gauzier**, **gauziest**)

gay *adjective*
1. Someone who is **gay** is homosexual. They are sexually attracted to people of the same sex as themselves. **2.** *Informal* Something that is **gay** is not fashionable or cool: *I think a mohawk is gay.* **3.** *Old-fashioned* **Gay** used to mean 'bright and cheerful': *a garden full of gay yellow daisies*; *a gay social occasion.*

gaze *verb* To **gaze** is to look long and steadily.
☐ **gaze**, *noun*

gazelle /*say* guh-**zel**/ *noun* a small, graceful antelope with large eyes.

gazette /*say* guh-**zet**/ *noun* an official government magazine containing lists of people the government has appointed, and so on.

> WORD HISTORY from the Italian name for a coin (the price of the gazette)

gear *noun*
1. a group of toothed wheels, or one of the wheels on its own, that connect with each other to pass on or change the movement of a machine, such as those that carry power from the engine to the wheels of a car. **2.** equipment: *cricket gear*; *camping gear.* **3.** *Rather informal* clothes: *Don't forget to bring some warm gear with you.*

gearbox *noun* a case in which the gears of a vehicle are enclosed.

gearstick *noun* a lever for engaging the gears in a car.

> OTHER WORDS for this are **gearlever** and **gearshift**.

gecko *noun* a small lizard which is active at night, with special pads on its toes which help it stick to things.

> WORD HISTORY from a Malay word that imitates the sounds these lizards make

Geiger counter /*say* **guy**-guh/ *noun* an instrument for measuring radioactivity, especially after the explosion of a nuclear bomb.

> WORD HISTORY named after the German physicist, Hans *Geiger*

gel /*say* jel/ *noun* a clear, sticky paste, such as the one that you spread lightly on your hair to hold it in shape.

> WORD HISTORY short for *gelatine*

gelatine *noun* a colourless, tasteless substance, used to make jellies and glues.

gelato /*say* juh-**lah**-toh/ *noun* (*plural* **gelatos** *or* **gelati**) a kind of ice-cream, made from cream, milk or water with fruit or nut flavouring.

> WORD HISTORY from the Italian word meaning 'frozen' or 'ice-cream'

gelding /*say* **gel**-ding/ *noun* a male animal that has had its sex organs removed, especially a horse.

gelignite /*say* **jel**-uhg-nuyt/ *noun* an explosive substance used in mining.

gem *noun* a stone used in jewellery, after it has been cut and polished.

> ANOTHER WORD for this is **gemstone**.

gender /*say* **jen**-duh/ *noun*
1. the condition of being either male or female: *The sports teams at school are worked out according to gender and age.* **2.** in the grammar of many languages, a set of classes to which nouns belong, such as masculine, feminine, and neuter.

> SEE the Grammar and Punctuation Guide appendix (for definition 2).

gene /*say* jeen/ *noun* one of the units in the body which is responsible for passing on characteristics, like blue eyes, from parents to their children.
☐ **genetic** /*say* juh-**net**-ik/, *adjective*: *a genetic disease.* –**genetically**, *adverb*

> ☑ SPELLING TIP Don't confuse the spelling of the plural **genes** with **jeans** (a kind of pants) which has the same sound. The word **gene** comes from the Greek word *genea* meaning 'breed' or 'kind'

genealogy /*say* jee-nee-**al**-uh-jee/ *noun* (*plural* **genealogies**) a study or record of the ancestors and relations in your family.
☐ **genealogist**, *noun* –**genealogical**, *adjective*

SEE ALSO **pedigree**, which has a similar meaning but it is used more often of animals.

☑ SPELLING TIP The word **genealogy** comes from the same Greek word as *gene* does. If you think of *gene* this will help you to remember that the vowel sound after the *n* is spelt *e* (though it may sound like it should be spelt *i*). The suffix *-logy* is used in many words relating to the study of something. Remember that in this word it has an *a* before it.

general *adjective*
1. concerning all or most people: *a general election.* **2.** common or widespread: *a general reaction of disappointment.* **3.** not limited to particular details or information: *I'll just tell you the general plan.*
–*noun* **4.** an officer of the highest rank in an army. **5.** a military commander: *Napoleon was a great general.*
–*phrase* **6. in general**, **a.** having to do with the whole group referred to. **b.** usually or commonly.
☐ **generally**, *adverb*

generate *verb* To **generate** something is to produce it or bring it into existence: *The Olympic Games generate a lot of interest.*

generation *noun*
1. all of the people born about the same time: *Our generation saw the first men on the moon.* **2.** the period of years, usually about 25 to 30, thought of as the difference between one generation of a family and another.

generator *noun* a machine for producing electricity.

generous *adjective* unselfish or ready to give freely: *That was generous of her to give up her seat.*
☐ **generosity**, *noun* –**generously**, *adverb*

WORD HISTORY from a Latin word meaning 'of noble birth'

genesis /*say* **jen**-uh-suhs/ *noun* (*plural* **geneses** /*say* **jen**-uh-seez/) a coming into being: *The genesis of the idea for the novel was his life in the tribe.*

NOTE When spelt with a capital, **Genesis** is the name of the first book of the Bible, which gives a story of the creation of the world.
WORD HISTORY from a Greek word meaning 'creation'

☑ SPELLING TIP *Tricky 'uh' sound*: the vowel sound in the middle is spelt *e*. Think of the word *gene* which has a related meaning (though not from the same origin) and matches the spelling of the first part of **genesis**.

genetically-modified *adjective*
1. having to do with an animal or plant which has had genes added or changed so as to produce characteristics that suit a particular purpose: *They are growing genetically-modified wheat that is less likely to be attacked by insects.* **2.** having to do with food produced from such an animal or plant.

THE ABBREVIATION is **GM**.

genetics /*say* juh-**net**-iks/ *noun* the science which studies the passing on of special characteristics from parents to their young.

NOTE Although it ends with an *s*, this word is singular, like *mathematics*: *Genetics is a very important part of science.*

genial /*say* **jee**-nee-uhl/ *adjective* A **genial** person has a warm and friendly manner.
☐ **genially**, *adverb*

☑ SPELLING TIP Remember the *gen* spelling (not *jeen* or *jean*) for the start of this word.

genie /*say* **jee**-nee/ *noun* a spirit in Arabian stories.

☑ SPELLING TIP Remember the *gen* spelling (not *jeen* or *jean*) for the start of this word.

genitals /*say* **jen**-uh-tuhlz/ *plural noun* the parts of the body which are used for sexual intercourse.

ANOTHER WORD for this is **genitalia** /*say* jen-uh-**tay**-lee-uh).

genius /*say* **jee**-nee-uhs/ *noun* a very talented or clever person.

☑ SPELLING TIP Remember the *gen* spelling (not *jeen* or *jean*) for the start of this word. Also remember the *us* ending which appears in some nouns that have come from Latin (where **genius** meant 'guardian spirit').

genocide /*say* **jen**-uh-suyd/ *noun* the planned killing of all the people belonging to one race or nation.
☐ **genocidal**, *adjective*

☑ SPELLING TIP Remember the *c* spelling for the 's' sound in this word. The suffix *-cide* means 'killer' or 'act of killing' and appears in several other words, such as *suicide*. It comes from the Latin word for 'kill'. Here it is joined to a form of *genos*, the Greek word for 'people'.

genre /*say* **zhon**-ruh/ *noun*
1. a kind or type. **2.** the category to which a piece of writing, music, film or art belongs, indicated by special features of its subject matter, form or language.

NOTE For definition 2, categories of genres include **narrative**, **drama**, **poetry**, **discussion**, **exposition** and so on.

genteel /*say* jen-**teel**/ *adjective* If someone is **genteel**, they are overly careful to be polite in their manners, speech and behaviour.
☐ **genteelly**, *adverb* –**gentility**, *noun*

ANOTHER WORD for this is **polite**.

gentile /*say* **jen**-tuyl/ *noun* someone who is not Jewish.

gentle *adjective*
1. kind and patient: *a gentle manner.* **2.** not rough or violent: *She was a gentle soul and wouldn't hurt a fly.* **3.** gradual: *We walked up a gentle hill.* **4.** soft or low: *a gentle voice.*
☐ **gentleness**, *noun* –**gently**, *adverb*

gentleman *noun* (*plural* **gentlemen**)
1. any man: *Gentlemen must not wear thongs into the club.* **2.** a man with polite manners: *He was such a gentleman – he insisted on walking her home.*

NOTE This word (as in definition 1) is used as a polite form of speech. In the past, this word meant 'a man born into a family with a high social standing' and a woman of the same kind was called a **gentlewoman**.

genuine /*say* **jen**-yooh-uhn/ *adjective*
1. Something that is **genuine** is true or real: *Their happiness was genuine*; *Is that a genuine ruby or a fake?* **2.** Someone who is **genuine** has real, not pretended, feelings: *You can believe everything he says – he is very genuine.*
☐ **genuinely**, *adverb* –**genuineness**, *noun*

A SIMILAR WORD (for definition 1) is **authentic**; (for definition 2) **sincere**.

☑ SPELLING TIP Don't forget the *e* at the end of **genuine**. Think of other words which have an *ine* spelling for an ending that sounds like 'uhn', such as *examine* and *imagine*.

geo- *prefix* a word part meaning 'the earth', as in *geography*, *geology*.

WORD HISTORY this prefix comes from Greek

geography /*say* jee-**og**-ruh-fee/ *noun* the study of the earth, including its land forms, peoples, climates, soils and plants.
☐ **geographer**, *noun* –**geographical**, *adjective*

geology /*say* jee-**ol**-uh-jee/ *noun* the study of the rocks which form the earth.
☐ **geological**, *adjective* –**geologist**, *noun* –**geological**, *adjective*

geometry /*say* jee-**om**-uh-tree/ *noun* the part of mathematics that studies shapes such as squares and triangles.
☐ **geometric**, *adjective* –**geometrical**, *adjective*

geranium /*say* juh-**ray**-nee-uhm/ *noun* a common garden plant usually with red, pink or purple flowers.

WORD HISTORY from a Greek word meaning 'crane's bill'

geriatric /*say* je-ree-**at**-rik/ *adjective* having to do with old people or their care: *a doctor specialising in geriatric medicine.*

germ *noun*
1. a tiny living thing which can only be seen with a microscope and which causes disease. **2.** the beginning of anything: *The germ of the movement for change was started by ordinary people.*

German measles *noun* See **rubella**.

German shepherd *noun* See **Alsatian**.

germinate *verb* To **germinate** is to begin to grow or develop: *These plants take longer to germinate*; *A secret desire began to germinate in her mind.*
☐ **germination**, *noun*

gesticulate /*say* jes-**tik**-yuh-layt/ *verb* If you **gesticulate**, you make movements with a part of your body, especially your hands, in order to express a feeling or idea.
☐ **gesticulation**, *noun*

☑ SPELLING TIP You will be able to spell **gesticulate** by sounding out its syllables, if you remember that it starts with a soft *g* (not a *j*) and that it has a *c* (not a *k*) in the middle. Rap it out as *ges + tic + u + late*.

gesture /*say* **jes**-chuh/ *noun*
1. a movement of part of your body to express a feeling or idea: *She flung the book across the table in a gesture of anger.* **2.** something done to express a feeling or idea: *The presentation of the gift was a gesture of our appreciation.*
–*verb* **3.** If you **gesture**, you express something by use of actions instead of words: *She gestured to us to wait for the car to pass.*

get *verb* (**gets**, **getting**, **got**, **has got**) To **get** is to **1.** obtain or receive something: *to get a fantastic Christmas present.* **2.** go somewhere and bring something back with you: *Could you get some milk?* **3.** hear something: *I didn't get the last bit of what you said – could you repeat it please?* **4.** reach someone: *Did you get her, or was the phone still engaged?* **5.** cause to be or do something: *Sonia wants to get her hair cut.* **6.** prepare or make something ready: *I think you can get breakfast yourselves.* **7.** arrive: *We got there too late.* **8.** become or grow: *We get tired if we watch television too late.* **9.** *Informal* to understand the meaning of something: *Do you get what I am telling you?*; *He still doesn't get it – he must be stupid.*
–*phrase* **10. get about**, **a.** to move about. **b.** of news and so on, to become known. **11. get ahead**, to make progress or be successful. **12. get** (**an idea**, **message**, etc.) **across**, to make (an idea, message, etc.) understood. **13. get at**, **a.** to reach: *I can't get at it – it's just out*

of my reach. **b.** to imply or suggest: *What are you getting at?* **14. get away**, to escape: *The fish got away.* **15. get away with**, to escape punishment for: *Unfortunately, they got away with the crime.* **16. get by**, to manage: *He didn't know how he'd get by without a car.* **17. get down to**, to work hard at. **18. get off**, to escape punishment. **19. get on**, **a.** to become old: *She's getting on now – you can see it in her slow walk.* **b.** to make progress: *He is getting on with his work.* **c.** to be friendly: *She gets on well with the rest of the class.* **20. get over**, **a.** to defeat or find a way around. **b.** to get well again after (a sickness): *She finally got over the flu.* **21. get round**, **a.** to get into favour with: *to get round your teacher.* **b.** to deal with: *to get round difficulties.* **22. get round to**, to come at last to: *to get round to washing the car.* **23. get through to**, **a.** to connect on the telephone with. **b.** to make understand: *I can't get through to her at all.* **24. get up**, **a.** to sit up or stand. **b.** to rise from bed. **25. get up to**, to take part in: *to get up to something bad.*

geyser /*say* **gee**-zuh, **guy**-zuh/ *noun* a hot spring that sometimes sends up a column of water and steam into the air.

WORD HISTORY from an Icelandic word meaning 'gush'

☑ SPELLING TIP *Tricky vowel sound*: the first vowel sound is spelt *ey* (which can be pronounced as either 'ee' or 'uy').

ghastly /*say* **gahst**-lee/ *adjective* (**ghastlier**, **ghastliest**) very bad or unpleasant: *a ghastly memory.*

☑ SPELLING TIP *Silent letter alert*: don't forget that there is an *h* following the *g*. Remember that you would feel **ghastly** if you saw a *ghost* (which starts with the same spelling).

gherkin /*say* **ger**-kuhn/ *noun* a small, pickled cucumber.

☑ SPELLING TIP *Silent letter alert*: don't forget that there is an *h* following the *g*. Apart from this, the spelling of **gherkin** is quite straightforward.

ghetto /*say* **get**-oh/ *noun* (*plural* **ghettos** *or* **ghettoes**) the part of a city where a group of similar people, such as poor people or people from another country, live together.

☑ SPELLING TIP *Silent letter alert*: don't forget that there is an *h* following the *g*. Also remember that there is a double *t* before the *o* ending. This ending occurs in many words which come from Italian, as **ghetto** does. It comes from the Italian name given to the Jewish quarter of Venice in the 16th century.

ghost /*say* gohst/ *noun*
1. the spirit of someone who has died, imagined as visiting living people. **2.** a very small amount or trace: *She hasn't a ghost of a chance*; *a ghost of a smile.*
☐ **ghostly**, *adjective* –**ghostliness**, *noun*

OTHER WORDS (for definition 1) are **apparition**, **phantom**, **spectre** and **spook** (*Informal*).

☑ SPELLING TIP *Silent letter alert*: don't forget that a ghostly *h* has slipped silently in after the *g* in **ghost** and it is followed by an *o* making a spooky 'oh' sound. The same ghostly *h* turns up in *ghastly* too.

giant *noun*
1. an imaginary creature that looks like a human but is much bigger and stronger. **2.** someone or something of great size, importance or ability: *a giant in the research world.*
–*adjective* **3.** extremely big: *a giant plant.*

NOTE A female giant can be called a **giantess**.

gibberish /*say* **jib**-uh-rish/ *noun* If somebody speaks **gibberish**, they speak quickly and without making any sense.

gibber /*say* **gib**-uh/ *noun* a stone or rock.

WORD HISTORY from an Aboriginal language of New South Wales called Dharug

gibbon *noun* a kind of small ape with long arms.

giblets /*say* **jib**-luhts/ *plural noun* the inside parts of a fowl, such as the heart and liver, usually cooked separately.

giddy *adjective* (**giddier**, **giddiest**) If you are **giddy**, you have the feeling of spinning around.
☐ **giddily**, *adverb* –**giddiness**, *noun*

A SIMILAR WORD is **dizzy**.

gift *noun*
1. something that is given as a present. **2.** a special ability: *He had a gift for making people feel comfortable.*
☐ **gifted**, *adjective*

A SIMILAR WORD (for definition 2) is **talent**.

gig[1] *noun* a light, two-wheeled carriage pulled by one horse.

gig[2] *noun* a job for a musician, often a booking for one show only.

gigabyte /*say* **gig**-uh-buyt/ *noun* a unit for measuring information stored by a computer, equal to 1024 megabytes.

THE SHORT FORM of this is **gig**.

gigantic /*say* juy-**gan**-tik/ *adjective* extremely big: *a gigantic tree*; *a gigantic sculpture in the shape of a banana.*

☑ SPELLING TIP The word **gigantic** comes from *gigas*, a Latin word meaning 'giant' which is why that extra *g* appears between the two syllables of the *giant* part of the word. The suffix *-ic* makes the meaning 'like a giant'.

giggle *verb* To **giggle** is to laugh in a silly way.
☐ **giggle**, *noun* –**giggler**, *noun* –**giggly**, *adjective*

gild *verb* (**gilds**, **gilding**, **gilded** *or* **gilt**, **has gilded** *or* **has gilt**) If you **gild** something, you cover it with a layer of gold or something gold-coloured.
☐ **gilding**, *noun*

gill *noun* the part of the body that fish and other sea creatures use for breathing.

gilt *adjective*
1. golden-coloured or covered with gold: *a gilt frame.*
–*noun* **2.** the gold or other material used in gilding.

☑ SPELLING TIP Don't confuse the spelling of **gilt** with **guilt** which sounds the same. **Guilt** is the feeling you have when you know you have done something wrong.

gimmick *noun* an unusual action or trick, usually to get attention.
☐ **gimmicky**, *adjective*

☑ SPELLING TIP *Double letter alert*: double *m*. Also remember that the ending is *ick* (not *ic*).

gin /*say* jin/ *noun* a strong alcoholic drink.

ginger *noun*
1. a plant root which is used in cooking as a spice and in medicine. **2.** a reddish-brown colour.
☐ **ginger**, *adjective*: *a ginger moustache.*

gingerly *adverb* with great care: *They walked gingerly among the broken glass.*

gingham /*say* **ging**-uhm/ *noun* a cotton cloth with a striped or checked pattern.

WORD HISTORY from a Malay word meaning 'striped'

gipsy /*say* **jip**-see/ *noun* See **gypsy**.

giraffe /*say* juh-**rahf**/ *noun* an African animal with spots, a very long neck and long legs.

NOTE The male is a **bull**; the female is a **cow**; the young is a **calf**.

☑ SPELLING TIP If you remember the sentence 'Giraffes instinctively reach all fresh food easily' and put the first letter of each word together you have **giraffe** with its one *r* and two *f*'s.

girder /*say* **ger**-duh/ *noun* a thick beam used as a support in building.

girl *noun* a female child or a young woman.
☐ **girlhood**, *noun* –**girlish**, *adjective*: *a girlish giggle.*

girlfriend *noun*
1. a woman or girl with whom someone has a steady romantic relationship: *My brother's girlfriend came to the film with us.* **2.** a female friend: *Leila came home from school with several girlfriends.*

girth /*say* gerth/ *noun*
1. the measurement around anything: *He needs specially made clothes because of his enormous girth.* **2.** a band placed under the stomach of a horse to hold a saddle or pack onto its back.

gist /*say* jist/ *noun* the essence or the essential meaning of something: *The gist of the email is that he can't come.*

give *verb* (**gives**, **giving**, **gave**, **has given**)
1. If you **give** something to someone, you offer it to them freely: *She gave me her book to read.* **2.** If you **give** someone money in return for something, you pay them: *I'll give you $25 for your old bike.* **3.** If something **gives** you a feeling, it causes you to experience it: *She gave the impression of being quite content.* **4.** If you **give** someone a right, opportunity or responsibility, you make it theirs: *I was given the job of watching the class.* **5.** If you **give** a party, you organise it and act as the host: *They gave a party to celebrate his return.* **6.** If you **give** someone information, you tell it to them: *to give an answer.*
–*phrase* **7. give away**, **a.** to give as a present. **b.** to allow to become known: *Don't give away any details that you want kept secret.* **8. give in**, to admit defeat. **9. give off**, to send out: *to give off fumes.* **10. give out**, **a.** to become worn out or used up: *The engine gave out.* **b.** to hand out. **11. give up**, **a.** to lose all hope. **b.** to stop: *She should give up smoking.* **c.** to stop fighting or resisting: *I give up – you've won.*
☐ **giver**, *noun*

given name *noun* the name that you have been given, distinct from your family name: *Her given names are Alice Elizabeth and her surname is Martin.*

ANOTHER TERM is **Christian name**.

glacial /*say* **glay**-shuhl, **glay**-see-uhl/ *adjective*
1. having ice. **2.** icy or cold as ice.
☐ **glacially**, *adverb* –**glaciate**, *verb* –**glaciation**, *noun*

glacier /*say* **glay**-see-uh, **glas**-ee-uh/ *noun* a river of ice which moves very slowly down a mountain.

glad *adjective* (**gladder**, **gladdest**)
1. happy or pleased.
–*phrase* **2. glad of**, grateful for: *We didn't think we would need cold drinks, but we were glad of them when it got hot.*
☐ **gladden**, *verb* –**gladly**, *adverb* –**gladness**, *noun*

glade *noun* an open space in a forest.

gladiator *noun* in ancient Rome, a man, often a slave, who fought other men or animals as a public entertainment.
☐ **gladiatorial**, *adjective*

glamour *noun* an exciting charm or beauty: *The movie world seems to be full of glamour.*
☐ **glamorous**, *adjective*

ANOTHER SPELLING is **glamor**.

glance *verb*
1. If you **glance** at something, you look at it quickly. **2.** If something **glances** off something else, it hits it and then goes off in a slightly different direction: *The bullet glanced off the side of the tree.*
☐ **glance**, *noun* –**glancing**, *adjective*

gland *noun* a part of the body that makes a substance that is used by another part of the body, such as the pancreas which produces substances which help in digestion.
☐ **glandular**, *adjective*

glare *noun*
1. a strong, bright light: *the glare of car headlights.* **2.** an angry look.
–*verb* **3.** If you **glare** at someone, you look at them angrily: *Dad glares at me when I get up late.*

glass *noun*
1. a hard, transparent substance used for such things as windows, bottles and drinking containers. **2.** something made of glass, such as a drinking container or a mirror.
☐ **glassy**, *adjective* looking like glass.

glasses *plural noun* two lenses in a frame which are worn over your eyes to help you see more clearly.

ANOTHER WORD for this is **spectacles**, although this is rather old-fashioned now.

glaze *verb*
1. If you **glaze** an area, you fit or cover it with glass. **2.** If you **glaze** something like pottery, you cover it with a thin coat of a clear shiny substance.
–*noun* **3.** a smooth, shiny coating or surface.
–*phrase* **4. glaze over**, to become glassy looking: *His eyes glazed over as soon as she started talking.*
☐ **glazier**, *noun* someone who fits glass into windows.

gleam *noun*
1. a flash of light: *the gleam of the torch*; *a gleam of interest in his eyes.* **2.** a soft light: *the gleam of polished wood.*
–*verb* **3.** If something **gleams**, it shines with light, often a soft light: *We cleaned the car until it gleamed.*
☐ **gleaming**, *adjective*

A SIMILAR WORD is **glimmer**.

glean *verb* If you **glean** something like information, you gather it, usually slowly and bit by bit: *We were finally able to glean that they had left the house secretly that night.*
☐ **gleaner**, *noun*

glee *noun* a showing of pleasure or a feeling of happiness.
☐ **gleeful**, *adjective* –**gleefully**, *adverb*: *to laugh gleefully.*

glen *noun* a small, narrow valley.

glide *verb* To **glide** is to move or make to move along smoothly.
☐ **glide**, *noun*

glider *noun* an aeroplane without an engine that flies by using air currents.

glimmer *noun*
1. a weak light which goes on and off. **2.** a slight suggestion: *Her encouragement gave us a glimmer of hope.*
–*verb* **3.** If something **glimmers**, it shines faintly or unsteadily: *The fire was glimmering in the distance.*
☐ **glimmering**, *noun*

A SIMILAR WORD is **gleam**.

glimpse *noun*
1. a quick sighting: *I caught a glimpse of him as he ran past.*
–*verb* **2.** If you **glimpse** something, you catch sight of it briefly: *From the car, we glimpsed the ocean through a break in the trees.*

glint *noun*
1. a flash of light: *At the bottom of the drawer, we could see the glint of coins.* **2.** a look showing amusement or a secret idea: *We could tell by the glint in her eyes that she was up to something.*

glisten /*say* **glis**-uhn/ *verb* If something **glistens**, it shines with a sparkling light: *The drops of rain glistened in the early morning light.*

☑ SPELLING TIP *Silent letter alert*: don't forget the silent *t* after the *s*.

glitter *verb* To **glitter** is to shine brightly: *The town glittered with Christmas lights.*
☐ **glitter**, *noun* –**glittery**, *adjective*

gloat *verb* If you **gloat**, you take great satisfaction in your own success or other people's failure: *They were gloating over their win.*
☐ **gloating**, *adjective*

globalisation *noun*
1. the process of becoming international: *the globalisation of the mining industry.* **2.** the development of a single worldwide economy and culture.

ANOTHER SPELLING is **globalization**.

global warming *noun* a noticeable increase in the temperature of the air around the earth's surface, thought by many to be caused by an increase in the amount of greenhouse gases being released into the atmosphere by human activities such as the burning of coal and oil to provide energy, fuel, etc.

globe *noun*
1. a round, ball-shaped map of the earth. **2.** anything shaped like a round ball. **3. the globe**, the earth: *People all over the globe were watching the Olympic Games.*
☐ **global**, *adjective*

A SIMILAR WORD (for definition 2) is **sphere**.
WORD HISTORY from a Latin word meaning 'round body', 'mass', or 'ball'

glockenspiel /*say* **glok**-uhn-speel, **glok**-uhn-shpeel/ *noun* a musical instrument with metal bars set in a frame, which you hit with hammers.

WORD HISTORY from the German words for 'bell' and 'play'

gloom *noun* darkness or dimness.
☐ **gloomy**, *adjective* –**gloominess**, *noun* –**gloomily**, *adverb*

glorious *adjective*
1. beautiful, wonderful, or delightful: *The view from the top of the mountain at sunset was glorious.* **2.** giving or having glory: *a glorious win for justice.*
☐ **gloriously**, *adverb* –**gloriousness**, *noun*

☑ SPELLING TIP Don't forget the *ous* ending. This common suffix means 'full of' so the basic meaning of **glorious** is 'full of glory'. The *y* in *glory* has changed to *i* following the rule that words ending in *y* change the *y* to an *i* when a word part is added.

glory *noun* (*plural* **glories**)
1. praise and honour. **2.** something that is a cause of pride or honour: *Instead of dwelling on past glories, they should be thinking of the future.* **3.** splendid or holy beauty: *hymns sung to the glory of God*; *the glory of the setting sun.*

gloss *noun*
1. the shine on the outside of something: *the gloss of satin.*
–*phrase* **2. gloss over**, to cover up or try to make seem unimportant: *He glossed over his mistakes.*
☐ **glossy**, *adjective* (**glossier**, **glossiest**) –**glossiness**, *noun*

glossary *noun* (*plural* **glossaries**) a list of special or difficult words about a particular subject, with their definitions: *There was a glossary of ten pages at the end of the book.*

glove *noun* a covering for your hand, usually with a separate part for each finger and for the thumb.

glow *noun*
1. the light given out by something extremely hot. **2.** brightness of colour. **3.** a pleasant warm feeling: *a glow of contentment.*
–*verb* **4.** If something **glows**, it gives out light or warmth: *The camp fire glowed in the dark night.*
☐ **glowing**, *adjective*

glow-worm *noun* a kind of insect whose body gives off light in the dark.

glucose *noun* a natural sugar which is found in plants and in some animal tissues, which supplies most of the energy that cells need.

WORD HISTORY from a Greek word meaning 'sweet'

glue *noun*
1. a paste used to stick things together.
–*verb* **2.** If you **glue** one thing to another, you stick them together with glue.
☐ **gluey**, *adjective*

glum *adjective* (**glummer**, **glummest**) unhappy or dejected.
☐ **glumly**, *adverb*

glut *noun* an oversupply: *They reduced the price of grapefruit because there was a glut of them.*

glutton *noun* someone who eats too much.
☐ **gluttonous**, *adjective* –**gluttony**, *noun*

gnarled /*say* nahld/ *adjective*
1. twisted and having many woody lumps: *She ran her hand over the gnarled bark of an old tree.* **2.** rough and worn by the weather: *The old man's face was gnarled and wrinkled.*

☑ SPELLING TIP *Silent letter alert*: don't forget the silent *g* at the start of **gnarled**. This word has been formed from *gnarl* (an outgrowth on a tree trunk or branch) plus the suffix *-ed*. It might help you to remember the silent *g* at the beginning if you think of it as looking just like the knotty shape of a *gnarl* that grows in unexpected places.

gnash /*say* nash/ *verb* If you **gnash** your teeth, you grind them together noisily, usually because you are angry or upset: *He gnashed his teeth thinking of how they had cheated him.*

gnat /*say* nat/ *noun* a kind of small insect with only one pair of wings.

gnaw /*say* naw/ *verb* To **gnaw** is to wear something away by continuous chewing or biting: *The dog was gnawing on a bone.*
☐ **gnawing**, *adjective* –**gnawing**, *noun*

gnome /*say* nohm/ *noun* a small being in fairytales, usually imagined as a little old man.

gnu /*say* nooh/ *noun* (*plural* **gnus** *or* **gnu**) See **wildebeest**.

☑ SPELLING TIP *Silent letter alert*: don't forget the silent *g* at the start of this word. It is not unusual for *gn* at the start of a word to make an 'n' sound (see the words above), but in **gnu** it tends to be surprising!

go *verb* (**goes**, **going**, **went**, **has gone**)
1. If you **go** somewhere, you move or travel from one place to another: *Let's go to the pictures.* **2.** If you **go** somewhere, you visit that place regularly: *Where do you go to school?* **3.** If something **goes** somewhere, it leads to there or can get as far as there: *The belt's too short to go around my waist.* **4.** If something **goes** somewhere, it belongs there or that is its usual spot: *The plates go on the second shelf.* **5.** If a vehicle **goes**, it is in motion: *How fast does this car go?* **6.** If a piece of machinery **goes**, it works properly: *If you put glue in the engine, it will stop going.* **7.** If you **go**, you leave: *I'd better go – it's getting late.* **8.** If something **goes**, it disappears: *My pen was here a minute ago but now it's gone.* **9.** If something such as food or money **goes**, it is used up. **10.** If someone or something **goes** a certain way, they become like that: *to go bald*; *to go mad.* **11.** If something **goes** in a certain way, it makes a particular sound or movement: *The gun went bang.*
–*noun* (*plural* **goes**) **12.** a turn: *How many goes have you had?*
–*phrase* **13. all the go**, in the current fashion. **14. from the word go**, from the very beginning. **15. go along with**, to accept or agree. **16. go back on**, to fail to keep: *to go back on a promise.* **17. go for**, **a.** to attack: *That dog will go for children.* **b.** to be attracted to: *to go for heavy metal music.* **c.** to aim for: *to go for the top job.* **d.** to apply to: *That rule goes for all of us.* **18. go in for**, to be interested in: *He goes in for stamp collecting.* **19. go off**, **a.** to explode: *The gun went off.* **b.** to become bad: *The meat has gone off.* **c.** to stop liking: *I've gone off fruit.* **20. on the go**, active and energetic.

goad *noun*
1. a stick with a pointed end used to prod cattle and other animals into moving.
–*verb* **2.** If someone uses a goad to drive cattle, they **goad** them. **3.** If you **goad** someone into doing something, you try to provoke them to do it: *The malicious boys goaded Harry into punching back at them.*

goal *noun*
1. an area, basket or something similar at which you aim the ball in sports such as football, basketball and others. **2.** the score made by doing this: *He tried hard but missed scoring a goal.* **3.** something you aim towards: *My goal is to be the first to get 100 in the maths test.*

goanna *noun* any of a number of large Australian lizards.

goat *noun* a small cud-chewing animal with horns, which is able to live in rocky mountainous areas and is used as a farm animal in many countries.

NOTE The male is a **billy goat**; the female is a **nanny goat**; the young is a **kid**.

gobble *verb* To **gobble** food is to swallow or eat it quickly in large pieces.

goblet *noun* a cup or glass with a stem and a base.

goblin *noun* an ugly elf in fairytales who usually makes trouble for people.

go-cart *noun*
1. See **billycart**. **2.** See **go-kart**.

god *noun*
1. a supernatural being who is believed to have the power to control human affairs or the world of nature and is worshipped or prayed to according to particular religious beliefs: *Some people believe in many gods.* **2.** someone or something which is given too much attention: *Money is his god.* **3. God**, in religions that believe in only one god, the highest being who is the maker and ruler of the universe.
☐ **godlike**, *adjective*

goddess /*say* **god**-es/ *noun* a female god.

godly *adjective* (**godlier**, **godliest**) following God's laws: *She led a godly life.*
☐ **godliness**, *noun*

goggles *plural noun* glasses with frames and side pieces used to protect your eyes from wind, dust, sunlight or water.

go-kart *noun* a small, light, low-powered car for racing.

ANOTHER SPELLING is **go-cart**.

gold *noun*
1. a precious yellow metal. **2.** things made of gold, like jewellery: *We handed over all our gold and money.* **3.** something highly valued: *Water was like gold in that dry place.*
☐ **gold**, *adjective*: *a gold watch*; *a gold sash.* –**golden**, *adjective*

goldfish *noun* (*plural* **goldfish** *or* **goldfishes**) a small and pretty fish, often kept in bowls or pools.

goldmine *noun*
1. a place where gold is mined. **2.** an enterprise that makes a lot of money: *My dad said the business was a goldmine.*
☐ **goldminer**, *noun* –**goldmining**, *noun*

golf *noun* an outdoor game in which a small ball is hit with special clubs around a set course.
☐ **golfer**, *noun*: *Golfers can move around the golf course in golf buggies.* –**golfing**, *noun*

gondola /*say* **gon**-duh-luh/ *noun* a long, narrow boat with high pointed ends, used on the canals of Venice in Italy.
☐ **gondolier**, *noun*

gong *noun* a round, flat piece of metal which is hit with a stick with a padded end to give a loud ringing sound.

good *adjective* (**better**, **best**) If something is **good** it is **1.** pleasant or enjoyable: *I went to a good party last Saturday.* **2.** of a high standard or quality: *a good performance.* **3.** suitable or right: *It was a good site to pitch a tent.* **4.** If someone is **good**, they behave morally or correctly. **5.** If a child is **good**, they are well-behaved. **6.** *Informal* If you say that you are **good**, you mean that you are in good health or that things are going quite well for you: *'How are you today?' 'Good, thanks.'* **7.** If you are **good** at something, you do it skilfully or successfully.
–*noun* **8.** advantage or benefit: *Mum said she was getting rid of the television for our own good.* **9.** excellent qualities or proper actions: *Look for good in others.* **10. goods**, **a.** possessions. **b.** products or articles that you can buy: *goods from a factory.*
–*phrase* **11. as good as**, almost: *Once we reach the corner, we are as good as there.* **12. for good**, for ever. **13. make good**, **a.** to fulfil or carry out: *to make good a promise.* **b.** to be successful.
☐ **goodness**, *noun*

SIMILAR WORDS (for definitions 1 and 2) are **fine**, **excellent**, **great** and **first-class**, which all mean 'very good'; (for definition 4) **decent**, **honest**, **upright**, **virtuous** and **saintly**. Note that if you describe someone as **saintly**, you mean that they are extremely good and unselfish, beyond what is usual for a human.

goodbye *interjection* a word you use when you leave someone.

WORD HISTORY a shortened form of 'God be with you'

google *verb* If you **google** something or somebody, you search the internet for information on that thing or person, especially using the Google search engine: *Mum googled the restaurant so she could look at the menu.*

WORD HISTORY trademark

goose *noun* (*plural* **geese**)
1. a large bird with webbed feet and a long neck, sometimes kept on farms. **2.** the female of this bird. **3.** a silly person: *She was a bit of a goose to set out on that walk without any water!*

NOTE The male is called a **gander**. A young goose is called a **gosling**.

gooseberry /*say* **gooz**-buh-ree/ *noun* (*plural* **gooseberries**) a small, sour-tasting, round berry.

goosebumps *plural noun* tiny lumps on the skin that appear when you are cold or frightened.

OTHER TERMS for this are **goose pimples** and **goose flesh**.

goosestep *noun* an unusual marching step in which the legs are swung high while the knees are kept straight and stiff.

gore[1] *noun* blood from a cut, especially when it has clotted: *wounds covered in gore.*
☐ **gory**, *adjective* (**gorier**, **goriest**)

gore[2] *verb* If an animal **gores** something or somebody, it pierces them with its horns or tusks: *She wouldn't cross the paddock because she was terrified of being gored by the bull.*

gorge *noun*
1. a narrow valley with steep rocky walls, often with a river running through it.
–*verb* **2.** If you **gorge** yourself, you eat large quantities of food.

WORD HISTORY from a French word meaning 'throat'

gorgeous /*say* **gaw**-juhs/ *adjective* If someone or something is **gorgeous**, they are very attractive or desirable.

WORD HISTORY from a French word meaning 'fashionable' or 'colourful'

☑ SPELLING TIP The letter *g* turns up twice in **gorgeous**, the first time with a hard sound and the second time with a soft sound indicated by the letter *e* which follows it. Rap it out as *gor+ ge+ ous*.

gorilla *noun* the largest kind of ape, found in Africa.

☑ SPELLING TIP *Single/double letter alert*: only one *r* but a double *l*. Think of 'an ill gorilla' to remind yourself of the double *l*. Also, don't confuse **gorilla** with **guerilla** or **griller** which both have a similar sound. A **guerilla** is a member of a small band of soldiers that makes surprise raids and attacks on the enemy. This may also be spelt **guerrilla**. A **griller** is the part of a stove or kitchen appliance which cooks meat by direct heat.

gosling *noun* a young goose.

NOTE The male is called a **gander**. The female is called a **goose**.

gospel *noun*
1. in Christianity, the teachings of Christ as written in the Bible.
–*phrase* **2. the gospel truth**, information which is completely true: *We didn't believe her story but it turned out to be the gospel truth.*
☐ **gospel**, *adjective*

ANOTHER FORM This word (as in definition 1) is often spelt with a capital letter.

gossamer /*say* **gos**-uh-muh/ *noun*
1. a fine cobweb lying on grass or bushes or floating in the air. **2.** any very fine material.
☐ **gossamer**, *adjective*

gossip *noun*
1. silly, and sometimes unkind, talk about other people's business. **2.** someone who talks gossip: *She is a great gossip.*
–*verb* **3.** If you **gossip**, you tell silly and sometimes untrue or unkind stories about other people.

gouge /*say* gowj/ *noun*
1. a sharp, curved tool used for making grooves in wood. **2.** a hole made by this tool.
–*verb* **3.** If you **gouge** something, you make a hole or a long cut in it with a sharp object: *They gouged out a tunnel through the mountain for a railway.*

> ☑ SPELLING TIP *Tricky vowel sound*: *ou* for the 'ow' sound. Also remember that there are two *g*'s in this word – one at the beginning with a hard sound and one near the end with a soft sound indicated by the letter *e* which follows it.

goulash /*say* **gooh**-lash/ *noun* a meat stew containing onions and paprika.

gourd /*say* gawd/ *noun*
1. the fruit of a climbing plant. **2.** the shell of this plant, dried and used as a bottle, bowl or container.

gourmet /*say* **gaw**-may, **goo**-uh-may/ *noun* someone who knows a lot about good food and drink.

> ☑ SPELLING TIP *Silent letter alert*: don't forget the *et* ending giving an 'ay' sound (the *t* is silent). **Gourmet** has this sound and this spelling because it comes from French, where it means 'wine taster'.

govern *verb* To **govern** is to rule by authority, such as laws.

governess *noun* especially in the past, a woman with the job of teaching children in their own homes.

government *noun*
1. the group of people who rule or govern a country or state. **2.** rule or control: *Different countries have different forms of government.*

governor *noun*
1. a. the representative of the king or queen in an Australian state. **b.** the person at the head of the government of a province or state in another country, as in the United States of America. **2.** someone in charge of a place or institution: *the governor of a prison*; *the governor of a bank.*
☐ **governorship**, *noun*

> ANOTHER FORM This word (as in definition 1) is spelt with a capital letter when you are writing the title of a particular person.

> ☑ SPELLING TIP The difficulty with this word is remembering the *or* ending. There are two common suffixes that are used to indicate that someone does something – *-er* and *-or*. In **governor**, it is the *-or* suffix that has been added to the word *govern*.

governor-general *noun* (*plural* **governor-generals** *or* **governors-general**) the main representative of the king or queen in Australia and some other British Commonwealth countries.

> ANOTHER FORM This is spelt with capital letters when you are writing the title of a particular person.

gown *noun*
1. a dress worn by women on important occasions. **2.** a loose, flowing piece of clothing worn by judges, lawyers, priests and others.

GPS *noun*
1. a navigation system that uses information from satellites to give the exact location of an object, such as a ship or car. **2.** a device that uses this system.

> NOTE This is a short form of **global positioning system**.

grab *verb* (**grabs**, **grabbing**, **grabbed**, **has grabbed**)
1. If you **grab** something, you take it suddenly: *The thief grabbed her bag.* **2.** *Informal* If something **grabs** you, it affects or interests you: *How does the idea of going to the beach grab you?*

> A SIMILAR WORD (for definition 1) is **snatch**.

grace *noun*
1. beauty of appearance or movement. **2.** favour or kindness: *by the grace of god.*
☐ **graceful**, *adjective* –**gracefully**, *adverb*

gracious /*say* **gray**-shuhs/ *adjective* showing kindness and good manners: *They were gracious enough to invite him in despite his shabby appearance*; *a gracious gesture.*
☐ **graciously**, *adverb*

grade *noun*
1. a stage or step on a scale of positions, quality or value: *He was promoted to a higher grade*; *Walking tracks are described in terms of grades of difficulty.* **2.** a class in a school arranged according to age and ability: *the fifth grade.*
–*verb* **3.** If you **grade** something, you rate it on some measure like quality or age: *The teachers graded us according to hopping ability and then put us into teams for the sack race.*
–*phrase* **4. make the grade**, to reach a desired standard.

grader *noun*
1. a vehicle with a blade in front, used for levelling roads. **2.** someone or something that sorts or groups: *an apple grader.*

gradient *noun*
1. the amount of slope or steepness in a road, railway or path: *The road went up the mountain in a steep gradient.* 2. a sloping surface: *Once we reached the gradient, we slowed down.*

gradual *adjective* happening slowly over a long period of time.
☐ **gradually**, *adverb*

graduate *noun* /*say* **graj**-ooh-uht/
1. someone who has passed a course of study at a university or college.
–*verb* /*say* **graj**-ooh-ayt/ 2. If you **graduate**, you successfully complete your course at university or college.
☐ **graduation**, *noun*

graffiti /*say* gruh-**fee**-tee/ *noun* drawings or words written without permission on walls in public places: *The bus shelter was full of graffiti.*

NOTE This word comes from Italian where it is a plural noun (meaning 'scratches'). However, in English it is usually considered singular and therefore is used with a singular verb: *Some graffiti is quite funny.*

☑ SPELLING TIP *Double/single letter alert*: double *f*, but only one *t*. **Graffiti** has this spelling because it comes from Italian where the letter *i* is a common ending for plural nouns.

graft *noun*
1. part of a plant placed into a small thin cut in another plant's stem, which then begins to grow as part of that plant. 2. a piece of living material cut by a doctor from one part of someone's body and placed somewhere else in their body: *She was so badly burnt she needed skin grafts.*
–*verb* 3. If you **graft** a plant, you insert a piece of it into another plant's stem to get the best qualities from both: *They grafted some mandarin shoots onto a lemon tree.*

grain *noun*
1. a small, hard seed of one of the cereal plants: *wheat grains.* 2. any small, hard particle: *a grain of sand.* 3. a very small amount of something: *If you had a grain of sympathy, you would look after him.* 4. the direction of the fibres in wood or cloth.
☐ **grainy**, *adjective* (**grainier**, **grainiest**) –**granular**, *adjective* –**granulate**, *verb*

gram *noun* a measure of weight in the metric system.

THE SYMBOL for this is **g**.

grammar *noun*
1. the parts of a language, such as sounds and words, and the way they are combined into phrases and sentences. 2. the description of this or a book containing such a description.
☐ **grammarian**, *noun* –**grammatical**, *adjective*

☑ SPELLING TIP There is a double *m* in this word but the part most people get wrong is the *ar* (not *er*) ending. Remember you have to put an *a* from the alphabet into **grammar** and you will get it right.

gramophone *noun Old-fashioned* a machine that reproduces sound from a record.

NOTE In more modern times, this kind of machine was called a **record-player**. Now most people have **CD players** or **MP3 players** instead.

granary /*say* **gran**-uh-ree/ *noun* (*plural* **granaries**) a building in which grain is stored.

grand *adjective*
1. important-looking: *a grand building centuries old.* 2. noble or fine: *a grand old man.* 3. complete: *the grand total.* 4. highest in importance: *a grand master of swimming coaching.*
☐ **grandeur** /*say* **gran**-juh/, *noun*

grandchild *noun* (*plural* **grandchildren**) the child of someone's daughter or son.

granddaughter *noun* a daughter of someone's son or daughter.

ANOTHER FORM is **grand-daughter**.

grandfather *noun* the father of someone's father or mother.

grandiose /*say* **gran**-dee-ohs/ *adjective* extremely grand or splendid: *He was always full of grandiose plans to make money.*
☐ **grandiosely**, *adverb* –**grandiosity**, *noun*

grandmother *noun* the mother of someone's father or mother.

grandparent *noun* a parent of one of your parents.

grandson *noun* a son of someone's son or daughter.

grandstand *noun* a building with seats rising in tiers, at a sports field or similar outdoor place of entertainment.

granite /*say* **gran**-uht/ *noun* a hard rock used for making statues or sculptures, and for some large buildings.

WORD HISTORY from a Latin word meaning 'grain'

grant *noun*
1. something which is given, such as land or money: *a grant for research into kidney disease.*
–*verb* 2. If someone **grants** something to you, they give or bestow it to you: *The governor-general granted him a pardon.*
–*phrase* 3. **take for granted**, to accept without questioning: *She takes all her opportunities for granted and doesn't realise how lucky she is.*

grape *noun* a small, round, green or purple fruit which grows in bunches on a climbing plant and is eaten, or used for making wine.
☐ **grapevine**, *noun*

grapefruit *noun* a large, round, yellow-skinned citrus fruit with sour juicy flesh.

graph /*say* graf, grahf/ *noun*
1. a diagram which shows the relationship between two or more things by dots, lines or bars.
–*verb* **2.** If you **graph** something, you represent it with dots, lines or bars so that it is easier to understand: *If you graph Australia's population over the last fifty years, you can see how much it has increased.*

graph- *prefix* a word part meaning 'writing', as in *graphic*.

WORD HISTORY this prefix comes from Greek

graphic *adjective*
1. If something is **graphic**, it is very detailed and clear: *He gave a graphic description of his dangerous and frightening night.* **2. Graphic** design is the creation of pictures and images to go with writing or to carry a message, rather than as pure art.
☐ **graphic**, *noun*: *a book with a lot of graphics.* –**graphically**, *adverb*

graphite /*say* **graf**-uyt/ *noun* a soft, blackish form of carbon used in pencils.

grapple *verb*
1. If you **grapple** with someone, you try to get hold of them when having a fight with them. **2.** If you **grapple** with a problem, you try your best to solve it.
–*noun* **3.** a tool with one or more claws used for hooking or holding something.

WORD HISTORY from an Old English word meaning 'seize'

grasp *verb*
1. If you **grasp** something, you take it very firmly in your hands and hold it tightly. **2.** If you **grasp** an idea, you understand it.
☐ **grasp**, *noun* –**grasping**, *adjective*

grass *noun*
1. a plant which you can grow to make a lawn. **2.** any of a number of plants with long narrow leaves, including bamboo, wheat, etc. **3.** *Informal* marijuana.
☐ **grassy**, *adjective* (**grassier**, **grassiest**)

grasshopper *noun* a type of plant-eating insect with large back legs for jumping.

grate[1] *noun*
1. a frame of parallel or crossing bars used as a cover or guard: *His ice-cream money rolled down the footpath and fell through a grate over the drain.* **2.** a frame of metal bars used to hold fuel in a fireplace: *Put some wood in the grate and we'll start a fire.*

ANOTHER WORD (for definition 1) is **grating**.

☑ SPELLING TIP Don't confuse the spelling of **grate** with **great** which has the same sound. **Great** has many meanings including 'large', and 'very good'.

grate[2] *verb*
1. To **grate** is to rub on something with a rough, unpleasant sound: *The two branches of the tree grated against each other in the wind.* **2.** To **grate** something is to rub it into small pieces against a surface with many sharp-edged openings: *We grate lots of cheese over our lasagne.*
–*phrase* **3. grate on**, to annoy: *Her habit of giggling all the time really grates on me.*
☐ **grater**, *noun*

☑ SPELLING TIP See **grate**[1].

grateful *adjective* feeling thankful or showing thanks.
☐ **gratefully**, *adverb* –**gratitude**, *noun*

grave[1] *noun* a hole dug in the earth for burying a dead body.

grave[2] *adjective*
1. If someone's face or expression is **grave**, they look solemn or without humour: *Her face was grave as she told them the bad news.* **2.** If something is **grave** it is **a.** serious or dangerous: *Suffering both drought and war, the country faced a grave situation.* **b.** important: *With the threat of war, the government had grave issues to discuss.*
☐ **gravely**, *adverb*

gravel *noun* small stones mixed with sand.
☐ **gravelly**, *adjective*

WORD HISTORY from a French word meaning 'little sandy shore'

☑ SPELLING TIP *Single letter alert*: only one *l* at the end. However, remember that you double the *l* when you make the adjective **gravelly**.

gravity *noun*
1. the force that attracts or causes everything to fall towards the centre of the earth. **2.** seriousness: *We realised the gravity of our situation when we saw that the tide had come in.*
☐ **gravitational**, *adjective*: *gravitational forces.*

WORD HISTORY from a Latin word meaning 'heaviness'

gravy *noun* a sauce made from the juices that come from meat during cooking, mixed with flour and water.

graze[1] *verb* To **graze** is to feed on growing grass: *The sheep were grazing on the hillside.*

graze[2] *verb*
1. To **graze** something is to touch it lightly in passing. **2.** To **graze** a part of your body is to rub the skin off it: *She slipped on the rocks and grazed her legs and arms.*
☐ **graze**, *noun*: *a graze on her knee.*

grazier *noun* a farmer who usually has a large area of land on which he grazes cattle or sheep.

grease *noun* /*say* grees/
1. melted animal fat. **2.** any fatty or oily substance. **3.** a substance used to keep machinery running smoothly.
–*verb* /*say* greez, grees/ **4.** If you **grease** something, you put grease or fat on or into it: *I greased the pan.*
□ **greasy**, *adjective* (**greasier**, **greasiest**)

great *adjective*
1. large: *a great mass of black clouds*; *Great herds of animals once roamed the plains.* **2.** unusual or extreme: *great sorrow.* **3.** notable or important: *a great fighter for justice.* **4.** very good or fine: *A great time was had by all.*
□ **greatly**, *adverb* –**greatness**, *noun*

☑ SPELLING TIP Don't confuse the spelling of **great** with **grate** which has the same sound. A **grate** is a frame of metal bars. To **grate** is to rub something, making a rough sound.

great white shark *noun* See **white shark**.

ANOTHER FORM is **great white**.

greed *noun* a great or unreasonable desire, especially for food or money.
□ **greedy**, *adjective* (**greedier**, **greediest**) –**greediness**, *noun* –**greedily**, *adverb*

green *adjective*
1. of the colour of the leaves of plants. **2.** not ripe: *a green mango.* **3.** in politics, to be concerned with environmental issues.
–*noun* **4.** a green colour. **5.** the part of a golf course surrounding a hole. **6.** the smooth level grass on which bowls is played. **7.** **greens**, green vegetables: *If you don't eat your greens, you can't have dessert.*
–*phrase* **8.** **green with envy**, wanting something very badly that someone else has: *Pete was green with envy about Eric's new bike.*

greengrocer *noun* someone who sells fresh vegetables and fruit.

greenhouse *noun* a building used for growing plants, which is made mainly of glass so that it will store the sun's heat.

greenhouse effect *noun* the increase in the temperature of the earth caused by its atmosphere acting as the glass of a greenhouse does and heating up everything on the earth; the increase may become greater as pollution adds more and more carbon dioxide to the atmosphere.

greenhouse gas *noun* a gas involved in the greenhouse effect.

greenie *noun* *Informal* someone who believes that the environment should be conserved and not damaged by cars on the roads, waste in the water, chopping down trees, farming using chemicals, etc.
□ **greenie**, *adjective*: *Our council is keen to have a greenie image.*

green screen *noun* an alternative to a blue screen which needs to be used under certain conditions.

SEE **blue screen**.

greet *verb* To **greet** someone is to welcome or receive them, usually with friendly words.

greeting *noun*
1. the act or words of someone who greets. **2.** **greetings**, a friendly message: *Pass on our greetings when you see them.*

gregarious /*say* gruh-**gair**-ree-uhs/ *adjective* fond of the company of other people.
□ **gregariously**, *adverb* –**gregariousness**, *noun*

A SIMILAR WORD is **sociable**.

☑ SPELLING TIP Remember the *ious* ending. The word **gregarious** comes from the Latin word *grex* (meaning 'flock'). The *x* has changed to a *g* and the suffix *-arious* ('having to do with') added.

gremlin *noun* a small, imaginary creature that is thought to cause trouble: *Our teacher said that a gremlin must be taking the chalk.*

grenade *noun* a small bomb thrown by hand or fired from a rifle.

WORD HISTORY from a Spanish word meaning 'pomegranate'

grevillea /*say* gruh-**vil**-ee-uh/ *noun* any of a number of types of Australian shrubs or trees, many of which have spiky, brightly coloured flowers.

NOTE The grevillea flower is sometimes called a **spider flower** because of its shape.

☑ SPELLING TIP *Tricky vowel sound*: remember that the vowel before the final *a* is *e* (not *i*). This word comes from the name of a Scottish botanist, CF *Greville* (died 1809). The *a* has been added to make it a scientific name.

grey *adjective*
1. If something is **grey**, it is of a colour between black and white. **2.** A **grey** day is dark and cloudy.
□ **grey**, *noun* –**greyness**, *noun*

greyhound *noun* a type of tall, slender dog used for racing.

grey nurse shark *noun* a common shark with a large stout body coloured grey on top and off-white underneath, and with long thin ripping teeth.

ANOTHER FORM is **grey nurse**.

greywater *noun* water that has been used in industry, or in houses for washing machines, showers, baths, handwashing, and so on, which can be used again for such activities as watering gardens and lawns.

grid *noun*
1. a grating of crossed bars. **2.** a network of cables and pipes supplying electricity, gas or water. **3.** a network of crossed lines on a map, designed to give fixed points of reference for finding a place easily. **4.** in mathematics, a pattern of evenly-spaced squares used in calculations.

griddle *noun* a flat, heavy pan for cooking on top of the stove.

grief /*say* greef/ *noun* great sadness: *My grandfather suffered enormous grief when my grandmother died.*

> ☑ SPELLING TIP *Tricky vowel sound*: *ie* to spell the 'ee' sound. This follows the rule that *i* comes before *e* except after *c*.

grievance /*say* **gree**-vuhns/ *noun* a feeling of anger or annoyance caused by something unfair that has happened.

grieve /*say* greev/ *verb*
1. If you **grieve** over something, you feel grief because of it: *They grieved for their dog after it died.* **2.** If something **grieves** you, you feel grief because of it: *Her sudden death grieved them terribly.*

> A SIMILAR WORD (for definition 1) is **mourn**.

grill *verb*
1. To **grill** food, especially meat, is to cook it by direct heat, as under a grill: *They grilled some tomatoes and fish.*
–*noun* **2.** a meal, mainly of meat, which has been grilled: *Dad cooked up a grill of sausages and chops for tea.* **3.** the part of a stove or kitchen appliance for cooking food by radiating direct heat towards it: *Put it under the grill for a few minutes.*

> ANOTHER WORD (for definition 3) is **griller**.

grille /*say* gril/ *noun* a screen of metal bars for a window, gate or the front of a car.

> ☑ SPELLING TIP Remember the *e* at the end of this word. Don't confuse it with **grill** which is a way of cooking food.

griller *noun* See **grill** (definition 3).

grim *adjective* (**grimmer**, **grimmest**)
1. If a situation is **grim**, it is extremely unpleasant or serious. **2.** If someone is **grim**, they are very serious because they are worried or upset about something or have an unpleasant job to do.

grimace /*say* **grim**-uhs, gruh-**mays**/ *verb* If you **grimace**, you twist your face so that it shows you are upset, angry, afraid or in pain.
☐ **grimace**, *noun*

> WORD HISTORY from a Spanish word meaning 'panic'

grime *noun* dirt, especially dirt that has collected on a surface: *A thick grime had built up in the old fridge.*
☐ **grimy**, *adjective*

grin *verb* (**grins**, **grinning**, **grinned**, **has grinned**)
1. To **grin** is to smile broadly.
–*phrase* **2. grin and bear it**, to suffer without complaining: *We had lost and we just had to grin and bear it.*
☐ **grin**, *noun*

grind *verb* (**grinds**, **grinding**, **ground**, **has ground**) To **grind** is to **1.** crush into fine particles: *to grind coffee beans.* **2.** produce by grinding: *stone ground flour.* **3.** rub two hard objects together, producing an unpleasant noise: *Don't grind your teeth like that!* **4.** smooth, shape or sharpen by rubbing with a tool: *a machine to grind and polish lenses*; *to grind an axe.*
–*noun* **5.** *Rather informal* hard or boring work: *She finds doing homework every night a real grind.*
☐ **grinder**, *noun*

grip *verb* (**grips**, **gripping**, **gripped**, **has gripped**)
1. If you **grip** something, you hold it very tightly: *She was afraid and gripped her mother's hand.*
–*noun* **2.** a firm hold.
–*phrase* **3. come** (or **get**) **to grips with**, to deal with: *to come to grips with a problem*; *to get to grips with an enemy.*
☐ **gripping**, *adjective* very interesting or exciting: *a gripping story.*

gripe *verb Informal* If somebody **gripes**, they complain or grumble: *He is always griping about something.*
☐ **gripe**, *noun*

grisly /*say* **griz**-lee/ *adjective* (**grislier**, **grisliest**) horrible or frightening: *It was such a grisly story we couldn't go to sleep.*
☐ **grisliness**, *noun*

> ☑ SPELLING TIP Remember that **grisly** is spelt with a single *s*. Don't confuse it with **grizzly** which sounds the same. **Grizzly** is the adjective from the verb **grizzle**, and can also be used to refer to an American brown bear. Also don't confuse **grisly** with **gristly** which sounds similar. **Gristly** is the adjective from the noun **gristle**.

gristle /*say* **gris**-uhl/ *noun* a firm, elastic tissue in animals or humans.
☐ **gristly**, *adjective*

> ANOTHER WORD for this is **cartilage**. **Cartilage** is the more formal scientific word.

> ☑ SPELLING TIP Remember the silent *t* in **gristle**. Don't confuse the adjective **gristly** /*say* **gris**-lee/ with **grisly** /*say* **griz**-lee/. Something that is **grisly** is frightening in a horrible way.

grit *noun*
1. fine, hard, stony particles. **2.** strength of character or courage: *Grit, guts and determination saw them through.*
–*verb in the phrase* (**grits**, **gritting**, **gritted**, **has gritted**) **3. grit your teeth**, to close your jaw firmly because you have something difficult or unpleasant to do.
☐ **gritty**, *adjective* (**grittier**, **grittiest**): *a gritty surface.*

grizzle *verb* If a child **grizzles** about something, they cry and complain in an annoying way.
☐ **grizzly**, *adjective*: *a grizzly child.*

groan *verb* If you **groan**, you make a long, deep sound expressing pain or sorrow.
☐ **groan**, *noun*

groceries *plural noun* food and other things bought for a household regularly: *Mum buys the groceries every week.*

NOTE **Groceries** used to be sold at a **grocer's** shop but now you usually buy them at a supermarket.

grog *noun Informal* alcoholic drink, particularly when cheap and of poor quality.

groggy *adjective* (**groggier**, **groggiest**) If you are **groggy**, you are not fully alert or able to function normally: *She was still groggy from the operation.*

groin *noun* the hollow where the legs join the body.

grommet *noun* a small tube put into the ear by a doctor to prevent ear infections: *The grommet helped Tom to hear better.*

groom *noun*
1. someone who looks after horses. **2.** See **bridegroom**.
–*verb* **3.** If you **groom** an animal, you clean it by brushing its coat. **4.** If you **groom** yourself, you take care that you are looking clean and tidy.

groomsman *noun* (*plural* **groomsmen**) a man who accompanies a bridegroom at his wedding.

groove *noun* a long, narrow cut made by a tool: *The wooden bowl was decorated with patterns of grooves.*

groovy *adjective Informal* **1.** exciting or satisfying. **2.** stylish or fashionable.

grope *verb* If you **grope** for something, you feel about for it because you cannot see it.
☐ **groper**, *noun* –**gropingly**, *adverb*

gross /*say* grohs/ *adjective*
1. If something is **gross**, it is offensive or extremely disgusting and unpleasant: *A squashed snail is gross.* **2.** If something is **gross**, it is extreme and unacceptable: *She treated him with a gross lack of courtesy.* **3.** If someone is **gross**, they are **a.** bad-mannered and offensive. **b.** very fat. **4.** An amount that is **gross** is the total amount of something. It can describe a sum of money before any deductions or costs are removed, or a weight including both the packaging and contents, or the vehicle and load.
☐ **grossly**, *adverb*: *grossly negligent.*

THE OPPOSITE (of definition 4) is **net**[2].

grotesque /*say* groh-**tesk**/ *adjective* very unnatural or ugly in shape, form or appearance: *His leg was so inflamed and swollen that it was grotesque to look at.*
☐ **grotesquely**, *adverb* –**grotesqueness**, *noun*

☑ SPELLING TIP Remember that the ending of **grotesque** is spelt *esque* (although it sounds like 'esk'). Another word with the *-esque* suffix is *picturesque*. These words come from French.

grotto *noun* (*plural* **grottoes** *or* **grottos**) a cave.

grotty *adjective* (**grottier**, **grottiest**) *Informal* dirty or unpleasant.

grouch *noun* (*plural* **grouches**) *Informal* someone who is always complaining or bad-tempered: *Don't be such an old grouch!*
☐ **grouchy**, *adjective* (**grouchier**, **grouchiest**) –**grouchiness**, *noun*

ground *noun*
1. firm or dry land: *They dropped to the ground.* **2.** earth or soil: *fertile ground.* **3.** the land surrounding a building or group of buildings: *The fete was held in the school grounds.* **4.** basis or reason: *What are the grounds for your complaint?*
–*phrase* **5. gain ground**, to make progress. **6. lose ground**, to lose what has been gained. **7. stand your ground**, to keep to your opinion.

group *noun*
1. a number of people or things gathered together and thought of as being connected in some way. **2.** a number of musicians who play together: *a rap group.*
–*verb* **3.** If you **group** things, you sort them into groups: *We grouped all the information we had according to how relevant it was.*
☐ **grouping**, *noun*

grouper *noun* a large fish found in warm seas.

grouse /*rhymes with* house/ *adjective Informal* very good.

grout *noun* a thin, coarse cement poured into the joints between tiles.

ANOTHER WORD for this is **grouting**.

grove *noun* a small group of trees.

grovel /*say* **grov**-uhl/ *verb* (**grovels**, **grovelling**, **grovelled**, **has grovelled**) To **grovel** is to **1.** behave in a way that shows clearly that you think of yourself as a worthless person. **2.** lie or move face down, especially in fear.
☐ **grovelling**, *adjective*: *a grovelling apology.*

grow *verb* (**grows**, **growing**, **grew**, **has grown**) To **grow** is to **1.** increase in size. **2.** develop: *In*

the story, the ugly duckling grew into a beautiful swan. **3.** become gradually: *Over the years he grew more and more wealthy.* **4.** cause to grow: *Mum grows herbs in the back garden.*
–*phrase* **5. grow on**, **a.** to gain an increasing influence, effect, and so on: *The idea grew on him that he could be prime minister one day.* **b.** to win the admiration of, bit by bit: *I didn't like the plan at first but it's beginning to grow on me.* **6. grow out of**, **a.** to become too big for. **b.** to develop from: *This tree grew out of a small seedling*; *The idea grew out of a small suggestion.* **7. grow up**, to become an adult.
☐ **grower**, *noun* –**grown**, *adjective*

growl *verb* To **growl** is to **1.** make a deep, angry sound. **2.** complain angrily.
☐ **growl**, *noun*

grown-up *noun Informal* someone who is fully grown.

ANOTHER WORD for this is **adult**.

growth *noun*
1. gradual increase or development: *He is pleased with the steady growth of his bank account.* **2.** something that grows or has grown: *Every spring there is a new growth of leaves on the bushes.*

☑ SPELLING TIP The spelling of **growth** will be easy if you see that it contains *grow* and the suffix *-th* (used to form words which refer to an action or condition).

grub *noun* the young or larva of some insects.

WORD HISTORY from a Middle English word meaning 'dig'

grubby *adjective* (**grubbier**, **grubbiest**) If something or someone is **grubby**, they are dirty or untidy: *a grubby house*; *a grubby child.*

grudge *noun* a feeling of anger caused by someone hurting or insulting you: *Because they snubbed her, she bore a grudge against them for years.*

gruel /*say* **grooh**-uhl/ *noun* a thin mixture of cereal, usually oats, cooked in water or milk.

gruelling /*say* **grooh**-uh-ling/ *adjective* very tiring: *a gruelling competition.*

gruesome /*say* **grooh**-suhm/ *adjective* causing feelings of horror: *The house had a gruesome history which terrified people when they heard it.*

☑ SPELLING TIP *Tricky vowel sound*: the first vowel sound is spelt *ue*. Remember that **gruesome** has nothing to do with anything which grew. The first part of the word, *grue*, is an old English word meaning 'to shudder' or 'shake'. Then there is the suffix *-some* (meaning 'tending to be' or 'tending to cause'). Some other words with this ending are *awesome* and *wholesome*.

gruff *adjective*
1. hoarse or low and harsh. **2.** rough or unfriendly: *His gruff approach did not win him any friends.*
☐ **gruffly**, *adverb* –**gruffness**, *noun*

grumble *verb* To **grumble** is to complain in a bad-tempered way.
☐ **grumble**, *noun*

grumpy *adjective* (**grumpier**, **grumpiest**) A **grumpy** person is bad-tempered.

grunt *verb* To **grunt** is to make a deep sound like a pig.
☐ **grunt**, *noun*

guarantee /*say* ga-ruhn-**tee**/ *noun*
1. a promise to replace or repair something if it is faulty: *Some new cars have three-year guarantees.* **2.** a promise: *He gave me a guarantee that he would turn up in time.*
–*verb* (**guarantees**, **guaranteeing**, **guaranteed**, **has guaranteed**) **3.** If you **guarantee** something, you promise it: *The builder guaranteed that he would finish the job before Christmas.*

☑ SPELLING TIP *Silent letter alert*: don't forget the *gua* beginning to the word, although the *u* is silent. Also remember there is a single *r* and the ending is spelt just as it sounds with *ee*, although this is a fairly unusual ending for a word. Another example is *employee*.

guard /*say* gahd/ *verb*
1. If you **guard** someone or something, you protect them from harm or damage. **2.** If you **guard** someone, you watch them to make certain that they do not escape.
–*noun* **3.** someone who protects or keeps watch. **4.** a careful watch: *He was put under guard around the clock.* **5.** something that guards from harm or injury: *Players are advised to wear a guard over their shins.*
–*phrase* **6. guard against**, to take steps to prevent: *to guard against illness.*

☑ SPELLING TIP *Silent letter alert*: don't forget the silent *u* after the *g*.

guardian /*say* **gah**-dee-uhn/ *noun*
1. someone who guards, protects or takes care of someone or something. **2.** someone who is appointed by law to take care of another person and their property.
☐ **guardianship**, *noun*

☑ SPELLING TIP *Silent letter alert*: **guardian** comes from the word *guard* plus the suffix *-ian*, a form of *-an* (meaning 'having to do with'). Like *guard*, it has a silent *u* following the *g*.

guava /*say* **gwah**-vuh/ *noun* a tropical American tree or shrub with a fruit that you can eat.

guerilla /*say* guh-**ril**-uh/ *noun* a member of a small band of soldiers which worries the enemy by surprise raids and attacks.
☐ **guerilla**, *adjective*: *guerilla attacks.*

ANOTHER SPELLING is **guerrilla**.

☑ SPELLING TIP This comes from the Spanish word *guerra* meaning 'war', which is why it can be difficult to spell. To make it more confusing, you can spell it in two ways – either with a single *r*, or with a double *r* – but in either case it has a double *l*. Also remember the *gu* spelling at the beginning. Don't confuse **guerilla** with **gorilla** which sounds the same. A **gorilla** is the largest kind of ape.

guess /*say* ges/ *noun*
1. a judgement or opinion formed without really knowing if it is true or not.
–*verb* **2.** If you **guess** something, you express an opinion knowing you might be wrong because you do not have all the facts.

guest /*say* gest/ *noun*
1. a visitor or someone who is entertained at your house. **2.** someone well-known who visits and performs at a club or show. **3.** someone who stays at a hotel.
☐ **guest**, *adjective*: *a guest speaker.*

guffaw /*say* gu-**faw**/ *verb* If you **guffaw**, you laugh loudly and noisily.
☐ **guffaw**, *noun*

guidance *noun* advice, guiding, or leadership.

guide /*say* guyd/ *verb*
1. If you **guide** someone somewhere, you show them the way or lead them there: *She guided me towards the open door.*
–*noun* **2.** someone who guides, often as a job. **3.** a book with information for travellers. **4.** a member of a worldwide youth movement for girls which provides organised activities which have the aim of promoting outdoor adventure, community service and care for the environment.

ANOTHER FORM This word (as in definition 4) is sometimes spelt with a capital letter. **Guides** used to be called **Girl Guides**.

guild /*say* gild/ *noun* an organisation or society of people who have similar jobs or interests.

☑ SPELLING TIP Don't confuse the spelling of **guild** with **gild** which has the same sound. To **gild** is to cover something with gold.

guile /*say* guyl/ *noun* cleverness or cunning in the way you deceive somebody.
☐ **guileful**, *adjective* clever and deceitful. –**guileless**, *adjective* frank or honest.

guillotine /*say* **gil**-uh-teen/ *noun*
1. a machine with a heavy blade that falls between two posts, used for cutting off the head of someone who has been sentenced to death. **2.** a machine with a long blade used for cutting the edges off paper.

☑ SPELLING TIP *Silent letter alert*: don't forget the silent *u* after the *g* in **guillotine**. Also remember that it has a double *l*, and that the ending is spelt *ine* (although it sounds like 'een'). Like many other words that have this ending with this sound, such as *routine*, **guillotine** comes from French. It is particularly unusual because it comes from a French name (the name of the French person who encouraged its use as a humane method of capital punishment during the French Revolution).

guilt /*say* gilt/ *noun*
1. the position of having committed a crime or being wrong: *His bloody hands made his guilt obvious to everyone.* **2.** a feeling that something is your fault: *She felt a lot of guilt about upsetting her friend so much.*
☐ **guilty**, *adjective*

☑ SPELLING TIP Don't confuse **guilt** with **gilt** which has the same sound. **Gilt** is the gold or other material used to decorate precious objects like vases.

guinea pig /*say* **gin**-ee/ *noun*
1. a short-eared, short-tailed animal used in scientific experiments and also commonly kept as a pet. **2.** someone used in experiments: *They used him as a guinea pig in the testing of the new drug.*

guise /*say* guyz/ *noun* the outside appearance, usually only pretended, of someone or something: *He appeared in commercials in the guise of a car salesman.*

guitar /*say* guh-**tah**/ *noun* a violin-shaped musical instrument with a long neck and strings which you play by pulling the strings or running your fingers across them.
☐ **guitarist**, *noun*

☑ SPELLING TIP *Silent letter alert*: don't forget the silent *u* after the *g*.

gulf *noun*
1. a part of an ocean which is partly bordered by land. **2.** a deep hollow in the surface of the earth. **3.** any wide separation: *The gulf between the families widened over time.*

gull *noun* See **seagull**.

gullet *noun* the tube-like part of the body by which the food and drink are passed from the back of the mouth to the stomach.

gullible *adjective* If you are **gullible**, you are easily deceived or cheated.
☐ **gullibly**, *adverb* –**gullibility**, *noun*

gully *noun* (*plural* **gullies**)
1. a small valley cut out of the earth by running water. **2.** a ditch or a gutter.

gulp *verb*
1. To **gulp** is to swallow quickly: *She gulped down a mouthful of tea as she ran towards the*

phone; He gulped with fear as he realised what lay ahead.
–*noun* **2.** an amount swallowed at one time.

gum[1] *noun*
1. a sticky liquid which comes out of plants or trees. **2.** a sticky flavoured sweet for chewing. **3.** a glue.

ANOTHER TERM (for definition 2) is **chewing gum**.

gum[2] *noun* the firm flesh in which your teeth sit.

NOTE This is often used in the plural: *I've got sore gums.*

gumboot *noun* a rubber boot sometimes reaching to your knee or thigh.

gum tree *noun* See **eucalyptus**.

gun *noun*
1. a weapon with a long metal tube for firing bullets or other ammunition. **2.** anything which is similar to a gun in its shape or in the way it is used: *a water gun.*
–*phrase* **3. stick to your guns**, to keep your position in an argument, when faced with opposition.
☐ **gunshot**, *noun*: *I think I heard a gunshot.* –**gunpoint**, *noun*: *He held them up at gunpoint.*

gunpowder *noun* a mixture of chemical powders that explodes when set off by a gun or by fire.

gunwale /*say* **gun**-uhl/ *noun* the upper edge of the side of a ship or boat.

ANOTHER SPELLING is **gunnel**.

gunyah /*say* **gun**-yuh/ *noun* an Aboriginal hut or temporary shelter in the bush, made from tree branches and bark.

ANOTHER WORD for this is **humpy**.
WORD HISTORY from an Aboriginal language of New South Wales called Dharug

guppy *noun* (*plural* **guppies**) a small, brightly coloured fish which is often kept in home aquariums.

WORD HISTORY named after a Trinidad clergyman, RJL *Guppy*, who sent the first recorded specimen to the British Museum

gurgle *verb*
1. If liquid **gurgles**, it flows with a noisy, bubbling sound. **2.** If someone **gurgles**, they make a sound like this.
☐ **gurgle**, *noun* –**gurgling**, *adjective*

guru /*say* **goo**-rooh/ *noun*
1. in Hinduism, a spiritual teacher. **2.** any wise and powerful teacher.

gush *verb*
1. If liquid **gushes**, it flows forcefully in large quantities: *Water was gushing from the burst main.* **2.** *Informal* If someone **gushes**, they express their enthusiasm or say good things about someone in such a strong way that it sounds silly.
☐ **gush**, *noun*: *a gush of water.* –**gushing**, *adjective*

gust *noun* a sudden, strong rushing, as of air: *Gusts of wind had covered the house in yellow dust.*

gusto *noun* hearty enjoyment.

gut *noun*
1. the intestines, the long digestive tube inside the body. **2.** the strong string made from the gut of an animal and used for things like violin strings or tennis racquet strings. **3. guts**, *Informal* **a.** the stomach: *to be kicked in the guts.* **b.** courage: *Has he got the guts to stand up to her?* **c.** most important part or contents: *The guts of the book is about his twenty years in jail.*

gutter *noun*
1. a passage, usually along the side of a street, for carrying away water. **2.** an open pipe along the edge of the roof of a building for carrying off water.

ANOTHER WORD (for definition 2) is **guttering**.

guttural /*say* **gut**-uh-ruhl/ *adjective* If a sound is **guttural**, it is harsh and made by someone using the back of their throat: *The old man spoke with a guttural voice.*

☑ SPELLING TIP *Tricky 'uh' sound*: remember that **guttural** has nothing to do with a gutter – the vowel following the double *t* is a *u* (not an *e*). It is spelt this way because the word comes from *guttur* (the Latin word for 'throat') plus the suffix *-al* (meaning 'having to do with' or 'like').

guy[1] *noun Informal* **1.** a man or a boy. **2. guys**, You can use **guys** to refer to people of either sex when they are in a group: *Do any of you guys want a swim?*; *bad guys and good guys.*

guy[2] *noun* a rope or wire attached to something to guide, steady or secure it.

guzzle *verb* If you **guzzle**, you eat or drink noisily and greedily.
☐ **guzzler**, *noun* someone who guzzles.

gym /*say* jim/ *noun*
1. a building or room specially equipped for gymnastics and sport: *She goes to the gym every afternoon because she wants to keep fit.* **2.** See **gymnastics**.

NOTE This word (as in definition 1) is short for **gymnasium**.

gymkhana /*say* jim-**kah**-nuh/ *noun* horseriding events with games and contests.

☑ SPELLING TIP *Letter 'y' alert*: the first vowel sound in **gymkhana** is spelt with a *y* (although it sounds like it should be spelt *i*). So the word starts with *gym* (not *jim*). This word comes from Hindustani *gendkhana*, meaning 'ball house', for games and sporting activities. This explains the silent *h* following the *k*.

gymnasium /*say* jim-**nay**-zee-uhm/ *noun* a building or room specially equipped for gymnastics and sport.

THE SHORT FORM of this is **gym** which is the word that you usually use.

☑ SPELLING TIP *Letter 'y' alert*: the first vowel sound in **gymnasium** is spelt with a *y* (although it sounds like it should be spelt *i*). This is the same in related words such as *gymnastics* and the short form *gym*. This is because all these words come from Greek. **Gymnasium** comes from the Greek word meaning 'naked' (in ancient times athletes were naked when they trained).

gymnast /*say* **jim**-nast/ *noun* someone especially trained and skilled in gymnastics.

gymnastics /*say* jim-**nas**-tiks/ *noun* the performance of exercises to develop flexibility, strength and agility.
☐ **gymnastic**, *adjective*

THE SHORT FORM of this is **gym**: *We do gym at school on Friday mornings.*

gyn- *prefix* a word part meaning 'woman' or 'female', as in *gynaecology*.

ANOTHER SPELLING is **gyno-**.
WORD HISTORY this prefix comes from Greek

gynaecology /*say* guy-nuh-**kol**-uh-jee/ *noun* the type of medical practice that is concerned with diseases that only affect women.
☐ **gynaecological**, *adjective* –**gynaecologist**, *noun*

ANOTHER SPELLING is **gynecology**.

☑ SPELLING TIP *Letter 'y' alert*: remember that the first part of this word is the prefix *gyn-* meaning 'woman' and is spelt with a *y*.

gypsy /*say* **jip**-see/ *noun* (*plural* **gypsies**)
1. someone who belongs to a people, once from India but now found mainly in Europe, who do not live in any one place but travel about.
2. someone who lives in an unusual way, especially someone who wanders about without a permanent home.

ANOTHER SPELLING is **gipsy**. Definition 1 is often spelt with a capital letter.
NOTE For definition 1, most of these people prefer to be called the **Romani** people which is their real name.
WORD HISTORY from a form of the word 'Egyptian'

gyrate /*say* juy-**rayt**/ *verb* If you **gyrate**, you whirl or move in a circular motion.
☐ **gyration**, *noun*

gyro- *prefix* a word part meaning 'ring', 'circle' or 'spiral', as in *gyroscope*.

WORD HISTORY this prefix comes from Greek

gyroscope /*say* **juy**-ruh-skohp/ *noun* a rotating wheel inside a frame which lets the wheel's axis keep its original direction even though the frame is moved around. It is used to help make such instruments as stabilisers in ships.

habit *noun* something that you do again and again, always in the same way: *It's his habit to walk the dog before breakfast.*
☐ **habitual**, *adjective*

habitat *noun* the place where a plant or animal naturally lives or grows.

habitation *noun* a home or place of living.
☐ **habitable**, *adjective*

hack[1] *verb*
1. To **hack** something is to cut or chop it with rough, heavy blows.
–*noun* **2.** a rough cut.
–*phrase* **3. hack into**, to gain unauthorised access, as to the information stored on a computer.
☐ **hacker**, *noun*

hack[2] *noun*
1. an old or worn-out horse. **2.** a riding horse kept for hire or ordinary riding. **3.** someone who does poor quality writing for a living.
–*verb* **4.** *Informal* If you **hack** something, you put up with it: *Can you hack sleeping on the floor for another night?*
☐ **hack**, *adjective*

hackles *plural noun* the hair on the back of a dog's neck.

haemo- *prefix* a word part meaning 'blood', as in *haemorrhage*.

ANOTHER SPELLING is **hemo-**.
WORD HISTORY this prefix comes from Greek

haemophilia /*say* hee-muh-**fil**-ee-uh/ *noun* a blood disorder in which you bleed a lot from small wounds because your blood does not clot normally. This disorder can be passed down from parent to child.
☐ **haemophiliac**, *noun*

ANOTHER SPELLING is **hemophilia**.

haemorrhage /*say* **hem**-uh-rij/ *noun*
1. a heavy flow of blood inside a person's body, such as from a damaged blood vessel.
–*verb* **2.** When someone **haemorrhages**, they have a haemorrhage.

ANOTHER SPELLING is **hemorrhage**.

☑ SPELLING TIP *Silent letter and double letter alert*: don't forget the silent *h* following the unusual double *r* spelling. Also notice that the main spelling of this word has *ae* in the first syllable for the 'e' sound (though you can also spell it with just *e*). The *ae* spelling is used in many medical words which come from Greek, as this word does.

hag *noun* an ugly old woman.

NOTE If you use this word to describe someone, you will offend them.

haggard /*say* **hag**-uhd/ *adjective* looking worn out from hunger, sickness or worry.

haggle *verb* To **haggle** is to discuss or argue about the price of something, with the aim of obtaining it more cheaply.

haiku /*say* **huy**-kooh/ *noun* a Japanese form of poem which has three lines and only seventeen syllables.

hail[1] *verb*
1. If you **hail** someone, you call out to them to greet them or get their attention: *He hailed her from across the road.* **2.** If you **hail** a vehicle, you wave or call out so that it stops to collect you: *to hail a taxi.*

hail[2] *noun*
1. a shower of small balls of ice from the clouds, like frozen rain. **2.** a shower of anything hard: *a hail of bullets.*
–*verb* **3.** When it **hails**, hail falls from the sky like rain.

hair *noun*
1. a fine, thread-like growth from the skin of people and animals: *Have you got hairs on the back of your hand?* **2.** the mass of these which cover the human head or the body of an animal: *I need to get my hair cut.*
–*phrase* **3. without turning a hair**, remaining calm and showing no emotion.
☐ **hairless**, *adjective*

☑ SPELLING TIP Don't confuse the spelling of **hair** with **hare** which sounds the same. A **hare** is a rabbit-like animal.

hairdresser *noun* someone whose job is to wash hair, cut it, colour it, and arrange it in a special way.
☐ **hairdressing**, *noun*

hairy *adjective* (**hairier**, **hairiest**)
1. covered with hair. **2.** *Informal* difficult: *a hairy problem.* **3.** *Informal* frightening: *a hairy drive.*

hajj /*say* hahj/ *noun* the annual pilgrimage to Mecca which every Muslim is supposed to make at least once in their lifetime.

OTHER SPELLINGS are **haj** and **hadj**.

hakea /*say* **hay**-kee-uh/ *noun* a type of Australian shrub or tree that has hard, woody fruit.

☑ SPELLING TIP *Tricky vowel sound*: remember that the vowel before the final *a* is *e* (not *i*). It will help if you know that this word was formed from *Hake*, the last name of a German man who encouraged the study of botany. The *a* at the end has been added to make it a scientific name.

halal /*say* **hal**-al/ *adjective* having to do with meat from animals that have been killed according to the special food rules of the Islamic religion.

WORD HISTORY from an Arabic word meaning 'lawful'

half /*say* hahf/ *noun* (*plural* **halves** /*say* hahvz/)
1. one of two equal parts into which anything can be divided.
–*phrase* **2. by half**, by a great deal or by too much: *too clever by half.*
☐ **half**, *adjective*: *at half speed.*

☑ SPELLING TIP *Tricky vowel sound*: don't forget the *l*. The *alf* spelling gives the 'ahf' sound.

half-brother *noun* a brother who is related to you through one parent only.

half-hearted *adjective* If you are **half-hearted** about something, you are not very eager or enthusiastic: *She made a half-hearted apology, then left.*
☐ **half-heartedly**, *adverb*

half-sister *noun* a sister who is related to you through one parent only.

halfway *adverb*
1. with half the distance covered: *to go halfway to a place.* **2.** to or at half the distance: *The rope reaches only halfway.*
–*adjective* **3.** in the middle, between two places or points: *the halfway mark.*

hall *noun*
1. a large building or room used for such things as public meetings or dances. **2.** a corridor or passage inside the front door of a house, from which you can get to the other rooms.

ANOTHER WORD (for definition 2) is **hallway**.

☑ SPELLING TIP Don't confuse the spelling of **hall** with **haul** which has the same sound. To **haul** something is to drag it along.

hallelujah /*say* hal-uh-**looh**-yuh/ *interjection* a cry which expresses praise to God.

WORD HISTORY a Hebrew word meaning 'praise ye Jehovah' (another name for God)

Halloween /*say* hal-uh-**ween**/ *noun* the night of 31 October, when children dress up in costumes and ask people for treats. The traditional idea is that if they don't get a treat, then they play a trick.

hallucination /*say* huh-looh-suh-**nay**-shuhn/ *noun* something which someone imagines they have seen or heard: *I saw a large, cool drink in front of me but it was just a hallucination.*
☐ **hallucinate**, *verb*

A SIMILAR WORD is **illusion**.

halo /*say* **hay**-loh/ *noun* (*plural* **haloes** *or* **halos**)
1. a ring of light surrounding the head of a holy person in paintings of saints or angels. **2.** a circle of light seen around the sun or moon.

haloumi /*say* huh-**looh**-mee/ *noun* a soft, firm cheese, originating in Greece, which has been preserved by being soaked in salty water.

ANOTHER SPELLING is **halloumi**.

halt *verb*
1. To **halt** is to stop moving forward. **2.** When you **halt** someone or something, you prevent them from moving forward or progressing.
☐ **halt**, *noun*

halter *noun* a rope or strap for leading or tying horses or cattle.

halve /*say* hahv/ *verb* To **halve** something is to **1.** divide it in two: *She halved the apple for the two boys.* **2.** cut it down or reduce it to half: *to halve the profits.*

ham *noun* salted or smoked meat from the upper part of a pig's leg.

hamburger *noun* a bread roll containing a fried, flattened piece of chopped up beef.

WORD HISTORY named after *Hamburg*, a town in Germany

hamlet *noun* a very small village.

hammer *noun*
1. a tool with a heavy metal head and a handle, used for banging nails into wood and for beating things. **2.** such a tool used for musical instruments like a gong or xylophone, or one of the inner parts of a piano that strike the strings to make sound.
–*verb* **3.** When you **hammer** a nail, you hit it with a hammer. **4.** If you **hammer** something, such as a door, you hit it repeatedly with your hand or fist.

hammerhead *noun* a shark with a head expanded sideways so that it looks like a double-headed hammer.

hammock *noun* a hanging bed made of canvas or net-like material.

☑ SPELLING TIP *Double letter alert*: double *m* in the middle. Also note that the ending is spelt *ock* (although it sounds like 'uhk'). Though it is not related to the meaning, you might try remembering that **hammock** contains two words: *ham* and *mock*.

hamper[1] *verb* To **hamper** someone or something is to hold them back: *Heavy rain hampered the start of the boat race.*

hamper[2] *noun* a large cane basket, sometimes with a cover, used to carry food: *We took a large hamper to the picnic.*

hamster *noun* a small, short-tailed animal belonging to the rat family, similar to a guinea pig.

hand *noun*
1. the end part of the arm below the wrist, used for touching and holding things. **2.** something like a hand: *the hands of a clock.* **3.** a worker: *a factory hand.* **4.** help or cooperation: *Give me a hand.* **5.** a side or point in an argument: *on the other hand.* **6.** a unit of measurement, about 10 centimetres, for giving the height of horses: *This horse is sixteen hands.* **7.** a burst of clapping for a performer: *Give him a big hand.* **8. hands**, power or control: *Your future is in your own hands.*
–*verb* **9.** If you **hand** something to someone, you deliver or pass it to them with your hand: *Hand me the book please.*
–*phrase* **10. at hand**, near or ready. **11. by hand**, using your own hands rather than a machine: *The computer was down so I had to write out the letter by hand.* **12. change hands**, to pass from one owner to another. **13. hand out**, to pass on by hand: *to hand out exam papers.* **14. hand over**, to give control and responsibility to someone else. **15. hands down**, totally, completely or very easily: *to win hands down.*

handbag *noun* a small bag women use for holding money and small articles.

handcuff *noun*
1. one of a pair of connected metal rings or bracelets put around someone's wrists to stop them using their hands.
–*verb* **2.** If you **handcuff** someone, you put handcuffs around their wrists: *to handcuff the prisoner.*

handicap *noun*
1. a physical disability. **2.** any disadvantage that makes success harder. **3.** a race or contest in which competitors are given an advantage or a disadvantage, in terms of weight to carry, distance to run, etc., in order to make their chances of winning equal. **4.** the disadvantage given to these competitors, such as the extra distance: *Last year's winner was given a handicap of three metres in this race.*
–*verb* (**handicaps**, **handicapping**, **handicapped**, **has handicapped**) **5.** If something **handicaps** you, it restricts you, or makes it harder for you to do something: *A shortage of water handicapped their efforts to put out the fire.*

handicraft *noun* an occupation or art in which you use your hands: *Weaving and pottery are handicrafts.*

☑ SPELLING TIP Remember that the letter in the middle joining together the two words *hand* and *craft* is an *i* (not a *y* as in the word *handy*).

handkerchief /*say* **hang**-kuh-cheef/ *noun* a small, square piece of cloth used for wiping or blowing your nose.

THE SHORT FORM of this is **hankie**.

☑ SPELLING TIP *Silent letter alert*: don't forget the *d* after the *n*. It will help if you see that **handkerchief** contains the word *hand*. The other part is *kerchief* (an old word meaning 'a cloth worn or carried on your body'), so the overall meaning is 'a cloth that you carry in your hand'. Rap it out as *hand+ ker+ chief*.

handle *noun*
1. a part of something, used to hold it by or open it with: *the handle of a knife*; *a door handle.*
–*verb* When you **handle** something, you **2.** touch or feel it with your hand: *Please don't handle the fruit.* **3.** use it: *Can you handle a spade?* **4.** manage or control it: *She handled the problem well.*

handlebars *plural noun* the curved bar at the front of a bike that you steer it with.

handsome /*say* **han**-suhm/ *adjective*
1. A **handsome** person is good-looking. **2.** Something **handsome** is large or generous: *a handsome gift.*
□ **handsomely**, *adverb*

NOTE This word (as in definition 1) is used mostly of men and boys.

☑ SPELLING TIP *Silent letter alert*: don't forget the *d* after the *n*. Also remember that the ending is spelt *some* (although it sounds like 'suhm'). The original meaning of the word was 'easy to handle' and it was formed by putting *hand* and *some* together. If you remember this, it will be a handy way to remember the *d*.

handwriting *noun* writing done by hand: *very neat handwriting.*
□ **handwritten**, *adjective*

handy *adjective* (**handier**, **handiest**)
1. If something is **handy**, it is useful or helpful: *This dictionary is very handy to have.* **2.** If something is **handy**, it is nearby and convenient: *Have you got a pen handy?* **3.** If someone is **handy**, they are skilled at using their hands, especially in doing jobs around the home.

hang *verb* (**hangs**, **hanging**, **hung** *or, for definition 2*, **hanged**, **has hung** *or, for definition 2*, **has hanged**)
1. When something **hangs**, it is attached or fixed to something at the top and dangles free at the bottom. **2.** To **hang** someone is to kill them by tying a rope around their neck and making their body hang in the air: *The bushranger Ned Kelly was hanged in 1880.*
–phrase **3. hang back**, to delay going on or continuing: *She hung back because she was afraid of what might happen.* **4. hang on**, to wait. **5. hang up**, to break off a telephone conversation.

NOTE Note that the usual past form of **hang** is **hung**, except when referring to death by hanging (definition 2), when the standard past form used to be **hanged**. However, nowadays, except in formal and legal use, the past form often used for this sense is **hung**.

hangar /*say* **hang**-uh/ *noun* a large building that aircraft are kept in.

☑ SPELLING TIP Notice the unusual *ar* ending. Don't confuse this word with **hanger**, something you hang things on.

hang-glider *noun*
1. a large type of kite which you hang on to as you fly through the air. **2.** the person who flies it.
☐ **hang-gliding**, *noun*

hangover *noun*
1. the feeling of sickness that comes after drinking too much alcohol. **2.** something remaining or left over.

hang-up *noun Informal* something which worries you and which you can't get off your mind: *She has a hang-up about her height.*

haphazard /*say* hap-**haz**-uhd/ *adjective* not tidily planned or organised: *a haphazard system*; *trees growing in haphazard clumps.*

happen *verb*
1. If something **happens**, it takes place or occurs, sometimes by chance. **2.** If you **happen** to do something, you have the luck or the occasion to do it: *I happened to look up just at the right time.*
☐ **happening**, *noun*

happy *adjective* (**happier**, **happiest**)
1. a feeling of pleasure or enjoyment: *You can't help being happy on such a sunny day.* **2.** very pleased about something: *I am happy that you have arrived so early.* **3.** fortunate or lucky: *a happy coincidence.*
☐ **happily**, *adverb* –**happiness**, *noun*

SIMILAR WORDS (for definition 1) are **cheerful** and **bright**: (for definition 2) **delighted**, **glad**, **thrilled** and **elated**. Note that **thrilled** and **elated** both mean 'extremely happy'.

harangue /*say* huh-**rang**/ *verb* If you **harangue** someone, you talk to them for a long time, usually in a loud voice, criticising them or trying to change their opinion: *He harangued the crowd about the need for a change of government.*
☐ **harangue**, *noun*

☑ SPELLING TIP *Single letter alert*: only one *r*. Also remember the silent *ue* at the end. **Harangue** has this spelling because it comes from French. Don't forget that you drop the final *e* when you add *-ed* or *-ing*.

harass /*say* huh-**ras**, **ha**-ruhs/ *verb* If someone **harasses** you, they keep annoying or worrying you: *Stop harassing me! I'll give you my answer when I've decided.*
☐ **harassment**, *noun*

WORD HISTORY from a French word meaning 'set a dog on'

☑ SPELLING TIP *Single/double letter alert*: only one *r*, but two *s*'s. You might think of this word as a pair with *embarrass* in which you have to remember the double *r*. 'It will embarrass me if you harass me' – two *r*'s in the first word, one *r* in the second.

harbour /*say* **hah**-buh/ *noun*
1. a sheltered area of water along a coastline where ships and boats can anchor and be protected from wind and waves. **2.** any shelter.
–verb **3.** To **harbour** someone who is wanted by the police is to let them stay secretly in your house: *to harbour a wanted criminal.*

ANOTHER SPELLING is **harbor**.

hard *adjective*
1. solid and firm to the touch: *Concrete is hard.* **2.** difficult to do: *a hard exam.* **3.** unpleasant: *to have a hard time.* **4.** needing much physical effort: *Digging gardens is hard work.*
–adverb **5.** with a lot of effort or energy: *to work hard.*
–phrase **6. hard up**, *Informal* not having much money.
☐ **hardness**, *noun*

SIMILAR WORDS (for definition 1) are **rigid** and **stiff**; (for definition 2) **complex**, **complicated**, **demanding**, **tough** and **tricky**; (for definition 5) **energetically**, **forcefully**, **intently** and **strongly**. THE OPPOSITE of definition 1 is **soft**; the opposite of definition 2 is **easy**.

hard disk *noun* a stiff disk with a magnetic coating, used for storing large amounts of computer data, originally built into a computer but now also available as an external memory storage facility.

COMPARE this with **floppy disk**.

hard drive *noun* a disk drive for a hard disk.

harden *verb*
1. When you **harden** something, or when something **hardens**, it becomes hard or harder: *The cold air hardened the wax*; *The glue slowly*

hardened. **2.** If someone **hardens**, they become tough, unfeeling or unkind: *I hardened my heart against the stray dog*; *Joan's feelings hardened when she saw the evidence.*

hardly *adverb*
1. almost not at all: *I can hardly hear you, the music is so loud.* **2.** probably not: *He would hardly come now, would he?*

hardship *noun* unpleasantness or suffering in the way you live: *They struggled through years of hardship during the drought.*

hardware *noun*
1. building materials or tools. **2.** the solid parts of a computer. **3.** the equipment needed for carrying out an activity: *military hardware.*

COMPARE definition 2 with **software**.

hardworking *adjective* If someone is **hard-working**, they put a lot of effort into their work.

ANOTHER FORM is **hard-working**.
SIMILAR WORDS are **diligent** and **industrious**.

hardy *adjective* (**hardier**, **hardiest**) able to stand up to harsh treatment or conditions.
□ **hardily**, *adverb*

hare *noun* a rabbit-like animal with long ears and long back legs.

☑ SPELLING TIP Don't confuse the spelling of **hare** with **hair** which has the same sound. **Hair** is what grows on your head.

harebrained *adjective* reckless or without sense.

harm *noun*
1. damage or hurt.
–*verb* **2.** If something **harms** you, it injures or hurts you: *You can pat the dog – she won't harm you.*
□ **harmful**, *adjective*: *a harmful disease.* –**harmless**, *adjective*: *The insect's sting was painful but harmless.*

harmonica /*say* hah-**mon**-ik-uh/ *noun* a small wind instrument with metal reeds, which you play by blowing.

ANOTHER TERM for this is **mouth organ**.

harmony *noun* (*plural* **harmonies**)
1. agreement in feelings, actions or ideas. **2.** a pleasing combination of musical notes sounding together.
□ **harmonic**, *adjective* –**harmonious**, *adjective* –**harmoniously**, *adverb* –**harmonise**, *verb*

ANOTHER SPELLING for **harmonise** is **harmonize**.
WORD HISTORY from a Greek word meaning 'a joining', 'agreement', or 'music'

harness *noun*
1. a set of leather straps and metal pieces that fit around a horse's head and body so that it can be ridden or used to pull a vehicle. **2.** a set of straps that fits around a person's body. It can be used to attach equipment to the person, or to hold the person in place for safety.
–*verb* **3.** When you **harness** a horse or other animal, you put a harness on it. **4.** If you **harness** something, you bring it under control and put it to work: *We need to harness the energy of the sun to produce electricity.*

harp *noun* a large musical instrument with a frame into which strings of different length are fixed. It is played by plucking the strings with your fingers.
□ **harpist**, *noun*

harpoon *noun*
1. a spear attached to a rope, used to catch large fish, whales, etc.
–*verb* **2.** If you **harpoon** a large fish or whale, you hit it with a harpoon.

harpsichord /*say* **hahp**-suh-kawd/ *noun* an old-fashioned musical instrument like a piano.
□ **harpsichordist**, *noun* a harpsichord player.

WORD HISTORY from the French words for 'harp' and 'string'

harsh *adjective*
1. rough and unpleasant: *a harsh voice.* **2.** cruel or severe: *a harsh winter.*
□ **harshly**, *adverb* –**harshness**, *noun*

harvest *noun*
1. the gathering or picking of crops.
–*verb* **2.** When you **harvest** a crop, you gather it in: *We're harvesting olives at present.*

hash[1] *noun*
1. a mixture of chopped, cooked meat and vegetables, fried and served with gravy or a sauce. **2.** a jumble or mess.
–*phrase* **3. make a hash of it**, to fail at or ruin something entirely.

WORD HISTORY from a French word meaning 'axe'

hash[2] *noun* the symbol (#) found on a computer keyboard, telephone keypad, etc.

hash brown *noun* a small mass of grated or mashed potato, fried until crisp.

hashtag *noun*
1. a special word, phrase, or group of letters or symbols added to a tweet (see **tweet**[2] definition 2) to show it is connected to a certain topic.
–*verb* **2.** To **hashtag** a tweet is to add such a word, phrase, or group of letters or symbols to show the tweet is connected to a certain topic.
□ **hashtagging**, *noun*

hassle *verb Informal* If you **hassle** someone, you worry or annoy them: *Stop hassling me about finishing my homework.*

haste *noun* hurried action: *His music practice was done in haste.*
☐ **hasty**, *adjective* (**hastier**, **hastiest**) –**hastily**, *adverb*

hasten /*say* **hay**-suhn/ *verb Rather old-fashioned* To **hasten** is to hurry: *She hastened to his side.*

☑ SPELLING TIP *Silent letter alert*: don't forget the silent *t* after the *s*. Remember that this word comes from *haste* (meaning 'speed') where you can hear the *t*.

hat *noun* a shaped covering for the head, usually worn when you are outside.

hatch[1] *verb*
1. If an egg **hatches**, the baby chick breaks out of it. **2.** To **hatch** a plan is to think of it or work it out.
☐ **hatchery**, *noun*

hatch[2] *noun* (*plural* **hatches**)
1. an opening in a floor, roof, or ship's deck. **2.** a cover for this.

hatchet *noun* a small, short-handled axe.

ANOTHER WORD for this is **tomahawk**.
WORD HISTORY from a French word meaning 'little axe'

hate *verb*
1. If you **hate** someone or something, you strongly dislike them.
–*noun* **2.** strong dislike. **3.** the object of hatred: *My pet hate is sewing.*
☐ **hatred**, *noun*

SIMILAR WORDS (for definition 1) are **detest** and **loathe**. They both mean 'to hate something very much'.

☑ SPELLING TIP Remember that when you form the noun **hatred** from **hate**, the *e* is dropped even though it still has the 'hayt' sound.

hate crime *noun*
1. criminal violence done to someone seen as belonging to a social or racial group hated by the attacker. **2.** an act of this violence.

hateful *adjective* so nasty or unpleasant as to cause a feeling of hate: *Stealing the old woman's money was a hateful thing to do.*

haughty /*say* **haw**-tee/ *adjective* (**haughtier**, **haughtiest**) A **haughty** person is arrogant and proud and looks down on others: *His haughty manner didn't fit in with the friendly atmosphere of the meeting.*
☐ **haughtily**, *adverb* –**haughtiness**, *noun*

WORD HISTORY from a French word meaning 'high'

☑ SPELLING TIP *Tricky vowel sound*: the first vowel sound is spelt *augh* (although it sounds like 'aw'). It might help if you think of some other words which you know well which have the same spelling for this sound, such as *daughter* and *naughty*.

haul *verb*
1. To **haul** is to pull hard: *to haul a heavy load*; *to haul on the rope.*
–*noun* **2.** a strong pull: *one haul of the rope.* **3.** the amount won, taken or caught at one time: *a haul of fish.*

☑ SPELLING TIP Don't confuse the spelling of **haul** with **hall** which has the same sound. A **hall** is a large assembly room.

haunch /*say* hawnch/ *noun* (*plural* **haunches**)
1. the fleshy part of a person's body around the hip. **2.** the back part of an animal.

haunt *noun*
1. a place visited often: *The cave was one of the bushranger's favourite haunts.*
–*verb* **2.** When a ghost or spirit is said to **haunt** a place, people think that it appears there regularly: *Some of the people in the town believe that a ghost haunts the old hotel.* **3.** If a thought **haunts** you, you cannot make it go away: *Memories of the accident haunted her for years.*
☐ **haunted**, *adjective* –**haunting**, *adjective*: *haunting beauty.* –**hauntingly**, *adverb*

have *verb* (**has**, **having**, **had**, **has had**) To **have** is to **1.** own: *I have a diamond ring.* **2.** possess: *I have an uncle in China.* **3.** possess as a characteristic: *to have red hair.* **4.** get, receive or take: *Can I have your attention?* **5.** experience: *to have a good time.* **6.** eat or drink: *to have a glass of water.* **7.** give birth to: *to have twins.*
–*phrase* **8. have on**, **a.** to be wearing. **b.** to have arranged: *What do you have on tomorrow?* **9. have to do with**, **a.** to have dealings with: *She will have nothing to do with me.* **b.** to concern: *This has nothing to do with you.*

SEE the Grammar and Punctuation Guide appendix.

haven *noun* a place of shelter or safety.

haven't a short form of *have not*.

haversack *noun Old-fashioned* a backpack.

havoc *noun*
1. great damage or destruction.
–*phrase* **2. play havoc with**, to destroy or totally disorganise: *The wind has played havoc with my hair.*

☑ SPELLING TIP The difficulty with **havoc** is its unusual ending. Remember that it is simple ☐ just *oc* (not *ock* or *uck*).

hawk[1] *noun* a hunting bird with a hooked beak and large claws.

hawk[2] *verb* To **hawk** things is to offer them for sale in the street or by calling at people's homes.

hay *noun* grass which has been cut and dried, used as animal feed.

hay fever *noun* an attack of watery eyes and sneezing caused by a reaction to pollen or other plant or animal material.

haywire *adjective* crazy or out of control.

hazard /*say* **haz**-uhd/ *noun* a risk or danger: *Smoking is a health hazard.*
□ **hazardous**, *adjective*

WORD HISTORY from an Arabic word for the die in a game of chance

☑ SPELLING TIP *Single letter alert*: only one *z*. Also remember that the ending is spelt *ard* (not *erd*). Some other words which have the same spelling for this sound are *lizard* and *wizard*.

haze *noun* bits of dust, smoke and so on which combine and look like a thin mist: *We could just see the top of the building through the haze.*
□ **hazy**, *adjective* (**hazier**, **haziest**)

hazel *noun*
1. a small tree which has light brown nuts that people eat. **2.** a greenish-brown colour.
□ **hazel**, *adjective*: *hazel eyes.*

he *pronoun* the male being talked about: *He said he'd come.*

SEE ALSO **him** and **his**.

head *noun*
1. the top part of a person's body with the brain, eyes, ears, nose and mouth; it is joined to the rest of the body by the neck. **2.** a similar part of an animal's body. **3.** the brain or mind: *Use your head!* **4.** the top or front part of anything: *the head of a page*; *the head of a procession.* **5.** a leader: *the head of the expedition.* **6.** a person or animal as one of a number: *ten head of cattle*; *How much a head do you charge for a banquet?* **7. heads**, the side of a coin with a picture of a head on it: *Heads or tails?*
–*verb* **8.** To **head** something is to be at the head of it: *to head the procession.* **9.** To **head** somewhere is to go towards it: *to head for home.*
–*phrase* **10. go to your head**, **a.** to make you confused. **b.** to make you too proud or pleased with yourself. **11. head off**, to get in front of and make change direction: *He was able to head off the goats before they reached the vegetable garden.* **12. lose your head**, to be so terrified that you can't think clearly. **13. over your head**, outside your understanding.
□ **head**, *adjective*: *the head teacher.*

headache *noun*
1. a pain in the head. **2.** *Informal* a troublesome or worrying problem: *This job has become a real headache.*

heading *noun* the title of a piece of writing, written at the top: *We found the information under the heading 'Birds of Prey'.*

headland *noun* a high piece of land which sticks out into a sea or lake.

A SIMILAR WORD is **promontory**.

head lice *plural noun* very small insects that can live in the hair and make the head itchy. They lay eggs called nits.

NOTE This is often shortened to **lice**.

headlight *noun* one of the powerful lights on the front of a vehicle.

headline *noun*
1. a heading at the top of a newspaper article, printed in large type, saying what the article is about. **2. headlines**, the main points to be covered in the news: *'Here are the headlines', said the TV news reader.*
□ **headline**, *adjective*: *a headline story.*

headlong *adverb* at great speed and with no control: *She raced headlong down the hill.*

headmaster *noun* the male principal of a school.

headmistress *noun* the female principal of a school.

headphones *plural noun* a listening device for a radio or CD player made of earphones held on by a band over your head.

ANOTHER WORD for this is **headset**.

headquarters /*say* **hed**-kwaw-tuhz, hed-**kwaw**-tuhz/ *noun* the place where the people in charge of a large organisation work: *police headquarters.*

THE ABBREVIATION is **HQ**.

headscarf *noun* (*plural* **headscarfs** *or* **headscarves**)
1. a scarf worn around the head. **2.** See **hijab**.

head start *noun* an advantage at the start of a race or competition: *She had too big a head start so I couldn't catch her.*

headstrong *adjective* A **headstrong** person is hard to control or determined to have their own way.

headway *noun* forward motion: *The swimmer made little headway against the strong current.*

heal *verb*
1. When a part of your body that has been injured **heals**, it becomes well and normal again. **2.** When someone or something **heals** you or **heals** part of your body, they make it healthy again: *The job of a doctor is to try to heal sick people*; *The ointment healed the cut on my leg almost straightaway.*
□ **healing**, *adjective*: *a healing touch.* –**healing**, *noun*

☑ SPELLING TIP Don't confuse the spelling of **heal** with **heel** which has the same sound. Your **heel** is the rounded back of your foot.

health /*say* helth/ *noun*
1. freedom from disease or sickness. **2.** the general state of your body: *in poor health.*
☐ **healthy**, *adjective* (**healthier**, **healthiest**) –**healthily**, *adverb*

☑ SPELLING TIP *Tricky vowel sound*: *ea* spelling for the 'e' sound. Think of the related word *heal* to remind you. Another word with this sound and spelling pattern is *wealth*.

heap *noun*
1. a group of things lying one on top of the other: *a heap of stones.* **2.** *Rather informal* a great quantity or number: *He has made a heap of money.*
–*verb* **3.** When you **heap** things, you put them in a heap: *to heap dead leaves*; *to heap up rubbish.*
–*phrase* **4. give someone heaps**, *Informal* to give someone a lot of insults or trouble.

hear *verb* (**hears**, **hearing**, **heard** /*say* herd/, **has heard**)
1. If you **hear** something, you are aware of a sound: *I heard a knock at the door.* **2.** If you **hear** that something is so, you are told or get information about it: *I hear there's going to be a meeting next week.*

☑ SPELLING TIP Don't confuse the spelling of **hear** with **here** which has the same sound. If you are **here**, you are in or at this place.

hearing *noun*
1. the ability to hear sounds: *Our grandmother is beginning to lose her hearing.* **2.** the opportunity to speak or be heard: *Please give our next speaker a polite hearing.* **3.** a session of an official investigation.
–*phrase* **4. out of hearing**, beyond the range within which a sound can be heard: *Tell me now, while she is out of hearing.*

hearsay *noun* gossip or rumour.

hearse /*rhymes with* verse/ *noun* a special car used in a funeral for carrying a coffin.

☑ SPELLING TIP *Tricky vowel sound*: don't forget that there is an *a* in **hearse**. Think of other words in which the letter combination *ear* makes an 'er' sound, such as *earn* or *learn*.

heart *noun*
1. the organ in the body that pumps the blood and keeps it going around the body. **2.** emotions, affections or feelings: *He won her heart.* **3.** courage or enthusiasm: *He showed plenty of heart when he went on to win the race.* **4.** the middle part of something: *the heart of the wood.* **5.** the most important part: *the heart of the matter.* **6.** a figure said to be shaped like a heart, such as on playing cards.
–*phrase* **7. by heart**, from memory: *to learn a poem off by heart.* **8. take heart**, to find new courage or strength. **9. take to heart**, to be deeply affected by: *Don't take their comments to heart.*

NOTE **Cardiac** is a medical word meaning 'having to do with the heart'.

☑ SPELLING TIP Remember the *e* in the spelling of **heart**.

hearten *verb* If something **heartens** you, it cheers you up or gives you courage: *We were heartened by the doctor's good news.*

hearth /*rhymes with* bath/ *noun* the floor of a fireplace, which usually extends a little way onto the floor of the room.

heart-rending *adjective* causing great sorrow.

hearty *adjective* (**heartier**, **heartiest**)
1. friendly, enthusiastic and sincere: *a hearty welcome*; *hearty approval.* **2.** large and satisfying: *a hearty meal.*
☐ **heartily**, *adverb*

heat *noun*
1. warmth or the quality of being hot. **2.** excitement or anger: *the heat of an argument.* **3.** a race or competition run to decide who will be in the final: *The first three in every heat will run in the final.*
–*verb* **4.** When you **heat** something, you make it become warm or hot: *You must heat the water first.*
–*phrase* **5.** to gradually become hotter: *Let's start our walk early, before the day heats up.*
☐ **heated**, *adjective*: *a heated room*; *a heated discussion.* –**heatedly**, *adverb* –**heating**, *noun* –**heater**, *noun*: *a gas heater.*

heath /*rhymes with* teeth/ *noun*
1. an area of open land with a lot of low shrubs growing on it. **2.** the small, low shrubs which grow on such land.

heathen /*say* **hee**-dhuhn/ *noun* (*plural* **heathen** *or* **heathens**) someone who does not believe in a religion, especially someone who does not believe in the Christian religion.
☐ **heathen**, *adjective*

A SIMILAR WORD is **pagan**.
NOTE **Heathen** is usually used in an insulting way.
WORD HISTORY from an Old English word for someone who lived on a heath

heather /*say* **hedh**-uh/ *noun* the shrubs called heath plants, usually with small, light purple flowers.

NOTE This is the word for these plants and the area in which they grow in Scotland. In Australia we talk about **heath**.

heat stroke *noun* a sickness caused by being in hot temperatures for too long, leading to weakness, headaches and dizziness, and sometimes more severe symptoms such as coma and death.

ANOTHER SPELLING is **heatstroke**.

heave /*say* heev/ *verb*
1. To **heave** something is to **a.** raise or lift it using effort or force: *The sailors heaved the anchor on board.* **b.** pull it: *They heaved on the ropes.* **2.** If something **heaves**, it rises and falls: *Her chest heaved after her race.*
□ **heave**, *noun*: *Give it a big heave.* –**heaving**, *adjective*

heaven /*say* **hev**-uhn/ *noun*
1. in some religions, a place where the divine being or beings live, and where good people are said to go when they die to enjoy everlasting happiness. **2.** a place or condition of great happiness or pleasure.
□ **heavenly**, *adjective*

ANOTHER FORM This word (as in definition 1) is often spelt with a capital letter.
NOTE **Celestial** is a word meaning 'having to do with heaven'.

heavens *interjection* an exclamation expressing surprise.

heavy /*say* **hev**-ee/ *adjective* (**heavier**, **heaviest**)
1. of great weight and, as a result, hard to lift or carry. **2.** larger or greater than usual: *heavy rain.* **3.** serious: *a heavy responsibility.* **4.** filled or weighed down: *The air was heavy with moisture*; *His heart was heavy with sorrow.*
–*noun* (*plural* **heavies**) **5.** *Informal* someone important in a particular area: *a political heavy.*
□ **heavily**, *adverb* –**heaviness**, *noun*

ANOTHER WORD (for definition 5) is **heavyweight**.

heavy metal *noun* a type of loud, fast rock music with emphasis on the use of electric guitars.

heckle *verb* To **heckle** someone is to repeatedly trouble them with annoying questions and remarks.
□ **heckler**, *noun*

hect- *prefix* a word part meaning '10^2 of a given unit', as in *hectare*.

ANOTHER SPELLING is **hecto-**.
WORD HISTORY this prefix comes from Greek

hectare /*say* **hek**-tair/ *noun* a unit of measurement of land in the metric system equal to 10 000 square metres, or about $2\frac{1}{2}$ acres.

THE SYMBOL for this is **ha**.

hectic *adjective* full of excitement and confusion: *a hectic trip.*

he'd a short form of *he had* or *he would*.

hedge *noun*
1. a row of bushes or small trees planted close together to form a fence.
–*verb* **2.** If you **hedge**, you avoid giving a direct answer or making a decision: *Stop hedging – just tell me whether you can do it or not.*

hedgehog *noun* a spiny, insect-eating animal, active at night, found mostly in Europe.

heed *verb*
1. To **heed** someone or something is to pay attention to them: *Please heed the warning signs.*
–*noun* **2.** careful attention: *You must pay heed to what I say.*

heel *noun*
1. the rounded back part of the foot, below the ankle. **2.** the part of a sock or shoe that fits over your heel.
–*phrase* **3. dig your heels in**, to stubbornly refuse to change your mind. **4. take to your heels**, to run away quickly.

☑ SPELLING TIP Don't confuse the spelling of **heel** with **heal** which has the same sound. To **heal** is to become well again.

heeler *noun* a dog trained to round up sheep or cattle by chasing them and biting at their heels.

hefty *adjective* (**heftier**, **heftiest**) A **hefty** person is big, strong and heavy.
□ **heftiness**, *noun*

heifer /*say* **hef**-uh/ *noun* a young cow that has not had a calf.

☑ SPELLING TIP *Tricky vowel sound*: remember that **heifers** 'eat in fields' to help you remember there is an *i* between the *e* and single *f* in this word.

height /*rhymes with* kite/ *noun*
1. the distance from bottom to top. **2.** a cliff or mountain top or other very high place. **3.** the greatest part or amount: *the height of the bushfire*; *the height of ignorance.*
□ **heighten**, *verb*: *Their excitement was heightened by the fireworks.*

☑ SPELLING TIP *Tricky vowel sound*: **height** comes from the adjective *high* and it sounds like *high* with a *t* added on. However, you have to remember that there is an *e* following the first *h*.

heir /*sounds like* air/ *noun* someone who inherits a dead person's money, property or title.

NOTE A woman who inherits can be called an **heiress**.

☑ SPELLING TIP Don't confuse **heir** with the **air** that you breathe, which has the same sound. **Heir** is related to other words such as *inherit*, *inheritance*, and *hereditary* whose meaning has to do the handing down of things from the older to the younger generation through time. All these words come from *heres*, the Latin word for an 'heir'. Think that 'humans eventually inherit riches' to help you remember the *h* at the beginning and the *eir* spelling.

heirloom /*say* **air**-loohm/ *noun* something valuable that is handed down from generation to generation in a family.

helicopter *noun* an aircraft without wings which flies by means of a large propeller on the top.

☑ SPELLING TIP *Single letter alert*: only one *l*. Also remember that the following vowel sound is spelt with an *i*.

heliport *noun* a place for helicopters to take off and land.

ANOTHER WORD for this is **helipad**.

helium /*say* **hee**-lee-uhm/ *noun* a gas which is lighter than air and is often used to fill balloons.

WORD HISTORY from a Greek word meaning 'sun'

hell *noun*
1. in some religions, a place where evil people are said to go for punishment after death. **2.** a place or condition of great unhappiness or difficulty.
□ **hellish**, *adjective*

ANOTHER FORM Definition 1 is often spelt with a capital letter.

he'll a short form of *he will*.

hello *interjection* an exclamation to greet someone or to answer the telephone.

OTHER SPELLINGS are **hallo** and **hullo**.

helm *noun* the wheel or handle which is used to steer a boat.
□ **helmsman**, *noun*

helmet *noun* a hard kind of hat worn to protect your head.

help *verb*
1. If you **help** someone, you do something to make what they are doing easier: *I can't carry all this luggage – please help me!* **2.** If someone or something **helps** something to happen, they do something that makes it more likely that it will happen: *The government is doing all it can to help the growth of the economy*; *This medicine should help her recovery.* **3.** If you cannot **help** doing something, you cannot keep yourself from doing it: *We couldn't help laughing.*
–*noun* **4.** someone or something that helps: *He was no help at all.*
–*phrase* **5. help out**, to help in a time of difficulty: *She is helping out while her friend is in hospital.* **6. help yourself to**, to take for yourself: *Help yourself to some more food.*
□ **helper**, *noun* –**helping**, *noun* a serving of food.

SIMILAR WORDS (for definition 1) are **aid** and **assist**; (for definition 2) **promote**, **advance** and **further**; (for definition 4) **aid**, **assistance**, **backing** and **support**. All of these words are more formal than **help**.

help desk *noun*
1. a service to customers to provide help. **2.** a section in an organisation that provides help with faults or difficulties to users of a computer system: *Jan could not log on to her computer so she rang the help desk.*

ANOTHER FORM of this is **helpdesk**.

helpless *adjective*
1. weak or unable to do anything. **2.** without help: *helpless victims of the earthquake.*
□ **helplessly**, *adverb* –**helplessness**, *noun*

helter-skelter *adverb* with great haste and confusion: *People and animals ran helter-skelter from the sudden downpour of rain.*

hem *noun*
1. a folded and sewn edge of material.
–*verb* (**hems**, **hemming**, **hemmed**, **has hemmed**) **2.** If you **hem** a piece of cloth, you fold back the edge of it and sew it: *to hem curtains.*
–*phrase* **3. hem in**, to surround or enclose: *Enemy soldiers hemmed the prisoners in.*

hemi- *prefix* a word part meaning 'half', as in *hemisphere*.

WORD HISTORY this prefix comes from Greek

hemisphere /*say* **hem**-uhs-fear/ *noun* half of a round shape, such as the earth: *When it's summer in the northern hemisphere it's winter in the southern hemisphere.*
□ **hemispherical**, *adjective*

hemp *noun* a plant which is grown for its strong fibres which are used to make rope and bags, and also for the leaves which are used as a drug.

hen *noun* a female chicken, especially one that is kept for eggs.

NOTE The male is called a **cock** or, for domestic chickens, a **rooster**.

henna *noun* a reddish-orange dye which is used to colour hair and to paint designs on the skin.

hepatitis /*say* hep-uh-**tuy**-tuhs/ *noun* a disease of the liver which makes the skin and the whites of the eyes turn yellow.

hepta- *prefix* a word part meaning 'seven' as in *heptagon*.

ANOTHER SPELLING is **hept-**.
WORD HISTORY this prefix comes from Greek

heptagon /*say* **hep**-tuh-gon/ *noun* a flat shape with seven sides.
□ **heptagonal** /*say* hep-**tag**-uh-nuhl/, *adjective*

her *pronoun* **1.** a form of the pronoun **she** used as the object of the verb in a sentence: *I'll ask her.* **2.** a form of **she** that shows something belongs to her: *her CD.*
☐ **hers**, *pronoun*: *that CD is hers.* –**herself**, *pronoun*: *She cut herself.*

herald *noun*
1. in the past, somebody whose job was to carry messages or announce coming events.
–*verb* **2.** To **herald** something is to be a sign that it is coming: *The storm heralded the start of a week of rain.*

heraldry /*say* **he**-ruhl-dree/ *noun* the investigation and recording of coats of arms and the histories of the families to which they belong.
☐ **heraldic**, *adjective*

herb *noun* a plant used in cooking or medicines: *Thyme, mint and rosemary are all herbs.*
☐ **herbal**, *adjective* –**herbalist**, *noun*

WORD HISTORY from a Latin word meaning 'grass'

herbivore /*say* **her**-buh-vaw/ *noun* an animal that eats plants.
☐ **herbivorous** /*say* her-**biv**-uh-ruhs/, *adjective*

COMPARE this with **carnivore**, **insectivore** and **omnivore**.

herd *noun*
1. a large group of animals: *a herd of cattle.*
–*verb* **2.** When you **herd** animals or people, you make them move together in a group: *to herd the sheep into the pen*; *She herded us into the dining room.*

☑ SPELLING TIP Don't confuse the spelling of **herd** with **heard** which has the same sound. **Heard** is the past form of the verb **hear**.

here *adverb*
1. in this place: *Put it here.* **2.** to or towards this place: *Come here!* **3.** at this point: *Here the speaker paused.*
–*phrase* **4. here and there**, in or to various places: *The fish darted here and there among the coral.*

☑ SPELLING TIP Don't confuse the spelling of **here** with **hear** which has the same sound. If you can **hear**, you are able to sense sounds through your ear.

hereditary /*say* huh-**red**-uh-tree/ *adjective* inherited or passed down from a parent to their young ones: *a hereditary disease*; *hereditary ownership of land.*

☑ SPELLING TIP Don't forget the *ary* ending of **hereditary** although the *a* is not pronounced. **Hereditary** is related to other words whose meaning has to do the handing down of things from the older generation to the younger generation through time. Think of *inherit*, *inheritance* and *heritage*. All these words come from *heres*, the Latin word for an 'heir' (someone who inherits something). This may help you to remember the *her* start to **hereditary**.

heredity /*say* huh-**red**-uh-tee/ *noun* (*plural* **heredities**) the passing on of characteristics from parents to their young ones: *Heredity is to blame for my red hair.*

heresy /*say* **he**-ruh-see/ *noun* (*plural* **heresies**) a belief, especially about religion, which goes against the things that people generally believe.
☐ **heretic**, *noun* –**heretical**, *adjective*

heritage *noun* something which is passed on to you because you have been born into a particular family or country.

A SIMILAR WORD is **inheritance**.

hermit *noun* someone who lives alone and keeps away from other people.
☐ **hermitage**, *noun*

WORD HISTORY from a Greek word meaning 'of the desert'

hernia *noun* the pushing out of an organ in the body, through a tear or opening in the tissue that surrounds it.

hero /*say* **hear**-roh/ *noun* (*plural* **heroes**)
1. someone who has done a very brave thing. **2.** the main character in a book, film or play.
☐ **heroic** /*say* huh-**roh**-ik/, *adjective* –**heroism** /*say* **he**-roh-iz-uhm/, *noun*

NOTE In the past, the term **hero** was used mainly to refer to men or boys, but nowadays it is used for women and girls as well, and the term **heroine** is used less often.

heroin /*say* **he**-ruh-wuhn/ *noun* an illegal drug which makes people feel they can't do without it once they have started.

WORD HISTORY from a Greek word for *hero* (the effect of the drug is supposed to make someone feel like a hero)

☑ SPELLING TIP Don't confuse the spelling of **heroin** with **heroine** (with an *e*) which has the same sound. A **heroine** is a brave woman.

heroine /*say* **he**-ruh-wuhn/ *noun*
1. a woman who has done a very brave thing. **2.** the female character who has the main part in a book, film or play.

☑ SPELLING TIP Remember the *e* at the end of **heroine**. Don't confuse it with **heroin** which has the same sound. **Heroin** is an illegal drug.

heron *noun* a water bird with long legs, a long neck and a long bill.

herpes /*say* **her**-peez/ *noun* an infection which causes small blisters to break out on the skin.

herring *noun* (*plural* **herrings** *or* **herring**) small fish which is caught in the seas of the northern hemisphere and eaten either fresh or pickled.

he's a short form of *he is* or *he has*.

hesitate *verb* To **hesitate** is to wait or pause before doing something, as when you are not sure if you should go on or when you are preparing yourself: *to hesitate before you speak*.
☐ **hesitancy**, *noun* –**hesitant**, *adjective* –**hesitantly**, *adverb* –**hesitation**, *noun*

hessian /*say* **hesh**-uhn/ *noun* strong, rough cloth often used to make sacks.

hetero- *prefix* a word part meaning 'other' or 'different', as in *heterosexual*.

WORD HISTORY this prefix comes from Greek

heterosexual /*say* het-uh-roh-**sek**-shooh-uhl/ *adjective* Someone who is **heterosexual** is sexually attracted to people of the opposite sex.
☐ **heterosexual**, *noun* –**heterosexuality**, *noun*

COMPARE this with **homosexual**.

hew *verb* (**hews**, **hewing**, **hewed**, **has hewn**) To **hew** wood or a tree is to chop or cut it.

hex *noun* an evil spell or charm.

hexa- *prefix* a word part meaning 'six', as in *hexagon*.

WORD HISTORY this prefix comes from Greek

hexagon /*say* **heks**-uh-gon/ *noun* a flat shape with six straight sides.
☐ **hexagonal** /*say* heks-**ag**-uh-nuhl/, *adjective*

hibernate /*say* **huy**-buh-nayt/ *verb* When animals **hibernate**, they sleep through the winter in a safe place.
☐ **hibernation**, *noun*

hibiscus /*say* huy-**bis**-kuhs/ *noun* a shrub or small tree with large, brightly coloured flowers.

hiccups /*say* **hik**-ups/ *plural noun* sudden movements in your chest that you cannot stop, which cause a quick taking in of breath and a short, sharp sound.

hide[1] *verb* (**hides**, **hiding**, **hid**, **has hidden**)
1. If you **hide** something, you keep it from being seen: *I hid her presents until it was her birthday*; *She hid her anger by keeping a steady smile on her face*. **2.** If you **hide**, you keep yourself from being seen: *They couldn't find him because he was hiding behind the fence*.

SIMILAR WORDS are **conceal**, **cover**, **screen**, **disguise**, **mask** and **camouflage**. Note that when you **cover** or **screen** something, you hide it by placing something over or in front of it. When you **disguise**, **mask** or **camouflage** something, you hide the way it looks by making it look or seem different: *The great detective disguised himself as a workman*; *She sprayed the room to mask the smell of cooking*; *She wears loose clothes to camouflage the fact that she is a little overweight*.

hide[2] *noun* the skin of an animal: *Cow hide is used to make leather shoes*.

hideous /*say* **hid**-ee-uhs/ *adjective*
1. very ugly: *a hideous monster*. **2.** shocking: *a hideous crime*.
☐ **hideousness**, *noun* –**hideously**, *adverb*

☑ SPELLING TIP *Tricky vowel sound*: the main difficulty in spelling **hideous** is remembering that the vowel following the *d* is an *e* (not an 'i'). Then there is the common adjective suffix *-ous*. If you rap it out as *hid+e+ous*, you'll get it right.

hiding *noun*
1. a severe beating as a punishment. **2.** a thorough defeat or loss in a game: *Our team gave them a hiding in the finals*.

hierarchy /*say* **huy**-uh-rah-kee/ *noun* (*plural* **hierarchies**) a system which arranges people or things in ranks from the highest to the lowest.
☐ **hierarchical**, *adjective*

☑ SPELLING TIP *Tricky vowel sound*: don't let the meaning and sound of this word trick you into thinking that it contains the word *high*. The letters *hie* spell the 'huy-uh' sounds at the beginning. Note that the end of the word is formed by the suffix *-archy* which means 'rule' or 'government'. This suffix comes from Greek and is found in several other words relating to government, such as *monarchy*.

hieroglyphics /*say* huy-ruh-**glif**-iks/ *plural noun* writing in which words or sounds are represented by pictures: *Egyptian hieroglyphics*.

☑ SPELLING TIP *Tricky vowel sounds*: the first vowel sound is spelt *ie* (not *ei*) and the 'i' sound in the second last syllable is spelt with a *y*. The best way to remember this difficult word is to split it into its two parts: *hiero* (from the Greek word for 'sacred') and *glyphics* (from the Greek word for 'carving').

high *adjective*
1. tall or far above the ground. **2.** measured from bottom to top: *a tree 20 metres high*. **3.** above the normal level or amount: *a high temperature*; *high prices*. **4.** (of sound) at the top of the range that humans can hear: *to sing in a high voice*. **5.** excited or happy: *The crowd was in high spirits as they waited for the match to start*. **6.** *Informal* affected by drugs or alcohol.
–*noun* **7.** *Informal* an excitedly happy state: *She was on a high for days after winning the prize*.
☐ **high**, *adverb*: *to jump high*. –**highly**, *adjective*: *highly dangerous*.

highlands *plural noun* the part of a country where there are mountains or high hills: *the Tasmanian highlands.*
☐ **highlander**, *noun*

highlight *noun*
1. the best, brightest or most outstanding part: *The highlight of the night was a fireworks display.*
–*verb* **2.** When you **highlight** something, you emphasise it or make it stand out: *His speech highlighted the problems faced by young people.*

highlighter *noun* a wide fluoro-coloured pen used to colour over special words or pictures that you want to be noticed.

high-pitched *adjective* in music, having a high sound. See **pitch** (definition 4): *a high-pitched voice.*

high-rise *adjective* A **high-rise** building is tall and narrow with many storeys.

highway *noun* a main road built to carry a lot of traffic.

highwayman *noun* (*plural* **highwaymen**) a robber, usually on horseback, who used to hold up travellers on the road.

NOTE This term was used mainly in Britain. In Australia, someone who robbed people as they travelled was called a **bushranger**.

hijab /*say* hij-**ahb**/ *noun* a scarf-like piece of clothing worn by many Muslim women which covers the hair, neck and shoulders, leaving the face uncovered.

ANOTHER SPELLING is **hejab**.
ANOTHER TERM for this is **headscarf**.

hijack *verb* If someone **hijacks** an aircraft or vehicle, they take control of it, usually for political or religious reasons, by using force and threats.
☐ **hijacker**, *noun*

☑ SPELLING TIP This word sounds as if someone is saying hello to a man called Jack. Of course, the meaning has nothing to do with this, and **hijackers** certainly are not that friendly. However, it may help you remember the spelling. In fact, the word **hijack** comes from *highwayman* (a robber on the roads in England in the old days) and *jack* (an old word meaning 'to hunt at night'). You can spell the word **highjack**, but the most usual spelling is **hijack**.

hike *noun*
1. a very long walk, usually done for pleasure: *We went on a hike across the island.* **2.** a sudden increase: *a hike in the price of milk.*
–*verb* **3.** To **hike** is to go on a long walk: *It took us three days to hike from the lake to the coast.*
☐ **hiker**, *noun* –**hiking**, *noun*

hilarious /*say* huh-**lair**-ree-uhs/ *adjective*
1. noisily cheerful. **2.** extremely funny: *a hilarious story.*
☐ **hilariously**, *adverb* –**hilarity**, *noun*

☑ SPELLING TIP *Single letter alert*: only one *l* (think of one *l* in *laugh* to remind you). Also remember that the vowel sound in the middle is spelt with just an *a* (although it sounds like 'air').

hill *noun*
1. a naturally raised part of the earth's surface, smaller than a mountain. **2.** a heap or pile made by humans or animals: *an ant hill.*
–*phrase* **3. over the hill**, *Rather informal* past the height of physical or other condition.

hillbilly *noun* someone living in the country, especially in the mountains away from other people.

NOTE This word was first used in American English. An Australian word with a similar meaning is **bushie**.

hilt *noun*
1. the handle of a sword or dagger.
–*phrase* **2. to the hilt**, completely.

him *pronoun* a form of **he** used after the verb in a sentence: *The dog belongs to him.*
☐ **himself**, *pronoun*: *He can go by himself.*

hind *adjective* placed behind or at the back: *Kangaroos have very strong hind legs.*

hinder /*say* **hin**-duh/ *verb* To **hinder** someone or something is to slow them down or make their way difficult: *Heavy traffic hindered our progress.*
☐ **hindrance**, *noun*

WORD HISTORY from an Old English word meaning 'behind' or 'back'

hindsight /*say* **huynd**-suyt/ *noun* the ability to understand what you should have done in an event, after it has happened: *With hindsight, it is easy to see where we made the mistake.*

Hinduism /*say* **hin**-dooh-iz-uhm/ *noun* the main religion of India, in which followers worship many gods and goddesses. Followers of Hinduism are called Hindus, and worship in a temple.
☐ **Hindu**, *adjective*: *the Hindu system of castes or social ranks.*

hinge *noun*
1. a movable joint, like the one which attaches a door to a door post, allowing the door to swing backwards and forwards.
–*verb* **2.** To **hinge** is to join with a hinge: *to hinge a door.*
–*phrase* **3. hinge on**, to depend: *Everything hinges on your decision.*

hint *noun*
1. a roundabout or indirect suggestion: *to drop a hint that you would like an invitation to the party.*
2. a piece of helpful advice.

–*verb* **3.** If you **hint** or **hint at** something, you mention it in a roundabout way: *She hinted that she would like to come.*

hinterland *noun* the land lying just inland from the coast: *The hinterland is very mountainous.*

hip *noun* the part at each side of the body, just below the waist, formed by the top of the pelvic bone.

hippie *noun* a person who belongs to a general movement that promotes peace and freedom from narrow social conventions, especially such a person living in the 1960s.

ANOTHER SPELLING is **hippy**.

hippopotamus /*say* hip-uh-**pot**-uh-muhs/ *noun* (*plural* **hippopotamuses** *or* **hippopotami** /*say* hip-uh-**pot**-uh-muy/) a large mammal with short legs and a heavy hairless body, that lives around lakes and rivers in Africa.

THE SHORT FORM of this is **hippo**. This is more suited to informal language.

☑ SPELLING TIP The word **hippopotamus** comes from Greek words meaning 'horse of the river'. If you rap out the syllables – *hip+po+pot+a+mus* – you should get the double *p* in the right place!

hire *verb* To **hire** something or someone is to pay money to use them or employ them: *to hire a car*; *to hire a butler.*
☐ **hire**, *noun*: *a car for hire.*

hire-purchase *noun* a way of buying expensive things like cars or furniture by making regular payments of money after you take the goods home.

COMPARE this with **lay-by**.

his *pronoun* the form of **he** you use when something belongs to him: *That hat is his*; *That is his dog.*

hiss *verb* If something or someone **hisses**, they make the sound 'ssss', like a snake, especially as a way of showing their dislike for something: *The audience hissed and booed when the wicked witch appeared.*
☐ **hiss**, *noun* –**hissing**, *noun*

historian *noun* someone who studies history and writes about it.

history *noun* (*plural* **histories**)
1. the events which have happened in the past, or the study of them. **2.** a description of important things which have happened in the past.
☐ **historic**, *adjective* –**historical**, *adjective*

WORD HISTORY from a Greek word meaning 'inquiry' or 'observation'

hit *verb* (**hits**, **hitting**, **hit**, **has hit**) To **hit** something is to **1.** touch it hard, as with your hand or something held in your hand. **2.** to move into something hard and at speed: *The truck hit a lamp post.* **3.** to knock against: *I hit my head*; *a branch hitting a roof.* **4.** reach or arrive at it: *to hit the heights of success.*
–*noun* **5.** a knock or blow. **6.** a success: *The play was a hit.* **7.** on a computer, **a.** a connection on the internet: *My home page has had 300 hits this week.* **b.** a successful search on the internet: *I searched the Web for 'Harry Potter' and got thousands of hits.*
–*phrase* **8. hit home**, to have the desired effect on someone. **9. hit it off**, *Rather informal* to get on well together: *We hit it off immediately.* **10. hit on**, to find by chance: *to hit on a good idea.* **11. hit the nail on the head**, *Rather informal* to state or sum up exactly. **12. hit the roof**, *Informal* to show extreme anger.
☐ **hit**, *adjective*: *a hit song.*

hitch *noun* (*plural* **hitches**)
1. a kind of knot that can be undone easily. **2.** something that makes progress difficult: *a hitch in our plans.*
–*verb in the phrase* **3. hitch up**, to pull up: *to hitch up your trousers.*

hitchhike *verb* To **hitchhike** is to travel free of charge by getting lifts in passing cars or trucks.
☐ **hitchhiker**, *noun* –**hitchhiking**, *noun*

ANOTHER WORD for this, especially in informal language, is **hitch**.

HIV *noun* the virus that causes AIDS.

WORD HISTORY made by joining the first letters of *human immunodeficiency virus*

hive *noun*
1. a place that bees live in.
–*phrase* **2. hive of activity**, a place full of busy people.

hives *noun* a rash, usually due to eating or touching something to which you are allergic: *Strawberries give me hives.*

hoard /*say* hawd/ *noun*
1. a secret store.
–*verb* **2.** If you **hoard** something, you save it up and hide it away in a secret place: *Squirrels hoard nuts for winter.*
☐ **hoarder**, *noun*

☑ SPELLING TIP Don't confuse the spelling of **hoard** with **horde** which has the same sound. A **horde** is a large group of people or animals.

hoarding *noun*
1. a large board for putting up advertisements or notices. **2.** a temporary fence made of boards around a building site.

hoarse /*say* haws/ *adjective* A **hoarse** voice sounds rough and low: *to shout until your voice becomes hoarse.*
☐ **hoarseness**, *noun*

☑ SPELLING TIP Don't confuse the spelling of **hoarse** with **horse** which has the same sound. A **horse** is a large, four-legged animal with hoofs.

hoax *noun* a trick or practical joke.
□ **hoaxer**, *noun*

hobble *verb* To **hobble** is to walk with difficulty: *to hobble around with a sore heel.*

hobby *noun* (*plural* **hobbies**) something that you are very interested in and enjoy doing when not at school or working: *My hobby is photography.*

hock *noun* the joint in the hind leg of a horse or similar animal, which acts in the same way as a human's ankle.

hockey *noun* a game played on a field or on ice in which two teams compete to hit a ball or disc into a goal using a stick with a curved end.

hoe *noun*
1. a garden tool with a long handle and flat thin blade, which you use to break up the soil.
–*verb* (**hoes**, **hoeing**, **hoed**, **has hoed**) **2.** When you **hoe**, you use a hoe to break up weeds or soil in the garden or in a field.
–*phrase* **3. hoe into**, *Informal* **a.** to eat heartily. **b.** to attack strongly, usually with words: *If your parents find out you have been late to school, they will hoe into you.* **c.** to take up with energy: *He hoed into his homework.*

hog *noun*
1. a pig. **2.** *Informal* someone who is greedy or dirty.
–*verb* (**hogs**, **hogging**, **hogged**, **has hogged**) **3.** *Informal* If you **hog** something, you take all of it in a greedy way: *The children tried to hog the visitor's attention*; *She loves to hog the limelight.*
–*phrase* **4. go the whole hog**, *Informal* to do something completely: *He went the whole hog and spent all his savings buying CDs.*

hoist *verb*
1. If you **hoist** something, you raise or lift it, often with the help of a machine or some other device. **2.** If you **hoist** a flag, you raise it on a pole.
–*noun* **3.** a machine or device for raising or lifting things.

hold[1] *verb* (**holds**, **holding**, **held**, **has held**) To **hold** something is to **1.** have it or keep it in your arms or hands. **2.** own it: *to hold some shares.* **3.** contain it: *This jug holds two litres.* **4.** fasten it: *Pegs hold washing on the line.* **5.** have or control it: *to hold a meeting.*
–*noun* **6.** a grip: *Take a firm hold.* **7.** control or influence: *She seems to have some sort of hold over them.*
–*phrase* **8. hold down**, to continue to hold even though there are difficulties: *to hold down a job.* **9. hold on**, **a.** to keep a firm hold on something. **b.** *Rather informal* to stop or wait: *Hold on! I can't keep up.* **10. hold out**, **a.** to last: *I hope the money holds out till Monday.* **b.** to refuse to give in. **11. hold up**, **a.** to delay. **b.** to rob.
□ **holder**, *noun*

hold[2] *noun* the part of a ship, below the deck, where goods are stored.

hold-up *noun*
1. a robbery. **2.** a delay.

hole *noun*
1. an opening through something. **2.** a hollow space. **3.** *Informal* a dirty or unpleasant place: *This waiting room is a hole.*
–*verb in the phrase* **4. hole up**, to stay somewhere, especially because you are hiding: *The escaped prisoner was holed up in a cave for several weeks*; *She is holed up in her room studying.*

holiday *noun*
1. a day's break from work or school, usually to celebrate or remember an important event: *We have a public holiday to celebrate New Year.* **2. holidays**, a much longer break from your daily work, school or studies.
–*verb* **3.** When you **holiday**, you take a holiday: *We usually holiday on the coast.*

ANOTHER WORD (for definition 2) is **vacation**.

☑ SPELLING TIP *Single letter alert*: only one *l*. This is because **holiday** comes from 'holy day' (the first holidays were special days in the Church's calendar). But remember that the *y* has changed to an *i*.

hollow *adjective*
1. having empty space inside: *a hollow log.* **2.** empty of meaning: *hollow promises.*
–*noun* **3.** a hole or a downward slope, especially in the ground.
–*verb* **4.** If you **hollow** or **hollow out** something, you make it hollow by removing the solid inside part: *to hollow out a log.*
□ **hollowness**, *noun*

holly *noun* a small tree with shiny, prickly leaves and bright red berries in winter.

holo- *prefix* a word part meaning 'whole' or 'entire', as in *holocaust*.

WORD HISTORY this prefix comes from Greek

holocaust /*say* **hol**-uh-kost, **hol**-uh-kawst/ *noun* great loss of life, especially when caused by a bad fire.

☑ SPELLING TIP **Holocaust** comes from Greek and is difficult to spell. Try remembering that it comes from the prefix *holo-* (meaning 'whole') and *caust* (meaning 'something burnt').

holster *noun* a leather case for a gun, worn on a belt.

holy *adjective* (**holier**, **holiest**)
1. sacred or kept only for a god or gods: *a holy festival.* 2. A **holy** person is religious: *a holy priest.*
☐ **holiness**, *noun*

☑ SPELLING TIP Don't confuse the spelling of **holy** with **holey** which has the same sound. Something is **holey** if it is full of holes.

homage /*say* **hom**-ij/ *noun* respect or honour: *to pay homage to a leader.*

home *noun*
1. the place where you live or were born: *My home is opposite a park*; *Darwin is my home.* 2. a house or other place that people live in. 3. a place where people can be cared for: *an old people's home.*
–*adverb* 4. to or at home: *to come straight home after school.*
–*phrase* 5. **at home**, a. in a familiar or comfortable situation: *They always make their guests feel at home.* b. familiar with or used to: *I'm quite at home with computers.* c. in sport, in your own town or grounds.
☐ **home**, *adjective*: *home team.* –**homemade**, *adjective*: *homemade jam.* –**homing**, *adjective*: *a homing pigeon.*

homely /*say* **hohm**-lee/ *adjective* (**homelier**, **homeliest**)
1. plain and simple: *homely food.* 2. not attractive or good-looking: *a homely face.*
☐ **homeliness**, *noun*

homeopathic /*say* hoh-mee-oh-**path**-ik/ *adjective* having to do with homeopathy.

ANOTHER SPELLING is **homoeopathic**.

homeopathy /*say* hoh-mee-**op**-uh-thee/ *noun* the method of treating disease with tiny amounts of a substance which would, if you gave it in larger amounts, cause symptoms just like those of the disease being treated.
☐ **homeopath** /*say* **hoh**-mee-uh-path/, *noun*

ANOTHER SPELLING is **homoeopathy**.

home page *noun* an introductory page to a website, from which you can go to all other parts of the site.

ANOTHER FORM of this is **homepage**.

homesick *adjective* unhappy and wanting to be at home.
☐ **homesickness**, *noun*

homestead *noun* the main house on a sheep or cattle station or a large farm.

home unit *noun* See **unit** (definition 3).

homework *noun* school work that is done at home.

homicide /*say* **hom**-uh-suyd/ *noun* the crime of killing someone on purpose.
☐ **homicidal**, *adjective*

☑ SPELLING TIP Remember the *c* spelling for the 's' sound in this word. The suffix *-cide* means 'killer' or 'act of killing' and appears in several other words, such as *suicide*. It comes from the Latin word for 'kill'. Here it is joined to a form of *homo*, the Latin word for 'man'.

hommos /*say* **hom**-uhs, **hoom**-uhs/ *noun* See **hummus**.

homo- *prefix* a word part meaning 'same', as in *homonym*.

WORD HISTORY this prefix comes from Greek

homogeneous /*say* hoh-muh-**jee**-nee-uhs/ *adjective* made up of parts which are all of the same or a similar kind: *a homogeneous chemical substance*; *a homogeneous group of people.*

ANOTHER FORM You can also use **homogenous** but note that this word (without the *e* before the *ous*) has a different pronunciation: huh-**moj**-uh-nuhs.

☑ SPELLING TIP The spelling will be easier if you see the words **homogeneous** and **homogenous** are formed. They begin with the prefix *homo-* (from the Greek word for 'the same'). The *gen* spelling of the middle section comes from the Greek word *genos* (meaning 'sort' or 'kind'). Replace the *os* with the English adjective suffix *-eous* for **homogeneous** or with *-ous* for **homogenous**.

homonym /*say* **hom**-uh-nim/ *noun* a word which has the same sound or the same spelling as another but has a different meaning.

☑ SPELLING TIP **Homonym** comes from Greek and is made up of two parts - the prefix *homo-* (meaning 'the same') and *nym* (meaning a 'word' or 'name'). You may know some other words that have this ending – *synonym* (a word with a similar meaning to another) and *antonym* (a word with the opposite meaning to another).

homosexual /*say* hoh-muh-**sek**-shooh-uhl/ *adjective* Someone who is **homosexual** has sexual feelings for people of the same sex as themselves.
☐ **homosexual**, *noun* –**homosexuality**, *noun*

COMPARE this with **heterosexual**.

honest /*say* **on**-uhst/ *adjective* truthful and fair.
☐ **honestly**, *adverb* –**honesty**, *noun*

honey /*rhymes with* funny/ *noun* a sweet, sticky liquid made by bees from the nectar of flowers.

honeycomb *noun* a wax structure with many rows of tiny separate spaces, made by bees for holding eggs, honey and pollen in the hive.

honeydew *noun* a sweet-flavoured, round melon with a smooth, pale green or yellow skin.

honeymoon *noun* a holiday spent by newly married couples shortly after their marriage ceremony.

honorary /*say* **on**-uh-ruh-ree/ *adjective* If someone is in an **honorary** position, they are not paid for doing that job: *the honorary secretary of the club.*

> ☑ SPELLING TIP This word is made up of *honour* plus the suffix *-ary* (meaning 'having to do with'). However, you have to remember that the *u* in *honour* has been left out. Several words that contain *our* change to *or* when they change their form. For example, the *u* in *humour* is left out when *humorous* is formed, and *glamour* becomes *glamorous*.

honour /*say* **on**-uh/ *noun*
1. fame or good reputation: *to bring honour to your family.* **2.** respect: *to be treated with honour.* **3.** honesty and high morals: *a person of honour.*
–*verb* **4.** If you **honour** someone, you respect them highly. **5.** If you **honour** an arrangement or a promise, you do what you have agreed to do.
–*phrase* **6. do honour to**, to show respect to. **7. on your honour**, accepting personal responsibility for your actions or the truthfulness of your words.
☐ **honourable**, *adjective*

> ANOTHER SPELLING is **honor**.

hood *noun*
1. a loose kind of hat, usually attached to a coat, which covers your head and neck. **2.** a folding roof for a car or baby's pram.
☐ **hooded**, *adjective*

hoodlum /*say* **hoohd**-luhm/ *noun* a rough destructive young person.

hoodwink *verb* If someone **hoodwinks** you, they deceive or trick you because you do not really understand what is happening.
☐ **hoodwinked**, *adjective* –**hoodwinker**, *noun*

hoof *noun* (*plural* **hoofs** *or* **hooves**) the hard covering which protects the feet of some animals such as horses, cows and pigs.

hook *noun*
1. a piece of metal or some other material bent or curved so as to hold or catch something. **2.** a blow in boxing, made with the arm bent.
–*verb* **3.** If you **hook** something, you attach or fasten it with a hook. **4.** If you **hook** a fish, you catch it with a hook on the end of a line. **5.** When you **hook** a ball, you hit it so it swerves to the left if you are right-handed, or to the right if you are left-handed.
–*phrase* **6. off the hook, a.** out of trouble. **b.** with the receiver lifted: *The telephone is off the hook.*
☐ **hooked**, *adjective*: *a hooked stick*; *hooked on sweets.*

hook-up *noun* a connection between radio or television stations or telephones.

hooligan *noun* a rough and noisy young person who causes trouble.
☐ **hooliganism**, *noun*

> A SIMILAR WORD is **hoon**.

hoop *noun* a ring or circular band made of wire, wood or plastic.

hop[1] *verb* (**hops**, **hopping**, **hopped**, **has hopped**)
1. To **hop** is to jump about on one foot.
–*noun* **2.** a hopping movement: *a hop, step and jump.*
–*phrase* **3. on the hop, a.** unprepared: *caught on the hop.* **b.** busy or moving.

hop[2] *noun* a climbing plant whose flowers are used to flavour beer.

hope *noun*
1. a wish or desire that something good will happen: *a hope for the future.* **2.** an expectation or likelihood: *no hope of getting there in time.*
–*verb* **3.** If you **hope** that something will happen, you want it to happen, especially something good: *I hope you feel better soon*; *I hope to study drama.*
☐ **hopeful**, *adjective* –**hopefulness**, *noun* –**hopeless**, *adjective* –**hopelessness**, *noun*

hopscotch *noun* a children's game in which the player hops from one square to another in a pattern of squares drawn on the ground without touching a line.

horde /*say* hawd/ *noun* a great crowd or number: *A horde of supporters welcomed the winning team home.*

> A SIMILAR WORD is **host**.

> ☑ SPELLING TIP Don't confuse the spelling of **horde** with **hoard** which has the same sound. A **hoard** is a secret supply collected over some period of time.

horizon /*say* huh-**ruy**-zuhn/ *noun*
1. the line where the earth or sea appears to meet the sky. **2.** the limit or boundary to knowledge: *Reading broadens your horizons.*

horizontal /*say* ho-ruh-**zon**-tuhl/ *adjective*
1. in line with the horizon: *The horizontal bar goes across and the vertical bar goes up.* **2.** lying down flat.
☐ **horizontally**, *adverb*

> COMPARE this with **vertical**.

hormone *noun* a chemical substance made by a gland in the body, which travels through the blood and affects other parts of the body.
☐ **hormonal**, *adjective*

> WORD HISTORY from a Greek word meaning 'setting in motion'

horn *noun*
1. a hard pointed growth on the forehead of animals like cows, sheep and deer. 2. the bone-like material making up horns. 3. a musical wind instrument: *a French horn.* 4. a device for sounding a warning signal: *to blow the car's horn.*
☐ **horny**, *adjective*

hornet *noun* a large wasp with a very painful sting.

horoscope /*say* **ho**-ruh-skohp/ *noun*
1. a diagram showing the position of the planets in the sky at a particular time and thought by some people to be a help in telling the future. 2. a telling of the future based on such a diagram.

☑ SPELLING TIP Let's hope that there is no *horror* when someone reads your **horoscope**. Remember that there is only one *r* in this word. It is made up of *horo* (from the Greek word for 'time') and the suffix *-scope* (from the Greek word for 'observe'). This suffix appears in the names of many things used for seeing, such as *telescope* and *microscope*.

horrendous *adjective* horrible and dreadful.

horrible *adjective*
1. frightening, shocking and disgusting: *horrible nightmares*; *the horrible truth.* 2. unpleasant: *a horrible meal*
☐ **horribly**, *adverb*

SIMILAR WORDS are **awful**, **dreadful**, **nasty**, **shocking** and **terrible**.

horrid *adjective* nasty or horrible.

horrify *verb* (**horrifies**, **horrifying**, **horrified**, **has horrified**) to shock or fill with horror: *The violent film horrified me.*
☐ **horrific**, *adjective* shocking. –**horrifying**, *adjective*

horror /*say* **ho**-ruh/ *noun* a strong feeling of fear or disgust: *a horror of spiders.*
☐ **horrific** /*say* ho-**rif**-ik, huh-**rif**-ik/, *adjective*

hors d'oeuvre /*say* aw-**derv**/ *noun* a small piece of food such as an olive, a nut or a savoury, served before a main meal.

NOTE We pronounce these words like this because they come from French.

horse *noun*
1. a large, four-legged animal, widely used by humans for riding, racing or pulling loads.
–*verb in the phrase* 2. **horse about** (or **around**), to act or play roughly.
☐ **horseback**, *noun*, *adjective*: *on horseback*; *a horseback rider.*

NOTE The female is a **mare**; the male is a **stallion**; the young is a **foal**.

horsepower *noun* a unit for measuring power in the imperial system: *a 50 horsepower engine.*

horseradish *noun* a plant whose strongly flavoured root is used in cooking.

horticulture /*say* **haw**-tuh-kul-chuh/ *noun* the growing of garden plants for their fruit, vegetables and flowers.
☐ **horticultural**, *adjective* –**horticulturalist**, *noun* –**horticulturist**, *noun*

☑ SPELLING TIP The spelling of **horticulture** will be easier if you see that it is made up of *horti* (a form of *hortus*, the Latin word for 'garden') and the suffix *-culture* (meaning 'cultivation'). Another word with this ending is *agriculture*.

hose *noun*
1. a long plastic tube for carrying water. 2. See **hosiery**.
–*verb* 3. If you **hose** something, you wet or water it with a hose: *She's hosing the garden.*

hosiery /*say* **hoh**-zuh-ree/ *noun* clothing for your legs and feet, such as socks or stockings.

ANOTHER WORD for this is **hose**.

☑ SPELLING TIP The tricky part to remember is the *si* in the middle which makes the single 'z' sound. **Hosiery** comes from the word *hose* which can mean 'an article of clothing for the legs, such as stockings or tights'.

hospice *noun* a hospital for patients who are dying, often run by a church.

hospital *noun* a place where sick and injured people are given medical treatment.
☐ **hospitalise**, *verb*

ANOTHER SPELLING for **hospitalise** is **hospitalize**.

hospitality /*say* hos-puh-**tal**-uh-tee/ *noun* kindness and generosity shown to guests.
☐ **hospitable**, *adjective*

host[1] /*rhymes with* most/ *noun*
1. someone who entertains guests: *The host of a party.* 2. an animal or plant on which a parasite lives: *A dog is host to many fleas.* 3. See **host computer**.
–*verb* 4. If you **host** a party or other social occasion, you are the host: *to host a dinner.*
☐ **hostess**, *noun*

host[2] /*rhymes with* most/ *noun* a great number or crowd: *a host of questions*; *a host of angels.*

A SIMILAR WORD is **horde**.

hostage /*say* **hos**-tij/ *noun* someone held prisoner by an enemy or terrorist until certain conditions are met or ransom money is paid.

host computer *noun* the key or central computer in a network on which a range of tasks can be performed which are not available to the other computers in the network.

ANOTHER FORM is **host**.

hostel *noun* a place where people can get a room to sleep for the night at a low cost.

WORD HISTORY from a French word meaning 'guest'

hostile *adjective* To be **hostile** is to be unfriendly or to act like an enemy.
□ **hostility**, *noun*

WORD HISTORY from a Latin word meaning 'enemy'

hot *adjective*
1. having a high temperature: *Be careful you don't burn yourself on the hot stove.* **2.** If you are **hot**, you feel that you are very warm. **3.** If food is **hot**, it has a lot of spices in it that produce a burning feeling on your tongue when you eat it. **4.** If news is **hot**, it is recent or fresh. **5.** If you have a **hot** temper, you are quick to get angry.
–phrase **6. not so hot**, *Rather informal* **a.** not very good: *He's not so hot at maths.* **b.** not very well: *I'm not feeling so hot.*

hot dog *noun* a long, red sausage served hot in a bread roll, usually with tomato sauce and sometimes mustard.

hotel *noun*
1. a place which provides accommodation and meals for paying guests. **2.** a place where people go to drink alcohol.
□ **hotelier**, *noun*

hotline *noun* a telephone line which connects people, especially those in an emergency, to special services that can give advice or organise help.

hotplate *noun* a metal plate on an electric stove or barbecue which can be heated and used to cook food.

hound *noun*
1. a dog, especially a hunting dog.
–verb **2.** If you **hound** someone, you keep on at them to do something.

hour *noun*
1. a unit of measurement of time equal to 60 minutes. **2.** a particular time: *The hour has come.* **3. hours**, the usual times for work or business: *Office hours are 8.30 a.m. to 5.30 p.m.*
–phrase **4. the eleventh hour**, the very last possible moment: *Don't leave it until the eleventh hour.*
□ **hourly**, *adjective* –**hourly**, *adverb*

hourglass *noun* an instrument for measuring time, consisting of two bulbs of glass joined by a narrow passage through which a quantity of sand runs in exactly an hour.

house *noun /say* hows/
1. a building where people live. **2.** a building for any purpose: *Parliament House*; *a house of worship.* **3.** a division of a school, made up of children from all classes, formed for sport and other competitions. **4.** the group of people forming a parliament or one of its divisions: *the upper house*; *the lower house.* **5.** a family seen as consisting of ancestors and descendants: *the royal house of Windsor.* **6.** an audience in a theatre: *The performers played to a full house.*
–verb /say howz/ **7.** If you **house** someone, you provide accommodation for them: *to house refugees.*
□ **housing**, *noun*

houseboat *noun* a boat which is fitted up for people to live on.

household *noun* all the people who live together in a house.
□ **household**, *adjective*: *household pets*; *household furniture.* –**householder**, *noun*

hovel *noun* a small, dirty house or hut.

hover */say* **hov**-uh/ *verb* To **hover** is to **1.** stay in one spot in the air as if hanging: *The helicopter hovered over the accident site.* **2.** stay close to: *Reporters were hovering around the hotel entrance all day, waiting for the film star to leave.*

hovercraft *noun* a vehicle which can travel over land or water, supported by the downward pressure of air that it produces.

how *adverb*
1. in what way or manner: *How did it happen?* **2.** to what degree or amount: *How late will you be?* **3.** in what state or condition: *How are you?*

however *conjunction*
1. in no matter what condition, state, or manner: *Go there however you like.*
–adverb **2.** no matter how far, much, and so on: *However hard he tries, he'll never win.* **3.** despite this: *It's raining. However, I would still like to go for a walk.*

howl *verb* To **howl** is to make a long, loud, crying noise like a dog or wolf.
□ **howl**, *noun*

hub *noun*
1. the centre part of a wheel. **2.** any busy or important centre: *This control tower is the hub of the airport.*

huddle *verb*
1. To **huddle** is to crowd closely together: *to huddle by the fire to keep warm.*
–noun **2.** a few people crowded together to discuss something in private: *They were in a huddle in the corner, whispering to each other.*

hue *noun* a colour or shade of colour: *the hues of the rainbow.*

huff *noun* a fit of temper.
□ **huffy**, *adjective*

hug *verb* (**hugs**, **hugging**, **hugged**, **has hugged**)
1. If you **hug** someone, you hold them tightly in

your arms, especially with affection. **2.** If a person or vehicle **hugs** something as they go along, they keep close to it: *The boat hugged the coastline.*
☐ **hug**, *noun*

A SIMILAR WORD (for definition 1) is **embrace**.

huge *adjective* very, very large: *a huge ocean.*
☐ **hugely**, *adverb* –**hugeness**, *noun*

hulk *noun* someone or something that is large, heavy or clumsy.
☐ **hulking**, *adjective*

hull *noun* the body or frame of a ship or boat.

hullabaloo /*say* hul-uh-buh-**looh**/ *noun* an uproar or loud noisy disturbance.

hum *verb* (**hums**, **humming**, **hummed**, **has hummed**)
1. When something **hums**, it makes a continuous low sound: *bees humming near the flowers*; *The room hummed with activity.* **2.** When you **hum**, you sing a tune with your lips closed, without saying the words.
☐ **hum**, *noun*

human *noun* a person; a man, woman or child.
☐ **human**, *adjective*: *the human eye.* –**humanly**, *adverb*: *humanly possible.*

ANOTHER TERM for this is **human being**.
WORD HISTORY from a Latin word meaning 'of a man'

humane /*say* hyooh-**mayn**/ *adjective* If you are **humane**, you show feelings of kindness and sympathy: *It would be humane to help him.*
☐ **humanely**, *adverb*

humanitarian /*say* hyooh-man-uh-**tair**-ree-uhn/ *adjective* concerned with helping people who live in bad conditions or are suffering: *humanitarian aid.*

humanity *noun*
1. all humans. **2.** sympathy and kindness towards other people and animals.

humankind *noun* all humans: *a discovery which benefited humankind.*

humble *adjective*
1. extremely modest, thinking of yourself as someone of no great importance: *He was too humble to expect the famous singer to notice him.* **2.** poor and lowly: *She rose from humble origins to be the president.*
☐ **humbly**, *adverb*

humdrum *adjective* dull and ordinary: *a humdrum existence.*

humid /*say* **hyooh**-muhd/ *adjective* moist and damp, especially when it is also warm: *a humid day.*
☐ **humidity**, *noun*

humiliate /*say* hyooh-**mil**-ee-ayt/ *verb* To **humiliate** someone is to cause them to feel ashamed or foolish: *His rude remarks humiliated her.*
☐ **humiliation**, *noun*

humility /*say* hyooh-**mil**-uh-tee/ *noun* the condition of being humble, usually a way of behaving that shows you do not think you are better than other people: *She had the humility to see that she was wrong and apologise.*

hummus /*say* **hoom**-uhs, **hom**-uhs/ *noun* a soft, paste-like food made from chickpeas, oil, lemon and garlic, originating in Middle Eastern cooking.

OTHER SPELLINGS are **hommos**, **hoummus** and **hoummos**.

☑ SPELLING TIP Notice that you can spell this word in several different ways, but that it always has a double *m*. Don't confuse it with **humus** (with one *m*) which is dark material in soil.

humour *noun* the quality of being funny or amusing: *a sense of humour*; *I know you think that show is funny, but I just can't see the humour in it.*
☐ **humorous**, *adjective* –**humorously**, *adverb*

ANOTHER SPELLING is **humor**.

☑ SPELLING TIP Notice that there is no *u* after the *o* in the adjective form **humorous**. It is common for words that contain *our* to change to *or* when they change their form. For example, the *u* in *glamour* is dropped when the word *glamorous* is formed, and *vigour* becomes *vigorous*.

hump *noun*
1. a large lump on the back: *a camel's hump.* **2.** a rounded rise in the ground or on a road: *a speed hump.*

humpy *noun* an Aboriginal bush shelter.

WORD HISTORY from an Aboriginal language of Queensland called Yagara

humus /*say* **hyooh**-muhs/ *noun* dark rich material in soil, formed by the rotting of animal and vegetable matter.

☑ SPELLING TIP Don't confuse the spelling of **humus** (single *m*) with **hummus** (double *m*) which is a kind of Middle Eastern food.

hunch *noun* (*plural* **hunches**) *Rather informal* a belief, usually without knowledge of the facts: *I had a hunch that something would happen.*

hundred *noun*
1. a cardinal number, ten times ten (10 × 10). **2.** a symbol for this number, as 100 or C.
☐ **hundred**, *adjective* –**hundredth**, *adjective*, *noun*

hunger *noun* an uncomfortable feeling of the need for food.
□ **hungry**, *adjective* (**hungrier**, **hungriest**) –**hungrily**, *adverb*

hunk *noun* a large piece with rough edges: *I broke off a hunk of bread.*

hunt *verb* To **hunt** is to **1.** chase animals for food or sport. **2.** search: *I hunted in my bag for a pen.*
□ **hunt**, *noun* –**hunter**, *noun*

NOTE A woman who hunts can be called a **huntress**.

huntsman *noun* (*plural* **huntsmen**)
1. a man who hunts animals, etc., to kill them for food or as a sport. **2.** See **tarantula** (definition 1).

hurdle *noun*
1. a movable fence over which horses or people have to jump in a race. **2.** something difficult that has to be done: *We still have many hurdles to overcome.*
–*verb* **3.** If you **hurdle** something, you jump over it: *She hurdled the fence with ease.*

hurl *verb* To **hurl** something is to throw it.

hurricane /*say* **hu**-ruh-kuhn/ *noun* a violent tropical storm with a very strong wind.

☑ SPELLING TIP *Double letter alert*: double *r*. You will remember this if you think of the double *r* in *hurry* – **hurricanes** are always in a hurry. Also remember that the final part is spelt *ane* (even though it sounds like 'uhn').

hurry *verb* (**hurries**, **hurrying**, **hurried**, **has hurried**) To **hurry** is to act quickly to save time: *Hurry or you will be late!*
□ **hurried**, *adjective* –**hurriedly**, *adverb* –**hurry**, *noun*

hurt *verb*
1. If someone or something **hurts** you, they cause pain or damage to part of your body: *You hurt me when you hit my arm*; *These new shoes are hurting my feet.* **2.** If you **hurt** someone, you cause physical or mental pain or damage to them: *My thoughtlessness hurt her.* **3.** If a part of you **hurts**, it is painful: *My arm hurts.*
□ **hurt**, *noun* –**hurtful**, *adjective*

hurtle *verb* If something **hurtles**, it moves quickly and often in an uncontrolled way: *The truck hurtled down the hill.*

husband *noun* the man to whom a woman is married.

hush *verb*
1. If you **hush** someone, you tell or signal them to be quiet: *The teacher hushed the class before the principal came in.*
–*phrase* **2. hush up**, to prevent from becoming known: *to hush up a scandal.*
□ **hush**, *noun*

husk *noun* the dry, outside covering of some fruits and seeds: *corn husk.*

husky[1] *adjective* (**huskier**, **huskiest**)
1. low and breathy: *a husky voice.* **2.** big and strong: *a husky lifesaver.*
□ **huskiness**, *noun*

husky[2] *noun* (*plural* **huskies**) a strong dog used to pull sledges over the snow.

hustle /*say* **hus**-uhl/ *verb*
1. If you **hustle** someone somewhere, you force or push them to make them move quickly: *Police hustled the prisoners through the crowd into the courtroom.* **2.** If you **hustle** someone, you try to get them to do what you want by putting pressure on them.

☑ SPELLING TIP *Silent letter alert*: don't forget the *st* (not double *s*) spelling. The *t* is silent.

hut *noun* a small, house-like shelter: *a beach hut.*

hutch *noun* (*plural* **hutches**) a coop or house for small animals: *a rabbit hutch.*

hybrid /*say* **huy**-bruhd/ *noun* an animal or plant that is the result of breeding between different types.
□ **hybridise**, *verb*

ANOTHER SPELLING for **hybridise** is **hybridize**.
WORD HISTORY from a Latin word for the young of a tame sow and a wild boar

hydrangea /*say* huy-**drayn**-juh/ *noun* a shrub which has large blue or pink flowers and loses its leaves in winter.

☑ SPELLING TIP You will notice the word *range* is hidden inside **hydrangea** – think of a range of different coloured flowers to help you remember the spelling. **Hydrangea** is made up of two Greek words: *hydr-* (a form of *hydro-* meaning 'water') and *angeia* meaning 'vessels' (the seeds are shaped like vessels), although the letter *i* has been dropped from this spelling.

hydrant *noun* a point where a hose can be connected to a water main.

☑ SPELLING TIP Remember that this word starts with *hydr-* (a form of the prefix *hydro-* meaning 'water').

hydraulic /*say* huy-**drol**-ik/ *adjective* worked or controlled by the pressure of a liquid such as water or oil: *hydraulic brakes.*
□ **hydraulically**, *adverb* –**hydraulics**, *noun*

☑ SPELLING TIP *Tricky vowel sound*: *au* for the 'o' sound in the middle. Also remember the *y* spelling in the first syllable. This is part of the prefix *hydr-* (a form of *hydro-* meaning 'water').

hydraulic fracturing *noun* in oil and gas mining, a process by which pressure from water mixed with chemicals and sand is used to make fractures in rock to release oil or gas.

ANOTHER WORD for this is **fracking**.

hydro- *prefix* a word part meaning 'water', as in *hydroplane*.

WORD HISTORY this prefix comes from Greek

hydro-electric *adjective* **Hydro-electric** power is electricity made by the energy of falling water.
☐ **hydro-electricity**, *noun*

hydrofoil *noun*
1. a ski-like attachment which raises the bottom of a boat above the surface of the water when a certain speed has been reached. **2.** a boat with hydrofoils.

hydrogen *noun* a gas which combines with oxygen to make water.

☑ SPELLING TIP The spelling of this word will be easier if you learn its two parts. If it made up of *hydro-* (meaning 'water') and *-gen* (a suffix used in the names of chemical substances that produce something).

hydroplane *noun* a light boat designed to skim along the surface of the water at high speed.

hydroponics *noun* the growing of plants with their roots in water rather than soil.

hyena /*say* huy-**ee**-nuh/ *noun* a dog-like animal that eats the flesh of dead animals.

☑ SPELLING TIP *Letter 'y' alert*: remember that *y* spells the 'uy' sound, and that there is a single *e* for the 'ee' sound in the middle of the word. Think that 'hyenas yawn every night automatically' to remind yourself of the sequence of letters. Like many words with a *y* spelling, **hyena** comes from the Greek word *hys* meaning 'hog'.

hygiene /*say* **huy**-jeen/ *noun*
1. the science of preserving health. **2.** the cleanliness necessary for preserving health.
☐ **hygienically**, *adverb*

☑ SPELLING TIP *Tricky vowel sound*: *ie* for the 'ee' sound in the second syllable. This follows the rule that *i* comes before *e* except after *c*. Also remember the *y* spelling in the first syllable, which is common in many words that come from Greek.

hymn /*say* him/ *noun* a religious song.

☑ SPELLING TIP Don't confuse **hymn** with the pronoun **him**, which has the same sound. Remember the *y* spelling for the 'i' sound and the silent *n* at the end of **hymn**.

hyper- *prefix* a word part meaning 'over', as in *hyperactive*.

WORD HISTORY this prefix comes from Greek

hyperactive *adjective* so active that you are restless and cannot settle down: *a hyperactive child.*
☐ **hyperactivity**, *noun*

THE SHORT FORM of this is **hyper**, which is used in informal language.

hyperlink *noun* on a computer, a word or image which is connected to another document or website, or to another place in the same document. You can click on the hyperlink to go to that other document or site.

hyphen /*say* **huy**-fuhn/ *noun* a short line (-) used to join the parts of words like 'part-time', or to join the parts of a word when it has to be broken at the end of a line.

SEE the Grammar and Punctuation Guide appendix.

☑ SPELLING TIP *Letter 'y' alert*: remember that **hyphen** is spelt with a *y* for the 'uy' sound and a *ph* for the 'f' sound, like many words from Greek.

hypno- *prefix* a word part meaning 'sleep', as in *hypnosis*.

WORD HISTORY this prefix comes from Greek

hypnosis /*say* hip-**noh**-suhs/ *noun* a sleep-like state brought about by cooperating with someone who is then able to control your mind and actions.
☐ **hypnotic** /*say* hip-**not**-ik/, *adjective*

☑ SPELLING TIP *Letter 'y' alert*: this word comes from Greek which is why is it has a *y* for the 'i' sound in the first syllable. It ends with the suffix *-osis* which is used in many words that come from Greek and relate to an action or a process, such as *diagnosis*.

hypnotise *verb*
1. To **hypnotise** someone is to put them under hypnosis: *The psychiatrist hypnotised the patient.*
2. If something or someone **hypnotises** you, they fascinate you so much that you can't think of anything else: *He was hypnotised by her beautiful singing.*
☐ **hypnotism**, *noun* –**hypnotist**, *noun*

ANOTHER SPELLING is **hypnotize**.

hypo- *prefix* a word part meaning 'under', as in *hypodermic*.

WORD HISTORY this prefix comes from Greek

hypochondria /*say* huy-puh-**kon**-dree-uh/ *noun* the state of being very anxious about your health or imagining yourself to be ill when you are not.
☐ **hypochondriac**, *adjective*, *noun*

☑ SPELLING TIP Notice the *ch* spelling for the 'k' sound in the middle of this word. If you remember this and also know the prefix *hypo-*, you will be able to spell this long word. This prefix means 'under' or 'less than'. Here it is part of an original Greek word meaning 'stomach', thought of as being under the ribs. People thought that sadness and worry came from that area of the body.

hypocrite /*say* **hip**-uh-krit/ *noun* someone who pretends that they have certain beliefs or morals that in reality they do not have.
☐ **hypocrisy**, *noun* –**hypocritical**, *adjective*

☑ SPELLING TIP Remember that this word ends with *e*, although the *ite* ending sounds like 'it'. The first part of the word *hypo* is part of a Greek word meaning 'actor' or 'pretender'.

hypodermic *adjective* injecting under the skin: *a hypodermic needle.*

☑ SPELLING TIP The spelling of this word will be easier if you can see that it is made of the prefix *hypo-* (meaning 'under') and *dermic* (a form of *derma*, the Greek word for 'skin').

hypotenuse /*say* huy-**pot**-uhn-yoohz/ *noun* the side opposite the right angle in a triangle.

☑ SPELLING TIP *Letter 'y' alert*: many words of Greek origin have a *y* spelling where you might expect an *i*, as **hypotenuse** does in the first syllable. It comes from Greek words meaning 'to stretch under'. The last syllable sounds like the word *use* and is spelt like it too.

hypothermia /*say* huy-puh-**therm**-ee-uh/ *noun* a dangerous condition, often caused by being exposed to cold weather, in which body temperature is lower than normal.
☐ **hypothermal**, *adjective*

hypothesis /*say* huy-**poth**-uh-suhs/ *noun* (*plural* **hypotheses** /*say* huy-**poth**-uh-seez/) something put forward as being true which is taken as a useful starting point for a discussion or scientific investigation.
☐ **hypothesise**, *verb* –**hypothetical** /*say* huy-puh-**thet**-ik-uhl/, *adjective*

ANOTHER SPELLING for **hypothesise** is **hypothesize**.

☑ SPELLING TIP The spelling of this word will be easier if you think of it as being made up of two parts, *hypo-* and *thesis*, even though you do not say it in this way. The prefix *hypo-* means 'under' or 'less' and *thesis* is a theory or idea. This links to the meaning of **hypothesis** in that it is a theory without complete evidence and so needs to be tested.

hysterical /*say* his-**te**-rik-uhl/ *adjective*
1. extremely and wildly emotional. **2.** laughing uncontrollably. **3.** *Rather informal* extremely amusing: *That film was hysterical.*
☐ **hysteria**, *noun*

☑ SPELLING TIP *Letter 'y' alert*: remember the *y* spelling for the 'i' sound in the first syllable. **Hysterical** comes from *hysterikos*, a Greek word meaning 'suffering in the womb (or uterus)'. (Women were believed to be the only ones who suffered from emotion like this!)

I *pronoun* the word that the speaker of a sentence uses about himself or herself before a verb: *I signed my name.*

SEE ALSO **me**, **my** and **mine**[2].

ibis /*say* **uy**-buhs/ *noun* (*plural* **ibises**) a bird like a heron with a long, thin, curved beak.

ice *noun*
1. frozen water.
–*verb* **2.** If you **ice** a cake, you spread icing over it.
□ **icy**, *adjective*: *an icy road.*

iceberg *noun* a large mass of ice broken off from a glacier and floating in the sea.

ice-cream *noun* a sweet, frozen food made with cream or milk.

ice-skate *noun*
1. a special boot with a blade running from the front of the sole to the back of the sole.
–*verb* **2.** When you **ice-skate**, you move on ice, wearing ice-skates.
□ **ice-skater**, *noun* a person who ice-skates.

NOTE This word is often shortened to **skate**.

icicle /*say* **uy**-sik-uhl/ *noun* a hanging tapering piece of ice formed by the freezing of water falling in drops.

☑ SPELLING TIP Remember that **icicles** are made of *ice*. So the first part of **icicle**, which sounds like 'uys', is spelt *ic* (*ice* without the *e*). Then you have to remember to add another *ic*, like another little drop of *ic*(*e*), and end with *le* (not *al*).

icing *noun* a mixture of sugar and water or other colourings or flavourings for covering cakes.

icon /*say* **uy**-kon/ *noun*
1. a religious picture or statue. **2.** someone or something that is very well known and regarded as a representative of their group or a symbol of something: *The soldier's hat has become a national icon.* **3.** in computers, a small picture or symbol on the screen that represents something that you want to do or a set of things that you want to find: *Select the calculator icon if you want to use the computer as a calculator.*

I'd a short form of *I would* or *I had.*

idea *noun*
1. a thought or picture in the mind. **2.** a clever plan.

ideal *noun*
1. an idea of something at its most perfect: *This is my ideal of a holiday!* **2.** a high aim or standard: *She works hard towards her ideals.*
□ **ideal**, *adjective*: *ideal behaviour.* –**idealise**, *verb* –**idealism**, *noun* –**idealist**, *noun* –**idealistic**, *adjective*

ANOTHER SPELLING for **idealise** is **idealize**.

identical *adjective* exactly alike: *identical twins.*
□ **identically**, *adverb*

identify *verb* (**identifies**, **identifying**, **identified**, **has identified**) To **identify** someone or something is to recognise or prove them as being a particular person or thing: *Can you identify which is your watch?*
□ **identifiable**, *adjective* –**identification**, *noun*: *to present your identification.*

identity *noun* (*plural* **identities**)
1. the condition of being a certain person or thing: *our national identity.* **2.** a well-known personality: *an identity in the music world.*

☑ SPELLING TIP This is one of a group of words that come from the Latin word part *identi-* meaning 'the same'. Others are *identical* and *identify*. (Think of *ID*, the abbreviation for *identity* and you have the first two letters to start you off.) In **identity**, the *-ty* suffix (meaning 'the quality of being') has been added.

idiom /*say* **id**-ee-uhm/ *noun* an expression, especially one having a meaning other than its literal one, such as *It's raining cats and dogs*.

idiosyncrasy /*say* id-ee-oh-**sink**-ruh-see/ *noun* (*plural* **idiosyncrasies**) a peculiarity of someone's character or behaviour: *One of her idiosyncrasies is twisting her hair when she is thinking.*
□ **idiosyncratic**, *adjective* –**idiosyncratically**, *adverb*

☑ SPELLING TIP The most difficult part of this word is the *asy* ending (not *acy*). Also remember the *y* spelling for the 'i' sound in the middle (from the Greek *syn-*). **Idiosyncrasy** comes from Greek where the *idios* means 'own' or 'private'.

idiot *noun* a very foolish or stupid person.
☐ **idiotic**, *adjective*

idle *adjective*
1. If someone is **idle**, they are not doing anything: *Let's find some work for these idle children.* **2.** If something is **idle**, it is not being used: *idle machinery; idle time.*
☐ **idleness**, *noun* –**idler**, *noun* –**idly**, *adverb*

idol */say* **uy**-duhl/ *noun*
1. a statue worshipped as a god. **2.** any person or thing that is greatly loved, sometimes too much and without any judgement: *a sporting idol.*
☐ **idolise**, *verb* –**idolatry** */say* uh-**dol**-uh-tree/, *noun*

ANOTHER SPELLING for **idolise** is **idolize**.

i.e. *abbreviation* short for *id est*, Latin words meaning 'that is': *Please bring all your linen with you, i.e. sheets and towels.*

if *conjunction*
1. on condition that: *I'll come if you want me to.*
2. even though: *If you did say it, I didn't hear you.*
3. whether: *I don't know if I can do it.*
–*phrase* **4. if only**, a phrase used when you are talking about something you wish for: *If only he would come!*

igloo *noun* a dome-shaped Inuit house built of blocks of hard snow.

NOTE **Igloo** is from an Inuit word for *house*.

ignite *verb* If something **ignites**, it catches fire.

ignition *noun*
1. the act of setting on fire. **2.** a system for setting on fire, especially that of the electrical sparks which ignite the fuel in the cylinders in a car engine.

ignoble *adjective* of low character and behaviour.
☐ **ignobly**, *adverb*

THE OPPOSITE is **noble**.

ignoramus */say* ig-nuh-**ray**-muhs/ *noun* someone who knows little or nothing.

ignorant *adjective*
1. uneducated or knowing very little about a particular subject. **2.** having no knowledge: *I am ignorant of his whereabouts.*
☐ **ignorance**, *noun*

ignore *verb* To **ignore** someone or something is to take no notice of them.

iguana */say* i-**gwah**-nuh/ *noun* a large lizard of tropical America.

WORD HISTORY from a Native American language

☑ SPELLING TIP Remember the *gu* spelling for the 'gw' sound in this word.

ill *adjective*
1. sick, unwell. **2.** bad: *an ill wind.*
–*noun* **3.** an evil: *the ills of our society.*
–*adverb* **4.** badly: *ill advised.*
–*phrase* **5. ill health**, bad health. **6. ill effects**, a harmful result: *the ill effects of eating too much.*
☐ **illness**, *noun*

I'll a short form of *I will*.

illegal *adjective* not allowed by the law: *It's illegal to drive a car without a licence.*
☐ **illegally**, *adverb* –**illegality**, *noun*

THE OPPOSITE is **legal**.

illegible *adjective* not able to be read: *illegible scribble.*
☐ **illegibility**, *noun*

THE OPPOSITE is **legible**.

illegitimate */say* il-uh-**jit**-uh-muht/ *adjective*
1. *Old-fashioned* born to parents who are not married to each other. **2.** against the law or not proper: *illegitimate business deals.*
☐ **illegitimacy**, *noun*

THE OPPOSITE is **legitimate**.

illicit */say* i-**lis**-uht/ *adjective* forbidden or not legal: *illicit alcohol.*

☑ SPELLING TIP Remember that *i* is the only vowel in this word. It turns up three times. Also remember that there is a *c* in **illicit** (for the 's' sound). This word is made up of the prefix *il-*, meaning 'not', and *licit*, an unusual word meaning 'allowed'.

illiterate *adjective* unable to read and write: *an illiterate peasant.*
☐ **illiteracy**, *noun*

THE OPPOSITE is **literate**.

illuminate */say* i-**looh**-muh-nayt/ *verb*
1. To **illuminate** something is to light it up: *A flash of lightning illuminated the sky.* **2.** To **illuminate** someone is to give knowledge to or inform them: *Could you illuminate me on the latest changes?*
☐ **illuminating**, *adjective* –**illumination**, *noun*

illusion */say* i-**looh**-zhuhn/ *noun* a false idea or hope: *illusions of becoming a film star.*
☐ **illusory**, *adjective*

illustrate */say* **il**-uhs-trayt/ *verb*
1. If you **illustrate** a story or a book, you provide pictures to go with the writing. **2.** If you **illustrate** something that you are saying, you give examples to make it clear: *She illustrated her theory about leadership with accounts of the lives of some famous explorers.*
☐ **illustration**, *noun* –**illustrative**, *adjective* –**illustrator**, *noun*

☑ SPELLING TIP *Double letter alert*: double *l*. Notice also that the following vowel sound is spelt with a *u*.

illustrious *adjective* famous or distinguished: *an illustrious woman in the nation's history.*

im- *prefix* a form of **in-** meaning **1.** not, as in *impatient* and *impotent*. **2.** into, as in *imprison*.

I'm a short form of *I am*.

image *noun*
1. a picture in the mind: *I have an image of my perfect holiday.* **2.** reflection: *her image in the mirror.* **3.** an exact likeness: *He is the image of his father.*

imagery /*say* **im**-ij-ree/ *noun* the metaphors, similes and other figures of speech we use to get an idea across to others.

imagination *noun* the ability to form pictures in your mind or to make up interesting stories.
☐ **imaginative**, *adjective*

imagine *verb*
1. If you **imagine** something, your mind forms a picture or idea about it: *Try to imagine that you're on a sailing boat.* **2.** If you **imagine** something, you believe that you are experiencing it, but it isn't real: *I must have imagined that conversation.*
☐ **imaginary**, *adjective*

imam /*say* i-**mahm**/ *noun* an Islamic religious leader.

imbecile /*say* **im**-buh-seel, **im**-buh-suyl/ *noun* someone who behaves in a very stupid way.
☐ **imbecile**, *adjective*

☑ SPELLING TIP Remember the *c* spelling for the 's' sound.

imitate *verb*
1. If you **imitate** someone, you copy the way they speak or behave, often as a way of making fun of them. **2.** If you **imitate** someone, you use them as a model because you want to be like them.
☐ **imitation**, *adjective*, *noun* –**imitative**, *adjective*

immaculate *adjective* absolutely clean.
☐ **immaculately**, *adverb*

immediate *adjective* happening straight away: *an immediate reaction.*
☐ **immediacy**, *noun* –**immediately**, *adverb*

☑ SPELLING TIP *Double letter alert*: double *m*. Also remember the *ate* ending.

immense *adjective* extremely large: *an immense appetite*; *an immense amount of time.*
☐ **immensely**, *adverb* –**immensity**, *noun*

immerse *verb* If you **immerse** something, you put it below the surface of a liquid: *She immersed her feet in the cool pond.*
☐ **immersion**, *noun*

WORD HISTORY from a Latin word meaning 'dipped'

immigrate *verb* To **immigrate** is to come to live in a new country.
☐ **immigrant**, *noun* –**immigration**, *noun*

☑ DO NOT CONFUSE this with **emigrate** which is to leave your country to go to a new country.

imminent *adjective* likely to happen at any moment.
☐ **imminence**, *noun* –**imminently**, *adverb*

☑ DO NOT CONFUSE **imminent** with **eminent** which describes a very important person. Remember that **imminent** starts with an *i* and has a double *m*.

immoral *adjective* wrong or morally bad: *an immoral war*; *immoral behaviour.*
☐ **immorality**, *noun* –**immorally**, *adverb*

immortal *adjective* living or lasting forever: *the immortal works of Shakespeare.*
☐ **immortalise**, *verb* –**immortality**, *noun*

ANOTHER SPELLING for **immortalise** is **immortalize.**
THE OPPOSITE of **immortal** is **mortal.**

immune *adjective*
1. protected from a disease: *He's immune to chickenpox now.* **2.** unaffected by: *She seemed immune to the criticism.*
☐ **immunise**, *verb* –**immunity**, *noun*

ANOTHER SPELLING for **immunise** is **immunize.**

imp *noun*
1. a little devil. **2.** a child who is a little naughty.
☐ **impish**, *adjective*

impact *noun* the hitting of one thing against another: *I heard the impact of the hail on the roof.*

impair *verb* To **impair** something is to damage or weaken it: *Rain impaired our enjoyment of the harbour cruise.*
☐ **impairment**, *noun*

A SIMILAR WORD is **spoil** which is less formal.

impartial /*say* im-**pah**-shuhl/ *adjective* not taking one side or the other: *an impartial judge.*
☐ **impartiality**, *noun* –**impartially**, *adverb*

SIMILAR WORDS are **objective**, **neutral**, **unbiased**, **even-handed** and **disinterested.**

☑ SPELLING TIP Remember the *tial* ending (giving a 'shuhl' sound).

impasse /*say* **im**-pahs/ *noun* a situation from which there is no way out.

☑ SPELLING TIP Remember the *e* at the end. This word is from French.

impassive *adjective* not showing any emotion: *The judge remained impassive as she listened to the evidence.*
☐ **impassively**, *adverb* –**impassivity**, *noun*

impatient *adjective*
1. unwilling to wait: *impatient for dinner.* 2. short-tempered: *She's often impatient with noisy children.*
☐ **impatience**, *noun* –**impatiently**, *adverb*

impeccable /*say* im-**pek**-uh-buhl/ *adjective* without any faults: *His behaviour was impeccable.*
☐ **impeccably**, *adverb*

☑ SPELLING TIP *Double letter alert*: double *c* (making a single 'k' sound). This word comes from the Latin *peccare* meaning 'to sin'. When the prefix *im-* (meaning 'not') is added, we get **impeccable** with the meaning 'not being able to sin or do wrong' or 'without fault'.

impede *verb* If you **impede** someone or something, you slow them down or block their way: *The work being done on the road impeded the traffic.*
☐ **impediment**, *noun*

imperial /*say* im-**pear**-ree-uhl/ *adjective*
1. Something that is **imperial** is connected with an empire: *the imperial throne.* 2. The **imperial system** is a system of weights and measures set up in Britain and used in Australia before the metric system was introduced.

imperious /*say* im-**pear**-ree-uhs/ *adjective* arrogant or bossy: *an imperious manner.*

impersonal *adjective* formal and official, not showing any personal emotion: *His printed reply was cool and impersonal.*

impersonate *verb* To **impersonate** someone is to pretend to be that person: *to impersonate a police officer.*
☐ **impersonation**, *noun* –**impersonator**, *noun*

impertinent *adjective* cheeky or rude.
☐ **impertinence**, *noun*

impetuous /*say* im-**pech**-ooh-uhs/ *adjective* acting quickly but thoughtlessly: *an impetuous shopper.*
☐ **impetuosity**, *noun* –**impetuously**, *adverb*

A SIMILAR WORD is **impulsive**.

☑ SPELLING TIP Remember the *tu* spelling in this word (which gives a 'chooh' sound). Also notice that **impetuous** ends with the common adjective suffix *-ous* (meaning 'full of'). The word literally means 'full of impetus (or force)'.

impetus /*say* **im**-puh-tuhs/ *noun*
1. a moving force, stimulus, or impulse: *Getting my own computer was the impetus to save money.* 2. the force or energy of a moving object.

implement *noun* /*say* **im**-pluh-muhnt/
1. a tool: *a gardening implement.*
–*verb* /*say* **im**-pluh-ment/ 2. To **implement** a plan is to put it into effect: *The revised timetable will be implemented from the beginning of next month.*
☐ **implementation**, *noun*

implicate /*say* **im**-pluh-kayt/ *verb* If someone is **implicated** in something, usually something bad, there is some indirect evidence or suggestion that they are involved in it: *All the footballers were implicated in the scandal, some by just being present at the time.*

implication *noun*
1. a possible result or effect: *The government decision will have implications for the farming industry.* 2. something that someone suggests is true, although in an indirect way: *I object to your implication that I haven't been doing my share of the work.*

implicit /*say* im-**plis**-uht/ *adjective*
1. absolute and without doubts: *implicit trust.* 2. suggested or implied but not actually stated: *an implicit agreement.*
☐ **implicitly**, *adverb*

☑ SPELLING TIP Remember the *c* spelling for the 's' sound. This word comes from the Latin *implicitus* meaning 'entangled' or 'involved'.

implore *verb* To **implore** is to ask with great feeling.
☐ **imploringly**, *adverb*

imply /*say* im-**pluy**/ *verb*
1. If you **imply** something, you suggest it without actually stating it clearly: *He didn't actually say it was my fault – but he implied it.* 2. If something **implies** something else, it means that because the first thing exists, the second thing probably also exists or will exist: *His refusal to answer any questions implied that he was guilty.*
☐ **implication**, *noun*

☑ DO NOT CONFUSE this word with **infer** which is to work something out by reasoning.

import *verb* /*say* im-**pawt**, **im**-pawt/
1. To **import** goods is to bring them in from another country.
–*noun* /*say* **im**-pawt/ 2. something that is brought in from another country. 3. meaning: *to get the full import of a statement.*
☐ **importation**, *noun*

COMPARE definitions 1 and 2 with **export**.

important *adjective*
1. having a great meaning or effect: *an important announcement*; *an important event.* 2. leading or powerful: *an important politician.*
☐ **importance**, *noun* –**importantly**, *adverb*

SIMILAR WORDS (for definition 1) are **significant**, **major** and **momentous**. Note that something that is **momentous** is very important; (for definition 1) **eminent**, **pre-eminent** and **prestigious**.

impose *verb*
1. If you **impose** something on someone, you force them to accept it, often by passing a law: *The government is planning to impose a new tax on businesses.* **2.** If someone **imposes** on you, they expect too much of you when they ask for favours.
☐ **imposition**, *noun*

imposing *adjective* making an impression on your mind: *an imposing waterfall*; *an imposing personality.*

impossible *adjective*
1. not able to be done: *It is impossible for anyone to jump that far.* **2.** not able to be, exist, or happen: *It's impossible for him to have done it – he was with me the whole day.* **3.** not able to be true: *an impossible story.* **4.** very difficult to handle, put up with, etc.: *They have been left in an impossible situation.*

THE OPPOSITE (of definitions 1 and 2) is **possible**.

impostor *noun* someone who deceives other people by pretending to be someone else.

impotent /*say* **im**-puh-tuhnt/ *adjective* lacking the power to do things: *an impotent law.*
☐ **impotence**, *noun*

☑ SPELLING TIP *Tricky 'uh' sound*: the middle vowel sound is spelt *o*. This will be easier to remember if you see that **impotent** is made up of the prefix *im-* (a form of *in-*, meaning 'not') and *potent* (meaning 'powerful' or 'strong').

impress *verb*
1. If someone or something **impresses** you, they attract your attention and make you think highly of them. **2.** If you **impress** something on someone, you emphasise it clearly to them: *She impressed on us the risks involved in climbing higher.*
☐ **impressive**, *adjective*

impression *noun*
1. a mark made by pressure: *the impression of a foot in the sand.* **2.** a strong effect made on the mind or feelings: *Her story made an impression on all who heard it.* **3.** a slight feeling or indication: *I had the impression she was lonely.*
☐ **impressionable**, *adjective*: *an impressionable child.* –**impressionistic**, *adjective*: *an impressionistic picture.*

imprint *verb* When something is **imprinted** in your memory or on your mind, it is fixed firmly there: *Her last words are imprinted on my mind.*

impromptu *adjective* made up or done on the spur of the moment: *an impromptu party.*

☑ SPELLING TIP Remember that the ending of **impromptu** is spelt with a *u* which is quite unusual in English. This is because it comes from the Latin phrase *in promptu*, meaning 'in readiness'. Another word ending in *u* is *menu*.

improve *verb*
1. To **improve** something is to make it better. **2.** To **improve** is to get better at doing something.
☐ **improvement**, *noun*

improvise /*say* **im**-pruh-vuyz/ *verb*
1. If you **improvise** something, you make it from whatever is available: *We improvised a picnic table by turning the boxes upside down.* **2.** If you **improvise** while speaking or performing music, you invent or make it up on the spot: *I hadn't prepared my speech so I had to improvise*; *to improvise a little tune.*
☐ **improvisation**, *noun*

impudent /*say* **im**-pyooh-duhnt/ *adjective* cheeky or rude.
☐ **impudence**, *noun* –**impudently**, *adverb*

impulse *noun* a sudden desire: *an impulse to yawn.*
☐ **impulsive**, *adjective*: *an impulsive act of generosity.* –**impulsiveness**, *noun*

in *preposition*
1. inside or within: *in the city*; *in politics.* **2.** within a certain period of time: *in ancient days*; *in ten minutes.* **3.** in a particular condition or situation: *in darkness*; *in love.*
–*adjective* **4.** fashionable: *That restaurant is in at the moment.*
–*phrase* **5. in for**, about to experience: *We are in for another hot day.* **6. in on**, having a share or a part of, especially something secret: *She's in on the plot*; *in on the secret.*

in- *prefix* a word part meaning **1.** not, as in *indecent*, *indispensable*, *independent*. **2.** in or into, as in *inhale*, *inland*.

WORD HISTORY this prefix comes from Old English and Middle English

inane *adjective* silly or senseless: *an inane comment.*
☐ **inanity**, *noun* (*plural* **inanities**) –**inanely**, *adverb*

inanimate *adjective* not living: *inanimate objects.*

THE OPPOSITE is **animate**.

inaugurate *verb* When you **inaugurate** an event or organisation, you have an opening ceremony for it.
☐ **inaugural**, *adjective*: *the inaugural broadcast of the new radio station.* –**inauguration**, *noun*

incandescent /*say* in-kan-**des**-uhnt/ *adjective* glowing with white heat.
☐ **incandescence**, *noun*

☑ SPELLING TIP *Silent letter alert*: don't forget the silent *c* following the *s*, just like in the word *scent*.

incapacitate /*say* in-kuh-**pas**-uh-tayt/ *verb* To **incapacitate** someone is to make them unable or unfit: *The fall incapacitated her.*
☐ **incapacitation**, *noun*

incarnate /*say* in-**kah**-nuht, in-**kah**-nayt/ *adjective* with a human body: *the devil incarnate.*
☐ **incarnation**, *noun*

incense[1] /*say* **in**-sens/ *noun* a substance which gives off a sweet smell when burnt.

☑ SPELLING TIP Remember the *c* spelling for the first 's' sound. You could think of a ceremony with smoke to remind you. **Incense** comes from the Latin word *incendere* meaning 'to set on fire'.

incense[2] /*say* in-**sens**/ *verb* If something **incenses** you, it makes you very angry.
☐ **incensed**, *adjective*

☑ SPELLING TIP See **incense**[1].

incentive *noun* something that encourages you and gives you a reason for doing something: *The thought of a cool swim at the end of the walk was an incentive for us to keep going.*

incessant /*say* in-**ses**-uhnt/ *adjective* continuing without stopping: *incessant chatter.*
☐ **incessantly**, *adverb*

☑ SPELLING TIP The word **incessant** is related to *cease*, meaning 'to stop'. (Something that is **incessant** never stops.) This will help you to remember the *c* which spells the first 's' sound in the word. You will also need to remember that the second 's' sound is spelt with a double *s*. Think of 'seagulls screeching incessantly' to remind yourself of the double *s*.

incest /*say* **in**-sest/ *noun* sexual intercourse between closely related people.
☐ **incestuous**, *adjective*

inch *noun* (*plural* **inches**)
1. a unit of length in the imperial system equal to 25.4 millimetres.
–*phrase* **2. within an inch of**, almost or very near to: *She came within an inch of being killed.*

WORD HISTORY from a Latin word meaning 'twelfth part'

incident *noun* an event or happening.
☐ **incidence**, *noun*: *The incidence of measles in the school was very low.* –**incidental**, *adjective* happening at the same time as something more important. –**incidentally**, *adverb*

incinerate /*say* in-**sin**-uh-rayt/ *verb* If you **incinerate** something, you burn it to ashes: *The truck was incinerated in the fire.*
☐ **incinerator**, *noun* a container for burning things in. –**incineration**, *noun*

incision *noun* a cut with a knife: *Make the first incision here.*

incisor /*say* in-**suy**-zuh/ *noun* a tooth in the front part of the jaw, used for cutting or biting.

incite *verb* If you **incite** someone to do something, you urge them on or stir them up to do it: *The speaker incited the crowd to riot.*
☐ **incitement**, *noun*

incline *noun* /*say* **in**-kluyn/
1. a fairly gentle slope in a surface.
–*verb* /*say* in-**kluyn**/ **2.** If something **inclines**, it slants or leans: *The old fence inclines inwards.* **3.** If you **incline** something, you make it slant or lean: *He inclined his head.*

inclined *adjective*
1. feeling in agreement: *Go if you feel inclined.*
–*phrase* **2. inclined to**, tending towards, often because of your character: *He is inclined to forget.*
☐ **inclination**, *noun*: *the inclination to read.*

include *verb* To **include** something is to contain it as a part: *The role includes both singing and dancing.*
☐ **inclusion**, *noun* –**inclusive**, *adjective*

incognito /*say* in-kog-**nee**-toh/ *adverb* with your name or appearance changed so you won't be recognised: *The spy travelled incognito.*

☑ SPELLING TIP This word looks unusual but you can spell it by sounding each of its parts. The most difficult part is the *ito* ending. This is a common ending in Italian words and **incognito** has come directly from Italian (from an original Latin word meaning 'unknown').

income *noun* the money someone earns from their work or investments.

income tax *noun* a tax which the government sets each year, based on how much money you earn.

incongruous /*say* in-**kong**-grooh-uhs/ *adjective* out of place or unsuitable: *His old T-shirt looked incongruous with his business suit.*
☐ **incongruity**, *noun* –**incongruously**, *adverb* –**incongruousness**, *noun*

☑ SPELLING TIP **Incongruous** is made up of the prefix *in-* meaning 'not' and *congruous* meaning 'in harmony' or 'compatible'. The ending is a bit tricky – after the *u* of *congru* there is the common adjective suffix *-ous*.

incorporate *verb* When you **incorporate** something, you include it and make it part of something else: *They incorporated some of our ideas into the design of the park.*
☐ **incorporation**, *noun*

incorrigible /*say* in-**ko**-ruh-juh-buhl/ *adjective* too bad to ever improve: *an incorrigible thief.*
□ **incorrigibly**, *adverb*

☑ SPELLING TIP This word is formed from the prefix *-in* (meaning 'not') and *corrigible*, an uncommon word meaning 'able to be corrected' which comes from the Latin word *corrigere* (meaning 'to correct'). You need to remember the double *r*, the soft *g* and the *-ible* ending.

increase *verb* /*say* in-**krees**/
1. If something **increases**, it becomes greater: *The population increases each year.* **2.** If you **increase** something, you make it greater: *He suddenly increased his speed and disappeared around the corner.*
–*noun* /*say* **in**-krees/ **3.** growth in amount or size: *an increase in wages.*
□ **increasing**, *adjective* –**increasingly**, *adverb*

THE OPPOSITE is **decrease**.

incredible *adjective* amazing, hard to believe: *incredible bravery*; *an incredible life.*
□ **incredibility**, *noun* –**incredibly**, *adverb*

incredulous /*say* in-**krej**-uh-luhs/ *adjective* not willing to believe something, usually because it is too surprising or shocking: *She explained her theory to an incredulous audience.*
□ **incredulity** /*say* in-kruh-**dyooh**-luh-tee/, *noun*

A SIMILAR WORD is **sceptical**.

☑ DO NOT CONFUSE the meaning of this word with **incredible**. These are related words but you use **incredulous** to describe the way a person feels about something, but you use **incredible** to describe something that is unbelievable or very good.

incriminate *verb* If something **incriminates** someone, it proves that they did something wrong.
□ **incriminatory**, *adjective* –**incriminating**, *adjective*: *incriminating evidence.*

WORD HISTORY from a Latin word meaning 'accused of a crime'

incubate /*say* **in**-kyooh-bayt/ *verb* To **incubate** eggs is to hatch them by keeping them warm: *The sparrow incubated her eggs by sitting on them*; *The pigeon breeder is incubating these eggs under a warm lamp.*
□ **incubator**, *noun* a machine that looks like a plastic box, for keeping premature babies at a constant temperature. –**incubation**, *noun*

WORD HISTORY from a Latin word meaning 'hatched' or 'sat on'

incur *verb* (**incurs**, **incurring**, **incurred**, **has incurred**) If you **incur** something unpleasant, you bring it upon yourself: *to incur a loss*; *to incur someone's anger.*

WORD HISTORY from a Latin word meaning 'run into'

indebted /*say* in-**det**-uhd/ *adjective*
1. owing money. **2.** feeling that you owe a debt of gratitude for help, a favour, or the like: *I'm indebted to you for taking care of my dog while I was on holiday.*
□ **indebtedness**, *noun*

☑ SPELLING TIP Remember that **indebted** contains the word *debt* with its silent *b*. It has the prefix *-in* before it and the suffix *-ed* at the end.

indecent *adjective* not proper or in good taste: *indecent language.*
□ **indecency**, *noun*

indeed *adverb* truly or in fact: *Indeed he did it.*

indelible *adjective* not able to be removed: *indelible ink*; *an indelible impression.*

indent *verb* To **indent** a line of writing is to set it in or back from the main part of the writing: *to indent the first line of a paragraph.*
□ **indentation**, *noun*

independent *adjective*
1. able to make up your own mind: *an independent thinker.* **2.** not needing or depending on the help of others: *When you grow up, you become independent of your parents*; *an independent country.*
□ **independence**, *noun*

A SIMILAR WORD (for definition 2) is **autonomous**. This is used in particular in relation to a country that is self-governing.

☑ SPELLING TIP See the note at **dependent** which will remind you of the *-ent* ending.

index /*say* **in**-deks/ *noun* (*plural* **indexes** *or* **indices** /*say* **in**-duh-seez/)
1. an alphabetical list of names, places or subjects in a book, showing their page numbers.
–*verb* **2.** If you **index** a book, you make an index for it.

index finger *noun* See **forefinger**.

indicate /*say* **in**-duh-kayt, **in**-di-kayt/ *verb*
1. If you **indicate** something to someone, you draw their attention to it, usually by pointing at it: *He indicated the places of interest on the map.* **2.** If something **indicates** that something is the case, it shows or suggests it to be true: *These good marks indicate that everyone has been working hard.*
□ **indication**, *noun* –**indicative** /*say* in-**dik**-uh-tiv/, *adjective*

indicator *noun* something that points to or shows something: *The fuel indicator showed we were nearly out of petrol.*

☑ SPELLING TIP Although this word comes from *indicate*, it has an *-or* ending. Remember that the *e* has been dropped and this ending added.

indifferent *adjective*
1. showing no interest or concern: *She was indifferent to my distress.* **2.** not very good: *He is an indifferent dancer*; *She is in indifferent health.*
☐ **indifference**, *noun*

indigenous /*say* in-**dij**-uh-nuhs/ *adjective*
1. relating to someone who belongs to a people who were the first people to live in a particular country: *Aboriginal and Torres Strait Islander people are the Indigenous people of Australia.* **2.** relating to plants or animals that live or grow naturally in a particular area or country, rather than being introduced from somewhere else: *Emus are indigenous to Australia but sparrows are not.*

ANOTHER FORM This word is usually spelt with a capital letter when it refers the original people of Australia, the Aboriginal and Torres Strait Islander people.

☑ SPELLING TIP Remember that **indigenous** has a soft *g* (to spell the 'j' sound) and that the following vowel sound is spelt *e* (not *i*). Finally there is the common adjective suffix *-ous*. It might help to rap it out as *in+dig+e+nous*.

indigestion /*say* in-duh-**jes**-chuhn/ *noun* pain in the stomach caused by difficulty in digesting food.

indignation /*say* in-dig-**nay**-shuhn/ *noun* anger at something you think is unjust or morally bad.
☐ **indignant**, *adjective*

indignity /*say* in-**dig**-nuh-tee/ *noun* (*plural* **indignities**) treatment which makes you feel embarrassed and foolish: *the indignity of being spoken to so rudely.*

indigo /*say* **in**-dig-oh/ *noun*
1. a blue dye. **2.** a deep blue colour.
–*adjective* **3.** of an indigo colour.

indirect *adjective*
1. not going in a straight line, or not taking the most direct course: *They took an indirect way home.* **2.** not directly caused by something: *She lost weight as an indirect result of worrying so much.* **3.** not saying something in a clear, straightforward way: *His comments were an indirect insult to me.*

indispensable *adjective* absolutely necessary.
☐ **indispensability**, *noun*

indisposed *adjective* slightly sick or unwell: *indisposed with an upset stomach.*
☐ **indisposition**, *noun*

individual *noun*
1. a single person or thing. **2.** a person: *a strange individual.*
☐ **individual**, *adjective*: *individual servings.* –**individuality**, *noun* –**individually**, *adverb*

indoctrinate *verb* If you **indoctrinate** someone, you instruct them so thoroughly that your ideas and beliefs are accepted without question.
☐ **indoctrination**, *noun*

indoors *adverb* inside a building: *You can move indoors if it starts to rain.*
☐ **indoor**, *adjective*: *indoor activities.*

THE OPPOSITE is **outdoors**.

induce *verb*
1. If you **induce** something, you cause it to happen: *This drink should induce sleep.* **2.** If you **induce** someone to do something, you persuade them to do it: *Can't I induce you to come to the party?*; *Nothing will induce me to change my mind.*
☐ **inducement**, *noun*

indulge *verb*
1. If you **indulge** someone, you allow them to do or have what they want: *His mother indulges him with too much pocket money.*
–*phrase* **2. indulge in**, to satisfy your own desire for: *to indulge in chocolates.*
☐ **indulgence**, *noun* –**indulgent**, *adjective*

industrious *adjective* hardworking: *an industrious student.*

A SIMILAR WORD is **diligent**.

industry *noun* (*plural* **industries**)
1. all businesses that produce things with machinery: *the growth of industry in Victoria.* **2.** a particular type of business that uses machinery: *the steel industry.* **3.** any large business activity: *the film industry.* **4.** hard and careful work.
☐ **industrial**, *adjective* –**industrialise**, *verb*: *to industrialise the economy.*

ANOTHER SPELLING for **industrialise** is **industrialize**.

inept *adjective* awkward or unskilful: *an inept apology*; *an inept attempt to make a cake.*
☐ **ineptitude**, *noun* –**ineptly**, *adverb* –**ineptness**, *noun*

inertia /*say* in-**er**-shuh/ *noun* sluggishness or lack of energy: *It was just inertia that stopped me from going to the beach with you.*

☑ SPELLING TIP The trick to overcoming the spelling of **inertia** is remembering the *tia* ending, for the 'shuh' sound. It has this ending because it comes from Latin (meaning 'lack of skill' or 'inactivity')

inevitable *adjective* not able to be avoided: *an inevitable result.*
☐ **inevitability**, *noun* –**inevitably**, *adverb*

infallible /*say* in-**fal**-uh-buhl/ *adjective*
1. never wrong: *an infallible judge of character.* 2. able to be depended on completely: *an infallible recipe*; *an infallible cure for hiccups.*
☐ **infallibility**, *noun* –**infallibly**, *adverb*

infamous /*say* **in**-fuh-muhs/ *adjective* having a very bad name or reputation: *an infamous murderer*; *Now you'll have a chance to try the infamous canteen food.*
☐ **infamy** /*say* **in**-fuh-mee/, *noun*

infant *noun* a baby or very young child.
☐ **infancy**, *noun* –**infantile**, *adjective* childish: *infantile behaviour.*

infantry *noun* soldiers who fight on foot with hand weapons.

infatuated *adjective* blindly or foolishly in love, usually temporarily.
☐ **infatuation**, *noun*

infect *verb*
1. To **infect** someone or something is to give germs or a disease to them: *He got chickenpox and infected the whole family*; *The wound was not cleaned and it became infected.* 2. To **infect** a group is to affect them in a certain way one by one: *Her happy mood infected the whole class.*
☐ **infected**, *adjective* –**infection**, *noun* –**infectious**, *adjective*

infer /*say* in-**fer**/ *verb* (**infers**, **inferring**, **inferred**, **has inferred**) If you **infer** that something is the case, you form an opinion after thinking about all the facts and information: *I inferred from his good mood that the exam had gone well.*
☐ **inference**, *noun*: *to draw an inference.*

☑ DO NOT CONFUSE this with **imply** which is to suggest something without actually stating it.

inferior *adjective*
1. of poor quality: *The clothes on sale at the market are very inferior.* 2. not as good or as valuable as someone or something else: *She is so good at everything that she makes me feel inferior.* 3. of a lower rank or position: *A captain is inferior to a major in the army.*
☐ **inferior**, *noun* –**inferiority**, *noun*

THE OPPOSITE is **superior**.

inferno *noun* (*plural* **infernos**) a place that seems like hell because of extreme heat or fire.

WORD HISTORY from an Italian word meaning 'hell' and before this from a Latin word meaning 'underground'

infest *verb* To **infest** a place or an area is to spread over it in great numbers: *Rats infest this part of the building.*
☐ **infestation**, *noun*

infidel /*say* **in**-fuh-del/ *noun* someone who doesn't accept a particular religious faith.
☐ **infidel**, *adjective*

NOTE This is an old-fashioned word that Christians and Muslims used of each other.

infiltrate *verb* If someone **infiltrates** a group or organisation, they join it and become involved in its activities in order to harm or destroy it.
☐ **infiltration**, *noun* –**infiltrator**, *noun*

infinite /*say* **in**-fuh-nuht/ *adjective* endless or without limits: *The ocean seemed infinite.*
☐ **infinitely**, *adverb* –**infinity**, *noun*

infinitive /*say* in-**fin**-uh-tiv/ *noun* the grammatical form of a verb usually indicated by 'to' in front of it, as in *I wanted to swim*.

SEE the Grammar and Punctuation Guide appendix.

infirm *adjective* weak in body or health.
☐ **infirmity**, *noun*

infirmary *noun* (*plural* **infirmaries**) a kind of hospital: *the school's infirmary.*

inflame *verb* To **inflame** someone is to make them angry or emotional: *The rebel leader inflamed the crowd with his fiery speech.*
☐ **inflammatory**, *adjective*

inflammable *adjective* If something is **inflammable**, it burns easily: *inflammable clothing.*
☐ **inflammability**, *noun*

NOTE Nowadays, the more usual word is **flammable**. This is because many people thought **inflammable** meant '*not* easily set on fire' because *in-* at the beginning of a word often does mean 'not', as in *inactive* and *insensitive*. This misunderstanding could have placed people in danger, so it was decided to use **flammable** to mean 'easily set on fire' and **nonflammable** as its opposite, meaning 'not likely to burn easily'.

☑ SPELLING TIP *Double letter alert*: double *m*, although it comes from the word *inflame*.

inflammation *noun* a red, painful, and often swollen area on the body, caused by an infection.
☐ **inflamed**, *adjective*

☑ SPELLING TIP *Double letter alert*: double *m*, although it comes from the word *inflame*.

inflate *verb*
1. If you **inflate** something such as a balloon or a tyre, you fill it with air or gas so that it becomes larger or firmer. 2. If prices **inflate**, they increase.
☐ **inflatable**, *adjective* –**inflated**, *adjective*: *an inflated tyre*; *an inflated ego.* –**inflation**, *noun* –**inflationary**, *adjective*

inflict *verb* To **inflict** something on someone is to cause them to suffer it: *The enemy inflicted heavy casualties on our troops.*
☐ **infliction**, *noun*

influence *noun* some force or power that affects or produces a change in someone or something else: *He is a good influence on his brother.*
☐ **influence**, *verb* –**influential**, *adjective*

☑ SPELLING TIP Remember that **influence** contains the word *flu* (an illness like a cold). This is not just a coincidence. Both *influenza* (the full name of *flu*) and **influence** come from the Latin word *influens* meaning 'flowing through'.

influenza *noun* a sickness caused by a virus which affects the nose and throat and causes high temperatures and tiredness.

THE SHORT FORM of this is **flu**.

☑ SPELLING TIP **Influenza** is the full name of *flu*, and so it contains that spelling inside it. It comes from the Latin word *influens* meaning 'flowing through', in the sense that **influenza** is a disease that is easy to catch. It has the *enza* ending because it has come into English through Italian.

influx *noun* a flowing in: *influx of new ideas*; *Every year there is an influx of campers at the start of the summer holidays.*

inform *verb* To **inform** someone is to give news or knowledge to them: *She informed us of the results.*
☐ **informant**, *noun* –**informative**, *adjective*

informal *adjective* relaxed or without ceremony or formality, as in a situation where you behave as you do with family and friends: *an informal visit*; *informal language.*
☐ **informality**, *noun* –**informally**, *adverb*

information *noun* knowledge or news: *tourist information.*

information report *noun* writing or speaking which gives facts on something.

information technology *noun* the use of computers to produce, store and obtain information.

THE ABBREVIATION is **IT**.

infra- *prefix* a word part meaning 'below' or 'beneath', as in *infra-red*.

WORD HISTORY this prefix comes from Latin

infra-red *noun* /*say* in-fruh-**red**/
1. the invisible part of the spectrum of light which has a wavelength longer than that of visible red light.
–*adjective* /*say* **in**-fruh-red/ **2.** having to do with the infra-red: *infra-red radiation.*

infringe *verb* If you **infringe** a law or rule, you disobey it.
☐ **infringement**, *noun*

WORD HISTORY from a Latin word meaning 'break off'

infuriate *verb* If someone or something **infuriates** you, they make you very cross.
☐ **infuriating**, *adjective* –**infuriation**, *noun*

infuse *verb* When you **infuse** something, such as tea leaves or dried herbs, you soak them in hot water to draw out the flavour.
☐ **infuser**, *noun* –**infusion**, *noun*

ingenious /*say* in-**jee**-nee-uhs/ *adjective*
1. cleverly made or invented: *an ingenious machine.* **2.** clever at working out ways of doing and making things: *an ingenious inventor.*
☐ **ingenuity**, *noun*

☑ SPELLING TIP Don't confuse the spelling of **ingenious** with **genius** which has a related meaning ('a very clever person'). Remember the **ingenious** ends with the adjective suffix *-ous*, while **genius** ends with *-us*, a noun suffix appearing in some words which have come from Latin.

ingot /*say* **ing**-guht/ *noun* a block of metal which has been melted and poured into a container that gives it shape when it goes cold.

WORD HISTORY from a Middle English word for a 'mould for metal'

ingrained *adjective* fixed firmly and deeply: *ingrained beliefs*; *ingrained dirt.*

ingratitude *noun* failure to be grateful.

ingredient *noun* one of the parts of a mixture or a whole: *an ingredient in a cake.*

☑ SPELLING TIP Remember that there is only one *e* before the *d* in **ingredient** (although it sounds like 'ee'). If you notice the word *red* is hidden inside **ingredient** that will remind you. Also remember that the ending is spelt *ient* (not *iant*).

inhabit *verb* (**inhabits**, **inhabiting**, **inhabited**, **has inhabited**) If people **inhabit** a place, they live there: *Aboriginal people inhabited Australia long before Europeans came.*
☐ **inhabitable**, *adjective* –**inhabitant**, *noun*

A SIMILAR WORD is **populate**.

inhale *verb* To **inhale** is to breathe in: *to inhale the cool mountain air*; *Inhale deeply to fill your lungs.*
☐ **inhalant**, *noun* –**inhalation**, *noun*

THE OPPOSITE is **exhale**.

inherit *verb* (**inherits**, **inheriting**, **inherited**, **has inherited**)
1. To **inherit** something is to receive it as a gift from someone who has died: *She inherited some money and a diamond ring from her aunt.* **2.** If you **inherit** a characteristic, you get it through

your parents: *He's inherited his mother's beautiful voice.*
☐ **inheritance**, *noun*

inhibit /*say* in-**hib**-uht/ *verb* (**inhibits**, **inhibiting**, **inhibited**, **has inhibited**) To **inhibit** someone or something is to hold them back: *Many people wore masks to inhibit the spread of the disease.*
☐ **inhibition** /*say* in-uh-**bish**-uhn/, *noun*

iniquity /*say* in-**ik**-wuh-tee/ *noun* (*plural* **iniquities**) wickedness: *We must never let such iniquity happen again.*
☐ **iniquitous**, *adjective*

initial /*say* in-**ish**-uhl/ *noun*
1. the first letter of a word or name: *His initials are J.B.*
–*adjective* **2.** having to do with the beginning or the first: *My initial reaction was one of shock, but then I got used to the idea.*
–*verb* (**initials**, **initialling**, **initialled**, **has initialled**) **3.** When you **initial** something, you write your initials on it: *to initial each correction.*
☐ **initially**, *adverb*: *I was initially surprised but then pleased.*

> ☑ SPELLING TIP Remember that **initial** ends in *tial*, making a 'shuhl' sound.

initiate /*say* in-**ish**-ee-ayt/ *verb*
1. To **initiate** something is to begin it or set it going: *We want to initiate an annual street party*; *Who initiated the fight?* **2.** To **initiate** someone is to admit them into a society or club with a formal ceremony.
☐ **initiation**, *noun* –**initiator**, *noun*

> ☑ SPELLING TIP Remember that **initiate** has a *ti* in the middle, making a 'shuh' sound, the same as in *initial*.

initiative /*say* in-**ish**-ee-uh-tiv/ *noun*
1. a first act or step: *to take the initiative.* **2.** readiness or ability to set something going.

> A SIMILAR WORD (for definition 2) is **enterprise**.

> ☑ SPELLING TIP Remember that **initiative** has a *ti* in the middle making a 'shuh' sound, the same as in *initial*.

inject *verb* If you **inject** something into someone or **inject** someone with something, you put it into their body using a needle and syringe: *The doctor injected the patient with the flu vaccine*; *The doctor injected the antibiotic into her arm.*
☐ **injection**, *noun*

injure *verb* If something **injures** you, it causes you some harm: *The rock injured my knee when I tripped*; *Lies can injure people.*
☐ **injury**, *noun* (*plural* **injuries**) –**injured**, *adjective* –**injurious**, *adjective*

injustice *noun*
1. something that is not fair or just: *He suffered many injustices growing up in such poverty.* **2.** lack of justice or fairness: *She is always angered by injustice.*

ink *noun* a dark, watery substance used for writing or printing.
☐ **inky**, *adjective*: *inky black*; *inky fingers.*

inkling *noun* a vague or uncertain idea: *I had an inkling that you might be planning a surprise party.*

inland *noun*
1. the inner part of a country, away from the coast or border: *a warm wind blowing from the inland.*
–*adverb* **2.** in or towards the inner part of a country: *We went inland.*
☐ **inland**, *adjective*

inlet *noun* a small, narrow bay.

inn *noun* a small hotel, especially one used by travellers in the past.
☐ **innkeeper**, *noun*

> WORD HISTORY from an Old English word meaning 'house'

innate *adjective* existing in a person from their birth: *innate goodness.*
☐ **innately**, *adverb* –**innateness**, *noun*

inner *adjective*
1. located inside something else: *the inner office*; *the inner ear.* **2.** personal: *I attempted to hide my inner feelings.*
☐ **innermost**, *adjective*

innings *plural noun* **1.** the turn of a member of a cricket team to bat. **2.** the whole team's turn at batting: *We made 136 in the first innings.*

innocent *adjective*
1. free from guilt or from having done anything wrong. **2.** not knowing a lot about life, especially about the bad side of life: *She was so innocent that he was able to trick her out of a fortune.* **3.** not intended to cause harm: *My question was perfectly innocent*; *innocent fun.*
☐ **innocence**, *noun* –**innocently**, *adverb*

innocuous /*say* in-**ok**-yooh-uhs/ *adjective* not harmful: *an innocuous comment.*
☐ **innocuously**, *adverb* –**innocuousness**, *noun*

> ☑ SPELLING TIP *Double/single letter alert*: a double *n* and a single *c* (similar to the word *innocent*). Think how something that is **innocuous** is 'not nasty' to help you remember the double *n*. Also don't forget that it ends with the common adjective suffix *-ous*.

innovation *noun* a new method, practice or custom.
☐ **innovate**, *verb* –**innovative**, *adjective* –**innovator**, *noun*

innuendo /*say* in-yooh-**en**-doh/ *noun* (*plural* **innuendos** *or* **innuendoes**) a remark that suggests something unpleasant about someone without actually spelling it out.

☑ SPELLING TIP *Double/single letter alert*: double *n*. Also note that it ends with *o*. The *endo* ending occurs in some words that have come from Latin or Italian.

innumerable /*say* in-**yooh**-muh-ruh-buhl/ *adjective* too many of to be counted: *innumerable reasons.*

inoculate /*say* in-**ok**-yuh-layt/ *noun* To **inoculate** a person or animal is to inject them with germs which give them a very mild form of a disease in order to protect them from that same disease later.
☐ **inoculation**, *noun* –**inoculator**, *noun*

A SIMILAR WORD is **vaccinate**.

☑ SPELLING TIP *Single letter alert*: only one *n* and one *c*.

input *noun* anything that is put into something to be used, especially by a machine.

inquest *noun* an official examination of the facts surrounding a death, to try to find out how the death occurred.

inquire *verb*
1. If you **inquire**, you ask for information: *'What should we do next?' I inquired*; *I need to inquire about the bus timetable.*
–*phrase* **2. inquire into**, to search or examine the details of: *to inquire into the cause of the explosion.*
☐ **inquirer**, *noun* –**inquiring**, *adjective* keen to learn new things: *an inquiring mind.* –**inquiringly**, *adverb*

ANOTHER SPELLING is **enquire**.

inquiry *noun* (*plural* **inquiries**) an investigation.

ANOTHER SPELLING is **enquiry**.

inquisitive *adjective* wanting to find out as much as possible about something: *The crashed car was surrounded by inquisitive onlookers.*
☐ **inquisition**, *noun* a thorough investigation and questioning. –**inquisitor**, *noun*

SIMILAR WORDS are **curious**, **inquiring**, **questioning**, **prying** and **nosy** (*Informal*). Note that **inquiring** and **questioning** describe someone who is eager to seek out knowledge. **Prying** and **nosy** both describe someone who is too interested in things that have nothing to do with them.

insane *adjective* seriously mentally ill and unable to function normally in society.
☐ **insanity**, *noun*

insatiable /*say* in-**say**-shuh-buhl/ *adjective* never having enough: *an insatiable appetite.*
☐ **insatiably**, *adverb*

☑ SPELLING TIP Remember the *t* in this word. Together with the following *i*, it gives an 'sh' sound. It might help if you see the word *sat* sitting inside **insatiable**, although this is not related to the meaning.

inscribe *verb* When you **inscribe** something, you write on it or cut letters into it: *The ring is inscribed with my grandfather's initials.*
☐ **inscription**, *noun*

inscrutable /*say* in-**skrooh**-tuh-buhl/ *adjective* mysterious or not easily understood: *an inscrutable expression on his face.*
☐ **inscrutability**, *noun*

☑ SPELLING TIP Remember the *u* spelling for the 'ooh' sound in the middle. There is no *screw* in this word which is made up of the prefix *in-* (meaning 'not') and a short form of *scrutari* (Latin for 'to search'), as well as the suffix *-able*. Rap it out as *in+scru+ta+ble*.

insect *noun* a small creature with its body clearly divided into three parts with three pairs of legs and usually two pairs of wings.

NOTE Some examples of **insects** are bees, ants and flies. Spiders and ticks are not **insects**.
WORD HISTORY from a Latin word meaning 'cut in or up' (from the way insects' bodies have three segments)

insecticide /*say* in-**sek**-tuh-suyd/ *noun* any chemical substance used to kill insects.
☐ **insecticidal**, *adjective*

☑ SPELLING TIP Remember the *c* spelling for the 's' sound in this word. The suffix *-cide* means 'killer' or 'act of killing' and appears in several other words, such as *suicide*. It comes from the Latin word for 'kill'.

insectivore /*say* in-**sek**-tuh-vaw/ *noun* a bird or animal that eats insects.
☐ **insectivorous** /*say* in-sek-**tiv**-uh-ruhs/, *adjective*

COMPARE this with **carnivore**, **herbivore** and **omnivore**.

insecure *adjective*
1. not firm or safe: *That tent peg looks insecure.*
2. afraid or unsure: *She feels insecure walking home at night by herself.*
☐ **insecurity**, *noun*

insensitive *adjective* lacking in feeling: *an insensitive approach to the problem.*

insert *verb* /*say* in-**sert**/
1. If you **insert** something into something else, you put the first thing inside the second thing: *Insert the plug into the hole.*
–*noun* /*say* **in**-sert/ **2.** something that is inserted: *an advertising insert in a newspaper*; *an insert for a shoe.*
☐ **insertion**, *noun*

inside *preposition /say* in-**suyd**/
1. on the inner side of: *inside the box.*
–*noun /say* **in**-suyd/ **2.** the inner part or side: *She put the label on the inside.* **3. insides**, *Informal* the stomach and intestines and other inner parts of the body.
–*phrase* **4. inside out**, **a.** with the inner side turned to face out. **b.** thoroughly or completely: *She knows her job inside out.*
☐ **inside**, *adjective*: *inside walls.* –**inside**, *adverb*: *to work inside.*

ANOTHER WORD (for definition 4a) is **within**.

insider attack *noun* an attack from a person within your own troops, police force, etc., usually an enemy who has infiltrated.

insight *noun* an understanding of the inner nature of someone or something: *I gained an insight into how the company was organised.*
☐ **insightful**, *adjective*

insignia /*say* in-**sig**-nee-uh/ *plural noun* badges or special marks that are worn by someone who holds a position or rank: *military insignia*; *The mayor wore chains and other insignia of her office.*

insinuate *verb*
1. If you **insinuate** something unpleasant, you suggest it without saying so outright: *I hope you are not insinuating that I cheated, just because I got a better mark than usual.* **2.** When you **insinuate** yourself into a position or organisation, you get into it gradually and slyly: *Almost without us noticing, she insinuated herself as the leader of the group.*
☐ **insinuation**, *noun*

insipid *adjective*
1. not having much taste: *a rather insipid fruit drink.* **2.** boring, or without interesting features: *a coat of an insipid cream colour.*

insist *verb* To **insist** is to demand firmly: *I insist that you leave.*
☐ **insistence**, *noun* –**insistent**, *adjective*

insolent /*say* **in**-suh-luhnt/ *adjective* insulting and rude: *an insolent remark.*
☐ **insolence**, *noun*

insomnia /*say* in-**som**-nee-uh/ *noun* a condition in which you have difficulty sleeping.
☐ **insomniac**, *noun* –**insomniac**, *adjective*

☑ SPELLING TIP You can spell **insomnia** by sounding out its parts. It will also help to see that it is made up of the prefix *in-* (meaning 'not') and a form of the Latin word *somnus* (meaning 'sleep'). Remember the *ia* ending which occurs in many words that have come from Latin, especially those that have to do with science or medicine.

inspect *verb* To **inspect** something is to look at it carefully to see whether it is in an acceptable state: *He inspected his food*; *Government officials came to inspect the school.*
☐ **inspection**, *noun* –**inspector**, *noun*

inspire *verb*
1. If someone **inspires** you, their success or enthusiasm encourages you to try to do the same as them: *I was inspired to go to university by my English teacher.* **2.** If something **inspires** a certain emotion in you, it causes you to feel it: *The beautiful weather inspired a much better mood.*
☐ **inspiration**, *noun* –**inspirational**, *adjective* –**inspirer**, *noun* –**inspiring**, *adjective*

install *verb*
1. If you **install** something such as a machine or a computer program, you put it into the place where it will be used and you get it ready for use. **2.** If someone is **installed** into a job or position, there is an official ceremony to mark their appointment.
☐ **installation**, *noun*

☑ SPELLING TIP *Double letter alert*: remember that the spelling of **install** is not tricky at all! There is a double *l* at the end, the same as in the word *stall.*

instalment *noun*
1. a single payment in a series which is meant to pay off a debt. **2.** a single part of a story being published in several parts one after the other.

☑ SPELLING TIP *Single letter alert*: only one *l*. The second *l* from the word *install* has been left off.

instance *noun* an example or case: *Losing his watch was just another instance of his carelessness.*

instant *noun*
1. a very short space of time. **2.** a particular point of time: *At that instant the phone rang.*
☐ **instant**, *adjective*: *instant relief*; *instant coffee.* –**instantaneous**, *adjective* –**instantaneously**, *adverb* –**instantly**, *adverb*

instead *adverb* in place of someone or something else: *He sent us instead.*

instep *noun* the arched upper part of the foot between the toes and ankle.

instinct *noun*
1. a natural tendency that is there when you are born: *a dog's instinct to bury bones.* **2.** a natural knowledge or skill: *She has an instinct for making friends.*
☐ **instinctive**, *adjective*

institute *verb*
1. To **institute** something is to set it up or establish it: *to institute a new government department*; *to institute rules of conduct.*
–*noun* **2.** an organisation or society set up to carry on a particular activity: *a literary institute.*

☐ **institution**, *noun* –**institutional**, *adjective* –**institutionalise**, *verb*: *to institutionalise a ceremony.* –**institutor**, *noun*

ANOTHER SPELLING for **institutionalise** is **institutionalize**.

instruct *verb*
1. If you **instruct** someone to do something, you tell or command them to do it: *He instructed us to wait here for him.* **2.** If you **instruct** someone about something or how to do something, you teach them: *The guide instructed us about safety rules.*
☐ **instruction**, *noun* –**instructive**, *adjective* –**instructor**, *noun*

instrument *noun*
1. a device or tool: *a dental instrument.* **2.** something made to produce musical sounds: *The violin is a stringed instrument.* **3.** an electrical device which gives information about the state of some part of an aeroplane, car or other vehicle: *The pilot checked the panel of instruments.*
☐ **instrumental**, *adjective* –**instrumentalist**, *noun*: *A violin player is an instrumentalist.*

insubordinate /*say* in-suh-**baw**-duh-nuht/ *adjective* not obeying those in authority.
☐ **insubordination**, *noun*

insulate *verb*
1. To **insulate** something electrical is to surround it with something that does not allow electricity to pass through in order to prevent people from getting electric shocks: *He used the plastic tape to insulate the cable.* **2.** To **insulate** a room or building is to put special material in the roof to keep in warmth in winter and keep out heat in summer.
☐ **insulation**, *noun*

WORD HISTORY from a Latin word meaning 'made into an island'

insulin /*say* **in**-shuh-luhn, **in**-syuhluhn/ *noun* a substance which the body produces to help it use the sugar in the food eaten.

NOTE If your body does not make enough insulin you get a disease called *diabetes*.
WORD HISTORY from a Latin word meaning 'island' (the gland in the body where insulin is made has lumps of tissue that look like islands)

insult *verb* /*say* in-**sult**/
1. To **insult** someone is to act or speak rudely or offensively to them.
–*noun* /*say* **in**-sult/ **2.** a rude or offensive action or remark.
☐ **insulting**, *adjective*

insure /*say* in-**shaw**/ *verb* If you **insure** something, you pay money to a company that will then pay a sum of money to you if the thing you have insured is stolen or damaged: *Most people insure their house and their car.*
☐ **insurance**, *noun*

☑ DO NOT CONFUSE **insure** with **ensure** or **assure**. To **ensure** that something happens is to make sure that it happens; to **assure** someone is to tell them that something is certainly true.

intact *adjective* not damaged, changed or disturbed in any way: *The statue survived the move intact.*

integer /*say* **in**-tuh-juh/ *noun* a whole number.

COMPARE this with **fraction**.
WORD HISTORY from a Latin word meaning 'untouched', 'whole', or 'entire'

☑ SPELLING TIP Remember the *ger* spelling for the 'juh' sound at the end.

integral /*say* **in**-tuh-gruhl/ *adjective* forming a necessary part of something: *Our pet dog is now an integral part of the family.*
☐ **integrally**, *adverb*

integrate *verb* If you **integrate** one thing into another thing, you bring them together to make a whole: *I try to integrate homework, sport and music into my normal school week*; *The club helps new families integrate into the town.*
☐ **integration**, *noun*

☑ SPELLING TIP Notice that that this word does not begin with the prefix *inter-*, as you might think. There is no *r* between the *e* and the *g*.

integrity /*say* in-**teg**-ruh-tee/ *noun* honesty and trustworthiness.

intellect *noun* the power of your mind to think, reason and understand: *to have a fine intellect.*
☐ **intellectual**, *adjective*, *noun* –**intellectuality**, *noun* –**intellectually**, *adverb*

A SIMILAR WORD is **intelligence**.

intelligence *noun*
1. the ability to learn, understand, and reason: *Use your intelligence to solve the problem.* **2.** good mental ability: *a woman of intelligence.*
☐ **intelligent**, *adjective*

☑ SPELLING TIP *Double letter alert*: double *l*. Also remember that the ending is spelt *ence* (not *ance*).

intend *verb* If you **intend** to do something, you plan to do it: *I intend to sleep in tomorrow.*
☐ **intended**, *adjective*: *the intended result.*

intense *adjective*
1. very great or severe: *intense pain*; *intense heat.* **2.** strongly and deeply felt: *intense love*; *intense hatred.* **3.** showing strong feeling: *an intense expression.*
☐ **intensely**, *adverb* –**intensify**, *verb* (**intensifies**, **intensifying**, **intensified**, **has intensified**) –**intensity**, *noun* –**intenseness**, *noun*

intensive *adjective* with a lot of attention or work: *intensive care of a seriously ill person.*

intent *adjective*
1. having your mind firmly fixed: *Joe was intent on finishing the computer game before he went to bed.*
–noun **2.** purpose, or what you intend: *She acted with good intent.*
☐ **intently**, *adverb*: *to stare intently.*

intention *noun* a firm plan or purpose.
☐ **intentional**, *adjective*

inter- *prefix* a word part meaning 'between' or 'among', as in *intercom*, *international*.

WORD HISTORY this prefix comes from Latin

interact *verb*
1. When people **interact** with each other, they communicate and work together. **2.** If things **interact**, they act together and have a combined effect: *The chemicals interacted to form a poisonous gas.*
☐ **interaction**, *noun* –**interactive**, *adjective*

intercept *verb* /*say* in-tuh-**sept**/
1. If you **intercept** something, you catch or stop it as it goes from one place to another: *to intercept a letter*; *I intercepted the ball as it was thrown.*
–noun /*say* **in**-tuh-sept/ **2.** an act of intercepting, such as gaining possession of the ball in a football game.
☐ **interception**, *noun* –**interceptor**, *noun*

interchange *verb* /*say* in-tuh-**chaynj**/
1. If you **interchange** two things, you cause them to change places: *I interchanged his name with mine so I would be further up the list.*
–noun /*say* **in**-tuh-chaynj/ **2.** an act of interchanging or sharing: *an interchange of ideas.* **3.** a point where it is possible to change from one form of public transport to another.
☐ **interchangeable**, *adjective* –**interchangeability**, *noun*: *the interchangeability of parts.*

intercom *noun* a system for sending spoken messages throughout a place such as a school or office.

WORD HISTORY short for *intercommunication system*

intercourse *noun*
1. See **sexual intercourse**. **2.** *Old-fashioned* exchange of ideas, thoughts and feelings between people: *Clubs provide a means of social intercourse.*

interest *noun*
1. the feeling you have when your attention is held by something: *to have an interest in frogs.* **2.** importance: *The winner's name was of great interest to us all.* **3.** extra money paid by the borrower of a sum, over and above the original amount borrowed, as a fee for the use of the money.
–verb **4.** When something **interests** you, it attracts your attention: *Does anything on the menu interest you?*
☐ **interested**, *adjective* –**interesting**, *adjective*

interfere *verb*
1. If someone **interferes** in something, they get involved in it without being asked when it really isn't any of their business. **2.** If something **interferes** with something else, it prevents it from working or functioning properly: *There is something interfering with the TV reception.*
☐ **interference**, *noun* –**interfering**, *adjective*

intergalactic /*say* in-tuh-guh-**lak**-tik/ *adjective* existing or happening between different galaxies in space: *intergalactic travel.*

interim /*say* **in**-tuh-ruhm/ *noun* an intervening period of time: *The movie didn't start until 6.30, so we decided to listen to CDs in the interim.*
☐ **interim**, *adjective* temporary.

WORD HISTORY from a Latin word meaning 'in the meantime'

interior *noun* an inner or inside area: *the interior of a house*; *the interior of the country.*
☐ **interior**, *adjective*: *an interior wall.*

THE OPPOSITE is **exterior**.

interjection *noun*
1. a word or phrase that is not part of a normal sentence but by itself expresses a feeling or reaction, such as *Goodbye*, *Ouch!* or *Thank you*. **2.** a remark made to interrupt a conversation or a speech.

SEE the Grammar and Punctuation Guide appendix.

interlude *noun*
1. a short period of time, especially of restfulness: *Meeting her friend for coffee was a welcome interlude in the busy day.* **2.** a short performance, especially of music between two acts of a play.

intermediate /*say* in-tuh-**mee**-dee-uht/ *adjective* occurring between other stages or levels: *He gave the answer first, and then explained the intermediate steps in his reasoning.*

☑ SPELLING TIP Remember that **intermediate** begins with the prefix *inter-* (meaning 'between'). Also remember that the ending is spelt *ate* (although it sounds like 'uht'). It might help to rap it out as *in + ter + me + di + ate*.

interminable /*say* in-**ter**-muh-nuh-buhl/ *adjective* without end: *interminable lectures.*
☐ **interminably**, *adverb*

intermission *noun* an interval, especially at the movies, concerts, etc.

intermittent *adjective* stopping and starting: *intermittent noise.*

☐ **intermittently**, *adverb*: *It has rained intermittently all day.*

☑ SPELLING TIP Remember that **intermittent** begins with the prefix *inter-* (meaning 'between'). Then you need to remember that the final part *mittent* has a double *t* in the middle and an *ent* ending.

intern[1] /*say* in-**tern**/ *verb* To **intern** someone is to keep them in an enclosed and guarded area, especially during wartime.
☐ **internment**, *noun*

intern[2] /*say* **in**-tern/ *noun*
1. a doctor who has recently finished university and is working full-time in a hospital. **2.** a person who is receiving practical experience in the workplace as a first step in a career.
☐ **intern**, *verb*

internal *adjective*
1. having to do with the inside: *the internal walls*; *internal bleeding.* **2.** happening within: *internal affairs of the company.*

THE OPPOSITE is **external**.

international *adjective* involving different countries or nations: *international sporting events.*
☐ **internationally**, *adverb*

internet *noun* the connection of computers all around the world so that you can share information.

ANOTHER FORM You can also spell this with a capital letter: **the Internet**.
THE SHORT FORM of this is **the Net** or **the net**.

internet cafe *noun* a place where you can pay to be connected to the internet, sometimes also selling coffee, tea and small meals.

internet service provider *noun* a company that provides access to the internet, usually for a monthly fee.

THE ABBREVIATION is **ISP**.

interplay *noun* the effect that various things have on each other: *the interplay between politics and the environment.*

interpret /*say* in-**ter**-pruht/ *verb* (**interprets**, **interpreting**, **interpreted**, **has interpreted**)
1. If you **interpret** something in a certain way, you understand it to be like that. You think that that is its meaning: *She interpreted my words as a compliment.* **2.** If you **interpret** for people who speak different languages, you repeat what each of them says, using the language of the other.
☐ **interpreter**, *noun* –**interpretation**, *noun*

A SIMILAR WORD (for definition 2) is **translate**.

interrogate /*say* in-**te**-ruh-gayt/ *verb* To **interrogate** someone is to question them closely to find out something: *The detectives interrogated the suspect.*
☐ **interrogation**, *noun* –**interrogator**, *noun*

interrupt *verb*
1. If you **interrupt** someone, you start speaking while they are still in the middle of saying something, or you disturb them while they are doing something. **2.** If you **interrupt** something, you stop it or disturb it before it is finished: *The lesson was interrupted by the fire alarm going off.*
☐ **interruption**, *noun* –**interruptive**, *adjective*

☑ SPELLING TIP Remember that **interrupt** begins with the prefix *inter-* (meaning 'between'). It is followed by the word part *rupt* (meaning 'broken) and so has a double *r*.

intersect *verb*
1. To **intersect** something is to cut or divide it by passing through or across it: *Walking tracks intersect the park.* **2.** If lines **intersect**, they cross: *There is a noticeboard where the paths intersect.*
☐ **intersection**, *noun*

intersperse *verb* When one thing is **interspersed** with one or more other things, these other things are scattered through it here and there: *a forest of eucalypts interspersed with wattle.*
☐ **interspersion**, *noun*

interstate *adjective* /*say* **in**-tuh-stayt/
1. between states: *an interstate spelling competition.*
–*adverb* /*say* in-tuh-**stayt**/ **2.** to or from another state: *I sent the parcel interstate.*

interval *noun*
1. the length of time between events: *There is an interval of four years between each Olympic Games.* **2.** a pause or break, especially halfway through a program of films or music. **3.** the space between things. **4.** the difference in pitch between two notes.

intervene *verb* To **intervene** is to step in, in order to change or solve something: *The teacher intervened in the argument.*
☐ **intervention**, *noun*

interview *noun*
1. a meeting in which someone is asked questions about something: *The winner gave an interview about the race*; *a job interview.*
–*verb* **2.** If you **interview** someone, you ask them questions: *The police interviewed three suspects about the crime.*
☐ **interviewer**, *noun*

☑ SPELLING TIP If you know how to spell the word *view* (something you look at), you will be able to spell **interview** which has the prefix *inter-* (meaning 'between') added at the start. The original idea of **interview** was 'seeing each other'.

intestine /*say* in-**tes**-tuhn/ *noun* the long tube that carries food from the stomach to the anus. The **large intestine** is the broader and shorter part, and the **small intestine** is the narrower and longer part.
☐ **intestinal**, *adjective*

ANOTHER FORM This is often used in the plural form, the **intestines**.

intimate /*say* **in**-tuh-muht/ *adjective*
1. very close: *intimate friends.* **2.** secret or deep: *an intimate conversation.* **3.** very thorough: *an intimate knowledge.*
–*noun* **4.** a close friend.
☐ **intimacy**, *noun* –**intimately**, *adverb*

intimidate *verb* If someone **intimidates** you, they scare or frighten you, often to make you do what they want: *Many witnesses withdrew their statements because they were intimidated by the gang.*
☐ **intimidated**, *adjective* –**intimidating**, *adjective* –**intimidation**, *noun*

into *preposition*
1. a word expressing **a.** movement or direction towards the inner part: *to run into the kitchen.* **b.** involvement or placement within: *to be well into a book.* **c.** change to new conditions, and so on: *to turn into a butterfly.* **2.** in mathematics, being the divisor of: *3 into 12 equals 4.*

intonation *noun* the pattern of changes of pitch in speech or music.

intoxicate /*say* in-**toks**-uh-kayt/ *verb* To **intoxicate** someone is to make them drunk.
☐ **intoxication**, *noun*

☑ SPELLING TIP If you know the word *toxic* (meaning 'poisonous'), you will be able to spell **intoxicate** which is based on it. Remember the *x* for the 'ks' sound in the middle.

intra- *prefix* a word part meaning 'within', as in *intravenous*.

WORD HISTORY this prefix comes from Latin

intransitive verb *noun* a verb like 'come' as in 'I want to come', that needs no object for it to make sense.

COMPARE this with **transitive verb**. Also see the Grammar and Punctuation Guide appendix.

intravenous /*say* in-truh-**vee**-nuhs/ *adjective* An **intravenous** medicine is given directly into the blood, through a needle put in a vein: *He's on an intravenous drip.*
☐ **intravenously**, *adverb*

intrepid *adjective* very brave: *an intrepid leader.*
☐ **intrepidly**, *adverb*

intricate /*say* **in**-truh-kuht/ *adjective* finely detailed: *intricate embroidery.*
☐ **intricacy**, *noun*

WORD HISTORY from a Latin word meaning 'entangled'

intrigue *verb* /*say* in-**treeg**/
1. To **intrigue** someone is to interest them or make them eager to learn more because of puzzling or unusual qualities: *The oddly shaped parcel intrigued me.*
–*noun* /*say* **in**-treeg/ **2.** a secret plan.
☐ **intriguing**, *adjective*

☑ SPELLING TIP The difficult part of **intrigue** is the *igue* ending (giving an 'eeg' sound). Another word with the same spelling for this sound is *fatigue*. They both come from French. Remember to drop the final *e* when you add *-ing* to make **intriguing**.

introduce *verb*
1. To **introduce** someone to someone else is to make the first person known to the second. **2.** To **introduce** an idea, topic, etc., is to speak or write about it for the first time.
☐ **introduction**, *noun* –**introductory**, *adjective*

intrude *verb* To **intrude** is to enter or force yourself in when you are not wanted or invited.
☐ **intruder**, *noun* –**intrusion**, *noun* –**intrusive**, *adjective*

intuition /*say* in-chooh-**ish**-uhn/ *noun* a strong feeling about something without any real reason that you know of: *My intuition tells me that she's telling the truth.*
☐ **intuitive** /*say* in-**tyooh**-uh-tiv/, *adjective*

☑ SPELLING TIP Remember that **intuition** has two separate *t*'s, neither of them giving a straightforward 't' sound. The first, after the *in*, gives a 'ty' or 'ch' sound, and the second, at the start of the *-tion* suffix, gives an 'sh' sound.

invade *verb* To **invade** is to **1.** attack and enter: *An army was sent to invade the neighbouring country.* **2.** force yourself in on: *to invade someone's privacy.*
☐ **invader**, *noun* –**invasion**, *noun*

invalid[1] /*say* **in**-vuh-lid/ *noun* someone who is sick or weak.
☐ **invalid**, *adjective*: *her invalid brother.*

invalid[2] /*say* in-**val**-uhd/ *adjective* not correct, especially legally: *an invalid election*; *an invalid contract.*

THE OPPOSITE is **valid**.

invaluable *adjective* Something **invaluable** has a value too great to be measured: *an invaluable carving*; *invaluable information.*

invent *verb* To **invent** something is to make it up: *She invented the story about her rich uncle.*
☐ **invention**, *noun* –**inventive**, *adjective* –**inventor**, *noun*

inverse *adjective* turned in the opposite position or direction.
☐ **inverse**, *noun* the opposite. –**inversely**, *adverb* –**invert**, *verb*

invertebrate /*say* in-**ver**-tuh-bruht/ *noun* an animal without a backbone: *A snail is an invertebrate.*
☐ **invertebrate**, *adjective*

COMPARE this with **vertebrate**.

☑ SPELLING TIP *Tricky 'uh' sound*: the vowel sound before the *b* is spelt *e*.

inverted comma *noun* See **quotation mark**.

invest *verb*
1. To **invest** money is to put it into something such as property, shares, or a small business in the hope of making a profit. **2.** To **invest** time or energy in something is to spend it working at that thing.
☐ **investment**, *noun* –**investor**, *noun*

investigate *verb* To **investigate** something is to look into it or examine it closely: *I saw smoke coming from the shed and went to investigate*; *The police investigated the theft.*
☐ **investigation**, *noun* –**investigator**, *noun*

invigorate *verb* To **invigorate** someone is to fill them with energy and strength: *We were invigorated by our swim.*
☐ **invigorating**, *adjective*

invincible /*say* in-**vin**-suh-buhl/ *adjective* unable to be defeated or beaten.
☐ **invincibly**, *adverb*

invisible *adjective*
1. unable to be seen because it is too small, too far away or behind something else, etc.: *Her hands were invisible, deep in her pockets*; *The particles were so small they were invisible to the human eye.* **2.** made in a special way that stops it from being seen: *invisible ink*; *The witch in the story made herself invisible.*

THE OPPOSITE is **visible**.

invite *verb*
1. If you **invite** someone, you ask them to do something with you as a social event. **2.** If you say someone **invites** something bad to happen, you mean that they act in a way which makes it very likely: *Her wild behaviour is inviting trouble.*
☐ **invitation**, *noun*

in-vitro fertilisation /*say* in-**vit**-roh/ *adjective* the process by which a woman's egg is fertilised outside her body (as in a laboratory) and then placed in her uterus to grow into a baby.

THE ABBREVIATION is **IVF**.
WORD HISTORY from Latin words meaning 'in glass'

invoice *noun*
1. a listing of things bought or work done, giving each price separately.
–*verb* **2.** To **invoice** someone is to send them an invoice, showing an amount of money to be paid.

involve *verb*
1. If something **involves** something else, the second thing is part of it or connected with it: *Repairing the wharf involved cancelling ferry services for a week.* **2.** If you **involve** someone in something, you cause them to take part in it: *I don't want to involve you in our quarrel.*
☐ **involvement**, *noun*

involved *adjective*
1. complicated; not easy to understand: *an involved explanation.* **2.** deeply interested: *involved in art.* **3.** closely connected or associated, especially romantically.

inward /*say* **in**-wuhd/ *adjective*
1. going towards the inside: *inward thoughts.*
–*adverb* **2.** towards the inside or interior: *The gate swung inward.*
☐ **inwardly**, *adverb*

ANOTHER FORM of the adverb (definition 2) is **inwards**.
THE OPPOSITE is **outward**.

iodine /*say* **uy**-uh-deen, **uy**-uh-duyn/ *noun* a chemical element which produces a purple antiseptic when heated.

☑ SPELLING TIP The word **iodine** comes from Greek and has an unusual *io* beginning. The *ine* ending is common in the names of chemical substances. Some other examples are *chlorine* and *morphine*.

ion /*say* **uy**-uhn/ *noun* a tiny particle, such as an atom, which has an electric charge.

☑ SPELLING TIP Don't confuse the spelling of **ion** with **iron** which has the same sound. **Iron** is a metallic element, and an **iron** is a tool for smoothing clothes.

IP address *noun* the unique identifying number that is given to each computer connected to the internet.

NOTE **IP** is a short form of **internet protocol**.

irate *adjective* very angry.

iris *noun* (*plural* **irises**)
1. the coloured part of the eye around the pupil.
2. a large, brightly coloured flower.

WORD HISTORY named after *Iris*, a messenger of the gods and goddess of the rainbow in Greek myths

irk *verb* If something **irks** you, it annoys or troubles you: *It irks me to see people leaving rubbish in the park.*
☐ **irksome**, *adjective*

iron /*say* **uy**-uhn/ *noun*
1. a metallic element used in the making of tools and machinery, and which is also found in some foods and is used by the body in the making of blood. 2. a tool which can be heated and used to smooth out clothes. 3. a golf club with an iron head.
–*verb* 4. When you **iron** clothes or sheets, you remove creases from them using an iron.
–*phrase* 5. **strike while the iron is hot**, to act quickly while the opportunity is still there.
☐ **iron**, *adjective*: *an iron rod*; *an iron will.* –**ironing**, *noun*

☑ SPELLING TIP Remember the silent *r* in **iron**. Don't confuse it with **ion** which has the same sound. An **ion** is a small particle of matter with an electric charge.

ironbark *noun* a gum tree with hard, dark grey bark.

irony /*say* **uy**-ruh-nee/ *noun* a humorous way of speaking in which the real meaning is the opposite of what is said: *'Great!' she said with irony when she saw the muddy paw prints on her white skirt.*
☐ **ironic**, *adjective* –**ironically**, *adverb*

irrational *adjective* not based on sound reasoning: *He has an irrational fear of cats.*
☐ **irrationally**, *adverb*

THE OPPOSITE is **rational**.

irregular *adjective*
1. uneven: *She sobbed with short irregular gasps*; *irregular intervals.* 2. not usual or normal.
☐ **irregularity**, *noun* –**irregularly**, *adverb*

THE OPPOSITE is **regular**.

irrelevant *adjective* Something that is **irrelevant** is not important because it is not connected with what you are saying or dealing with: *Let's not get distracted by irrelevant issues*; *His remarks were irrelevant to the subject.*

THE OPPOSITE is **relevant**.

irresistible *adjective* so tempting that you cannot fight against it: *an irresistible idea*; *irresistible flavours.*
☐ **irresistibility**, *noun* –**irresistibleness**, *noun* –**irresistibly**, *adverb*

irresponsible *adjective* not careful or able to be trusted: *an irresponsible driver.*
☐ **irresponsibility**, *noun* –**irresponsibleness**, *noun* –**irresponsibly**, *adverb*

THE OPPOSITE is **responsible**.

irrigate *verb* To **irrigate** land is to supply it with water using a system of canals and pipes.
☐ **irrigation**, *noun*

irritable *adjective* easily annoyed: *I try to keep out of his way when he is tired and irritable.*
☐ **irritability**, *noun*

☑ SPELLING TIP *Double letter alert*: double *r* (just as there is in *irritate*). You might think of the phrase 'irritable people react rapidly' to remind you of the double *r*.

irritate *verb*
1. If someone or something **irritates** you, they annoy you or make you cross. 2. If something **irritates** a part of your body, it makes it sore or itchy: *The dust irritates my nose and makes me sneeze.*
☐ **irritated**, *adjective* –**irritating**, *adjective*: *an irritating noise.* –**irritation**, *noun*

is *verb* the third person singular present tense indicative of the verb **be**.

NOTE For an explanation of *indicative*, see **mood**[2]. See also the Grammar and Punctuation Guide appendix.

Islam /*say* **iz**-lam, **iz**-lahm/ *noun* a world religion based on the teachings of the prophet Mohammed and set down in the holy book of Islam, the Koran, which teaches that its followers should live their lives according to the wishes of Allah (God). Followers of Islam are called Muslims, and worship in a mosque.
☐ **Islamic**, *adjective*: *Islamic teachings.*

island /*say* **uy**-luhnd/ *noun* a piece of land completely surrounded by water.
☐ **islander**, *noun*

☑ SPELLING TIP *Silent letter alert*: don't forget the *s* after the *i*. You might remember that you can swim all the way around an **island** to remind you of the silent *s*.

isle /*rhymes with* mile/ *noun* a small island.

☑ SPELLING TIP *Silent letter alert*: don't forget the *s* between the *i* and the *l*. Don't confuse the spelling of **isle** with **aisle** which has the same sound. An **aisle** is a clear path between seats.

isn't a short form of *is not*.

iso- *prefix* a word part meaning 'equal', as in *isosceles*.

WORD HISTORY this prefix comes from Greek

isobar /*say* **uy**-suh-bah/ *noun* a line drawn on a weather map, connecting all the places that have the same air pressure.

isolate *verb* If you **isolate** something, you keep it separate or apart from other things: *Scientists have managed to isolate the virus responsible for the strange disease.*
☐ **isolated**, *adjective* –**isolation**, *noun*

☑ SPELLING TIP *Single letter alert*: only one *s*. Also remember that the middle vowel is spelt *o*.

Though unconnected to the meaning, it will help if you notice that **isolate** contains the words *is* and *late* with an o**isolated** between them.

isosceles /*say* uy-**sos**-uh-leez/ *adjective* An **isosceles** triangle has two equal sides.

☑ SPELLING TIP *Silent letter alert*: don't forget the *c* after the second *s*. Also remember the *es* ending, giving an 'eez' sound. **Isosceles** comes from Greek and is made up of *iso-* (a word part meaning 'equal') and *skeles* (a form of the word for 'leg').

issue /*say* **ish**-ooh, **ish**-yooh, **is**-yooh/ *noun* **1.** something sent or given out. **2.** something published or sent out at a certain time: *We will put your letter in next week's issue.* **3.** an important topic of discussion. **4.** a complaint or objection: *do you have an issue with this decision?* –*verb* **5.** When you **issue** something, you send or give it out: *to issue a statement*; *to issue rations.* –*phrase* **6. at issue**, in disagreement: *The point at issue is how much we'll be paid.* **7. issues**, unresolved psychological problems: *She has issues which she needs to work through.* **8. take issue**, to disagree: *They took issue over their wages.*

☑ SPELLING TIP Remember the double *s* spelling for the 'sh' sound in this word. A similar word is *tissue*.

isthmus /*say* **is**-muhs/ *noun* a narrow strip of land, with water on both sides, joining two larger pieces of land.

WORD HISTORY from a Greek word meaning 'narrow passage' or 'neck'

☑ SPELLING TIP *Silent letter alert*: don't forget the *th* after the *s*. Not just one silent letter but two, making this word have an unusual number of consonants coming together!

it *pronoun* someone or something being talked about whose sex is not known or that does not have a sex: *Did you see who it was?*; *A smile is a wonderful thing. It can really brighten your day.*

SEE ALSO **its**.

IT *noun* See **information technology**.

italics /*say* uh-**tal**-iks, uy-**tal**-iks/ *plural noun* printing which slopes to the right (as *italics*), which is often used for emphasis.
□ **italic**, *adjective*

itch *verb* **1.** If a part of your body **itches**, it has an annoying feel that makes you want to scratch it. **2.** If you **itch** to do something, you are very eager to do it: *I'm itching to get home.*
□ **itch**, *noun* (*plural* **itches**) –**itchy**, *adjective* (**itchier**, **itchiest**) –**itchiness**, *noun*

item /*say* **uy**-tuhm/ *noun* **1.** one thing, especially among a number: *There are eight items on my list.* **2.** a piece of news: *Her name is mentioned in an item on the back page.*
□ **itemise**, *verb*

ANOTHER SPELLING for **itemise** is **itemize**.

itinerant /*say* uy-**tin**-uh-ruhnt/ *adjective* An **itinerant** person travels from place to place, especially to find work.
□ **itinerant**, *noun*

itinerary /*say* uy-**tin**-uh-ree/ *noun* (*plural* **itineraries**) the program or plan of a journey, listing places to be visited, times of journeys and so on.

☑ SPELLING TIP *Tricky 'uh' sound*: *e* spelling for the middle vowel sound. Also don't forget the *ary* ending (although the *a* is not pronounced). It might help to rap it out as *it+ in+ er+ ary*.

it'll a short form of *it will*.

its *pronoun* the form of **it** you use when something belongs to a thing or animal: *The dog gnawed its bone.*

it's a short form of *it is* or *it has*.

I've a short form of *I have*.

ivory *noun* **1.** the valuable white tusk of elephants. **2.** a creamy white colour. –*adjective* **3.** of a creamy white colour: *ivory skin.*

ivy *noun* a climbing plant with smooth, shiny, leaves.

jab *verb* (**jabs**, **jabbing**, **jabbed**, **has jabbed**) If you **jab** someone or something, you push them with something sharp or pointed: *The nurse jabbed the needle in so hard that it hurt*; *The sharp end of the wood jabbed into my stomach.*
☐ **jab**, *noun*

jabiru /*say* jab-uh-**rooh**/ *noun* a type of white stork found in Australia with a green-black head, neck and tail.

jacaranda *noun* a tall tree with pale purple flowers.

WORD HISTORY from a South American language

jack *noun*
1. a tool used for lifting up heavy weights, such as a car. **2.** a playing card that has a picture of the knave (or prince) on it.
–*verb in the phrase* **3. jack up**, **a.** to lift with a jack. **b.** *Informal* to refuse to do something: *She finally jacked up when they asked her to work seven days a week.*

jackal /*say* **jak**-uhl/ *noun* a wild dog of Asia and Africa which hunts in packs at night.

jackaroo *noun* a young man who is learning the work of a cattle or sheep station.

ANOTHER SPELLING is **jackeroo**.

jacket *noun*
1. a short coat. **2.** a book's paper cover which can be taken off. **3.** the skin of a potato.

jackhammer *noun* a tool which is used to break up rocks and concrete by hammering at them.

jack-in-the-box *noun* a toy figure on a spring which jumps out of its box when the lid is opened.

jackknife *noun* (*plural* **jackknives**)
1. a large knife whose blade folds into its handle. **2.** a dive in which you bend your body so that your hands briefly touch your toes before you hit the water.
–*verb* **3.** To **jackknife** is to bend or fold up, like a jackknife: *The semitrailer hit a tree and jack-knifed.*

jackpot *noun* the biggest prize that you can win in a lottery or other competition.

jade *noun* a precious, green stone.
☐ **jade**, *adjective*

jaded *adjective* worn out with tiredness: *to feel jaded with the heat.*

jaffle *noun* a sandwich cooked by being pressed between two hot metal plates.

jagged /*say* **jag**-uhd/ *adjective* rough and sharp-edged: *The outline of the mountain peak was jagged against the sky.*

jaguar /*say* **jag**-yooh-uh/ *noun* a large, fierce, spotted cat found in tropical America.

☑ SPELLING TIP Remember the *uar* ending (no *y*). You can think of it as standing for 'U-turn and retreat' – just what you should do if you come across a **jaguar**!

jail *noun*
1. the place where prisoners are kept while they serve their sentence.
–*verb* **2.** If a person is **jailed**, they are put into jail.
☐ **jailer**, *noun*

ANOTHER SPELLING is **gaol**.
NOTE We used to think of *jail* as an American spelling but it is now so common that *gaol* is becoming outdated.

jam[1] *verb* (**jams**, **jamming**, **jammed**, **has jammed**)
1. If something **jams**, it becomes stuck: *The window has jammed and we can't close it.* **2.** To **jam** something is to push or force it into a space tightly: *You can't jam anything else into the case unless you take something out.*
–*noun* **3.** people or things crowded together: *There is a traffic jam at the intersection and nobody can move.* **4.** *Rather informal* a difficult situation: *He got into a jam trying to do two jobs at the same time.*

jam[2] *noun* a food made of fruit and sugar which you spread on bread.

jamb /*say* jam/ *noun* the side piece of a doorway or window.

☑ SPELLING TIP *Silent letter alert*: remember the silent *b* at the end. Don't confuse this word with **jam**.

jamboree *noun* a large gathering of Scouts.

janitor *noun* a caretaker.

January /*say* **jan**-yooh-uh-ree/ *noun* the first month of the year, with 31 days.

THE ABBREVIATION is **Jan**.
WORD HISTORY from a Latin word meaning 'the month of Janus'; Janus was the Roman god of

doors and gates, who was drawn with two faces looking in opposite directions

jar[1] *noun* a glass container, usually round and with a wide opening at the top.

jar[2] *verb* (**jars**, **jarring**, **jarred**, **has jarred**) If something **jars** you, it **1.** jolts or shakes you about roughly or painfully: *Every jolt over the rough road jarred against his bones.* **2.** upsets or shocks you: *It jarred his self-confidence to be told that he was no longer wanted on the team.*

jargon /*say* **jah**-guhn/ *noun* the words used only by people in a particular job or group: *medical jargon.*

jarrah *noun* a large tree found in western Australia with a hard, dark red wood.

WORD HISTORY from an Aboriginal language of Western Australia called Nyungar

☑ SPELLING TIP *Double letter alert*: double *r*. Also remember the *ah* ending. Several other words that come from Aboriginal languages, such as *galah*, have this spelling.

jaunt /*say* jawnt/ *noun* a short journey, usually made for fun: *How would you like to come for a jaunt?*

jaunty /*say* **jawn**-tee/ *adjective* (**jauntier**, **jauntiest**) lively and confident: *His jaunty approach relaxed everybody.*
☐ **jauntily**, *adverb* –**jauntiness**, *noun*

javelin /*say* **jav**-uh-luhn/ *noun* a spear which is thrown in sporting contests.

jaw *noun* one of the two bones between the chin and nose which contain the teeth.

jaywalk *verb* If you **jaywalk**, you cross a street carelessly, not using a pedestrian crossing.

jazz *noun*
1. a type of music, first played by African Americans, with complex melodies and rhythms, often characterised by the performers making up or varying the music as they play.
–*phrase* **2. jazz up**, to make brighter or more exciting: *We'll jazz up the school hall with balloons and streamers.*
☐ **jazz**, *adjective*: *jazz tunes.* –**jazzy**, *adjective*

jealous /*say* **jel**-uhs/ *adjective*
1. wanting what someone else has: *Pete was very jealous of Charlie's new bike.* **2.** angry or upset because someone you like seems to like someone else: *She got very jealous when her best friend played with other people.*
☐ **jealously**, *adverb* –**jealousy**, *noun*

jeans *plural noun* trousers made of denim.

☑ SPELLING TIP Don't confuse the spelling of **jeans** with **genes** which has the same sound. **Genes** are the units in the body which are responsible for passing on physical characteristics, like blue eyes, from parents to their children.

jeep *noun* a small, strong car, often used for driving in rough conditions.

jeer *verb*
1. To **jeer** at someone is to make fun of or insult them.
–*noun* **2.** an insult.
☐ **jeering**, *noun*

jelly *noun* (*plural* **jellies**) a soft sweet food which sets firm but shakes a little when it is moved.

jellyfish *noun* (*plural* **jellyfish** *or* **jellyfishes**) a soft-bodied sea animal, especially one with an umbrella-shaped body and long tentacles.

jeopardy /*say* **jep**-uh-dee/ *noun* danger: *The school excursion is in jeopardy because insurance costs so much.*
☐ **jeopardise**, *verb* to risk.

ANOTHER SPELLING for **jeopardise** is **jeopardize**.

☑ SPELLING TIP *Silent letter alert*: don't forget the *o* before the *p*.

jerk *noun*
1. a sudden rough movement. **2.** *Informal* a stupid or annoying person.
–*verb* **3.** If you **jerk** something, you pull it suddenly and roughly.
☐ **jerky**, *adjective* –**jerkiness**, *noun* –**jerkily**, *adverb*

jersey *noun*
1. a long-sleeved top, often worn by members of a sporting team as a uniform. **2. Jersey**, a breed of cattle which produces rich milk.

WORD HISTORY from the island of *Jersey*, in the English Channel, where the cows came from and where the knitted fabric originally used for the tops was produced

jest *noun*
1. a joke.
–*verb* **2.** If you **jest**, you say something as a joke; you are not speaking seriously.
☐ **jesting**, *adjective* –**jestingly**, *adverb*

jester *noun* a clown who entertained a king or queen in medieval times: *They were entertained by a new court jester.*

jet[1] *noun*
1. a fast, narrow flow of liquid or gas coming out of a small hole: *The fire crew directed the jet of water at the flames.* **2.** the opening for a jet of liquid or gas: *The jets for the spa were blocked.* **3.** See **jet plane**.

jet[2] *noun* a hard black coal which is polished and used to make things like buttons and jewellery.

jet engine *noun* an engine that pushes out a stream of liquid or gas behind it, the force of which sends the vehicle forward.

jet plane *noun* an aircraft which is powered by engines that work by having hot gas forced at high speed through an opening at the back.

THE SHORT FORM of this is **jet**.

jetty *noun* (*plural* **jetties**) a long structure, sticking out into a river or the sea, that boats or ships can be tied to.

SIMILAR WORDS are **pier** and **wharf**.

Jew *noun*
1. a person descended from the Hebrews. **2.** a person whose religion is Judaism.
☐ **Jewish**, *adjective*

jewel /*say* **jooh**-uhl/ *noun* a precious stone, such as a diamond or ruby, which has been cut in a special shape.
☐ **jeweller**, *noun* –**jewellery**, *noun*

☑ SPELLING TIP *Tricky vowel sound*: notice the unusual group of letters *ewe* making the 'ooh' sound.

jib *verb* (**jibs**, **jibbing**, **jibbed**, **has jibbed**)
1. If an animal like a horse **jibs**, it will not move forwards, but stops suddenly because it is frightened.
–*phrase* **2. jib at**, to be unwilling to do: *She always jibs at any dirty work.*

A SIMILAR WORD (for definition 1) is **baulk**.

jiffy *noun* (*plural* **jiffies**) *Rather informal* a very short time: *It only took a jiffy to get things together.*

jig *noun*
1. a very energetic dance.
–*verb* (**jigs**, **jigging**, **jigged**, **has jigged**) **2.** If somebody **jigs**, they move energetically up and down or to and fro, or they dance a jig.

jigsaw *noun*
1. a narrow saw for cutting curves. **2.** a jigsaw puzzle.

jigsaw puzzle *noun* a puzzle made up of many differently shaped pieces which fit together to form a picture.

jillaroo *noun* a young woman who is learning the work of a cattle or a sheep station.

jingle *noun*
1. a ringing sound, as if made by many small bells. **2.** a bright, simple song such as those used in radio or television commercials.
–*verb* (**jingles**, **jingling**, **jingled**, **has jingled**) **3.** If something **jingles**, it makes high tinkling sounds like bells or coins knocking together.

jinx *noun* someone or something which is thought to bring bad luck.

job *noun*
1. a piece of work. **2.** paid employment.
–*phrase* **3. a good job**, a lucky state of affairs: *It was a good job that the weather cleared up for the sports carnival.*

jockey *noun* someone who professionally rides horses in races.

jocular /*say* **jok**-yuh-luh/ *adjective* joking or playful: *They made a jocular comment on his lack of hair.*
☐ **jocularity**, *noun*

jodhpurs /*say* **jod**-puhz/ *plural noun* riding trousers which are close-fitting below the knee.

☑ SPELLING TIP *Silent letter alert*: don't forget the *h*. Also remember that the ending is spelt *urs* (not *ers*). The spelling of **jodhpurs** is unusual because it is named after *Jodhpur*, a place in India.

joey *noun* a young animal, especially a young kangaroo which is carried in its mother's pouch.

jog *verb* (**jogs**, **jogging**, **jogged**, **has jogged**)
1. To **jog** is to run or go along at a slow regular speed. **2.** If you **jog** something, you push it: *He accidentally jogged the flimsy table and it collapsed*; *She jogged my arm and passed over the book.*
☐ **jog**, *noun*

jogger *noun*
1. a person who jogs for exercise. **2.** a type of shoe suitable for jogging as an exercise.

join *verb*
1. If you **join** one thing to another or **join** things together, you put them together so that they are connected. **2.** If things **join**, they come together and become united. **3.** If you **join** someone, you meet up with them: *You go ahead – I'll join you later.* **4.** If you **join** someone in something, you take part in an activity with them: *If everyone joins us, we'll have enough for two teams.* **5.** If you **join** an organisation, you become a member of it: *to join the Scouts.*
–*phrase* **6. join up**, to become a member of one of the armed forces.
☐ **join**, *noun*: *a neat join.*

SIMILAR WORDS (for definition 1) are **connect**, **combine**, **link** and **unite**.

joiner *noun* someone who makes wooden furniture and wooden structures in houses such as window frames.
☐ **joinery**, *noun* the work a joiner does.

joint *noun*
1. the place where two things or parts are joined: *The pain seemed to be right in the knee joint.* **2.** a cut of meat: *Mum asked the butcher for a joint of lamb.*
–*phrase* **3. out of joint**, out of position.

□ **joint**, *adjective*: *a joint undertaking.* –**jointed**, *adjective*: *a doll with jointed arms and legs.* –**jointly**, *adverb*

joist *noun* a length of wood or metal used to support floors, ceilings or other structures.

joke *noun*
1. something which is said or done to make people laugh.
–*verb* (**jokes**, **joking**, **joked**, **has joked**) 2. If you **joke**, you act or speak in a playful way not meaning to be serious at all.
□ **joker**, *noun* –**jokingly**, *adverb*

jolly *adjective* (**jollier**, **jolliest**) *Rather old-fashioned* good-humoured and full of fun: *The party was a jolly occasion and everybody had a good time.*

jolt *verb* To **jolt** something is to bump or shake it roughly.
□ **jolt**, *noun*

jostle /*say* **jos**-uhl/ *verb* If people **jostle**, they push roughly or rudely: *At the Christmas sale, everybody was jostling to get to the sale bins.*

> ☑ SPELLING TIP *Silent letter alert*: don't forget the *st* (not double *s*) spelling. The *t* is silent.

jot *verb* (**jots**, **jotting**, **jotted**, **has jotted**)
1. If you **jot** something down, you write it quickly in note form: *She jotted the details down on a scrap of paper.*
–*noun* 2. a little bit: *Allie doesn't like him one jot.*
□ **jotter**, *noun* –**jotting**, *noun*

joule /*say* joohl/ *noun* a measure of work or energy.

> THE SYMBOL for this is **J**.
> WORD HISTORY named after a British physicist, JP *Joule*, who lived from 1818-89

journal /*say* **jer**-nuhl/ *noun*
1. a newspaper or magazine. 2. a daily record of events.

> ☑ SPELLING TIP If you remember that this word means 'a *daily* record' and that it contains *jour*, the French word for 'day', you should be all right with the spelling. Its origins are Latin but it has come into English from French, which is why it is spelt like this.

journalist /*say* **jer**-nuhl-uhst/ *noun* someone who writes, edits or produces newspapers and magazines, or news and current affairs programs on television and radio.
□ **journalism**, *noun*

> ☑ SPELLING TIP **Journalist** comes from the word *journal*, so, as with *journal*, you need to remember that it contains *jour*, the French word for 'day'.

journey /*say* **jer**-nee/ *noun*
1. the act of travelling between two places, especially by land: *Drivers on long journeys should stop every two hours.*
–*verb* 2. If you **journey** from one place to another, you travel there: *They journeyed for hours without seeing anyone.*

> ☑ SPELLING TIP This word comes from the idea of a trip made in a day. If you think of this, and can see that it contains *jour*, the French word for 'day', the spelling will be easier. Also remember the *ey* ending.

joust /*say* jowst/ *noun* in medieval times, a contest in which two knights riding horses used lances to fight one another.

jovial /*say* **joh**-vee-uhl/ *adjective* cheerful and friendly.
□ **joviality**, *noun* –**jovially**, *adverb*

> ☑ SPELLING TIP The spelling will be easier if you can see that this word comes from *Jove* (a name for Jupiter, the supreme Roman god), with the *e* changed to *i* and the adjective suffix *-al* (meaning 'having to do with') added. The idea behind this word comes from astrology in which someone born under the planet Jupiter was thought to have a cheerful personality.

jowl *noun* a fold of flesh which hangs below the cheek or jaw.

joy *noun*
1. great happiness or pleasure: *On seeing the ocean for the first time, she felt a sudden rush of joy.* 2. a source of happiness: *That baby is his pride and joy.*
□ **joyful**, *adjective* –**joyfully**, *adverb* –**joyless**, *adjective* –**joyous**, *adjective* –**joyously**, *adverb*

joystick *noun*
1. the control stick of an aircraft. 2. a lever used to control the movement of the cursor and other images in computer games.

jube *noun* a chewy fruit-flavoured lolly made with gelatine.

jubilant /*say* **jooh**-buh-luhnt/ *adjective* extremely happy or joyful: *They were jubilant at reaching the peak.*
□ **jubilantly**, *adverb* –**jubilation**, *noun*

> ☑ SPELLING TIP *Tricky 'uh' sounds*: the middle vowel sound is spelt *i* and the last one is spelt *a* (giving an *ant*, not *ent* ending.) Imagine a 'jubilant ant' to remind yourself.

jubilee /*say* jooh-buh-**lee**/ *noun* a celebration, especially of the anniversary of something which happened a long time ago.

> ☑ SPELLING TIP *Tricky 'uh' sound*: the middle vowel sound is spelt *i*. Also remember the *ee* ending.

Judaism /*say* **jooh**-day-iz-uhm/ *noun* the religion of the Jewish people, based on the writings of the Old Testament and the teachings of the rabbis, which say that there is only one God. Followers

of Judaism are called Jews, and worship in a synagogue.
☐ **Judaic**, *adjective*: *Judaic teachings.*

judge *noun*
1. someone whose job is to hear and decide cases in a court of law. **2.** someone who gives an opinion or a decision on the winner of a contest or competition.
–*verb* (**judges**, **judging**, **judged**, **has judged**) **3.** If you **judge** someone or something, you make a decision based on information that you have: *Farmers have to judge which crops to grow; The magistrate will judge what the punishment should be.*

judgement *noun*
1. an opinion or conclusion: *His judgement was hasty and he was sorry afterwards.* **2.** the ability to make right decisions: *Her judgement is always spot on.* **3.** the decision in a court case: *The guilty judgement was decided very quickly.*

ANOTHER SPELLING is **judgment**.

judicial /*say* jooh-**dish**-uhl/ *adjective* having to do with judges or law courts: *They asked for a judicial opinion on the matter.*
☐ **judiciary**, *noun* the system of courts and judges. –**judicially**, *adverb*

☑ SPELLING TIP Remember that the ending is *icial* giving an 'ishuhl' sound. Another word with this ending is *official*. Think of a 'judicial official'.

judicious /*say* jooh-**dish**-uhs/ *adjective* showing good or wise judgement.
☐ **judiciously**, *adverb*

judo *noun* a Japanese art of self-defence which is practised as a sport.

WORD HISTORY from a Japanese word meaning 'soft way'

jug *noun* a container that holds liquids, usually with a handle and pouring lip.

juggle *verb* To **juggle** objects is to throw them into the air and keep them moving by catching and throwing them without dropping any.
☐ **juggler**, *noun*

juice *noun* the liquid part of a plant, especially fruit: *tomato juice.*
☐ **juicy**, *adjective* (**juicier**, **juiciest**)

jukebox *noun* a coin-operated machine which plays music and songs that you select.

July *noun* the seventh month of the year, with 31 days.

THE ABBREVIATION is **Jul** or **Jy**.
WORD HISTORY named after the Roman general and statesman *Julius* Caesar, who was born in this month

jumble *noun*
1. a confused mixture. **2.** a state of confusion or lack of order.
–*verb* **3.** If you **jumble** things, you mix them so they turn into a confused mass: *I jumbled everything together in the drawer so Mum wouldn't see her present.*

jumbo *noun*
1. a very large jet plane, or anything bigger than usual. **2.** *Informal* an elephant.
☐ **jumbo**, *adjective*: *a jumbo box of chocolate frogs.*

jumbuck *noun Old-fashioned* a sheep.

NOTE We know this word only because it's in the song 'Waltzing Matilda'. It is not used in ordinary language any more.

jump *verb*
1. If you **jump**, you move up suddenly, leaving the ground and moving your whole body through the air. **2.** If you **jump** somewhere, you move there quickly: *She jumped off the tram at the very last minute.* **3.** If you **jump** from fright or surprise, you make a quick, sudden movement: *The noise was so loud I jumped.* **4.** If something such as the temperature or a cost **jumps**, it increases suddenly by a big amount.
–*noun* **5.** a leap. **6.** a sudden move from one state or thing to another: *a jump in price.*
–*phrase* **7. jump at**, accept eagerly: *She jumped at the chance of a new job.* **8. jump on** (or **upon**), to scold: *They jumped on her for copying other people's work.*

SIMILAR WORDS (for definitions 1 and 2) are **leap**, **spring** and **bound**.

jumper *noun* a piece of warm clothing worn on the top half of the body, often over other clothes.

OTHER WORDS for this are **pullover** and **sweater**.

jumpy *adjective* (**jumpier**, **jumpiest**) nervous or frightened in mood or behaviour: *We were very jumpy because we knew they were a hard team to beat.*
☐ **jumpily**, *adverb* –**jumpiness**, *noun*

junction /*say* **junk**-shuhn/ *noun* the place where two or more things, especially roads or railway tracks, meet or cross.

juncture *noun*
1. a particular point in time: *At that juncture, she thought it best to leave the room.* **2.** the junction or joining point of two things.

June *noun* the sixth month of the year, with 30 days.

THE ABBREVIATION is **Jun**.
WORD HISTORY named after the Roman goddess *Juno*, the wife of Jupiter, the head god

jungle *noun* the thick trees and plants which grow in warm, slightly wet, tropical conditions.

junior *adjective* If someone is **junior** to someone else, they are younger or lower in rank than them: *a junior member of staff.*
☐ **junior**, *noun*

THE OPPOSITE is **senior.**

junk *noun* old or unwanted things.

junket *noun* a milk pudding made by setting sweetened warm milk.

junk food *noun* food that is not healthy: *He eats too much junk food and is getting fat.*

junkie *noun Informal* a drug addict.

junk mail *noun* unwanted emails, usually advertisements.

junta /*say* **jun**-tuh/ *noun* a small group of people ruling a country, especially as the result of a revolution.

WORD HISTORY from Spanish, from a Latin word meaning 'joined'

jurisdiction /*say* jooh-ruhs-**dik**-shuhn/ *noun* If a person or legal body has **jurisdiction** in a particular matter, they have the power or authority to make a judgement about it: *The industrial court does not have jurisdiction to decide on that kind of dispute.*

jury *noun*
1. a group of people chosen from the public to hear arguments for and against an accused person so that they can decide whether that person is innocent or guilty of what they are being accused of. **2.** a group chosen to judge a competition and award prizes.
☐ **juror**, *noun*: *The jurors all agreed that the man was guilty.*

just *adjective*
1. based on right: *We supported them because we thought it was a just cause.*
–*adverb* **2.** by a very little: *Alison just beat Marjorie, but only by a few metres.* **3.** exactly: *Nanda did just what the teacher said.* **4.** only: *He is just a dog – he cannot understand you.*

justice *noun*
1. what is right and fair: *They trust his sense of justice.* **2.** judgement by a court of law.
–*phrase* **3. do justice to**, **a.** to show in favourable terms: *The colour of that dress does not do justice to your eyes.* **b.** to deal with properly: *We didn't have the time to do justice to the exhibition.*

justice of the peace *noun*
1. In Australia, a **justice of the peace** is a person who has the authority to supervise someone making an official oath or declaration, or to certify that instruments work correctly. **2.** In Britain, a **justice of the peace** is a type of magistrate.

THE ABBREVIATION is **JP**.

justify *verb* (**justifies**, **justifying**, **justified**, **has justified**) To **justify** something is to try to defend it or show it to be right: *Can Bill justify taking the bike without asking?*
☐ **justifiable**, *adjective* –**justifiably**, *adverb* –**justification**, *noun*

jut *verb* (**juts**, **jutting**, **jutted**, **has jutted**) If something **juts** out, it sticks out: *Be careful of that branch jutting out across the path*; *The bed juts into the doorway.*

jute *noun* a strong fibre which is used for making rope or sacks.

WORD HISTORY from a Sanskrit word meaning 'a braid of hair'

juvenile /*say* **jooh**-vuh-nuyl/ *adjective*
1. having to do with, or for young people: *a juvenile court.* **2.** acting as if you are younger than you are: *juvenile behaviour*; *Don't be so juvenile!*
☐ **juvenile**, *noun*

☑ SPELLING TIP *Tricky 'uh' sound*: the middle vowel sound is spelt *e*. **Juvenile** comes from *juvenis*, the Latin word for 'a young person'.

juxta- *prefix* a word part meaning 'near' or 'close by', as in *juxtaposition*.

WORD HISTORY this prefix comes from Latin

juxtapose /*say* juks-tuh-**pohz**, **juks**-tuh-pohz/ *verb* If you **juxtapose** things, you place them close together: *Her painting was interesting because it juxtaposed several different shapes and colours.*
☐ **juxtaposition**, *noun*

kaftan *noun* See **caftan**.

kaleidoscope /*say* kuh-**luy**-duh-skohp/ *noun* a tube with mirrors and pieces of coloured glass in one end, which shows different patterns when it is turned around.
☐ **kaleidoscopic**, *adjective*

☑ SPELLING TIP This word has several difficult parts. Concentrate on the *ei* spelling for the 'uy' sound in the second syllable. Also notice that it ends with the suffix *-scope* which appears in the names of many instruments for seeing through, such as *telescope* and *microscope*.

kanga cricket *noun* a type of cricket for children that uses a softer ball and a plastic bat.

kangaroo *noun* an Australian animal with a small head, short front limbs, and a large tail and back legs for jumping. Kangaroos belong to a class of animals called marsupials.

WORD HISTORY from an Aboriginal language of Queensland called Guugu Yimidhirr

karaoke /*say* ka-ree-**oh**-kee/ *noun* singing along to a video and the background music of a song. The singer reads the words to the song displayed on a video screen.

☑ SPELLING TIP Remember that there is no *i* or *y* in this word. That sound is spelt by the second *a*. The word **karaoke** comes from two Japanese words – *kara* meaning 'absent' and *oke* meaning 'orchestra'. It might help to rap it out as *ka* + *ra* + *o* + *ke*.

karate /*say* kuh-**rah**-tee/ *noun* a Japanese form of self-defence which uses only hands, elbows, feet and knees as weapons.

☑ SPELLING TIP **Karate** comes from Japanese where it means 'empty hand'. Let the *e* for '*empty* remind you that **karate** ends with an *e* (where you might expect a *y* or *ie*).

karri *noun* a gum tree from western Australia with very hard long-lasting wood.

WORD HISTORY from an Aboriginal language of Western Australia called Nyungar

kauri /*say* **kow**-ree/ *noun* a tall New Zealand cone-bearing tree, which is valued for its wood and its resin.

WORD HISTORY from a Maori word

kayak /*say* **kuy**-ak/ *noun* a light canoe, like the skin-covered hunting canoe made by Inuit people.

☑ SPELLING TIP Remember the *ay* spelling for the 'uy' sound. This word has an unusual spelling because it comes from the Inuit language, but it has a pattern that will help you remember it: *y* in the middle, with *ka* before it and the reverse, *ak*, after it.

kebab *noun*
1. See **doner kebab**. **2.** See **shish kebab**.

keel *noun*
1. a long piece of wood or metal which stretches along the bottom of a ship, holding it together.
–*verb in the phrase* **2. keel over**, to turn over or upside down: *The tent keeled over in the strong winds.*

keen *adjective* To be **keen** is to be **1.** strong or intense in things like feelings or senses: *He has a keen interest in the social habits of mosquitoes*; *She has a keen eye for colour.* **2.** full of enthusiasm: *We were keen to start the game.* **3.** sharp: *a keen blade*; *a keen mind.*
–*phrase* **4. keen on**, liking a great deal: *She's very keen on this new rock group.*
☐ **keenly**, *adverb* –**keenness**, *noun*

keep *verb* (**keeps**, **keeping**, **kept**, **has kept**)
–*verb* **1.** If someone or something **keeps** in a particular state or place, they remain in that state or place: *to keep still*; *to keep healthy*; *to keep faith with someone.* **2.** If someone or something **keeps** an action going, they continue to do it: *They kept walking for hours*; *The wind kept blowing.* **3.** If you **keep** something, you do not give it away: *Our cat had kittens – we kept one and gave the rest away.* **4.** If you **keep** someone from doing something, or something from happening, you prevent them doing it or prevent it from happening: *We must fix the fence to keep the dog from getting out.* **5.** If you **keep** a promise or appointment, you carry out what you said you would, or you do what was arranged: *He kept his promise that he would take us to the beach.* **6.** If you own animals and look after them, you **keep** them: *We keep chooks.* **7.** If you **keep** a record of something, you write it down: *She kept a diary of her trip.* **8.** If food **keeps**, it remains good: *The butter and milk will keep in the fridge.*
–*noun in the phrase* **9. earn one's keep**, to make enough money to cover the cost of the

basic needs of living, like food and somewhere to live. **10. for keeps**, *Informal* permanently or forever: *We will be friends for keeps.*
–*verb in the phrase* **11. keep at**, to continue in: *Try to keep at your homework.* **12. keep on**, to continue or persist: *She kept on running in spite of the heat.* **13. keep to**, to follow or stick to: *to keep to an agreement*; *to keep to the truth.* **14. keep up**, to have an equal rate of speed or progress with another: *We are going to work quickly so you will have to concentrate if you want to keep up.*
☐ **keeper**, *noun*

keeping *noun*
1. care or possession: *He gave his pets into my keeping during his absence.*
–*phrase* **2. in keeping with**, suitable for: *The ornate furnishings were not in keeping with the simple home.*

keepsake *noun* something kept to remember a person or event by: *Her grandmother gave her a little silver clock for a keepsake.*

keg *noun* a barrel, especially for beer.

kelp *noun* large greenish-brown seaweed: *Lots of kelp was strewn on the beach.*

kelpie *noun* a breed of dog used on Australian farms for rounding up sheep and cattle.

kennel *noun* a house or shelter built for a dog.

kerb *noun* the line of stones or concrete at the edge of a street.

kernel *noun*
1. the inner part of a nut which you can eat. **2.** a grain, as of wheat or corn.

kerosene *noun* a liquid used as a fuel for lighting, heating and for engines.

THE SHORT FORM of this, used especially in informal language, is **kero**.

ketchup *noun* a sauce, usually made with tomatoes.

NOTE This word is used more in American English.

kettle *noun* a container with a spout, a lid and a handle, used for boiling water.

kettledrum *noun* a drum with a skin stretched over a brass or copper bowl.

key *noun*
1. a small, specially shaped piece of metal that can open a lock. **2.** something which helps you to read or understand such things as a map, a code, or a puzzle. **3.** one of the notes on a piano. **4.** the set of notes, starting and ending on one particular note, used to make up a piece of music: *This sonata is in the key of A minor.* **5.** one of a set of parts pressed in working a typewriter or computer terminal.
–*verb in the phrase* **6. key in**, to enter information into a computer by using a keyboard: *to key in the latest figures.*
☐ **key**, *adjective* main or important: *key information.*

keyboard *noun* a row or set of keys such as on a piano, typewriter or computer.

key card *noun*
1. See **cash card**. **2.** a card, usually made of plastic, which has a magnetic strip that enables you to open a door or operate machinery.

key signature *noun* the sharps or flats placed after the clef to show what key a piece of music is in.

COMPARE this with **time signature**.

khaki /*say* kah-**kee**, **kah**-kee/ *noun* a greenish-brown colour, used especially for soldiers' uniforms.
☐ **khaki**, *adjective*

☑ SPELLING TIP *Silent letter alert*: don't forget the *h*. Also remember the *i* ending. The spelling of **khaki** is unusual because it comes from Hindi.

kibbutz /*say* kib-**oots**/ *noun* (*plural* **kibbutzim** /*say* kib-**oot**-sim, kib-oot-**seem**/) an Israeli farming settlement whose management, work and products are shared.
☐ **kibbutznik**, *noun* someone who lives and works on a kibbutz.

WORD HISTORY from a Modern Hebrew word meaning 'gathering'

☑ SPELLING TIP *Double letter alert*: two *b*'s in the middle.

kick *verb*
1. When a person or animal **kicks**, they use their foot to hit out: *That horse kicks*; *to kick a ball.*
–*noun* **2.** a hit with the foot. **3.** *Informal* a feeling of pleasure or satisfaction: *Being congratulated by the principal gave our class a real kick.*
–*phrase* **4. kick on**, *Informal* to continue: *Will we kick on or is it time to stop?* **5. kick yourself**, to be annoyed with yourself: *We kicked ourselves for taking the wrong turn.*
☐ **kicker**, *noun* –**kicking**, *noun*

kid[1] *noun*
1. a young goat. **2.** *Informal* a child.

NOTE Although informal, definition 2 is used very widely.

kid[2] *verb* (**kids**, **kidding**, **kidded**, **has kidded**) To **kid** someone is to tease or trick them: *Laura was kidding when she said she had won the lottery.*

kidnap *verb* (**kidnaps**, **kidnapping**, **kidnapped**, **has kidnapped**) To **kidnap** someone is to take them away by force and hold them prisoner until money is paid, or some other condition is met.
☐ **kidnapper**, *noun*

kidney *noun* one of the two bean-shaped organs in the body which get rid of waste from the blood.

kikuyu /*say* kuy-**kooh**-yooh/ *noun* a tough grass which is used for lawns and pasture.

kill *verb*
1. When someone or something **kills** a person, animal or plant, they cause them to die: *Spiders kill insects for food*; *Fifty people were killed in the plane crash.* **2.** To **kill** something is to destroy it or end it: *The storm killed any ideas about a game of cricket.*
–*phrase* **3. kill time**, to occupy yourself with something to make time pass.
☐ **kill**, *noun* –**killer**, *noun* –**killing**, *noun*

SIMILAR WORDS (for definition 1) are **murder**, **assassinate**, **slaughter** and **massacre**. Note that to **murder** is to kill someone deliberately. To **assassinate** is to murder an important person, often for political reasons. To **slaughter** or to **massacre** is to kill a large number of people. **Slaughter** can also mean 'to kill animals for their meat'.

kill switch *noun* a switch which shuts down a device, machine, etc., instantly, without going through the normal procedures for shutting down.

kiln *noun* a big oven or furnace for baking bricks or pottery.

kilo /*say* **kee**-loh/ *noun* (*plural* **kilos**) See **kilogram**.

kilo- *prefix* a word part meaning 10^3 of a given unit, as in *kilogram*, *kilometre*.

WORD HISTORY this prefix comes from Greek

kilobyte /*say* **kil**-uh-buyt/ *noun* a unit for measuring information stored by a computer, equal to 1024 bytes.

kilogram /*say* **kil**-uh-gram/ *noun* a measure of weight in the metric system equal to 1000 grams.

THE SYMBOL for this is **kg**.
THE SHORT FORM of this is **kilo**. It is a little more informal.

☑ SPELLING TIP *Tricky 'uh' sound*: the middle vowel sound is spelt *o*. Learn the prefix *kilo-* (which means 'thousand') and you will be able to spell not only **kilogram** but other words which include it, such as *kilometre*.

kilojoule /*say* **kil**-uh-joohl/ *noun* a metric measure of work or energy equal to 1000 joules or the amount of food needed to produce it.

THE SYMBOL for this is **kJ**.

kilometre /*say* **kil**-uh-mee-tuh, kuh-**lom**-uh-tuh/ *noun* a measure of length in the metric system equal to 1000 metres.

THE SYMBOL for this is **km**.

kilowatt /*say* **kil**-uh-wot/ *noun* 1000 watts.

THE SYMBOL for this is **kW**.

kilt *noun* a short, pleated skirt of tartan cloth, sometimes worn by men from the Scottish Highlands.

kimono /*say* **kim**-uh-noh, kuh-**moh**-noh/ *noun* a wide-sleeved Japanese piece of clothing which is tied at the waist.

kin *noun* your relatives: *All of my kin are coming to stay.*
☐ **kin**, *adjective*

kind[1] *adjective* friendly and wanting to help people.
☐ **kindly**, *adverb* –**kindness**, *noun*

kind[2] *noun*
1. a type or sort: *What kind of animal is that?*; *Fighting in the playground is the kind of behaviour that gets us into trouble.*
–*phrase* **2. a kind of** (**something**), something like the thing named but not quite exact: *They used the shed as a kind of house.*

kindergarten /*say* **kin**-duh-gah-tuhn/ *noun* a school or class for very young children which prepares them for primary school.

☑ SPELLING TIP *Tricky 'uh' sound*: the middle vowel sound is spelt *er*. This is because this part of the word is *kinder*, the German word for 'children' (in German *er* makes the plural of some words). Added to it is *garten*, the German word for 'garden'. Don't get confused and put a *d* in place of the *t*.

kindle *verb*
1. If somebody or something **kindles** a fire, they start it burning: *Sparks blown from the fire kindled the dry bush and started a bushfire.* **2.** When something causes a feeling, you say it **kindles** it: *Seeing a falling star one night kindled our interest in astronomy.*

kindling *noun* the twigs and other material used to start a fire.

kinetic /*say* kuh-**net**-ik/ *adjective* having to do with movement.

king *noun*
1. a man, from a royal family, who rules over a country or empire. **2.** someone who is powerful or important: *a media king*; *He is a king among men.* **3.** a playing card with a picture of a king on it. **4.** the chess piece whose capture ends the game.
☐ **kingly**, *adjective* –**king-size**, *adjective*

ANOTHER FORM This word (as in definition 1) is spelt with a capital letter when you are writing the title of a particular person.

kingdom *noun*
1. a country or government ruled over by a king or queen. **2.** a division of nature, especially one of

the three great divisions of natural objects, animal, vegetable or mineral.

kingfisher *noun* a bird with a strong beak which eats reptiles, insects and small fish which they catch by diving.

kink *noun*
1. a wrinkle or fault. **2.** an unusual taste or desire.
☐ **kinky**, *adjective* (**kinkier**, **kinkiest**)

kinship *noun* relationship by family or other ties: *Caroline felt a sense of kinship with them*; *Different cultures have different systems of kinship.*

kinship name *noun* See **skin name**.

kiosk */say* **kee**-osk/ *noun* a small shop or stall which sells such things as newspapers, cigarettes and small items of food.

> ☑ SPELLING TIP The most difficult part is the *ki* opening (giving a 'kee' sound). This word is unusual because it comes from a Turkish word meaning 'pavilion'.

kipper *noun* a dried fish, usually herring or salmon, which has been salted and smoked.

kiss *verb* If you **kiss** someone or something, you touch or press them with your lips, as a sign of greeting, affection, and so on.
☐ **kiss**, *noun*

kit *noun*
1. a set of tools, supplies or parts for a special purpose: *a medical kit*; *a repair kit.* **2.** a set of parts to be put together: *a kit to build a classic model train.*

kitchen *noun* the room or place where food is cooked and prepared.

kite *noun*
1. a light frame covered by a thin material, which is flown in the wind at the end of a long string. **2.** a medium-sized hawk with long wings and tail.

kitten *noun* a young cat.

kiwi *noun*
1. a New Zealand bird with thick legs and a long thin bill, which cannot fly. **2.** *Informal* a person from New Zealand.

> ANOTHER FORM This word (as in definition 2) is also spelt with a capital letter.

kiwifruit *noun* a small, oval, hairy fruit with green flesh.

> ANOTHER FORM is **Kiwi fruit**.

kleptomaniac */say* klep-tuh-**may**-nee-ak/ *noun* a person with an uncontrollable urge to steal things.
☐ **kleptomania**, *noun*

knack */say* nak/ *noun* the skill for doing a particular thing.

> ☑ SPELLING TIP *Silent letter alert*: don't forget the *k* at the start. You will notice that it ends with a *k* too, as part of the common *ck* combination for a 'k' sound.

knapsack */say* **nap**-sak/ *noun Old-fashioned* a backpack.

knave */say* nayv/ *noun*
1. *Old-fashioned* a dishonest man or boy. **2.** See **jack** (definition 2).
☐ **knavish**, *adjective* –**knavishly**, *adverb*

> ☑ SPELLING TIP Don't confuse the spelling of **knave** with **nave** which sounds the same. Remember the silent *k* at the start of **knave**. A **nave** is part of a church.

knead */say* need/ *verb* To **knead** dough is to press and fold it with your hands.

> ☑ SPELLING TIP Don't confuse the spelling of **knead** with **need** which has the same sound. To **need** something is to want it urgently.

knee */say* nee/ *noun* the joint between your upper and lower leg.

kneecap *noun* the flat movable bone which covers the knee joint.

kneel */say* neel/ *verb* (**kneels**, **kneeling**, **knelt** *or* **kneeled**, **has knelt** *or* **has kneeled**) To **kneel** is to go down on your knees.

knell */say* nel/ *noun* a slow bell ringing for a death or funeral.

knickerbockers */say* **nik**-uh-bok-uhz/ *plural noun* loose short trousers which are gathered in at the knees.

> WORD HISTORY named after Diedrich *Knickerbocker*, the imaginary author of Washington Irving's book *The History of New York* which had illustrations of people wearing loose pants like the ones Dutch people wore in about 1800

knickers */say* **nik**-uhz/ *plural noun* underpants, usually for women.

knick-knack */say* **nik**-nak/ *noun* a small ornament.

knife */say* nuyf/ *noun* (*plural* **knives**)
1. a tool with a sharp blade for cutting.
–*verb* (**knifes**, **knifing**, **knifed**, **has knifed**) **2.** If somebody **knifes** another person, they stab them with a knife.

knight */say* nuyt/ *noun*
1. in medieval times, a man of noble birth who promised to serve and fight for a king. **2.** an honour given by a king or queen to a man for service to his country. He then uses the title 'Sir'. **3.** a chess piece shaped like a horse's head.
–*verb* **4.** If a king or queen **knights** a man, they give him that honorary title for service to the

country: *He was knighted for his service in the war.*
☐ **knighthood**, *noun* –**knightly**, *adjective*

☑ SPELLING TIP Don't confuse **knight** with **night**, the time of darkness, which has the same sound. Remember that **knight** starts with a silent *k*.

knit /*say* nit/ *verb* (**knits**, **knitting**, **knitted**, **has knitted**)
1. If you **knit**, you make something to wear out of wool using long needles or a special machine. **2.** If someone or something **knits**, they join or become closely joined: *The plaster cast must stay on your leg till the bones knit*; *The tragedy had knitted the family more closely together.*
☐ **knitter**, *noun* –**knitting**, *noun*

☑ SPELLING TIP Don't confuse **knit** with **nit** which has the same sound. A **nit** is the egg or young of an insect, such as a louse, living in human hair. Remember that **knit** starts with a silent *k*.

knob /*say* nob/ *noun*
1. a round handle such as on a drawer or door. **2.** a rounded lump: *a knob of plasticine.*
☐ **knobby**, *adjective* –**knobbly**, *adjective*

knock /*say* nok/ *verb*
1. If someone or something **knocks** on a door or window, they tap it to let people inside know they are there: *You must knock before you enter.* **2.** If you **knock** something, you bump it: *She accidentally knocked the vase and spilt the water.* **3.** *Informal* If you **knock** someone or something, you criticise or find fault with them: *Why do you always knock my ideas?*
–*phrase* **4. knock off**, *Informal* **a.** to stop an activity, especially work: *to knock off at 5 o'clock.* **b.** to steal: *to knock off some lollies.* **5. knock someone out**, to hit someone so hard that they lose consciousness. **6. knock up**, **a.** to put together quickly or roughly: *to knock up a model of the building.* **b.** to score: *to knock up points.*
☐ **knock**, *noun*

knockout *noun*
1. the act of knocking someone unconscious. **2.** *Informal* something or someone who is extremely attractive or successful.

knot /*say* not/ *noun*
1. a piece of something like thread or string tied tightly into a lump or knob, or two pieces tied together in the same way. **2.** a fault or join in the grain of wood. **3.** a measure of speed, used especially for ships, equal to about 1.85 kilometres an hour.
–*verb* (**knots**, **knotting**, **knotted**, **has knotted**)
4. If you **knot** something like thread or string, you tie it in a knot.
☐ **knotty**, *adjective*

☑ SPELLING TIP Don't confuse **knot** with **not** which has the same sound. Remember that **knot** starts with a silent *k*.

know /*say* noh/ *verb* (**knows**, **knowing**, **knew**, **has known**)
1. If you **know** something, you understand it to be true or a fact. You are certain in your mind about it: *He knew that the dog had been there when he left.* **2.** If you **know** something, you have learned it and can do it: *I know how to cook.* **3.** If you **know** a person or a place, you are familiar with them.
–*noun in the phrase* **4. in the know**, having inside knowledge.
☐ **known**, *adjective*: *a known fact.*

☑ SPELLING TIP Don't confuse the spelling of **know** with **no**, or the spelling of **knew** with **new** which has the same sound. Remember that **know** and its various forms start with a silent *k*.

know-all *noun Informal* someone who thinks or says they know everything about a particular subject.

knowledge /*say* **nol**-ij/ *noun* what is or can be known: *His knowledge about working with timber is amazing*; *The tribe survived the drought through their knowledge of waterholes in the area.*
☐ **knowledgeable**, *adjective*

knuckle /*say* **nuk**-uhl/ *noun* a finger joint, especially the bottom joint where the finger meets the rest of the hand.

koala /*say* koh-**ah**-luh/ *noun* a furry, grey, Australian animal without a tail, which lives and feeds in certain types of gum trees. Koalas belong to a class of animals called marsupials.

WORD HISTORY from an Aboriginal language of New South Wales called Dharug

komodo dragon *noun* a very big lizard of the island of Komodo in Indonesia.

kookaburra *noun* an Australian bird of the kingfisher family whose call sounds like human laughter.

WORD HISTORY **Kookaburra** comes from an Aboriginal language of New South Wales called Wiradjuri

☑ SPELLING TIP *Double letter alert*: two *o*'s and two *r*'s. There are also two separate *k*'s in **kookaburra** but no *c*. It may help to remember that **kookaburras** belong to the kingfisher family.

Koori /*say* **koo**-ree/ *noun* an Aboriginal person from New South Wales or Victoria.
☐ **Koori**, *adjective*: *Koori art.*

ANOTHER SPELLING is **Koorie**.
WORD HISTORY from an Aboriginal language of New South Wales called Awabakal

Koran /*say* kaw-**rahn**, kuh-**rahn**/ *noun* the holy book of Islam, which Muslims believe came directly from Allah through the prophet Mohammed.

ANOTHER SPELLING is **Qur'an**.
WORD HISTORY from an Arabic word meaning 'reading' or 'recitation'

kosher /*say* **koh**-shuh, **ko**-shuh/ *adjective* prepared according to the special food rules of the Jewish religion: *kosher sausages.*

WORD HISTORY this word comes from Hebrew

kowari /*say* kuh-**wah**-ree/ *noun* a small, yellow-brown animal with a black bushy tail that lives in the Australian desert. It is endangered.

WORD HISTORY from an Aboriginal language of South Australia called Diyari

kowtow *verb* To **kowtow** is to **1.** kneel touching the forehead to the ground in respect or worship. **2.** try very hard to please, especially in an over-eager way: *Everyone kowtowed to the leader of the group except Fred.*

WORD HISTORY from a Chinese word meaning 'knock the head'

☑ SPELLING TIP If you remember that *ow* appears twice in this word, you will have no trouble with the spelling. Just add *k* before the first one, and *t* before the second. This word is unusual because it comes from a Chinese word meaning 'knock-head'.

kudos /*say* **kyooh**-dos/ *noun* good reputation or fame: *Andrew got all the kudos from the team winning the game because he scored the last goal.*

kumquat /*say* **kum**-kwot/ *noun* See **cumquat**.

kung-fu /*say* koong-**fooh**, kung-**fooh**/ *noun* a Chinese form of karate.

kurrajong *noun* a flowering tree of eastern Australia whose bark was traditionally used by Aboriginal people to make fishing line and fishing nets.

WORD HISTORY from an Aboriginal language of New South Wales called Dharug

kylie /*say* **kuy**-lee/ *noun* a boomerang with one side flat and the other curved.

WORD HISTORY from an Aboriginal language of Western Australia called Nyungar

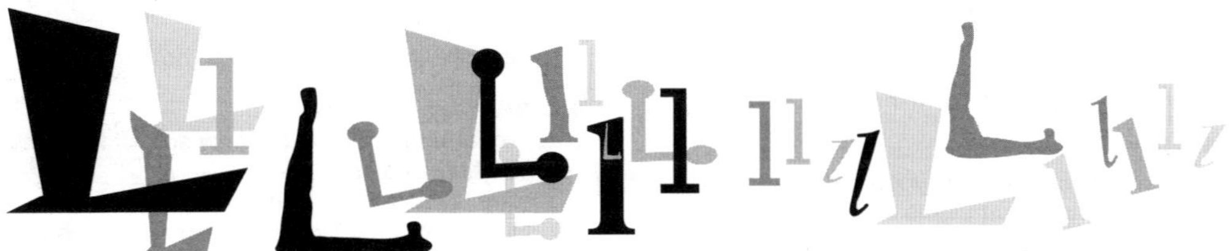

label *noun*
1. a piece of paper or material put on something to show what it is, who owns it, or where it is going: *We put a label on our work so the teacher would know who did it.*
–*verb* (**labels**, **labelling**, **labelled**, **has labelled**)
2. If you **label** something, you put a label on it to show what it is, who owns it, or where it is going.

☑ SPELLING TIP Remember that the ending of **label** is spelt *el* (not *le*). The more common ending is *le* but there are a lot of *el* words, such as *angel*, *camel* and *kennel*. Also remember that the single *l* at the end is doubled when you add *-ed* or *-ing*.

laboratory /*say* luh-**bo**-ruh-tree/ *noun* (*plural* **laboratories**) a building or room for doing scientific tests or for making chemicals or medicines.

☑ SPELLING TIP The original meaning of **laboratory** was a workshop. This might help you remember that the first part of the word is spelt *labor* (a form of the word *labour* meaning 'work'). Also remember that the ending is *ory* although the *or* is not pronounced.

laborious /*say* luh-**baw**-ree-uhs/ *adjective* needing a lot of effort: *a laborious climb.*
☐ **laboriously**, *adverb*

labour *noun*
1. hard or tiring work: *Nobody likes the labour involved in digging clay soil.* **2.** people who are employed to do such work, especially when organised into trade unions: *Labour and management are meeting for talks today.* **3.** the process of giving birth to a baby, during which the baby gradually is pushed out from its mother's body: *My mother was in labour for eight hours before she gave birth to me.*
–*verb* **4.** If a person **labours**, they work very hard at some job or task.
☐ **labourer**, *noun*

ANOTHER SPELLING is **labor**.

labrador *noun* a kind of large dog with short golden or black hair.

WORD HISTORY named after *Labrador*, a peninsula in Canada, where the breed first came from

labyrinth /*say* **lab**-uh-rinth/ *noun* a twisting set of passages in which it is hard to find your way.

A SIMILAR WORD is **maze**.

☑ SPELLING TIP *Tricky 'uh' sound*: the middle vowel sound is spelt with a *y*! As with many other words with a difficult *y* spelling, **labyrinth** comes from Greek. In ancient Greek legend, there was one particular Labyrinth, a maze inhabited by a monster called the Minotaur.

lace *noun*
1. a material with a fine, net-like design of threads: *She wore a lace veil.* **2.** a cord for pulling and holding something together: *My little brother still can't tie up his shoe laces.*
–*verb* **3.** To **lace** your shoes is to fasten them around your feet by tying the laces.
☐ **lacy**, *adjective* (**lacier**, **laciest**)

lacerate /*say* **las**-uh-rayt/ *verb* If something **lacerates** you, it tears you roughly or cuts you: *My leg was lacerated on the reef.*
☐ **lacerated**, *adjective* –**laceration**, *noun*

☑ SPELLING TIP Remember the *c* spelling for the 's' sound in this word.

lack *noun*
1. a shortage or absence of something you need or want: *My grandmother showed a total lack of interest in my tadpoles*; *A lack of money means we can't have a holiday this year.*
–*verb* **2.** To **lack** something is to be without it: *He lacks the knowledge to use the computer properly.*
☐ **lacking**, *adjective*

laconic /*say* luh-**kon**-ik/ *adjective* using few words: *He was moody and gave only laconic replies.*
☐ **laconically**, *adverb*

lacquer /*say* **lak**-uh/ *noun*
1. a clear coating put on something to protect it or to make it shiny.
–*verb* **2.** If you **lacquer** something, such as a piece of furniture, you cover it with a substance to protect it or make it shiny.
☐ **lacquered**, *adjective*

☑ SPELLING TIP Remember that the 'k' sound in the middle is spelt by *c* followed by *qu*, not *ck* as you might think. Also notice the *er* ending.

lactate *verb* If a female animal or human **lactates**, they produce milk for a baby.
☐ **lactation**, *noun*

WORD HISTORY from a Latin word meaning 'to give milk'

lad *noun* a boy or young man.

ladder *noun*
1. a structure made of wood, metal or rope, with rungs or steps you use to climb up or down. **2.** a line in a stocking or pair of tights where the stitches have come undone.

ladle *noun*
1. a cup-shaped spoon with a long handle, used for serving liquids.
–*verb* **2.** If you **ladle** a liquid, you use a ladle to serve it from its container: *The soup was dripping as she ladled it into the bowls.*

lady *noun* (*plural* **ladies**)
1. a woman. **2.** a woman who is polished in appearance and manners: *My father told my sister to act more like a lady.*

NOTE **Lady**, as in definition 1, is a polite way of referring to a woman, as in *Ladies and gentlemen, could I have your attention please* or *Could you please tell the lady over there that it is her turn now.* Some older people think that this is the best and most polite way to refer to a woman on all occasions. However, the usual word is **woman** and most women now prefer this.

ladybird *noun* a small winged beetle, usually with an orange back spotted with black.

lag /lag/ *verb* (**lags**, **lagging**, **lagged**, **has lagged**)
If someone or something **lags**, they fail to keep up with others: *The lame horse was lagging behind.*

lager /*say* **lah**-guh/ *noun* a kind of beer.

lagoon *noun* a pool of shallow water, often separated from the sea by low banks of sand.

lair *noun* the home or shelter of a wild animal.

lake *noun* a large area of water surrounded by land.

laksa *noun* a food consisting of fine, spicy rice noodles, vegetables, meat, etc., served in a soup, originating in Malaysian cooking.

lama /*rhymes with* farmer/ *noun* a Buddhist priest or monk.

☑ SPELLING TIP Don't confuse this with **llama** which has the same sound, but starts with a double *l*. A **llama** is a kind of animal.

WORD HISTORY from a Tibetan word

lamb *noun* a young sheep or its meat.

☑ SPELLING TIP *Silent letter alert*: don't forget the silent *b* at the end.

lame *adjective*
1. If a person or animal is **lame**, they have something wrong with their foot or leg that causes them to walk unevenly. **2.** A **lame** excuse is a weak or poor one.
☐ **lamely**, *adverb* –**lameness**, *noun*

lament /*say* luh-**ment**/ *verb*
1. To **lament** is to feel or show sorrow for someone who has died.
–*noun* **2.** a poem or song expressing sorrow.
☐ **lamentable**, *adjective* –**lamentation**, *noun*

laminate *verb*
1. If a material is **laminated**, it is separated or split into thin sheets or layers. **2.** If you **laminate** something, you cover it with a thin layer of some material.
☐ **laminate**, *adjective* –**laminated**, *adjective* –**lamination**, *noun*

lamington *noun* a square of sponge cake covered with chocolate icing and grated coconut.

WORD HISTORY thought to be named after Baron *Lamington*, governor of Queensland 1895–1901

lamp *noun* a kind of light, often one which you can move or carry around: *There was a lamp beside the bed.*

lance *noun*
1. a long spear once used as a weapon by soldiers on horses.
–*verb* **2.** To **lance** an infected sore is to cut it open with a sharp instrument: *The doctor lanced the patient's boil and put antiseptic on it.*

land *noun*
1. the part of the earth's surface not covered by water. **2.** a particular area of ground: *The land the school owns extends to the river.* **3.** a country or nation: *a land of sweeping plains.*
–*verb* **4.** To **land** is to arrive at the land or shore. **5.** To **land** is to come to rest in any place or position: *The kite landed in the pond.* **6.** *Rather informal* To **land** something is to gain or obtain it: *She landed an A for her maths test.*
–*phrase* **7. land on your feet**, to be successful in a situation which might have gone badly.

land claim *noun*
1. a claim for ownership of land. **2.** a claim by an Aboriginal community for ownership of land under native title.

landing *noun*
1. the act of landing: *The skydiver got ready for landing by opening his parachute.* **2.** the area at the top or bottom of a flight of stairs: *On the landing was a suitcase to be carried down.* **3.** the end of an aeroplane's journey: *On landing, the plane taxied slowly over the tarmac.*

landline *noun* a telephone that receives signals from another telephone through cables under or above the ground, rather than through the air as a mobile phone does.

landlord *noun* someone who owns and rents out land, houses, flats or rooms.

NOTE The term **landlord** used to refer to a man, but now can refer to either a man or a woman. For a woman you can also use the term **landlady**.

landlubber *noun* someone who is not used to boats or sailing.

WORD HISTORY from *land* and *lubber* (a word used in some parts of Britain to mean 'a clumsy person')

landmark *noun*
1. something on land that is easily seen and is used as a sign to travellers: *The lighthouse on the hill is a landmark in the area.* **2.** an event that stands out as important: *The Eureka rebellion was a landmark in Australian history.*

landscape *noun*
1. what you see when you look across the land: *The landscape is very flat around here.* **2.** a painting or photograph of an area of land.
–*verb* **3.** If someone **landscapes** an area of land, they design and create an attractive park or garden.

landslide *noun*
1. the sliding down of a mass of rocks and soil from a steep slope. **2.** an easy win in an election: *The government was re-elected in a landslide.*

lane *noun*
1. a narrow passage or road between fences, walls or houses. **2.** a strip of road marked out for a single line of vehicles. **3.** a strip marked out on a running track or swimming pool for one runner or swimmer in a race. **4.** the narrow alley on which the ball is bowled in tenpin bowling.

language /*say* **lang**-gwij/ *noun*
1. the arrangement of words we use when we speak and write. **2.** any set of signs or symbols used to pass on information: *We made up a secret language to communicate with*; *various computer languages.* **3.** the language of a particular country or group of people: *Because she was born near the border of France and Germany, she speaks both languages.*

☑ SPELLING TIP The *gu* spelling for the 'gw' sound in the middle is the tricky bit here. It might help if you remember that **language** comes from *langue* (the French word for 'tongue' or 'language'). The *e* had been dropped and the noun suffix *-age* added. The French word comes from the earlier Latin word *lingua* which explains the spelling of words related to language such as *linguistics*.

languid /*say* **lang**-gwuhd/ *adjective* If someone or something moves or acts in a **languid** way, they appear weak, tired or slow-moving: *She spoke in a languid voice*; *We spent a languid afternoon on the beach.*
☐ **languidly**, *adverb*

languish /*say* **lang**-gwish/ *verb* If someone or something **languishes**, they remain in an unpleasant or unwanted situation: *He was left to languish in jail.*

lank *adjective* Hair that is **lank** is straight and lifeless.
☐ **lankness**, *noun*

lanky *adjective* (**lankier**, **lankiest**) Someone who is **lanky** is tall and thin, often in a rather awkward way.
☐ **lankiness**, *noun*

lantana /*say* lan-**tah**-nuh/ *noun* a plant with yellow or orange flowers, which has become an annoying weed in warm, wet parts of Australia.

lantern *noun* an enclosed light, protected from wind and rain, especially one that can be carried around.

lap[1] *noun* the front of your body from your waist to your knees, when you are sitting down: *The soup spilt onto her lap.*

lap[2] *noun*
1. a single round of a racing track or a single length of a swimming pool.
–*verb* (**laps**, **lapping**, **lapped**, **has lapped**) **2.** If you **lap** a competitor in a race, you pass them when they are one lap behind you.

lap[3] *verb* (**laps**, **lapping**, **lapped**, **has lapped**)
1. When water **laps**, it hits something in small, gentle waves: *The sea was lapping against the pier.* **2.** When an animal **laps**, it uses its tongue to drink: *The cat greedily lapped up the milk.*

lapel /*say* luh-**pel**/ *noun* the part of a coat collar that is folded back over your chest.

☑ SPELLING TIP *Single letter alert*: only one *p* and one *l*.

lapse *noun*
1. a failure in the working of or the supply of something: *There was a major lapse in protocol at the opening of the match when the wrong national anthem was sung.* **2.** the passing of time: *After a short lapse, the radio transmission came on again.*
–*verb* **3.** To **lapse** is to pass slowly or gradually into a particular state: *Andy lapsed into a long silence.*

laptop *noun* a very small computer that can be carried around.

larceny /*say* **lah**-suh-nee/ *noun* (*plural* **larcenies**) the stealing of someone else's goods.
☐ **larcenous**, *adjective*

lard *noun* pig fat melted down for use in cooking.

larder *noun Old-fashioned* a room or cupboard where food is kept.

A SIMILAR WORD which is still in use is **pantry**.

large *adjective*
1. being of more than usual size, amount or range: *I'm hoping for a very large present.*
–*phrase* **2. at large, a.** free: *Unfortunately, the prisoner has escaped and is now at large.* **b.** as a whole: *The community at large would benefit by cutting down on water consumption.*
☐ **largely**, *adverb* mainly: *The success of the party was largely due to your efforts.* –**largeness**, *noun*

THE OPPOSITE (of definition 1) is **small**.

lark[1] *noun* a kind of bird that lives in northern areas of the world and is known for its singing while flying.

lark[2] *noun Informal* something done for fun or as a joke: *We put toothpaste on her chair as a lark.*

larrikin /*say* **la**-ruh-kuhn/ *noun* someone, usually young, who behaves in a noisy, wild way.
☐ **larrikinism**, *noun*

☑ SPELLING TIP *Tricky 'uh' sound*: the vowel sound in the middle is spelt *i*. Also remember the double *r*.

larva /*say* **lah**-vuh/ *noun* (*plural* **larvae** /*say* **lah**-vee/) the young of any insect which changes the form of its body before becoming an adult: *the larvae of bees.*
☐ **larval**, *adjective*

WORD HISTORY from a Latin word meaning 'ghost', 'skeleton' or 'mask'.

☑ SPELLING TIP Don't confuse the spelling of **larva** with **lava** which sounds the same. **Lava** is hot, melted rock from a volcano.

laryngitis /*say* la-ruhn-**juy**-tuhs/ *noun* a soreness and swelling in the larynx that often makes you lose your voice for a while.

☑ SPELLING TIP If you know the spelling of *larynx* (see the next entry), you will only need to remember to change the *x* to a *g* and add the suffix *-itis*. This suffix (*itis*) is used in many medical words referring to an inflammation, such as *tonsillitis* and *appendicitis*.

larynx /*say* **la**-rinks/ *noun* (*plural* **larynges** /*say* luh-**rin**-jeez/ *or* **larynxes**) the box-like space at the top of the windpipe that contains the vocal cords which are used for speaking.
☐ **laryngeal** /*say* la-ruhn-**jee**-uhl/, *adjective*

ANOTHER TERM for this is **voice box**. This is a less scientific term.

☑ SPELLING TIP Remember that two letters from the very end of the alphabet are involved here – *y* in the middle of the word (giving an 'i' sound) and *x* at the end. The word **larynx** comes from Greek.

lasagne /*say* luh-**sahn**-yuh/ *noun*
1. a type of pasta cut into rectangular sheets. **2.** a food made with this, often with mince meat, tomato and cheese between layers of the pasta.

☑ SPELLING TIP *Silent letter alert*: don't forget the *g* before the *n*. Because this word comes from Italian, you don't hear the *g* but it makes the *n* sound as if it has a *y* following it. So, although you hear the last part of the word as 'ahnyuh', remember that the spelling is *agne*.

laser /*say* **lay**-zuh/ *noun* a device which produces a very narrow beam of intense light.

WORD HISTORY an acronym made by joining the first letters of the words *light amplification* by *stimulated emission* of *radiation*

lash *noun*
1. the cord part of a whip. **2.** a blow with a whip or something similar: *The prisoner received ten lashes.* **3.** See **eyelash**.
–*verb* **4.** If you **lash** someone or something, you strike them with a whip or something similar. **5.** If you **lash** things, you tie them up with a rope or cord.

lass *noun Old-fashioned* a girl or young woman.

lasso /*say* las-**ooh**/ *noun* (*plural* **lassos** *or* **lassoes**)
1. a long rope with a loop at one end which tightens when pulled, used to catch horses and other animals.
–*verb* (**lassoes**, **lassoing**, **lassoed**, **has lassoed**) **2.** To **lasso** an animal is to catch it with a lasso.

☑ SPELLING TIP *Single letter alert*: the ending is the difficult bit – just a single *o* for the 'ooh' sound.

last[1] *adjective*
1. coming after everything else in time, order or place. **2.** the latest or the most recent: *last Easter.*
–*adverb* **3.** after all the others: *Last in the procession came the brass band.*
–*noun* **4.** something or someone that is at the end: *Who was the last out of the pool?*
–*phrase* **5. at last**, finally, or after a long time: *At last the pups were born.*
☐ **lastly**, *adverb*

last[2] *verb* If something **lasts**, it goes on or continues: *The speeches seemed to last for a long time.*
☐ **lasting**, *adjective*

latch *noun* (*plural* **latches**)
1. a bar which slides or falls into a slot, used to keep a door or gate closed.
–*verb* **2.** To **latch** something is to close or fasten it with a latch.
–*phrase* **3. latch on to**, *Informal* to understand: *Once you latch onto computers, they seem easy.*

late *adjective* (**later**, **latest**)
1. coming or continuing after the usual or proper time: *The carnival got off to a late start because of the storm.* **2.** far advanced in time: *They didn't*

turn up until the late afternoon. **3.** recently dead: *the late Mrs Patel.*
–*adverb* **4.** after the usual or proper time: *We mustn't be late.*
–*phrase* **5. of late**, recently: *The temperatures have been extremely hot of late.*
☐ **lately**, *adverb*: *The car's been running better lately.* –**lateness**, *noun*

latent *adjective* present but not active or able to be seen: *a latent problem*; *Who knows what latent talents you might have!*
☐ **latency**, *noun*

A SIMILAR WORD is **dormant**.

lateral *adjective* of or having to do with the side: *vertical and lateral movement.*
☐ **laterally**, *adverb*

lathe /*say* laydh/ *noun* a machine which holds and turns a piece of wood or metal while it is being cut or shaped.

lather /*rhymes with* gather/ *noun*
1. a mass of bubbles made from soap and water. **2.** froth caused by heavy sweating: *The horse was in a lather from running so far.*
–*verb* **3.** If soap **lathers**, it forms a foam or froth when it is wet with water. **4.** If you **lather** yourself, you rub your body with soap and water until they form a lather.

latitude *noun* the distance, measured in degrees, by which a point on the earth is north or south of the equator.
☐ **latitudinal**, *adjective*

COMPARE this with **longitude**.

☑ SPELLING TIP *Single letter alert*: there is no double *t* in this word – each of the two times the letter appears it is single.

latter *adjective*
1. You use **latter** to refer to the second of two things mentioned: *He spoke about drugs in sport and about sporting heroes, but more about the latter topic.*
–*noun* **2. the latter**, the last of two people or things that you mention: *If I had to eat either prunes or prawns, I would choose the latter.*

THE OPPOSITE (of definition 1) is **former**; the opposite (of definition 2) is **the former**.

lattice /*say* **lat**-uhs/ *noun* a frame made of crossed wooden or metal strips with diamond-shaped spaces in between, used as a screen or as a support for plants.

laugh /*say* lahf/ *verb*
1. If you **laugh** you make the sounds that show amusement, happiness, or scorn.
–*phrase* **2. laugh off**, to treat lightly or with scorn: *You can't just laugh off these matters.*
☐ **laugh**, *noun* –**laughable**, *adjective* –**laughably**, *adverb* –**laughter**, *noun*

SIMILAR WORDS (for definition 1) are **chuckle**, **chortle**, **cackle**, **giggle**, **titter**, **snigger** and **guffaw**. All these words refer to different kinds of laughter. To **chuckle** or **chortle** is to laugh in a quiet, amused way, especially when you are thinking privately about something funny or are feeling satisfied. To **cackle** is to laugh with a harsh, broken sound, a bit like a hen makes when laying an egg. To **giggle** is to laugh repeatedly in a quiet way that can sound a bit silly or annoying, either from amusement or from shyness or nervousness. To **titter** or **snigger** is to laugh in a quiet and half covered-up way, especially in an unkind way because you are making fun of somebody: *She tripped as she reached the stage and some people in the audience tittered.* To **guffaw** is to laugh loudly and suddenly at something that is very funny. There are many expressions with a similar meaning, such as **burst into laughter**, **collapse with laughter**, **dissolve into laughter** and **roar with laughter**. Expressions meaning to keep on laughing, sometimes even when you don't want to, include **have hysterics**, **have the giggles**, **have a fit of the giggles** and **not be able to keep a straight face**.

launch[1] /*say* lawnch/ *noun* (*plural* **launches**) a strong open boat, usually with a motor.

WORD HISTORY from the Portuguese word for 'an open boat'

☑ SPELLING TIP *Tricky vowel sound*: *au* for the 'aw' sound.

launch[2] /*say* lawnch/ *verb* To **launch** something is to **1.** send it into the water: *He launched the boat from off the trailer.* **2.** send it up into the air: *to launch a spacecraft.* **3.** set it going or start it: *The election campaign will be launched after the Christmas break.*
☐ **launch**, *noun* (*plural* **launches**): *a missile launch.* –**launcher**, *noun*

WORD HISTORY from the French word for 'a lance'

☑ SPELLING TIP See **launch**[1].

laundromat *noun* a public laundry with washing machines and dryers which you operate by putting coins in the slot of each machine.

WORD HISTORY began as a trademark in the United States

laundry /*say* **lawn**-dree/ *noun*
1. clothes that are ready to be washed or have been washed. **2.** a business where people pay to have their clothes washed. **3.** a room in a house for washing clothes.
☐ **launder**, *verb*: *He laundered his shirt and hung it up.*

☑ SPELLING TIP *Tricky vowel sound*: *au* for the 'aw' sound. You will notice that the last three letters spell the word *dry* – very suitable for a **laundry**!

laurel /*say* **lo**-ruhl/ *noun*
1. a small evergreen tree with leaves that are used as a herb in cooking. **2.** the leaves of this tree made into a wreath, used as a sign of victory. –*phrase* **3. rest on your laurels**, to be happy with what you have already done and not want to try for any more achievements.

☑ SPELLING TIP *Tricky vowel sound*: *au* spelling for the 'o' sound in the first syllable. Also remember the *el* ending.

lava /*say* **lah**-vuh/ *noun*
1. the hot liquid rock which comes out of a volcano. **2.** the hard rock formed when this becomes cool and solid.

☑ SPELLING TIP Don't confuse the spelling of **lava** with **larva** which sounds the same. **Larva** is the young of any insect that changes the form of its body before becoming an adult.

lavatory /*say* **lav**-uh-tree/ *noun* (*plural* **lavatories**) a toilet.

☑ SPELLING TIP Remember that the ending is *ory* although the *or* is not pronounced.

lavender *noun*
1. a small shrub with pale purple flowers that have a strong but pleasant smell. **2.** a pale bluish-purple colour.
–*adjective* **3.** pale bluish-purple.

lavish *adjective*
1. If you are **lavish**, you are very generous: *She was always lavish in giving gifts*; *lavish support.* **2.** If something is **lavish**, it is large or luxurious: *a lavish apartment.*
–*verb* **3.** If you **lavish** something on someone, you give it to them in generous quantities: *He lavished much attention on his grandchildren.*
☐ **lavishly**, *adverb* –**lavishness**, *noun*

law *noun*
1. a rule or set of rules, especially those made by a government or ruler. **2.** the area of knowledge or work that has to do with these rules: *property law*; *family law.* **3.** a statement describing what always happens under certain conditions: *the law of decreasing returns.*
☐ **lawful**, *adjective* –**lawfully**, *adverb* –**lawless**, *adjective* –**lawlessly**, *adverb*

☑ SPELLING TIP Don't confuse the spelling of **law** with **lore** which sounds the same. **Lore** is learning or knowledge about a particular subject.

lawn *noun* an area of mown, grass-covered land, usually part of a garden.

WORD HISTORY from a French word meaning 'wooded ground'

lawyer /*say* **law**-yuh, **loy**-yuh/ *noun* someone whose work is to give advice about the law and to argue for people in law courts.

SEE ALSO **barrister** and **solicitor**.

☑ SPELLING TIP To get this spelling right you have to remember that a **lawyer** knows about the *law*. This will give you the first three letters (which some people say more like the sound 'loy'). Then add *yer* and you're there.

lax *adjective*
1. careless or not strict: *Security was lax and many thefts occurred.* **2.** loose or relaxed: *Let your arms go lax.*
☐ **laxity**, *noun*

laxative *noun* a medicine for helping waste matter to pass from the bowels easily and without pain.
☐ **laxative**, *adjective*

lay[1] *verb* (**lays**, **laying**, **laid**, **has laid**)
1. If you **lay** something somewhere, you place it there so that it is lying flat: *She laid the sick bird in a shoe box.* **2.** To **lay** a table for a meal, you put on it the things you will need to eat the meal, such as knives and forks. **3.** When a hen produces an egg from its body, you say it **lays** an egg. **4.** If someone **lays** plans, they plan something carefully or prepare a certain plan of action. **5.** If someone **lays** a bet, they gamble money on what they think will happen.
–*phrase* **6. lay off**, **a.** to dismiss from a job: *The boss laid off five workmen.* **b.** *Informal* to stop: *We asked the neighbours to lay off playing their music so loudly.* **7. lay out**, **a.** to arrange in order, or prepare. **b.** *Informal* to spend: *They laid out a fortune for the wedding.*

☑ DO NOT CONFUSE **lay** with **lie**. To **lie** is to *be* in a flat position, while to **lay** something somewhere is to *put* it there in a flat position. It can be confusing because the words have a similar meaning. To make things even more confusing, **lay** is also the form of **lie** that you use when the lying down action was in the past: *I lay on the bed for the whole afternoon*. Compare that with **laid**, from **lay**, as in: *She laid the plates on the table.*

lay[2] *verb* the past tense of **lie**[2].

lay-by *noun*
1. a system of buying something by paying out part of the cost and then making further payments until it has been fully paid for and may be collected: *He used lay-by to purchase the refrigerator.*
–*verb* **2.** If somebody **lay-bys** an item, they make payments over time until it is fully paid for: *Do you want to take it now or lay-by it?*

COMPARE this with **hire-purchase**.

layer *noun* a single thickness or coating: *a sandwich with three layers of filling*; *a layer of lacquer.*

layout *noun* the way something is arranged: *The new layout of the classroom has the teacher in the middle.*

lazy *adjective* (**lazier**, **laziest**)
1. If someone is **lazy**, they do not want to work hard or do things that take energy: *She was too lazy to help with the dishes.* **2.** To be **lazy** is to be slow-moving: *a lazy swimming style.* **3.** A **lazy** time is not spent in work or effort: *a lazy holiday spent relaxing in the sun.*
□ **laze**, *verb*: *to laze around in the shade.* –**lazily**, *adverb* –**laziness**, *noun*

SIMILAR WORDS (for definition 1) are **idle** and **indolent**; (for definition 3) **leisurely** and **unhurried**.

☑ SPELLING TIP *Tricky vowel sound*: the letter *a* alone spells the 'ay' sound.

lead[1] /*say* leed/ *verb* (**leads**, **leading**, **led**, **has led**)
1. To **lead** someone is to go in front and show them the way, often in a particular direction or to a particular place: *She led the Scouts through the bush.* **2.** To **lead** people is to be in charge of them: *James was chosen to lead the team.* **3.** To **lead** a discussion is to control the way it develops: *She led an interesting debate on the need to cut down on the use of plastic bags.*
–*noun* **4.** the front position: *to be in the lead.* **5.** amount or distance ahead: *a lead of a whole lap.* **6.** a strap for holding an animal: *a dog lead.* **7.** a discovery that might show who did something: *The discovery of the car was a major lead.*
–*phrase* **8. lead someone on**, to make someone continue in a foolish belief or action. **9. lead to**, **a.** to be a way of getting to: *The next track leads to the river.* **b.** to cause something to happen: *The discovery of how to split the atom led to the development of nuclear energy.*

ANOTHER WORD (for definition 6) is **leash**.

lead[2] /*say* led/ *noun* a heavy bluish-grey metal.
□ **lead**, *adjective*

☑ SPELLING TIP *Tricky vowel sound*: notice the *ea* spelling for the 'e' sound. Don't confuse this word with **led** which has the same sound. **Led** is the past form of **lead**[1]: *He led the walkers through the bush.*

leaded petrol /*say* **led**-uhd/ *noun* petrol that contains tiny bits of lead which can harm you and the environment.

COMPARE this with **unleaded petrol**.

leader /*say* **leed**-uh/ *noun*
1. someone or something that leads. **2.** an article in a newspaper that gives an opinion on events happening at the moment: *The leader in today's paper argued for the farmers and against the government.* **3.** the main violinist in an orchestra, who helps the conductor.
□ **leadership**, *noun*

ANOTHER WORD (for definition 2) is **editorial**.

leaf *noun* (*plural* **leaves**)
1. the flat, usually green, part of a plant that grows out from its stem. **2.** a page of a book. **3.** a thin sheet of metal: *lettering in gold leaf.*
–*phrase* **4. leaf through**, to turn the pages of. **5. take a leaf out of someone's book**, to follow someone's example. **6. turn over a new leaf**, to begin new and better behaviour.
□ **leafy**, *adjective* (**leafier**, **leafiest**) –**leafless**, *adjective*

leaflet *noun* a small sheet of printed information: *They handed out leaflets advertising the school concert.*

A SIMILAR WORD is **pamphlet**.

league /*say* leeg/ *noun*
1. a group of people, countries or organisations who have made an agreement between themselves.
–*phrase* **2. in league**, having an agreement, often to do something bad: *It turned out the robbers and some of the bank staff were in league with each other.*

☑ SPELLING TIP *Silent letter alert*: don't forget the *ue* at the end. This word has come from French, originally from the Latin word *legare* meaning 'to bind'.

leak *noun*
1. a hole or crack that lets liquid or gas in or out accidentally: *The bag of ice had a leak and there was water everywhere.* **2.** the amount of liquid or gas that escapes through a leak: *Was it a bad gas leak?* **3.** the giving out of secret information: *a deliberate leak of sensitive information.*
–*verb* **4.** If a container or a pipe **leaks**, it lets liquid or gas escape through a crack or a hole: *A gas pipe was leaking and there was a terrible smell in the kitchen.* **5.** If gas or liquid **leaks**, it escapes through a hole or crack: *There must be gas leaking from somewhere.*
□ **leakage**, *noun* –**leaky**, *adjective* (**leakier**, **leakiest**) –**leakiness**, *noun*

☑ SPELLING TIP Don't confuse **leak** with **leek** which sounds the same but is spelt with a double *e*. A **leek** is a vegetable.

lean[1] *verb* (**leans**, **leaning**, **leaned** *or* **leant** /*say* lent/, **has leaned** *or* **has leant**) To **lean** is to **1.** be in a sloping position: *The wind made the trees all lean to the east.* **2.** move your body so that it bends in a particular direction: *He leaned down to pat the dog*; *She leaned over and snatched the book out of my hands.* **3.** If you **lean** on something, you rest your body there for support: *I was so tired that I had to lean on the railing.* **4.** If you **lean** something somewhere you rest it there for support: *She leaned the ladder against the wall*; *He leaned his hand on her shoulder.*

SIMILAR WORDS (for definition 1) are **slant**, **slope**, **tilt**, **tip** and **list**. Note that **list** usually refers to a ship leaning towards one side because of damage.

lean[2] *adjective*
1. thin: *a lean person.* **2.** with little or no fat: *lean bacon.*
☐ **leanness**, *noun*

leap *verb* (**leaps**, **leaping**, **leapt** *or* **leaped**, **has leapt** *or* **has leaped**)
1. To **leap** is to jump or move quickly: *The goat leapt up the rocks*; *He had to leap from the window.* **2.** To **leap** something is to jump over it: *The horse leapt the fence and galloped away.*
–*phrase* **3. leap at**, to accept eagerly: *She leapt at the chance of winning a bike.*
–*noun* **4.** a jump. **5.** a sudden rise: *a leap in the cost of houses.*

leap year *noun* a year containing 366 days which occurs every fourth year, with the extra day on 29 February.

learn *verb* (**learns**, **learning**, **learned** *or* **learnt**, **has learned** *or* **has learnt**) To **learn** is to **1.** come to have knowledge of or skill in: *We learned about the history of flying at school today*; *I would like to learn skating.* **2.** get knowledge or skill: *Babies learn very quickly.*
☐ **learner**, *noun*

learned /*say* **lern**-uhd/ *adjective* A **learned** person has a lot of knowledge from study: *A number of learned people were at the conference.*
☐ **learnedly**, *adverb*

SIMILAR WORDS are **educated**, **knowledgeable** and **well-informed**.

lease /*rhymes with* peace/ *noun*
1. a written agreement which gives someone the right to use land, live in a building or use a car in return for rent.
–*verb* **2.** If somebody **leases** something like a house or a car from another person, or that person **leases** it to them, they pay money to that person for the use of it: *They will lease a car for their holiday*; *My uncle will lease out his house while he works overseas.*
☐ **lessee**, *noun* –**lessor**, *noun*

leash *noun*
1. a strap for holding a dog.
–*verb* **2.** If you **leash** an animal, you control it by putting a leash on.

ANOTHER WORD (for definition 1) is **lead**[1] (definition 6).

least *adjective*
1. in the smallest quantity, degree, amount or number: *She received the least amount of all*; *At the least sign of danger, he panics.*
–*pronoun* **2.** the smallest quantity, amount or degree: *James ate the least*; *That is the least I can do to help.*
–*adverb* **3.** in or to the smallest range or degree: *least attractive.*
–*phrase* **4. at least**, **a.** at the lowest calculation or judgement: *At the canteen, it costs at least a dollar to get lunch.* **b.** at any rate: *Your measles look awful but at least you'll get some sympathy.*

NOTE **Least** is the superlative form of **little**. See also **less**.

leather /*say* **ledh**-uh/ *noun* the skin of animals prepared by tanning, used to make such things as shoes, bags and clothes.
☐ **leathery**, *adjective*

☑ SPELLING TIP *Tricky vowel sound*: *ea* for the 'e' sound.

leatherjacket *noun* a flat fish with a large spine and a roughened skin that can be removed in one piece like a jacket.

leave[1] *verb* (**leaves**, **leaving**, **left**, **has left**)
1. If you **leave** a place you go away from it: *We had to leave the classroom.* **2.** To **leave** is to go away: *I can't wait to leave.* **3.** If you **leave** something in a particular place or condition you let it remain there or in that state: *Leave my things alone!*; *He accidentally left the tap on.* **4.** If someone **leaves** property to you, they give it to you for use after they have died: *I hope my grandmother leaves me her car.*

A SIMILAR WORD (for definition 4) is **bequeath**. This is a more formal word.

leave[2] *noun*
1. permission: *She applied for leave to change her roster.* **2.** the time during which someone has permission to be absent: *My mum has applied for a month's leave.*

lecture *noun*
1. a speech that is given before an audience or a class in order to teach or inform: *a lecture on the decreasing number of frogs in the world.* **2.** a long talk from someone who is angry about something you have done: *My dad gave me a long lecture about the importance of doing my homework on time.*
–*verb* **3.** If someone **lectures**, they give a prepared talk on a particular topic to inform other people.
☐ **lecturer**, *noun*

WORD HISTORY from a Latin word meaning 'read'

ledge *noun* a narrow, flat shelf sticking out from something upright: *The key is on the ledge.*

ledger /*say* **lej**-uh/ *noun* an account book used to record money that is paid out and paid in.

☑ SPELLING TIP Remember the *dg* spelling for the 'j' sound.

lee *noun* a side or part that is sheltered or turned away from the wind: *in the lee of a sheltering wall.*
☐ **lee**, *adjective* –**leeward**, *adjective*, *adverb*

leech *noun* (*plural* **leeches**) a small worm that sucks the blood of humans or animals and was once used by doctors to take blood from sick people.

leek *noun* a vegetable that tastes like an onion and has a white bulb and wide green leaves.

> ☑ SPELLING TIP Don't confuse **leek** with **leak** which sounds the same but is spelt with *ea*. A **leak** is a hole or crack that lets something out.

leer *noun*
1. an unpleasant kind of smile.
–*verb* 2. If somebody **leers**, they smile at someone unpleasantly, often in a sexually suggestive way.

leeway *noun*
1. the distance by which a ship or plane is blown off course by the wind. 2. extra space, time or money that allows freedom of action and choice: *If we take more money with us, it gives us more leeway to buy a better present.*

left[1] *adjective*
1. The **left** side of something or someone is the side which is turned toward the west when they are facing north: *In Australia, cars drive on the left side of the road.*
–*noun* 2. the left side: *Cars drive on the left in Australia but in Europe, they drive on the right.* 3. **the left**, a political party or group that believes in the equal distribution of wealth and supports workers rather than companies.

> ANOTHER FORM This word (as in definition 3) is sometimes spelt with a capital letter.
> THE OPPOSITE is **right**.

left[2] *verb* the past tense and past participle of **leave**[1].

leg *noun*
1. one of the two parts of a person's body used for support and for walking. 2. one of the parts of the body of an animal, bird or insect that is used for walking. 3. one of the supports of a piece of furniture: *Don't sit on that chair – it has a broken leg.* 4. one of the divisions of a journey, race or competition: *We gained in the last leg of the race.*
–*phrase* 5. **not have a leg to stand on**, to have no good reason or excuse. 6. **pull someone's leg**, to tease or make fun of someone.
☐ **leggy**, *adjective* –**legless**, *adjective*

legacy *noun* (*plural* **legacies**)
1. a gift of money or property made after someone's death through their will: *He was able to leave a legacy of some land to each of his children.* 2. anything that is handed down from the past or happens as a result of something in the past: *His large stomach was the legacy of too many meals of greasy chips.*
☐ **legatee**, *noun* someone who is given a legacy.

legal /*say* **lee**-guhl/ *adjective*
1. allowed or decided by law: *a legal question.* 2. associated with law: *legal chambers.*
☐ **legalise**, *verb*: *to legalise gambling.* –**legality**, *noun* –**legally**, *adverb*

> ANOTHER SPELLING for **legalise** is **legalize**.

legend /*say* **lej**-uhnd/ *noun* a story that comes from long ago in the past and which is thought by many people to be at least partly true.
☐ **legendary**, *adjective*

legible /*say* **lej**-uh-buhl/ *adjective* If something is **legible**, it can be read easily: *The letter couldn't be delivered because the address was hardly legible.*
☐ **legibility**, *noun* –**legibly**, *adverb*

> THE OPPOSITE is **illegible**.

> ☑ SPELLING TIP Look out for the *-ible* ending (not *-able*) and the soft *g* giving the 'j' sound.

legion /*say* **lee**-juhn/ *noun*
1. a unit of soldiers in the ancient Roman army. 2. a large group of soldiers. 3. a great number: *A legion of film stars were at the awards.*
☐ **legionary**, *noun* –**legionary**, *adjective*

legislation /*say* lej-uhs-**lay**-shuhn/ *noun* a law or all the laws made: *Parliament passed new legislation designed to increase national security.*
☐ **legislate**, *verb* –**legislator**, *noun*

legislature /*say* **lej**-uhs-lay-chuh/ *noun* an organisation, such as a parliament, that makes laws.
☐ **legislative**, *adjective*

legitimate /*say* luh-**jit**-uh-muht/ *adjective*
1. following accepted law, regulations or principles: *a legitimate government*; *a legitimate business.* 2. genuine or based on sensible reasons: *She has a legitimate concern about the safety in the park.*
☐ **legitimacy**, *noun*

leisure /*say* **lezh**-uh/ *noun*
1. time that is free from work.
–*phrase* 2. **at leisure**, without hurry.
☐ **leisureliness**, *noun* –**leisurely**, *adjective*

> ☑ SPELLING TIP *Tricky vowel sound*: *ei* spelling for the 'e' sound in the first syllable

lemon *noun* a yellow fruit with a sour taste.
☐ **lemon**, *adjective* –**lemony**, *adjective*

lemonade *noun* a fizzy soft drink made with lemons, sugar and water.

lend *verb* (**lends**, **lending**, **lent**, **has lent**) To **lend** something to someone is to let them have it for a short time: *I can lend you this book but I want it back in a few days.*
☐ **lender**, *noun*

> NOTE If you **lend** something to someone, you give them the **loan** of it.
> COMPARE this with **borrow**.

length *noun*
1. the measure of something from end to end: *The length of the pool is 50 metres.* **2.** a piece of something long: *a length of wood.*
–*phrase* **3. at length**, **a.** in full detail: *He told us about his exploits at length.* **b.** at last or finally: *'I'll go if I have to', she said at length.*
☐ **lengthen**, *verb* –**lengthy**, *adjective* –**lengthiness**, *noun*

☑ SPELLING TIP Remember **length** is formed from *long* and so it has a *g* in it.

lenient /*say* **lee**-nee-uhnt/ *adjective* If you are **lenient**, you don't treat someone as harshly as they deserve. You let them off.
☐ **lenience**, *noun* –**leniency**, *noun*

☑ SPELLING TIP *Tricky vowel sound*: there is only *e* spelling the 'ee' sound in the first syllable.

lens *noun* (*plural* **lenses**) a piece of curved glass used for bringing together or spreading light rays, usually so as to make objects look larger or for use in glasses to correct bad sight.

lentil *noun* a small, flattened seed used as food, similar to a bean.

☑ SPELLING TIP Remember the *il* ending.

leopard /*say* **lep**-uhd/ *noun* a large, fierce, spotted animal of the cat family.

NOTE The male is a **leopard**; the female is a **leopardess**; the young is a **cub**.

☑ SPELLING TIP *Tricky vowel sound*: *eo* for the 'e' sound in the first syllable. This is because the word comes from *leo*, the Latin word for 'lion'. Also remember there is an *r* in the last syllable.

leotard /*say* **lee**-uh-tahd/ *noun* a close-fitting piece of clothing worn for dancing or doing exercises.

WORD HISTORY named after a French acrobat, Jules *Léotard*

leper /*say* **lep**-uh/ *noun* someone who has leprosy.

leprechaun /*say* **lep**-ruh-kawn/ *noun* a fairy in Irish folk stories, in the shape of a little man.

☑ SPELLING TIP **Leprechaun** is an Irish word which comes from words meaning a 'little body'. The most difficult part is the last syllable where you have to remember the *ch* spelling for the 'k' sound and the *au* spelling for the 'aw' sound. It sounds like the corn that you eat but it is spelt quite differently.

leprosy /*say* **lep**-ruh-see/ *noun* an infectious disease which can cause sores on the skin and the loss of feeling in parts of the body.

lesbian /*say* **lez**-bee-uhn/ *noun* a woman who has sexual feelings for other women.
☐ **lesbian**, *adjective*

less *adverb*
1. to a smaller degree or in a smaller amount: *The teacher said the other class was less noisy.*
–*adjective* **2.** smaller in amount: *less hope*; *less time.*

OTHER FORMS This is the comparative form of **little**. See also **least**.
NOTE Many people say that **fewer** as an adjective should be used with things you can count and **less** with things you can't, as in 'You should eat less sugar and fewer biscuits'.

lessen *verb* To **lessen** is to become or make less or smaller in amount or severity: *Her anger lessened when she heard the whole story*; *Honey lessens the pain of a bee sting.*

lesson *noun*
1. the time during which a student or a class is taught one subject. **2.** anything that you learn, or from which you learn: *a lesson in knitting*; *The lesson we learned was to keep a low profile.*

let *verb* (**lets**, **letting**, **let**, **has let**)
1. To **let** someone do something is to allow or permit them to do it. **2.** To **let** a room, house, etc., is to rent it out.
–*phrase* **3. let alone** or **let be**, to stop annoying, arguing with and so on. **4. let down**, to disappoint: *She let us down by not doing as she was asked.* **5. let go**, **a.** to stop holding onto someone or something. **b.** *Informal* to freely express anger or other emotion. **6. let know**, to inform or tell: *Would you let her know that I came.* **7. let off**, **a.** to excuse. **b.** to make explode: *The fireworks were let off over the harbour.* **8. let off steam**, to express your anger or other strong emotion in a free and harmless manner. **9. let out**, **a.** to tell: *He let out our secret.* **b.** to make larger: *to let out the waist of a skirt.* **c.** to give out: *He let out a laugh.* **d.** to free: *to let a bird out of a cage.*

lethal /*say* **lee**-thuhl/ *adjective* Something **lethal** causes death: *Petrol sniffing is a lethal practice.*

lethargy /*say* **leth**-uh-jee/ *noun* a state of sleepy laziness: *We had to shake ourselves out of our lethargy and get moving.*
☐ **lethargic**, *adjective*: *The hot weather made him feel lethargic.*

let's a short form of *let us*.

letter *noun*
1. a message in writing or printing, addressed to a person or group. **2.** one of the signs used in writing and printing to stand for a speech sound: *There are 26 letters in the alphabet.*

lettuce *noun* a plant with large green leaves which are used in salads.

☑ SPELLING TIP Notice the ending is *uce* (not *ice*).

leukaemia /*say* looh-**kee**-mee-uh/ *noun* a disease in which the body produces too many white blood cells and which can cause death.

ANOTHER SPELLING is **leukemia**.
WORD HISTORY from a Greek word meaning 'white'

levee /*say* **lev**-ee/ *noun*
1. a raised bank of earth and sand built up by a river during floods. **2.** a bank built to keep a river from overflowing.

☑ SPELLING TIP Don't confuse **levee** with **levy** which sounds the same but is spelt with a *y* at the end. A **levy** is an amount of money which has to be paid. **Levee** is spelt with a double *e* ending because it comes from French.

level *adjective*
1. If something is **level** it is even, or has no part higher than another. **2.** If the ground, or a surface, is **level** it is horizontal, not sloping. **3.** If people are **level** they are equal in some way: *In terms of ambition, they are level.*
–*noun* **4.** a horizontal or level position or surface. **5.** a rank, whether high or low: *He was employed at a low level but rose through the ranks.* **6.** an instrument for finding out whether something is exactly flat or horizontal.
–*verb* (**levels**, **levelling**, **levelled**, **has levelled**) **7.** If you **level** something, you make it smooth or even.
☐ **leveller**, *noun*

lever /*say* **lee**-vuh/ *noun*
1. a bar supported at one point along its length, which lifts a weight at one end when you press or pull down the other.
–*verb* **2.** If you **lever** something, you use a lever to lift it.
☐ **leverage**, *noun*

levitate *verb* To **levitate** is to rise or float in the air as if by magic.
☐ **levitation**, *noun*

levity *noun* a lack of seriousness in the way you think and behave.

levy /*say* **lev**-ee/ *noun* (*plural* **levies**)
1. an amount of money which has to be paid: *There was a levy on everyone who wanted to use the road.*
–*verb* (**levies**, **levying**, **levied**, **has levied**) **2.** If a government or some other institution **levies** a tax or some other money to be paid, they demand that people pay it.

☑ SPELLING TIP Don't confuse **levy** with **levee** which sounds the same but is spelt with *ee* at the end. A **levee** is a raised bank of earth and sand built up by a river during floods.

liability /*say* luy-uh-**bil**-uh-tee/ *noun* (*plural* **liabilities**)
1. something or someone that causes difficulty rather than being helpful: *Having a pet can be a liability when you want to go on holidays.* **2.** legal responsibility: *It was my fault and I accept liability.* **3.** **liabilities**, debts; obligations to make payments.

COMPARE definition 3 with **asset** (definition 3).

liable /*say* **luy**-uh-buhl/ *adjective*
1. likely: *Tom is liable to turn up unexpectedly.* **2.** legally responsible: *The council was found liable and had to pay costs.*

liaison /*say* lee-**ay**-zuhn, lee-**ay**-zon/ *noun* a connection or communication between people or groups: *The council works in liaison with some local groups to organise bush regeneration.*
☐ **liaise** /*say* lee-**ayz**/, *verb* to communicate and act together with: *The school had to liaise with the police to have the road closed for the fete.*

☑ SPELLING TIP *Tricky vowel sound*: this word has an unusual grouping of vowels – two *i*'s, with an *a* between them.

liar *noun* someone who tells lies.

☑ SPELLING TIP Don't confuse the spelling of **liar** with **lyre** which has the same sound. A **lyre** is an ancient stringed musical instrument.

libel /*say* **luy**-buhl/ (in the past, in Australia)
–*noun* **1.** a written or printed statement which damages someone's reputation: *The football star sued the magazine for libel.*
–*verb* (**libels**, **libelling**, **libelled**, **has libelled**) **2.** If a publication like a newspaper **libels** someone, it publishes something which damages their reputation: *The footballer said the newspaper libelled him by saying he had bought his way into the team.*
☐ **libeller**, *noun* –**libellous**, *adjective* –**libellously**, *adverb*

COMPARE this with **slander**, but note that nowadays, in the Australian legal system, there is no difference between libel and slander – they are both simply regarded as defamation.
WORD HISTORY from a Latin word meaning 'book'

liberal *adjective*
1. tolerant, or accepting of the beliefs and opinions of other people: *Her liberal approach suits her work with many different cultural groups.* **2.** If someone is **liberal**, they are generous: *They were liberal in their support for the charity function.*
☐ **liberality**, *noun* –**liberally**, *adverb*

☑ SPELLING TIP Remember the *e* in the middle of **liberal**. You have to put it in the spelling although it is often not pronounced.

liberate *verb* To **liberate** someone is to set them free: *The soldiers liberated the citizens of the city.*
☐ **liberation**, *noun* –**liberator**, *noun*

liberty *noun* (*plural* **liberties**)
1. freedom from imprisonment, or from a cruel or foreign government. **2.** freedom to do, think, or speak as you choose.
–*phrase* **3. at liberty**, free, or having permission to do a particular thing. **4. take a liberty**, to behave in a way that is rude or disrespectful.

library /*say* **luh**-bree/ *noun* (*plural* **libraries**)
1. a room or building where books and other reading or study materials are kept for people to use or borrow. **2.** a collection of books, films, records or music: *Dad has every song by the Beatles in his record library.*

WORD HISTORY from a Latin word meaning 'book'

☑ SPELLING TIP Don't forget that the ending of **library** is *ary* although the *ar* is usually not pronounced. Try remembering that there are two separate *r*'s (for 'relax and read') in this word.

lice *plural noun* (*singular* **louse**) small wingless insects which live in the hair or skin, suck blood and make your head itchy.

NOTE The most common kind of **lice** are found on the head or in the hair. These are also called **head lice**.

licence /*say* **luy**-suhns/ *noun*
1. official permission to do something, or an official piece of paper showing this permission: *a licence to export native timbers.* **2.** uncontrolled freedom of behaviour: *My father believes that too much licence leads to chaos.*

☑ SPELLING TIP Remember that this noun is spelt with a *c* in the last syllable. The related verb is spelt with an *s*: *Is she licensed to drive?*.

license /*say* **luy**-suhns/ *verb* To **license** someone is to give official permission to them: *Is he licensed to drive trucks?*
☐ **licensee**, *noun*: *hotel licensee.*

☑ SPELLING TIP Remember that this verb is spelt with a *s* in the last syllable. The related noun is spelt with an *c*: *a driving licence*.

lichen /*say* **luy**-kuhn/ *noun* a moss-like plant that grows in patches, usually on rocks or tree trunks.

☑ SPELLING TIP Notice the *ch* spelling for the 'k' sound. Don't confuse this word with **liken** which has the same sound. To **liken** something to something else is to see how it is similar.

lick *verb*
1. If you **lick** something, you rub your tongue on it, sometimes in order to wet it, or as a way of eating it: *You have to lick the back of the stamp or it won't stick*; *She licked the jam off the spoon.* **2.** *Informal* To **lick** someone is to defeat them: *We stand a good chance of licking the next team.*
☐ **lick**, *noun*

licorice /*say* **lik**-uh-rish, **lik**-rish, **lik**-uh-ruhs/ *noun* a sweet-tasting substance made from the root of a plant and used in making sweets and some medicines.

ANOTHER SPELLING is **liquorice**.

lid *noun*
1. a movable top for covering a container. **2.** See **eyelid**.

lie[1] *noun*
1. something that is not true, said by someone who knows it is not true.
–*verb* (**lies**, **lying**, **lied**, **has lied**) **2.** If you **lie**, you tell a lie.

lie[2] *verb* (**lies**, **lying**, **lay**, **has lain**)
1. To **lie** is to rest in a flat horizontal position: *The baby foal was lying on the grass.* **2.** If something **lies** somewhere it is to be found or located in that place: *The land lies at the foot of the mountain.*

☑ DO NOT CONFUSE **lie** with **lay**. To **lay** something somewhere is to *put* it there, while to **lie** is to *be* in a flat position. To make things even more confusing, **lay** is also the form of **lie** that you use when the lying down action was in the past: *I lay on the bed for the whole afternoon*. **Laid** is the past form of **lay**. So you have to be careful about which **lay** you are using.

lieutenant /*say* lef-**ten**-uhnt/ *noun* an officer in the army or navy, lower in rank than a captain.

WORD HISTORY from a French word meaning 'holding a place'

☑ SPELLING TIP This word does not look the way it is pronounced. You have to remember the group of three vowels *ieu* which give an 'ef' sound. In American English, the word is pronounced 'looh-**ten**-uhnt', so there is not so much difficulty.

life *noun* (*plural* **lives**)
1. the condition that makes animals and plants different from dead things and from other objects like rocks, water, machines and so on. **2.** the time you are alive, from your birth to your death: *She lived her whole life in the one house.* **3.** living things as a group: *Our planet supports every form of life.* **4.** activity or interest: *Her eyes were full of vitality and life.*
☐ **lifeless**, *adjective*

lifeboat *noun* a boat carried on a large ship and used if the ship sinks or catches fire.

life cycle *noun* the development of a living thing from the beginning of its life to the time it becomes an adult.

lifeguard *noun* someone employed at a place where people swim to rescue anyone in difficulty and give first aid to those in distress.

lifesaver *noun* someone who makes sure that people swim at the safe part of a beach and who rescues swimmers in difficulty, usually working as part of a voluntary organisation rather than being paid.
☐ **lifesaving**, *noun*, *adjective*

lifetime *noun* the period of time that someone's life continues, from birth until death: *In his* *lifetime he had seen the quiet village become a huge city.*

lift *verb*
1. To **lift** something is to raise or bring it upwards.
–noun **2.** a moving platform or cage for bringing people from one level of a building to another. **3.** a free ride in a vehicle: *We offered our friends a lift with us.*

ANOTHER WORD (for definition 2) is **elevator**.

lift-off *noun* the moment when a rocket or spaceship leaves the ground.

light[1] *noun*
1. a form of radiation produced by some objects such as the sun or a fire: *the light of the sun.* **2.** one of those things which give off light: *a street light.* **3. lights**, the set of coloured lights used to control traffic at street corners: *The lights have turned green.*
–verb (**lights**, **lighting**, **lit** *or* **lighted**, **has lit** *or* **has lighted**) **4.** If you **light** a fire, you set it burning. **5.** If you **light** a place, you shine light on it: *We lit the dark passageway with some candles.*
–phrase **6. bring to light**, to discover. **7. in the light of**, taking into account: *In the light of the latest discoveries, the police feel sure the crimes are related.* **8. light up**, **a.** to make brighter: *The good news lit up their faces.* **b.** to become bright with light or colour: *The bridge lit up with fireworks.* **9. shed light on**, to explain: *The discovery shed light on the mysterious happenings.*
☐ **light**, *adjective*: *light blue.* –**lightness**, *noun*

light[2] *adjective*
1. of little weight: *a light suitcase.* **2.** small in amount, force or depth: *a light fall of snow*; *a light snack.* **3.** not heavy or serious: *light music.* **4.** cheerful: *They went forward with light hearts.*
–phrase **5. make light of**, to treat as being of little importance: *Don't make light of our problems!*
☐ **lightly**, *adverb* –**lightness**, *noun*

lighthouse *noun* a tower with a strong light that warns passing ships of any dangerous rocks nearby or under the surface.

lightning *noun* a sudden flash of light in the sky caused by electricity in the air during a storm.

light-year *noun* the distance travelled by light in one year, used in measuring distances between stars.

like[1] *adjective*
1. Something or someone that is **like** another thing or person is similar to them or able to be compared with them in some way: *She is very like her mother*; *Your house is like ours – it has the bedrooms upstairs.*
–noun **2.** something that is similar: *pens, pencils and the like.*
☐ **liken**, *verb*: *to liken the moon to an orange.* –**likeness**, *noun*

like[2] *verb*
1. If you **like** someone you feel affection for them: *I like my cousins very much.* **2.** If you **like** something you find it pleasant or enjoyable: *I like cricket*; *I like sleeping under the stars.*

likely *adjective* (**likelier**, **likeliest**)
1. If something is **likely**, it is probable. You think that it will happen or it is true: *Do you think a storm's likely?*; *He must have missed the bus. That's the most likely reason for him not being here.* **2.** If someone is **likely** to do something, they will probably do it: *They're likely to be back soon, now it's getting dark.*
–adverb **3.** probably: *She will very likely win.*
☐ **likelihood**, *noun*

lilac /*say* **luy**-luhk/ *noun*
1. a purple or white flower with a pleasant smell, made up of a cluster of small flowers close together. **2.** a pale purple colour.
–adjective **3.** pale purple.

lilt *noun* a sound that has a light rhythmic swing: *She spoke with a pleasant lilt in her voice.*
☐ **lilting**, *adjective*

lily *noun* a plant with a bulb and a funnel-shaped flower which can be found in many colours.

lima bean /*say* **luy**-muh/ *noun* a kind of bean with a broad, flat seed that you can eat.

limb *noun*
1. a person's arm or leg, or the similar part of an animal's body, such as a wing. **2.** a large or main branch of a tree.

☑ SPELLING TIP *Silent letter alert*: don't forget the *b* at the end.

limber *phrase* **limber up**, to do some exercises before a race or the like, in order to stretch your muscles and warm up your body: *She limbered up by stretching her arms and legs.*

limbo *noun*
1. in the past in the Roman Catholic religion, the place where people were thought to go who were not wicked enough to go to hell but not quite good enough to go to heaven.
–phrase **2. in limbo**, in a situation where nothing is decided or resolved.

ANOTHER FORM Definition 1 is often spelt with a capital letter.

lime[1] *noun* a white powder obtained by heating limestone, that is used in making cement.

lime[2] *noun* a small greenish-yellow citrus fruit.
☐ **lime**, *adjective*

limelight *noun* a situation in which someone gets a lot of attention from other people, the public, the media, and so on: *She has been in the limelight ever since she appeared in her first film.*

limerick /*say* **lim**-uh-rik/ *noun* a funny rhyming poem of five lines.

WORD HISTORY named after *Limerick*, a county in the Republic of Ireland

limestone *noun* a soft, white, chalky rock.

limit *noun*
1. the end or furthest part: *We had reached the limits of Mum's tolerance.* **2.** a boundary or line that you should not pass: *No logging is allowed within the limits of the national park.*
–*verb* (**limits, limiting, limited, has limited**) **3.** If somebody **limits** someone or something, they restrict them by fixing limits: *The school has limited the areas we can play football in.*
–*phrase* **4. off limits**, having access forbidden.
☐ **limited**, *adjective* –**limitation**, *noun*

limousine /*say* **lim**-uh-zeen, lim-uh-**zeen**/ *noun* a kind of car, usually large and comfortable, especially one driven by a paid driver.

☑ SPELLING TIP *Tricky 'uh' sound*: the middle vowel sound is spelt *ou*. **Limousine** has this spelling because the word comes from French. It is based on the name of the town Limousin.

limp[1] *verb* To **limp** is to walk with difficulty because of an injured leg or foot.
☐ **limp**, *noun*: *He walks with a limp.*

limp[2] *adjective* not stiff or firm: *limp material.*
☐ **limply**, *adverb* –**limpness**, *noun*

limpet *noun* a cone-shaped shellfish that sticks very firmly to rocks.

limpid *adjective* clear or transparent: *Blossoms floated on the limpid surface of the water.*
☐ **limpidly**, *adverb*

line[1] *noun*
1. a thin mark made on paper, wood or some other surface. **2.** something arranged like a line: *a line of soldiers*; *lines of pine trees.* **3.** a wrinkle on someone's face. **4.** a strip of railway track: *Men are working on the line.* **5. lines**, the words of an actor's part in a play: *He forgot his lines and had to be prompted.* **6.** a type of goods which a shop sells: *a new line in confectionery.* **7.** a continuous stretch of length, straight or curved, without breadth or thickness: *The line of people wound out of the bank and around the corner.*
–*phrase* **8. in line, a.** behaving as expected. **b.** with a good chance: *in line for a promotion.* **9. line up, a.** to take a position in a line or queue. **b.** to bring into a line. **10. out of line**, not according to standard practice or agreement.

line[2] *verb* To **line** something is to cover the inside of it: *to line a drawer with paper*; *to line a dress with satin.*
☐ **liner**, *noun* –**lining**, *noun*

linen /*say* **lin**-uhn/ *noun*
1. cloth made from flax. **2.** articles made from linen or cotton, such as sheets.
☐ **linen**, *adjective*

liner *noun* a large passenger ship.

linesman *noun* (*plural* **linesmen**)
1. a sports official who helps a referee or umpire decide if the ball has landed inside or outside one of the lines on the field of play. **2.** someone who puts up or repairs telephone or electric power lines.

linger *verb*
1. If you **linger** somewhere, you stay for longer than usual or when you really ought to go: *I lingered at the cafe and nearly missed my train.* **2.** If something such as a smell or a memory **lingers**, it stays around and does not immediately go away.
☐ **lingering**, *adjective*

lingerie /*say* **lon**-zhuh-ray/ *noun* women's underwear or nightwear.

☑ SPELLING TIP **Lingerie** comes from a French word and in English we have tried to give it a French sound. It comes from *linge* meaning 'linen'. When you add an *r* to this you get *linger*. But don't *linger* in your **lingerie** too long because you need to add an *ie* to complete its spelling.

linguistics /*say* ling-**gwis**-tiks/ *noun* the study of language, including sounds, words and grammar.
☐ **linguist**, *noun* someone who studies language. –**linguistic**, *adjective*: *linguistic analysis.*

☑ SPELLING TIP Like *language*, this word has a *gu* spelling for the 'gw' sound. It comes from *lingua*, the Latin word for 'language'.

liniment *noun* an oily liquid for rubbing on bruises, sprains or sore muscles.

☑ SPELLING TIP *Single letter alert*: only one *n* in the first syllable. Also notice that the vowel on either side of it is an *i*.

link *noun*
1. one of the separate rings which make up a chain. **2.** anything which is a joining or connecting part: *The link between us is that we both went to the same kindergarten.*
–*verb* **3.** If something **links** things or people, it joins them together.

linoleum /*say* luy-**noh**-lee-uhm/ *noun* a floor covering made of a mixture of oil, cork and a kind of resin pressed into a strong, cloth backing.

A SHORT FORM of this is **lino**.

linseed *noun* the seed of the flax plant from which an oil is made.

lion *noun*
1. a large, honey-coloured member of the cat family, living in Africa and southern Asia.
–*phrase* **2. the lion's share**, the largest share or part of anything.

NOTE The male is a **lion**; the female is a **lioness**; the young is a **cub**.

lip *noun*
1. one of the dark areas of raised skin around the edge of the mouth. **2.** an edge of something: *the lip of the volcano*; *the lip of the cup.*

lipstick *noun* a cosmetic for colouring the lips.

liquefied natural gas *noun* a gas formed naturally in the earth, liquefied to make it easier to transport and store, then usually turned back into a gas and used as a fuel.

THE ABBREVIATION is **LNG**.

liquefy /*say* **lik**-wuh-fuy/ *verb* (**liquefies**, **liquefying**, **liquefied**, **has liquefied**) If something **liquefies**, it becomes liquid: *The chocolate liquefied in the heat of the car.*
☐ **liquefier**, *noun*

☑ SPELLING TIP Remember that the second vowel sound in **liquefy** is spelt with an *e*, not an *i* as you might think as this word comes from *liquid*.

liqueur /*say* luh-**kyooh**-uh, luh-**ker**/ *noun* a type of strong alcoholic liquor made in many flavours.

☑ SPELLING TIP This word, which comes from French, is a difficult one to spell, especially because it has a lot of vowels coming together. You just have to memorise the *queur* spelling at the end.

liquid *noun* any substance like water that can be poured: *What's this liquid in the bottom of the pan?*
☐ **liquid**, *adjective*

COMPARE this with **solid** and **gas**[1] (definition 1).

liquidate *verb*
1. If someone **liquidates** a debt, they settle it or pay it off. **2.** If a company is **liquidated**, its assets are sold to pay for its debts and it is closed down. **3.** If somebody **liquidates** another person, they get rid of them, especially by killing them.
☐ **liquidation**, *noun*: *The company will have to go into liquidation.* –**liquidator**, *noun*

liquid paper *noun* a thin, white paint that is used to cover written or typed mistakes on paper.

ANOTHER TERM for this is **white-out**.

liquor /*sounds like* licker/ *noun* a strong alcoholic drink such as brandy or whisky.

liquorice /*say* **lik**-uh-rish, **lik**-rish, **lik**-uh-ruhs/ *noun* See **licorice**.

lisp *noun*
1. the inability to pronounce the sound 's', making it sound like the 'th' in *thin*.
–*verb* **2.** If somebody **lisps**, they pronounce 's' in this way.

list[1] *noun*
1. a set of the names of things written down one under the other: *a list of everyone going on the excursion*; *a shopping list.*
–*verb* **2.** If you **list** things, you write them down one under the other: *We listed all the things we wanted for Christmas.*
☐ **listing**, *noun*

list[2] *verb* If a ship **lists**, it leans to one side: *Tossed by furious waves, the ship was listing dangerously.*
☐ **list**, *noun*

listen /*say* **lis**-uhn/ *verb*
1. If you **listen**, you pay careful attention to something that you can hear: *I love listening to music.* **2.** If you **listen** to what someone says, you take notice of it and are influenced by it.
☐ **listener**, *noun*

☑ SPELLING TIP *Silent letter alert*: don't forget the silent *t* following the *s*.

listless *adjective* having no energy or interest in anything.
☐ **listlessly**, *adverb* –**listlessness**, *noun*

literal *adjective*
1. If words are used in a **literal** way, they are given their most basic meaning: *When you say that something frightened you so much that you almost 'jumped out of your skin', you do not mean it in a literal way.* **2.** If a translation of another language is **literal**, the exact words of the language are translated.
☐ **literally**, *adverb*

literary *adjective* having to do with books and literature of a high standard: *a literary magazine.*

literate /*say* **lit**-uh-ruht/ *adjective* able to read and write.
☐ **literacy**, *noun*

THE OPPOSITE is **illiterate**.

literature *noun*
1. books, poems, plays and other forms of writing of a high standard: *Our teacher said the books in airport lounges were not usually good literature.* **2.** what is written about a particular subject: *The literature on European history is vast.*

lithe /*say* luydh/ *adjective* To be **lithe** is to bend easily and spring back into shape: *Ballerinas are always lithe and graceful.*
☐ **lithely**, *adverb*

litmus /*say* **lit**-muhs/ *noun* a blue colouring matter obtained from certain lichens. In alkaline solutions litmus turns blue, in acid solutions it turns red. Strips of paper soaked in a solution of litmus are used for this test.

NOTE A **litmus test** can refer generally to any event or action which decides matters one way or the other.

litre /*rhymes with* beater/ *noun* a measure of liquid in the metric system.

THE SYMBOL for this is **L** or **l**.
WORD HISTORY from a Greek word meaning 'pound'

litter *noun*
1. things, especially rubbish, scattered about. **2.** a number of baby animals born at the same time: *The mother dog had a litter of four to care for.*
–*verb* **3.** If somebody **litters** an area, they spoil it by scattering rubbish in it. **4.** If material of any sort **litters** an area, it is scattered around there.
☐ **litterbug**, *noun* someone who leaves rubbish around a place.

little *adjective*
1. (**littler**, **littlest**) small in size: *a little boy.* **2.** (**less**, **least**) not much or small in amount: *little hope.* **3.** (**less**, **least**) short or brief: *a little time.*
–*phrase* **4. make little of**, to treat as unimportant.

live[1] /*rhymes with* give/ *verb* To **live** is to **1.** be alive or have life. **2.** have your home in a particular place: *She lived in Germany for six months.*
–*phrase* **3. live on**, to keep alive by feeding on, without eating anything else: *He lives on fruit and vegetables.*

live[2] /*rhymes with* dive/ *adjective*
1. A **live** person, plant or animal is living or alive. **2.** Something **live** is **a.** broadcast or televised as it is being performed: *The match will be telecast live.* **b.** charged with electricity: *Careful of the wires – they're live!* **c.** unexploded: *a live land mine.*
–*adverb* **3.** of a radio or television program, broadcast at the time of its happening: *This race is brought to you live from the Olympic swimming pool.*

THE OPPOSITE (of definition 2) is **dead**.

livelihood /*say* **luyv**-lee-hood/ *noun* a way of earning money to live: *There is no livelihood in mining those hills any more.*

lively /*say* **luyv**-lee/ *adjective* (**livelier**, **liveliest**) full of energy or spirit: *lively discussions.*
☐ **liveliness**, *noun*

liver /*rhymes with* giver/ *noun* the part of the body that makes bile which helps digest food.

livestock /*say* **luyv**-stok/ *noun* all the animals kept on a farm or station such as horses, cattle and sheep.

livid /*say* **liv**-uhd/ *adjective*
1. If someone is **livid**, they are extremely angry: *I was livid when I found out she had lied to me.* **2.** If something is **livid**, it is dark with bruising: *Her knee was puffy and livid.*

living /*say* **liv**-ing/ *adjective*
1. alive: *All living things need water.*
–*noun* **2.** the money necessary to live: *to earn a living.*
–*phrase* **3. in living memory**, for as long as people can remember. **4. the living image**, the exact likeness or copy: *He's the living image of his father.*

living room *noun* a room in a home where people can relax and be together. It might have such things as comfortable chairs, a television set and a stereo in it.

ANOTHER TERM for this is **lounge room**.

lizard *noun* a reptile with a long body, four legs and a tail.

llama /*rhymes with* farmer/ *noun* a South American animal related to the camel and used for carrying loads.

☑ SPELLING TIP *Double letter alert*: two *l*'s at the start. The second *l* is silent. Don't confuse this with **lama** (with a single *l*) which is a Buddhist monk or priest.

load *noun*
1. something carried. **2.** the quantity carried: *a load of fertiliser.*
–*verb* **3.** If you **load** someone or something, you put something on or in them: *Mum loaded up Dad with all the picnic plates*; *The builders loaded the trailer with the rubbish*; *Load the camera first.*
–*phrase* **4. get a load of**, *Informal* to look at or listen to with attention.

loaf[1] *noun* (*plural* **loaves**)
1. an amount of bread or cake baked in a particular shape. **2.** any food made into a loaf shape: *a meat loaf.*

loaf[2] *verb*
1. To **loaf** is to do nothing when you should be working: *He loafs around all day and never helps.*
–*noun* **2.** a restful, lazy time.

loam *noun* loose, very fertile soil.
☐ **loamy**, *adjective*

loan *noun*
1. the giving of something to be used for a short time before being returned to the owner: *Would you like a loan of our cricket bat?* **2.** money given for a short time, usually to be paid back with interest: *a loan from the bank.*
–*phrase* **3. on loan**, lent for a period of time.

☑ SPELLING TIP Don't confuse the spelling of **loan** with **lone** which has the same sound. **Lone** means 'not with anyone' or 'standing apart'.

loath /*rhymes with* both/ *adjective* If you are **loath** to do something, you are not willing or not inclined to do it: *I am loath to tell her because she can't keep a secret.*

loathe /*say* lohdh/ *verb* If you **loathe** someone or something, you hate them.
☐ **loathing**, *noun* –**loathsome**, *adjective*

☑ SPELLING TIP *Tricky vowel sound*: *oa* for the 'oh' sound. Also remember the *e* at the end.

lob *verb* (**lobs**, **lobbing**, **lobbed**, **has lobbed**) To **lob** something, such as a ball, is to hit or throw it high into the air.
☐ **lob**, *noun*

lobby *noun* (*plural* **lobbies**)
1. an entrance hall. **2.** a group of people trying to get support for a particular cause: *a lobby for saving the forests.*
–*verb* **3.** To **lobby** a government is to try to influence the decisions it makes.
☐ **lobbyist**, *noun*

lobe *noun*
1. a roundish part which stands out, as of an organ, leaf, and so on. **2.** the soft, hanging, lower part of the ear.
☐ **lobed**, *adjective*

lobster *noun* a crustacean with ten legs and a long tail, which turns pink when cooked.

local *adjective*
1. If something is **local**, it **a.** has to do with a particular place: *local history.* **b.** has to do with the area you are living in rather than the whole town or state: *the local library*; *the local council chambers.* **2.** A **local** anaesthetic acts on only part of the body.
–*noun* **3.** someone who lives in a particular place: *The fire in the park was reported by some locals.*
☐ **localise**, *verb* –**locality**, *noun*: *a pleasant locality.*

ANOTHER SPELLING for **localise** is **localize**.

locate *verb*
1. If you **locate** something, you look for it and manage to find out where it is: *I finally located the library.* **2.** If something is **located** somewhere, that is where it is: *The library is located behind the school.*
☐ **location**, *noun*

loch /*say* lok/ *noun* (*plural* **lochs**) a lake.

☑ SPELLING TIP Remember the *ch* ending for the 'k' sound. **Loch** sounds like this because it is a Scottish word. Don't confuse it with **lock** which has the same sound. A **lock** is something you use to fasten a door and so on.

lock[1] *noun*
1. a device for fastening a door, gate, lid or drawer, which needs a key to open it. **2.** a part of a canal with gates at each end allowing ships to be raised from one level to another.
–*verb* **3.** If you **lock** something or it **locks**, you fasten it or it becomes fastened: *Lock the door before you leave*; *The gate blew shut and locked.* **4.** If you **lock** something or somebody somewhere, you shut or put them into a place of safety or imprisonment: *Lock your jewellery in the safe*; *They locked him away for years.*

lock[2] *noun*
1. a short length or curl of hair: *He kept a lock of her hair in his wallet.* **2. locks**, the hair of your head: *She wanted to shave off her golden locks because she thought it would feel cooler in summer.*

locker *noun* a cupboard that may be locked, especially one for your own use.

locket *noun* a small case for a picture or lock of hair, usually worn on a chain hung around your neck.

lockjaw *noun* See **tetanus**.

locksmith *noun* someone who makes or mends locks and keys.

locomotive /*say* loh-kuh-**moh**-tiv/ *noun* the engine which pulls railway carriages or trucks.
☐ **locomotion**, *noun*

locust /*say* **loh**-kuhst/ *noun* a type of grasshopper which moves from one place to another in large numbers and destroys crops.

lodge *noun*
1. a building used as a holiday house: *We booked into a wilderness lodge.*
–*verb* To **lodge** is to **2.** board or live for a while in someone else's home. **3.** be fixed or caught in something: *A nail had lodged in my bike tyre.*
☐ **lodger**, *noun* –**lodgings**, *noun*

loft *noun* the space in a building between the roof and the ceiling.

lofty *adjective* (**loftier**, **loftiest**)
1. reaching high into the air: *lofty peaks.* **2.** noble or high in character: *His lofty ideals are based on a concern for justice.* **3.** proud or haughty: *We found her lofty manner a bit hard to take.*

log *noun*
1. a large branch or the trunk of a tree which has fallen or been cut down. **2.** the daily record of a journey or flight kept by the captain of a ship or an aircraft.
–*verb* (**logs**, **logging**, **logged**, **has logged**) **3.** To **log** trees is to cut them down.
–*phrase* **4. log in** (or **on**), to begin a session on a computer, usually by typing in your name and a password. **5. log off** (or **out**), to end a session on a computer.
☐ **logger**, *noun* –**logging**, *noun*

loganberry *noun* (*plural* **loganberries**) a large, dark red berry you can eat, or the plant it grows on.

WORD HISTORY named after the Californian man who first grew them, JH *Logan* (1841–1928)

logbook *noun* a book in which the record of a journey made by a ship or plane is entered.

logic /*say* **loj**-ik/ *noun* correct reasoning: *There is no logic to what you say.*
☐ **logical**, *adjective* –**logically**, *adverb* –**logician** /*say* luh-**jish**-uhn/, *noun*

logo /*say* **loh**-goh/ *noun* a design that identifies a company or brand.

loin *noun*
1. the part of a person's body between the lowest rib and the top of either thigh. 2. a cut of meat from the similar part of a four-legged animal: *a loin of lamb.*

loiter *verb* To **loiter** is to move about aimlessly or stay in the one place for too long: *The police were suspicious of the man who had been loitering outside the shop.*
☐ **loiterer**, *noun*

loll *verb* To **loll** is to 1. lean in a relaxed manner: *He lolled in the old lounge chair.* 2. hang loosely: *The rag doll's head lolled around.*

lollipop *noun* a kind of boiled sweet, often fixed to the end of a stick.

> ☑ SPELLING TIP This word is made up of *lolly* and *pop*, but you have to remember that the *y* at the end of *lolly* has changed to an *i*.

lolly *noun* (*plural* **lollies**) a sweet, especially a boiled one.

lone *adjective* If someone or something is described as **lone**, they are on their own, or they are the only one in a particular situation: *the lone survivors.*
☐ **lonesome**, *adjective*

> ☑ SPELLING TIP Don't confuse the spelling of **lone** with **loan** which sounds the same. A **loan** is when you give something to someone to be used for a short time and then returned.

lonely *adjective* (**lonelier**, **loneliest**)
1. If you are **lonely**, you feel sad because you miss the company of other people: *It's easy to be lonely in a big city.* 2. If a place is **lonely**, few people go there: *a lonely bush track.*
☐ **loneliness**, *noun*

long[1] *adjective*
1. having a great distance from one end to the other: *a long walk.* 2. lasting a great amount of time: *a long day.* 3. having a lot of words: *a long book.* 4. having a stated distance or time: *a journey seventy kilometres long*; *a lecture two hours long.*
–*adverb* 5. for a great amount of time: *He stayed long into the night.* 6. for or during a certain amount of time: *How long will the lecture last?*
–*phrase* 7. **before long**, soon. 8. **in the long run**, in the final result.

> A SIMILAR WORD (for definitions 2 and 3) is **lengthy**. Note that **lengthy** can sometimes have the sense of being too long: *He couldn't follow her lengthy explanation.*

long[2] *verb in the phrase* **long for**, to want or desire something very much: *She longed for her independence.*
☐ **longing**, *noun* –**longingly**, *adverb*

> A SIMILAR EXPRESSION is **yearn for**.

longitude /*say* **long**-guh-tyoohd/ *noun* the distance, measured in degrees, by which a point on the earth is east or west of Greenwich in England.
☐ **longitudinal**, *adjective*

> COMPARE this with **latitude**.

longwinded *adjective* talking for too long or using more words than necessary: *His speech was so longwinded that we fell asleep.*
☐ **longwindedness**, *noun*

look *verb* To **look** is to 1. use your eyes in order to see. 2. examine by searching: *to look through all the records.* 3. try to find by searching: *I haven't found your CD yet, but I'll keep looking*; *He looked for the lost dog for hours.* 4. appear or seem: *The house looked as if no-one had lived there for years.* 5. face towards: *The building looks north.*
–*noun* 6. the act of looking: *a look of inquiry.* 7. **looks**, general appearance: *good looks.*
–*phrase* 8. **look after**, to take care of. 9. **look down on**, to think badly of. 10. **look forward to**, to expect with pleasure. 11. **look out**, to be on guard or be watchful: *to look out for cheats.* 12. **look up to**, to admire or respect.

lookout *noun*
1. a watch kept for something that may come or happen. 2. someone who keeps such a watch. 3. a place from which a watch is kept. 4. a place high up where you can admire the view.

loom[1] *noun* a machine or device for weaving yarn or thread into material.

> WORD HISTORY from an Old English word meaning 'tool' or 'implement'

loom[2] *verb* If something **looms** it appears in vague outline, especially in a large or frightening form: *The horse appeared to baulk as the highest hurdle loomed in front.*

> WORD HISTORY from a Swedish word meaning 'move slowly'

loop *noun*
1. a more or less oval shape twisted in a piece of string, wool or something similar. 2. anything shaped like this: *a loop in the road.*
–*verb* 3. If something **loops**, it makes or forms a loop: *The road looped around the hills.*

loophole *noun* a way or means of escape.

loose /*say* loohs/ *adjective*
1. not fastened: *She wore her hair loose to the party.* 2. not bound together: *a loose leaf publication.* 3. not in a container: *loose odds and ends.* 4. not tight: *a loose rope.* 5. not fitting tightly: *These pants are loose.*
–*verb* 6. To **loose** someone or something is to free them from check or control.
–*phrase* 7. **at a loose end**, having nothing to do. 8. **on the loose**, free from check or control: *a prisoner on the loose.*
☐ **loosely**, *adverb* –**loosen**, *verb*

☑ SPELLING TIP Remember the double *o* in **loose**. Don't confuse it with **lose** (spelt with one *o* and pronounced *loohz*). When you **lose** something, you can't find it. You could remind yourself of the spelling of **loose** by thinking that something that is **loose** has extra space and so there is room for the double *o*.

loot *noun*
1. anything that has been stolen.
–*verb* 2. If somebody **loots** a building or **loots** things from a building, they steal things especially in times of war or unrest.
☐ **looter**, *noun* –**looting**, *noun*

lop *verb* (**lops**, **lopping**, **lopped**, **has lopped**) If you **lop** something, you cut off the top part of it: *The council lopped the street tree.*
☐ **lopper**, *noun*

lope *verb* If you **lope**, you move with long, easy steps: *He loped onto the stage, full of confidence.*
☐ **lope**, *noun*: *at a lope.*

lopsided *adjective*
1. leaning to one side: *The pole was lopsided after the car hit it.* 2. larger or heavier on one side than the other: *The weight shifted so that the truck was lopsided.*
☐ **lopsidedly**, *adverb* –**lopsidedness**, *noun*

lord *noun*
1. in Britain, a man with an especially high position in society, who has the word **Lord** as part of his title. 2. in Australia, part of the title of some important positions: *the Lord Mayor of Sydney.*
☐ **lordly**, *adjective*

lore *noun* learning or knowledge, especially on a particular subject: *tribal lore*; *Local lore has it that he was born in this house.*

☑ SPELLING TIP Don't confuse **lore** with **law** which sounds the same. A **law** is a rule made by a government.

lorikeet *noun* a small, brightly coloured parrot that has a brush-like tongue for feeding on nectar.

lorry *noun* (*plural* **lorries**) a motor vehicle with a back part for carrying goods.

ANOTHER WORD for this is **truck** (definition 1) which is more common.

lose /*say* loohz/ *verb* (**loses**, **losing**, **lost**, **has lost**)
1. If you **lose** something, it is missing and you do not know where it is: *I've lost my glasses again.* 2. If you **lose** something, you no longer have it because it has been destroyed: *We lost our home in the fires.* 3. If you **lose** a member of your family, they die: *They lost both of their parents in a car accident.* 4. If you **lose** something, you no longer have it: *She lost her enthusiasm.* 5. If you **lose** something such as a match, race, argument, war or court case, you do not win it. 6. If a business **loses** money, it makes a loss rather than a profit. 7. If your watch **loses** time, the time it shows is earlier than it really is.
–*phrase* 8. **lose face**, to lose worth or position by having a mistake or foolish action made public. 9. **lose out**, to miss out on something: *All the black jelly beans had gone and so I lost out.*
☐ **loser**, *noun*

☑ SPELLING TIP Don't confuse **lose** with **loose** (spelt with a double *o* and pronounced *loohs*). If something is **loose**, it is not tight.

loss *noun*
1. the losing of something: *the loss of his hair*; *the loss of her trust.* 2. something that is lost.
–*phrase* 3. **a dead loss**, a completely useless person or thing. 4. **at a loss**, confused or uncertain: *He was at a loss as to what to do.*

lost *adjective*
1. If something is **lost**, it is no longer in your possession. 2. If you are **lost**, you do not know the way. 3. If time is **lost**, it is wasted or not used.

NOTE This word comes from the verb **lose**.

lot *noun*
1. a large number. 2. a general situation that is typical of someone's life, especially when it is bad: *Never having enough money seems to be her lot.* 3. the drawing of an object from a hat or box to decide something by chance: *We chose who would do classroom duty by lot.*
–*phrase* 4. **a lot**, much: *That is a lot better.* 5. **the lot**, the whole amount.

lotion *noun* a liquid that you use to heal, clean, or nourish your skin.

WORD HISTORY from a Latin word meaning 'a washing'

lottery *noun* (*plural* **lotteries**) a kind of raffle in which the prize is usually money.

lotto *noun* a gambling game in which you select numbers and win money if all or most of these numbers are drawn by chance.

lotus /*say* **loh**-tuhs/ *noun* a kind of flower which grows in water, originally from Asia and Egypt.

loud *adjective*
1. noisy and able to be heard very clearly: *The TV's too loud.* 2. having very strong, bright colours: *The magazine attracted attention with its loud cover.*
–*phrase* 3. **out loud**, so that it can be heard: *Say that again out loud!*
☐ **loudly**, *adverb* –**loudness**, *noun*

SIMILAR WORDS (for definition 1) are **deafening**, **ear-splitting**, **blaring**, **raucous**, **shrill**, **booming** and **resonant**. These all describe a sound that is very loud. If a noise is **deafening** and **ear-splitting**, it is so loud that it could almost make you deaf or cause you pain. **Blaring**, **raucous** and **shrill** all refer to sounds that are loud and harsh in various ways (*a blaring car* *radio, raucous laughter, a shrill, high-pitched whistle*). **Booming** and **resonant** usually describe a voice that is loud and deep and able to be heard from a distance.

loudspeaker *noun* a device which turns electronic signals into sounds, as in a radio or public address system.

THE SHORT FORM of this is **speaker**.

lounge *noun*
1. a long, padded seat for two or more people, with a back and two sides.
–*verb* 2. If you **lounge** in a comfortable chair, you relax into it.

OTHER WORDS (for definition 1) are **couch**, **sofa** and **settee**.

lounge room *noun* See **living room**.

louse /*rhymes with* house/ *noun* singular of **lice**.

lousy /*say* **low**-zee/ *Informal*
–*adjective* (**lousier**, **lousiest**)
1. mean or hateful: *That was a lousy trick to steal their wedding presents.*
–*phrase* 2. **feel lousy**, to feel sick or unwell.

lout *noun* a rough, rude and sometimes violent young man.
□ **loutish**, *adjective*

love *noun*
1. strong or warm feelings of affection. 2. sexual desire. 3. strong liking: *love of music.* 4. no score in tennis and similar games: *The score is 30 love – the server is 30 and the opponent is nil.*
–*verb* 5. If you **love** someone, you have strong feelings of affection for them: *My grandmother brought me up and I love her dearly.* 6. If you **love** doing something, you like doing it very much: *He loves watching horror films.*
–*phrase* 7. **in love with**, feeling deep affection for, as for someone you want to marry: *They are in love with each other.* 8. **make love**, to have sexual intercourse.
□ **loveable**, *adjective* –**lover**, *noun*

SIMILAR WORDS AND EXPRESSIONS (for definition 5) are **adore**, **worship**, **idolise**, **dote on**, **think the world of** and **cherish**. Note that all of these mean 'to love very much'. To **idolise** someone is to love them in a way that makes you see nothing wrong at all about them. To **dote on** someone can be to love them so much that you seem a bit silly. To **cherish** someone or something is to take care of them well because you love them so much.

lovely *adjective* (**lovelier**, **loveliest**)
1. having a beautiful appearance or personality.
2. be very pleasant: *a lovely picnic.*

low[1] *adjective*
1. not far above the ground, floor or base: *a low shelf.* 2. lying below the average level: *low tide*; *low ground.* 3. small in amount: *It was a low price because of the sale.* 4. deep in pitch: *The low notes of the cello contrasted with the melody of the violins.* 5. not loud: *He spoke in a low voice.* 6. less high in rank, quality or importance: *She started in a low position in the company but now she is a manager.* 7. depressed or dejected: *She's been feeling low ever since she failed the exam.*
□ **low**, *adverb* –**lowly**, *adjective*

low[2] *verb Old-fashioned or in literature* When cattle **low**, they make a soft mooing sound.
□ **low**, *noun* –**lowing**, *noun*

lower *verb*
1. If you **lower** something, you make it less in amount or degree: *They lowered their prices to sell the stock more quickly*; *The temperature is lowered until the gas becomes liquid.* 2. If you **lower** your voice, you make it less loud. 3. If you **lower** something, you move it downwards: *They lowered the rope to the next climber.* 4. If you **lower** your eyes, you look downwards: *She lowered her eyes when he came into the room.*
–*adjective* 5. The **lower** part of something is the part nearer the bottom: *I sat on the lower deck of the ferry.*

THE OPPOSITE (of definitions 1–4) is **raise**.

lower case *adjective* If letters are **lower case**, they are small letters, such as *a*, *b*, *c*, and so on.

COMPARE this with **upper case** and **capital** (definition 2).

loyal *adjective* Someone is **loyal** when they do not change in their friendship, support or love for someone or something: *A dog is a loyal companion*; *to be loyal to a team.*
□ **loyally**, *adverb* –**loyalty**, *noun*

lozenge /*say* **loz**-uhnj/ *noun* a small sweet, usually used to soothe a sore throat.

WORD HISTORY from a Persian word meaning 'stone slab'

Ltd *abbreviation* short for *Limited.*

NOTE This is used after the name of a company to show that the people holding shares in it lose only the money they have invested in it if the company gets into debt, often with 'Pty' coming before it. See **Pty**.

lubricate /*say* **looh**-bruh-kayt/ *verb* To **lubricate** a machine is to oil the moving parts of it, so that they will move more easily.
□ **lubricant**, *noun* –**lubrication**, *noun* –**lubricative**, *adjective*

lucerne /*say* **looh**-suhn/ *noun* a plant used to feed cattle.

lucid /*say* **looh**-suhd/ *adjective*
1. clear or easy to understand: *Her presentation was extremely lucid and everyone understood it.* 2. rational or having clear understanding: *The*

player was still lucid despite a severe blow to the head.
☐ **lucidity**, *noun* –**lucidly**, *adverb*

luck *noun*
1. something which happens to a person by chance: *It was just luck that we managed to score the goal a minute before full-time.* **2.** good luck: *She wished me luck.*
☐ **lucky**, *adjective* (**luckier**, **luckiest**) –**luckily**, *adverb* –**luckless**, *adjective*

lucrative /*say* **looh**-kruh-tiv/ *adjective* producing good profits or paying well: *Buffalo hunting is a hazardous but lucrative career.*

ludicrous /*say* **looh**-duh-kruhs/ *adjective* so silly as to cause laughter: *Sally looked ludicrous dressed as an egg.*

lug *verb* (**lugs**, **lugging**, **lugged**, **has lugged**) If you **lug** something somewhere, you drag or take it there with great difficulty, usually because it is heavy: *Don't tell me I've lugged all these heavy books over here for nothing!*

luggage *noun* the bags and other containers you use when travelling.

A SIMILAR WORD is **baggage**.

☑ SPELLING TIP *Double letter alert*: two *g*'s. **Luggage** comes from the word *lug* meaning 'to drag' so think of yourself 'lugging around luggage' and you will remember the double *g*.

lukewarm *adjective*
1. a bit warm: *lukewarm water.* **2.** not very enthusiastic: *a lukewarm audience.*

ANOTHER WORD (for definition 1) is **tepid**.

lull *noun*
1. a period of calm: *the lull before the storm.*
–*verb* **2.** If you **lull** someone, you make them feel calm and settled: *She lulled the baby to sleep*; *We mustn't be lulled into a false sense of security.*

lullaby /*say* **lul**-uh-buy/ *noun* (*plural* **lullabies**) a song sung to put a baby to sleep.

lumber[1] *verb* To **lumber** is to move clumsily or heavily: *The huge bear lumbered through the forest.*

lumber[2] *noun* wood cut up into boards.

ANOTHER WORD for this is **timber** (definition 1). The word **lumber** is used mainly in American English.

lumberjack *noun* someone whose job is to cut down trees.

NOTE This term is mostly used in American English.

luminous /*say* **looh**-muh-nuhs/ *adjective* If something is **luminous**, it shines in the dark, or reflects light well: *The road signs have a special luminous surface.*
☐ **luminosity**, *noun*

☑ SPELLING TIP It will help if you think of the basic meaning of **luminous** as being 'full of light'. Then see that it comes from *lumen* (the Latin word for 'light'), with the *e* changed to *i*, and the suffix *-ous* (meaning 'full of') added. The word *illuminate* also contains *lumin* because it means 'to light up'.

lump *noun*
1. a mass of solid matter: *a lump of clay.* **2.** a swelling: *a lump on the head.*
–*phrase* **3. have a lump in the throat**, to feel as if you're about to cry.
☐ **lump**, *adjective*: *a lump sum of money.* –**lumpy**, *adjective* –**lumpiness**, *noun*

lunar /*rhymes with* sooner/ *adjective* Something **lunar** has to do with the moon: *There's going to be a lunar eclipse next Friday.*

lunatic /*say* **looh**-nuh-tik/ *noun* someone who is mad.
☐ **lunacy**, *noun* –**lunatic**, *adjective*: *a lunatic idea.*

☑ SPELLING TIP Surprisingly, this word comes from *luna*, the Latin word for 'moon'. People used to think that madness was related to the moon.

lunch *noun* (*plural* **lunches**)
1. a light meal eaten in the middle of the day.
–*verb* **2.** When people eat a meal in the middle of the day, they **lunch**.

ANOTHER WORD (for definition 1), when you want to sound more formal, is **luncheon**.

luncheon /*say* **lunch**-uhn/ *noun* See **lunch**.

lung *noun* either of the two bag-like parts of the body in the chest of humans and some other animals, used for breathing.

lunge *verb* To **lunge** is to make a sudden forward movement or attack: *He lunged forward and managed to catch the ball*; *She lost her temper and lunged at him.*
☐ **lunge**, *noun*: *She made a lunge at him.*

lurch[1] *noun* (*plural* **lurches**)
1. a sudden or unsteady movement either to one side or forwards.
–*verb* **2.** If you **lurch**, you stagger in a sudden or unsteady movement, either to one side or forwards: *He lurched into the bathroom.*

lurch[2] *noun in the phrase* **leave someone in the lurch**, to leave someone in a helpless situation: *He quit his job suddenly and left the company in the lurch.*

lure *noun*
1. something that attracts: *The supermarket chain offered a lure of cheaper petrol.* **2.** a device used to attract fish.

–*verb* **3.** If you **lure** somebody or something, you attempt to attract them with something to encourage them to act in a way they would not normally: *My friend lured me away from my homework with talk of going to the beach.*

lurid /*say* **looh**-ruhd/ *adjective*
1. shining with an unnatural glare: *She was wearing a bright red dress and dripping with lurid jewellery.* **2.** horrifying or frightening: *We were terrified by his lurid stories of underworld life.*

lurk *verb* To **lurk** is to stay or move about secretly: *He was always lurking in the background.*

luscious /*say* **lush**-uhs/ *adjective* tasting extremely pleasant: *We had a luscious lunch of crayfish.*
☐ **lusciously**, *adverb* –**lusciousness**, *noun*

☑ SPELLING TIP Remember the *sci* spelling in this word, giving the 'sh' sound. The origin of this word is thought to be related to *delicious*. So remember the opening letters *lus* and then add on the *cious* ending of *delicious*.

lush *adjective* If plants are **lush**, they are very green and growing well: *The cattle grew fat on the lush pasture.*

lust *noun*
1. strong desire: *His lust for power never diminished.* **2.** uncontrolled sexual desire.
–*verb* **3.** If somebody **lusts** for someone or something, they strongly desire them.
☐ **lustful**, *adjective*

lustre /*say* **lust**-uh/ *noun* shining brightness: *The lustre of a pearl is quite beautiful.*
☐ **lustrous**, *adjective*

☑ SPELLING TIP *Tricky 'uh' sound*: this is one of those words like *centre* and *theatre* where the 'uh' sound at the end is spelt *re*.

lute /*rhymes with* boot/ *noun* an old-fashioned musical instrument with strings like a guitar.
☐ **lutenist**, *noun*

luxuriant /*say* lug-**zhooh**-ree-uhnt/ *adjective* strong in growth: *The luxuriant forest was thick with ferns and hanging vines.*
☐ **luxuriance**, *noun* –**luxuriantly**, *adverb*

luxury /*say* **luk**-shuh-ree/ *noun* (*plural* **luxuries**)
1. anything that makes life extremely pleasant or comfortable. **2.** enjoyment of costly food, clothing, and living generally: *I think I deserve a little luxury.*
☐ **luxurious**, *adjective*

lychee /*say* **luy**-chee/ *noun* a fruit consisting of a thin, easily broken shell enclosing a sweet, jelly-like flesh and a single seed.

WORD HISTORY from a Chinese word

lynch /*rhymes with* finch/ *verb* To **lynch** someone is to put them to death, usually by hanging, without a trial: *They had to get him straight into the police van or the mob would have lynched him.*
☐ **lynching**, *noun*

WORD HISTORY named after Captain William *Lynch* (1742–1820) of the United States, who was the first to do this

lynx /*sounds like* links/ *noun* a type of wild cat with long limbs and a short tail.

☑ SPELLING TIP *Letter 'y' alert*: note the *y* spelling for the 'i' sound in this word.

lyre /*say* **luy**-uh/ *noun* a stringed musical instrument of ancient Greece.

☑ SPELLING TIP *Letter 'y' alert*: note the *y* in the spelling of this word. Don't confuse it with **liar** which has the same sound. A **liar** tells lies.

lyrebird *noun* a type of Australian bird which can mimic other sounds and is known for the long beautiful tails which the males display when courting the females.

☑ SPELLING TIP This bird can make all sorts of sounds, but it is not a *liar*. Remember that the first part of its name is the word *lyre*. It was given this name because people thought the lovely feathers of the male bird looked like the ancient Greek instrument.

lyric /*say* **li**-rik/ *adjective*
1. having the form and musical quality of a song: *a lyric style.*
–*noun* **2.** a lyric poem. **3. lyrics**, the words of a song: *Can you remember the lyrics of the first song?*
☐ **lyricist** /*say* **li**-ruh-suhst/, *noun* someone who writes lyrics. –**lyrically**, *adverb* –**lyricism** /*say* **li**-ruh-siz-uhm/, *noun*

ANOTHER WORD (for definition 1) is **lyrical**.

☑ SPELLING TIP *Letter 'y' alert*: note the *y* in the spelling of this word, giving an 'i' sound. This word comes from Greek and is based on the name of the musical instrument, the *lyre*.

Mabo *noun* a decision made by the High Court of Australia in 1992 which declared that Australia was not unoccupied at the time of British settlement, thus allowing Aboriginal and Torres Strait Islander people the right to claim title to land and water where they have had uninterrupted connection.

NOTE This is a short way of saying **Mabo judgement** or **Mabo decision**.
WORD HISTORY named after Eddie Koiki Mabo (1936–1992), a Torres Strait Islander from Murray (Mer) Island

macabre /*say* muh-**kahb**, muh-**kah**-buh, muh-**kah**-bruh/ *adjective* horrible in a gruesome way: *macabre murders.*

☑ SPELLING TIP You can say the ending of **macabre** in several different ways, but remember that the spelling is always *re*.

macadamia /*say* mak-uh-**day**-mee-uh/ *noun* an edible nut with a very hard shell. The macadamia tree is found in eastern Australia and South-East Asia.

macaroni *noun* thick, short tubes of pasta which are boiled and served in a sauce.

WORD HISTORY from an Italian word, and, before that, a Greek word meaning 'food of broth and pearl barley'

☑ SPELLING TIP *Single letter alert*: all the letters are single. Also notice the *i* which is common in words that have come from Italian that are plural in form. Think of the names of some other pastas, such as *spaghetti* and *ravioli*.

macaw /*say* muh-**kaw**/ *noun* a colourful, tropical American parrot with a long tail and a harsh voice.

machete /*say* muh-**shet**-ee/ *noun* a large knife with a broad blade used for slashing thick plants.

WORD HISTORY from a Spanish word meaning 'hammer'

☑ SPELLING TIP Remember the *ete* ending, giving the sound 'et-ee'.

machine /*say* muh-**sheen**/ *noun*
1. a device which is made up of parts that work together and which is used to perform work of some kind: *a washing machine.*
–*verb* **2.** To **machine** something is to make it or do it by machine: *She machined the buttonholes, but did the embroidery on the collar by hand.*
☐ **machinist**, *noun*

machine gun *noun* a gun which repeatedly fires bullets while the trigger is held.

machinery /*say* muh-**sheen**-uh-ree/ *noun*
1. machines in general: *Machinery has made our lives easier.* **2.** the parts of a machine: *the machinery of a clock.*

macho /*say* **mach**-oh, **much**-oh/ *adjective* strongly masculine.

mackerel *noun* a shiny, greenish fish which is used for food.

macramé /*say* muh-**krah**-mee/ *noun* the craft of making things by knotting thread or cord in patterns.

☑ SPELLING TIP Notice that the final letter is an *e* with an accent on it, giving the 'ee' sound. This is because **macramé** comes from French (from an original Turkish word meaning 'tablecloth'). Like other words with an accent, you sometimes see it spelt without it –**macrame**.

mad *adjective*
1. mentally ill or insane: *She went mad.* **2.** angry: *He gets mad if you tease him.* **3.** wild or excited: *They went mad on the dance floor.*
–*phrase* **4. like mad**, *Rather informal* with great speed: *to run like mad.*
☐ **madden**, *verb* –**madly**, *adverb* –**madness**, *noun*

SIMILAR WORDS (for definition 1) are **insane**, **crazy**, **deranged**, **loony**, **loopy**, **barmy** and **nutty**. The last four of these are informal words that are often used in a not very serious way to refer humorously to someone who is a bit mad or silly. There are many informal phrases with a similar meaning which include **mad as a hatter**, **mad as a meat axe**, **off your rocker**, **round the twist** and **round the bend**.

madam /*say* **mad**-uhm/ *noun* (*plural* **madams** *or* **mesdames** /*say* may-**dam**, may-**dahm**/) a polite form of address to a woman: *May I help you, madam?*

ANOTHER FORM When you begin a letter 'Dear Madam', you usually use a capital letter.
WORD HISTORY it comes from the French words 'ma dame' which mean 'my lady'

magazine *noun*
1. a paper containing news, stories and advertisements, usually issued once a week or once a month. 2. a place where explosives are kept.

maggot *noun* the small, white grub which turns into a fly or other similar insect, often found on decaying flesh or food.
☐ **maggoty**, *adjective*

magic *noun*
1. a power which some people believe can make things happen that would normally be impossible: *In the fairytale, the witch used magic to turn the boy into a frog*; *Modern science has explained many things that people used to think happened by magic.* 2. an act in which seemingly impossible tricks are done for entertainment.
☐ **magic**, *adjective* –**magical**, *adjective* –**magically**, *adverb*

magician /*say* muh-**jish**-uhn/ *noun* someone who practises magic or magic tricks.

> ☑ SPELLING TIP Remember that this word comes from *magic* and has a *c* in it, even though the sound has changed. The noun suffix *-ian* (meaning 'having to do with') has been added. A word with a similar pattern is *musician* (from *music*).

magistrate /*say* **maj**-uhs-trayt/ *noun* someone who acts as a judge in some less important court cases: *He had to appear before a magistrate for not paying his speeding fine.*

magma *noun* the very hot molten or liquid rock under the solid crust of the earth's surface.

magnanimous /*say* mag-**nan**-uh-muhs/ *adjective* nobly unselfish and generous: *What a magnanimous gesture to let me have your ticket to the concert.*
☐ **magnanimity** /*say* mag-nuh-**nim**-uh-tee/, *noun* –**magnanimously**, *adverb*

magnate /*say* **mag**-nayt, **mag**-nuht/ *noun* someone who is very powerful and successful, especially in business.

magnesium *noun* a light silver-white metal.

magnet *noun*
1. a piece of metal which has the special power of being able to pull other metal objects towards it. 2. anything that attracts something else.
☐ **magnetic**, *adjective* –**magnetically**, *adverb* –**magnetism**, *noun*

magnetic tape *noun* tape which is used to record sound for a tape recorder, pictures for a video cassette, or data for a computer.

magnificent /*say* mag-**nif**-uh-suhnt/ *adjective*
1. beautiful in a way that gives a feeling of importance: *magnificent architecture.* 2. excellent: *a magnificent meal.*
☐ **magnificence**, *noun* –**magnificently**, *adverb*

> A SIMILAR WORD is **splendid**.

> ☑ SPELLING TIP *Tricky 'uh' sound*: the vowel sound after the *f* is spelt *i*. If you remember this, and also that the *s* sound is spelt with a *c* (just as in *cent*, the unit of money), you will not have any problems sounding out the parts of this word.

magnify *verb* (**magnifies**, **magnifying**, **magnified**, **has magnified**)
1. When a lens **magnifies** something, it makes it look bigger than it really is: *The microscope magnified the cells so that we could see their structure more clearly.* 2. If you **magnify** something, you make it seem more important than it really is.
☐ **magnification**, *noun* –**magnifier**, *noun*

magnitude *noun*
1. size: *What is the magnitude of the angle?* 2. greatness or importance: *It took a few days for the magnitude of the disaster to sink in.*

magnolia *noun* a tree with white or dark pink flowers.

> WORD HISTORY named after P *Magnol* (1638–1715), French botanist

magpie *noun* a black and white bird with a large beak, which is found throughout Australia and New Guinea.

mahjong /*say* mah-**zhong**/ *noun* a game of Chinese origin, usually for four players, with 136 (or sometimes 144) tiles, counters, and dice.

mahogany /*say* muh-**hog**-uh-nee/ *noun* a hard, reddish-brown wood, used for making furniture.

maid *noun*
1. *Old-fashioned* a girl or unmarried woman. 2. a female servant.

> ☑ SPELLING TIP Don't confuse the spelling of **maid** with **made** which has the same sound. **Made** is the past tense and past participle of **make**.

maiden *noun Old-fashioned* a young, unmarried woman.

maiden name *noun* the family name a woman had before she was married, if she has later taken her husband's family name.

mail *noun*
1. letters and packages sent by post.
–*verb* 2. When you **mail** a letter or parcel, you send it by post.
☐ **mail**, *adjective*: *the mail run.*

> ☑ SPELLING TIP Don't confuse the spelling of **mail** with **male** which has the same sound. **Male** describes a man or boy, or an animal of the masculine gender.

maim *verb* To **maim** someone is to damage or cripple them: *These bombs can maim innocent children.*
☐ **maimed**, *adjective*

main *adjective*
1. If something is described as **main**, it is the most important thing: *The main difference between them is their size.*
–*noun* **2.** the largest pipe in a gas or water system.
☐ **mainly**, *adverb*

☑ SPELLING TIP Don't confuse the spelling of **main** with **mane** which has the same sound. A **mane** is the long hair growing on the neck of an animal like a horse or a lion.

mainland *noun* a large land mass, seen as the biggest in comparison with the islands around it.

mainstream *noun* the chief trend or tendency in an area: *in the mainstream of popular music.*

maintain *verb*
1. To **maintain** something is to keep it in good condition: *to maintain a car*; *to maintain a friendship.* **2.** To **maintain** something you have achieved is to hold onto it: *to maintain a lead in a race.*
☐ **maintenance**, *noun*

maize *noun* a tall cereal plant with heads of yellow grain.

WORD HISTORY from a West Indian language called Taino

☑ SPELLING TIP Notice the *i* in this word. Don't confuse it with **maze** which has the same sound. A **maze** is something complicated that you have to find your way through.

majesty *noun* (*plural* **majesties**)
1. greatness or dignity: *We were overwhelmed by the majesty of the vast night sky.* **2. Your Majesty**, the form of address for a king or queen.
☐ **majestic**, *adjective* –**majestically**, *adverb*

major *noun*
1. an officer in the army.
–*adjective* **2.** If something is **major**, it is serious or important: *a major problem.*

THE OPPOSITE (of definition 2) is **minor**.

majority /*say* muh-**jo**-ruh-tee/ *noun*
1. the greater number or more than half: *The majority of the class voted for her, so she won.* **2.** the age at which the law says you are an adult and can vote in elections.

THE OPPOSITE is **minority**.

major scale *noun* any musical scale which has semitones between the third and fourth notes and between the seventh and eighth notes.

COMPARE this with **minor scale**.
NOTE Such a scale is said to be in a **major key**.

make *verb* (**makes**, **making**, **made**, **has made**)
1. If you **make** something, you bring it into being: *My mother makes all my clothes.* **2.** You say you **make** certain actions when you do them: *I need to make a quick telephone call*; *We haven't yet made a decision.* **3.** If something **makes** you a certain way, it causes you to be in that state: *The medicine made her sleepy.* **4.** If someone or something **makes** you do something, they cause you to do it: *Sad movies always make me cry.* **5.** If someone or something **makes** you do something, they force you to do it: *My parents always make me eat up my vegetables.* **6.** If you **make** money, you earn or gain it. **7.** If you **make** a friend, someone becomes your friend. **8.** If you **make** something that you aim for, you succeed in achieving it: *He made the finals of the long jump.* **9.** If two numbers **make** a certain number, they add up to it. That is their total: *5 and 6 make 11, and 7 makes 18, and 4 makes 22.* **10.** If someone or something will **make** something, they have the necessary qualities to turn into it: *This material would make a really nice dress.*
–*noun* **11.** a type or brand: *What make of car does she drive?*
–*phrase* **12. make a face**, to twist up your face to show disgust, etc. **13. make believe**, to pretend. **14. make up**, **a.** to form or complete: *We need three more players to make up a team.* **b.** to invent: *We made up the game ourselves*; *to make up an excuse.* **c.** to become friendly again after an argument. **d.** to apply cosmetics to: *She made up her face.*
☐ **maker**, *noun*

SIMILAR WORDS (for definition 1) are **create**, **devise**, **build**, **construct**, **assemble**, **manufacture** and **produce**. When you **create** and **devise** something, you have the idea for how to make it, or you make it for the first time. When you **build**, **construct** or **assemble** something, especially something large or complicated, you make it by putting parts together. When someone **manufactures** or **produces** something, they make it to be sold. To **produce** something can also be to make it by a natural process or to cause it: *Bees produce honey*; *Painting the wall yellow has produced a nice effect.*

makeshift *noun* something used in place of something else: *I didn't have an umbrella, so I used a newspaper as a makeshift.*
☐ **makeshift**, *adjective*: *a makeshift protection.*

make-up *noun*
1. a product put on your face with the aim of making it attractive-looking: *Mum's in the bathroom putting her make-up on.* **2.** all the different things which go together to make something: *the make-up of a business organisation*; *She has a strange emotional make-up.*

mal- *prefix* a word part meaning 'bad' as in *maltreat, malnutrition*.

WORD HISTORY this prefix comes from Latin

malapropism /*say* **mal**-uh-prop-iz-uhm/ *noun* a word used by mistake for a similar-sounding word, so that the effect is funny: *It is a malapropism to say 'Beethoven wrote nine sympathies' since the right word is 'symphonies'.*

WORD HISTORY named after Mrs *Malaprop*, a character in a play, who misused words in this way

malaria /*say* muh-**lair**-ree-uh/ *noun* an illness which gives you fever and which is spread by mosquitoes.

male *adjective* of the same sex as a man: *the male deer is a stag.*
☐ **male**, *noun*: *the male of the species.*

THE OPPOSITE is **female**.

☑ SPELLING TIP Don't confuse the spelling of **male** with **mail** which has the same sound. **Mail** is all the letters and parcels that are sent by post.

malevolent /*say* muh-**lev**-uh-luhnt/ *adjective* full of ill will: *a malevolent glare.*
☐ **malevolence**, *noun* –**malevolently**, *adverb*

malice /*say* **mal**-uhs/ *noun* the desire to harm or hurt someone: *the malice of your enemy.*
☐ **malicious**, *adjective* –**maliciously**, *adverb*

malignant /*say* muh-**lig**-nuhnt/ *adjective*
1. A tumour or lump in the body is **malignant** when it is the kind that can grow or spread to cause serious illness and death. **2.** To be **malignant** is to be mean or evil: *a malignant look.*
☐ **malignancy**, *noun*

THE OPPOSITE is **benign**.

☑ SPELLING TIP *Tricky 'uh' sound*: the first vowel sound is spelt *a*. See **mal-**.

mall /*say* mawl, mal/ *noun* an area without traffic where people can walk and shop.

☑ SPELLING TIP Note that the usual pronunciation of **mall** is the same as that of **maul**. Don't confuse the spelling of these words. To **maul** someone or something is to attack them savagely.

malleable /*say* **mal**-ee-uh-buhl/ *adjective* easily worked into a different shape: *This plastic is quite malleable when warm.*
☐ **malleability**, *noun*

mallee *noun* a wiry Australian gum tree which has several thin stems which grow from a large underground root.
☐ **the mallee**, *noun* country where these trees grow.

WORD HISTORY probably from an Aboriginal language of Victoria called Wembawemba

mallet *noun*
1. a hammer made of wood. **2.** the wooden stick used to hit the ball in some games, such as polo.

malnutrition /*say* mal-nyooh-**trish**-uhn/ *noun* illness caused by not having enough food.

☑ SPELLING TIP The spelling of **malnutrition** will be easier if you can see that it is made up of the prefix *-mal* (meaning 'bad' or 'wrong') and the word *nutrition*. Remember that in *nutrition*, as in many other words, the final sound 'shuhn' is spelt *tion*.

malt *noun* grain which is used in making beer and whisky.

maltreat *verb* If you **maltreat** someone or something, you treat them roughly or cruelly.
☐ **maltreatment**, *noun*

malware /*say* **mal**-wair/ *noun* computer software that has been created to damage or destroy computers and computer systems, such as a virus.

☑ SPELLING TIP The spelling of **malware** will be easier if you see that it is a combination of the words *mal*(*icious*) and (*soft*)*ware*.

mammal /*say* **mam**-uhl/ *noun* an animal whose young feeds on its mother's milk.
☐ **mammalian** /*say* muh-**may**-lee-uhn/, *adjective*

WORD HISTORY from a Latin word meaning 'of the breast'

mammoth *noun*
1. a type of large, hairy elephant with long, curved tusks, that died out a long time ago.
–*adjective* **2.** extremely big: *a mammoth job.*

man *noun* (*plural* **men**)
1. a grown-up male human being. **2.** human beings in general: *When did man find out how to use fire?* **3.** a piece in a game such as chess or draughts.
–*verb* (**mans**, **manning**, **manned**, **has manned**)
4. If you **man** something, such as a machine or a particular service, you are in charge of operating it: *My sister is manning the information desk.*
☐ **manly**, *adjective* –**manned**, *adjective*

NOTE Another word for definition 2 is **mankind**. However, it is becoming less common now to use either **man** or **mankind** in this sense, that is, including women and children. It is better to say **humans**, **humanity** or **humankind**, as in *a disease dangerous to humans* and *a discovery that will benefit all humanity.*

manage *verb*
1. If you **manage** to do something, you succeed in doing it, although often with difficulty or

narrowly: *Did you manage to finish in time?* **2.** If someone **manages** a business or activity, they control or take charge of it: *My mother manages a bookshop.*
□ **manageable**, *adjective*

management *noun*
1. the running of something: *The old couple left the management of the farm to their son-in-law.* **2.** the people who run something, such as a business or hotel.

manager /*say* **man**-uh-juh/ *noun*
1. someone who runs a business. **2.** someone who looks after the business interests of an entertainer or a sporting team.
□ **managerial** /*say* man-uh-**jear**-ree-uhl/, *adjective*

NOTE A woman who runs a business can be called a **manageress**.

mandarin /*say* man-duh-**rin**/ *noun* a small, soft-skinned, orange-coloured citrus fruit.

ANOTHER SPELLING is **mandarine**.

mandatory /*say* **man**-duh-tree/ *adjective* required or essential: *A life sentence is mandatory for some types of crime.*

SIMILAR WORDS are **compulsory**, **imperative** and **obligatory**.

mandolin /*say* man-duh-**lin**/ *noun* a musical instrument with a pear-shaped wooden body and metal strings which you pluck.

☑ SPELLING TIP *Tricky 'uh' sound*: the middle vowel sound is spelt *o*. Notice that the last four letters, including this *o*, are the same as those in the name of another musical instrument – the *violin*.

mane *noun* the long hair on a male lion's head or along the neck of a horse.

☑ SPELLING TIP Don't confuse the spelling of **mane** with **main** which has the same sound. The **main** thing is the most important or biggest thing.

mange /*say* maynj/ *noun* a skin disease, mainly of animals, in which the skin becomes rough and red and loses its hair.
□ **mangy**, *adjective* (**mangier**, **mangiest**)

manger /*say* **mayn**-juh/ *noun* a box from which cattle or horses eat.

mangle *verb* To **mangle** something is to crush, cut, or ruin it.

mango *noun* (*plural* **mangoes** *or* **mangos**) a sweet, yellow tropical fruit.

mangrove *noun* a tree which grows thickly along the water's edge, sending up roots through the wet earth or sand.

manhole *noun* a covered hole, as in a footpath or ceiling, that you can climb through to get at pipes and wires.

mania /*say* **may**-nee-uh/ *noun*
1. great enthusiasm or excitement: *a mania for football.* **2.** a violent or excitable form of mental illness.
□ **manic** /*say* **man**-ik/, *adjective* –**maniac** /*say* **may**-nee-ak/, *noun* –**maniacal** /*say* muh-**nuy**-uh-kuhl/, *adjective*

manicure *noun* care and treatment of the hands and fingernails.
□ **manicurist**, *noun* someone who does manicures.

manifesto *noun* (*plural* **manifestos** *or* **manifestoes**) a public statement by a government or group, setting out its ideas or goals: *The party issued its manifesto.*

manipulate /*say* muh-**nip**-yuh-layt/ *verb*
1. If you **manipulate** something, you control it in a skilful way: *to manipulate a kite with strings*; *to manipulate the canoe through the rapids.* **2.** If you **manipulate** someone, you influence them cleverly and unfairly to do what you want: *He manipulates his family with his tantrums.* **3.** To **manipulate** the body is to press and move it with the hands, as a chiropractor does: *to manipulate the spine.*
□ **manipulation**, *noun* –**manipulative**, *adjective* –**manipulator**, *noun*

mankind *noun* human beings in general.

SEE the note at **man**.

mannequin /*say* **man**-uh-kuhn, **man**-uh-kwuhn/ *noun*
1. a human-sized figure used to model clothes in a shop window or to fit clothes while they are being made. **2.** someone who wears new clothes to show them to customers.

☑ SPELLING TIP *Double letter alert*: two *n*'s. **Mannequin** comes from a Dutch word meaning 'little man' but you have to remember that the *n* in *man* has been doubled. Also remember that the middle vowel sound is spelt *e*.

manner *noun*
1. a way of being or doing: *a formal manner.* **2. manners**, behaviour or way of behaving: *good manners*; *bad manners.*
□ **mannerism**, *noun*: *a strange mannerism of nodding his head.*

manoeuvre /*say* muh-**nooh**-vuh/ *noun*
1. a clever move: *The team won with a brilliant manoeuvre that ended at the try line.* **2. manoeuvres**, military exercises: *soldiers out on manoeuvres.*
–*verb* **3.** When you **manoeuvre** something, you move it using care or skill: *We manoeuvred the new washing machine into the space beside the laundry cupboard.*

☐ **manoeuvrability**, *noun* –**manoeuvrable**, *adjective*

☑ SPELLING TIP *Tricky vowel sound*: this is a very difficult word to spell because of the group of three vowels *oeu* which give the 'ooh' sound. This is the beginning of the word part *oeuvre* which is the French word for 'work'. **Manoeuvre** has come into English from French. Its origins are the Latin words *manu operare* meaning 'to work by hand'.

manor *noun* a large British country house with its land, originally the home of a lord.

☑ SPELLING TIP Don't confuse the spelling of **manor** with **manner** which has the same sound. Your **manner** is your way of being or doing things.

manse *noun* the house that a member of the clergy lives in.

mansion *noun* a very large house.

manslaughter /*say* **man**-slaw-tuh/ *noun* the accidental killing of someone.

mantelpiece *noun* the shelf above a fireplace.

☑ SPELLING TIP **Mantelpiece** is made up of two words: *mantel* which is the frame around the opening of a fireplace, and *piece*. The tricky bit is remembering the *el* spelling at the end of *mantel*. In fact, it can also be spelt *mantle* but the *el* spelling is the most common and the one to remember.

mantis /*say* **man**-tuhs/ *noun* (*plural* **mantises** *or* **mantes** /*say* **man**-teez/) a long, stick-like, brown or green insect which holds its front legs folded up as if in prayer.

ANOTHER NAME for this is **praying mantis**.

mantle *noun*
1. a loose cloak or cover. **2.** in geology, the layer of the earth between the crust and the core, consisting of solid rock.

manual *adjective*
1. If something is described as **manual**, it is done by a person instead of a machine: *manual work.*
–*noun* **2.** a book which tells you how to do or use something. **3.** a car which has gears that you change with a gear lever, rather than automatically.
☐ **manually**, *adverb*

☑ SPELLING TIP The spelling of this word will be easier if you can see that it is made up of *manu* (the Latin word for 'by hand') and the suffix *-al*.

manufacture *verb*
1. If a company **manufactures** something, they make it with machines in a factory.
–*noun* **2.** the making of goods by hand or by machinery, especially on a large scale.
☐ **manufacturer**, *noun* –**manufacturing**, *adjective*, *noun*

☑ SPELLING TIP The original meaning of **manufacture** was the making of things by hand. The spelling will be easier if you can see that is made up of *manu* (the Latin word for 'by hand') and *facture* (from *facere*, Latin for 'to make'). Several words come from this same Latin word. Think, for example, of *factory*.

manure *noun* animal waste, especially when used as fertiliser.

manuscript *noun* a book, letter, or piece of music, written by hand.
☐ **manuscript**, *adjective*

many *adjective* (**more**, **most**)
1. a large number of people or things: *Many customers have complained about the delay*; *Many people were killed in the war.* **2.** relatively large in number: *Many of the children were away sick*; *Five may be too many.*
–*phrase* **3. a good** (or **great**) **many**, a large number.

Maori /*say* **mow**-ree/ *noun* one of the people who have lived in New Zealand for many centuries.

WORD HISTORY from a Maori word meaning 'of the usual kind'

map *noun*
1. a drawing of an area showing where certain things are, such as towns, roads, mountains and borders.
–*verb* (**maps**, **mapping**, **mapped**, **has mapped**)
2. To **map** an area is to make a map of it.
–*phrase* **3. put on the map**, to make famous or widely known: *The discovery of gold put the town on the map.* **4. wipe off the map**, to destroy completely: *Whole cities were wiped off the map.*

maple *noun* a tree that grows in cold countries, used for its wood and the sweet juice it makes.

mar *verb* (**mars**, **marring**, **marred**, **has marred**)
To **mar** something is to spoil it: *Finding half a caterpillar in my salad marred my enjoyment of the meal.*

marathon *noun*
1. a long-distance foot race, officially of 42 195 metres. **2.** something that takes a long time and often a lot of effort.
☐ **marathon**, *adjective*: *a marathon match.*

WORD HISTORY named after the Greek plain of *Marathon* from which a runner took news of a Greek victory in 490 BC to Athens, 42 kilometres away

marauding /*say* muh-**raw**-ding/ *adjective* going from place to place looking for things to steal or people to attack: *They were scared to sail there because of marauding pirates.*

☑ SPELLING TIP *Tricky vowel sound*: *au* spelling for the 'aw' sound. Also notice the *a* spelling for the 'uh' sound in the first syllable.

marble *noun*
1. a hard limestone of various colours, used in building and sculpture. **2.** a small glass ball used in a game.
☐ **marble**, *adjective* –**marbled**, *adjective*

march *verb*
1. When soldiers **march**, they walk in time with regular steps and swing their arms. **2.** When people **march** somewhere, they walk as an organised and disciplined body: *We marched around the oval in single file.* **3.** If you **march** somewhere, you go there in a determined and angry mood: *She marched into the room and demanded an apology.*
–*noun* (*plural* **marches**) **4.** the act of marching: *We joined the march.* **5.** the distance covered by a march: *The coast is two days' march away.* **6.** an energetic piece of music with a strong rhythm suited to marching.
☐ **marcher**, *noun*

March *noun* the third month of the year, with 31 days.

THE ABBREVIATION is **Mar.**
WORD HISTORY from a Latin word meaning 'the month of Mars', after the planet *Mars*

mare /*rhymes with* hair/ *noun* a fully grown female horse.

NOTE The male is a **stallion** or **stud**.

margarine /*say* mah-juh-**reen**/ *noun* a butter-like spread made from vegetable oil.

☑ SPELLING TIP *Tricky 'uh' sound*: the middle vowel is spelt *a*. Think of spreading **margarine** on *a* slice of toast.

margin *noun* an edge or border, such as the blank space beside the writing on a page.
☐ **marginal**, *adjective* –**marginally**, *adverb*

marijuana /*say* ma-ruh-**wah**-nuh/ *noun* a drug made from the dried leaves and flowers of the Indian hemp plant.

ANOTHER SPELLING is **marihuana**.
ANOTHER WORD for this is **cannabis**.

☑ SPELLING TIP The 'w' sound in **marijuana** is spelt with *ju* or *hu* because it comes from Spanish. Also remember that the middle vowel sound is spelt *i* and it ends with an *a*.

marinate *verb* When you **marinate** food, you add flavour to it by soaking it in a spicy liquid before cooking.
☐ **marinade**, *noun* the liquid used for marinating.

marine *adjective*
1. having to do with the sea: *The reef is full of wonderful marine life*; *She trained as a marine biologist.*
–*noun* **2.** a soldier who serves on a ship and on land.

marionette /*say* ma-ree-uh-**net**/ *noun* a puppet which is worked by strings attached to its limbs.

maritime /*say* **ma**-ruh-tuym/ *adjective* having to do with ships and sailing: *Have you visited the maritime museum?*

mark *noun*
1. something like a spot, line, scratch or stain on anything. **2.** a sign which tells something about an object, such as who made it or who owns it. **3.** a symbol, such as a letter of the alphabet, used to judge behaviour or work: *a good mark for an exam.* **4.** a target: *His arrow hit the mark.* **5.** the place from where you start when you are in a race: *Get on your marks!* **6.** in Australian Rules football, the action of taking a catch.
–*verb* **7.** If you **mark** something, you make a mark on it. **8.** When something **marks** an occasion or event, it is a special feature of that occasion or event: *My parents marked my first day at school by planting a tree in our garden.* **9.** When someone **marks** your work, they judge its value by giving it a number or a symbol: *Has the teacher marked our essays yet?*
–*phrase* **10. make your mark**, to become famous or successful.
☐ **marker**, *noun* –**marking**, *noun*

market *noun*
1. a place where things are bought and sold, often at many different stalls. **2.** the demand for goods: *There's not much of a market for raincoats in the desert.* **3.** current price or value: *a rising market.*
–*verb* (**markets**, **marketing**, **marketed**, **has marketed**) **4.** When you **market** something, you sell it: *to market a new brand of soft drink.* .

marketing *noun* the selling of a product in an organised way, usually including advertising.

marlin *noun* a large, powerful fish with an upper jaw like a spear.

marmalade /*say* **mah**-muh-layd/ *noun* a jam made of citrus fruits, such as oranges and grapefruit.

WORD HISTORY from a Greek word meaning 'honey apple'

☑ SPELLING TIP *Tricky 'uh' sound*: the middle vowel sound is spelt *a*. Remember you need three *a*'s to make **marmalade** properly. Apart from this, you should have no trouble sounding out the parts of this word.

maroon /*say* muh-**rohn**, muh-**roohn**/ *adjective* dark brownish-red.
☐ **maroon**, *noun*

marooned /*say* muh-**roohnd**/ *adjective* left in a place from which you cannot get away, especially one that is surrounded by water: *The boat's engine broke down and we were marooned on the island.*

marquee /*say* mah-**kee**/ *noun* a big tent used for outdoor parties, circuses and so on.

> ☑ SPELLING TIP Notice the 'qu' spelling for the 'k' sound and the *ee* ending. **Marquee** is spelt like this because it comes from French.

marriage celebrant *noun* someone who is authorised by the government to marry people.

marrow *noun*
1. the soft substance inside bones which is important in producing red blood cells. **2.** a large white, yellow or green vegetable.

marry /*say* **ma**-ree/ *verb* (**marries**, **marrying**, **married**, **has married**)
1. If you **marry** someone, you become their husband or wife. **2.** If a person with special authority **marries** a man and a woman, he or she performs the ceremony by which they become husband and wife.
☐ **marriage** /*say* **ma**-rij/, *noun* –**married**, *adjective*

> ☑ SPELLING TIP Notice that the *y* at the end of **marry** changes to an *i* when the suffix *-age* is added to make the noun **marriage**. You do not hear this as an extra syllable when you say the word **marriage**, so you have to remember it is there.

marsh *noun* low-lying, wet land.
☐ **marshy**, *adjective*

> SIMILAR WORDS are **bog** and **swamp**.

marshal *noun*
1. someone who organises the activities at a show or other public occasion.
–*verb* (**marshals**, **marshalling**, **marshalled**, **has marshalled**) **2.** If you **marshal** a group of people, you gather them together and organise them into rows or ranks: *to marshal the troops.*

> ☑ SPELLING TIP *Single letter alert*: only one *l* at the end. However, remember that you double the *l* when you add *-ed* or *-ing*. Don't confuse the spelling with **martial** which has the same sound. Something that is **martial** has to do with fighting or war.

marshmallow *noun* a soft sweet made from gelatine, sugar and flavouring.

marsupial /*say* mah-**sooh**-pee-uhl/ *noun* a mammal such as a kangaroo which keeps and feeds its young in a pouch for a few months after birth.

> WORD HISTORY from a Latin word meaning 'pouch'

martial /*say* **mah**-shuhl/ *adjective* having to do with war or fighting: *martial tactics.*

> ☑ SPELLING TIP Remember the *tial* spelling for the 'shuhl' sound at the end. Don't confuse **martial** with **marshal** which has the same sound. To **marshal** people is to gather them together.

martial arts *plural noun* sports such as judo and kung-fu which have developed from fighting but don't use weapons and are based on self-defence.

martyr /*say* **mah**-tuh/ *noun*
1. someone who is killed or suffers a great deal for the sake of their beliefs. **2.** someone who goes to great trouble for others, just so they can feel pleased with themselves and receive the pity of others.
☐ **martyrdom**, *noun*

> ☑ SPELLING TIP *Letter 'y' alert*: the ending is spelt *yr* (not *er*). As with many words with a *y* spelling, this word comes from Greek.

marvel *noun*
1. something which causes happiness and surprise.
–*verb* (**marvels**, **marvelling**, **marvelled**, **has marvelled**) **2.** If you **marvel** at something, you are filled with admiration and surprise: *I marvel at your ability to concentrate with all this noise.*
☐ **marvellous**, *adjective* –**marvellously**, *adverb*

> ☑ SPELLING TIP Notice the ending is *el*, not *le*. Also remember that you double the final *l* when you add *-ous*, *-ed* or *-ing*.

marzipan /*say* **mah**-zuh-pan/ *noun* a sweet made of crushed almonds and sugar.

> ☑ SPELLING TIP *Tricky 'uh' sound*: the middle vowel sound is spelt *i* (you will notice it makes the word *zip* inside the word **marzipan**).

mascara *noun* a substance used to colour the eyelashes.

> WORD HISTORY from a Spanish word meaning 'a mask'

mascot *noun* something which is thought to bring good luck.

masculine /*say* **mas**-kyuh-luhn/ *adjective* If someone or something is **masculine**, they have qualities or characteristics which are thought to be typical of men.
☐ **masculinity**, *noun*

> THE OPPOSITE is **feminine**.

mash *verb* If you **mash** something, you crush it so that it becomes a soft mass: *Mash the banana.*
☐ **mashed**, *adjective*

mask *noun*
1. a covering for your face, worn as a disguise or for protection.

–*verb* **2.** If you **mask** something, you hide or disguise it: *to mask your identity.*
☐ **masked**, *adjective*

mason *noun* someone who builds or works with stone.
☐ **masonry**, *noun*

masquerade /*say* mas-kuh-**rayd**, mahs-kuh-**rayd**/ *noun*
1. a party at which the guests wear clothes or costumes that make them look like someone else, such as a famous person or a person from another time. **2.** a false show: *It was just a masquerade of kindness.*
–*verb* **3.** If you **masquerade** as something, you disguise yourself as that thing: *He managed to meet the famous actor by masquerading as a photographer.*

☑ SPELLING TIP Remember the *qu* spelling for the 'k' sound. This word is based on *masque*, the French word 'mask'.

mass[1] *noun*
1. a quantity of matter of no particular shape or size: *a mass of hair*; *an ice mass.* **2.** a large number or quantity: *a mass of applications*; *a mass of people.* **3.** the amount of matter in a body.
–*verb* **4.** When large numbers of people or things **mass** somewhere, they group there.

mass[2] *noun* a religious service in the Roman Catholic and some other Christian churches.

ANOTHER FORM You can also spell this with a capital letter.

massacre /*say* **mas**-uh-kuh/ *noun*
1. the killing of a large number of people.
–*verb* **2.** If someone **massacres** a large number of people, they kill them in a cruel and violent way.

A SIMILAR WORD (for definition 1) is **carnage**.

☑ SPELLING TIP Remember that a **massacre** is the killing of a lot or a *mass* of people. The tricky bit is the *re* (not *er*) ending. Other words like this are *centre* and *theatre*.

massage /*say* **mas**-ahzh/ *noun*
1. the act of rubbing and pressing the body, to relax it or improve health.
–*verb* **2.** If someone **massages** a part of your body, they give you a massage: *to massage a stiff neck.*
☐ **masseur** /*say* mas-**er**/, *noun* –**masseuse** /*say* mas-**erz**/, *noun*

massive *adjective* large and heavy: *a massive load.*
☐ **massively**, *adverb*

SIMILAR WORDS are **colossal**, **enormous**, **gigantic**, **huge** and **vast**.

mass media *plural noun* radio, television, newspapers, and magazines, by which information is passed on to large numbers of people.

mass-produce *verb* To **mass-produce** something is to make it in large quantities with machines in factories: *to mass-produce cars.*
☐ **mass-production**, *noun*

mast *noun*
1. a tall pole rising from the deck of a ship to support the sails. **2.** any upright pole: *a radio mast.*

master *noun*
1. someone who has control over others: *the ship's master.* **2.** someone who has special skill: *He is a master of disguise.* **3.** the owner of a dog or other animal.
–*verb* **4.** When you **master** something, you get control of it: *to master French*; *to master your temper.*
☐ **masterly**, *adverb* –**mastery**, *noun*

masterpiece *noun* the most excellent piece of work of an artist, musician or writer.

masturbate *verb* To **masturbate** is to rub the genitals to produce a pleasant sexual sensation.
☐ **masturbation**, *noun*

mat *noun*
1. a piece of material of some kind used to cover the floor or part of it: *a bath mat*; *a rubber mat.* **2.** a small piece of material for putting under a plate or the like.
–*verb* (**mats**, **matting**, **matted**, **has matted**) **3.** If something like hair **mats**, it becomes thick and messy.
☐ **matting**, *noun*

match[1] *noun* (*plural* **matches**) a short, thin piece of wood tipped with a chemical substance which produces fire when you scrape it on a rough surface.

match[2] *noun* (*plural* **matches**)
1. someone or something that equals or looks like another in some way. **2.** a contest or game: *a football match.*
–*verb* **3.** If things **match**, they agree exactly: *Those saucers don't match the cups.* **4.** If you **match** two people, you have them in opposition to each other: *The two brothers were matched against each other in the sprint final.*

mate *noun*
1. a friend. **2.** the male or the female of a pair of animals: *the fox and its mate.*
–*verb* **3.** When animals **mate**, a male and a female come together to have sexual intercourse and make babies.

NOTE People you share things with are described as mates, as in *flatmate*, *workmate*, *classmate*.

material *noun*
1. the substance which is used to make something: *writing material*; *building materials.* **2.** cloth: *curtain material.*

–*adjective* **3.** having to do with things with a physical existence, rather than ideas, thoughts, emotions and so on: *Some people think that material possessions, such as money, houses and cars, are more important than love.*
☐ **materialism**, *noun*

materialise *verb* When someone or something **materialises**, they appear in a physical shape: *We heard footsteps, but it was several seconds before the face of a young boy materialised at the window.*

ANOTHER SPELLING is **materialize**.

maternal *adjective* having to do with or behaving like a mother: *my maternal grandfather*; *maternal pride.*
☐ **maternity**, *noun*

mathematics /*say* math-uh-**mat**-iks/ *noun* the science dealing with numbers and the size of things: *Mathematics is my favourite subject.*
☐ **mathematical**, *adjective* –**mathematician** /*say* math-uh-muh-**tish**-uhn/, *noun*

NOTE This word is often shortened to **maths**. In American English the abbreviated form is **math**.

matilda *noun Old-fashioned* a swag.

NOTE You now only hear this word in the song 'Waltzing Matilda', which is an expression meaning 'going about as a swagman'.

matinee /*say* **mat**-uh-nay/ *noun* an afternoon performance of a play or showing of a film.

☑ SPELLING TIP This comes from a French word (meaning 'morning'), which is why it has the *ee* spelling at the end, giving an 'ay' sound.

matri- *prefix* a word part meaning 'mother', as in *matriarch*.

WORD HISTORY this prefix comes from Latin

matriarch /*say* **may**-tree-ahk/ *noun* (*plural* **matriarchs**) a woman leader in a family, tribe or any field of activity.
☐ **matriarchal**, *adjective* –**matriarchy**, *noun*

☑ SPELLING TIP The spelling will be easier if you see that **matriarch** is made up of the prefix *matri-* (from the Latin word for 'mother') and the suffix *-arch* which means 'chief' or 'ruler'. This suffix comes from Greek and is found in several other words relating to rulers and government, such as *monarch*.

matrimony /*say* **mat**-ruh-muh-nee/ *noun* the state of being married.
☐ **matrimonial**, *adjective*

matron /*say* **may**-truhn/ *noun*
1. *Old-fashioned* a middle-aged, married woman. **2.** formerly, the most important nurse who is in charge in some hospitals.
☐ **matronly**, *adjective*

NOTE For definition 2, the official term these days is usually **director of nursing** or a similar term.

matt *adjective* having a dull surface: *matt paint.*

☑ SPELLING TIP Note that this word is usually spelt with a double *t* at the end, although it can also be spelt **mat**. Don't confuse it with **mat**, something to cover the floor.

WORD HISTORY from a French word meaning 'dead'

matter *noun*
1. the substance of which things are made. **2.** a particular kind of substance: *vegetable matter.* **3.** an affair or subject: *a matter of the heart.* **4.** trouble or difficulty: *Do you mind if I use your phone, there's something the matter with mine.*
–*verb* **5.** If someone or something **matters**, they are of importance to you.
–*phrase* **6. as a matter of fact**, actually.

matter-of-fact *adjective* ordinary, not excited or imaginative: *a matter-of-fact tone.*

mattock *noun* a tool for loosening the soil, like a pick but with a blade instead of a point.

mattress *noun* a case filled with soft material, often reinforced with springs, used as a bed.

mature /*say* muh-**tyooh**-uh/ *adjective*
1. A **mature** animal or plant is fully grown and developed: *The mature fruit is harvested in autumn.* **2.** A **mature** person is fully adult. Generally they are at least in their twenties. **3.** If someone behaves in a **mature** way, they have a sensible and serious attitude to life. **4. Mature** fruit, cheese or wine is ripe or has developed its full flavour.
–*verb* **5.** When an animal or plant **matures**, it becomes fully grown and developed.
☐ **maturation**, *noun* –**maturity**, *noun*

matzo /*say* **mat**-soh/ *noun* (*plural* **matzos**) a biscuit made of bread without yeast, eaten by Jewish people during the Feast of the Passover.

NOTE Another name for bread made without yeast is **unleavened bread**.

maul *verb* If an animal **mauls** you, it injures you by tearing at you with its claws and teeth.

☑ SPELLING TIP Don't confuse the spelling of **maul** with **mall** which has the same sound. A **mall** is an area without traffic where people can stroll and shop.

mauve /*say* mohv/ *adjective* light purple.

maxim *noun* a saying containing a general truth or rule: *'Don't count your chickens before they hatch' is a well-known maxim.*

ANOTHER WORD for this is **proverb**.

maximum *noun* (*plural* **maximums** *or* **maxima**) the greatest number or amount possible: *This lift holds a maximum of 16 people.*
□ **maximum**, *adjective* –**maximise**, *verb*

ANOTHER SPELLING for **maximise** is **maximize**.
THE OPPOSITE of **maximum** is **minimum**.

may *verb*
1. If you say something **may** happen, you mean that it could possibly happen: *It may rain tomorrow – there are quite a few dark clouds around.* **2.** If you say that something **may** be true, or **may** have happened, you mean that it could possibly be true or could have happened: *He is a terrible liar but what he says about his sister may be true.* **3.** If you **may** do something, you are allowed to do it: *You may come in.*

NOTE This verb is always used with another verb in the form **I may** or **I might**. See *modal verbs* in the Grammar and Punctuation Guide appendix.

May *noun* the fifth month of the year, with 31 days.

maybe *adverb* possibly: *It's not like her to be late – maybe she slept in.*

mayhem *noun* disorder or confusion.

WORD HISTORY from a French word meaning 'injury'

mayonnaise /*say* may-uh-**nayz**/ *noun* a thick, cold sauce made from eggs and oil and eaten with salad.

☑ SPELLING TIP *Double letter alert*: two *n*'s. Also remember the *aise* ending. It is spelt like this because it has come into English straight from French.

mayor /*say* mair/ *noun* the person elected to lead a city.
□ **mayoral**, *adjective* –**mayoress**, *noun*

NOTE The wife of a **mayor** can be called a **mayoress**. This term is also sometimes used for a woman who is a mayor but **mayor** is the usual term for either a man or a woman in this position.

☑ SPELLING TIP Don't confuse the spelling of **mayor** with **mare** which has the same sound. A **mare** is a female horse.

maze *noun* a confusing and complicated arrangement of many crossing paths or lines that you have to find a way through.

me *pronoun* the form of the pronoun **I** you use after a verb: *Take me with you.*

meadow *noun* a small field.

NOTE This word is used mostly in poetic language.

meagre /*say* **mee**-guh/ *adjective* small and not enough to satisfy: *a meagre meal.*

☑ SPELLING TIP *Tricky vowel sound*: *ea* for the 'ee' sound. Also remember the *re* (not *er*) ending. Other words like this are *centre* and *theatre*.

meal[1] *noun* food served at more or less fixed times each day: *Breakfast is the first meal of the day.*

meal[2] *noun* grain which has been ground or crushed.
□ **mealy**, *adjective* soft, dry and crumbly.

mean[1] *verb* (**means**, **meaning**, **meant** /*say* ment/, **has meant**) To **mean** is to **1.** intend: *I mean to visit them tomorrow.* **2.** be a sign of or indicate: *'Dim sum' means 'little heart'*; *Those black clouds mean trouble.*

☑ SPELLING TIP Remember that the past form **meant** keeps the spelling *mean* (with *t* added), even though the pronunciation changes so that it sounds like 'ment'.

mean[2] *adjective*
1. unwilling to share or give anything away. **2.** unkind: *What a mean thing to say!*

SIMILAR WORDS (for definition 1) are **miserly**, **penny-pinching**, **ungenerous**, **stingy** (*Informal*) and **tight** (*Informal*).

mean[3] *noun*
1. something halfway between two end points. **2.** in mathematics, the average.
□ **mean**, *adjective*

meander /*say* mee-**an**-duh/ *verb* When someone or something **meanders**, they wind or wander about: *My sister spent hours meandering about the market looking at earrings*; *The track meandered through the forest.*

meaning *noun* what is referred to or indicated by something: *I don't know the meaning of this word*; *The teacher explained the meaning of the poem to us.*
□ **meaningful**, *adjective* –**meaningless**, *adjective*

means *plural noun* **1.** a method or way used to reach an end: *a means of transport.* **2.** a supply of money: *Our means are quite enough for our needs.*
–*phrase* **3. by all means**, certainly: *Go, by all means.* **4. by means of**, by the use of: *He got his good results by means of hard work.*

NOTE Although this is a plural noun, definition 1 is usually followed by a singular verb: *The means is not as important as the end result.*

meanwhile *adverb* at the same time: *My sister was inside doing her homework. Meanwhile, her friends were playing outside.*

☑ SPELLING TIP You won't have any problems with spelling this word if you can see that it is made up of two words you know well: *mean* (in the sense of **mean³**) and *while* (remember the silent *h*).

measles *noun* a type of infectious disease occurring mostly in children, with a fever and rash.

WORD HISTORY from a German word meaning 'a spot'

measure /*say* **mezh**-uh/ *noun*
1. the size or quantity of something. **2.** an agreed unit or standard: *A litre is a measure of volume.* **3.** a means to an end: *to take measures to prevent flood damage.*
–*verb* **4.** When you **measure** something, you decide the size or quantity of it, usually by using a special instrument such as a ruler or scales.
–*phrase* **5. measure up to**, to be suitable for.
☐ **measurable**, *adjective* –**measurement**, *noun*

SIMILAR WORDS (for definition 4) are **calculate**, **estimate**, **gauge** and **survey**. **Estimate** has the sense of a rough, not exact measurement. **Gauge** can have the same meaning or it can mean to measure certain things with particular instruments: *Airports have instruments to gauge the wind rate.* **Survey** in this sense has the specific meaning of measuring the form and boundaries of land.

☑ SPELLING TIP *Tricky vowel sound*: *ea* for the 'e' sound in the first syllable. Also remember the *sure* ending which sounds like *shuh*. Think of other words with this spelling and sound, such as *pleasure* and *treasure*.

meat *noun* the flesh of animals when used for food.

☑ SPELLING TIP Don't confuse the spelling of **meat** with **meet** which has the same sound but is spelt with a double *e*. To **meet** someone is to come across them, either by accident or by arrangement.

mechanic /*say* muh-**kan**-ik/ *noun* a person who repairs machinery.

mechanical /*say* muh-**kan**-i-kuhl/ *adjective*
1. having to do with or worked by machinery or tools. **2.** like a machine: *to speak in a mechanical way.*

mechanise /*say* **mek**-uhn-uyz/ *verb* If an industry **mechanises**, it changes its means of production to the use of machines: *Mechanising the dairy industry meant the milking of cows could be done much more efficiently.*
☐ **mechanisation**, *noun*

ANOTHER SPELLING is **mechanize**.

mechanism /*say* **mek**-uhn-iz-uhm/ *noun* a piece of machinery.

medal *noun* a metal disc or cross given as a reward for bravery or as a prize.
☐ **medallist**, *noun*

☑ SPELLING TIP Don't confuse the spelling of **medal** with **meddle** which has the same sound. To **meddle** is to interfere with something that doesn't concern you. Note that **medal** ends with *al* but that the *l* is doubled when the word **medallist** is formed.

medallion *noun* a large medal.

meddle *verb* To **meddle** is to concern yourself with something that is none of your business.
☐ **meddler**, *noun* –**meddlesome**, *adjective* –**meddling**, *adjective*

☑ SPELLING TIP Don't confuse the spelling of **meddle** with **medal** which has the same sound. A **medal** is given as a reward for bravery or as a prize.

media *plural noun* the means of communication, including radio, television, newspapers and magazines.

NOTE This word is actually the plural of **medium** but it can be treated as a singular or plural noun. For example, in *The media encourages violence*, it is singular; in *The media are to blame for the loss of the election*, it is plural. It is mainly used as a plural when different forms of media, such as radio, television, newspapers, etc., are being referred to.

median *adjective* coming in the middle: *We had managed to get across one side of the highway and were stuck on the median strip.*

mediate *verb* If someone **mediates** between people or groups who are arguing, they try to get them to agree: *He was asked to mediate in the dispute between the two employees.*
☐ **mediator**, *noun* someone who mediates. –**mediation**, *noun*

medical *adjective* having to do with medicine or its practice: *The talk was full of medical jargon that we couldn't understand.*
☐ **medically**, *adverb*

medication *noun* drugs taken to treat an illness: *You must not take these tablets if you are taking another medication.*
☐ **medicate**, *verb*

medicine /*say* **med**-uh-suhn, **med**-suhn/ *noun*
1. a substance used in treating disease: *cough medicine.* **2.** the art or science of treating disease: *skilled in medicine.*
☐ **medicinal** /*say* muh-**dis**-uh-nuhl/, *adjective*: *a medicinal drug.*

☑ SPELLING TIP Remember that there is an *i* in the middle of **medicine** (after the *d*), although you sometimes do not hear it when the word is pronounced. If you think of the adjective form **medical**, you should remember the *i*.

medieval /*say* med-ee-**eev**-uhl/ *adjective* Something **medieval** belongs in the Middle Ages, that is, from about the fifth to the fifteenth century in Europe: *a medieval castle.*

ANOTHER SPELLING is **mediaeval**.

mediocre /*say* mee-dee-**oh**-kuh/ *adjective* To be **mediocre** is to be neither good nor bad: *mediocre abilities.*
□ **mediocrity** /*say* mee-dee-**ok**-ruh-tee/, *noun*

☑ SPELLING TIP The difficulty here is the *ocre* (giving the sound of 'ohkuh'). Particularly remember that the final part is *re* (not *er*). Other words like this are *centre* and *theatre*.

meditate *verb* To **meditate** is to think long and deeply: *to meditate on a problem.*
□ **meditation**, *noun* –**meditative**, *adjective*

medium *noun* (*plural* **media** *or* **mediums**)
1. the way in which something is done or communicated: *an advertising medium*; *the medium of television.* **2.** the material or method used by an artist: *A potter works in the medium of clay.* **3.** (*plural* **mediums**) someone who claims to be able to communicate with the spirits of dead people. –*adjective* **4.** average in size, degree, quality, and so on: *a man of medium height.*

medley *noun* a mixture: *He played a medley of tunes on the flute.*

meek *adjective* humbly patient or submissive: *He was too meek to complain about the poor service.*
□ **meekly**, *adverb* –**meekness**, *noun*

meet *verb* (**meets**, **meeting**, **met**, **has met**)
1. If you **meet** someone, you come together in the same place with them, either by chance or by arrangement: *I met my friend in the street.* **2.** If you **meet** someone, you are there to greet them when they arrive. **3.** If you **meet** someone, you are introduced to them for the first time. **4.** If a group of people **meet**, they gather together for a reason: *Let's meet again to discuss it in more detail.* **5.** When things **meet**, they come together or join: *Remember to turn right where the track meets the main road.* **6.** If you **meet** a need, you satisfy it.

☑ SPELLING TIP Don't confuse the spelling of **meet** with **meat** which has the same sound. **Meat** is the flesh of animals when used for food.

meeting *noun* a coming together of people for a purpose: *a meeting of the computer club*; *a business meeting.*

SIMILAR WORDS are **gathering**, **assembly**, **conference**, **convention**, and **summit**. A **conference** or **convention** is a large meeting where people discuss something important for several days, such as business, politics or an academic subject. A **summit** is a important meeting between the government leaders of powerful countries: *The leaders of the Western nations held a summit to discuss environmental policies.*

mega- *prefix* a word part meaning 'great' or 'huge', as in *megastar*, *megabucks*.

WORD HISTORY this prefix comes from Greek

megabyte /*say* **meg**-uh-buyt/ *noun* a unit for measuring information stored by a computer, equal to 10 000 000 bytes.

megafauna /*say* **meg**-uh-faw-nuh/ *noun* a group of very large animals, especially those that are extinct, such as giant kangaroos and giant wombats.

megalomania /*say* meg-uh-luh-**may**-nee-uh/ *noun* a mental illness in which the patients falsely believe they are great and powerful.
□ **megalomaniac**, *noun*

megaphone *noun* a funnel-shaped device for increasing or directing sound.

megawatt *noun* a unit of electrical power, equal to one million watts.

THE SYMBOL for this is **MW**.

melancholy /*say* **mel**-uhn-kol-ee/ *noun* a feeling of sadness.
□ **melancholic**, *adjective*: *a melancholic outlook.* –**melancholy**, *adjective*: *a melancholy tune.*

melanin /*say* **mel**-uh-nuhn/ *noun* the dark colouring in the skin.

melanoma *noun* (*plural* **melanomas** *or* **melanomata**) a malignant tumour formed from cells containing dark pigments, especially in skin.

ANOTHER TERM for this is **skin cancer**.
WORD HISTORY from Greek words meaning 'black' and 'tumour'

melee /*say* mel-**ay**/ *noun* a noisy and confused situation sometimes involving fighting.

☑ SPELLING TIP *Tricky vowel sound*: *ee* for the 'ay' sound at the end. **Melee** is spelt like this because it has come into English straight from French. Other words with this spelling for the same sound, also from French, are *entree* and *fiancé*.

mellow *adjective*
1. smooth and pleasing, such as a colour, taste or sound: *a mellow voice*; *a mellow flavour.* **2.** softened by time: *a mellow attitude to life.* –*verb* **3.** When something **mellows**, it becomes more mellow: *Wine mellows with age.*
□ **mellowness**, *noun*

melodrama *noun* a play in which the characters make their emotion much more obvious than in real life.
□ **melodramatic**, *adjective*

WORD HISTORY from a Greek word meaning 'music drama'

melody /*say* **mel**-uh-dee/ *noun* a tune.
☐ **melodic** /*say* muh-**lod**-ik/, *adjective* –**melodious** /*say* muh-**loh**-dee-uhs/, *adjective* –**melodiously**, *adverb*

melon *noun* a large, juicy fruit with a thick skin.

melt *verb* To **melt** is to **1.** make or become liquid with heat: *The snow melted in the spring.* **2.** disappear gradually: *The rider melted into the mist.* **3.** fill with feelings of affection: *His heart melted.*

member *noun*
1. each of the people forming a society, parliament, or other group. **2.** a part of a whole, such as a limb of your body.
☐ **membership**, *noun*

membrane *noun* a thin sheet or film covering a part of the body or part of a plant.
☐ **membranous**, *adjective*

memento *noun* (*plural* **mementos** *or* **mementoes**) something that acts as a reminder of what is past: *We brought back some shells as a memento of our holiday at the beach.*

☑ SPELLING TIP A **memento** has a lot to do with *memory*, and nothing to do with a *moment*, which is why it begins with *mem*. Don't make the common mistake of spelling it 'momento'.

memo /*say* **mem**-oh, **mee**-moh/ *noun* (*plural* **memos**) a note of something to be remembered: *The manager sent around a memo about next week's meeting.*

WORD HISTORY short for *memorandum*

memoirs /*say* **mem**-wahz/ *plural noun* a record of the life and times of somebody based on their personal experience.

A SIMILAR WORD is **autobiography**.

memorable *adjective* worth remembering.

memorial *noun* something to make people remember a person or event: *a memorial to a great leader.*

memory /*say* **mem**-uh-ree/ *noun*
1. the ability to store things in your mind and remember them when needed. **2.** something remembered: *a memory of home.* **3.** part of a computer in which information is stored until needed.
–*phrase* **4. in memory of**, in order to make people remember: *a monument in memory of those who died in the war.*
☐ **memorise**, *verb* to learn by heart: *to memorise a speech.* –**memorisation**, *noun*

ANOTHER SPELLING for **memorise** is **memorize**.

☑ SPELLING TIP *Tricky 'uh' sound*: the ending of **memory** is *ory* (not *ary*). It might help if you think of *ory* being part of the word *story* – a memory is like a story from the past.

memory stick *noun* See **USB drive**.

menace *noun*
1. something or someone dangerous. **2.** a threatening attitude: *to speak with menace.* **3.** *Rather informal* someone or something that is annoying: *That child is a real menace!*
–*verb* **4.** If someone or something **menaces** you, they threaten you: *I was menaced by a growling dog in the park.*
☐ **menacing**, *adjective*

menagerie /*say* muh-**naj**-uh-ree/ *noun* a collection of wild or unusual animals, especially for show.

mend *verb*
1. If you **mend** something that is broken or not working properly, you fix it or set it right. **2.** If a part of the body is broken or hurt, it **mends** as it gets better: *Her broken ankle is mending.*
–*phrase* **3. on the mend**, improving in health.

menial *adjective* having to do with or fit for servants: *As the cleaner, he had to do all sort of menial tasks.*
☐ **menial**, *noun* a servant.

meningitis /*say* men-uhn-**juy**-tuhs/ *noun* a disease which causes the lining of the brain to swell up.

menopause *noun* the time in a woman's life when her monthly periods stop altogether.
☐ **menopausal**, *adjective*

menstruate /*say* **men**-strooh-ayt/ *verb* When a female **menstruates**, she has a flow of blood from the womb, usually monthly.
☐ **menstrual**, *adjective* –**menstruation**, *noun*

mental *adjective* having to do with the mind: *I formed a mental picture of the scene*; *He suffers from a mental illness.*
☐ **mentality**, *noun* –**mentally**, *adverb*

mention *verb* If you **mention** something, you speak or write about it briefly: *She mentioned that her mother was sick.*
☐ **mention**, *noun*

mentor *noun* a wise and trusted adviser: *His mentor had been generous in giving advice and assistance over the years.*

WORD HISTORY from *Mentor*, friend of the Greek hero Odysseus and guardian of his household when he went to Troy

menu *noun*
1. a list of the dishes served at a meal or in a restaurant. **2.** in computers, a list of choices presented by a computer program.

mercenary /*say* **mer**-suhn-ree/ *adjective*
1. A **mercenary** person works only for money: *He has a mercenary attitude to his painting.*
–*noun* (*plural* **mercenaries**) **2.** a soldier who is paid to fight in a foreign army.

merchandise /*say* **mer**-chuhn-duys/ *noun* goods for sale.

☑ SPELLING TIP Despite the sound, there is no *ice* in **merchandise**. Remember that the end is spelt *ise*.

merchant *noun* someone who buys and sells goods.
☐ **merchant**, *adjective*

mercury *noun* a silvery metallic element which is liquid instead of solid at ordinary temperatures.

ANOTHER WORD for this, now old-fashioned, is **quicksilver**.
WORD HISTORY named after the planet *Mercury* because long ago the symbol for the planet was used for the metal as well

mercy *noun* (*plural* **mercies**) kindness shown by not punishing someone or not being cruel.
☐ **merciful**, *adjective* –**merciless**, *adjective*

mere *adjective* being nothing more than: *She is a mere two days old.*
☐ **merely**, *adverb*

merge *verb* To **merge** is to unite or mix together: *The two groups merged.*
☐ **merger**, *noun*

meridian /*say* muh-**rid**-ee-uhn/ *noun* a line of longitude.

meringue /*say* muh-**rang**/ *noun* a mixture of sugar and beaten whites of eggs used in cakes and sweets.

☑ SPELLING TIP A **meringue** takes its name from a type of cake made in the German city of Mehringen but has come into English from French which is why it has the unusual *ingue* spelling for the 'ang' sound.

merino /*say* muh-**ree**-noh/ *noun* (*plural* **merinos**) a type of sheep that has very fine wool.

WORD HISTORY from a Latin word meaning 'of the larger sort'

merit *noun*
1. excellence: *a poem of merit.* **2. merits**, the qualities or features of something or someone, whether good or bad: *to judge each applicant on their merits.*
–*verb* (**merits**, **meriting**, **merited**, **has merited**) **3.** If you **merit** something, you deserve it: *This essay merits a high mark.*

mermaid *noun* an imaginary sea creature, a woman from the waist up and a fish from the waist down.
☐ **merman**, *noun*

WORD HISTORY from the Latin word for 'lake' added to the word *maid*

merry *adjective* (**merrier**, **merriest**) cheerful and happy.
☐ **merriment**, *noun* –**merrily**, *adverb* –**merry-making**, *noun*

merry-go-round *noun* a circular platform with wooden horses or the like on it, which goes around and which you ride on for fun.

OTHER WORDS for this are **roundabout** and **carousel**.

mesh *noun* a netting of some kind: *caught in the mesh of a fishing net.*
☐ **enmesh**, *verb*: *to enmesh a trapped animal.*

mesmerise *verb* If something **mesmerises** you, it completely holds your attention: *We were mesmerised by the sight of the snake swallowing the frog.*
☐ **mesmerisation**, *noun*

ANOTHER SPELLING is **mesmerize**.
WORD HISTORY named after FA *Mesmer*, an 18th century German doctor who used to hypnotise people (the old meaning of **mesmerise** was 'to hypnotise')

mess *noun*
1. a dirty or untidy state. **2.** a difficult or confused state: *My history project is in a mess.* **3.** a room to eat in, especially in the army.
–*phrase* **4. mess about** (or **around**), *Informal* to waste time doing useless things.
☐ **messy**, *adjective* (**messier**, **messiest**) –**messiness**, *noun* –**messily**, *adverb*

message *noun*
1. information sent from one person to another. **2.** the meaning of something such as a book or what it tries to teach you.
–*verb* **3.** To **message** someone is to communicate with them by a text message.
–*phrase* **4. get the message**, to understand.

messenger *noun* someone who carries a message.

☑ SPELLING TIP *Double letter alert*: two *s*'s, just the same as in the related word *message*.

meta- *prefix* a word part meaning 'change', as in *metamorphosis*.

WORD HISTORY this prefix comes from Greek

metabolism /*say* muh-**tab**-uh-liz-uhm/ *noun* all the processes and chemical changes happening in any living thing.

metal *noun* an element which is shiny, able to be shaped or worked, and is often a good conductor of electricity: *Iron, copper and gold are metals.*
☐ **metallic**, *adjective* –**metalwork**, *noun*

☑ SPELLING TIP Don't confuse the spelling of **metal** with **mettle** which has the same sound. To be on your **mettle** is to try to do your very best.

metamorphosis /*say* met-uh-**maw**-fuh-suhs/ *noun* (*plural* **metamorphoses** /*say* met-uh-**maw**-fuh-seez/) a change from one form to another: *the metamorphosis of a tadpole into a frog.*
☐ **metamorphic**, *adjective*

☑ SPELLING TIP The spelling of this difficult word will be easier if you can see that it is made up of the prefix *meta-* (meaning 'change'), *morph* (a form of *morphe*, the Greek word for 'form') and the suffix *-osis* (used to make nouns that have to do with a process or condition).

metaphor /*say* **met**-uh-fuh, **met**-uh-faw/ *noun* a figure of speech in which something is spoken of as if it were something else: *'She is a rock in a stormy sea' is a metaphor.*
☐ **metaphorical**, *adjective* –**metaphorically**, *adverb*

COMPARE this with **simile**.

meteor /*say* **mee**-tee-aw, **mee**-tee-uh/ *noun* a small piece of dust or rock from outer space which burns brightly after entering the earth's atmosphere.

☑ SPELLING TIP There are three syllables in this word – *me* + *te* + *or*. It comes from a Greek word meaning 'phenomenon in the heavens'. It has nothing to do with 'meat' or 'meeting' someone!

meteorite /*say* **mee**-tee-uh-ruyt/ *noun* a mass of stone or metal that has reached the earth from outer space.

meteorology /*say* mee-tee-uh-**rol**-uh-jee/ *noun* the study of weather and climate.
☐ **meteorological**, *adjective* –**meteorologist**, *noun*

meter *noun* an instrument that measures, especially one that measures the amount of gas, electricity or water passing through it.

☑ SPELLING TIP Remember that **meter** ends with *er*. Don't confuse it with **metre** which is a unit of measurement of length.

method *noun* a way of going about something, especially an orderly way: *a method for doing an experiment.*
☐ **methodical**, *adjective* –**methodically**, *adverb*

methylated spirits *noun* a liquid used for cleaning and sometimes as a fuel.

meticulous /*say* muh-**tik**-yuh-luhs/ *adjective* careful about small details: *There has to be meticulous maintenance of planes so that they are safe.*
☐ **meticulously**, *adverb*

WORD HISTORY from a Latin word meaning 'fearful'

metre[1] /*say* **mee**-tuh/ *noun* a unit of measurement of length in the metric system.

THE SYMBOL for this is **m**.

☑ SPELLING TIP Remember that **metre** ends with *re*. Don't confuse it with **meter** which is an instrument for measuring gas, etc.

metre[2] /*say* **mee**-tuh/ *noun* the regular arrangement of stressed and unstressed syllables in poetry.
☐ **metrical**, *adjective*

☑ SPELLING TIP See **metre**[1].

metric *adjective* **Metric** measurements are expressed in terms of the international standard system based on the number 10 which uses units such as metres, kilometres, kilograms and litres.

metric system *noun* a system of measurement originally based on the metre.

metronome /*say* **met**-ruh-nohm/ *noun* an instrument that can be set to beat at a fixed rate and so give the right speed of performance for a piece of music.

metropolitan /*say* met-ruh-**pol**-uh-tuhn/ *adjective* having to do with a large city.
☐ **metropolis** /*say* muh-**trop**-uh-luhs/, *noun* a large city.

mettle *noun*
1. the quality of someone's character, especially when spirited or brave: *This job will give you a chance to prove your mettle.*
–*phrase* **2. on your mettle**, eager to do your best.
☐ **mettlesome**, *adjective*

☑ SPELLING TIP Don't confuse the spelling of **mettle** with **metal** which has the same sound. A **metal** is a hard substance like gold, silver, copper or iron.

mezzanine /*say* **mez**-uh-neen, mez-uh-**neen**/ *noun* a balcony-like floor in a building, usually between the ground floor and the next.

micro- *prefix* a word part meaning **1.** very small, as in *microscopic*, *microchip*. **2.** making bigger or stronger, as in *microscope*, *microphone*.

WORD HISTORY this prefix comes from Greek

microbe *noun* a tiny living creature which is so small that it can only be seen under a microscope, and which sometimes carries disease.

microchip *noun* a minute square which contains electronic circuits, used in a computer, watch, or electronic game.

NOTE The prefix 'micro-' meaning 'very small' indicates that this is even smaller than an ordinary electronic **chip**.

microfiche /*say* **muy**-kroh-feesh/ *noun* a sheet of transparent plastic about the size of a filing card which may have many pages of print on it that can be read with a special projector.

microfilm *noun* a photographic film with very small images which can be enlarged when projected, used for storing information.

microorganism *noun* a microscopic animal or vegetable organism.

microphone /*say* **muy**-kruh-fohn/ *noun* an instrument which changes sound waves into electrical waves, often used in equipment that makes sounds louder or records them on a tape recorder.

☑ SPELLING TIP *Tricky 'uh' sound*: the middle vowel sound is spelt *o*. It will help if you see that this is part of the prefix *micro-*. This prefix has two meanings – 'very small' or 'magnifying or increasing' – but it is the second meaning that is used here. The stem of the word, *phone*, is a word you know well. It is used in the names of instruments that have to do with sound, like this word and *telephone*. Both of the word parts come from Greek.

microscope /*say* **muy**-kruh-skohp/ *noun* an instrument used for looking at extremely tiny things that you normally cannot see.
☐ **microscopic**, *adjective*: *microscopic bacteria.*

☑ SPELLING TIP *Tricky 'uh' sound*: the middle vowel sound is spelt *o*. It will help if you see that this is part of the prefix *micro-*. This prefix has two meanings – 'very small' or 'magnifying or increasing' – but it is the second meaning that is used here. The stem of the word, *scope*, is used in the names of instruments used for viewing, like this word and *telescope*. Both of the word parts come from Greek.

microwave oven *noun* a type of oven which heats or cooks food very quickly by passing high-speed waves through it.

mid- *prefix* a word part meaning 'middle', as in *midnight*.

midday *noun* twelve o'clock in the middle of the day.

middle *noun* a halfway point: *the middle of the oval*; *the middle of a song.*
☐ **middle**, *adjective*

midget *noun* a very small person or thing.
☐ **midget**, *adjective*: *a midget submarine.*

midnight *noun* twelve o'clock at night.

midriff *noun* the part of the body between the chest and the waist.

midwife /*say* **mid**-wuyf/ *noun* (*plural* **midwives** /*say* **mid**-wuyvz/) a nurse specially trained to help a woman while she is giving birth to a baby.
☐ **midwifery** /*say* mid-**wif**-uh-ree/, *noun*

might[1] *verb*
1. the past tense of the verb **may**. **2.** If you say you **might** do something, you mean that it is possible that you will: *We might come if the weather clears up.*

NOTE This is always used with another verb. See *modal verbs* in the Grammar and Punctuation Guide appendix.

☑ SPELLING TIP Don't confuse the spelling of **might** with **mite** which has the same sound. A **mite** is a small insect.

might[2] *noun* power or force: *I pushed at the door with all my might, but it wouldn't open.*

☑ SPELLING TIP See **might**[1].

mighty *adjective*
1. powerful: *a mighty force*; *a mighty emperor.*
2. extremely large: *a mighty ocean.*

migraine /*say* **muy**-grayn, **mee**-grayn/ *noun* a very bad headache which makes you feel ill.

☑ SPELLING TIP The first part of this word may be pronounced 'muy' or 'mee' but it is spelt *mi* in either case. If you also remember the *aine* ending, particularly the final *e* (a **migraine** is your 'enemy'), you won't find spelling this word a pain in the head! It is spelt like this because it comes from French.

migrant *noun* someone who leaves their own country to go and live in another.

migrate *verb*
1. If people **migrate**, they move from one country to go and live in another country. **2.** When animals **migrate**, they go to a different area for part of the year.
☐ **migration**, *noun*: *the migration of arctic birds.* –**migratory**, *adjective*

mild *adjective*
1. gentle: *a mild voice.* **2.** not severe: *mild pain.*
3. not sharp or strong: *a mild flavour.*
☐ **mildly**, *adverb* –**mildness**, *noun*

mildew *noun* a coating or growth which appears on slightly wet cloth, paper, leather and other materials.
☐ **mildewy**, *adjective*

mile *noun* a unit of length in the imperial system equal to about 1.6 kilometres.
☐ **mileage**, *noun*

WORD HISTORY from a Latin word meaning 'a thousand'

militant *adjective* fighting or ready to fight, especially for a cause: *There was trouble between the government and a militant trade union.*
☐ **militancy**, *noun* –**militant**, *noun* –**militantly**, *adverb*

military *adjective* having to do with soldiers: *a military band.*

militia /*say* muh-**lish**-uh/ *noun* a group of part-time citizen soldiers.

milk *noun*
1. the white liquid produced by female mammals to feed their young, especially cow's milk. The milk of the cow and some other animals is used for food for humans.
–*verb* **2.** If you **milk** a cow or other female mammal, you get milk from the udder of that animal.
☐ **milky**, *adjective*

mill *noun*
1. a building with machinery for crushing grain into flour. **2.** a small machine for crushing food into powder: *a coffee mill*; *a pepper mill.* **3.** a factory, especially one for spinning or weaving: *a woollen mill.*
–*phrase* **4. run of the mill**, very common or usual.
☐ **miller**, *noun*

millennium *noun* a period of 1000 years.

WORD HISTORY from Latin words meaning 'a thousand' and 'year'

☑ SPELLING TIP *Double letter alert*: double *l* and double *n*. The double *n* is the one you have to concentrate on remembering, as many people make a mistake with this.

millet *noun* a cereal grain grown in Asia and southern Europe.

milli- *prefix* a word part expressing a thousandth part of a given unit, as in *millilitre*.

millibar *noun* a metric unit of measurement for air pressure, especially in the atmosphere.

THE SYMBOL for this is **mb**.

☑ SPELLING TIP *Double letter alert*: two *l*'s in the prefix *milli-* which means 'thousandth'. In this word, this prefix is joined to the word *bar*. It can also be joined to other measurement words to make a word meaning a thousandth part of that measurement, as you can see in *milligram*, *millilitre* and *millimetre*.

milligram *noun* a unit of measurement in the metric system equal to one thousandth of a gram.

THE SYMBOL for this is **mg**.

millilitre *noun* a unit of measurement in the metric system equal to one thousandth of a litre.

THE SYMBOL for this is **ml** or **mL**.

millimetre *noun* a unit of measurement in the metric system equal to one thousandth of a metre.

THE SYMBOL for this is **mm**.

milliner /*say* **mil**-uh-nuh/ *noun* someone who makes or sells hats.

million *noun* a cardinal number, one thousand times one thousand, 1 000 000 or 10^6.
☐ **million**, *adjective* –**millionth**, *adjective*, *noun*

millionaire *noun* someone who has a million dollars or more.

☑ SPELLING TIP All you have to remember here is the *aire* ending joined to the familiar word *million*. The ending is spelt in this way because it comes from French.

millipede *noun* a small creature like a caterpillar with a long body made up of many parts, most of which have two pairs of legs.

☑ SPELLING TIP The spelling of **millipede** will be easier if you see that it is made up of the prefix *milli-* (which comes from the Latin word for 'thousand') and the word ending *-pede* (from the Latin word for 'foot'). So, while a *centipede* is meant to have 100 feet, the **millipede** is said to have even more!

mime *noun*
1. a form of acting in which the actors tell the story by using movements of their body and face instead of words. **2.** a play in which the performers use this form of acting.
–*verb* **3.** If you **mime** something, you communicate it using movements of your face and body instead of words: *She mimed a question to me from the opposite railway platform.*

mimic /*say* **mim**-ik/ *noun*
1. someone who is good at copying the voice and movements of others.
–*verb* (**mimics**, **mimicking**, **mimicked**, **has mimicked**) **2.** If you **mimic** someone, you copy their voice and actions.
☐ **mimicry** /*say* **mim**-uh-kree/, *noun*

☑ SPELLING TIP Remember that this word ends in *ic* (not *ick*). However, when you add *-ed* or *-ing*, the *k* is added.

mince *verb*
1. If you **mince** something, you chop it up into very small pieces.
–*noun* **2.** meat that has been finely chopped up.

mind *noun*
1. the part of you that thinks and feels, using judgement, memory, and so on. **2.** intelligence, understanding or mental ability. **3.** your opinion or what you think or feel: *to speak your mind.*
–*verb* **4.** If you **mind** someone or something, you look after them: *to mind the children*; *to mind my place.* **5.** If you tell someone to **mind** something, you are warning them to be careful about it: *Mind the floor – it's slippery.*
–*phrase* **6. make up your mind**, to come to a decision. **7. stick in your mind**, to stay in your memory: *His words stuck in my mind for years.*

☐ **mindful**, *adjective*: *mindful of the feelings of others.*

mine[1] *noun*
1. a large hole dug in the ground to remove precious stones, coal and the like. **2.** a rich store of anything: *The internet is a mine of information.* **3.** a bomb placed underground or in the sea.
–*verb* **4.** When you **mine** for precious stones, coal and the like, you remove them from the ground by digging a mine: *to mine for diamonds.*

mine[2] *pronoun* one of the forms of **I** and **me** that you use to show that something belongs to you: *That CD is mine*; *a cousin of mine.*

miner[1] *noun* someone who works in a mine.

> ☑ SPELLING TIP Don't confuse the spelling of **miner** with **minor**. These words have the same sound, but note the different endings. Something that is **minor** is not large or important.

miner[2] *noun* a type of bird with a yellow beak and yellow or yellow-brown legs: *We have lots of noisy miners in our yard.*

> ☑ SPELLING TIP See **miner**[1].

mineral *noun* a substance such as stone, ore or coal which is obtained by mining.
☐ **mineral**, *adjective*

mineral water *noun* water containing dissolved mineral salts and gases.

minestrone /*say* min-uh-**stroh**-nee/ *noun* a soup made with vegetables, herbs, pasta, and so on.

> WORD HISTORY from Italian, from a Latin word meaning 'serve' or 'wait on'

mingle *verb*
1. If something **mingles** with something else, it becomes mixed with it: *sugar mingled with some sand.* **2.** If you **mingle**, you move among a group of people, for example at a party, and talk to them.

mini- *prefix* a word part meaning 'small' or 'miniature', as in *minibus*.

> WORD HISTORY this prefix comes from Latin and is a short form of *miniature*

miniature /*say* **min**-uh-chuh/ *noun*
1. a very small copy or model of something: *The model castle is a miniature of the real thing.* **2.** a very small painting, especially a portrait.
☐ **miniature**, *adjective*

> ☑ SPELLING TIP *Silent letter alert*: don't forget the *i* after the *n*. Although you cannot hear the second *i*, remember that this word contains *mini*, used in many words that have to do with smallness.

minibus *noun* a motor vehicle that is big enough to carry roughly twice the number of passengers that a normal car can carry.

minim *noun* a note in music equal to half a semibreve in length.

> WORD HISTORY from a Latin word meaning 'least' or 'smallest'

> ☑ SPELLING TIP Notice that the two vowel sounds in this word are both spelt *i*. The second is the tricky one to remember.

minimum *noun* (*plural* **minimums** *or* **minima**)
1. the smallest number or amount possible: *You'll need a minimum of $20 spending money.* **2.** the lowest number.
☐ **minimise**, *verb* –**minimum**, *adjective*

> ANOTHER SPELLING for **minimise** is **minimize**.
> THE OPPOSITE of **minimum** is **maximum**.

> ☑ SPELLING TIP **Minimum** comes from the Latin word *minimus* which means 'least' or 'smallest'. Just think of a 'mini mum' and you won't go wrong.

miniskirt *noun* a very short skirt.

minister /*say* **min**-uh-stuh/ *noun*
1. a member of parliament who is in charge of a government department. **2.** a priest in some branches of the Christian church.
–*verb* **3.** To **minister** to someone is to give them service, care, or help: *She ministered to homeless people.*
☐ **ministerial** /*say* min-**uh**-stear-ree-uhl/, *adjective*

mink *noun*
1. an animal that looks like a weasel and lives part of the time in water. **2.** the valuable fur of this animal.

minor *adjective*
1. not very serious or important: *She suffered only minor injuries.*
–*noun* **2.** someone who is under the legal adult age.

> THE OPPOSITE (of definition 1) is **major**.

> ☑ SPELLING TIP Don't confuse the spelling of **minor** with **miner**. These words have the same sound, but note the different endings. A **miner** is someone who works in a mine, or a kind of bird.

minority *noun* (*plural* **minorities**)
1. the smaller part or number, or less than half. **2.** a group of people whose views are different to the views of most other people: *Most people clapped, but a minority booed.*

> THE OPPOSITE is **majority**.

minor scale *noun* any musical scale which has a semitone between the second and third notes, between the fifth and sixth notes and between the seventh and eighth notes.

NOTE Such a scale is said to be in a **minor key**. COMPARE this with **major scale**.

minstrel *noun* a musician in the Middle Ages who sang or recited poetry while playing an instrument.

WORD HISTORY from a French word meaning 'servant'

mint[1] *noun*
1. a herb with leaves that are used in cooking. **2.** a peppermint.

mint[2] *noun*
1. a place where money is made by the government.
–*verb* **2.** To **mint** money is to make it in a mint: *to mint coins.*
–*adjective in the phrase* **3. in mint condition**, new or looking like new: *She takes such good care of her bike that it is still in mint condition, even though she has been using it for three years.*

minus *preposition* **Minus** is used to show that one number or quantity is subtracted or taken away from something else. In writing mathematical equations the **minus sign** (−) is used to represent this word, as in '15−7=8': *Fifteen minus seven equals eight.*

THE OPPOSITE is **plus**.

minuscule /*say* **min**-uhs-kyoohl/ *adjective* tiny.

SIMILAR WORDS are **microscopic** and **minute**.

☑ SPELLING TIP *Tricky 'uh' sound*: the vowel sound in the middle is spelt *u* (not *i*). Remember that **minuscule** comes from the Latin word *minus* (meaning 'less'), and not from the prefix *mini-* (meaning 'small').

minute[1] /*say* **min**-uht/ *noun*
1. a sixtieth part of an hour. **2.** any short space of time: *Don't go, I'll be there in a minute.* **3. minutes**, the official record of what has been discussed in a meeting.

minute[2] /*say* muy-**nyooht**/ *adjective* extremely small: *The figures in the hot air balloon far above looked minute.*

miracle *noun*
1. an event which cannot be explained by natural or scientific facts or arguments, believed to be caused by a supernatural power. **2.** a surprising or remarkable thing: *It will be a miracle if she finds the ring she lost at the beach.*
☐ **miraculous**, *adjective* –**miraculously**, *adverb*

mirage /*say* muh-**rahzh**/ *noun* a false vision in which someone sees distant things as much closer than they really are, or even sees things that are not there at all.

WORD HISTORY from a French word meaning 'look at (yourself) in a mirror'

mire /*rhymes with* buyer/ *noun*
1. wet, swampy ground. **2.** deep mud.
☐ **miry**, *adjective*

mirror *noun*
1. glass that has been treated so that you can see yourself reflected in it. **2.** something that gives a true picture of something else: *That film was a mirror of my grandmother's life.*
–*verb* **3.** When something **mirrors** something else, it reflects it, as if in a mirror: *trees mirrored in the water*; *Her face mirrored her emotion.*

mirth *noun* amusement and laughter: *His eyes twinkled with mirth.*
☐ **mirthful**, *adjective*

mis- *prefix* a word part meaning **1.** failure, as in *misfire*. **2.** wrong, as in *mishap*, *mislead*. **3.** not, as in *mistrust*.

WORD HISTORY this prefix comes from Old English

misadventure *noun*
1. bad luck or a piece of ill fortune. **2.** an accident or mishap.

misbehave *verb* To **misbehave** is to behave badly: *Out teacher said she was embarrassed when some of the class misbehaved while we were on an excursion.*
☐ **misbehaviour**, *noun*

miscarriage *noun*
1. the failure to get the right result or decision: *a miscarriage of justice.* **2.** the birth of a dead baby, especially early in a pregnancy.
☐ **miscarry**, *verb* (**miscarries**, **miscarrying**, **miscarried**, **has miscarried**)

miscellaneous /*say* mis-uh-**lay**-nee-uhs/ *adjective* A **miscellaneous** group is made up of things of several different kinds: *The store room contained a miscellaneous collection of junk.*
☐ **miscellaneously**, *adverb* –**miscellany** /*say* muh-**sel**-uh-nee/, *noun*

☑ SPELLING TIP *Silent letter alert*: don't forget the *c* after the *s* (which begins the word *cell* hidden in the word *miscellaneous*). Also remember the ending is *eous* (not the more common *ious*). It might help to rap it out: *mis+cell+an+e+ous.*

mischief /*say* **mis**-chuhf/ *noun*
1. behaviour meant to tease or annoy. **2.** harm, injury or trouble.
☐ **mischievous** /*say* **mis**-chuh-vuhs/, *adjective*

☑ SPELLING TIP *Tricky 'uh' sound*: the second vowel sound is spelt *ie*. Remember also that that the ending of the adjective **mischievous** is *vous* – without an *i* although some people say the word incorrectly by making it into two syllables with an 'ee-uhs' sound.

miser /*say* **muy**-zuh/ *noun*
1. someone who is obsessed with storing up money. **2.** someone who is mean and greedy.
☐ **miserly**, *adjective*

miserable /*say* **miz**-ruh-buhl/ *adjective*
1. Someone who is **miserable** is very unhappy or uncomfortable. **2.** Something **miserable** causes unhappiness or discomfort: *miserable living conditions.* **3.** mean; not generous: *a miserable amount of pocket money.*
☐ **miserably**, *adverb*

☑ SPELLING TIP Don't forget the *e* in the middle, although you do not hear it when the word is pronounced. It will help if you remember that this word comes from *misery* where you can hear the middle syllable with the *e* spelling. The final *y* has been dropped and the suffix *-able* added. Rap it out as *mis+er+a+ble*.

misery /*say* **miz**-uh-ree/ *noun* (*plural* **miseries**) great unhappiness.

misfire *verb*
1. If something like a gun **misfires**, it fails to fire or explode properly. **2.** If something like a plan **misfires**, it goes wrong or it fails.

misfit *noun* someone who does not fit in or get along well with other people.

misfortune *noun* bad luck: *It was just misfortune that we missed the train.*

misgiving *noun* a feeling of doubt or worry.

mishap /*say* **mis**-hap/ *noun* an unlucky accident: *I had a mishap on the way to school – I dropped my bag and my drink bottle spilt everywhere.*

☑ SPELLING TIP *Single letter alert*: only one *s*. It will help if you can see that this word is made up of the prefix *mis-* (meaning 'mistaken' or 'wrong') and *hap* (an old word for a 'happening').

misjudge *verb* (**misjudges**, **misjudging**, **misjudged**, **has misjudged**) If you **misjudge** something, you do not assess it correctly: *He misjudged the distance that he had to throw the ball.*
☐ **misjudgement**, *noun*

ANOTHER SPELLING for **misjudgement** is **misjudgment**.

mislay *verb* (**mislays**, **mislaying**, **mislaid**, **has mislaid**) If you **mislay** something, you cannot find it because you cannot remember where you put it: *My dad is always mislaying his glasses.*

mislead *verb* (**misleads**, **misleading**, **misled**, **has misled**)
1. If someone or something **misleads**, they lead or guide wrongly: *The real estate agent misled her as to what her house was worth*; *The sign was very unclear – it misled us into taking the wrong turn.* **2.** If someone **misleads** you, they influence you badly or lead you into error or into doing something that is wrong: *His parents were worried that he would get into trouble because his friends were misleading him.*
☐ **misleading**, *adjective* –**misleadingly**, *adverb*

miss[1] *verb* To **miss** is to **1.** fail to hit, meet, catch, see, hear and so on: *to miss a shot in tennis*; *to miss a bus*; *to miss a film.* **2.** fail to attend: *to miss school for several days.* **3.** notice or feel sad about the absence or loss of someone or something: *We missed our dog when he died.*
–*phrase* **4. miss out on**, to fail to receive, especially something you particularly want: *My sister was disappointed because she missed out on a place at university.*
☐ **miss**, *noun*

miss[2] *noun*
1. Miss, a title put before an unmarried woman's name. **2.** a form of address for an unmarried woman or for any young woman.

NOTE Some women prefer the title **Ms** because it makes no reference to whether they are married or not.

missile /*say* **mis**-uyl/ *noun* an object or weapon that can be thrown or shot.

☑ SPELLING TIP *Double letter alert*: two *s*'s.

missing *adjective* If someone or something is **missing**, they are not where they should be and cannot be found: *The missing shoe eventually turned up under the bed.*

mission *noun*
1. a group of people sent out, usually to another country, to do government or religious work. **2.** a duty someone is sent to carry out: *He had thirty days to complete his mission.*

WORD HISTORY from a Latin word meaning 'a sending'

missionary /*say* **mish**-uhn-ree/ *noun* (*plural* **missionaries**) someone sent out, often to another country, on religious work.

mist *noun*
1. a cloud-like collection of water vapour, like a very thin fog.
–*verb* **2.** If something **mists**, it becomes covered with mist: *His eyes misted when he thought of happier days*; *The windows misted in the rain.*
☐ **misty**, *adjective* –**mistily**, *adverb*

mistake *noun*
1. an action or decision that is wrong or has an unwanted result.
–*verb* (**mistakes**, **mistaking**, **mistook**, **has mistaken**) **2.** If you **mistake** someone or something for another person or thing, you wrongly believe them to be someone or something

different: *I mistook her for a very old friend – which was very embarrassing!*
☐ **mistaken**, *adjective* –**mistakenly**, *adverb*

SIMILAR WORDS (for definition 1) are **error**, **slip**, **slip-up**, **blunder**, **boo-boo** (*Informal*) and **misjudgement**. A **slip** or a **slip-up** is a small mistake, while a **blunder** is usually a big mistake.

mister *noun Rather informal* a form of address for a man: *Excuse me, Mister, can you tell me the time?*

NOTE **Mister** (spelt with a capital letter) is the full form of **Mr** but only the abbreviation is used these days.

mistletoe /*say* **mis**-uhl-toh/ *noun* a plant with small, white berries which feeds and grows on the branches of other trees, and is often used for Christmas decorations.

mistress *noun*
1. a female owner of an animal like a dog or a horse. **2.** a female teacher in charge of a particular subject or department at school. **3.** a woman who has a sexual relationship with a man who is married to someone else. **4.** in the past, a woman in charge of everyone in a house.

mistrust *noun*
1. suspicion, or a lack of trust or confidence.
–*verb* **2.** If you **mistrust** someone, you have a lack of trust or confidence in them.
☐ **mistrustful**, *adjective* –**mistrustfully**, *adverb*

misunderstanding *noun*
1. a failure to understand correctly: *Because of a misunderstanding, everyone went to different pizza places.* **2.** a disagreement or argument: *They had a major misunderstanding and are not speaking to each other.*
–*verb* (**misunderstands**, **misunderstanding**, **misunderstood**, **has misunderstood**) **3.** If you **misunderstand** someone or something, you do not understand them: *They misunderstand her – she really is very nice!*; *Dad misunderstood what the policeman said and backed into the parking meter.*

misuse *noun* /*say* mis-**yoohs**/
1. wrong use: *They said there had been a misuse of public money.*
–*verb* /*say* mis-**yoohz**/ **2.** To **misuse** something is to use it in the wrong way: *She told us not to misuse the computer by sending rude messages on it.*

mite *noun* a tiny creature, like a very small spider, which lives in food like cheese or flour or feeds off plants and animals.

☑ SPELLING TIP Don't confuse the spelling of **mite** with **might** which has the same sound. **Might** is power.

mitre /*say* **muy**-tuh/ *noun*
1. the tall, pointed hat worn by a bishop. **2.** the angle cut at the ends of two pieces of wood which are then joined together.

mitten *noun* a kind of glove which covers the four fingers together and the thumb separately.

mix *verb*
1. If you **mix** things, you combine them in the same place, so that it is not easy to separate them out again: *Mix the butter and sugar until they are creamy.* **2.** If you **mix** something, you make it by combining two or more things: *We mixed a special drink of lemonade and ice-cream.* **3.** If you **mix** socially, you meet people and relate to them.
–*phrase* **4. mix with**, to be friends with or associate with.
☐ **mix**, *noun* –**mixer**, *noun*

mixed signals *plural noun* a communication of intentions or feelings which contradict each other.

mixture *noun*
1. something made up of mixed or combined things. **2.** in chemistry and physics, two or more substances, not chemically united, mixed in no fixed proportion to each other.

mix-up *noun* a muddle or confused state of things.

moan *noun*
1. a long, low sound of sorrow or pain. **2.** any similar sound: *the moan of trucks descending the hill.*
–*verb* **3.** If you **moan**, you let out a long, low sound of sorrow or pain.
☐ **moaning**, *noun*

moat *noun* a long, deep, wide hole, usually filled with water, that ran around a town or castle to help protect it from the enemy, especially in medieval Europe.

mob *noun*
1. a large crowd which is sometimes rowdy or violent.
–*verb* (**mobs**, **mobbing**, **mobbed**, **has mobbed**) **2.** To **mob** someone is to crowd around them: *Thousands of fans mobbed the team when they returned victorious.*

mobile *adjective*
1. If something is **mobile**, it is not fixed in one place but can be moved around and used in different places: *There was a mobile barrier around the playground.*
–*noun* **2.** a hanging decoration made up of delicately balanced movable parts. **3.** See **mobile phone**.
☐ **mobility**, *noun*

mobile phone *noun* a telephone that you can carry around with you and use anywhere.

THE SHORT FORM of this is **mobile**: *I can't find my mobile.*

mobilise *verb* If someone **mobilises** a particular group, they make them ready for duty or use: *to mobilise the army*; *to mobilise a peacekeeping force.*
☐ **mobilisation**, *noun*

ANOTHER SPELLING is **mobilize**.

moccasin /*say* **mok**-uh-suhn/ *noun* a shoe made completely of soft leather.

WORD HISTORY from a Native American language

☑ SPELLING TIP *Double/single letter alert*: double *c* but only one *s*.

mock *verb*
1. If you **mock** someone, you make fun of them. –*adjective* **2.** If something is described as **mock**, it is not the real thing, but is made to seem like it: *mock cream.*
☐ **mockery**, *noun* –**mocking**, *adjective*: *a mocking laugh.*

modal verb *noun* a type of auxiliary verb which indicates how probable something is (as in 'I *might* come', 'The sun *will* rise') or how necessary something is (as in 'He *should* speak up', 'The court *must* decide').

SEE the Grammar and Punctuation Guide appendix.

mode *noun* a method or way: *a mode of dressing.*
☐ **modal**, *adjective* –**modality**, *noun*

model *noun*
1. a copy of something, usually in a smaller size, to show what the real thing looks like or how it works: *My brother loves making scale models of ships.* **2.** something that is used as an example to copy: *My mother always said my elder brother was a model of politeness.* **3.** someone who poses for a photographer or painter. **4.** someone who is employed to wear new clothes and display them at fashion shows and in magazines.
–*verb* (**models**, **modelling**, **modelled**, **has modelled**) **5.** If you **model** something out of a substance such as clay, you form the substance into a shape: *In preschool, we modelled all sorts of things from clay.* **6.** If you **model** something on something else, you copy it: *I modelled my style of writing on the teacher's.*
☐ **model**, *adjective*: *a model train.*

modem /*say* **moh**-dem, **moh**-duhm/ *noun* a device that changes data stored in one computer into a form which can be sent over telephone lines to another computer.

WORD HISTORY made from part of the words *modulator demodulator*

moderate *adjective* /*say* **mod**-uh-ruht/
1. If something is **moderate** in amount or size, it is not very great or very small: *The car suffered moderate damage in the smash, but it can be fixed.*
–*verb* /*say* **mod**-uh-rayt/ **2.** If you **moderate** something, you cause it to become less extreme or severe: *Mum told me to moderate my language.*
☐ **moderately**, *adverb* –**moderation**, *noun* –**moderator**, *noun*

modern *adjective*
1. belonging to the present or the recent past: *modern art.* **2.** new and up-to-date in its style.
☐ **modernise**, *verb* –**modernisation**, *noun*

ANOTHER SPELLING for **modernise** is **modernize**.

modest *adjective*
1. If someone is **modest**, they do not talk loudly about their abilities or achievements: *She's a great athlete but she's too modest to talk about it.* **2.** If something is **modest**, it is not large or expensive: *a modest house.*
☐ **modestly**, *adverb* –**modesty**, *noun*

modify *verb* (**modifies**, **modifying**, **modified**, **has modified**)
1. If you **modify** something, you change it slightly to improve it: *After early trials they modified the design.* **2.** To **modify** a word is to limit or add more detail to its meaning: *Verbs are modified by adverbs.*
☐ **modification**, *noun*

modulate *verb*
1. If you **modulate** something, you tone it down or adjust it. **2.** If you **modulate** your voice, you change the pitch or loudness when you speak.
☐ **modulation**, *noun*

module *noun* a part of something which can be separated from the rest and be used on its own.

mohawk *noun* a hairstyle in which the head is shaved leaving a strip of upright hair along the centre of the scalp from the forehead to the back of the neck.

WORD HISTORY from the name of a Native American people

moist *adjective* slightly wet: *moist soil.*
☐ **moisten**, *verb* –**moistness**, *noun* –**moisture**, *noun* –**moisturise**, *verb*

ANOTHER SPELLING for **moisturise** is **moisturize**.

molar *noun* one of the large teeth at the back of the mouth used for crushing food.
☐ **molar**, *adjective*

molasses *noun* the syrup taken from raw sugar.

mole[1] *noun* a small spot on the skin, which is usually dark and slightly raised.

mole[2] *noun*
1. a small, furry animal that feeds on insects and lives mainly underground. **2.** a person who has a job in the government of the enemy in order to act as a spy.

molecule /*say* **mol**-uh-kyoohl/ *noun* the smallest unit or particle into which something can be divided without changing its features: *A molecule of water is made up of two atoms of hydrogen and one atom of oxygen.*
☐ **molecular** /*say* muh-**lek**-yuh-luh/, *adjective*

molest /*say* muh-**lest**/ *verb* If someone **molests** another person, **1.** they assault them sexually. **2.** they annoy or interfere with them so as to hurt them.
☐ **molestation**, *noun*

mollify *verb* (**mollifies**, **mollifying**, **mollified**, **has mollified**) If someone **mollifies** another person, they make them calmer or less angry: *Only Mum could mollify Dad when he was so enraged.*

SIMILAR WORDS are **appease** and **placate**.
WORD HISTORY from a Latin word meaning 'soften'

mollusc /*say* **mol**-uhsk/ *noun* an animal with a soft body in a hard shell, such as a snail or oyster.

WORD HISTORY from a Latin word meaning 'soft' (used about a thin-shelled nut)

☑ SPELLING TIP Remember that the last letter is a *c* (not *k*).

mollycoddle *verb* If you **mollycoddle** someone, you treat them too carefully or tenderly: *In pre-school, they mollycoddle you a bit, but in primary, you have to do more for yourself.*

molten *adjective* made liquid by heat: *molten metal.*

moment *noun*
1. a very short space of time: *Just give me a moment and I'll get it done.* **2.** the present or another particular time: *Mum said she was busy for the moment.*

momentary /*say* **moh**-muhn-tree/ *adjective* lasting for only a moment: *Jacky felt a momentary sense of guilt.*
☐ **momentarily**, *adverb*

momentum /*say* muh-**men**-tuhm/ *noun* the force with which something is moving.

monarch /*say* **mon**-uhk, **mon**-ahk/ *noun* (*plural* **monarchs**) a ruler of a country who inherits the position, such as a king or queen.
☐ **monarchy**, *noun*

☑ SPELLING TIP The spelling will be easier to remember if you see that **monarch** is made up of *mon* (a form of the prefix *mono-*, meaning 'one') and *-arch* (a suffix meaning 'ruler'). In the related word **monarchy**, the form of the suffix has changed to *archy*, meaning 'rule' or 'government'. These suffixes are found in several other words relating to rulers and government, such as *matriarch*, *patriarch*, *anarchy* and *hierarchy*.

monastery /*say* **mon**-uhs-tree/ *noun* (*plural* **monasteries**) a place where a group of monks live and work.

Monday *noun* the second day of the week.

THE ABBREVIATION is **Mon**.
WORD HISTORY from an Old English word meaning 'moon's day'

money *noun* (*plural* **moneys** *or* **monies**)
1. metal coins or banknotes. **2.** property or wealth: *He was ultimately destroyed by his love of money.*
☐ **monetary**, *adjective*

money order *noun* an order for payment which can be exchanged for money at a post office.

mongoose *noun* (*plural* **mongooses**) a small, furry animal found in India, noted for its ability to kill snakes.

mongrel /*say* **mung**-gruhl/ *noun* a plant or animal, especially a dog, that is a mix of different breeds or kinds.

☑ SPELLING TIP *Tricky vowel sound*: the first vowel is an *o* (although it sounds like it would be a *u*). And notice it has an *el* ending.

monitor *noun*
1. a student who has particular jobs to help the teacher. **2.** something that keeps a check or gives warning. **3.** a screen which displays information about an electrical machine. **4.** a screen which displays images from a camera. **5.** a computer screen. **6.** a kind of large lizard which is popularly believed to give warning if crocodiles are near.
–*verb* **7.** If you **monitor** someone, you check on their progress.

monk /*rhymes with* sunk/ *noun* a male member of a religious group living away from the rest of the world.

monkey *noun* (*plural* **monkeys**) an animal that has a long tail and lives in trees in tropical areas.

mono- *prefix* a word part meaning 'alone' or 'single', as in *monologue*, *monorail*, *monotone*.

WORD HISTORY this prefix comes from Greek

monocle *noun* a glass lens for one eye only.

monogamy /*say* muh-**nog**-uh-mee/ *noun* marriage to one person at a time.
☐ **monogamous**, *adjective*

☑ SPELLING TIP This word will be easier to spell if you see that it is made up of the prefix *mono-* (meaning 'one') and *gamy* (a word part coming from the Greek word for 'marriage'). See also **bigamy** and **polygamy** which contain this same word part.

monogram *noun* a design made up of two or more letters, usually your initials.

monolith *noun* a single, huge rock or stone, such as Uluru.
☐ **monolithic**, *adjective*

monologue /*say* **mon**-uh-log/ *noun* a long talk by one person.

☑ SPELLING TIP *Silent letter alert*: don't forget the silent *ue* at the end. It is spelt in this way because it comes from French. The ending *logue* with the same sound turns up in several words that have to do with speaking, including **monologue**'s partner word, *dialogue*, which is a conversation between two people.

monopoly /*say* muh-**nop**-uh-lee/ *noun* (*plural* **monopolies**) the complete control of something, especially the supply of a product or service.
☐ **monopolise**, *verb* –**monopolisation**, *noun*

ANOTHER SPELLING for **monopolise** is **monopolize**.

monorail *noun* a train that runs on one rail.

monotone *noun* a series of spoken or sung sounds in one unchanging tone: *He delivered his speech in a monotone and sent us to sleep.*

monotony /*say* muh-**not**-uh-nee/ *noun* lack of change or variety, which produces boredom.
☐ **monotonous**, *adjective*

monotreme *noun* an egg-laying mammal. The platypus and the echidna, found in Australia and nearby regions, are the only examples.

☑ SPELLING TIP **Monotremes** are *extremely* unusual and interesting animals. The *treme* in *extreme* might help you to remember the spelling of the end of **monotreme**. In fact the word is made up of the prefix *mono-* (meaning 'one') and *treme* (a form of *trema*, the Greek word for 'hole') – a **monotreme** has only one opening for its digestive and sexual organs.

monsoon *noun*
1. a strong wind of the Indian Ocean and Indonesia. **2.** a season of heavy rainfall.
☐ **monsoonal**, *adjective*

WORD HISTORY from an Arabic word meaning 'season' or 'seasonal wind'

monster *noun*
1. someone or something that is frighteningly cruel. **2.** someone or something extremely large.
☐ **monster**, *adjective*: *monster rats.*

monstrous *adjective*
1. extremely large: *He has a monstrous ego.* **2.** frightful or shocking: *A monstrous sight met them when they opened the door.*
☐ **monstrosity**, *noun* (*plural* **monstrosities**) –**monstrously**, *adverb*

montage /*say* mon-**tahzh**/ *noun* a picture, painting or film in which bits taken from other sources are blended or added.

COMPARE this with **collage**.

month *noun*
1. any of the twelve parts into which the year is divided. **2.** a period of about four weeks or 30 days.
☐ **monthly**, *adjective*, *adverb*

monument *noun*
1. something made in memory of a person or event, such as a statue. **2.** something from the past, such as an ancient building: *the monuments remaining from ancient South American civilisations.*
☐ **monumental**, *adjective* –**monumentally**, *adverb*

moo *noun*
1. the sound a cow makes.
–*verb* **2.** To **moo** is to make this sound.

mood[1] *noun* the way you feel at a particular time: *Her friendly smile immediately put him in a good mood*; *a holiday mood.*

mood[2] *noun* a set of verb forms which explain the action described by a verb **1.** the **indicative mood** describes a certainty: *He will go.* **2.** the **imperative mood** describes a command: *Go!* **3.** the **subjunctive mood** describes a wish or a desire: *Were I able to go, I would.*

SEE the Grammar and Punctuation Guide appendix.

moody *adjective* (**moodier**, **moodiest**)
1. angry or unhappy: *Do you know what happened to make him so moody?* **2.** changeable in mood or feelings: *Elena is so moody – you never know how she'll be from one day to the next!*
☐ **moodily**, *adverb* –**moodiness**, *noun*

A SIMILAR WORD (for definition 2) is **temperamental**.

moon *noun*
1. the round body that circles the earth every month and can be seen as a light in the sky at night. **2.** this body as it appears at different stages of the month: *You don't catch many fish at the time of the full moon.*
☐ **moonlight**, *noun*

NOTE **Lunar** is a scientific word meaning 'having to do with the moon'.

moor[1] *noun* especially in Britain, an open area of rather wet, wild land, usually covered with low, rough, plant growth.

☑ SPELLING TIP Don't confuse the spelling of **moor** with **more** which has the same sound. **More** is the opposite of *less*.

moor[2] *verb* If you **moor** a ship, you make it stay in the same position with ropes or an anchor.
☐ **mooring**, *noun* –**moorings**, *plural noun*

> ☑ SPELLING TIP See **moor**[1].

moose *noun* (*plural* **moose**) a large animal of the deer family.

mop *noun*
1. a loose bundle of cloth or strings fixed to the end of a stick, and used for washing floors or dishes. **2.** a thick mass: *a mop of tangled seaweed.*
–*verb* (**mops**, **mopping**, **mopped**, **has mopped**) **3.** If you **mop** a floor, you use a mop to wash it.

mope *verb* If you **mope**, you are in a dull, unhappy mood.

mopoke *noun* a kind of owl found in Australia and New Zealand.

> WORD HISTORY named after the sound it makes

moral *adjective*
1. having to do with the knowledge of what is right and wrong: *We had to think about whether it was moral to steal medicine for a dying child.* **2.** acting according to the rules of what is thought to be right, especially in sexual behaviour.
–*noun* **3.** the lesson taught by story or experience: *The moral is: 'Two wrongs don't make a right'.* **4. morals**, beliefs or ways of behaviour that have to do with right and wrong.
☐ **moralistic**, *adjective* –**morality**, *noun* –**morally**, *adverb*

morale /*say* muh-**rahl**/ *noun* a cheerful and confident state of mind: *His morale was very low after he lost his job.*

moratorium *noun* (*plural* **moratoriums**) any official delay, such as in making a political decision.

morbid *adjective* If someone is **morbid**, they show a lot of interest in things such as death, disease and injury: *The crash site attracted a crowd of morbid onlookers.*
☐ **morbidity**, *noun* –**morbidly**, *adverb* –**morbidness**, *noun*

more *adjective*
1. in greater quantity, measure, degree, or number: *more cake*; *more speed*; *more people.*
–*adverb* **2.** in or to a greater degree: *He can eat more quickly than anyone else I have ever seen.*

morgue /*say* mawg/ *noun* a place where the bodies of dead people are kept until their funerals.

> ANOTHER WORD for this is **mortuary**.

> ☑ SPELLING TIP *Silent letter alert*: don't forget the silent *ue* at the end. The word **morgue** is spelt in this way because it comes from French. (It was originally the name of the building in Paris where dead bodies were taken.)

morning *noun*
1. the beginning of day. **2.** the first part of the day, from dawn, or from 12 o'clock at night, to 12 o'clock in the day.
☐ **morning**, *adjective*: *morning sun.*

> ANOTHER WORD (for definition 1) is **dawn** (definition 1).

moron /*say* **maw**-ron/ *noun Informal* someone who is stupid.
☐ **moronic**, *adjective*

> NOTE If you call someone a **moron**, you will offend them.

> ☑ SPELLING TIP Remember that both the vowels in **moron** are *o*'s.

morose /*say* muh-**rohs**/ *adjective* bad-tempered or gloomy because of unhappiness.
☐ **morosely**, *adverb* –**moroseness**, *noun*

morphine /*say* **maw**-feen/ *noun* a strong drug used to stop pain.

> WORD HISTORY from a Greek word for 'the strange forms people see in dreams'; *Morpheus* was the Greek god of dreams

morse code *noun* a system of signalling in which different groups of short and long sounds or flashes of light, called dots and dashes, stand for each letter in a word.

> WORD HISTORY named after Samuel *Morse* (1791–1872), the American inventor of the telegraph system and of morse code

morsel *noun* a very small piece or amount, especially of food.

mortal *adjective*
1. When people and living creatures are described as **mortal**, it means that one day they will die: *When the hero in the film died, we realised he was mortal after all.* **2.** A **mortal** wound or injury is so severe that it causes death. **3.** A **mortal** enemy hates you enough to kill you.
–*noun* **4.** a human being.
☐ **mortally**, *adverb*: *mortally wounded.*

mortality *noun*
1. the condition of being mortal or human: *Serving in the war made him acutely aware of his mortality.* **2.** death or rate of death: *AIDS in the early days had a frightening rate of mortality.*

mortar[1] *noun*
1. a heavy bowl in which food or other substances are ground to a powder with a pestle. **2.** a short cannon designed to fire shells to a great height.

mortar[2] *noun* a mixture of lime or cement, sand and water, used for joining bricks together.

mortarboard *noun* a square-shaped cap sometimes worn by teachers and university graduates.

mortgage /*say* **maw**-gij/ *noun* a loan in which property is used as security and given over if the loan is not repaid to the lender.

☑ SPELLING TIP *Silent letter alert*: don't forget the *t* before the *gage* ending. The *t* is there because **mortgage** is made up of *mort* (the French word for 'dead') and *gage* (a word meaning 'pledge' which also turns up in *engage*).

mortify *verb* (**mortifies**, **mortifying**, **mortified**, **has mortified**) If someone **mortifies** you, they embarrass you severely or hurt your feelings or pride: *He was mortified when they told everybody what he had done.*
☐ **mortification**, *noun*

mortuary *noun* (*plural* **mortuaries**) a place where the bodies of dead people are kept until their funerals.

ANOTHER WORD for this is **morgue**.

mosaic /*say* moh-**zay**-ik/ *noun* a picture or pattern made of small pieces of different coloured stone or glass.

mosque /*say* mosk/ *noun* a place of worship for Muslims.

☑ SPELLING TIP Don't forget the *que* spelling for the 'k' sound. **Mosque** is spelt in this way because it has come into English from French. It comes originally from an Arabic word.

mosquito /*say* muh-**skee**-toh/ *noun* (*plural* **mosquitoes** *or* **mosquitos**) a small flying insect, the female of which sucks the blood of animals and humans. Some types, by doing this, pass on some diseases, such as malaria.

☑ SPELLING TIP Remember the *qu* for the 'k' sound. This word comes from Spanish where the *ito* ending can mean 'small'. The literal meaning of this word in Spanish is 'small fly'.

moss *noun* a plant with very small leaves that grows in patches on rather wet ground, tree trunks or rocks.
☐ **mossy**, *adjective*

most *adjective*
1. in the greatest quantity, degree, amount or number: *the most votes.*
–*pronoun* **2.** the greatest quantity, amount or degree: *Ann ate the most.*
–*adverb* **3.** in or to the greatest range or degree: *It was the most awful time in his whole life.*
☐ **mostly**, *adverb*

motel *noun* a roadside hotel which provides a place for travellers to stay and parking for their cars.

moth *noun* a flying insect, similar to a butterfly, that is active at night.

mothball *noun* a small ball of a chemical substance which is stored with clothes to kill moths.

mother *noun*
1. a female parent.
–*verb* **2.** To **mother** someone is to treat them protectively or tenderly: *She's still mothering him even though he's 47 years old and a firefighter!*
☐ **motherhood**, *noun* –**motherliness**, *noun* –**motherly**, *adjective*

mother-in-law *noun* (*plural* **mothers-in-law**) the mother of someone's husband or wife.

mother-of-pearl *noun* the hard, shiny lining of some shells, used to make things look pretty.

motif /*say* moh-**teef**/ *noun*
1. an idea that is repeated in various ways all through a piece of writing or music or in the work of an artist. **2.** a part of a design that is repeated, such as in cloth.

motion *noun*
1. movement or the power of movement. **2.** an idea put forward at a meeting to be voted on: *There was a motion put forward at the school council meeting about removing junk food from the canteen.*
–*verb* **3.** If you **motion** someone to do something, you direct them by a movement of the hand or head: *The teacher motioned to us to be quiet during the speech.*

motive *noun* a strong reason for doing something: *We had a strong motive to help with the cooking because we knew that we would get to eat the brownies.*
☐ **motivated**, *adjective* –**motivation**, *noun* –**motivate**, *verb*

motley *adjective* made up of different parts or colours: *There was a motley collection of things in the bottom drawer, including an empty jam jar and a burst balloon.*

motocross *noun* cross-country motorcycle racing.

motor *noun*
1. an engine, especially that of a car or boat. **2.** a device which receives and changes energy from some natural source in order to use it to drive machinery, and so on.
☐ **motorise**, *verb*: *to motorise a tool.*

ANOTHER SPELLING for **motorise** is **motorize**.

motorbike *noun* See **motorcycle**.

motorcade *noun* a procession of cars.

motorcycle *noun* a large, heavy bicycle with an engine.
☐ **motorcyclist**, *noun*

ANOTHER WORD for this is **motorbike**.

motorist *noun* someone who drives a car.

motorway *noun* a road on which traffic can travel fast.

OTHER WORDS for this are **expressway** and **freeway**.

mottled *adjective* covered with different coloured spots or patches: *a horse with mottled colouring; a curtain mottled with light.*

motto *noun* (*plural* **mottoes** *or* **mottos**) a short saying, often taken as summing up the aims or beliefs of a particular organisation or group: *The motto of our school is 'And gladly learn'.*

mould[1] /*rhymes with* bold/ *noun*
1. a hollow form which gives shape to melted or soft material which hardens inside it: *Pour the mixture into a jelly mould.*
–*verb* **2.** To **mould** something is to give a particular shape or character to it.

mould[2] /*rhymes with* bold/ *noun* a furry growth on something that is wet or is decaying: *Some of the food at the back of the fridge had mould growing on it.*
□ **mouldy**, *adjective* (**mouldier**, **mouldiest**)

moult /*rhymes with* bolt/ *verb* When birds or animals **moult**, they lose their feathers or fur and grow a new covering: *Dingoes moult most in August and September.*

mound *noun*
1. a pile: *We jumped into the mound of sand.* **2.** a small hill: *The park is just over that mound in the distance.*

mount *verb* If you **mount** something, you **1.** go up it: *She mounted the ladder.* **2.** get up on it: *At the rodeo, they mounted the bulls in a small fenced area.* **3.** fix it on or in a position or setting: *The ruby was mounted at the centre of a circle of tiny diamonds.* **4.** If something like prices **mount**, they rise or increase: *Prices of houses are mounting monthly.*
–*noun* **5.** a horse for riding. **6.** a backing or setting: *We should put this photograph on a white mount.*

mountain *noun*
1. a large, natural, raised part of the earth, higher than a hill. **2.** something like this in size, shape or amount: *There was a mountain of food at the wedding.*
□ **mountainous**, *adjective* –**mountaineer**, *noun* a person who climbs mountains.

ANOTHER FORM This is sometimes called a **mount,** especially in a name, such as in *Mount Kosciuszko.*

☑ SPELLING TIP See the note at **captain** about words ending in *ain.*

mourn /*say* mawn/ *verb* If you **mourn**, you feel or show sorrow, especially over someone's death or the loss of something: *He mourned the death of his wife.*
□ **mourner**, *noun* –**mournful**, *adjective* –**mournfully**, *adverb* –**mourning**, *noun*

mouse *noun*
1. (*plural* **mice**) a small animal with sharp teeth and a long tail. **2.** (*plural* **mouses** or **mice**) in computers, a small object which you hold and move to position the cursor on the computer screen.

moussaka /*say* moo-**sah**-kuh/ *noun* a food made with layers of minced lamb, tomatoes and eggplant, with a thick white sauce on top, originating in Greece, Turkey and other countries near them.

☑ SPELLING TIP *Double letter alert*: double *s* following the *ou*. Also note the single *k* in the last part of the word.

mousse /*say* moohs/ *noun* a food made of whipped cream, beaten eggs, gelatine and a sweet or savoury flavouring: *salmon mousse with dill sauce.*

WORD HISTORY from a French word meaning 'froth'

☑ SPELLING TIP Don't confuse the spelling of **mousse** with **moose** which sounds the same. A **moose** is a large kind of deer.

moustache /*say* muh-**stahsh**/ *noun* the hair that grows on the upper lip of a man.

☑ SPELLING TIP *Tricky 'uh' sound*: the first vowel sound is spelt *ou*. Another difficult part is the *ache* spelling for the 'ahsh' sound at the end. **Moustache** is spelt in this way because it comes from French (originally from a Greek word meaning 'upper lip').

mouth *noun* /*say* mowth/
1. the opening in the face used for eating, drinking and talking. **2.** an opening in anything. **3.** the place where a river flows into the sea.
–*verb* /*say* mowdh/ **4.** If you **mouth** a word or sentence, you move your lips as if you were speaking but you do not make a sound: *She mouthed the words of the song.*
–*phrase* **5. down in the mouth**, unhappy.

mouthful *noun* as much as you can fit into your mouth at one time.

mouth organ *noun* a harmonica, a small wind instrument played by blowing.

mouthpiece *noun* the part of a wind instrument which you blow into or the part of a telephone which you speak into.

move *verb*
1. If someone or something **moves**, it is not still: *Something was moving in the bushes.* **2.** If someone or something **moves**, it changes position. It goes somewhere else: *Could you move to one side, please?* **3.** If you **move** something, you

put it somewhere else: *Who's moved my bag?* **4.** If you **move**, you leave the place where you are living and go and live somewhere else. **5.** If something **moves** you, it makes you feel an emotion: *Hearing the old songs moved my grandmother to tears.*
–*noun* **6.** a movement or change of position. **7.** a player's turn in a game: *It's my move, not yours!*
–*phrase* **8. get a move on**, *Rather informal* hurry up. **9. move in**, to settle into a house. **10. move out**, to leave a house. **11. on the move**, moving.
☐ **movable**, *adjective*

ANOTHER SPELLING for **movable** is **moveable**.

movement *noun*
1. a moving or changing from one place or position to another. **2.** an organised group of people working towards a particular goal: *the movement for democracy.* **3.** one of the parts of a long piece of music: *The audience clapped wildly at the end of the third movement.*

movie *noun* a film: *Have you seen all the 'Lord of the Rings' movies?*

mow *verb* (**mows**, **mowing**, **mowed**, **has mowed** *or* **has mown**)
1. If you **mow** grass or grain, you cut it so that only a short part of the stems or leaves remain.
–*phrase* **2. mow down**, to knock down: *The advancing army was mown down by enemy fire.*

mozzarella /*say* mot-suh-**rel**-uh/ *noun* a soft, white cheese which melts easily and is often used as a pizza topping.

WORD HISTORY from an Italian word meaning 'a slice'

☑ SPELLING TIP *Double/single letter alert*: double *z* and double *l*, but only one *r*.

MP3 *noun* a type of digital sound file, commonly used on the internet to store musical data.

ANOTHER FORM is **mp3**.

MP3 player *noun* a portable electronic device that downloads, stores, and plays MP3s.

Mr /*say* **mis**-tuh/ *noun* a title put before a man's name.

NOTE This is short for **Mister**, which is never written in full before a name any more.

Mrs /*say* **mis**-uhz/ *noun* a title put before a married woman's name.

NOTE This is short for **Mistress**, which is never used in full before a name any more. Many women prefer to use the title **Ms**, which does not say whether or not the woman is married.

Ms /*say* muhz/ *noun* a title put before a woman's name, whether married or unmarried.

NOTE Many women now use *Ms* as a title, preferring it because it does not say whether or not they are married. Compare **Miss** and **Mrs**.

much *adjective* (**more**, **most**)
1. in great quantity, amount, measure or degree: *much work.*
–*pronoun* **2.** a great quantity or amount: *Much of this is true.*
–*phrase* **3. make much of**, **a.** to treat as of great importance: *The newspapers made much of the error.* **b.** to treat with attention or affection: *We made much of our old grandfather on his birthday.*

muck *noun*
1. filth or dirt, especially when moist: *You've got some kind of muck all over your clothes.*
–*verb in the phrase Informal* **2. muck about** (or **around**), to waste time doing nothing important. **3. muck out**, to remove muck from: *to muck out the stables.* **4. muck up**, **a.** to spoil. **b.** to misbehave.
☐ **muck-up**, *noun* a mess or muddle. –**mucky**, *adjective*

mucus /*say* **myooh**-kuhs/ *noun* thick liquid which builds up in the nose and throat when you have a cold.
☐ **mucous** /*say* **myooh**-kuhs/, *adjective*

☑ SPELLING TIP Notice that the noun **mucus** ends in *us*, while the adjective **mucous** ends in *ous*.

mud *noun* wet, soft, sticky earth.
☐ **muddy**, *adjective* (**muddier**, **muddiest**) –**muddy**, *verb* (**muddies**, **muddying**, **muddied**, **has muddied**)

muddle *noun*
1. anything which is confused and not in order.
–*verb* **2.** If you **muddle** something, you confuse it or you make it so it is out of order: *He was so nervous, he muddled his speech*; *Now I've muddled all my clothes up and I can't find anything.*

mudguard *noun* a cover for the wheel of a car or bicycle to stop mud and water splashing up.

muesli /*say* **myoohz**-lee/ *noun* breakfast cereal made from a mixture of oats, chopped fruit, nuts, etc.

☑ SPELLING TIP *Tricky vowel sound*: the first vowel sound is spelt *ue*, giving a 'yooh' sound. Also notice the *i* ending. The word **muesli** is spelt like this because it from the German that is spoken in Switzerland.

muff *noun* a rolled up piece of fur or woollen material into which you can put your hands for warmth.

muffin *noun*
1. a type of flat, round bread which is split in two and toasted. **2.** a type of small, sweet cake.

muffle *verb* To **muffle** something is to deaden the sound of it: *He muffled the sound of the horn by putting his hand inside the bell.*
☐ **muffled**, *adjective*

muffler *noun*
1. a device which fits onto the exhaust pipe of a car to deaden the noise of the engine. **2.** a thick, warm scarf.

mug *noun*
1. a large drinking cup. **2.** *Informal* someone's face. **3.** *Informal* someone who is easily fooled.
–*verb* (**mugs**, **mugging**, **mugged**, **has mugged**) **4.** If someone **mugs** you, they attack and rob you.
☐ **mugger**, *noun* –**mugging**, *noun*: *My father suffered a mugging in the city.*

muggy *adjective* (**muggier**, **muggiest**) unpleasantly warm and wet: *It was a muggy Monday morning and we all felt tired and sticky.*

mulberry /*say* **mul**-buh-ree/ *noun* (*plural* **mulberries**)
1. a tree which has sweet, dark-purple fruit like blackberries, and leaves which are eaten by silkworms. **2.** the fruit of this tree.

☑ SPELLING TIP *Single letter alert*: only one *l*.

mulch *noun*
1. straw, grass clippings, leaves or similar material spread on gardens to protect and feed the plants.
–*verb* **2.** If you **mulch** a garden, you put mulch on it.

mule *noun* an animal produced by a female horse and a male donkey.
☐ **mulish**, *adjective* stubborn or obstinate.

NOTE The male is a **jackass**; the female is a **mare**; the young is a **foal**.

mulga *noun* a type of wattle tree found in dry inland areas of Australia. Cattle like to eat its leaves.

WORD HISTORY from Aboriginal languages of New South Wales called Yuwaalaraay and Kamilaroi

mulgara *noun* a small marsupial that looks like a mouse with a black, hairy tail. It lives in the Australian desert and is endangered.

WORD HISTORY from an Aboriginal language of South Australia called Wangganguru

mull *verb in the phrase* **mull over**, If you **mull over** something, you think about it: *They mulled over the guest list for weeks.*

mullet *noun* (*plural* **mullets**)
1. a type of fish commonly found in the rivers and sea around Australia. **2.** *Informal* a type of hairstyle for men, long at the back and cut short on the top and sides.

multi- *prefix* a word part meaning 'many', as in *multiracial*, *multitude*.

WORD HISTORY this prefix comes from Latin

multicultural *adjective* having to do with a society which contains several large groups of people of different cultures or ethnic backgrounds.
☐ **multiculturalism**, *noun*

multimeter /*say* **mul**-tee-mee-tuh/ *noun* an instrument for testing electrical equipment, which measures voltage, current and resistance.

multinational *adjective* involving many different countries: *a multinational business company.*

multiple *adjective*
1. If things are described as **multiple**, there are several of them: *He suffered multiple fractures to his legs in the accident.*
–*noun* **2.** a number formed by multiplying one number by another: *10, 15 and 20 are multiples of 5.*

multiply *verb* (**multiplies**, **multiplying**, **multiplied**, **has multiplied**)
1. When something **multiplies**, it increases greatly in number or amount: *Rabbits multiply more quickly than many other animals.* **2.** When you **multiply** one number by another, you add up as many lots of the first number as there are of the second number: *13 multiplied by 9 equals 117.*
☐ **multiplication**, *noun*

multiracial *adjective* having people of many different races or nationalities.

multiskill *verb* If you **multiskill**, you take part in multiskilling.
☐ **multiskilled**, *adjective*

multiskilling *noun* the development of a number of skills from which workers may earn a livelihood.

ANOTHER FORM is **multi-skilling**.

multitude /*say* **mul**-tuh-tyoohd/ *noun* a large number of items or people: *We received a multitude of complaints.*
☐ **multitudinous** /*say* mul-tuh-**tyooh**-duh-nuhs/, *adjective*

☑ SPELLING TIP *Tricky 'uh' sound*: the middle vowel sound is spelt *i*. It will help if you can see that this is part of the prefix *multi-* meaning 'many'.

mum[1] *noun Informal* mother.

ANOTHER FORM is **mummy**, especially among children.
NOTE You use these words when you are talking about your mother in a rather informal way, or when you are addressing your mother: *My mum is rather tall. Can we watch television, Mummy?*

mum[2] *adjective in the phrase* **keep mum**, saying nothing: *We all kept mum about the surprise party.*

mumble *verb* If someone **mumbles**, they do not speak clearly so that it is difficult to understand what they say: *He mumbled some excuse.*

mumbo jumbo *noun* meaningless words, especially when thought to have a magical effect.

mummy[1] *noun* (*plural* **mummies**) a dead body that has been specially treated to stop it from decaying: *The museum had a special Egyptian display including some mummies.*

WORD HISTORY from a Persian word meaning 'asphalt'

mummy[2] *noun* See **mum[1]**.

mumps *noun* an infectious disease caused by a virus which makes the glands around the mouth and neck very sore and swollen: *I could only swallow ice-cream when I had mumps.*

munch *verb* If you **munch** something, you chew it noisily: *He was in trouble for munching chocolate bars in class.*

mundane *adjective* ordinary or boring: *Choir practice can be mundane at times.*

WORD HISTORY from a Latin word meaning 'of the world'

municipality /*say* myooh-nuh-suh-**pal**-uh-tee/ *noun* a district which has its own local government: *We have some good parks in our municipality.*
☐ **municipal**, *adjective*: *the municipal library.*

munitions *plural noun* weapons and ammunition used in war.

mural *noun* a picture painted on a wall or ceiling.

murder *noun*
1. the crime of intentionally killing someone. **2.** *Informal* a very hard or unpleasant job: *It's murder trying to look after my little sister!*
–*verb* **3.** If someone **murders** a person, they intentionally kill them.
☐ **murderer**, *noun* –**murderous**, *adjective*

murky *adjective* (**murkier**, **murkiest**) dark and difficult to see through: *a murky sewer tunnel*; *We peered into the murky water beneath.*
☐ **murk**, *noun* –**murkiness**, *noun*

murmur *noun*
1. a soft sound or conversation: *A low murmur started as soon as he entered the court.*
–*verb* (**murmurs**, **murmuring**, **murmured**, **has murmured**) **2.** If someone or something **murmurs**, they make a soft, low sound: *He murmured some quiet advice into my ear*; *The wind murmured softly in the palms.*
☐ **murmuring**, *adjective*

☑ SPELLING TIP Notice that the ending is *ur* (not *er*). This will be easy to remember if you see that **murmur** is made up of two lots of the letter combination *mur*.

Murri /*say* **mu**-ree/ *noun* an Aboriginal person from northern New South Wales or Queensland.
☐ **Murri**, *adjective*: *Murri traditions.*

WORD HISTORY from the Kamilaroi language of New South Wales

muscle /*say* **mus**-uhl/ *noun*
1. the parts of the body which give it the strength and power to move. **2.** strength or force: *It takes a lot of muscle to lift a piano.*
☐ **muscly**, *adjective* –**muscular**, *adjective* –**muscularity**, *noun*

WORD HISTORY from a Latin word meaning 'little mouse' (because when you flex your muscles so that they ripple, it looks as if a little mouse is running up and down).

☑ SPELLING TIP *Silent letter alert*: don't forget the silent *c* after the *s*. Don't confuse this word with **mussel** which has the same sound. A **mussel** is a type of shellfish.

muse[1] *verb* If someone **muses**, they meditate or are lost in thought: *Tom was musing on what life might be like without sisters.*

A SIMILAR WORD is **ponder**.

muse[2] *noun* a person who inspires a creative force in someone.

WORD HISTORY from the nine *Muses* who, in stories of Ancient Greece, were the goddesses in charge of writing, painting and science

museum *noun* a place where rare and interesting things are displayed.

mush *noun*
1. a thick liquid: *If you cook vegetables too long, they turn to mush.* **2.** *Informal* something, such as a film or book, with a great deal of emotion.
☐ **mushy**, *adjective* (**mushier**, **mushiest**)

mushroom *noun*
1. a type of fungus with a round top growing on a stem, which grows very quickly in slightly wet soil and which you can eat.
–*verb* **2.** If something **mushrooms**, it spreads or grows quickly: *New suburbs are mushrooming in the outer parts of the city.*

COMPARE definition 1 with **toadstool**.

music *noun*
1. sounds combined together using melody, rhythm and harmony to express ideas and feelings. **2.** written notes and signs which represent sounds and can be sung or played on a musical instrument.

musical *adjective*
1. producing music or like music: *At the musical evening, I had to play the trumpet.* **2.** fond of

music or able to play an instrument or sing well: *Helen has a very musical way of playing the violin.*
☐ **musical**, *noun* a play or film with a lot of singing and dancing. –**musically**, *adverb*

musician /*say* myooh-**zish**-uhn/ *noun* someone who plays or composes music.
☐ **musicianship**, *noun*

☑ SPELLING TIP Remember that this word comes from *music* and has a *c* in it, even though the sound has changed. The noun suffix *-ian* (meaning 'having to do with') has been added. A word with a similar pattern is *magician* (from *magic*).

music sticks *plural noun* two wooden sticks which are hit together rhythmically to make music, often used in Aboriginal music.

ANOTHER TERM for this is **song sticks**.

musk *noun* a liquid with a strong smell produced by certain animals, and used in perfume.
☐ **musky**, *adjective* (**muskier**, **muskiest**)

musket *noun* an old-fashioned type of gun from which the modern rifle has developed.
☐ **musketeer**, *noun* a soldier armed with a musket.

Muslim *noun* a person whose religion is Islam.
☐ **Muslim**, *adjective*: *Muslim law.*

ANOTHER SPELLING is **Moslem**.
WORD HISTORY from an Arabic word meaning 'submission' or 'someone who accepts Islam'

muslin /*say* **muz**-luhn/ *noun* a soft, fine cotton material.

mussel *noun* a type of shellfish which has two black shells hinged together and which you can eat.

☑ SPELLING TIP Don't confuse the spelling of **mussel** with **muscle** which has the same sound. Your **muscles** are the parts of your body which give it the ability to move.

must *verb*
1. Must is used to express the fact that you have to do something: *I must get to school on time.* **2. Must** is used to say that something is desirable or advisable: *You must book the seats now or you'll miss out.* **3. Must** can be used to show that you feel certain about something: *They must be mad to try that trick again!* **4. Must** is used when you are talking about something that is probable: *You must feel like a cool drink on such a hot day.*
–*noun* **5.** something that is thought to be necessary: *If you've seen the first two films, the third one is a must.*

NOTE This is always used with another verb. See *modal verbs* in the Grammar and Punctuation Guide appendix.

mustard *noun* a yellow-brown powder made from the seeds of a plant, which is used as a hot spice with food.

muster *verb*
1. If a number of people **muster**, they gather into a group: *We all had to muster beside the school buses.*
–*noun* **2.** a gathering up or rounding up into a group.
–*phrase* **3. pass muster**, to come up to a certain standard: *Our shoes have to be shining to pass muster with our mum.*

WORD HISTORY from a Latin word meaning 'show'

mustn't /*say* **mus**-uhnt/ a short form of *must not*.

musty *adjective* (**mustier**, **mustiest**) having an unpleasant smell because there is no fresh air: *After being closed for the weekend, the classroom is always musty on Monday.*
☐ **mustiness**, *noun*

mutate *verb* If something **mutates**, it changes from one appearance, kind, or quality, to another: *Animals have mutated to adapt to the demands of the environment they live in.*
☐ **mutant**, *adjective*

NOTE This term is used mainly in biology and other sciences.

mutation *noun*
1. a plant or animal which becomes different in appearance or nature because of a change in genes. **2.** the process of changing.

mute *adjective*
1. silent: *a mute stare.* **2.** unable to speak, as from birth on.
–*noun* **3.** something which can be put in or on a musical instrument to soften the sound.
☐ **mutely**, *adverb*

NOTE The use of this term as in definition 2 is not common any more and may be offensive. You can use another term such as **speech-impaired**.

mutilate /*say* **myooh**-tuh-layt/ *verb* If someone or something **mutilates** a person or thing, they seriously injure or damage them: *A mine left over from the war mutilated both his legs.*
☐ **mutilation**, *noun* –**mutilator**, *noun*

mutiny /*say* **myooh**-tuh-nee/ *noun* (*plural* **mutinies**)
1. rebellion against authority, especially by sailors or soldiers against their officers.
–*verb* (**mutinies**, **mutinying**, **mutinied**, **has mutinied**) **2.** If a person or people **mutiny**, they revolt against the authority over them.
☐ **mutinous**, *adjective*

mutter *verb* If you **mutter**, you speak in a low voice that is hard to understand.
☐ **mutter**, *noun*

mutton *noun* the meat from a sheep.

mutual /*say* **myooh**-chooh-uhl/ *adjective* shared or common: *They have a mutual interest in native bees.*
☐ **mutuality**, *noun* –**mutually**, *adverb*

☑ SPELLING TIP Remember the *t* in this word. With the *u* following it has a 'ch' sound and you don't hear the *t*.

muzzle *noun*
1. the jaws, mouth and nose of an animal. **2.** a small wire cage which can be fastened over an animal's mouth to stop it biting. **3.** the open front end of a gun.
–*verb* **4.** If you **muzzle** an animal, you put a strap or a small cage over its mouth to stop it biting. **5.** If you **muzzle** a person, you try to stop them saying something.

ANOTHER WORD (for definition 1) is **snout**.

my *pronoun* the form of the pronoun **I** and **me** that you use before a noun to show that something belongs to you: *my new thongs.*

myopia /*say* muy-**oh**-pee-uh/ *noun* a condition of the eyes which stops you from clearly seeing things in the distance.
☐ **myopic** /*say* muy-**op**-ik/, *adjective*

myriad /*say* **mi**-ree-uhd/ *noun* a very great number: *There was a myriad of delicious morsels to eat.*
☐ **myriad**, *adjective*: *the myriad stars in the sky.*

☑ SPELLING TIP *Letter 'y' alert*: the first vowel sound is spelt *y* (not *i*). Like many words which have this kind of *y* spelling, **myriad** comes from Greek (from the word for 'ten thousand'). Also remember the *ad* ending.

myrrh /*say* mer/ *noun* a sticky gum which tastes bitter but which can be used to make incense and perfume.

☑ SPELLING TIP *Silent letter alert*: don't forget the silent *h* at the end. This is only one of the difficulties with this unusual word. Remember the *y* spelling of the vowel sound, and the double *r*.

mystery /*say* **mis**-tree/ *noun* (*plural* **mysteries**) something that is puzzling, secret or cannot be explained: *the mystery of Mona Lisa's smile.*
☐ **mysterious**, *adjective*: *It was a mysterious phone call – no-one knew who the speaker was.*

☑ SPELLING TIP *Letter 'y' alert*: the first vowel sound is spelt *y* (not *i*). Many words that come from Greek have this kind of *y* spelling. Also remember that there is another *y* (not *ey*) spelling the 'ee' sound at the end. This *y* changes to an *i* in the adjective **mysterious**.

mystic /*say* **mis**-tik/ *noun* someone who is concerned with spiritual matters.
☐ **mystical**, *adjective* –**mysticism** /*say* **mis**-tuh-siz-uhm/, *noun*

mystify /*say* **mis**-tuh-fuy/ *verb* (**mystifies**, **mystifying**, **mystified**, **has mystified**) If something **mystifies** you, you find it puzzling and difficult to understand.

myth /*rhymes with* pith/ *noun* an ancient story about gods, brave people and supernatural happenings, which may try to explain natural events like the weather, sunrise and sunset and so on.
☐ **mythical**, *adjective* –**mythological**, *adjective* –**mythology**, *noun*

☑ SPELLING TIP *Letter 'y' alert*: the vowel sound is spelt *y* (not *i*). Many words that come from Greek have this kind of *y* spelling. **Myth** comes from the Greek word meaning 'legend', 'story' or 'word'.

naan /*say* nahn/ *noun* a flat, round bread, originating in Indian cooking.

> ☑ SPELLING TIP *Double letter alert*: remember the double *a*. In fact, you can spell this word with one *a*, but the most common spelling is **naan**.

nab *verb* (**nabs**, **nabbing**, **nabbed**, **has nabbed**) *Rather informal* If you **nab** someone, you catch or grab them suddenly.

nachos *noun* a snack made from corn chips with tomato, chilli, and melted cheese on top.

> WORD HISTORY from Mexican Spanish

nag[1] *verb* (**nags**, **nagging**, **nagged**, **has nagged**) If somebody **nags** another person, they keep complaining, finding fault or making demands of them: *My brother nagged my mother until she bought him some diving gear.*
☐ **nagger**, *noun*

nag[2] *noun Rather informal* a horse, especially one that is old or worn out.

nail *noun*
1. a long, thin piece of metal with one pointed end. You use nails to join together pieces of wood by hitting them through the two layers of wood with a hammer. **2.** the hard, horny part on the end of each finger and toe: *Her nails were painted a bright red.*
–*verb* **3.** If you **nail** something somewhere, you fix it there with nails: *It took a while to nail the carpet down.*

naive /*say* nuy-**eev**, nah-**eev**/ *adjective* If someone is **naive**, they do not understand the real nature of people or the world. They are often too willing to believe that people are good or truthful: *His statement that life is always fair was naive.*
☐ **naively**, *adverb* –**naivety**, *noun*

> SIMILAR WORDS are **innocent**, **inexperienced**, **unsophisticated** and **gullible**. Note that a **gullible** person is easily deceived or cheated.

> ☑ SPELLING TIP Remember that the beginning of this word is spelt *na* (although it is often said as 'nuy'). Immediately after comes the *ive* ending (giving an 'eev' sound). This brings the vowels *a* and *i* together, but not as a sound pair. **Naive** is spelt in this way because it comes from French. This is why you sometimes see it spelt with an accent over the *i*: **naïve**.

naked /*say* **nay**-kuhd/ *adjective* unclothed or bare: *He was naked to the waist*; *The comet was clear to the naked eye.*
☐ **nakedness**, *noun*

name *noun*
1. what someone or something is called. **2.** reputation or fame: *The band took only a year to make its name.*
–*verb* **3.** If somebody **names** somebody or something, they give them a name: *They named him Aloysius*; *What did they name the new star?*

nanny *noun* (*plural* **nannies**) a person, usually a woman, who is employed to look after the children of a family in their home.

nanny goat *noun* a female goat.

> NOTE The male is a **billy goat**.

nap *verb* (**naps**, **napping**, **napped**, **has napped**) If you **nap**, you have a short sleep.
☐ **nap**, *noun*

napalm /*say* **nay**-pahm, **na**-pahm/ *noun* a substance which is mixed with petrol and used in flame throwers and fire bombs.

> ☑ SPELLING TIP *Tricky vowel sound*: don't forget the *l*. The *alm* spelling gives the 'ahm' sound.

nape *noun* the back of the neck.

napkin *noun* a serviette.

nappy *noun* (*plural* **nappies**) a piece of cloth or a pad of paper fastened round a baby's waist and legs to contain the waste matter from its body.

> ANOTHER WORD for this is **diaper**. **Diaper** is used more in American English.

narcissism /*say* **nah**-suh-siz-uhm/ *noun* love of yourself, especially love of your own appearance.
☐ **narcissistic**, *adjective*

> WORD HISTORY from *Narcissus*, a handsome young man in Greek myths, who fell in love with his own reflection in water and was changed into a narcissus plant

> ☑ SPELLING TIP There are lots of 's' sounds in this word. But don't think that someone who indulges in **narcissism** is a *sissy* because you have to remember that there is a *c* spelling for

the first 's' sound. The next is spelt with a double *s* and then there is the *ism* ending.

narcotic *noun* any drug which can relieve pain and make you sleepy.
□ **narcotic**, *adjective*

WORD HISTORY from a Greek word meaning 'making stiff or numb'

narrate *verb* If you **narrate** a story, you tell it.
□ **narration**, *noun* –**narrator**, *noun*

narrative /*say* **na**-ruh-tiv/ *noun* a story of events, experiences, and so on, in speech or writing.

narrow *adjective*
1. not wide: *narrow street.* **2.** only just achieved: *a narrow miss.* **3.** not interested in or not understanding behaviour, ideas or customs that are different from your own: *Our leader has a very narrow view on many important issues.*
–*verb* **4.** To **narrow** is to become less wide.
□ **narrowly**, *adverb*

ANOTHER WORD (for definition 3) is **narrow-minded**.

nasal *adjective*
1. In medical or technical language, **nasal** refers to the nose: *a nasal drip*; *the nasal cavity.* **2.** If someone has a **nasal** voice, they make speech sounds using the air in their nose as well as their mouth: *Her nasal whine was very annoying.*
□ **nasally**, *adverb*

nasty *adjective* (**nastier**, **nastiest**)
1. If something is **nasty**, it is unpleasant or disgusting: *a nasty piece of business*; *a nasty appearance.* **2.** If someone is **nasty** they are unkind or cruel: *My mum's boss is thoroughly nasty.*
□ **nastily**, *adverb* –**nastiness**, *noun*

nation *noun*
1. a large group of people living in one country under one government: *The leaders of most of the world's nations attended the conference.* **2.** a group of people who have the same customs, history, and language, even though they may not have their own government: *an elder of the Arrernte nation.*
□ **national**, *adjective* –**nationally**, *adverb*

nationalise *verb* If a government **nationalises** a particular private industry, it brings it under public ownership or government control: *The point of nationalising medical services is so that everybody's health can be looked after.*
□ **nationalisation**, *noun*

ANOTHER SPELLING is **nationalize**.

nationalism *noun* love of your own country: *There was a surge of nationalism in the face of threatened war.*
□ **nationalist**, *noun* –**nationalistic**, *adjective*

nationality *noun* (*plural* **nationalities**) membership or connection that someone has with a country: *We are proud of our Australian nationality.*

A SIMILAR WORD is **citizenship**.

native *adjective*
1. Your **native** town or country is the place where you were born. **2.** If something is **native** to a particular country or place, it originally came from there: *Koalas are native to Australia.*
–*noun* **3.** someone born in a particular place: *a native of Greece.*

native title *noun* the right of an Aboriginal or Torres Strait Islander person to land or water that they have maintained connection with.

nativity *noun* (*plural* **nativities**)
1. birth. **2. the Nativity**, the birth of Jesus Christ.

natural *adjective*
1. Something that is **natural** is normal. It is what you would expect: *It's only natural that you're upset.* **2.** If something, such as behaviour or a certain skill, is **natural**, you were born with it and you did not need to learn it: *She has a natural talent for singing.* **3. Natural** surroundings or physical features are not artificial or created by people: *We sheltered in a natural harbour.* **4.** If you say that someone is **natural** or behaves in a **natural** way, you mean that they behave in a relaxed and simple way without any pretence.
□ **naturally**, *adverb*

naturalise *verb* If a country **naturalises** a person, they make them a full citizen of that country: *Andreas was very proud to be naturalised as an Australian citizen.*
□ **naturalisation**, *noun*

ANOTHER SPELLING is **naturalize**.

nature *noun*
1. the world around us, made up of earth, sky and sea, along with animals and plants, especially when untouched by human beings: *There is no end to the wonders of nature.* **2.** the fundamental qualities of a person or thing: *She has a kind nature*; *The nature of jelly is to be wobbly.*
□ **naturalist**, *noun*

naught /*say* nawt/ *noun Old-fashioned* nothing.

WORD HISTORY from Old English words meaning 'no' and 'thing'

☑ SPELLING TIP *Tricky vowel sound*: Notice the *augh* for the 'aw' sound. Don't confuse this word with **nought** which has the same sound and a related meaning. **Nought** is the sign in maths (0) which stands for zero.

naughty /*say* **naw**-tee/ *adjective* (**naughtier**, **naughtiest**) badly behaved.
□ **naughtiness**, *noun*

☑ SPELLING TIP *Tricky vowel sound*: the first vowel sound is spelt *augh* (although it sounds like 'aw'). It might help if you think of other words with the same spelling for this sound, such as *caught* and *daughter*.

nausea /*say* **naw**-see-uh, **naw**-zee-uh/ *noun* a feeling of wanting to be sick.
☐ **nauseous**, *adjective*

☑ SPELLING TIP *Tricky vowel sound*: the first vowel sound is spelt *au* (although it sounds like 'aw'). Remember also that the ending is *ea* (not *ia*). Like many medical words, **nausea** comes from Greek.

nautical *adjective* If something is **nautical**, it has to do with ships, sailors or sailing.

nautilus /*say* **naw**-tuh-luhs/ *noun* a kind of sea creature with a spiral shell divided into many parts.

WORD HISTORY from a Greek word meaning 'sailor'

naval *adjective* having to do with a navy: *naval forces*; *naval commander.*

☑ SPELLING TIP Don't confuse the spelling of **naval** with **navel** which has the same sound but ends with *el* instead of *al*. Your **navel** is the small, round hollow in your stomach.

navel *noun* the small, round hollow in the middle of the stomach.

☑ SPELLING TIP Don't confuse the spelling of **navel** with **naval** which has the same sound but ends with *al* instead of *el*. Something that is **naval** has to do with a navy.

navigate *verb* To **navigate** is to steer or direct on a course: *to navigate through stormy seas.*
☐ **navigable**, *adjective* –**navigation**, *noun* –**navigator**, *noun*

navy *noun* (*plural* **navies**)
1. the part of a country's armed forces that is trained to fight at sea. **2.** a very dark blue colour, as of a naval uniform.
–*adjective* **3.** of a navy colour.

ANOTHER TERM (for definition 2) is **navy blue**.

NB *abbreviation* short for *nota bene*, Latin words meaning 'note well'.

ANOTHER FORM is **n.b.**
NOTE This is usually used in writing to make you notice a particular piece of important information.

near *adverb*
1. at or to a short distance: *She stood near, waiting for them to finish.*
–*adjective* **2.** being at a short distance in place or time: *She went to the nearest house.* **3.** less distant: *the near side.*
–*verb* **4.** If someone or something **nears** a place, they come closer to it: *They finally neared their destination.*
☐ **nearby**, *adjective* –**nearby**, *adverb*

nearly *adverb* almost: *She nearly fainted.*

neat *adjective*
1. If someone is **neat**, they are tidy in their habits and careful about their appearance. **2.** If something is **neat**, it is tidy and in good order: *My bedroom never seems to stay neat for long.* **3.** *Informal* If you say something is **neat**, you mean that it is very clever or you like it very much: *That's a neat idea!*
☐ **neatly**, *adverb* –**neatness**, *noun*

nebula /*say* **neb**-yuh-luh/ *noun* (*plural* **nebulae** /*say* **neb**-yuh-lee/ *or* **nebulas**) a cloud-like patch in the night sky, usually consisting of a group of stars.

WORD HISTORY from a Latin word meaning 'mist', 'cloud' or 'vapour'

nebulous *adjective* cloudy or vague: *Trees on the bank were dark and nebulous shapes*; *nebulous hopes and expectations.*
☐ **nebulously**, *adverb*

necessary /*say* **nes**-uh-se-ree/ *adjective*
1. If something is **necessary**, you need it: *all the necessary ingredients.* **2.** If it is **necessary** to do something, it is important that you do it.
–*noun* (*plural* **necessaries**) **3.** something necessary: *Nothing but necessaries were carried.*
☐ **necessarily**, *adverb*

SIMILAR WORDS (for definition 2) are **essential**, **crucial** and **vital**. Note that these words all mean 'absolutely necessary'.

☑ SPELLING TIP *Single/double letter alert*: one *c* but two *s*'s. Think that 'in the classroom school socks are **necessary**' to remind you of this.

necessity /*say* nuh-**ses**-uh-tee/ *noun* (*plural* **necessities**)
1. something that cannot be done without: *A water flask is a necessity when you are walking in summer.* **2.** the state of being in need or difficulty: *In the grip of compelling necessity, he struggled to climb the cliff.*
☐ **necessitate**, *verb*: *His situation necessitated drastic action.*

neck *noun*
1. the part of the body of a human or animal which joins the head to the trunk. **2.** any narrow connecting part: *the neck of a guitar*; *the neck of a decanter.*
–*phrase* **3. neck and neck**, completely even in a race. **4. stick your neck out**, to act, speak and so on, so as to leave yourself open to criticism or risk.

necklace /*rhymes with* reckless/ *noun* a string of beads or other ornament worn round your neck.

nectar /*say* **nek**-tuh/ *noun*
1. a sweet liquid produced by plants and made into honey by bees. **2.** any pleasant-tasting drink.

nectarine *noun* a kind of peach with a smooth skin.

need *noun*
1. something that you have to have: *The chief need of the refugees is clean water.* **2.** an urgent want: *The teacher said there was a need for improvement in our maths.*
–*verb* **3.** If you **need** something, you have a need for it: *Mum needed some assistance in changing the tyre.* **4.** If you **need** to do something, you have to do it: *We need to buy her a present.*
–*phrase* **5. in need of**, in a situation where something is needed: *a country in need of financial aid.*
☐ **needy**, *adjective* (**needier**, **neediest**) –**needful**, *adjective* –**needless**, *adjective*

needle *noun*
1. a small, thin, pointed tool, usually made of metal and with a hole at one end for thread, used for sewing. **2.** a thin metal or plastic stick used for knitting. **3.** a pointer on a dial: *a speedometer needle.* **4.** a thin tube sharp enough to pierce your skin, used for giving injections. **5.** anything sharp and shaped like a needle: *We walked on a carpet of pine needles.*

negative *adjective*
1. A **negative** answer to a question is one that says 'no'. **2.** A **negative** number is smaller than nothing.
–*noun* **3.** an answer or opinion that says or means 'no'. **4.** a photographic film which is used to make prints and has the light and dark of the picture the opposite way to how it really is.
☐ **negation**, *noun* –**negativity**, *noun*

THE OPPOSITE is **positive**.

neglect *verb*
1. To **neglect** something is to pay no attention to it: *She neglected to clean up after her painting.* **2.** To **neglect** a person or an animal is to fail to look after them.
☐ **neglect**, *noun*: *the neglect of a child.* –**neglectful**, *adjective*

negligee /*say* **neg**-luh-zhay/ *noun* a woman's nightdress, especially one made of thin material.

☑ SPELLING TIP *Tricky 'uh' sound*: the middle vowel sound is spelt *i*. Also remember the *ee* ending, giving an 'ay' sound. This is because **negligee** comes from French, surprisingly from the word for 'neglected' (in the sense of 'not given much thought or attention').

negligent /*say* **neg**-luh-juhnt/ *adjective* If someone is **negligent**, they do not take enough care over what they are doing: *A young man was charged with negligent driving.*
☐ **negligence**, *noun*

☑ SPELLING TIP *Tricky 'uh' sound*: **negligent** comes from the word *neglect* but notice the vowel after the *gl* has changed from *e* to *i*.

negligible /*say* **neg**-luh-juh-buhl/ *adjective* unimportant enough to be ignored: *In such a small town, distances are negligible.*
☐ **negligibly**, *adverb*

☑ SPELLING TIP *Tricky 'uh' sound*: as in other words formed from *neglect*, the vowel after the *gl* has changed from *e* to *i*. Also remember that there are two separate *g*'s in this word – the first with a hard sound, the second soft – and the *ible* ending.

negotiate /*say* nuh-**goh**-shee-ayt/ *verb* To **negotiate** is to arrange by discussion: *The hotel had to negotiate a solution with neighbouring properties about the noise on Saturday nights.*
☐ **negotiable**, *adjective* –**negotiation**, *noun*

☑ SPELLING TIP Remember that the letter *t* turns up twice in this word. The first time it gives a 'sh' sound. You could also rap it out as *ne+go+ti+ate* to remember the two *t*'s.

neigh /*say* nay/ *noun*
1. the sound a horse makes.
–*verb* **2.** When a horse **neighs**, it makes a distinctive loud noise.

☑ SPELLING TIP *Tricky vowel sound*: the vowel sound is spelt *eigh* (although it sounds like 'ay'). It might help if you think of other words with the same spelling for this sound, such as *eight* and *weigh*.

neighbour /*say* **nay**-buh/ *noun* someone who lives near you.
☐ **neighbourhood**, *noun* –**neighbourly**, *adjective* –**neighbouring**, *adjective*

ANOTHER SPELLING is **neighbor**.

☑ SPELLING TIP Most **neighbours** talk, rather than *neigh* like a horse. However, *neigh* forms the first part of this word. In this case, it comes from the Old English word meaning 'near'.

neither /*say* **nuy**-dhuh, **nee**-dhuh/ *adjective*
1. not one nor the other: *Neither colour suits me – I look awful in both orange and purple.*
–*pronoun* **2.** not the one nor the other: *Neither of the colours looks good on me.*
–*conjunction* **3.** not either: *Neither my brother nor I like cabbage.*

NOTE Definition 3 is always used with **nor**.

☑ SPELLING TIP There are two ways of saying **neither**, but only one way of spelling it. The first vowel sound is spelt *ei* whether you pronounce it as 'uy' or 'ee'.

neon *noun* a gas which gives off light when an electric current is put through it, and so is used in lights.

nephew /*say* **nef**-yooh, **nev**-yooh/ *noun* the son of a person's brother or sister, or of their husband's or wife's brother or sister.

NOTE The daughter of a person's brother or sister is their **niece**.

☑ SPELLING TIP Remember that there is no *v* in this word, although one of the ways in which you can say it has a 'v' sound. Concentrate on the *ph* for either an 'f' or a 'v' sound.

nepotism /*say* **nep**-uh-tiz-uhm/ *noun* the favouring of a relation or friend by giving them a job or promotion.

WORD HISTORY from an Italian word meaning 'nephew'

nerd *noun Informal* a person who prefers to spend their time working on a computer or studying and who takes little or no part in social activities.

nerve *noun*
1. a fibre or bundle of fibres that carries messages from the brain to other parts of the body, giving the ability to move and feel. **2.** courage, especially when you are facing a difficult situation: *It took all her nerve to go and see the principal.* **3. nerves**, nervousness or shakiness: *We tried to think about other things to settle our nerves.*

nervous *adjective*
1. worried or frightened, especially about something that is going to happen: *The thought of going up the ladder made him very nervous.* **2.** having to do with the system of nerves in the body.
□ **nervously**, *adverb* –**nervousness**, *noun*

SIMILAR WORDS (for definition 1) are **anxious**, **apprehensive**, **tense**, **edgy** and **jittery** (*Rather informal*). You can also say that you **have butterflies (in your stomach)** when you feel nervous.

nest *noun*
1. a shelter built or a place used by a bird to hatch its eggs and bring up its young.
–*verb* **2.** When a bird **nests**, it builds and then settles in a nest where it hatches and brings up its young: *A magpie is nesting outside my window.*
□ **nestling**, *noun* a young bird.

net[1] *noun*
1. a material made of fine threads knotted or woven together with holes in between: *a mosquito net.* **2.** a fabric like this, made of cord or rope: *a fishing net.* **3.** a piece of net used in some sports, such as tennis. **4. the Net**, See **internet**.
–*verb* (**nets**, **netting**, **netted**, **has netted**) **5.** To **net** something, such as fish, is to catch it in a net.

net[2] *adjective*
1. If a weight is **net**, it does not include packaging: *The net weight of this jam is 250 grams.* **2.** If an amount of money is **net**, costs have been taken out of it: *net profit.*
–*verb* (**nets**, **netting**, **netted**, **has netted**) **3.** If you **net** a certain amount you are left with the amount gained after the costs have been taken out.

ANOTHER SPELLING is **nett**.

netball *noun*
1. a game played by two teams of seven players, in which the players must try to throw the ball through a hoop attached to a pole at the opponents' end of the court. **2.** the ball used in this game.
□ **netballer**, *noun*

nett *adjective* See **net**[2].

nettle *noun* a plant with hairs on its leaves and stem, which can sting and cause red itchy spots on your skin if you touch it.

network *noun*
1. a net-like arrangement of connected lines or passages: *a network of drainage ditches.* **2.** a group of radio or television stations, sometimes having the same owner, which have formal arrangements to share programs. **3.** a system of computers, printers, etc., which are connected by cables so that they can transfer information to one another.

neurotic /*say* nyooh-**rot**-ik/ *adjective* on edge and behaving strangely, because of a disorder of the mind.
□ **neurotic**, *noun* a neurotic person. –**neurotically**, *adverb*

☑ SPELLING TIP *Tricky vowel sound*: *eu* for the 'yooh' sound. This word is based on *neuron*, the Greek word for a kind of nerve.

neuter /*say* **nyooh**-tuh/ *adjective* neither masculine nor feminine.

neutral /*say* **nyooh**-truhl/ *adjective*
1. If a person or country remains **neutral** in an argument or war, they do not support one side or the other: *Switzerland was neutral in World War II.* **2.** If someone remains **neutral** in a discussion or debate, they do not enter into the argument: *She took a neutral position in the discussion.* **3.** If someone's voice is **neutral**, they speak without emotion.
–*noun* **4.** a person or country that does not take sides in a war. **5.** the position of gears in a car where they are not ready to be driven by the engine.
□ **neutrality**, *noun* –**neutralise**, *verb*

ANOTHER SPELLING for **neutralise** is **neutralize.**

☑ SPELLING TIP *Tricky vowel sound*: *eu* for the 'yooh' sound.

neutron *noun* a very tiny particle present in the nucleus of an atom, having the same mass as a proton but no charge.

SEE ALSO **electron** and **proton**.

never *adverb*
1. not ever: *I'll never tell you the secret.* 2. not at all: *Fighting never solves anything.*

never-never *noun*
1. *Informal* desert country where hardly anyone lives.
–*adjective in the phrase* 2. **never-never land**, an imaginary place where everything is pleasant and exciting.

new *adjective*
1. recently arrived, obtained or come into being: *a new girl in the class*; *Our new car is red.* 2. fresh or unused: *Turn to a new page.*
☐ **newness**, *noun*

news *noun*
1. a report of something that has just happened.
–*phrase* 2. **bad news**, *Informal* someone or something from whom nothing good is to be expected: *Don't bother going to see that film – it's really bad news.*

newsagency *noun* a shop where you can buy things such as newspapers, pens, magazines and books.
☐ **newsagent**, *noun* someone who runs a newsagency.

newspaper *noun* a printed publication issued at regular times, usually daily or weekly, and commonly containing news, discussion, features, and advertisements.

newt *noun* a small salamander.

next *adjective*
1. immediately following: *the next day.* 2. nearest: *the next room.*
–*adverb* 3. in the nearest place: *Can I sit next to you?*

next of kin *noun* your nearest relation or relations.

nib *noun* the writing point of a pen.

nibble *verb* If you **nibble** food, you bite off small bits from it: *We nibbled the biscuits in our sleeping bags so no-one could hear.*
☐ **nibble**, *noun*

nice *adjective*
1. pleasing or enjoyable: *What a nice weekend that was!* 2. kind or pleasant: *He was very nice and helped us push the car.* 3. showing great accuracy, skill or exactness: *a nice analysis of the problem.*
☐ **nicely**, *adverb* –**niceness**, *noun*

SIMILAR WORDS (for definition 1) are **excellent**, **exceptional**, **first-class**, **marvellous**, **sensational**, **terrific**, **cool** (*Informal*) and **top** (*Informal*). Note that all of these words mean 'extremely nice'; (for definition 2) **agreeable**, **considerate**, **courteous**, **helpful**, **polite** and **thoughtful**.

niche /*say* neesh, nich/ *noun*
1. a small hollow set into something like a wall: *A statue of Venus stood in a niche in the wall.* 2. a place or position suitable for a person or thing: *The new airline has found its own niche in the industry.*

☑ SPELLING TIP Notice that there are two ways to say this word. Whichever one you use, the main thing to remember about the spelling is the *che* ending. **Niche** is spelt like this because it comes from French.

nick *noun*
1. a small cut.
–*verb* 2. To **nick** yourself is to cut yourself slightly.
3. *Informal* To **nick** something is to steal it.
–*phrase* 4. **in the nick of time**, at the last possible moment. 5. **nick off**, *Informal* to leave or disappear.

nickel *noun* a hard, silvery white metal.

nickname *noun*
1. a name used instead of your real name.
–*verb* 2. If you **nickname** a person, you give them a name different to their real name: *They nicknamed him 'the Kangaroo' because he was so good at jumping.*

nicotine /*say* nik-uh-**teen**, **nik**-uh-teen/ *noun* a poisonous substance in tobacco.

WORD HISTORY named after Jacques *Nicot*, who introduced tobacco into France in 1560

☑ SPELLING TIP *Tricky 'uh' sound*: the middle vowel is spelt *o*. Also remember that a *c* alone (not *ck*) spells the 'k' sound.

niece /*say* nees/ *noun* the daughter of a person's brother or sister, or of their husband's or wife's brother or sister.

NOTE The son of a person's brother or sister is their **nephew**.

☑ SPELLING TIP *Tricky vowel sound*: *ie* to spell the 'ee' sound. This follows the rule that *i* comes before *e* except after *c* (when making an 'ee' sound). Another word with a similar spelling pattern is *piece* (meaning a 'bit').

nifty *adjective* (**niftier**, **niftiest**) *Informal* 1. clever: *That was pretty nifty the way she bargained for the car she wanted.* 2. stylish: *My dad looked really nifty in his new suit.*

night *noun* the time of darkness between sunset and sunrise.

nightcap *noun*
1. a drink, especially a hot one, you have before going to bed. 2. a cap people used to wear to bed.

nightingale /*say* **nuy**-ting-gayl/ *noun* a small European bird known for its beautiful singing, especially at night.

nightly *adjective*
1. coming, happening or active at night: *the nightly penguin parade.*
–adverb **2.** every night: *The penguins emerge from the sea nightly.*

nightmare *noun*
1. a very frightening dream. **2.** any very upsetting or frightening experience.
☐ **nightmarish**, *adjective*

nil *noun* nothing: *His income at present is nil.*

nimble *adjective*
1. able to move quickly and easily: *Jacky is nimble on his feet and loves to dance.* **2.** quick in understanding: *With her nimble mind, she answered the questions quickly and correctly.*
☐ **nimbleness**, *noun* –**nimbly**, *adverb*

nimbus /*say* **nim**-buhs/ *noun* (*plural* **nimbi** /*say* **nim**-buy/ *or* **nimbuses**) a rain cloud.

COMPARE this with **cirrus** and **cumulus**.
WORD HISTORY from a Latin word meaning 'rainstorm' or 'thunder-cloud'

nine *noun*
1. a cardinal number, eight plus one (8 + 1). **2.** a symbol for this number, as 9 or IX.
☐ **nine**, *adjective* –**ninth**, *adjective*, *noun*

nineteen *noun*
1. a cardinal number, ten plus nine (10 + 9). **2.** a symbol for this number, as 19 or XIX.
☐ **nineteen**, *adjective* –**nineteenth**, *adjective*, *noun*

ninety *noun* (*plural* **nineties**)
1. a cardinal number, nine times ten (9 × 10). **2.** a symbol for this number, as 90 or XC. **3. nineties**, the numbers from 90 to 99 of a series, especially with reference to the years of a person's age, or the years of a century: *He's in his nineties.*
☐ **ninetieth**, *adjective*, *noun* –**ninety**, *adjective*

nip *verb* (**nips**, **nipping**, **nipped**, **has nipped**)
1. to take a small bite or pinch.
–noun **2.** a pinch. **3.** a small bit of anything.
–phrase **4. nip off**, *Informal* to move or go away suddenly or quickly: *He nipped off as soon as the main part of the ceremony was over.*

nipple *noun*
1. part of your breast and in women the part from which a baby sucks milk. **2.** something like this, such as the mouthpiece of a baby's bottle.

nippy *adjective* (**nippier**, **nippiest**)
1. very chilly or cold: *A nippy southerly was blowing up.* **2.** active or nimble: *Spot is still a puppy and very nippy and lively.*

niqab /*say* nik-**ahb**/ *noun* a veil worn by some Muslim women, covering the face but leaving the area around the eyes uncovered.

nirvana /*say* ner-**vah**-nuh/ *noun* in Buddhism, the final state of happiness when freedom from human emotions and concerns is achieved.

nit *noun*
1. the egg of an insect such as a louse. **2.** the young of such an insect, especially when it is living in human hair.

nitrogen /*say* **nuy**-truh-juhn/ *noun* a colourless gas with no smell which forms 78 per cent of the air around us.
☐ **nitrogenous** /*say* nuy-**troj**-uh-nuhs/, *adjective*

nix *noun Informal* nothing.

no *interjection* **1.** a word used to express denial, disagreement, or refusal such as in an answer, or to add force to an earlier negative: *No, you cannot have another piece of cake!*
–adjective, *adverb* **2.** not any: *I have no money with me*; *He's feeling no better.*

No. *abbreviation* short for *number*.

noble *adjective*
1. A **noble** person belongs to the ruling class of a country, or that which once ruled: *the noble families of Europe.* **2.** Someone who is **noble** has high principles: *It was noble of her to take the full responsibility and be punished instead of her brother.*
☐ **nobility**, *noun* –**nobly**, *adverb*: *He nobly sacrificed himself.* –**nobleman**, **noblewoman**, *noun*

nobody *pronoun* **1.** no person: *There was nobody in the room.*
–noun (*plural* **nobodies**) **2.** a person of no importance: *I was angry when I heard her call my friend a nobody.*

ANOTHER WORD (for definition 1) is **no-one.**

nocturnal /*say* nok-**ter**-nuhl/ *adjective* Animals that are **nocturnal** are usually active at night and sleep during the day.
☐ **nocturnally**, *adverb*

nod *verb* (**nods**, **nodding**, **nodded**, **has nodded**)
1. To **nod** is to lower and raise your head in a short, quick movement especially in agreement, greeting, command, and so on: *Su Li nodded in agreement*; *They all nodded as the princess walked past.*
–phrase **2. nod off**, to go to sleep.
☐ **nod**, *noun*: *He gave a nod.*

node *noun*
1. a knot or lump, especially one that is found in some parts of the body. **2.** a joint in the stem of a plant, especially where a leaf grows.
☐ **nodal**, *adjective* –**nodose**, *adjective*

nodule *noun* a small rounded mass or lump.
☐ **nodular**, *adjective*

noise *noun* any kind of sound, especially a sound which is too loud or which you do not like.

☐ **noisy**, *adjective* (**noisier**, **noisiest**) –**noisiness**, *noun* –**noisily**, *adverb*

nomad *noun*
1. a member of a race or tribe that moves from one area to another hunting, food-gathering, or allowing their animals to feed. **2.** anyone who generally travels about.
☐ **nomadic**, *adjective*

WORD HISTORY from a Greek word meaning 'roaming' (like cattle)

nominal *adjective*
1. having to do with a noun: *a nominal clause.* **2.** in name only: *the nominal head of the organisation.*

nominate *verb* To **nominate** someone is to name them as a candidate in an election: *Six people were nominated for captain.*
☐ **nomination**, *noun* –**nominator**, *noun* –**nominee**, *noun*

non- *prefix* a word part meaning 'not', as in *non-essential*, *non-government*.

WORD HISTORY this prefix comes from Latin

nonagon /*say* **non**-uh-gon/ *noun* a flat shape with nine straight sides.
☐ **nonagonal** /*say* non-**ag**-uh-nuhl/, *adjective*

nonchalant /*say* **non**-shuh-luhnt/ *adjective* calm and indifferent: *He shrugged his shoulders in a nonchalant way.*
☐ **nonchalance**, *noun* –**nonchalantly**, *adverb*

☑ SPELLING TIP Remember that there is a *ch* spelling in this word, giving a 'sh' sound. Also notice that the ending is *ant* (not *ent*).

non-committal *adjective* If you are **non-committal**, you do not show your opinion or decision so that you will not be held to it: *It's no good being non-committal – we have to know where you stand!*

nonconformist *noun* a person who refuses to accept the usual or expected ideas, customs or ways of living.
☐ **nonconformity**, *noun*

nondescript *adjective* very ordinary-looking, without any easily recognised qualities.

none /*rhymes with* bun/ *pronoun* **None** means 'not one' or 'not any': *None of the hats fitted her*; *None of us wants to go.*

nonentity /*say* non-**en**-tuh-tee/ *noun* someone of no importance: *The prime minister was at the party, but most of the people were nonentities.*

nonfiction *noun* something written about real people and events that actually happened.

THE OPPOSITE is **fiction**.

nonflammable *adjective* If something is **nonflammable**, it is not easily set on fire.

THE OPPOSITE is **flammable**. The term **inflammable** also has the opposite meaning to **nonflammable**, but it is not used much nowadays. See the note at **flammable**.

nonplussed /*say* non-**plust**/ *adjective* puzzled.

☑ SPELLING TIP This word is actually the past form of the verb *nonplus*, meaning 'to surprise and confuse'. It has doubled its *s* before adding *-ed* in the usual way. If you remember this, you will have no trouble spelling the ending.

non-renewable resource *noun* a supply of something, such as oil, gas and coal, that is needed in everyday life to make power and which, once used, cannot be naturally replaced or restored.

COMPARE this with **renewable resource**.

nonsense /*say* **non**-suhns/ *noun*
1. words that are silly or without meaning. **2.** silly ideas or behaviour: *Stop that nonsense!*; *What you are suggesting is nonsense.*
☐ **nonsensical** /*say* non-**sen**-sik-uhl/, *adjective*

noodle *noun* a type of flour and egg paste cut in long thin strips, often served in soups or with a sauce.

nook *noun*
1. a corner, especially in a room. **2.** any small, private or hidden place.

noon *noun* twelve o'clock in the daytime.

no-one *pronoun* no person: *No-one has been here since yesterday.*

ANOTHER WORD for this is **nobody** (definition 1).

noose *noun* a loop with a sliding knot which tightens as the rope is pulled.

nor *conjunction* **Nor** is used **1.** after *neither* to mention something else that is also negative: *He could neither read nor write.* **2.** after a negative statement to introduce another negative: *I don't want to go, nor does my brother.*

norm *noun* a standard or model that you judge everything else by.

normal *adjective*
1. ordinary or usual: *Why can't you come down the stairs the normal way?*
–*phrase* **2. back to normal**, back to the usual way of doing things: *After the fires, life took a long time to get back to normal.*
☐ **normalcy**, *noun* –**normality**, *noun* –**normally**, *adverb*

THE OPPOSITE is **abnormal**.

north *noun* the direction which is to your right when you face the setting sun or the west.

☐ **north**, *adjective*, *adverb* –**northerly**, *adjective*: *northerly winds.* –**northern**, *adjective*

NOTE The opposite direction is **south**.

nose *noun*
1. the part of the face used for breathing and smelling. 2. a sense of smell: *You must have a good nose to have smelt the fires from such a distance.*
–*verb* 3. If a vehicle **noses** its way, it moves or pushes forward in a certain direction, sometimes with difficulty: *The fire truck nosed its way down the trails towards the fire.*
–*phrase* 4. **on the nose**, *Informal* **a.** smelly, especially because something has decayed. **b.** unpleasant or giving a bad feeling: *His offer is on the nose.* 5. **turn your nose up**, to not accept something you don't like, especially when you really ought to be grateful. 6. **under your nose**, *Informal* in an obvious place.

nostalgia /*say* nos-**tal**-juh/ *noun* a longing for the past and all the things that belonged to it.
☐ **nostalgic**, *adjective* –**nostalgically**, *adverb*

☑ SPELLING TIP The tricky part is the *gia* ending which sounds like 'juh'. **Nostalgia** comes from Greek and is made up of two parts – a short form of *nostos* meaning 'return home' and *algia* meaning 'pain'.

nostril *noun* one of the two openings of the nose.

nosy *adjective* (**nosier**, **nosiest**) If someone is **nosy**, they are interested in things that are not their business.

not *adverb* a word which shows a negative or opposite: *You must not do that*; *It's not far.*

notable *adjective*
1. important or worthy of noticing: *a notable success.*
–*noun* 2. an important person.
☐ **notability**, *noun* –**notably**, *adverb*

notation *noun* a way of writing down things like music or dance by using signs or symbols, such as notes or lines to stand for sounds or marks to stand for movement: *musical notation.*

notch *noun* (*plural* **notches**)
1. a small sharp cut on an edge or surface.
–*verb* 2. If you **notch** something like a piece of wood, you make notches in it: *Every birthday, we notch the side of the garage door to show how tall we are.*
–*phrase* 3. **notch up**, to score in a game or something like that: *We notched up three wins at the beginning of the season.*

note *noun*
1. something written down to make you remember something. 2. a short letter. 3. paper money: *He counted out the notes.* 4. importance or fame: *After thirty years recording, he is a person of note in the music world.* 5. a musical sound, or the sign or symbol you use to write it down on paper.
–*verb* 6. If you **note** something, you observe it: *She noted that he looked quite ill.* 7. If you **note** something, you write it down so that you will remember it: *She noted down everything she was told about the computer program for future reference.*
–*phrase* 8. **take note of**, to pay attention to.

ANOTHER WORD (for definition 3) is **banknote**.

noted *adjective* famous or honoured: *a noted scientist.*

nothing /*say* **nu**-thing/ *noun*
1. You use **nothing** to refer to a complete absence of something: *We have nothing left to eat*; *Say nothing.*
–*phrase* 2. **for nothing**, free of charge. 3. **next to nothing**, very little.

notice *noun*
1. a sign or note giving a warning or some information. 2. a statement that an agreement or arrangement is going to end: *The family was given only a month's notice to leave the house*; *He was depressed because he had been given notice – his job ended at the end of the week.* 3. interested attention: *Their activities came to the notice of the police.*
☐ **notice**, *verb* –**noticeable**, *adjective*: *a noticeable difference.* –**noticeably**, *adverb*

noticeboard *noun* a board where you put notices and information of general interest, such as one in a central position in a school, office, etc.

notify *verb* (**notifies**, **notifying**, **notified**, **has notified**) If somebody **notifies** you of something, they inform or tell you, especially in an official way: *The manager informed us that the game had been cancelled.*
☐ **notifiable**, *adjective* –**notification**, *noun*

notion *noun*
1. an idea, often not very clear in your mind: *Makiko had a notion that she could somehow train the dog to be obedient.* 2. an idea that is silly or not practical: *It's a crazy notion to think they can climb the mountain in this weather!*
☐ **notional**, *adjective*

notorious /*say* nuh-**taw**-ree-uhs/ *adjective* If someone is **notorious**, they are famous or well-known for something bad: *He's notorious for his wild parties.*
☐ **notoriety** /*say* noh-tuh-**ruy**-uh-tee/, *noun* –**notoriousness**, *noun*

nougat /*say* **nooh**-gah/ *noun* a hard paste-like sweet, usually white or pink and containing almonds or other nuts.

☑ SPELLING TIP *Silent letter alert*: don't forget the silent *t* at the end. Also remember the *ou* spelling for the 'ooh' sound. The word **nougat** comes from French.

nought /*say* nawt/ *noun* the symbol '0', or zero.

> ☑ SPELLING TIP *Tricky vowel sound*: Notice the *ough* for the 'aw' sound (just like in the word *ought*). Don't confuse **nought** with **naught** which has the same sound and a related meaning. **Naught** is an old-fashioned word for 'nothing'.

noun *noun* a type of word which names something, commonly divided into proper nouns like 'Kosciuszko' and common nouns like 'endurance' or 'explorer'.

> SEE **abstract noun**, **collective noun**, **common noun**, **concrete noun**, **proper noun**. See also the Grammar and Punctuation Guide appendix.

nourish /*say* **nu**-rish/ *verb* To **nourish** someone or something is to give them enough food to make them grow.
☐ **nourishing**, *adjective* –**nourishment**, *noun*

novel[1] *noun* a long imaginative story which fills a whole book.
☐ **novelist**, *noun*

novel[2] *adjective* new or different: *Our novel scheme for making money was doing foot rubs for tired shoppers.*

novelty *noun* (*plural* **novelties**)
1. newness or strangeness: *We enjoyed our trip to Venice, especially the novelty of riding in a gondola.* **2.** a new or different experience: *It was a novelty for her to be alone.* **3.** a new or unusual article in a shop: *The shop was filled with gifts and novelties.*

November *noun* the 11th month of the year, with 30 days.

> THE ABBREVIATION is **Nov.**
> WORD HISTORY from a Latin word for the ninth month of the early Roman year

novice /*say* **nov**-uhs/ *noun* someone who is new to the type of work or activity they are doing.

now *adverb*
1. at the present time or moment: *He's here now.* **2.** immediately or at once: *now or never.* **3.** at the time or moment only just past: *I saw him just now in the street.*
–*phrase* **4. now and again** or **now and then**, occasionally.

nowadays *adverb* in these times: *Nowadays it's much quicker to travel to Europe.*

nowhere *adverb* in, at, or to no place: *My shoes seem to be nowhere – they have completely disappeared.*

noxious /*say* **nok**-shuhs/ *adjective*
1. harmful or hurtful: *noxious fumes from the factory.* **2.** declared harmful by law and meant to be destroyed: *Lantana is a noxious weed.*
☐ **noxiously**, *adverb*

nozzle *noun* the end of a pipe or hose through which you can spray water.

nuance /*say* **nyooh**-ons, nyooh-**ahns**/ *noun* a slight variation of colour, meaning, expression or feeling: *We knew every nuance of her voice and could tell that she was worried.*

nuclear /*say* **nyooh**-klee-uh/ *adjective* having to do with processes involving the nucleus of the atom.

> ☑ SPELLING TIP Remember the spelling of *nucleus* and see that **nuclear** is formed from this word (with the *us* ending changed to *ar*). Another way to remember the spelling of **nuclear** is that if you reverse the first two letters you get the word *unclear*.

nuclear energy *noun* See **atomic energy**.

nuclear power *noun* power created by processes involving the nucleus of the atom.

nuclear reactor *noun* a machine for producing nuclear energy.

nuclear waste *noun* the harmful substances that remain after the production of atomic energy.

nuclear weapon *noun* any weapon that uses atomic energy to make it explode.

nucleus /*say* **nyooh**-klee-uhs/ *noun* (*plural* **nuclei** /*say* **nyooh**-klee-uy/ *or* **nucleuses**)
1. the central part or thing about which other parts or things are grouped: *The guitar players were the nucleus of a new band.* **2.** in biology, the central part of a living cell. **3.** in physics, the central core of an atom, consisting of protons and neutrons.

> ☑ SPELLING TIP This was originally the Latin word for 'nut' (something at the centre). This will help you to remember that the beginning is spelt *nu* (although it sounds like the word *new*). Also remember the *eus* ending.

nude *adjective*
1. If someone or something is **nude**, they are unclothed or naked.
–*noun* **2.** an unclothed human figure, especially one that an artist has painted.
☐ **nudism**, *noun* –**nudist**, *noun* –**nudity**, *noun*

nudge *verb* To **nudge** someone or something is to give them a small push with your arm.
☐ **nudge**, *noun*

nugget *noun* a lump of something, especially of gold, found in the ground.

nuisance /*say* **nyooh**-suhns/ *noun* someone or something that is very annoying.

> ☑ SPELLING TIP *Tricky vowel sound*: *ui* to spell the 'yooh' sound. You could remind yourself that someone who is a **nuisance** is utterly irritating.

null *adjective in the phrase* **null and void**, having no legal force or effect: *Many voting forms disappeared and the election was declared null and void.*
☐ **nullify**, *verb* (**nullifies**, **nullifying**, **nullified**, **has nullified**) If something **nullifies** another thing, it affects it so that it is useless or has no effect: *The scientists' opinions nullified the stories spreading about the sightings of aliens.*
–**nullification**, *noun*

nulla-nulla *noun* a heavy wooden club which was traditionally used by Aboriginal people in fighting and hunting.

WORD HISTORY from an Aboriginal language of New South Wales called Dharug

numb */rhymes with* sum*/ adjective*
1. If a part of your body is **numb**, it has no feeling in it.
–*verb* **2.** If something **numbs** you or some part of you, it has the effect of stopping feeling: *The cold had numbed his fingers and toes*; *The awful news numbed my parents and they couldn't think straight.*
☐ **numbness**, *noun*

☑ SPELLING TIP *Silent letter alert*: don't forget the *b* at the end.

numbat *noun* a small Australian marsupial which feeds on insects, especially termites. It has red and brown fur with white stripes on its back, a long bushy tail and a long pointed nose. It is endangered.

WORD HISTORY from an Aboriginal language of Western Australia called Nyungar

number *noun*
1. the sum or total of a collection of things: *What's the final number of people coming to the swimming carnival?* **2.** a collection or quantity, usually large: *We're expecting quite a number to attend.* **3.** See **numeral**. **4.** the particular numeral or figure given to something to fix its place in a list or series: *I am always number 38 on the class roll because my surname starts with 'Z'.* **5.** in grammar, the number of persons or objects a noun, pronoun or verb refers to. **6.** a song, especially on a concert program: *The first two numbers in the concert were put on by the senior classes.*
–*verb* To **number** is to **7.** mark with a number. **8.** count, saying the numbers one by one: *The teacher numbered us off as we went into the aquatic centre.*

SEE the Grammar and Punctuation Guide appendix (for definition 5).

numberplate *noun* a flat metal strip which shows the registration number of your car.

numeral *noun* a sign used to represent a number: *the numeral 9.*
☐ **numeral**, *adjective*

numerate */say* **nyooh**-muh-ruht*/ adjective* having basic skills in maths.
☐ **numeracy**, *noun*

numerator *noun* the number which is written above the line in a fraction to show how many parts of the whole are taken: *In the fraction ¾ 3 is the numerator.*

COMPARE this with **denominator**.

numerical */say* nyooh-**me**-rik-uhl*/ adjective* Something **numerical** has to do with numbers.

numerous *adjective* very many: *Numerous ants had got into the picnic basket.*

nun *noun* a woman who has given herself up to a religious life, usually in a convent.

Nunga */say* **nung**-guh*/ noun* an Aboriginal person from southern South Australia.
☐ **Nunga**, *adjective*: *Nunga traditions.*

WORD HISTORY from an Aboriginal language of South Australia

nuptial */say* **nup**-shuhl*/ adjective* having to do with marriage or the marriage ceremony: *nuptial vows.*
☐ **nuptials**, *plural noun* a marriage ceremony.

nurse *noun*
1. someone who looks after sick people, usually in a hospital.
–*verb* **2.** To **nurse** someone is to look after them in time of sickness: *Some patients are more difficult to nurse than others.* **3.** To **nurse** a baby is to hold it in your arms. **4.** To **nurse** something is to look after it carefully so as to help it grow: *Dad decided to nurse the exotic orchids in the hotter temperature of the greenhouse*; *For years, he nursed a terrible desire for revenge.*

nursery *noun* (*plural* **nurseries**)
1. a room or place for babies. **2.** a place where plants can be bought.

nursery rhyme *noun* a short simple poem or song for young children.

nurture */say* **ner**-chuh*/ verb*
1. If someone **nurtures** a young child or a young plant, they care for all its needs while it is growing. **2.** If someone **nurtures** enterprises or people undertaking particular activities, they do what is needed to ensure their success: *She nurtured the prisoners' art group for years.*
☐ **nurture**, *noun* –**nurturing**, *adjective*

nut *noun*
1. a dry fruit consisting of a kernel that you can eat inside a hard shell. **2.** the kernel itself. **3.** a small metal block with a hole which has a thread in it, allowing it to be screwed on to the end of a bolt. **4.** *Informal* someone who is strange or foolish.

nutmeg *noun* a spice made from the seed of a tree that grows in tropical countries.

nutrient /*say* **nyooh**-tree-uhnt/ *noun* a substance that provides food and energy: *Dad says there are more nutrients in a cardboard box than in most junk food.*
☐ **nutrient**, *adjective*

☑ SPELLING TIP Remember that the beginning of this word is spelt *nu* (although it sounds like the word *new*). Also remember the *ent* (not *ant*) ending. Think of *e* for 'eating' to remind yourself of this.

nutrition /*say* nyooh-**trish**-uhn/ *noun* eating or eating habits: *Athletes have to be aware of a few basic rules of nutrition.*
☐ **nutritional**, *adjective* –**nutritionist**, *noun* –**nutritious**, *adjective*

nuzzle *verb* To **nuzzle** someone or something is to touch or rub them with the nose: *The dog nuzzled its rescuer with its big, wet nose.*

nylon /*say* **nuy**-lon/ *noun* a strong synthetic material used in making clothes, stockings, brushes, and so on.

WORD HISTORY trademark

☑ SPELLING TIP *Letter 'y' alert*: the first vowel sound is spelt *y*, giving an 'uy' sound.

nymph /*say* nimf/ *noun*
1. a goddess, pictured as a beautiful young woman living in the sea, woods or mountains.
2. a young wingless insect.

☑ SPELLING TIP *Letter 'y' alert*: the vowel sound is spelt *y*, giving an 'i' sound. Like many words with a *y* spelling, **nymph** comes from Greek. Also remember the *ph* giving the final 'f' sound.

Nyungar /*say* **nyoong**-ah/ *noun* an Aboriginal person from south-western Australia.
☐ **Nyungar**, *adjective*: *Nyungar culture.*

ANOTHER SPELLING is **Noongar**.
WORD HISTORY from the Nyungar language of Western Australia

oaf *noun* someone who is clumsy, stupid or rude.
☐ **oafish**, *adjective*

WORD HISTORY from an Old English word meaning 'elf'

oak *noun* a tree that is famous for its hard wood.
☐ **oaken**, *adjective*

oar /*rhymes with* for/ *noun* a long pole with a wide, flattened end, used for rowing a boat.

☑ SPELLING TIP Don't confuse the spelling of **oar** with the other three words that sound the same. You use **or** to connect alternative words, phrases or clauses; **ore** is a rock or mineral which is mined for the metal it contains; **awe** is a feeling of great respect.

oasis /*say* oh-**ay**-suhs/ *noun* (*plural* **oases** /*say* oh-**ay**-seez/) a place in the desert where there is water and trees can grow.

oath *noun*
1. a very solemn promise to do something: *He made them swear an oath of loyalty.* **2.** a saying which uses God's name or that of some other powerful or holy thing in order to express the strongest anger, disgust, bitterness, etc.: *He uttered an oath at the sight of the animals killed by drought.*

oats *plural noun* a cereal which is used to make porridge or to feed horses.

obedient *adjective* If you are **obedient**, you follow someone else's wishes or commands: *The adults were impressed because the children were clean, well-trained and obedient.*
☐ **obedience**, *noun* –**obediently**, *adverb*

☑ SPELLING TIP *Tricky vowel sound*: the second vowel sound is spelt with a single *e* (although you say it as 'ee'). This is because **obedient** has been formed from the word *obey*.

obelisk *noun* a tall pillar of stone, put up as a monument.

WORD HISTORY from a Greek word meaning 'a pointed pillar'

obese /*say* oh-**bees**/ *adjective* extremely fat.
☐ **obesely**, *adverb*

obesity /*say* oh-**bee**-suh-tee/ *noun* a medical condition in which too much body fat affects the person's health.

obey /*say* oh-**bay**/ *verb* If you **obey** someone, you do as you are told.

obituary /*say* uh-**bich**-uh-ree/ *noun* a notice, usually in a newspaper, saying that someone has died and often including a short account of their life and achievements.

☑ SPELLING TIP You have to remember the *uary* ending because the two vowels *u* and *a* are not sounded separately when you say the word. Other words that have this ending are *January* and *February*.

object *noun* /*say* **ob**-jekt/
1. something which can be seen or felt: *On the ground there was a curious-looking object.* **2.** the reason or purpose: *Our object was to get to the airport on time.* **3.** the person or thing which receives the action of a verb, as 'glasses' does in the sentence *He's lost his glasses*.
–*verb* /*say* uhb-**jekt**/ **4.** If you **object** or if you **object** to something, you say you do not agree, or that you do not like something: *They were going to build new flats on the vacant land, but many people objected*; *The coach objected to the interference of one of the parents.*
☐ **objector**, *noun*

COMPARE definition 3 with **subject** (definition 4). Also see the Grammar and Punctuation Guide appendix.

objection *noun* an argument against something.

objectionable *adjective* unpleasant or offensive: *His language was full of objectionable descriptions of other people.*
☐ **objectionably**, *adverb*

objective *noun*
1. something to work towards: *Our objective was to find enough people to fill two teams.*
–*adjective* **2.** If someone is **objective**, they are able to think about a question or situation fairly, without being influenced by how they feel personally: *They had to make an objective assessment as to whether their club could keep going.*
☐ **objectively**, *adverb* –**objectivity**, *noun*

THE OPPOSITE (of definition 2) is **subjective**.

objective case *noun* the form of a noun or pronoun which shows it is the object of a verb, such as 'her' in the sentence *The dog licked her.*

SEE the Grammar and Punctuation Guide appendix.

obligation *noun* something which should be done out of duty or gratitude: *Since we were their guests, we had an obligation to be polite.*
☐ **obligatory**, *adjective* required.

oblige /*say* uh-**bluyj**/ *verb*
1. If you **oblige** someone, you do them a favour: *The actor obliged the photographers by appearing in a costume from the film*; *I would be obliged if you would hold open the door.*
–*phrase* **2. be obliged to**, **a.** to have to, out of duty or need, or by law: *The pilot was obliged to make a forced landing.* **b.** to be grateful for someone's kindness: *She felt obliged to them for their generosity.*
☐ **obliging**, *adjective*

WORD HISTORY from a Latin word meaning 'bind' or 'tie around'

oblique /*say* uh-**bleek**/ *adjective*
1. indirect: *The bullocks took an oblique course to the other side of the river*; *Her family let her know with oblique remarks that they did not approve!* **2.** sloping; not horizontal or perpendicular: *an oblique shaft of sunlight.*
☐ **obliquely**, *adverb*

☑ SPELLING TIP Remember that the ending of **oblique** is spelt *ique* (although it sounds like 'eek'). Think of some other words that have the same spelling for this sound, such as *antique* and *unique*.

obliterate /*say* uh-**blit**-uh-rayt/ *verb* To **obliterate** something is to wipe it out or destroy it: *All their possessions had been obliterated in the fire.*
☐ **obliteration**, *noun*

oblivious *adjective* not remembering or not noticing: *They appeared oblivious of the normal rules of politeness*; *She seemed oblivious to the rain*; *Everyone else was very upset by what was happening but she remained oblivious.*
☐ **oblivion**, *noun* –**obliviously**, *adverb*

NOTE This word is often followed by *of* or *to*.

oblong *noun* a four-sided shape which is longer than it is wide, and which has four right angles.
☐ **oblong**, *adjective*

obnoxious /*say* uhb-**nok**-shuhs/ *adjective* disagreeable or nasty: *Her presence was obnoxious to them*; *There was an obnoxious odour in the air.*
☐ **obnoxiously**, *adverb*

WORD HISTORY from a Latin word meaning 'exposed to harm'

oboe /*say* **oh**-boh/ *noun* a tube-shaped woodwind instrument with two reeds that you blow through.
☐ **oboist** /*say* **oh**-boh-uhst/, *noun*

obscene /*say* uhb-**seen**/ *adjective*
1. expressing something about sex in a rude and offensive way. **2.** shocking and offensive: *The film was full of obscene language.*
☐ **obscenity** /*say* uhb-**sen**-uh-tee/, *noun* –**obscenely**, *adverb*

☑ SPELLING TIP *Silent letter alert*: don't forget the silent *c* after the *s*, just like in the word *scene*.

obscure *adjective*
1. uncertain or unclear: *What he said was quite obscure and no-one knew what he meant.* **2.** not prominent or well-known: *They were travelling to an obscure tropical island.*
–*verb* **3.** If something **obscures** another thing, it makes it obscure: *Low dark clouds obscured the sky.*
☐ **obscurely**, *adverb* –**obscurity**, *noun*

observant *adjective* watchful or alert: *An observant neighbour noticed that the front door was open and called the police.*
☐ **observantly**, *adverb*

observatory /*say* uhb-**zerv**-uh-tree/ *noun* (*plural* **observatories**) a building equipped with powerful telescopes for looking at the stars, planets and weather patterns.

observe *verb*
1. If you **observe** someone or something, you watch them carefully: *We had to observe a life-saving demonstration so we could help people in trouble.* **2.** If you **observe** something, you notice it: *At the shops, we observed that the newsagency had closed down.* **3.** If someone **observes** a law or rule, they obey it: *Noriko was sent off the field for not observing the rules.*
☐ **observation**, *noun* –**observer**, *noun*

obsession *noun* a strong idea or feeling which controls someone's behaviour: *Accumulating more and more money is his obsession.*
☐ **obsessed**, *adjective* –**obsessive**, *adjective*

obsolete /*say* ob-suh-**leet**/ *adjective* no longer being used: *Faxes are becoming obsolete now that everyone sends emails.*
☐ **obsolescence** /*say* ob-suh-**les**-uhns/, *noun*

☑ SPELLING TIP *Tricky 'uh' sound*: the second vowel sound is spelt *o*. Also remember the *ete* ending (which sounds like 'eet'). Other words with a similar pattern include *concrete* and *complete*.

obstacle *noun* something which is in your way or which delays you.

obstetrics /*say* ob-**stet**-riks/ *noun* the type of medical practice that is concerned with caring for pregnant women before, during and after the birth of their babies.
☐ **obstetric**, *adjective* –**obstetrician** /*say* ob-stuh-**trish**-uhn/, *noun*

obstinate *adjective* If someone is **obstinate**, they are stubborn or not willing to change their mind, even though they may be wrong.
□ **obstinacy**, *noun* –**obstinately**, *adverb*

obstreperous /*say* uhb-**strep**-uh-ruhs/ *adjective* resisting control in a noisy way: *He was obstreperous about having to go to bed and flew into a tantrum.*
□ **obstreperously**, *adverb*

☑ SPELLING TIP This word is long, but not really difficult to spell if you remember that there are no double letters and that the ending is *erous*. Try rapping it out as *ob+strep+er+ous*.

obstruct *verb*
1. If something **obstructs** a road or a passageway, it blocks it so that things cannot move freely: *A fallen tree obstructed our way.* **2.** If someone or something **obstructs** an action, they make it difficult to carry it out: *The police obstructed the attempts of the crowd to reach the prisoner*; *His heavy clothes obstructed his attempts to swim.*
□ **obstruction**, *noun* –**obstructive**, *adjective*

obtain *verb* If you **obtain** something, you get or own it: *He obtained the award for 'Best Helper of the Week'.*
□ **obtainable**, *adjective*

obtuse /*say* uhb-**tyoohs**/ *adjective* An **obtuse** person is stupid or slow to understand: *He was too obtuse to realise the situation was getting out of hand.*
□ **obtusely**, *adverb* –**obtuseness**, *noun*

☑ SPELLING TIP Remember the *use* ending (which sounds like 'oohs').

obtuse angle *noun* an angle greater than 90° but less than 180°.

obvious *adjective* If something is **obvious**, you notice it or understand it easily.
□ **obviously**, *adverb*

SIMILAR WORDS are **clear**, **evident**, **plain** and **apparent**.
WORD HISTORY from a Latin word meaning 'in the way' or 'meeting'

occasion /*say* uh-**kay**-zhuhn/ *noun*
1. a particular time or event: *The teacher said that on this occasion she would give us extra time to get our homework done.* **2.** a special or important event: *The wedding was a happy occasion.* **3.** an opportunity: *We used the fact of our parents going out as an occasion to watch more television.*
–*phrase* **4. rise to the occasion**, to show yourself able to meet the needs of a particular job or situation: *Our team rose to the occasion and we ended up winning.*
□ **occasional**, *adjective* happening sometimes: *occasional emails.* –**occasionally**, *adverb*

☑ SPELLING TIP *Double/single letter alert*: double *c* but only one *s*. Also remember that the middle vowel sound is spelt with a single *a* (although you say it as 'ay'). Rap it out as *oc+cas+i+on* to help you get it right.

occult /*say* **ok**-ult, uh-**kult**/ *adjective*
1. Occult knowledge has to do with secret practices, as in magic, witchcraft or astrology.
–*noun* **2. the occult**, practices relating to this knowledge.

occupation *noun*
1. your usual job or employment: *My uncle wants to go into the occupation of teaching.* **2.** the possession of a place, either legally or illegally: *The builders finish this week and we expect to be in occupation next week.* **3.** the taking over of a country or other area by force.

☑ SPELLING TIP *Double/single letter alert*: double *c* but only one *p*, just as in *occupy* from which **occupation** is formed.

occupy *verb* (**occupies**, **occupying**, **occupied**, **has occupied**)
1. If people **occupy** a place, they live or work there. **2.** If something **occupies** a place, it takes up space there. **3.** When a foreign force **occupies** a country, it attacks it and takes control. **4.** If you **occupy** yourself in doing something, that is how you spend your time: *My grandfather used to occupy himself with calligraphy.*
□ **occupant**, *noun* –**occupancy**, *noun*

☑ SPELLING TIP *Double/single letter alert*: double *c* but only one *p*. Think of a 'crammed classroom with lots of pupils occupying it' to help you remember the spelling of **occupy**.

occur /*say* uh-**ker**/ *verb* (**occurs**, **occurring**, **occurred**, **has occurred**)
1. To **occur** is to happen: *The accident occurred about midnight.*
–*phrase* **2. occur to**, to come into the mind of: *It occurred to us that we should write about our adventures.*
□ **occurrence** /*say* uh-**ku**-ruhns/, *noun*

☑ SPELLING TIP *Double/single letter alert*: double *c* but only one *r* at the end. However, when you add *-ed* or *-ing*, or make the word **occurrence**, the *r* is doubled. Notice also that there is a change in the way you say **occurrence** but the spelling of the second vowel sound remains *u*.

ocean /*say* **oh**-shuhn/ *noun* one of the large areas of salt water between continents, such as the Atlantic Ocean or the Pacific Ocean.
□ **oceanic** /*say* oh-shee-**an**-ik, oh-see-**an**-ik/, *adjective*

ochre /*say* **oh**-kuh/ *noun*
1. a yellowish clay used in paints and dyes. **2.** a yellowish or reddish colour.
□ **ochre**, *adjective*

☑ SPELLING TIP Remember the *ch* spelling for the 'k' sound and the *re* spelling at the end. It might help if you think of other words which you know well with the same spelling for this sound, such as *centre* and *theatre*.

ocker *noun Informal* **1.** an Australian person thought of as not having much education and with rather rough manners: *What an ocker – he's only comfortable in thongs!* **2.** an Australian person who has the qualities that people think of as being Australian, such as good humour, helpfulness, and being able to overcome difficulties: *He was a true ocker – just helping his mate!*
☐ **ocker**, *adjective* very Australian: *an ocker sense of humour.*

OTHER SPELLINGS are **occa** or **okker**.

o'clock *adverb* of or by the clock: *We had to assemble at the buses before ten o'clock.*

octagon /*say* **ok**-tuh-gon/ *noun* a flat shape with eight straight sides.
☐ **octagonal** /*say* ok-**tag**-uh-nuhl/, *adjective*

octave /*say* **ok**-tiv/ *noun*
1. the eight note distance between two musical notes of the same name but different pitch. **2.** these two notes played together.

octet *noun*
1. a group of eight. **2.** a piece of music for eight voices or eight instruments.

October *noun* the tenth month of the year, with 31 days.

THE ABBREVIATION is **Oct**.
WORD HISTORY from the Latin name for the eighth month of the early Roman year

octopus *noun* (*plural* **octopuses**) a soft-bodied sea animal which has eight arms with suckers on them.

WORD HISTORY from a Greek word meaning 'eight-footed'

OD /*say* oh **dee**/ *noun*, *verb* (**OD's or ODs, OD'ing, OD'd, has OD'd**) See **overdose**.

odd *adjective*
1. Something or someone that is **odd** is strange or unusual. **2. Odd** numbers are ones which cannot be divided by two. For example, one, three, five and seven are odd numbers. **3.** If two things are **odd**, they do not match: *He was wearing odd socks.*
–*phrase* **4. odd jobs**, the various small jobs that you have to do to maintain a property or keep things running smoothly.
☐ **oddity**, *noun* (*plural* **oddities**)

THE OPPOSITE (of definition 2) is **even**.

odds *plural noun* **1.** the chances of something happening, such as a horse winning a race: *They have impossible odds stacked against them*; *By behaving all day, we increased the odds that we would be let out early.*
–*phrase* **2. at odds**, in disagreement: *Mum was at odds with the lady next door about what sort of fence to put up.* **3. odds and ends**, unimportant things of different types that you deal with together: *We keep our odds and ends in a locker.*

ode *noun* a song or poem praising something: *We had to compose an ode to small things.*

odious *adjective* hateful or disgusting: *Cleaning the toilets is an odious job.*
☐ **odium**, *noun* hatred.

odour *noun* a smell: *There was a very odd odour in the kitchen.*
☐ **odorous**, *adjective*

ANOTHER SPELLING is **odor**.

oesophagus /*say* uh-**sof**-uh-guhs/ *noun* (*plural* **oesophagi** /*say* uh-**sof**-uh-guy/) the tube that connects the back of the mouth with the stomach.

ANOTHER SPELLING is **esophagus**.
ANOTHER WORD for this is **gullet**.

of *preposition* a word indicating: **1.** substance or contents: *a packet of sugar*; *a lump of wood.* **2.** cause or reason: *to die of hunger.* **3.** distance or separation from: *within a metre of the house.* **4.** belonging, possession or association: *the queen of England*; *the property of us all.*

off *adverb*
1. away from a position occupied, or from an attachment: *He got off the seat*; *The handle has come off.* **2.** to or at a distance away: *Summer is only a week off.* **3.** less: *ten per cent off.* **4.** away from normal employment: *Dad has two weeks off at Christmas.*
–*preposition* **5.** away from: *to fall off a ladder.* **6.** distant from: *off the beaten track.*
–*adjective* **7.** stopped or no longer in effect: *The agreement is off.* **8.** not as good as usual: *an off year for apples.* **9.** *Rather informal* unwell: *Wyn felt a bit off after eating the oysters.* **10.** bad or unfit for eating: *The meat is off.*
–*phrase* **11. be off**, to go away or leave. **12. off and on** or **on and off**, occasionally: *It works on and off.* **13. off your food**, not hungry because you are ill.

offal *noun* animal intestines and other parts which are usually thrown away, or other organs such as the brain, liver and tripe which are used as food.

off-colour *adjective*
1. unwell or sick. **2.** in bad taste: *I didn't laugh at the off-colour joke.*

ANOTHER SPELLING is **off-color**.

offence *noun*
1. a wrong action or crime: *a speeding offence.* 2. an insult, or other action that has hurt or harmed someone: *The building was an offence to any standard of beauty*; *Don't take offence – she didn't mean to be rude.*

offend *verb*
1. To **offend** someone is to annoy them or make them angry: *Jiro is always offending people – he never thinks before he speaks!* 2. If you **offend**, you do wrong or commit a crime: *This is the third time she has offended.*
☐ **offender**, *noun*

offensive *adjective*
1. displeasing or disgusting: *It was a totally offensive film and many people walked out!* 2. insulting: *To deliberately ignore them was totally offensive.* 3. attacking: *offensive operations to remove enemy ground forces.*
–*noun* 4. an attack: *They launched a fresh offensive against the guerillas.*
☐ **offensively**, *adverb*

offer *verb*
1. If you **offer** someone something, you ask them if they would like to have it: *to offer guests something to drink.* 2. If you **offer** to do something, you say that you are willing to do it, usually without being asked: *She offered to help me.* 3. If you **offer** a certain amount of money for something, you say that you are willing to pay that price.
–*noun* 4. an act of offering, or something which is offered. 5. a suggestion or proposal: *an offer of marriage*; *a business offer.*
☐ **offering**, *noun*

> ☑ SPELLING TIP Notice that you do not double the final *r* when you add *-ed* or *-ing*, following the rule that the consonant remains single if the final syllable is not stressed.

offhand *adjective* vague or casual, sometimes in a rude way: *The receptionist was very offhand and many clients objected.*

office *noun*
1. a place where you work or do business. 2. a place where you go to buy tickets or get information. 3. rank or duty: *She takes the responsibilities of her office very seriously.*

officer *noun*
1. someone who holds a rank in the army, navy, air force, police force or similar organisation. 2. someone chosen to do an important job in a particular organisation: *My mother is the publicity officer for a computer company.*

official /*say* uh-**fish**-uhl/ *noun* someone who has authority to do a particular job.
☐ **official**, *adjective* –**officially**, *adverb* –**officiate** /*say* uh-**fish**-ee-ayt/, *verb*: *to officiate at a ceremony.*

> ☑ SPELLING TIP Notice the spelling of the last part of this word – *cial* (giving the sound 'shuhl'). Other words with this pattern are *artificial* and *superficial*.

offline *adjective* not connected to the internet or to a network of other computers: *Most of the suburb was offline after a cable was accidentally cut by a machine working on the road.*

off-peak *adjective* having to do with a time when there is less activity or lower demand: *We always ring overseas in off-peak times.*

off-putting *adjective* discouraging or unfriendly: *A 'Beware of vicious dogs' sign outside the house was very off-putting.*

offset /*say* **of**-set, of-**set**/ *verb* (**offsets**, **offsetting**, **offset**, **has offset**) If you **offset** something or someone, you balance the bad result coming from it against the good result of something else: *We will offset our losses this year against the good income of the previous year.*

offsider *noun* a partner or friend.

offspring *noun* (*plural* **offspring**) the children or young of a particular parent.

often /*say* **of**-uhn, **of**-tuhn/ *adverb* If something happens **often**, it happens frequently: *I often walk to school.*

> ☑ SPELLING TIP *Silent letter alert*: if you say this word as in the first pronunciation, you have to remember that there is a silent *t* after the *f*. If you think 'of-ten' **often**, you will never forget!

ogle *verb* If somebody **ogles** another person, they look at them, especially with sexual interest.

ogre /*say* **oh**-guh/ *noun* an imaginary monster of popular stories, often one which likes to eat people.

> ☑ SPELLING TIP Remember that the ending is *re* (not *er*).

ohm /*rhymes with* home/ *noun* a measure of electrical resistance.

> WORD HISTORY named after a German scientist, GS *Ohm* (1787–1854)

oil *noun*
1. a fatty liquid made from animal or vegetable fats, which is used in cooking. 2. a thick, black liquid made from petroleum which is used to run and maintain machinery.
–*verb* 3. If you **oil** a surface, you apply oil to it to preserve it: *We oiled the wood of our outdoor furniture.*
☐ **oily**, *adjective*

oilskin *noun*
1. a cloth treated with oil to make it waterproof so that it can be used for rainwear. 2. a piece of

clothing made of this, as one worn for fishing, sailing, riding, etc.

ointment *noun* a soft, thick, oily mixture used for healing your skin.

okay *Informal*
–*adjective* **1.** all right or satisfactory: *We felt okay once we were on the train.*
–*adverb* **2.** well or correctly: *The traffic moved okay considering it was a holiday weekend.*
–*noun* **3.** approval: *He gave the plan the okay.*
–*verb* **4.** If someone **okays** a request, they agree to it: *Mum okayed our trip to the beach.*

ANOTHER FORM is **OK**.

okra /*say* **ok**-ruh, **ohk**-ruh/ *noun* a small green vegetable used in soups and chutneys.

WORD HISTORY from a West African language

old *adjective*
1. If someone is **old**, they have lived for a long time. **2.** If something is **old**, it has existed for a long time: *We explored the old part of the city.* **3.** If something is **old**, it belongs to a time before the present: *Our old dog was small but our new dog is a big, heavy breed.* **4.** An **old** friend is someone you have been friends with for a long time. **5.** If you say someone is a certain number of years **old**, you mean that they have lived for that length of time: *The woman pulled from the earthquake rubble was 97 years old.*

SIMILAR WORDS (for definition 1) are **aged**, **elderly**, **mature** and **senior**; (for definition 2) **ancient** and **antique**; (for definition 3) **former**, **past** and **previous**.

old-fashioned *adjective* belonging to an earlier time or style: *Her ideas are so old-fashioned – she needs to catch up with the times.*

SIMILAR WORDS are **out-of-date**, **outdated**, **dated**, **obsolete**, **antiquated** and **archaic**. Something that is **obsolete** is no longer useful or in use because it has been replaced by something more modern: *Typewriters have become obsolete now that everyone has a computer.* Something that is **antiquated** or **archaic** is very old-fashioned and needs to be replaced by something more modern (*antiquated machinery*, *an archaic law*).

oligarchy /*say* **ol**-uh-gah-kee/ *noun* a type of government in which a few people have all the power.

☑ SPELLING TIP The spelling will be easier if you see that **oligarchy** is made up of the prefix *olig-* (a short form of *oligo-*, meaning 'a few') and the suffix *-archy* which means 'rule' or 'government'. Both these word parts come from Greek. The suffix *-archy* is found in several other words relating to government, such as *monarchy*.

olive *noun*
1. a tree which grows in warm countries, or its fruit which can be eaten or crushed for its oil. **2.** a yellowish-green or brownish-green colour.
☐ **olive**, *adjective*

ollie *noun* a manoeuvre using a skateboard or snowboard where the board is driven into the air from a flat surface without the hands holding it, often to jump over stairs or other obstacles.

Olympic Games *plural noun* Competitions in sports such as running, swimming, jumping, shooting, etc, between most countries of the world, taking place over a period of several weeks, and held every four years, each time in a different country.

ombudsman /*say* **om**-buhdz-muhn/ *noun* an official whose job is to look into people's complaints against the government.

WORD HISTORY from a Swedish word meaning 'commissioner'

omelette /*say* **om**-luht/ *noun* a food made of eggs beaten and fried in a pan.

ANOTHER SPELLING is **omelet**.
WORD HISTORY from a French word meaning 'a thin plate'

omen /*say* **oh**-muhn/ *noun* a sign of good or bad luck to come.

ominous /*say* **om**-uh-nuhs/ *adjective* threatening: *We thought we were safe in the deserted house but then we heard an ominous creaking.*
☐ **ominously**, *adverb*

☑ SPELLING TIP The spelling of this word will be easier if you see that it is made up of *omen* (a sign of bad luck coming), with the *e* changed to an *i*, and the suffix *-ous* (meaning 'full of').

omit *verb* (**omits**, **omitting**, **omitted**, **has omitted**)
1. To **omit** something is to leave it out: *You will have to omit some of the sugar so it's not so sweet.* **2.** To **omit** to do something is to fail to do it: *I omitted to tell you to bring some food.*

omni- *prefix* a word part meaning 'all', as in *omnivorous*.

WORD HISTORY this prefix comes from Latin

omnibus *noun*
1. *Old-fashioned* a bus. **2.** a book of collected stories or writings by one writer or by different writers but about one particular subject.

omnipotent /*say* om-**nip**-uh-tuhnt/ *adjective* To be **omnipotent** is to have the power to do all things: *Being in charge made him feel omnipotent.*
☐ **omnipotence**, *noun*

omniscient /*say* om-**nis**-ee-uhnt, om-**nish**-uhnt/ *adjective* knowing everything: *Not being omniscient, how could they know all the happenings on the other side of the planet?*
☐ **omniscience**, *noun*

☑ SPELLING TIP *Silent letter alert*: don't forget the *c* following the *s* (as in the word *science*). **Omniscient** is made up of the prefix *omni-* (meaning 'all') and *scient* (a form of the Latin word *sciens* meaning 'knowing', which is also the origin of *science*).

omnivore /*say* **om**-nuh-vaw/ *noun* an animal that eats both animals and plants.

COMPARE this with **carnivore**, **herbivore** and **insectivore**.

omnivorous /*say* om-**niv**-uh-ruhs/ *adjective* **1.** eating both animals and plants: *We had to list the animals as herbivorous, carnivorous or omnivorous.* **2.** taking in everything, as with your mind: *Yusef is an omnivorous reader and is now reading books on the history of railways.*

on *preposition* a word indicating: **1.** position above and in contact with a surface: *on the desk.* **2.** situation or place: *a house on the river*; *a scar on the face*; *the person on the left.* **3.** time or occasion: *on Saturday.* **4.** what something is about: *an essay on animals.*
–*adverb* **5.** on yourself or itself: *She put her coat on.* **6.** forwards: *further on.* **7.** into active operation: *to turn the light on.*
–*adjective* **8.** If a device is **on**, it is operating or in use: *The computer is on.* **9.** If an event is **on**, it is occurring: *What's on tomorrow?*
–*phrase* **10. get on to**, **a.** to work on: *You need to get on to that project.* **b.** to make contact with: *We had to get on to a plumber.* **11. have yourself on**, *Informal* to think yourself better than you really are. **12. on and off** or **off and on**, occasionally.

once *adverb*
1. at a time in the past: *Hardly anyone owned a car once.* **2.** a single time: *The mail is delivered once a day.*
–*conjunction* **3.** if ever or whenever: *There'll be trouble once she finds out the truth.*
–*noun* **4.** a single occasion: *Once is enough.*
–*phrase* **5. all at once** or **at once**, **a.** suddenly. **b.** immediately. **c.** at the same time: *Three things happened all at once.* **6. once in a while**, occasionally.

ANOTHER WORD (for definition 1) is **formerly**.

one *noun*
1. the number I.
–*adjective* **2. One** describes a single thing or person: *Take one tablet in the morning and two at night.* **3. One** can mean 'single' or 'only': *The rose was the one flower she was not allowed to pick.*
–*pronoun* **4. One** refers to a single thing or person: *One of the books had been damaged.* **5. One** refers to a person or thing of a particular type, often something that has already been mentioned: *This is one of the best movies I've ever seen.*

NOTE Something that is number one or comes before all others is the **first**.

onion /*say* **un**-yuhn/ *noun* a white vegetable with a white, brown or purple skin and a strong smell and taste, used in cooking.

☑ SPELLING TIP An **onion** is a rather ordinary vegetable, but it has a tricky spelling, particularly as it does not sound as if it begins with an *o*. You could try thinking of it as being made up of two lots of *on* joined by an *i* in the middle.

online *adjective*
1. directly linked to a computer. **2.** connected to the internet: *Once you are online, you can send emails.* **3.** having a site on the internet: *The newspaper is online and you can get the daily news from there.*

ANOTHER FORM is **on-line**.

onlooker *noun* someone who watches something: *The police asked the onlookers to move away from the accident scene.*

A SIMILAR WORD is **spectator**.

only *adverb*
1. alone or without others: *I only have one chip left.* **2.** just: *If Santa would only bring me a new bike!* **3.** as recently as: *He was here only a moment ago.*
–*adjective* **4.** If you are an **only** child, you do not have any brothers or sisters.
–*conjunction* **5.** but: *I would have kept silkworms, only I wasn't allowed.*

onomatopoeia /*say* on-uh-mat-uh-**pee**-uh/ *noun* the use of a word or words which sound like the thing or sound they are describing, such as *whoosh*, *bubbling* or *purr*.
☐ **onomatopoeic**, *adjective*

☑ SPELLING TIP This long word comes from Greek and has a difficult spelling. Rap the first part out as *on* + *o* + *ma* + *ta*, then concentrate on learning the group of vowels at the end – *oeia* to spell the 'ee-uh' sound.

onset *noun* a beginning: *The rain heralded the onset of the wet season.*

onslaught /*say* **on**-slawt/ *noun* a fierce rush or attack.

☑ SPELLING TIP *Tricky vowel sound*: the second vowel sound is spelt *augh* (although it sounds like 'aw'). It might help if you think of some other words which you know well which have the same spelling for this sound, such as *daughter* and *naughty*.

onto *preposition* to a place or position on: *Move the books onto the table*; *They loaded the goods onto the truck.*

onus /*say* **oh**-nuhs/ *noun* a duty or responsibility: *The onus is on you to get everything ready in time.*

WORD HISTORY from a Latin word meaning 'load' or 'burden'

onwards *adverb* towards a point ahead or in front.

ANOTHER FORM is **onward**.

ooze *verb*
1. If liquid **oozes** it flows out very slowly: *Oil was oozing out of the side of the tank.* **2.** If something **oozes** it releases a liquid slowly: *The tree was oozing sap.*

opal *noun* a valuable gem having beautiful patterns of different colours.

opaque /*say* oh-**payk**/ *adjective* If something is **opaque**, it does not let light through and you cannot see through it.

COMPARE this with **transparent** and **translucent**.

☑ SPELLING TIP Remember the *aque* spelling for the 'ayk' sound at the end of this word. **Opaque** was spelt *opake* in old English, but the spelling was changed to be more like the French word.

open *adjective*
1. not shut or locked. **2.** not limited or enclosed: *an open competition.* **3.** not blocked: *an open path.* **4.** friendly: *His open personality charmed everybody.*
–*verb* **5.** To **open** something is to make it become open: *Could you open the door and let some air in?* **6.** If something **opens**, it becomes open of its own accord: *These flowers open in the morning and close at night.* **7.** If something like a shop or business **opens**, it starts to operate: *We opened last year and haven't looked back*; *The restaurant opens at six o'clock.*
–*phrase* **8. in the open**, outside. **9. open up**, **a.** to make ready for use: *to open up new land.* **b.** to begin firing: *The artillery opened up.*
☐ **opening**, *noun* –**openly**, *adverb*: *to speak openly about difficult things.* –**openness**, *noun*

open-minded *adjective* able to accept new and different ideas.

opera *noun* a play which is sung to music.
☐ **operatic**, *adjective*

WORD HISTORY from a Latin word meaning 'a work'

operate *verb*
1. If you **operate** something or it **operates**, it works: *She can't operate the coffee machine*; *The washing machine isn't operating properly.* **2.** If a doctor **operates** on a patient, they perform surgery: *They operated for nearly ten hours to save the man's hand.*

operating system *noun* in computers, the program which establishes the connection between the user and the hardware of the computer and which allows all other programs to be run.

operation *noun*
1. the way that something works. **2.** working order: *The ghost train isn't in operation.* **3.** a medical treatment on someone's body, in which the doctor cuts into the patient. **4.** a military mission.
☐ **operational**, *adjective*

operative *adjective*
1. working or functional: *The trailer brakes were fully operative again.* **2.** having force or effect: *The agreement becomes operative at the end of two years.*

operator *noun*
1. someone who works a machine: *a computer operator*; *a tow truck operator.* **2.** someone who runs a big business: *an international air freight operator.*

opinion *noun* what you think or decide: *Nobody is ever interested in my opinion.*
☐ **opinionated**, *adjective*

☑ SPELLING TIP *Single letter alert*: only one *p*. Also remember that there is no *y*. The 'y' sound is spelt by the *i* in the *ion* ending.

opium *noun* a drug made from the juice of a type of poppy, which is used in medicines to lessen pain.

WORD HISTORY from a Greek word meaning 'juice'

opponent *noun* someone who is on the opposite side to you in a fight or competition.

☑ SPELLING TIP *Double/single letter alert*: double *p* but only one *n*.

opportunity /*say* op-uh-**tyooh**-nuh-tee/ *noun* (*plural* **opportunities**) a suitable time or occasion: *We waited for an opportunity to interrupt.*

☑ SPELLING TIP *Double letter alert*: double *p*. Also remember that the second vowel sound is spelt *or*, although it sounds like 'uh'.

oppose *verb* To **oppose** something is to resist or fight it: *Kate opposes the increase in the number of cars on the road, because it is bad for the environment.*

opposite *adjective*
1. Two things which are **opposite** are completely different: *They have opposite views on politics.* **2.** If one thing is **opposite** another, it is directly facing it: *The newsagency is opposite the bank.*
☐ **opposite**, *noun*: *They say that opposites attract.*

☑ SPELLING TIP *Double/single letter alert*: double *p* but only one *s*. Also remember that the vowel in between them is an *o*. It will help if you remember that **opposite** has been formed from the word *oppose*. You could also try thinking of **opposite** as being 'the perfect position for the other side'.

opposition *noun*
1. resistance or a fight: *We're expecting opposition to our ideas.* 2. the opposing side: *The opposition has been weakened by his behaviour.*

oppress *verb*
1. If something **oppresses** someone, it causes difficulty for them and weighs them down: *The lack of space in their unit oppressed them.* 2. If someone who is powerful **oppresses** people, he or she treats them cruelly or unfairly: *Workers in the factories were often oppressed by their employers.*
☐ **oppression**, *noun* –**oppressor**, *noun*

A SIMILAR WORD (for definition 2) is **tyrannise**.

☑ SPELLING TIP *Double letter alert*: double *p* and double *s*.

op shop *noun* a shop that sells second-hand goods, run by a charity.

NOTE This is a short form of **opportunity shop**.
ANOTHER TERM for this is **thrift shop**.

opt *verb*
1. To **opt** is to choose: *We had a choice of learning several languages. I opted for German.*
–*phrase* 2. **opt out**, to decide not to join in or continue with: *Helen wasn't feeling well, so she opted out of playing tennis.*

optical *adjective* having to do with seeing: *optical fibres*; *optical products.*

optician /*say* op-**tish**-uhn/ *noun* someone who makes or sells glasses.

COMPARE this with **optometrist**.

optimism *noun* hopefulness or the habit of expecting that things will turn out well: *It is a sign of optimism to look at the size of the doughnut instead of the size of the hole.*
☐ **optimistic**, *adjective* –**optimistically**, *adverb*

THE OPPOSITE is **pessimism**.

option *noun* a choice: *What are my options?*
☐ **optional**, *adjective*

optometrist /*say* op-**tom**-uh-truhst/ *noun* someone who tests your eyesight and, if necessary, prescribes glasses to improve it.
☐ **optometry**, *noun*

COMPARE this with **optician**.

opulent /*say* **op**-yuh-luhnt/ *adjective* rich or wealthy.
☐ **opulence**, *noun* wealth. –**opulently**, *adverb* richly.

opus /*say* **oh**-puhs/ *noun* a work, especially a musical composition.

NOTE The plural is **opera** but it is not often used in this way. The usual meaning of **opera** is a single play set to music.

or *conjunction*
1. **Or** is used to connect a number of different things: *Would you like juice or water?*; *We haven't got a car or a television*; *Let's meet on Saturday or Sunday.* 2. **Or** is used with numbers to show that you mean an approximate quantity: *There were about nine or ten of us*; *It'll cost fifty or sixty dollars.*
–*phrase* 3. **or else**, If you tell someone to do something **or else** something unpleasant will happen, you are warning them that they should do as you say: *We have to finish our vegetables or else we can't have pudding.*

oracle /*say* **o**-ruh-kuhl/ *noun*
1. someone who answers difficult questions or reveals the future: *The oracle at Delphi in Ancient Greece gave messages that could not be proved either right or wrong.* 2. a difficult saying given by such an oracle.
☐ **oracular**, *adjective*

oral *adjective*
1. spoken: *The oral test will be harder for him than the written one because he is shy.* 2. having to do with the mouth or taken by mouth: *oral hygiene.*

☑ DO NOT CONFUSE **oral** with **aural**, which means 'having to do with hearing or listening'.

orange *noun*
1. a round, reddish-gold citrus fruit. 2. a reddish-gold colour.
☐ **orange**, *adjective*: *orange juice*; *orange socks.*

orangutan /*say* uh-**rang**-uh-tan/ *noun* a large ape found in Indonesia, which climbs trees.

OTHER SPELLINGS are **orang-utan** and **orang-outang**.
WORD HISTORY from a Malay word meaning 'man of the woods'

orator /*say* **o**-ruh-tuh/ *noun* a public speaker, especially a skilful one.
☐ **oratorical**, *adjective*

orbit *noun*
1. the curved path or line of flight followed by a planet or satellite around the earth or sun.
–*verb* (**orbits**, **orbiting**, **orbited**, **has orbited**)
2. If a body **orbits** another one, it goes around it: *The moon orbits the earth.*
☐ **orbital**, *adjective*

orchard /*say* **aw**-chuhd/ *noun* a farm where fruit trees are grown.

orchestra /*say* **aw**-kuhs-truh/ *noun* a large group of players of musical instruments.

orchid /*say* **aw**-kuhd/ *noun* a plant which grows in warm climates and which produces a beautiful flower with an unusual shape.

ordain *verb*
1. to appoint to the church as a priest or minister. **2.** to order or declare: *Kings in the past had the power to ordain that someone should be killed.*
☐ **ordination**, *noun*

ordeal /*say* aw-**deel**, **aw**-deel/ *noun* a severe test or difficulty: *The marathon was an ordeal for us.*

order *noun*
1. a command. **2.** the proper arrangement of things: *Get some order into your room and you will be able to find things.* **3. a.** a request to make or supply something, usually for money: *to place an order for shoes.* **b.** the goods bought: *Your order has arrived.* **c.** a written request to pay money or deliver goods. **4.** the way things are placed in relation to each other: *I couldn't find what I wanted because the books weren't in the right order.* **5.** a lawful state or behaviour: *The police tried to restore order.*
–*verb* **6.** If you **order** someone to do something, you tell them that they must do it: *The commander ordered the troops to advance.* **7.** If you **order** something, you make a request for it to be made or supplied: *Mum has ordered a new CD player but it is not in the shop yet.*
–*phrase* **8. a tall order**, *Informal* a difficult job. **9. call to order**, to establish quiet and order among a group of people at a meeting or so on. **10. in order**, properly arranged. **11. out of order**, not working properly.
☐ **orderly**, *adjective* tidy and in order. –**orderliness**, *noun*

SIMILAR WORDS (for definition 6) are **command**, **demand**, **insist** and **require**.

ordinal number *noun* a number which tells you the place of a thing in a series, such as 'third' in *the third finger* or 'eleventh' in *the eleventh player*.

COMPARE this with **cardinal number**.

ordinance *noun* a rule or regulation: *The council issued an ordinance closing the park at dusk.*

ordinary /*say* **aw**-duh-nuh-ree/ *adjective*
1. If something is **ordinary**, it is similar to other things of the same type. There is nothing special about it: *The letter came in an ordinary plain envelope.* **2.** If something is **ordinary**, it is of rather poor quality: *The food was very ordinary.*
☐ **ordinarily**, *adverb* –**ordinariness**, *noun*: *the ordinariness of life.*

SIMILAR WORDS (for definition 1) are **average**, **nondescript**, **run-of-the-mill**, **standard**, **unremarkable** and **routine**. Note that **routine** refers to actions, etc., that are usual or ordinary: *Let's follow the routine procedures.*

ore *noun* a rock or mineral which contains a metal that is valuable enough to be mined.

WORD HISTORY from an Old English word meaning 'brass'.

☑ SPELLING TIP Don't confuse the spelling of **ore** with the other three words that sound the same. You use **or** to connect alternative words, phrases or clauses; you use an **oar** for rowing a boat; **awe** is a feeling of great respect mixed with fear.

oregano /*say* o-ruh-**gah**-noh/ *noun* a herb of the mint family, used in cooking.

organ *noun*
1. a musical instrument with pipes and one or more keyboards. **2.** a part of the body which has a particular job, such as the heart which pumps blood or the liver which makes bile. **3.** a part of an organisation that performs a particular role: *A small committee is the policy-making organ of the party.*
☐ **organist**, *noun* someone who plays the organ.

organic /*say* aw-**gan**-ik/ *adjective*
1. having to do with living things or their organs. **2.** describing parts that are organised in a complete structure. **3.** having to do with farming without chemicals: *They only use organic fertilisers.*
☐ **organically**, *adverb*

organisation *noun*
1. the skilful arrangement or running of something. **2.** a group which runs something. **3.** something which is run or managed.
☐ **organisational**, *adjective*

ANOTHER SPELLING is **organization**.

organise *verb*
1. If you **organise** something, you make arrangements for it to happen. You plan it: *We're organising a birthday party.* **2.** If you **organise** things, you tidy them up and put them in particular places so that people can find them easily: *The room's a lot tidier since I organised my books.*
☐ **organiser**, *noun*

ANOTHER SPELLING is **organize**.

organism *noun* any form of animal or plant life.

orgasm *noun* the moment of greatest pleasure in sexual intercourse.
☐ **orgasmic**, *adjective*

orgy /*say* **aw**-jee/ *noun* (*plural* **orgies**) wild or drunken feasting, or other uncontrolled behaviour.

orient *verb* See **orientate**.

oriental *adjective* If something is **oriental**, it comes from or has to do with Asia.

orientate /say **o**-ree-uhn-tayt, **aw**-ree-uhn-tayt/ *verb*
1. If you **orientate** something, you aim or direct it: *The health scheme is heavily orientated to improving diets.* **2.** If you **orientate** yourself, you change to suit a new situation: *Department stores attempt to orientate themselves to the changing demands of customers.*
□ **orientated**, *adjective* –**orientation**, *noun*

ANOTHER WORD for this is **orient**.

orienteering *noun* a sport in which you have to find your way as quickly as possible over a difficult course, using maps and compasses.

origami *noun* the art of folding paper into interesting shapes.

WORD HISTORY from a Japanese word

origin *noun* where something or someone comes from: *What is the origin of throwing salt over your left shoulder for luck?; She lives in Australia now, but Hungary is her country of origin.*
□ **originate**, *verb*: *The sport of surfing originated in Hawaii.* –**origination**, *noun*

original /say uh-**rij**-uh-nuhl/ *adjective* If something is **original** it is **1.** first or earliest: *The original copy of the music has never been found.* **2.** newly thought up or invented, especially without a model: *It was such an original idea we all voted for it.*
–*noun* **3.** the earliest or first form from which copies are made: *All the originals are kept in the library.* **4.** a work which has not been copied from anything else.
□ **originality**, *noun* –**originally**, *adverb*

☑ SPELLING TIP The main thing to remember is the *g* giving the 'j' sound, as in the word *origin*. Try rapping it out as *or*+*ig*+*in*+*al*.

ornament *noun* /say **aw**-nuh-muhnt/
1. an object or decoration which is meant to be beautiful rather than useful.
–*verb* /say **aw**-nuh-ment/ **2.** If you **ornament** something, you decorate it.
□ **ornamental**, *adjective*

ornate *adjective* covered with beautiful things to look showy or fine: *The city was filled with buildings of ornate architecture.*
□ **ornately**, *adverb*

ornithology /say aw-nuh-**thol**-uh-jee/ *noun* the study of birds and bird life.
□ **ornithologist**, *noun*

☑ SPELLING TIP This difficult-looking word comes from *ornis*, the Greek word for 'bird', with the *s* changed to *th* and the suffix *-ology* (meaning 'the study of') added. Think of other words with this ending, such as *biology*, *geology* and *zoology*.

orphan *noun* someone, especially a child, whose parents have died.

orphanage *noun* a place where children without parents live.

orthodontist *noun* someone whose job is to straighten your teeth.
□ **orthodontics**, *noun*

orthodox *adjective* If something is **orthodox**, it is in accordance with the methods or ideas that are most widely accepted: *Australians are moving away from the orthodox hot Christmas dinner.*
□ **orthodoxy**, *noun*

orthopaedics /say aw-thuh-**pee**-diks/ *noun* the type of medical treatment that corrects or cures any problems or diseases of your spine and bones.
□ **orthopaedic**, *adjective* –**orthopaedist**, *noun*

ANOTHER SPELLING is **orthopedics**.

oscillate /say **os**-uh-layt/ *verb* If something **oscillates**, it moves or swings to and fro: *The satellite dish was oscillating on the control tower.*
□ **oscillation**, *noun* –**oscillator**, *noun*

☑ SPELLING TIP *Silent letter alert*: don't forget the silent *c* after the *s*. Also remember that the middle vowel sound is spelt *i* and that the *l* is doubled. Think of getting *ill* from too much **oscillating** to help you remember this part.

osmosis *noun* the movement of liquid from a cell in which there is a concentrated solution across the cell wall to a cell in which there is a less concentrated solution, so that in the end the solutions will be of equal concentration.

WORD HISTORY from a Greek word meaning 'a thrusting'

ostentatious *adjective* Something that is **ostentatious** is meant to impress people but is too showy: *He made an ostentatious display of the medals he had been awarded; ostentatious gold jewellery.*
□ **ostentation**, *noun* –**ostentatiously**, *adverb* –**ostentatiousness**, *noun*

NOTE Some words with an opposite meaning are **modest** and **discreet**.

osteopathy /say os-tee-**op**-uh-thee/ *noun* a method of treating injuries to bones and muscles by putting pressure on them to bring them back into their proper place.
□ **osteopath** /say **os**-tee-uh-path/, *noun* –**osteopathic**, *adjective*

ostracise /say **os**-truh-suyz/ *verb* If you **ostracise** someone, you exclude them, or send them away, especially as a punishment: *It was unfair of the team to ostracise him because he played badly.*
□ **ostracism**, *noun*

ANOTHER SPELLING is **ostracize**.

ostrich *noun* (*plural* **ostriches**) a large bird of Africa which runs fast but cannot fly.

other *adjective*
1. Other people or things are ones that are different from or additional to the ones already mentioned: *It's a small car and we only have room for Sam and one other person.* **2.** If you say you did something the **other** day or the **other** week, you mean that you did it fairly recently: *I swam at the pool the other day.*
–*pronoun* **3.** the other one: *I don't want that dress – I like the other better.* **4.** some other person or thing: *I'll see you some time or other.*
–*phrase* **5. every other**, every alternate: *We go to pottery classes every other week.*

otherwise *adverb*
1. if things had been different: *I might otherwise have come.* **2.** in other ways: *an otherwise happy life.*

> ☑ SPELLING TIP The spelling of this word will be quite easy if you see that it is made up of *other* with the suffix *-wise*. This suffix does not mean 'knowledgeable' but is a form of *ways* used in words having to do with direction or the way something is done.

otter *noun* a furry water animal of Europe and North America, with webbed feet and a flattened tail.

ought /*say* awt/ *verb* If you **ought** to do something, then you have some responsibility to do it: *I really ought to do my homework.*

> ☑ SPELLING TIP *Tricky vowel sound*: *ough* for the 'aw' sound. This letter combination occurs in many other words, such as *bought* and *fought*.

ounce *noun* a measure of weight in the imperial system equal to about 29 grams.

> THE SYMBOL for this is **oz**.

> ☑ SPELLING TIP *Tricky vowel sound*: the vowel sound is spelt *ou*, as in some other words such as *bounce* and *pounce*.

our *pronoun* the form of the pronoun **we** that you use when something belongs to us: *Mind our places while we go to the canteen.*
☐ **ours**, *pronoun*: *Hey, those seats are ours!*

oust /*say* owst/ *verb* If you **oust** someone from a position or place, you push them out or expel them: *He was ousted from the council after a disagreement.*

out *adverb*
1. away from a place, position, state, and so on: *out of the room.* **2.** completely or to the end: *to dry out.*
–*adjective* **3.** incorrect: *He was out in his calculations.* **4.** not burning or giving light: *The fire is out.* **5.** unconscious: *The boxer was out for five minutes.* **6.** finished: *before the week is out.*
–*preposition* **7.** through as an exit: *out the door.* **8.** outside: *out the back.*

outback *noun* the remote parts of the country or bush, far from the cities and the coast.
☐ **outback**, *adjective*: *an outback adventure.* –**outback**, *adverb*: *to go outback.*

outboard *adjective* on the outside of a boat or plane: *an outboard engine.*

outbreak *noun* a sudden beginning or happening: *There has been an outbreak of food poisoning from polluted oysters.*

outburst *noun* a sudden bursting or pouring out: *There was an outburst of clapping when she came onto the stage.*

outcast *noun* someone who is not accepted by people in a society.

outcome *noun* a result: *Do you know the outcome of the discussions?*

outcry *noun* (*plural* **outcries**) a strong expression of anger about something, especially by many people: *There was an outcry when they took chips off the list in the canteen.*

outdoors *adverb* outside a building, in the open air: *Dad said the party had to be outdoors.*
☐ **outdoor**, *adjective*: *outdoor furniture.*

outer *adjective* located outside something else: *My friend lives in an outer suburb.*
☐ **outermost**, *adjective*

outfit *noun*
1. a set of clothes or equipment needed for an activity: *My doll has more outfits than I do.* **2.** a group associated with a particular undertaking: *He's part of a new construction outfit.*
–*verb* (**outfits**, **outfitting**, **outfitted**, **has outfitted**) **3.** To **outfit** someone is to provide them with clothes for a particular activity: *Mum took me to be outfitted for my soccer clothes.*

outgoing *adjective*
1. friendly and sociable: *Su Li is warm, outgoing and humorous.* **2.** departing or going out: *The outgoing president gave a very long speech.*

outing *noun* a journey taken for fun: *A good outing would be to the cinema.*

outlandish *adjective* strange and irregular: *outlandish clothes*; *outlandish behaviour.*

outlaw *noun*
1. a criminal, especially in earlier times one who had been cut off from the protection of the law.
–*verb* **2.** If the government **outlaws** a behaviour, it makes it illegal: *English kings once outlawed bowling.*

outlay *noun* /*say* **owt**-lay/
1. money, time or energy spent in getting something.
–*verb* /*say* owt-**lay**/ (**outlays**, **outlaying**, **outlaid**, **has outlaid**) **2.** If you **outlay** something like

money, time or energy, you spend it in order to achieve something: *The government outlaid $4 000 000 to start the project.*

outlet *noun*
1. an opening or way for letting something out: *The drain is connected to the stormwater outlet*; *He finds an outlet for his energy in the local gym.* **2.** a shop or market: *My mum was looking for a retail outlet that sold hand-painted cards.*

outline *noun*
1. a line showing the shape of something: *We had to draw the outline of a rabbit.* **2.** a short description giving only the most important points: *The police asked for an outline of what had happened.*
–*verb* **3.** If you **outline** something, you give the most important facts about it. **4.** If someone or something is **outlined**, their shape is seen, usually with a lighter colour behind them: *She could see a group of people outlined against the blue of the sea.*

outlook *noun*
1. a view: *The house had an outlook over the bush.* **2.** an attitude or point of view: *He has an optimistic outlook on life.* **3.** what is likely to happen in the future: *The financial outlook is not good.*

outpatient *noun* a patient who comes to a hospital for medical treatment but does not have to stay.

outpost *noun*
1. a group of soldiers stationed away from the main army. **2.** a settlement far away from the main town: *The outpost consisted of a couple of sheds.*

output *noun*
1. something that is produced: *The output is about 500 000 units a week.* **2.** the information that a computer can put out, based on the information that has been put in.

outrage *noun*
1. something that shocks or offends people. **2.** a feeling of very strong anger.
☐ **outrageous**, *adjective* –**outrageously**, *adverb*

outright *adverb*
1. completely or totally: *My uncle failed the driving test outright when he backed up onto the footpath.* **2.** immediately: *The committee rejected him outright when he turned up late for the interview.*
☐ **outright**, *adjective*: *outright victory.*

outset *noun* the beginning or start: *Let's get it straight right from the outset who's going to be boss!*

outside *preposition*
1. on the outer side of: *Put your muddy shoes outside the back door.*
–*noun* **2.** the outer part or side: *The paint is peeling on the outside of the house*; *On the outside the group looks organised but actually it isn't.*
–*phrase* **3. an outside chance**, a very small chance: *There's an outside chance that you'll make the train if you run.*
☐ **outside**, *adjective*: *outside walls*; *outside interests.* –**outside**, *adverb*: *to play outside.* –**outsider**, *noun*

outskirts *plural noun* the outer areas: *We reached the outskirts of the city towards night.*

outspoken *adjective* If you are **outspoken**, you say openly what you think even if it offends people.
☐ **outspokenly**, *adverb* –**outspokenness**, *noun*

outstanding *adjective*
1. standing out from all others in skill: *What an outstanding debater!* **2.** not settled or finished: *Unfortunately, there are some outstanding debts to be paid.*
☐ **outstandingly**, *adverb*

outward *adjective*
1. on the outside: *His outward appearance was quite smart.*
–*adverb* **2.** towards the outside or exterior: *The door opens outward.*
☐ **outwardly**, *adverb*

ANOTHER FORM of the adverb (definition 2) is **outwards**.
THE OPPOSITE is **inward**.

outwit *verb* (**outwits**, **outwitting**, **outwitted**, **has outwitted**) If you **outwit** someone, you beat them by being more clever or tricky than they are: *She outwitted the security guard by pretending she was one of the family.*

oval *adjective*
1. shaped like an egg.
–*noun* **2.** an oval shape. **3.** a field for playing sport on.

ovary *noun* (*plural* **ovaries**) the part of a female's body that produces eggs for reproduction.

WORD HISTORY from a Latin word meaning 'egg'

ovation *noun* cheers and enthusiastic applause: *There was a standing ovation for her as she ran towards the finishing line.*

oven /*say* **uv**-uhn/ *noun* a closed-in space, usually part of a stove, used for cooking and heating food.

over *preposition*
1. above in place or position: *a roof over our heads.* **2.** above and to the other side of: *to jump over a wall.* **3.** above in power: *The manager is over the supervisor.* **4.** on or upon: *Put a cloth over the food.* **5.** across: *to go over a bridge.* **6.** more than: *over a kilometre.*
–*adverb* **7.** in repetition: *two times over.*
–*phrase* **8. all over**, **a.** everywhere. **b.** finished and done with. **c.** typical of: *That's him all over.*

9. over and above, in addition to: *What he did was over and above his duty.*
☐ **overly**, *adverb*: *She's overly eager to become my friend.*

overall *adjective /say* **oh**-vuhr-awl/
1. from one extreme limit of a thing to another: *the overall length of a bridge.* **2.** with everything included: *an overall price.*
–*adverb /say* oh-vuhr-**awl**/ **3.** covering or including everything: *the situation viewed overall.*

☑ SPELLING TIP The spelling of this word will be quite easy if you see that it is simply made up of *over* and *all* joined together.

overalls *plural noun* a pair of trousers with a flap covering your chest, fastened by shoulder straps.

overawe *verb* If something **overawes** you, it fills you with fear and respect: *She was overawed by the number of people who had come to hear her sing.*

overbalance *verb* If you **overbalance**, you are unable to keep your balance and you fall over: *He overbalanced and fell off the wall.*

overbearing *adjective* Someone who is **overbearing** is proud and bossy.

☑ SPELLING TIP The spelling of this word will be quite easy if you see that it is made up of *over* and *bearing* joined together. Remember that this comes from one of the meanings of the word *bear* (not *bare*), which is 'to weigh down or press on'.

overboard *adverb*
1. over the side of a boat or ship into the water: *He jumped overboard and swam for shore.*
–*phrase* **2. go overboard**, *Rather informal* to be too enthusiastic: *They went overboard when they put up their prices – they're far too high!*

overcast *adjective* cloudy and grey: *The overcast weather was depressing.*

overcome *verb* (**overcomes**, **overcoming**, **overcame**, **has overcome**)
1. If you **overcome** something, such as a fear or a problem, you deal with it successfully: *I finally overcame my anxiety.* **2.** If an emotion **overcomes** you, it is suddenly so strong that you have to give way to it: *Exhaustion finally overcame them and they had to stop for the night.*

overdo *verb* (**overdoes**, **overdoing**, **overdid**, **has overdone**) If you **overdo** something, you do too much of it: *I overdid enjoying myself at the party and now I feel rather full.*

overdose *noun /say* **oh**-vuh-dohs/
1. a dose of a drug that is large enough to either kill the person who takes it, or make them seriously ill.
–*verb /say* oh-vuh-**dohs**/ **2.** If somebody **overdoses**, they take a dangerously large dose of a drug: *He overdosed on heroin.*

ANOTHER TERM for this, used in informal language, is **OD**.

overdue *adjective* late or past the proper time: *Babies that are overdue often have wrinkled skin when they are born.*

overflow *verb /say* oh-vuh-**floh**/
1. If a body of water **overflows**, it flows or runs over: *The bath overflowed when we left the taps on*; *At the height of the rains, the river overflowed.*
–*noun /say* **oh**-vuh-floh/ **2.** a flood: *the overflow of a river.* **3.** the area of land covered by water in times of flood.

overgrown *adjective* covered with weeds and long grass.
☐ **overgrowth**, *noun*

overhang *verb /say* oh-vuh-**hang**/ (**overhangs**, **overhanging**, **overhung**, **has overhung**)
1. To **overhang** something is to hang over it: *A white gum overhung the cliff.*
–*noun /say* **oh**-vuh-hang/ **2.** a part that sticks out and hangs over something: *We sheltered under the rocky overhang.*
☐ **overhanging**, *adjective*

overhaul *verb /say* oh-vuh-**hawl**/
1. If you **overhaul** something, you check, take apart, and repair it: *We sent the car to the mechanic to be overhauled.*
–*noun /say* **oh**-vuh-hawl/ **2.** a thorough checking and repairing of something: *It's time our computer system had an overhaul.*

overhead *adverb /say* oh-vuh-**hed**/
1. straight above and up in the air: *We watched the ceiling fans spinning overhead.*
–*adjective /say* **oh**-vuh-hed/ **2.** in a position straight above and up in the air: *Overhead wires are ugly.*

overheads */say* **oh**-vuh-hedz/ *plural noun* the fixed costs involved in running a business.

overhear *verb* (**overhears**, **overhearing**, **overheard**, **has overheard**) If you **overhear** someone speaking to someone else, you hear what they say, usually without them knowing: *Ann overheard a very interesting conversation that she was not meant to hear.*

overlap *verb /say* oh-vuh-**lap**/ (**overlaps**, **overlapping**, **overlapped**, **has overlapped**)
1. If one thing **overlaps** another, it partly covers it.
–*noun /say* **oh**-vuh-lap/ **2.** something partly covering something else: *I trimmed back the overlap of the material.*

overlook *verb* To **overlook** something is to **1.** miss or ignore it: *Josh overlooked the time he was supposed to turn up*; *Luckily the teacher said she would overlook our mess that time.* **2.** look down over it: *Our school overlooks the shops.*

overpass *noun* a bridge for cars or pedestrians, which crosses over a busy road.

overpower *verb* If you **overpower** someone, you defeat them with your greater strength: *The wrestler overpowered his opponent.*
□ **overpowering**, *adjective*: *Allie had an overpowering sensation of fear.*

overrun *verb* (**overruns**, **overrunning**, **overran**, **has overrun**) If people or things **overrun** an area, they spread or swarm all over it: *The mice overran all of the grain crops in the district.*

overseas *adverb* /*say* oh-vuh-**seez**/
1. to a part of the world which lies at the other side of a sea: *She dreamed of going overseas one day.*
–*adjective* /*say* **oh**-vuh-seez/ **2.** having to do with a part of the world across the sea: *overseas travel.*

oversee *verb* (**oversees**, **overseeing**, **oversaw**, **has overseen**) If a person **oversees** something like an event or group of people, they supervise or manage it: *My job was to oversee the class while the teacher went to a meeting.*
□ **overseer**, *noun* a supervisor or person in charge.

overt /*say* oh-**vert**, **oh**-vert/ *adjective* not hidden or secret, but out in the open: *There was no overt violence in the film.*
□ **overtly**, *adverb*

overtake *verb* (**overtakes**, **overtaking**, **overtook**, **has overtaken**)
1. If you **overtake** someone or something, you catch up to them and pass them: *The red car overtook us.* **2.** If something **overtakes** you, it affects you suddenly and often unpleasantly: *She was overtaken by a terrible feeling of illness and had to go home.*

overthrow *verb* /*say* oh-vuh-**throh**/ (**overthrows**, **overthrowing**, **overthrew**, **has overthrown**)
1. To **overthrow** a ruler or a government is to defeat or put an end to their rule by force: *They are predicting that the president will be overthrown soon.*
–*noun* /*say* **oh**-vuh-throh/ **2.** the situation when the ruler or government is removed by force: *Elections were held soon after the overthrow of the president.*

overtime *noun* extra time worked before or after the usual working hours: *She applied for overtime to save up for the trip.*
□ **overtime**, *adjective*

overture *noun* music played before the start of an opera, ballet or musical show.

overturn *verb*
1. If something **overturns**, it turns onto its side or upside down: *The high winds caused the boat to overturn.* **2.** If someone in authority **overturns** a decision, they state that the original decision is wrong: *The judges in the upper court overturned the lower court decision.*

overwhelm /*say* oh-vuh-**welm**/ *verb*
1. If something **overwhelms** you, it affects you so much that you cannot function properly: *The scenes from the earthquake overwhelmed us.* **2.** To **overwhelm** someone is to defeat them: *The army overwhelmed the enemy.*
□ **overwhelming**, *adjective*: *an overwhelming feeling of sorrow.*

> ☑ SPELLING TIP *Silent letter alert*: don't forget the silent *h* after the *w*, as in many other words, such as *where* and *wheel*.

overwrought /*say* oh-vuh-**rawt**/ *adjective* worked up with excitement or worry.

> ☑ SPELLING TIP *Silent letter alert*: this word is made up of *over* and *wrought*. The second is the difficult part, starting with the silent *w* at the beginning. Also remember the *ough* spelling for the 'or' sound. *Wrought* is the old-fashioned form of the past participle of *work*, so **overwrought** literally means 'overworked'.

ovulate *verb* When a woman **ovulates**, she releases eggs from her ovaries.
□ **ovulation**, *noun*

ovum /*say* **oh**-vuhm/ *noun* (*plural* **ova**) one of the cells produced by a female which can join with a sperm to develop into a new organism.

> WORD HISTORY from the Latin word meaning 'egg'

owe *verb*
1. If you **owe** money to someone, you are in their debt for the amount you borrowed from them. **2.** If you say that you **owe** someone something, you mean you know that you should give it to them: *Sam owes the teacher an apology.* **3.** If you **owe** something to someone or something, you have it because of that person or thing: *They owed their safety to the courageous fire crew.*

owing *adjective*
1. Something that is **owing** is due to be paid or given back: *My friend reminded me that there was still some money owing to her.*
–*phrase* **2. owing to**, because of: *The boat was hard to launch owing to the steepness of the river bank.*

owl *noun* a bird with large eyes, which feeds mostly at night on small animals like birds and frogs.

own *verb*
1. If you **own** something, it belongs to you.
–*adjective* **2.** If something is your **own**, it belongs to you: *They are my own paints.*
–*noun* **3.** something belonging to yourself: *I am lucky to have paints of my own.*
–*phrase* **4. own up**, to admit.
□ **owner**, *noun* –**ownership**, *noun*

A SIMILAR WORD (for definition 1) is **possess**.

ox *noun* (*plural* **oxen**) a bull, which has been castrated, used to pull loads.

oxygen /*say* **ok**-suh-juhn/ *noun* a gas with no colour or smell which is a necessary part of the air we breathe.

oyster *noun* a shellfish you can eat, having a two-part shell with a rough, sharp edge.

Oz *noun Informal* Australia.

ozone /*say* **oh**-zohn/ *noun* a form of oxygen with three atoms to the molecule, having a peculiar smell.

☑ SPELLING TIP You can think of **ozone** as being made of *o* plus *zone* which will make the spelling easier. In fact, it comes from *ozein*, the Greek word for 'smell'.

ozone depletion *noun* a thinning of the ozone layer caused by the release into the atmosphere of certain gases that break down and destroy the ozone.

ozone layer *noun* a layer of ozone in one of the outer parts of the earth's atmosphere, which partly blocks the harmful rays of the sun.

ANOTHER WORD for this is **ozonosphere**.

pace *noun*
1. a single step or the distance covered by it. 2. speed or rate of movement: *the pace at which you are travelling.*
–*verb* 3. When you **pace**, you walk with regular steps: *The prisoner paced back and forth in his cell.* 4. When you **pace** something, you measure it by paces: *We paced the length of the hall to work out how many rows of chairs we could fit in.*

pacemaker *noun*
1. someone or something that sets the pace, usually in a race. 2. a medical instrument placed in someone's body when their heart is diseased and needs help to keep it beating at the right rate.

pacific /*say* puh-**sif**-ik/ *adjective* peaceful or peace-loving.

pacifism /*say* **pas**-uh-fiz-uhm/ *noun* opposition to war or violence of any kind.
☐ **pacifist**, *noun*

pacify /*say* **pas**-uh-fuy/ *verb* (**pacifies**, **pacifying**, **pacified**, **has pacified**) If you **pacify** someone, you make them peaceful or calm: *She pacified the whimpering child by letting him pat the puppy.*
☐ **pacification**, *noun*

pack *noun*
1. a parcel or bundle of things wrapped or tied up. 2. a load carried on the back of people or animals: *The weary hikers took off their packs while they rested in the shade.* 3. a group of animals living and hunting together: *a pack of wolves.* 4. a group of people or things: *a pack of thieves*; *a pack of lies.* 5. a complete set: *a pack of playing cards.*
–*verb* 6. When you **pack** something, you put it into a suitcase, parcel or box: *Don't close the suitcase – I haven't packed my shoes yet.* 7. If people **pack** into a place, they press in or cram together: *The crowd packed into the stadium.*
–*phrase* 8. **pack off**, to send away in a hurry: *She packed them off to the country.*
☐ **packed**, *adjective* –**packer**, *noun*

package *noun*
1. a parcel or a bundle.
–*verb* 2. When you **package** something, you put it into packages: *to package tomatoes.*

packet *noun* a small pack or package of anything.

pact *noun* an agreement: *We made a pact to finish our homework before we watched television.*

pad[1] *noun*
1. a piece of soft material used to give comfort, protection or shape to something. 2. a number of sheets of paper held together at one edge. 3. the soft part on the underneath of the feet of animals like dogs, cats, foxes, and so on. 4. a flat area that helicopters and sometimes spacecraft take off from. 5. *Informal* a place where someone lives, especially a single room.
–*verb* (**pads**, **padding**, **padded**, **has padded**) 6. If you **pad** something, you use a pad or pads to make it more comfortable or to fill out hollow spaces: *to pad a chair.*

ANOTHER TERM (for definition 2) is **writing pad.**

pad[2] *verb* (**pads**, **padding**, **padded**, **has padded**) If a person or animal **pads**, they walk with soft footsteps: *She padded down the corridor in her socks.*

paddle[1] *noun*
1. a short oar which you use in moving a small boat, such as a canoe, through the water.
–*verb* 2. When you **paddle** a boat, you move it through the water using a paddle: *to paddle a canoe.*

paddle[2] *verb* If you **paddle** in shallow water, you wet your feet in it up to your ankles.

paddleboarding *noun* the activity or sport of riding a stand-up paddleboard.

ANOTHER NAME for this is **paddleboard surfing.**

paddock *noun* a large area of land which has been fenced and is used for grazing sheep or other animals.

☑ SPELLING TIP *Double letter alert*: double *d*. To remember this and the spelling of the end of the word, you can try thinking of it being made up of *pad* and *dock* though these words are not related to the meaning.

pademelon /*say* **pad**-ee-mel-uhn/ *noun* a type of small wallaby.

ANOTHER SPELLING is **paddymelon.**

padlock *noun* a removable lock with a curved metal bar, used to lock gates, etc.

pad thai /*say* pad **tuy**/ *noun* a food made from rice noodles, stir-fried with ingredients such as beef, tofu and vegetables, originating in Thai cooking.

☑ SPELLING TIP *Silent letter alert*: don't forget the silent *h* following the *t*, as in *Thailand* from where this food comes.

paediatrician /*say* pee-dee-uh-**trish**-uhn/ *noun* a doctor who specialises in treating children's illnesses.
□ **paediatric** /*say* pee-dee-**at**-rik/, *adjective* –**paediatrics**, *noun*

ANOTHER SPELLING is **pediatrician**.

paedophile /*say* **ped**-uh-fuyl, **peed**-uh-fuyl/ *noun* an adult who engages in sexual activities with children.

ANOTHER SPELLING is **pedophile**

paella /*say* puy-**el**-uh/ *noun* a food made from rice, chicken, shellfish and vegetables, originating in Spanish cooking.

pagan /*say* **pay**-guhn/ *noun* someone who does not follow one of the major accepted religions.
□ **pagan**, *adjective*: *a pagan practice.* –**paganism**, *noun*

page[1] *noun*
1. one of the sheets of paper making up a book, magazine, letter, and so on. **2.** one side of one of these sheets. **3.** See **web page**.

page[2] *noun*
1. a boy servant or an attendant.
–*verb* **2.** If you **page** someone, you try to find them in a hotel, hospital, shop, and so on, by calling out their name on a microphone or public address system.

pageant /*say* **paj**-uhnt/ *noun*
1. a colourful public show, often including a procession of people in costume. **2.** any showy display.

☑ SPELLING TIP Remember the *e* before the *ant* (which you don't hear when you say the word). It may help to think of **pageant** as broken into two parts – *page* and *ant* – although these words are not related to its meaning.

pagoda /*say* puh-**goh**-duh/ *noun* in India, Myanmar, China, etc., a temple or sacred building, shaped like a tower.

pail *noun* a bucket.

☑ SPELLING TIP Don't confuse the spelling of **pail** with **pale** which has the same sound. **Pale** describes something which is whitish or colourless.

pain *noun*
1. suffering or hurt felt when you are injured or sick, or when you are unhappy. **2.** such a feeling in a particular part of the body: *a sharp pain in the stomach.* **3. pains**, very careful efforts: *Take great pains with your homework.*
–*verb* **4.** If something **pains** you, it makes you feel upset or distressed: *It pains me that you care so little about your friends.*
□ **painful**, *adjective* –**painfully**, *adverb*

☑ SPELLING TIP Don't confuse the spelling of **pain** with **pane** which has the same sound. A **pane** is a single piece of glass, usually in a window.

painstaking *adjective* extremely careful: *painstaking work.*

paint *noun*
1. a liquid colouring substance that you can put on a surface to give it colour.
–*verb* **2.** When you **paint** something, you cover it with paint: *We put paper on the floor before we painted the bookshelves*; *My little brother painted his face.* **3.** When you **paint** a picture of someone or something, you make an image of them using paint: *She painted the view from her window.*
□ **painting**, *noun*

painter[1] *noun*
1. an artist who paints pictures. **2.** someone whose work is painting walls, fences, and so on.

painter[2] *noun* a rope for tying a boat to a ship, wharf, and so on.

pair *noun* (*plural* **pairs** *or* **pair**)
1. two things of the same kind that go together: *a pair of socks.* **2.** a combination of two parts joined together to make a single thing: *a pair of jeans.* **3.** two people, things or animals thought of as connected to each other in some way: *a happily married pair.*

WORD HISTORY from a Latin word meaning 'equal'.

☑ SPELLING TIP Don't confuse the spelling of **pair** with **pear** or **pare**, both of which have the same sound. A **pear** is a kind of fruit. When you **pare** an apple, you peel off the skin.

pal *noun Rather informal* a friend.
□ **pally**, *adjective*

WORD HISTORY from a Gypsy word meaning 'brother'

palace *noun* the official home of a king, queen, or other very important person.

palatable /*say* **pal**-uh-tuh-buhl/ *adjective* reasonably pleasant to taste.

palate /*say* **pal**-uht/ *noun*
1. the roof of the mouth. **2.** the sense of taste.

palatial /*say* puh-**lay**-shuhl/ *adjective* large and grand, like a palace.
□ **palatially**, *adverb*

pale *adjective* (**paler**, **palest**)
1. not strong or bright in colour: *a pale light*; *a pale blue shirt.* **2.** having a whitish or colourless

appearance: *Are you sick? You look very pale.*
☐ **palely**, *adverb* –**paleness**, *noun*

☑ SPELLING TIP Don't confuse the spelling of **pale** with **pail** which has the same sound. A **pail** is a bucket.

palette /*say* **pal**-uht/ *noun* a thin board, usually with a thumb hole at one end, used by artists to mix colours on.

☑ SPELLING TIP *Single letter alert*: only one *l*. Also notice the *ette* ending. It is spelt in this way because it comes from French. Some other words with an *ette* ending are *cassette* and *serviette*. Don't confuse the spelling of **palette** with **pallet** which has the same sound. A **pallet** is a movable base for storing or moving things.

palindrome /*say* **pal**-uhn-drohm/ *noun* a word or sentence which reads the same either backwards or forwards, such as the sentence *Madam, I'm Adam*.

WORD HISTORY from a Greek word meaning 'running back'

paling *noun* a long, pointed piece of wood, as in a fence.

palisade /*say* pal-uh-**sayd**/ *noun* a fence of tall pointed sticks set firmly in the ground as a protection around a fort or camp.

☑ SPELLING TIP *Single letter alert*: only one *l* and one *s*.

pall[1] /*say* pawl/ *noun*
1. a cloth for spreading over a coffin. **2.** something that covers with darkness or gloominess: *A pall of dust hung over the road.*

pall[2] /*say* pawl/ *verb* If something **palls**, it becomes tiring or boring: *Going swimming early every morning was great fun at first, but the excitement soon palled.*

pallbearer *noun* someone who carries the coffin at a funeral.

pallet *noun* a movable base on which things are placed when being stored or moved from place to place in a factory.

☑ SPELLING TIP *Double/single letter alert*: double *l* and only one *t* at the end. Don't confuse the spelling of **pallet** with **palette** which is a thin board an artist uses for paints.

pallid *adjective* pale or lacking in colour.
☐ **pallor**, *noun* unusual paleness caused by fear, illness, and so on.

palm[1] /*say* pahm/ *noun* the part of the inside of the hand that reaches from the wrist to the beginning of the fingers.

☑ SPELLING TIP *Tricky vowel sound*: remember the *l* in this word. The *alm* spelling gives an 'ahm' sound.

palm[2] /*say* pahm/ *noun* See **palm tree**.

☑ SPELLING TIP See **palm**[1].

palmistry /*say* **pah**-muh-stree/ *noun* the telling of someone's fortune or character by the length and pattern of the lines on the palm of their hand.
☐ **palmist**, *noun* someone who reads palms.

palmtop *noun* a personal computer that is small enough to be held in the hand.

palm tree *noun* a tall plant with no branches, but a set of large leaves at the top.

ANOTHER FORM You can also call this a **palm**.

palomino /*say* pal-uh-**mee**-noh/ *noun* (*plural* **palominos**) a tan or cream-coloured horse with a white mane and tail.

ANOTHER SPELLING is **palamino**.
WORD HISTORY from a Spanish word meaning 'like a dove'

palpitate *verb* If your heart **palpitates**, it beats much faster than normal.
☐ **palpitation**, *noun*

palsy /*say* **pawl**-zee/ *noun* See **cerebral palsy**.

paltry /*say* **pawl**-tree/ *adjective* small or worthless: *a paltry few cents.*

pamper *verb* To **pamper** a person or animal is to look after them very well, sometimes so much that it is not good for them: *He pampers his children by giving them chocolates.*

pamphlet /*say* **pam**-fluht/ *noun*
1. a very small paper-covered book. **2.** a single sheet of paper with advertisements printed on it.
☐ **pamphleteer**, *noun*

☑ SPELLING TIP Remember the *ph* spelling for the 'f' sound. Otherwise this word is spelt as it sounds.

pan *noun* a broad, shallow, open dish, which is usually used for cooking.

pancake *noun* a thin, flat cake made of batter, cooked in a frying pan.

pancreas /*say* **pang**-kree-uhs/ *noun* a gland near the stomach which produces important hormones and helps digestion.
☐ **pancreatic** /*say* pang-kree-**at**-ik/, *adjective*: *pancreatic juices.*

panda *noun* a large, black-and-white, bear-like animal which is found mainly in China.

pandemonium /*say* pan-duh-**moh**-nee-uhm/ *noun* wild and noisy confusion.

WORD HISTORY from *Pandemonium*, the name the English poet John Milton (1608–1674) gave to the capital of Hell

pander *verb* If you **pander** to someone, you indulge them.
□ **panderer**, *noun*

pane *noun* a single plate or sheet of glass, usually part of a window.

☑ SPELLING TIP Don't confuse the spelling of **pane** with **pain** which has the same sound. **Pain** is hurt or suffering.

panel *noun*
1. a separate piece set into a ceiling, door or wall, that is sometimes raised above or sunk below the main surface. **2.** a thin, flat piece of wood. **3.** a separate piece of material set into a dress. **4.** a part of a machine on which controls are fixed: *the instrument panel of an aeroplane.* **5.** a group of people chosen to form a jury, or brought together to discuss matters, judge competitions and so on.

pang *noun* a sudden, short, sharp feeling of mental or physical pain: *a pang of remorse*; *a pang of hunger.*

panic *noun*
1. a sudden fear, sometimes without an obvious reason.
–*verb* (**panics**, **panicking**, **panicked**, **has panicked**) **2.** If you **panic**, you feel panic: *I panicked when the lights went out.*

WORD HISTORY from a Greek word meaning 'having to do with or caused by *Pan*', the god of the forests in Greek myths who was thought to inspire wild feelings

☑ SPELLING TIP Don't **panic**! All you have to do is remember that this word ends in *ic* (not *ick*). However, when you add *-ed* or *-ing*, the *k* is added.

panorama /*say* pan-uh-**rah**-muh/ *noun*
1. a view over a wide area: *The panorama was dotted with dams, farmhouses and apple trees.* **2.** a continually changing scene: *Sally made a collage representing the panorama of her whole life.*
□ **panoramic** /*say* pan-uh-**ram**-ik/, *adjective*

☑ SPELLING TIP *Tricky 'uh' sound*: the middle vowel sound is spelt *o*. Also remember that there are no double letters in this word. It is made of the prefix *pan-* (meaning 'all') and a form of *horama* (the Greek word for 'view'). Another word which includes this form of the Greek word is *diorama*.

pansy *noun* (*plural* **pansies**) a garden plant with white, yellow or purple flowers.

pant *verb*
1. If you **pant** after exercise, you breathe hard and quickly.
–*noun* **2.** a sudden short breath.
□ **panting**, *adjective*

panther *noun* a leopard, especially a black one.

NOTE The male is a **panther**; the female is a **pantheress**; the young is a **cub**.

pantihose *noun* a piece of close-fitting women's underwear, covering from the waist to the feet, made out of stocking material.

ANOTHER SPELLING is **pantyhose**.
ANOTHER WORD for this is **tights**.
NOTE This word is always used as a plural, with a plural verb: *My pantihose are getting worn out.*

pantomime /*say* **pan**-tuh-muym/ *noun* a play in which the actors use actions and not words to tell the story.

☑ SPELLING TIP *Tricky 'uh' sound*: the middle vowel sound is spelt *o* (sometimes this word is shortened to *panto*). You can remember the spelling by seeing that this letter joins together two words *pant* and *mime*. The prefix *pant-* is in fact a form of *pan-* meaning 'all' and *mime* has the sense of 'imitate'. The idea behind **pantomime** was someone who imitated everyone.

pantry *noun* (*plural* **pantries**) a room or cupboard in which food is kept.

WORD HISTORY from a Latin word meaning 'bread'

pants *plural noun* **1.** trousers. **2.** underpants, especially women's.

papacy /*say* **pay**-puh-see/ *noun* (*plural* **papacies**)
1. the office or position of the pope in the Roman Catholic church. **2.** the period during which a particular pope rules.

papal /*say* **pay**-puhl/ *adjective* having to do with the pope: *a papal decree.*

paparazzo /*say* pa-puh-**raht**-soh, pah-puh-**raht**-soh/ *noun* (*plural* **paparazzi**) a photographer who persistently searches for or follows famous people in order to photograph them and sell the photographs to the media.

☑ SPELLING TIP *Single/double letter alert*: all letters are single except for the double *z*. This is an Italian word and comes from the surname of a photographer who behaved like this in a famous film called *La dolce vita* (1960).

papaya /*say* puh-**puy**-yuh/ *noun* a pawpaw, especially the kind with reddish flesh.

paper *noun*
1. a material made from wood, usually in thin sheets for writing or printing on, or wrapping

things in. **2.** a newspaper. **3.** a written examination.
–*phrase* **4. on paper**, in theory rather than in practice: *It looks fine on paper, but will it work?*

paperback *noun* a book with a soft paper cover, usually cheaper than one with a hard cover.

papier-mâché /*say* pay-puh-**mash**-ay/ *noun* a substance made of paper pulp sometimes mixed with glue and other materials and used when wet to make models, boxes, and so on which become hard and strong when dry.

☑ SPELLING TIP This is difficult because the spelling remains the same as in French (where it means 'chewed paper') but the pronunciation has changed to become English. So remember that the first part is spelt *papier* (not *paper*) and the second part ends with *ché*, giving a 'shay' sound. You may see this spelt without the French accents as **papier-mache**.

pappadum /*say* **pap**-uh-dum/ *noun* a thin crisp wafer bread, made from spiced potato or rice flour, originating in Indian cooking.

OTHER SPELLINGS are **pappadam** and **poppadum**.

paprika /*say* **pap**-ri-kuh, puh-**pree**-kuh/ *noun* powder made from a red pepper, used as a spice.

papyrus /*say* puh-**puy**-ruhs/ *noun* (*plural* **papyri** /*say* puh-**puy**-ruy/)
1. a tall water plant. **2.** material for writing on made out of this plant, used by the ancient Egyptians, Greeks and Romans. **3.** an ancient document written on this material.

par *noun*
1. an equal level: *His French is on a par with his sister's.* **2.** an average or normal amount: *below par*; *above par.*

parable /*say* **pa**-ruh-buhl/ *noun* a short story used to teach a truth or moral lesson.

parabola /*say* puh-**rab**-uh-luh/ *noun* in geometry, a special kind of even curve, like the path of an object when it is thrown forward into the air and falls back to the earth.
□ **parabolic** /*say* pa-ruh-**bol**-ik/, *adjective*

☑ SPELLING TIP *Single letter alert*: only one *r* and one *b*. There are no double letters in this word.

parachute /*say* **pa**-ruh-shooht/ *noun*
1. a large piece of cloth which opens out in a round shape, used to slow down the fall of someone jumping from an aircraft.
–*verb* **2.** When someone **parachutes**, they jump from an aircraft using a parachute: *The soldiers parachuted into enemy territory.*
□ **parachutist**, *noun*

parade *noun*
1. a gathering of soldiers, students, and so on, usually for display. **2.** a group of people marching in the street to celebrate something.
–*verb* **3.** If a group of people **parade**, they walk together in a parade, or to make a display: *The demonstrators paraded down the street.* **4.** If you **parade** something you are proud of, you show it to people: *The cricket team paraded their trophy.*

A SIMILAR WORD (for definition 1) is **procession**.

paradigm /*say* **pa**-ruh-duym/ *noun* a pattern or example: *Dad regards his elder brother as the paradigm of a successful businessman.*

☑ SPELLING TIP Remember that there is a *g* in the last syllable of this word – the *igm* spelling gives an 'uym' sound. **Paradigm** has this unusual spelling because it comes from Greek.

paradise *noun* a place of great beauty or pleasure.

WORD HISTORY from a Persian word meaning 'enclosure'

☑ SPELLING TIP Notice that the ending is *ise* (not *ice*) – remember that we don't expect there to be cold and ice in **paradise**!

paradox *noun*
1. a statement which is true although it contains two seemingly opposite ideas, such as the statement 'You have to be cruel to be kind'. **2.** someone or something which seems to show opposite ideas.
□ **paradoxical**, *adjective* –**paradoxically**, *adverb*

paragon /*say* **pa**-ruh-guhn/ *noun* someone or something excellent enough to copy: *'She is the paragon of all virtues!' he said enthusiastically.*

paragraph *noun* a block of writing dealing with a particular subject or point and beginning on a new line.

parakeet *noun* a kind of small parrot, such as the budgerigar, usually with a long pointed tail.

ANOTHER SPELLING is **parrakeet**.

parallel /*say* **pa**-ruh-lel/ *adjective*
1. If two lines are **parallel**, they are the same distance from each other at every point along the way: *the parallel lines of a railway track.*
–*noun* **2.** a line parallel with another. **3.** a comparison showing likeness: *Historians like to draw parallels between modern happenings and events in ancient times.*

☑ SPELLING TIP *Single/double letter alert*: only one *r*, then a double *l*, then a single *l* at the end. Remember single – double – single.

parallelogram /*say* pa-ruh-**lel**-uh-gram/ *noun* a four-sided figure whose opposite sides are parallel to each other.

paralysis /*say* puh-**ral**-uh-suhs/ *noun* (*plural* **paralyses** /*say* puh-**ral**-uh-seez/) an inability to move.
☐ **paralyse**, *verb* –**paralytic** /*say* pa-ruh-**lit**-ik/, *adjective*

☑ SPELLING TIP *Letter 'y' alert*: remember that *y* spells the vowel sound following the *l* (a *y* also appears in the verb form **paralyse**). Also don't forget the *is* ending.

paramedical *adjective* having to do with people or services that help the medical profession: *A paramedical team gave the accident victims external heart massage.*

parameter /*say* puh-**ram**-uh-tuh/ *noun* one of a set of variable qualities.

paramount *adjective* above all others in rank, authority or importance.

paranoid *adjective* full of fears about things which are made up or imagined.
☐ **paranoia** /*say* pa-ruh-**noy**-uh/, *noun*

parapet *noun* a wall at the edge of a roof, bridge, or the like, to stop things from falling off it.

paraphernalia /*say* pa-ruh-fuh-**nay**-lee-uh/ *plural noun* goods, equipment, baggage or other articles, especially unnecessary ones.

☑ SPELLING TIP *Tricky 'uh' sound*: the vowel sound following the *ph* (not *f*) is spelt *er*. Also remember that the 'ay' sound before the *l* is spelt with a single *a*. Try rapping it out as *pa+ra+pher+nal+i+a*.

paraphrase *verb* To **paraphrase** something is to put it in different words so that it is easier to understand.
☐ **paraphrase**, *noun*

paraplegic /*say* pa-ruh-**plee**-jik/ *noun* someone who has lost the use of the lower part of their body.
☐ **paraplegia**, *noun* –**paraplegic**, *adjective*

parasite /*say* **pa**-ruh-suyt/ *noun*
1. an animal or plant which lives on or in another from which it obtains its food: *Lice are parasites.* **2.** someone who lives on the money earned by other people without doing anything in return.
☐ **parasitic** /*say* pa-ruh-**sit**-ik/, *adjective*

parasol *noun* a small sun umbrella.

WORD HISTORY from Latin words meaning 'guard against the sun'

paratrooper *noun* a soldier who reaches the fighting in a war by landing from an aeroplane by parachute.

parcel /*say* **pah**-suhl/ *noun*
1. a package or wrapped bundle of goods.
–*verb* (**parcels**, **parcelling**, **parcelled**, **has parcelled**) **2.** When you **parcel** something, you wrap it up into a parcel: *She parcelled up some warm clothes to send to her nephew in the mountains.*

☑ SPELLING TIP *Single letter alert*: only one *l* at the end. However, when you add *-ed* or *-ing*, the *l* is doubled. Also remember the *c* spelling for the 's' sound in the middle.

parch *verb* If something **parches**, it makes or becomes very dry: *The sun parched the already brown earth*; *Her throat had become so parched that it hurt.*
☐ **parched**, *adjective*

parchment *noun*
1. the skin of sheep, goats or similar animals prepared as a material to write on. **2.** paper which looks like this.

pardon *noun*
1. forgiveness, especially for a crime.
–*verb* **2.** To **pardon** someone is to forgive them and not punish them: *I will pardon your misbehaviour on this occasion, but don't let it happen again.*
☐ **pardonable**, *adjective*

pare /*rhymes with* hair/ *verb* If you **pare** something, **1.** you peel or cut off the outer layer of it: *We pared the charcoal from the outside of the burnt potatoes.* **2.** you cut it down or make it less: *The work crew had been pared down to just a few men.*

☑ SPELLING TIP Don't confuse the spelling of **pare** with **pair** or **pear**, both of which have the same sound. Two things that go together are a **pair**. A **pear** is a kind of fruit.

parent *noun* a father or a mother.
☐ **parentage**, *noun* –**parental**, *adjective* –**parenthood**, *noun*

parenthesis /*say* puh-**ren**-thuh-suhs/ *noun* (*plural* **parentheses** /*say* puh-**ren**-thuh-seez/)
1. a word or group of words to describe or explain something else, marked off by commas, brackets or dashes, such as 'a peach and an apple' in *I packed some fruit – a peach and an apple – and then left.* **2.** one of the upright brackets ( ) often used to mark off such a word or group of words.

SEE the Grammar and Punctuation Guide appendix.

parish *noun* in the organisation of some Christian churches, a district which has its own church and priest or minister.
☐ **parishioner**, *noun*

park *noun*
1. an area of land set aside for public use and kept in good order by the local government: *a city park*; *a national park.*
–*verb* **2.** If you **park** a vehicle, you leave it standing somewhere.
☐ **parking**, *noun*

parka *noun* a warm waterproof jacket with a hood.

parley *noun* (*plural* **parleys**) a talk or discussion, especially between people who are fighting each other.

parliament /*say* **pah**-luh-muhnt/ *noun* the national gathering of people elected to make the laws for a country or state.
□ **parliamentarian**, *noun* –**parliamentary**, *adjective*

ANOTHER FORM This is often spelt with a capital letter.
WORD HISTORY from an Old French word meaning 'talking'

☑ SPELLING TIP *Silent letter alert*: don't forget the *i* before the middle *a*. Try rapping it out as *parl* + *i* + *a* + *ment*.

parlour *noun*
1. *Old-fashioned* a formal room in a house for entertaining visitors. **2.** a room where customers of certain businesses are attended to: *a beauty parlour.*

ANOTHER SPELLING is **parlor**.

parmesan *noun* a hard, dry, pale yellow cheese, often used for grating.

WORD HISTORY named after the city of *Parma* in Northern Italy

parody /*say* **pa**-ruh-dee/ *noun* (*plural* **parodies**)
1. a humorous copy of a serious piece of writing or music.
–*verb* (**parodies**, **parodying**, **parodied**, **has parodied**) **2.** If you **parody** a serious piece of writing or music, you imitate it in such a way as to ridicule it: *He made the audience laugh by parodying other singers.*

parole *noun*
1. the early freeing of a prisoner on the condition that they will behave well: *He will be eligible for parole in two years.*
–*verb* **2.** If a prisoner is **paroled**, they are put on parole.

WORD HISTORY from a French word meaning 'word', as in 'to give one's word'

paroxysm /*say* **pa**-ruhk-siz-uhm/ *noun* a sudden violent fit: *a paroxysm of coughing.*

☑ SPELLING TIP Don't have a **paroxysm** about the number of consonants coming together at the end of this word. Remember that one of them is a *y* giving a vowel 'i' sound. Not surprisingly, this difficult word comes from Greek.

parquet /*say* **pah**-kay/ *adjective* made of short pieces of wood fitted together to form a pattern: *A colourful rug was in the centre of the parquet floor.*
□ **parquet**, *noun* –**parquetry**, *noun*

parrot *noun* a brightly coloured bird with a hooked bill which can be taught to imitate human speech.

parry *verb* (**parries**, **parrying**, **parried**, **has parried**) If someone **parries** a question, they turn aside from it or avoid it.

WORD HISTORY this comes from fencing where it is a tactic to avoid the thrust of an opponent's sword

parse *verb* To **parse** a sentence is to describe it by telling the parts of speech of each word in it: *We had to parse the sentence that the teacher wrote on the board.*

parsley *noun* a garden herb used as a garnish or to season food.

parsnip *noun* a whitish root vegetable that is shaped like a carrot.

parson *noun* a member of the clergy.
□ **parsonage**, *noun* a parson's house.

part *noun*
1. a piece or amount that is less than the whole of something. **2.** a replacement piece for something worn out or broken: *My grandfather still loves his old car, even though it's difficult to find parts for it these days.* **3.** a share in something, such as work, a duty, and so on: *to do your part.* **4.** an actor's role: *a part in a play.*
–*verb* **5.** When you **part** something, you separate it into two parts: *We parted the bushes and peered through the gap*; *to part your hair.*
–*phrase* **6. part with**, to give up: *I had to part with my old desk, because it would not fit into the new room.* **7. take someone's part**, to defend or support someone: *He took my part in the argument.*
□ **partly**, *adverb* –**parting**, *noun*

SIMILAR WORDS (for definition 1) are **portion**, **section**, **segment**, **bit** and **fraction**. Note that a **portion** is a part or share of something: *If I cut this apple in two, we can both have a portion.* A **segment** is a part or division and is often used to refer to one of the parts into which a piece of fruit or a pie can be divided. A **fraction** is a small part or amount: *We drove here in a fraction of the time it usually takes.*

partial /*say* **pah**-shuhl/ *adjective*
1. not complete or whole: *He suffers from partial deafness.* **2.** showing unfair support or favouritism: *We thought the referee was being partial in his decisions.*
□ **partiality**, *noun* –**partially**, *adverb*

participate /*say* pah-**tis**-uh-payt/ *verb* If you **participate** in an activity, you take part in it: *to participate in a discussion.*
□ **participant**, *noun* –**participation**, *noun*

participle /*say* **pah**-tuh-sip-uhl/ *noun*
1. a word formed from a verb and used as an adjective, such as 'laughing' in *a laughing child* or

'added' in *added sugar*. **2.** a word formed from a verb and used in compound verbs, such as 'laughing' in *the child has been laughing* or 'added' in *I have added*.
☐ **participial** /*say* pah-tuh-**sip**-ee-uhl/, *adjective*

SEE the Grammar and Punctuation Guide appendix.

☑ SPELLING TIP *Tricky vowel sound*: the middle vowel sound is spelt *i*. Also remember that the following letter is a *c* and that the ending is *le*.

particle *noun* a very small bit: *a particle of dust.*

particular /*say* puh-**tik**-yuh-luh/ *adjective*
1. single, or one, rather than all: *I am only interested in that particular style.* **2.** more than usual or special: *Please pay particular attention to these instructions.*
–*noun* **3.** a point or detail: *The map was accurate in every particular.*
–*phrase* **4. in particular**, especially: *There is one film in particular that I want to see.*
☐ **particularly**, *adverb*

partition *noun*
1. a separating wall. **2.** a division into shares or parts: *The partition of India into India and Pakistan took place in 1947.*
–*verb* **3.** When you **partition** something, you divide it into parts.

partner *noun*
1. someone who shares or takes part in something with someone else: *a business partner*; *a tennis partner.*
–*verb* **2.** When you **partner** someone, you are their partner in a game or at a social occasion: *Joe partnered Louise to the formal.*
☐ **partnership**, *noun*

part of speech *noun* any of the main types of words in a language, such as *noun*, *pronoun*, *verb*, *adjective*, *adverb*, *preposition*, *conjunction* or *interjection*.

SEE the Grammar and Punctuation Guide appendix.

partridge *noun* a European bird that is hunted and eaten.

part-time /*say* **paht**-tuym/ *adjective* taking or working fewer than all the usual working hours: *She has a part-time job at the chemist.*
☐ **part-time** /*say* paht-**tuym**/, *adverb*: *She works part-time.*

COMPARE this with **full-time**.

party *noun* (*plural* **parties**)
1. a social gathering, often to celebrate something: *a birthday party.* **2.** a group of people who hold the same political beliefs.

pass *verb*
1. If you **pass** somewhere, you move through or along, following a route that you are meant to take: *We passed over the bridge and turned left.* **2.** If you **pass** something, you go past it: *The bus passed us on the road.* **3.** If you **pass** something, such as an exam or test, you are successful in it. **4.** If you **pass** something to someone, you give it to them, often by hand. **5.** If time **passes**, it goes by.
–*noun* **6.** a narrow path or road through a low part in a mountain. **7.** a piece of paper that shows you are allowed to do something or go somewhere: *a boarding pass*; *a train pass.* **8.** the handing or throwing of a ball to another player in some ball games. **9.** the passing of an examination.
–*phrase* **10. pass away**, to die. **11. pass off**, to cause to be accepted or received in disguise: *I passed my older brother off as my boyfriend.* **12. pass out**, to lose consciousness. **13. pass up**, to refuse or turn down: *to pass up an opportunity to study overseas.*
☐ **passable**, *adjective*

passage *noun* a way for going through to some other place: *a passage from the street to the back of the house*; *a passage through the reef.*

passenger *noun* someone who travels on a ship, aircraft, bus or other vehicle.

☑ SPELLING TIP *Double letter alert*: double *s*. Also remember the *er* ending.

passion *noun*
1. any strong feeling or emotion, especially love or anger: *Their relationship was full of passion for the first few years.* **2.** a strong interest or enthusiasm: *One of her many passions was basketball.*
☐ **passionate**, *adjective*

WORD HISTORY from a Latin word meaning 'suffering'

passionfruit *noun* (*plural* **passionfruit**) a small purplish fruit, the seeds and pulp of which you can eat.

passive *adjective*
1. If you are **passive**, you let things happen without taking any action yourself. **2.** If you say a sentence or a verb is **passive**, you mean that the person doing the action is not the subject of the sentence or the verb. *I was hit by the ball* is passive because 'the ball' is doing the hitting but is not the subject.
☐ **passively**, *adverb*

COMPARE definition 2 with **active** (definition 3). Also see the Grammar and Punctuation Guide appendix.

passport *noun* a government document which shows who you are and where you come from, which you need to travel to foreign countries.

password *noun* a secret word or expression that allows you to get into a place or a computer system where others are not allowed.

past *adjective*
1. happening or existing before the present time: *The cellar was dug out by the past owners.*
–*noun* **2.** time gone by: *in the past.*
–*adverb* **3.** by: *The train sped past.*

SEE ALSO **past tense**.

pasta /*say* **pahs**-tuh, **pas**-tuh/ *noun* a food made from flour, water and sometimes egg, shaped in different forms which have their own name, such as spaghetti and ravioli, and cooked by boiling, then usually served with a sauce.

paste *noun*
1. a glue used for sticking things onto other surfaces. **2.** something made into a soft, smooth mass: *toothpaste*; *tomato paste.*
–*verb* **3.** When you **paste** something, you stick it to a surface using paste: *to paste a label onto a jar.*

pastel /*say* **pas**-tuhl/ *noun*
1. a soft pale colour. **2.** a crayon, or a drawing made with crayons.
☐ **pastel**, *adjective*

pasteurise /*say* **pahs**-chuh-ruyz/ *verb* To **pasteurise** milk is to destroy germs in it by heating it to a very high temperature.
☐ **pasteurisation**, *noun*

ANOTHER SPELLING is **pasteurize**.
WORD HISTORY named after Louis *Pasteur* (1822–1895), a French chemist

pastie /*say* **pas**-tee, **pahs**-tee/ *noun* (*plural* **pasties**) a type of pie filled with meat and vegetables.

ANOTHER SPELLING is **pasty**.

pastime *noun* something you do to make time pass pleasantly: *The best pastime at the beach is looking in rock pools.*

☑ SPELLING TIP *Single letter alert*: only one *s*. Although this word is formed from *pass* and *time*, the second *s* in *pass* has been dropped.

pastor *noun* a member of the clergy.

WORD HISTORY from a Latin word meaning 'shepherd'

pastry *noun* a mixture of flour, water and fat cooked as a crust for pies and tarts.

past tense *noun* the form of a verb which shows that something has already happened such as 'fell' in *it fell off* and 'has fallen' in *it has fallen off*.

SEE the Grammar and Punctuation Guide appendix.

pasture *noun* land suitable for cattle or sheep to graze on: *The sheep are in the pasture.*

pasty /*say* **pay**-stee/ *adjective* whitish or sick-looking: *I knew she was not well when I saw her pasty face.*

pat[1] *verb* (**pats**, **patting**, **patted**, **has patted**) If you **pat** someone or something, you touch them lightly with the palm or fingers of your hand several times: *Mum patted me on the back and congratulated me*; *John patted the dog on its head*; *'Sit here', she said, patting the seat beside her.*
☐ **pat**, *noun*

pat[2] *adjective*
1. exactly to the point: *He had a pat answer for every question they asked.*
–*adverb* **2.** exactly or perfectly: *We had to learn all our multiplication tables off pat by the end of the week.*

patch *noun* (*plural* **patches**)
1. a piece of material used to mend a hole or a weak place. **2.** a piece of material used to cover a cut or sore. **3.** a small piece: *a patch of grass*; *a patch of sunlight.*
–*verb* **4.** If you **patch** something, you fix it or make it strong with a patch or patches: *to patch a hole in your jeans.*
–*phrase* **5. not a patch on**, *Informal* not nearly as good as. **6. patch up**, **a.** to repair, often in a quick, temporary way: *to patch up a break in a pipe.* **b.** to settle or smooth over: *to patch up a quarrel.*

patchwork *noun* a type of work in which pieces of different coloured or shaped cloth are sewn together.

pâté /*say* **pat**-ay, **pah**-tay/ *noun* a food like a paste or spread made out of finely minced liver, meat, fish, and so on.

WORD HISTORY from a French word, which is why it has accents on two of the letters

patent /*say* **pay**-tuhnt/ *noun* permission given by a government to an inventor, authorising them to be the only one allowed to make or sell an invention.

patent leather *noun* leather with a very shiny surface.
☐ **patent-leather**, *adjective*

paternal *adjective* having to do with or behaving like a father: *my paternal grandmother*; *paternal pride.*
☐ **paternalism**, *noun*

path *noun* a narrow way for walking: *a garden path.*

pathetic *adjective*
1. causing feelings of pity or sadness: *a pathetic sight.* **2.** *Rather informal* of poor quality: *What a pathetic excuse!*
☐ **pathetically**, *adverb*

pathologist /*say* puh-**thol**-uh-juhst/ *noun* a doctor who is an expert in the effects of diseases on the body.
☐ **pathological**, *adjective* –**pathology**, *noun*

patient /*say* **pay**-shuhnt/ *noun*
1. someone who is being treated by a doctor or is in a hospital.

–*adjective* **2.** If you are **patient**, you are willing to wait calmly for something to happen: *a patient customer.* **3.** If you are **patient** with someone, you are kind and tolerant even when they are slow or make mistakes.
☐ **patience**, *noun* –**patiently**, *adverb*

☑ SPELLING TIP Remember the *ti* spelling in the middle. These letters together make the 'sh' sound.

patio /*say* **pat**-ee-oh, **pay**-shee-oh/ *noun* (*plural* **patios**) an outdoor living area joined to a house.

☑ SPELLING TIP Notice that there are two ways of saying this word. If you say it in the first way, you should have no trouble with the spelling. If you say it in the second way, you will have to remember the *t* spelling for the 'sh' sound.

patriarch /*say* **pay**-tree-ahk/ *noun* (*plural* **patriarchs**) a male leader in a family, tribe or any field of activity.
☐ **patriarchal**, *adjective* –**patriarchy**, *noun*

☑ SPELLING TIP The spelling will be easier if you see that **patriarch** is made up of the prefix *patri-* (from the Latin word for 'father') and the suffix *-arch* which means 'chief' or 'ruler'. This suffix comes from Greek and is found in several other words relating to rulers and government, such as *monarch*.

patriot /*say* **pay**-tree-uht, **pat**-ree-uht/ *noun* someone who loves their country and is loyal to it.
☐ **patriotic**, *adjective* –**patriotism**, *noun*

patrol /*say* puh-**trohl**/ *verb* (**patrols**, **patrolling**, **patrolled**, **has patrolled**) To **patrol** a place is to go around it regularly to make certain there is no trouble: *Guards patrol this building.*
☐ **patrol**, *noun*

☑ SPELLING TIP *Single letter alert*: only one *l* at the end. But remember that you double the *l* when you add *-ed* or *-ing*.

patron /*say* **pay**-truhn/ *noun*
1. a regular customer of a hotel, shop, cinema, or similar place. **2.** a supporter or helper: *a patron of art.*
☐ **patronage**, *noun*

patronise /*say* **pat**-ruh-nuyz/ *verb*
1. If you **patronise** a shop or a business, you are its customer: *Mum has been patronising that hairdressing salon for years.* **2.** If you **patronise** a person, you treat them kindly, but as if they are inferior: *I hate the way he patronises us just because we don't know as much as he does.*
☐ **patronising**, *adjective*

ANOTHER SPELLING is **patronize**.

patter[1] *verb* If someone or something **patters**, it strikes or moves with quick, light tapping sounds: *She was pattering around in pyjamas and slippers*; *We could hear the rain pattering on the iron roof.*
☐ **patter**, *noun*: *the patter of footsteps.*

patter[2] *noun* rapid speech or chatter, especially of a salesman or entertainer: *Mum said not to take any notice of what he said – it was just sales patter*; *He kept us laughing with his amusing patter between songs.*

pattern *noun*
1. a particular arrangement of forms and colours. **2.** a model or example: *a paper pattern for a dress.* **3.** a design or figure that's repeated over and over: *a number pattern in mathematics.*
☐ **patterned**, *adjective*

☑ SPELLING TIP *Double letter alert*: double *t* in the middle. Also remember the *r* in the last part of this word which you do not hear when it is pronounced.

paunch /*say* pawnch/ *noun* (*plural* **paunches**) the belly or abdomen, usually a particularly large and rounded one: *He crossed his hands over his paunch and leaned contentedly back into the lounge.*
☐ **paunchy**, *adjective* –**paunchiness**, *noun*

pause /*say* pawz/ *noun*
1. a short rest or stop when you're speaking or doing something.
–*verb* **2.** When you **pause**, you stop what you are doing for a moment: *to pause for breath.*

pave *verb* To **pave** an area is to put something such as bricks on the ground to make it firm and level to walk on.

pavement *noun* a paved path at the side of a road.

pavilion /*say* puh-**vil**-yuhn/ *noun* an open shelter in a park or amusement area.

☑ SPELLING TIP *Single letter alert*: only one *l*.

pavlova *noun* a dessert made of a large, round soft-centred meringue covered with whipped cream and topped with fruit.

WORD HISTORY named after Anna *Pavlova* (1885–1931), a Russian ballerina

paw *noun*
1. the foot of an animal with nails or claws.
–*verb* **2.** When an animal **paws** something, it hits at it with its paw: *The kitten pawed me playfully.*

☑ SPELLING TIP Don't confuse the spelling of **paw** with **pour**, **poor** or **pore**, all of which have the same sound. You can **pour** a liquid from one container to another. Someone who is **poor** does not have much money or property. A **pore** is a small hole in your skin. To **pore** over something is to read or study it carefully.

pawn[1] *verb* If someone **pawns** something they own, they leave it with a person (a **pawnbroker**)

who lends them money on the basis that if they pay the money back before the item is sold, they can have their property back.
☐ **pawnshop**, *noun*

pawn² *noun* one of the pieces of lowest value in chess.

pawpaw *noun* a large fruit with yellow or reddish flesh which grows in tropical parts of Australia and in Asia.

ANOTHER SPELLING is **papaw**.
SEE ALSO **papaya**.

pay *verb* (**paying**, **paid**, **has paid**)
1. If you **pay** money to someone, you give them money in exchange for something they are selling or have done for you: *Did you pay her for our drinks?* **2.** If it **pays** to do something, it is worthwhile to do it: *It pays to do the right thing.* **3.** To **pay** is to suffer or be punished: *to pay for a crime.*
–noun **4.** money one is paid for working.
–phrase **5. pay off**, **a.** to pay the full amount of a debt. **b.** to give a profit, or prove to be worthwhile: *The gamble paid off.*
☐ **payable**, *adjective* –**payback**, *noun* –**payment**, *noun*

PC *noun* See **personal computer**.

PE *noun* sport and other forms of exercise, usually done at school.

WORD HISTORY short for *physical education*

pea *noun* a small, round, green seed which grows in a pod, used as a vegetable.

peace *noun*
1. freedom from war. **2.** calm, quiet or stillness: *peace of mind*; *the peace of the countryside.*
☐ **peaceable**, *adjective* –**peaceful**, *adjective*

☑ SPELLING TIP Don't confuse the spelling of **peace** with **piece** which has the same sound. A **piece** is a bit or part of something.

peach *noun* (*plural* **peaches**) a round, sweet, pinkish-yellow fruit with a single seed and furry skin.

peacock *noun* a type of bird noted for the colourful eye-like pattern on its tail feathers.

NOTE The male is a **peacock**; the female is a **peahen**; the young is a **chick**.

peak *noun*
1. the pointed top of a mountain. **2.** the highest or greatest point: *the peak of her career.*
–verb **3.** When something **peaks**, it reaches its highest point: *The temperature peaked at 39°*; *The flooded river peaked during the night.*
☐ **peaked**, *adjective*

☑ SPELLING TIP Don't confuse the spelling of **peak** with **peek** which has the same sound but is spelt with a double *e*. To **peek** is to take a quick look at something.

peal *noun*
1. a loud, long sound of bells. **2.** any other loud, long sound: *a peal of laughter.*
–verb **3.** If bells **peal**, they sound out one after the other to make a musical sound.

☑ SPELLING TIP Don't confuse the spelling of **peal** with **peel** which has the same sound but is spelt with a double *ee*. To **peel** an apple is to remove its skin.

peanut *noun* a small nut which ripens in a pod underground and which you can eat.

pear *noun* a thin-skinned, pale green or brownish fruit, round at its base and growing smaller towards the stem.

☑ SPELLING TIP Don't confuse the spelling of **pear** with **pair** or **pare** which have the same sound. A **pair** consists of two things that go together, like shoes. You **pare** an apple when you peel the skin off.

pearl /*rhymes with* curl/ *noun* a shiny, round, usually white growth, found in some oysters and used in jewellery.
☐ **pearly**, *adjective* (**pearlier**, **pearliest**)

☑ SPELLING TIP *Tricky vowel sound*: remember the *ea* spelling for the vowel sound. Don't confuse the spelling of **pearl** with **purl** which sounds the same. **Purl** is a stitch used in knitting.

peasant /*say* **pez**-uhnt/ *noun* someone who lives and works on land owned by someone else, keeping animals and growing crops to feed their own family.
☐ **peasantry**, *noun*

NOTE This word is only used about past times or of people in developing countries.

peat *noun*
1. soil which consists of partially rotted leaves, roots, grasses and similar matter in marshy areas. **2.** blocks of this, dried and used as fuel.

pebble *noun* a small, smooth, rounded stone.
☐ **pebbly**, *adjective* (**pebblier**, **pebbliest**)

pecan /*say* **pee**-kan, pee-**kan**/ *noun* a sweet, oily nut which grows on trees in America, and which you can eat.

peck *verb*
1. If a bird **pecks**, it uses its beak to bite or to eat something: *The hens pecked the grain.* **2.** If you **peck** at something, you eat just a bit of it, usually because you are not very hungry.
☐ **peck**, *noun*

pectoral *adjective* having to do with or located in the chest: *pectoral muscles.*

peculiar /*say* puh-**kyooh**-lee-uh, puh-**kyooh**-lyuh/ *adjective*
1. If someone or something is **peculiar**, they are strange or unusual.
–*phrase* **2. peculiar to**, If something is **peculiar to** a person or a group of people, it has to do with that person or that group only: *The habit of writing letters rather than sending emails is peculiar to people of an older age group.*
☐ **peculiarly**, *adverb* –**peculiarity**, *noun* (*plural* **peculiarities**)

☑ SPELLING TIP Remember the *iar* (not *ier*) ending. Another word with this ending is *familiar*. If you remember that, you should feel familiar with this spelling.

pedal *noun*
1. a lever worked by the foot: *a brake pedal*; *a sewing machine pedal*; *a bicycle pedal.*
–*verb* (**pedals**, **pedalling**, **pedalled**, **has pedalled**) **2.** If you **pedal** something like a bicycle or piano, you push the pedals with your feet.

☑ SPELLING TIP Don't confuse the spelling of **pedal** with **peddle** which has the same sound. To **peddle** something is to sell small quantities of it to individual buyers.

peddle *verb* To **peddle** goods is to take them around from place to place in order to sell them.
☐ **peddler**, **pedlar**, *noun*

pedestal *noun*
1. a support for a statue or the like. **2.** the supporting base of a column.

pedestrian /*say* puh-**des**-tree-uhn/ *noun*
1. someone who travels on foot: *I joined a crowd of pedestrians who were waiting to cross the street.*
–*adjective* **2.** dull or commonplace: *pedestrian writing.*

☑ SPELLING TIP *Single letter alert*: only one *d*. **Pedestrian** comes from *pedes*, the Latin word for 'feet'.

pedigree *noun* a line of direct relationship, showing, for example, the parents, grandparents, and so on, used mainly to show the breeding history of an animal: *My dog has a long pedigree.*
☐ **pedigreed**, *adjective*

peek *verb* To **peek** is to look at something quickly, especially something that you are not meant to see: *Mum said not to peek at the Christmas presents.*
☐ **peek**, *noun*

A SIMILAR WORD is **peep**.

☑ SPELLING TIP Don't confuse the spelling of **peek** with **peak** which has the same sound. A **peak** is the top of a mountain.

peel *noun*
1. the skin of a fruit. **2.** the outer layer of anything.
–*verb* **3.** When you **peel** something, you take off its skin, rind or outer layer: *to peel a banana.* **4.** To **peel** is to come off: *The paint is peeling where the water soaked through the wall.*
–*phrase* **5. keep your eyes peeled**, *Informal* to keep a close watch.
☐ **peelings**, *plural noun*

☑ SPELLING TIP Don't confuse the spelling of **peel** with **peal** which has the same sound. When bells **peal**, they ring out.

peep *verb* To **peep** at something is to look at it through a small opening or from a hiding place.
☐ **peep**, *noun*

peer[1] *noun* someone of your own age or at the same stage in life as you are.
☐ **peerless**, *adjective* unable to be equalled: *peerless beauty.*

☑ SPELLING TIP Don't confuse the spelling of **peer** with **pier** which has the same sound. A **pier** is a jetty where boats pull up.

peer[2] *verb* If you **peer** at something, you look at it closely in order to see it clearly.

☑ SPELLING TIP See **peer**[1].

peevish *adjective* cross or easily annoyed.

peg *noun*
1. a small wooden, metal or plastic pin used to fasten things, to hang things on, or to mark a place: *a clothes peg*; *a tent peg*; *a hat peg*; *a surveyor's peg.*
–*verb* (**pegs**, **pegging**, **pegged**, **has pegged**) **2.** When you **peg** something, you fasten it with a peg: *to peg clothes on the line.*
–*phrase* **3. take someone down a peg**, to humble someone: *That girl needs taking down a peg.*

pejorative /*say* puh-**jo**-ruh-tiv/ *adjective* expressing disapproval: *I called her a bookworm, but I didn't mean it to be pejorative.*
☐ **pejoratively**, *adverb*

pelican *noun* a large, web-footed seabird with a pouch hanging beneath its bill for holding the fish it catches.

pellet *noun*
1. a small, rounded piece of anything: *a paper pellet*; *a pellet of food.* **2.** a small bullet fired from a shotgun.

pelmet *noun* an ornamental covering which hides a curtain rail.

pelt[1] *verb*
1. If you **pelt** someone or something, you throw objects at them: *to pelt stones at a post.* **2.** If rain **pelts** down, it comes down heavily.

pelt[2] *noun* the skin taken from a dead animal to be made into leather.

pelvis *noun* the ring of bone made up of the lower part of the backbone and the two hip bones, and the space it forms.
☐ **pelvic**, *adjective*

pen[1] *noun*
1. an instrument for writing with ink.
–*verb* (**pens**, **penning**, **penned**, **has penned**)
2. When you **pen** a letter or note, you write it.

pen[2] *noun*
1. an enclosure for animals on a farm.
–*verb* (**pens**, **penning**, **penned**, **has penned**)
2. When you **pen** an animal, you put it in a pen: *to pen the sheep for the night.*

penal /*say* **pee**-nuhl/ *adjective* having to do with the punishment of crimes: *The island was a penal settlement.*

penalty *noun* (*plural* **penalties**)
1. the price you pay for breaking a law or rule. **2.** a free kick, throw, etc., allowed in some sports to one team or player because an opponent has broken a rule.

penance /*say* **pen**-uhns/ *noun* a punishment you agree or offer to accept to show you are sorry for doing wrong.

pencil *noun*
1. a thin, pointed piece of wood enclosing a stick of graphite or crayon and used for writing or drawing.
–*verb* (**pencils**, **pencilling**, **pencilled**, **has pencilled**) **2.** If you **pencil** a note or a symbol, you write or draw it with a pencil.

pendant *noun* a hanging piece of jewellery such as a necklace.
☐ **pendant**, *adjective* hanging.

> ☑ SPELLING TIP Remember that the ending is *ant* (not *ent*). Think of an ant hanging from the bottom of a **pendant** to remind you.

pendulum /*say* **pen**-juh-luhm/ *noun* a weight swinging backward and forward, which makes some clocks work.

penetrate /*say* **pen**-uh-trayt/ *verb* If something **penetrates** something, it pierces it or breaks through it: *The arrow penetrated the target*; *Light penetrated the shadows.*
☐ **penetrable**, *adjective* –**penetrating**, *adjective*: *a penetrating stare*; *a penetrating mind.* –**penetratingly**, *adverb* –**penetration**, *noun*

penfriend *noun* someone, usually in another country, you have become friends with through writing letters.

penguin /*say* **peng**-gwuhn/ *noun* a bird which cannot fly, has webbed feet and lives in or near the cold southern parts of the world.

> WORD HISTORY from Old French words meaning 'white head'

penicillin /*say* pen-uh-**sil**-uhn/ *noun* a strong germ-fighting substance used in medicine.

> ☑ SPELLING TIP *Single/double letter alert*: only one *n* but a double *l*. Also note the *c* spelling for the 's' sound. This is a difficult word. It might help to think of the word *pencil*. Put an *i* in the middle between the *pen* and the *cil* and add *lin* at the end, and you have **penicillin**.

peninsula /*say* puh-**nin**-shuh-luh/ *noun* a long piece of land sticking out into the sea.
☐ **peninsular**, *adjective*

> WORD HISTORY from Latin words meaning 'almost an island'

penis /*say* **pee**-nuhs/ *noun* the part of a male's body with which he urinates and has sexual intercourse.

penitent /*say* **pen**-uh-tuhnt/ *adjective* feeling sorry for doing something wrong and willing to put things right.
☐ **penitence**, *noun* –**penitently**, *adverb*

> A SIMILAR WORD is **repentant**.

penitentiary /*say* pen-uh-**ten**-shuh-ree/ *noun* a jail or prison.

penknife *noun* (*plural* **penknives**) a small knife with one or more blades that fold into the handle so that it can be carried safely in a pocket.

> ANOTHER WORD for this is **pocketknife**.
> WORD HISTORY this kind of knife was once used to clean and mend the kind of old-fashioned pens which were made from feathers

pennant *noun* a triangular flag, used as a signal on ships or as an award in a sporting event.

penny *noun* (*plural* **pennies** *or* **pence**) a coin worth only a small amount, used in Britain and some other countries.
☐ **penniless**, *adjective* very poor; having no money: *They were penniless when they arrived in the country.*

pension *noun* a fixed regular payment made in consideration of old age, poverty, injury or loss, past services, etc.
☐ **pensioner**, *noun*

pensive *adjective* seriously or sadly thoughtful: *She seemed pensive and we knew something was wrong.*
☐ **pensively**, *adverb*

pentagon /*say* **pen**-tuh-gon/ *noun* a flat shape with five straight sides.
☐ **pentagonal** /*say* pen-**tag**-uh-nuhl/, *adjective*

penthouse *noun* a separate flat on the roof or top storey of a building.

penultimate /*say* puh-**nul**-tuh-muht/ *adjective* next to the last: *In the word 'happiness', 'ness' is* *the ultimate syllable and 'pi' is the penultimate syllable.*

people *noun*
1. humans in general. 2. all the members of a tribe, ethnic group or nation: *an island people*; *nomadic peoples.* 3. the members of a particular group: *the people of a village*; *working people.*

NOTE **People** is a collective noun and does not have a plural form, except for definition 2 when the plural **peoples** is used.

people smuggling *noun* an illegal trade in which people are transported from one country to another country which they are not authorised to enter as immigrants.
□ **people smuggler**, *noun*

pepita /*say* puh-**pee**-tuh/ *noun* a pumpkin seed which has been shelled, roasted and salted: *I often have a handful of pepitas for an afternoon snack.*

WORD HISTORY from a Spanish word meaning 'little seed'

pepper *noun*
1. a spice with a hot taste, made from the dried fruit of a tropical plant. 2. a capsicum.
□ **peppery**, *adjective*

peppermint *noun*
1. a garden herb grown for its strong-tasting, strong-smelling oil. 2. a sweet flavoured with peppermint.

perceive *verb*
1. If you **perceive** something, you notice it by means of your senses, such as sight or hearing, or by your understanding: *Perceiving that she wanted to be alone, I quietly left the room.* 2. If people **perceive** something or someone in a particular way, they think about them in a certain way: *He is generally perceived to be a fine speaker.*
□ **perceivable**, *adjective*

per cent *adverb* for or out of every hundred: *The price has increased by ten per cent, so instead of costing $100, it now costs $110.*

ANOTHER FORM is **percent**.
THE SYMBOL for this is %.

percentage *noun*
1. a number which shows the rate in every hundred: *I got seven out of ten – or, as a percentage, seventy.* 2. a part or proportion: *A large percentage of the atmosphere is nitrogen.*

perception /*say* puh-**sep**-shuhn/ *noun*
1. the act of perceiving or the ability to perceive: *Sorry I'm late again, my perception of time is not good*; *Some birds have very good visual perception.* 2. the ability to understand the inner nature of something quickly and clearly: *His decisions are usually correct because he has good perception.* 3. understanding or knowledge: *Have you any perception of the trouble you've caused?*
□ **perceptive**, *adjective*

perch[1] *noun* (*plural* **perches**)
1. a rod for birds to roost on.
–*verb* 2. If someone or something **perches**, they settle or rest on a perch or something similar: *Martin perched on the edge of his chair*; *A kookaburra perching in the tree carefully watched the lizard below.*

perch[2] *noun* (*plural* **perches** *or* **perch**) any of a number of types of Australian fish that you can eat.

percolate *verb*
1. If liquid **percolates** through a substance, it passes through it: *The ground was so hard that the first rains could not percolate through it.* 2. If something **percolates**, it spreads or becomes known gradually: *Laughter and music percolated through the house*; *News of her departure gradually percolated through the school.*
□ **percolator**, *noun* a coffee-maker in which boiling water is percolated through ground coffee.
–**percolation**, *noun*

A SIMILAR WORD is **filter**.

percussion /*say* puh-**kush**-uhn/ *noun*
1. the hitting of one thing against another. 2. musical instruments, such as drums and cymbals, that you play by hitting or shaking them.
□ **percussionist**, *noun*

percussion instrument *noun* a musical instrument, such as a drum, cymbal, or piano, which produces notes when it is struck.
□ **percussionist**, *noun*

perennial /*say* puh-**ren**-ee-uhl/ *adjective*
1. Something **perennial** lasts for a long time or continually comes back: *a perennial joke*; *a perennial nuisance.* 2. A **perennial** plant has a life cycle of more than two years.
–*noun* 3. a perennial plant.
□ **perennially**, *adverb*

COMPARE definition 3 with **annual** (definition 2).

perentie /*say* puh-**ren**-tee/ *noun* the largest Australian lizard, dark in colour with large pale yellow spots.

ANOTHER SPELLING is **perenti**.
WORD HISTORY from an Aboriginal language of South Australia called Diyari

perfect *adjective* /*say* **per**-fuhkt/
1. without fault or correct in every detail: *Very few people get a perfect score.* 2. undamaged or complete: *in perfect condition.* 3. so good that it could not possibly be better: *The weather has been perfect all week.* 4. completely suitable: *I have found the perfect dress to wear to the party*; *That would be a perfect present for her.* 5. complete or absolute: *She is a perfect stranger to me.*

I have never seen her before. **6.** having to do with the form of a verb which shows that something continues up to the present (*I have seen*), to some point in the past (*I had seen*), or into the future (*I will have seen*).
–*verb /say* per-**fekt**/ **7.** If you **perfect** something, you improve it until you have got it exactly right: *He perfected his command of Japanese.*
☐ **perfectly**, *adverb* –**perfection**, *noun* –**perfectionist**, *noun*

SEE the Grammar and Punctuation Guide appendix (for definition 6).

perforate */say* **per**-fuh-rayt/ *verb* If you **perforate** something, you make a hole or holes in it: *The boxes had been perforated so that the chickens inside could breathe.*
☐ **perforated**, *adjective* –**perforation**, *noun*

perform *verb*
1. If you **perform**, you appear in public in something such as a play: *She is performing in the school play every night this week.* **2.** If you **perform** a play, you present it: *We decided to perform Shakespeare's 'Romeo and Juliet'.* **3.** If you **perform** a job, you do it: *He has always performed his duties diligently.* **4.** To **perform** is to behave or do something in a certain way: *She didn't perform well in the exam because she was sick.*
☐ **performance**, *noun* –**performer**, *noun*

perfume *noun*
1. a liquid prepared so that it gives out a pleasant smell. **2.** a pleasant smell: *the perfume of roses.*

pergola */say* puh-**goh**-luh, **per**-guh-luh/ *noun* a shelter formed of bars supported on posts, over which climbing plants are grown.

perhaps *adverb* maybe or possibly: *Perhaps he'd come if he knew it was a party.*

peril *noun* danger or risk: *They have braved great perils in search of adventure.*
☐ **perilous**, *adjective*

perimeter */say* puh-**rim**-uh-tuh/ *noun*
1. the outside edge of a shape or area: *the perimeter of a lake.* **2.** the length of this edge.

period *noun*
1. any division of time: *long periods of sunshine.* **2.** a particular division of time or history: *the colonial period in India.* **3.** the monthly flow of blood from the uterus of a girl or woman, or the time when this happens. **4.** in geology, the main division of a geological era, shown in the earth's crust by the layers of rocks laid down.
☐ **periodic**, **periodical**, *adjective* –**periodically**, *adverb*

periphery */say* puh-**rif**-uh-ree/ *noun* the outside edge of an area or thing: *Some very odd people were standing on the periphery of the crowd.*
☐ **peripheral**, *adjective* not central in importance. –**peripherally**, *adverb*

periscope *noun* an instrument made of a tube with an arrangement of mirrors, used to see something from a position below or behind it: *the periscope of a submarine.*

perish *verb*
1. If someone **perishes**, they die, usually in a sudden or unnatural way: *The climbers perished in the snow.* **2.** If a material **perishes**, it rots or decays: *This leather is no good any more – it has perished.*
☐ **perishable**, *adjective*

perjury */say* **per**-juh-ree/ *noun* the crime of telling a lie while under an oath: *She was charged with perjury because she lied in the witness box.*

☑ SPELLING TIP *Tricky vowel sound*: remember the *u* in the *ury* ending (not *ary* or *ery*). Like the word *jury* itself, this word comes from the Latin word *jurare*, meaning 'to swear an oath'.

perk[1] *verb in the phrase* **perk up**, to feel better and become more cheerful.
☐ **perky**, *adjective*

perk[2] *noun Informal* an extra benefit or payment that someone gets in a job, in addition to their normal salary: *One of the perks of the job is free overseas trips.*

permanent */say* **per**-muh-nuhnt/ *adjective* to last for a very long time or forever: *a permanent water supply*; *a permanent limp.*
☐ **permanence**, *noun* –**permanency**, *noun* –**permanently**, *adverb*

THE OPPOSITE is **temporary**.

☑ SPELLING TIP *Tricky 'uh' sound*: the vowel sound in the middle is spelt with an *a*. Try thinking that there is a *mane* in this word. This will also help you remember the *ent* ending.

permeate */say* **per**-mee-ayt/ *verb* If something **permeates**, it passes or spreads through: *As the tide came in, a feeling of fear permeated the group in the cave.*
☐ **permeable**, *adjective* able to be passed through, especially by liquids: *a permeable membrane.*

permission *noun* the act of permitting or allowing someone to do something.

permissive *adjective* allowing freedom, especially in sexual or moral matters: *Some people think our society has become too permissive.*
☐ **permissively**, *adverb* –**permissiveness**, *noun*

permit *verb /say* puh-**mit**/ (**permits**, **permitting**, **permitted**, **has permitted**)
1. To **permit** someone to do something is to allow them to do it: *Swimming is permitted in this area only.*

–*noun* /*say* **per**-mit/ **2.** an official certificate that gives permission.

A SIMILAR WORD (for definition 2) is **licence** (definition 1).

peroxide /*say* puh-**rok**-suyd/ *noun* a chemical that is often used to bleach or lighten hair.
☐ **peroxide**, *adjective*: *They jeered at his peroxide blond hair.*

perpendicular /*say* per-puhn-**dik**-yuh-luh/ *adjective*
1. upright or vertical: *a perpendicular pole.* **2.** meeting a line or surface at right angles.
☐ **perpendicular**, *noun*: *on the perpendicular.*

perpetrate *verb* If someone **perpetrates** a wrong action such as a deception or crime, they carry it out: *They perpetrated a hoax that fooled everybody.*
☐ **perpetration**, *noun* –**perpetrator**, *noun*

perpetual /*say* puh-**pech**-ooh-uhl/ *adjective*
1. lasting for ever: *the perpetual changing of the seasons.* **2.** continuing without a break: *I get tired of his perpetual complaints.*
☐ **perpetually**, *adverb*

☑ SPELLING TIP Remember the *t* in this word. With the *u* following it has a 'ch' sound and you don't hear the *t*.

perplex /*say* puh-**pleks**/ *verb* If something or someone **perplexes** you, they puzzle you: *We were perplexed by his mysterious behaviour.*
☐ **perplexed**, *adjective* –**perplexing**, *adjective* –**perplexity**, *noun*

SIMILAR WORDS are **confuse** and **bewilder**.

persecute /*say* **per**-suh-kyooht/ *verb* If someone **persecutes** you, they harm you or treat you unjustly, often because of religious or political beliefs: *The regime was accused of persecuting ethnic minorities.*
☐ **persecution**, *noun* –**persecutor**, *noun*

persevere /*say* per-suh-**vear**/ *verb* To **persevere** is to continue in spite of difficulty: *I will persevere with this question until I get it right.*
☐ **perseverance**, *noun*

A SIMILAR WORD is **persist**.

persimmon /*say* **per**-suh-muhn, puh-**sim**-uhn/ *noun* a red or orange plum-like fruit.

WORD HISTORY from an Algonquian (a language of some Native American Indian peoples) word meaning '(artificially) dried fruit'

persist *verb* To **persist** is to **1.** continue doing something, often in spite of difficulty: *He persisted ringing the bell until someone answered.* **2.** go on and on: *The pain persisted for hours.*
☐ **persistence**, *noun* –**persistent**, *adjective* –**persistently**, *adverb*

A SIMILAR WORD (for definition 1) is **persevere**.

person *noun*
1. a human being. **2.** a type of verb or pronoun form that shows the difference between the speaker (**first person**), the person spoken to (**second person**), and anyone or anything spoken about (**third person**).
–*phrase* **3. in person**, with the person actually present: *She delivered the note in person.*

SEE the Grammar and Punctuation Guide appendix (for definition 2).

personage *noun* a person, especially someone important.

personal *adjective*
1. private or having to do with a particular person: *a personal opinion*; *personal belongings.* **2.** directed to a particular person in a rude way: *I take that as a personal insult!*
☐ **personally**, *adverb*

personal computer *noun* a small computer that can be placed on a desk or table.

THE ABBREVIATION is **PC**.

personality *noun* (*plural* **personalities**)
1. the qualities of character that make someone a particular person, different from everyone else: *She's got a very friendly personality.* **2.** strong and interesting qualities of character: *I don't know why she wants to marry him – he has no personality at all.* **3.** someone who is well-known: *a television personality.*

A SIMILAR WORD (for definition 3) is **celebrity**.

personify *verb* (**personifies**, **personifying**, **personified**, **has personified**)
1. To **personify** something is to give a human nature or form to it: *Ancient legends personified mountains, lakes, animals and trees, so that each one was given a human shape and nature.* **2.** To **personify** some quality is to provide a perfect example of it: *The two characters in the play personified good and evil.*
☐ **personification**, *noun*

personnel /*say* per-suh-**nel**/ *noun* the group of people working for a particular organisation.

☑ SPELLING TIP *Double letter alert*: double *n*. Don't confuse this word with **personal** (meaning 'private'). Both of them contain the word *person* but in **personnel** the *n* is doubled and the ending is *el*. It is spelt like this because it comes from French.

perspective *noun*
1. the appearance of distance as well as height and width, produced on a flat surface, such as in a painting: *Your drawing of the street has a good perspective.* **2.** a mental point of view: *I now have a new perspective on the problem.*

–*phrase* **3. in perspective**, with a proper balance: *You should keep things in perspective, rather than concentrating on the one bad thing she did.*

perspire *verb* To **perspire** is to get rid of a salty liquid through the pores of your skin.
□ **perspiration**, *noun*

ANOTHER WORD for this is **sweat** (definition 1).

persuade /*say* puh-**swayd**/ *verb* If you **persuade** someone to do something, you talk to them and get them to agree to do it, although at first they do not want to: *We persuaded Yusef to come to the beach with us.*
□ **persuasive**, *adjective*

☑ SPELLING TIP Remember that there is no *w* in **persuade**. The letters *su* spell the 'sw' sound.

persuasion *noun*
1. the act or power of persuading. **2.** a belief, especially religious: *Our society includes people of many different persuasions.*

pert *adjective*
1. confident and cheeky: *a pert child.* **2.** attractive in an energetic way: *a pert smile.*
□ **pertly**, *adverb* –**pertness**, *noun*

pertinent *adjective* having to do with the matter being discussed or thought about: *Please only ask questions that are pertinent to what we are discussing.*
□ **pertinence**, *noun* –**pertinently**, *adverb*

A SIMILAR WORD is **relevant**.

perturb *verb* If something **perturbs** you, it disturbs or worries you greatly: *Seeing how big the kids on the other side were perturbed us.*
□ **perturbation**, *noun*

☑ SPELLING TIP Remember that there are two separate *r*'s in this word, the first following an *e* and the second following a *u*.

perverse *adjective* deliberately going against what is expected or wanted: *Because of his perverse behaviour, he was sent out of the room.*
□ **perversely**, *adverb* –**perverseness**, *noun* –**perversity**, *noun*

pervert *noun* /*say* **per**-vert/
1. someone who has unusual or unpleasant sexual habits.
–*verb* /*say* puh-**vert**/ **2.** to turn away from the right path: *The men were accused of perverting the course of justice.*
□ **perversion**, *noun* –**perverted**, *adjective*

pessimism /*say* **pez**-uh-miz-uhm/ *noun* the habit of expecting that things will turn out badly.
□ **pessimist**, *noun* –**pessimistic**, *adjective*

THE OPPOSITE is **optimism**.

☑ SPELLING TIP *Double letter alert*: double *s* for the first 's' sound (think of a 'sad sack' to remind you). Also remember that the 'uh' sound in the middle is spelt with an *i*.

pest *noun*
1. a small animal or insect, such as a rat or cockroach, which damages food or crops. **2.** *Rather informal* someone or something that is annoying: *Little brothers can be a real pest.*
□ **pestilent**, *adjective*

pester *verb* If someone **pesters** you, they annoy you by disturbing you when you are busy or by keeping on asking you to do something.

pesticide /*say* **pest**-uh-suyd/ *noun* a chemical for killing animals that are dangerous or harmful.

☑ SPELLING TIP Remember the *c* spelling for the 's' sound in this word. The suffix *-cide* means 'killer' or 'act of killing' and appears in several other words, such as *suicide*. It comes from the Latin word for 'kill'.

pestle /*say* **pes**-uhl/ *noun* a short tool with a round end, used for breaking up and grinding substances in a mortar.

WORD HISTORY from a Latin word meaning 'pounded'

☑ SPELLING TIP *Silent letter alert*: don't forget the *st* (not double *s*) spelling. The *t* is silent.

pesto *noun* a thick sauce made of pine nuts, garlic, basil, cheese and oil, mixed into a paste, originating in Italian cooking.

WORD HISTORY from an Italian word meaning 'paste'

pet *noun*
1. an animal that you keep in your home and treat with affection. **2.** a person who is given special attention: *teacher's pet.*
–*verb* (**pets**, **petting**, **petted**, **has petted**) **3.** If you **pet** someone, you touch them in an affectionate way, for example by giving them kisses and loving pats: *She petted the child until his sobs ceased.*

petal *noun* any of the soft floral leaves of a flower which are usually of a colour other than green.

☑ SPELLING TIP Remember that the ending is *al*.

petite /*say* puh-**teet**/ *adjective* small and delicate: *a petite woman.*

☑ SPELLING TIP Remember that the ending is *ite*, giving an 'eet' sound. This is because **petite** comes from French.

petition *noun*
1. a formal request, especially to someone or a group in power: *We signed a petition to the government.*

–*verb* **2.** If you **petition** someone, you send a petition to them: *to petition the council for a new park.*
☐ **petitioner**, *noun*

petrify *verb* (**petrifies**, **petrifying**, **petrified**, **has petrified**)
1. If something **petrifies** you, it makes you stiff or unable to move with fear. **2.** If something is **petrified**, it is changed into stone or something like stone: *Over millions of years the tree trunk had been petrified into a rock.*
☐ **petrifaction**, *noun*

petrol *noun* a liquid made from petroleum, used widely as a fuel in engines.

petroleum *noun* an oily liquid, usually obtained from under the ground, and used to make petrol or other fuels.

☑ SPELLING TIP This is where *petrol* comes from, so if you know how to spell this word, with its *ol* (not *el*) ending, you are almost there. Just remember that the ending of **petroleum** is *eum* (not *ium*).

petticoat *noun* a light, skirt-like piece of clothing sometimes worn under dresses by women and girls.

ANOTHER WORD for this is **slip** (definition 6).

petty *adjective* (**pettier**, **pettiest**)
1. If something is **petty**, it is of little importance: *petty problems.* **2.** If someone is **petty**, they are concerned with unimportant things or show narrow ideas and interests: *a petty attitude.*
☐ **pettily**, *adverb* –**pettiness**, *noun*

A SIMILAR WORD (for definition 1) is **trivial**.

petulant *adjective* showing or feeling impatient annoyance, especially over something unimportant: *'Well, I don't care anyway', she said in a petulant voice.*
☐ **petulance**, *noun* –**petulantly**, *adverb*

pew *noun* a long, plain seat in a church.

pewter *noun* a special mix of metals, including tin, used for making dishes and so on.

phalanger /*say* fuh-**lan**-juh/ *noun* one of the Australian marsupials which live in trees and which have tails that can wrap around branches, such as cuscuses and brush-tailed possums.

phantom *noun*
1. an image appearing in a dream or in the mind only. **2.** a ghost.

pharmacy /*say* **fah**-muh-see/ *noun* (*plural* **pharmacies**)
1. the preparing and giving out of drugs used in medicine: *My sister is studying pharmacy at university.* **2.** a shop selling medicines; a chemist's shop.
☐ **pharmacist**, *noun*

☑ SPELLING TIP Remember that there is no *s* in **pharmacy** and that it has nothing to do with a farm. Concentrate on the *ph* beginning and the *acy* ending.

pharynx /*say* **fa**-rinks/ *noun* (*plural* **pharynxes** *or* **pharynges** /*say* fuh-**rin**-jeez/) the tube which connects the mouth and nose passages with the throat.

☑ SPELLING TIP *Letter 'y' alert*: remember the *y* in the second syllable of this word, spelling the 'i' sound. Like many words having to do with medicine or the body, **pharynx** comes from Greek.

phase *noun*
1. a stage of change or development: *the final phase of the war.*
–*phrase* **2. phase in**, to introduce gradually so as to fit into a system, and so on: *to phase in wearing hats to school.* **3. phase out**, to take out gradually from a system or way of doing things: *to phase out school uniforms.*

pheasant /*say* **fez**-uhnt/ *noun* a kind of large, long-tailed bird, often eaten as food.

phenomenon /*say* fuh-**nom**-uh-nuhn/ *noun* (*plural* **phenomena**)
1. anything which is seen or able to be seen: *A tsunami is a natural phenomenon.* **2.** something or someone that is outside the ordinary.
☐ **phenomenal**, *adjective* –**phenomenally**, *adverb*

phial /*say* **fuy**-uhl/ *noun* a small glass container for liquids: *The phial was three quarters full.*

☑ SPELLING TIP Don't confuse **phial** with **file** which has almost the same sound. A **file** is a folder or something you use for smoothing and grinding. Concentrate on saying **phial** with two syllables (as shown in the pronunciation guide) to help you remember that it has two vowels in the middle – an *i* and then an *a*.

philately /*say* fuh-**lat**-uh-lee/ *noun* the collecting and studying of postage stamps.
☐ **philatelic** /*say* fil-uh-**tel**-ik/, *adjective* –**philatelist**, *noun*

☑ SPELLING TIP This rather difficult word comes from Greek. Remember the *ph* spelling for the 'f' sound at the start. This will be easier if you see the **philately** starts with the prefix *phil-* (meaning 'love of'). Notice that this prefix appears in several of the following words. The other difficult part is the *ely* ending.

philharmonic *adjective* a term meaning 'fond of music', used in the names of some musical societies, choirs or orchestras.

philistine /*say* **fil**-uh-stuyn/ *noun* someone who does not like or is not interested in beautiful things

such as paintings, sculpture or music, and is proud to be that way.
☐ **philistine**, *adjective* –**philistinism**, *noun*

WORD HISTORY named after the people of *Philistia*, an ancient country on the east coast of the Mediterranean Sea, who were thought to be barbarians

philosophy /*say* fuh-**los**-uh-fee/ *noun* (*plural* **philosophies**)
1. the search for knowledge and the answers to questions such as 'Why do I exist?' and 'What is the purpose of life?'. **2.** a system of rules or principles by which you live: *Her philosophy was to always look for good in a person.*
☐ **philosopher**, *noun* –**philosophical**, *adjective* –**philosophise**, *verb*: *to philosophise about life.*

ANOTHER SPELLING for **philosophise** is **philosophize**.
WORD HISTORY from a Greek word meaning 'love of knowledge'

phishing /*say* **fish**-ing/ *noun* a type of internet fraud where an email that is supposed to be from a legitimate organisation, such as a bank, is actually from somebody trying to trick the receiver of the email into revealing personal information, such as credit card details, which they can then use to their own advantage.

WORD HISTORY from the idea of *fishing* with the *f* replaced with *ph*, standing for 'password harvesting'

phlegm /*say* flem/ *noun* thick mucus in your nose, throat or lungs, often as a result of a cold.
☐ **phlegmy**, *adjective*

☑ SPELLING TIP *Silent letter alert*: don't forget the silent *g* before the *m*. Also remember the *ph* spelling which makes an 'f' sound, as in many other words.

phlegmatic /*say* fleg-**mat**-ik/ *adjective* calm in a situation where other people might get angry, excited, frightened, etc.

phobia /*say* **foh**-bee-uh/ *noun* a very strong fear: *a phobia about flying.*
☐ **phobic**, *adjective*

NOTE This word is often joined with another word part to indicate fear of that particular thing, as in *claustrophobia* which means 'fear of being shut in a small space' or *arachnophobia* which means 'fear of spiders'.

phoenix /*say* **fee**-niks/ *noun* a mythical bird of great beauty, said to burn on a funeral pyre and then to rise from the ashes young again.

☑ SPELLING TIP *Tricky vowel sound*: *oe* for the 'ee' sound.

phone *noun* See **telephone**.

phonetics *noun* the study of the sounds used in speaking.
☐ **phonetic**, *adjective*: *phonetic symbols.* –**phonetically**, *adverb*

phoney *adjective Informal* false or not real: *a phoney banknote.*

phosphorescent /*say* fos-fuh-**res**-uhnt/ *adjective* shining or giving out light without getting hot.
☐ **phosphorescence**, *noun*

☑ SPELLING TIP This word is formed from *phosphorus*. The *us* ending has been dropped and the suffix *-escent* (meaning 'doing' or 'becoming') has been added. Remember the silent *c* in this suffix, just as in the word *scent*.

phosphorus /*say* **fos**-fuh-ruhs/ *noun* a chemical element which is used in making match heads, detergents and garden fertilisers.
☐ **phosphate**, *noun* a garden fertiliser made from phosphorus.

☑ SPELLING TIP Remember that the letter combination *ph* (giving an 'f' sound) appears twice in **phosphorus**. Also remember the *us* ending. This word comes from Greek where it was formed by joining *phos* (meaning 'light') and *-phoros* (meaning 'bringing'). The ending was changed when it became part of Latin where *us* is a common ending.

photo *noun* (*plural* **photos**) See **photograph**.

photobomb *verb*
1. To **photobomb** is to put yourself, accidentally or on purpose, into the way of a photograph that is being taken of someone or something else, so that you appear in the photograph in a funny or distracting way.
–*noun* **2.** a photograph in which someone appears unexpectedly in a funny or distracting way.
☐ **photobombing**, *noun*

photocopy *noun* (*plural* **photocopies**)
1. an exact copy of a page of writing or pictures, made by a machine using a special camera and paper which reacts to light.
–*verb* (**photocopies**, **photocopying**, **photocopied**, **has photocopied**) **2.** When you **photocopy** a page of writing or pictures, you make a photocopy of it.
☐ **photocopier**, *noun* a machine that makes photocopies.

ANOTHER WORD for this is **photostat**.

photogenic *adjective* looking attractive in photographs.

photograph *noun*
1. an image produced by the chemical effect of light on a light-sensitive surface such as film.
–*verb* **2.** When you **photograph** someone or something, you use a camera to take a photograph of them.
☐ **photographer**, *noun* –**photographic**,

adjective –**photography**, *noun* the art of taking photographs.

THE SHORT FORM (of definition 1) is **photo**.

photosynthesis /*say* foh-toh-**sin**-thuh-suhs/ *noun* the making of carbohydrates (sugars) by plants from carbon dioxide and water in the presence of light and chlorophyll (the green colouring in plants).

phrase *noun*
1. a small group of words that go together, usually without a complete verb. **2.** a group of musical notes which go together to form part of a tune.

SEE the Grammar and Punctuation Guide appendix (for definition 1).

phylum /*say* **fuy**-luhm/ *noun* (*plural* **phyla** /*say* **fuy**-luh/) one of the main groups into which biologists classify animals and plants: *Sea sponges are in a phylum of their own.*

☑ SPELLING TIP *Letter 'y' alert*: remember the *phy* spelling at the start of this word. Don't get confused by thinking that this word is related to *file*. **Phylum** comes from a Greek word meaning 'tribe'.

physical *adjective*
1. having to do with things you can see and touch: *our physical surroundings.* **2.** having to do with the human body: *The athlete has great physical strength.*
☐ **physically**, *adverb*: *physically fit.*

physician /*say* fuh-**zish**-uhn/ *noun* a medical doctor, especially one who does not do surgery.

physics *noun* the science of heat, light, electricity, magnetism, motion, and other forms of matter and energy.
☐ **physicist**, *noun*

physiology /*say* fiz-ee-**ol**-uh-jee/ *noun* the science that has to do with the bodies of living things and how they work.
☐ **physiological**, *adjective* –**physiologist**, *noun*

physiotherapy *noun* the treatment of disease and injuries by physical means such as massage and exercise.
☐ **physiotherapist**, *noun*

physique /*say* fuh-**zeek**/ *noun* the shape of someone's body: *a muscular physique.*

☑ SPELLING TIP **Physique** comes from French where it is an adjective meaning 'physical'. This should help you to remember the *phys* beginning. The *ique* ending, which sounds like 'eek', appears in several other words that have come from French, such as *antique* and *technique*.

pi /*rhymes with* my/ *noun* the number you always get, 3.141 592+, when you divide the circumference of a circle by its diameter, expressed by the symbol π.

piano[1] *noun* (*plural* **pianos**) a large musical instrument played by striking keys which are connected to hammers which then strike metal strings.
☐ **pianist**, *noun*

WORD HISTORY short for the Italian word *pianoforte*

piano[2] *adverb* softly.
☐ **pianissimo**, *adverb* very softly.

THE OPPOSITE is **forte**[2] (written as **f**).
NOTE This is an instruction in music where it is written as **p** (or **pp** for *pianissimo*). Like most musical instructions, it comes from Italian.

piccolo /*say* **pik**-uh-loh/ *noun* (*plural* **piccolos**) a small flute with a very high sound.

☑ SPELLING TIP *Double/single letter alert*: double *c* but only one *l*. Also notice the *o* ending. **Piccolo** is spelt like this because it comes from Italian (meaning 'small').

pick[1] *verb*
1. If you **pick** something or someone, you choose them: *to pick a place to go on holiday*; *He was picked for the basketball team.* **2.** If you **pick** flowers or fruit, you gather them from where they are growing. **3.** If someone **picks** a lock they use something apart from the right key to open it.
–*noun* **4.** a choice or selection: *Take your pick.* **5.** See **plectrum**.
–*phrase* **6. pick at**, to eat almost none of: *to pick at your food.* **7. pick holes in**, to find fault with. **8. pick on**, to tease or criticise. **9. pick out**, **a.** to choose. **b.** to see separately from surrounding things. **c.** to make out: *Can you pick out the meaning of the code?* **d.** to take out by picking. **10. pick up**, **a.** to call for: *My mother will pick me up from school.* **b.** to learn easily, without special teaching: *Did you pick up any French when you were in New Caledonia?* **c.** to get well again.
☐ **picker**, *noun*

pick[2] *noun* a tool made up of a metal bar with sharp ends, fitted to a wooden handle and used for breaking up hard ground.

ANOTHER WORD for this is **pickaxe**.

picket *noun*
1. a pointed wooden fence post. **2.** a group of members of a trade union who prevent access to their place of work during a strike.

pickle *noun*
1. an onion or other vegetable preserved in vinegar or salt water.
–*verb* **2.** To **pickle** a food is to preserve it in vinegar or salt water.
☐ **pickled**, *adjective*: *pickled onions.*

pickpocket *noun* someone who steals things out of people's pockets or bags, etc., in public places.

picnic *noun*
1. a meal eaten in the open air, usually in pleasant surroundings such as the country, a park, a beach, etc.
–*verb* (**picnics**, **picnicking**, **picnicked**, **has picnicked**) **2.** When people **picnic**, they eat a picnic: *to picnic in the park.*

☑ SPELLING TIP Remember that this word ends in *ic* (not *ick*). However, when you add *-ed* or *-ing*, the *k* is added.

pictogram *noun*
1. a written symbol representing something by a simple drawing of it, or of something associated with it, and not by its name or the sound of its name. **2.** a chart on which information is represented by symbols.

ANOTHER NAME (for definition 1) is **pictograph**.

picture *noun*
1. a drawing, painting, photograph or something similar. **2.** someone or something that looks very beautiful: *The baby looks a picture when he is asleep like that.* **3. the pictures**, the cinema: *Do you want to go to the pictures tomorrow? There's a good film on.*
–*verb* **4.** When you **picture** something, you imagine it in your mind: *I can't really picture him getting up early every morning for swimming training*; *Can you picture the scene?*

☑ SPELLING TIP Don't confuse the spelling of **picture** with **pitcher** which has a similar sound. In baseball, a **pitcher** is the player who throws the ball.

picturesque /*say* pik-chuh-**resk**/ *adjective* pretty or charming: *It was a picturesque setting for a film.*
□ **picturesquely**, *adverb*

☑ SPELLING TIP The basic meaning of **picturesque** is 'like a picture'. You know the spelling of *picture*, so all you need to remember is the *-esque* suffix (meaning 'like' or 'in the style of') in place of the final *e*. This suffix gives an 'esk' sound because it comes from French. Another word with this ending is *grotesque*.

pidgin /*say* **pij**-uhn/ *noun* a language based on a mixture of other languages and used by people who have no other language in common.

☑ SPELLING TIP Don't confuse the spelling of **pidgin** with **pigeon** which has the same sound. A **pigeon** is a kind of bird.

pie *noun* a pastry case filled with fruit, vegetables, or meat and baked in an oven.

piebald *adjective* A **piebald** animal is covered with patches of black and white or other colours: *She was riding a piebald pony.*

piece *noun*
1. a bit or part of something. **2.** a single thing: *a piece of fruit.*
–*phrase Informal* **3. a piece of cake**, something that is very easy to achieve. **4. a piece of your mind**, strong criticism: *He deserves a piece of your mind after that disgraceful behaviour.* **5. go to pieces**, to lose emotional or physical control of yourself.

☑ SPELLING TIP Don't confuse **piece** with **peace** which has the same sound. **Peace** is freedom from war or trouble.

piecemeal *adverb* piece by piece or in untidy stages.
□ **piecemeal**, *adjective*

pied /*rhymes with* side/ *adjective* covered with different coloured patches: *A pied butcherbird visits our yard.*

WORD HISTORY from the word *magpie*, as this bird has black-and-white feathers

pier /*rhymes with* here/ *noun*
1. a jetty built out into the water, that you can tie a boat to or fish from. **2.** one of the wooden or concrete supports which are driven into the ground to hold up a bridge.

ANOTHER WORD (for definition 2) is **pile^2**.

☑ SPELLING TIP Don't confuse the spelling of **pier** with **peer** which has the same sound. To **peer** at something is to look at it closely.

pierce *verb* If something sharp **pierces** an object, it makes a hole in it and goes into or through it: *The arrow pierced the target*; *Headlights pierced the darkness.*

☑ SPELLING TIP *Tricky vowel sound*: *ier* spelling for the 'ear' sound. This follows the rule that *i* comes before *e* except after *c*.

piety /*say* **puy**-uh-tee/ *noun* deep honour and respect for religion.

pig *noun*
1. a farm animal with a flat snout and curly tail, which is kept for its meat. **2.** *Informal* someone who is dirty, selfish or greedy.

NOTE The male is a **boar**; the female is a **sow**; the young is a **piglet**.

pigeon /*say* **pij**-uhn/ *noun* a small-headed, usually grey bird which is often found in cities.

☑ SPELLING TIP Remember that there is a *pig* in this word, but with the *g* giving a 'j' sound which you might think would be spelt *dg*. Also remember the silent *e* before the *on* ending. Don't confuse **pigeon** with **pidgin** which has the same sound. **Pidgin** is a language based on a mix of other languages.

pigeonhole *noun* a small compartment for papers in an old-fashioned desk, cabinet, etc.

piggyback *noun*
1. a ride on the back or shoulders or someone else.
–*verb* 2. When you **piggyback** someone, you give them a piggyback.

pig-headed *adjective* stupidly stubborn or obstinate.

piglet *noun* a baby pig.

pigment *noun*
1. a coloured powder which can be mixed with water to make paint. 2. the substance which gives animals and plants colour.
☐ **pigmentation**, *noun*

pigsty *noun* (*plural* **pigsties**)
1. a place where pigs are kept. 2. *Informal* any dirty or untidy place: *You should tidy up your room – it's a real pigsty.*

ANOTHER WORD (for definition 1) is **piggery**.

pigtail *noun* a bunch of tied-up hair hanging from the side or back of the head.

pike[1] *noun* a large, fierce freshwater fish of the Northern Hemisphere.

pike[2] *verb Informal* If you **pike**, or if you **pike** on someone, you let them down by not keeping to an arrangement, especially an arrangement to meet them or go out with them: *We were all annoyed with him for piking and not coming to the party.*
☐ **piker**, *noun*

pikelet *noun* a small sweet pancake, often eaten with butter and jam.

pilchard /*say* **pil**-chuhd/ *noun* a kind of small fish.

pile[1] *noun*
1. a number of things put on top of each other. 2. a large amount or number: *The pile of clothes on my bedroom floor has got bigger.*
–*verb in the phrase* 3. **pile up**, to collect together: *My little brother was piling up mud to make channels for the water.*

pile[2] *noun* a long, heavy beam driven into the ground to support a bridge or building.

SIMILAR WORDS are **pier** and **pylon**.

pile[3] *noun* the raised surface of carpet, towels, velvet and similar material.

pilfer *verb* If someone **pilfers** something, they steal small amounts of it: *Someone has been pilfering food out of the kitchen.*
☐ **pilferer**, *noun*

pilgrim *noun* someone who makes a long journey to visit a holy place.
☐ **pilgrimage**, *noun*

WORD HISTORY from a Latin word meaning 'foreigner'

pill *noun* a small, round, flat object containing medicine, to be swallowed whole.

ANOTHER WORD for this is **tablet** (definition 1).

pillage *verb* To **pillage** is to rob brutally and violently, as in war: *When the city collapsed, the soldiers pillaged the houses.*
☐ **pillage**, *noun* –**pillager**, *noun*

A SIMILAR WORD is **plunder**.

pillar *noun* a column which supports part of a building.

☑ SPELLING TIP Remember the *ar* (not *er*) ending. Think of other words with this ending, such as *collar* and *dollar*.

pillion *noun* the passenger seat behind the driver's seat on a motorcycle.
☐ **pillion**, *adjective*: *a pillion passenger.*

WORD HISTORY from a Latin word meaning 'skin' or 'pelt'

pillow *noun* a bag filled with soft material to rest your head on when you are in bed.

pilot *noun*
1. someone who flies an aircraft. 2. someone who steers a ship into or out of port.
–*verb* 3. When someone **pilots** an aircraft or a ship, they act as its pilot.
–*adjective* 4. done as an experiment: *They are trying a pilot scheme this year.*

pimple *noun* a small swelling filled with pus, usually on the face.
☐ **pimply**, *adjective*

pin *noun*
1. a thin piece of metal with a sharply pointed end, used to fasten things together. 2. any type of fastener that looks or works like a pin. 3. a bottle-shaped object used in tenpin bowling.
–*verb* (**pins**, **pinning**, **pinned**, **has pinned**) 4. When you **pin** something or someone in a position, you fasten it there or hold it securely there: *Pin this badge on your coat*; *The police pinned the robber to the floor.*

PIN *noun* a group of numbers or letters you use to show who you are when you are doing something like getting money from an automatic teller machine.

ANOTHER FORM You can also say **PIN number**.
WORD HISTORY an acronym made by joining the first letters of *Personal Identification Number*

pinafore *noun* a dress with no sleeves and a low neck, worn over other clothes, often as a school uniform or apron.

pinball *noun* a game played on a sloping board, in which a ball, driven by a spring, hits pins or bumpers which electronically record the score.

pincers *plural noun* **1.** a tool with a pair of hinged parts, used for pulling nails out of wood. **2.** the claws of crabs, lobsters, and some insects, which can be brought together to hold things.

pinch *noun* (*plural* **pinches**)
1. a painful squeeze. **2.** the very small amount that you can hold between your finger and thumb: *a pinch of salt.*
–verb **3.** If you **pinch** a part of a person, you press or squeeze it between your thumb and finger: *She pinched him on the cheek.* **4.** *Informal* To **pinch** is to steal: *Someone has pinched my lunch!*

pine[1] *noun*
1. an evergreen tree with needle-like leaves and cones instead of flowers. **2.** the wood of this tree: *The table is made from pine.*

pine[2] *verb*
1. If you **pine**, you have an intense longing, or you yearn for someone or something: *Sarah had been away for a year and was pining for all the things she loved at home.*
–phrase **2. pine away**, to become sick from grief and longing: *After he died, she pined away.*

pineapple *noun* a large tropical fruit which has sweet yellow flesh inside and a rough outer skin.

pine nut *noun* a small nut that can be eaten, found in the cone of several kinds of pine tree.

ping-pong *noun* See **table tennis**.

pinion[1] *noun* a small toothed wheel which locks together with a toothed bar or larger wheel, used in machinery.

pinion[2] *noun*
1. a bird's wing or feather.
–verb **2.** To **pinion** a bird is to cut off part of a bird's wing to stop it flying away. **3.** To **pinion** a person is to prevent them escaping by tying back their arms and hands.

pink[1] *adjective*
1. of a colour that is between red and white; pale red.
–noun **2.** a pink colour.

pink[2] *verb* If you **pink** something like material, you cut it in a zigzag pattern.
☐ **pinking shears**, *noun* scissors with notched blades for cutting a zigzag line.

pinnacle /*say* **pin**-uh-kuhl/ *noun*
1. a high, pointed mountain top. **2.** the highest point of anything: *the pinnacle of fame.*

pint *noun* a measure of liquid in the imperial system equal to almost 600 millilitres.

pin-up *noun* a picture of a favourite person, pinned or stuck up on a wall.

pioneer *noun*
1. someone who first goes into an area, opening the way for others to follow: *a pioneer in unknown territory*; *a pioneer of modern music.*
–verb **2.** Someone who **pioneers** an activity or process is the first, or one of the first, to do it: *to pioneer digital photography.*

pious /*say* **puy**-uhs/ *adjective* deeply religious.
☐ **piously**, *adverb*

pip[1] *noun* the small seed of an apple, orange or similar fruit.

pip[2] *noun* a short, high sound such as the ones used as time signals on the radio.

pipe *noun*
1. a hollow tube for carrying water, gas and so on. **2.** a hollow tube or stem with a small bowl at the end used for smoking tobacco. **3.** a tube through which you can pump air to make musical notes, such as in an organ.
–verb **4.** To **pipe** a liquid or a gas is to transport it using a pipe: *to pipe water to the house.*
–phrase Informal **5. pipe down**, to keep quiet: *Pipe down or someone will hear us!* **6. pipe up**, to start talking suddenly.
☐ **pipeline**, *noun* a pipe for carrying gas, oil or water over a long distance.

pipi *noun* a shellfish that burrows in the sand and that is good to eat.

piping *noun*
1. a system of pipes such as for the plumbing of a house. **2.** the shrill sound made by birds. **3.** a thin strip of material for trimming the edges of cushions or clothes.
–adverb in the phrase **4. piping hot**, very hot.

piquant /*say* **peek**-uhnt, pee-**kont**/ *adjective* If food or drink is **piquant**, it is pleasantly spicy and sharp-tasting.

pique /*rhymes with* week/ *verb*
1. If someone or something **piques** you, it annoys and upsets you: *It piqued Mrs Brown that her friends hadn't commented on her brand new curtains.* **2.** If something **piques** your curiosity, it excites or stimulates it: *The subject of galactic travel piqued his curiosity.*
–noun **3.** anger or hurt feelings: *She's had a fit of pique about not getting into the team.*

> ☑ SPELLING TIP Remember the *ique* spelling of the 'eek' sound in this word which comes from French. Don't confuse with **peak** or **peek** both of which have the same sound. A **peak** is the top of a mountain. To **peek** is to take a quick look at something.

piranha /*say* puh-**rah**-nuh/ *noun* a small South American fish which swims in schools that attack animals, including people, and eat their flesh at great speed.

☑ SPELLING TIP *Silent letter alert*: don't forget the *h* before the final *a*. **Piranha** is spelt in this way because it comes from Portuguese.

pirate *noun*
1. someone who attacks and robs ships at sea.
–*verb* **2.** If someone **pirates** something that someone else has invented, designed or composed, they use that person's ideas without permission: *It is illegal to pirate CDs and videos.*
☐ **piracy**, *noun*

pirouette /*say* pi-rooh-**et**/ *noun*
1. a quick turn in a dance, often on tiptoe.
–*verb* **2.** To **pirouette** is to perform this movement: *She pirouetted happily around the room.*

☑ SPELLING TIP *Tricky vowel sound*: *ou* for the 'ooh' sound in the middle syllable. This and the *ette* ending show that this word comes from French, where it means 'a spinning top'.

pistil *noun* the part of a flower that holds the seeds.

☑ SPELLING TIP Remember the end of this word is spelt *il*. Don't confuse it with **pistol** which is a kind of gun. If you think of a **pistil** as bursting 'into life' and a **pistol** as taking someone 'out of life', that may remind you of the different endings.

pistol *noun* a gun with a short barrel that fits into a special holder or holster.

☑ SPELLING TIP Remember the end of this word is spelt *ol*. Don't confuse it with **pistil** which is part of a flower. See the spelling tip at **pistil**.

piston *noun* a rod or disc inside a tube which is pumped up and down and is used in engines.

pit[1] *noun*
1. a large hole in the ground, such as a mine. **2.** a small hollow in the surface: *The little pits in the sand were traps made by insects for ants to fall into.* **3.** the space in front of and beneath the stage in a theatre where the orchestra sits. **4.** an area beside a car racing track where the cars are repaired and filled with petrol.
–*verb* (**pits**, **pitting**, **pitted**, **has pitted**) **5.** If something **pits** a surface, it makes hollows or holes in it: *His face is pitted from years of acne.* **6.** To **pit** one person against another is to set them in opposition: *We were unevenly pitted against last year's winners.*
☐ **pitted**, *adjective*

pit[2] *noun*
1. the stone of a fruit such as a peach or a cherry.
–*verb* (**pits**, **pitting**, **pitted**, **has pitted**) **2.** If you **pit** a fruit, you remove the stone from it: *Pit the olives and stuff them with cheese.*

pita *noun* a small, flat, round pocket of bread which you can open up and fill with food.

ANOTHER SPELLING is **pitta**.
OTHER FORMS You can also call this **pita bread** or **pitta bread**.
WORD HISTORY from a Greek word meaning 'a cake'

pitch *verb*
1. If you **pitch** something such as a ball, you throw it quite hard at something: *He pitched the ball straight at the stumps.* **2.** If you **pitch** a tent, you set it up so that it is upright and ready to be used: *We pitched our tents beside the stream.*
–*noun* (*plural* **pitches**) **3.** a throw, especially in baseball and softball. **4.** the quality of a musical note thought of in terms of its highness or lowness. **5.** the area for playing sport, particularly the area between the wickets in cricket. **6.** the degree of slope: *the steep pitch of the roof.*
–*phrase Rather informal* **7. pitch in**, to join in doing something: *The work will be done more quickly if we all pitch in.* **8. pitch into**, **a.** to attack, using words or action. **b.** to begin to do: *They pitched into the washing up straight after the meal.*

pitcher[1] *noun* in baseball and softball, the player who throws the ball to the batter.

☑ SPELLING TIP Don't confuse the spelling of **pitcher** with **picture** which has a similar sound. A **picture** is a drawing, painting or photo.

pitcher[2] *noun* a container which you use to store and pour liquids: *a pitcher of orange juice.*

☑ SPELLING TIP See **pitcher**[1].

pitchfork *noun* a large fork used for lifting and tossing hay.

pitfall *noun* an unexpected trap: *He warned her of the pitfalls of buying such an old house.*

pith *noun*
1. soft, loose substance such as that between the skin and the flesh of an orange and some other citrus fruits. **2.** the most important part.
☐ **pithy**, *adjective*: *a pithy remark.*

pitiful *adjective*
1. causing or deserving pity. **2.** unsuccessful or worthless: *a pitiful attempt.*
☐ **pitifully**, *adverb*

pitta *noun* See **pita**.

pittance *noun* a very small amount of money.

pity *noun*
1. deep sympathy for the suffering or sorrow of other people. **2.** a cause for sorrow: *What a pity that you can't stay longer.*
–*verb* (**pities**, **pitying**, **pitied**, **has pitied**) **3.** If you **pity** someone, you feel pity for them.
☐ **pitiable**, *adjective*

pivot *noun*
1. someone or something on which something turns or depends.
–*verb* 2. If someone or something **pivots**, they turn, as if on a pivot: *She pivoted quickly to see who was behind her.*
☐ **pivotal**, *adjective*

☑ SPELLING TIP *Single letter alert*: only one *v* and one *t*. Notice that you do not double the *t* when you add *-ed* or *-ing*, following the rule that the consonant remains single if the final syllable is not stressed.

pixel *noun* the smallest element of a graphic image which can be produced on a VDU.

pixie *noun* a small fairy.

pizza /*say* **peet**-suh/ *noun* a thin dough base covered with tomato, olives, grated cheese or similar savoury foods and baked in an oven.

WORD HISTORY from an Italian word meaning 'pie'

placard *noun* a large notice or poster put up in a public place.

placate *verb* If you **placate** someone, you make them calm when they have been angry or upset: *It took a long while to placate Dad after the broken window incident.*
☐ **placatory**, *adjective*

A SIMILAR WORD is **appease**.

place *noun*
1. a particular area or part of space: *The beach is a good place to be on a hot day*; *That is the place for the cups and saucers.* 2. situation: *What would you do if you were in my place?* 3. the page or passage you are up to when reading: *I kept my finger on my place.* 4. a short street, court or square. 5. position in a race: *second place.*
–*verb* 6. When you **place** something somewhere, you put or set it there: *I placed the book on my desk.* 7. If you can **place** someone, you can remember them: *I can't place that name, but I may recognise the face.*
–*phrase* 8. **in place of**, instead of. 9. **out of place, a.** not in the proper position. **b.** unsuitable. 10. **take place**, to happen.
☐ **placement**, *noun*

ANOTHER FORM When definition 4 is the name of a street, you spell it with a capital letter and its abbreviation is **Pl**.
SIMILAR WORDS (for definition 1) are **location**, **position**, **spot** and **site**. Note that a **site** is the particular place where something has happened or is going to happen, or the place where something is or will be built (*the site of a famous battle, a good site for an airport*).

placenta /*say* pluh-**sen**-tuh/ *noun* the organ which gives food and oxygen to a baby in its mother's womb.
☐ **placental**, *adjective*: *The calf was still wet with placental fluid.*

WORD HISTORY from a Greek word meaning 'flat cake'

placid /*say* **plas**-uhd/ *adjective* calm or peaceful.
☐ **placidity**, *noun* –**placidly**, *adverb*

plagiarism /*say* **play**-juh-riz-uhm/ *noun* the taking of someone else's ideas or way of expressing them, as in writing, art, etc., and using them as if they were your own.
☐ **plagiarise**, *verb*

ANOTHER SPELLING for **plagiarise** is **plagiarize**.

plague /*say* playg/ *noun*
1. any serious disease which spreads very quickly. 2. a very large number of any pest: *a plague of mice.*
–*verb* 3. If someone or something **plagues** you, they are annoying and you cannot get rid of them.

☑ SPELLING TIP Remember the *ague* spelling for the 'ayg' sound at the end of this word. Think of a word you know with the same sound and ending, like *vague*.

plaid /*rhymes with* dad/ *noun* tartan cloth.

plain *adjective*
1. clearly seen, heard or understood. 2. simple and uncomplicated. 3. not beautiful.
–*noun* 4. a large, flat area of land.
☐ **plainly**, *adverb*

☑ SPELLING TIP Don't confuse the spelling of **plain** with **plane** which has the same sound. A **plane** is an aeroplane, a flat surface, or a tool for smoothing wood.

plaintiff *noun* a person who brings a court case against someone else known as the defendant.

plaintive *adjective* complaining or sorrowful: *'Has anyone seen my mouse?' he asked in a plaintive voice.*
☐ **plaintively**, *adverb*

plait /*say* plat/ *verb* To **plait** hair is to wind three or more strands of it together.
☐ **plait**, *noun*

☑ SPELLING TIP *Tricky vowel sound*: *ai* spelling for the 'a' sound. The *i* is there because this word once was pronounced 'playt'. The pronunciation has changed but the spelling has not!

plan *noun*
1. a program or design for how something should be done or made: *Have you finalised your plans for the day?*; *First we drew a plan of the castle, then we made it out of cardboard and glue.* 2. a system of payment for a mobile phone or internet service: *The plan comes with a new phone.*
–*verb* (**plans**, **planning**, **planned**, **has planned**) 3. When you **plan** something, you work out a plan or a scheme for it: *I have planned every day*

of my holiday. **4.** When someone **plans** a building or other structure, they draw a diagram of how it should be.

plane[1] *noun*
1. a level: *Their conversation was on such a high plane that I couldn't follow it.* **2.** a flat or level surface. **3.** a winged machine which is driven through the air by its propellers or jet engines.
☐ **plane**, *adjective*: *A square is a plane figure.*

NOTE Definition 3 is a shortened form of **aeroplane**.

☑ SPELLING TIP Don't confuse the spelling of **plane** with **plain** which has the same sound. This can be especially confusing as the meaning of **plain** as a noun is related to definition 2 of **plane**. You use **plane** for a flat surface, especially in maths or geometry. You use **plain** for a large area of ground: *the plains of Africa.*

plane[2] *noun*
1. a tool for smoothing wood.
–*verb* **2.** If you **plane** a piece of wood, you smooth it with a plane.

☑ SPELLING TIP See **plane**[1].

planet *noun* any of the large bodies in space turning around the sun or around any star.
☐ **planetary**, *adjective*

plank *noun* a long, flat piece of timber thicker than a board.

plankton *noun* the mass of very tiny plants and animals which drift at or near the surface of the water.

plant *noun*
1. a living thing which grows in the ground and which cannot move around. **2.** the machinery and equipment connected with an industry.
–*verb* **3.** To **plant** something is to put it in the ground to grow.

plantation *noun* a farm, especially in tropical areas where crops such as rubber, sugar, or bananas are grown.

plaque /*say* plahk, plak/ *noun*
1. a metal plate, such as one fastened to a wall, with a name, profession or memorial date on it. **2.** a coating on teeth which causes decay.

☑ SPELLING TIP Remember the *aque* spelling for the end of this word. **Plaque** is spelt like this because it comes from French.

plasma *noun*
1. the liquid part of blood which contains the blood cells. **2.** a type of gas which can be used to display light on some types of electronic screens.

plasma TV *noun* a television which has a screen that uses plasma (definition 2) to display images.

OTHER NAMES for this are **plasma television** and **plasma**.

plaster *noun*
1. a thick mixture of lime, sand and water, used to cover walls and ceilings. **2.** a fine white powder which swells and sets rapidly when mixed with water and is used in making moulds. **3.** a bandage soaked in such a mixture, which is put around a broken limb to hold it in place. **4.** a covering for a small cut or sore.
–*verb* **5.** To **plaster** a wall or ceiling is to cover it with a smooth layer of plaster. **6.** If you **plaster** a surface with something, you cover the surface with a lot of it: *He has plastered his bedroom wall with pictures of rock stars.*
☐ **plasterer**, *noun*

ANOTHER NAME (for definition 2) is **plaster of Paris**.

plastic /*say* **plas**-tik/ *noun* a substance which can be shaped when soft and then hardened.
☐ **plastic**, *adjective* –**plasticity** /*say* plas-**tis**-uh-tee/, *noun*

plasticine /*say* **plas**-tuh-seen/ *noun* a soft substance used for modelling figures.

WORD HISTORY trademark

plate *noun*
1. a flat, round dish for food. **2.** a thin, flat sheet of metal. **3.** a full-page picture in a book. **4.** a support for teeth, often for false teeth.

plateau /*say* **plat**-oh/ *noun* (*plural* **plateaus** *or* **plateaux** /*say* **plat**-ohz/) a large, flat stretch of high ground.

☑ SPELLING TIP *Tricky vowel sound*: *eau* spelling for the 'oh' sound at the end. **Plateau** has this spelling because it comes from French. Another word like this is *bureau*.

platelet /*say* **playt**-luht/ *noun* one of many small discs in the blood which help it to clot in wounds.

platform *noun*
1. a raised floor, as in a hall or theatre, for public speakers or performers. **2.** the raised area beside the tracks at a railway station. **3.** a computer operating system or a telecommunications system.

platinum /*say* **plat**-uh-nuhm/ *noun* a greyish-white metallic element, used especially for making chemical and scientific equipment and in jewellery.

WORD HISTORY from a Spanish word meaning 'silver'

platitude *noun* an expression which has been used too many times, especially one spoken as if it were fresh and wise: *Saying 'school is the best time of your life' is a platitude.*
☐ **platitudinous**, *adjective*

platonic *adjective* having to do with a love that is deep but not expressed physically: *They had a platonic relationship.*
☐ **platonically**, *adverb*

WORD HISTORY named after the Greek philosopher *Plato* (about 427–347 BC)

platoon *noun* a group or unit of soldiers.

platter *noun* a large plate used for serving food.

platypus /*say* **plat**-uh-poos/ *noun* (*plural* **platypuses**) an Australian animal with webbed feet and a bill like a duck's, which lays eggs and feeds its young with its own milk.

☑ SPELLING TIP *Tricky 'uh' sound*: the vowel sound in the middle is spelt with a *y*. Also remember that there is a single *s* only at the end of the word. The final word part, *pus*, has nothing to do with a cat, but comes from *pous*, the Greek word for 'foot'. The first part comes from *platus*, Greek for 'flat'. So the name that was given to this animal means 'flat-footed'.

plausible /*say* **plawz**-uh-buhl/ *adjective* believable or reasonable: *They didn't think her story about being sick was plausible because she looked so well.*
☐ **plausibility**, *noun* –**plausibly**, *adverb*

play *noun*
1. activity for fun or relaxation. **2.** a story which can be acted out by actors in a theatre. **3.** light, rapid movement: *the play of moonlight on the waves.*
–*verb* **4.** To **play** a role is to act it out: *She is playing a convict in the performance.* **5.** To **play** a game is to take part in it: *I play cricket.* **6.** When children **play** they take part in enjoyable activities for fun: *Let's go outside and play.* **7.** To **play** a musical instrument is to perform on it: *Seth plays the guitar.* **8.** To **play** a CD, tape, etc., is to make it produce the sound recorded on it.
–*phrase* **9. play down**, to lessen the importance of.
☐ **player**, *noun* –**playful**, *adjective* –**playfully**, *adverb* –**playfulness**, *noun*

playground *noun*
1. an area set aside for children to play in, especially one with equipment such as swings, slides and so on. **2.** the open area around school buildings.

playwright /*say* **play**-ruyt/ *noun* someone who writes plays.

ANOTHER WORD for this is **dramatist**.

☑ SPELLING TIP Although a **playwright** writes plays, you have to remember that the last part of the word is spelt *wright*. This is an old-fashioned word for 'someone who makes or build things'.

plaza *noun* an open space or square in a town.

plea *noun* a request made with strong and sincere feeling.

plead /*say* pleed/ *verb* (**pleads**, **pleading**, **pleaded** *or* **plead** /*say* pled/, **has pleaded** *or* **has plead** /*say* pled/) To **plead** is to **1.** ask with great feeling. **2.** say whether you are innocent or guilty in a court case.

pleasant /*say* **plez**-uhnt/ *adjective* agreeable or pleasing: *a pleasant meal*; *a pleasant afternoon.*
☐ **pleasantly**, *adverb*

☑ SPELLING TIP *Tricky vowel sound*: *ea* for the 'e' sound in the first syllable. This will be easy if you remember that **pleasant** things are things that *please* you.

please *verb*
1. If you **please** someone, you make them happy or satisfied: *The news of her win pleased us all.*
–*interjection* **2.** an expression you use when you are politely asking to be given something or to have something done: *Can I have another sandwich, please*; *Stop that noise, please.*
☐ **pleased**, *adjective* –**pleasing**, *adjective*

pleasure /*say* **plezh**-uh/ *noun* enjoyment or happiness.
☐ **pleasurable**, *adjective*

☑ SPELLING TIP *Tricky vowel sound*: *ea* for the 'e' sound in the first syllable. As with *pleasant*, remember that **pleasure** comes from things that *please* you. Also remember the *sure* ending which sounds like 'zhuh'. Think of other words with this spelling and sound, such as *measure* and *treasure*.

pleat /*rhymes with* meet/ *noun*
1. a pressed or stitched fold in trousers or a skirt.
–*verb* **2.** To **pleat** cloth is to make pleats in it.
☐ **pleated**, *adjective*

plectrum *noun* (*plural* **plectrums**) a small piece of wood, plastic or metal, used to pluck the strings of instruments such as the guitar or banjo.

ANOTHER WORD for this is **pick**.

pledge *noun*
1. a promise made very seriously. **2.** something given as a guarantee that you will return a loan: *She left a ring as a pledge.*
–*verb* (**pledges**, **pledging**, **pledged**, **has pledged**) **3.** When you **pledge** to do something, you make a solemn promise to do it: *He pledged to take care of his little brother.*

A SIMILAR WORD (for definitions 1 and 3) is **vow**.

plentiful *adjective* great in amount or number: *With plentiful rain, the crops were growing well.*
☐ **plentifully**, *adverb*

plenty *noun* an amount or supply which is large or all that is needed: *Eat as much food as you* *like – we have plenty*; *We have plenty of time to catch the bus.*

pliable *adjective* flexible or easily bent: *He rubbed oil into the leather until it was soft and pliable.*
☐ **pliability**, *noun* –**pliably**, *adverb*

pliers /*say* **pluy**-uhz/ *plural noun* a tool used for holding things, pulling out nails, etc., and for twisting or cutting wire.

plight *noun* a state or situation, usually bad: *The plight of the flood victims was desperate.*

plod *verb* (**plods**, **plodding**, **plodded**, **has plodded**) To **plod** is to go or continue in a slow, steady and unexciting way: *He plodded off to do his study.*
☐ **plodder**, *noun*

plot[1] *noun*
1. a secret plan, especially to do something illegal. **2.** the story of a novel or play.
–*verb* (**plots**, **plotting**, **plotted**, **has plotted**) **3.** If someone **plots** to do something, they plan secretly to do it: *The robbers plotted to break into the factory at night.* **4.** When you **plot** something, you mark it out or map it: *to plot the route on a map*; *to plot the position of the ship.*

plot[2] *noun* a small piece of ground: *a vegetable plot.*

plough /*rhymes with* now/ *noun*
1. a tool with a curved blade for digging the soil.
–*verb* **2.** To **plough** soil is to dig it with a plough: *The farmer began ploughing the field at dawn.*
–*phrase* **3. plough into**, to attack energetically. **4. plough through**, to work steadily at: *We had to plough through the washing up before we could go swimming.*

☑ SPELLING TIP *Tricky vowel sound*: *ough* for the 'ow' sound (as in some other words, such as *bough*). This word is actually spelt **plow** in American English, but in Australian English the spelling **plough** is the most common so this is the one you should learn.

ploy *noun* a scheme or trick to gain an advantage over someone: *As part of his ploy to inherit the family wealth, he assumed the identity of a long-lost cousin.*

pluck *verb*
1. If you **pluck** a flower or fruit, you pull at it and remove it: *to pluck a strawberry.* **2.** If you **pluck** a stringed instrument, you play notes on the strings by pulling at them with your fingers or by using a plectrum.
–*noun* **3.** courage.
☐ **plucky**, *adjective* (**pluckier**, **pluckiest**) full of courage.

plug *noun*
1. an object designed to fit into an opening in a container to stop liquid flowing out. **2.** something used to block a hole. **3.** the connection which you put into an electrical power point.
–*verb* (**plugs**, **plugging**, **plugged**, **has plugged**) **4.** If you **plug** something, you stop it up: *to plug a leaking tank.* **5.** *Informal* If someone **plugs** something, such as a film or book, they mention it often as a kind of advertisement: *The radio keeps plugging that new show.*

plum *noun* a soft, purplish-coloured, smooth-skinned fruit related to, but larger than the cherry.

plumage /*say* **plooh**-mij/ *noun* the feathers covering a bird's body.

plumb /*rhymes with* mum/ *noun*
1. a lead weight on a string, used in measuring depth or as a test of uprightness. **2.** an exactly upright or perpendicular line or position: *You must get the corner poles plumb, or the whole wall will be wrong.*
–*adverb* **3.** in an upright position. **4.** exactly: *plumb on time.*

ANOTHER WORD (for definition 1) is **plumbline**.

☑ SPELLING TIP *Silent letter alert*: don't forget the *b* at the end. Don't confuse the word with **plum**, a type of fruit, which has the same sound.

plumber /*say* **plum**-uh/ *noun* someone who puts into a building the pipes and fixtures which are used to carry water and waste, and fixes them when something goes wrong.
☐ **plumbing**, *noun*

☑ SPELLING TIP *Silent letter alert*: don't forget the silent *b* following the single *m*. Think of a burst pipe to remind you of the *b*.

plume *noun* a feather, especially a long or showy one.

plummet *verb* (**plummets**, **plummeting**, **plummeted**, **has plummeted**) To **plummet** is to fall straight and fast, as something heavy does.

☑ SPELLING TIP *Double/single letter alert*: double *m* and only one *t*. Notice that you do not double the *t* when you add *-ed* or *-ing*, following the rule that the consonant remains single if the final syllable is not stressed.

plump *adjective* rather fat, but in a pleasant, round shape.

plunder *verb* To **plunder** is to rob violently, as in war: *The villagers were plundered of all their possessions and food.*
☐ **plunder**, *noun*

A SIMILAR WORD is **pillage**.

plunge *verb* To **plunge** is to **1.** jump suddenly into water: *It is lovely to plunge into a pool on a hot day.* **2.** fall suddenly from a high position: *The car plunged off the cliff.* **3.** To **plunge** something or someone into a liquid or into a certain situation is to push them there suddenly and strongly: *She plunged her burnt hand into the cool water*; *The news plunged us into despair.*
–*noun* **4.** a sudden rush or move. **5.** a fall, especially sudden or head first.

–*phrase* **6. take the plunge**, to start to do something that is difficult or important, after having hesitated to do it.
□ **plunger**, *noun*

plural *adjective* The **plural** form of a word shows that it refers to more than one person or thing: *'Clothes' is a plural noun.*
□ **plural**, *noun*: *'Cats' is the plural of 'cat'.* –**plurality**, *noun*

SEE the Grammar and Punctuation Guide appendix.

plus *preposition*
1. Plus is used to show that one number or quantity is added to something else. In writing mathematical equations the **plus sign** (+) is used to represent this word, as in $2+3=5$: *Two plus three equals five.*
–*noun* **2.** an added advantage: *Good weather is a definite plus for a holiday.*

plush *adjective* rich, fine or costly.

plutonium /*say* plooh-**toh**-nee-uhm/ *noun* a radioactive element which is obtained from uranium, and is a powerful source of energy.

ply[1] *verb* (**plies**, **plying**, **plied**, **has plied**)
1. If you **ply** something, you use or do it, especially busily: *The rider was plying his whip*; *ships plying their trade between ports.* **2.** If you **ply** a person with something, you supply them continuously with it: *The journalist plied him with question after question.* **3.** If forms of transport like ships **ply** an area, they travel or cross it: *Ships continually ply the seas between Australia and Papua New Guinea*; *The airline will ply the new route in September.*

ply[2] *noun* (*plural* **plies**) a strand or a thickness: *My grandmother knitted a baby dress with wool of a very fine ply.*

plywood *noun* board made of thin layers of wood stuck together.

p.m. *abbreviation* short for *post meridiem*, Latin words meaning 'after noon', covering the period between 12 o'clock in the middle of the day and 12 o'clock at night: *I get home at 4 p.m.*

ANOTHER FORM is **pm**.

pneumatic /*say* nyooh-**mat**-ik/ *adjective* worked by air or air pressure: *a pneumatic pump.*
□ **pneumatically**, *adverb*

☑ SPELLING TIP *Silent letter alert*: don't forget the silent *p* at the beginning. It is part of the tricky *pneu* spelling of the start of the word, which sounds like 'nyooh'. **Pneumatic** comes from *pneuma*, the Greek word for 'wind'.

pneumonia /*say* nyooh-**mohn**-yuh/ *noun* a serious illness caused by an inflammation of the lungs which makes it difficult to breathe.

☑ SPELLING TIP *Silent letter alert*: don't forget the silent *p* at the beginning. It is part of the tricky *pneu* spelling of the start of the word, which sounds like 'nyooh'. **Pneumonia** comes from *pneumon*, the Greek word for 'lung'.

poach[1] *verb* If you **poach** something, you cook it in liquid just below boiling point: *We poached some eggs for breakfast.*

poach[2] *verb* If someone **poaches**, they hunt or fish without permission on someone else's property.
□ **poacher**, *noun* someone who poaches.

pocket *noun*
1. a cloth fold or pouch sewn into a piece of clothing, designed for holding things. **2.** a small area of something: *a pocket of air*; *a pocket of resistance.*
–*verb* (**pockets**, **pocketing**, **pocketed**, **has pocketed**) **3.** If you **pocket** something, you put it in your pocket, especially dishonestly: *She pocketed all the change.*
–*phrase* **4. line your pockets**, to make money by dishonest means. **5. out of pocket**, without money or having made a loss.

pocket money *noun*
1. money that parents regularly give their children, often in return for the performance of household chores. **2.** money that can be used to pay for small personal needs.

pod[1] *noun* the long container in which seeds grow: *a pea pod.*

pod[2] *noun* a small group of animals, especially of seals or whales.

podcast *verb* (**podcasts**, **podcasting**, **podcast** *or* **podcasted**, **has podcast** *or* **has podcasted**)
1. To **podcast** a radio or television program is to send it over the internet as a computer file that can be downloaded and stored to be played later on a computer or an MP3 player.
–*noun* **2.** the digital file of a radio or television program: *If you would like to listen to this program again, you can download the podcast from our website.*
□ **podcast**, *adjective* –**podcasting**, *noun*, *adjective*

podium /*say* **poh**-dee-uhm/ *noun* a small platform for a public speaker or the conductor of an orchestra.

WORD HISTORY from a Greek word meaning 'foot'

poem *noun* a piece of writing set out in a special way, often with lines that match in length, rhythm or rhyme.

poetry *noun*
1. writing or speaking in the form of a poem or poems: *She writes poetry.* **2.** beauty of expression: *poetry in motion.*
□ **poet**, *noun* –**poetic**, *adjective*

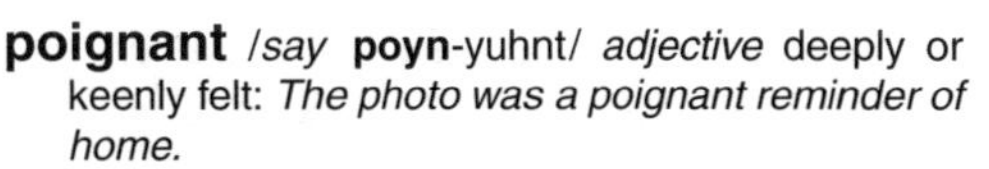

poignant /*say* **poyn**-yuhnt/ *adjective* deeply or keenly felt: *The photo was a poignant reminder of home.*
☐ **poignancy**, *noun*

☑ SPELLING TIP *Silent letter alert*: don't forget the silent *g* before the *n*. Also remember that the ending is *ant* (not *ent*). This word comes from French.

point *noun*
1. a sharp end: *the needle's point.* **2.** a written dot, as in punctuation or decimals. **3.** the level or place in a process at which something happens: *boiling point.* **4.** the main thing: *The point of the party was to get to know our new neighbours.* **5.** a unit for scoring in a game.
–*verb* **6.** If someone **points** in a particular direction, they use their finger to show the way there. A sign can also **point** somewhere: *I asked which woman was her mother and she pointed to the one at the end of the row*; *The arrow points west.* **7.** If you **point** something, you aim it: *She pointed the gun at his head.*
–*phrase* **8. make a point of**, insist upon. **9. on** (or **upon**) **the point of**, close to: *on the point of deciding.* **10. point of view**, the opinion or attitude that someone has about a particular matter. **11. to the point**, related to the issue.
☐ **pointed**, *adjective* –**pointer**, *noun*

point-blank *adjective* aimed or fired at very close range: *He fired at them at point-blank range.*
☐ **point-blank**, *adverb*: *He refused point-blank to go along with the plan.*

poise *noun* confidence and calmness when dealing with people and situations.
☐ **poised**, *adjective*

poison *noun*
1. a substance which causes death or illness if you swallow it.
–*verb* **2.** To **poison** someone or something is to kill or harm them with poison.: *to poison weeds.*
☐ **poisonous**, *adjective*

poke *verb*
1. If you **poke** someone or something, you push them with your finger or with something you hold in your hand: *She poked the spider with a stick to see if it was still alive.* **2.** If you **poke** something somewhere, you push it there, usually through a narrow opening: *He poked the letter under the door.* **3.** If something **pokes** out, it shows or appears from behind something else: *He poked his head around the corner and offered us a cup of tea.*
–*phrase* **4. poke fun at**, to make fun of.
☐ **poke**, *noun*

poker[1] *noun* a metal rod for poking or stirring the fire in a fireplace.

poker[2] *noun* a card game in which the players bet money on the value of the cards they are holding.

poky *adjective* (**pokier**, **pokiest**) not having much space; cramped: *It was a poky tent – no room to stretch out.*

pole[1] *noun* a long, thin piece of wood or other material: *a flag pole.*

pole[2] *noun*
1. each of the extreme points of the axis of the earth, or of any round body.
–*phrase* **2. poles apart**, having completely opposite or widely different opinions, interests, and so on.
☐ **polar**, *adjective* –**polarity**, *noun*

police *noun*
1. members of a force employed by a state or nation to keep order and to protect life and property.
–*verb* **2.** If someone **polices** something, such as a place, crowd, law, etc., they protect it and keep it in order.
☐ **policeman**, **policewoman**, *noun*

policy[1] /*say* **pol**-uh-see/ *noun* (*plural* **policies**) a plan of action: *It is a good policy not to join in other people's arguments*; *The premier announced a new education policy.*

policy[2] /*say* **pol**-uh-see/ *noun* (*plural* **policies**) a signed agreement with an insurance company.

polio /*say* **poh**-lee-oh/ *noun* a disease, now rare, causing paralysis.

WORD HISTORY short for **poliomyelitis**.

polish *noun*
1. a paste or liquid which gives a shine when it is rubbed on: *floor polish.* **2.** fineness or stylishness: *She writes with polish.*
–*verb* **3.** When you **polish** something, you make it shiny by rubbing: *to polish the car.* **4.** To **polish** something is to put the final touches to it: *I want to polish the last paragraph a little more before I hand in my essay.*
–*phrase* **5. polish off**, to finish: *There was some food left over but Dad polished it off in no time.*
☐ **polished**, *adjective* –**polisher**, *noun*

polite *adjective*
1. having good manners: *It's not polite to reach across people at the table.* **2.** behaving well to other people: *Even though she was very angry she tried to remain polite.*
☐ **politely**, *adverb* –**politeness**, *noun*

THE OPPOSITE is **impolite** or **rude**.

political asylum *noun* the protection that a country gives to a person who has fled their own country because they fear being persecuted for their race, religion or political opinions, or because of war.

politics /*say* **pol**-uh-tiks/ *noun*
1. the management of the affairs of a country or state. **2.** methods used to gain power or success: *He hates the politics of his job.*

☐ **political**, *adjective* –**politician** /*say* pol-uh-**tish**-uhn/, *noun*

NOTE You can treat this noun as singular or plural.

☑ SPELLING TIP Remember that the ending of **politician** is spelt *ician*. Many other words have this spelling for an 'ishuhn' sound, such as *electrician* and *musician*.

polka *noun* a quick and lively dance.

poll *noun*
1. a counting of votes or opinions. **2. the polls**, the place where votes are taken.

☑ SPELLING TIP Don't confuse the spelling of **poll** with **pole** which has a similar sound. A **pole** is a long, thin piece of wood, or one of the extremities of the axis of the earth.

pollen *noun* the yellowish seed dust of flowers.

WORD HISTORY a Latin word meaning 'fine flour' or 'dust'

pollinate *verb* Bees **pollinate** flowers when they carry pollen to them so that they can produce seeds.
☐ **pollination**, *noun*

pollute *verb* If something **pollutes** the environment, it makes the earth, water or air dirty or harmful: *Rubbish washed into the city drains pollutes the harbour.*
☐ **polluted**, *adjective* –**pollution**, *noun*

polo *noun* a ball game on horseback, between two teams using long wooden mallets and a wooden ball.

poltergeist /*say* **pol**-tuh-guyst/ *noun* a troublesome ghost or spirit who shows its presence by making noises and moving things about.

☑ SPELLING TIP *Tricky vowel sounds*: *er* for the 'uh' sound in the middle, and *ei* for the 'uy' sound in the last syllable. This word breaks the rule that *i* comes before *e* except after *c* because it comes from German – from *poltern* (meaning 'to make a disturbance') and *geist* (meaning 'ghost').

poly- *prefix* a word part meaning 'much' or 'many', as in *polygamy*.

WORD HISTORY this prefix comes from Greek

polygamy /*say* puh-**lig**-uh-mee/ *noun* marriage to more than one person at a time.
☐ **polygamist**, *noun* –**polygamous**, *adjective* –**polygamously**, *adverb*

☑ SPELLING TIP This word will be easier to spell if you see that it is made up of the prefix *poly-* (meaning 'many') and *gamy* (a word part coming from the Greek word for 'marriage'). See also **bigamy** and **monogamy** which contain this same word part.

polygon /*say* **pol**-ee-gon/ *noun* a flat shape with many straight sides.

polythene *noun* a firm, light plastic which is used for containers, packing and insulation.

pomegranate /*say* **pom**-uh-gran-uht/ *noun* a thick-skinned, pinkish fruit which has edible seeds and flesh.

☑ SPELLING TIP *Single letter alert*: only one *m* followed by an *e* (this part of the word comes from *pome* meaning 'fruit of the apple family'). Also remember the *ate* spelling at the end – as you can eat **pomegranates**, remembering *ate* shouldn't be too hard.

pommel *noun* the rounded part at the front of a saddle.

Pommy *adjective* (*plural* **Pommies**) *Informal* an English person.

ANOTHER FORM of this is **Pom**. Both forms can also be spelt with a small letter.
NOTE Some people find the use of this word offensive.

pomp *noun* splendid display, as in a ceremony.

pompom *noun* a ball made of wool or other thread, often put on hats or caps as an ornament.

pompous *adjective* Someone who is **pompous** speaks or behaves as if they think they are very important.
☐ **pomposity**, *noun* –**pompously**, *adverb*

poncho *noun* (*plural* **ponchos**) a cloak with a hole in the centre to put your head through.

pond *noun* an area of water smaller than a lake.

ponder *verb* To **ponder** something is to think about it deeply or carefully: *to ponder the problem.*

ponderous *adjective*
1. large and heavy. **2.** serious and dull: *His ponderous speeches send most people to sleep.*
☐ **ponderously**, *adverb*

pontiff *noun* a pope.
☐ **pontifical**, *adjective*

pontificate /*say* pon-**tif**-uh-kayt/ *verb* If someone **pontificates**, they speak in a pompous manner.

pontoon *noun* a floating structure used to support a temporary bridge or as a place where boats can tie up.

pony *noun* (*plural* **ponies**) a small horse.

ponytail *noun* a hairstyle in which the hair is tied in a loose bunch at the back of the head.

poo *noun Informal* faeces.

poodle *noun* a dog with thick, curly hair often trimmed to a special shape.

pool[1] *noun*
1. a small area of still water, especially one made for swimming in. 2. a small collection of any liquid: *a pool of blood.*

pool[2] *noun*
1. a combination of possessions, money or services for the use of everyone in a group: *Mum and Dad and some other parents have formed a car pool so that they can take turns in driving us all to school.* 2. the sum of money that can be won in some gambling games. 3. a kind of billiards game.
–*verb* 4. If a group of people **pool** something, such as money, equipment or knowledge, they allow it to be collected and put together for a particular use: *On the last night of the camp we pooled our remaining food for a makeshift feast.*

poop /*rhymes with* loop/ *noun* an enclosed space at the back part of a ship, above the main deck.

poor *adjective*
1. having very little money or belongings: *a poor student.* 2. of bad quality: *He's in poor health*; *Her exam results were very poor.* 3. unfortunate or unlucky: *You poor thing, it must be really painful.*
–*noun* 4. **the poor**, the people who are poor.

NOTE If you are very poor, you are suffering from **poverty**.

☑ SPELLING TIP Note the *oor* spelling for the 'aw' sound in **poor**. Don't confuse it with **pour**, **paw**, or **pore** which all have the same sound. You can **pour** a liquid from one container to another. A **paw** is the foot of an animal. A **pore** is one of the small holes in your skin that sweat passes out through. To **pore** over something is to read it carefully.

pop[1] *verb* (**pops**, **popping**, **popped**, **has popped**)
1. If something **pops**, it makes a short explosive sound. 2. If someone **pops**, they come, go or move quickly or suddenly: *Mum popped into the shop for the paper*; *Pop the butter in the fridge.*
–*noun* 3. a short explosive sound.

pop[2] *noun* See **pop music**.

popcorn *noun* grain which bursts open and swells up when heated and is then eaten.

pope /*say* pohp/ *noun* the bishop of Rome as head of the Roman Catholic Church.
□ **papal** /*say* **pay**-puhl/, *adjective*

ANOTHER FORM This is spelt with a capital letter when you are writing the title of a particular person.

pop music *noun* a type of modern music, based on rock music but with a wider appeal, usually with singing and a simple rhythm.
□ **pop**, *adjective*: *pop group.*

ANOTHER FORM You can also call this **pop**: *Do you like pop?*

poppadum /*say* **pop**-uh-dum/ *noun* See **pappadum**.

poppy *noun* (*plural* **poppies**) a plant with showy flowers of various bright colours.

popular *adjective*
1. liked by many people: *a popular school captain*; *popular music.* 2. having to do with the people in general: *There is popular support for his polices.*
□ **popularity**, *noun* –**popularly**, *adverb*

populate *verb* If people **populate** a place, they live there: *People from many different countries populate Australia.*

A SIMILAR WORD is **inhabit**.

population *noun* the people living in a country, town or other area.

populous *adjective* having a large number of people: *NSW and Victoria are the most populous states of Australia.*

pop-up *adjective*
1. having parts that unfold into a shape, or that appear suddenly: *a pop-up card.* 2. having to do with a shop, restaurant, bar, etc., open for a brief time only, often for a specific marketing purpose.

porcelain /*say* **paw**-suh-luhn/ *noun* a kind of fine china, used for dishes and ornaments.

☑ SPELLING TIP *Tricky vowel sounds*: *ain* for the 'uhn' sound at the end. There are some other difficult parts in this word. Remember the *c* spelling for the 's' sound and the *e* spelling for the 'uh' sound in the middle. **Porcelain** is spelt in this way because it comes from French. The French word came from an Italian word *porcellana* which means 'cowrie shells'. These shells are thick and white, like dishes made of china.

porch *noun* (*plural* **porches**) a covered area at an entrance to a building.

porcupine *noun* a small animal covered with stiff, sharp spines, found in Europe, Africa, and North America.

pore[1] *verb* If you **pore** over something, you read it or study it carefully: *He pored over the sports pages.*

☑ SPELLING TIP Don't confuse the spelling of **pore** with **pour**, **paw** or **poor**, all of which have the same sound. You can **pour** a liquid from one container to another. A **paw** is the foot of an animal. If someone is **poor**, they don't have much money or property.

pore[2] *noun* a very small opening, especially in the skin, for liquid to be taken in or come out through: *Sweat comes out through your pores.*

☑ SPELLING TIP See **pore**[1].

pork *noun* the meat of a pig.

pornography /*say* paw-**nog**-ruh-fee/ *noun* art, photography or writing that is thought to be offensive.
□ **pornographer**, *noun* –**pornographic**, *adjective*

☑ SPELLING TIP Don't confuse the first part of this word with *pawn* which is a chess piece. **Pornography** comes from *porne*, the Greek word for 'prostitute'.

porous *adjective* A **porous** material or substance has a lot of tiny holes or spaces and so allows water or air to pass through it: *If you add sand to the soil, it will become more porous.*
□ **porousness**, *noun*

porpoise /*say* **paw**-puhs/ *noun* a sea animal with a rounded nose, usually blackish on top and paler beneath, which often jumps out of the water. A **porpoise** is a kind of dolphin.

WORD HISTORY from a Latin word meaning 'hogfish'

porridge *noun* oats cooked with water or milk, often eaten for breakfast.

☑ SPELLING TIP Remember the *idge* spelling at the end (not *age* or *ige*). You could think of making a *ridge* in your **porridge** with a spoon to remind you of this spelling.

port[1] *noun*
1. a sheltered part of the coast where ships load and unload. **2.** a town with such a sheltered area of water.

port[2] *noun* the left-hand side of a ship or an aircraft when you are facing the front.

THE OPPOSITE is **starboard**.

port[3] *noun*
1. an opening, such as a porthole in a ship. **2.** a connection point in a computer for the entry or exit of data.

port[4] *noun* a suitcase or school bag.

NOTE This word is a short from of *portmanteau*, a kind of suitcase that opens into two halves. The word *portmanteau* is from French.

portable *adjective* able to be easily carried or moved: *We bought my grandmother a portable phone for Christmas.*
□ **portability**, *noun*

portal *noun*
1. a door, gate, or entrance, especially a grand one, as in a palace. **2.** a means of access. **3.** See **web portal**.

WORD HISTORY from a Latin word meaning 'gate'

porter *noun* someone whose job is carrying bags or other loads: *a hotel porter.*

portfolio *noun*
1. a case for carrying loose papers or letters. **2.** the duties of a minister in a government: *The prime minister gave her the health portfolio.* **3.** a collection of an artist's drawings, photographs, etc., which may be shown as examples of their work.

porthole /*say* **pawt**-hohl/ *noun* a round opening like a window in the side of a ship that gives light and air.

portion *noun*
1. a part or share of something.
–*verb in the phrase* **2. portion out**, to divide into shares: *to portion out the cherries.*

portly *adjective* large and stout.
□ **portliness**, *noun*

portrait /*say* **pawt**-ruht/ *noun*
1. a painting, drawing or photograph of someone, especially of their face. **2.** a written or spoken description: *a portrait of life in ancient Rome.*
□ **portraiture**, *noun*

portray *verb* If you **portray** someone in a certain way, you represent them as being like that, either in speech, or in a book, film or play: *In the book, she was portrayed as a rather weak character.*
□ **portrayal**, *noun*

pose *verb*
1. If you **pose** for a photograph, you stand in a particular way or in a particular place so that someone can take a picture of you. **2.** If someone **poses** as someone else, they pretend to be that person: *to pose as a policeman.* **3.** To **pose** a question, is to ask a question. **4.** If something **poses** a problem or a threat, it causes one: *The virus can pose a serious danger to the elderly.*
□ **pose**, *noun* –**poser**, *noun*

posh *adjective Rather informal* stylish, expensive-looking, or suggesting a high social class: *a posh dress*; *a posh accent.*

position *noun*
1. a place or location: *He has not left his position beside the pool all day.* **2.** proper place: *I helped move the desks back into position.* **3.** the manner in which something is placed or arranged: *The position of the desks is all wrong.* **4.** a situation or state: *She knows a lot about plants, so is in a good position to help plan the school garden.* **5.** rank or standing: *Mum has a high position in her company.* **6.** a job: *He has applied for a position as a landscape gardener.* **7.** a point of view: *I can see your position – I just don't agree with it.*
–*verb* **8.** If you **position** something, you put it in a particular position: *He positioned his chair right in front of the TV.*

positive *adjective*
1. If you say you are **positive** about something, you mean that you are certain or sure: *The*

witness was positive that the car was yellow. **2.** If you feel **positive** about something, you are enthusiastic. **3.** If you have a **positive** attitude, you think about what you can do rather than what you cannot. **4.** A **positive** answer to a question or statement shows agreement or approval. **5.** A **positive** number is greater than zero.
☐ **positively**, *adverb*: *positively rude.* –**positiveness**, *noun*

posse /*say* **pos**-ee/ *noun* a group of men that helps a sheriff keep law and order.

NOTE This word is mainly used in America.

☑ SPELLING TIP *Single letter alert*: a single *e* spells the 'ee' sound at the end. This comes from the Latin verb form *posse*, meaning 'to be able'.

possess *verb*
1. To **possess** something is to own it or have it: *to possess a mobile phone*; *to possess a sense of humour.* **2.** If something **possesses** you, it takes control of you: *She was possessed by a sudden urge to giggle.*
☐ **possessor**, *noun*

possessed *adjective* If you are **possessed**, you are taken over by a strong feeling, madness or a seemingly supernatural force: *She screamed as though possessed.*

possession *noun*
1. ownership or the act of possessing: *He was charged with being in possession of illegal drugs.* **2.** something possessed: *My dog is more of a friend than a possession.*

possessive *adjective* wanting to possess or control something or someone all by yourself.
☐ **possessively**, *adverb* –**possessiveness**, *noun*

possessive case *noun* the form of a noun or pronoun which shows ownership, such as 'his', in the phrase *his hat*, which is the possessive case of 'he'.

SEE the Grammar and Punctuation Guide appendix.

possible *adjective*
1. If something is **possible**, it can be done: *It's possible to fix the problem.* **2.** If something is **possible**, it may happen: *It's possible I'll be back early today.* **3.** If something is **possible**, it could be true or correct but you do not know for sure: *It's possible that he's left already.*
☐ **possibility**, *noun* (*plural* **possibilities**) –**possibly**, *adverb*

THE OPPOSITE (of definition 1) is **impossible**.

possum *noun* an Australian marsupial that lives in trees, has a long tail for climbing and is active at night.

post[1] *noun*
1. an upright piece of wood or metal used as a support: *He put in a few posts to support the fence.* **2.** a post marking the start or finish of a race.
–*verb* **3.** If you **post** a notice, you attach information to something like a wall for people to see: *The teacher posted details about the competition on the noticeboard.*

post[2] *noun*
1. a job or duty: *My dad has been offered a post in another town.* **2.** the place where the duty is done: *The guard is not permitted to leave his post under any circumstances.*
–*verb* **3.** If someone **posts** a person to a position, they send them there for a position or a duty: *The department has posted him to a teaching job in the country.*

post[3] *noun*
1. delivery of letters or other mail. **2.** the letters themselves. **3.** the system of carrying letters and other mail. **4.** on the internet, a single message in a forum.
–*verb* **5.** If you **post** something, you send it by post: *She posted us a card from Switzerland.* **6.** If you **post** something on the internet you send a message electronically to a forum.
☐ **postage**, *noun* the cost of sending something by post. –**postal**, *adjective*

post- *prefix* a word part meaning 'behind' or 'after', as in *posthumous*, *postscript*.

WORD HISTORY this prefix comes from Latin

postcard *noun* a card for sending to someone by post, usually with a photograph or picture of a place on one side and space for writing on the other side.

postcode *noun* a group of numbers, or in some countries letters, forming part of an address to help speed the delivery of letters.

poster *noun* a large picture or notice.

posterior *adjective*
1. from or at the back: *The X-ray gave a posterior view of the lung.*
–*noun* **2.** *Informal* your bottom.

posterity /*say* pos-**te**-ruh-tee/ *noun* the generations of people who will live in the future: *Our duty to posterity is to care for the planet.*

posthumous /*say* **pos**-chuh-muhs/ *adjective* published, given or happening after someone's death: *He was awarded a posthumous award for bravery.*
☐ **posthumously**, *adverb*

☑ SPELLING TIP The spelling of this word will be easier if you can see that it is made up of the prefix *post-* (coming from Latin and meaning 'after') and *humous* (from *humus*, the Latin word for 'ground'). Thinking of the *post-* prefix will help you to remember there is a *t* after the *s* (not *ch* as you might think from the pronunciation).

post-mortem *noun* the medical examination of a dead body.
☐ **post-mortem**, *adjective*

ANOTHER WORD for this is **autopsy**.

☑ SPELLING TIP Remember the *em* (not *um*) ending. This comes from the Latin words meaning 'after death'.

postpone *verb* If you **postpone** an event, you put it off to a later time: *I postponed my dentist's appointment until next week.*
☐ **postponement**, *noun*

A SIMILAR WORD is **defer**.

postscript *noun* an extra message written on the end of a finished and signed letter.

THE ABBREVIATION is **PS**. You write these letters at the beginning of the message you are adding to your letter.

posture *noun* the position of your body: *a kneeling posture.*

posy *noun* (*plural* **posies**) a small, neatly arranged bunch of flowers.

pot *noun*
1. a container, usually round and deep: *a cooking pot*; *a flower pot.*
–*verb* (**pots**, **potting**, **potted**, **has potted**)
2. When you **pot** a plant, you put it into a pot filled with earth: *to pot seedlings.*

potato *noun* (*plural* **potatoes**) a white plant root which you can eat as a vegetable.

potent *adjective* powerful or strong: *Our football team is a pretty potent mix with all the experience they have.*
☐ **potency**, *noun*

potential /*say* puh-**ten**-shuhl/ *noun* possible or likely ability: *He is a writer with a lot of potential.*
☐ **potential**, *adjective*: *a potential success.* –**potentiality**, *noun* –**potentially**, *adverb*

pothole /*say* **pot**-hohl/ *noun* a hole in the ground, especially one in a road.

potion *noun Old-fashioned* a drink, especially medicine, or one that is poisonous or magical in some way.

potoroo *noun* a small, long-nosed animal with a pointed head that lives in thick grass, and sleeps during the day and comes out at night.

WORD HISTORY from an Aboriginal language of New South Wales called Dharug

potpourri /*say* pot-**poo**-uh-ree, poh-puh-**ree**/ *noun*
1. a mixture of dried flower petals used to give a perfume. **2.** any collection or mixture of different things: *The immigrants were a potpourri of people from many different walks of life.*

☑ SPELLING TIP *Double letter alert*: double *r*. This is only one of the unusual things about the ending of this word. You just have to memorise the spelling of *pourri*. This word comes French where it literally means 'rotten pot'.

potter[1] *noun* someone who shapes dishes, pots, and so on, out of clay, and then hardens them by baking.
☐ **pottery**, *noun*

potter[2] *verb* To **potter** around is to busy or occupy yourself without getting much done: *My grandparents spent the morning pottering in the garden.*

potty *noun* (*plural* **potties**) a pot used as a toilet, especially for small children.

pouch *noun* (*plural* **pouches**)
1. a small bag used for carrying things like money. **2.** a part of the body shaped like a bag or pocket: *the pouch of a kangaroo*; *pouches of skin beneath the eyes.*

poultry /*say* **pohl**-tree/ *noun* birds such as chickens, turkeys, ducks, and geese, which are used as food or for egg production.

☑ SPELLING TIP *Tricky vowel sound*: remember that it is *ou*, not just *o*, in the first syllable.

pounce *verb* To **pounce** on something is to move suddenly and take hold of it: *The cat pounced on the mouse*; *He pounced on the ball.*
☐ **pounce**, *noun*

pound[1] *verb*
1. If you **pound** something, you hit it hard and many times, and possibly crush it into small pieces or a powder. **2.** If your heart **pounds**, it beats violently. **3.** To **pound** along is to run with quick, heavy steps: *They pounded through the tunnel.*

pound[2] *noun*
1. a measure of weight in the imperial system equal to just under half a kilogram. **2.** a unit of money used in Britain and in some other countries.

THE SYMBOL for definition 1 is **lb** (*pl.* **lbs**).
THE SYMBOL for definition 2 is **£**.

pound[3] *noun* a place where animals are sheltered or kept, especially if they are homeless.

pour *verb*
1. If you **pour** liquid, you let it run out of a container: *I poured the syrup all over the pudding.* **2.** If it **pours** with rain, it rains very heavily. **3.** If people **pour** somewhere, a lot of them go there quickly: *The audience poured out of the hall.* **4.** If someone **pours** money into a business or something they want to do, they invest a large amount in an attempt to succeed.

☑ SPELLING TIP Note the *our* spelling for the 'aw' sound in **pour**. Don't confuse it with **poor**, paw, or **pore**, all of which have the same sound. If someone is **poor**, they don't have much money or property. A **paw** is the foot of an animal. A **pore** is one of the small holes in your skin that sweat comes out through. To **pore** over something is to read or study it carefully.

pout *verb* To **pout** is to push out the lips showing disappointment or unwillingness.
□ **pout**, *noun*

poverty *noun*
1. the condition of being poor: *She spent most of her life in poverty.* **2.** a shortage of something needed or wanted: *a poverty of ideas.*

powder *noun*
1. the very small loose bits of something dry that has been crushed or ground: *a powder of dust; tablets crushed to a powder.*
–*verb* **2.** If you **powder** something, you crush it into a powder: *He powdered the tablet and put it into the cat's food.* **3.** If you **powder** yourself, you cover your body, or a part of your body, with powder: *She powdered her nose.*
□ **powdered**, *adjective*: *powdered milk.* –**powdery**, *adjective*

A SIMILAR WORD (for definition 2) is **pulverise**.

power *noun*
1. the ability to do something. **2.** control over others, especially the control that rulers or governments have: *The power he has in his new position is enormous.* **3.** strength or force: *a punch with a lot of power.* **4.** in mathematics, the number that is the result of multiplying a number by itself one or more times: *Nine is the second power of three, and twenty-seven is the third power of three.* **5.** energy or force that can be used for doing work: *electrical power.*
–*verb* **6.** If something **powers** a machine, it supplies it with electricity or some other form of power to make it function.
□ **powerful**, *adjective*

power point *noun* a device, usually on a wall, to plug electrical power leads into.

practical *adjective*
1. Something that is **practical** has to do with actual practice or action, rather than ideas: *A theory can often lead to a practical outcome.* **2.** Someone who is **practical** is interested in and good at work which has an immediate use, such as making or fixing things: *He was so practical, he could fix anything.* **3.** Someone who is being **practical** is being sensible and realistic: *She is being practical when she says that the weather won't necessarily be sunny.*
□ **practicality**, *noun*

practically *adverb*
1. in a practical way: *She approaches problems very practically.* **2.** nearly or almost: *After walking for three hours, we were practically there.*

practice *noun*
1. actual action or performance: *There are laws against the practice of cruelty to animals; The plan did not work well in practice.* **2.** an action or performance that is repeated regularly to improve skill: *I do my piano practice every morning.* **3.** the usual way of doing something: *It is their practice to take the phone off the hook during a meal so they can talk without being interrupted.* **4.** the business of someone such as a doctor or lawyer.
□ **practicable**, *adjective* capable of being actually done or put into practice.

☑ SPELLING TIP See also **practise** and remember that the noun **practice** ends with *ice* while the verb **practise** ends with *ise*. This is the pattern with other pairs of words with these endings, for example *advice* (noun) and *advise* (verb). Try thinking that *ice* is a noun as a way to remember that the noun forms of these words ends with *ice*. In American English, both the verb and the noun are usually spelt **practice**.

practise *verb* To **practise** is to **1.** do or carry out as a usual habit: *You should practise good manners at home.* **2.** work in as a profession: *He wants to practise in sports medicine.* **3.** do or perform repeatedly in order to improve skill: *She has been practising the same scale for five minutes now!*
□ **practised**, *adjective*

☑ SPELLING TIP See **practice**.

practitioner /*say* prak-**tish**-uh-nuh/ *noun* someone working in a practice, particularly a doctor: *She was a practitioner of herbal medicine.*

☑ SPELLING TIP Remember that there are two separate *t*'s in this word. If you ignore the *er* ending for a moment, you will be able to see the common suffix *-ition* which has the sound 'ishuhn'.

pragmatic *adjective* thinking about the results or usefulness of actions: *She is essentially pragmatic and does whatever it takes to get results.*
□ **pragmatically**, *adverb*

prairie /*say* **prair**-ree/ *noun* a flat, grassy, treeless plain, especially in America and Canada.

WORD HISTORY from a Latin word meaning 'meadow'

praise *verb* If you **praise** someone or something, you say that you admire and approve of them.
□ **praise**, *noun*

pram *noun* a small four-wheeled baby carriage which you push along.

prance *verb* If someone **prances**, they move with more action than is necessary, often because they are showing off to other people.

prank *noun* a playful trick.

prattle *verb* If somebody **prattles**, they chatter in a stupid way.
☐ **prattle**, *noun*

prawn *noun* a small shellfish used for food.

ANOTHER WORD for this, especially in American English, is **shrimp**.

pray *verb*
1. If you **pray**, you talk to the god that you believe in, often to ask for help or to be forgiven for something that you have done wrong. **2.** If you say that you **pray** that something happens, you mean you really want it to happen because you feel very strongly about it: *I pray that he gets well soon.*

☑ SPELLING TIP Don't confuse the spelling of **pray** with **prey** which has the same sound. If an animal or bird **preys** on something, it hunts and eats it.

prayer /*say* prair/ *noun* a communication with the god that you believe in, often a request to ask for help or forgiveness: *She said a prayer for her daughter's safety.*

praying mantis *noun* See **mantis**.

pre- *prefix* a word part meaning 'before', as in *preliminary*.

WORD HISTORY this prefix comes from Latin

preach *verb* To **preach** is to talk about religious or moral subjects: *The priest preaches every Sunday.*
☐ **preacher**, *noun*

preamble /*say* pree-**am**-buhl/ *noun* an introduction explaining the purpose of the book or document which follows.

precarious /*say* pruh-**kair**-ree-uhs/ *adjective* If something is **precarious**, there is a strong possibility that something will go wrong with it: *Move that plate away from the edge of the table – it looks a bit precarious.*
☐ **precariously**, *adverb*

precaution *noun* something done in advance to prevent problems: *They took chains as a precaution for driving in the snow.*
☐ **precautionary**, *adjective*

precede /*say* pree-**seed**/ *verb* To **precede** someone or something is to go before them, as in place, order, or position: *A guard of police on motorbikes preceded the presidential car.*
☐ **preceding**, *adjective*

☑ SPELLING TIP Remember that the ending of this word is *cede* (not *ceed*). Don't confuse it with the similar word **proceed** which means 'to go forward or continue'. **Precede** is made up of the prefix *pre-* (meaning 'before') and *cede* (from *cedere*), a Latin word meaning 'to go'. It might help if you remember there are three *e*'s in **precede** but none of them are next to each other.

precedent /*say* **pree**-suh-duhnt, **pres**-uh-duhnt/ *noun* an event or case which may be used as an example for future action: *Kate thought it was not a good idea to set a precedent of doing too well in exams.*

☑ SPELLING TIP *Tricky vowel sounds*: notice that there is only one vowel in this word – *e* – and it appears three times. **Precedent** comes from the verb *precede*. Don't confuse it with **president** although it can be said in way that sounds the same as this word.

precept /*say* **pree**-sept/ *noun* a rule of action: *He lives by the precept of acting to others as he would like them to act to him.*

precinct /*say* **pree**-singkt/ *noun*
1. a place or area with definite limits: *There is a post office in the shopping precinct.* **2.** the surrounding area: *As we left the precincts of the War Memorial, we saw a very small plaque which we hadn't noticed before.*

precious *adjective* of great value: *Water is a precious commodity*; *His collection of fossils is very precious to him.*

precipice /*say* **pres**-uh-puhs/ *noun* a steep cliff.
☐ **precipitous** /*say* pruh-**sip**-uh-tuhs/, *adjective*

☑ SPELLING TIP Remember that there are two separate *c*'s in this word, each time giving an 's' sound. Also remember the *e* at the end. Try rapping it out as *pre* + *ci* + *pice*.

precipitate /*say* pruh-**sip**-uh-tayt/ *verb*
1. To **precipitate** something is to bring it about quickly: *Her suggestion precipitated a new surge of interest.* **2.** If water vapour in the atmosphere **precipitates**, it changes from vapour into dew, rain, or snow.
☐ **precipitation**, *noun*

precis /*say* **pray**-see/ *noun* (*plural* **precis** /*say* **pray**-seez/) a summary, usually a brief piece of writing containing the main points of a larger written work.

A SIMILAR WORD is **summary**.

☑ SPELLING TIP *Silent letter alert*: don't forget the *is* ending where the *s* is silent. There are several other tricky bits to this word, which comes from French. Remember that the letter *e* alone spells the 'ay' sound and that this is followed by a *c* for the 's' sound.

precise /*say* pruh-**suys**/ *adjective* exact: *The brochure gave precise instructions on how to use the glue.*
☐ **precisely**, *adverb* – **precision**, *noun*

preclude *verb* If something **precludes** you from doing something, it makes it impossible for you to do it: *The sheer cliff we had come to precluded us from going any further; The fact that he was hopeless at maths precluded him from doing engineering.*

precocious /*say* pruh-**koh**-shuhs/ *adjective* more advanced than others of the same age: *Anyone who composes music at the age of four, like Mozart, is precocious.*
☐ **precociously**, *adverb* –**precociousness**, *noun* –**precocity** /*say* pruh-**kos**-uh-tee/, *noun*

☑ SPELLING TIP Notice that there are two separate *c*'s in this word, the first one giving a 'k' sound and the second a 'sh' sound. **Precocious** literally means 'before being cooked', so when someone does something that is **precocious**, they do it at too early a stage. The word is made up of the prefix *pre-* (meaning 'before') and *cocious* (coming from *coquere*, Latin for 'to cook').

predatory /*say* **pred**-uh-tuh-ree/ *adjective* A **predatory** animal hunts other animals for food: *A predatory bird soared high above looking for prey.*
☐ **predator**, *noun*

predecessor /*say* **pree**-duh-ses-uh/ *noun* someone who had the job before someone else: *Governor Macquarie arrived in Australia shortly after his predecessor had left.*

predicament /*say* pruh-**dik**-uh-muhnt/ *noun* a difficult or dangerous situation.

predicate /*say* **pred**-uh-kuht/ *noun* the word or words which say something about the subject of a sentence, such as 'ate a rabbit' in the sentence *The snake ate a rabbit*.

SEE the Grammar and Punctuation Guide appendix.

predict *verb* If you **predict** the future, you tell what is going to happen.
☐ **predictable**, *adjective* –**prediction**, *noun*

SIMILAR WORDS are **forecast** and **prophesy**.

predominate *verb* To **predominate** is to **1.** be stronger or more important: *The choir items predominate in the concert – the dancing group is only on the stage twice.* **2.** control or lead: *Her ideas predominate discussions because she knows her facts so well.*
☐ **predominance**, *noun* –**predominant**, *adjective*

pre-eminent *adjective* To be **pre-eminent** is to be at a much higher level in a particular area than others: *He is a pre-eminent heart surgeon.*
☐ **pre-eminence**, *noun*

preen *verb*
1. When birds **preen** their feathers, they clean them with their beak.
–*phrase* **2. preen yourself**, to be obviously pleased with your appearance or your achievements.

prefabricate *verb* If a company **prefabricates** a product, it makes it in a factory in parts, ready for putting together somewhere else at a later time: *The bridge was prefabricated and then transported in huge pieces to the river site.*
☐ **prefabrication**, *noun*

preface /*say* **pref**-uhs/ *noun*
1. an introduction or statement at the front of a book, explaining its purpose.
–*verb* **2.** If you **preface** something you say or do with something else, you do that thing first: *She prefaced her remarks with an apology for being late.*
☐ **prefatory** /*say* **pref**-uh-tree/, *adjective*: *The prefatory material was much easier to understand than the book was!*

prefect *noun* an older student with certain responsibilities in a school.

prefer /*say* pruh-**fer**/ *verb* (**prefers**, **preferring**, **preferred**, **has preferred**) If you **prefer** something, you like it more than another thing: *Dogs prefer playing with balls rather than sticks.*
☐ **preferable** /*say* **pref**-uh-ruh-buhl/, *adjective* –**preference** /*say* **pref**-uh-ruhns/, *noun*

☑ SPELLING TIP Notice that although you double the final *r* of **prefer** when you add *-ed* or *-ing*, the *r* remains single in the words **preferable** and **preference**. This is because the stress is these words has moved to the first syllable, and so follows the rule that the consonant remains single if the final syllable is not stressed.

prefix *noun* a word part which is put in front of a word to make a new word with a new meaning, such as *extra-* in *extraordinary* (*extra-* has been put in front of *ordinary*).

COMPARE this with **suffix**.
WORD HISTORY from a Latin word meaning 'fixed before'

pregnant *adjective* If a woman is **pregnant**, she is going to have a baby.
☐ **pregnancy**, *noun*

prehistoric *adjective* belonging to the time before history was written or records were kept.

prejudice /*say* **prej**-uh-duhs/ *noun*
1. an opinion unfairly formed beforehand, without reason or proof. **2.** harm or unfair treatment which is caused by an opinion like this.
☐ **prejudiced**, *adjective*

☑ SPELLING TIP Remember that there is no *d* before the *j* in this word, although it can sound as if there is. It will help if you know that the basic meaning of **prejudice** is 'judgement made in advance or too early'. It is made up of the prefix *pre-* (meaning 'before' or 'in advance') and *judice* (a form of *judicium*, the Latin word for 'judgement'.

preliminary /*say* pruh-**lim**-uhn-ree/ *adjective* Something that is **preliminary** comes before the main matter: *The preliminary talk was about how to introduce ourselves.*

> ☑ SPELLING TIP Remember the *ary* ending. You usually don't hear the *a* when the word is pronounced.

prelude /*say* **prel**-yoohd/ *noun* 1. something that comes before: *A sore throat is often a prelude to the flu.* 2. a short piece of music written for an instrument.

premature /*say* **prem**-uh-chuh, prem-uh-**tyooh**-uh/ *adjective* If something is **premature**, it happens before it ought to or before it usually does: *It was premature to open a bank account before I had any money.*
☐ **prematurely**, *adverb*

premeditate *verb* To **premeditate** an action is to plan it beforehand.
☐ **premeditation**, *noun*

premier /*say* **prem**-ee-uh/ *adjective* 1. of top quality or the best of its kind: *The premier football team is doing a tour of the country.*
–*noun* 2. the leader of a state government in Australia.
☐ **premiership**, *noun*

> ANOTHER FORM This word (as in definition 2) is spelt with a capital letter when you are writing the title of a particular person.

premiere /*say* prem-ee-**air**/ *noun* 1. the first public performance of a play, film, or something similar.
–*verb* 2. If a public performance **premieres**, it appears for the first time: *A new production of 'Peter Pan' is premiering next week.*

premises /*say* **prem**-uh-suhz/ *plural noun* a building or house with the land belonging to it: *There was a big sign with the words 'Keep off these premises.'.*

premium /*say* **pree**-mee-uhm/ *noun* 1. a bonus, gift or additional sum. 2. a payment made for insurance.

premonition /*say* prem-uh-**nish**-uhn/ *noun* a feeling that something is about to happen, usually something bad.

> ☑ SPELLING TIP *Tricky 'uh' sound*: the second vowel sound is spelt *o*. This will be easier to remember if you see that **premonition** is made up of the prefix *pre-* (meaning 'before') and *monition* (from *monere*, Latin for 'to warn').

preoccupied *adjective* If someone is **preoccupied**, they are completely taken up in thought: *The teacher was preoccupied and did not hear the bell.*
☐ **preoccupation**, *noun*

prepare *verb* 1. To **prepare** something is to make or get it ready: *We helped prepare the hall for the choir presentation.* 2. If you **prepare** yourself for something, you make yourself ready for it and able to deal with it: *We prepared ourselves for bad news.*
☐ **preparation**, *noun* –**prepared**, *adjective*: *Mum says that when she has her make-up on she feels prepared for anything.* –**preparatory**, *adjective*

preposition /*say* prep-uh-**zish**-uhn/ *noun* a word placed before a noun to show its relation to other words in the sentence.

> SEE the Grammar and Punctuation Guide appendix.

preposterous *adjective* absurd or far from what is normal or sensible: *He had some preposterous idea of capturing light in bottles and selling it to people who wanted to tan fast.*
☐ **preposterously**, *adverb*

prerogative /*say* pruh-**rog**-uh-tiv/ *noun* a right or privilege: *Sally said it was her party and her prerogative to choose who would come.*

> ☑ SPELLING TIP Note that the beginning of this word is the prefix *pre-*, not *per*, though some people pronounce it in this way.

preschool *noun* a place where some young children go for a year or so before they start primary school.

prescribe *verb* If someone **prescribes** something, they order it for use as a treatment: *I'll ask the doctor to prescribe something to help my awful itch.*

prescription *noun* a written order by a doctor to a chemist for medicine.

presence *noun* attendance or being in a place: *His presence is sometimes a nuisance.*

present[1] /*say* **prez**-uhnt/ *adjective* To be **present** is to be 1. happening or existing now: *The present class monitor is Clive.* 2. being in a place: *Everyone was present except for Nicole.*

> SEE ALSO **present tense**.

present[2] *verb* /*say* pruh-**zent**/ 1. To **present** something is to hand it over, especially in a formal way: *A champion ex-swimmer presented the trophies.*
–*noun* /*say* **prez**-uhnt/ 2. something given, such as a gift: *birthday presents.*
☐ **presentation**, *noun* –**presenter**, *noun*: *the presenter of the late-night show.*

presentable *adjective* fit to be seen: *My dad's beard looked pretty scruffy and he had to clip it so he would look presentable.*
☐ **presentably**, *adverb*

presently *adverb*
1. in a short time: *Don't look up at the sun – the eclipse will happen presently.* **2.** at this time: *Presently, my best friend is Sophie.*

present tense *noun* the form of a verb which shows that something is happening or exists now, such as 'eat' in *I eat muesli* and 'am eating' in *I am eating and can't talk to you.*

SEE the Grammar and Punctuation Guide appendix.

preservative *noun* a chemical substance that prevents something, such as food, from going bad: *This fruit juice contains no preservatives.*

preserve /*say* pruh-**zerv**/ *verb*
1. To **preserve** food is to treat it a special way to keep it from going bad: *to preserve fish by smoking.*
–*noun* **2.** something that is preserved, especially fruit made into a jam: *apricot preserve.*
□ **preservation**, *noun* –**preservative**, *noun*

preside *verb* If someone **presides** at a meeting or assembly, they are in charge of it and control it: *They asked him to be chairperson and preside at the meeting of club members.*

president *noun*
1. the person who holds the highest political position in a republic. **2.** someone chosen to have control over the meetings of a society or something similar.
□ **presidential**, *adjective*

ANOTHER FORM This word (as in definition 1) is spelt with a capital letter when you are writing the title of a particular person.

press *verb*
1. If you **press** something, you push it to act on it in some way: *Mary pressed the front door bell.* **2.** If you **press** something against something else, you push it against it: *She pressed up against the other people to make more room.* **3.** If you **press** something, you squeeze it: *Mum pressed my arm and told me not to worry.* **4.** If you **press** clothes, you iron them. **5.** If someone **presses** you to do something, they try hard to get you to do it.
–*noun* **6.** a machine used for printing. **7. the press**, newspapers, magazines and so on, or the people who write for them.

pressure /*say* **presh**-uh/ *noun*
1. the weight or force with which something presses on something else: *The tomatoes squashed under the pressure of the potatoes.* **2.** a force applied to something, measured as so much weight on a unit of area: *We had to increase the pressure in the tyres.* **3.** continual worry: *It is a pressure having to do homework every night.*
–*verb* **4.** If you **pressure** someone to do something, you use force to persuade them to do it: *They pressured me to join the team.*

pressurise *verb* If an internal area like the cabin of a plane is **pressurised**, its air pressure is kept at normal pressure rather than what is outside.

ANOTHER SPELLING is **pressurize**.

prestige /*say* pres-**teezh**/ *noun* high reputation or standing: *He thought the expensive car would add to his prestige.*
□ **prestigious**, *adjective*

☑ SPELLING TIP The main difficulty here is the *ige* which is pronounced as 'eezh'. This is because **prestige** comes from French.

presume /*say* pruh-**zyoohm**/ *verb*
1. If you **presume** something, you believe it to be true because it seems obvious, even though you might not be certain: *'I presume you want something to eat', said my mum.* **2.** To **presume** to do something is to be bold enough to do it: *She never presumed to open her mouth, let alone suggest anything.*
□ **presumption** /*say* pruh-**zump**-shuhn/, *noun*

A SIMILAR WORD (for definition 1) is **assume**.

pretence *noun*
1. a false show: *Her humility is a pretence – she is really quite vain!* **2.** a pretended reason: *All that talk about the phone being broken was a pretence – he just couldn't be bothered to call!*

☑ SPELLING TIP Remember that the end of this word is *tence*, not *tense*. The spelling **pretense** is used in American English but **pretence** is the standard spelling in Australian English.

pretend *verb*
1. If you **pretend** that something is the case, you try to make other people believe that it is true, even though it is not: *I pretended to be pleased to see her.* **2.** If you **pretend** to do something, you act as though you are doing it but you do not really do it: *She pretended to ring her friend but she really called up her own number.* **3.** If you **pretend** that something is the case, you think for a while about how things would be if it was true, even though you know that it isn't really: *When I was a little girl, I used to pretend that I was a princess.*

pretentious /*say* pruh-**ten**-shuhs/ *adjective* having an exaggerated outward show of importance, wealth and so on.
□ **pretentiously**, *adverb*

pretty *adjective* (**prettier**, **prettiest**)
1. pleasant or attractive.
–*adverb* **2.** rather or quite: *The party was pretty amazing!*
□ **prettily**, *adverb* –**prettiness**, *noun*

pretzel *noun* a small, crisp salted biscuit, often in the shape of a knot.

WORD HISTORY from a German word

prevail *verb* To **prevail** is **1.** to win: *The opposition team were the strong favourites, but, in the end, we prevailed.* **2.** to be general or frequent: *Some unusual ideas about Australia used to prevail – for instance, that kangaroos regularly bounded along city streets.*
–*phrase* **3. prevail upon**, to persuade successfully: *We prevailed on them to contribute to the school library fund.*

prevalent /*say* **prev**-uh-luhnt/ *adjective* widespread: *Snakes seem to be more prevalent this summer.*
☐ **prevalence**, *noun*

prevaricate /*say* pruh-**va**-ruh-kayt/ *verb* If you **prevaricate**, you speak in a way which tries to avoid the point by trickery: *The journalist asked a third time – but still the politician prevaricated.*
☐ **prevarication**, *noun*

prevent *verb* If you **prevent** someone from doing something or **prevent** something from happening, you make certain that they do not do it or it does not happen: *The club prevented people who weren't members from coming in*; *Dad swerved the car and just managed to prevent an accident.*
☐ **prevention**, *noun* –**preventive**, *adjective*

preview *noun* a showing of a film or show, or a small part of it, before the public is allowed to see it.

previous *adjective* happening before: *On her previous visit, she had got lost.*
☐ **previously**, *adverb*

prey /*rhymes with* may/ *noun*
1. an animal hunted for food by another: *Snakes can swallow prey much bigger than you would think.* **2.** A **bird of prey** is one which hunts smaller birds and animals.
–*verb in the phrase* **3. prey on**, to hunt and eat: *Hyenas prey on animals that are sick or diseased.*

> ☑ SPELLING TIP Don't confuse the spelling of **prey** with **pray** which has the same sound. When someone **prays**, they talk to the god they believe in.

price *noun*
1. the amount of money for which something is bought or sold.
–*verb* **2.** If someone **prices** goods, they determine what price they will be.

priceless *adjective* having a value beyond all price: *My grandmother is always telling me how priceless it is to have good health.*

prick *noun*
1. a small hole made by a needle or something else sharp. **2.** the feeling of being pricked.
–*verb* **3.** If you **prick** something, you pierce a small hole in it.
–*phrase* **4. prick up your ears**, to start listening, especially to something of particular interest.

prickle *noun* a sharp point, especially on a plant.
☐ **prickly**, *adjective*

pride *noun*
1. well-earned pleasure or satisfaction: *He takes pride in his work.* **2.** a high, or too high, opinion of your own position or importance. **3.** a group of lions.
–*verb in the phrase* **4. pride yourself on**, to take well-earned pleasure or satisfaction in: *We prided ourselves on doing a very good group project.*

priest *noun* someone whose job is to perform religious ceremonies.
☐ **priestess**, *noun* –**priesthood**, *noun* –**priestly**, *adjective*

> ☑ SPELLING TIP *Tricky vowel sound*: *ie* spelling for the 'ee' sound. This follows the rule that *i* comes before *e* except after *c*.

prig *noun* someone who is too concerned about doing the right thing and who thinks they are the only one doing things properly.
☐ **priggish**, *adjective* –**priggishly**, *adverb*

prim *adjective* (**primmer**, **primmest**) stiff and very proper in manner.
☐ **primly**, *adverb*

primary *adjective*
1. If something is **primary**, it is first in order or importance: *The primary reason for exercising is for your health.* **2. Primary** education is the first stage of school, usually for children between the ages of five and eleven.
☐ **primarily**, *adverb*

primate /*say* **pruy**-mayt/ *noun* any mammal of the group that includes humans, apes and monkeys.

prime *adjective*
1. of the first importance or quality: *prime time television*; *prime cuts of meat.*
–*noun* **2.** the period or condition of greatest energy and health: *As a netballer, she is now in her prime.*

prime minister *noun*
1. the leader of the federal government in Australia. **2.** the leader of the government in some other countries.

> ANOTHER FORM This is spelt with capital letters when you are writing the title of a particular person.

prime number *noun* a number which can be divided only by itself and 1.

primer /*say* **pruy**-muh/ *noun* the first coat of paint used to prepare a surface for the next coat.

primeval /*say* pruy-**meev**-uhl/ *adjective* belonging to the earliest period of the earth: *primeval forms of life.*

> WORD HISTORY from a Latin word meaning 'young'

☑ SPELLING TIP Notice the *eval* ending of this word. Don't confuse it with the word *evil* (meaning 'wicked').

primitive /*say* **prim**-uh-tiv/ *adjective* belonging to an early stage of development: *Sharpened stones are an example of primitive tools.*

prince *noun* a son or near male relation of a king or queen.
☐ **princely**, *adjective*

ANOTHER FORM This is spelt with a capital letter when you are writing the title of a particular person.

princess *noun*
1. a daughter or near female relation of a king or queen. **2.** someone married to a prince.

ANOTHER FORM This is spelt with a capital letter when you are writing the title of a particular person.

principal /*say* **prin**-suh-puhl/ *adjective*
1. main or leading: *The principal actors were very good but the others were disappointing.*
–*noun* **2.** the head of a school.

☑ SPELLING TIP Remember the *al* ending in **principal** – make the **principal** your *pal*. Don't confuse it with **principle** which has the same sound. A **principle** is a general truth or rule.

principle /*say* **prin**-suh-puhl/ *noun*
1. a general truth or rule: *Shop owners often state the principle that the customer is always right.* **2.** a basic belief, teaching, or opinion: *the principles of Islam.* **3.** an inner sense of right behaviour: *He is a person of principle.*
–*phrase* **4. in principle**, having to do with the basic ideas or principles: *I accept your plan in principle.* **5. on principle**, according to a personal rule for right behaviour: *He doesn't eat meat on principle.*

☑ SPELLING TIP Remember the *le* ending in **principle**. Don't confuse it with **principal** which has the same sound.

print *verb*
1. To **print** a publication is to make copies of it by pressing an inked surface onto paper or other material: *The book was printed in Hong Kong.* **2.** If you **print**, you write in separate letters rather than in cursive script: *We had to print our name in full and then sign.*
–*phrase* **3. in print**, **a.** published: *My aunt's book is finally in print.* **b.** of a book, still able to be bought from the publisher: *The book is no longer in print, so we have to look in second-hand stores.* **4. out of print**, of a book, sold out by the publisher.

printer *noun*
1. a person who is in the business of printing books, newspapers and so on. **2.** in computers, a device which gives out information in printed form.

printout *noun* information printed by a computer so that it can be read.

prior *adjective*
1. earlier: *Sandra thinks that in a prior life she may have been a belly dancer.*
–*phrase* **2. prior to**, before: *The plan was to have a snack prior to going to the pictures.*

☑ SPELLING TIP Remember the *or* (not *er*) ending. It might help if you think of the *or* in *before* – a word which has a similar meaning to **prior**.

priority /*say* pruy-**o**-ruh-tee/ *noun* the right to go before someone or something else, because of urgency or importance: *The sickest people will be given priority.*

prise /*say* pruyz/ *verb* If you **prise** something open, you manage to get it open although it is quite firmly stuck. Often you have to use something as a lever to open it: *After Mum had shaken the paint, she prised open the lid with a screwdriver.*

☑ SPELLING TIP Remember that **prise** is always spelt with *ise* (not *ize*). Don't confuse it with **prize** which sounds the same. A **prize** is a reward for success and to **prize** something is to value it highly.

prism /*say* **priz**-uhm/ *noun* a transparent object, usually of glass and with triangular ends, used for breaking light down into the colours of the rainbow.
☐ **prismatic**, *adjective*

WORD HISTORY from a Greek word meaning 'something sawed'

prison *noun* a place where people are kept locked up as a punishment for a crime.
☐ **imprison**, *verb* –**imprisonment**, *noun* –**prisoner**, *noun*

ANOTHER WORD for this is **jail**.

private *adjective*
1. If something is **private**, it belongs to someone and is for their use only: *We could not look any further because it was private property.* **2.** If something is **private**, it is secret: *The letter was marked 'private'.*
–*noun* **3.** a soldier of the lowest rank.
☐ **privacy**, *noun* –**privately**, *adverb*

A SIMILAR WORD (for definitions 1 and 2) is **personal**.
THE OPPOSITE (of definition 1) is **public**.

privet *noun* an evergreen tree or shrub introduced into Australia from Europe, which is now thought to be a pest because it grows over areas of native bush.

privilege /*say* **priv**-uh-lij/ *noun* a special right or advantage enjoyed by only a limited number of people: *The sign said that it was a privilege to view the penguins and people should look after the site.*
☐ **privileged**, *adjective*

☑ SPELLING TIP *Tricky 'uh' sound*: the middle vowel sound is spelt with an *i*. Also remember that there is no *d* in this word. The ending *ege* gives the 'ij' sound. This part of the word comes from *lex*, the Latin word for 'law', forms of which are spelt with a *g*, as in *legal*.

prize *noun*
1. a reward for winning a race or competition. **2.** something won in a lottery or raffle.
–*verb* **3.** If you **prize** something, you value it highly: *Elspeth prizes the trophies she has won in debating.*

☑ SPELLING TIP Don't confuse the spelling of **prize** with **prise** which is to force something open, usually with a lever.

pro- *prefix* a word part meaning 'in favour of': *There were a number of pro-war speakers.*

THE OPPOSITE is **anti-**.
WORD HISTORY this prefix comes from Latin

probable *adjective* likely to happen or be true.
☐ **probably**, *adverb*

probation *noun*
1. a period of trial: *Her employment will start with three month's probation after which a decision will be made about permanent employment.* **2.** a system of punishment in which certain people who have broken the law can stay free on condition of good behaviour: *He was convicted of minor drug charges and put on a year's probation.*
☐ **probationary**, *adjective*

probe *verb* To **probe** something is to examine or search it thoroughly: *The doctor probed the lump with his fingers.*
☐ **probe**, *noun*

problem *noun*
1. something which is difficult or uncertain: *His health is a problem*; *We have had problems with the computer lately – it has not been working well.* **2.** a question to be answered: *The teacher set us a very tricky problem.*
☐ **problematic**, *adjective*

procedure /*say* pruh-**see**-juh/ *noun*
1. a way of doing something: *The procedure for choosing a school captain is for each class to nominate someone and then for the whole school to vote.* **2.** writing or speaking which tells how to do or make something step by step. **3.** a surgical operation or other medical technique.

ANOTHER FORM (of definition 3) is **medical procedure**.

☑ SPELLING TIP *Tricky vowel sound*: the middle vowel sound is spelt with a single *e*. This word comes from *proceed* but remember that one of the *e*'s has been dropped.

proceed /*say* pruh-**seed**/ *verb*
1. To **proceed** is to move forward, especially after stopping. **2.** If some activity **proceeds**, it goes on or continues.

☑ SPELLING TIP Note that the ending is *ceed*. The *ee* spelling is not difficult, but you have to be careful not to confuse it with words with a related meaning which are spelt with *cede*, such as *precede*.

proceeding *noun*
1. behaviour or way of acting: *What was the reason for such a strange proceeding?* **2. proceedings**, records of the activities and meetings of a club or society: *She took notes of all the proceedings in shorthand.*

proceeds /*say* **proh**-seedz/ *plural noun* money brought in from a sale, business, etc.

process *noun*
1. a series of actions carried out for a particular purpose: *The process for selecting the cricket team has begun.*
–*verb* **2.** If you **process** something, you prepare or treat it in some way: *The film is processed at a local lab.*
☐ **processor**, *noun*

☑ SPELLING TIP *Single/double letter alert*: one *c* (giving an 's' sound) and double *s* at the end.

procession /*say* pruh-**sesh**-uhn/ *noun* an orderly line of people, cars or floats moving along in a ceremony or as a show.

A SIMILAR WORD is **parade**.

☑ SPELLING TIP *Single/double letter alert*: one *c* (giving an 's' sound) and double *s*. Remember that this word is formed from *process* with the suffix *-ion* added. It has nothing to do with a session.

proclaim *verb* To **proclaim** something is to announce it formally and publicly: *The prime minister proclaimed a holiday to celebrate the victory.*
☐ **proclamation**, *noun*

procrastinate *verb* If you **procrastinate**, you put off doing something until another time.
☐ **procrastination**, *noun*

procreate *verb* If a male and female **procreate**, they produce offspring.
☐ **procreation**, *noun*

procure *verb* If you **procure** something, you obtain it: *Once we knew what food could be procured, we planned the menu.*
☐ **procurable**, *adjective*

prod *verb* (**prods**, **prodding**, **prodded**, **has prodded**) If you **prod** someone or something, you push them with something such as your finger or a stick.
☐ **prod**, *noun*

prodigal *adjective* wasteful or extravagant: *Don't lend him anything – he tends to be prodigal as soon as he has money in his pocket.*

prodigious /*say* pruh-**dij**-uhs/ *adjective* Something **prodigious** is extremely great in size, amount or force: *a prodigious appetite.*

prodigy /*say* **prod**-uh-jee/ *noun* (*plural* **prodigies**) someone, especially a child, who has talent far greater than is normal: *He was a prodigy in chess from a very early age.*

produce *verb* /*say* pruh-**dyoohs**/
1. To **produce** something means to create it, grow it, or make it: *Rabbits produce so many offspring that they are a major problem for farmers.* **2.** To **produce** something is to cause it or make it happen: *The new treatment is producing very good effects in some patients.* **3.** If you **produce** something, you bring it out of somewhere in order to show it to someone: *She produced a torn ticket from her pocket.* **4.** If someone **produces** a play or film, they organise and manage the business side.
–*noun* /*say* **prod**-yoohs/ **5.** farm or natural products: *They should be proud of their produce considering the drought they have been through.*
☐ **producer**, *noun* –**production**, *noun* –**productive**, *adjective* –**productivity**, *noun*

product *noun*
1. something made or brought into existence: *There are many more products on supermarket shelves than there used to be.* **2.** in mathematics, the result you get by multiplying two or more numbers together. **3.** in chemistry, a substance obtained from another substance through chemical change.

profane /*say* pruh-**fayn**/ *adjective* showing deep lack of respect for religion.
☐ **profanely**, *adverb* –**profanity** /*say* pruh-**fan**-uh-tee/, *noun*

WORD HISTORY from a Latin word meaning 'outside the temple'

profess *verb* If you **profess** something, you declare or show it, but you may not be sincere: *Sophie professed to be my friend but behind my back she was talking about me.*

profession *noun*
1. an area of work in which advanced and special knowledge of a subject is needed: *His mother wants him to go into a profession and be an accountant or a lawyer.* **2.** the people in a profession taken as a whole: *The profession of dentistry has welcomed the new preventive dental scheme.* **3.** an announcement, whether true or false: *Just be a bit careful about her profession of loyalty.*
☐ **professionalism**, *noun* –**professionally**, *adverb*

☑ SPELLING TIP *Single/double letter alert*: one *f* and double *s*.

professional *adjective*
1. following an occupation to earn a living from it: *I want to be a professional tennis player when I grow up.* **2.** belonging to a profession: *a professional association.* **3.** of high quality: *Her performance was very professional.*
☐ **professional**, *noun* –**professionalism**, *noun* –**professionally**, *adverb*

THE OPPOSITE (of definition 1) is **amateur**.

professor /*say* pruh-**fes**-uh/ *noun* a university teacher of the highest rank.
☐ **professorial** /*say* prof-uh-**saw**-ree-uhl/, *adjective*

☑ SPELLING TIP *Single/double letter alert*: one *f* and double *s*. Also notice the *or* (not *er*) ending.

proffer *verb* If you **proffer** something, you place it before someone for them to accept: *My mother proffered ten dollars to pay for the lunch but her friend insisted on paying.*

☑ SPELLING TIP *Double letter alert*: double *f* in the middle. Think of the related word *offer*. Also notice that, as with *offer*, you do not double the final *r* when you add *-ed* or *-ing*, following the rule that the consonant remains single if the final syllable is not stressed.

proficient /*say* pruh-**fish**-uhnt/ *adjective* skilled or expert: *Once we were proficient in hitting the ball back, we learned how to aim wherever we wanted on the court.*
☐ **proficiency**, *noun* –**proficiently**, *adverb*

profile *noun*
1. a line which shows the outer shape of a face, especially from a side view. **2.** a drawing, painting, or photograph of the side view of a face. **3.** a short account of someone's life and character: *We had to write a short profile of ourselves on our first day in the new class.*
–*phrase* **4. keep a low profile**, to act so as not to be noticed.

profit *noun*
1. money made from selling something at a higher price than you paid for it. **2.** advantage or benefit: *There is some profit in studying before an exam.*
–*verb* (**profits**, **profiting**, **profited**, **has profited**) **3.** If you **profit** from something, you gain from it: *Ultimately, we profited from going the longer way because we saw so much more.*
☐ **profitable**, *adjective* –**profiteer**, *noun*

☑ SPELLING TIP Don't confuse the spelling of **profit** with **prophet** which has a similar sound. A **prophet** is a teacher or leader, especially someone in Biblical times who spoke on behalf of God. Also notice that you do not double the final *t* of **profit** when you add *-ed* or *-ing*, following the rule that the consonant remains single if the final syllable is not stressed.

profound *adjective* very deep: *She had a profound love of the outback.*
☐ **profoundly**, *adjective*: *profoundly deaf.* –**profundity**, *noun*

profuse /*say* pruh-**fyoohs**/ *adjective* plentiful: *They offered profuse thanks to their rescuers.*
☐ **profusely**, *adverb* –**profusion**, *noun*

progeny /*say* **proj**-uh-nee/ *noun* offspring or descendants: *The progeny of a male lion and a female tiger is called a 'liger'.*
☐ **progenitor**, *noun* an ancestor.

prognosis /*say* prog-**noh**-suhs/ *noun* (*plural* **prognoses** /*say* prog-**noh**-seez/) a doctor's opinion on how a disease will develop.

program *noun*
1. a plan to be followed: *My mum follows a strict exercise program.* **2.** a list of items and performers in a concert or play. **3.** a particular entertainment or production: *We disagreed about what program to watch at 8 o'clock.* **4.** a set of instructions that makes a computer perform a task.
–*verb* (**programs**, **programming**, **programmed**, **has programmed**) **5.** If you **program** a machine or a system, you set it up to work in a certain way: *Dad asked me to program the video so we could all see what we wanted.*
☐ **programmer**, *noun* Someone whose job it is to write programs for a computer is called a **programmer** or a **computer programmer**.

ANOTHER SPELLING (for definitions 1–3) is **programme**. For the meaning to do with computers (definition 4), the spelling **program** alone is used.
WORD HISTORY from a Greek word meaning 'a public notice in writing'

progress *noun* /*say* **proh**-gres/
1. advance or improvement: *Has there been any progress in their talks?*
–*verb* /*say* pruh-**gres**/ **2.** If someone or something **progresses**, it advances or improves: *Now that the infection has subsided, she is progressing well.*
–*phrase* /*say* **proh**-gres/ **3. in progress**, going on or under way: *Work on the bridge will be in progress for another year.*
☐ **progression**, *noun*

progressive *adjective* If someone is **progressive**, they favour or make changes or improvements: *There were the usual arguments between the progressive and the conservative sides.*
☐ **progressively**, *adverb*

prohibit *verb* (**prohibits**, **prohibiting**, **prohibited**, **has prohibited**) To **prohibit** something is to forbid it by a law or rule: *We are prohibited from leaving the school grounds without a note from home.*
☐ **prohibition**, *noun* –**prohibitive**, *adjective*

project *noun* /*say* **proh**-jekt, **proj**-ekt/
1. a planned piece of work: *The project for March is to totally replant the school garden.* **2.** a special piece of work that you do for school, usually by researching something: *For our project, we can choose between bridges or fire ants.*
–*verb* /*say* pruh-**jekt**/ **3.** To **project** something is to throw it forward or up high: *Joseph didn't project his voice enough in the play and we could only hear Mary and the shepherds.* **4.** If something **projects**, it sticks out: *The table projects too far into the hall.* **5.** If someone **projects** a film, they show it on a screen.
☐ **projection**, *noun*

projectile /*say* pruh-**jek**-tuyl/ *noun* something thrown or fired with great force.

A SIMILAR WORD is **missile**.

projector *noun* a piece of equipment for showing a film or a slide on a screen.

☑ SPELLING TIP Remember the *or* (not *er*) ending. You could think of 'on screen' for *o* to remind you.

proliferate /*say* pruh-**lif**-uh-rayt/ *verb* If something **proliferates**, it grows by multiplying: *Swimming pools have proliferated in many suburbs.*
☐ **proliferation**, *noun*

☑ SPELLING TIP *Single letter alert*: one *l* and one *f* (as in the word *life* which is hidden inside **proliferate** but not related to its meaning). There are no double letters in this word.

prolific *adjective* producing plentifully: *a prolific passionfruit vine*; *a prolific goal-scorer.*

prologue /*say* **proh**-log/ *noun*
1. a speech at the beginning of a play. **2.** anything that introduces something else: *Hurting my tooth while eating breakfast was the prologue to a day of disasters!*

☑ SPELLING TIP *Silent letter alert*: don't forget the silent *ue* at the end. It is spelt in this way because it comes from French. The ending *logue* with the same sound turns up in several words that have to do with speaking, including *dialogue* and *monologue*.

prolong *verb* To **prolong** something is to make it last longer: *If only we could prolong our holiday!*
☐ **prolongation**, *noun* –**prolonged**, *adjective*

promenade /*say* prom-uh-**nahd**/ *noun*
1. an unhurried walk, especially in a public place. 2. a place where people walk to and fro, especially next to a beach.

ANOTHER WORD (for definition 2) is **esplanade**.

prominent /*say* **prom**-uh-nuhnt/ *adjective*
1. If someone is **prominent**, they are important or well known: *a prominent local lawyer.* 2. If something is **prominent**, it is very noticeable: *The posters were placed in prominent positions around the city.*
□ **prominence**, *noun* –**prominently**, *adverb*

☑ SPELLING TIP Remember the *ent* (not *ant*) ending. If you see that **prominent** has the word *mine* hidden in it (although it is not related to the meaning), you will be able to remember the *e* in the ending.

promiscuous /*say* pruh-**mis**-kyooh-uhs/ *adjective* having many sexual partners.
□ **promiscuity**, *noun* –**promiscuously**, *adverb*

promise *noun*
1. an announcement or statement that you will do, or keep from doing something. 2. signs of future excellence: *Our new dog shows a lot of promise – he can already shake hands.*
–*verb* 3. If you **promise** something, you state that something will happen or not happen in the future.
□ **promising**, *adjective*: *an extremely promising dog.*

promontory /*say* **prom**-uhn-tree/ *noun* (*plural* **promontories**) a high point of land or rock sticking out into the sea.

☑ SPELLING TIP *Tricky 'uh' sound*: the middle vowel sound is spelt with an *o*. Also remember that the ending is *ory* although you do not hear the *o* when you say the word. If you remember that **promontory** has three *o*'s inside it, you should get the spelling right.

promote *verb*
1. To **promote** someone is to raise or advance them in rank or position: *Our teacher has been promoted to be deputy principal.* 2. To **promote** something is to try to increase its sales by advertising: *They are going to promote their new corn products at the show.*
□ **promotion**, *noun* –**promotional**, *adjective*

prompt *adjective*
1. immediate: *Mum got a prompt response when she complained about the phone.*
–*verb* 2. To **prompt** someone is to encourage them to act: *A desire to help prompted him to speak.* 3. If you **prompt** an actor in a play, you tell them the next words to say when they have forgotten them.
□ **prompter**, *noun* –**promptitude**, *noun* –**promptly**, *adverb*

prone *adjective*
1. If you are **prone** to something, you often suffer from it: *Anna is prone to tooth decay and should be very careful about cleaning her teeth.* 2. If you are **prone** to do something, you have a tendency to do it often: *He is prone to talk about himself rather too much.* 3. If you are **prone**, you are lying on your front.

prong *noun* a thin, sharp point on a fork.

pronoun *noun* a word which stands for a noun, such as *I, she, them, it, those* or *who*.

SEE the Grammar and Punctuation Guide appendix.

pronounce /*say* pruh-**nowns**/ *verb* If you **pronounce** a word, you say it in a certain way: *Some words in other languages are hard for us to pronounce.*
□ **pronunciation** /*say* pruh-nun-see-**ay**-shuhn/, *noun*

pronounced *adjective* strongly marked: *Since the accident, Steve has had a pronounced limp.*

proof *noun* something that shows a thing is true.

proofread *verb* (**proofreads**, **proofreading**, **proofread**, **has proofread**) If you **proofread** a piece of writing, you read it in order to find and mark mistakes to be corrected: *Mum proofread my speech and made quite a few changes.*
□ **proofreader**, *noun*

prop *noun*
1. a stick, pole, beam or other support. 2. a person or thing serving as a support.
–*verb* (**props**, **propping**, **propped**, **has propped**) 3. If you **prop** something on or against another thing, you support it by resting it on the other thing.
–*phrase* 4. **prop up**, to support or prevent from falling: *We propped up the broken window with a piece of wood.*

propaganda /*say* prop-uh-**gan**-duh/ *noun* information which is used to try to make you believe a certain point of view: *My dad said the book was full of anti-government propaganda.*

☑ SPELLING TIP *Single letter alert*: there are no double letters in this word. You should be able to work out the spelling of **propaganda** because it is spelt as it sounds, but it looks unusual because it comes from Italian (originally from the Latin name of a committee of cardinals set up in 1622 by Pope Gregory XV to help spread the Christian faith).

propagate *verb*
1. If someone or something **propagates**, they increase or multiply: *My grandfather propagates orchids*; *In the heat, the plants propagated rapidly.* 2. If a person **propagates** something like information, they spread it: *I don't know*

who propagated the story that I could do triple somersaults.
☐ **propagation**, *noun*

propel /*say* pruh-**pel**/ *verb* (**propels**, **propelling**, **propelled**, **has propelled**) To **propel** something is to drive it forwards: *Some vehicles are propelled by diesel fuel*; *She took him by the arm and propelled him forward.*

> ☑ SPELLING TIP *Single letter alert*: only one *l* at the end. However, the *l* is doubled when you add *-ed* or *-ing*.

propellant *noun* the fuel used to propel a rocket.

propeller *noun* a device with turning blades used for driving an aircraft or ship.

> ☑ SPELLING TIP *Single/double letter alert*: the second *p* is single, but there is a double *l*. Also notice the *er* (not *or*) ending. Try rapping it out as *pro+ pel+ ler*.

proper *adjective* To be **proper** is to be **1.** appropriate or polite: *We have to eat in the proper way all the time, not just when we have visitors.* **2.** correct in behaviour, often too much so: *She was so proper that she made people feel slightly uncomfortable.* **3.** real or genuine: *I want proper food, not just peanuts!*
☐ **properly**, *adverb*

proper noun *noun* a noun that is the name of a particular place, person or thing, such as *Canberra*, *Shakespeare* or *the Eiffel Tower*.

> NOTE Proper nouns are spelt with a capital letter.
> COMPARE this with **common noun**. Also see the Grammar and Punctuation Guide appendix.

property *noun* (*plural* **properties**)
1. something that is owned: *There is a very big box for lost property at our school.* **2.** a piece of land or building that may be owned.

prophecy /*say* **prof**-uh-see/ *noun* (*plural* **prophecies**)
1. a statement telling what is going to happen in the future. **2.** a message from a god.

> ☑ SPELLING TIP Remember the *ph* spelling for the 'f' sound and the *ecy* ending. Remember too that the noun **prophecy** takes the *c* and the verb **prophesy** takes the *s*.

prophesy /*say* **prof**-uh-suy/ *verb* (**prophesies**, **prophesying**, **prophesied**, **has prophesied**) If you **prophesy** something, you predict that it will be so: *James prophesied that he would catch the biggest fish ever.*

> ☑ SPELLING TIP Remember the *ph* spelling for the 'f' sound and the *esy* ending. Don't confuse this verb with the noun **prophecy**.

prophet /*say* **prof**-uht/ *noun*
1. someone who speaks on behalf of a god. **2.** someone who predicts the future. **3.** a great teacher or leader.
☐ **prophetic**, *adjective*

> ☑ SPELLING TIP Remember the *ph* spelling for the 'f' sound in this word. Don't confuse the spelling of **prophet** with **profit** which has a similar sound. **Profit** is the money you make from selling something at a higher price than you paid for it.

proportion /*say* pruh-**paw**-shuhn/ *noun*
1. the relation or comparison of one thing to another according to its size, number, and so on: *The proportion of boy babies born to girl babies is slightly larger.* **2.** a proper or correct relationship between things: *You must draw the horse's head so that it is in proportion to the body.* **3.** a part, compared to the whole: *We all promised to give a proportion of our time to help.*
☐ **proportional**, *adjective* –**proportionate**, *adjective*

> ☑ SPELLING TIP *Tricky 'uh' sound*: the first vowel sound is spelt with an *o*. The prefix is *pro-* (not *pre-*) which means 'for' or 'having to do with'. So the literal meaning is 'having to do with (each person's) share or portion'.

propose *verb*
1. If someone **proposes** a certain plan or idea, they suggest it: *The coach proposed an extra training night.* **2.** If you **propose** to do something, you intend to do it. **3.** If a man **proposes** to a woman, he asks her to marry him.
☐ **proposal**, *noun* –**proposition**, *noun*

propound *verb* If you **propound** something, you put it forward to be considered, accepted, or acted on: *Of course, everybody was propounding their own theory.*

proprietor /*say* pruh-**pruy**-uh-tuh/ *noun* the person who owns a business or a property.
☐ **proprietary**, *adjective* –**proprietorship**, *noun*

propriety /*say* pruh-**pruy**-uh-tee/ *noun* good manners or proper behaviour.

propulsion /*say* pruh-**pul**-shuhn/ *noun* a force which moves something forward: *The missile was under rocket propulsion.*

prosaic /*say* proh-**zay**-ik/ *adjective* dull and unimaginative.
☐ **prosaically**, *adverb*

> ☑ SPELLING TIP **Prosaic** comes from the Latin word *prosa* meaning 'prose'. If you remember to add the *ic* suffix, which means 'having the properties of', you get **prosaic**.

proscribe *verb* If someone **proscribes** something, they forbid it: *Olympic athletes know that all forms of drug-taking are proscribed.*

☑ DO NOT CONFUSE **proscribe** with **prescribe**, which is to order something as a treatment for someone.

prose *noun* ordinary written or spoken language rather than poetry.

prosecute /*say* **pros**-uh-kyooht/ *verb* To **prosecute** someone is to accuse them before a court of law.
□ **prosecution**, *noun*

☑ SPELLING TIP *Tricky 'uh' sound*: the middle vowel sound is spelt with an *e*. It could help if you see that the words 'cute prose' occur in reverse order in this word. Rap it out as *pro+se+cute*.

proselyte /*say* **pros**-uh-luyt/ *noun* a convert or someone who has changed from one opinion to another.

☑ SPELLING TIP *Letter 'y' alert*: remember the *yte* spelling at the end (not *ite*). This word comes from Greek.

prospect *noun*
1. something looked forward to or expected, especially something successful: *The prospect of having the rest of the day off because the temperature was 40 degrees pleased everybody.* **2.** someone who may be a customer, contestant, and so on: *Our neighbour is always looking for likely prospects to marry her sons.* **3.** a view or a scene.
–*verb* **4.** To **prospect** is to search for gold or other minerals.
□ **prospective**, *adjective* –**prospector**, *noun*

prospectus *noun* a statement or pamphlet which advertises something new or gives more details about things like a school, university or commercial company.

prosperous *adjective* successful or wealthy: *He owns a few mining companies and is very prosperous.*
□ **prosperity**, *noun*

prostitute *noun* someone who has sexual intercourse with someone else for money.
□ **prostitution**, *noun*

prostrate *adjective* lying with your body flat, because you are tired or sick: *She had collapsed in the heat and was prostrate on the floor.*

protagonist /*say* pruh-**tag**-uh-nuhst/ *noun* the main character in a story or play.

protect *verb* To **protect** someone is to keep them safe from injury, danger or annoyance.
□ **protection**, *noun* –**protective**, *adjective* –**protector**, *noun*

SIMILAR WORDS are **guard**, **defend**, **shelter** and **shield**. Note that to **shelter** is to provide a place where someone can be safe or a covering for someone or something: *They sheltered the escapees in their garage*; *He put a handkerchief over his head to shelter it from the sun.* **Shield** is very similar and is used in relation to protecting someone by putting something between them and danger: *He shielded the child with his own body.*

protectorate /*say* pruh-**tek**-tuh-ruht/ *noun* a country protected and controlled by another stronger state.

protégé /*say* **proh**-tuh-zhay/ *noun* someone who is protected or supported by someone else.

☑ SPELLING TIP *Tricky 'uh' sound*: the middle vowel has the unusual spelling of *e* with an accent on it. There is another of these at the end of the word, this time giving the sound 'ay'. **Protégé** is spelt like this because it comes from the French word for 'protect'.

protein /*say* **proh**-teen/ *noun* any of a group of substances which are present in such foods as meat and cheese, and which are important to our diet.

☑ SPELLING TIP *Tricky vowel sound*: *ei* for the 'ee' sound in the last syllable. This does not fit in with the rule that *i* comes before *e*, except after *c*. That is because **protein** has come from the Greek word *proteios*, meaning 'primary'.

protest *noun* /*say* **proh**-test/
1. an objection or expression of disapproval.
–*verb* /*say* pruh-**test**/ **2.** If you **protest**, you make an objection or you express disapproval about something: *We protested about the highway being taken through our suburb.*
□ **protester**, *noun* –**protestation**, *noun*

protocol /*say* **proh**-tuh-kol/ *noun* the rules of behaviour and ceremony used on official occasions involving royalty, heads of state, diplomats, etc.

☑ SPELLING TIP *Tricky 'uh' sound*: the middle vowel sound is spelt *o*.

proton *noun* a very tiny particle present in the nucleus of every atom, the number of protons being different for each element. It has a type of energy which balances the energy of an electron.

NOTE The energy of a proton is called **positive**.
SEE ALSO **neutron** and **electron**.

prototype /*say* **proh**-tuh-tuyp/ *noun* the original or the model of something which is later copied.

☑ SPELLING TIP *Tricky 'uh' sound*: the middle vowel sound is spelt *o*. You will remember this if you see that **prototype** is made up of *proto-*, a prefix meaning 'original' (from *protos*, the Greek word for 'first'), and the word *type*.

protract *verb* If you **protract** something, you draw it out or lengthen it in time: *We protracted the time* *it took for the washing up so there was less time left for our piano practice.*

protractor *noun* an instrument used to measure or mark off angles.

protrude *verb* To **protrude** is to stick out.
☐ **protrusion**, *noun*

proud *adjective*
1. If you are **proud**, you are pleased about something that you have achieved: *We were really proud to come second in the relay.* **2.** If you are **proud**, you hold a very high opinion of yourself: *She's too proud to apologise for her mistake.*
☐ **proudly**, *adverb*

prove /*say* proohv/ *verb* (**proves**, **proving**, **proved**, **has proved** *or* **has proven**)
1. If you **prove** something, you show that it is true by presenting convincing facts: *You say that he's a liar, but can you prove it?* **2.** If something **proves** to be the case, it becomes clear that it is so: *To our surprise, he proved to be an excellent tennis player.*
☐ **proven**, *adjective*: *proven ability.*

☑ SPELLING TIP *Tricky vowel sound*: there is no double *o*. The spelling *ove* makes the 'oohv' sound, as it does in other words such as *move*.

proverb *noun* a short, popular, usually wise saying that has been used by people for a long time, such as *A bird in the hand is worth two in the bush.*
☐ **proverbial**, *adjective*

provide *verb*
1. If you **provide** something, you supply it: *Food and drink was to be provided.*
–*phrase* **2. provide for, a.** to support someone financially: *My family undertook to provide for an exchange student.* **b.** to allow for something in your planning: *Building two extra classrooms will provide for a growing population.*
☐ **provider**, *noun* –**providence**, *noun* –**provident**, *adjective*

province /*say* **prov**-uhns/ *noun* a division of a country or region.
☐ **provincial**, *adjective*

provision *noun*
1. a part of a document setting out a particular matter. **2.** the providing or supplying of something such as food. **3.** an arrangement made beforehand. **4. provisions**, supplies of food and other necessities.

provisional *adjective* temporary: *They said she could stay but only on a provisional basis.*
☐ **provisionally**, *adverb*

provoke *verb*
1. If something **provokes** a certain reaction, it causes it to happen: *His joke provoked loud laughter.* **2.** If someone **provokes** you, they intentionally say or do something that they know will make you angry.
☐ **provocation**, *noun* –**provocative**, *adjective*

prowess /*say* **prow**-es, prow-**es**/ *noun* outstanding ability or skill: *We were impressed by her athletic prowess.*

☑ SPELLING TIP Remember that there is a *w* in the middle of this word.

prowl *verb* To **prowl** is to go about quietly, as if in search of prey or something to steal.
☐ **prowl**, *noun*

proximity *noun* nearness in place, time and so on.

proxy *noun* (*plural* **proxies**) someone who is officially allowed to act for someone else: *We have someone standing in as proxy for the principal while she is away.*

prude *noun* someone who is overly modest or proper.

prudence *noun* carefulness that comes from good sound judgement.
☐ **prudent**, *adjective*

prune[1] *noun* a dried plum.

prune[2] *verb* To **prune** a plant is to cut branches off it, usually so that it grows better.

pry *verb* (**pries**, **prying**, **pried**, **has pried**) If someone **pries**, they look or search with too much curiosity: *She pried once too often and was caught snooping where she shouldn't be.*
☐ **prying**, *adjective*

PS *abbreviation* postscript.

NOTE This is often used at the end of a letter, before a message that has been added on.

psalm /*say* sahm/ *noun* a sacred song, hymn or poem.

WORD HISTORY from a Greek word meaning 'a song sung to the harp'

☑ SPELLING TIP *Silent letter alert*: there are two letters that you do not hear in this word – the *p* at the start, and the *l* before the *m*.

pseudonym /*say* **syooh**-duh-nim/ *noun* an invented name used instead of your real name.

ANOTHER WORD for an invented name used by a writer is **pen-name**.

☑ SPELLING TIP *Silent letter alert*: don't forget the silent *p* before the *s* at the beginning. There are several other difficulties with this word, which comes from Greek. It will help if you can see that it is made up of two parts – the prefix *pseudo-* (meaning 'false') and *nym* (meaning a 'word' or 'name').

psychiatry /*say* suh-**kuy**-uh-tree/ *noun* the study and treatment of mental illness.
☐ **psychiatric**, *adjective* –**psychiatrist**, *noun*

☑ SPELLING TIP *Silent letter alert*: don't forget the silent *p* before the *s* at the beginning. Also remember the *y* following the *s*. This word begins with the prefix *psycho-* with the *o* dropped. This means 'having to do with the mind' and comes from the Greek word for 'breath', 'mind' or 'soul'. If you learn this difficult prefix, you will also be able to spell related words, such as *psychology* and *psychic*.

psychic /*say* **suy**-kik/ *adjective* If someone is **psychic**, they apparently have supernatural mental powers, such as the ability to see the future or to know what other people are thinking.
□ **psychic**, *noun*

psychology /*say* suy-**kol**-uh-jee/ *noun* the study of the mind, how it works, and why people behave as they do.
□ **psychological**, *adjective* –**psychologist**, *noun*

psychosomatic /*say* suy-koh-suh-**mat**-ik/ *adjective* having to do with an illness of the body which is caused by or made worse by the person's emotional state.

p.t.o. *abbreviation* please turn over.

Pty /*say* pruh-**pruy**-uh-tree/ *abbreviation* short for *Proprietary.*

NOTE This is added to the name of a company to show that there is only a small number of people holding shares in it, often followed by 'Ltd'. See **Ltd**.

pub *noun Rather informal* a hotel.

NOTE A **pub** is usually the kind of hotel where people go for a drink, a meal and possibly to listen to music.
WORD HISTORY short for *public house*

puberty /*say* **pyooh**-buh-tee/ *noun* the stage of physical development when someone is first able to produce children.

pubic /*say* **pyooh**-bik/ *adjective* having to do with the lower part of your abdomen where the genitals are.

public *adjective*
1. having to do with or used by the people of a community or the people as a whole: *Public libraries are meant to be used by everyone*; *She thinks public transport should be the main form of transport instead of the private car.*
–*noun* **2.** the people of a community.
□ **publicly**, *adverb*

publican *noun* the owner or manager of a hotel.

publication *noun*
1. the publishing of a book, magazine, newspaper or other printed work. **2.** something which is published.

publicity /*say* pub-**lis**-uh-tee/ *noun* any advertisement, information and so on which is meant to attract the attention of the public: *We need a lot more publicity for the school fete.*

public relations *noun* the methods used to give the public a good impression of a particular business or company.

THE ABBREVIATION is **PR**.

publish *verb* If someone **publishes** what someone else has written, they prepare and issue it as a book or magazine in printed copies for sale to the public.
□ **publisher**, *noun*

puce /*say* pyoohs/ *adjective* dark purplish-brown.

WORD HISTORY from a French word meaning 'flea'

pucker *verb* If something **puckers**, it gathers into small folds or wrinkles: *The material had puckered where the machine had pulled it too tight.*
□ **pucker**, *noun*

pudding /*say* **pood**-ing/ *noun* a soft, sweet food usually served as a dessert.

puddle *noun* a small pool of liquid, such as dirty water left after rain.

puff *noun*
1. a short, quick sending out of air, wind or breath. **2.** a light pastry with a sweet or savoury filling: *a curry puff.*
–*verb* **3.** If someone or something **puffs**, they send out air in puffs.
–*phrase* **4. puff up**, to become swollen.
□ **puffed**, *adjective* –**puffy**, *adjective* (**puffier**, **puffiest**): *Her eyes were puffy from crying.*

puffin *noun* a seabird found in the northern Atlantic, with a body like a duck and a narrow, brightly coloured bill.

pug *noun* a small dog with a smooth coat, wrinkled face, snub nose and a tightly curled tail.

pugnacious /*say* pug-**nay**-shuhs/ *adjective* tending to quarrel or fight.
□ **pugnaciously**, *adverb*

pull *verb*
1. If you **pull** something, you get a firm hold on it and draw it towards you in order to move it: *Pull this lever to operate the machine.* **2.** If a person, animal or vehicle **pulls** something, they hold on to it or are tied to it and make it move along behind them: *The old horse was slowly pulling the heavy cart.* **3.** If you **pull** yourself somewhere, you hang onto something and use it to help you move yourself up or away: *By holding onto the rope she managed to pull herself from the river onto the bank.*
–*phrase* **4. pull in**, to move a vehicle to the side of the road in order to stop. **5. pull off**, *Informal* to succeed in gaining or performing something: *I*

was worried about how my performance would go, but I managed to pull it off. **6. pull up**, to stop. **7. pull yourself together**, to regain your self-control. **8. pull your weight**, to take a full and fair share of work, responsibility, and so on.
☐ **pull**, *noun*

SIMILAR WORDS (for definition 2) are **drag**, **haul** and **tow**.

pull-down menu *noun* a computer menu which appears on a computer screen when its title is selected and which offers a list of choices from which the computer user can select one by clicking so as to determine the next action or screen page.

ANOTHER TERM for this is **drop-down menu**.

pulley /*rhymes with* bully/ *noun* a wheel or system of wheels with ropes or chains, used to lift heavy things.

pullover *noun* a piece of warm clothing for the top half of the body.

OTHER WORDS for this are **jumper** and **sweater**.

pulmonary /*say* **pul**-muhn-ree, **pool**-muhn-ree/ *adjective* having to do with the lungs: *The pulmonary artery takes blood from the lungs to the body.*

pulp *noun*
1. the soft, juicy part of a fruit. **2.** any soft, wet mass: *The newspaper had been left out in the rain and had turned to pulp.*
–*verb* **3.** If you **pulp** something, you reduce it to pulp: *The books were pulped so the paper could be recycled.*

pulpit /*say* **pool**-puht/ *noun* a raised platform in a church where the priest or minister stands to give a sermon.

☑ SPELLING TIP Remember that the ending is *it* (not *et*).

pulsate /*say* pul-**sayt**/ *verb* If something **pulsates** it beats or throbs rhythmically, like your heart.
☐ **pulsation**, *noun*

pulse *noun*
1. the regular beating in the arteries caused by the pumping of blood by the heart. **2.** any regular beat.

pulverise *verb* If you **pulverise** something, you pound or grind it into dust or powder: *Flour is made by pulverising wheat or other grain.*

ANOTHER SPELLING is **pulverize**.

puma /*say* **pyooh**-muh/ *noun* a large animal of the cat family found in America.

OTHER TERMS for this are **cougar** and **mountain lion**.

pumice /*say* **pum**-uhs/ *noun* a light, spongy form of volcanic stone used for polishing things.

☑ SPELLING TIP *Single letter alert*: only one *m*. Also remember that the ending is *ice* (not *ace* or *is*). You could think of a **pumice** stone as looking like a white mouse, and you can find the word *mice* in **pumice**.

pummel *verb* (**pummels**, **pummelling**, **pummelled**, **has pummelled**) If you **pummel** something, you beat it with rapid blows of the fists.

pump *noun*
1. a device that forces a liquid or gas in or out of something.
–*verb* **2.** If you **pump** a liquid or gas, you force it to go in a certain direction using a pump: *Steam trains used to use water pumped from the lake.*
–*phrase* **3. pump up**, to fill with air: *I have to pump up the tyres before I take the bike out.*

pumpkin *noun* a large, roundish, yellow-orange vegetable, sometimes with green skin.

pun *noun* a play on words which sound like each other but are different in meaning, as in the sentence *Our photography shop is a developing business* where *developing* has two meanings.

punch[1] *noun* (*plural* **punches**)
1. a hit or blow, especially with your fist. **2.** a strong or forceful effect.
–*verb* **3.** If you **punch** someone or something, you hit them with your fist: *I was so angry that I wanted to punch him on the nose.*

punch[2] *noun* (*plural* **punches**) a device for making holes in tickets, leather or similar materials.

punch[3] *noun* a drink made of water, fruit juice, pieces of fruit and sometimes wine, rum or other spirits.

punctilious /*say* punk-**til**-ee-uhs/ *adjective* being very exact about doing things correctly: *The judge was punctilious in following legal procedure.*

punctual /*say* **punk**-chooh-uhl/ *adjective* If someone is **punctual**, they are always on time for meetings and appointments.
☐ **punctuality**, *noun* –**punctually**, *adverb*

☑ SPELLING TIP Remember the *t* in this word. With the *u* following it has a 'ch' sound and you don't hear the *t*.

punctuation /*say* punk-chooh-**ay**-shuhn/ *noun* marks used in writing in order to make the meaning clear: *Commas, full stops and question marks are important marks of punctuation.*
☐ **punctuate**, *verb*

puncture *verb* If someone or something **punctures** something such as a balloon or a tyre, they make a hole in it with something pointed.
☐ **puncture**, *noun*: *a puncture in a tyre.*

pundit /*say* **pun**-duht/ *noun* someone who knows a lot about a subject.

pungent /*say* **pun**-juhnt/ *adjective* having a sharp taste or smell: *The pungent odour of acid hurt my nostrils.*
☐ **pungency**, *noun* –**pungently**, *adverb*

WORD HISTORY from a Latin word meaning 'pricking'

punish *verb* If you **punish** someone, you make them suffer in some way because they have done something wrong: *The only way to punish him is to take his skateboard away.*
☐ **punishment**, *noun*

punk *noun*
1. one of a group of young people whose appearance is characterised by mainly black clothes with silver studs and chains, ear and face piercings, and spiky hair. **2.** See **punk music**.
☐ **punk**, *adjective*

punk music *noun* a type of loud, fast, heavy rock music with songs with aggressive lyrics.

ANOTHER FORM You can also call this **punk**: *Do you like punk?*

punnet *noun* a small, shallow box or basket for small fruits, especially berries.

punt[1] *noun* a shallow-bottomed boat with square ends usually driven by pushing with a pole against the bottom of the river.

punt[2] *noun*
1. a kick which you give to a dropped football before it has hit the ground.
–*verb* **2.** When you **punt** a football, you give it a punt: *He punted the ball over the heads of the opposing players.*

punt[3] *noun* a bet: *I took a punt on Mum letting me go after all and said yes.*
☐ **punter**, *noun*

puny /*say* **pyooh**-nee/ *adjective* (**punier**, **puniest**)
1. small and weak. **2.** of little importance: *He made a few puny attempts at helping and then disappeared.*

pup *noun* a young dog, or the young of some other kinds of animals, such as seals: *There were seal pups on the rocks.*

ANOTHER FORM A young dog can also be called a **puppy** (*plural* **puppies**).

pupa /*say* **pyooh**-puh/ *noun* (*plural* **pupae** /*say* **pyooh**-pee/) an insect in the cocoon between the larval and fully grown adult stages.
☐ **pupal**, *adjective*

WORD HISTORY from a Latin word meaning 'girl', 'doll' or 'puppet'

pupil[1] *noun* someone who is being taught.

pupil[2] *noun* the small, dark spot on the iris of the eye, which grows larger to allow in more light and smaller to keep out light that is too bright.

puppet *noun*
1. a doll or figure or some kind which is moved by wires or your hand, usually on a small stage. **2.** a person who is controlled by others, or a government that is controlled by the government of a stronger country: *He described his small country as a puppet of America.*
☐ **puppeteer**, *noun* –**puppetry**, *noun*

ANOTHER WORD (for definition 1) is **marionette**.

purchase /*say* **per**-chuhs/ *verb*
1. If you **purchase** something, you buy it: *Our family has purchased a new car.*
–*noun* **2.** something which is bought.
☐ **purchaser**, *noun*

☑ SPELLING TIP Remember that the beginning is *pur* (not *per*). Try thinking that a woman uses her purse to **purchase** things. Also remember the *ase* (not *ace* or *is*) ending.

purdah *noun* the costume worn by some Muslim women, consisting of black clothing, a covering for the face, black gloves, and black shoes.

pure *adjective*
1. If something is **pure**, it is not mixed with anything else: *a pure dingo*; *pure fruit juice.* **2.** If something is **pure**, it is clean and healthy: *the pure waters of a mountain stream.* **3.** If something such as a colour or sound is **pure**, it is clear and bright. **4. Pure** can also mean 'nothing other than': *It was pure chance that I happened to meet her.*
☐ **purely**, *adverb* –**purification**, *noun* –**purify**, *verb* –**purity**, *noun*

puree /*say* **pyooh**-ray/ *verb* (**purees**, **pureeing**, **pureed**, **has pureed**) If you **puree** fruit or vegetables, you cook them and then sieve or beat them until they are soft and creamy.
☐ **puree**, *noun* –**pureed**, *adjective*

☑ SPELLING TIP Remember the double *e* at the end, giving the 'ay' sound. **Puree** is spelt like this because it comes from French. You can also use the spelling **purée** (with the accent on the first *e*), which is how it is spelt in French.

purgative /*say* **per**-guh-tiv/ *noun* a medicine causing emptying or cleansing of the bowels.
☐ **purgative**, *adjective* cleansing or purging.

purgatory /*say* **per**-guh-tree/ *noun*
1. a place of temporary punishment where some Christians believe you go after death but before you go to heaven. **2.** any place or situation in your life which causes a lot of suffering.

ANOTHER FORM This word (as in definition 1) is often spelt with a capital letter.

purge /*say* perj/ *verb* To **purge** something is to purify it or get rid of what is unwanted or not good.

puritan /*say* **pyooh**-ruh-tuhn/ *noun* someone who tries to be very pure and strict in moral and religious matters.
☐ **puritan**, *adjective* having to do with puritans. –**puritanical**, *adjective* behaving like a puritan. –**puritanism**, *noun*

purl *noun*
1. a stitch used in knitting.
–*verb* **2.** If someone who is knitting **purls**, they do a purl stitch: *Knit 1, purl 1 – continue like this until the end of the row.*

☑ SPELLING TIP Don't confuse the spelling of **purl** with **pearl** which sounds the same. A **pearl** is a white jewel.

purple *adjective* of a dark, reddish-blue colour.
☐ **purple**, *noun*

purpose /*say* **per**-puhs/ *noun*
1. the reason something is done or made: *The purpose of a dishwasher is to make washing up quicker and easier.*
–*phrase* **2. on purpose**, intentionally.
☐ **purposeful**, *adjective* determined.

purr *verb*
1. A cat **purrs** when it makes a low, continuous sound, usually when it is contented. **2.** A person is said to **purr** when they are expressing their total enjoyment of something: *'This is the life!', she purred as she stretched out in the hammock.*
☐ **purr**, *noun*

purse *noun*
1. a small bag for carrying money.
–*verb* **2.** If you **purse** your lips, you draw them tightly into folds or wrinkles because you do not like something.

purser *noun* a ship's officer who looks after the accounts.

pursue /*say* puh-**syooh**/ *verb*
1. If someone **pursues** someone or something, they follow them in order to catch them. **2.** If you **pursue** something such as an aim or a dream, you try to achieve it.
☐ **pursuer**, *noun* –**pursuit**, *noun*

☑ SPELLING TIP Remember that the beginning is *pur* (not *per*). Also notice the *sue* and remember that this changes to *suit* when the noun **pursuit** is formed (the same spelling as for a set of clothes).

pus /*rhymes with* bus/ *noun* the yellowish-white substance in a boil or sore.
☐ **pussy** /*say* **pus**-ee/, *adjective*

☑ SPELLING TIP *Single letter alert*: remember that this word ends with a single *s*. Don't confuse it with **puss** (pronounced with an 'oo' sound, not an 'u'), a word you can use for a cat.

push *verb*
1. If you **push** something, you use force on it to make it move forward: *I had to push the door hard to make it open*; *Don't push anyone into the pool – it can be dangerous.* **2.** If you **push** something, you make it move along in front of you as you go forward: *I had to get off and push the bike up the hill.* **3.** If you **push** somewhere, you get there by pressing things or people out of the way so that you can squeeze through: *She somehow managed to push to the front of the crowd.* **4.** If someone **pushes** you to do something, they try very hard to get you to do it: *My father is pushing me to accept the scholarship.*
–*phrase* **5. push on**, to continue or go forward.
☐ **push**, *noun*

pushover *noun* something easily done.

push-up *noun* an exercise in which you raise your body from a lying down position by pushing against the floor with your hands.

ANOTHER TERM for this is **press-up**.

puss *noun Informal* a cat.

ANOTHER FORM is **pussy** (*plural* **pussies**). You usually use these words when you are talking to, or calling a cat.

☑ SPELLING TIP *Double letter alert*: remember that **puss** ends with a double *s*. Don't confuse it with **pus** (pronounced to rhyme with 'bus'), which is the yellowish-white substance in a boil or sore.

pussyfoot *verb Informal* To **pussyfoot** around is to act uncertainly as if afraid to make a decision.

pustule /*say* **pus**-tyoohl/ *noun* a pimple.
☐ **pustulant**, *adjective* –**pustular**, *adjective*

put *verb* (**puts**, **putting**, **put**, **has put**)
1. If you **put** something somewhere, you move it from somewhere else and leave it in that place: *Could you put the racquets in the garage when you finish?* **2.** If you **put** something to someone, you suggest it to them: *We put a proposal to the teacher.*
–*phrase* **3. put down**, **a.** to stamp out: *The captain was not able to put down the mutiny.* **b.** to kill as an act of kindness: *We got the vet to put down our dog when he got very old and sick.* **c.** to cause someone to feel ashamed or foolish: *They put her down all the time just because she has no fashion sense.* **4. put forward**, to suggest: *to put forward a plan.* **5. put off**, to decide to do something later on, rather than immediately. **6. put up with**, to tolerate: *I don't know how you put up with his constant chattering.*

putrid /*say* **pyooh**-truhd/ *adjective* decaying or rotten, especially when having a horrible smell.

putt /*rhymes with* but/ *verb* To **putt** in golf is to hit the ball gently along the green towards the hole.
☐ **putter**, *noun*

putty *noun* a kind of cement used for fixing glass into frames or filling holes in wood.

WORD HISTORY from a French word meaning 'a potful'

puzzle *noun*
1. a toy or game which entertains by giving you an interesting problem to solve. **2.** something that is difficult to understand: *How my 'Aliens from Space' game got into the back of the kitchen cupboard is a complete puzzle to me.*
–*verb* **3.** If someone or something **puzzles** you, it confuses you or is difficult to understand.
☐ **puzzled**, *adjective* –**puzzlement**, *noun* –**puzzling**, *adjective*

pygmy /*say* **pig**-mee/ *noun*
1. one of a group of African people who are very small. **2.** any small, dwarf-like person or thing.

ANOTHER SPELLING is **pigmy**.

pyjamas /*say* puh-**jah**-muhz/ *plural noun* loose trousers and jacket worn in bed.

THE SHORT FORM of this is **PJs**.

☑ SPELLING TIP *Letter 'y' alert*: the first vowel sound is spelt with a *y*. The spelling with an *a* is used in American English but **pyjamas** is the standard spelling in Australian English. The word is unusual because it comes from the Hindi words for 'leg' and 'clothing'.

pylon /*say* **puy**-lon/ *noun*
1. a tall tower made of metal for carrying electric or telephone wires. **2.** one of the two tall structures on either side of the end of a bridge.

pyramid /*say* **pi**-ruh-mid/ *noun* a structure with a square base and with sides sloping to a point, such as the extremely large stone ones built by the ancient Egyptians.

☑ SPELLING TIP *Letter 'y' alert*: the first vowel sound is spelt with a *y*. Like many words with a *y* spelling, **pyramid** comes from Greek.

pyre /*rhymes with* fire/ *noun* a pile of wood used for burning dead bodies in some countries.

☑ SPELLING TIP *Letter 'y' alert*: the vowel sound is spelt with a *y*. See the note at **pyromania**.

pyromania /*say* puy-ruh-**may**-nee-uh/ *noun* a great desire to set things on fire.
☐ **pyromaniac**, *noun* –**pyromaniacal** /*say* puy-roh-muh-**nuy**-uh-kuhl/, *adjective*

☑ SPELLING TIP *Letter 'y' alert*: the first vowel sound is spelt with a *y*. This is part of the prefix *pyro-* which comes from Greek and means 'having to do with fire'. If you learn it, you will be able to spell not only **pyromania** but also related words such as *pyrotechnics*.

pyrotechnics *noun* the art of making and using fireworks.
☐ **pyrotechnic**, *adjective* –**pyrotechnist**, *noun*

python /*say* **puy**-thuhn/ *noun* a large snake which crushes its prey but is not venomous.

☑ SPELLING TIP *Letter 'y' alert*: the first vowel sound is spelt with a *y*. Also remember that the ending is *on* (not *en*). Like many words with a *y* spelling, **python** comes from Greek. In Greek myth, the *Python* was a huge snake killed by the god Apollo.

quack[1] *noun* the sound a duck makes.

WORD HISTORY an imitation of the sound

quack[2] *noun* someone with no proper medical training who tricks sick people into believing there is a cure for them.
□ **quackery**, *noun*

A SIMILAR WORD is **charlatan**.

quadrangle /*say* **kwod**-rang-guhl/ *noun* a square or rectangular courtyard surrounded by buildings.

quadrant /*say* **kwod**-ruhnt/ *noun* a quarter of a circle.

quadrilateral /*say* kwod-ruh-**lat**-ruhl/ *noun* a closed, flat figure with four sides.
□ **quadrilateral**, *adjective*

quadrille /*say* kwuh-**dril**/ *noun* a dance where four couples dance in a square pattern.

☑ SPELLING TIP Remember the ending – *ille* for the 'il' sound. This is because **quadrille** comes from French (originally from a Spanish word meaning 'company' or 'troop').

quadruped /*say* **kwod**-ruh-ped/ *noun* an animal with four feet.
□ **quadruped**, *adjective*

☑ SPELLING TIP *Tricky 'uh' sound*: the vowel sound in the middle is spelt with a *u*. The other parts of this word are quite easy to work out, especially if you remember that the prefix *quad-* means 'four', and the word part *ped* is a form of the Latin word for 'foot'.

quadruple /*say* kwod-**rooh**-puhl/ *verb*
1. If you **quadruple** something, you multiply it by four.
–*adjective* **2.** made up of four parts. **3.** four times bigger.
□ **quadruple**, *noun*

quadruplet /*say* kwod-**roohp**-luht/ *noun* one of four children born at the same time to the same mother.

THE SHORT FORM of this is **quad**.

quaff /*say* kwof/ *verb* If you **quaff** a drink, you drink it quickly.

☑ SPELLING TIP *Tricky vowel sound*: the vowel sound is spelt with an *a*, although it gives an 'o' sound. Think of some of the other words you know that start with *qua* and have a 'kwo' sound, such as *quantity* and *quality*.

quagmire /*say* **kwog**-muy-uh/ *noun* a muddy patch of ground: *The field is a quagmire after yesterday's heavy rain.*

SIMILAR WORDS are **bog** and **swamp**.

☑ SPELLING TIP *Tricky vowel sound*: the first vowel sound is spelt with an *a*, although it gives an 'o' sound. Think of some of the other words you know that start with *qua* and have a 'kwo' sound, such as *quantity* and *quality*. Also remember that **quagmire** has a single *g*.

quail[1] *noun* a small bird that builds its nest on the ground.

quail[2] *verb* If you **quail**, you suddenly feel afraid: *I quailed at the thought of crossing the gorge on the flimsy footbridge.*

quaint *adjective* rather unusual and old-fashioned: *a quaint little cottage.*
□ **quaintly**, *adverb* –**quaintness**, *noun*

quake *verb* If you **quake**, you tremble or shake: *to quake with fear*; *The building quaked as the full force of the storm hit.*
□ **quake**, *noun* an earthquake.

qualify /*say* **kwol**-uh-fuy/ *verb* (**qualifies**, **qualifying**, **qualified**, **has qualified**)
1. If you **qualify** for a certain type of work or profession, you pass the exams necessary in order to do it: *My sister is studying to work as a doctor – she'll qualify next year.* **2.** If you **qualify** for something, you are suitable or right for it according to a set of rules: *To qualify for the prize, your entry must arrive before the end of the month.* **3.** If someone **qualifies** a statement, they add something further which changes or limits it in some way: *She qualified her story by saying she wasn't sure of all the facts.*
□ **qualification**, *noun* –**qualified**, *adjective*

quality /*say* **kwol**-uh-tee/ *noun* (*plural* **qualities**)
1. a feature or characteristic: *The quality of sameness about the landscape depressed him*; *Her voice has a ringing quality.* **2.** value or worth: *a film of quality.*
–*adjective* **3.** of fine or good quality: *quality shoes.*

qualm /*say* kwahm/ *noun* a slightly guilty feeling: *We were left to clean up, so we had no qualms about finishing off the cake as well.*

WORD HISTORY from an Old English word meaning 'torment', 'pain' or 'plague'

☑ SPELLING TIP *Tricky vowel sound*: don't forget the *l*. The *alm* spelling gives the 'ahm' sound.

quandary /*say* **kwon**-dree/ *noun* (*plural* **quandaries**) confusion about what is the best thing to do: *I'm in a quandary about what to wear to this party.*

quandong /*say* **kwon**-dong/ *noun* an Australian tree with fruit which you can eat raw or make into jams and jellies.

quantity /*say* **kwon**-tuh-tee/ *noun* (*plural* **quantities**) an amount or measure: *I got the quantities of milk and flour wrong, so my cake was more like a pudding.*
☐ **quantify**, *verb* (**quantifies**, **quantifying**, **quantified**, **has quantified**)

quarantine /*say* **kwo**-ruhn-teen/ *noun*
1. the separating of people or animals from others for a certain period of time to make certain they don't spread a disease to others.
–*verb* **2.** To **quarantine** a person or animal is to put them into quarantine.

☑ SPELLING TIP *Single letter alert*: only one *r*. Also remember the *ine* ending.

quarrel /*say* **kwo**-ruhl/ *noun*
1. an angry argument.
–*verb* (**quarrels**, **quarrelling**, **quarrelled**, **has quarrelled**) **2.** If two people **quarrel**, they have a quarrel: *Friends shouldn't quarrel.*
☐ **quarrelsome**, *adjective*

☑ SPELLING TIP *Double/single letter alert*: double *r* (think of how you 'rant and rave' when you **quarrel**), but only one *l* at the end. Remember that the *l* is doubled when you add *-ed* or *-ing* but not when you add the suffix *-some* to make the adjective **quarrelsome**. Note the spelling of this suffix which means 'tending towards' or 'involving'. Some other words that include it are *awesome* and *wholesome*.

quarry[1] /*rhymes with* sorry/ *noun* (*plural* **quarries**)
1. a large, open pit where stone used for building is got out of the ground: *a marble quarry.*
–*verb* (**quarries**, **quarrying**, **quarried**, **has quarried**) **2.** To **quarry** stone is to remove it from a quarry.

quarry[2] /*rhymes with* sorry/ *noun* (*plural* **quarries**) an animal or bird that is being hunted or chased: *The dogs tracked down their quarry.*

quarter /*say* **kwaw**-tuh/ *noun*
1. one of the parts you get when you divide something equally into four: *a quarter of an orange.* **2.** a particular area in a town: *the industrial quarter.* **3. quarters**, a place to live: *the officers' quarters.*
–*verb* **4.** To **quarter** something is to divide it into four equal parts. **5.** To **quarter** someone is to provide them with a place to live or sleep: *The soldiers were quartered in the barracks.*

quarterdeck *noun* the upper deck of a ship between the mast and the stern, used by the officers.

quartermaster *noun* a military officer in charge of food, clothing, housing and equipment.

quartet /*say* kwaw-**tet**/ *noun*
1. a group of four people, especially musicians or singers. **2.** a musical piece for four voices or four performers: *a quartet for string instruments.*

quartz /*say* kwawts/ *noun* a common mineral which has many different forms and colours, used in making very accurate clocks and watches, etc.

quasi- /*say* **kwah**-zee/ *prefix* a word part meaning 'resembling' or 'as though', as in *quasi-official*.

WORD HISTORY this prefix comes from Latin

quaver *noun*
1. a shaking or trembling voice: *The nervous child answered in a quaver.* **2.** a musical note which is half as long as a crotchet.
–*verb* **3.** If someone's voice **quavers**, it trembles: *Her voice quavered when she talked about her old dog.*
☐ **quavery**, *adjective*

quay /*say* kee/ *noun* a place beside the water where ships are loaded and unloaded or ferries pick up and drop off passengers.

☑ SPELLING TIP *Tricky vowel sound*: *ay* spells the 'ee' sound. Don't confuse **quay** with **key** which has the same sound. A **key** is most often a small piece of metal that can open a lock, a piece on a piano or computer keyboard, etc.

queasy *adjective* (**queasier**, **queasiest**) If you are **queasy**, you feel as if you are going to be sick.

queen *noun*
1. a woman who is the ruler of a country. **2.** the wife of a king. **3.** the large egg-laying female of such creatures as bees, ants, and termites. **4.** a playing card with a picture of a queen on it. **5.** the most powerful chess piece.
☐ **queenly**, *adjective*

ANOTHER FORM This word (as in definitions 1 and 2) is spelt with a capital letter when you are writing the title of a particular person.

queer *adjective*
1. strange: *a queer sensation.* **2.** unwell: *I feel queer.*
☐ **queerly**, *adverb*

WORD HISTORY from a Greek word meaning 'cross' or 'oblique'

quell *verb* If you **quell** something, you stop or calm it: *to quell an argument*; *to quell your nervousness*; *to quell an uneasy stomach.*

quench *verb* To **quench** something is to **1.** put it out: *to quench the flames.* **2.** satisfy it or make it less: *He drank a large glass of water to quench his thirst.*

querulous /*say* **kwe**-ruh-luhs/ *adjective* irritable and complaining.
☐ **querulously**, *adverb*

query /*say* **kwear**-ree/ *noun* (*plural* **queries**)
1. a question. **2.** a doubt or problem: *a query about the telephone bill.*
–*verb* **3.** If you **query** something, you ask a question about it because you think it is wrong or inaccurate.

> ☑ SPELLING TIP *Tricky vowel sound*: *er* (not *eer*) spells the 'ear' sound. Also remember that the ending is *y* (not *ey*).

quest *noun* a search: *a quest for knowledge*; *a talent quest.*

question *noun*
1. a request for information: *Do you have any questions about the new timetable?* **2.** a doubt or problem: *There is some question as to which day he will arrive.*
–*verb* **3.** When you **question** someone, you ask them one or more questions: *The police questioned the witnesses to the accident.* **4.** If you **question** something, you raise doubts about whether it is true or worthwhile: *Are you questioning my honesty?*; *Some of the class questioned the purpose of the exercise.*
–*phrase* **5. out of the question**, impossible.
☐ **questionable**, *adjective* possibly not true or accurate.

> ☑ SPELLING TIP Remember that the *s* is followed by a *tion* ending. There is no *ch* although you can sometimes hear that sound when people say the word. Try rapping it out as *ques*+*ti*+*on*.

question mark *noun* a mark of punctuation (?) put at the end of a written question.

> SEE the Grammar and Punctuation Guide appendix.

questionnaire /*say* kwes-chuhn-**air**, kes-chuhn-**air**/ *noun* a list of questions set out on a printed form with spaces for the answers to be written in.

> ☑ SPELLING TIP *Double letter alert*: the *n* at the end of the *question* part of the word is doubled. Also remember the *aire* ending. **Questionnaire** has this spelling because it comes from French. This is also why some people say it with a 'kes' instead of a 'kwes' sound at the beginning.

queue /*say* kyooh/ *noun*
1. a line or file of people, cars or animals waiting in turn for something: *We joined the end of the queue.*
–*verb* **2.** When you **queue** for something, you wait in a queue: *to queue for lunch.*

> ☑ SPELLING TIP *Tricky vowel sound*: the unusual letter combination *eue* makes the 'yooh' sound. Also notice that *qu* makes a 'k' (not 'kw') sound at the start of the word. This is because **queue** comes from French. (It was based on the Latin word for 'tail' – because a **queue** is often shaped like a tail). Don't confuse it with **cue** which has the same sound. A **cue** is a signal for something to happen, or a stick used to hit the balls in billiards.

quibble *verb* If you **quibble**, you argue over things that do not matter: *The twins quibbled over whose turn it was to clear the table.*

quiche /*say* keesh/ *noun* a tart filled with a mixture of cooked eggs, cream and cheese, often eaten cold.

> ☑ SPELLING TIP The *qu* at the start gives a 'k' (not 'kw') sound and the *iche* spelling sounds like 'eesh' because this word comes from French.

quick *adjective*
1. fast or rapid: *a quick flick of the wrist*; *a quick runner.* **2.** done, completed or happening in a short time: *a quick trip.*
–*noun* **3.** the sensitive skin under your nails: *His nails were bitten down to the quick.*
☐ **quicken**, *verb*: *to quicken your pace.* –**quickly**, *adverb* –**quickness**, *noun*

quicksand *noun* wet sand which traps anyone or anything that falls into it and sucks them down.

quid *Informal*
–*noun* **1.** one pound in money, used before decimal currency was introduced.
–*phrase* **2. for quids**, for anything: *I wouldn't do it for quids.*

quiet /*say* **kwuy**-uht/ *adjective*
1. still or silent: *The lake is quiet.* **2.** calm and peaceful: *a quiet day*; *a quiet village.* **3.** shy: *The new girl is rather quiet.*
–*noun* **4.** calmness or peace.
☐ **quieten**, *verb* –**quietly**, *adverb*

> ☑ SPELLING TIP Don't confuse the spelling of **quiet** with **quite** which sounds similar. **Quite** means 'completely' or 'fairly'.

quill *noun*
1. a large feather from the wing or tail of a bird. **2.** an old-fashioned pen, made from a goose's feather.

quilt *noun* a light, warm cover for a bed, filled with feathers.

quince *noun* a sour yellow fruit, rather like a large pear, which is so hard it has to be cooked before you can eat it.

quinine /*say* **kwin**-een, kwuh-**neen**/ *noun* a bitter medicine used to treat malaria.

quintet *noun*
1. a group of five people, especially musicians or singers. 2. a musical piece for five voices or five performers.

quintuple */say* kwin-**tyooh**-puhl/ *verb*
1. If you **quintuple** something, you multiply it by five.
–*adjective* 2. made up of five parts. 3. five times bigger.
☐ **quintuple**, *noun*

quintuplet */say* kwin-**tup**-luht/ *noun* one of five children born at the same time to the same mother.

quip *noun*
1. a clever or sarcastic remark.
–*verb* (**quips**, **quipping**, **quipped**, **has quipped**) 2. If you **quip**, you utter a quip: *'That will be the day!' she quipped.*
☐ **quipster**, *noun*

quirk *noun*
1. a particular habit or way of acting: *a quirk of his nature.* 2. a sudden twist or turn: *a quirk of fate.*
☐ **quirky**, *adjective* (**quirkier**, **quirkiest**) odd or eccentric.

quit *verb* (**quits**, **quitting**, **quit** *or* **quitted**, **has quit**, **has quitted**) To **quit** is to cease doing something or to leave: *Quit fooling around!*; *to quit a job.*

quite */say* kwuyt/ *adverb* 1. completely: *You are quite wrong.* 2. fairly or reasonably: *quite pleasant.*

> ☑ SPELLING TIP Don't confuse the spelling of **quite** with **quiet** which sounds similar. To be **quiet** is to be still or silent.

quiver[1] *verb* To **quiver** is to shake slightly: *to quiver with excitement*; *The grass quivered in the breeze.*
☐ **quiver**, *noun*

quiver[2] *noun* a case for holding arrows.

quixotic */say* kwik-**sot**-ik/ *adjective* having romantic ideas about doing brave and wonderful deeds.

> WORD HISTORY from *Don Quixote*, the hero of a Spanish novel (written in 1605), who was always trying to do good

quiz *noun* (*plural* **quizzes**)
1. a test to see how much you know about a particular subject: *a magazine quiz on general knowledge*; *a music quiz.*
–*verb* (**quizzes**, **quizzing**, **quizzed**, **has quizzed**) 2. If you **quiz** someone, you ask them a lot of questions to try to find out about something.

> ☑ SPELLING TIP *Single letter alert*: only one *z* at the end. However, remember that the *z* is doubled when you make the plural **quizzes** or add the verb endings *-ed* or *-ing*.

quizzical *adjective* showing in a friendly fashion that you think something is surprising, strange or funny: *He gave a quizzical look when she marched in with a mohawk.*

> ☑ SPELLING TIP *Double letter alert*: double *z*.

quoits */say* koyts/ *plural noun* a game played by throwing rings made of stiff rope over a peg on the ground.

quokka */say* **kwok**-uh/ *noun* a small wallaby, just larger than a cat, with rounded ears and a short face.

> WORD HISTORY from an Aboriginal language of Western Australia called Nyungar

> ☑ SPELLING TIP *Double letter alert*: double *k*.

quoll *noun* a marsupial with a long tail and spots, about the size of a cat.

> ANOTHER TERM for this is **native cat**.
> WORD HISTORY from an Aboriginal language of Queensland called Guugu Yimidhirr

quorum */say* **kwaw**-ruhm/ *noun* the number of people that have to be at a meeting before decisions can be made.

quota *noun* the share that you are entitled to: *There is a quota on how many fish you can catch here each day.*

quotation *noun*
1. a passage copied exactly from a book or speech. 2. a price given for carrying out a job: *He has given us a quotation for painting the school hall.*

> THE SHORT FORM of this is **quote**.

quotation mark *noun* one of the punctuation marks (' ') or (" ") used before and after a quotation, as in *'We studied "Hamlet" at school', she said.*

> ANOTHER TERM for this is **inverted comma**.
> SEE the Grammar and Punctuation Guide appendix.

quote *verb*
1. If you **quote** someone's words, you repeat exactly what they said or wrote: *The teacher quoted an ancient Chinese proverb to the class.*
2. If someone **quotes** you a certain price for a job, they tell you that is how much you will have to pay for it to be done: *The other garage quoted less for the same job.*
–*noun* 3. See **quotation**.

quotient */say* **kwoh**-shuhnt/ *noun* the number or result you get when one number is divided by another: *In the sum 15 ÷ 3, the quotient is 5.*

> SEE ALSO **divisor** and **dividend** (definition 1).

> ☑ SPELLING TIP Remember that there is a *t* followed by an *i* in the middle of this word, although the sound that you hear is 'sh'. Try rapping it out as *quot+i+ent*.

Qur'an */say* kaw-**rahn**, kuh-**rahn**/ *noun* See **Koran**.

rabbi /*say* **rab**-uy/ *noun* a Jewish priest or leader.

☑ SPELLING TIP *Double letter alert*: double *b*. Also notice that the ending is a simple *i*. This word comes from Hebrew.

rabbit *noun* a small, long-eared, burrowing animal.

NOTE The male is a **buck**; the female is a **doe**; the young is a **kit**.

rabble *noun* a noisy, violent crowd.

rabies /*say* **ray**-beez/ *noun* an infectious brain disease leading to death that is spread to people by the bite of a dog or of some other animal which has the disease.
☐ **rabid**, *adjective*

WORD HISTORY from a Latin word meaning 'madness' or 'rage'

☑ SPELLING TIP *Single letter alert*: only one *b*. Also remember the *ies* ending, giving an 'eez' sound. In fact, this word is the same as *babies* but with an initial *r* instead of a *b* – although the meaning is very different!

race[1] *noun*
1. a contest of speed. **2.** any kind of competition. –*verb* **3.** To **race** is to run or move very quickly: *We raced home from school so that we would be in time for the TV show.* **4.** To **race** someone is to compete with them to cover a distance in the shortest time: *I'll race you to the bus stop!*
☐ **racing**, *noun*

race[2] *noun* a group of tribes or nations thought to have the same ancestors, the same language and culture, or the same skin colour.

racial /*say* **ray**-shuhl/ *adjective*
1. having to do with or typical of a race: *people of different racial origins.* **2.** having to do with relations between people of different races: *racial equality.*
☐ **racially**, *adverb*

racism /*say* **ray**-siz-uhm/ *noun*
1. the belief that one race of people is better than any other. **2.** unpleasant or violent behaviour towards people of a particular race.
☐ **racist**, *noun*, *adjective*

ANOTHER WORD for this is **racialism**.

rack *noun*
1. a structure of bars or wires for holding things. –*verb* **2.** If pain or fever **racks** your body, it causes you great suffering.

racket[1] *noun*
1. a loud, confused noise. **2.** an illegal business or way of making money: *He runs a racket cheating people of their money by telling them they are donating to a charity.*

racket[2] *noun* See **racquet**.

raconteur /*say* rak-on-**ter**/ *noun* someone who is very good at telling interesting and amusing stories, especially true ones.

☑ SPELLING TIP Remember the *-eur* spelling at the end of this word. This ending occurs in several words that have come from French and means 'someone who does something', as in *amateur* and *chauffeur*. **Raconteur** is formed from *raconter*, the French word meaning 'to tell' or 'to relate'.

racquet /*say* **rak**-uht/ *noun* a bat with a netting of nylon or cord stretched across a frame, which is used in tennis and similar games.

ANOTHER SPELLING is **racket**.

☑ SPELLING TIP Notice that you can spell this word in two ways. The first one is the more difficult to remember because it uses *qu* following the *c* for the 'k' sound. This is because it comes from French. The *ck* spelling in the second spelling choice is more straightforward and is now an acceptable spelling for the bat that you use in tennis.

radar *noun*
1. a system which tells you the position and speed of objects like cars, ships or aircraft, by sending out radio waves and measuring the time the echo takes to come back and the direction it comes from. –*phrase* **2. under the radar**, entirely escaping attention.

WORD HISTORY an acronym made by joining the first letters of the words *ra*(*dio*) *d*(*etecting*) *a*(*nd*) *r*(*anging*)

radial /*say* **ray**-dee-uhl/ *adjective* arranged like rays or radii.

radiant /*say* **ray**-dee-uhnt/ *adjective*
1. If something is **radiant**, it shines or sends out rays: *the radiant light of the sun.* **2.** If someone or something is **radiant**, they are bright with happiness: *She glowed with radiant joy.*
☐ **radiance**, *noun* –**radiantly**, *adverb*

radiate *verb* To **radiate** is to **1.** spread out like rays from a centre. **2.** send out in rays: *We stood next to the camp fire which radiated warmth and comfort.*

radiation *noun* the sending and spreading out of rays, particles or waves, especially by a radioactive substance: *The nuclear tests have exposed many people to harmful radiation.*

radiator *noun*
1. an electric room heater with a rod or rods which become red-hot. **2.** a device which cools the engine of a motor vehicle.

radical *adjective*
1. If a person or group is **radical**, they hold extreme beliefs, especially political beliefs relating to the need for great change in society: *Many of us didn't agree with her radical views.* **2.** If something is **radical**, it goes to the root or basic nature of something: *There's been a radical improvement at our school since the new classrooms were built.*
–*noun* **3.** someone who holds or follows radical ideas and beliefs.
□ **radically**, *adverb*

A SIMILAR WORD (for definition 3) is **extremist**.
WORD HISTORY from a Latin word meaning 'root'

radio *noun* (*plural* **radios**)
1. the sending of electrical signals through the air to a set which receives them: *Radio was a sensation when it first came into people's homes.* **2.** a device for picking up radio broadcasts: *We turned on the radio for the news.*

ANOTHER WORD (for definition 2) is **wireless** (definition 1), but this is now old-fashioned.

radioactivity *noun* the ability of some substances, like uranium, to release harmful radiation.
□ **radioactive**, *adjective*

radish *noun* a small, hot-tasting, red-skinned vegetable which is eaten raw in salads.

radium *noun* a naturally occurring radioactive element, sometimes used to treat cancer.

radius /*say* **ray**-dee-uhs/ *noun* (*plural* **radii** /*say* **ray**-dee-uy/ *or* **radiuses**)
1. a straight line going from the centre of a circle to its circumference or edge. **2.** a circular area around some point: *Kids who live outside a one-kilometre radius of the school can get a bus pass.*

raffia *noun* a fibre obtained from the leaves of a palm tree, used in weaving mats, baskets, and in other items.

raffle *noun*
1. a lottery in which the prizes are usually goods, not money.
–*verb* **2.** To **raffle** goods is to run a lottery in which they are the prizes: *At the school fete, they raffled a BMX bike to raise funds for the new hall.*

raft *noun* a floating platform, often made of branches of trees or bamboo, for carrying goods or people on the water.

rafter *noun* a sloping piece of wood forming part of the structure of a roof.

rag *noun*
1. an old, torn piece of cloth that you use for cleaning. **2.** *Informal* a newspaper or magazine, especially one thought to be of low quality.

rage *noun*
1. strong anger: *He was in a rage because the computer was not working again.*
–*verb* **2.** If a person **rages**, they speak or act in a way that shows that they are very angry.
–*phrase* **3. all the rage**, *Informal* fashionable or popular.

ragged /*say* **rag**-uhd/ *adjective* If clothes are **ragged**, they are old and torn or worn to rags.

raid *noun*
1. a sudden attack: *There was a police raid at the club last night.*
–*verb* **2.** If police or soldiers **raid** a place, they force their way in to look for someone or something.

rail *noun*
1. a rod or bar used as a support or barrier. **2.** the railway: *If more people travelled by rail, there would be less congestion on the roads.* **3. rails**, the railway lines that a train runs on.
□ **railing**, *noun*: *There were clothes hanging from the railing outside the house.*

railway *noun*
1. the track or way laid with parallel metal rails for trains to run on. **2.** all these tracks together with their trains, buildings and land.

rain *noun*
1. water falling from the sky in drops.
–*verb* **2.** If it **rains**, drops of water fall from the sky. **3.** If things **rain**, they fall like rain: *Stones rained down from the cliff.*
–*phrase* **4. rain cats and dogs**, to rain heavily.
□ **rainfall**, *noun* –**rainy**, *adjective*

☑ SPELLING TIP Don't confuse the spelling of **rain** with **rein** which has the same sound. A **rein** is a strap used by a rider to guide a horse. There is another word with the same sound, **reign** (definition 1), which is the period during which a king or queen rules.

rainbow *noun* an curved band of colours that appears in the sky when the sun is shining after rain.

rainforest *noun* thick forest in fairly warm to very hot areas which have heavy rainfall.

raise *verb* To **raise** something is to **1.** lift it up into a higher position. **2.** increase it: *The supermarket has raised its prices again.* **3.** If you **raise** something such as money, you get it together or collect it: *Our class raised a hundred dollars for the victims.* **4.** When someone **raises** children,

they look after them until they are grown up: *My grandmother raised a large family.* **5.** If you **raise** a certain topic or subject, you begin to talk or ask a question about it: *When the teacher was in a good mood, we raised the question of being allowed to leave early.*
–*noun* **6.** an increase in pay.

raisin *noun* a dried, sweet grape.

WORD HISTORY from a Latin word meaning 'cluster of grapes'

☑ SPELLING TIP Remember that the ending is *in* (not *on*). Try thinking of the word *raising* (lifting up) and leave off the *g*.

rake *noun*
1. a long-handled gardening tool used for gathering cut grass and leaves or for levelling and smoothing the ground.
–*verb* **2.** If you **rake** an area of ground, you use a rake either to collect grass and leaves, or to smooth the ground.

rally *verb* (**rallies**, **rallying**, **rallied**, **has rallied**)
1. To **rally** people is to bring them together: *Let's rally everyone and clean up the playground!* **2.** When people **rally**, they come together: *Everyone rallied around to help in the disaster.* **3.** If someone or something **rallies**, they get stronger: *She didn't begin to rally until she started taking the new medicine*; *Share prices have rallied.*
–*noun* (*plural* **rallies**) **4.** a public meeting to discuss an important or worrying topic. **5.** a long exchange of strokes in tennis and similar games. **6.** a car competition testing skill rather than speed.

ram *noun*
1. a male sheep. **2.** a device for battering or forcefully pushing something aside or down.
–*verb* (**rams**, **ramming**, **rammed**, **has rammed**) To **ram** is to **3.** hit with great force: *The bike rammed into the telegraph post.* **4.** force down by heavy blows: *Ram as much into the buckets as you can.*

NOTE For definition 1, the female is a **ewe**.

RAM /*say* ram/ *noun* computer memory from which each item can be accessed or found equally quickly.

WORD HISTORY an acronym made by joining the first letters of *Random Access Memory*

ramble *verb*
1. If you **ramble**, you walk unhurriedly: *I love rambling across the rocks at the beach.* **2.** If you **ramble** when you speak, you talk at length in a rather confused fashion: *He's always rambling on about keeping ferrets.*
☐ **ramble**, *noun* –**rambler**, *noun* –**rambling**, *adjective*

ramp *noun* a sloping surface connecting two levels: *They backed the boat down to the ramp.*

WORD HISTORY from a French word meaning 'creep', 'crawl' or 'climb'

rampage *noun* /*say* **ram**-payj/
1. violent or angry behaviour: *The mob's rampage ended suddenly.*
–*verb* /*say* ram-**payj**/ **2.** If people **rampage**, they move or act violently and angrily.
–*phrase* **3. on the rampage**, roaming around to do violence.

rampant /*say* **ram**-puhnt/ *adjective* happening widely in an uncontrolled way: *Extra police are needed in that area because crime is rampant there.*

rampart /*say* **ram**-paht/ *noun* a mound of earth used as a fortification or defence.

ramshackle *adjective* shaky or likely to collapse: *We found the ramshackle ruins of an old gold-mining site.*

ranch *noun* (*plural* **ranches**) a large farm or station for keeping cattle, horses or sheep.

NOTE This word is especially used in America.

rancid /*say* **ran**-suhd/ *adjective* having a sour, unpleasant smell or taste from lack of freshness: *We caught some yabbies with some rancid meat.*
☐ **rancidity**, **rancidness**, *noun*

☑ SPELLING TIP Remember the *cid* ending, especially the *c* for the 's' sound.

R & B *noun* See **rhythm and blues**.

random *adjective*
1. not following any order or pattern: *Every day, the teachers make a random selection of kids to do garbage duty.*
–*phrase* **2. at random**, without a plan or purpose: *We wandered into several different shops at random.*
☐ **randomly**, *adverb*

range *noun*
1. a line or row of mountains. **2.** a large area of land, especially one used for sport like shooting or golf. **3.** the distance that a bullet or rocket can travel. **4.** the limits within which there can be differences: *He is shorter than the normal range for height for boys of his age.* **5.** a collection or variety: *There is a range of hen varieties that you can see at the show.* **6.** a kind of large cooking stove.
–*verb* To **range** is to **7.** vary or change within stated limits: *Opinions ranged from 'boring' to 'absolutely fantastic'.* **8.** go or move: *Some birds range between continents in their breeding cycle.*

ranger *noun* someone who looks after a national park, a nature reserve, and so on.

rank[1] *noun*
1. official position or grade: *the rank of colonel.* **2.** social class: *She thinks her posh accent*

makes her sound like a person of rank. **3.** a row or line: *The penguins seemed to be marching up onto the beach in ranks.*
–*verb* **4.** If you **rank** things, you place them in an order: *We had to rank the designs from most interesting down to the least interesting.*

rank[2] *adjective*
1. growing too tall or coarse: *rank weeds.* **2.** having a strong unpleasant taste or smell: *the rank smell of cabbage being cooked.*
☐ **rankly**, *adverb*

rankle *verb* If something **rankles**, it irritates or upsets you, usually over some period of time: *It still rankles that I was punished unfairly.*

ransack *verb* To **ransack** a place is to search for something in it, leaving it in an untidy state: *The thieves ransacked the room, looking for money*; *They ransacked the tent looking for the torch.*

ransom *noun* a price, usually money, which must be paid for the return of someone who has been kidnapped or captured in war.

rant *verb* To **rant** is to speak loudly or angrily.

rap[1] *verb* (**raps**, **rapping**, **rapped**, **has rapped**) To **rap** is to hit with a quick, light blow: *She rapped smartly on the door.*
☐ **rap**, *noun*

rap[2] *noun*
1. a type of modern music in which the words are spoken rather than sung. **2.** a spoken part for such music.
–*verb* (**raps**, **rapping**, **rapped**, **has rapped**) **3.** to utter a verbal improvisation as part of a rap performance.

> ANOTHER FORM You can also say **rap music** for definition 1.

rapacious /*say* ruh-**pay**-shuhs/ *adjective* very greedy.
☐ **rapaciously**, *adverb* –**rapacity** /*say* ruh-**pas**-uh-tee/, *noun*

rape *noun*
1. the crime of having sexual intercourse with someone against their will.
–*verb* **2.** If someone **rapes** another person, they have sexual intercourse with them against their will.
☐ **rapist**, *noun*

rapid *adjective*
1. fast or quick: *We decided to make a rapid exit.*
–*noun* **2. rapids**, a part of a river where the current runs very swiftly.
☐ **rapidity**, *noun* –**rapidly**, *adverb*

rapier /*say* **ray**-pee-uh/ *noun* a sword with a long, thin, pointed blade.

rap music *noun* See **rap**[2].

rapport /*say* ruh-**paw**/ *noun* a friendly feeling between people: *Josie and I have a good rapport and can talk about anything.*

> ☑ SPELLING TIP *Silent letter alert*: don't forget the silent *t* at the end. **Rapport** has this spelling and pronunciation because it comes from French.

rapt *adjective*
1. deeply occupied with your own thoughts and unaware of what is going on around you: *He seems rapt in a world of his own.* **2.** overpowered by strong feelings: *We were rapt to see the DVD when we got home from school.*

> ☑ SPELLING TIP Don't confuse the spelling of **rapt** with **rapped** (the past form of the verb **rap**, to hit or knock sharply or lightly) or with **wrapped** (the past form of **wrap**, to fold material or paper around someone or something).

rapture *noun* great joy or happiness.
☐ **rapturous**, *adjective* –**rapturously**, *adverb*

rare[1] *adjective*
1. A **rare** thing is unusual or not common: *It was a rare sighting of the bird.* **2.** If air is described as **rare**, it is thin because it has less oxygen which makes it harder for people to breathe: *The climb was more demanding at the top in the rare mountain air.*
☐ **rarefied**, *adjective* thin or limited: *The rarefied air made it hard to breathe*; *In the rarefied atmosphere of the laboratory, he was lonely.*
–**rarely**, *adverb*

> ☑ SPELLING TIP Notice that the adjective **rarefied** is spelt with an *e* in the middle, although you might think it would be an *i* as in many words with an *ify* or *ified* ending. Just remember to keep the *e* from the end of **rare**.

rare[2] *adjective* If cooked meat is **rare**, it has only been cooked for a short time so that it is still very red inside: *I would like my steak rare, please.*
☐ **rareness**, *noun* –**rarity**, *noun*

rascal *noun*
1. *Old-fashioned* a dishonest person. **2.** a mischievous child.

> WORD HISTORY from a Latin word meaning 'scratch'

rash[1] *adjective*
1. If someone is **rash**, they act too quickly and without thinking. **2.** If an action is **rash**, it is done without thinking about what might happen: *a rash plunge into the ocean at night.*
☐ **rashly**, *adverb* –**rashness**, *noun*

rash[2] *noun* red, itchy spots or patches on the skin.

rasher *noun* a thin slice of bacon.

rasp /*say* rahsp, rasp/ *noun*
1. a coarse metal file.
–*verb* **2.** If something **rasps** something, they scrape or rub it roughly, sometimes making a

grating sound: *You could hear the saw rasping against the tree trunk.*

raspberry /*say* **rahz**-bree/ *noun* (*plural* **raspberries**) a soft, juicy, reddish-purple berry.

☑ SPELLING TIP *Silent letter alert*: don't forget the *p* following the *s*. Think of **raspberry** as made up of two words – *rasp* and *berry*.

rat *noun*
1. a long-tailed animal similar to, but larger than, a mouse. **2.** *Informal* someone who leaves a friend who is in trouble.

rate *noun*
1. speed: *If we learn the words at the rate of 20 a week, we will finish the whole spelling list by November.* **2.** a charge or payment: *The interest rate on the loan is 10% per year.* **3. rates**, the tax paid by people who own land to their local council.
–*verb* **4.** If you **rate** something or someone, you consider their value, quality or suitability.
–*phrase* **5. at any rate**, in any case. **6. at this rate**, if things go on like this.

rather *adverb*
1. to a certain degree: *rather annoying.*
–*phrase* **2. rather than**, instead of: *I would like a CD of my favourite group rather than a book.*

ratify *verb* (**ratifies**, **ratifying**, **ratified**, **has ratified**) If a person or group **ratifies** something, they confirm or approve it: *The committee ratified his decision immediately.*
□ **ratification**, *noun* –**ratifier**, *noun*

rating *noun* the value or standing that someone or something has.

ratio /*say* **ray**-shee-oh/ *noun* the relationship between two amounts or quantities expressed in the lowest possible whole numbers: *The male–female ratio of kids in our school is about 4 to 3.*

ration /*rhymes with* fashion/ *noun*
1. a fixed amount allowed to one person or group: *I think my ration of pavlova was definitely smaller than the others.*
–*verb* **2.** If you **ration** something, you share it out as a ration.

rational *adjective*
1. If a decision is **rational**, it is sensible or reasonable. **2.** If someone is **rational**, they are in possession of their reason: *They questioned whether he was rational when he turned up to work in a kilt.*
□ **rationally**, *adverb*

rattle *verb*
1. To **rattle** is to make, or cause something to make, a series of repeated short, sharp sounds: *I could hear the keys rattling in the tin*; *They rattled their cutlery to show they were hungry.* **2.** *Rather informal* If you say something **rattles** you, you mean that it causes you to become upset: *It really rattled him when he thought he was going to miss the plane.*
–*noun* **3.** a number of repeated short, sharp sounds. **4.** a baby's toy which makes a noise like this.

rattlesnake *noun* a venomous American snake that has a tail with horny rings at the end of it, which makes a rattling sound when shaken.

raucous /*say* **raw**-kuhs/ *adjective* harsh-sounding: *James is known for his raucous belly laughs.*
□ **raucously**, *adverb*

ravage *verb* If something **ravages** someone or something, it damages or devastates them: *The years had ravaged her once-beautiful face.*
□ **ravages**, *plural noun*: *The ravages of war had destroyed much of the city.*

rave *verb* If someone **raves**, they talk in a wildly excited way, usually because they are very enthusiastic, very ill, or very angry: *She raved about the wonderful movie*; *She was raving when the fever was at its worst.*
□ **rave**, *noun* –**raver**, *noun* –**ravings**, *plural noun*: *the ravings of a mentally ill person.*

raven /*say* **ray**-vuhn/ *noun* a large, shiny, black bird with a harsh call.

ravenous /*say* **rav**-uh-nuhs/ *adjective* extremely hungry.
□ **ravenously**, *adverb*

ravine /*say* ruh-**veen**/ *noun* a long, deep, narrow valley, especially one made by a river.

ravioli /*say* rav-ee-**oh**-lee/ *plural noun* small pieces of pasta, cut square or otherwise, with a filling as of meat or cheese.

WORD HISTORY from Italian, from a Latin word meaning 'turnip' or 'beet'

ravishing *adjective* very beautiful.
□ **ravishingly**, *adverb* –**ravishment**, *noun*

raw *adjective*
1. If food is **raw**, it is not cooked: *Some vegetables are good to eat raw.* **2.** If something is **raw**, it is in its natural state and has not been treated: *raw silk thread*; *raw wood.* **3.** If you say that someone is **raw**, you mean that they are awkward and not experienced: *Give him a chance – he's only a raw recruit!* **4.** If your skin is **raw**, it is very painful and sore: *My feet are raw from running on the concrete without sneakers.*
□ **rawness**, *noun*

☑ SPELLING TIP Don't confuse the spelling of **raw** with **roar** which has the same sound. To **roar** is to make a loud, deep sound, like lions do.

ray *noun*
1. a beam of light. **2.** a small amount: *She was able to shed a ray of light on the mystery.*

rayon *noun* an artificial fabric, similar to silk.

raze *verb* To **raze** something is to knock it down level to the ground: *Much of the city was razed by the attack.*

> ☑ SPELLING TIP Don't confuse **raze** with **raise** ('to lift up') which has a similar sound. Remember the *z* spelling and sound in **raze**. Some other words spelt like this are *daze*, *haze* and *laze*.

razor *noun* a sharp-edged instrument or a small electrical instrument for shaving hair from the skin.

> WORD HISTORY from a French word meaning 'scrape' or 'shave'

re- *prefix* a word part meaning **1.** again, as in *rearrange*. **2.** back, as in *return*.

> WORD HISTORY this prefix comes from Latin

reach *verb*
1. If you **reach** a place or a stage, you arrive there: *We reached Darwin early in the morning*; *He's reached his teenage years.* **2.** If you **reach** something, you can touch it, especially by stretching out your arm and hand as far as you can: *Can you reach the top shelf?* **3.** If something **reaches** a certain place or level, it goes all the way to it: *The flood waters reached almost to the centre of the town.*
☐ **reach**, *noun* (*plural* **reaches**)

react /*say* ree-**akt**/ *verb*
1. If you **react** to something, you behave in a particular way as a result of it. **2.** When chemicals **react** with each other they cause each other to change in some way when they are combined: *The salt reacted with the silver and gradually corroded it.*
☐ **reactive**, *adjective* –**reactor**, *noun*

reaction /*say* ree-**ak**-shuhn/ *noun*
1. something done as a result of an action by someone or something else: *His reaction to doing badly was to have another go.* **2.** a chemical change.

read /*say* reed/ *verb* (**reads**, **reading**, **read** /*say* red/, **has read**)
1. If you **read** something that is written, you look at it and understand it: *I always read the back of the cereal label to see if there is a competition going.* **2.** If you **read** something to someone, you say the words out loud: *He spent a lot of time reading books to his grandmother after she lost her sight.* **3.** If you **read** anything, you understand it: *She could read the situation as soon as she entered the room.* **4.** If a computer **reads** something, it takes in information: *You need an extra program to read that disk.*
☐ **readable**, *adjective* –**reader**, *noun* –**reading**, *noun*

> ☑ SPELLING TIP Don't confuse the spelling of **read** with **reed** which has the same sound but is spelt with *ee*. A **reed** is a kind of tall grass. Notice that the spelling of **read** remains the same in the past forms even though the sound changes. Don't confuse this form of the word with the colour **red**.

ready *adjective* (**readier**, **readiest**)
1. completely prepared: *Are you ready for school?* **2.** quick: *He's always got a ready answer to every question.*
–*phrase* **3. ready to**, likely at any moment to: *an egg ready to hatch.*
☐ **readily**, *adverb* –**readiness**, *noun*

real *adjective*
1. true or actual: *She is a real friend!*; *Reality TV is supposed to be about real life.* **2.** not artificial: *The jewels in her ring are all real.*

> ☑ SPELLING TIP Don't confuse the spelling of **real** with **reel**, which has the same sound but is spelt with *ee*. A **reel** is a cylinder onto which thread or something similar is wound; to **reel** is to sway or stagger.

real estate *noun* land and the buildings on it.

realise *verb* If you **realise** something, you become aware of it for the first time: *I've just realised that it's his birthday.*
☐ **realisation**, *noun*

> ANOTHER SPELLING is **realize**.

realism *noun*
1. the facing of life as it really is. **2.** painting nature or writing about life as it really is.
☐ **realist**, *noun* –**realistic**, *adjective* –**realistically**, *adverb*

> THE OPPOSITE is **idealism**.

reality /*say* ree-**al**-uh-tee/ *noun* (*plural* **realities**)
1. the state or fact of being real: *You have to face up to the reality of death.* **2.** a real thing or fact: *The accident was a reality, not a dream.*

reality TV *noun* a television program format which uses actual film of events as they occur, often in a situation that has been set up especially for the program in which ordinary people are chosen for the show rather than professional actors.

really *adverb*
1. in reality: *to see things as they really are.* **2.** truly: *a really honest man*; *I really want to go.* **3.** indeed: *Really, this is too much.* **4.** extremely: *really hot.*

realm /*say* relm/ *noun*
1. a kingdom. **2.** a particular area of interest or knowledge: *the realm of nature.*

> ☑ SPELLING TIP *Tricky vowel sound*: *ea* to spell the 'e' sound.

ream *noun*
1. a standard quantity of paper equal to 500 sheets. **2. reams**, *Informal* a large quantity: *I have reams of homework.*

reap *verb*
1. To **reap** crops is to cut and gather them in. **2.** If you **reap** a benefit or reward, you get it as a return for something: *He couldn't wait to reap the benefit of his work and travel overseas.*
☐ **reaper**, *noun*

A SIMILAR WORD (for definition 1) is **harvest**.

rear[1] *noun*
1. the back of anything. **2.** the buttocks.
☐ **rear**, *adjective*: *We wound up the rear window so the dog couldn't jump out.*

A SIMILAR WORD is **posterior**.

rear[2] *verb*
1. If you **rear** children, you look after and support them: *People used to rear much bigger families than now.* **2.** If an animal **rears**, it rises up on its back legs: *The funnel-web spider reared back and looked more menacing than ever.*

reason *noun*
1. the cause of an action or happening. **2.** a statement or explanation of these causes. **3.** the ability to use your mind to form opinions. **4.** sound judgement or good sense.
–*verb* **5.** To **reason** is to argue in a sensible way: *If you reason with people, you get a lot further than by yelling at them.*
–*phrase* **6. it stands to reason**, it is obvious. **7. within reason**, within the limits of what is sensible: *You can buy some new clothes – as long as the cost is within reason.*
☐ **reasoning**, *noun*: *logical reasoning.*

reasonable *adjective*
1. If you say that someone is **reasonable**, you mean that they behave in a sensible and just way: *Our teacher is very reasonable and doesn't expect us to do too much homework.* **2.** If a decision is **reasonable**, it is based on good sense: *a reasonable choice.* **3.** If the price of something is **reasonable**, it is fair and not too high: *They get a lot of customers because they sell their stock at reasonable prices.* **4.** If something is of a **reasonable** standard, it is fairly good: *She's made reasonable progress in her studies this year.*
☐ **reasonably**, *adverb*: *reasonably priced.*

reassure /*say* ree-uh-**shaw**/ *verb* If you **reassure** someone, you give them confidence: *The doctor reassured her that her mother would get better.*
☐ **reassurance**, *noun*

rebate /*say* **ree**-bayt/ *noun* the return of part of an amount of money you have already paid out for something: *Under the new scheme, we got a rebate on our water bill.*

rebel *noun* /*say* **reb**-uhl/
1. someone who fights the government or resists those in authority: *The rebels were hiding out somewhere in the town.*
–*verb* /*say* ruh-**bel**/ (**rebels**, **rebelling**, **rebelled**, **has rebelled**) **2.** If a person **rebels**, they reject the authority of whoever is in charge and fight them: *The party members rebelled against the leader.*
☐ **rebellion**, *noun* –**rebellious**, *adjective*

rebound *verb* /*say* ruh-**bownd**/
1. To **rebound** is to bounce or spring back: *The tennis ball rebounded on the elastic rope.*
–*noun* /*say* **ree**-bownd/ **2.** the action of rebounding: *The rebound of the ball caught her by surprise.*

rebuff *verb* If someone **rebuffs** you, they do not accept your offers or suggestions: *The music teacher rebuffed our offer to compose a new school song.*
☐ **rebuff**, *noun*

A SIMILAR WORD is **snub**.

rebuke /*say* ruh-**byoohk**/ *verb* To **rebuke** someone is to scold them or show that you disapprove of their actions.
☐ **rebuke**, *noun*

recall *verb* /*say* ruh-**kawl**/
1. If you **recall** something, you remember it: *Angela couldn't recall his name.* **2.** To **recall** a person or a group is to order them to come back to do some job or duty: *The committee was recalled to discuss the new developments.*
–*noun* /*say* **ree**-kawl/ **3.** ability to remember: *She has total recall of many events in her childhood.*

recede /*say* ruh-**seed**/ *verb*
1. If something or someone **recedes**, they move further away until they disappear: *We watched the hikers ascend the mountain until they receded into the distance.* **2.** If a man's hair is **receding**, he is starting to lose hair at the front of his head.

receipt /*say* ruh-**seet**/ *noun*
1. a signed piece of paper proving that you have received goods sent and paid money for them. **2.** the receiving of something: *The company promised to send the printer on receipt of our cheque.* **3. receipts**, money received, especially in a shop: *The accountant is checking the receipts and expenses for last year.*

☑ SPELLING TIP *Silent letter alert*: don't forget the *p* before the final *t*. It is there because the word comes from *recipere*, the Latin word for 'receive', which has a past form *receptus*. Also notice the *ei* spelling for the 'ee' sound. This follows the rule that *i* comes before *e*, except after *c*.

receive /*say* ruh-**seev**/ *verb*
1. To **receive** something is to get or be given it: *We received a big surprise when we got to school.* **2.** The way you are **received** is how people treat you when you go to be with them: *He was received with wild applause when he walked onto the stage.*
☐ **recipient** /*say* ruh-**sip**-ee-uhnt/, *noun*

☑ SPELLING TIP Remember the *ei* spelling for the 'ee' sound. This follows the rule that *i* comes before *e*, except after *c*.

receiver *noun*
1. someone or something that receives: *The receiver of the package has to sign a receipt for it; He was charged with being a receiver of stolen goods.* **2.** someone who is appointed to take over a bankrupt company. **3.** the player receiving the balls served in tennis and similar games.

recent *adjective* If something is **recent**, it happened a short time ago: *A recent poll suggested people were very concerned about the environment.*
☐ **recently**, *adverb*

receptacle /*say* ruh-**sep**-tik-uhl/ *noun* a container or something that holds things: *There is a separate receptacle for recyclable waste.*

☑ SPELLING TIP Notice the *c* spelling for the 's' sound. It will help if you remember that this word is related to *receive* (both coming from the Latin *recipere*). Also remember the *cle* ending. Other words with this ending are *miracle* and *spectacle*.

reception *noun*
1. a formal party in honour of someone: *After the wedding ceremony, we had the reception.* **2.** an office or desk where hotel guests or callers are met and looked after. **3.** the result or act of receiving or being received: *We get good satellite reception; What a reception – I think I'll arrive again!*

receptionist *noun* someone employed in an office or hotel to look after callers or guests.

receptive *adjective* willing to listen to an idea and act on it: *Our class was receptive to the idea that we should help the younger kids.*

recess /*say* ruh-**ses**, **ree**-ses/ *noun*
1. a part of a room where the wall is set back for shelves or cupboards. **2.** a short time or break when school or work stops: *We arranged to meet at recess.*

recession *noun* a time when business affairs in a nation are bad and many people do not have a job.

recipe /*say* **res**-uh-pee/ *noun* any formula, especially a list of the food items needed and the instructions telling you how to cook something.

☑ SPELLING TIP The main thing to notice is the single *e* at the end giving the 'ee' sound. Also remember the *c* spelling for the 's' sound. It will help if you know that **recipe** comes from the Latin word *recipere*, meaning 'to receive'. The original use of the word **recipe** was as the instruction 'Receive!' written on medical prescriptions.

reciprocal /*say* ruh-**sip**-ruh-kuhl/ *adjective* given, felt or done by two people, each to the other: *Mum has a reciprocal arrangement with our neighbour about driving us all to school – Mum does it one day and Mrs Jones does it the next.*
☐ **reciprocally**, *adverb* –**reciprocate**, *verb*

☑ SPELLING TIP Remember the *c* spelling for the 's' sound near the beginning of the word. But the main thing to notice is the single *ocal* ending. Rap it out as *re+cip+ro+cal*.

recital /*say* ruh-**suy**-tuhl/ *noun*
1. a concert or entertainment given by one performer or by the pupils of one teacher. **2.** a long explanation or statement: *We listened to a recital of Annabelle's problems.*

recite *verb* If you **recite** something such as a poem, you say it out loud, usually without reading it because you have learned it by heart: *At the concert we had to recite our favourite poem.*
☐ **recitation**, *noun*

reckless *adjective*
1. If someone is **reckless**, they do not care about danger to the point where it is foolish: *Some of his sailing exploits have made him seem reckless.* **2.** If an action is **reckless**, it shows a careless attitude: *He was charged with reckless driving.*
☐ **recklessly**, *adverb* –**recklessness**, *noun*

reckon *verb*
1. *Rather informal* If you say you **reckon** that something is the case, you mean that you think that is how it is: *I reckon he'll come if you ask him.* **2.** If you **reckon** an amount, you calculate it: *I reckoned the total cost to be over a thousand dollars.*
☐ **reckoning**, *noun*

reclaim *verb*
1. To **reclaim** land is to make it suitable for farming or some other use: *The land was reclaimed for new housing.* **2.** To **reclaim** something is to get it back: *She is keen to reclaim her position as the fastest swimmer in the school.*
☐ **reclamation**, *noun*

recline *verb* To **recline** is to lean or lie back.

recluse /*say* ruh-**kloohs**/ *noun* someone who lives alone and does not mix with other people.
☐ **reclusive**, *adjective*

recognise /*say* **rek**-uhg-nuyz/ *verb*
1. If you **recognise** someone or something, you know who they are, usually because you have seen them before: *We recognised him immediately because of the bald head.* **2.** If you **recognise** a fact, you know that it is true, and admit this: *The principal recognised that we had a reason for feeling upset.*
☐ **recognisable**, *adjective* –**recognition**, *noun*

ANOTHER SPELLING is **recognize**.

recoil *verb*
1. If you **recoil**, you draw back in fright or horror: *He recoiled when he saw the disaster scene.* **2.** If a gun or a rifle **recoils**, it springs back when it is

fired: *The rifle recoiled against his shoulder when he fired it.*
☐ **recoil**, *noun*

recollect /*say* rek-uh-**lekt**/ *verb* If you **recollect** something, you remember it or bring it back to your mind.
☐ **recollection**, *noun*

recommend /*say* rek-uh-**mend**/ *verb*
1. If someone **recommends** something to you, they tell you that it is extremely good or useful: *This book was recommended to me by a friend.* **2.** If someone **recommends** a certain course of action, they encourage you to follow it: *The doctor recommended total rest for a week.*
☐ **recommendation**, *noun*

A SIMILAR WORD (for definition 1) is **commend**.

recompense /*say* **rek**-uhm-pens/ *verb* If you **recompense** someone, you make a repayment to them for something: *They recompensed us for the money we had paid out.*
☐ **recompense**, *noun*

A SIMILAR WORD is **compensate**.

☑ SPELLING TIP Notice the *c* (not *ck*) spelling. In spite of the way you say this word, it is made up of the prefix *re-* (meaning 'again') and *compense* (from the Latin *compensare*, meaning 'to weigh one thing against another').

reconcile /*say* **rek**-uhn-suyl/ *verb*
1. If you **reconcile** two things or people that do not agree with each other, you bring them into agreement: *My big brother is trying to reconcile the social life that he wants with the fact that he has no money.* **2.** If two people **reconcile**, they agree to settle differences that were between them: *After years of not talking, my aunts have finally reconciled.* **3.** If you **reconcile** yourself to something, you are no longer opposed to it: *My best friend and I have reconciled ourselves to being in different classes.*
☐ **reconciliation**, *noun*

A SIMILAR WORD (for definition 2) is **conciliate**.

☑ SPELLING TIP Notice the *c* (not *ck*) spelling in the first part of **reconcile**. In spite of the way you say this word, it is made up of the prefix *re-* (meaning 'again') and *concile* (from the Latin *conciliare*, meaning 'to bring back').

recondition *verb* To **recondition** something is to repair it or bring it back to a good condition: *We had our washing machine reconditioned.*

reconnoitre /*say* rek-uh-**noy**-tuh/ *verb* If you **reconnoitre**, you look carefully at something in order to gain useful information before taking action: *Somebody has to reconnoitre the area to find where it is best to camp*; *We sent James out to reconnoitre.*
☐ **reconnoitre**, *noun*

WORD HISTORY from a French word meaning 'recognise'

☑ SPELLING TIP Remember that the ending is *re* (not *er*). The *re* ending is found in several nouns, such as *centre* and *theatre*, but is unusual in verbs.

reconstitute *verb* If you **reconstitute** something, you form it or make it again: *The milk was reconstituted by adding water to the dried milk powder.*
☐ **reconstitution**, *noun*

record *verb* /*say* ruh-**kawd**/
1. If you **record** something that happens, you write it down at that time so that you can refer to it later if you need to. **2.** If you **record** music, or other sounds, you put it on a tape or CD in order to be able to replay it.
–*noun* /*say* **rek**-awd/ **3.** something that has been recorded in writing or print. **4.** a disc, usually plastic, on which music has been recorded. **5.** the best performance so far in a sport or any other activity: *He was aiming to beat the 200 metre record.* **6.** a self-contained piece of data on a computer database.
–*adjective* /*say* **rek**-awd/ **7.** being greater in number, degree or quality than all others: *record sales.*
☐ **recorded**, *adjective* –**recording**, *noun*

recorder *noun*
1. an official who keeps records. **2.** a machine for recording sound, especially on magnetic tape. **3.** a type of wooden or plastic flute that you play by holding it to your mouth in a vertical position.

recount *verb* /*say* ruh-**kownt**/
1. To **recount** something is to tell it: *We sat around the camp fire recounting the adventures of the day.*
–*noun* /*say* **ree**-kownt/ **2.** writing or speaking which explains exactly how things happened.

recover /*say* ruh-**kuv**-uh/ *verb*
1. To **recover** something is to regain or get it again: *We never recovered our stolen car.* **2.** To **recover** is to get well again after being sick.
☐ **recovery**, *noun*

recreation /*say* rek-ree-**ay**-shuhn/ *noun* a game, hobby or sport which is an enjoyable change from your daily work.

☑ SPELLING TIP Notice the *c* (not *ck*) spelling. In spite of the way you say this word, it begins with the prefix *re-* (meaning 'again'). It comes from the Latin word *recreare* meaning 'to renew' (in the sense of refreshing yourself, which is what **recreation** does for you).

recruit /*say* ruh-**krooht**/ *noun*
1. someone who has just joined the army, navy or air force. **2.** someone who has just joined any organisation or group: *We've got a new recruit for our gardening club.*

–*verb* **3.** To **recruit** someone is to get them to join an organisation, especially a military one: *The army is recruiting new members*; *The team has to recruit new players.*
☐ **recruitment**, *noun*

rectangle *noun* a four-sided shape with all its angles being right angles.
☐ **rectangular**, *adjective*

NOTE A **rectangle** is usually thought of as having two sides of one length and two sides of another, that is, the same as an **oblong**. Note, however, that a **square** is also a **rectangle** because all its angles are right angles.

rectify *verb* (**rectifies**, **rectifying**, **rectified**, **has rectified**) To **rectify** something is to make or put it right: *The newspaper rectified the incorrect story by printing an apology the next day.*
☐ **rectification**, *noun*

rectum *noun* (*plural* **rectums** *or* **recta**) the short final section of the large intestine leading to the anus.
☐ **rectal**, *adjective*

recuperate /*say* ruh-**kooh**-puh-rayt/ *verb* If you **recuperate**, you recover from sickness or exhaustion.
☐ **recuperation**, *noun* –**recuperative**, *adjective*

recur /*say* ree-**ker**/ *verb* (**recurs**, **recurring**, **recurred**, **has recurred**) If something **recurs**, it happens again: *Her headaches keep recurring.*
☐ **recurrence** /*say* ruh-**ku**-ruhns/, *noun* –**recurrent**, *adjective*

WORD HISTORY from a Latin word meaning 'run back'

recycle *verb* To **recycle** things that have already been used is to process them or change them in some way so that they can be used again: *Our council now recycles most glass and plastic bottles.*
☐ **recyclable**, *adjective*

red *adjective*
1. If something is **red**, it has the colour of a ripe tomato.
–*noun* **2.** a red colour.
–*phrase* **3. see red**, to become very angry.
☐ **redden**, *verb* –**redness**, *noun*

red-back *noun* a small, very venomous Australian spider, coloured dark brown to black, usually with a red or orange streak on its back.

red blood cell *noun* a red corpuscle in the blood, which carries oxygen to cells in the body.

redeem *verb* If you **redeem** yourself after doing something bad or unpleasant, you do something good which makes people pleased with you again: *After being rude to all his friends, he tried to redeem himself by apologising.*
☐ **redeemable**, *adjective* –**redeemer**, *noun* –**redemption**, *noun*

red-handed *adjective* To catch someone **red-handed** is to catch them in the actual act of doing something wrong: *They investigated the noise and caught the thief red-handed.*

NOTE This adjective always follows the noun it describes.

red herring *noun* a false clue or something that takes your attention away from what is really important: *The claim that a change in climate is causing the river to dry up is just a red herring. The real trouble is the pollution from the factory.*

reduce *verb*
1. If you **reduce** something, you make it lower, less or fewer: *We have to try and reduce the number of spelling mistakes in our writing.* **2.** If you **reduce** someone or something to a worse condition, you bring them to it: *The loss of her doll reduced the little girl to tears.*
☐ **reduction**, *noun*

redundant *adjective*
1. If something is **redundant**, it is no longer needed: *Records are becoming redundant now that everyone buys CDs.* **2.** If an employee is made **redundant**, they are dismissed from their job because the employer no longer needs someone to do that job.
☐ **redundancy**, *noun* –**redundantly**, *adverb*

reed *noun*
1. a tall straight-stemmed grass growing in wet, soft land. **2.** a musical pipe made from a reed or something like it. **3.** a small, flat piece of cane or metal set in the mouthpiece of some wind instruments such as a clarinet, which vibrates when you blow into it.

☑ SPELLING TIP Don't confuse the spelling of **reed** with **read** which has the same sound but is spelt with *ea*. You **read** books and newspapers.

reef *noun* a line of rock, sand or coral at or near the surface of the ocean.

reef knot *noun* a kind of double knot which does not slip.

reek *verb* To **reek** is to have a strong unpleasant smell: *The football change room reeked of sweaty clothes.*
☐ **reek**, *noun*

reel[1] *noun*
1. a cylinder or wheel-like device onto which something is wound: *a reel of fishing line.*
–*verb* **2.** To **reel** is to wind on a reel: *My uncle reckoned he reeled in a monster of a fish.*
–*phrase* **3. reel off**, to say or write in a smooth rapid way: *She can reel off her multiplication tables without even thinking!*

☑ SPELLING TIP Don't confuse the spelling of **reel** with **real** which has the same sound but is spelt with *ea*. Something is **real** if it is true or genuine.

reel[2] *verb* To **reel** is to move unsteadily, especially from a blow, or a feeling that you are spinning out of control.

☑ SPELLING TIP See **reel**[1].

reel[3] *noun* a lively Scottish dance or the music for it.

☑ SPELLING TIP See **reel**[1].

refer /*say* ruh-**fer**/ *verb* (**refers**, **referring**, **referred**, **has referred**)
1. If you **refer** to someone or something, you mention them: *The teacher referred to a couple of people who had done extra good work.* **2.** If you **refer** to a book or other publication, you look something up in it in order to find out certain information: *You need to refer to a dictionary!* **3.** If someone such as a doctor **refers** a patient to another doctor, they ask the other doctor to see their patient.
□ **referral**, *noun*: *I was given a referral to see an ear, nose and throat specialist.*

referee *noun*
1. someone who makes certain that the rules in a sporting match are followed. **2.** someone who decides or settles matters which are being argued about.
–*verb* (**referees**, **refereeing**, **refereed**, **has refereed**) **3.** If someone **referees** a sporting match, they control it and make sure that the rules are followed.

ANOTHER WORD for this is **umpire**.

☑ SPELLING TIP *Single letter alert*: only one *f*, but remember the double *ee* at the end. This will be easier to remember if you see that **referee** is made up of the word *refer* and the suffix *-ee* (which is from French and is used in words for a person who receives something, or, as in this word, does something).

reference /*say* **ref**-ruhns/ *noun*
1. a mention: *Your speech should include a reference to the volunteers.* **2.** a book or a place in a book or other writing where information may be found: *The medical references are on the bottom shelf.* **3.** the act of looking for information: *The library is there for general reference by everybody.* **4.** a letter giving a description of someone's character and abilities: *Could you write me a reference for the job, please.*
–*adjective* **5. Reference** books are books such as dictionaries or encyclopedias in which you can look up facts or information about a particular topic.
–*phrase* **6. with reference to**, having to do with: *With reference to the excursion, do we have to take sleeping bags?*

NOTE This comes from the verb **refer**.

☑ SPELLING TIP Don't forget that there are four *e*'s in **reference**. Be careful about the second one, because you usually do not hear it when you say the word. This will be easier to remember if you see that it is made up of the word *refer* and the noun suffix *-ence*.

referendum *noun* (*plural* **referendums** *or* **referenda**) a public vote taken on a question of government or law.

refine *verb* To **refine** something is to make it more fine or pure: *When oil is refined, a number of side products are made.*
□ **refinement**, *noun* –**refinery**, *noun* (*plural* **refineries**): *a sugar refinery.*

refined *adjective*
1. A **refined** person has polite manners and likes cultural activities, such as those related to the arts, literature, and so on. **2.** A **refined** substance has been made fine or pure: *refined sugar.*

reflect *verb*
1. If a surface **reflects** light, the light shines back from it: *The moon reflects the light of the sun.* **2.** If a mirror or other surface **reflects** someone or something, it shows an image of it: *The smooth surface of the lake reflected the trees and the clouds.* **3.** If you say that something **reflects** something else, you mean that it shows its influence: *His good playing reflects all those hours of practice.* **4.** If you **reflect** on something, you think carefully about it: *I need more time to reflect on the problem.*
□ **reflection**, *noun* –**reflective**, *adjective* –**reflector**, *noun*

reflex /*say* **ree**-fleks/ *noun* an action done without thinking as a reaction to something: *It was pure reflex for her to hit back like that.*
□ **reflex**, *adjective*

reflexive pronoun *noun* a pronoun which refers back to the subject of a clause or sentence. For example, in the sentence *The dog was scratching itself*, the reflexive pronoun 'itself' refers back to 'the dog'.

SEE the Grammar and Punctuation Guide appendix.

reflexive verb *noun* a verb whose subject and object are identical, such as 'saw' in the sentence *I saw myself in the mirror*, which has the subject *I* and the object *myself*, that is, one and the same person.

SEE the Grammar and Punctuation Guide appendix.

reform *verb*
1. To **reform** someone or something is to change them so that they are better: *If you don't reform your table manners, you won't be taken out to dinner*; *The public transport system needs to be reformed.* **2.** If someone **reforms**, they give up their bad behaviour or habits.
□ **reform**, *noun* –**reformation**, *noun* –**reformed**, *adjective*: *a reformed thief.* –**reformer**, *noun*

refrain[1] *verb* If you **refrain** from doing something, you keep yourself back or stop yourself doing it: *Anna is trying to refrain from eating so much chocolate.*

WORD HISTORY from a Latin word meaning 'to bridle'

refrain[2] *noun* a line or verse that is repeated regularly in a song or poem: *The boys were supposed to join in for the refrain but they didn't.*

ANOTHER WORD for this is **chorus** (definition 1).

refresh *verb* If something **refreshes** you, it gives you back your strength and energy after you have become tired: *Swimming in the cold mountain stream refreshed us all.*
☐ **refreshing**, *adjective*: *a refreshing shower.*

refreshment *noun* something that refreshes, especially food and drink or a light meal: *Refreshments were served at the end of the concert.*

refrigerate /*say* ruh-**frij**-uh-rayt/ *verb* To **refrigerate** food is to keep it cold or frozen to keep it from going bad.
☐ **refrigeration**, *noun*

refrigerator /*say* ruh-**frij**-uh-ray-tuh/ *noun* a special appliance or room where food and drink are kept cool.

THE SHORT FORM of this is **fridge**.

☑ SPELLING TIP Remember that there is no *d* in this word (although there is in the short form *fridge*). In **refrigerator**, the *g* alone makes the 'j' sound. Also notice that the ending is *or* (not *er*). Rap it out as *re+ frig+ er+ a+ tor.*

refuge /*say* **ref**-yoohj/ *noun*
1. shelter or protection from danger or trouble: *They ran to a neighbour's house for refuge.* **2.** a place that gives shelter or protection: *a refuge for homeless men.*

A SIMILAR WORD is **sanctuary**.

refugee /*say* ref-yooh-**jee**/ *noun* someone who escapes to another country for safety, especially because of war or persecution.

refund *verb* /*say* ruh-**fund**/
1. To **refund** money is to give it back: *The shop refunded our money because the game broke in the first week.*
–*noun* /*say* **ree**-fund/ **2.** money paid back: *With the refund, I bought another game instead.*

refurbish *verb* If you **refurbish** a place, you do it up so that it seems new again: *Mum wants to refurbish her office.*

A SIMILAR WORD is **renovate**.

refuse[1] /*say* ruh-**fyoohz**/ *verb*
1. If you **refuse** to do something, you say you will not do it: *She refused to come to my party.* **2.** If you **refuse** something, you do not accept it: *I was surprised she refused my invitation without a good reason.*
☐ **refusal**, *noun*

refuse[2] /*say* **ref**-yoohs/ *noun* rubbish: *The beach was covered with refuse after the wild storm.*

refute *verb* If you **refute** something, you prove it to be false: *It wasn't hard to refute everything that he said.*
☐ **refutation**, *noun*

regain *verb* If you **regain** something, you get it back again: *We had a rest to regain our strength.*

regal *adjective* having to do with or like a king or queen: *The regal party was met at the airport by the prime minister*; *Beside the river stood regal red gums.*
☐ **regality**, *noun* –**regally**, *adverb*

regard *verb*
1. If you **regard** someone or something in a certain way, that is how you think of them: *Our family regards every holiday as a chance to do something different.* **2.** If you **regard** someone, you look at them: *The shop owner regarded the intruders with a mixture of anger and fear.*
–*noun* **3.** thought or attention: *Have some regard for the family involved.* **4.** a feeling of kindness or liking: *Everybody has immense regard for the contribution of the lifesavers.* **5. regards**, expressions of respect or friendship: *Pass on my regards when you see him.*
–*phrase* **6. with** (or **in**) **regard to**, having to do with or concerning: *The principal's decision with regard to the new rules is final.*
☐ **regardless**, *adverb*: *We are determined to go swimming regardless of the weather.*

regatta *noun* a meeting for boat races.

regenerate *verb* To **regenerate** something is to make or develop it again, especially in a better form or condition: *The city centre has been regenerated and is now clean and full of smart, new shops.*
☐ **regeneration**, *noun*: *a campaign for bush regeneration.*

regent /*say* **ree**-juhnt/ *noun* someone who rules a kingdom while the king or queen is sick or too young.
☐ **regency**, *noun*

WORD HISTORY from a Latin word meaning 'ruling'

reggae /*say* **reg**-ay/ *noun* a type of modern music, originating in the West Indies in the 1970s, with a strong bass part and guitar chords played on the unaccented beat.

regime /*say* ray-**zheem**/ *noun* a system of rule or government: *Everybody is criticising the strictness of the new regime.*

NOTE This is also spelt **régime** (with an accent on the first *e*) because it comes from French.

regiment *noun* /*say* **rej**-uh-muhnt/
1. a division of an army consisting of two or more battalions.
–*verb* /*say* **rej**-uh-ment/ **2.** To **regiment** things or people is to impose a system on them or to organise them: *Angela was never one to be regimented.*
☐ **regimental**, *adjective* –**regimentation**, *noun*

region *noun*
1. any part or area: *In some regions, health facilities are scarce.* **2.** an area of the earth with particular features: *the hot desert regions of Australia.*
☐ **regional**, *adjective*

register *noun*
1. a list of names, belongings, or events, kept as a record: *The club has to present a register of all its assets.* **2.** a machine which records information: *The cash registers were ringing continually.* **3.** the musical range of a voice or instrument: *The soprano has a high register.*
–*verb* **4.** If you **register** something such as your car, you record the details of it on an official list: *Cars have to be registered each year.* **5.** If something **registers** an effect, it shows it or indicates it: *The polls have registered an increasing concern over health matters.*
☐ **registration**, *noun*

registrar *noun*
1. someone who keeps records. **2.** a doctor in a hospital who is training to be a specialist.
☐ **registry**, *noun* (*plural* **registries**)

regress *verb* If you **regress**, you move or go back: *Whenever he is stressed, he regresses to the behaviour of a baby.*
☐ **regression**, *noun* –**regressive**, *adjective* –**regressively**, *adverb*

regret *verb* (**regrets**, **regretting**, **regretted**, **has regretted**)
1. If you **regret** something, you are sorry about it, or wish that you had not done it: *Everybody regretted that they had been so mean to him.*
–*noun* **2.** a feeling of loss or disappointment or of being sorry about something you have done.
☐ **regretful**, *adjective* –**regretfulness**, *noun* –**regrettable**, *adjective*

regular *adjective* Something is **regular** if **1.** it always happens at the same time: *The regular school assembly is at 9 o'clock on Tuesdays.* **2.** it follows a pattern or happens at fixed times: *We have a regular bus service to our school.* **3.** it is usual or normal: *She always wants to follow regular procedure and not try anything different.* **4.** it is even or well-balanced: *Her smile revealed beautifully regular teeth.*
–*noun* **5.** *Informal* a regular visitor or customer: *Take no notice of him – he's just a regular who drops in all the time!*
☐ **regularity**, *noun* –**regularly**, *adverb*

regulate *verb* To **regulate** people or situations is to control or change them so that a rule or standard is kept to: *The state government has regulated the speed that cars drive at outside school grounds.*
☐ **regulative**, *adjective* –**regulator**, *noun* –**regulatory**, *adjective*

regulation *noun*
1. a rule or law: *council regulations.* **2.** control, or correction and adjustment: *The meter provides regulation of the water flow.*

rehabilitate *verb* To **rehabilitate** someone is to help return them to normal activities, especially after an illness or accident, or after having been in prison: *They have brought in a new scheme to help rehabilitate drug addicts*; *They argued about whether the main aim of prison was to punish or to rehabilitate criminals.*
☐ **rehabilitation**, *noun*

rehearse /*say* ruh-**hers**/ *verb* To **rehearse** is to practise in private before giving a public performance.
☐ **rehearsal**, *noun*

☑ SPELLING TIP *Tricky vowel sound*: don't forget that there is an *a* in **rehearse**. Think of other words in which the letter combination *ear* makes an 'er' sound, such as *earn* or *learn*.

reign /*say* rayn/ *noun*
1. the time during which a king or queen rules or holds the position of ruler.
–*verb* **2.** When a king or queen **reigns**, they rule or hold the position of ruler: *Queen Victoria reigned for 64 years.*

☑ SPELLING TIP *Tricky vowel sound*: remember the *eign* spelling in this word, giving an 'ayn' sound. The *g* is left over from the Latin origins of the word (*regnum*, meaning 'rule'). Don't confuse **reign** with **rain** or **rein** which both sound the same. **Rain** is water falling from the sky. A **rein** is a strap which a rider uses to guide a horse.

reimburse /*say* ree-im-**bers**/ *verb* If you **reimburse** someone, you pay them back: *The teacher will be reimbursed for the costs of the excursion.*
☐ **reimbursement**, *noun*

A SIMILAR WORD is **refund**.

rein /*say* rayn/ *noun*
1. one of the long, thin straps which a rider uses to direct a horse or other animal. **2.** any kind of control or check: *The chairman had to keep a firm rein on the proceedings of the meeting.*
–*verb in the phrase* **3. rein in** (or **back**), **a.** to use the reins to guide the movements of (a horse). **b.** to control (a person or thing): *The chairman had to rein in the direction of the discussion.*

WORD HISTORY from a Latin word meaning 'hold back'

☑ SPELLING TIP Don't confuse **rein** with **rain** or **reign** which both sound the same. **Rain** is water falling from the sky. The **reign** of a king or queen is the time during which they rule.

reincarnation /*say* ree-in-kah-**nay**-shuhn/ *noun* the return of the soul after death in a new body or form, a process which some people believe happens.

reindeer /*say* **rayn**-dear/ *noun* (*plural* **reindeer** *or* **reindeers**) a kind of deer with large antlers, which lives in the cold northern areas of the world.

☑ SPELLING TIP Although it might rain a lot where **reindeers** come from, this is not related to the spelling of the word. The *rein* part comes from the original language, Old Norse (the old language of Scandinavia). However, it might help to think of the word *rein* (a strap a rider uses to guide a horse) and imagine Santa Claus in his sleigh, guiding his **reindeers** with reins.

reinforce /*say* ree-in-**faws**/ *verb* To **reinforce** something is to strengthen it, by adding something: *Extra sand bags were needed to reinforce the banks of the flooded river.*
☐ **reinforcement**, *noun*

reject *verb* /*say* ruh-**jekt**/
1. To **reject** something is refuse to accept it or to disagree with it: *I totally reject your argument*; *The patient's body rejected the new kidney soon after the transplant.*
–*noun* /*say* **ree**-jekt/ **2.** someone or something that has been rejected: *In this pile are the photographs I want to keep; in that pile are the rejects.*
☐ **rejection**, *noun*

rejoice *verb* If you **rejoice**, you feel great joy: *The whole community rejoiced when the miners were found alive.*

rejoinder *noun* a spoken answer or response: *The teacher's rejoinder was short and to the point.*

rejuvenate /*say* ruh-**jooh**-vuh-nayt/ *verb* If something **rejuvenates** someone, it makes them feel young or energetic again: *Swimming in the fresh ocean water rejuvenated them.*
☐ **rejuvenation**, *noun*

relapse *verb* /*say* ruh-**laps**/
1. To **relapse** is to return or fall back: *He relapsed into his bad ways.*
–*noun* /*say* **ree**-laps/ **2.** an act of going back to a bad condition, especially a return to illness after starting to get better.

relate *verb*
1. If you say that one thing **relates** to another, you mean that the two things are connected: *What you say relates to what I said earlier.* **2.** If someone **relates** something to something else, they connect the two things in their mind: *The police related his absence to the time of the murder.* **3.** If you **relate** to someone or to someone's experience, you understand them and therefore you can communicate well with them: *I can relate to what he's going through.* **4.** If you **relate** something to someone, you tell them.

related *adjective*
1. associated or connected: *The long drought and the increase in sales of farms are related.* **2.** part of the same family.

relation *noun*
1. the way things or people are connected: *There is a relation between rain patterns and movements of flocks of birds.* **2.** a family relative: *We invited a hundred of our friends and relations to the wedding.*
☐ **relationship**, *noun*

relative *noun*
1. someone who is part of your family: *We only see some of our relatives at Christmas.*
–*adjective* **2.** You use **relative** to describe how something is in comparison with something else: *Compared to many countries, Australia enjoys relative prosperity.*
☐ **relatively**, *adverb* –**relativity**, *noun*

A SIMILAR WORD (for definition 2) is **comparative**.

relax *verb*
1. If you **relax**, you stop working or worrying and you do something that you find pleasant or restful. **2.** If you **relax** part of your body, you let it go loose: *In this exercise you stretch your arm, relax it, then stretch it again.* **3.** To **relax** a rule is to be less strict about it: *The new school principal decided to relax the uniform rules a bit.*
☐ **relaxation**, *noun*

relay *noun* /*say* **ree**-lay/
1. a group which takes its turn with others to keep some activity going: *The guests arrived in relays for their breakfast.* **2.** a team race in which each member runs or swims a part of the distance.
–*verb* /*say* ruh-**lay**, **ree**-lay/ **3.** To **relay** something is to pass or carry it forward: *I had to relay a message from our teacher to a classroom at the other end of the school.*

release *verb*
1. To **release** a person or animal is to set them free: *He is to be released from prison next week*; *Because of the fire, we were released from homework.* **2.** To **release** information is to make it public: *The news was released at midday.*
–*noun* **3.** the act of releasing: *His release is a worry to many people.* **4.** a statement, news story, and so on, released to the public: *a press release.*

relent *verb* If you **relent**, you soften or become more forgiving than you meant to be: *My mother finally relented and let me go to the movies.*
☐ **relentless**, *adjective* never giving up or stopping: *relentless heat.*

relevant /*say* **rel**-uh-vuhnt/ *adjective* If something is **relevant** to a subject, it is connected with it: *Just tell me the relevant facts and leave the rest out.*
☐ **relevance**, *noun* –**relevancy**, *noun*

A SIMILAR WORD is **pertinent**.

☑ SPELLING TIP *Tricky 'uh' sound*: the middle vowel sound is spelt *e*. Also remember that the ending is *ant* (not *ent*). Try thinking of the word *van* is hiding inside the word **relevant**.

reliable *adjective* If someone or something is **reliable**, you can trust them and depend on them: *Josh is often asked to take messages because he is so reliable*; *Our car is old but it is still reliable.*
☐ **reliability**, *noun* –**reliably**, *adverb*

SIMILAR WORDS are **dependable**, **trustworthy** and **responsible**. Note that most of these words can be used to describe a person or thing (*a trustworthy friend*, *a dependable car*); however, **responsible** can only be used about a person who is able to be trusted with duties or responsibilities: *We are looking for a hardworking, responsible person to do this job.*

reliant /*say* ruh-**luy**-uhnt/ *adjective* having trust, or depending: *The chickens are reliant on the mother hen for warmth.*
☐ **reliance**, *noun*

relic *noun* something left over from the past: *The museum has thousands of relics from past civilisations.*

relief *noun*
1. freedom or release from pain, unhappiness or worry: *He sighed with relief when he heard that his house was not affected by the fire.* **2.** something that gives relief or help: *After the disaster, several charities organised relief for the victims.* **3.** someone who replaces someone else in a job or on a duty: *She stayed until the relief arrived.* **4.** a figure or shape carved so that it stands out above its background. **5.** in physical geography, the change of the land surface in any area from that of a level surface.

☑ SPELLING TIP Remember the *ie* spelling for the 'ee' sound. This follows the rule that *i* comes before *e*, except after *c*.

relieve *verb*
1. If something **relieves** an unpleasant feeling, it makes it less unpleasant: *This tablet will relieve the pain*; *Their fears were relieved when the children returned safely.* **2.** If someone or something **relieves** you of a difficulty or an unpleasant feeling, you no longer have to experience it: *The massage relieved him of tension.* **3.** If you **relieve** someone who is on duty, you replace them: *Mrs Johnson is coming to relieve our teacher while she does a special course.*

religion *noun*
1. belief in a god or gods. **2.** the way this belief is expressed in a particular system of worship: *There are many religions throughout the world.*
☐ **religious**, *adjective*

WORD HISTORY from a Latin word meaning 'fear of the gods' or 'sacredness'

relinquish /*say* ruh-**ling**-kwish/ *verb* If you **relinquish** something, you give it up or put it aside: *We have had to relinquish our plans for going on holidays*; *The prime minister decided to relinquish the leadership and not stand at the next election.*
☐ **relinquisher**, *noun* –**relinquishment**, *noun*

relish *noun*
1. a liking or enjoyment of something: *We looked at the party table with relish.* **2.** something that adds taste to food, such as a sauce: *The tomato relish was a great hit!*
–*verb* **3.** If you **relish** something, you like or enjoy it: *We relished the idea of a short day on Friday.*

WORD HISTORY from a French word meaning 'what is left' or 'remainder'

reluctant *adjective* If you are **reluctant** to do something, you do not want to do it: *We were reluctant to go out because it was so cold.*
☐ **reluctance**, *noun* –**reluctantly**, *adverb*

rely /*say* ruh-**luy**/ *verb* (**relies**, **relying**, **relied**, **has relied**)
1. If you **rely** on someone, you trust that they will do what you want them to do: *I'm relying on you to come so I won't be on my own.* **2.** If you **rely** on someone or something, you need them or depend on them for something: *I rely on public transport to get to school.*

remain *verb*
1. If you **remain** somewhere or in a certain condition, you stay there: *to remain at the beach until sunset*; *to remain determined.* **2.** If something **remains**, it is left over: *Only a small amount of water remained in the dam.*
☐ **remaining**, *adjective*

remainder *noun* what remains or is left: *Can we have the remainder of the food?*; *If you take 8 from 20, the remainder is 12.*

remains *plural noun* **1.** what is left: *The fire left few remains.* **2.** someone's dead body: *His remains were buried at sea.*

remark *verb* To **remark** is to something say in a casual way: *She remarked that she had seen Jodie at the shops.*
☐ **remark**, *noun* –**remarkable**, *adjective* –**remarkably**, *adverb*

remedy /*say* **rem**-uh-dee/ *noun* (*plural* **remedies**)
1. a cure for a disease. **2.** something that corrects anything that is wrong or bad: *There isn't a simple remedy for his continual bad behaviour.*

–*verb* (**remedies**, **remedying**, **remedied**, **has remedied**) **3.** To **remedy** something is to correct or fix it: *A snack remedied our hunger pangs.*
☐ **remedial**, *adjective*

remember *verb* To **remember** is to bring back to or keep in your mind: *I can't remember her mobile number.*
☐ **remembrance**, *noun*

remind *verb* To **remind** someone is to make them remember: *Remind me to get a new train pass before school goes back.*
☐ **reminder**, *noun*

reminiscence /*say* rem-uh-**nis**-uhns/ *noun* a story you tell about the past, or thoughts you have about something in the past: *His reminiscences about the Antarctic were fascinating.*
☐ **reminisce** /*say* rem-uh-**nis**/, *verb*: *She spends her days reminiscing about when she was young.* –**reminiscent**, *adjective*

☑ SPELLING TIP *Silent letter alert*: don't forget the silent *c* following the *s*. If you think of the adjective **reminiscent** and notice it contains the word *scent* – something which often brings back memories – that will remind you to include the *c* in **reminiscence**.

remiss /*say* ruh-**mis**/ *adjective* careless or negligent: *The teacher said we had been remiss in performing our class duties.*

remnant *noun* a part or amount that is left: *Fern fossils are remnants of plants that grew millions of years ago.*

remorse *noun* the sorrow or regret you feel when you have done something wrong: *She felt deep remorse for the trouble she had caused her family.*
☐ **remorseful**, *adjective* –**remorseless**, *adjective*

remote *adjective*
1. far away or distant: *Sometimes I think I would like to live on a remote planet.* **2.** slight: *There is only a remote chance that I will be a tennis champion.*
–*phrase* **3. remote control**, **a.** the control of a machine or system by means of electrical, radio, or mechanical signals from a point outside the machine or system: *The toy plane is operated by remote control.* **b.** a device used to operate such a system: *Do you know where the remote control for the TV is?*
☐ **remotely**, *adverb* –**remoteness**, *noun*

remove *verb*
1. If you **remove** something, you take it off or away: *Please remove the plates from the table!* **2.** If someone is **removed** from their position, they are dismissed: *Not many people knew why the conductor was removed.*
☐ **removable**, *adjective* –**removal**, *noun* –**removalist**, *noun*

renal /*say* **ree**-nuhl/ *adjective* having to do with the kidneys.

rend *verb* (**rends**, **rending**, **rent**, **has rent**) If you **rend** something, you pull or tear it violently.

render *verb* To **render** is to **1.** cause to be or become: *Her condition rendered her unable to speak.* **2.** give: *They offered to render whatever assistance they could.* **3.** perform: *They asked the school band to render a few pieces to open the awards ceremony.* **4.** cover with a coat of plaster: *The walls were rendered and later painted.*
☐ **rendering**, *noun* –**rendition**, *noun*: *He gave a rendition of a very funny song.*

rendezvous /*say* **ron**-day-vooh, ron-day-**vooh**/ *noun* (*plural* **rendezvous** /*say* **ron**-day-voohz, ron-day-**voohz**/)
1. a meeting which has been arranged at an earlier time and which is sometimes secret: *The lovers organised a rendezvous.* **2.** a meeting place: *He was waiting at the rendezvous to meet her.*

☑ SPELLING TIP *Silent letter alert*: don't forget the silent *z* in the middle of this word (where *ez* makes an 'ay' sound) nor the silent *s* at the end. Also remember the *en* spelling in the first syllable, which you say as 'on'. All this is because **rendezvous** comes directly from French. It is made up of two words – *rendez* (meaning 'present' or 'appear') and *vous* (meaning 'you'), with the sense of a command: 'Present yourself!'

renew *verb*
1. If you **renew** something, you begin it again: *I will have to renew my loan at the library.* **2.** If you **renew** a supply of something, you build it up again: *We have to renew the ink cartridge in the printer.*
☐ **renewal**, *noun*

renewable resource *noun* a supply of something in nature, such as the sun, wind and tides, which can make power and which does not run out.

COMPARE this with **non-renewable resource**.

renounce *verb* If you **renounce** something, you give it up or put it aside: *My dad says that he has renounced smoking for ever.*
☐ **renunciation**, *noun*

renovate *verb* To **renovate** something is to repair it or bring it back to good condition: *My grandparents are renovating their unit.*
☐ **renovation**, *noun* –**renovator**, *noun*

renown *noun* fame: *His renown is based on his huge gifts to charity.*
☐ **renowned**, *adjective*

rent *verb*
1. To **rent** something to someone is to allow them to use it in return for regular payment: *The landlords want to rent the house to a family.* **2.** To **rent**

something such as a property is to pay its owner for being able to use it, usually for a fairly long time: *The family rented the house for three years.* –*noun* **3.** payment that is made regularly for a house, flat or other property that you use.
☐ **rental**, *noun*

repair *verb*
1. If you **repair** something that is broken, you bring it back to good condition: *Dad's trying to repair Nanna's favourite chair.*
–*noun* **2.** the work of repairing: *What will the repair cost?* **3.** condition: *My old bike is in a state of bad repair at the moment.*
☐ **repairable**, *adjective*

SIMILAR WORDS (for definition 1) are **fix**, **mend**, **restore** and **renovate**. Note that to **restore** or to **renovate** something old is to repair, clean or decorate it so that it looks like it would have looked when new: *This firm specialises in restoring antique furniture*; *We are going to renovate our kitchen.*

reparation /*say* rep-uh-**ray**-shuhn/ *noun*
1. the making up for doing something wrong or harmful: *The victim is demanding reparation.* **2.** something done or money paid as reparation: *The reparation will be in the order of thousands.*

A SIMILAR WORD is **compensation**.

repay *verb* (**repays**, **repaying**, **repaid**, **has repaid**) To **repay** something is to pay it back.
☐ **repayment**, *noun*

repeal *verb* If a government **repeals** something like a law, it officially puts an end to it.
☐ **repeal**, *noun*

repeat *verb*
1. If you **repeat** something, you say or do it again: *She repeated her maths tables over and over again until she could say them off by heart.*
–*noun* **2.** something that is repeated, such as a television program, that has been shown before: *Is it a repeat or a new series?*
☐ **repeated**, *adjective* –**repeatedly**, *adverb*

repel *verb* (**repels**, **repelling**, **repelled**, **has repelled**)
1. If one thing **repels** another, it drives or forces the other thing away from it: *The troops repelled the invading army with grenades*; *This spray repels mosquitoes.* **2.** If something **repels** you, it disgusts you: *The bad smell repelled them.*
☐ **repellent**, *adjective*: *insect repellent.* –**repelling**, *adjective*

☑ SPELLING TIP *Single letter alert*: only one *l* at the end. However, the *l* is doubled when you add *-ed* or *-ing* or make the word *repellent*.

repent *verb* If you **repent** something, you regret or feel sorry for it: *Sarah repented her nastiness as soon as she had said the words*; *She repented that she had treated the new girl so badly.*
☐ **repentance**, *noun* –**repentant**, *adjective*

repertoire /*say* **rep**-uh-twah/ *noun* the plays, musical pieces or other items which an entertainer such as an actor or musician is prepared to perform in public: *Her repertoire is small but it is more quality than quantity.*

☑ SPELLING TIP Remember the unusual *oire* ending, giving a 'wah' sound. This is because **repertoire** comes from French (originally from a Latin word meaning 'inventory' or 'catalogue').

repetition *noun*
1. the act of repeating: *Dad's continual repetition of the same jokes drives us all mad.* **2.** the thing which is repeated: *I think the story on the radio was a repetition of one yesterday.*
☐ **repetitious**, *adjective* –**repetitive**, *adjective*

replace *verb*
1. When someone or something **replaces** another person or thing, they take their place: *I will replace the vase I broke*; *He replaced the main actor, who was sick.* **2.** If you **replace** something, you put it back where it was before: *Please replace all the books on the shelf when you have finished reading them.*
☐ **replacement**, *noun*

replay *noun*
1. a previously tied match or game that is played again to decide the winner. **2.** a repeat, especially on television, of the important parts of a game, often straight after they have happened.

replenish *verb* If you **replenish** a supply, you refill or restore it: *We had to replenish the paper supply for the printer.*
☐ **replenishment**, *noun*

replica /*say* **rep**-lik-uh/ *noun* an exact copy: *They sailed around the world on a replica of Captain Cook's ship, the 'Endeavour'.*
☐ **replicate**, *verb* –**replication**, *noun*

reply *verb* (**replies**, **replying**, **replied**, **has replied**) To **reply** is to give an answer: *He didn't reply because he had gone to sleep*; *Have you replied to the email yet?*
☐ **reply**, *noun* (*plural* **replies**)

report *noun*
1. writing or speaking which gives information about something. **2.** an account of a meeting, an event, or someone's progress at work or school.
–*verb* **3.** If you **report** something that has happened, you tell someone about it officially: *Did you report the theft to the police?* **4.** If you **report** someone for doing something wrong, you make a formal complaint against them to someone in authority: *My teacher reported me to the principal for failing to do my homework.* **5.** If you **report** for work, you arrive and present yourself to the person in charge: *The soldier reported to his commanding officer.*

reporter *noun* someone who works for a newspaper, or for radio or television, gathering and describing the news.

repose *noun*
1. peaceful rest: *He maintained there should be a time for work – and a time for repose.*
–*verb* 2. If you **repose**, you rest: *She was reposing on a velvet lounge.*

repossess *verb* If someone **repossesses** goods, they take them back, usually because payments have not been made on time: *All the new furniture was repossessed.*
☐ **repossession**, *noun*

represent *verb*
1. If you **represent** someone or something, you act for them: *Our house captain represented us at the awards and received our swimming trophy.* 2. If a sign or symbol **represents** something, people understand that that's what it means: *A picture of a dove represents peace.* 3. To **represent** something is to show or describe it: *The unusual orange and purple abstract painting represented people's frustration at the confusion of modern life.*
☐ **representation**, *noun* –**representative**, *adjective*, *noun*

repress *verb* To **repress** a feeling is to keep it under control by effort or force: *She repressed her urge to speak her mind and tried to remain calm.*
☐ **repressed**, *adjective* –**repression**, *noun* –**repressive**, *adjective*

reprieve /*say* ruh-**preev**/ *noun*
1. a delay or cancellation, especially in carrying out a punishment: *She may be given a reprieve because of her remorse over the crime.*
–*verb* 2. If a person is **reprieved** from something like a punishment, they are able to avoid it: *He was reprieved from the death sentence but was given life imprisonment.*

☑ SPELLING TIP Remember that **reprieve** has *ie* (to spell the 'ee' sound) following the *r*. This follows the rule that *i* comes before *e* except after *c*.

reprimand *noun*
1. a scolding, especially from someone in charge.
–*verb* 2. If someone in authority **reprimands** you, they scold you.

reprisal *noun* an act which causes hurt or damage to someone in retaliation for something they have done.

reproach *noun* (*plural* **reproaches**)
1. blame or disapproval: *Dad was full of reproach when we got home late.*
–*verb* 2. If you **reproach** someone, you blame them: *Mum reproached me for suggesting the game in the first place.*
☐ **reproachful**, *adjective* –**reproachfully**, *adverb*

reproduce *verb*
1. To **reproduce** something is to make a copy of it: *The factory where Mum works reproduces all kinds of antique furniture.* 2. When animals or plants **reproduce**, they produce new ones of their own kind.
☐ **reproducer**, *noun* –**reproduction**, *noun* –**reproductive**, *adjective*

reprove /*say* ruh-**proohv**/ *verb* If someone **reproves** you, they scold or blame you for some behaviour: *The principal reproved us for our bad behaviour.*
☐ **reproof**, *noun*

NOTE This is a very formal word.

☑ SPELLING TIP *Tricky vowel sound*: there is no double *o*. The spelling *ove* makes the 'oohv' sound, as it does in *prove* and other words such as *move*.

reptile *noun* a cold-blooded animal, such as a lizard or snake, that lays eggs and moves close to or on the ground.
☐ **reptilian**, *adjective*

republic *noun* a nation in which the leader is not a person who inherits the position, such as a king or queen. A republic usually has a president as its head.

WORD HISTORY from a Latin word meaning 'public matter'

republican *adjective*
1. having to do with a republic: *A republican government does not have a king or queen.* 2. favouring a republican form of government.
☐ **republican**, *noun*

repugnant *adjective* unpleasant or distasteful: *She finds the thought of eating meat repugnant.*
☐ **repugnance**, *noun*

repulse *verb*
1. If an army **repulses** an attack, it drives it back. 2. If you **repulse** something, you reject or refuse it: *She repulsed all his approaches and he eventually gave up.* 3. If someone or something **repulses** you, they disgust you.
☐ **repulse**, *noun*

A SIMILAR WORD is **repel**.

repulsive *adjective* disgusting: *a repulsive habit*; *a repulsive smell.*
☐ **repulsion**, *noun*

reputable /*say* **rep**-yuh-tuh-buhl/ *adjective* able to be trusted: *My uncle is looking for a good position with a reputable firm.*
☐ **reputably**, *adverb*

reputation *noun*
1. the way in which people regard someone or something: *His reputation as a bowler has suffered due to his recent poor performances.* 2. honesty or good name: *She spoiled her reputation.*

reputed *adjective* supposed or thought to be: *The police investigation centred on the reputed crime boss.*
☐ **repute**, *noun* –**reputedly**, *adverb*

request *noun*
1. the act of asking. 2. the thing asked for.
–*verb* 3. If you **request** something, you ask for it politely: *I've requested a copy of the book but haven't received it yet.*

requiem /*say* **rek**-wee-uhm/ *noun* a church service, especially in the Roman Catholic Church, where prayers are said for someone who has died.

> ☑ SPELLING TIP Notice the *em* ending. **Requiem** is a form of the Latin word for 'rest'. (It is the first word in the Latin mass for the dead.)

require /*say* ruh-**kwuy**-uh/ *verb* To **require** is to 1. need: *I require two people to help me.* 2. demand: *She requires silence.*
☐ **requirement**, *noun*

> ☑ SPELLING TIP Remember the *qu* spelling for the 'kw' sound.

rescue *verb* To **rescue** someone or something is to save them from danger or destruction.
☐ **rescue**, *noun* –**rescuer**, *noun*

research *noun*
1. close study or investigation in order to understand or learn more about a subject.
–*verb* 2. If you **research** a subject, you make close study of it or you carry out an investigation in order to understand or learn more about it: *We are researching the development of film.*
☐ **researcher**, *noun*

resemble *verb* If a person or a thing **resembles** another, they look like each other: *They all said the baby resembled his father.*
☐ **resemblance**, *noun*

resent *verb* If you **resent** something, you have very strong feelings against it and it makes you angry: *She resented the way he always interrupted.*
☐ **resentful**, *adjective* –**resentment**, *noun*

reservation *noun*
1. something which has been held or set aside for you, such as seats in a theatre or a room in a hotel. 2. a doubt: *The choir teacher had reservations about Clive's singing so Clive turned the pages instead.*

reserve *verb*
1. If you **reserve** something, you arrange in advance to use it: *We had to reserve seats two months before the concert.* 2. If you **reserve** something, you keep it for later use: *Mum used some of the lemon peel in the cake, and reserved some for the icing.*
–*noun* 3. someone or something kept as a replacement, especially an extra member of a sports team. 4. public land set aside for a special use, especially as a park or wildlife sanctuary.
☐ **reserve**, *adjective*

reserved *adjective*
1. kept or set aside: *reserved tickets.* 2. shy and not wanting to talk about yourself: *Her reserved nature stops her making friends easily.*

reservoir /*say* **rez**-uh-vwah/ *noun*
1. a place where water is stored. 2. a container, especially for oil or gas.

> ☑ SPELLING TIP *Tricky 'uh' sound*: the middle vowel sound is spelt *er*. This will be easier to remember if you see that **reservoir** is related to the word *reserve*. The *e* has been dropped and the suffix *-oir* added. You need also to remember the spelling of this word part, which comes from French, which is why it sounds like 'wah'.

reshuffle *verb* If you **reshuffle** something, you change it around: *Our coach reshuffled the playing positions halfway through the game.*
☐ **reshuffle**, *noun*

reside *verb* To **reside** is to live in a particular place, especially over a long period: *They resided in a very grand house at the end of a long tree-lined drive.*

residence *noun*
1. the place where someone lives, especially a large house: *the governor-general's residence.* 2. the act of living in a place: *They took up residence there about 20 years ago.*
☐ **resident**, *noun* –**residential**, *adjective*

residue /*say* **rez**-uh-dyooh/ *noun* what is left after a process like burning or chemical change: *The burnt papers left a residue of ash.*
☐ **residual** /*say* ruh-**zij**-ooh-uhl/, *adjective*

> A SIMILAR WORD is **remainder**.

resign /*say* ruh-**zuyn**/ *verb*
1. If someone **resigns** from a job or position, they officially say that they are leaving it: *She had an argument with her boss and immediately resigned.* 2. If you **resign** yourself to something unpleasant, you accept it because you know there is nothing you can do to change it: *She resigned herself to never seeing him again.*
☐ **resignation**, *noun*: *She handed in her resignation.* –**resigned**, *adjective*

> ☑ SPELLING TIP Remember the *g* in this word. The letter combination *ign* gives the 'uyn' sound, as in the word *sign*.

resilient *adjective* able to become strong, healthy or happy again after an illness or misfortune: *He showed how resilient he was by returning to work a few days after the accident.*
☐ **resilience**, *noun* –**resiliently**, *adverb*

resin *noun* a sap produced by some plants, which can be used in medicines and varnishes.
☐ **resinous**, *adjective*

resist *verb*
1. If you **resist** something that you would like to do, you stop yourself doing it: *I have to resist the temptation to buy new clothes all the time.* 2. To **resist** someone or something is to fight against them: *We will resist any invasion of our country; He said that he would resist all attempts to make him change his mind.*
☐ **resistance**, *noun* –**resistant**, *adjective*

resolute *adjective* firm or determined: *Halimah was resolute in her determination to succeed.*
☐ **resolutely**, *adverb*

resolution *noun*
1. a decision, especially one made by a group or committee: *The new resolution means that after-school care will be free.* **2.** determination or firmness: *His grim face reflected his resolution to beat his opponent.*

resolve *verb* If you **resolve** something, you **1.** decide it: *We resolved to go to the beach.* **2.** solve or settle it: *We couldn't resolve our argument.*
☐ **resolve**, *noun* determination.

resonant /*say* **rez**-uh-nuhnt/ *adjective*
1. resounding or ringing: *The bells were resonant in the early morning air.* **2.** deep and rich in tone: *The sergeant's resonant voice boomed out.*
☐ **resonance**, *noun* –**resonantly**, *adverb*

resonate *verb* If something **resonates**, it rings or resounds: *The sound of the bells resonated through the church.*
☐ **resonation**, *noun*

resort /*say* ruh-**zawt**/ *verb*
1. If you **resort** to some action, you fall back on it in time of necessity: *I resorted to buying the same presents for everybody because I ran out of time.*
–*noun* **2.** a holiday place: *a beach resort.* **3.** someone or something turned to for help: *She was my last resort.*

resound *verb* To **resound** is to be filled with a loud sound: *Outside the hall, the air resounded with the sounds of the music from inside.*
☐ **resounding**, *adjective* –**resoundingly**, *adverb*

resource /*say* ruh-**zaws**, ruh-**saws**, **ree**-saws/ *noun*
1. something that can give you support or help: *The internet is a good resource for finding some kinds of information.* **2.** something, such as money, property, or workers, that can be used to give benefit to a company or institution: *The transport system needs a lot more resources to work effectively.* **3.** something existing in nature that can be used to give benefit to many people or to a country: *Australia has many mineral resources.*
☐ **resourceful**, *adjective*: *She is a resourceful person who can always fix up problems.*

A SIMILAR WORD (for definition 2) is **asset**.

NOTE This word (as in definitions 2 and 3) is often used in the plural form.

NOTE For definition 2, see also **non-renewable resource** and **renewable resource**.

☑ SPELLING TIP Notice **resource** contains the word *source*. Don't confuse the spelling of this part of the word with **sauce** (something tasty that you put on food).

respect *noun*
1. an opinion you have of someone that they are worthy of being admired and honoured. **2.** politeness or consideration: *He was put outside the classroom for lack of respect to the teacher.* **3.** a matter or detail: *In many respects it would have been better if he hadn't come.*
–*verb* **4.** If you **respect** someone, you think highly of them: *She is respected for her integrity.* **5.** If you **respect** someone's wishes, rights or ways of doing things, you allow them to have those wishes, rights or ways of doing things, even though you may not agree with them: *Some journalists often don't respect the privacy of public figures.*
☐ **respected**, *adjective*: *He is a respected psychologist.* –**respectful**, *adjective*

SIMILAR WORDS (for definition 1) are **regard**, **esteem** and **reverence**. Note that **reverence** is a feeling of very deep respect and affection.

respectable *adjective*
1. If someone or something is **respectable**, they are good or worthy of respect, especially in the sense of being socially acceptable: *Her parents said she should be sure to marry a respectable man.* **2.** If something is **respectable**, it is fairly good: *The school fete raised a respectable amount of money.*
☐ **respectability**, *noun*

respective *adjective* having to do with each one: *They were all snoozing at their respective desks.*
☐ **respectively**, *adverb*: *Tim and Anna chose a peach and a pear respectively. That is, Tim chose the peach and Anna chose the pear.*

respiration *noun* breathing: *At swimming classes, we learned a bit about artificial respiration.*

respond *verb* If you **respond** to something, you react to it by doing or saying something: *Angela responded 'yes' without even thinking*; *They responded positively*; *I do not expect them to respond to my suggestion.*

response *noun*
1. a reply in words or actions: *The televised singing competition had a tremendous response from the public.* **2.** a reaction: *Her response to his rudeness was to ignore him.*
☐ **responsive**, *adjective*

responsibility *noun* (*plural* **responsibilities**) a duty or care: *It is my responsibility to look after the dog and the goldfish.*

responsible *adjective*
1. If you are **responsible** for something, you are in charge of it and it is your job or duty to look after it properly: *You are responsible for your pets.* **2.** If you are **responsible** for something that has happened, you caused it to happen or let it happen: *Are you responsible for breaking this vase?* **3.** If you say that someone is **responsible**, you mean that you can trust them to do things properly. They are reliable: *She is very responsible for*

her age. **4.** A **responsible** job or position involves important duties or decisions.
☐ **responsibly**, *adverb*

rest[1] *noun*
1. a time during which you are not active and can relax. **2.** a short time off, especially from something tiring or troubling. **3.** a stopping of movement: *The car came to rest on the embankment.* **4.** the time of silence between notes in music. **5.** a support: *Give her a cushion as an arm rest.* –*verb* **6.** If you **rest**, you sleep, lie down, or relax for a while. **7.** If you **rest** something somewhere, you let it lie or lean there: *They rested their tired bodies on the soft cushions on the floor.* **8.** If something **rests** on a particular thing, it depends on it: *Do you realise that her future career rests on your decision?* **9.** If something **rests** somewhere, it stays or lies there: *The crown rested on a blue cushion*; *She let her eyes rest on the beautiful scene.*
☐ **restful**, *adjective* –**restfulness**, *noun* –**restless**, *adjective* –**restlessness**, *noun*

rest[2] *noun* everyone or everything left over: *There was only space for ten and the rest missed out.*

restaurant /*say* **res**-tuh-ront/ *noun* a place where meals are served to customers.

> ☑ SPELLING TIP *Tricky 'uh' sound*: the middle vowel sound is spelt *au*. Also remember the *ant* ending (which gives the 'ont' sound). This is because the word **restaurant** comes from French (from a word meaning literally 'restore' but used in the sense of 'provide food for').

restitution *noun* a paying back of something to someone who has suffered a loss or injury, as compensation.

restore *verb*
1. If you **restore** something that has gone away or been lost, you give or bring it back: *The police were able to restore the stolen car to the owner*; *It was impossible to restore the feeling of serenity that had been there.* **2.** If you **restore** something old, you bring it back to its original or good condition: *He has a passion for restoring veteran cars.*
☐ **restoration**, *noun* –**restorer**, *noun*

restrain *verb* To **restrain** is to control or prevent: *We couldn't restrain our screams of delight when we saw the trampoline in the backyard.*
☐ **restrained**, *adjective* –**restraint**, *noun*

restrict *verb* To **restrict** something is to limit it: *Some diets restrict the fat that people eat and others restrict the carbohydrates.*
☐ **restricted**, *adjective* –**restriction**, *noun* –**restrictive**, *adjective*: *restrictive clothing.*

result *noun*
1. the effect of an action or event. **2.** the answer to a sum. **3.** a mark in an examination: *She was very happy with her results.*
–*verb* **4.** If something **results** in a particular way. it ends in that way: *The match resulted in a draw*; *The accident resulted in the deaths of two people.*
☐ **resulting**, *adjective*: *The storm and the resulting damage cost many millions.*

resume *verb* If you **resume** an activity, you start it again: *We resumed our search in the rock pools when the tide went out.*
☐ **resumption**, *noun*

resurrect /*say* rez-uh-**rekt**/ *verb*
1. If you **resurrect** something, you bring it back into use: *I'll have to resurrect my old pink dress for the dance.* **2.** To be **resurrected** is to be brought back to life after death, a process that people in some religions believe in.
☐ **resurrection**, *noun*

resuscitate /*say* ruh-**sus**-uh-tayt/ *verb* If you **resuscitate** someone who is unconscious or close to death, you make them start breathing again: *The lifesavers taught us how to resuscitate people.*
☐ **resuscitation**, *noun*

> ☑ SPELLING TIP *Silent letter alert*: don't forget the silent *c* after the second *s*. There are no double letters in this word. The first 's' sound is spelt by a single *s*, the second by the *sc* combination. Try rapping it out as *re* + *sus* + *ci* + *tate*.

retail *verb*
1. To **retail** something is to sell single items of it to the final buyer and user. **2.** If something **retails** at a certain price, it is sold at that price.
☐ **retail**, *noun*, *adjective* –**retailer**, *noun*

> COMPARE this with **wholesale**.

retain *verb* If you **retain** something, you **1.** keep it: *Dad wants to retain his old car as long as possible.* **2.** remember it: *I can't retain that sort of useless information.* **3.** If something is **retained**, it is held in place: *Millions of litres of water are retained by the dam wall.*
☐ **retainer**, *noun*

retaliate *verb* If you **retaliate**, you do something unpleasant to someone who has done something unpleasant to you: *Of course the dog will retaliate if anyone kicks it.*
☐ **retaliation**, *noun*

retard *verb* To **retard** something is to cause it to slow down: *The fallen trees on the track retarded our progress.*
☐ **retardation**, *noun* –**retarded**, *adjective*

retch *verb* If you **retch**, you almost vomit.

retina /*say* **ret**-uh-nuh/ *noun* (*plural* **retinas** *or* **retinae** /*say* **ret**-uh-nee/) the coating on the back part of the eyeball which receives the image of what you see.
☐ **retinal**, *adjective*

> WORD HISTORY from a Latin word meaning 'net'

retire *verb* If someone **retires**, they **1.** leave their job permanently, especially because they are

getting older. **2.** go away from other people, especially to go to bed: *She always retires before 8 o'clock.* **3.** stop playing in a sporting match early, usually because they are injured: *The footballer had to retire from the game after his ankle was badly hurt.*
□ **retired**, *adjective* –**retirement**, *noun*

retort *noun*
1. a quick or sharp reply.
–*verb* **2.** If you **retort**, you make a quick or sharp reply: *'Don't even try!' she retorted.*

retrace *verb* If you **retrace** something, you go over it again: *Try and retrace what you did that day*; *She retraced her steps hoping to find her earring.*
□ **retraceable**, *adjective*

retract *verb*
1. If something **retracts**, it draws back in: *The headlights of some cars are able to retract.* **2.** If someone **retracts** something they have said, they say that it was not true or they should not have said it.
□ **retractable**, *adjective* –**retraction**, *noun*

retread *verb* /*say* ree-**tred**/
1. To **retread** a tyre is to renew the part of a wheel or tyre that touches the road.
–*noun* /*say* **ree**-tred/ **2.** a tyre that has been renewed in this way.

retreat *noun*
1. a movement away from a difficult or dangerous situation, usually in war: *The commander decided to order a retreat.* **2.** a place which is sheltered or far away: *What we need is a little retreat in the country.*
–*verb* **3.** To **retreat** is to move back away from something that threatens you: *The burrowing crab retreated as soon as my shadow crossed its path.*

retrench *verb* If a company **retrenches** someone, it dismisses them from their work because they are no longer needed.
□ **retrenchment**, *noun*

retrieve /*say* ruh-**treev**/ *verb* If you **retrieve** something, you **1.** get it or bring it back: *We managed to retrieve the coin that had fallen through the grating.* **2.** deal with or save it: *By her quick talking she managed to retrieve a very embarrassing situation.*
□ **retrievable**, *adjective* –**retrieval**, *noun*

☑ SPELLING TIP Remember that **retrieve** has *ie* (to spell the 'ee' sound) following the *r*. This follows the rule that *i* comes before *e* except after *c*.

retriever *noun* a type of dog that can be trained to bring back to the hunter birds and small animals which have been shot.

retro- *prefix* a word part meaning 'backwards', as in *retrospective*.

WORD HISTORY this prefix comes from Latin

retrospective *adjective*
1. having to do with or coming from the past: *The retrospective display included all of the old farming machinery.* **2.** taking effect from a date before the present: *Retrospective compensation was paid to the victims.*
□ **retrospective**, *noun* –**retrospectively**, *adverb*

return *verb*
1. If you **return** somewhere, you go or come back there: *They returned home very late*; *The fete committee keeps returning to the same old ideas.* **2.** If you **return** something, you give or send it back: *Did you return the library book?*
–*noun* **3.** an act of returning: *Mum has been away for a week and we are all looking forward to her return*; *The tennis player's return of serve was amazing to see.* **4.** a profit from money invested: *Do you get a good return if you leave your money in a bank?*
□ **return**, *adjective*: *the return trip.*

reunion *noun* a special meeting, usually of a family, or of people who have not seen each other for a long time.

☑ SPELLING TIP Remember that there is no *y* in this word. It is made up of the prefix *re-* and the word *union*.

rev *noun*
1. a turning round or revolution, usually of an engine.
–*verb* (**revs**, **revving**, **revved**, **has revved**) **2.** *Informal* To **rev** a car engine is to increase its speed by pressing on the accelerator.

WORD HISTORY a shortened form of *revolution*

reveal *verb* If you **reveal** something, you show it or make it known: *I promise not to reveal a thing!*
□ **revealing**, *adjective* –**revelation**, *noun*

reveille /*say* ruh-**val**-ee/ *noun* the signal sounded on a bugle or drum to wake up soldiers in the morning.

☑ SPELLING TIP **Reveille** comes from the French word for 'Wake up!'. It is difficult because the spelling does not match the way you say it. Concentrate on remembering the *eille* spelling.

revenge *noun* the hurt or damage done to pay someone back for the bad things they have done to you.

SIMILAR WORDS are **retaliation** and **vengeance**.

revenue /*say* **rev**-uh-nyooh/ *noun* the money a government makes from taxes and other sources.

☑ SPELLING TIP The tricky bit is the *ue* which gives a 'yooh' sound. Think of other words with this ending, such as *avenue*, *due* and *value*.

reverberate *verb* If a sound **reverberates**, it echoes over and over again.
☐ **reverberation**, *noun*

revere /*say* ruh-**vear**/ *verb* If you **revere** someone, you feel deep respect for them.

reverence *noun* great respect: *She spoke of her grandfather's achievements with reverence.*
☐ **reverent**, *adjective* –**reverential**, *adjective*

Reverend *noun* the title of a member of the clergy: *the Reverend John Smith.*

reverse *noun*
1. the opposite: *He thought that thunder came before lightning but then realised that the reverse was true.* **2.** the back or rear of anything. **3.** a gear which drives a car backwards.
–*verb* **4.** If you **reverse**, you turn back, or drive backwards: *Dad reversed down the steep drive very slowly.* **5.** If you **reverse** something, you put it in the opposite direction: *Do you think there is any chance they will reverse their decision?*
☐ **reversal**, *noun* –**reverse**, *adjective* –**reversible**, *adjective*

revert *verb* If you **revert** to an earlier state, you go back to it: *In thunderstorms, our dog reverts to coming inside and hiding under the table – that's what he did when he was a puppy.*
☐ **reversion**, *noun*

review *noun*
1. writing or speaking which describes and gives an opinion of something, such as a film, a performance, or an art show. **2.** a magazine which contains articles about recent happenings or discoveries, often in a particular area of interest: *an architectural review.* **3.** an examination: *They demanded a review of what had happened.*
–*verb* **4.** To **review** something is to examine or look at it: *The tax officers were brought in to review the accounts.* **5.** To **review** a book, play, and so on, is to write an article stating your opinion of it. **6.** If you **review** something, you think about it again possibly to arrive at a different decision: *In view of the criticism, they have decided to review their conclusions.*
☐ **reviewer**, *noun*

☑ SPELLING TIP Remember that **review** contains the word *view*. Don't confuse it with **revue** which sounds the same. A **revue** is a show that makes fun of recent events.

revise *verb*
1. If you **revise** something, you examine it and make any changes that you think are necessary. **2.** If you **revise** a subject for an examination, you go over your work and learn it: *We have to revise our spelling lists for the last three weeks.* **3.** If you **revise** your opinion about someone or something, you change your opinion about them: *I used to like her, but I have revised my opinion.*
☐ **revision**, *noun*

revive *verb*
1. If someone **revives**, they become conscious again: *She felt a bit dizzy when she first revived.* **2.** If you **revive** someone who has been unconscious, you return them to consciousness. **3.** If you **revive** after feeling tired and worn out, you regain your energy. **4.** If you **revive** something, you bring it back into use or custom: *Mum is reviving her exercise routine – again!*
☐ **revival**, *noun*

revoke /*say* ruh-**vohk**/ *verb* To **revoke** something like a law or a permission is to take it back or cancel it: *His probation was revoked and he was returned to prison.*
☐ **revocation** /*say* rev-uh-**kay**-shuhn/, *noun*

revolt *verb*
1. If someone **revolts** against something or someone, they rebel or rise up against them in an effort to defeat those who have power over them: *Some members of the cabinet revolted the prime minister's ruling on the issue.* **2.** If something **revolts** you, it disgusts you: *The scenes of the aftermath of the war revolted us.*

revolution *noun*
1. a complete change: *There has been a revolution in communications since the invention of computers.* **2.** a complete change of government or a system of government, often through violence: *There was a revolution in France in 1789.*
☐ **revolutionise**, *verb*

ANOTHER SPELLING for **revolutionise** is **revolutionize**.

revolutionary *adjective*
1. having to do with a complete change or revolution: *He was known for his revolutionary ideas.*
–*noun* (*plural* **revolutionaries**) **2.** someone who supports a revolution.

revolve *verb* If something **revolves**, it turns in a circle or moves in an orbit: *Jupiter has 16 satellites revolving around it.*

revolver *noun* a gun with a turning barrel holding a number of bullets, which fires once for each pull of the trigger.

revue /*say* ruh-**vyooh**/ *noun* a musical show with songs, dances and items which make fun of recent events or popular trends.

☑ SPELLING TIP Remember the *ue* ending. Don't confuse the spelling of **revue** with **review** which sounds the same. A **review** is an article which describes and gives you an opinion of a book, film, and so on.

reward *noun*
1. something given or received in return for work or help. **2.** money offered to encourage people to give information about a crime or lost property.
–*verb* **3.** To **reward** someone is to give them something for their work or service.
☐ **rewarding**, *adjective*

rhapsody /*say* **rap**-suh-dee/ *noun* (*plural* **rhapsodies**) a poem or piece of music that is romantic in style.
☐ **rhapsodic** /*say* rap-**sod**-ik/, *adjective*

rhetoric /*say* **ret**-uh-rik/ *noun* speaking or writing that is exaggerated in style.
☐ **rhetorical** /*say* ruh-**to**-rik-uhl/, *adjective*

rheumatism /*say* **rooh**-muh-tiz-uhm/ *noun* a disease affecting the joints or muscles.
☐ **rheumatic**, *adjective*

☑ SPELLING TIP *Silent letter alert*: don't forget the silent *h* following the *r* at the start. The other challenge is the *eu* spelling for the 'ooh' sound. The stem of this word is *rheum* which comes from a Greek word meaning 'stream'. In ancient times, the disease of **rheumatism** was thought to be caused by having too much watery liquid in the body.

rhinoceros /*say* ruy-**nos**-uh-ruhs/ *noun* a large, thick-skinned animal of Africa and Asia, with one or two horns on its nose.

THE SHORT FORM of this is **rhino**.

☑ SPELLING TIP *Silent letter alert*: don't forget the silent *h* following the *r* at the start. Also remember the *c* spelling for the *s* sound and the *os* (not *ous*) ending. **Rhinoceros** is formed of two parts: the prefix *rhino-* (meaning 'having to do with the nose' from the Greek *rhis* for 'nose') and *keras*, the Greek word for 'horn'.

rhododendron /*say* roh-duh-**den**-druhn/ *noun* a large evergreen shrub with pink, purple or white flowers.

WORD HISTORY from a Greek word meaning 'rose tree'

☑ SPELLING TIP *Silent letter alert*: don't forget the silent *h* following the *r* at the start. Also remember that the second vowel sound, which sounds like 'uh', is spelt with an *o*. Try rapping this long word out as *rho*+*do*+*den*+*dron*.

rhombus /*say* **rom**-buhs/ *noun* (*plural* **rhombuses** *or* **rhombi** /*say* **rom**-buy/) a parallelogram with four equal sides and angles that are not right angles.

☑ SPELLING TIP *Silent letter alert*: don't forget the silent *h* following the *r* at the start. Also remember the *us* ending which appears in some nouns that come from Latin, as **rhombus** does.

rhubarb /*say* **rooh**-bahb/ *noun* a plant whose stalks are cooked with sugar and water to make a dessert.

☑ SPELLING TIP *Silent letter alert*: don't forget the silent *h* following the *r* as part of the *rhu* (not *roo*) start of this word.

rhyme /*say* ruym/ *noun*
1. an agreement or a likeness in the sounds at the end of words, as in 'mist' and 'fist'. **2.** a word which rhymes with another. **3.** a poem that has rhymes.
–*verb* **4.** If a word **rhymes** with another one, its ending sounds the same.
–*phrase* **5. rhyme or reason**, understandable explanation: *There was no rhyme or reason for the changed rules.*

☑ SPELLING TIP *Silent letter alert*: don't forget the silent *h* following the *r* at the start. The other challenge is the *y* spelling for the vowel sound. You might think this word would be spelt *rime* and this is in fact an old spelling of the word. However the one to learn now is **rhyme**. Try thinking 'red hyenas yodel most evenings' as a way of remembering it.

rhythm /*say* **ridh**-uhm/ *noun*
1. the pattern of beats in music or speech. **2.** an even or regular movement: *The drums kept up a throbbing rhythm that you wanted to dance to.*
☐ **rhythmic**, **rhythmical**, *adjective* –**rhythmically**, *adverb*

☑ SPELLING TIP *Silent letter alert*: don't forget the silent *h* following the *r* at the start, as in *rhyme*. This is an unusual looking word because it has no vowels other than the *y* for the 'i' sound. The final *m* follows straight after the *th*. See the suggestion at *rhyme* and change it to 'red hyenas yodel to horrify monsters.

rhythm and blues *noun* a type of modern music, based originally on the blues but usually with a quicker tempo and more complex rhythms.

THE ABBREVIATION is **R & B**.

rib *noun* one of the set of curved bones partly enclosing the chest.

ribbon *noun*
1. a long, thin piece of material that can be used to tie something up or to decorate things: *We decorated the hall with red and white ribbons.* **2.** an award for success in a competition.

rice *noun* white or brown seeds or grain grown in warm, wet climates and widely used for food.

rice paper *noun* a thin, almost transparent paper that can be eaten, made from the rice plant and used to wrap around fillings in Asian cooking.

rich *adjective*
1. If a person or a country is **rich**, they have a great deal of everything, especially money: *He has inherited a lot of money and is very rich.* **2.** If something is **rich**, it is strong and fine in quality, such as materials, sounds, smells and colours: *We loved the rich colours of the clothes the Indian women wore.* **3.** If food is **rich**, it contains a lot of things, such as butter, cream, eggs, and so on, which can fill you up quickly: *I couldn't eat much of the soup – it was too rich.* **4.** If soil is **rich**, it

contains a lot of substances which help plants to grow well.
–*noun* **5. riches**, wealth.
☐ **richly**, *adverb* –**richness**, *noun*

SIMILAR WORDS (for definition 1) are **wealthy**, **affluent** and **prosperous**. There are also many informal expressions used to describe a person who is extremely rich, including **loaded**, **rolling in it** and **made of money**.

rickety *adjective* weak or shaky: *The rickety old verandah was sagging under the weight of the roof.*

☑ SPELLING TIP *Single letter alert*: only one *t*.

rickshaw *noun* a light cart drawn by one or two men, which is used in some Asian countries to carry passengers.

WORD HISTORY from a Japanese word meaning 'man-powered carriage'

ricochet /*say* **rik**-uh-shay/ *noun*
1. the movement of an object, such as a bullet, when it hits something, bounces off, and keeps travelling in another direction.
–*verb* (**ricochets**, **ricocheting**, **ricocheted**, **has ricocheted**) **2.** If a thing **ricochets**, it hits something, bounces off and flies off in another direction.

☑ SPELLING TIP *Tricky 'uh' sound*: the middle vowel sound is spelt *o*. This is only one of the difficulties with this word. Remember the *c* spelling for the 'k' sound and the *chet* ending which gives a 'shay' sound. As with other words like *ballet* that have a silent *t* at the end, **ricochet** comes from French.

ricotta *noun* a soft cottage cheese with a mild taste, made from whey.

WORD HISTORY from an Italian word meaning 'cooked again'

☑ SPELLING TIP *Single/double letter alert*: one *c* (giving a 'k' sound) and double *t*.

rid *verb* (**rids**, **ridding**, **rid**, **has rid**) If you **rid** a place of something unpleasant or unwanted, you completely remove that thing from the place: *We rid the house of cockroaches eventually*; *You must try to rid your mind of these suspicious thoughts.*
☐ **riddance**, *noun*

riddle[1] *noun*
1. a cleverly worded question usually asked as a joke. **2.** any puzzling thing or person.

riddle[2] *verb* If something is **riddled** with something, it has many of those things in it: *The house was riddled with white ants*; *The dead man's shirt was riddled with bullet holes.*

ride *verb* (**rides**, **riding**, **rode**, **has ridden**)
1. If you **ride** an animal or a vehicle, you sit on it and control it while in motion: *She was so proud when she learned how to ride a horse.* **2.** To **ride** is to travel or be carried along: *We rode in the ferry on the way home.*
–*noun* **3.** a short journey: *Do you want to come for a ride?*
–*phrase* **4. take for a ride**, to deceive or trick: *They really took her for a ride when they sold her a piece of the Harbour Bridge!*
☐ **ride**, *noun* –**rider**, *noun*

☑ SPELLING TIP Don't confuse the spelling of the past tense **rode** with **road** or **rowed**, both of which have the same sound. A **road** is a way for cars to drive on. **Rowed** is the past form of the verb **row**, to move using oars.

ridge *noun*
1. a long, narrow range of mountains. **2.** any long, narrow, raised part of something: *the ridges on a shell.*

ridicule *verb* If someone **ridicules** you, they make fun of you: *We were reprimanded for ridiculing the new boy and his funny clothes.*
☐ **ridicule**, *noun*: *Their ridicule annoyed me.*

ridiculous /*say* ruh-**dik**-yuh-luhs/ *adjective* If something is **ridiculous**, it is very silly or foolish: *The idea may sound ridiculous, but I actually think it will work*; *Where did you get that ridiculous hat?*
☐ **ridiculously**, *adverb*

SIMILAR WORDS are **absurd** and **ludicrous**.

☑ SPELLING TIP *Tricky 'uh' sound*: the first vowel sound is spelt with an *i*. Also remember that there are no double letters in this word and that there is a *c* alone for the 'k' sound. Rap it out as *rid*+*ic*+*u*+*lous*.

rife *adjective* common or widespread: *The deadly disease was rife in some areas.*

rifle *noun* a gun that is held against the shoulder, with a long barrel which is specially designed to give spin to the bullet so its flight will be more accurate.

rift *noun*
1. a narrow opening or crack: *a rift in the mountains.* **2.** a breaking down in the friendly relations between people or countries.

rig *verb* (**rigs**, **rigging**, **rigged**, **has rigged**) To **rig** something is to **1.** equip it with the necessary ropes and lines: *A man was standing on a platform rigged with thick ropes.* **2.** control it dishonestly: *The contest must have been rigged!*
–*phrase* **3. rig up**, to put together or in proper working order: *They rigged up the microphone system so that everybody could hear.*
☐ **rig**, *noun* –**rigging**, *noun*: *A sailor climbed the rigging.*

right *adjective*
1. fair and good: *I hope he makes the right decision.* **2.** correct: *'Santa Claus' is the right answer.* **3.** not left: *Face north, turn right and you will be looking east.* **4.** straight or upright: *She insisted on putting things right before she went.*

–*noun* **5.** what is fair and good: *I am sure that right will prevail!* **6.** a fair claim: *They have a right to have their views heard.* **7.** the right side: *I live to the right of the fire station.* **8. the right**, the people with the more conservative opinions in a political system.
–*adverb* **9.** to the right side: *Turn right and then you will be there.* **10.** directly or straight: *right to the bottom.* **11.** exactly or immediately: *I want you here right now!*
–*verb* If you **right** something, you **12.** put it in an upright or proper position: *They were asked to go and right all the chairs that had been knocked over.* **13.** correct it or make up for it: *It is possible to right this wrong but it may take some time.*
☐ **rightly**, *adverb*

ANOTHER FORM This word (as in definition 8) is often spelt with a capital letter.

☑ SPELLING TIP Don't confuse the spelling of **right** with **write**, or **rite** which both sound the same. To **write** is to form letters or words with a pen or something similar. A **rite** is a ceremony, often a religious one.

right angle *noun* an angle of 90°.

righteous /*say* **ruy**-chuhs/ *adjective* good and upright: *He was a righteous man and respected by all.*
☐ **righteously**, *adverb* –**righteousness**, *noun*

☑ SPELLING TIP This word is formed from *right* with the suffix *-eous* (not *-ious*) added. Think of *right* to help you to remember the *t* spelling although the sound you hear is 'ch'.

rigid /*say* **rij**-uhd/ *adjective*
1. stiff and unmoving: *She held herself rigid and hoped they would pass by without noticing her.* **2.** strict or unbending: *Her ideas on society were rigid in the extreme.*
☐ **rigidity**, *noun* –**rigidly**, *adverb*

rigour *noun*
1. strictness: *They will be punished in accordance with the rigour of the law.* **2.** hardship or severity: *They had many stories of the rigours of six months in the Antarctic.*
☐ **rigorous**, *adjective*

ANOTHER SPELLING is **rigor**.

rim *noun* the outer edge, especially of a circular or round object: *the rim of a volcano*; *the rim of a cup.*

rind *noun* a fairly thick and firm skin, as of some fruits, plants, cheeses, etc.: *lemon rind.*

ring[1] *noun*
1. a circular band for wearing on the finger: *a friendship ring.* **2.** a circular line or shape: *I drew a ring in the sand.* **3.** an enclosed area for sporting competitions, not necessarily circular: *The boxers faced each other from the opposite corners of the ring.*
–*verb* **4.** If something **rings** an area, it runs in a circle around it: *The road ringed the city.*

ring[2] *verb* (**rings**, **ringing**, **rang**, **has rung**)
1. To **ring** is to give out a clear musical sound: *The bells rang out over the valley*; *Her voice rang out from the kitchen.* **2.** If you **ring** a bell or something similar, you make it sound, especially as a signal: *We had better ring the alarm.* **3.** To **ring** someone is to telephone them: *He must have forgotten to ring.*
–*phrase* **4. ring a bell**, to bring back a memory or to seem familiar: *Her face rings a bell but I don't remember her name.* **5. ring up**, to telephone.
☐ **ring**, *noun*

ringbark *verb* To **ringbark** a tree is to cut away a ring of bark from its trunk in order to kill it by cutting off the flow of sap.

ringer[1] *noun* a station hand, especially a stockman or drover.

ringer[2] *noun*
1. the fastest shearer of a group. **2.** anyone who is the fastest or best at anything.

ring-in *noun Informal* someone or something taking the place of another at the last moment.

ringlet *noun* a long curl of hair shaped like a corkscrew.

ringmaster *noun* someone in charge of a circus performance.

ringtone *noun*
1. the sound you hear that tells you the telephone you are calling is ringing. **2.** the sound, sometimes a tune, that a mobile phone makes to let the owner know that someone is ringing in: *We can all tell when Danny gets a call because his ringtone is a laughing baby.*

ringworm *noun* a skin disease with ring-shaped patches, caused by a fungus.

rink *noun*
1. a sheet of ice prepared for skating. **2.** a smooth floor for rollerskating.

rinse *verb*
1. If you **rinse** something, you wash it lightly in clean water to remove scraps of food or soap.
–*noun* **2.** a liquid for colouring hair that lasts for a short time.

riot /*say* **ruy**-uht/ *noun*
1. a disturbance of the peace by a group of people. **2.** wild confusion or lack of order.
–*verb* **3.** If people **riot**, they disturb the peace with wild confusion and disorder: *When food became very scarce, the people rioted.*
☐ **rioter**, *noun* –**riotous**, *adjective*

WORD HISTORY from a Latin word meaning 'roar'

rip[1] *verb* (**rips**, **ripping**, **ripped**, **has ripped**)
1. If something **rips**, it tears or becomes torn in a rough way.

–phrase **2. rip off**, *Informal* to charge too much: *They must have ripped me off – I should have more change.*
☐ **rip**, *noun* a tear: *a rip in my jeans.*

rip² *noun* a fast current in the sea, especially one at a beach.

ripe *adjective* If a crop or fruit is **ripe**, it is ready for harvesting, picking or eating: *ripe cherries.*
☐ **ripen**, *verb* –**ripeness**, *noun*

ripple *verb*
1. To **ripple** a liquid is to make small waves on it: *The wake from the boat rippled the surface of the lake.*
–noun **2.** a small wave.

rise *verb* (**rises**, **rising**, **rose**, **has risen**)
1. To **rise** is to get up or get out of bed. **2.** If someone **rises**, they stand up. **3.** If something **rises**, it goes upwards, or swells up: *The mountain rose ahead of them*; *The noise of the music rose as the night progressed*; *The cake didn't rise because we forgot the eggs.*
–noun **4.** an upward movement: *We are expecting a rise in temperature tomorrow.* **5.** an upward slope: *A slight rise led up to the house.*
–phrase **6. give rise to**, to cause or produce: *The decision has given rise to a lot of arguments.*

risk *noun*
1. the possibility of being injured, hurt or losing something.
–verb **2.** If you **risk** something, you take a chance that you might lose it or be hurt in some way.
☐ **risky**, *adjective* (**riskier**, **riskiest**)

risotto /*say* ruh-**zot**-oh/ *noun* a food made of rice mixed with meat, fish or vegetables and flavoured with cheese or other flavourings, originating in Italian cooking.

> ☑ SPELLING TIP *Single/double letter alert*: one *s* and double *t*.

rissole *noun* a fried ball or small cake of chopped up food: *a salmon rissole.*

rite *noun* a ceremony, especially a religious one.

> ☑ SPELLING TIP Don't confuse the spelling of **rite** with **right** or **write**, both of which have the same sound. Something that is **right** is good or fair. To **write** is to form letters or words with a pen or something similar.

ritual /*say* **rich**-ooh-uhl/ *noun*
1. a set procedure for a religious or other ceremony. **2.** an often repeated series of actions: *We went through the same old ritual of my little sister not eating her vegetables and my dad getting mad.*

> ☑ SPELLING TIP Remember the *t* in this word. With the *u* following it has a 'ch' sound and you don't hear the *t*.

rival *noun*
1. someone who is aiming at the same thing as another person: *He had worked out who were likely to be his most serious rivals in the 200 metres.*
–verb (**rivals**, **rivalling**, **rivalled**, **has rivalled**) **2.** If somebody **rivals** you in a particular area, they have proved to be just as good as you: *James is not as good as Isabelle in some subjects, but he rivals her in maths.*
☐ **rivalry**, *noun* (*plural* **rivalries**)

river *noun* a large natural body of water flowing over the land along a winding course.

rivet *noun*
1. a metal pin or bolt for holding flat pieces of metal together.
–verb (**rivets**, **riveting**, **riveted**, **has riveted**) **2.** To **rivet** something is to fasten it with a rivet. **3.** If someone is **riveted** by something, they have their whole attention fixed on it: *We were riveted by the performance of the tightrope walker.*
☐ **riveting**, *adjective*: *a riveting mystery series.*

road *noun* a way or track suitable for cars, people and animals to travel along.

> ☑ SPELLING TIP Don't confuse the spelling of **road** with **rode** or **rowed**, both of which have the same sound. **Rode** is the past tense of the verb **ride**, to sit on an animal or vehicle and control it. **Rowed** is the past form of the verb **row**, to move using oars.

roadie *noun Informal* someone who looks after the sound equipment for a pop or rock group on tour.

road train *noun* a very large vehicle, consisting of a truck towing a number of trailers, usually used for carrying cattle.

roadway *noun* the part of the road that people drive on.

roam *verb* If you **roam**, you walk or travel with no particular purpose: *We spent the whole day roaming all over our uncle's farm.*

roar *verb*
1. If something **roars**, it makes a loud, deep noise like the noise made by a lion: *When lions roar, they can be heard five kilometres away*; *'Just keep away from here!' he roared.* **2.** If you **roar** with laughter, you laugh loudly.
☐ **roar**, *noun*: *the roar of the wind in a storm.*

> ☑ SPELLING TIP Don't confuse the spelling of **roar** with **raw** which has the same sound. If food is **raw**, it hasn't been cooked.

roast *verb* If you **roast** food, you bake it in an oven or sometimes cook it over a fire on a spit.

rob *verb* (**robs**, **robbing**, **robbed**, **has robbed**) If you **rob** someone, you steal from them, often using force.
☐ **robber**, *noun* –**robbery**, *noun* (*plural* **robberies**)

robe *noun* a long, loose piece of outer clothing worn by men or women.

NOTE This is often used in the plural, as in *ceremonial robes*.

robin *noun*
1. any of a group of Australian birds with brightly coloured breasts. **2.** a European bird with a red breast, often painted on Christmas cards.

robot *noun* a machine programmed to do a job which is usually done by a person.

WORD HISTORY first used in the play *RUR* by the Czech writer Karel Capek (1890–1938)

robust /*say* **roh**-bust, ruh-**bust**/ *adjective* strong: *She was in robust health after her holiday*; *He had a robust confidence in his ability to succeed.*

rock[1] *noun*
1. a large mass of stone. **2.** a stone of any size.
☐ **rocky**, *adjective*

rock[2] *verb*
1. If something **rocks** or you **rock** it, it moves from side to side or to and fro: *We put a bit of paper under the leg of the table to stop it rocking*; *She rocked the pram backwards and forwards.*
–*noun* **2.** See **rock music**.

rock art *noun* a kind of Aboriginal art in which pictures are made on rock surfaces by painting or drawing on or cutting out sections of rock.

rocker *noun*
1. one of the curved pieces on which a cradle or a rocking chair rocks. **2.** a rocking chair.
–*phrase* **3. off one's rocker**, *Informal* crazy or insane.

rockery *noun* (*plural* **rockeries**) part of a garden where you grow plants in between rocks.

rocket *noun*
1. a cylinder full of something that will explode, fired into the air as a signal or as a firework. **2.** a space vehicle driven by hot gas that shoots out from the rear.
–*verb* (**rockets**, **rocketing**, **rocketed**, **has rocketed**) **3.** To **rocket** is to move rapidly like a rocket: *Susie rocketed to fame after her first movie release.*

rockmelon *noun* a sweet-flavoured, round melon with orange flesh and a hard, rough skin.

ANOTHER WORD for this is **cantaloupe**.

rock music *noun* a type of music that developed from rock'n'roll, usually with a heavy regular rhythm and the use of electric guitars.

ANOTHER FORM You can also call this **rock**: *My favourite music is rock* .

rock'n'roll *noun*
1. a type of popular music originating in the 1950s and early 1960s, usually with simply worded songs, a strong beat, and the use of electric guitars. **2.** a style of dance performed to this music.

ANOTHER FORM is **rock-and-roll**.

rod *noun* a long stick of wood, metal or other material.

rodent *noun* one of a group of animals, including rats, mice, and guinea pigs, with sharp teeth.

WORD HISTORY from a Latin word meaning 'gnawing'

rodeo /*say* **roh**-dee-oh, roh-**day**-oh/ *noun* an event in which people compete or display skills in riding horses, lassoing cattle, and so on.

WORD HISTORY from a Spanish word meaning 'cattle ring'

roe *noun*
1. the mass of eggs inside a female fish. **2.** the sperm of the male fish.

rogue /*say* rohg/ *noun*
1. *Old-fashioned* a dishonest person. **2.** someone who plays tricks for fun.
☐ **roguish** /*say* **roh**-gish/, *adjective* mischievous.

☑ SPELLING TIP Don't forget the *ue* at the end. The spelling *ogue* gives an 'ohg' sound in this word.

role *noun*
1. the part or character that an actor plays. **2.** the expected or usual part played in life: *The role of school captain involves setting an example and representing the school.*

roll *verb*
1. If something **rolls**, it moves along, turning over and over: *The ball rolled along the ground.* **2.** You can also say that something **rolls** if it moves along on wheels: *The pram rolled off the path into a flower bed.* **3.** If you **roll** something with a rolling cylinder, you press or flatten it: *They rolled their grass tennis court with a huge concrete roller.* **4.** If you **roll** something that bends easily, you make it into the shape of a cylinder by wrapping it around and around itself: *For the party, we made sushi by rolling seaweed around rice and raw fish.* **5.** If something such as a ship **rolls**, it moves slowly from side to side rather than up and down.
–*noun* **6.** a piece of paper, material or food made into the shape of a cylinder: *a roll of kitchen paper.* **7.** a list or register: *a class roll.* **8.** a low continuous sound: *First there was a crack of lighting and then a long roll of thunder.* **9.** a small loaf of bread with a round or long shape, meant to be eaten by one person: *Do you want a sandwich or a roll?*
–*phrase* **10. roll in**, to arrive or appear in large numbers: *Entries for the competition are rolling in.* **11. roll up**, **a.** to make into the shape of a cylinder: *to roll up a sleeping bag.* **b.** to come along: *to roll up to a concert.*

roller *noun*
1. a cylinder or wheel on which something is rolled along. **2.** a cylinder used for flattening: *a tennis court roller.* **3.** a cylinder around which something is rolled: *heated hair rollers.*

rollerblade *noun*
1. a type of rollerskate with narrower wheels that are positioned in a straight line from the front of the sole to the back of the sole.
–*verb* **2.** When you **rollerblade**, you move swiftly on the ground, wearing rollerblades.
☐ **rollerblader**, *noun* a person who rollerblades.

roller-coaster *noun* a turning, sloping, steep railway in an amusement park with open cars, which you can ride on for the thrill of speed and rapid turns.

rollerskate *noun*
1. a kind of skate running on small wheels or rollers.
–*verb* **2.** To **rollerskate** is to move along on rollerskates.

rollicking *adjective* jolly and carefree: *His rollicking laugh could be heard all over the camp.*

ROM /*say* rom/ *noun* computer memory which can be read but not changed.

WORD HISTORY an acronym made by joining the first letters of *Read Only Memory*

romance /*say* ruh-**mans**, **roh**-mans/ *noun*
1. feelings of great love and affection or behaviour suited to those feelings: *There is still romance between my grandparents.* **2.** a novel or movie about people falling in love. **3.** a love affair.
☐ **romantic**, *adjective* –**romantically**, *adverb*

Roman numerals *plural noun* the numbers used by the ancient Romans, and still used for some purposes, as for royal titles and chapter headings in books, for example *George VI* (for *George the Sixth*).

romp *verb*
1. If someone **romps**, they play in an active, noisy way: *The kids who couldn't swim were allowed to romp in the babies' pool.*
–*phrase* **2. romp in**, to win easily.

roo *noun Informal* a kangaroo.

roof *noun* (*plural* **roofs** *or* **rooves**)
1. the top covering of a building or car. **2.** the upper surface of a hollow space: *From the roof of the cave hung thousands of small bats.*
–*phrase* **3. hit the roof**, *Informal* to become very angry.
☐ **roofing**, *noun*

rook[1] *noun* a black European crow that nests in groups in tall trees.

rook[2] *noun* a chess piece which can only travel in straight lines.

ANOTHER NAME for this is **castle**.

rookery *noun* (*plural* **rookeries**)
1. a place where there are a lot of rooks' nests. **2.** a breeding place for other birds or animals: *The penguins waddled up the beach towards the rookery.*

room *noun*
1. a part of a building separated by walls from other parts. **2.** space: *Is there room for one more?*
☐ **roomy**, *adjective* spacious.

roost *noun*
1. a resting place for birds at night.
–*verb* **2.** When birds **roost**, they perch on something like a branch to rest for the night.

rooster *noun* an adult male chicken.

ANOTHER WORD for this is **cock**.
NOTE The female is a **hen**.

root *noun*
1. the part of a plant which usually grows downwards into the soil and supplies the plant with food and water. **2.** the origin or beginning: *The root of the problem is that Jane is jealous of Shona.* **3.** a number which, when multiplied by itself a certain number of times, produces a given quantity: *4 is the square root of 16 and the cube root of 64.* **4. roots**, a feeling of belonging: *She maintains her roots will always be in the country despite living in the city for years.*
–*verb* **5.** When a plant **roots**, it sends down roots and begins to grow: *The onion on our school nature table has started to root.* **6.** If someone or something is **rooted** somewhere, they are fixed there as if by roots: *Justin stood rooted to the ground in surprise.*
–*phrase* **7. root out**, **a.** to pull up by the roots: *We had to root out the weeds.* **b.** to remove completely: *They are trying to root out the drug dealers.* **8. take** (or **strike**) **root**, **a.** to send out roots and begin to grow. **b.** to become fixed or established: *Once the idea took root, everybody wanted to get involved.*
☐ **rootless**, *adjective*

SEE ALSO **square root** and **cube root** (for definition 3).

rope *noun*
1. a strong, thick cord made of twisted fibre or wire.
–*verb* **2.** To **rope** something is to tie it up with a rope.

ropeable *adjective Rather informal* angry.

ANOTHER SPELLING is **ropable**.

rosary *noun* (*plural* **rosaries**)
1. a string of beads used for counting a series of prayers, usually in the Roman Catholic Church. **2.** the series of prayers that are said.

rose[1] *noun*
1. a garden flower, usually brightly coloured and sweet-smelling with thorny stems, growing on a small shrub.
–*adjective* **2.** of a deep pink colour.

rose[2] *verb* the past tense of **rise**.

rosella *noun* a parrot with bright red, green and blue feathers, common in Australia.

WORD HISTORY from *Rose Hill*, an early settlement in NSW

rosemary *noun* a plant with a strong smell, used in cooking.

WORD HISTORY from a Latin word meaning 'dew of the sea'

rosette *noun* a decoration made of ribbons tied so as to look like the petals of a rose.

rosin /*say* **roz**-uhn/ *noun* resin made from the dried sap of pine trees, used for rubbing on violin bows, etc.

roster *noun* a list of people's names and the times they are on duty: *We have a roster for the washing up at home.*

rostrum *noun* (*plural* **rostrums** *or* **rostra**) a raised platform for a speaker or the conductor of an orchestra.

rosy *adjective* (**rosier**, **rosiest**)
1. If something is **rosy**, it is a rich pink colour: *a rosy sky.* **2.** If you say that a situation looks **rosy**, you mean that it has turned out well or that it is likely to turn out well: *Things have improved and the future looks rosy.*

rot *verb* (**rots**, **rotting**, **rotted**, **has rotted**)
1. To **rot** is to make or go bad: *Water has rotted our back step*; *Our back step has rotted.*
–*noun* **2.** a type of disease that makes things decay or go bad: *dry rot in timber*; *foot rot in sheep.* **3.** *Informal* nonsense or rubbish: *What rot – I've never heard anything so unlikely!*

rotate *verb* To **rotate** is to **1.** turn round like a wheel. **2.** go, or cause to go, through a series of changes: *It makes sense to rotate crops so that soil nutrients are replenished.*
☐ **rotation**, *noun*

rote *noun in the phrase* **learn by rote**, to learn something by repeating it over and over until you know it.

rotisserie /*say* roh-**tis**-uh-ree/ *noun* a skewer which turns round and round in an oven, for cooking chickens and other food.

☑ SPELLING TIP *Single/double letter alert*: one *t* but double *s*. Also notice the *erie* ending. **Rotisserie** is from a French word meaning 'roasting place'.

rotten *adjective*
1. If something is **rotten**, it has gone bad and is decaying: *I can't eat this meat – it's rotten.* **2.** *Informal* If you say that something is **rotten**, you mean that it is of a very low standard: *She is a rotten piano player.* **3.** *Informal* You can use **rotten** to describe something that you are not pleased with: *This rotten bike keeps on getting a flat tyre.* **4.** If you say that you feel **rotten**, you mean that you feel very sick.

rotund /*say* roh-**tund**/ *adjective* plump and rounded: *She was a rotund lady with a big jolly laugh.*
☐ **rotundity**, *noun* –**rotundness**, *noun*

rouge /*say* roohzh/ *noun*
1. pinkish-red make-up used on the cheeks.
–*verb* **2.** If someone **rouges** their cheeks, they colour them with pinkish make-up.

NOTE This word comes from French.

rough /*say* ruf/ *adjective*
1. If something is **rough**, its surface is uneven. **2.** If you say that someone is **rough**, you mean that they use force or physical pressure in order to get things done: *The police were rough in the way they handled the protesters.* **3.** If something such as a calculation or drawing is **rough**, it is not exact but only approximate: *He drew a rough map of the area for the tourist.* **4.** If you say that someone is having a **rough** time, you mean that life is very difficult for them at the moment: *Her family is having a rough time because her father lost his job.* **5.** If the sea is **rough**, there are many large waves due to strong winds or a storm.
–*verb in the phrase* **6. rough it**, to make do without the usual home comforts: *We are roughing it while builders are replacing the roof.*
☐ **roughen**, *verb* –**roughly**, *adverb* –**roughness**, *noun*

THE OPPOSITE (of definition 1) is **smooth**.

☑ SPELLING TIP Remember that there is no *f* in **rough** – the spelling *ough* gives the 'uf' sound, as it does in some other words like *enough* and *tough*.

roughage /*say* **ruf**-ij/ *noun* the fibre in food that you cannot digest.

roulette /*say* rooh-**let**/ *noun* a gambling game in which players bet on a small ball which runs around a spinning wheel.

☑ SPELLING TIP *Tricky vowel sound*: the first vowel sound is *ou* (not *oo*). Also remember the *ette* ending as in some other words that have come from French such as *serviette* and *cigarette*.

round *adjective*
1. If something is **round**, it is shaped like a circle or a ball. **2.** If you do a **round** trip, you travel somewhere and then return to where you started from.
–*noun* **3.** a group or number of things: *The premiers held a round of talks.* **4.** a period of boxing or wrestling: *The boxing match didn't get past the first round.* **5.** a song for several singers, each joining in one after the other.
–*adverb* **6.** in a circular direction: *The trapeze artist spun round and round.* **7.** here and there:

We were just walking round doing nothing. **8.** in some other direction: *Turn round and then you will see it.*
–*verb in the phrase* **9. round out**, to add more detail to. **10. round up**, to gather people or animals together: *Everyone was rounded up for the last event in the carnival – the fun swim.*

roundabout *noun*
1. a circular intersection for controlling traffic. **2.** See **merry-go-round**.
–*adjective* **3.** going somewhere or saying something in a long, indirect way: *They told him in a roundabout way that he wasn't invited.*

rounders *plural noun* a game like baseball, played with a soft ball.

NOTE This word takes a singular verb, as in *Rounders is good fun.*

rouse[1] /*rhymes with* cows/ *verb*
1. If someone or something **rouses** you, they wake you up: *The sudden thumping on the door roused me.* **2.** If something **rouses** you to have a feeling, it stirs that feeling up in you: *Injustice always rouses me to anger.*
☐ **rousing**, *adjective*: *a rousing song.*

ANOTHER WORD for this is **arouse**.

rouse[2] /*rhymes with* mouse/ *verb in the phrase* **rouse on**, to criticise someone and speak angrily to them, but not in a very serious way: *Mum roused on our grandfather for spending too much money on us.*

rout /*rhymes with* out/ *verb* If an army or a sporting team **routs** its opposition, it defeats it completely.
☐ **rout**, *noun* a total defeat.

route *noun*
1. /*sounds like* root/ a way or road from one place to another: *The bus takes two different routes from here to town.* **2.** /*rhymes with* out/ in computers, a connecting path, such as that between two host computers in a network.
☐ **router**, *noun*

☑ SPELLING TIP Don't confuse the spelling of **route** with **root** which sounds the same when you use it with the meaning of definition 1. A **root** is the part of a plant that grows down into the earth.

routine /*say* rooh-**teen**/ *noun*
1. something which is always done in the same way or at the same time or place: *My routine is to have breakfast before I get dressed.*
–*adjective* **2.** You can say that something such as a job is **routine** if it is boring and repetitive.

rove *verb* If you **rove**, you wander or roam: *She spent the year after she finished school roving around Europe.*
☐ **rover**, *noun*

row[1] /*rhymes with* go/ *noun* a line of people or things.

row[2] /*rhymes with* go/ *verb* To **row** is to move a boat using the oars: *We rowed the boat down the river*; *It was fun learning to row.*
☐ **rower**, *noun* –**rowing**, *noun*

☑ SPELLING TIP Don't confuse the spelling of the past tense **rowed** with **rode** or **road**, both of which have the same sound. **Rode** is the past tense of the verb **ride**, to sit on an animal or vehicle and control it. A **road** is a way for cars to drive on.

row[3] /*rhymes with* how/ *noun*
1. a noisy argument or fight. **2.** shouting and loud noise: *A row broke out when the crowd found they couldn't get tickets.*

rowdy /*rhymes with* cloudy/ *adjective* (**rowdier**, **rowdiest**) wild and noisy: *The crowd turned rowdy when they were forbidden entry.*
☐ **rowdily**, *adverb* –**rowdiness**, *noun*

rowlock /*say* **rol**-uhk/ *noun* one of the metal rings that support the oars in a rowing boat.

☑ SPELLING TIP Remember that this word is made up of *row* and *lock*, even though it does not sound like this. Don't confuse its spelling with *rollick*, as in the word **rollicking**.

royal *adjective* having to do with a king or queen: *the royal jewels.*
☐ **royalist**, *noun*

royalty *noun*
1. kings, queens and members of their families. **2.** a share of the profits made from their work, paid to an inventor, author or composer.

☑ SPELLING TIP Remember that this word is formed from *royal* with the suffix *-ty* added. This will remind you of the *al* spelling, although you sometimes don't hear the *a* when the word is said.

RSVP *abbreviation* short for *répondez s'il vous plaît*, which is French for 'please reply'.

NOTE You usually write this on an invitation. It means the person you are inviting should let you know if they intend to come or not.

rub *verb* (**rubs**, **rubbing**, **rubbed**, **has rubbed**)
1. If you **rub** something, you press down on it and move back and forth: *It didn't matter how much I rubbed, I couldn't get the shoe polish out of my shirt.*
–*noun* **2.** an ointment. **3.** a mixture of spices and herbs to be applied to meat before cooking.
–*phrase* **4. rub down**, to rub so as to smooth or clean: *The painter rubbed down the wall before he started.* **5. rub off on**, to be passed on to, especially as a result of close contact: *His love of music rubbed off on her.* **6. rub out**, to clean off by rubbing: *We had to rub out our spelling mistakes and correct them.*

rubber *noun*
1. elastic material made from the thick sap of a tropical tree (**rubber tree**), used to make things

like car tyres, bouncing balls and elastic bands. **2.** a small piece of soft rubber used to rub out pencil marks.
☐ **rubbery**, *adjective*

ANOTHER WORD (for definition 2) is **eraser**.

rubbish *noun*
1. useless unwanted material to be thrown away. **2.** nonsense: *He was full of rubbish as usual!*

ANOTHER WORD (for definition 1) is **refuse**[2]. This is a more formal word.

rubble *noun* rough pieces of broken stone or brick.

rubella /*say* rooh-**bel**-uh/ *noun* a disease which gives you a temperature and a rash and is usually not serious except in the case of a woman who is pregnant because her unborn baby can be affected.

ANOTHER NAME is **German measles**.
WORD HISTORY from a Latin word meaning 'reddish'

ruby *noun* (*plural* **rubies**) a precious stone of a rich red colour.
☐ **ruby**, *adjective*

rucksack *noun* a backpack.

rudder *noun* a flat, vertical, movable plate at the back of a boat or an aircraft, used for steering.

ruddy *adjective* (**ruddier**, **ruddiest**) having a healthy red colour: *a ruddy complexion* .

rude *adjective* bad-mannered or not polite: *a rude person*; *a rude answer.*
☐ **rudely**, *adverb* –**rudeness**, *noun*

THE OPPOSITE is **polite**.
SIMILAR WORDS are **cheeky**, **impertinent**, **impudent** and **insolent**. Note that **cheeky** describes someone who is rude in a mischievous way and is usually used about children in an affectionate way. **Impertinent**, **impudent** and **insolent** describe someone who is rude in a deliberate and disrespectful way.

ruffian *noun* someone who is rough or rowdy: *I like him but he's a bit of a ruffian.*

ruffle *verb*
1. If someone or something **ruffles** anything, they spoil its calmness or smoothness: *We knew it wasn't the time to ruffle Mum's temper*; *The breeze ruffled her hair.*
–*noun* **2.** a frill on a skirt, blouse or curtains.
☐ **ruffled**, *adjective*

rug *noun*
1. a thick, warm covering for sleeping. **2.** a small piece of floor covering.

Rugby football *noun* See **Rugby Union** and **Rugby League**.

WORD HISTORY named after *Rugby* school in Warwickshire, England, where the game was developed

Rugby League *noun* one of the two forms of Rugby football, played by teams of 13 players each.

THE SHORT FORM of this is **League**.

Rugby Union *noun* one of the two forms of Rugby football, played by teams of 15 players each.

THE SHORT FORM of this is **Union**.

rugged /*say* **rug**-uhd/ *adjective*
1. If something like land is **rugged**, it is very rocky and uneven, and has very few plants growing on it. **2.** If you say that someone is **rugged**, you mean that they are very strong or tough and able to cope with things.
☐ **ruggedly**, *adverb*

ruin *verb*
1. To **ruin** something is to destroy it: *The rain ruined the sports carnival.*
–*noun* **2.** complete destruction: *The old building was falling into ruin*; *That single decision was the ruin of her!* **3. ruins**, the remains of fallen buildings: *You can see many ruins from the ancient world in countries such as Italy and Greece.*
☐ **ruination**, *noun* –**ruined**, *adjective*

rule *noun*
1. an instruction about behaviour, actions, and so on: *You can't play until you know the rules.*
–*verb* **2.** If someone **rules** a country, they govern and control the affairs of the country: *The idea of a democracy is that the people rule through their representatives.* **3.** If someone **rules**, they make a decision that others have to take notice of: *The boss ruled that personal emails had to stop.*
–*phrase* **4. as a rule**, usually: *We walk to school as a rule.* **5. rule out**, to say publicly something is not possible: *The council has ruled out dogs without leads in the park.*
☐ **ruling**, *noun*, *adjective*

ruler *noun*
1. someone who rules or governs. **2.** a strip of wood or plastic with a straight edge, used for measuring and drawing straight lines.

rum *noun* a strong alcoholic drink made from sugar cane.

rumble *noun*
1. a deep, rolling sound: *the rumble of traffic on the highway.*
–*verb* **2.** To **rumble** is to make a deep, rolling sound: *Heavy trucks rumbled along the road from the mine.*

ruminate /*say* **rooh**-muh-nayt/ *verb*
1. If cattle **ruminate**, they chew their cud. **2.** If someone **ruminates**, they consider something very carefully or they meditate: *You shouldn't*

have said that to her – she will ruminate about it for days!
☐ **ruminant**, *noun* an animal that chews its cud.

rummage *verb* If you **rummage**, you search by moving everything around: *She rummaged through her bag again but her key wasn't there.*

WORD HISTORY from a French word meaning 'stow goods in the hold of a ship'

☑ SPELLING TIP *Double letter alert*: double *m*. Also remember the *age* ending (which sounds like 'ij').

rummy *noun* a card game in which you put cards into matching sets and ordered groups.

rumour *noun*
1. a story that spreads round which may or may not be true.
–verb **2.** If something is **rumoured**, it is spread or reported by rumour: *It was rumoured that Ella Jane had won the prize, but no-one was sure.*

ANOTHER SPELLING is **rumor**.
A SIMILAR WORD (for definition 2) is **gossip**.

rump *noun*
1. the back part of a cow, horse or similar animal. **2.** meat taken from this part.

rumple *verb* If you **rumple** something, you crush or mess it up: *They jumped all over the bed and rumpled the covers.*
☐ **rumple**, *noun* a crease or wrinkle.

rumpus *noun* a loud noise and commotion.

run *verb* (**runs**, **running**, **ran**, **has run**)
1. If you **run**, you move quickly on your feet, usually because you are in a hurry or in a race. **2.** If something such as a road **runs** somewhere, it goes there: *The new road runs from the coast to the top of the mountain.* **3.** If you **run** something over or through an object, you pass it lightly or quickly over or through that thing: *She ran her fingers over the raised lettering on the card.* **4.** If something such as a machine is **running**, it is turned on or working. **5.** If someone **runs** something such as a business, they are in charge of it: *My uncle runs a bookshop.* **6.** If a train or bus **runs** somewhere, it goes there regularly at a fixed time. **7.** If a liquid **runs** somewhere, it flows there: *Tears ran down her cheeks.* **8.** If you **run** the risk of something unpleasant happening, you take the risk that it might happen: *If you sunbake without sunscreen, you run the risk of burning.* **9.** If someone or something **runs** late, they are behind time or late, often because of unforeseen circumstances: *We were running late because we had to go back for our towels.*
–noun **10.** the action of running: *She goes for a run every morning.* **11.** a journey: *a run to the mountains.* **12.** a pen for animals: *The baby lambs were kept in a small run.* **13.** a score in cricket: *We need twenty runs to win.* **14.** a series of happenings: *a run of coincidences.*
–phrase **15. in the long run**, in the end: *In the long run, it made no difference who came first.* **16. run across**, to meet or find unexpectedly. **17. run into**, **a.** to meet unexpectedly: *Guess who I ran into?* **b.** to hit: *Dad ran into the car in front.* **18. run out**, **a.** to use up completely: *We've run out of food.* **b.** to be all used up: *The food has run out.* **19. run over**, **a.** of a car, driver, and so on, to knock down and injure. **b.** to go outside a limit: *to run over a time limit.* **20. run short**, **a.** to become scarce or nearly used up: *Water was beginning to run short because of the drought.* **b.** to have almost nothing of something left: *We're running short of bread.* **21. run through**, to practise: *to run through a speech.* **22. run up**, **a.** to collect or build up: *to run up a large bill.* **b.** to make, especially quickly: *to run up a dress.*

runaway *adjective*
1. happening at a very fast pace or out of control: *runaway price increases.* **2.** very easy: *The fete was a runaway success and made lots of money.*
☐ **runaway**, *noun* someone who has escaped or run away.

rung[1] *noun* one of the steps of a ladder.

rung[2] *verb* the past participle of **ring**[2].

run-in *noun* a disagreement or argument: *They had a run-in over whose turn it was to do the car pool.*

runner *noun*
1. someone who runs well and competes in races. **2.** one of the smooth strips of wood on which a drawer slides.

runner-up *noun* someone who comes second in a contest.

running *adjective*
1. able to run or suitable for running: *Is your computer up and running yet?* **2.** flowing: *a cool running stream.* **3.** in a row: *For three days running, the trains have been delayed.*
–noun **4.** management or organisation: *the running of the club was mostly up to me.*
–phrase **5. running writing**, writing where all the letters of a word are joined together.

running sheet *noun* a list of the order in which events will take place, as for a day's filming for a film or television show.

runny *adjective* (**runnier**, **runniest**)
1. If something is **runny**, it is softer than usual and tends to flow like a liquid: *This ice-cream's nice but it's a bit runny.* **2.** If someone has a **runny** nose, mucus is flowing from it: *He's got a sore throat and a runny nose.*

runt *noun* an animal that is the smallest in their group: *The runt of the litter got squashed.*

runway *noun* a long, level strip, often with a special hard surface, on which aeroplanes land and take off.

ANOTHER WORD for this is **airstrip**.

rupture *verb* If something **ruptures**, it breaks or bursts: *The water tank ruptured.*
☐ **rupture**, *noun*

rural *adjective* Something which is **rural** has to do with the countryside or farming: *They love rural life.*

ruse /*rhymes with* shoes/ *noun* a dishonest trick or scheme.

rush[1] *verb*
1. If someone or something **rushes**, they move or do something in a great hurry: *Clare rushed out of the room when the phone rang*; *My brother rushes through the washing up and never does it properly.* **2.** If you **rush** into something, you hurry into doing it or make a decision too quickly: *They rushed into buying the house and later wished they had got something larger.*
–*noun* **3.** a time of great hurry and movement: *There was a rush to buy the cheap mobiles at the sale.*

rush[2] *noun* a type of long grass that grows in wet ground along river banks.

rust *noun*
1. the red or orange coating which forms on the surface of iron as a reaction to air and water.
–*verb* **2.** If something **rusts**, it becomes covered with this orange coating.
☐ **rusty**, *adjective* (**rustier**, **rustiest**)

rustic *adjective* having to do with, or suitable for the country rather than the city: *rustic life*; *rustic furniture.*

rustle /*say* **rus**-uhl/ *verb*
1. If things **rustle**, they make a series of slight, soft sounds as they rub gently together: *The leaves were rustling in the wind.*
–*phrase* **2. rustle up**, *Informal* to make or get by energetic action: *Let's rustle up some breakfast.*
☐ **rustle**, *noun*

☑ SPELLING TIP *Silent letter alert*: don't forget the *st* (not double *s*) spelling. The *t* is silent.

rut *noun*
1. a groove made in the ground by the wheels of a vehicle.
–*phrase* **2. in a rut**, doing the same thing all the time.

ruthless /*say* **roohth**-luhs/ *adjective* If someone is **ruthless**, they are very harsh or cruel and will do anything to get their own way: *He was ruthless in business and only cared about making money for himself.*
☐ **ruthlessness**, *noun* –**ruthlessly**, *adverb*

rye *noun* a grain which grows like wheat and is ground into flour.
☐ **rye**, *adjective*: *rye bread.*

☑ SPELLING TIP Don't confuse the spelling of **rye** with **wry** which sounds the same. **Wry** humour is funny in a clever but unemotional way, often about something unpleasant.

Sabbath *noun*
1. the seventh day of the week, Saturday, which is the day of worship for Jews and for some Christians. **2.** the first day of the week, Sunday, which is the day of worship for most Christians.

sabotage /*say* **sab**-uh-tahzh/ *noun*
1. damage done on purpose to stop someone else being successful: *an act of sabotage on his rival's computer.*
–*verb* **2.** If a piece of equipment is **sabotaged**, it is damaged on purpose as a protest or to weaken an enemy: *The rebels sabotaged the bridge to stop the enemy advance.* **3.** To **sabotage** a plan or meeting is to deliberately prevent it from having a successful result: *to sabotage an election campaign.*
☐ **saboteur** /*say* sab-uh-**ter**/, *noun*

☑ SPELLING TIP *Tricky 'uh' sound*: the middle vowel sound is spelt with an *o*. Also remember the *age* ending for the 'ahzh' sound. **Sabotage** has this sound and spelling because it comes from French.

sabre /*say* **say**-buh/ *noun* a heavy, slightly curved, one-edged sword.

☑ SPELLING TIP Remember the *a* spelling for the 'ay' sound and the *re* spelling at the end. It might help if you think of other words which you know well with the same spelling for this sound, such as *centre* and *theatre*.

saccharin /*say* **sak**-uh-ruhn/ *noun* a sweet chemical used instead of sugar.
☐ **saccharine**, *adjective*: *saccharine sweet.*

☑ SPELLING TIP *Double letter/silent letter alert*: notice the double *c*, followed by a silent *h*, all of which gives a 'k' sound.

sachet /*say* **sash**-ay/ *noun* a small, sealed package or bag used to contain small quantities of something.

☑ SPELLING TIP *Silent letter alert*: don't forget the silent *t* at the end – the *et* spelling makes an 'ay' sound. Other words with this ending are *ballet* and *beret*. They all come from French.

sack *noun*
1. a large bag made of strongly woven material. **2.** *Informal* dismissal from your job: *He was given the sack.*
–*verb* **3.** *Informal* If an employer **sacks** someone, they fire them.

sacrament /*say* **sak**-ruh-muhnt/ *noun* an important Christian religious ceremony, such as marriage.
☐ **sacramental**, *adjective*

sacred /*say* **say**-kruhd/ *adjective* holy or worthy of religious respect: *a sacred city.*
☐ **sacredly**, *adverb* –**sacredness**, *noun*

sacrifice /*say* **sak**-ruh-fuys/ *verb*
1. In some religions, if something such as an animal is **sacrificed**, it is killed and offered to the gods in a religious ceremony. **2.** If you **sacrifice** something, you give it up, usually in order to gain something else for yourself or for someone else: *He sacrificed his chance of winning to help his friend.*
☐ **sacrifice**, *noun* –**sacrificial** /*say* sak-ruh-**fish**-uhl/, *adjective*

☑ SPELLING TIP *Tricky 'uh' sound*: the middle vowel sound is spelt with an *i*. Also remember the *c* spelling for the 'k' sound. **Sacrifice** comes from the same Latin word as *sacred*, because the original meaning of the word related to the killing of a person or animal as part of a religious ceremony. Rap it out as *sac+ri+fice*.

sacrilege /*say* **sak**-ruh-lij/ *noun* lack of respect for holy objects or places.
☐ **sacrilegious** /*say* sak-ruh-**lij**-uhs/, *adjective*

☑ SPELLING TIP *Tricky 'uh' sound*: the middle vowel sound is spelt with an *i*. Also remember that there is no *d* in this word. The ending *ege* gives the 'ij' sound. This part of the word comes from *legere*, a Latin word meaning 'to take possession of'. The beginning *sacri* is related to **sacrifice**.

sad *adjective* (**sadder**, **saddest**)
1. If you are **sad**, you are not happy. You are upset about something: *Seeing his sad face, I knew that he must have failed the exam.* **2.** If an event is **sad**, it makes you feel sad.
☐ **sadden**, *verb*: *The dreadful news saddened me.* –**sadly**, *adverb* –**sadness**, *noun*

SIMILAR WORDS are **unhappy**, **miserable**, **sorrowful** and **mournful**.
THE OPPOSITE is **happy**.

saddle *noun*
1. a seat for the rider of a horse. **2.** the seat on a bicycle.
–*verb* **3.** If you **saddle** a horse or pony, you put a saddle on it so you can ride it. **4.** If you **saddle**

someone with a problem or job, you burden them with it so that it becomes their responsibility.
☐ **saddler**, *noun*

safari /*say* suh-**fah**-ree/ *noun* (*plural* **safaris**) a journey involving camping in the wild, usually to view wildlife, and, in the past, to hunt it.

WORD HISTORY from Swahili, an African language

safe *adjective*
1. free from danger or risk: *We are safe now.* **2.** careful in avoiding danger: *a safe driver.* **3.** away from danger: *in a safe place.*
–*noun* **4.** a metal box that you keep money, jewels or valuable papers in.
☐ **safely**, *adverb* –**safety**, *noun*

SIMILAR WORDS (for definition 1) are **immune**, **protected**, **secure** and **sheltered**.

safe sex *noun* sexual practices in which precautions are taken to prevent the spread of disease, especially AIDS, through sexual intercourse.

safflower *noun* a plant with large orange-red flowers which is grown for the oil you can get from its seeds.

saffron *noun* an orange-coloured powder made from flowers, which is used to colour food.

sag *verb* (**sags**, **sagging**, **sagged**, **has sagged**) If something **sags**, it bends down, especially in the middle: *The branch sagged under the weight of our bodies.*
☐ **sag**, *noun*

saga /*say* **sah**-guh/ *noun*
1. a long novel about the lives of a family or group of people. **2.** any long story.

sage[1] *noun* a very wise person.
☐ **sage**, *adjective*: *She gave me sage advice.*

sage[2] *noun* a herb used for seasoning in cooking.

sago /*say* **say**-goh/ *noun* a food consisting of small pearl-like grains made from the soft inside of the trunk of various palm trees, often used in puddings.

sail *noun*
1. a sheet of material which catches the wind and makes a boat move through the water. **2.** a journey in a ship or boat: *We went for a sail last weekend.*
–*verb* **3.** When a boat moves on water, it **sails**. **4.** If you **sail** on a boat or a ship, you travel on it. **5.** If you **sail** a boat, you cause it to move over water, using sails: *They sailed their yacht through rough seas.* **6.** If something **sails** somewhere, it moves there smoothly and rather quickly: *White clouds were sailing overhead.*
–*phrase* **7. set sail**, to start a journey. **8. under sail**, with the sails set.
☐ **sailing**, *noun* –**sailor**, *noun*

☑ SPELLING TIP Don't confuse the spelling of **sail** with **sale** which has the same sound. A **sale** is when something such as a house is sold.

sailboard *noun* a light-weight surfboard with a mast and sail, on which the rider stands to control the sail.

saint *noun*
1. someone who has been formally recognised as being holy by the Christian church. **2.** a very good person.
☐ **sainthood**, *noun* –**saintly**, *adjective*

NOTE This word (as in definition 1) can be shortened to **St** and used as a title, as in *St John*.

sake *noun*
1. benefit or good: *He did his best in the race for the school's sake.*
–*phrase* **2. for the sake of**, for the purpose of: *For the sake of peace, let's shake hands.*

salad *noun*
1. a food made up of raw vegetables such as greens, tomatoes, and celery. **2.** other raw or cooked food, cut up and mixed together and served cold: *fruit salad*; *pasta salad.*

☑ SPELLING TIP *Single letter alert*: only one *l* in the middle. Notice also that the vowel on either side of the *l* is an *a*.

salamander /*say* **sal**-uh-man-duh/ *noun* a type of amphibian with a tail, which lives in the water when very young, but later lives on land.

salami /*say* suh-**lah**-mee/ *noun* a kind of sausage with a strong salty taste.

salary *noun* (*plural* **salaries**) the regular pay people get for their jobs, especially for office work.

sale *noun*
1. the act of selling: *the sale of a boat.* **2.** a special selling at a low price: *a sale of shoes*; *The end of year sales always attract crowds of eager buyers.*
–*phrase* **3. for sale** or **on sale**, able to be bought: *His boat is for sale*; *Her latest CD is on sale now.*
☐ **salesperson**, **salesman**, **saleswoman**, *noun*

☑ SPELLING TIP Don't confuse the spelling of **sale** with **sail** which has the same sound. A **sail** is the part of a boat which catches the wind and makes it move through the water.

saline /*say* **say**-luyn, **say**-leen/ *adjective* containing or tasting like salt: *Water returning to the river from irrigated land is more saline than the water taken out.*
☐ **salinity**, *noun*

saliva /*say* suh-**luy**-vuh/ *noun* the watery liquid in the mouth, which helps in swallowing food and beginning to digest it.

☐ **salivate**, *verb*: *The dog salivated when it saw the bone.*

sallow *adjective* If a person or their skin is **sallow**, their skin has a sickly yellowish colour: *We could tell from her sallow appearance that she was not well.*

salmon /*say* **sam**-uhn/ *noun* (*plural* **salmons** *or* **salmon**) a sea and freshwater food fish with pink flesh, found near the mouths of large rivers, or in lakes.

> ☑ SPELLING TIP *Silent letter alert*: don't forget the silent *l* before the *m*. Rap it out as *sal* + *mon*.

salon /*say* **sal**-on/ *noun* a fashionable shop: *a dress salon*; *a hair salon.*

saloon *noun* a well-furnished room, as in a hotel, passenger ship, etc.

salsa *noun*
1. a spicy sauce made from tomatoes and chilli, originating in Mexican cooking. **2.** a type of dance music originating in Central America and blending Cuban rhythms with jazz and rock music.

salt /*say* solt, sawlt/ *noun*
1. white crystals obtained from seawater and used to flavour or preserve food. **2.** a chemical compound formed from the reaction of an acid with an alkali.
–*phrase* **3. take with a grain of salt**, to have little belief in: *He often exaggerates so I take everything he says with a grain of salt.*
☐ **saltwater**, *adjective*: *a saltwater crocodile.*
–**salty**, *adjective* (**saltier**, **saltiest**)

> NOTE The scientific name for definition 1 is **sodium chloride**.

saltbush *noun* a plant which can grow in very dry parts of Australia and which horses and cattle can eat when there is no grass.

saltcellar *noun* a container for salt, used at a meal table.

salutary /*say* **sal**-yuh-tree/ *adjective*
1. health-giving or wholesome: *the salutary effect of eating less fatty food and more fruit.* **2.** beneficial or doing good: *The teacher said it would be a salutary lesson for him to stand outside the room for a while.*

salute *verb* If you **salute** someone, you bring your right hand up to your forehead sharply as a formal sign of respect: *The soldier saluted his commanding officer.*
☐ **salutation**, *noun* –**salute**, *noun*

salvage *noun*
1. the saving of a ship or its load when it has been damaged or sunk.
–*verb* **2.** If you **salvage** something, you recover or save it: *She managed to salvage a few possessions after the fire.*

salvation *noun*
1. the act of saving. **2.** the cause or means of saving: *The lost hikers' salvation appeared in the form of an old truck approaching slowly along the sandy track.*

salvo *noun* (*plural* **salvoes**) the firing of guns a number of times, often as a salute.

> WORD HISTORY from a Latin word meaning 'be in good health'

sambal /*say* **sam**-bahl/ *noun* a spicy paste made from hot chillies and used to flavour food, originating in Indonesian cooking.

same *adjective*
1. exactly alike: *I have the same jeans as you.* **2.** referring to only one thing, time, place, etc. and not to different ones: *We go to the same school.* **3.** referring to something that has already been mentioned: *He has a bad temper and his brother has exactly the same problem.*
–*pronoun* **4.** the same person or thing: *She's the same as ever.*
–*phrase* **5. all the same**, **a.** even so: *All the same, I do think you should come.* **b.** unimportant: *Whether you come or not is all the same to me.* **6. just the same**, **a.** in the same way: *She parts her hair just the same as she's always done.* **b.** even so: *I will come just the same.*

sample *noun*
1. a part or piece which shows what the whole is like: *a sample of his music.*
–*verb* **2.** When you **sample** something, you test or judge it by a sample: *I'd better sample that cake to make sure it's all right.*
–*adjective* **3.** acting as a specimen: *a sample packet.*

> A SIMILAR WORD (for definition 1) is **specimen**.

samurai /*say* **sam**-yuh-ruy/ *noun* (*plural* **samurai**) a Japanese fighter who lived in medieval times.

> ☑ SPELLING TIP *Tricky vowel sound*: *ai* to spell the 'uy' sound at the end. This word comes from Japanese.

sanatorium *noun* (*plural* **sanatoriums** *or* **sanatoria**) a hospital for sick people who need to rest and be treated for a time, especially in a healthy climate.

> ANOTHER SPELLING is **sanitarium**.

sanctify *verb* (**sanctifies**, **sanctifying**, **sanctified**, **has sanctified**) To **sanctify** something is to make it holy or set it apart as holy.
☐ **sanctification**, *noun*

sanction *verb*
1. If someone **sanctions** something, they give it their approval or support.
–*noun* **2.** permission or support for something, given by someone in authority: *The principal gave*

her sanction to the idea of charity day. **3. sanctions**, actions exercised by a number of countries against another country to force that country to obey some legal requirement.

NOTE You will notice that the two noun definitions of **sanction** (definitions 2 and 3) seem to have almost opposite meanings. The basic meaning is allowing or agreeing to something (from the Latin word *sancire* meaning 'to give formal approval to'). This applies also to definition 3 because this meaning of **sanction** developed from the idea of a group of nations making an agreement to take such action.

sanctuary /*say* **sangk**-chuh-ree/ *noun* (*plural* **sanctuaries**)
1. a holy place. **2.** a place of safety: *a wildlife sanctuary.* **3.** protection given to someone running away from danger or cruel treatment.

A SIMILAR WORD (for definitions 2 and 3) is **refuge**.

☑ SPELLING TIP Remember the *u* before the *ary* ending, which you often do not hear when the word is pronounced. Rap it out as *sanc+tu+ar+y.*

sand *noun*
1. fine grains of rocks that have been broken up or worn away.
–*verb* **2.** To **sand** something is to smooth or polish it with sandpaper.
☐ **sandy**, *adjective* (**sandier**, **sandiest**)

sandal *noun* a kind of shoe made of a flat sole fastened to the foot with straps.

☑ SPELLING TIP Remember that the ending is *al* (not *el* or *le*). Think of other words with this ending, such as *capital* or *metal.*

sandalwood *noun* a sweet-smelling wood used for carving ornaments, or burnt as incense.

sandpaper *noun*
1. a strong paper coated with a layer of sand and used for smoothing rough surfaces.
–*verb* **2.** If you **sandpaper** a surface, you rub it with sandpaper to make it smoother.

sandshoe *noun* a canvas shoe with a rubber sole, usually worn for sport.

sandstone *noun* a type of rock formed from sand.

sandwich *noun* (*plural* **sandwiches**) two slices of bread with a cold filling between them.

☑ SPELLING TIP *Silent letter alert*: don't forget the silent *d* following the *n*. Think of this word in two parts – *sand* and *wich* (remember *witch*-without the *t*). In fact, the word comes from the name of an English lord, the Earl of Sandwich (1718–1792) who is said to have eaten sandwiches rather than stop playing gambling games to have a full meal.

sane *adjective*
1. If someone is **sane**, they are not mad. Their mind is normal and healthy. **2.** A **sane** decision is one that is based on common sense and reason.
☐ **sanely**, *adverb* –**sanity**, *noun*

sanitary /*say* **san**-uh-tree/ *adjective* having to do with cleanliness or care in preventing disease: *sanitary procedures.*

☑ SPELLING TIP Remember the *ary* ending, although you do not usually hear the *a* when the word is pronounced. It might help if you notice the word *tar* is hiding inside **sanitary**.

sap[1] *noun* the juice circulating in a plant.

sap[2] *verb* (**saps**, **sapping**, **sapped**, **has sapped**) To **sap** something, such as strength or ability, is to weaken or destroy it gradually: *Continual outbreaks of fire had sapped the ability of the bush to regenerate.*

sapling *noun* a young tree.

sapphire /*say* **saf**-uy-uh/ *noun* a clear blue gem.
☐ **sapphire**, *adjective*

sarcasm /*say* **sah**-kaz-uhm/ *noun* the saying of harsh and bitter things, especially by using the trick of saying the opposite of what you really mean, so as to hurt someone's feelings.
☐ **sarcastic**, *adjective* –**sarcastically**, *adverb*

sarcophagus /*say* sah-**kof**-uh-guhs/ *noun* (*plural* **sarcophagi** /*say* sah-**kof**-uh-guy/ *or* **sarcophaguses**) a stone coffin.

sardine /*say* sah-**deen**/ *noun* a young fish, often cooked and tinned in oil.

sardonic *adjective* sarcastic or mockingly scornful: *She listened to their weak excuses with a sardonic sneer.*

sari /*say* **sah**-ree/ *noun* a long piece of cotton or silk material worn by a Hindu woman, which is draped around the body with one end over the head or shoulders.

sarong /*say* suh-**rong**/ *noun* a piece of clothing consisting of a length of cloth wrapped around the body like a skirt, or around the whole body like a dress, worn as part of traditional dress by people in parts of Asia and the Pacific, especially Malaysia and Indonesia, and elsewhere as casual or beach clothing.

sash[1] *noun* a long band of cloth worn round your waist or over your shoulder.

sash[2] *noun* a window frame which slides up and down.

sashimi /*say* suh-**shee**-mee/ *noun* a Japanese food made of raw fish.

satanic /*say* suh-**tan**-ik/ *adjective* extremely wicked.

NOTE This is from **Satan**, the name of the devil.

satay /*say* **sah**-tay/ *noun* a food made up of small pieces of meat cooked on a skewer and covered with a hot peanut sauce, originating in Indonesian and Malaysian cooking.

satchel *noun* a bag made of something like leather or canvas with a shoulder strap, such as one used for carrying schoolbooks.

satellite *noun*
1. a body in space, such as a moon, which moves around a larger one, such as a planet. **2.** an object sent into orbit around the earth or around another planet to send information back to earth.

> ☑ SPELLING TIP *Single/double letter alert*: the *t* is single both times it appears, the *l* is doubled.

satin *noun* a very smooth, shiny cloth.
☐ **satin**, *adjective*

satire /*say* **sat**-uy-uh/ *noun*
1. the use of sarcasm or humour to draw people's attention to something which is silly or bad. **2.** any poem, book or play, etc., which does this.
☐ **satiric** /*say* suh-**ti**-rik/, *adjective* –**satirical**, *adjective*: *satirical writing.* –**satirise** /*say* **sat**-uh-ruyz/, *verb*: *to satirise a situation.* –**satirist**, *noun*

> ANOTHER SPELLING for **satirise** is **satirize**.

satisfy *verb* (**satisfies**, **satisfying**, **satisfied**, **has satisfied**)
1. If you are **satisfied** with someone or something, you are happy because they have done or given you what you want or expect: *I am more than satisfied with your work so far.* **2.** If you are **satisfied** about something, you believe that it is true: *I am satisfied that you are telling the truth.* **3.** If someone or something **satisfies** you, they give you enough of what you want or need: *The cold drink satisfied his thirst.*
☐ **satisfaction**, *noun* –**satisfactory**, *adjective*: *a satisfactory solution.* –**satisfied**, *adjective*: *a satisfied customer.*

saturate *verb* If someone or something becomes **saturated**, they get wet right through, usually from rain.
☐ **saturated**, *adjective* –**saturation**, *noun*

Saturday *noun* the seventh day of the week.

> THE ABBREVIATION is **Sat.**
> WORD HISTORY from an Old English word meaning 'day of Saturn'

satyr /*say* **say**-tuh, **sat**-uh/ *noun* a kind of god in ancient Greek mythology, pictured as part goat and part human.

> ☑ SPELLING TIP *Tricky vowel sound*: the ending is spelt *yr*, giving an 'uh' sound.

sauce *noun* a liquid food put on other food as a flavouring.

> ☑ SPELLING TIP Don't confuse the spelling of **sauce** with **source** which has the same sound. The **source** of something is where it comes from.

saucepan *noun* a cooking container with a lid and a long handle.

saucer *noun* a small, round plate used under a cup.

sauna /*say* **saw**-nuh/ *noun* a room with a kind of steam bath in which you become clean by perspiring a lot.

> ☑ SPELLING TIP *Tricky vowel sound*: *au* to spell the 'aw' sound. Also remember the *a* ending. **Sauna** is spelt like this because it comes from Finnish.

saunter /*say* **sawn**-tuh/ *verb* If you **saunter**, you walk in an unhurried way: *sauntering along the beach.*
☐ **saunter**, *noun*

sausage *noun* finely chopped up meat with seasonings or preservatives packed into a thin skin.

sausage roll *noun* a roll of baked pastry filled with sausage meat.

sauté /*say* **soh**-tay/ *verb* (**sautés**, **sautéing**, **sautéed**, **has sautéed**) If you **sauté** food, you brown or cook it gently in a pan with a little fat.

> ☑ SPELLING TIP *Tricky vowel sounds*: *au* spelling for the 'oh' sound. Also notice the accent over the *e* at the end which gives it an 'ay' sound. This is because **sauté** comes from French.

savage *adjective*
1. untamed or wild: *a savage animal.* **2.** fierce or cruel: *savage punishment.*
☐ **savagely**, *adverb* –**savagery**, *noun*

savanna /*say* suh-**van**-uh/ *noun* a grassland area with some trees scattered about.

> ANOTHER SPELLING is **savannah**. Notice that the *n* is doubled, whichever spelling you use.

save *verb*
1. If you **save** someone, you help them escape from a difficult or dangerous situation. **2.** If you **save** money, you keep it rather than spend it. **3.** If you **save** something such as time, money or energy, you make certain that you are careful in your actions so that you have time, money or energy left over.
–*phrase* **4. save up**, to put aside money: *to save up for a computer game.*
☐ **savings**, *plural noun*: *I'm going to use my savings to buy a new computer.*

saviour /*say* **sayv**-yuh/ *noun* someone who saves, rescues or delivers: *They hoped the new president would be the saviour of their country.*

> ANOTHER SPELLING is **savior**.

savour /*say* **say**-vuh/ *verb* If you **savour** something, you taste or smell it, especially with pleasure: *We savoured the wonderful whiffs of spices coming from the kitchen and couldn't wait for dinner to start.*
☐ **savour**, *noun*

ANOTHER SPELLING is **savor**.

savoury /*say* **say**-vuh-ree/ *adjective*
1. Savoury food tastes spicy or salty tasting rather than sweet.
–*noun* (*plural* **savouries**) **2.** a tasty, bite-sized piece of food on a small biscuit or piece of bread.

ANOTHER SPELLING is **savory**.

saw[1] *noun*
1. a cutting tool with sharp teeth on a thin blade.
–*verb* (**saws**, **sawing**, **sawed**, **has sawn** *or* **has sawed**) **2.** If you **saw** something, you cut it with a saw: *It took two men to saw down the massive old tree.* **3.** If you **saw**, you cut something as a saw does: *He sawed away at the tough steak.*

☑ SPELLING TIP Don't confuse the spelling of **saw** with **sore** or **soar**, both of which have the same sound. If part of your body is **sore**, it hurts. To **soar** is to fly upwards, or to rise to a great height.

saw[2] *verb* the past tense of **see**.

saxophone /*say* **saks**-uh-fohn/ *noun* a wind instrument with a curved brass body.
☐ **saxophonist** /*say* saks-**of**-uh-nuhst/, *noun*

say *verb* (**says**, **saying**, **said**, **has said**)
1. If you **say** something, you speak: *What did you say?* **2.** If you **say** something, you express yourself in words: *Have you got anything to say?*
–*noun* **3.** a turn to speak: *Can I have my say now?*

saying *noun*
1. something wise that is often said.
–*phrase* **2. go without saying**, to be very obvious.

A SIMILAR WORD (for definition 1) is **proverb**.

scab *noun* the hard top which forms over a sore when it is healing.

scabbard /*say* **skab**-uhd/ *noun* a holder for the blade of a sword or dagger.

scaffold *noun*
1. a structure for people to stand on when they are doing work on a building. **2.** in the past, a raised platform on which criminals who had received a death sentence were killed by hanging or having their head cut off.

ANOTHER WORD (for definition 1) is **scaffolding**.

scald /*rhymes with* called/ *verb*
1. If you **scald** yourself, you burn yourself with boiling water or steam: *Be careful with that kettle – don't scald yourself!* **2.** If you **scald** milk, you bring it to the boil.
–*noun* **3.** a burn caused by hot liquid or steam.
☐ **scalding**, *adjective*

scale[1] *noun*
1. one of the thin, flat plates which form the covering of fish and some other animals. **2.** any thin coating that comes away from a surface.
–*verb* **3.** When you **scale** a fish, you remove its scales: *The fish needs to be scaled before cooking.*
☐ **scaly**, *adjective* (**scalier**, **scaliest**)

scale[2] *noun*
1. a set of marks along a line for measuring: *a temperature scale.* **2.** a marked line on a map showing how to measure distances. **3.** size, compared to something else: *Everything in the new shopping mall is on a larger scale.* **4.** a series of musical notes going up or down at fixed intervals, usually one that begins on a particular note: *the scale of C major.*
–*verb* **5.** To **scale** something is to climb it: *to scale a cliff.*

scales *plural noun* a weighing machine.

scallop /*say* **skol**-uhp/ *noun*
1. a type of edible shellfish which has two wavy shells. **2.** a thin slice of potato battered and deep-fried. **3.** one of the regular curves along the edge of pastry or cloth.

ANOTHER TERM (for definition 2) is **potato scallop**.

scalp *noun* the skin of the head where the hair grows.

scalpel *noun* a small, very sharp knife used by doctors in operations.

scam *noun Informal* a trick, especially one that makes money.

scamp *noun Rather old-fashioned* a rascal or mischievous person.

scamper *verb* If a person or animal **scampers** away, they run or hurry away quickly: *The mouse scampered into its hole.*
☐ **scamper**, *noun*

scan *verb* (**scans**, **scanning**, **scanned**, **has scanned**)
1. If you **scan** something that is written, you read it very quickly in order to get the main facts from it: *to scan a letter.* **2.** If you **scan** something, you look at it very closely in order to get information: *She eagerly scanned his face to see what he was feeling.* **3.** If a machine **scans** something, it reads it electronically to gather information.
–*noun* **4. a.** an examination of part of the body done by an electronic beam being passed over that part to produce an image of it: *a lung scan.* **b.** the image of a part of the body produced in this way.

scandal *noun*
1. talk about someone's behaviour, often harmful to their reputation. 2. an event that shocks people because they think it involves wrong behaviour.
□ **scandalous**, *adjective* –**scandalously**, *adverb*

☑ SPELLING TIP Remember that the ending is *al* (not *el* or *le*). Think of other words with this ending, such as *capital* or *metal*.

scanner *noun*
1. a machine that looks at printed information like text, a picture, or a barcode, and puts it directly into a computer. 2. a machine that passes an electronic beam over part of the body in order to produce an image of it, used as a medical test.

scant *adjective* If something is **scant**, there is not enough of it: *scant information.*

scapegoat *noun* someone who is made to bear the blame for others.

scar *noun*
1. a mark left on the skin by a healed sore or burn.
–*verb* (**scars**, **scarring**, **scarred**, **has scarred**)
2. If something **scars** you, it leaves a scar on your skin: *The cut scarred his face.*

scarce /*say* skairs/ *adjective*
1. not enough to fill the need. 2. rarely seen or found: *Leather-covered books are scarce now.*
□ **scarcity**, *noun* (*plural* **scarcities**)

scarcely *adverb* barely or not quite: *We were scarcely home and the phone rang.*

scare *verb*
1. To **scare** someone is to frighten them.
–*noun* 2. a sudden fright, sometimes for no reason. 3. widespread fear or worry: *a scare about a new flu epidemic.*
□ **scared**, *adjective* –**scary**, *adjective* (**scarier**, **scariest**)

scarecrow *noun* a figure dressed in old clothes, put up to frighten birds away from crops.

scarf *noun* (*plural* **scarfs** *or* **scarves**) a piece of material worn around your neck or head to keep you warm or to look nice.

scarlet *adjective* of a bright red colour.
□ **scarlet**, *noun*

WORD HISTORY from a Persian word meaning 'a rich cloth'

scathing /*say* **skay**-dhing/ *adjective* meant to hurt your feelings by criticising you: *Her scathing attack surprised them all.*
□ **scathingly**, *adverb*

☑ SPELLING TIP Remember the *a* spelling for the 'ay' sound. This is because **scathing** comes from the verb *scathe* (a now rare word meaning 'to criticise').

scatter *verb*
1. If you **scatter** something, you spread it or parts of it all over a place: *She scattered her books all over my room.* 2. If a group of people **scatters**, they spread out over a wide area.
□ **scatter**, *noun* –**scattered**, *adjective* –**scattering**, *noun*

scavenger *noun*
1. someone who searches through rubbish for useful things. 2. an animal which eats flesh from dead animals.
□ **scavenge**, *verb*

scene /*sounds like* seen/ *noun*
1. a place where something happens: *the scene of the accident.* 2. a view or a picture of a view. 3. one of the divisions of a play. 4. a real or imaginary event, especially one described in writing. 5. a noisy show of excitement or anger in front of other people.

☑ SPELLING TIP *Silent letter alert*: don't forget the silent *c* after the *s*. Also remember the *ene* spelling for the 'een' sound. Take care with the spelling of this word and don't confuse it with **seen** (the past participle of the word *see*, as in *I have seen you somewhere before*).

scenery /*say* **seen**-uh-ree/ *noun* (*plural* **sceneries**)
1. the natural features of a place: *beautiful coastal scenery.* 2. painted boards and structures put on a stage to show the place where a play is meant to take place.

☑ SPELLING TIP *Silent letter alert*: don't forget the silent *c* after the *s*. Also remember the *ery* ending. This will be easier if you remember that **scenery** comes from the word *scene*.

scent /*sounds like* sent/ *noun*
1. a pleasant smell: *the scent of roses.* 2. the particular smell of an animal or person which allows other animals to follow them. 3. a liquid you put on your skin to make you smell good: *a bottle of scent.*
–*verb* 4. If an animal **scents** something, it recognises it or is aware of it because of its scent.

☑ SPELLING TIP *Silent letter alert*: don't forget the silent *c* after the *s*. Don't confuse **scent** with **sent** or **cent**, both of which have the same sound. **Sent** is the past form of the verb *send*. A **cent** is a unit of money.

sceptic /*say* **skep**-tik/ *noun* someone who does not believe things that most other people accept without question.
□ **sceptical**, *adjective* –**sceptically**, *adverb* –**scepticism** /*say* **skep**-tuh-siz-uhm/, *noun*

sceptre /*say* **sep**-tuh/ *noun* a rod carried by a king or queen, as a symbol of royal power.

☑ SPELLING TIP *Silent letter alert*: don't forget the silent *c* after the *s*. Also remember the *re* (not *er*) ending. Some other words with this ending are *centre* and *theatre*.

schedule /*say* **shej**-oohl, **skej**-oohl/ *noun* **1.** a plan which shows you how something is to be carried out and sets out when each stage is to be done. **2.** a list of things to be done.
–*verb* **3.** If something is **scheduled** to happen, plans have been made for it to happen: *We are scheduled to leave on Friday morning*; *There are ten operations scheduled for today.*

☑ SPELLING TIP Remember the *sch* spelling for the opening of this word, which some people say as 'sh' and some as 'sk'. Think of the *sch* spelling as being the same as the beginning of *school*.

scheme /*say* skeem/ *noun* **1.** a plan of action: *a scheme for raising money.* **2.** a secret plan: *a scheme to rob the bank.*
☐ **scheming**, *adjective*

☑ SPELLING TIP Remember the *sch* spelling for the opening 'sk' sound, as at the start of *school*. Also notice the *eme* spelling for the 'eem' sound.

schizophrenia /*say* skit-suh-**free**-nee-uh/ *noun* a serious mental illness in which the way a person thinks and feels does not match what is really happening.
☐ **schizophrenic** /*say* skit-suh-**fren**-ik/, *noun*, *adjective*

scholar /*say* **skol**-uh/ *noun* **1.** someone who is studying. **2.** a learned person: *a history scholar.*
☐ **scholarly**, *adjective*

☑ SPELLING TIP Remember the *sch* spelling for the opening 'sk' sound, as at the start of *school*. This word comes from the same Greek origin as *school*. Take one *o* out, keep the single *l* and add the *ar* ending, and you have **scholar**.

scholarship /*say* **skol**-uh-ship/ *noun* **1.** a sum of money won by a student which helps to pay school or university fees. **2.** knowledge gained by study: *The depth of her scholarship is evident in her lectures.*

☑ SPELLING TIP See **scholar**.

scholastic /*say* skuh-**las**-tik/ *adjective* having to do with schools, students or education: *His scholastic record was brilliant.*

☑ SPELLING TIP See **scholar**.

school[1] *noun* **1.** a place where children are taught. **2.** the children who go to a school: *A quarter of the school was away sick this week.* **3.** lessons in a particular activity: *a horseriding school.*
☐ **schooling**, *noun*

school[2] *noun* a large number of fish swimming together.

WORD HISTORY from a Dutch word meaning 'school' or 'multitude'

schooner /*say* **skooh**-nuh/ *noun* a sailing ship with two or more masts.

☑ SPELLING TIP Remember the *sch* spelling for the opening 'sk' sound, as at the start of *school*.

science /*say* **suy**-uhns/ *noun* **1.** the study of the physical world in an organised way, by measuring, testing and experimenting. **2.** knowledge gained in this way. **3.** a particular branch of this study: *the science of zoology.*
☐ **scientific**, *adjective* –**scientist**, *noun*

☑ SPELLING TIP *Silent letter alert*: don't forget the silent *c* following the *s* at the start. Also notice that the *ie* after the *c* does not appear to follow the normal rule of *i* before *e* except after *c*. This is because the *i* and the *e* are part of two separate syllables in this word, rather than going together to make an 'ee' sound. **Science** comes from *scientia*, the Latin word for 'knowledge'.

science fiction *noun* a form of fiction which uses scientific knowledge in its story, setting, and so on, in an imaginative way.

THE SHORT FORM of this is **sci-fi**.

scissors /*say* **siz**-uhz/ *plural noun* a cutting instrument made of two blades joined together: *My scissors need sharpening.*
☐ **scissor-like**, *adjective*

ANOTHER TERM for this is a **pair of scissors**. Note that this is always used as a singular, as opposed to **scissors** by itself, which is always plural.

☑ SPELLING TIP *Silent letter alert*: don't forget the silent *c* following the *s*. Also remember the double *s* in the middle – you will notice that there are four *s*'s altogether in **scissors**.

scoff *verb* If you **scoff** at someone, you mock them: *They scoffed at us for losing the match.*

scold *verb* If you **scold** someone for doing something wrong, you speak to them angrily: *He scolded me for losing my key again.*
☐ **scolding**, *noun*: *a good scolding.*

SIMILAR WORDS are **reprimand**, **rebuke** and **admonish**.

scoliosis /*say* skol-ee-**oh**-suhs/ *noun* a condition in which a person's spine curves from side to side, often developing during adolescence because of growth spurts during that time.

scone /*rhymes with* gone/ *noun* a small, light, plain cake usually eaten with butter and jam and often served hot.

WORD HISTORY from a Dutch word meaning 'fine bread'

scoop *noun*
1. a cup-shaped spoon. 2. an amount of something held by or taken out by a scoop: *two scoops of ice-cream.* 3. the bucket of a machine used for drawing up earth, sand, etc. 4. a hollow made by a scoop. 5. a news story published or broadcast before any other newspaper, radio or television station.
–*verb* 6. When you **scoop** something, you take it up or out with a scoop, or by using your hands as a scoop: *to scoop ice-cream into a bowl*; *She scooped up handfuls of water to splash over her face.*

scooter *noun*
1. a small vehicle, usually a child's toy, with two wheels, one in front of the other, and a board between them on which you stand. 2. a kind of small motorcycle.

ANOTHER TERM (for definition 2) is **motor scooter**.

scope *noun*
1. range or reach: *That question is beyond the scope of my knowledge.* 2. space or room: *scope for improvement.*

scorch *verb*
1. If you **scorch** something, you burn it slightly, often with an iron: *It is easy to scorch clothes while ironing in front of the television.* 2. If a source of heat **scorches** something, it causes it to dry up with heat: *The sun scorched the desert vegetation.*
☐ **scorch**, *noun* (*plural* **scorches**) a burn on the surface.

score *verb*
1. If players **score** in a game or match, they make points for themselves or for their team. 2. If you **score** for a game or match, you are the person who keeps a record of the number of points each side makes. 3. If you **score** something, you cut it or mark it with a sharp utensil such as a knife: *The desk tops were deeply scored.*
–*noun* 4. the number of points gained in an examination or competition. 5. a written or printed piece of music.
☐ **scorer**, *noun*

scorn *noun*
1. a strong feeling that something or someone is not good enough for you to approve of or respect: *She treated our suggestion with scorn.*
–*verb* 2. If you **scorn** a person or thing, you look on them with scorn: *She scorned his attempt at an apology.*
☐ **scornful**, *adjective*

scorpion *noun* a small, hard-shelled animal with a long, narrow tail that ends in a poisonous sting.

scoundrel /*say* **skown**-druhl/ *noun* a wicked and immoral person.

scour /*rhymes with* flower/ *verb* If you **scour** something, you clean it by rubbing it hard, usually in soap and water.

scout *noun*
1. someone sent to find out information, especially about an enemy. 2. a member of a worldwide youth movement, which provides organised activities with the aim of promoting outdoor adventure, community service and care for the environment.
–*verb* 3. When you **scout** for something, you investigate it and gather information about it: *He went ahead to scout out the path*; *Scout around and see if you can find a spare table.*

ANOTHER FORM You can also spell definition 2 with a capital letter.

scowl *verb* If you **scowl**, you have an angry look on your face.
☐ **scowl**, *noun*

scrabble *verb* If an animal or person **scrabbles**, they scratch or scrape with their claws or hands: *We could hear rats scrabbling in the roof*; *He scrabbled through his pocket for the right coins.*

scramble *verb*
1. If you **scramble** over something such as a hill or rough ground, you climb awkwardly, feeling your way with your hands. 2. If you **scramble** to get somewhere or do something, you move quickly and clumsily: *The students scrambled to their feet.* 3. If you **scramble** eggs, you beat them with milk and cook them in a pan.
–*noun* 4. a hurried climb or movement over rough ground. 5. a confused attempt by many people to get something all at once: *There was a scramble for the door as soon as the bell went.*

scrap[1] *noun*
1. a small piece: *Have you got a scrap of paper?* 2. anything useless or worn out, especially old metal. 3. **scraps**, bits of anything left over from any activity, especially a meal: *scraps of material*; *Give your dinner scraps to the dog.*
–*adjective* 4. consisting of scraps: *It was thrown onto the scrap heap.*
–*verb* (**scraps**, **scrapping**, **scrapped**, **has scrapped**) To **scrap** something is to 5. make it into scrap: *The old ship was finally scrapped for metal.* 6. put it aside as useless: *They scrapped the idea altogether.*

scrap[2] *noun Rather informal* a fight or quarrel.

scrape *verb*
1. If you **scrape** something, you knock it against something else, often causing a little damage such as the removal of part of its surface or skin: *The child scraped her knees when she fell.* 2. If something **scrapes** against something else, it produces an unpleasant noise: *The chalk scraped on the blackboard.*
–*noun* 3. the act or sound of scraping. 4. a scraped place. 5. an awkward situation.

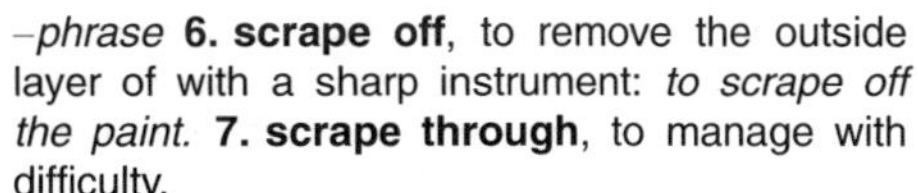

–*phrase* **6. scrape off**, to remove the outside layer of with a sharp instrument: *to scrape off the paint.* **7. scrape through**, to manage with difficulty.
☐ **scraper**, *noun*

scratch *verb*
1. If something sharp **scratches** you, it rubs against you and cuts your skin slightly: *Be careful of that piece of wire – it may scratch you.* **2.** If you **scratch** yourself, you rub your fingernails against a part of your body, usually because it is itchy. **3.** If you **scratch** an object, you damage it with something that leaves small cuts on it: *to scratch the surface.*
–*phrase* **4. from scratch**, from the beginning or from nothing. **5. up to scratch**, of a satisfactory standard: *Your homework is not up to scratch.*
☐ **scratch**, *noun* (*plural* **scratches**) –**scratchy**, *adjective* (**scratchier**, **scratchiest**)

scrawl *verb* If you **scrawl** something, you write it quickly and untidily, so that it is hard to read: *She scrawled a note and left it on the kitchen table before rushing out.*
☐ **scrawl**, *noun* –**scrawled**, *adjective*: *a scrawled message.*

scrawny *adjective* (**scrawnier**, **scrawniest**) thin and bony: *Those big jeans make you look a bit scrawny.*

scream *verb*
1. To **scream** is to make a loud, piercing cry or sound: *to scream with pain.*
–*noun* **2.** such a cry or sound. **3.** *Informal* someone or something that is very funny: *That girl is a scream – she's always doing something ridiculous.*

screech *verb* To **screech** is to make a harsh, high noise: *Cockatoos screeched from the treetops; The car screeched to a stop.*
☐ **screech**, *noun* (*plural* **screeches**)

screen *noun*
1. a large, flat surface on which a film can be shown. **2.** the part of a television set or computer terminal on which the image appears. **3.** a frame covered with wire netting, placed over a window to keep out insects. **4.** a covered frame or a curtain used to hide something or to protect something. **5.** anything that shelters or hides: *They stood behind a screen of shrubs.*
–*verb* **6.** To **screen** a film is to show it on a screen: *This is a guide to the movies being screened next week.*

screw *noun*
1. a small, thin, pointed piece of metal with a flat head and a spiral thread used for joining things, such as pieces of wood, together.
–*verb* **2.** When you **screw** something, you turn it: *Don't forget to screw the lid on.* **3.** If you **screw** something into a particular position, you fasten it in place with screws: *He screwed the name of the house to the front door.* **4.** If you **screw** something into a particular shape or direction, you twist or squeeze it like that: *He screwed the piece of paper into a ball and threw it in the bin; She screwed up her nose at the disgusting smell.*

screwdriver *noun* a tool which fits into the end of a screw and is turned to drive the screw in or take it out.

scribble *verb* If you **scribble** something, you write it quickly and carelessly.
☐ **scribble**, *noun* –**scribbler**, *noun*

scribe *noun* someone who used to make copies of books before the invention of printing.

script *noun*
1. the written dialogue for the actors to say in a play or film. **2.** writing done by hand.

scripture *noun* a collection of sacred writing in any religion.
☐ **scriptural**, *adjective*

NOTE This is often used in the plural, as in *a reading from the scriptures.*
WORD HISTORY from a Latin word meaning 'writing'

scroll *noun* a roll of parchment or paper, especially one with writing on it.

scrotum /*say* **skroh**-tuhm/ *noun* the pouch of skin in males which contains their testicles.

scrounge *verb Informal* If you **scrounge** for something, you obtain it by borrowing, begging or stealing: *We scrounged around the camp sites for wood to start a fire.*
☐ **scrounger**, *noun*

scrub[1] *verb* (**scrubs**, **scrubbing**, **scrubbed**, **has scrubbed**)
1. If you **scrub** something, you rub it hard with a brush, soap and water in order to clean it. **2.** *Rather informal* If you **scrub** an event, you get rid of it or stop it: *We had to scrub the basketball game because of illness.*
☐ **scrub**, *noun*

scrub[2] *noun*
1. low trees or shrubs growing closely together. **2.** a large area covered with scrub, as in the Australian bush.

scruff *noun* the back of the neck.

scruffy *adjective* (**scruffier**, **scruffiest**) dirty, shabby and uncared for.

scrum *noun*
1. a way of restarting the play in a game of Rugby football, in which some of the players pack together and push, one side against the other, until the ball is thrown in and someone kicks it out to other members of the team. **2.** the formation of players in a scrum.

ANOTHER WORD for this is **scrummage**.

scrumptious /*say* **skrum**-shuhs/ *adjective Informal* very tasty: *a scrumptious dessert.*

scrupulous /*say* **skroohp**-yuh-luhs/ *adjective*
1. careful or exact in every detail: *After having her teeth out, Anna had to be scrupulous in her oral hygiene.* **2.** being strict about doing what is right: *He is absolutely scrupulous – he would never use his clients' money illegally.*
☐ **scruple**, *noun* a doubt that you have about a matter of deciding between right and wrong: *He had no scruples about exploiting the poor old woman.* –**scrupulously**, *adverb*

scrutinise /*say* **skrooh**-tuh-nuyz/ *verb* If you **scrutinise** something, you examine it closely and carefully.
☐ **scrutiny**, *noun* (*plural* **scrutinies**)

ANOTHER SPELLING is **scrutinize.**

scuba /*say* **skooh**-buh/ *noun* a system that lets a diver breathe air through a mouthpiece connected by tubes to a container of air.

WORD HISTORY an acronym made by joining the first letters of *self-contained underwater breathing apparatus*

scuff *verb*
1. If you **scuff** with your feet, you scrape with them: *He scuffed the ground with his toe.* **2.** If something is **scuffed**, it has a mark on it from scraping: *Her shoes were scuffed and dirty*; *scuffed linoleum.*

scuffle *noun*
1. a fight which is usually not much more than a little pushing and shoving: *There was a scuffle over who was first in the queue.*
–*verb* **2.** To **scuffle** is to push and shove in a confused way.
☐ **scuffling**, *noun*

scullery *noun* (*plural* **sculleries**) a small room in some old houses where the rough, dirty kitchen work was done.

sculpture *noun*
1. the art or work of making figures or designs in marble, clay, bronze or similar materials. **2.** something made this way.
☐ **sculpt**, *verb* –**sculptor**, *noun* –**sculptural**, *adjective*

scum *noun* a thin layer of froth or dirt on the top of a liquid.

scungies *plural noun* short pants worn by women or girls over underwear and under a skirt while doing sport or exercise.

WORD HISTORY trademark

scurry *verb* (**scurries**, **scurrying**, **scurried**, **has scurried**) If you **scurry**, you move quickly: *We all scurried for cover when we heard them coming.*
☐ **scurry**, *noun*

scurvy *noun* a disease marked by swollen and bleeding gums, blue spots on the skin, inability to stand, and so on, caused by not eating enough food with vitamin C in it.

scuttle *verb* To **scuttle** is to run with quick steps: *The mouse scuttled away.*
☐ **scuttle**, *noun*

scythe /*say* suydh/ *noun* a tool with a long, curved blade joined at an angle to a long handle: *He used a scythe to cut the long grass.*

☑ SPELLING TIP *Silent letter alert*: don't forget the silent *c* following the *s* at the start. Also remember the *y* spelling in this difficult word.

sea *noun*
1. the salt waters that cover most of the earth's surface. **2.** a particular part of these waters, usually near or almost surrounded by land: *the Mediterranean Sea.* **3.** a large quantity: *a sea of troubles.*
–*phrase* **4. at sea**, **a.** out on the ocean. **b.** uncertain or confused.

☑ SPELLING TIP Don't confuse the spelling of **sea** with **see** which has the same sound but is spelt with *ee*. You **see** things with your eyes.

sea anemone /*say* uh-**nem**-uh-nee/ *noun* a sea animal which stays in one place and catches food with tentacles growing on top of its tube-shaped body.

seafarer *noun* a traveller on the sea.
☐ **seafaring**, *adjective*

seafood *noun* food which comes from the sea, such as fish, squid and shellfish.

seagull *noun* a bird, usually white with a grey back and wings and a harsh cry, which lives near the sea.

ANOTHER WORD for this is **gull.**

seahorse *noun* a small fish with a curved tail and a head shaped like a horse's.

seal[1] *noun*
1. a design pressed into a piece of wax, or a stamp (definition 3) with such a design, used for making official something that has been written. **2.** a piece of wax for closing an envelope or piece of writing which has to be broken before the contents can be read. **3.** anything used to close something.
–*verb* **4.** If you **seal** something, you close it so that it is very difficult to open again: *He sealed the envelope.* **5.** If you **seal** a road, you cover it with tar. **6.** If you **seal** someone's fate, you decide it: *His fate was sealed – the judge pronounced him guilty.*

seal[2] *noun* a sea animal with smooth fur, a long rounded body and large flippers.

NOTE The male is a **bull**; the female is a **cow**; the young is a **pup**.

sea level *noun* the average level of the sea, used as a base to measure height: *The mountain peak is 2000 metres above sea level.*

sea lion *noun* a type of large seal which has white hair on the back of its neck.

seam *noun*
1. the line where two pieces of material have been joined together: *The skirt has a seam on either side.* **2.** a thin layer of a different kind of rock or mineral in the ground: *a coal seam.*

☑ SPELLING TIP Don't confuse the spelling of **seam** with **seem** which has the same sound but is spelt with *ee*. To **seem** a certain way is to appear to be that way.

seaman *noun* (*plural* **seamen**) a sailor.
☐ **seamanship**, *noun*

seance /*say* **say**-ons/ *noun* a meeting of people who are trying to contact the spirits of dead people.

☑ SPELLING TIP This word comes from French, where it means 'a sitting'. The spelling is difficult because it is pronounced in a French way. Notice that the letter *e* alone spells the 'ay' sound in the first syllable, and that *ance* spells the 'ons' sound.

seaplane *noun* a plane with floats, which can land on water.

sear *verb* To **sear** something is to **1.** burn or blacken the outside of it: *The fire had seared the bark of the trees.* **2.** cause it to dry up or wither: *The sun had seared the land and every living thing on it.*
☐ **searing**, *adjective*: *searing heat.*

search *verb*
1. If you **search** for something, you look carefully for it. **2.** If you **search** a place, you try to find something in it: *to search the desk for a book.*
☐ **search**, *noun* (*plural* **searches**) –**searcher**, *noun*

☑ SPELLING TIP *Tricky vowel sound*: remember the *a* in this word. The letter combination *ear* spells the 'er' sound, as in many other words such as *earn* and *learn*.

search warrant *noun* an order by a court which allows the police to search someone's house, usually for stolen goods.

seasickness *noun* a feeling of sickness in the stomach, or vomiting caused by the movement of a ship at sea.
☐ **seasick**, *adjective*

season *noun*
1. one of the four divisions of the year: spring, summer, autumn, and winter. **2.** a period of time characterised by a particular type of weather pattern: *wet season*; *dry season.* **3.** a period of time, especially when it is connected with some event or activity: *the football season*; *It's been a good season for mangoes.*
–*verb* **4.** If you **season** food, you add flavour to it: *She seasons her cooking with pepper and herbs.*
☐ **seasonal**, *adjective* –**seasoning**, *noun*

seat *noun*
1. something for sitting on: *a car seat.* **2.** a part for sitting on: *the seat of a chair*; *the seat of your pants.* **3.** a centre of some activity: *the seat of government.* **4.** the right to sit in parliament: *She will stand for a seat in the next election.*
–*verb* **5.** If you **seat** yourself somewhere, you sit on a seat there: *She seated herself beside the fire.* **6.** If a building or vehicle **seats** a certain number of people, it has seats for that number: *The hall seats 1000.*
☐ **seated**, *adjective* –**seating**, *noun*

seatbelt *noun* a belt attached to the seat of a vehicle or plane which you put around you to hold you safely in place if there is a sudden stop or accident.

ANOTHER TERM for this is **safety belt**.

sea urchin *noun* a sea animal with a round, spiky shell.

seaweed *noun* any plant that grows in the ocean.

secateurs /*say* **sek**-uh-tuhz, sek-uh-**terz**/ *plural noun* gardening shears for clipping and pruning.

seclude *verb* To **seclude** yourself is to shut yourself away: *She secluded herself in the library so she could read in peace.*
☐ **secluded**, *adjective* quiet and private. –**seclusion**, *noun*

second[1] *adjective*
1. next after the first. **2.** additional: *a second attempt.* **3.** alternate: *every second day.*
☐ **second**, *noun*

second[2] *noun* one sixtieth part of a minute of time.

secondary /*say* **sek**-uhn-dree/ *adjective*
1. Something that is **secondary** is less important than something else or comes from something else. **2. Secondary** industry is industry that involves the processing of primary products such as wool, oil, and wheat: *Secondary industries like clothing and food processing are important for the economy.* **3. Secondary** education is the second stage of school, after primary education, usually for children aged between twelve and eighteen.

☑ SPELLING TIP Remember that **secondary** is made up of the word *second* and the suffix *-ary*, although you do not usually hear the *a* in the ending.

second-hand /*say* **sek**-uhnd-hand, sek-uhnd-**hand**/ *adjective* owned and used by someone else before you buy it: *a second-hand bike.*

□ **second-hand** /*say* sek-uhnd-**hand**/, *adverb*: *They bought the car second-hand.*

secret *adjective*
1. done or made without others knowing: *a secret meeting.* **2.** designed to escape notice: *a secret pocket.*
–*noun* **3.** something hidden or concealed. **4.** a mystery: *the secrets of nature.*
–*phrase* **5. in secret**, with no-one else knowing.
□ **secrecy**, *noun* –**secretive**, *adjective* –**secretly**, *adverb*

secretary /*say* **sek**-ruh-tree/ *noun* (*plural* **secretaries**) someone whose job is to write letters, keep records or make telephone calls for an employer.
□ **secretarial** /*say* sek-ruh-**tair**-ree-uhl/, *adjective*

☑ SPELLING TIP Although there is nothing secret about a **secretary**, it will help with the spelling of the word if you think of it as being made up of *secret* and the suffix *-ary* (although you do not usually hear the *a* in the ending). In fact, **secretary** does come from the Latin word for 'secret', and was used originally in the sense of 'a person who is trusted to keep secrets'.

secrete /*say* suh-**kreet**/ *verb*
1. If a part of your body or a plant **secretes** something, it produces it: *The pancreas is a gland that secretes hormones that help in digestion*; *Gum trees secrete a resinous gum.* **2.** If someone or something **secretes** something, they hide it away: *We think the man at the end of the street has got a fortune secreted away somewhere in his house.*

sect *noun* a religious group, especially one which has broken away from a larger group.
□ **sectarian**, *adjective*

section *noun*
1. a part or division of something. **2.** a picture of how something would look if you cut it from top to bottom and showed the inside.

sector *noun*
1. a part of a circle which is between two straight lines going from the centre to the outer edge.
2. a large division or an area of activity: *He used to work in the public sector but now has a job with a private firm.*

secular /*say* **sek**-yuh-luh/ *adjective* If an institution, literature or music is **secular** it is not based on religious or spiritual things: *Some of my friends go to secular schools and some go to church schools*; *a secular wedding.*

secure *adjective*
1. free from care or danger. **2.** firmly fastened or in place. **3.** in safe keeping: *Your secret will be secure with me.*
–*verb* When you **secure** something, you **4.** make it safe from attack, harm or loss: *We secured the house before we left.* **5.** get it after a lot of effort: *We finally secured tickets to the concert.*
□ **securely**, *adverb* –**security**, *noun*: *a feeling of security.*

sedan /*say* suh-**dan**/ *noun* a car with four doors, which seats from four to six people.

WORD HISTORY from a Latin word meaning 'seat'

sedate *adjective*
1. Sedate behaviour is calm and steady: *We walked along at a sedate pace.*
–*verb* **2.** To **sedate** someone is to calm them or put them to sleep by means of sedatives.
□ **sedation**, *noun*

sedative *noun* a drug which lessens pain or excitement.
□ **sedative**, *adjective* calming or soothing.

sediment *noun*
1. solid material that falls to the bottom of a liquid. **2.** in geology, mineral or organic material laid down or deposited by water, ice, or air.
□ **sedimentary**, *adjective* –**sedimentation**, *noun*

A SIMILAR WORD (for definition 1) is **dregs**. However, note that **dregs** is a plural word, while **sediment** is singular.

seduce *verb* If someone **seduces** another person, they persuade that person to have sex with them.
□ **seducer**, *noun* –**seduction**, *noun* –**seductive**, *adjective* –**seductively**, *adverb*

see *verb* (**sees**, **seeing**, **saw**, **has seen**)
1. If you **see** something, you are aware of it when you look at it with your eyes: *Can you see anything without your glasses?* **2.** If you **see** something or why something is a certain way, you understand it or you understand why that is how it is: *I see what you mean.* **3.** If you **see** a film or television show, you watch it. **4.** If you **see** that something is the case, you understand that it is the case after looking at it and thinking about it: *I can see you're tired.* **5.** If you **see** someone, you meet them or visit them: *I have to see the doctor at 6 p.m.*
–*phrase* **6. see through**, **a.** to detect: *She saw through the disguise.* **b.** to stay until the end of: *He always sees a job through.*

☑ SPELLING TIP Don't confuse the spelling of **see** with **sea** which has the same sound but is spelt with *ea*. A **sea** is a large stretch of water.

seed *noun* (*plural* **seeds** *or* **seed**)
1. the part produced by a plant from which a new plant grows. **2. seeds**, the beginnings or start: *the seeds of his doubts.*

seedling *noun* a young plant.

seedy *adjective* (**seedier**, **seediest**)
1. shabby and untidy: *They stayed in a seedy motel which had seen better days.* **2.** *Informal*

unwell: *After eating and drinking so much, he felt quite seedy.*

seek *verb* (**seeks**, **seeking**, **sought**, **has sought**) **1.** To **seek** something or someone is to try to find them: *to seek a cure*; *to seek work.* **2.** To **seek** to do something is to try to do it: *to seek to help.*

seem *verb* If something **seems** to be a certain way, it appears or looks to be that way: *She seems to have put on weight*; *The noise seemed to come from next door.*
☐ **seeming**, *adjective* –**seemingly**, *adverb*

☑ SPELLING TIP Don't confuse the spelling of **seem** with **seam** which has the same sound but is spelt with *ea*. A **seam** is the line where two pieces of material like fabric or metal have been joined together.

seep *verb* To **seep** is to flow out slowly: *Oil was seeping from the engine.*
☐ **seepage**, *noun*

seer *noun* someone who can see into the future.

NOTE This word is used in literature rather than ordinary language.

seesaw *noun*
1. a long piece of wood balanced in the middle, so that the child sitting at one end rises when the child at the other end goes down.
–*verb* **2.** To **seesaw** is to move backwards and forwards between two different conditions: *She has been seesawing between happiness and sadness lately.*

seethe /*say* seedh/ *verb*
1. If water **seethes**, it bubbles and foams: *Through the porthole, we watched the ocean seething.* **2.** If a person **seethes**, they are excited or disturbed: *Mum was seething with anger when she saw what we had done in the kitchen.*

segment *noun* /*say* **seg**-muhnt/
1. a small piece: *a segment of orange.*
–*verb* /*say* seg-**ment**/ **2.** To **segment** something is to separate it into pieces: *She segmented the orange and shared it out.*
☐ **segmentation**, *noun*

segregate *verb* To **segregate** a group of people is to set or keep them apart from others: *Apartheid in South Africa was a system that segregated white people and black people.*
☐ **segregation**, *noun*

seize /*say* seez/ *verb*
1. If you **seize** something, you take hold of it quickly and firmly: *He seized the bag and ran off.* **2.** If a machine **seizes**, it stops working because it gets too hot: *Without oil the engine will seize.*
☐ **seizure**, *noun*

A SIMILAR WORD (for definition 1) is **grab**.

☑ SPELLING TIP *Exception to rule*: remember that **seize** is spelt with *ei*, breaking the rule that *i* comes before *e*, except after *c*.

seldom *adverb* rarely or not often: *It seldom rains here.*

select *verb*
1. If you **select** something, you choose it from a group of similar things.
–*adjective* **2.** carefully chosen: *a select few.* **3.** of special value or excellence: *Only select fruit is sold here.*
☐ **selection**, *noun* –**selective**, *adjective* –**selectively**, *adverb*

self *noun* (*plural* **selves**) Your **self** is you, taking in everything that makes you what you are, such as your body, your mind, your character and your intelligence.

self- *prefix* a word part showing action directed towards yourself, as in *self-service*.

self-confidence *noun* belief in your own ability: *His failure was a blow to his self-confidence.*
☐ **self-confident**, *adjective*

self-contained *adjective*
1. keeping your thoughts to yourself. **2.** having within it all that is necessary: *Their flat is small but self-contained – it has its own kitchen and bathroom.*

self-control *noun* the ability to stop yourself from doing something: *He showed a lot of self-control in not punching back.*
☐ **self-controlled**, *adjective*

self-defence *noun* the ability to protect yourself against attack.

selfie *noun Informal* a photograph someone has taken of himself or herself using a digital device, such as a smart phone, usually with the intention of posting it on a social network.

selfish *adjective* thinking only of your own interests: *a selfish person*; *selfish behaviour.*
☐ **selfishly**, *adverb* –**selfishness**, *noun*

self-raising flour *noun* flour with baking powder already added to it, so that it makes bread or cakes rise.

self-service *adjective* having to do with a shop or restaurant where the customers serve themselves and then pay a cashier.

sell *verb* (**sells**, **selling**, **sold**, **has sold**)
1. If you **sell** something, you exchange it for money: *He sold his bike.* **2.** If a shop, etc., **sells** a particular thing, people can buy it there: *Do you sell envelopes here?*
☐ **seller**, *noun*

semaphore /*say* **sem**-uh-faw/ *noun*
1. a system for signalling messages using flags. –*verb* 2. To **semaphore** is to use the semaphore system for signalling.

☑ SPELLING TIP Remember the *ph* spelling for the 'f' sound. The suffix *-phore* comes from Greek and appears in some scientific words, where it means 'bearing' or 'producing'. It has been added to *sema* which comes from the Greek word for 'signal'.

semen /*say* **see**-muhn/ *noun* liquid containing sperm, which is produced by a male's testicles.

WORD HISTORY from a Latin word meaning 'seed'

semi- *prefix* a word part meaning 'half', as in *semidetached*.

WORD HISTORY this prefix comes from Latin

semibreve *noun* a musical note which is four crotchets long.

semicircle *noun* a half circle.
☐ **semicircular**, *adjective*

semicolon *noun* a mark of punctuation (;) which is used to show more of a break between parts of a sentence than a comma does, as in *He entered the house; he picked up the bag; he left the house*.

SEE the Grammar and Punctuation Guide appendix.

semidetached *adjective* partly separate, used especially about two houses sharing one wall while remaining separate from other buildings.

seminary /*say* **sem**-uhn-ree/ *noun* a college for training Roman Catholic priests.
☐ **seminarian**, *noun*

semiquaver *noun* a musical note which is equal to half a quaver.

semitone *noun* half a tone, or the difference between the notes which are next to each other on the piano.

semitrailer *noun* a large, powerful truck which consists of a motor and cabin to which a long trailer is connected.

semolina /*say* sem-uh-**lee**-nuh/ *noun* the large hard bits of wheat grain left over after the fine flour has been separated, used in making some kinds of pasta and sweet foods.

WORD HISTORY from a Latin word meaning 'fine flour'

senate /*say* **sen**-uht/ *noun*
1. one of the houses of the Australian parliament. 2. one of the law-making bodies in some other countries.
☐ **senator**, *noun*

ANOTHER FORM This is spelt with a capital letter when referring to a particular body: *the Australian Senate*. The related word **senator** is spelt with a capital when writing the title of a particular person.

☑ SPELLING TIP Remember that the ending of **senator** is *or* (not *er*). The *-or* suffix appears in many words that have come from Latin. In ancient Rome the **senators** were the members of the highest ruling body.

send *verb* (**sends**, **sending**, **sent**, **has sent**)
1. If you **send** something to someone, you arrange for it to be given or delivered to them: *I sent him a long letter.* 2. If you **send** someone somewhere, you tell them to go there: *My mother sent me to the shop to buy some food.* 3. If something **sends** you into a particular physical or emotional state, it causes you to get into that state: *Classical music sends him to sleep.*
–*phrase* 4. **send up**, to make fun of, usually by copying: *It is mean of them to send up her accent.*
☐ **sender**, *noun*

senile /*say* **sen**-uyl, **seen**-uyl/ *adjective* weak in body or mind because of old age.
☐ **senility**, *noun*

senior *adjective* If someone is **senior** to someone else, they are older or of greater importance: *the senior students in a school*; *a senior lecturer.*
☐ **senior**, *noun* –**seniority**, *noun*

sensation *noun*
1. feeling: *It was so cold that I lost all sensation in my toes*; *It caused a burning sensation in her mouth*; *I had the strange sensation that I'd been there before.* 2. a cause or feeling of excitement: *The new show is a sensation*; *His surprise announcement caused a sensation.*
☐ **sensational**, *adjective* –**sensationally**, *adverb*

sense *noun*
1. one of the powers or abilities by which we taste, touch, hear, see, and smell: *a sense of smell.* 2. any physical or mental feeling or ability: *a sense of humour*; *a sense of relief.* 3. the ability to think and act sensibly and intelligently: *Show some sense in this situation*; *He has plenty of common sense.* 4. meaning: *I can't get the sense of this paragraph.*
–*verb* 5. If you **sense** something, you become aware of it or realise that it is going to happen: *We sensed that something was wrong.*
☐ **senseless**, *adjective*

sensible *adjective* full of good sense: *What a sensible girl to draw a map before they started.*
☐ **sensibility**, *noun* the ability to feel. –**sensibly**, *adverb*

☑ SPELLING TIP Remember that the ending is the suffix *-ible* (not *-able*). You could think of *i* for *intelligent* to remind yourself.

sensitive *adjective*
1. If someone is **sensitive**, they show an awareness of other people's feelings and needs. **2.** If you are **sensitive** about something, you easily get upset when it is mentioned: *She was sensitive about being short.* **3.** If a subject or issue is **sensitive**, it needs to be handled carefully because strong emotions are involved: *a sensitive issue.*
□ **sensitivity**, *noun* (*plural* **sensitivities**) –**sensitively**, *adverb*

sensory *adjective* having to do with feeling: *For a while after the crash, he had no sensory awareness*; *They have put in a sensory display at the museum, where you smell, touch and listen to things.*

sensual *adjective* having to do with feeling or with your senses: *The cooling swim was a sensual pleasure after the heat of the day.*
□ **sensualist**, *noun* –**sensuality**, *noun* –**sensually**, *adverb*

sentence *noun*
1. a group of words which form a complete statement, question, or exclamation, such as *I rang the bell*. **2.** the punishment of a criminal: *He received a sentence of five years' jail.*
–*verb* **3.** When a judge **sentences** a criminal, he or she decides what their punishment will be: *The judge sentenced him to five years' imprisonment.*

SEE the Grammar and Punctuation Guide appendix (for definition 1).

sentiment /*say* **sen**-tuh-muhnt/ *noun*
1. an attitude or opinion: *Sentiment is growing against the new railway timetable.* **2.** a tender feeling or emotion, as love, pity, etc.: *'There is no room for sentiment in business', the director barked.*

☑ SPELLING TIP *Tricky 'uh' sound*: the vowel sound after the *t* is spelt with an *i*.

sentimental /*say* sen-tuh-**men**-tuhl/ *adjective* showing or having to do with tender feelings, such as pity, romantic love and nostalgia: *sentimental tears*; *a sentimental film.*
□ **sentimentality**, *noun* –**sentimentally**, *adverb*

☑ SPELLING TIP *Tricky 'uh' sound*: the vowel sound after the *t* is spelt with an *i*, as in *sentiment*. Rap this word out as *sen+ti+men+tal*.

sentinel *noun* a soldier who acts as a lookout.

sentry *noun* (*plural* **sentries**) a soldier who stands guard to keep people out.

separate *verb* /*say* **sep**-uh-rayt/
1. If you **separate** two things, you move them or divide them so that they are no longer together: *Separate the white from the yolk of the egg.* **2.** If two or more things or people **separate**, they move apart after having been together for some time: *They walked down the street and separated at the corner.*
–*adjective* /*say* **sep**-ruht/ **3.** not connected: *a separate room.*
□ **separable**, *adjective* –**separately**, *adverb* –**separation**, *noun*

☑ SPELLING TIP *Tricky 'uh' sound*: the middle vowel sound is spelt with an *a*. Try thinking that **separate** has 'a rat' inside it.

September *noun* the ninth month of the year, with 30 days.

THE ABBREVIATION is **Sep** or **Sept**.
WORD HISTORY from a Latin word for the seventh month in the early Roman calendar

septet *noun*
1. any group or set of seven. **2.** a musical piece for seven voices or seven performers.

septic *adjective* infected with germs: *a septic wound.*

sepulchre /*say* **sep**-uhl-kuh/ *noun* a tomb or grave.

NOTE This word is used in literature rather than ordinary language.

☑ SPELLING TIP Remember the *ch* spelling for the 'k' sound and the *re* spelling at the end. It might help if you think of other words which you know well with the same spelling for this sound, such as *centre* and *theatre*.

sequel /*say* **see**-kwuhl/ *noun*
1. a book or film which continues on from an earlier work. **2.** anything which follows or results from something.

sequence /*say* **see**-kwuhns/ *noun* a series of things following each other.
□ **sequential** /*say* suh-**kwen**-shuhl/, *adjective*

☑ SPELLING TIP *Tricky vowel sound*: notice the single *e* spelling for the 'ee' sound in the first syllable. Also remember that there is *qu* for the 'kw' sound.

sequin /*say* **see**-kwuhn/ *noun* a small shiny disc sewn as a decoration onto bags, evening clothes or fancy dress.
□ **sequined**, *adjective*

serenade /*say* se-ruh-**nayd**/ *noun*
1. music traditionally played or sung by a lover under his loved one's window at night.
–*verb* **2.** To **serenade** someone is to play or sing a serenade for them.

☑ SPELLING TIP *Tricky 'uh' sound*: the middle vowel sound is spelt with an *e*. Also remember that there is only one *r*. It is like the word *serene* with the final *e* dropped and *ade* added.

serene *adjective* calm and peaceful.
□ **serenely**, *adverb* –**serenity**, *noun*

☑ SPELLING TIP Remember that the ending is *ene* (not *een*). Some other words with the same spelling for this sound are *convene* and *gangrene*.

serf *noun* someone who in feudal times was not free but was thought of as belonging to the land that a lord owned, and was sold with it.

☑ SPELLING TIP Don't confuse the spelling of **serf** with **surf** which has the same sound. **Surf** is the waves which break along the shore.

sergeant /*say* **sah**-juhnt/ *noun*
1. an officer in the army who ranks next above a corporal. **2.** a police officer of middle rank, just above a constable.

☑ SPELLING TIP This is a particularly tricky word to spell. Remember the unusual *er* spelling in the first syllable for the 'ah' sound, and the fact that there is both an *e* and an *a* in the *eant* ending (which you might think would be just *ent* or *ant*). To remind you, rap it out in three syllables as *ser*+*ge*+*ant*.

serial /*say* **sear**-ree-uhl/ *noun* a story that is published or broadcast regularly in separate parts.
☐ **serial**, *adjective*

☑ SPELLING TIP Don't confuse **serial** with **cereal** which has the same sound. A **cereal** is the breakfast food made from grain.

series /*say* **sear**-reez/ *noun* (*plural* **series**)
1. a number of things or events arranged or happening in a certain order or pattern. **2.** a set of something: *This stamp is one of a series showing famous writers.* **3.** a number of programs on radio or television which are connected in some way, either by subject matter or by being about the same group of people: *Have you been watching that new series about pirates on TV?* **4.** in geology, a division of a system of rocks, marked by sedimentary deposits formed during a geological epoch.

serious /*say* **sear**-ree-uhs/ *adjective*
1. thoughtful and not cheerful: *The judge had a serious expression on his face.* **2.** sincere and not joking: *Is she serious about leaving?* **3.** important or needing a lot of thought: *Getting married is a serious matter.* **4.** giving cause for concern or worry: *The injured man is in a serious condition.*
☐ **seriously**, *adverb* –**seriousness**, *noun*

sermon *noun*
1. a serious talk, usually one preached in church: *Yesterday's sermon was about loving your neighbour.* **2.** a long boring speech: *I got a sermon from my parents on why I should help more around the house.*

serpent *noun Old-fashioned* a snake.

serrated /*say* suh-**ray**-tuhd/ *adjective* having notches or teeth along its edge: *A bread knife has a serrated blade.*
☐ **serrate**, *verb* –**serration**, *noun*

☑ SPELLING TIP *Double letter alert*: double *r*. Think of the 'rough ridges' of a **serrated** edge to remind you.

serum /*say* **sear**-ruhm/ *noun* (*plural* **serums** *or* **sera**) a clear, pale yellow liquid that separates from blood when it clots.

servant *noun* someone who works for or is in the service of someone else.

serve *verb*
1. If you **serve** customers in a shop, you supply them with what they want: *My first job was serving customers in a bookshop.* **2.** If you **serve** food or drink to people, you give it to them: *Dad got up from the table to serve dessert.* **3.** If you **serve** something or someone, you work for them: *to serve your country.* **4.** In tennis and similar ball games, when you **serve**, you throw the ball up in the air and hit it to begin play. **5.** If something **serves** a particular purpose, it is used for that purpose: *This rock can serve as a seat.* **6.** If something **serves** a particular place or people, it supplies their need: *The library serves the school community.*
☐ **serving**, *noun*: *to ask for an extra serving.* –**serve**, *noun*: *a fast tennis serve.*

server *noun*
1. a computer or program which provides services to another computer by a network. **2.** the player who puts the ball in play in tennis and similar games.

service *noun*
1. a helpful act: *We did her a service by mowing the lawn.* **2.** the supplying of something either useful to, or needed by, a large group of people: *a telephone service*; *a bus service.* **3.** a department of public employment or the group of people in it: *the diplomatic service.* **4.** the way food is served: *The service in this restaurant is efficient and polite.* **5.** the act of getting a car or other machinery into good order: *She took the car for a service.* **6.** a religious ceremony: *a church service.* **7.** the act of serving a ball in tennis or similar ball games. **8. the services**, the military armed forces.
–*verb* **9.** To **service** a car or other piece of machinery is to make it fit for use: *The mechanic serviced our car.*

serviceable *adjective* useful: *His work clothes were serviceable and suitable for farm jobs.*
☐ **serviceably**, *adverb*

service provider *noun* See **internet service provider**.

service station *noun* a place where you can buy petrol and oil for motor vehicles, and where mechanical repairs are sometimes carried out.

OTHER TERMS for this are **petrol station** and **garage**.

serviette *noun* a piece of cloth or paper, used during a meal to wipe your lips and hands and to protect your clothes.

OTHER TERMS for this are **napkin** and **table napkin**.

☑ SPELLING TIP *Double letter alert*: double *t*. Note that this is part of the suffix *-ette* that appears in several words that have come from French and usually refers to something that is small or female. Some other words with this ending are *cigarette* (small) and *usherette* (female).

sesame /*say* **ses**-uh-mee/ *noun* a tropical plant, whose small seeds are used for food and oil.

☑ SPELLING TIP *Single letter alert*: only one *s* in the middle. Also remember the single *e* at the end making the 'ee' sound. This word comes from Greek.

session *noun*
1. the sitting or meeting together of a court, council or parliament. **2.** a period of time for any particular activity: *a discussion session.*

set *verb* (**sets**, **setting**, **set**, **has set**)
1. To **set** something in a particular place or position is to put it there: *She set the photo on her desk.* **2.** If something **sets** you doing something, it causes you to start doing it: *His question set me remembering the night of the party.* **3.** If a teacher **sets** an examination, they make up the questions which go into it. **4.** If the sun **sets**, it goes down behind the horizon: *The sun rises in the east and sets in the west.* **5.** If you **set** the table, you put on it the things you will need for the meal, such as knives and forks, plates and glasses. **6.** If something soft or runny **sets**, it becomes hard: *You will have to use the glue quickly before it sets.* **7.** If you **set** something, you change it to what you want: *Have you set the alarm clock?*
–*noun* **8.** a number of things that are used together, or form a collection: *a set of chess pieces.* **9.** a radio or television receiver. **10.** a group of games that make up one of the divisions of a tennis match. **11.** a number of pieces of scenery arranged together, used for a play or film. **12.** in mathematics, any collection of numbers or objects which have something in common.
–*phrase* **13. set off**, **a.** to explode: *to set off a bomb.* **b.** to begin a journey. **14. set out**, **a.** to arrange. **b.** to explain carefully. **c.** to start a journey.
☐ **set**, *adjective*: *a set routine*; *set to go.*

setback *noun* something that holds you back or slows down your progress.

set square *noun* a flat piece of wood or plastic in the shape of a right-angled triangle, used in drawing technical things like plans for buildings.

settee /*say* set-**ee**/ *noun* a long, padded seat for two or more people, with a back and two sides.

OTHER WORDS for this are **couch**, **lounge** and **sofa**.

setting *noun*
1. the surroundings of anything: *The setting was perfect for a murder mystery – grey and forbidding.* **2.** the time and place in which a play or film takes place. **3.** a group of things such as a knife, fork, and plate, used to set someone's place at the table.

settle *verb*
1. If someone or something **settles**, they sink down: *Her head settled into the soft pillows.* **2.** If people **settle** a fight or a disagreement, they put an end to it. **3.** If you **settle** your affairs or your business, you put them in order. **4.** If you **settle** a bill or an account, you pay it. **5.** If you **settle** somewhere, you go there intending to stay for a long time: *The family finally settled on the eastern coast.*
–*phrase* **6. settle down**, **a.** to put to bed. **b.** to begin to do serious work. **c.** to begin to live an ordered life, especially after marrying.
☐ **settlement**, *noun*

settler *noun* someone who settles in a new country: *The early settlers first had to find a water supply.*

set-up *noun*
1. organisation or arrangement: *Once you understand the set-up of the computer files, you will know where to put documents.* **2.** *Informal* something which has been arranged dishonestly. **3.** *Informal* a trap.
☐ **set-up**, *adjective*

seven *noun*
1. a cardinal number, six plus one (6 + 1). **2.** the symbol for this number, as 7 or VII.
☐ **seven**, *adjective* –**seventh**, *adjective*, *noun*

seventeen *noun*
1. a cardinal number, ten plus seven (10 + 7). **2.** the symbol for this number, as 17 or XVII.
☐ **seventeen**, *adjective* –**seventeenth**, *adjective*, *noun*

seventy *noun* (*plural* **seventies**)
1. a cardinal number, ten times seven (10 × 7). **2.** the symbol for this number, as 70 or LXX. **3. seventies**, the numbers from 70 to 79 of a series, especially with reference to the years of a person's age, or the years of a century.
☐ **seventieth**, *adjective*, *noun* –**seventy**, *adjective*

sever /*say* **sev**-uh/ *verb* If you **sever** something or if it is severed, it is cut right off: *to sever communications.*
☐ **severance**, *noun*

several /*say* **sev**-ruhl/ *adjective* not many, but more than two: *After several attempts he gave up.*

☑ SPELLING TIP Remember that the middle vowel is spelt *e* although you usually don't hear it when the word is pronounced. Also remember that the ending is *al* (with one *l* only). Rap it out as *sev+ er+ al*.

severe /*say* suh-**vear**/ *adjective*
1. harsh or extreme: *a severe penalty.* **2.** stern: *a severe expression.* **3.** serious: *severe damage.* **4.** simple, plain, and without decoration: *a severe uniform.*
☐ **severely**, *adverb* –**severity** /*say* suh-**ve**-ruh-tee/, *noun*

sew /*say* soh/ *verb*
1. To **sew** is to make stitches with a needle and thread. **2.** If you **sew** clothes, you make or repair them with a needle and thread.
☐ **sewing**, *noun*

☑ SPELLING TIP Notice the *ew* spelling of this word. Don't confuse it with **so** or **sow**, both of which have the same sound. **So** means 'therefore'. To **sow** seed is to scatter it on the ground.

sewage /*say* **sooh**-ij/ *noun* waste matter, such as human urine and excrement, that is carried away from buildings by underground pipes, etc.: *The pipe was blocked with sewage.*

☑ SPELLING TIP Remember the *ew* for the 'ooh' sound. Also don't confuse this word with **sewerage** (extra *er* in the middle) which is the removal of such matter by pipes.

sewer /*say* **sooh**-uh/ *noun* pipes, usually underground, and linked to other such pipes to carry away waste water and waste matter: *Our cousins in the country have finally had the sewer connected.*

☑ SPELLING TIP Remember the *ew* for the 'ooh' sound.

sewerage /*say* **sooh**-rij/ *noun* the removal of waste water and waste matter using sewers: *The government minister deals with water and sewerage.*

☑ SPELLING TIP *Silent letter alert*: don't forget the *e* following the *w* which you don't hear when the word is pronounced. Also remember the *ew* for the 'ooh' sound. Don't confuse this word with **sewage** which is the waste matter that is taken away by **sewerage**.

sex *noun*
1. one of the two divisions of either male or female in humans and animals. **2.** the characteristic or condition of being either male or female. **3.** See **sexual intercourse**.

sexist *adjective* If someone has a **sexist** attitude, they judge a person by their sex rather than by their own qualities.
☐ **sexism**, *noun* –**sexist**, *noun*

sextant *noun* an instrument which measures the angles between the sun, moon, stars and earth, to help sailors work out their position.

sextet *noun*
1. any group or set of six. **2.** a musical piece for six voices or six performers.

sexual *adjective* having to do with sex.
☐ **sexually**, *adverb* –**sexuality**, *adjective*

sexual harassment *noun* unwanted sexual advances, usually made by a man towards a women, especially in the workplace.

sexual intercourse *noun* a sexual act between two people, usually one in which a man's penis enters a woman's vagina.

OTHER FORMS You can also call this **intercourse** or **sex**.

sexy *adjective* (**sexier**, **sexiest**)
1. attractive in a way that appeals to others sexually. **2.** having a great concern with sex: *a sexy film.* **3.** *Informal* exciting or trendy: *My brother has just bought a sexy new car and everyone wants a ride.*
☐ **sexily**, *adverb*

shabby *adjective* (**shabbier**, **shabbiest**)
1. very worn: *Mum's slippers were looking shabby so we bought a new pair for her birthday.* **2.** wearing old or very worn clothes: *a shabby old man.* **3.** mean or unfair: *That was a pretty shabby trick to hide her clothes while she was swimming.*
☐ **shabbily**, *adverb*

shack *noun* a small roughly built house.

shackle *noun*
1. a ring of iron, usually one of a pair, for holding the wrist or ankle of a prisoner or slave. **2.** anything that stops someone's free thought or action.

shade *noun*
1. a slight darkness or an area of slight darkness caused by the blocking off of rays of light. **2.** a darker or lighter kind of one colour: *His room was painted in several shades of blue.*
–*verb* **3.** If you **shade** something, you protect it from heat or light: *We shaded our eyes against the glare.* **4.** If you **shade** an area in a drawing, you make it darker.
☐ **shady**, *adjective* (**shadier**, **shadiest**)

shadow *noun*
1. the dark figure or dark area made by something blocking out light. **2.** slight darkness from lack of light.
–*verb* **3.** If someone **shadows** you, they follow you to every place you go: *The detective's task was to shadow the suspect.*
☐ **shadowy**, *adjective*

shaft *noun*
1. a long pole or rod: *the shaft of a drill; the shaft of a spear.* **2.** a ray or beam: *a shaft of moonlight.* **3.** a passage that is like a well, or an enclosed

vertical or sloping space: *a lift shaft*; *a mine shaft.*

shaggy *adjective* (**shaggier**, **shaggiest**) If hair or fur is **shaggy**, it is long and untidy: *The dog's eyes were hidden by its shaggy coat.*

shake *verb* (**shakes**, **shaking**, **shook**, **has shaken**)
1. If you **shake** something or someone, you move them sharply backwards and forwards or up and down: *Shake the bottle before drinking the medicine.* **2.** If something **shakes**, it moves sharply backwards and forwards or up and down: *The windows shook when the plane flew by*; *The girls were shaking with laughter.* **3.** If your voice **shakes** when you are angry, afraid or upset, it is unsteady. **4.** If something **shakes** you, it makes you feel upset and unsafe: *The old man looked quite shaken by his fall.* **5.** If something **shakes** your beliefs, you become uncertain about them because of it: *The war shook his faith in human nature.*
□ **shake**, *noun* –**shaken**, *adjective* –**shaky**, *adjective* (**shakier**, **shakiest**) –**shakily**, *adverb* –**shakiness**, *noun*

shale *noun* a rock that breaks easily into flat pieces.
□ **shaly**, *adjective* (**shalier**, **shaliest**)

shall *verb* You can use **shall** **1.** when you are emphasising that you will do a particular thing in the future: *I shall go tomorrow.* **2.** in questions when you are asking someone's advice or opinion about something: *Shall I pour you a juice?*

NOTE This is always used with another verb. See *modal verbs* in the Grammar and Punctuation Guide appendix.

shallot /*say* shuh-**lot**/ *noun* an onion-like plant used for flavouring in cooking and as a vegetable.

shallow *adjective*
1. not very deep: *The shallow end of the pool is for small children.* **2.** without any serious thought: *a shallow argument.* **3.** concerned with unimportant things: *a shallow person.*
–*noun* **4. the shallows**, the shallow part of a river, sea, etc.
□ **shallowness**, *noun*

sham *noun*
1. something that is not what it appears to be.
–*verb* (**shams**, **shamming**, **shammed**, **has shammed**) **2.** To **sham** is to pretend: *He shammed illness to avoid going to school.*

SIMILAR WORDS (for definition 1) are **fraud** and **fake**.

shame *noun*
1. a mentally painful feeling that comes after you know you have said or done something wrong or silly. **2.** a loss of honour: *Their poor behaviour brought shame to the school.* **3.** a pity or something to be sorry about: *It's a shame you can't stay for the party.*
–*verb* **4.** If something **shames** you, it causes you to feel shame: *Their bad manners shamed their parents.* **5.** If you **shame** someone into doing something, you force them to do it by making them feel shame: *He shamed her into apologising.*
□ **shameful**, *adjective* –**shameless**, *adjective*

shampoo *noun*
1. a liquid soap, especially for the hair.
–*verb* (**shampoos**, **shampooing**, **shampooed**, **has shampooed**) **2.** If you **shampoo** your hair, you wash it with shampoo.

shamrock *noun* a bright green plant with three small leaves grouped on one stem: *The Irish contestant had a green jacket with a white shamrock embroidered on the pocket.*

shandy *noun* (*plural* **shandies**) a drink which is a mixture of beer with either ginger beer or lemonade.

shanghai[1] /*say* **shang**-huy, shang-**huy**/ *verb* (**shanghais**, **shanghaiing**, **shanghaied**, **has shanghaied**) To **shanghai** someone is to force them to join a ship as a member of the crew.

WORD HISTORY short for 'to ship to *Shanghai*' (a seaport in China)

shanghai[2] /*say* **shang**-huy/ *noun* See **catapult** (definition 1).

shanty[1] *noun* (*plural* **shanties**) a roughly built hut, cabin, or house.

shanty[2] *noun* (*plural* **shanties**) a sailors' song, usually sung in rhythm to the work they are doing.

shape *noun*
1. the outer form of something or someone. **2.** proper order: *It took us ages to get the house back into shape after the party.* **3.** condition: *The business is in bad shape.*
–*verb* **4.** When you **shape** something, you give it a definite form, shape or character: *The sculptor carefully shaped the neck of the figure.*
–*phrase* **5. shape up**, to develop: *The choir is shaping up well.*
□ **shapely**, *adjective* (**shapelier**, **shapeliest**) –**shapeless**, *adjective*

share *noun*
1. the part given to or owned by someone. **2.** each of the equal parts into which the ownership of a company is divided: *She bought 250 shares in the company.*
–*verb* **3.** When you **share** something with one or more people, you divide it into parts with each person receiving a part: *We shared the lemonade between the five of us.* **4.** When one or more people **share** something, they use it or enjoy it together: *I share a room with my sister.*

shark *noun* any of various kinds of large fish, some of which are very fierce and dangerous to humans, and which have soft skeletons and five to seven pairs of gill openings.

sharp *adjective*
1. having a very thin edge which can cut: *a sharp knife.* 2. having a very fine point: *a sharp needle*; *sharp teeth.* 3. very clear and distinct: *a sharp picture.* 4. alert and quick to notice: *a sharp mind.* 5. keen or sensitive: *a sharp nose*; *sharp ears.* 6. sudden and hard: *a sharp blow.* 7. unpleasant and painful: *a sharp wind*; *a sharp pain*; *sharp pangs of jealousy.* 8. happening suddenly: *a sharp bend in the road.*
–*adverb* 9. exactly: *at three o'clock sharp.*
–*noun* 10. a. a note that is one semitone above a given note. b. the music sign (♯) which raises a note by a semitone when it is placed before it.
☐ **sharply**, *adverb* –**sharpness**, *noun* –**sharpen**, *verb*: *to sharpen a pencil.* –**sharpener**, *noun*

THE OPPOSITE (of definition 10) is **flat**[1] (definition 10).

shashlik *noun* See **shish kebab**.

shatter *verb*
1. If something **shatters**, it breaks into lots of small pieces: *The windscreen of the car was shattered in the accident.* 2. If you say that someone is **shattered** by something, you mean they are so upset by it that they cannot function properly: *He was shattered by the accident.*
☐ **shattering**, *adjective*: *shattering news.*

shave *verb* (**shaves**, **shaving**, **shaved**, **has shaved** *or* **has shaven**)
1. If someone **shaves**, they remove hair by using a razor or an electric shaving device. 2. If you **shave** off part of something, you cut off very thin layers of it.
–*noun in the phrase* 3. **a close shave**, a narrow miss or escape.
☐ **shave**, *noun* –**shaver**, *noun*

shawl *noun* a piece of material worn as a covering for the shoulders or head, usually by women.

she *pronoun* the female being talked about: *Ann was certain – she hated eating bananas.*

SEE ALSO **her** and **hers**.

sheaf *noun* (*plural* **sheaves**)
1. one of the bundles into which cereal plants like wheat and rye are bound after they are cut in the field. 2. any bundle, group or collection: *The swimmer had collected a sheaf of national records.*

shear *verb* (**shears**, **shearing**, **sheared**, **has sheared** *or* **has shorn**)
1. To **shear** a sheep is to cut all the wool off it.
–*noun* 2. **shears**, large scissors or another similar cutting tool.
☐ **shearer**, *noun*

☑ SPELLING TIP Don't confuse the spelling of **shear** with **sheer** which has the same sound but is spelt with *ee*. **Sheer** describes material which is very thin, or something such as cliff that is very steep. To **sheer** is to swerve.

sheath /*say* sheeth/ *noun* (*plural* **sheaths**)
1. a covering for the blade of a sword, knife, and so on. 2. any similar covering.

shed[1] *noun* a simple or roughly built building used for storing equipment or sheltering animals.

shed[2] *verb* (**sheds**, **shedding**, **shed**, **has shed**)
1. To **shed** something liquid is to pour it out or let it fall: *to shed blood*; *to shed tears.* 2. To **shed** light, sound, or a smell is to give or send it out: *The candle shed a soft glow.* 3. To **shed** something is to put or throw it off: *A snake regularly sheds the outer layer of its skin.*

she'd a short form of *she would* or *she had.*

sheep *noun* (*plural* **sheep**) an animal which is kept for its meat and thick wool.

NOTE The male is a **ram**; the female is a **ewe**; the young is a **lamb**.

sheep dip *noun* a deep trough containing a liquid which kills harmful insects on sheep as they are driven through it.

sheepdog *noun* a dog bred to work at rounding up sheep.

sheepish *adjective* embarrassed: *She looked a bit sheepish when her mistake was discovered.*

sheer[1] *adjective*
1. so thin that you can see through it: *The material was so sheer she was worried that people could see straight through.* 2. absolute, or unmixed with anything else: *By sheer good fortune, we got a parking place.* 3. very steep: *We could not see a way to climb up the sheer cliff.*
☐ **sheer**, *adverb* very steeply: *The cliff rose sheer from the sea below.*

☑ SPELLING TIP Don't confuse the spelling of **sheer** with **shear** which has the same sound but is spelt with *ea*. To **shear** a sheep is to cut off its wool.

sheer[2] *verb* To **sheer** is to swerve or change course: *The birds sheered away over the top of the wall.*
☐ **sheer**, *noun* a swerve.

☑ SPELLING TIP See **sheer**[1].

sheet *noun*
1. a large piece of cloth used on a bed, usually one of two, one under you and the other over you. 2. any layer or covering: *a sheet of water.* 3. a broad, thin piece of something: *a sheet of glass*; *a sheet of paper.*

shelf *noun* (*plural* **shelves**)
1. a thin, flat piece of wood, glass, or something similar, fixed horizontally to a wall or in a frame and used for holding things like books, plates

and cups, etc. **2.** a narrow, flat surface: *a shelf of rock.*
☐ **shelving**, *noun*

shell *noun*
1. the hard outer covering of things like nuts, eggs, and certain animals. **2.** something like a shell: *Now that the shell of the building is up, we can see what the finished structure will look like.* **3.** a hollow bullet-like case filled with explosives, to be fired from a large gun.
–*verb* **4.** When you **shell** things like nuts, eggs and peas, you remove the hard outer shell from them: *to shell prawns.*
–*phrase* **5. shell out**, *Informal* to hand over or pay up.

she'll a short form of *she will*.

shellfish *noun* (*plural* **shellfish** *or* **shellfishes**) an animal such as an oyster or lobster which has a shell and lives in water, but is not a fish in the usual sense.

shelter *noun*
1. protection from bad weather, danger and so on: *We took shelter from the storm.* **2.** a place of safety and protection: *a bomb shelter.*
–*verb* **3.** If you **shelter** in a place, you take shelter there: *We sheltered from the storm in a cave.* **4.** If you **shelter** someone, you give them shelter: *Friends and neighbours sheltered the families made homeless by the bushfire.*

shelve *verb* If you **shelve** something, you **1.** place it on a shelf or shelves: *Shelve the books in alphabetical order so we can find them later.* **2.** stop considering or thinking about it: *Let's shelve the problem and have a swim instead.*

shepherd /*say* **shep**-uhd/ *noun*
1. someone who looks after sheep.
–*verb* **2.** If you **shepherd** someone, you take care of them or guard them, especially when moving along: *The teacher shepherded her class onto the train.*

☑ SPELLING TIP *Silent letter alert*: don't forget the silent *h*. Remember that the job of a **shepherd** is to herd sheep, so the word is made up of *shep* (*sheep* with one *e* dropped) and *herd*.

sherbet *noun* a sweet, fizzy powder that you can eat dry or use to make a fizzy drink.

WORD HISTORY from an Arabic word meaning 'a drink'

sheriff *noun*
1. in Australia, an officer of the law who has duties such as organising juries. **2.** in America, the person in charge of making certain the laws are obeyed in a particular area.

☑ SPELLING TIP *Double/single letter alert*: only one *r* and double *f* at the end. Think of a 'fighting fit **sheriff**' to remind you of the double letter.

sherry *noun* (*plural* **sherries**) a strong sweet or dry wine.

she's a short form of *she is* or *she has*.

shield /*say* sheeld/ *noun*
1. a flat piece of metal, leather, or wood, carried to protect your body in war. **2.** anything used for protection: *He wore several layers of clothes as a shield against the freezing cold.*
–*verb* **3.** If you **shield** yourself from something, you protect yourself with a shield or something you are using as a shield: *He shielded his eyes with his hands.*

☑ SPELLING TIP Remember the *ie* spelling for the 'ee' sound. This follows the rule that *i* comes before *e* except after *c*.

shift *verb*
1. If you **shift** something, you move it from one place to another.
–*noun* **2.** a change or move: *a shift in the wind's direction.* **3.** the period of work done by each group of workers in a place, such as a hospital, which operates day and night: *My mother works the night shift on the hospital telephones.* **4.** a straight, narrow dress.

shifty *adjective* (**shiftier**, **shiftiest**) deceitful, untrustworthy: *I didn't like his shifty eyes.*

shilling *noun* a silver coin, used in the past in Australia and Britain.

shimmer *verb* If something **shimmers**, it shines or gleams with a soft, unsteady light.

shin *noun*
1. the front part of the leg between the knee and the ankle.
–*verb* (**shins**, **shinning**, **shinned**, **has shinned**) **2.** To **shin** up something is to climb it using your hands and your feet: *He shinned up the tree to get a better view.*

shine *verb* (**shines**, **shining**, **shone** *or* **shined**, **has shone**)
1. If something **shines**, it gives out a light: *a light shining in the darkness.* **2.** If you **shine** a light somewhere, you point or direct it there in order to see something: *She shone the torch around the room.* **3.** If you **shine** something such as metal or shoes, you polish them: *She shined the silver dish until it sparkled.*
–*phrase* **4. shine at**, to be very good at: *She can't dance but she shines at ball games.*
☐ **shine**, *noun* –**shiny**, *adjective* (**shinier**, **shiniest**)

SIMILAR WORDS (for definition 1) are **glow** and **gleam**.

☑ SPELLING TIP Note that **shine** loses its *e* when the adjective **shiny** is formed.

shingle *noun* a thin piece of wood, slate and so on, used in rows to cover the roofs and sides of houses.

shingles *noun* a painful skin disease which affects the nerves in the body.

ship *noun*
1. a large boat for carrying people or goods over deep water.
–*verb* (**ships**, **shipping**, **shipped**, **has shipped**)
2. To **ship** goods is to send them by ship, train or truck.

shipment *noun* a load of goods shipped at one time.

shipshape *adjective* neat: *Make sure your room is shipshape before the visitors come.*

shiralee /*say* shi-ruh-**lee**, **shi**-ruh-lee/ *noun* See **swag**.

shire *noun* a local government area.

shirk *verb* If you **shirk** something, you get out of doing it: *Nobody shirked their duty – they all worked ten hours a day.*
☐ **shirker**, *noun*

shirt *noun* a piece of clothing for the upper part of the body, usually with buttons down the front, a collar, and long or short sleeves.

shish kebab *noun* small pieces of meat cooked on a skewer, usually with vegetables such as onion and capsicum.

> OTHER WORDS for this are **kebab** and **shashlik**.
> WORD HISTORY from the Turkish words for 'skewer' and 'roast meat'

shiver *verb* To **shiver** is to shake with fear, cold or excitement.
☐ **shiver**, *noun* –**shivery**, *adjective*

shoal[1] *noun* a bank of sand under shallow water.

shoal[2] *noun* a group of fish swimming together.

shock[1] *noun*
1. a sudden and violent fright or upset. 2. pain and injury caused by an electric current passing through the body.
–*verb* 3. If you **shock** someone, you cause them to to feel sudden fright or disgust.
☐ **shocking**, *adjective*: *shocking news.*

shock[2] *noun* a thick, bushy mass: *an unruly shock of black hair.*

shoddy *adjective* (**shoddier**, **shoddiest**) bad or made badly: *It was a pretty shoddy table – it fell apart when any weight was on it.*
☐ **shoddily**, *adverb* –**shoddiness**, *noun*

shoe *noun*
1. a covering, usually made of leather, for your foot.
–*verb* (**shoes**, **shoeing**, **shod**, **has shod**) 2. To **shoe** a horse is to attach new shoes to its hoofs.
–*phrase* 3. **in someone's shoes**, in the position or situation of another: *I wouldn't like to be in his shoes.*

shoot *verb* (**shoots**, **shooting**, **shot**, **has shot**)
1. If someone **shoots**, they fire a bullet from a gun: *Hands up or I'll shoot!* 2. If someone **shoots** someone or something, they kill or injure them with a bullet from a gun or with some other weapon. 3. To **shoot** a film is to make it. 4. If someone or something **shoots** somewhere, they go there very quickly and suddenly: *When she left, he shot after her.*
–*noun* 5. a new growth on a plant.
☐ **shooter**, *noun*

shop *noun*
1. a building where goods are sold.
–*verb* (**shops**, **shopping**, **shopped**, **has shopped**) 2. If you **shop**, you buy things from a shop.
–*phrase* 3. **shop around**, to visit a number of shops comparing quality and price before buying. 4. **talk shop**, to discuss your trade, profession, or business.
☐ **shopping**, *noun* –**shopkeeper**, *noun*

shoplift *verb* If someone **shoplifts**, they steal goods from a shop while pretending to be a customer.
☐ **shoplifter**, *noun* –**shoplifting**, *noun*

shore *noun* the land along the edge of a sea, lake, large river, etc.

> ☑ SPELLING TIP Don't confuse the spelling of **shore** with **sure** which has the same sound. If someone is **sure** of something, they are certain or confident of it.

short *adjective*
1. not long: *a short piece of string*; *a short time.* 2. not tall. 3. angry in your speech: *He was short with me after the argument.* 4. not having enough: *We are short of water.*
–*adverb* 5. If someone or something stops **short**, they stop suddenly: *We stopped short when we came to the cliff.* 6. If something falls **short**, it does not go the full length: *The ball fell short of the goal.*
–*noun* 7. **shorts**, short trousers, not reaching below your knee.
–*phrase* 8. **cut short**, to interrupt, or end suddenly. 9. **in short**, in a few words. 10. **short for**, being a shortened form of: *'Email' is short for 'electronic mail'.*
☐ **shorten**, *verb* –**shortness**, *noun*

shortage *noun* a lack in amount: *With the sudden rain, there was a shortage of umbrellas.*

shortbread *noun* a thick biscuit made with a lot of butter.

short circuit *noun* a fault in an electrical circuit causing the current to flow between two points only instead of through the whole circuit.

shortcoming *noun* a failure or fault: *His major shortcoming is a lack of modesty.*

short cut *noun* a shorter or quicker way: *The taxi driver knew the area well and took a short cut to our place.*

shortening *noun* fat, such as butter, margarine, or lard, used in making pastry.

shorthand *noun* a system of fast writing using lines, curves and dots instead of letters.
☐ **shorthand**, *adjective*

shortly *adverb* soon: *The train will be leaving shortly.*

short-sighted *adjective*
1. A **short-sighted** person is not able to see things clearly that are far away. **2.** A plan that is **short-sighted** does not take the future into account: *a short-sighted policy.*
☐ **short-sightedness**, *noun*

ANOTHER WORD (for definition 1) is **myopic**. This a more formal, technical word.

short-tempered *adjective* A **short-tempered** person becomes angry easily.

shot *verb*
1. the past tense and past participle of **shoot**.
–*noun* **2.** the shooting of a gun, bow, or other weapon: *He hit the target with his first shot.* **3.** bullets or other lead ammunition. **4.** the heavy metal ball thrown in shot-put contests. **5.** a stroke or throw in sports: *a shot at goal.* **6.** *Rather informal* a try, attempt or guess. **7.** an injection: *a tetanus shot.* **8.** a photograph: *I took some shots with my new camera.*
–*phrase* **9. like a shot**, immediately, or very quickly.

shotgun *noun* a gun that fires a lot of small bits of metal, used for shooting animals.

shot-put /*say* **shot**-poot/ *noun*
1. the sport of throwing a heavy metal ball as far as possible. **2.** the ball itself.
☐ **shot-putter**, *noun* –**shot-putting**, *noun*

should /*rhymes with* wood/ *verb*
1. If you **should** do something, you ought to do it: *We should go home now.* **2.** You use **should** in questions when you are asking for advice or information: *Who should I talk to about my exams?* **3.** You use **should** when you are giving advice about something: *I should ring her if I were you.*

NOTE **Should** is the past tense of **shall**. It is always used with another verb. See *modal verbs* in the Grammar and Punctuation Guide appendix.

shoulder /*rhymes with* holder/ *noun*
1. the part of the body that joins the neck to the arm.
–*verb* **2.** If you **shoulder** someone or something, you push them with your shoulder: *He shouldered the opposition player out of the way.* **3.** If you **shoulder** something, you support or carry it on your shoulders: *to shoulder a load.*
–*phrase* **4. give the cold shoulder to**, to ignore or treat coldly.

shoulderblade *noun* the flat bone that forms the back part of the shoulder.

ANOTHER WORD for this is **scapula**, which is the more formal, medical term.

shouldn't a short form of *should not*.

shout *verb* To **shout** is to call or cry out loudly.
☐ **shout**, *noun*

SIMILAR WORDS are **yell**, **bellow** and **roar**.

shove /*say* shuv/ *verb* To **shove** is to push roughly.
☐ **shove**, *noun*

shovel /*say* **shuv**-uhl/ *noun*
1. a tool with a wide, flat metal part on a long wooden handle, used for moving material such as sand and soil.
–*verb* (**shovels**, **shovelling**, **shovelled**, **has shovelled**) **2.** If you **shovel** something, such as sand or soil, you move it with a shovel.

☑ SPELLING TIP Remember that this word comes from *shove* (meaning 'to push') where *ove* spells the 'uv' sound, the same as in *love*. **Shovel** ends with a single *l*, but this is doubled when you add *-ed* or *-ing*.

show *verb* (**shows**, **showing**, **showed**, **has showed** *or* **has shown**)
1. If something **shows** that a particular thing is the case, it gives information that makes people understand this: *This picture of our house shows that it has a red roof; His exam result showed that he hadn't studied enough.* **2.** If you **show** something to someone, you give it to them or you lead them to it so that they can see it: *Show me your new dress.* **3.** If you **show** someone how to do something, you do it for them or explain it to them: *I'll show you how to ride a bicycle.* **4.** If you **show** someone somewhere, you lead them there: *The waiter showed them to their seats.* **5.** If you **show** a particular emotion or feeling, you behave in a way that allows others to see how you feel: *to show affection.*
–*noun* **6.** a public showing or exhibition: *an art show.* **7.** an entertainment, such as a play or television program. **8.** a false showing or pretence: *He was bored but he made a show of interest.*
–*phrase* **9. show off**, **a.** to show proudly: *He showed off his new bike.* **b.** to behave so as to get attention or praise for yourself: *Stop showing off!* **10. show up**, **a.** to make stand out clearly: *White clothes show up dirt.* **b.** to appear or arrive: *He didn't show up till after dinner.* **c.** to reveal: *The shoddy work showed up his carelessness.*
☐ **showy**, *adjective*: *a showy display of bright flowers.* –**showiness**, *noun* –**showily**, *adverb*

A SIMILAR WORD (for definitions 1, 6 and 8) is **display**.

showdown *noun* an open showing of disagreements, in order to clear up a situation: *The coach had a showdown with Col after he was late for training three sessions in a row.*

shower *noun*
1. a brief fall of rain. **2.** a fall of anything in large numbers: *a shower of sparks*; *a shower of questions.* **3.** the part of a bathroom where you stand to wash yourself: *He stood in the shower.* **4.** the use of such a shower to wash yourself: *I'll have a shower before dinner.*
–*verb* **5.** If you **shower** someone or something, you wet them with a shower: *He showered us with the hose.* **6.** When you **shower**, you wash yourself in a shower. **7.** To **shower** someone with things is to give them a lot of those things: *She was showered with compliments after her performance.*
☐ **showery**, *adjective*

show-off *noun* someone who behaves so as to get attention or praise.

showroom *noun* a room where goods for sale are shown.

shrapnel *noun* the small parts of an exploded cannon shell or other projectile weapon: *A piece of shrapnel lodged in his leg.*

WORD HISTORY named after the inventor H *Shrapnel* (1761–1842), an officer in the British army

shred *noun*
1. a narrow strip cut or torn off: *The curtains were ripped to shreds by the gale.* **2.** a very small bit: *There's not a shred of food in the house*; *The police did not find a shred of evidence against her.*
–*verb* (**shreds**, **shredding**, **shredded**, **shred**, **has shredded** *or* **has shred**) **3.** If you **shred** something, you cut or tear it into shreds: *to shred carrots.*
☐ **shredder**, *noun* –**shredded**, *adjective*: *shredded paper.*

shrew *noun*
1. a small, long-nosed mammal that looks like a mouse, and eats insects. **2.** a very bad-tempered woman.
☐ **shrewish**, *adjective*

NOTE If you use this word (as in definition 2) to describe someone, you will offend them.

shrewd *adjective* clever, and with good practical judgement: *a shrewd businessperson.*
☐ **shrewdly**, *adverb* –**shrewdness**, *noun*

A SIMILAR WORD is **astute**.

shriek /*say* shreek/ *noun*
1. a loud, sharp, high noise: *a shriek of excitement*; *the shriek of a whistle.*
–*verb* **2.** When you **shriek**, you utter a shriek: *The children shrieked with laughter when the clown tripped over.*

☑ SPELLING TIP *Tricky vowel pair*: *ie* spelling for the 'ee' sound, following the rule that *i* comes before *e*, except after *c*.

shrill *adjective* A **shrill** sound or voice is loud and high.
☐ **shrilly**, *adverb* –**shrillness**, *noun*

shrimp *noun* a kind of prawn.

shrine *noun* a sacred or holy place: *a shrine of remembrance for those killed in the war.*

shrink *verb* (**shrinks**, **shrinking**, **shrank**, **has shrunk** *or* **has shrunken**)
1. If something **shrinks**, it becomes smaller: *Woollen clothes shrink if washed in hot water.* **2.** If someone **shrinks** back, they draw back: *The timid kitten shrank away from my hand.*
☐ **shrinkable**, *adjective* –**shrinkage**, *noun*

shrivel *verb* (**shrivels**, **shrivelling**, **shrivelled**, **has shrivelled**) To **shrivel** is to dry up and wrinkle: *The seedlings shrivelled under the scorching sun*; *She has shrivelled with age.*

shroud *noun*
1. a cloth for wrapping a dead body in. **2.** something which covers and hides like a cloth: *a shroud of secrecy.*
–*verb* **3.** To **shroud** is to cover or hide: *Thick dark clouds shrouded the stars.*

shrub *noun* a small, low, tree-like plant.
☐ **shrubby**, *adjective* (**shrubbier**, **shrubbiest**)

shrug *verb* (**shrugs**, **shrugging**, **shrugged**, **has shrugged**) If you **shrug**, you raise and lower your shoulders to show doubt, scorn or lack of interest.
☐ **shrug**, *noun*

shudder *verb* To **shudder** is to shake suddenly from fear or cold.
☐ **shudder**, *noun*

shuffle *verb*
1. If you **shuffle**, you move along slowly without lifting your feet: *The old man shuffled across the road.* **2.** If you **shuffle** cards, you move them so as to change their order.
☐ **shuffle**, *noun* –**shuffler**, *noun*

shun *verb* (**shuns**, **shunning**, **shunned**, **has shunned**) If you **shun** someone or something, you avoid them: *She shuns the noisy bus and prefers to walk to school.*

shunt *verb*
1. To **shunt** a train is to move it from one line of rails to another: *The train was to be shunted to the yards for maintenance.* **2.** To **shunt** someone aside is to turn them aside or out of the way: *He was shunted from the top job to a lower position.*
–*noun* **3.** the act of shunting; a move. **4.** in

medicine, a tube inserted into the body to connect two liquid-carrying structures that are not normally connected.

shut *verb* (**shuts**, **shutting**, **shut**, **has shut**)
1. If you **shut** something that is open, you close it: *Shut the window*; *She finished reading the book and shut it*; *He shut his eyes.*
–*phrase* **2. shut down**, to close down or stop for a while: *The service station shuts down at night.* **3. shut in**, to keep in: *to shut a bird in a cage.* **4. shut off**, to stop the flow of: *to shut off electricity.* **5. shut out**, to keep out or bar: *She shut him out of her room.* **6. shut up**, *Informal* to stop talking.
☐ **shut**, *adjective*: *The door's shut*; *The shop is shut for the night.*

shutter *noun*
1. a movable wooden cover for the outside of a window. **2.** a part of a camera which opens and shuts over the lens to allow light through to the film.
☐ **shuttered**, *adjective*

shuttle *noun*
1. the part of a loom that carries the thread backwards and forwards in weaving. **2.** a frequent transport service running directly between two points. **3.** See **space shuttle**.

ANOTHER TERM (for definition 2) is **shuttle service**.
WORD HISTORY from an Old English word meaning 'a dart' or 'an arrow'

shuttlecock *noun*
1. a thin rounded piece of plastic with feathers attached to it, which is hit from one player to another over a net as a game. **2.** this game.

shy *adjective* If someone is **shy**, they feel **1.** anxious or not relaxed with other people. **2.** easily frightened.
–*verb* (**shies**, **shying**, **shied**, **has shied**) **3.** If an animal **shies**, it moves suddenly back or aside: *The pony shied when the fireworks went off.*
☐ **shyly**, *adverb* –**shyness**, *noun*

A SIMILAR WORD (for definition 1) is **bashful**; (for definition 2) **timid**.

sibling *noun* a brother or sister.

sick *adjective*
1. If you are **sick**, you are ill or have a disease. **2.** If you feel **sick**, you feel like vomiting. **3.** You can use **sick** to refer to something that is for sick people: *sick leave.* **4.** If a story or joke is **sick**, it treats disgusting things in a light manner: *a sick sense of humour.*
–*phrase* **5. be sick**, to vomit. **6. be sick of**, to be annoyed or fed up with: *I am sick of your complaining.*
☐ **sickness**, *noun* –**sicken**, *verb* –**sickening**, *adjective*

OTHER WORDS (for definition 2) are **nauseous** and **nauseated**.

sick bay *noun* the place that you go to if you are ill or injured while you are at school.

sickie *noun Informal* a day taken off work with pay or off school because of real or pretended sickness.

sickle *noun* a curved, short-handled tool for cutting grass or grain.

sickly *adjective* (**sicklier**, **sickliest**)
1. unhealthy or getting sick easily: *He was a sickly man who seemed to catch any disease around.* **2.** having to do with sickness: *We noticed the sickly smell as soon as we went into the room.* **3.** making you feel sick: *The new drink had too much sugar in it and was quite sickly.*
☐ **sickliness**, *noun*

side *noun*
1. one of the outer edges or lines of something, usually not the top, bottom, front, or back: *the side of a car*; *the side of a square.* **2.** one of the two surfaces of a material like paper or cloth: *You can write on both sides of the paper.* **3.** either half of the body: *I've got a pain in my side.* **4.** the space next to someone or something: *She stood at his side.* **5.** one of two or more groups that are against each other: *Whose side are you on?* **6.** a position or way of thinking about something: *to look at a question from all sides.* **7.** a part or area: *the south side of a city.*
–*verb in the phrase* **8. side with** (or **against**), to place yourself with or against a side or a party to support or oppose an issue.
☐ **side**, *adjective*: *a side door.*

sideboard *noun* a piece of furniture with shelves and drawers for holding things like plates and cups.

sideshow *noun* a small show that is part of a larger fair or circus.

sidestep *verb* (**sidesteps**, **sidestepping**, **sidestepped**, **has sidestepped**) If you **sidestep** something, you **1.** step to one side to avoid it: *Everybody sidestepped the squashed thing on the footpath.* **2.** avoid it: *Angela sidestepped the problem and thought about other things.*

sideways *adverb*
1. from or to the side of something: *to look sideways.* **2.** with the side going first or forwards: *A crab moves sideways.*
☐ **sideways**, *adjective*: *a sideways glance.*

sidle *verb* If you **sidle**, you move sideways, usually hoping not to be noticed: *The singer made a joke about the people who were sidling into the hall late.*

siege /*say* seej/ *noun* the surrounding of a place in order to capture it: *The castle was under siege for weeks but the king would not surrender.*

☑ SPELLING TIP *Tricky vowel pair*: *ie* spelling for the 'ee' sound, following the rule that *i* comes before *e*, except after *c*.

siesta /*say* see-**es**-tuh/ *noun* a rest in the middle of the day.

WORD HISTORY this word comes from Spanish and originally from a Latin word meaning 'sixth (hour)' or 'midday'

sieve /*say* siv/ *noun*
1. a container with holes at the bottom, used for straining liquids or separating thick from thin, or large from small.
–*verb* **2.** When you **sieve** a liquid or powder, you pass it through a sieve: *to sieve the flour.*

ANOTHER WORD (for definition 2) is **sift** (definition 1).

☑ SPELLING TIP *Tricky vowel sound*: Although the spelling of **sieve** follows the rule that *i* comes before *e* except after *c*, you have to concentrate on remembering the *ie* because the sound you hear is 'i'.

sift *verb*
1. If you **sift** something, such as flour, you put it through a sieve in order to make it smooth and fine. **2.** If you **sift** something, you search through it very carefully: *to sift the evidence.*

ANOTHER WORD (for definition 1) is **sieve** (definition 1).

sigh *verb* If you **sigh**, you let out a deep breath, sometimes as a release of tension or an expression of pleasure or sadness: *She sighed with relief.*
□ **sigh**, *noun*

sight *noun*
1. the ability to see. **2.** something which is seen or should be seen: *The full moon rising was a beautiful sight.*
–*verb* **3.** When you **sight** someone or something, you get sight of them: *We sighted several horses on the other side of the river*; *to sight land.*
–*phrase* **4. a sight**, something that looks strange or unattractive: *He looked a sight, all covered in mud.* **5. in sight of**, in a position where it is possible to see: *The weary walkers were finally in sight of home.* **6. on sight**, as soon as you see a thing.
□ **sighting**, *noun*: *a sighting of a famous actor.*

ANOTHER WORD (for definition 1) is **vision** (definition 1).

☑ SPELLING TIP Don't confuse the spelling of **sight** with **site** which has the same sound. A **site** is the land where something is built or where something has happened.

sightseeing *noun* travelling around an area looking at objects and places of interest.

sign /*say* suyn/ *noun*
1. anything that shows that something exists or is likely to happen: *Sailors know that birds are a sign that land is near.* **2.** a mark, figure, or symbol used to stand for a word, idea, or mathematical value: *a dollar sign*; *an equals sign.* **3.** a movement that expresses an idea or feeling: *She made a sign for me to follow her.* **4.** a notice that gives information, warns or advertises: *a 'danger' sign.*
–*verb* **5.** To **sign** a document is to write your signature on it: *to sign a card.*
–*phrase* **6. sign up, a.** to enter the military services. **b.** to take on by a signed agreement: *The club signed up two new players.*

☑ SPELLING TIP Remember the *g* in **sign**. Don't confuse it with **sine** which is a mathematical term used in trigonometry. In **sign** the letter combination *ign* gives the 'uyn' sound. It comes from the Latin word *signum*. If you remember this, you will be able to spell other words which have *sign* in them, such as *design* and *resign*.

signal /*say* **sig**-nuhl/ *noun*
1. any action or object that warns, points a direction, or gives an order: *The bell was our signal to leave*; *a traffic signal.* **2. signals**, the waves by which sound or pictures are sent in radio and television.
–*verb* (**signals**, **signalling**, **signalled**, **has signalled**) **3.** When you **signal** to someone, you make a signal to them: *He signalled for me to join him.* **4.** If you **signal** something, you make it known by a signal: *She signalled her impatience by tapping her foot.*

signature /*say* **sig**-nuh-chuh/ *noun*
1. the way you write your own name. **2.** in music, the sign or signs written at the beginning of a piece of music to tell its key and time.

☑ SPELLING TIP *Tricky 'uh' sound*: the middle vowel sound is spelt *a*. Think of the word *nature* which is hidden in this word.

signet *noun* a raised engraved design used as an official stamp or set into a finger ring.

significant /*say* sig-**nif**-uh-kuhnt/ *adjective*
1. important: *a significant event in a country's history.* **2.** full of meaning: *a significant look.*
□ **significantly**, *adverb* –**significance**, *noun*

signify /*say* **sig**-nuh-fuy/ *verb* (**signifies**, **signifying**, **signified**, **has signified**) To **signify** something is to **1.** be a sign of it: *Fever signifies illness.* **2.** make it known by signs: *He signified his anger with a frown.*
□ **signification**, *noun*

silence *noun*
1. absence of any sound or noise.
–*verb* **2.** When you **silence** someone or something, you stop them talking or making a sound: *She tapped her glass to silence the audience before she began speaking.*

silent *adjective*
1. To be **silent** is to be soundless: *The room was silent as she entered.* **2.** If someone is **silent**, they do not speak: *I asked him a question but he remained silent.* **3.** A letter is **silent** if it is not pronounced: *In the word 'knee' the letter 'k' is silent.*
☐ **silently**, *adverb*

silhouette /*say* sil-ooh-**et**/ *noun* a drawing which has an outer line filled in with black, like a shadow.

☑ SPELLING TIP *Silent letter alert*: don't forget the silent *h* following the single *l*. Another difficulty is the *ou* spelling for the 'ooh' sound. As the *ette* ending tells you, this word comes from French. It is named after a French author and politician, Etienne de *Silhouette* (1709–1767).

silicon *noun* an element found in minerals and rocks, used in making such things as glass and steel.

silk *noun* a soft, shiny cloth made from the threads of the cocoon of the silkworm.
☐ **silk**, *adjective* –**silken**, *adjective* –**silky**, *adjective* (**silkier**, **silkiest**) –**silkiness**, *noun*

silk-screen *noun*
1. a way of printing in which ink is passed over a stencil attached to a screen of silk or other fine cloth.
–*verb* **2.** If you **silk-screen** material, you print it using the silk-screen technique.

silkworm *noun* a kind of caterpillar which spins a fine, soft thread to make a cocoon.

sill *noun* a flat piece of wood or other material beneath a window or door.

silly *adjective* (**sillier**, **silliest**) foolish or stupid.
☐ **silliness**, *noun*

SIMILAR WORDS are **idiotic**, **inane**, **nonsensical**, **ridiculous** and **senseless**.

silo /*say* **suy**-loh/ *noun* (*plural* **silos**) a tower-like building for storing grain.

WORD HISTORY from a Greek word for a pit to keep grain in

silt *noun* earthy matter like very fine sand which is carried by running water and then left behind as sediment.

silver *noun*
1. a white metal used for making things like jewellery, coins, etc. **2.** things made from silver or similar metal, such as coins or knives and forks: *With the silver and our best glasses, the table was a grand sight.*
☐ **silver**, *adjective* –**silvery**, *adjective*

silverfish *noun* (*plural* **silverfish** *or* **silverfishes**) a small wingless insect which feeds on paper and some fabrics, and so damages books and household goods.

SIM card *noun* a card in a mobile phone that allows the identification of that phone from its signals and the correct directing of other signals to it.

WORD HISTORY short for *Subscriber Identity Module*

similar *adjective* having a general likeness: *The children are wearing similar clothes*; *Your bike is similar to mine, but not exactly the same.*
☐ **similarity**, *noun* –**similarly**, *adverb*

simile /*say* **sim**-uh-lee/ *noun* a figure of speech which points out a likeness between two generally unlike things, as in the sentences *She swims like a fish*, and *He's as cunning as a fox.*

COMPARE this with **metaphor**.

☑ SPELLING TIP *Tricky 'uh' sound*: the vowel sound after the *m* is spelt with an *i*, so an *i* appears on either side of the *m*. If you relate this word to **similar** you will get a clue to the spelling. Drop the *ar* ending and just add an *e* (not *ee* or *ie*) to get **simile**.

simmer *verb*
1. To **simmer** something is to cook it in a liquid just below boiling point. **2.** If someone **simmers**, they are full of strong, barely controlled feelings: *Everyone was simmering with anger by the time he finished speaking.*
–*phrase* **3. simmer down**, to become calm or calmer.

simper *verb* If you **simper**, you smile in a silly or unnatural way: *She is so annoying the way she sits there simpering at the teacher!*
☐ **simper**, *noun*

simple *adjective*
1. If something is **simple**, it is easy to do or to understand. **2.** If something is **simple**, it is plain rather than decorative or complicated: *a simple black dress*; *to lead a simple life.* **3.** If you say someone is **simple**, you mean that they are mentally weak. **4.** The **simple** form of a verb is the most basic one-word form: *'Sat' is the simple past tense of 'sit'.*
☐ **simpleness**, *noun* –**simplicity**, *noun*

SEE the Grammar and Punctuation Guide appendix (for definition 4).

simpleton *noun Rather old-fashioned* a foolish person.

simplify *verb* (**simplifies**, **simplifying**, **simplified**, **has simplified**) To **simplify** something is to make it easier or more simple.
☐ **simplification**, *noun*

simplistic *adjective* so simple as to lose accuracy: *She gave a simplistic account of the causes of the war.*
☐ **simplistically**, *adverb*

simply *adverb*
1. in a plain or easy to understand way: *He spoke simply*; *She dressed simply.* **2.** merely: *He's not ill, he's simply resting.* **3.** completely: *He is simply terrible in the role of Hamlet.*

simulate /*say* **sim**-yuh-layt/ *verb*
1. If you **simulate** a behaviour, you make a pretence of it: *She simulated helplessness to get people's attention.* **2.** To **simulate** something is to imitate or make a copy of it: *Outside the pool shop was an artificial waterfall flowing down simulated sandstone rocks.*
☐ **simulator**, *noun* a device used in training or experiments that simulates movement or flight. –**simulation**, *noun*

simulcast /*say* **sim**-uhl-kahst/ *noun* a program broadcast on both television and radio at the same time.

> ☑ SPELLING TIP Remember the *ul* spelling in the middle of this word. It will help if you see that **simulcast** is formed by a blend of the words *simultaneous* and *broadcast*.

simultaneous /*say* sim-uhl-**tay**-nee-uhs/ *adjective* happening at the same time.
☐ **simultaneously**, *adverb*

> ☑ SPELLING TIP Notice the *eous* (not *ious*) ending. **Simultaneous** things happen at the 'same time' – words that both end with *e* so that may remind you of the *eous* ending.

sin *noun*
1. an act or behaviour which is strongly disapproved of by society or which breaks a religious law.
–*verb* (**sins**, **sinning**, **sinned**, **has sinned**) **2.** If someone **sins**, they do something which is believed to be a sin.
☐ **sinful**, *adjective*

since *adverb*
1. from then until now: *We have been good friends ever since we started school.* **2.** between a particular past time and the present time: *He refused at first, but has since agreed.*
–*preposition* **3.** counting from: *since noon.*
–*conjunction* **4.** because: *Since you like animals so much we will go to the zoo.*
–*phrase* **5. long since**, a long time ago: *The park has long since gone – there is a block of flats there now.*

sincere *adjective* having and expressing true feelings, saying what you mean.
☐ **sincerity**, *noun* –**sincerely**, *adverb*

sinew /*say* **sin**-yooh/ *noun* a cord of strong body substance joining a muscle to a bone.

> ANOTHER WORD for this is **tendon**.

sing *verb* (**sings**, **singing**, **sang**, **has sung**) When you **sing**, you use your voice to produce words to a tune: *See if you can sing this song.*
☐ **singer**, *noun* –**singing**, *noun*

singe /*say* sinj/ *verb* If you **singe** something, you burn it slightly.

single *adjective*
1. If you refer to a **single** thing, you are referring to only one thing: *a single reason.* **2.** If someone is **single**, they are not married. **3.** If you describe something as being **single**, you mean that it is for one person only: *a single room in a hotel.*
–*verb in the phrase* **4. single out**, to choose alone: *They singled her out for praise.*
☐ **single**, *noun* –**singleness**, *noun*

single-handed *adverb* by working alone: *She wrote the computer program single-handed.*
☐ **single-handedly**, *adverb*

singlet /*say* **sing**-luht/ *noun* a piece of clothing which looks like a sleeveless T-shirt.

singsong *adjective* with a regular up-and-down pattern in the tone: *The singsong music in the background was driving Dad crazy.*

singular *noun*
1. If a noun is in the **singular**, it indicates that there is only one thing. For example, the singular of *houses* is *house* and the singular of *children* is *child*.
–*adjective* **2.** If something is **singular**, it is unusual: *a person of singular appearance.*
☐ **singularly**, *adverb* –**singularity**, *noun*

> SEE the Grammar and Punctuation Guide appendix (for definition 1).

sinister *adjective* suggesting a threat of evil: *a sinister laugh*; *a sinister figure.*

sink *verb* (**sinks**, **sinking**, **sank**, **has sunk**)
1. If something **sinks**, it goes down gradually, especially in water: *The ship sank to the bottom of the ocean*; *We sank to our knees so that we could not be seen.* **2.** If you **sink** something, you cause it to go down, usually in water: *They sometimes sink old ships to make artificial reefs for fish.*
–*noun* **3.** a basin with a water supply and drain, especially in a kitchen.
–*phrase* **4. sink in**, to become understood: *The importance of her news at last sank in.*
☐ **sunken**, *adjective*: *a sunken ship.*

sinker *noun* a weight, usually of lead, for making a fishing line sink below the surface.

sinuous /*say* **sin**-yooh-uhs/ *adjective* winding like a snake: *the sinuous course of an old river bed.*

sinus /*say* **suy**-nuhs/ *noun* one of the hollow cavities in the skull, connecting with the nose.

sip *verb* (**sips**, **sipping**, **sipped**, **has sipped**) To **sip** a liquid is to drink it in small mouthfuls.
☐ **sip**, *noun*

siphon /*say* **suy**-fuhn/ *noun*
1. a tube through which liquid flows up over the edge of a higher container to a lower one, using

the force of gravity to draw the water out at the lower end.
–*verb* **2.** If you **siphon** a liquid, you pass it through a siphon: *We siphoned the water from the tub of the broken washing machine.*

ANOTHER SPELLING is **syphon**.
WORD HISTORY from a Greek word meaning a 'pipe'

sir *noun*
1. a respectful or formal word used when speaking to a man. **2. Sir**, the title of a man who has been knighted.

sire *noun* the male parent of an animal.

siren *noun* a device that makes a loud warning sound, used on ambulances, police cars, and so on.

sissy *noun* (*plural* **sissies**) *Informal* a coward.

sister *noun*
1. a female relative who has the same parents as you. **2.** *Old-fashioned* a fully qualified nurse. **3.** a nun.
☐ **sisterhood**, *noun*

sister-in-law *noun* (*plural* **sisters-in-law**)
1. the sister of someone's husband or wife. **2.** the wife of someone's brother. **3.** the wife of the brother of someone's husband or wife.

sit *verb* (**sits**, **sitting**, **sat**, **has sat**)
1. If you **sit**, you put your buttocks on a surface such as a chair or seat and support your body there: *Sit down – there's a chair over there.* **2.** If something **sits** somewhere, it rests there: *He left his plate sitting on the table in the dining room.*
–*phrase* **3. sit around**, to spend time wastefully: *He spent the entire holiday sitting around watching television.* **4. sit for**, **a.** to do: *to sit for an exam.* **b.** to pose for: *to sit for a photograph.*
☐ **sitting**, *noun*

site *noun*
1. the piece of land on which something is or will be built: *The house was specially designed for the sloping site.* **2.** a place where something happens or has happened: *the site of the battle.* **3.** See **website**.

☑ SPELLING TIP Don't confuse the spelling of **site** with **sight** which has the same sound. Your **sight** is your ability to see things.

situate *verb* To **situate** something is to place it in a position: *Early settlers situated their camps on banks of rivers; The hospital is situated on the outskirts of the town.*

situation *noun*
1. a position in relation to the surroundings: *The house has a good situation on the side of a hill.* **2.** a state of affairs: *This situation is very worrying.*

☑ SPELLING TIP Remember that there is neither a *ch* nor a *sh* spelling in this word but there are two separate *t*'s. The first *t* with the following *u* gives a 'chooh' sound, and the second *t* forms part of the *tion* ending which gives a 'shuhn' sound.

six *noun*
1. a cardinal number, five plus one (5 + 1). **2.** a symbol for this number, as 6 or VI.
☐ **six**, *adjective* –**sixth**, *adjective*, *noun*

sixteen *noun*
1. a cardinal number, ten plus six (10 + 6). **2.** a symbol for this number, as 16 or XVI.
☐ **sixteen**, *adjective* –**sixteenth**, *adjective*, *noun*

sixty *noun* (*plural* **sixties**)
1. a cardinal number, ten times six (10 × 6). **2.** a symbol for this number, as 60 or LX. **3. sixties**, the numbers from 60 to 69 of a series, especially with reference to the years of a person's age, or the years of a century.
☐ **sixtieth**, *adjective*, *noun* –**sixty**, *adjective*

size *noun*
1. the length, height and breadth of something. **2.** the degree to which something is small or large: *the size of the problem.*
–*verb in the phrase* **3. size up**, to judge the worth or nature of: *Anna quickly sized up the situation and decided that more help was needed.*

sizeable *adjective* quite big.
☐ **sizeably**, *adverb*

sizzle *verb* To **sizzle** is to make a sound while frying: *The bacon is sizzling in the pan.*

skate *noun*
1. a boot with a blade attached to the bottom, which you wear to move on ice. **2.** a rollerskate.
–*verb* **3.** When you **skate**, you move swiftly wearing skates: *to skate on ice.*
☐ **skater**, *noun*

skateboard *noun* a narrow, wooden board on rollerskate wheels, on which you stand to ride.

skein /*say* skayn/ *noun* a length of thread or yarn wound in a coil.

☑ SPELLING TIP *Exception to rule*: this word does not fit in with the rule that says *i* comes before *e* except after *c*. This is because that rule only works when the sound is 'ee' as in *believe*. Notice that in **skein** the sound is 'ay' so the rule does not apply.

skeleton /*say* **skel**-uh-tuhn/ *noun* all the bones of a human or animal body, connected together.
☐ **skeletal** /*say* **skel**-uh-tuhl, skuh-**lee**-tuhl/, *adjective*

WORD HISTORY from a Greek word meaning 'dried up'

☑ SPELLING TIP *Tricky 'uh' sound*: the middle vowel sound is spelt *e*. Don't 'let on' but there is a **skeleton** inside each one of us, just as the words *let on* are hidden inside the word **skeleton**.

sketch *noun* (*plural* **sketches**)
1. a drawing or painting done roughly or quickly.
2. any rough plan.
–*verb* 3. When you **sketch** something, you make a sketch of it: *to sketch a design.*
□ **sketchy**, *adjective* (**sketchier**, **sketchiest**)

skewer *noun*
1. a long pin of wood or metal, especially one for holding meat while it is being cooked.
–*verb* 2. If you **skewer** something, you push a skewer through it.

ski *noun*
1. one of the two long, thin pieces of metal, wood or plastic onto which you fix your boots so as to move about on snow.
–*verb* (**skis**, **skiing**, **ski'd** *or* **skied**, **has ski'd** *or* **has skied**) 2. When you **ski**, you travel on or use skis.
□ **skier**, *noun*

skid *verb* (**skids**, **skidding**, **skidded**, **has skidded**) If a vehicle **skids**, it slides forward or sideways in an uncontrolled way because its wheels are not holding firmly to the road surface: *The car skidded on the sandy track.*
□ **skid**, *noun*

skill *noun* the ability to do something well.
□ **skilful**, *adjective* –**skilfully**, *adverb* –**skilfulness**, *noun* –**skilled**, *adjective*

☑ SPELLING TIP Note that **skill** loses one of its *l*'s when the adjective **skilful** is formed. And, as usual, the suffix *-ful* (meaning 'full of') is spelt with one *l*. So be a **skilful** speller and remember that the *l* is single both times it appears in this word.

skillet *noun* a small frying pan.

skim *verb* (**skims**, **skimming**, **skimmed**, **has skimmed**)
1. If you **skim** something, you remove its top layer: *to skim the cream off the milk.* 2. If something **skims** a surface, it moves quickly just above it, or just lightly touching it: *The birds skimmed the surface of the lake.* 3. If you **skim** something, such as a book or newspaper, you read through it very quickly, without paying much attention to the detail.

skim milk *noun* milk from which the cream has been removed.

ANOTHER FORM is **skimmed milk**.

skimpy *adjective* (**skimpier**, **skimpiest**) hardly big enough: *Mum said Jo's clothes were too skimpy.*
□ **skimp**, *verb* –**skimpily**, *adverb* –**skimpiness**, *noun*

skin *noun*
1. the outer covering of an animal or human.
2. any surface layer: *banana skin.*
–*verb* (**skins**, **skinning**, **skinned**, **has skinned**)
3. If you **skin** something, you remove the skin from it: *to skin a banana.* 4. If you **skin** part of your body, you injure it by scraping off some of the skin: *I skinned my knee when I fell off my bike.*

skin cancer *noun* See **melanoma**.

skindiving *noun* underwater swimming for which you use a snorkel, mask and flippers.
□ **skindiver**, *noun*

skink *noun* any of many different lizards, usually small and with smooth scales.

skin name *noun* a name which identifies an Aboriginal person to a particular kinship group.

ANOTHER NAME for this is **kinship name**.

skinny *adjective* (**skinnier**, **skinniest**) very thin.
□ **skinniness**, *noun*

skip *verb* (**skips**, **skipping**, **skipped**, **has skipped**)
1. If you **skip**, you spring or jump lightly from one foot to the other. 2. If you **skip** with a rope, you jump over a moving rope. 3. If you **skip** something, you leave it out: *I skipped the introduction and started reading the first chapter*; *You shouldn't skip breakfast.*
□ **skip**, *noun*: *a hop, skip and jump.*

skipper *noun* the captain of a ship or a team.

skirmish *noun*
1. a small battle. 2. any short exchange of arguments between people: *There were a number of skirmishes between the pop star and the photographers.*

WORD HISTORY from a German word for 'shield'

skirt *noun* a piece of outer clothing, worn by women and girls, that hangs from the waist.

skirting board *noun* a board running around a room at the base of the walls.

skit *noun* a short play or other piece of writing which makes fun of something.

skite *Informal*
–*noun* 1. someone who boasts a lot.
–*verb* 2. If someone **skites**, they boast a lot: *He is always skiting about how good he is at swimming.*

skittle *noun*
1. a bottle-shaped piece of wood, that people try and knock down with a ball as part of a game.
2. **skittles**, this game.
–*verb* 3. To **skittle** something or someone is to knock them over: *That motorbike almost skittled me.*

skivvy *noun* (*plural* **skivvies**) a close-fitting piece of clothing of knitted material, with long sleeves and a high collar.

skulk *verb* If someone **skulks**, they stay nearby, trying not to let anyone know they are there, often for an evil or cowardly reason: *Did you see anyone skulking around the place earlier?*

skull *noun* the bony structure of the head, enclosing the brain and supporting the face.

skullcap *noun* a cap with no brim, fitting closely to the head, especially one worn by a Jewish man or boy.

ANOTHER WORD for this, when worn by a Jewish person, is **yarmulke**.

skunk *noun* a small, furry, North American animal that frightens off its attackers by letting out a bad smell.

WORD HISTORY from a Native American language

sky *noun* (*plural* **skies**) the area of the clouds or the upper air.

skydiving *noun* the sport of falling from an aircraft for some distance before opening a parachute.
☐ **skydiver**, *noun*

skylight *noun* a flat window in a roof, designed for letting light in.

skyscraper *noun* a very tall building, especially an office block.

slab *noun* a large, flat piece: *a concrete slab.*

slack *adjective*
1. loose: *a slack rope.* **2.** not willing to work or be active: *They were too slack to help with the painting.*
☐ **slackly**, *adverb* –**slacken**, *verb* –**slackness**, *noun*

slacks *plural noun* long trousers.

slag *noun* the waste material from a mine, or from metal-bearing rock when it is melted down.

slalom /*say* **slay**-luhm, **slah**-luhm/ *noun* a skiing race with a winding course.

slam *verb* (**slams**, **slamming**, **slammed**, **has slammed**)
1. If a door **slams** or if you **slam** a door, it shuts very noisily and with a lot of force. **2.** If you **slam** an object somewhere, you put it there with a lot of force.

slander *noun*
1. a false spoken statement which damages someone's reputation or good name.
–*verb* **2.** To **slander** someone is to speak slander about them.
☐ **slanderous**, *adjective*

COMPARE this with **libel**, but note that nowadays, in the Australian legal system, there is no difference between libel and slander – they are both simply regarded as defamation.

slang *noun* informal language that is not acceptable in formal use.
☐ **slangy**, *adjective* (**slangier**, **slangiest**)

slant *noun*
1. a slope. **2.** an appearance or point of view: *His account gave a different slant to the morning's events.*
–*verb* **3.** If something **slants**, it slopes: *His handwriting slants backwards*; *Sunlight slanted through the branches.* **4.** If facts or information are **slanted**, they are presented in a way that favours a particular point of view or attracts a particular type of people: *a slanted account of the accident*; *The book is slanted towards tourists.*
☐ **slanted**, *adjective* –**slantwise**, *adverb*

slap *noun*
1. a quick hit, especially with the open hand.
–*verb* (**slaps**, **slapping**, **slapped**, **has slapped**)
2. To **slap** someone is to give them a slap.

slapstick *noun* rough and noisy comedy.

slash *verb* To **slash** something is to **1.** cut it violently and unevenly: *I slashed my foot on a piece of broken bottle*; *The election posters had been slashed with a knife.* **2.** reduce it greatly: *to slash prices.*
☐ **slash**, *noun* –**slasher**, *noun*

slat *noun* a long strip of wood or metal: *the slats of a blind.*

slate *noun* a dark bluish-grey rock which breaks easily into flat pieces and is used on roofs and floors.

slaughter /*say* **slaw**-tuh/ *verb*
1. If people are **slaughtered**, they are murdered in large numbers, often in a violent way: *The invading army slaughtered innocent civilians.* **2.** If animals are **slaughtered**, they are killed for their meat: *to slaughter cattle.*
☐ **slaughter**, *noun*

☑ SPELLING TIP *Tricky vowel sound*: the first vowel sound is spelt *augh* (although it sounds like 'aw'). It might help if you think of other words with the same spelling for this sound, such as *naughty* and *daughter*.

slave *noun*
1. someone who works without being paid and is the prisoner of someone else.
–*verb* **2.** To **slave** is to work very hard, like a slave.
☐ **slavery**, *noun* –**slavish**, *adjective*

slay *verb* (**slays**, **slaying**, **slew**, **has slain**) To **slay** someone is to kill them violently.

sleazy *adjective* (**sleazier**, **sleaziest**) If a person or place is **sleazy**, they are untidy and dirty.
☐ **sleaziness**, *noun*

sledge *noun* a vehicle designed to slide over the snow.

ANOTHER WORD for this is **sled**.

sledgehammer *noun* a large, heavy hammer.

sleek *adjective* smooth and shiny: *sleek fur.*
☐ **sleekness**, *noun*

sleep *verb* (**sleeps**, **sleeping**, **slept**, **has slept**)
1. To **sleep** is to rest with your eyes closed and your mind unconscious: *I slept well last night.*
–*phrase* **2. sleep in**, to sleep later than usual.
☐ **sleep**, *noun* –**sleepy**, *adjective* (**sleepier**, **sleepiest**) –**sleepiness**, *noun* –**sleepless**, *adjective*: *a sleepless night.*

sleeper *noun*
1. a wooden, concrete, or metal beam on which railway lines rest. **2.** a small ring worn in a pierced ear to prevent the hole from closing.

sleepover *noun* a night spent at a friend's home: *James had a sleepover and invited ten friends.*

sleet *noun*
1. rain mixed with snow or hail.
–*verb* **2.** When it **sleets**, rain mixed with snow or light hail falls.

sleeve *noun* the part of a piece of clothing that covers the arm.
☐ **sleeveless**, *adjective*

sleigh /*sounds like* slay/ *noun* a vehicle with two long pieces of wood or metal instead of wheels, for travelling over the snow, especially one pulled by animals.

OTHER WORDS for this are **sled** and **sledge**.

☑ SPELLING TIP *Tricky vowel sound*: the vowel sound is spelt *eigh* (although it sounds like 'ay'). It might help if you think of other words with the same spelling for this sound, such as *eight* and *weigh*. Don't confuse the spelling of **sleigh** with **slay** which has the same sound. To **slay** someone is to kill them.

slender *adjective* thin; having only slight thickness: *a slender girl*; *a slender branch.*
☐ **slenderness**, *noun*

sleuth /*rhymes with* tooth/ *noun* a detective.

☑ SPELLING TIP *Tricky vowel sound*: the vowel sound is spelt *eu* (although it sounds like 'ooh').

slice *noun*
1. a piece of food which has been cut from a larger piece: *slice of meat*; *a slice of bread.*
–*verb* **2.** When you **slice** something, you cut it into slices: *to slice bread.*
☐ **sliced**, *adjective*

slick *adjective*
1. Someone who is **slick** has an attractive and smooth manner, but is not sincere: *a slick salesman.* **2.** If something such as a play or film is **slick**, it is well-made but does not have deep meaning.
–*noun* **3.** a shiny patch of oil on water.

slide *verb* (**slides**, **sliding**, **slid**, **has slid**)
1. To **slide** is to move along smoothly: *He slid the drawer open*; *to slide down the slope.*
–*noun* **2.** a sliding movement: *She slipped on the wet floor and went for a slide.* **3.** a transparent photograph which can be shown on a screen using a projector. **4.** a thin sheet of glass used for holding things that you look at under a microscope.

slight *adjective*
1. If something is **slight**, there is only a small amount of it: *He walks with a slight limp*; *She doesn't have the slightest interest in sport.* **2.** If someone is **slight**, their body is small compared to other people.
–*verb* **3.** If you **slight** someone, you ignore them or treat them rudely by not giving them your attention.
–*noun* **4.** an insult.
☐ **slightly**, *adverb*: *slightly late.*

slim *adjective* (**slimmer**, **slimmest**)
1. thin: *a slim boy*; *slim legs.* **2.** slight; not great or large: *a slim chance.*
–*verb* (**slims**, **slimming**, **slimmed**, **has slimmed**) **3.** To **slim** is to lose weight by diet and exercise.

slime *noun* slippery wet matter, usually unpleasant: *Slugs leave a trail of slime.*
☐ **slimy**, *adjective* (**slimier**, **slimiest**) –**sliminess**, *noun*

☑ SPELLING TIP Note that **slime** loses its *e* when the adjective **slimy** is formed.

sling *noun*
1. a piece of cloth looped around your neck to support your arm if it is injured. **2.** an old-fashioned weapon for throwing stones, made of a leather strap which is swung quickly round and round before releasing the stone.
–*verb* (**slings**, **slinging**, **slung**, **has slung**) **3.** If you **sling** something, you throw it, usually in a careless way: *to sling a stone*; *to sling a coat across your shoulders.*

slingshot *noun* See **catapult** (definition 1).

slink *verb* (**slinks**, **slinking**, **slunk**, **has slunk**) If someone or something **slinks**, they creep quietly so as not to be noticed: *He slunk away when he realised that he was in big trouble.*

slip *verb* (**slips**, **slipping**, **slipped**, **has slipped**)
1. If you **slip**, your foot slides on something smooth and you lose your balance. **2.** If something **slips**, it suddenly slides away from its previous position: *The wet soap slipped from my hands.* **3.** If you **slip** something somewhere, you slide it there quickly: *She slipped the note into her bag.* **4.** If you **slip** somewhere, you go there quickly and not for very long: *I'll just slip upstairs and wash my hands.*

–*noun* **5.** a mistake: *to make a slip in adding up the bill.* **6.** a petticoat. **7.** a small sheet or piece: *a slip of paper.*
–*phrase* **8. let slip**, to say or reveal without meaning to.

slipper *noun* a soft, comfortable shoe for wearing indoors.

slippery *adjective* so smooth or oily that it is hard to hang onto or to walk or drive on without sliding.

slippery dip *noun* a steeply sloping, smooth metal structure which children slide down for play.

ANOTHER TERM for this is **slippery slide**.

slit *noun*
1. a long, straight cut or opening.
–*verb* (**slits**, **slitting**, **slit**, **has slit**) **2.** If you **slit** something, you cut it apart or open it along a line: *to slit open an envelope.*

slither *verb* To **slither** is to slide along like a snake.

sliver /*rhymes with* river/ *noun* a small thin piece: *a sliver of wood.*

slob *noun Informal* someone who is lazy, coarse and very untidy.

NOTE This word is used as an insult.
WORD HISTORY from an Irish word meaning 'mud'

slobber *verb* To **slobber** is to let saliva flow from your mouth, especially over food.
☐ **slobbery**, *adjective*

slog *verb* (**slogs**, **slogging**, **slogged**, **has slogged**)
1. If you **slog** something, such as a ball, you hit it hard.
–*phrase* **2. slog away at**, to work very hard at.
☐ **slog**, *noun*: *a hard slog.*

slogan /*say* **sloh**-guhn/ *noun* a clever saying that gets people's attention, used to advertise something.

slop *verb* (**slops**, **slopping**, **slopped**, **has slopped**) If you **slop** a liquid, you make it fall out of a container in a careless way: *He slopped his drink into the saucer.*

slope *noun*
1. a line or surface which is higher at one end than the other; a line or surface that is neither horizontal nor vertical: *the floor had a gentle slope*; *climbing the steep slope.* **2.** the angle of a sloping line or surface: *a slope of 20 degrees*; *the slope of a roof.* **3. slopes**, a hilly area near a mountain range: *It is raining on the eastern slopes.*
–*verb* **4.** To **slope** is to be higher at one end than the other: *The hill slopes steeply.*
☐ **sloping**, *adjective*

sloppy *adjective* (**sloppier**, **sloppiest**)
1. wet and runny: *sloppy mud.* **2.** too sentimental: *It was such a sloppy film we were all crying in the end – or laughing!* **3.** loose or untidy: *sloppy clothes*; *She has a sloppy approach to her work.*
☐ **sloppily**, *adverb* –**sloppiness**, *noun*

slosh *verb*
1. If you **slosh** a liquid, you pour, stir, or spread it in a careless way: *I sloshed the bucket of water onto the path.* **2.** To **slosh** is to walk through a liquid, making it fly about noisily: *to slosh around in the mud.*

slot *noun* a small narrow hole or opening: *I pushed the letter through the slot.*

sloth /*rhymes with* both, cloth/ *noun*
1. great laziness. **2.** a slow, clumsy mammal which lives in the jungles of South America.
☐ **slothful**, *adjective*

slouch *verb* To **slouch** is to walk or sit without holding yourself up straight.
☐ **slouching**, *adjective*: *a slouching walk.*

slouch hat *noun* an army hat made of soft felt with the brim designed to be turned up on one side.

slovenly /*say* **sluv**-uhn-lee/ *adjective* dirty, careless and untidy.
☐ **slovenliness**, *noun*

slow *adjective*
1. If someone or something is **slow**, they take a long time: *a slow train.* **2.** If a clock or watch is **slow**, it is behind the right time: *My watch is two minutes slow.*
–*verb* **3.** If someone or something **slows**, they get slower: *He slowed down towards the end of the race.*
☐ **slowly**, *adverb* –**slowness**, *noun*

sludge *noun* soft muddy substance: *After the floods, the houses were filled with sludge.*
☐ **sludgy**, *adjective*

slug[1] *noun*
1. a creature like a snail but without a shell. **2.** a small bullet.

slug[2] *verb* (**slugs**, **slugging**, **slugged**, **has slugged**) *Informal* To **slug** someone is to **1.** hit them hard: *I wanted to slug the bully on the nose.* **2.** charge them far too much: *They slugged us for the tickets, but I really wanted to see the show.*
☐ **slug**, *noun*

ANOTHER WORD (for definition 1) is **slog** (definition 1).

sluggish *adjective* moving slowly with no energy.
☐ **sluggishly**, *adverb* –**sluggishness**, *noun*

sluice /*say* sloohs/ *noun* a channel for water, fitted with a gate to control the water flow.

☑ SPELLING TIP *Tricky vowel sound*: the vowel sound is spelt *ui* (although it sounds like 'ooh'). Also remember the *ce* (not *s* or *se*) ending.

slum *noun* a dirty, overcrowded part of a city in which poor people live.
☐ **slummy**, *adjective* (**slummier**, **slummiest**)

slumber *noun*
1. deep sleep.
–*verb* **2.** To **slumber** is to sleep deeply.

NOTE This word is used in literature rather than ordinary language.

slump *verb* To **slump** is to drop heavily and loosely: *to slump into a chair.*

slur *noun*
1. unclear sound or speech. **2.** harm done to someone's good name, often caused by an unkind or unjust remark: *a slur on his reputation.*
–*verb* (**slurs**, **slurring**, **slurred**, **has slurred**) **3.** If you **slur** your speech, you pronounce words in a way that is not clear.

slush *noun* snow which is partly melted.
☐ **slushy**, *adjective*

sly *adjective* tricky or deceitful.
☐ **slyly**, *adverb*

smack[1] *verb in the phrase* **smack of**, to have a touch of: *Her reaction smacked of jealousy.*
☐ **smack**, *noun*

smack[2] *verb*
1. If you **smack** something or someone, you hit them with your open hand.
–*phrase* **2. smack your lips**, to make a noise with your lips as if you are looking forward to eating something good.
☐ **smack**, *noun*

small *adjective*
1. not large: *The house is quite small but it's comfortable.* **2.** not great in importance or value: *It's only a small problem, nothing to worry about.*
–*phrase* **3. small letters**, letters of the alphabet which are not capitals, as *a*, *b*, *c*, etc.
☐ **smallish**, *adjective*

SIMILAR WORDS (for definition 1) are **little**, **tiny** and **minute**. Both **tiny** and **minute** describe something that is extremely small.
ANOTHER TERM for **small letters** (definition 3) is **lower case**.

smallpox *noun* a serious infectious disease with a rash which leaves deep scars.

smart *adjective*
1. If someone is **smart**, they are clever or intelligent. **2.** If clothes are **smart**, they are tidy and fashionable.
–*verb* **3.** If a cut **smarts**, it stings or hurts.
☐ **smartly**, *adverb* –**smarten**, *verb*: *to smarten yourself up.*

smart phone *noun* a mobile phone with access to the internet and which can be used like a personal computer.

ANOTHER FORM of this is **smartphone**.

smash *verb*
1. If you **smash** something, you break it by dropping it, knocking it or throwing it: *The burglars entered the house by smashing the glass in the kitchen window.* **2.** If something **smashes**, it breaks, making a loud noise: *The plate smashed into tiny pieces as it hit the cement floor.*
–*noun* **3.** a loud noise of something hitting. **4.** a recording, film, or play that is a great success.

ANOTHER TERM (for definition 4) is **smash-hit**.

smear *noun*
1. a dirty mark or stain: *a smear of paint.* **2.** something bad said about you.
–*verb* **3.** If you **smear** a surface, you rub or spread something dirty on it: *She smeared the glass with her greasy fingers.* **4.** If you **smear** someone, you say bad things about them: *to smear his good name.*

smell *noun*
1. what you sense through your nose: *a sense of smell*; *food with a strong smell.*
–*verb* (**smells**, **smelling**, **smelt** *or* **smelled**, **has smelt** *or* **has smelled**) **2.** If you **smell** something, you sense it through your nose: *I can smell the sea.* **3.** If something **smells**, it gives off a smell: *Dinner smells delicious*; *This milk smells bad.* **4.** If you say that something **smells**, you can mean that it has a bad smell: *Your feet smell.*
☐ **smelly**, *adjective* (**smellier**, **smelliest**)

SIMILAR WORDS are **odour**, **scent**, **fragrance**, **aroma** and **bouquet**. Note that **odour** and **scent**, like **smell**, can refer to a smell that is neither good nor bad. **Odour** can also refer to a bad smell (*the odour of unwashed bodies*), while **scent** can refer to a pleasant smell (*the scent of flowers*). **Fragrance**, **aroma** and **bouquet** all refer to pleasant smells; a **fragrance** is a sweet smell (*the fragrance of perfume*), an **aroma** is a special smell (*the aroma of fresh coffee*), and a **bouquet** is the special smell of wine.

smelt *verb* To **smelt** ores like iron is to melt or refine them in order to obtain their valuable metal.
☐ **smelter**, *noun* the place where this is done.

smile *verb* If you **smile**, you show that you are happy or amused by curving the corners of your mouth upwards.
☐ **smile**, *noun*

smirk *verb* To **smirk** is to smile in a condescending or knowing way.
☐ **smirk**, *noun*

smith *noun* someone who makes things out of metal.

NOTE This word is usually found in combination with another word which shows which metal the person works with, as in *goldsmith, silversmith* and *blacksmith* (a blacksmith makes things out of iron).

smithereens /*say* smidh-uh-**reenz**/ *plural noun* tiny pieces: *My new glass ornament has broken into smithereens.*

☑ SPELLING TIP *Tricky 'uh' sound*: the middle vowel sound is spelt *e* (altogether there are three *e*'s in this word). Apart from this, you should be able to work out the spelling of **smithereens**. The origin of this unusual word is not known.

smock *noun* a long, loose shirt worn on top of your clothes to stop them getting dirty.

smog *noun* a dirty cloud of smoke and fog.
□ **smoggy**, *adjective*

WORD HISTORY formed by blending *smoke* + *fog*

smoke *noun*
1. the cloud of gas and tiny particles given off when something burns: *The fire in the mountains filled the air with smoke.*
–*verb* **2.** If something is **smoking**, it gives off smoke: *The fire is smoking.* **3.** If someone **smokes** a cigarette or cigar, they breathe in its smoke while holding it between their lips.
–*phrase* **4. go** (or **end**) **up in smoke**, **a.** to be burnt up completely. **b.** to end or disappear without coming to anything: *His career ended up in smoke.*
□ **smoky**, *adjective* (**smokier**, **smokiest**)

smokescreen *noun* anything used to hide the truth or what you are really doing: *Her excuse was simply a smokescreen.*

smoking ceremony *noun* an Aboriginal ceremony in which green leaves from local plants are burnt, creating smoke which is said to cleanse and heal the area, as, for example, when someone has died.

smooth *adjective*
1. If a surface is **smooth**, it is even, with no bumps or lumps. **2.** If a liquid is **smooth**, it has an even consistency, with no lumps in it. **3.** If someone is **smooth**, their manner is so polished and polite that they can seem not sincere: *a smooth talker.*
–*verb* **4.** When you **smooth** something, you make it level or even: *They smoothed the ground for the new oval.*
□ **smoothly**, *adverb*

THE OPPOSITE (of definition 1) is **rough**.

smorgasbord /*say* **smaw**-guhz-bawd/ *noun* a meal where you help yourself to a great variety of food laid out on a table.

☑ SPELLING TIP This word is unusual because it comes from Swedish where it means 'sandwich board'. The main thing to remember is that the ending is *bord* (without the *a* that appears in the English word *board*).

smother /*rhymes with* brother/ *verb*
1. If you **smother**, you die because you cannot get enough air. **2.** If you **smother** something with some substance or material, you cover it all over with it: *She smothered her cake with cream.* **3.** If you **smother** someone with love or attention, you give them too much of it. **4.** If you **smother** a fire, you put it out by covering it with something so that it cannot get any oxygen.

smoulder /*rhymes with* folder/ *verb* To **smoulder** is to burn slowly giving off smoke but no flame.

SMS *noun*
1. a message in words or a shortened form of words, sent to someone's mobile phone where it can be read on the screen of the phone.
–*verb* (**SMS's**, **SMS'ing**, **SMS'ed**, **has SMS'ed**) **2.** To **SMS** a message or information is to send it by an SMS. **3.** To **SMS** someone is to send them an SMS: *I'll SMS you about the date of the party.*

OTHER TERMS (for definition 1) are **SMS message** and **text message**.
WORD HISTORY short for *Short Messaging Service*

smudge *noun*
1. a dirty mark or stain without a clear edge.
–*verb* **2.** If you **smudge** something, you mark it with a smudge: *I smudged polish on the windscreen when I was cleaning the car.* **3.** If something is **smudged**, it is marked with a smudge or smudges: *The firefighter's face was smudged with soot.*

smug *adjective* If someone is **smug**, they are very pleased with themselves: *You were right, but there's no need to be so smug about it!*
□ **smugly**, *adverb*

WORD HISTORY from a Dutch word meaning 'neat'

smuggle *verb* To **smuggle** something somewhere is to take it there secretly and illegally: *They were caught smuggling rare fossils out of the country.*
□ **smuggler**, *noun* –**smuggling**, *noun*

SEE ALSO **people smuggling**.

smut *noun*
1. a smudge of soot or dirt **2.** offensive or obscene talk.
□ **smutty**, *adjective* (**smuttier**, **smuttiest**)

snack *noun*
1. a small, quick meal: *a snack after school.* **2.** *Informal* something that is very easy to do: *That puzzle was a snack.*

snag[1] *noun*
1. something sharp or rough sticking out from somewhere, such as a branch from a tree trunk

lying on the bottom of a river. **2.** a problem or difficulty: *a snag in our plans.*
–*verb* (**snags**, **snagging**, **snagged**, **has snagged**) **3.** If you **snag** something, you catch it on something sharp: *to snag your sleeve on a nail.*

snag[2] *noun Informal* a sausage.

snail *noun* a small, slow-moving animal with a soft body and a spiral shell, often found in gardens.

snake *noun* a long creature covered with scales and having no legs, which moves by sliding along the ground.

snap *verb* (**snaps**, **snapping**, **snapped**, **has snapped**)
1. If something **snaps**, it suddenly breaks, making a loud cracking sound: *The wind snapped a big branch off the tree.* **2.** If you **snap** your fingers, you rub your thumb and middle finger together, making a sharp sound. **3.** If a dog **snaps** at you, it tries to bite you. **4.** If you **snap** at someone, you speak to them in a sharp, angry way: *His mother snapped at him to get out of bed.*
–*noun* **5.** a sudden sharp sound or movement.
–*adjective* **6.** sudden: *a snap decision.*
–*phrase* **7. snap up**, to take quickly: *to snap up a bargain.*

snapper *noun* (*plural* **snapper** *or* **snappers**) a large fish of warm seas which is good to eat.

snapshot *noun* an informal photograph taken quickly.

snare *noun*
1. a trap for catching birds and small animals.
–*verb* **2.** If you **snare** an animal, you catch it in a trap.

snarl[1] *verb* If an animal **snarls**, it makes an angry or fierce sound.
☐ **snarl**, *noun*

snarl[2] *noun*
1. a tangle or knot.
–*verb* **2.** If something like thread or hair **snarls**, it becomes tangled: *The fishing line snarled and it took a long time to untangle.*

snatch *verb*
1. If you **snatch** something, you take it very quickly: *She snatched the letter out of his hands and quickly started to read it.* **2.** If someone **snatches** something from you, they steal it.
–*noun* (*plural* **snatches**) **3.** a sudden motion to grab something: *He made a snatch at her bag.* **4.** a scrap or small part: *I could only hear snatches of the conversation.*

sneak *verb* (**sneaks**, **sneaking**, **sneaked**, **has sneaked**)
1. If you **sneak** somewhere, you go there quietly and secretly, without letting others know about it: *She sneaked out to the party while her parents were asleep.* **2.** If you **sneak** something somewhere, you try to take it there without anyone seeing you: *I sneaked the puppy into my room.* **3.** If you **sneak** something, you take something that you should not be taking: *to sneak a look*; *to sneak a chocolate.*
–*noun* **4.** *Informal* someone who you think acts in a secretive or disloyal way, especially someone who reports that someone else has broken the rules in some way: *That sneak saw Jack writing on the blackboard and went and told the teacher straightaway.*
☐ **sneaky**, *adjective* (**sneakier**, **sneakiest**) –**sneakily**, *adverb*

ANOTHER FORM of the past form **sneaked**, especially in informal language, is **snuck**.

sneaker *noun* a running shoe with a rubber sole.

sneer *verb* If you **sneer** at someone, you make your dislike or disgust for them obvious by what you say to them or how you look at them.
☐ **sneer**, *noun* –**sneering**, *adjective* –**sneeringly**, *adverb*

sneeze *noun*
1. a sudden noisy explosion of air, mostly through your mouth, often caused by an itching inside your nose.
–*verb* **2.** When you **sneeze**, air blows noisily out of your mouth and nose.

sniff *verb* To **sniff** is to breathe in through the nose in a short, sharp burst: *The dog sniffed the tree*; *to sniff with a cold.*
☐ **sniff**, *noun*

sniffle *verb*
1. If you **sniffle**, you sniff continually because you have a cold or are trying not to cry.
–*noun* **2. the sniffles**, a cold with a runny nose.

snigger *verb* If you **snigger**, you laugh to yourself about someone in an unkind or unpleasant way: *What are you sniggering about – can't you see she's upset?*
☐ **snigger**, *noun*

snip *verb* (**snips**, **snipping**, **snipped**, **has snipped**) If you **snip** something, you cut it, usually with one quick action of the scissors: *Snip this loose thread.*
☐ **snip**, *noun*

sniper *noun* someone who shoots from a place which is hidden or a long way from the target.

snivel *verb* (**snivels**, **snivelling**, **snivelled**, **has snivelled**)
1. If you **snivel**, you sniffle noisily while you are crying. **2.** If you say that someone is **snivelling**, you mean that they are crying and complaining, maybe about something unimportant.

snob *noun* someone who looks down on people who are not wealthy, important, or clever.
☐ **snobbery**, *noun* –**snobbish**, *adjective*

snooker *noun* a game like billiards, played with balls of many colours.

snoop *verb* If someone **snoops**, they go around in a secretive way trying to find out about other people and their concerns.
☐ **snoopy**, *adjective* (**snoopier**, **snoopiest**)

snooze *Rather informal*
–*noun* **1.** a rest or short sleep.
–*verb* **2.** When you **snooze**, you sleep lightly for a short time.

snore *verb* If you **snore**, you breathe with a loud rumbling noise while you are sleeping.
☐ **snore**, *noun*

snorkel *noun*
1. a tube through which you can breathe air as you swim face downwards in the water.
–*verb* (**snorkels**, **snorkelling**, **snorkelled**, **has snorkelled**) **2.** When you **snorkel**, you swim under the water using a snorkel: *We snorkelled along the reef.*

WORD HISTORY from a German word

snort *verb* If a person or animal **snorts**, they breathe out noisily through their nose: *We could hear the pigs snorting as they ate.*
☐ **snort**, *noun*

snout *noun* the long nose of an animal.

ANOTHER WORD for this is **muzzle** (definition 1).

snow *noun*
1. white, frozen rain drops that fall to the ground.
–*verb* **2.** When it **snows**, snow falls from the sky.
–*phrase* **3. be snowed under**, to have too much to deal with: *I'm snowed under with work at the moment.*
☐ **snowy**, *adjective*

snowball *noun*
1. a pile of snow pressed into a ball.
–*verb* **2.** If anything **snowballs**, it piles up at a very fast rate: *Contributions to the disaster fund have snowballed since the special TV program.*

snowboard *noun*
1. a board for gliding over the snow, which resembles a surfboard in that the rider stands on it, the feet being strapped to it as with skis.
–*verb* **2.** to glide over the snow on a snowboard.
☐ **snowboarder**, *noun* –**snowboarding**, *noun*

snowman *noun* (*plural* **snowmen**) a human-like figure made of hard packed snow.

snub *verb* (**snubs**, **snubbing**, **snubbed**, **has snubbed**)
1. If you **snub** someone, you show dislike or contempt for them, especially by ignoring them.
–*noun* **2.** an instance of this: *I consider that a deliberate snub – he looked straight through me!*
–*adjective* **3.** short and turned up at the tip: *Gordon thought Arabella's little snub nose was cute.*

A SIMILAR WORD (definitions 1 and 2) is **rebuff**.

snug *adjective* (**snugger**, **snuggest**) comfortable and warm: *Our little cabin was snug despite the wind and rain.*

snuggle *verb* If you **snuggle** somewhere, you get warm and comfortable, usually by rolling your body closer to another person or thing.

so *adverb*
1. in the way shown or described: *Do it so.* **2.** as told or described: *Is that so?* **3.** to that degree: *Do not walk so fast.* **4.** very: *You are so kind.* **5.** for this reason: *Bananas are nutritious, so you should eat them often.* **6.** about that number or amount: *a day or so ago.*
–*phrase* **7. and so on** (or **forth**), and the rest: *You'll have to bring your own plates, knives, forks and so on.* **8. so-so**, only fair: *I'm feeling so-so today.*

soak *verb*
1. To **soak** is to lie in liquid or leave something in liquid for a long time: *I love soaking in a hot bath*; *She soaked the frying pan overnight to make it easier to clean.* **2.** If a liquid **soaks** something, it makes it very wet: *We were soaked by the sudden rain.*
–*phrase* **3. soak up**, to take in or absorb.
☐ **soak**, *noun*

soap *noun*
1. a substance made out of fat, used for washing yourself or cleaning things.
–*verb* **2.** If you **soap** yourself, you rub soap on your body to wash yourself.
☐ **soapy**, *adjective*

soap opera *noun* a television series which tells a story about people's lives and problems, often in an over-emotional way.

THE SHORT FORM of this is **soap**.
WORD HISTORY the name grew from the fact that soap manufacturers used to sponsor this type of entertainment

soar *verb* To **soar** is to **1.** fly upwards. **2.** fly at a great height without moving the wings very much: *The pelican soared high above the bay.* **3.** rise to a great height: *Huge trees soar from the valley floor*; *Our hopes soared*; *Costs are soaring.*

☑ SPELLING TIP Don't confuse the spelling of **soar** with **saw** or **sore**, both of which have the same sound. A **saw** is a cutting tool; **saw** is also the past tense of the verb **see**. If part of your body is **sore**, it hurts or feels painful.

sob *verb* (**sobs**, **sobbing**, **sobbed**, **has sobbed**) If someone **sobs**, they cry with so much emotion that they cannot control the sound of their breathing: *He ran out of the room sobbing.*
☐ **sob**, *noun*

sober *adjective*
1. If a person is **sober**, they are not drunk. **2.** If something is **sober**, it is quiet and serious: *We left the meeting in a sober mood.*
☐ **soberly**, *adverb* –**sobriety**, *noun*

soccer *noun* a form of football played with a round ball which the players kick but in general are not allowed to touch with their hands or arms.

sociable /*say* **soh**-shuh-buhl/ *adjective* friendly, or wanting to be with other people.
☐ **sociability**, *noun* –**sociableness**, *noun* –**sociably**, *adverb*

> ☑ SPELLING TIP Remember that this word is related to *society*. This will remind you of the *ci* spelling, the sound of which has changed to 'sh' in **sociable**.

social *adjective*
1. Something that is **social** relates to the organisation of society or the way society operates: *social justice.* **2.** An activity that is **social** relates to people meeting each other in their free time: *His social life doesn't leave him much time for study.* **3. Social** standing is the position of people in society in terms of class or wealth or power: *They come from different social backgrounds – he comes from a wealthy family and her family does not have much money.* **4.** If someone is **social**, they like going out and mixing with people all the time.
☐ **socially**, *adverb* –**socialise**, *verb*: *to socialise at a party.*

> ANOTHER SPELLING for **socialise** is **socialize**.

socialism /*say* **soh**-shuhl-iz-uhm/ *noun* the political belief that all industry and wealth should be owned and controlled by the people as a whole.
☐ **socialist**, *noun*

> COMPARE this with **capitalism** and **communism**.

social network *noun*
1. a supportive group of friends and relatives, or people you know with similar interests to yours, who are connected with other groups of their own friends and relatives in complex arrangements. **2.** a group of friends, relatives, or acquaintances who interact with each other online.
☐ **social networker**, *noun* –**social networking**, *noun*

society /*say* suh-**suy**-uh-tee/ *noun* (*plural* **societies**)
1. people as a whole: *human society.* **2.** people as a group in which there are divisions according to birth, education, and area of work: *the middle class of society.* **3.** a group of people with a common interest: *a society for coin collectors.* **4. high society**, that part of society in which people have wealth and status.

sociology /*say* soh-see-**ol**-uh-jee/ *noun* the study of the development and organisation of human society.
☐ **sociologist**, *noun*

sock[1] *noun*
1. a piece of clothing that you wear under a shoe, covering the foot and the ankle and sometimes reaching up to the knee.
–*phrase* **2. pull your socks up**, to make more effort.

sock[2] *verb Informal* To **sock** someone is to hit them hard.
☐ **sock**, *noun*

socket *noun*
1. a hollow area which holds some part or thing: *an eye socket.* **2.** a device on the wall into which you put an electric cord.

sod *noun* a piece of grass which has been cut or torn out of a lawn.

soda *noun*
1. See **soda water**. **2.** a drink made with soda water, fruit juices, and ice-cream.

> WORD HISTORY from an Arabic word

soda water *noun* a fizzy drink made by filling water with bubbles of carbon dioxide.

> THE SHORT FORM of this is **soda**.

sodden *adjective* soaked with a liquid: *Who left their sodden towel on the bathroom floor?*

sodium /*say* **soh**-dee-uhm/ *noun* a soft, silver-white, metallic element found in salt.

sofa *noun* a long, padded seat for two or more people, with a back and two sides.

> OTHER WORDS for this are **couch**, **lounge** and **settee**.

soft *adjective*
1. easily cut or pressed out of shape. **2.** smooth and pleasant to touch: *Feel the soft wool of my scarf.* **3.** low in sound: *I could hardly hear her, she has such a soft voice.* **4.** not harsh or too bright: *soft light.* **5.** gentle or pitying: *a soft heart.*
☐ **softly**, *adverb* –**soften**, *verb*

softball *noun* a form of baseball played with a larger, softer ball which is pitched underarm.
☐ **softballer**, *noun*

soft drink *noun* a drink which has no alcohol in it and is usually fizzy.

software *noun* the programs used to control the functions of a computer.

> COMPARE this with **hardware** (definition 2).

soggy *adjective*
1. If something is **soggy**, it is soaked or thoroughly wet: *soggy ground.* **2.** If food is **soggy**, it

is wet and heavy, like bread when it is not cooked enough.

soil[1] *noun* ground or earth, especially of the kind plants can grow in.

soil[2] *verb* To **soil** something is to make it dirty or stained: *The animals drinking in the dam had soiled and muddied the water*; *Their clothes were soiled with the grime of the mines.*
☐ **soiled**, *adjective*

solar *adjective*
1. having to do with the sun: *a solar eclipse.* **2.** operated or produced by the heat of the sun: *solar fuel.*

solar energy *noun* energy derived from the sun, as for home heating, industrial use, etc.

solar heating *noun* the use of energy from the sun to heat water or air in a building.

solar system *noun* the sun together with all the planets, moons, and so on, which turn around it.

solder *noun*
1. an alloy which can be melted easily and used to join other metals together.
–*verb* **2.** If someone **solders** metals, they join them together or repair them with solder.
☐ **solderer**, *noun*

soldier *noun*
1. someone who serves in an army.
–*phrase* **2. soldier on**, to continue doing something you have started in spite of difficulties.
☐ **soldierly**, *adjective*

sole[1] *adjective* If something is **sole**, it is the only one: *I am the sole person in the class who wears glasses.*
☐ **solely**, *adverb*: *solely in charge.*

> ☑ SPELLING TIP Don't confuse the spelling of **sole** with **soul** which has the same sound. Some people believe that you have a **soul**, a spiritual part of you, contrasted with your body.

sole[2] *noun* the underneath or bottom of the foot or of a shoe.

> ☑ SPELLING TIP See **sole**[1].

sole[3] *noun* (*plural* **soles**) any of a number of types of flat-bodied fish which are good to eat.

> ☑ SPELLING TIP See **sole**[1].

solemn /*say* **sol**-uhm/ *adjective*
1. If someone or something is **solemn**, they are very serious, rather than cheerful or without care: *Seeing her solemn face, I knew that something was wrong.* **2.** A **solemn** promise or agreement is one that is very sincere, usually made after serious thought.
☐ **solemnity** /*say* suh-**lem**-nuh-tee/, *noun* –**solemnly**, *adverb*

> ☑ SPELLING TIP *Silent letter alert*: don't forget the silent *n* at the end.

solicitor /*say* suh-**lis**-uh-tuh/ *noun* a lawyer who advises people about legal matters and prepares cases to be presented in court.

> COMPARE this with **barrister**.

> ☑ SPELLING TIP Remember that there are no double letters in this word and that the first and last vowel sounds are spelt *o* (the last making the *or* ending) and the middle two are both *i*. So the only vowels that appear are *i*'s and *o*'s.

solid *adjective*
1. having length, breadth, and thickness: *A solid shape has three dimensions.* **2.** wholly or entirely made out of (something): *solid chocolate.* **3.** strong and not easily damaged: *a solid person*; *a solid wall.*
–*noun* **4.** something solid. **5. solids**, food that is not in liquid form.
☐ **solidify**, *verb* –**solidity**, *noun* –**solidly**, *adverb*

> COMPARE definition 4 with **gas**[1] (definition 1) and **liquid**.

solidarity /*say* sol-uh-**da**-ruh-tee/ *noun* a united front presented by members of a group with strongly held common ideas and interests.

soliloquy /*say* suh-**lil**-uh-kwee/ *noun* (*plural* **soliloquies**) talking to yourself when you are alone or when you are pretending to be alone, as in a play: *The teacher read out the famous soliloquy from Shakespeare's 'Hamlet'.*

> ☑ SPELLING TIP To spell the first part of this difficult word, think of *solo* (meaning 'alone') and change it to *soli*. Then concentrate on the unusual *quy* ending for the 'kwee' sound. **Soliloquy** comes from two Latin words – *solus*, meaning 'alone', and *loqui*, meaning 'to speak'. Another word based on *loqui* is *colloquial*.

solitary /*say* **sol**-uh-tree/ *adjective*
1. quite alone. **2.** the only one: *A solitary tree remained.*

solitude /*say* **sol**-uh-tyoohd/ *noun* a state of being alone: *When my dog feels like solitude, it goes under the house.*

solo *noun*
1. a musical performance by one person.
–*adjective* **2.** performed or done alone: *a solo item*; *a solo flight.*
–*adverb* **3.** alone: *He flew solo.*
☐ **soloist**, *noun* someone who performs a solo.

solstice *noun* one of the two times each year when the sun is furthest away from the equator and the longest or shortest day occurs. The first comes on about June 21, when the sun enters the sign of Cancer (in the Southern Hemisphere, the

winter solstice) and the other comes on about December 22, when the sun enters the sign of Capricorn (the **summer solstice**).

soluble /*say* **sol**-yuh-buhl/ *adjective*
1. able to be dissolved: *Gargle some soluble aspirin.* **2.** able to be solved: *I am sure that the problem must be soluble.*
☐ **solubility**, *noun*

THE OPPOSITE is **insoluble**.

solution *noun*
1. the solving of, or answer to a problem. **2.** a substance which is made up of one chemical, usually a solid, spread perfectly through another chemical, usually a liquid: *Salt can be dissolved in water to make a solution.*

solve *verb* If you **solve** something such as a problem or question, you find the answer to it.

solvent *noun*
1. a liquid substance that can dissolve other substances: *You need a solvent to get the old paint off.*
–*adjective* **2.** having enough money to be able to pay your debts: *They hope the business will still be solvent after losing so much money in investments.*
☐ **solvency**, *noun* the ability to pay your debts.

sombre /*say* **som**-buh/ *adjective* dark or serious in a way that makes you feel sad: *a sombre colour scheme of brown and black*; *a sombre occasion.*

☑ SPELLING TIP Remember the ending is *re* (not *er*). Some other words with this ending are *centre* and *theatre*.

sombrero /*say* som-**brair**-roh/ *noun* (*plural* **sombreros**) a broad-brimmed hat worn in Spain, Mexico and some other countries.

WORD HISTORY from a Spanish word meaning 'shade'

some *adjective*
1. having to do with a number or quantity when it is not important to say exactly how many or how much: *Some friends are coming to dinner*; *I'll have some tea, please.* **2.** quite a few: *I haven't seen him now for some years.* **3.** a little: *There's still some hope that we will win the contest.* **4.** part of a thing rather than all of it: *We'll keep some of the cake for tomorrow.*
–*pronoun* **5.** certain people, or things, that are not named: *Some think he is dead.* **6.** an unstated number, amount, and so on, that is marked out from the rest: *Some of this work is good.*

☑ SPELLING TIP Don't confuse the spelling of **some** with **sum** which has the same sound. A **sum** is a calculation in arithmetic.

somebody *pronoun* **1.** some person: *Somebody took my book.*
–*noun* (*plural* **somebodies**) **2.** a person of some importance: *He thinks he is somebody.*

ANOTHER WORD for this is **someone**.

somehow *adverb* in some way not yet known or specified: *This is somehow wrong*; *We'll have to get the work finished somehow.*

someone *pronoun* some person: *Someone let the bird out.*

ANOTHER WORD for this is **somebody** (definition 1).

somersault /*say* **sum**-uh-sawlt, **sum**-uh-solt/ *noun*
1. a gymnastic movement in which you roll your body completely, heels over head.
–*verb* **2.** If you **somersault**, you perform a somersault.

☑ SPELLING TIP You may feel hot after doing **somersaults**, but this word has nothing to do with the season of summer, nor anything to do with salt. It comes from French, originally from two Latin words meaning 'over' and 'leap'. Try splitting it into its two parts and memorising them ☐ *somer*, then *sault* (like *salt* but with a *u* added in).

something *pronoun* You use **something** to refer to a thing, activity or quality, without saying exactly what you are referring to: *You might find something to eat in the refrigerator*; *Why don't you do something about this mess?*

sometimes *adverb* occasionally or on some occasions: *I watch TV sometimes.*

somewhere *adverb*
1. You use **somewhere** to refer to a place, without saying exactly where: *to get lost somewhere.* **2.** You also use **somewhere** to refer to a stage in a situation, without saying exactly where: *'What page are you up to in the book?' 'Oh, somewhere in the middle.'.*

son *noun*
1. the male child of someone. **2.** a man looked upon as having been affected by a particular thing: *a son of the land.*

sonar /*say* **soh**-nah/ *noun* a device or method for finding depth under water by measuring the time it takes to receive an echo from a sound.

WORD HISTORY an acronym made by joining the first letters of the words *so*(*und*) *n*(*avigation*) *a*(*nd*) *r*(*anging*)

sonata /*say* suh-**nah**-tuh/ *noun* a musical composition with three or four movements in different styles.

song *noun*
1. a short musical composition with words. **2.** musical sounds produced by birds.

sonic *adjective*
1. having to do with sound waves. 2. having to do with the speed of sound.

son-in-law *noun* (*plural* **sons-in-law**) the husband of someone's daughter.

sonnet *noun* a poem of fourteen lines in which the lines have to rhyme in a certain way.

sonorous /*say* **son**-uh-ruhs/ *adjective* sounding deep, loud and rich: *The double bass has a sonorous sound.*
☐ **sonority**, *noun*

sook /*rhymes with* book/ *noun Rather informal* someone who is shy, timid or cowardly.
☐ **sooky**, *adjective* (**sookier**, **sookiest**)

soon *adverb* within a short time: *She will be back soon.*

soot /*rhymes with* foot/ *noun* the black substance which sticks to the inside of a chimney when coal, wood, oil, or other fuels are burnt.
☐ **sooty**, *adjective* (**sootier**, **sootiest**)

soothe /*say* soohdh/ *verb*
1. If you **soothe** someone who is upset, you calm them. 2. If something **soothes** pain, it makes the pain less severe: *This ointment will soothe the pain of that burn.*
☐ **soothing**, *adjective*

sophisticated /*say* suh-**fis**-tuh-kay-tuhd/ *adjective*
1. wise and experienced in the interests and pleasures of the world. 2. finely detailed or complicated: *sophisticated machinery.*
☐ **sophistication**, *noun*

☑ SPELLING TIP If you remember that *ph* spells the 'f' sound in **sophisticated**, as it does in many words, you should have no trouble sounding out this rather long word.

soporific /*say* sop-uh-**rif**-ik/ *adjective* causing sleep or sleepiness.

sopping *adjective* very wet.

soppy *adjective* (**soppier**, **soppiest**) *Rather informal* too sentimental: *a soppy love story.*

soprano /*say* suh-**prah**-noh/ *noun* (*plural* **sopranos**) a woman or boy who sings with a high voice.
☐ **soprano**, *adjective*: *a soprano voice.*

NOTE The range of a **soprano** is the highest of the singing voices, above **alto**, **tenor**, **baritone** and **bass**.

sorbet /*say* **saw**-bay/ *noun* a frozen dessert made with fruit and whites of eggs.

☑ SPELLING TIP *Silent letter alert*: remember the silent *t* at the end – the *et* spelling makes an 'ay' sound. Other words with this ending are *ballet* and *bouquet*. They all come from French.

sorcery /*say* **saw**-suh-ree/ *noun* magic, especially when used for evil purposes.
☐ **sorcerer**, *noun*

NOTE A woman who does sorcery can be called a **sorceress**.

sordid *adjective*
1. morally mean or nasty: *a sordid story of murder and betrayal.* 2. dirty or filthy: *the sordid back streets of the city.*
☐ **sordidness**, *noun*

sore *adjective*
1. If a part of your body is **sore**, it hurts: *a sore throat.* 2. *Informal* If you say you are **sore** about something, you mean you are very angry or upset about it.
–*noun* 3. a sore spot or place on your body.

☑ SPELLING TIP Don't confuse the spelling of **sore** with **saw** or **soar**, both of which have the same sound. A **saw** is a cutting tool; **saw** is also the past tense of the verb **see**. To **soar** is to fly upwards.

sorrow *noun* sadness, or the feeling of being sorry.
☐ **sorrowful**, *adjective*

sorry *adjective* (**sorrier**, **sorriest**)
1. feeling sad because you have done something wrong. 2. feeling pity.
–*interjection* 3. an exclamation of apology.

SIMILAR WORDS (for definition 1) are **regretful**, **contrite**, **penitent**, **remorseful** and **repentant**. These words are all more formal than **sorry**.

sort *noun*
1. a particular kind or type: *Cockatoos are a sort of parrot.*
–*verb* 2. When you **sort** people or things, you arrange or group them according to type or kind: *I sorted the socks into pairs.*
–*phrase* 3. **sort of**, in some way: *I sort of think we should go, even though we can't stay long.*

SOS /*say* es-oh-**es**/ *noun* an urgent call for help: *The ship sent an SOS by radio.*

WORD HISTORY probably chosen because the Morse code for these letters is clear and easy, but some people say the letters stand for 'Save Our Souls'

soufflé /*say* **sooh**-flay/ *noun* a light baked food, made fluffy with beaten whites of eggs, and with flavouring, such as cheese or fruit, etc., added.

☑ SPELLING TIP The tricky part is the *é* spelling for the 'ay' sound at the end. The accent on the letter is the clue that this word comes from French, which also explains the pronunciation. You will also see this word spelt without the accent, but the sound of the *e* remains the same.

soul */say* sohl/ *noun*
1. the unseen or spiritual part of a person which some people believe stays alive after their body dies. **2.** a human being: *He's a kind old soul.* **3.** See **soul music**.
☐ **soulless**, *adjective* without spirit: *a soulless city.*

☑ SPELLING TIP Remember the *ou* spelling for the 'oh' sound. Don't confuse **soul** with **sole** which has the same sound. Your **sole** is the underneath part of your foot.

soul music *noun* a type of modern African-American music with songs about emotions and the singer's personal experience.

ANOTHER FORM You can also call this **soul**: *Do you like soul?*

sound[1] *noun*
1. something heard as a result of waves in the air reaching your ear. **2.** the effect on your ears of a particular sound: *the sound of music.*
–*verb* **3.** If something **sounds**, it makes a noise: *The door bell sounded.* **4.** To **sound** something is to cause it to make a sound: *Sound the alarm.* **5.** If something **sounds** a particular way to you, that is what you feel it means when you hear or read it: *That sounds interesting.*

sound[2] *adjective*
1. healthy or in good condition: *a sound heart.* **2.** unbroken or deep: *sound sleep.* **3.** trustworthy or good: *sound advice.*

sound[3] *verb*
1. To **sound** the depth of water is to measure or try its depth by letting down a lead weight on the end of a line.
–*phrase* **2. sound out**, to try by indirect ways to find the feelings of: *He asked me to sound her out about which film she would like to go to.*

sound[4] *noun* a narrow stretch of water joining two larger bodies of water or between an island and the mainland.

sound system *noun* a machine that consists of a CD player, cassette recorder, and radio.

soundtrack *noun*
1. the strip beside a moving picture film which carries the sound recording. **2.** the songs and music of a film recorded on a compact disc, cassette, etc.

soup *noun* a liquid food flavoured with meat, fish, or vegetables, which is usually served hot.

WORD HISTORY from a French word meaning 'soup' or 'broth'

sour *adjective*
1. having an acid taste, such as that of lemons. **2.** cross or irritable: *What a sour face!*
–*verb* **3.** To **sour** something, such as a friendship or mood, is to make it become less friendly or enjoyable: *Their bitter argument soured the atmosphere of the party.*
☐ **sourish**, *adjective*

source *noun*
1. the place or thing from which something comes: *Those countries are the main source of the world's oil.* **2.** the beginning or place of origin of a river: *The river has its source in the mountains.* **3.** a book, person, or statement which supplies information: *That book was one of the primary sources of my history essay*; *We heard it from a reliable source.*

☑ SPELLING TIP Remember the *our* spelling for the vowel sound. Don't confuse **source** with **sauce** which has the same sound. A **sauce** is a cooked liquid used to flavour food.

south *noun* the direction which is to your left when you face the setting sun in the west.
☐ **south**, *adjective*, *adverb* –**southerly**, *adjective*: *southerly winds.* –**southern**, *adjective*

NOTE The opposite direction is **north**.

Southern Cross *noun* the constellation you can see in the southern sky whose four chief stars are in the shape of a cross.

souvenir */say* sooh-vuh-**near**/ *noun* something you keep as a memory of a place or event.

☑ SPELLING TIP Remember the *ou* spelling for the 'ooh' sound, and the rather unusual *ir* ending. **Souvenir** comes from French, where it means 'to remember'.

souvlaki */say* soohv-**lah**-kee/ *noun* a food made with diced lamb and vegetables on skewers, originating in Greek cooking.

sovereign */say* **sov**-ruhn/ *noun* a king or queen.
☐ **sovereign**, *adjective* –**sovereignty**, *noun*

ANOTHER WORD for this is **monarch**.

☑ SPELLING TIP A **sovereign** is someone who rules or reigns, and you can see that the word *reign* appears as the last part of **sovereign**, although it sounds like 'ruhn'. Remember the *eign* spelling of *reign* and you will also be able to spell **sovereign**. Rap it out as *sov+e+reign*.

sow[1] */rhymes with* go/ *verb* (**sows**, **sowing**, **sowed**, **has sown** *or* **has sowed**) To **sow** seeds is to scatter them in the earth so they can grow: *We need to sow the seeds before the rain.*

☑ SPELLING TIP Don't confuse the spelling of **sow** with **so** or **sew**, both of which have the same sound. **So** means 'therefore'. To **sew** is to stitch something with a needle and thread.

sow[2] */rhymes with* how/ *noun* an adult female pig.

NOTE The male is a **boar**.

soybean *noun* the seed of an Asian plant which can be eaten as a bean or used for oil.

OTHER FORMS are **soy** and **soya bean**.

soy sauce *noun* a salty, dark brown sauce, made by fermenting soybeans in brine.

ANOTHER FORM is **soya sauce**.

spa *noun*
1. a place where there is a flow of mineral water from the earth. **2.** a bath or swimming pool which has heated bubbly water pumped into it.

space *noun*
1. the continuous openness in which everything exists: *There is space all around us.* **2.** the space outside the earth's atmosphere: *to launch a satellite into space.* **3.** a part or area of space: *I have space in my bag for your books*; *Your CD player doesn't take up much space.* **4.** the distance between things: *We put the candles at equal spaces along the path.* **5.** a blank area on a surface: *Write your name then leave two lines space.* **6.** a period of time: *He went into the house and after a space of just a few minutes we saw the light go out.*
–*verb* **7.** If you **space** items or people, you arrange them with spaces in between: *Space the seedlings so that they have room to grow.*

ANOTHER TERM (for definition 2) is **outer space**.

spacecraft *noun* a vehicle that can travel in space.

spaceship *noun* a spacecraft that has a crew.

space shuttle *noun* a spacecraft that carries people and equipment between earth and a satellite, and which can land and be used again.

THE SHORT FORM of this is **shuttle**.

spacious /*say* **spay**-shuhs/ *adjective* having a lot of space or room: *a spacious kitchen.*
☐ **spaciousness**, *noun*

A SIMILAR WORD is **roomy**.

spade[1] *noun* a tool for digging, with a long handle and a metal blade that you push into the ground with your foot.

spade[2] *noun* a black shape like an upside-down heart with a stem, used on some playing cards.

spaghetti /*say* spuh-**get**-ee/ *noun* a kind of pasta formed into long, thin, rounded strips.

☑ SPELLING TIP *Silent letter alert*: don't forget the silent *h* following the *g*. Also remember the *i* ending. **Spaghetti** is spelt like this because it comes from Italian.

spam *noun* junk mail sent to large numbers of people, usually advertising things that people are not interested in.

WORD HISTORY from *spam*, a trademark name for a kind of precooked tinned meat, this meat having featured in a British television comedy sketch in which every item on a cafe menu contained it

span *noun*
1. the distance between the two furthest edges or ends of something: *the span of a bridge*; *the span of your hand.* **2.** the full stretch of anything: *Humans have a longer life span than animals.*
–*verb* (**spans**, **spanning**, **spanned**, **has spanned**) **3.** To **span** something is to stretch over or across it: *The bridge spans the river*; *The story spans two centuries.*

spangle *noun* a small piece of something that glitters: *Their costumes were sparkling with sequins, glitter and spangles.*
☐ **spangled**, *adjective*

spaniel /*say* **span**-yuhl/ *noun* a kind of dog with a long silky coat and ears that hang down.

☑ SPELLING TIP Remember the *iel* ending, in which *i* gives the 'y' sound. Rap it out as *span*+ *i*+ *el*.

spank *verb* To **spank** a child is to hit them, usually as a punishment, with an open hand.
☐ **spank**, *noun* –**spanking**, *noun*

spanner *noun* a tool for holding and turning something, such as a nut on a bolt.

spar[1] *noun* a strong pole, such as a mast on a ship.

spar[2] *verb* (**spars**, **sparring**, **sparred**, **has sparred**)
1. If two people **spar**, they punch each other lightly or make punching movements: *The boxer practised for the big fight by sparring with other fighters.* **2.** If two people **spar**, they argue verbally but not particularly seriously: *They were sparring again about who was the better fisherman.*
☐ **spar**, *noun*

spare *verb*
1. If someone **spares** a person or thing, they decide not to harm or destroy them: *I was going to punish you but I have decided to spare you.* **2.** If you **spare** someone an unpleasant experience, you protect them from it, making it possible for them to avoid it: *Getting a lift to school spared me having to catch the bus.* **3.** If you **spare** someone something, you let them have it: *Can you spare me one of your pencils?*
–*adjective* **4.** If you have a **spare** thing, you have an extra one, in case you need it: *a spare tyre.* **5.** If something is **spare**, it is not being used at the moment. It is free to be used by someone: *Here's a spare seat.* **6.** Time that is **spare** is free for you to use how you want to.
–*noun* **7.** something that is extra: *The battery is flat and we haven't got a spare.*
–*phrase* **8. to spare**, more than is needed and so can be used by someone else or in another way:

Have some of our food. We have plenty to spare; We found we had half an hour to spare when we arrived at the cinema so we had a look in the bookshop.

spark *noun*
1. a tiny piece of burning material thrown up by a fire. **2.** a sudden escape of electricity, usually with a flash of light. **3.** a small showing of something: *a spark of intelligence.*
–verb **4.** To **spark** something is to set it going: *The photograph sparked his interest in learning more about the old house.*

sparkle *verb* To **sparkle** is to **1.** shine with many little flashes of light. **2.** be bright and energetic: *The conversation sparkled.*
☐ **sparkle**, *noun*

A SIMILAR WORD (for definition 1) is **glitter**.

spark plug *noun* a device in an engine that gives out an electric charge which sets fire to the fuel in each cylinder.

sparrow *noun* a small brown bird.

sparse *adjective* small in number and amount and thinly spread out over an area: *a sparse population; Dad has sparse hair.*
☐ **sparsely**, *adverb* –**sparseness**, *noun* –**sparsity**, *noun*

spasm /*say* **spaz**-uhm/ *noun*
1. a sudden tightening of the muscles in part of the body. **2.** a sudden, short burst of something such as an emotion or an activity: *a spasm of fear.*
☐ **spasmodic**, *adjective*: *Over the years his writing has had spasmodic success.*

spastic *noun*
1. *Old-fashioned* someone who has cerebral palsy. **2.** *Informal* someone who you think is foolish or clumsy.

NOTE **Spastic** used to be the usual term for referring to a person with cerebral palsy, but it is now regarded as offensive by many people, especially because of the insulting way the term is used in definition 2.

spate *noun* a large number of things occurring in a short time: *There has been a spate of robberies in our street.*

spatial /*say* **spay**-shuhl/ *adjective* having to do with space: *He has no spatial sense and keeps bumping into things.*

☑ SPELLING TIP Although **spatial** comes from the word *space*, you have to remember that the *c* has changed to a *t*, so that the ending is spelt *tial*. You could think of the astronaut who *spat* in space to remind you of the *t*.

spatula /*say* **spach**-uh-luh/ *noun* a tool with a flat, bendable blade, used for mixing or spreading such things as food or paint.

☑ SPELLING TIP Remember the *t* in this word. With the *u* following it has a 'ch' sound and you don't hear the *t*.

spawn *noun* a mass of eggs given out by fish, frogs, and other water creatures.

WORD HISTORY from a Latin word meaning 'expand'

speak *verb* (**speaks**, **speaking**, **spoke**, **has spoken**)
1. When you **speak**, you say words using your voice: *Be quiet – let me speak!* **2.** If you **speak** to someone, you talk to them: *I spoke to him on the phone yesterday.* **3.** If you **speak** a certain language, you are able to carry on a conversation in that language because you understand it: *Does anyone speak Dutch?* **4.** If you **speak** at a meeting or party, you make a speech.

speaker *noun*
1. someone who speaks, especially before an audience. **2.** the person who controls the meeting of a house of parliament.

ANOTHER FORM This word (as in definition 2) is often spelt with a capital letter.

spear *noun*
1. a weapon which consists of a long pole with a sharp pointed end.
–verb **2.** To **spear** something is to pierce it with a spear or with some other pointed instrument: *He was speared in the leg; I speared a sausage with my fork.*

spear gun *noun* a gun that throws out a spear when fired, used in underwater fishing.

special *adjective*
1. of a particular or distinct kind: *a special bus fare on the weekend; a new DVD with special features.* **2.** more important than others of the same kind: *We save the good plates for special occasions.*
–noun **3.** something which is sold at a cheap price.
☐ **specially**, *adverb*

specialise *verb* If someone **specialises** in something, they spend most of their time on this one thing, especially in their work or study: *a shop specialising in electronic games; He's going to specialise in radio journalism when he goes to university.*
☐ **specialised**, *adjective*

ANOTHER SPELLING is **specialize**.

specialist *noun* someone who studies or is good at a particular subject or area of work, particularly a doctor: *She is a specialist in childhood diseases.*

speciality /*say* spesh-ee-**al**-uh-tee/ *noun* See **specialty**.

specialty /*say* **spesh**-uhl-tee/ *noun* a particular kind of study, work or product that someone specialises in: *My older sister's specialty is the marine biology of tropical regions*; *The library's specialty is in languages.*

ANOTHER WORD for this is **speciality**.

species /*say* **spee**-seez, **spee**-sheez/ *noun* (*plural* **species**) one of the groups into which animals and plants are divided according to their characteristics.

specific /*say* spuh-**sif**-ik/ *adjective*
1. one particular thing from a group of a similar kind: *a specific paint colour.* **2.** exact and clear: *Can you be more specific about the time you left?*
☐ **specifically**, *adverb*

specification /*say* spes-uh-fuh-**kay**-shuhn/ *noun*
1. the act of specifying: *The next phase of the project is specification of everybody's roles.* **2.** an item in a detailed description of the measurements and materials to be used for something you plan to make: *We had to submit the building specifications to the council for approval.*

specify /*say* **spes**-uh-fuy/ *verb* (**specifies**, **specifying**, **specified**, **has specified**) If you **specify** something, you state the details of it clearly and exactly: *Please specify how long it will take you.*

specimen /*say* **spes**-uh-muhn/ *noun* a single thing or part taken as being typical of a whole group or mass: *The painting hanging in the dining room is a good specimen of her style*; *The doctor took a specimen of my blood for tests.*

speck *noun* a small spot or bit: *a blue sky with specks of cloud*; *a speck of dirt.*
☐ **specked**, *adjective*

speckle *noun*
1. a small spot or mark.
–*verb* **2.** To **speckle** is to mark with speckles: *The quartz rock was speckled with gold dust.*
☐ **speckled**, *adjective*

spectacle *noun*
1. a large public show or display: *The fireworks were a great spectacle.* **2. spectacles**, See **glasses**.
–*phrase* **3. make a spectacle of yourself**, to disgrace yourself in front of others by doing something foolish or undignified.

spectacular /*say* spek-**tak**-yuh-luh/ *adjective* having to do with a display or sight which is unusual in a very exciting and impressive way: *a spectacular ice-skating show*; *a spectacular view of the mountains.*
☐ **spectacularly**, *adverb*

SIMILAR WORDS are **striking**, **dazzling** and **breathtaking**.

spectator *noun* someone who watches something: *spectators at a basketball game.*

spectre /*say* **spek**-tuh/ *noun* a ghost.
☐ **spectral**, *adjective*

OTHER WORDS for this are **apparition**, **phantom** and **spook** (*Informal*).

☑ SPELLING TIP Remember the *re* (not *er*) ending. Some other words with this ending are *centre* and *theatre*.

spectrum *noun*
1. the band of colours which is produced when white light passes through a prism: *Red, orange, yellow, green, blue, indigo, and violet are colours of the spectrum.* **2.** a range of ideas, beliefs, or types: *a broad spectrum of views.*

WORD HISTORY from a Latin word meaning 'appearance' or 'form'

speculate *verb* If you **speculate** about something, you have an opinion about it without certain knowledge: *We speculated on how many people would be at the party.*
☐ **speculation**, *noun* –**speculative**, *adjective* –**speculator**, *noun*

speech *noun* (*plural* **speeches**)
1. the ability to speak. **2.** a talk given in front of an audience: *The visiting astronaut made a speech at our school assembly.* **3.** the way someone speaks: *Her mouth was numb from the dentist's injection so her speech was a bit difficult to understand.*

speed *noun*
1. quickness in moving, going, or doing something.
–*verb* (**speeds**, **speeding**, **sped** *or* **speeded**, **has sped** *or* **has speeded**) To **speed** is to **2.** move quickly: *He sped on his way.* **3.** drive a vehicle faster than is allowed by law.
–*phrase* **4. speed up**, to go or do more quickly.
☐ **speedy**, *adjective* (**speedier**, **speediest**) –**speedily**, *adverb* –**speedster**, *noun*

speed camera *noun* a computerised camera positioned to monitor traffic and photograph the numberplate of any vehicle that drives faster than the maximum legal speed.

speedometer /*say* speed-**om**-uh-tuh/ *noun* an instrument on a vehicle that shows how fast it is travelling.

spell[1] *verb* (**spells**, **spelling**, **spelt** *or* **spelled**, **has spelt** *or* **has spelled**)
1. If you **spell** a word, you write or say its letters in order: *Long words can be hard to spell.*
–*phrase* **2. spell out**, to explain clearly: *Surely you can understand what I've told you without me having to spell it out.*
☐ **spelling**, *noun*

spell[2] *noun*
1. a group of words that is thought to have magic power: *The wizard whispered a spell, then sprinkled a purple powder into the fire.* **2.** a strong power to attract: *She has him in her spell.*

spell[3] *noun*
1. a period of work: *She had a long spell of duty at the hospital.* **2.** *Informal* a short period of anything: *We need a spell of rain.* **3.** a period of rest: *We were promised a spell as soon as we had finished all the exercises.*

spend *verb* (**spends**, **spending**, **spent**, **has spent**)
1. To **spend** money is to pay it out: *I spent all my pocket money buying lollies.* **2.** To **spend** time in a certain way is to do something during that time: *We spent the evening at the movies.* **3.** To **spend** energy and so on is to use it to do something: *She spent a lot of effort to make the show a success.*
☐ **spender**, *noun*

spendthrift *noun* someone who spends their money wastefully.

sperm *noun* one of the cells produced by a male, that can join with an egg or ovum to develop into a new organism.

spew *verb Informal* To **spew** is to vomit.

sphere /*say* sfear/ *noun*
1. something completely round in shape, such as a ball or a planet. **2.** an area of activity: *Music is his main sphere of interest.*
☐ **spherical** /*say* **sfe**-rik-uhl/, *adjective*

spice *noun*
1. a substance made from a plant, which is used to flavour or preserve food: *Nutmeg is a spice.* **2.** something that adds interest: *She added bits of gossip to give her speech some spice.*
–*verb* **3.** To **spice** food is to add spice to it.
–*phrase* **4. spice up**, to make more interesting or exciting: *She made up some gory details to spice up her story.*
☐ **spicy**, *adjective* (**spicier**, **spiciest**) –**spiciness**, *noun* –**spiced**, *adjective*: *spiced nuts.*

WORD HISTORY from a Latin word meaning 'species'

☑ SPELLING TIP Notice the spelling of the adjective form **spicy**. The *e* at the end of **spice** is dropped before adding the *y*.

spider *noun* an eight-legged creature, like an insect but without wings, which usually spins a web and is sometimes venomous.
☐ **spidery**, *adjective*

spike *noun*
1. a sharp pointed piece or part: *The bush had long spikes on its branches.* **2. spikes**, a pair of shoes with sharp metal pieces on the bottom, worn by runners or other athletes to stop them from slipping.
☐ **spiky**, *adjective* (**spikier**, **spikiest**)

spill *verb* (**spills**, **spilling**, **spilt** *or* **spilled**, **has spilt** *or* **has spilled**) If you **spill** a liquid or if it **spills**, it accidentally flows over the edge of its container: *She spilt her cup of coffee on her skirt*; *The milk spilt all over the kitchen floor.*
☐ **spill**, *noun*: *an oil spill.* –**spillage**, *noun*

spin *verb* (**spins**, **spinning**, **spun**, **has spun**) To **spin** is to **1.** make thread by twisting and winding fibres, such as cotton or wool. **2.** turn or make turn around and around very fast: *The wheel is spinning*; *She spun on her heel to face us.*
–*phrase* **3. spin out**, to make last a long time: *to spin out money*; *to spin out sympathy.*
☐ **spin**, *noun* –**spinner**, *noun* –**spinning**, *noun*

spinach /*say* **spin**-ich/ *noun* a plant with large green leaves which are eaten as a vegetable.

☑ SPELLING TIP *Single letter alert*: only one *n* in **spinach**. Also remember that the ending is *ach*.

WORD HISTORY from an Arabic word

spindle *noun*
1. a rod used to twist or wind the thread in spinning. **2.** a part of a machine which turns round or on which something turns.

spindly *adjective* long and thin: *He was tall and spindly and looked as though he could have done with a good meal*; *spindly gum trees.*

spine *noun*
1. the column of bones in the back. **2.** a stiff, spiky part on an animal or plant, such as an echidna. **3.** the part of a book's cover that holds the front and back together.
☐ **spinal**, *adjective* –**spiny**, *adjective* –**spineless**, *adjective*

spinifex /*say* **spin**-uh-feks/ *noun* a kind of spiny grass.

spinnaker /*say* **spin**-uh-kuh/ *noun* a large triangular sail.

☑ SPELLING TIP *Double letter alert*: two *n*'s. Also remember that there is no *c* in this word. The *k* alone (not *ck*) makes the 'k' sound.

spinning wheel *noun* a machine for spinning consisting of a spindle turned around by a large wheel which is driven by your hand or foot.

spin-off *noun* an object, product, or undertaking that has come into being as a result of something larger or more important: *As a spin-off, they are making a program about how the film was produced.*

spinster *noun* a woman who has not been married.

spiny anteater *noun* See **echidna**.

spiral *noun*
1. a curve that winds around and around away from a centre: *a spring in the shape of a spiral.*
–*verb* (**spirals**, **spiralling**, **spiralled**, **has spiralled**) 2. When something **spirals**, it moves in the shape of a spiral: *Smoke spiralled into the sky.*
☐ **spiral**, *adjective*: *a spiral staircase.*

spire *noun* a tall, pointed part of a building, usually on a roof or tower: *Ahead we could see the spire of the cathedral.*

spirit *noun*
1. someone's soul. 2. a supernatural being. 3. temper or character: *a man with a generous spirit.* 4. feeling or mood: *team spirit*; *the spirit of celebration.* 5. general meaning or intention: *the spirit of an agreement.* 6. energetic courage: *I like him for his spirit.* 7. **spirits**, **a.** the state of your mind: *She is in high spirits today.* **b.** strong alcoholic drink.
☐ **spirited**, *adjective*

spiritual /*say* **spi**-ruh-chooh-uhl, **spi**-ruh-chuhl/ *adjective*
1. having to do with or interested in the spirit rather than the body: *She says that listening to music is a spiritual experience for her.* 2. having to do with holy, religious, or supernatural things: *He is the spiritual leader of his people, but not their political leader.*
☐ **spirituality**, *noun*

THE OPPOSITE (of definition 1) is **worldly**.

☑ SPELLING TIP Remember that **spiritual** comes from the word *spirit*. This will remind you that it includes the letter *t* although, with the *u* following, it has a 'ch' sound and you don't hear the *t*.

spit[1] *verb* (**spits**, **spitting**, **spat**, **has spat**)
1. To **spit** is to force out saliva from your mouth: *In some countries, it is not considered rude to spit in public.* 2. If you **spit** something out, you send it out from your mouth: *He spat out the mouthful of food when he realised what was in it.* 3. If rain **spits**, it falls in light scattered drops: *We could hear the rain spitting on the roof.* 4. If something **spits**, it makes a noise like spitting: *Turn the heat down if the oil starts to spit.*
–*noun* 5. saliva, especially when spat out.

spit[2] *noun*
1. a sharp pointed rod which is pushed through meat for roasting it over a fire or grilling it in an oven. 2. a narrow area of land jutting out into the water.

spite *noun*
1. a bad-tempered wish to annoy or hurt someone else: *I think she broke my pen out of spite.*
–*verb* 2. If someone does something to **spite** you, they do it deliberately to annoy or upset you: *She ate the last strawberry just to spite him.*
–*phrase* 3. **in spite of**, without taking notice of: *She went to school in spite of feeling unwell.*
☐ **spiteful**, *adjective*

A SIMILAR WORD (for definition 1) is **malice**.

splash *verb*
1. If you **splash** a liquid somewhere, you throw it there: *He splashed a bucket of water onto the fire.* 2. If you **splash** around in water, you cause some of it to fly up into the air. 3. If a liquid **splashes** something or onto something, it hits it and separates into many small drops: *The mud splashed us when the car drove past.*
–*noun* 4. the act or sound of splashing. 5. a mark made by splashing. 6. a patch of colour or light: *Her bright jacket was a splash of red among the dull grey uniforms.*
–*phrase* 7. **make a splash**, to be widely noticed: *The group made a splash with their first CD.*
☐ **splashy**, *adjective*

splendid *adjective*
1. beautiful in a way that makes you pay attention and feel admiration: *a splendid building.* 2. extremely good: *a splendid idea.*
☐ **splendidly**, *adverb* –**splendour**, *noun*

ANOTHER SPELLING for **splendour** is **splendor**.

splice *verb* To **splice** is to join things together by twisting threads, as in joining ropes, etc., or by overlapping pieces, especially as with timber, or film and tape.

splint *noun* a flat piece of something stiff which is used to hold a broken bone in place so that it can heal properly.

splinter *noun*
1. a long, thin, sharp piece broken off from something hard, such as wood, metal or glass.
–*verb* 2. If something **splinters**, it splits or breaks into splinters: *The wood has splintered with age.*

split *verb* (**splits**, **splitting**, **split**, **has split**) To **split** something is to 1. break it apart, especially from end to end: *He split the watermelon in two.* 2. divide it up in any way: *We split the money among all of us who were involved.* 3. *Informal* When someone **splits**, they leave in a hurry.
–*noun* 4. the act of splitting. 5. a break or division caused by splitting: *a split in a dress*; *a split in public opinion.*
–*phrase* 6. **split up**, to break up from a relationship or stop being friends. 7. **the splits**, an exercise in which you spread your legs apart along the floor until they stretch out at right angles to your body.

splurge *verb* To **splurge** money is to spend it wastefully or on a luxury: *He splurged all his money on taking his friends to a fancy restaurant.*
☐ **splurge**, *noun*

WORD HISTORY formed by blending *splash* and *surge*

splutter *verb*
1. If someone **splutters**, they talk quickly or in a confused way: *'How could you even think of doing that?' she spluttered.* **2.** If something **splutters**, it makes noises like spitting or popping: *The fat was spluttering in the pan*; *The car finally spluttered into life.*
☐ **splutter**, *noun* –**splutterer**, *noun*

spoil *verb* (**spoils**, **spoiling**, **spoiled** *or* **spoilt**, **has spoiled** *or* **has spoilt**)
1. If you **spoil** something, you damage it so that it becomes less valuable, useful or enjoyable. **2.** If you **spoil** someone, you ruin their character by giving them whatever they want.
☐ **spoilt**, *adjective*: *a spoilt child.*

spoke[1] *noun* one of the rods, bars, or wires that connect the outer part of a wheel to the centre, as on a bicycle or steering wheel.

spoke[2] *noun* the past tense of **speak**.

spokesperson *noun* someone who speaks for someone else.
☐ **spokesman**, **spokeswoman**, *noun*

sponge /*say* spunj/ *noun*
1. a material with lots of holes for soaking up liquid, used especially for wiping and cleaning. **2.** a kind of sea creature whose rubbery, absorbent skeleton can be used for washing and cleaning. **3.** a light cake made from well-beaten eggs, flour and sugar.
–*verb* **4.** If you **sponge** something, you wash or wipe it clean with a sponge: *Dad sponged the baby's face.* **5.** *Informal* To **sponge** off someone is to live at their expense: *He never spends his own money, he just sponges off us.*
☐ **spongy**, *adjective* (**spongier**, **spongiest**)

☑ SPELLING TIP Remember that the vowel sound in this word is spelt with an *o*, although it sounds like 'u'.

sponsor *noun*
1. a person or group who supports someone or something, often with money.
–*verb* **2.** If someone **sponsors** a person or group, they act as a sponsor for them.
☐ **sponsorship**, *noun*

spontaneous *adjective* happening naturally and often unexpectedly: *There was a spontaneous outpouring of affection for her when her illness was made known.*
☐ **spontaneity**, *noun* –**spontaneously**, *adverb*

spoof *noun Rather informal* a humorous imitation: *The play was a spoof on the royal family.*

spook *Informal*
–*noun* **1.** a ghost: *That old house looks as if it's full of spooks.*
–*verb* **2.** To **spook** a person or animal is to frighten them: *The shadow spooked the horse.*
☐ **spooked**, *adjective* –**spooky**, *adjective* (**spookier**, **spookiest**)

OTHER WORDS (for definition 1), used especially in formal language, are **apparition**, **phantom** and **spectre**.

spool *noun* the cylinder or bobbin on which something, such as wire, thread or film, is wound.

spoon *noun* a utensil with a rounded end attached to a handle, which is used for stirring or lifting food.

spoor /*say* spaw/ *noun* the track left by a wild animal.

☑ SPELLING TIP Don't confuse the spelling of **spoor** with **spore** which has the same sound. A **spore** is a plant reproductive cell.

sporadic /*say* spuh-**rad**-ik/ *adjective* irregular and not very frequent: *I have made sporadic attempts to get full marks in spelling.*
☐ **sporadically**, *adverb*

A SIMILAR WORD is **occasional**.

spore *noun* a reproductive cell produced by some plants.

sporran *noun* the pouch of fur worn by Scottish Highlanders at the front of the kilt.

WORD HISTORY from a Gaelic word, a language of the ancient Celtic people and their modern ancestors in Ireland and Scotland

sport *noun*
1. something done for pleasure or exercise, usually needing some physical skill or effort. **2.** *Informal* someone who is fair-minded or good-natured: *She's a real sport.*
☐ **sporting**, *adjective*: *a sporting chance.* –**sports**, *adjective*: *sports department*; *sports shoes* –**sporty**, *adjective* (**sportier**, **sportiest**) –**sportsman**, *noun* –**sportswoman**, *noun*

ANOTHER TERM (for definition 2) is a **good sport**.
THE OPPOSITE (of definition 2) is a **bad sport**.

spot *noun*
1. a small, usually round, mark: *There's a spot on your tie.* **2.** a place: *The jetty is a good spot for fishing.*
–*verb* (**spots**, **spotting**, **spotted**, **has spotted**) **3.** To **spot** something is to mark or stain it: *You have spotted the tablecloth.* **4.** If you **spot** someone or something, you see or notice them: *to spot someone in a crowd.*
–*phrase* **5. on the spot**, **a.** immediately: *She bought it on the spot.* **b.** in an awkward situation: *Her question put him on the spot.* **6. soft spot**, a special sympathy or affection: *a soft spot for small animals.* **7. tight spot**, a difficult or dangerous situation.
☐ **spotted**, *adjective* –**spotty**, *adjective* (**spottier**, **spottiest**)

spotlight *noun*
1. a strong lamp with a narrow beam, such as those used in the theatre or attached to cars.

–*phrase* **2. in the spotlight**, in a situation in which you get a lot of attention from other people, such as the public, the media, and so on: *Her sister is famous and now she thinks it's her turn to be in the spotlight.*

spouse /*rhymes with* house/ *noun* someone's husband or wife.

spout *noun* a narrow tube or lip-like part of a container from which water or other contents are poured.

sprain *verb* If you **sprain** a joint in your body, you twist or bend it accidentally so that it swells and bruises: *She sprained her ankle.*
☐ **sprain**, *noun*

sprawl *verb*
1. If you **sprawl** somewhere, you sit or lie in a very relaxed way with your limbs stretched out: *After a swim we sprawled out on the sand.* **2.** If something **sprawls**, it stretches or spreads out untidily: *The new suburbs are sprawled along the highway.*
–*noun* **3.** a scattered or irregular grouping of something: *urban sprawl.*

spray *noun*
1. a fine stream of droplets, such as one thrown by a wave or jet of water.
–*verb* **2.** To **spray** something is to send a spray onto it: *Mum sprayed the flowers in the vase to keep them fresh.*

spread *verb* (**spreads**, **spreading**, **spread**, **has spread**)
1. If you **spread** something, you put it out flat or arrange it over a surface so that you can see or use all of it: *She spread the wet coat over a chair to dry.* **2.** If you **spread** a substance on a surface, you put a thin layer of it over the surface: *to spread some jam on the bread.* **3.** If something **spreads**, it reaches or covers a wider area: *The rash started on her arm and spread to her whole body.*
–*noun* **4.** anything which is spread on bread, such as jam or soft cheese. **5.** *Rather informal* a large meal.

spree *noun*
1. a time of fun: *They went on a spree after their final exams.* **2.** an extravagant outing: *We went on a spending spree in the computer shop.*

sprightly /*say* **spruyt**-lee/ *adjective* lively and energetic: *a sprightly dance*; *a sprightly old man.*

> ☑ SPELLING TIP Remember the *ight* spelling for the 'uyt' sound in this word. Other words which are spelt in a similar way are *nightly* and *brightly.* Don't confuse the first part of the word with **sprite** which has the same sound. A **sprite** is a kind of fairy.

spring *verb* (**springs**, **springing**, **sprang** *or* **sprung**, **has sprung**)
1. To **spring** is to move or jump upwards with sudden energy: *to spring out of bed*; *The dog sprang into her waiting arms.* **2.** If something **springs** up, it comes up or starts: *New crazes are always springing up at school.*
–*noun* **3.** a leap or jump. **4.** a coil of wire which bounces back to its original shape after being stretched. **5.** the season of the year, following winter, when the weather starts to get warmer and new flowers and leaves appear on plants. **6.** the ability to bounce back: *The old couch hasn't much spring left.* **7.** a flow of water from the ground: *a hot spring.*
☐ **spring**, *adjective* –**springy**, *adjective* –**springiness**, *noun*

springboard *noun* a board with a lot of bounce in it, used for diving or vaulting.

spring roll *noun*
1. a deep-fried roll of thin dough containing a savoury filling, originating in Chinese cooking. **2.** a roll of raw vegetables and seafood or tofu, wrapped in rice paper and eaten cold, originating in Vietnamese cooking.

> WORD HISTORY in Chinese tradition, this is eaten at the spring festival

sprinkle *verb*
1. If you **sprinkle** something such as powder or liquid over something, you throw or scatter small amounts of it over the thing: *He sprinkled some soy sauce over the meat.* **2.** If it is **sprinkling**, it is raining gently.
☐ **sprinkle**, *noun* –**sprinkler**, *noun*

sprint *verb* To **sprint** is to race at top speed, especially over a short distance.
☐ **sprint**, *noun* –**sprinter**, *noun*

sprite *noun* a small fairy.

sprocket *noun* a toothed wheel that fits into a chain, such as the one on a bicycle.

sprout *verb*
1. To **sprout** is to grow, or send up shoots: *to sprout plants from seed*; *The old onions have sprouted.*
–*noun* **2.** a shoot.

spruce[1] *noun* an evergreen tree with fine, needle-like leaves, and cones.

spruce[2] *adjective*
1. stylish or smart: *Once he had put on his suit, he looked quite spruce and presentable.*
–*verb in the phrase* **2. spruce up**, to smarten something up: *You'd better spruce up your room for the visitors!*

spry *adjective* (**spryer**, **spryest**) nimble or active: *My grandfather puts his spry condition down to eating carrots.*
☐ **spryly**, *adverb*

spud *noun Informal* a potato.

> WORD HISTORY from a Middle English word for 'a kind of knife'

spunk *noun Informal* **1.** courage. **2.** someone who is good-looking, especially in a sexually attractive way.
□ **spunky**, *adjective* (**spunkier**, **spunkiest**)

spur *noun*
1. a sharp instrument worn on the heel of a riding boot to make a horse go faster. **2.** anything which encourages you to do something. **3.** something looking like a spur, such as the horny piece on some birds' feet, or a high piece of land rising up to a mountain range.
–*verb* (**spurs**, **spurring**, **spurred**, **has spurred**) **4.** To **spur** is to urge on: *The thought of food spurred them on.*
–*phrase* **5. on the spur of the moment**, suddenly or without preparation.

spurn /*say* spern/ *verb* If you **spurn** someone or something, you turn them away with scorn: *She spurned his offer of help.*

spurt *verb*
1. If a liquid **spurts** out of something, it comes out suddenly in a forceful stream: *Water spurted from the broken pipe.*
–*noun* **2.** a sudden rush: *a spurt of activity.*

spy *noun* (*plural* **spies**)
1. someone who secretly watches and reports on the activities of others.
–*verb* (**spies**, **spying**, **spied**, **has spied**) **2.** to see: *I spied his tall figure racing along the platform.*
–*phrase* **3. spy on**, to watch secretly.
□ **spying**, *noun*

spyware *noun* software that is installed on your computer without you knowing to gather information about which internet sites you visit: *Spyware can be secretly installed during a free download.*

squabble /*rhymes with* wobble/ *noun*
1. a small unimportant quarrel: *It was a stupid squabble about which colour jelly we should make.*
–*verb* **2.** If people **squabble**, they quarrel about something unimportant: *My Mum hates it when my sister and I squabble in the car.*

squad /*rhymes with* rod/ *noun* a small group taking part in a shared activity: *a squad of drivers*; *the cheer squad.*

squadron /*say* **skwod**-ruhn/ *noun* a fighting unit in the armed forces, especially in the air force or navy.

squalid /*say* **skwol**-uhd/ *adjective* dirty or filthy: *The squalid living conditions in the slum shocked us.*

> ☑ SPELLING TIP *Single letter alert*: only one *l*. Also remember that the first vowel sound is spelt *a* (not *o*). Think of putting 'a lid' on anything **squalid** to remind you how to spell the last four letters.

squall *noun* a sudden strong wind which dies away rapidly.

squalor /*say* **skwol**-uh/ *noun* dirt and poverty.

> ☑ SPELLING TIP Note the *or* ending. This is not one of those words where there can be either an *our* or *or* ending. It is always spelt *or*.

squander /*say* **skwon**-duh/ *verb* If you **squander** something, you spend or use it wastefully: *He squandered all his pocket money on pinball machines and now he's got nothing to show for it.*

square *noun*
1. a shape with four equal sides and four right angles. **2.** an open public place in a town. **3.** an instrument which is used to draw and check right angles. **4.** a number multiplied by itself: *The square of 3 is 9, (3×3).* **5.** *Rather informal* someone who is old-fashioned in what they like and the way they look.
–*verb* **6.** To **square** something is to make it straight or square. **7.** To **square** a number is to multiply it by itself: *If you add 2 and 2 then square the result, you get 16.*
□ **square**, *adjective*: *a square box*; *a square metre.* –**square**, *adverb* –**squarely**, *adverb*

square metre *noun* a unit of measurement of area, equal to a square which measures one metre on each side.

> THE SYMBOL is $\mathbf{m^2}$ or **sq. m.**

square root *noun* the number which, when multiplied by itself, gives the stated number: *The square root of 25 is 5.*

squash[1] /*say* skwosh/ *verb*
1. If you **squash** something, you flatten or crush it: *The wheel squashed his hat*; *The army squashed the rebellion.*
–*noun* **2.** a game for two players with racquets and a small rubber ball, played in a small court with four walls. **3.** a fizzy fruit drink.

squash[2] /*say* skwosh/ *noun* a round vegetable like a marrow.

squat /*say* skwot/ *verb* (**squats**, **squatting**, **squatted**, **has squatted**) To **squat** is to **1.** rest in a position close to the ground with the knees bent and the back more or less straight, resting on the front of the feet. **2.** live without permission on land or property which you do not own.
–*adjective* **3.** short and with a heavy build or square shape: *a squat old man*; *a squat building.*
□ **squat**, *noun* –**squatness**, *noun*

> ☑ SPELLING TIP Remember that the vowel sound is spelt *a* (not *o*).

squatter /*say* **skwot**-uh/ *noun*
1. in early colonial times in Australia, a person who settled on land without permission in order to farm sheep and cattle, and who was later given a

government lease to stay. **2.** someone who lives without permission in a place they do not own.

squaw *noun* a woman of a Native American people, especially a wife.

> NOTE Most people now find the use of this word offensive.
> WORD HISTORY from an Algonquian (a Native American language) word for 'woman'

squawk *verb* If someone or something squawks, they make a loud unpleasant cry: *The smaller birds started to squawk when they saw the crows.*
☐ **squawk**, *noun*

squeak *verb* To **squeak** is to make a high noise: *The rusty hinge squeaked as I pushed open the door*; *Mice squeak.*
☐ **squeak**, *noun* –**squeaky**, *adjective* (**squeakier**, **squeakiest**) –**squeakily**, *adverb*

squeal *verb* To **squeal** is to make a sudden high noise that lasts for a while: *to squeal in pain*; *The tyres squealed as the car went around the corner.*
☐ **squeal**, *noun*

squeeze *verb*
1. If you **squeeze** something, you press it firmly together: *to squeeze someone's hand.* **2.** If you **squeeze** something, you press it in order to get a liquid or a soft substance out of it: *She squeezed the remaining toothpaste out of the tube.*
–*noun* **3.** a tight fit: *We should all be able to fit around the table, but it will be a bit of a squeeze.* **4.** a small amount of something got by squeezing: *a squeeze of lemon.*
–*phrase* **5. a tight squeeze**, a difficult situation.

squid *noun* a sea animal with a soft body, ten tentacles and no backbone.

> ANOTHER NAME for this is **calamari**, especially when it is used as food.

squint *verb*
1. If you **squint** at something, you look at it with your eyes partly closed: *The strong light made him squint.*
–*noun* **2.** an eye condition in which it is hard to turn both eyes in the same direction at the same time.
☐ **squinting**, *adjective*

squire *noun*
1. an English country gentleman. **2.** in medieval times in Britain and Europe, a young nobleman attending a knight.

squirm /*say* skwerm/ *verb* If you **squirm**, you wriggle, often because you feel uncomfortable or embarrassed about something: *I couldn't get comfortable in bed and was squirming for hours*; *We squirmed when we realised how silly we had made ourselves look.*

> ☑ SPELLING TIP Even though the basic meaning of **squirm** is to wriggle like a worm, there is no *worm* in the spelling. Remember the *qu* spelling for the 'kw' sound, and be firm in your mind about the *irm* ending.

squirrel *noun* a bushy-tailed animal found in Europe, Asia, and North America, which lives in trees and stores nuts.

> ☑ SPELLING TIP *Double/single letter alert*: double *r* (think of a **squirrel** being a 'rodent relative' to remind you), but only one *l* at the end.

squirt *verb* If a liquid **squirts**, or you **squirt** a liquid, it comes out of a small hole in a thin, fast stream: *Shampoo squirted out of the bottle*; *I squirted some cream on my sunburn.*

stab *verb* (**stabs**, **stabbing**, **stabbed**, **has stabbed**)
1. To **stab** something or someone is to cut, pierce, or push them with a pointed weapon or with something similar: *My brother always stabs a potato with his fork.*
–*noun* **2.** a sudden painful blow or feeling: *a stab of remorse.* **3.** *Informal* an attempt: *Now you have a stab at it.*
☐ **stabbing**, *adjective*

stable¹ *noun* a place where horses are kept and fed.

stable² *adjective* firm and steady: *stable foundations*; *a stable temperature.*
☐ **stabilise**, *verb*: *to stabilise the situation.* –**stabiliser**, *noun* –**stability**, *noun*

> ANOTHER SPELLING for **stabilise** is **stabilize**.

staccato /*say* stuh-**kah**-toh/ *adverb* with the notes very short and detached from each other.

> NOTE This is used as an instruction in music.

> ☑ SPELLING TIP *Double letter alert*: double *c* in the middle. This is because the word **staccato** comes from Italian, like most musical instructions.

stack *noun*
1. a large pile of things on top of each other. **2.** a tall chimney. **3.** a large number or quantity: *There were a stack of people there.*
–*verb* **4.** When you **stack** things, you pile them one on top of the other: *We stacked the mats in the corner of the hall.* **5.** If someone **stacks** a deck of cards, they arrange them unfairly.
☐ **stacked**, *adjective*

stadium *noun* a large, often enclosed, sports ground, designed to hold many people.

staff *noun*
1. the people who work in a business or in a place like a school or hospital. **2.** a large stick or rod.
–*verb* **3.** To **staff** a business or organisation is to provide it with the people who work there: *On the weekends, the bookshop is staffed mainly by university students working part-time.*
☐ **staff**, *adjective*: *staff entrance.*

stag *noun* a male deer.

> NOTE The female is a **doe**.

stage *noun*
1. a raised floor, usually in a theatre, on which public performances take place. **2.** a step in a process: *Breaking the eggs is the first stage in making an omelette.* **3.** a period of development: *We are still in the early stages of planning.*
–*verb* **4.** To **stage** something is to carry it out or perform it: *to stage a robbery*; *to stage an opera.*

stagecoach *noun* (*plural* **stagecoaches**) a coach drawn by horses, used in the past to transport passengers and goods, running regularly over a fixed route.

stagger *verb*
1. To **stagger** is to walk, move or stand unsteadily: *He staggered away from the scene of the accident.* **2.** If you **stagger** events, you arrange them so they do not occur at the same time: *The dining room staggers meal times into three sittings.* **3.** To **stagger** someone is to shock them: *We were staggered by the results.*
☐ **stagger**, *noun* –**staggering**, *adjective*: *staggering news.*

stagnant *adjective* If water is **stagnant**, it is not flowing and is dirty: *It would be a big mistake to drink from a stagnant pond.*
☐ **stagnancy**, *noun*

stagnate /*say* **stag**-nayt, stag-**nayt**/ *verb*
1. If water **stagnates**, it stops running or flowing: *The creek has stagnated into muddy waterholes.* **2.** If a person **stagnates**, they become bored and inactive: *He feels he is stagnating in that job.*
☐ **stagnation**, *noun*

stain *noun*
1. a mark that is hard to remove. **2.** a clear colouring, such as that used on wood.
–*verb* **3.** To **stain** something is to make or leave a mark on it: *The spilt coffee stained the carpet.* **4.** To **stain** something made of wood is to colour it with a stain.
☐ **stained**, *adjective*

stair *noun* one of a series of steps.

> ☑ SPELLING TIP Don't confuse the spelling of **stair** with **stare** which has the same sound. To **stare** at someone is to look directly at them for a long time with your eyes wide open.

staircase *noun* a series of steps with its banister.

stake[1] *noun*
1. a stick which is often pointed at one end: *She put in stakes to support the vine.* **2. the stake**, in the past, a thick pole that a person was tied to while being burnt to death, as a form of punishment: *She died at the stake.*
–*verb in the phrase* **3. stake a claim**, to claim a right to something: *He has staked his claim to a share of the profits.* **4. stake out**, to surround, in order to keep watch or make a surprise attack: *to stake out a building.*

> ☑ SPELLING TIP Don't confuse the spelling of **stake** with **steak** which has the same sound. A **steak** is a thick slice of meat or fish.

stake[2] *noun*
1. the amount bet in a race or game: *The stakes were high.* **2.** a personal interest or involvement: *He has a stake in the shop.*
–*verb* **3.** To **stake** money or some other thing that is valuable is to risk it, as in a bet.
–*phrase* **4. at stake**, at risk: *A lot is at stake.*

> ☑ SPELLING TIP See **stake**[1].

stalactite /*say* **stal**-uhk-tuyt/ *noun* a stick of limestone or other material that forms, little by little, on the roof of a cave from dripping water.

stalagmite /*say* **stal**-uhg-muyt/ *noun* a stick of limestone or other material that forms, little by little, on the floor of a cave, formed from water dripping from above.

stale *adjective* not fresh or new.

stalemate *noun* a situation where no progress can be made.

> WORD HISTORY from chess, where any move by the king would place him under direct attack and end the game

stalk[1] /*rhymes with* fork/ *noun* the stem of a plant.

> ☑ SPELLING TIP Notice the *alk* ending. Don't confuse **stalk** with **stork** which has the same sound. A **stork** is a kind of bird.

stalk[2] /*rhymes with* fork/ *verb*
1. If one animal **stalks** another, it follows it quietly and carefully before attacking: *The lion was stalking an antelope.* **2.** If a person **stalks**, they walk slowly and proudly: *She stalked out of the room in a rage.* **3.** If a person **stalks** another person, they **a.** follow them secretly and constantly. **b.** harass them on social media, etc.

> ☑ SPELLING TIP See **stalk**[1].

stall[1] *noun*
1. a stand, tent, or table where goods are sold, such as at a market. **2.** a part of a building on a farm where a horse or cow is kept. **3. the stalls**, the front seats on the ground floor of a theatre.
–*verb* **4.** If an engine **stalls**, it stops, especially without warning: *He stalled the car*; *After the engine stalled we drifted in to shore with the tide.*

stall[2] *verb* If you **stall** someone, you put them off or get out of doing what they want for a time: *Stall the visitors until next week.*

stallion /*say* **stal**-yuhn/ *noun* a male horse that has not been castrated, especially one kept for breeding.

NOTE The female is a **mare**.

stamen /*say* **stay**-muhn/ *noun* the part of a flower that produces the pollen.

WORD HISTORY from a Latin word meaning 'thread'

stamina /*say* **stam**-uh-nuh/ *noun* physical power or strength, especially to fight off tiredness or sickness.

stammer *noun*
1. a speech problem in which someone repeats a sound in a word several times: *He has a slight stammer.*
–*verb* **2.** If someone **stammers**, they speak with a stammer: *He sometimes stammers when he is nervous.*

A SIMILAR WORD is **stutter**.

stamp *noun*
1. a small label which is sticky on one side, printed by the government for attaching to letters or documents. **2.** an official mark showing something is the real thing or has been approved. **3.** a block or instrument, usually of rubber, with a design on it which will make a mark on something when pressed onto it.
–*verb* **4.** If you **stamp** a mark on an object or if you stamp an object, you put a mark on it using a stamp: *The official stamped my passport.* **5.** If you **stamp** your foot, you place it hard on the ground: *She stamped her foot to get the class's attention.*
–*phrase* **6. stamp out**, to put an end to: *to stamp out crime.*

stampede *noun*
1. a sudden scattering or frenzied flight of a group of animals or people, often in fright.
–*verb* **2.** To **stampede** is to scatter or run in a stampede.

stance *noun*
1. the position of the body while standing: *a dancer's stance.* **2.** a way of thinking: *I don't agree with her stance on that issue.*

stand *verb* (**stands**, **standing**, **stood**, **has stood**)
1. To **stand** is to take or keep an upright position on your feet. **2.** If a law or rule **stands**, it remains unchanged: *My decision stands in spite of your arguments.* **3.** If something **stands** somewhere, it is placed or situated there: *The shed stands beside a clump of trees.* **4.** If you cannot **stand** someone or something, you cannot bear them.
–*noun* **5.** a small structure used to display goods. **6.** a building with many seats for watching races, sports events, etc. **7.** a structure to support something: *a music stand.* **8.** opposition to, or support for a cause: *He took a stand against the war.*
–*phrase* **9. stand by, a.** to wait or be ready. **b.** to help: *I'll stand by him.* **c.** to keep to: *She always stands by her promises.* **10. stand for, a.** to represent: *A policeman stands for the law.* **b.** to become a candidate for: *to stand for public office.* **11. stand in**, to act in place of someone else. **12. stand up for**, to defend the cause of. **13. stand up to, a.** to remain in good condition in spite of: *to stand up to hard wear.* **b.** to oppose, especially bravely: *to stand up to the enemy.*

standard *noun*
1. anything taken as a rule or basis for comparing other things. **2.** a level of excellence or achievement: *a high standard of living.* **3.** a flag, emblem, or symbol.
–*adjective* **4.** used as a standard or rule: *standard spelling.* **5.** normal, acceptable, or average: *Bella is the standard height for that breed of dog.*
☐ **standardise**, *verb* –**standardisation**, *noun*

ANOTHER SPELLING for **standardise** is **standardize**.

stand-by *noun* (*plural* **stand-bys**) someone or something kept ready to be used when needed or in an emergency.

stand-in *noun* any substitute, but especially one used to replace someone for a short time in a play or film.

standing *noun*
1. position, status or reputation: *He was given the contract because of his standing in the computer world.* **2.** duration or length of existence or membership: *She is a friend of long standing.*
–*adjective* **3.** in an upright position. **4.** continuing without stopping or changing: *The government has a standing commitment to fund health and education.*

standstill *noun* a stop or halt: *Work came to a standstill.*

stand-up paddleboard *noun* a surfboard designed so that the rider stands up on it and propels and steers it with a paddle.

THE ABBREVIATION is **SUP**.

stanza *noun* a group of lines of poetry arranged in a pattern or verse.

WORD HISTORY from a Latin word meaning 'standing'

staple[1] *noun*
1. a piece of wire driven into papers with a special tool and bent to hold them together. **2.** a U-shaped piece of metal with pointed ends for driving into a surface such as wood.
–*verb* **3.** When you **staple** something, you fasten it to something else or secure it in place using a staple.
☐ **stapler**, *noun*

staple[2] *noun* an important item, especially a food which is always used or needed.
☐ **staple**, *adjective*: *a staple food.*

star *noun*
1. any of the large bodies in space like our sun, which we see as bright points of light in the night sky. **2.** a shape which looks like a star in the sky, with five or six points which look like rays of light. **3.** someone who is excellent in something or who is famous in an art or profession, especially the movies: *She is a film star.*
–*adjective* **4.** best: *He is the star player in the team.*
–*verb* (**stars**, **starring**, **starred**, **has starred**) **5.** If someone **stars** in a show, play or film, they are the leading performer in it: *What was the first film that Nicole Kidman starred in?*
☐ **starred**, *adjective* –**starry**, *adjective* (**starrier**, **starriest**)

starboard /*say* **stah**-buhd/ *noun* the right-hand side of a ship when you are facing the front or bow of the ship.

THE OPPOSITE is **port**[2].

starch *noun*
1. a white, tasteless substance found in foods like potatoes and rice. **2.** a preparation of this used to stiffen clothes and materials.
–*verb* **3.** If you **starch** clothes, you stiffen them with starch: *to starch shirts.*

stare *noun*
1. a long fixed look, especially with the eyes wide open.
–*verb* **2.** If you **stare** at something, you look at it directly for a long time: *to stare in amazement*; *She stared at me in a very rude way.*

SIMILAR WORDS (for definition 2) are **gaze**, **gape** and **gawk** (*Informal*).

☑ SPELLING TIP Don't confuse the spelling of **stare** with **stair** which has the same sound. A **stair** is one of a series of steps.

starfish *noun* (*plural* **starfish** *or* **starfishes**) a sea animal with a body in the shape of a star.

stark *adjective*
1. bare, plain or harsh: *Their living conditions were stark and primitive.* **2.** complete or total: *a stark contrast.*
–*phrase* **3. stark naked**, completely naked.
☐ **starkly**, *adverb*

starling *noun* a noisy bird with dark, shiny feathers.

start *verb*
1. If you **start** to do something, you do something you were not doing before and keep doing it: *The baby started crying.* **2.** If something **starts** or if you **start** it, it happens from a particular time: *It started raining just as we were leaving.* **3.** If you **start** an engine or vehicle, or if it **starts**, it begins to work: *to start the car.* **4.** If you **start**, your body makes a sudden, sharp movement because something has surprised or frightened you: *I had just fallen asleep when a loud noise made me start.*
–*noun* **5.** a beginning. **6.** the first part of anything: *the start of a book.* **7.** a sudden, quick movement of your body: *I woke with a start.* **8.** a lead or advantage over other competitors: *I gave her a ten second start before I dived into the pool.*

starter *noun*
1. someone who gives the signal to start a race. **2.** anyone who is a competitor in a race or contest. **3.** the first course in a meal: *What would you like for a starter?*
–*phrase* **4. for starters**, *Rather informal* as a beginning: *I'll read the instructions for starters.*

startle *verb* If something such as a noise **startles** you, it surprises or frightens you a little: *The loud noise startled the baby.*
☐ **startled**, *adjective*: *a startled expression.* –**startling**, *adjective*: *startling news.*

starve *verb*
1. To **starve** is to die or cause to die from hunger: *Sometimes animals starve during a drought.* **2.** *Rather informal* If you say you are **starving**, you mean that you are very hungry.
☐ **starvation**, *noun*

state *noun*
1. the condition of someone or something: *a state of unhappiness.* **2.** a tense, excited, or nervous condition: *She has got herself into quite a state about her concert performance.* **3.** a large division of a country, having its own government: *Victoria is a state of Australia.* **4.** a nation: *Several states refused to sign the United Nations resolution.*
–*adjective* **5.** A **state** occasion is a ceremonial public event organised by a government: *The great writer was given a state funeral.*
–*verb* **6.** If you **state** something, you say or write it in a formal way.

SIMILAR WORDS (for definition 6) are **declare** and **assert**.

stately *adjective* (**statelier**, **stateliest**) formal and splendid: *a stately palace*; *a stately procession.*
☐ **stateliness**, *noun*

statement *noun*
1. the stating or declaring of facts or ideas. **2.** the thing or things stated: *Can you change the wording of that statement so that it sounds more friendly?*

statesman *noun* (*plural* **statesmen**) someone who is skilled in, or whose work is, directing the affairs of the government.
☐ **statesmanship**, *noun*

static *adjective*
1. staying still or not changing: *a static image*; *His painting style remained static in the latter years of his life.* **2.** having to do with electricity which is not flowing, especially that caused by friction.
–*noun* **3.** noise or interference with sound waves, such as crackling caused by electrical activity in the air.

station *noun*
1. a place at which a train regularly stops. **2.** the end of a bus route. **3.** the place or the equipment used for broadcasting radio or television. **4.** a rural property for raising sheep or cattle.
–*verb* **5.** If someone is **stationed** at a place, they are put there for a particular reason: *A guard was stationed at each gate.*

stationary /*say* **stay**-shuhn-ree/ *adjective* not moving: *She ran to the stationary car and opened the door.*

☑ SPELLING TIP Remember the *ary* ending in **stationary**. Don't confuse it with **stationery**, which is writing materials.

stationery /*say* **stay**-shuhn-ree/ *noun* writing paper and writing materials such as pens and pencils.
☐ **stationer**, *noun*

☑ SPELLING TIP Remember the *ery* ending in **stationery**. Don't confuse it with **stationary**. To be **stationary** is to be still or not moving. Think that **stationery** includes envelopes, so that is the word with the *ery* ending.

station wagon *noun* a car which has extra space behind the back seat, and a door at the back.

statistics /*say* stuh-**tis**-tiks/ *plural noun* the science which deals with the collection, ordering, and use of information in the form of numbers and amounts.
☐ **statistical**, *adjective* –**statistician** /*say* stat-uhs-**tish**-uhn/, *noun*

statue /*say* **stach**-ooh/ *noun* an image of a person or animal made out of stone, wood or bronze.
☐ **statuesque** /*say* stach-ooh-**esk**/, *adjective*: *a woman with a statuesque figure.*

☑ SPELLING TIP Remember the second *t* in this word. With the *u* following it has a 'ch' sound and you don't hear the *t*.

stature /*say* **stach**-uh/ *noun*
1. someone's height. **2.** achievement or distinction reached by someone: *She is a person of high stature in the computing business.*

☑ SPELLING TIP Remember that the ending is *ture*, although you hear a 'ch' sound (*chuh*). **Stature** is related to the word *state* (they both come from the Latin word *stare* meaning to 'stand' or 'be'). Think of *state*, take off the final *e* and add *ure* for the spelling.

status /*say* **stay**-tuhs, **stat**-uhs/ *noun*
1. someone's social or professional position, rank, or importance. **2.** the state or condition of something.

staunch[1] /*say* stawnch/ *verb* To **staunch** the flow of blood from a cut is to stop it bleeding.

staunch[2] /*say* stawnch/ *adjective* loyal or steadfast: *a staunch friend.*
☐ **staunchly**, *adverb*

stave *noun*
1. a thin, narrow, curved piece of wood that is part of the side of a barrel or tub. **2.** the set of five horizontal lines used in music, on which the notes are written.
–*verb in the phrase* (**staves**, **staving**, **staved** *or* **stove**, **has staved** *or* **has stove**) **3. stave in**, to break a hole in: *The whole structure had been staved in by a heavy blunt instrument.* **4. stave off**, to put off or prevent: *The tennis player was able to stave off the strong challenge of his opponent.*

ANOTHER WORD (for definition 2) is **staff**.

stay[1] *verb* To **stay** is to **1.** remain in a place. **2.** continue to be: *to stay clean.*
–*phrase* **3. stay put**, to remain where placed.
☐ **stay**, *noun*: *a short stay.*

stay[2] *noun* a support, especially used to keep something steady.

STD *noun* any disease which is picked up by having sexual intercourse with someone who is already infected with it.

WORD HISTORY short for *sexually transmitted disease*

stead /*rhymes with* bed/ *noun*
1. place or position: *She felt ill so she sent Maggie in her stead.*
–*phrase* **2. stand in good stead**, to be useful: *The extra dried fruit and nuts stood us in good stead on the second day.*

☑ SPELLING TIP *Tricky vowel sound*: *ea* spelling for the 'e' sound.

steadfast /*say* **sted**-fahst, **sted**-fuhst/ *adjective* firmly fixed, constant, or unchanging: *They made a steadfast commitment to stick by us whatever happened.*

☑ SPELLING TIP *Tricky vowel sound*: **steadfast** contains the word *stead*, with its *ea* spelling for the 'e' sound.

steady /*say* **sted**-ee/ *adjective* (**steadier**, **steadiest**)
1. continuing in an even way and without interruption, not changing very much: *His progress in class is steady.* **2.** firm and not moving: *This ladder isn't steady.*
–*verb* (**steadies**, **steadying**, **steadied**, **has steadied**) **3.** If you **steady** something, you hold it steady: *I steadied the boat so Mum could step aboard.*
–*adverb* **4.** in a firm or regular manner.
☐ **steadily**, *adverb* –**steadiness**, *noun*

☑ SPELLING TIP *Tricky vowel sound*: as in the word *stead*, there is an *ea* spelling for the 'e' sound, as in some other words such as *ready*.

steak /*say* stayk/ *noun* a thick slice of meat or fish.

> ☑ SPELLING TIP Don't confuse the spelling of **steak** with **stake** which has the same sound. A **stake** is a stick with a pointed end, or the amount bet in a race or game.

steal *verb* (**steals**, **stealing**, **stole**, **has stolen**)
1. If you **steal** something from someone, you take it from them without asking them for it and without intending to return it: *He got caught stealing someone's handbag.* **2.** If you **steal** somewhere, you go there very quietly, trying not to be noticed: *He stole up on us out of the dark.*
–*noun* **3.** *Informal* something obtained cheaply or below its true value: *We got our new computer for a special price – it was a real steal.*
☐ **stealing**, *noun*: *Stealing is a crime.*

> ☑ SPELLING TIP Don't confuse the spelling of **steal** with **steel** which has the same sound but is spelt with *ee*. **Steel** is iron mixed with other metals and carbon to make it very hard and strong.

stealth /*say* stelth/ *noun* hidden or secret action or behaviour.
☐ **stealthy**, *adjective* –**stealthily**, *adverb*

steam *noun*
1. a colourless gas or vapour produced by boiling water and used for driving machinery and for heating.
–*verb* **2.** If something is **steaming**, it is giving off steam: *a steaming bowl of soup.* **3.** When you **steam** food, you cook it using steam: *to steam the rice.*
–*phrase* **4. let off steam**, to release or let go of stored-up feelings. **5. run out of steam**, to lose power or energy. **6. steam up**, to become covered with steam: *The bathroom windows had all steamed up.*
☐ **steamer**, *noun* –**steamy**, *adjective* (**steamier**, **steamiest**)

steam engine *noun* an engine which is powered by steam, especially a locomotive.

steamroller *noun*
1. a heavy vehicle with a large roller, used for crushing and levelling rocks and earth in road-making. **2.** an extremely strong force which crushes anything in its path.

steed *noun Old-fashioned* a horse, especially one for fast riding.

steel *noun*
1. iron mixed with carbon and other metals so that it is very hard and strong.
–*verb* **2.** If you **steel** yourself, you prepare yourself to handle or manage something unpleasant: *She steeled herself before picking up the dead rat.*
☐ **steely**, *adjective*: *a steely gaze.*

> ☑ SPELLING TIP Don't confuse the spelling of **steel** with **steal** which has the same sound but is spelt with *ea*. To **steal** is to take something that does not belong to you.

steep[1] *adjective*
1. having a sharp slope: *a steep hill.* **2.** extremely high: *a steep price.*

steep[2] *verb*
1. If something **steeps**, it soaks or lies soaking in water or other liquid: *The lemon leaves should steep in the hot liquid for about five minutes.* **2.** If a person or place is **steeped** in something, they are filled with it: *We found an area steeped in the history of the goldmining times.*

steeple *noun* a tall tower attached to a church.

steeplechase *noun* a horserace over a course which has obstacles such as jumps and ditches.

steer[1] *verb* To **steer** a boat or vehicle is to direct its course by using a rudder or wheel.
☐ **steering**, *noun*

steer[2] *noun* a castrated male of the cattle family, especially one raised for beef.

stellar *adjective* having to do with a star or stars.

stem[1] *noun*
1. the central stalk of a plant that grows upwards from the root. **2.** the stalk which supports or joins a flower, leaf, or fruit to a plant. **3.** a long, thin part like the stem of a plant: *The stem of the glass broke in the dishwasher.*
–*verb* (**stems**, **stemming**, **stemmed**, **has stemmed**) **4.** If something **stems** from somewhere, it originates or comes from there: *The idea for the collage stemmed from our holiday in the outback.*

stem[2] *verb* (**stems**, **stemming**, **stemmed**, **has stemmed**) If you **stem** something, you stop, check, or dam it up: *They stemmed the leakage from the tin with some tape.*

stem cell *noun* a non-specialised cell that is taken from an organism early in its development and which has the ability to divide and develop into any cell type found in the body, such as a blood cell or a muscle cell.

stench *noun* a very bad smell, especially of something decaying.

> A SIMILAR WORD is **stink**.

stencil /*say* **sten**-suhl/ *noun*
1. a thin sheet of paper, cardboard or metal with designs or letters cut out of it. **2.** the actual letters or designs produced.
–*verb* (**stencils**, **stencilling**, **stencilled**, **has stencilled**) **3.** If someone **stencils** letters or designs, they print them using a stencil.

> WORD HISTORY from a Latin word meaning 'spark'

step *noun*
1. a movement made by lifting your foot and putting it down again in a new position. **2.** the

distance measured by one such movement: *It took me twenty steps to cross the road.* **3.** a move or action: *One of you has to take the first step.* **4.** a support for your foot in going up or coming down: *We had to climb hundreds of steps to get to the viewing platform.*
–*verb* (**steps**, **stepping**, **stepped**, **has stepped**) **5.** If you **step** somewhere, you move there by taking a step: *Bella stepped into the elevator.*

step- *prefix* a word part which tells you that someone is related to another person because of the remarriage of a parent, rather than by birth.

NOTE Someone can have a **step-parent**, **step-mother**, **step-father**, **step-sister**, **step-brother**, **step-child**, **step-daughter** and **step-son**.

stepladder *noun* a ladder which has flat steps instead of rungs and a pair of hinged legs to keep it upright.

steppe /*say* step/ *noun* a large plain, especially one without trees.

☑ SPELLING TIP *Double letter alert*: two *p*'s, followed by a final *e*. Although this word sounds the same as *step*, its spelling is different. This is because it comes from Russian (where it actually means 'step').

stereo /*say* **ste**-ree-oh, **stear**-ree-oh/ *noun* (*plural* **stereos**) a radio, CD, recording system, or the like, equipped to reproduce stereophonic sound.
☐ **stereo**, *adjective*

stereophonic /*say* ste-ree-uh-**fon**-ik, stear-ree-uh-**fon**-ik/ *adjective* using two channels and two speakers to send out sound.

stereotype *noun* a too simple and conventional idea or image, used to label or define people: *He thinks that all people from the country wear checked shirts, but that's just a stereotype.*

sterile /*say* **ste**-ruyl/ *adjective*
1. If something is **sterile**, it is free from germs. **2.** If a person or animal is **sterile**, they are unable to reproduce.
☐ **sterility**, *noun* –**sterilise**, *verb*: *to sterilise a needle.* –**sterilisation**, *noun*

ANOTHER SPELLING for **sterilise** is **sterilize**.

sterling *adjective*
1. having to do with British money. **2.** being of a certain standard quality of silver. **3.** made of this sterling silver: *a sterling bracelet.* **4.** thoroughly excellent: *He has done sterling service.*

stern[1] *adjective*
1. firm or strict: *He kept a stern watch over his children.* **2.** hard, harsh, or severe: *They were given a stern warning not to trespass again.*

stern[2] *noun* the back part of anything, but especially of a ship or boat.

stethoscope /*say* **steth**-uh-skohp/ *noun* an instrument used by doctors to listen to the sounds made by the heart and lungs.

stew *noun*
1. food cooked by stewing, especially a meal of meat and vegetables cooked together. **2.** *Informal* a state of worry or fuss: *He has got himself into a stew over the exams.*
–*verb* **3.** If food is **stewed**, it is cooked for a long time over slow heat. **4.** *Informal* If a person **stews** about something, they worry about it.

steward *noun*
1. someone who looks after others in a club or on a ship or aircraft. **2.** someone who manages someone else's affairs or property.

NOTE For definition 1, a woman who has this job can be called a **stewardess**, but this is now rather old-fashioned.

stick[1] *noun*
1. a branch or long thin piece of wood, sometimes used for a special purpose: *a digging stick.* **2.** something shaped like a stick: *a carrot stick.*

stick[2] *verb* (**sticks**, **sticking**, **stuck**, **has stuck**)
1. If you **stick** something pointed into something, you push it in or through that thing: *Of course the balloon burst when you stuck the pen into it!* **2.** If you **stick** something somewhere, you put it into a place or position: *It is not a good idea to stick your head out of a train window.* **3.** If you **stick** something onto something, you fasten it into position by piercing or gluing: *He stuck the note onto the wall to remind him.* **4.** If something **sticks**, it stays attached as if by glue: *The mud stuck to her shoes.*
–*phrase* **5. stick around**, to stay nearby. **6. stick by** (or **to**) (or **with**), to remain loyal to. **7. stick out**, **a.** to stand out, or be in the way. **b.** to be obvious or conspicuous: *The facts stick out a mile.* **c.** to endure. **8. stick together**, to remain friendly, loyal, and so on, to one another. **9. stick up for**, to speak or act in favour of.

sticker *noun* a label which is sticky on one side, usually with an advertisement or other message printed on it.

stick insect *noun* an insect, usually without wings, with a long, thin, twig-like body.

sticky *adjective* (**stickier**, **stickiest**)
1. Something **sticky** is adhesive or gluey. **2. Sticky** weather is hot and wet: *It was so sticky we felt like a shower.* **3.** *Informal* A **sticky** situation is awkward or difficult to deal with.
☐ **stickily**, *adverb* –**stickiness**, *noun*

stickybeak *Informal*
–*noun* **1.** someone who is eager to learn about things that are not their concern.
–*verb* **2.** If somebody **stickybeaks**, they try to find out about things that are not their business: *Stop stickybeaking!*

stiff *adjective*
1. hard or firm and not easily bent. **2.** not moving or working easily: *All the drawers were stiff from years of not being used.* **3.** not able to move easily: *Her limbs felt stiff when she got up from the cold ground.* **4.** severe or hard to deal with: *He was given a stiff penalty for his driving offence.*
–*noun* **5.** *Informal* a dead body.
☐ **stiff**, *adverb*: *scared stiff.* –**stiffen**, *verb* –**stiffly**, *adverb* –**stiffness**, *noun*

stifle /*say* **stuy**-fuhl/ *verb*
1. If you **stifle** something like a laugh or a cough, you stop yourself from doing it: *She stifled another yawn and hoped that nobody noticed.* **2.** If someone in power **stifles** something like a revolt or an uprising, they suppress or crush it: *The government tried to stifle any attempt at opposition.* **3.** If you say you feel **stifled**, you mean that you feel suffocated: *We were stifled by the rules and regulations we had to follow.*
☐ **stifling**, *adjective*: *stifling weather.*

stigma *noun* a mark of shame or disgrace or a stain on someone's reputation.

stile *noun* a step or steps for climbing over a fence where there is no gate.

> ☑ SPELLING TIP Don't confuse the spelling of **stile** with **style** which sounds the same. A **style** is a particular kind or type of something.

stiletto /*say* stuh-**let**-oh/ *noun*
1. a dagger with a narrow pointed blade. **2.** a high, very narrow heel on a woman's shoe.

> WORD HISTORY from the Latin word for a pointed instrument

still[1] *adjective*
1. without movement: *The air was still and hot – not a breeze stirred in the trees.* **2.** with no sound or noise: *'Be still!' the teacher roared.*
–*noun* **3.** a single photographic picture taking from a movie.
–*adverb* **4.** up to or even at this time: *I can't believe she is still wearing that old dress!* **5.** without sound or movement: *Stand still and don't move!*
–*verb* **6.** If someone **stills** a situation, they make it become calm, quiet or still: *He was eventually able to still the players.*
☐ **stillness**, *noun*

still[2] *noun* equipment for distilling a liquid, especially a liquor.

stilt *noun*
1. a high supporting post under a building. **2. stilts**, a pair of poles used for walking on, each with a support for your foot at some distance above the ground.

stilted *adjective* not at ease or relaxed: *His stilted manner made everybody uncomfortable.*

stimulant /*say* **stim**-yuh-luhnt/ *noun* something that increases wakefulness or quickens some process in the body, such as a medicine or food.

stimulate /*say* **stim**-yuh-layt/ *verb* If something **stimulates** you, it makes you feel excited or enthusiastic: *A short break always stimulates me to perform better.*
☐ **stimulation**, *noun* –**stimulator**, *noun* –**stimulating**, *adjective*: *a stimulating conversation.*

stimulus /*say* **stim**-yuh-luhs/ *noun* (*plural* **stimuli** /*say* **stim**-yuh-luy, **stim**-yuh-lee/ *or* **stimuluses**) something that starts action, effort, or thought: *The sound of the ambulance was the stimulus that started the dog barking.*

sting *verb* (**stings**, **stinging**, **stung**, **has stung**)
1. If something such as an insect **stings** you, it pricks you, causing a sharp pain: *He screamed when the wasp stung his neck.* **2.** If a part of your body **stings**, you feel a sharp pain there: *Jay's eyes were stinging because some soap got in.* **3.** If someone's remarks **sting** you, they hurt your feelings.
–*noun* **4.** an act of stinging. **5.** the sore or pain caused by stinging. **6.** a sharp-pointed, often venomous organ of insects and other animals, able to cause sharp pain: *The wasp had a very long sting.*
☐ **stinger**, *noun* –**stinging**, *adjective*: *stinging remarks.*

stingray *noun* a type of fish with a flat body and a long tail armed with a bony spine near the base.

stingy /*say* **stin**-jee/ *adjective* (**stingier**, **stingiest**) A **stingy** person is mean about spending money.

stink *verb* (**stinks**, **stinking**, **stank**, **has stunk**)
1. To **stink** is to give off a bad smell.
–*noun* **2.** a bad smell.
–*phrase* **3. kick up a stink**, *Informal* to get angry or make a big fuss of something: *They kicked up a stink when they were booted out of the competition.*

stir *verb* (**stirs**, **stirring**, **stirred**, **has stirred**)
1. When you **stir** a liquid, you move it around inside a container with something such as a spoon or stick: *Stir the paint well before use.* **2.** If someone **stirs**, they move slightly: *The cat stirred briefly and then went back to sleep.* **3.** If the wind **stirs** an object, it causes it to move a little. **4.** If something **stirs** you, it makes you feel excitement or some other strong emotion: *The playing of the national anthem stirred everybody.* **5.** *Informal* If someone is **stirring**, they are teasing or intentionally trying to cause an argument: *Don't listen to him, he's just stirring.*
–*noun* **6.** the act or sound of stirring or moving. **7.** excitement: *Her arrival caused quite a stir.*
☐ **stirrer**, *noun* –**stirring**, *adjective* emotionally rousing: *a stirring speech.*

stir-fry *verb* (**stir-fries**, **stir-frying**, **stir-fried**, **has stir-fried**)

1. To **stir-fry** food is to fry it lightly while stirring it. –*noun* (*plural* **stir-fries**) 2. a food prepared by stir-frying: *We're having a stir-fry for dinner tonight.*

stirrup /*say* **sti**-ruhp/ *noun* a loop or ring of metal hung from the saddle of a horse to support the rider's foot.

> ☑ SPELLING TIP *Double letter alert*: double *r* (think of riding ring) in the middle of **stirrup**.

stitch *noun* (*plural* **stitches**)
1. a complete movement of a threaded needle through a piece of material: *A stitch in time saves nine.* 2. the loop of thread left in the material: *Her stitches were tiny and neat.* 3. one complete movement with the needles in knitting. 4. a sudden sharp pain, especially between your ribs: *Ouch! I've got a stitch!*
–*verb* 5. If you **stitch** something, you use a needle and thread to join or work on material.
–*phrase* 6. **in stitches**, laughing uncontrollably: *The whole audience was in stitches for most of the film.*

stoat *noun* a type of weasel which has a brown coat of fur in summer, found in Europe, Asia and North America.

> NOTE The white winter coat of the stoat, which can be used to make coats and so on, is called **ermine**.

stock *noun*
1. the total quantity of goods kept by a business shop for selling to customers. 2. a quantity of something kept for future use: *In the pantry was a stock of tinned and bottled food.* 3. a tribe, family, or race: *You can tell from her red hair that she comes from Irish stock.* 4. liquid in which meat, fish, vegetables, and so on have been cooked, often used as a base for sauces or soups. 5. the shares of a business company.
–*verb* 6. If someone **stocks** a place, they put provisions or equipment there: *The new shop is stocked with lots of unusual things.* 7. If a shop or business **stocks** a product, they have it available to sell. 8. If a person **stocks** a farm or property, they put stock like cattle and sheep onto it.
–*phrase* 9. **take stock**, to make a judgement about a situation: *They realised they were getting lost, so they stopped to take stock.*
☐ **stock**, *adjective*: *stock items.* –**stockist**, *noun*: *I've found a stockist of that delicious jam.*

stockade *noun* a strong wooden barrier built for defence.

stock exchange *noun* a place where the stocks and shares of business companies are bought and sold.

stocking *noun* a tight-fitting item of clothing that covers the foot and leg.

stockman *noun* (*plural* **stockmen**) someone whose job is to look after the animals, especially the cattle, on a property.

stockpile *verb* To **stockpile** something is to save it up in large amounts for future use: *The farmer had stockpiled a huge barn of hay for the dry months.*
☐ **stockpile**, *noun*

stock-still *adverb* without moving at all: *I had to stand stock-still while Mum pinned up the hem.*

stocktake *noun*
1. an event where all products or assets in a shop or business are counted and written down: *At the end of the year, we need to do a stocktake of all the goods in the shop.* 2. an appraisal of your condition or progress.
☐ **stocktaking**, *noun*: *The shop is closed for stocktaking.* –**stocktaker**, *noun*

stocky *adjective* (**stockier**, **stockiest**) short, solid, and strong: *The bricklayer was a stocky man who could carry a large pile of bricks with ease.*

stoke *verb* If you **stoke** a fire, you add fuel to it or move burning pieces together so that they burn better.

stole[1] *verb* the past tense of **steal**.

stole[2] *noun* a long, wide scarf worn around your shoulders for warmth.

stomach /*say* **stum**-uhk/ *noun* (*plural* **stomachs**) the bag-like organ in the body that receives food after it is swallowed, and starts to digest it.

> WORD HISTORY from a Greek word meaning 'throat'

stone *noun*
1. the hard substance which rocks are made of: *The cold stone was good to lean against in the heat.* 2. a piece of rock. 3. a gem: *This diamond is a beautiful stone for a ring.* 4. the hard seed inside a cherry, peach, plum or similar fruit. 5. a measure of weight in the imperial system equal to a little more than six kilograms.
–*verb* 6. To **stone** someone is to throw stones at them: *The rioters stoned the police.* 7. To **stone** fruit is to take out the stone.
☐ **stone**, *adjective*: *a stone wall.* –**stony**, *adjective*: *a stony track*; *a stony stare.*

stoned *adjective Informal* 1. so affected by a drug, especially marijuana, as to be in an abnormal, relaxed state. 2. *Old-fashioned* very drunk.

stonefish *noun* (*plural* **stonefish** *or* **stonefishes**) a venomous tropical fish, looking like a piece of coral or rock, with spines which can give you a painful sting, sometimes causing death.

stool *noun* a seat with no arms or back.

stoop *verb* To **stoop** is to 1. bend your head and shoulders forward. 2. do something that is

not worthy of you: *She stooped to thieving small things from her friends.*
☐ **stoop**, *noun*

stop *verb* (**stops**, **stopping**, **stopped**, **has stopped**)
1. If you **stop** doing something that you have been doing, you no longer do it: *They stopped complaining.* **2.** If you **stop** something happening, you prevent it from happening or continuing to happen: *We stopped the cat from getting out at night.* **3.** If a process or an activity **stops**, it comes to an end: *As soon as the rain stops, we'll go shopping.* **4.** If someone or something that is moving **stops**, or if something stops them, they no longer move: *We stopped to look at the strange insects climbing up the tree.* **5.** If a device such as a clock **stops** or if you stop it, it no longer works or is switched off. **6.** If you **stop** somewhere, you stay there for a while before you continue to travel or move somewhere else.
–*noun* **7.** a finish or end: *We had to put a stop to the game when the bell rang.* **8.** the place where a bus, tram or other vehicle stops to pick up and set down passengers.
–*phrase* **9. stop by**, to call somewhere for a short time on the way to another place.
☐ **stoppage**, *noun*

stopper *noun* something that fits into the top of a bottle to close it.

stopwatch *noun* (*plural* **stopwatches**) a watch which can be stopped and started by pressing a button, used for timing races and so on.

storage *noun* room to keep things in: *You can put your furniture in our shed as there is plenty of storage there.*
☐ **storage**, *adjective*

☑ SPELLING TIP You will have no trouble with the spelling of this word if you see that it is made up of *store* (with the *e* dropped) and the suffix *-age* (used in nouns referring to a state or condition).

store *noun*
1. things put away for use in the future: *a store of food.* **2.** a place for keeping a supply of things: *The office manager is in the equipment store.* **3.** a shop: *the general store.*
–*verb* **4.** If you **store** things, you put them away for future use: *Our dog stores his bones at the bottom of the yard.*
–*phrase* **5. in store**, coming soon: *The carnival organisers have a surprise in store for all the participants.*

storey *noun* (*plural* **storeys**) a floor or level in a house or building.
☐ **-storey**, *adjective*: *a multi-storey car park.*

A SIMILAR WORD is **floor**.
WORD HISTORY from a French word meaning 'build'.

☑ SPELLING TIP Remember the *e* in **storey**. Don't confuse it with **story**, which is the telling of something that has happened.

stork *noun* a large bird with long legs and a long beak, which feeds in shallow water.

☑ SPELLING TIP Don't confuse the spelling of **stork** with **stalk** which has the same sound. A **stalk** is the stem of a plant; to **stalk** something is to follow it quietly and carefully.

storm *noun*
1. a violent change in the weather bringing wind, rain, thunder and lightning. **2.** a strong reaction: *a storm of protest.*
–*verb* **3.** If you **storm** somewhere, you go there very noisily and angrily: *She stormed out of the meeting.* **4.** If people **storm** a place, they attack it: *The drug squad stormed the club.*
–*phrase* **5. take by storm**, **a.** to take by military attack. **b.** to be a great success in: *He has taken the tennis world by storm since he won the Australian Open.*
☐ **stormy**, *adjective* (**stormier**, **stormiest**) –**storminess**, *noun*

story *noun* (*plural* **stories**)
1. the telling of something that has happened, either made up or in real life: *a story about pirates.* **2.** a lie or fib.

stout *adjective*
1. rather overweight: *a stout, determined-looking woman.* **2.** strong and heavy: *She felt a bit more confident holding a stout piece of wood.*

stove *noun* a device which uses wood, gas or electricity to produce heat for cooking or warming a room.

stow /*rhymes with* so/ *verb* To **stow** something is to pack it or store it away: *We stowed all our old clothes into boxes.*

stowaway /*say* **stoh**-uh-way/ *noun* someone who hides on a ship or aircraft so they do not have to pay.

straddle *verb* If you **straddle** something, you sit or stand on it with one leg on each side: *One of us straddled the creek and helped the little ones over.*

straggle *verb* To **straggle** is to **1.** wander about in a scattered fashion or to come in at the end: *We straggled in twos and threes back into the classroom.* **2.** grow or spread untidily: *A huge pumpkin vine straggled over the yard.*
☐ **straggler**, *noun* –**straggly**, *adjective* (**stragglier**, **straggliest**)

straight /*say* strayt/ *adjective*
1. Something **straight** is not bent or curved. **2.** Someone who is **straight** is honest and trustworthy: *You can trust him completely – he is straight.* **3.** A **straight** action or expression is a serious one: *Can you keep a straight face while I*

tell you a joke?; We were given a straight talk about how to behave.
–*adverb* **4.** without bending, curving, or twisting: *The highway runs straight for miles through the scrub.* **5.** in the proper order: *We had to get our rooms straight for the visitors.* **6.** directly or immediately: *We promised to go straight over.*
□ **straighten**, *verb*: *to straighten a tie.*

☑ SPELLING TIP Remember the *aight* spelling for the 'ayt' sound in **straight**. Don't confuse it with **strait**, which is a narrow channel connecting two large bodies of water.

straight angle *noun* an angle of 180°.

straightaway *adverb* at once: *Alice realised straightaway that something strange had happened to her.*

straightforward *adjective*
1. If someone is **straightforward**, they are honest and open. **2.** If something is **straightforward**, it is not difficult or complicated: *It is a straightforward problem and shouldn't take long to solve.*
□ **straightforwardly**, *adverb*

strain[1] *verb*
1. To **strain** is to pull, push, or stretch hard or too far: *Ashley strained a muscle running in the cross-country race.* **2.** To **strain** a liquid is to pour it through something with many small openings so that any bits that are bigger than the holes are left behind: *We had to strain the tea because there were too many leaves in it.*
–*noun* **3.** great effort, pressure or stress: *It was a big strain carrying the heavy pack up the mountain; Engineers have to calculate the strain that a bridge will bear.* **4. strains**, musical sounds: *They marched along accompanied by loud strains from the band.*

strain[2] *noun* breed or family line: *My favourite strain of chook is the one with fluffy legs.*

strainer *noun* a device that allows water to go through while keeping back the solid material: *a tea strainer.*

strait *noun* a narrow strip of water connecting two large bodies of water: *The ship reached Tasmania after crossing Bass Strait.*

☑ SPELLING TIP Don't confuse the spelling of **strait** with **straight** which has the same sound. Something that is **straight** is not bent or curved.

straitjacket *noun* a coat which is wrapped around mentally ill people to restrain them if they are acting violently enough to hurt themselves or others.

ANOTHER SPELLING is **straightjacket**.

☑ SPELLING TIP Note that, although you can also spell this word **straightjacket**, the main spelling is **straitjacket**. This may seem strange as you would think that this kind of jacket is meant to keep you *straight*. In fact, it is to keep you restricted. This is the basic meaning of *strait* which comes from *strictus*, the Latin word for 'bound'.

straitlaced *adjective* If someone is **straitlaced**, they are rather strict and proper about the way people should behave: *They were very straitlaced and we had to watch what we said.*

☑ SPELLING TIP Remember that the first part of this word is spelt *strait*. You cannot spell it *straight*, although the two spellings are allowed for **straitjacket**. See the spelling tip there.

strand *noun*
1. one of the threads which are twisted together to form a rope, cord, wire, and so on. **2.** a single thread in cloth. **3.** a lock of hair. **4.** a string of pearls, beads, and so on.

stranded *adjective*
1. If a sea animal is **stranded**, it is washed up on the beach and cannot get back into the water: *People could not get the stranded whales back to sea.* **2.** If a person is **stranded**, they are alone and helpless: *When his engine cut out, Cyril was stranded in the middle of the harbour.*

strange *adjective* If something is **strange** it is **1.** peculiar or unusual: *He had a strange way of talking.* **2.** not seen or heard of before: *That part of the world is strange to me.*
□ **strangely**, *adverb* –**strangeness**, *noun*

SIMILAR WORDS (for definition 1) are **abnormal**, **bizarre**, **extraordinary**, **peculiar**, **remarkable** and **unusual**; (for definition 2) **foreign**, **unfamiliar** and **unknown**.

stranger *noun*
1. someone you have not met before: *The tall man at the front door was a stranger to us.* **2.** someone who is new to a place: *I am a stranger here – can you tell me the way to the station?*

strangle *verb* To **strangle** someone is to kill them by squeezing their throat and cutting off the air supply.
□ **stranglehold**, *noun* a hold in wrestling where the opponent's breathing is stopped. –**strangler**, *noun*

ANOTHER WORD for this is **strangulate**.

strap *noun*
1. a strip of leather or cloth used for tying or holding things in place: *You will have to put a strap around your broken suitcase.*
–*verb* (**straps**, **strapping**, **strapped**, **has strapped**) **2.** If you **strap** something, you tie or hold it in place with a strap or straps: *They strapped the blankets to their saddles.*

strapping *adjective* tall and strong: *The coach said we were all strapping young things and should be able to do 20 laps of the sportsground.*

strategy /*say* **strat**-uh-jee/ *noun* (*plural* **strategies**)
1. a plan or scheme which sets out how to achieve a goal. 2. the planning and directing of military operations in war.
☐ **strategic**, *adjective* –**strategically**, *adverb* –**strategist**, *noun*

stratum /*say* **strah**-tuhm/ *noun* (*plural* **strata**) a layer or level: *The rock strata in the cliff were different colours.*

WORD HISTORY from a Latin word meaning 'something spread out'

straw *noun*
1. a thin, hollow tube through which you can suck a drink. 2. cut dried stems of wheat, corn or other grain.
–*phrase* 3. **the last straw**, a final act or event which makes it impossible to deal with a situation.

strawberry *noun* (*plural* **strawberries**) a small, juicy, red fruit which has many tiny seeds on its surface.

stray *verb*
1. To **stray** is to leave the right path and get lost.
–*noun* 2. an animal found without its owner.
☐ **stray**, *adjective*: *a stray dog*; *It was just a stray thought and probably not worth considering.*

streak *noun*
1. a long, thin mark or line: *I got a streak of yellow on my shirt from the new paint.*
–*verb* 2. To **streak** something is to mark it with streaks. 3. If something **streaks** somewhere, it moves there very quickly: *We had a glimpse of someone streaking behind the building.*
☐ **streaky**, *adjective* (**streakier**, **streakiest**)

stream *noun*
1. a small narrow river. 2. a continuous flow: *The bookshop had a stream of requests for the new novel.*
–*verb* 3. If things or people **stream**, they move like a stream: *The crowd streamed into the pavilion.* 4. To **stream** a digitised form of media content is to transmit it in a constant flow (see **streaming**).

streamer *noun* a long strip of brightly coloured paper.

streaming *noun* the process of sending digital data to a computer in a constant flow so that it can be processed and displayed as it is being received, rather than being stored and then displayed when all the data has been received.

streamlined *adjective* shaped to move quickly and smoothly through air or water.

street *noun*
1. a road lined with buildings. 2. the people who live in a street: *Our street gets together every Christmas for a party.*

strength *noun* the quality of being strong: *It took the strength of four men to move the piano*; *He has his tea only half strength.*
☐ **strengthen**, *verb*: *That will strengthen her determination.*

☑ SPELLING TIP Remember **strength** is formed from *strong* and so it has a *g* in it.

strenuous /*say* **stren**-yooh-uhs/ *adjective* hard and tiring and often quite unpleasant: *It was strenuous work, hot and exhausting.*

A SIMILAR WORD is **arduous**.

stress *noun*
1. great importance: *They laid stress on the need for secrecy.* 2. emphasis on a word, or part of a word, when it is pronounced: *French people often put the stress on the end of the word instead of the beginning.* 3. difficulty in relaxing due to too much emotional or physical effort over a long time.
–*verb* 4. If you **stress** something to someone, you let them know that it is important that they take note of it: *She stressed that I had to be on time.* 5. If you **stress** a part of a word, you put more emphasis on it.
☐ **stressed**, *adjective*

stressful *adjective* causing a person to feel tense and anxious: *The thought of giving a speech to a hall full of people was very stressful.*

stretch *verb*
1. If a soft or elastic object **stretches**, or if you **stretch** it, it becomes longer, wider or tighter without breaking: *We stretched a net across the tennis court.* 2. If something **stretches** over an area, distance or time, it reaches over that area, distance or time: *The ocean stretches to the horizon.* 3. If you **stretch**, you extend your limbs in such a way that your muscles tighten. 4. If a job **stretches** you, it makes you use all your energy or abilities.
–*noun* (*plural* **stretches**) 5. the action of stretching: *to have a yawn and a stretch.* 6. a continuous spread or period of time: *a stretch of land*; *a stretch of ten years.*
–*phrase* 7. **stretch out**, to lie down at full length.
8. **stretch your legs**, to go for a walk.
☐ **stretchy**, *adjective*

stretcher *noun* a light frame covered with canvas for carrying sick or injured people.

strew *verb* (**strews**, **strewing**, **strewed**, **has strewn**) If you **strew** things, you scatter or throw them everywhere: *They strewed the floor with rags to soak up the water.*

stricken *adjective* struck down or overcome: *Poor Sandra was stricken with measles during the holidays.*

NOTE This word comes from the verb **strike**.

strict *adjective*
1. Someone who is **strict** demands that you behave well and obey the rules: *She is a strict teacher but I still like her.* 2. To be **strict** is to be complete or total: *Do you promise strict loyalty?*
☐ **strictly**, *adverb*

stride *noun*
1. a big step forward: *It takes me 20 strides to get from one end of the house to the other.*
–*verb* (**strides**, **striding**, **strode**, **has stridden**) 2. If you **stride**, you walk with big steps: *He strode into the room glaring.*

strife *noun*
1. fighting and disagreement: *There's been a bit of strife in our family lately.*
–*phrase* 2. **in strife**, *Rather informal* in trouble: *I'm expecting to be in strife over my spelling.*

strike *verb* (**strikes**, **striking**, **struck**, **has struck**)
1. If you **strike** something or someone, you hit them: *She struck the ball with the racquet.* 2. To **strike** is to attack: *Be careful – she could strike when you least expect it!* 3. If you **strike** something, you find it or come across it: *Prospectors sometimes work for years without striking gold.* 4. If you **strike** a match, you light it.
–*noun* 5. a hit or blow. 6. a work stoppage, usually against low pay and poor working conditions.
☐ **striking**, *adjective*: *Her dark good looks were very striking.*

string *noun*
1. a thread or cord. 2. a row or line of things: *a string of railway carriages.* 3. one of the pieces of wire stretched across a violin, guitar or similar instrument, which produces musical sounds when it is made to vibrate. 4. **strings**, musical instruments with strings, especially those played with a bow.
–*verb* (**strings**, **stringing**, **strung**, **has strung**) 5. If someone **strings** an instrument, they fit strings onto it. 6. If you **string** things like beads onto a string, you slip them on.
–*phrase* 7. **pull strings**, to try to get some benefit for yourself or someone else by using the influence of a position or someone you know. 8. **string along** (or **on**), to deceive in a series of lies or tricks: *They strung her along for months.* 9. **string out**, to spread out or lengthen: *The crowd strung out along the length of the street to watch the parade; She tried to string out the conversation as long as she could.*
☐ **stringed**, *adjective*: *stringed instruments.*

stringent /*say* **strin**-juhnt/ *adjective* strict or severe: *The principal took stringent measures to prevent truancy.*

strip[1] *verb* (**strips**, **stripping**, **stripped**, **has stripped**)
1. If you **strip** something, you remove it or take it away: *We stripped the wallpaper from the wall.* 2. If you **strip**, you take off all your clothes.
☐ **stripper**, *noun*

strip[2] *noun* a long, narrow piece or area: *She bound up her leg with a strip of material; a strip of green along the river.*

stripe *noun* a long, narrow band of a different colour from the rest of a thing: *Our uniform is green with white stripes.*
☐ **striped**, *adjective*

strive *verb* (**strives**, **striving**, **strove**, **has striven**) To **strive** is to try hard or struggle: *She is striving to win the medal at the end of the year; to strive against time.*

strobe *noun* a device which gives out a series of brilliant flashes of light.

stroganoff /*say* **strog**-uh-nof/ *noun* a food made from meat cooked in a sauce of sour cream and mushrooms, originating in Russian cooking.

> ☑ SPELLING TIP *Double letter alert*: double *f* at the end. This word has an unusual spelling because it comes from the name of Count Paul *Stroganoff*, a Russian diplomat in the 19th century.

stroke[1] *noun*
1. a hit or blow. 2. the hitting of something with a stick, bat, etc., especially in sport. 3. a single complete movement of the arm when swimming: *Your left stroke is too weak.* 4. a style of swimming: *My favourite stroke is freestyle.* 5. an action or event: *She had a stroke of good luck when she started that job.* 6. a sudden break in the circulation of blood in the brain which can cause paralysis or other disabilities.

stroke[2] *verb* If you **stroke** something or someone, you pass your hand over them gently.
☐ **stroke**, *noun*

stroll *verb* To **stroll** is to walk slowly.
☐ **stroll**, *noun*

stroller *noun* a light, collapsible chair on wheels, used for carrying small children.

strong *adjective*
1. having great power or effect: *There is strong support for her among those who know her.* 2. not easily broken: *a strong rope.* 3. having a lot of flavour or smell: *a strong fishy smell.*
–*adverb* 4. in number: *The army was 10 000 strong.*
☐ **strongly**, *adverb*

stronghold *noun* a fortress.

structure *noun*
1. something that has been built or put together: *The most beautiful structure in Sydney is the Opera House.* 2. the way something is put together: *The structure of the central mail exchange is very complicated.*
–*verb* 3. To **structure** a group of things or people is to organise them into a structure: *He structured the department so that everybody knew what their role was and who they were responsible to.*
☐ **structural**, *adjective*

struggle *verb* If you **struggle**, you fight or work very hard: *They struggled up the steep hill; She struggled hard to learn the language of her new country.*
□ **struggle**, *noun* –**struggler**, *noun*

strum *verb* (**strums**, **strumming**, **strummed**, **has strummed**) To **strum** an instrument is to play it by running your fingers across the strings: *I can't play any notes on the guitar, I can only strum.*

strut[1] *verb* (**struts**, **strutting**, **strutted**, **has strutted**) To **strut** is to walk a little too proudly, with your back straight and your chin pushed forward.
□ **strut**, *noun*

A SIMILAR WORD is **swagger**.

strut[2] *noun* a wooden or metal bar that supports part of a building.

stub *noun*
1. a short end piece: *My pencil is worn down to a stub.*
–*verb* (**stubs**, **stubbing**, **stubbed**, **has stubbed**) **2.** If you **stub** your toe, you accidentally hit it against something hard.

stubble *noun*
1. the short stems left in the ground after wheat or rice has been harvested. **2.** the short, stiff hairs growing on the face of a man who has not shaved for a few days.
□ **stubbly**, *adjective*

stubborn /*say* **stub**-uhn/ *adjective* A **stubborn** person is determined not to give way or change their mind.
□ **stubbornly**, *adverb* –**stubbornness**, *noun*

A SIMILAR WORD is **obstinate**.

stuck-up *adjective Informal* snobbish or conceited.

stud[1] *noun* a small knob or button sticking out from a surface: *My football boots have studs.*

stud[2] *noun* a farm where horses or cattle are kept for breeding.

student *noun* someone who is studying, especially at a school, college or university.

studio /*say* **styooh**-dee-oh/ *noun*
1. the work room of an artist or musician. **2.** a place where films or radio and television programs are made.

study /*say* **stud**-ee/ *verb* (**studies**, **studying**, **studied**, **has studied**)
1. To **study** is to spend time learning. **2.** To **study** something is to look at it closely: *They studied the map carefully to see where they were.*
–*noun* (*plural* **studies**) **3.** the careful learning of a subject. **4.** a room with a desk and books for studying.
□ **studious** /*say* **styooh**-dee-uhs/, *adjective*

stuff *noun*
1. the material from which things are made: *All soft toys are filled with stuff that won't hurt babies.* **2.** *Informal* belongings: *We had to pick up all their stuff when they left.*
–*verb* **3.** To **stuff** a container is to fill it tight with something: *to stuff clothes in a drawer.* **4.** *Informal* If you **stuff** yourself, you fill yourself with food.
□ **stuffed**, *adjective*: *stuffed cushions.*

stuffing *noun*
1. material used for filling. **2.** a tasty mixture put inside a chicken or other poultry before it is cooked.

stuffy *adjective* (**stuffier**, **stuffiest**)
1. A room is **stuffy** if it does not have enough air: *The computer room is often stuffy in the morning.* **2.** A **stuffy** person is very stiff and proper, and easily shocked.
□ **stuffiness**, *noun*

stumble *verb* To **stumble** is to **1.** nearly fall over. **2.** walk unsteadily. **3.** act or speak in an unsteady way.

stump *noun*
1. a short part left after the main part has been cut off: *He ate his lunch sitting on an old tree stump.*
–*verb* **2.** *Informal* If you are **stumped**, you have no idea of the answer: *How they had got there had me stumped!*
□ **stumpy**, *adjective* (**stumpier**, **stumpiest**)

stun *verb* (**stuns**, **stunning**, **stunned**, **has stunned**) To **stun** someone is to **1.** make them unconscious: *Hitting his head against the rock stunned him.* **2.** shock or surprise them: *It stunned me to learn how much the bike cost.*
□ **stunning**, *adjective*

WORD HISTORY from an Old English word meaning 'resound' or 'crash'

stunt[1] *verb* To **stunt** the growth of something is to slow it down: *My dad says watching too much television stunts the brain.*

stunt[2] *noun*
1. a spectacular and often dangerous performance. **2.** something done to attract publicity or attention.

stuntman *noun* someone who is paid to perform dangerous acts, especially as a stand-in for a film actor.

stupefy /*say* **styooh**-puh-fuy/ *verb* (**stupefies**, **stupefying**, **stupefied**, **has stupefied**) If something **stupefies** you, it **1.** makes you unable to think clearly: *By the end of the long lecture, we were stupefied with boredom.* **2.** astounds or amazes you greatly: *We were stupefied to hear who had committed the murder.*
□ **stupefaction**, *noun*

stupendous *adjective* amazingly good: *It was a stupendous party.*
☐ **stupendously**, *adverb*

stupid *adjective*
1. not clever or quick to understand: *He seemed quite stupid and didn't have a clue what I was talking about.* **2.** showing a lack of good sense: *The man said he had been stupid to smoke for so many years.*
☐ **stupidity**, *noun* –**stupidly**, *adverb*

stupor /*say* **styooh**-puh/ *noun* a state in which the mind or senses are deadened or not working, as a result of illness or drugs.

☑ SPELLING TIP Note the *or* ending. This is not one of those words where there can be either an *our* or *or* ending. It is always spelt *or*.

sturdy *adjective* (**sturdier**, **sturdiest**) If someone or something is **sturdy**, they are strong and not easily hurt or damaged: *The pony has sturdy legs*; *You'll need sturdy boots to go hiking.*
☐ **sturdily**, *adverb* –**sturdiness**, *noun*

sturgeon /*say* **ster**-juhn/ *noun* a large fish found in the northern areas of the world, the eggs of which can be salted and eaten as caviar.

stutter *noun*
1. a speech problem in which the rhythm of speech is blocked and the first sound in a word is often repeated.
–*verb* **2.** If someone **stutters**, they speak with a stutter.

A SIMILAR WORD is **stammer**.

sty[1] *noun* (*plural* **sties**) a pen for pigs.

sty[2] *noun* See **stye**.

stye *noun* (*plural* **sties**) a small, red and painful swelling on the skin at the edge of the eye.

ANOTHER SPELLING is **sty**.

style *noun*
1. a particular kind or type, especially of music, art, architecture and so on: *a painting in a modern style*; *a reggae style of music.* **2.** a way of doing something: *JK Rowling's style of writing*; *a relaxed style of living.* **3.** a graceful or fashionable way of doing things.
–*verb* **4.** To **style** something in a particular way is to make it conform to a specific style: *She wants her hair styled like Nicole Kidman's.*
☐ **stylish**, *adjective*

☑ SPELLING TIP Notice the *y* in **style**. Don't confuse it with **stile** which sounds the same. A **stile** is a step or a set of steps for climbing over a fence.

stylus /*say* **stuy**-luhs/ *noun* (*plural* **styli** /*say* **stuy**-luy/ *or* **styluses**) a pointed tool for drawing or writing.

☑ SPELLING TIP *Letter 'y' alert*: the first vowel is spelt by a *y* (not an *i*). This is similar to the spelling of the word *style* though these two words are unrelated in origin.

suave /*say* swahv/ *adjective* Someone **suave** is charming and smooth in manner: *His suave manner impressed people into thinking he was very knowledgeable.*

☑ SPELLING TIP *Tricky vowel sound*: *ua* spelling for the 'wah' sound. The phrase 'smooth, unworried and very elegant' might help you to remember.

sub *noun* a short form of: **1.** submarine. **2.** subscription. **3.** substitute.

sub- *prefix* a word part meaning 'under', as in *submarine*.

WORD HISTORY this prefix comes from Latin

subconscious /*say* sub-**kon**-shuhs/ *noun* the part of your mind below consciousness or awareness: *There are often very surprising things in your subconscious.*
☐ **subconscious**, *adjective*

☑ SPELLING TIP Remember the *sci* spelling in this word. See **conscious**.

subdivide /*say* **sub**-duh-vuyd, sub-duh-**vuyd**/ *verb* To **subdivide** something, such as land, is to divide it again into smaller divisions.
☐ **subdivision**, *noun*

subdue *verb*
1. If something **subdues** you, it calms you by making your feelings less intense: *to subdue an excited child by speaking gently.* **2.** To **subdue** someone is to use force to bring them under control: *Guards managed to subdue the violent prisoner.*

subject /*say* **sub**-jekt/ *noun*
1. a matter under discussion: *The subject of our discussion was how to rustle up some more players.* **2.** a branch of study: *My favourite subject is art.* **3.** something chosen by an artist for painting. **4.** the part of a sentence about which something is said, such as 'the goldfish bowl' in the sentence *The goldfish bowl sat in the laundry.*
–*phrase* **5. subject to, a.** open to or likely to receive: *He was often subject to questioning about his accent.* **b.** depending on: *Our plans for an all-night party are subject to Mum's agreement.*

COMPARE definition 4 with **object** (definition 3). Also see the Grammar and Punctuation Guide appendix.

subjective *adjective* A **subjective** view is one that relates entirely to one individual and their personal likes and dislikes: *I don't agree with that – that's just your subjective opinion.*

THE OPPOSITE is **objective**.

subjective case *noun* the form of a noun or pronoun which shows it is the subject of a verb such as 'They' in the sentence *They love eating brownies after school*.

SEE the Grammar and Punctuation Guide appendix.

sublime /*say* suh-**bluym**/ *adjective*
1. uplifting in thought, language, bearing, and so on: *sublime music.* **2.** attracting the mind with a sense of greatness or power: *The scenery up in the mountains was sublime.* **3.** perfect: *It was a sublime moment when she was awarded the highest prize.*

submarine /*say* **sub**-muh-reen, sub-muh-**reen**/ *adjective*
1. under water: *a submarine volcano.*
–*noun* **2.** a type of ship that can travel under water.

submerge *verb* If something **submerges** or you **submerge** it, it goes under the surface of the water: *We watched as the submarine submerged and then we could see it no more.*
☐ **submersion**, *noun*

submissive *adjective* giving in obediently without asking questions or standing up for yourself: *She is too submissive and people tend to take advantage of her.*

submit *verb* (**submits**, **submitting**, **submitted**, **has submitted**)
1. If you **submit** to something, you accept or give in to it because you do not have enough strength or authority to resist it. **2.** If you **submit** something such as an entry or plan to someone, you send it to them in the hope that they will accept it.
☐ **submission**, *noun*

subordinate /*say* suh-**baw**-duh-nuht/ *adjective* Someone or something **subordinate** is placed in or belongs to a lower order or rank: *a subordinate committee*; *In the army, a captain is subordinate to a major.*
☐ **subordinate**, *noun* –**subordination**, *noun*

subscription *noun*
1. a payment you make for club membership, a series of concert tickets, a regular magazine, an internet access, or something similar. **2.** an amount of money given: *They are asking for subscriptions to a flood appeal.*
☐ **subscribe**, *verb*

subsequent /*say* **sub**-suh-kwuhnt/ *adjective* happening later: *Subsequent events showed his story to be true.*
☐ **subsequently**, *adverb*

subside *verb* If something **subsides**, it sinks to a lower level: *The foundations have subsided and the house has big cracks in it*; *Eventually the hilarity subsided.*
☐ **subsidence**, *noun*

subsidiary /*say* suhb-**sij**-uh-ree/ *noun* something less important: *The small company is a subsidiary of the large one.*

☑ SPELLING TIP Remember the *d* spelling in this word (although the sound you hear is 'j'). Rap it out as *sub+sid+i+a+ry.*

subsidy /*say* **sub**-suh-dee/ *noun* (*plural* **subsidies**) a supporting payment made by a government or other organisation: *a subsidy to sugar farmers.*
☐ **subsidise**, *verb*: *to subsidise sugar farmers.*

ANOTHER SPELLING for **subsidise** is **subsidize**.

subsist *verb* If people **subsist**, they continue to live or stay alive, especially when food and other needs are in short supply: *By the time help got to them, they were subsisting on what they could find in the bush.*
☐ **subsistence**, *noun*

substance *noun*
1. anything of which a thing is made. **2.** the main or basic part: *The substance of the lecture had to do with refugees.*

substantial /*say* suhb-**stan**-shuhl/ *adjective* large or solid: *He lost a substantial fortune in the market crash.*

substantiate /*say* suhb-**stan**-shee-ayt/ *verb* If you **substantiate** a story or a theory, you provide evidence to back it up.

substitute /*say* **sub**-stuh-tyooht/ *noun*
1. someone or something acting in place of another.
–*verb* **2.** If you **substitute** one thing for another, it takes the other one's place: *The recipe works just as well if you substitute margarine for butter.*
☐ **substitution**, *noun*

☑ SPELLING TIP *Tricky 'uh' sound*: the middle vowel sound is spelt *i*.

subterfuge /*say* **sub**-tuh-fyoohj/ *noun* a plan or trick used to hide or avoid something.

subterranean /*say* sub-tuh-**ray**-nee-uhn/ *adjective* underground: *The ants build subterranean passages far below the surface.*

☑ SPELLING TIP *Double letter alert*: double *r*. It will help if you see that this is part of the word part *terra*, from the Latin word for 'land' (found also in words such as *terracotta*, *terrain* and *terrestrial*). Before this comes the prefix *sub-*, meaning 'under'. Also remember that the ending is *ean* (not *ian*).

subtitle *noun*
1. a second and less important title of a book or play. **2.** **subtitles**, the words written at the bottom

of a film or television screen to help people who would otherwise have difficulty understanding what is being said.
☐ **subtitled**, *adjective*: *The film is subtitled.*

subtle /*say* **sut**-uhl/ *adjective* Something **subtle** is **1.** so fine or slight as to not be obvious or clear: *There was a subtle change in the music as the tempo slowed down ever so slightly.* **2.** skilful or clever: *The detective's subtle approach enabled him to find out important secrets.*
☐ **subtlety**, *noun* (*plural* **subtleties**) –**subtly**, *adverb*

WORD HISTORY from a Latin word meaning 'fine' or 'delicate'

☑ SPELLING TIP *Silent letter alert*: don't forget the silent *b* before the *t*. Rap it out as *sub+ tle* to remind yourself.

subtract *verb* If you **subtract** one number from another, you calculate what sum is left after you take one number away from the other number. For example, if you subtract 16 from 30, you get 14.
☐ **subtraction**, *noun*

suburb *noun* an area of a city with its own shopping centre, school and other facilities: *a wealthy suburb*; *a neighbouring suburb.*
☐ **suburban**, *adjective*

subway *noun* a passage under a street or railway for people to walk through.

succeed /*say* suhk-**seed**/ *verb* To **succeed** is to **1.** do or achieve what you have attempted: *My big brother has finally succeeded in passing his driving test.* **2.** come after and take the place of: *The principal who is succeeding our last one used to be a sports teacher.*
☐ **succession**, *noun*: *three goals in succession.* –**successor**, *noun*: *Who will be David's successor as captain?*

☑ SPELLING TIP *Double letter alert*: double *c* and double *e*.

success /*say* suhk-**ses**/ *noun*
1. a good or desired result. **2.** someone who has achieved a great deal in their field.
☐ **successful**, *adjective* –**successfully**, *adverb*

succulent /*say* **suk**-yuh-luhnt/ *adjective* juicy: *The mango is a succulent piece of fruit.*
☐ **succulence**, *noun*

☑ SPELLING TIP *Double letter alert*: Notice that it is double *c*, not *ck* at the end of the first syllable. So don't be a sucker and think that **succulent** food is something that you suck!

succumb /*say* suh-**kum**/ *verb* To **succumb** is to give in: *She succumbed to temptation and ate the whole chocolate*; *He succumbed to tiredness and fell asleep.*

☑ SPELLING TIP *Silent letter alert*: don't forget the silent *b* at the end (similar to that in *dumb* and *plumb*). Also notice that both the vowels in this word are *u*'s.

such *adjective* **Such** is used to **1.** introduce things or qualities which are like others of that kind: *Such gems are very valuable.* **2.** emphasise how much: *It was such a delicious meal.*
–*phrase* **3. such as**, for example: *He likes outdoor sports such as tennis and football.*

suck *verb*
1. If you **suck** something, you pull on it with the muscles of your mouth, usually in order to get some liquid out of it: *The orphaned lamb is learning how to suck from a bottle.* **2.** If something **sucks** a substance in a particular direction, it draws it there with a strong force: *The leaves were sucked down the drain in the storm.* **3.** If you are **sucked** into a situation, or you get **sucked** into it, you become involved in it although you do not want to: *Don't get sucked into an argument with her – just ignore her remarks.*
☐ **suck**, *noun*

sucker *noun*
1. *Informal* someone who is easily tricked: *Don't be a sucker and believe everything she tells you.* **2.** a part on the body of some insects and some animals, such as frogs and octopuses, that allow them to stick to surfaces.

suckle *verb* If a new-born baby **suckles**, it takes milk from its mother's breast.

suction *noun* the power of sucking produced when the pressure of the air inside something is less than the outside pressure.

sudden *adjective* Something **sudden** happens quickly and without warning.
☐ **suddenly**, *adverb* –**suddenness**, *noun*

suds *plural noun* soapy water with bubbles.

sue *verb* To **sue** someone is to bring a legal action against them: *He wants to sue the companies who have promoted smoking for years.*

suede /*say* swayd/ *noun* a soft leather with a slightly furry surface.

☑ SPELLING TIP Remember that there is no *w* in **suede**. The letters *ue* spell the 'way' sound. **Suede** comes from the French word for the country Sweden, originally in the phrase 'gloves of Sweden' which were made of this material.

suet /*say* **sooh**-uht/ *noun* a hard, dry fat surrounding the kidneys of animals and used in cooking.

suffer *verb*
1. If you **suffer** pain, or if you **suffer**, you feel severe pain in your body or in your mind for long periods: *She suffers a lot of pain because of her headaches.* **2.** If you **suffer** from an illness, you often feel pain or something unpleasant because of it: *He's been suffering from epilepsy since he*

was a child. **3.** If you **suffer** from a painful or unpleasant experience, you are temporarily affected by it rather badly: *After the accident she suffered from shock.* **4.** If you **suffer** an experience that is painful or unpleasant, you are in a situation in which it happens to you: *The army suffered heavy losses in the battle*; *He suffered the rough ride without complaining.* **5.** If something **suffers**, for example because it has not been given any attention, its quality or condition becomes worse: *His relationship with his family has suffered because he has been away a lot.*
□ **suffering**, *noun* –**sufferer**, *noun*: *The new drug offers relief to headache sufferers.*

suffice /*say* suh-**fuys**/ *verb* If something **suffices**, it is enough: *For dessert, anything chocolate will suffice.*

sufficient /*say* suh-**fish**-uhnt/ *adjective* all that is needed.
□ **sufficiency**, *noun* –**sufficiently**, *adverb*

suffix *noun* a word part added to the end of a word to make a new word with a new meaning, such as *-able* in *perishable* (*-able* has been added to *perish*).

COMPARE this with **prefix**.

suffocate /*say* **suf**-uh-kayt/ *verb*
1. To **suffocate** someone is to kill them by stopping them from breathing: *He suffocated his victim with a cushion.* **2.** To **suffocate** is to die from lack of air.
□ **suffocating**, *adjective* –**suffocation**, *noun*

☑ SPELLING TIP *Double letter alert*: double *f*. Also notice that the following vowel sound is spelt *o*. Think what a 'fearful and frightening ordeal' it would be to **suffocate** to remind you.

suffuse /*say* suh-**fyoohz**/ *verb* If colour, light, warmth, or so on **suffuses** something, it spreads evenly throughout it: *A blush of embarrassment suffused her face*; *The sky was suffused with orange light.*

sugar *noun* a sweet substance made mainly from cane and beet and used widely in food.
□ **sugary**, *adjective*

sugar cane *noun* a tall grass of tropical and warm regions, with a jointed stem from which we get sugar.

suggest /*say* suh-**jest**/ *verb* If you **suggest** something, you put forward an idea or plan: *The teacher suggested we divide into groups.*

☑ SPELLING TIP *Double letter alert*: double *g* spelling for the 'j' sound.

suggestible *adjective* If someone is **suggestible**, they are easily influenced: *Angie is so suggestible, you can get her to do anything.*

suggestion *noun*
1. an idea or plan put forward for someone to consider: *He made a suggestion that the meeting finish early*; *She made some good suggestions about how we could improve our kitchen.* **2.** something that indicates that something is true without being definite: *There is a suggestion that the crime was related to drugs.* **3.** a slight sign of something: *carrot soup with just a suggestion of ginger.*

SIMILAR WORDS (for definition 1) are **recommendation**, **proposition** and **proposal**.

suggestive *adjective* If something like an action or a presentation is **suggestive**, it suggests something, especially something that is not proper: *The ads were taken off TV because people thought they were too suggestive.*

suicide /*say* **sooh**-uh-suyd/ *noun*
1. the act of intentionally killing yourself: *The police feel it was a suicide.*
–*verb* **2.** If someone **suicides**, they kill themselves.
□ **suicidal**, *adjective*

☑ SPELLING TIP Remember the *c* spelling for the 's' sound in this word. The suffix *-cide* means 'killer' or 'act of killing' and appears in several other words, such as *homicide* and *insecticide*. It comes from the Latin word for 'kill'. Here it is joined to *sui*, a Latin word meaning 'of yourself'.

suit *noun*
1. a set of clothes meant to be worn together. **2.** one of the four sets in a pack of cards.
–*verb* **3.** If you say that something **suits** you, you mean that it is convenient for you or you like it: *Would 2.30 p.m. suit you?*; *This cool weather really suits me.* **4.** If something such as your clothing **suits** you, it makes you look good: *Blue suits me better than green.*
□ **suited**, *adjective*

suitable *adjective*
1. fitting or convenient: *Choose a time suitable to you.* **2.** right for the occasion: *I just don't have any suitable clothes!*
□ **suitability**, *noun* –**suitably**, *adverb*

suitcase *noun* a bag for carrying clothes and other things when you travel.

suite /*sounds like* sweet/ *noun* a series or set, especially of furniture or rooms.

☑ SPELLING TIP Remember that there is no *w* in **suite**. Don't confuse it with **sweet** which describes something that is not sour. **Suite** comes from French.

sukiyaki /*say* soo-kee-**ah**-kee/ *noun* a food made of fried meat, vegetables, onions, etc., usually cooked with soy sauce, originating in Japanese cooking.

sulfur /*say* **sul**-fuh/ *noun* See **sulphur**.

sulk *verb* If you **sulk**, you feel bad-tempered and upset because you feel that you have been unfairly treated.
☐ **sulky**, *adjective* (**sulkier**, **sulkiest**) –**sulkiness**, *noun*

sullen *adjective* angry, silent and bad-mannered.
☐ **sullenness**, *noun*

sulphur /*say* **sul**-fuh/ *noun* a yellow nonmetallic element used in gunpowder, matches and other things.
☐ **sulphuric**, *adjective* –**sulphurous**, *adjective* –**sulphureous**, *adjective*

NOTE Traditionally **sulphur** is the British spelling and **sulfur** the American one. In technical and scientific writing **sulfur** is now standard throughout the world, although the **sulphur** spelling is still the usual one in general use in Australian English.

sultan *noun* a ruler in some Islamic countries.
☐ **sultanate**, *noun*

WORD HISTORY from an Arabic word meaning 'king', 'ruler' or 'power'

sultana *noun*
1. a dried seedless grape. **2.** a wife or close female relative of a sultan.

sultry *adjective* hot and humid: *It was too sultry to do anything active.*
☐ **sultriness**, *noun*

sum *noun*
1. a total: *The sum of 45 and 55 is 100.* **2.** an exercise or problem in arithmetic. **3.** an amount: *She had a small sum of money with her.*
–*verb in the phrase* (**sums**, **summing**, **summed**, **has summed**) **4. sum up**, **a.** to add up. **b.** to express in a shortened form: *To sum up, he wants us to work harder.* **c.** to form an opinion about: *She tends to sum up people according to how they are dressed.*

summary *noun* (*plural* **summaries**) a short statement in speech or writing which gives the main points of something.
☐ **summarise**, *verb* –**summarily**, *adverb*

ANOTHER SPELLING for **summarise** is **summarize**.
SIMILAR WORDS are **precis** and **synopsis**. These words, especially **precis**, usually refer to a written summary of a longer piece of writing.

summer *noun* the warmest season of the year, following spring.
☐ **summery**, *adjective*

summit *noun* the top or highest point, especially of a mountain: *It took hours to reach the summit.*

summon *verb* To **summon** someone is to send for them officially: *The principal summoned all those who had been involved.*

summons *noun* (*plural* **summonses**) an order to appear at a particular place, especially an official order to appear at a court of law.

sumptuous /*say* **sump**-chooh-uhs/ *adjective* rich and luxurious: *He lives a sumptuous life – nothing is too good for him!*

☑ SPELLING TIP Remember the *tu* spelling in this word (which gives a 'chooh' sound).

sun *noun*
1. the star which is the centre of our solar system and which gives light and warmth to the earth. **2.** sunshine: *Do you want to sit in the shade or in the sun?*
☐ **sunny**, *adjective* (**sunnier**, **sunniest**) –**sunless**, *adjective* –**sunlight**, *noun*

NOTE An adjective meaning 'having to do with the sun' is **solar**.

sunbake *verb* If you **sunbake**, you lie or sit in the sun in order to become tanned.

ANOTHER WORD for this is **sunbathe**.

sunburn *noun* painful reddening of the skin caused by being burnt by the heat of the sun.
☐ **sunburnt**, *adjective*

sundae /*sounds like* **sun**-day/ *noun* an ice-cream served with flavoured syrup and chopped nuts.

☑ SPELLING TIP Remember the *ae* spelling at the end of this word. Don't confuse it with **Sunday**, the day of the week, which has the same sound.

Sunday *noun* the first day of the week.

sundial *noun* an instrument which tells the time by the shadow of the sun on its face, which is marked in hours like a clock.

sunflower *noun* a tall plant with big yellow flowers and seeds which you can eat.

sunglasses *plural noun* glasses with darkened lenses to protect your eyes from sunlight.

sunrise *noun* the appearance of the sun above the horizon in the morning, or the time when this happens.

sunscreen *noun* a cream or lotion that you rub onto your skin to protect it from getting damaged by the rays of the sun.

OTHER WORDS for this are **blockout** and **sunblock**.

sunset *noun* the disappearance of the sun below the horizon at night, or the time when this happens.

sunshine *noun*
1. the light of the sun. **2.** cheerfulness or brightness: *Their grandchildren brought sunshine into their life.*

sunspot *noun*
1. one of the dark patches on the surface of the sun which are believed to affect some things on earth, such as the weather. **2.** a discolouration and roughening of part of the skin, usually caused by too much exposure to the sun.

sunstroke *noun* a sickness with weakness and a high temperature caused by being in the sun for too long.

suntan *noun* brownness of the skin caused by being out in the sun.
□ **suntanned**, *adjective*

super *adjective*
1. of a superior quality: *a super issue of the magazine.* **2.** *Informal* extremely good or pleasing: *Dad and Mum said they had a super time – we thought it was pretty cool too.*

super- *prefix* a word part meaning 'over', 'beyond' or 'superior to', as in *supernatural*, *supervisor.*

WORD HISTORY this prefix comes from Latin

superannuation /*say* sooh-puh-ran-yooh-**ay**-shuhn/ *noun* money set aside to support someone when they stop working.

superb *adjective* excellent or splendid: *It was a superb athletic performance.*

supercilious /*say* sooh-puh-**sil**-ee-uhs/ *adjective* proud and scornful: *He gave the giggling teenagers a look of supercilious disdain.*
□ **superciliously**, *adverb* –**superciliousness**, *noun*

SIMILAR WORDS are **contemptuous** and **disdainful**.

☑ SPELLING TIP The most difficult part of this word is the *c* spelling for the 's' sound in the middle. **Supercilious** people often have the habit of raising their eyebrows (as well as looking down their noses!) – and in fact the word comes from *supercilium*, Latin for 'eyebrow' (from *super*, meaning 'above' or 'upper' and *cilium*, meaning 'a hair'). Look out for the word part *super* with the same meaning in the following words.

superficial /*say* sooh-puh-**fish**-uhl/ *adjective*
1. Something that is **superficial** is rather obvious or easy to understand. It is not very important, serious or thorough: *It was a rather superficial description of the situation. It didn't cover the some of the main problems.* **2.** If you describe someone as being **superficial**, you mean that you do not think they have much depth of character. They are not interested in serious or important matters. **3. Superficial** injuries, wounds or damage are not very deep or serious. They are only on the surface. **4.** A **superficial** similarity or likeness is one that is obvious when you look at something rather carelessly or quickly.
□ **superficiality**, *noun* –**superficially**, *adverb*

☑ SPELLING TIP You will recognise the first part of **superficial** as the word *super.* Here it is a prefix meaning 'on' or 'above' (the surface). Also notice the spelling of the last part – *cial* (giving the sound 'shuhl'). Other words with this pattern are *artificial* and *official*.

superfluous /*say* sooh-**per**-flooh-uhs/ *adjective* more than is needed: *There is plenty of food – any more would be superfluous.*
□ **superfluity**, *noun* –**superfluously**, *adverb* –**superfluousness**, *noun*

superintendent *noun* someone who supervises work, a business, or a building.
□ **superintend**, *verb*

☑ SPELLING TIP Remember that the ending is *ent* (not *ant*).

superior *adjective*
1. higher in position or rank: *In the army, a major is superior to a captain*; *You take an appeal from a lower court to a superior court.* **2.** better or of higher quality: *superior understanding.* **3.** thinking that you are better than other people: *He annoys everyone with his superior attitudes.*
–*noun* **4.** someone who is higher in rank than you: *They have to salute their superiors.*
□ **superiority**, *noun*

THE OPPOSITE is **inferior**.

superlative /*say* sooh-**per**-luh-tiv/ *adjective*
1. of the highest or best kind: *The physicist has a superlative ability to understand extremely difficult concepts.* **2.** having to do with the form of an adjective or adverb which expresses the greatest degree of comparison: *'Reddest' is the superlative form of 'red' and 'most abnormally' is the superlative form of 'abnormally'.*
□ **superlatively**, *adverb*

COMPARE definition 2 with **comparative** (definition 3). See also the Grammar and Punctuation Guide appendix.

supermarket *noun* a large self-service shop selling food and other household goods.

supernatural *adjective* Something **supernatural** cannot be explained in terms of the laws of nature: *We thought the blinking lights high in the sky had to be something supernatural.*
□ **supernatural**, *noun*: *The supernatural has always interested me.*

superpower *noun* a very rich and powerful nation.

supersonic *adjective* Something **supersonic** moves faster than the speed of sound: *supersonic velocity.*

superstar *noun* a singer or actor who is extremely famous.

superstition /*say* sooh-puh-**stish**-uhn/ *noun* a belief about the meaning of a thing or event that does not stem from reason or sensible thought: *She never steps on the lines of the footpath because of a silly superstition.*
☐ **superstitious**, *adjective* –**superstitiously**, *adverb*

supervise *verb* If you **supervise** an activity, or the people involved in it, you make certain that everything is done properly: *Who will supervise the class while the teacher is away?*
☐ **supervision**, *noun* –**supervisor**, *noun* –**supervisory**, *adjective*

supper *noun* a light meal eaten in the evening.

supplant *verb* If you **supplant** someone, you take their place: *Mike has supplanted Ben as the school's best batter.*

supple *adjective* Something **supple** bends easily: *a supple young tree*; *You're more supple than me – can you crawl under the table and get the cord?*
☐ **suppleness**, *noun*

supplement *noun* /*say* **sup**-luh-muhnt/
1. something added to complete or correct: *The book has a supplement listing addresses of health organisations.* **2.** an extra part of a newspaper on a particular subject: *a real estate supplement.*
–*verb* /*say* **sup**-luh-ment/ **3.** If you **supplement** something, you add something to it: *They want to supplement the fund by appealing for extra donations.*
☐ **supplemental**, *adjective* –**supplementary**, *adjective* –**supplementation**, *noun*

supply /*say* suh-**pluy**/ *verb* (**supplies**, **supplying**, **supplied**, **has supplied**)
1. To **supply** something is to provide it: *The council supplies the residents with seedlings*; *They supply seedlings to the residents.*
–*noun* (*plural* **supplies**) **2.** an amount of something provided or available for use: *The truck was delivering a supply of sheets.* **3. supplies**, a store of materials, food, and so on: *Her job was to top up the office supplies.*
☐ **supplier**, *noun*

WORD HISTORY from a Latin word meaning 'fill up'

support *verb*
1. To **support** something is to hold it up: *Four steel pylons support the bridge.* **2.** If you **support** someone, you give help or strength to them: *Her family are supporting her through her problems*; *That fact does not support your argument at all!* **3.** If you **support** a group or organisation, you believe in and help them: *This community supports its football team.* **4.** If you **support** a family, you supply them with money or other things needed for living: *Mum had to fill out a form saying how many children she supported.*
–*noun* **5.** the providing of support: *Can you offer any support?* **6.** someone or something that gives support: *Without its supports, the tent is just a bit of cloth.*
☐ **supporter**, *noun* –**supportive**, *adjective*

suppose *verb* If you **suppose** that something is the case, you think it is probably true: *I suppose we have to finish our maths before we can go to sport.*
☐ **supposition**, *noun*

supposed *adjective* /*say* suh-**pohzd**, suh-**poh**-zuhd/
1. If something is **supposed**, it is thought to be probable: *We didn't believe his supposed defection.*
–*phrase* /*say* suh-**pohzd**/ **2. supposed to**, expected or meant to: *We are supposed to do homework four nights of the week.*
☐ **supposedly** /*say* suh-**poh**-zuhd-lee/, *adverb*

suppress *verb* To **suppress** something is to **1.** put an end to it: *The school suppressed all the attempts to have a disco in the hall.* **2.** keep it inside or hidden: *I suppressed my feelings and tried to smile*; *The news was suppressed until the morning.*
☐ **suppression**, *noun* –**suppressive**, *adjective* –**suppressor**, *noun*

☑ SPELLING TIP *Double letter alert*: double *p* and then double *s* at the end. Rap it out as *sup+press*.

supreme /*say* suh-**preem**/ *adjective*
1. highest in position or power: *the supreme policy-making group.* **2.** extreme: *He showed supreme bravery diving into the flooded river.*
☐ **supremacy** /*say* suh-**prem**-uh-see/, *noun*

sure /*say* shaw/ *adjective*
1. certain, or confident: *I am sure that Matt would be a good player.* **2.** firm: *He thought he was on a sure thing, siding with Pete.* **3.** never missing: *She shoots the ball with a sure aim every time.*
–*adverb* **4.** *Informal* surely or certainly: *She was sure lucky to pick that one!*
–*phrase* **5. for sure**, as a certainty. **6. make sure**, to be certain.
☐ **sureness**, *noun*

☑ SPELLING TIP Don't confuse the spelling of **sure** with **shore** which has the same sound. The **shore** is the land along the edge of the sea or a lake.

surely /*say* **shaw**-lee/ *adverb* **1.** firmly or steadily: *Slowly but surely she worked towards her goal.* **2.** almost certainly: *They will surely respond to the plea for help.*

surf *noun*
1. the waves which break along the shore.
–*verb* **2.** If you **surf** as a sport, you lie or stand on a surfboard and let the surf carry you along: *They all go surfing every morning.* **3.** To **surf** the internet is to look for information on it.
☐ **surfer**, *noun* –**surfing**, *noun*

☑ SPELLING TIP Don't confuse the spelling of **surf** with **serf** which has the same sound. A **serf** was a peasant in medieval times.

surface *noun*
1. the outer part or side of anything: *The surface of the gem was smooth and translucent*; *When you throw the dice, the upper surface tells you how many to move.* **2.** the top, especially of water or other liquid: *The surface of the lake was glassy.* **3.** outside appearance: *Amy appears confident on the surface, but that is hiding a lot of uncertainty.*
–*verb* **4.** To **surface** is to rise to the top: *They were there when I dived into the pool, but when I surfaced I couldn't see them.*

surfboard *noun* a long, narrow board used to ride waves towards the shore.

surge *noun*
1. a wave-like rush or forward movement: *She felt a surge of hope*; *A surge of people pressed on the gates.*
–*verb* **2.** If something **surges**, it rushes forwards or upwards in waves or like waves: *The horses surged as a mass from the starting gates.*

surgeon /*say* **ser**-juhn/ *noun* a doctor who does surgery.

☑ SPELLING TIP Remember the *g* spelling for the 'j' sound. Also notice that the ending is *eon*, although you do not hear the *e* when the word is pronounced. You could think of the sentence 'Surgeons use red gloves every other night' to remind you of the order of the letters.

surgery *noun*
1. the treatment of diseases or injuries by using instruments to cut into the body. **2.** a doctor's or dentist's rooms where patients go for treatment.
□ **surgical**, *adjective*

surly *adjective* (**surlier**, **surliest**) unfriendly and bad-tempered: *He was a surly man and people avoided him.*

surname *noun* someone's family name.

☑ SPELLING TIP Remember that the first part is spelt *sur* (not *sir*). The word part *sur* comes from the French word for 'over' or 'above'.

surpass *verb* To **surpass** something or someone is to be better than them: *The relay team we put together surpassed all the other ones entered in the race.*

surplus /*say* **ser**-pluhs/ *noun* an amount that is more than what is needed or used: *There was a surplus of sausages at the barbecue.*
□ **surplus**, *adjective*

surprise *verb*
1. If something **surprises** you, it gives you a small shock because it is unexpected or unusual: *He surprised her by arriving early.* **2.** If you **surprise** someone, you find them or appear before them when they do not expect it: *We surprised the burglar in the act of robbing our house.*
–*noun* **3.** something that surprises: *Going out for tea was a great surprise.* **4.** the feeling of being surprised: *We could see the surprise in her face.*
–*adjective* **5.** sudden and unexpected: *a surprise attack.*
□ **surprising**, *adjective* –**surprisingly**, *adverb*

SIMILAR WORDS (for definition 1) are **amaze**, **astonish** and **astound**. These words all mean 'to surprise greatly'.

☑ SPELLING TIP Remember that there is an *r* in the first part of this word, so that the first syllable is spelt *sur*. Also note that there is no *ize* spelling choice for the last part of this word, as there is in some other words ending in *ise*. **Surprise** must always end in *ise*.

surrender *verb*
1. To **surrender** is to stop fighting or resisting: *They forced the enemy to surrender.* **2.** If you **surrender** to a feeling, you allow it to control you: *He surrendered to despair.* **3.** To **surrender** something is to give it up to the ownership or power of someone else: *We had to surrender our water pistols to the teacher.*
□ **surrender**, *noun*

surround *verb* To **surround** something is to go around it completely: *Bush surrounds the farm house.*
□ **surrounding**, *adjective*: *a farm and its surrounding fields.*

surroundings *plural noun* everything that is around or near someone or something: *She is used to living in city surroundings.*

A SIMILAR WORD is **environment**.

surveillance /*say* suh-**vay**-luhns/ *noun* a watch kept over someone, especially someone who is suspected of doing something wrong: *The police have had him under surveillance for several weeks.*

☑ SPELLING TIP *Tricky vowel sound*: *ei* spelling for the 'ay' sound. Also remember the double *l*. **Surveillance** comes from French where *veiller* means 'to watch'. The prefix *sur-* is the French word for 'on' or 'over'.

survey *verb* /*say* ser-**vay**, **ser**-vay/
1. If you **survey** something, you examine it carefully: *They surveyed the maps carefully to decide the best route to take.* **2.** If someone **surveys** an area of land, they measure it in order to draw a map of it that shows things such as the location of its boundaries.
–*noun* /*say* **ser**-vay/ **3.** a detailed investigation of something, particularly one that involves asking many questions, or in which things are carefully measured: *a survey of the flooded area*; *They did*

a survey to see the way people would vote. **4.** a report or map made after surveying.
☐ **surveyor**, *noun*

☑ SPELLING TIP **Survey** is made up of the prefix *sur-*, meaning 'over' or 'above', and *vey*, from the Latin word *videre* meaning 'to see'. This will help you remember the ending is *ey* (not *ay*).

survive *verb* To **survive** is to remain alive or in existence, especially after someone else's death, or after something ending or dying out: *Only one climber survived the avalanche*; *Interest in his music still survives despite his death 50 years ago.*
☐ **survival**, *noun* –**surviving**, *adjective* –**survivor**, *noun*

susceptible /*say* suh-**sep**-tuh-buhl/ *adjective* easily affected: *He is susceptible to coughs and colds.*
☐ **susceptibility**, *noun*

☑ SPELLING TIP Notice the *sc* spelling in this word (not double *s*). Also remember that the ending is *ible* (not *able*). Rap it out as *sus+cep+ti+ble*.

sushi *noun* a food made from cooked rice and raw fish wrapped in seaweed, originating in Japan.

suspect *verb* /*say* suh-**spekt**/
1. If you **suspect** something, you think that it is likely to be true: *I suspect you are right.* **2.** If you **suspect** something, you feel doubt about it. You do not trust it: *I can't help suspecting her motives.* **3.** If you **suspect** someone of doing something wrong, you think that they are guilty of it.
–*noun* /*say* **sus**-pekt/ **4.** someone who is suspected, especially of a crime: *The police are holding one suspect.*
–*adjective* /*say* **sus**-pekt/ **5.** open to suspicion: *Your story is very suspect.*

suspend *verb*
1. To **suspend** something is to hang it by joining it to something above: *The trapeze rope was suspended from the very top of the tent.* **2.** If you **suspend** an action, you put it off until a later time: *Work was suspended when it became dark.* **3.** Students who are **suspended** are removed from school for a time for bad behaviour.

suspender *noun* an elastic strap with fasteners to hold up stockings.

suspense *noun* an anxious state of mind caused by having to wait to find something out: *We were in suspense wondering who would win the jackpot.*
☐ **suspenseful**, *adjective*

suspension *noun*
1. a suspending or being suspended. **2.** a liquid in which very small parts of a solid substance are mixed but not dissolved. **3.** the system of springs and so on used in a vehicle to stop jolts being felt inside or damaging the engine.

suspicion /*say* suhs-**pish**-uhn/ *noun*
1. the feeling of suspecting: *They regarded her with suspicion.* **2.** the condition of being suspected: *He is being held under suspicion of murder.* **3.** a slight sign: *There was just a suspicion of laughter in his voice.*
☐ **suspicious**, *adjective* –**suspiciously**, *adverb*

sustain *verb*
1. To **sustain** something is to continue it or keep it going for a period of time: *The movie about creatures from black holes in space sustained our interest for two hours.* **2.** If something **sustains** you, it gives you strength and keeps you going: *The fact the coach believed in us sustained the team for the whole season.* **3.** If you **sustain** something such as a shock or an injury, you experience it.

sustainable *adjective*
1. able to be sustained or kept going. **2.** able to continue for a long time without damaging the environment: *Using renewable resources is an important step in sustainable economic development.*

swab /*say* swob/ *noun* a piece of soft material, often on a stick, used for cleaning parts of the body, such as the mouth, or applying a medicine and so on.

swaddle /*say* **swod**-uhl/ *verb* To **swaddle** someone is to wrap them up tightly with clothes or strips of cloth: *They swaddled the baby in the pink hospital blankets.*

swag *noun*
1. a bundle or roll of belongings carried on the shoulders by someone travelling in the bush. **2.** a rolled up mattress, used for camping. **3.** *Informal* a large number of quantity: *a swag of presents.*

ANOTHER WORD (for definition 1), used in the past, was **shiralee**.

swagger *verb* If someone **swaggers**, they walk in a defiant or insolent way: *He told them the business wasn't big enough for him and then swaggered out of the room.*
☐ **swagger**, *noun*

A SIMILAR WORD is **strut**.

swagman *noun* (*plural* **swagmen**) in past times and occasionally now, a man who camps and walks through the Australian bush, carrying everything he owns in a bundle on his shoulders: *Once a jolly swagman camped by a billabong.*

swallow[1] /*say* **swol**-oh/ *verb*
1. To **swallow** something is to take it into the stomach through the throat. **2.** *Informal* If you **swallow** a story, you believe it without questioning it.
–*phrase* **3. swallow up**, to use up or take over something so that it doesn't exist separately any more: *Christmas presents for my family swallowed up all my pocket money.*; *They were*

worried that the opening of the supermarket would swallow up many of the small shops in the district.
☐ **swallow**, *noun*: *It took a few swallows to get the pills down.*

swallow[2] /*say* **swol**-oh/ *noun* a small bird with long wings and a forked tail.

swamp /*say* swomp/ *noun*
1. an area of very wet and soft land.
–*verb* **2.** If something **swamps** a place, it floods or soaks it with water: *I forgot to turn the tap off and swamped the bathroom floor*; *A huge wave swamped the fishing boat.* **3.** If you are **swamped** by things, you have more of them than you can manage: *I've been swamped with work.*
☐ **swampy**, *adjective*

A SIMILAR WORD (for definition 1) is **marsh**.

swan /*say* swon/ *noun* a large waterbird with a long, thin neck, either black or white in colour.

NOTE The male is a **cob**; the female is a **pen**; the young is a **cygnet**.

swank *noun Informal* showy smartness in appearance or behaviour: *She marched in, full of confidence and swank.*
☐ **swanky**, *adjective* (**swankier**, **swankiest**): *a swanky hotel.*

swap /*say* swop/ *verb* (**swaps**, **swapping**, **swapped**, **has swapped**) To **swap** something is to exchange it for something else: *Would you like to swap your sausage roll for my ham sandwich?*
☐ **swap**, *noun*

swarm /*rhymes with* form/ *noun*
1. a large group of bees. **2.** a large number of people or things, especially when moving together.
–*verb* **3.** If people or things swarm, they move in large numbers: *Where we live, bees often swarm in November*; *Crowds swarmed around to get as close as they could to the singers.*
–*phrase* **4. swarm with**, to be covered or filled with: *The hot summer night was swarming with insects.*

swarthy /*say* **swaw**-dhee/
(**swarthier**, **swarthiest**) dark in skin colour.
☐ **swarthiness**, *noun*

swastika /*say* **swos**-tik-uh/ *noun* an ancient symbol or ornament in the form of a cross with its ends bent at right angles: *The swastika was adopted as a symbol by Hitler's Nazi Party.*

☑ SPELLING TIP The last part of this word has nothing to do with a sticker (a label that you can stick on to things). The spelling of this part of the word is *stika*. **Swastika** comes from a Sanskrit word meaning 'wellbeing'.

swat /*say* swot/ *verb* (**swats**, **swatting**, **swatted**, **has swatted**) If you **swat** something such as an insect, you hit it with a flat object: *She tried to swat the fly with her newspaper.*
☐ **swatter**, *noun*

swathe /*say* swaydh/ *verb* To **swathe** someone or something is to wrap them up loosely with strips of material or other wrappings: *The artist swathed the statues in pink silk.*

sway *verb*
1. If someone or something **sways**, they swing or move slowly from side to side: *The tops of the trees swayed gently in the breeze*; *He was swaying in his seat as he listened to the music.* **2.** If someone or something **sways** you, they influence what you do: *Her forceful argument swayed many to change their vote.*
–*noun* **3.** a swaying movement.

swear *verb* (**swears**, **swearing**, **swore**, **has sworn**) To **swear** is to **1.** make a very serious promise or oath: *Do you swear never to tell anyone my secret?*; *She swore to be loyal to the cause.* **2.** use language that is generally thought to be unpleasant or rude: *Tim was sent out of the classroom because he was swearing at his friend.*
–*phrase* **3. swear by**, **a.** to name some sacred being or thing as your witness for an action or statement: *She swore by everything sacred that she would not leave him.* **b.** to have confidence in: *My mum swears by Don – she says he's the best builder!* **4. swear in**, to admit to office or service by administering an oath: *The president will be sworn in next Monday.*
☐ **swear**, *adjective*: *a swear word.* –**swearer**, *noun*

sweat /*say* swet/ *verb*
1. If you **sweat**, a salty liquid comes out through your skin: *Walking under the midday sun made us sweat.*
–*phrase* **2. sweat on**, *Informal* to be very anxious about: *We are sweating on the fitness of our best player.*
☐ **sweat**, *noun* –**sweaty**, *adjective*

ANOTHER WORD (for definition 1) is **perspire**.

sweater /*say* **swet**-uh/ *noun* a warm top which is often worn over other clothes.

OTHER WORDS for this are **jumper** and **pullover**.

sweatshirt *noun* a loose, light top.

sweep *verb* (**sweeps**, **sweeping**, **swept**, **has swept**)
1. If you **sweep** a floor or similar surface, you clean it by pushing the dirt off it with a broom or brush: *We had to sweep the kitchen floor after we made such a mess cooking the cake.* **2.** If you **sweep** things off something, you remove them with a quick, swinging movement: *She swept the books off her chair and onto the floor.* **3.** If a force **sweeps** something along, it pushes it along quickly: *The wind swept the rubbish down the street.* **4.** If something **sweeps** through a place, it

moves or spreads through it quickly: *The crowd swept into the stadium.*
–*noun* **5.** the act of sweeping: *Could you give the floor a sweep, please.* **6.** a swinging movement: *He dismissed them with a sweep of his arm.* **7.** a long, curved area of land or water: *From our window we could see the whole sweep of the bay.*
☐ **sweeper**, *noun* –**sweeping**, *adjective*: *sweeping changes.*

sweet *adjective*
1. having a pleasant taste like that of sugar or honey. **2.** being pleasant in any way: *It was sweet of her to help*; *The baby animals were so sweet.*
–*noun* **3.** a small piece of sweet food: *Each of the children was given a bag of sweets.* **4. sweets**, a dessert.
☐ **sweeten**, *verb* –**sweetly**, *adverb* –**sweetness**, *noun*

ANOTHER WORD (for definition 3) is **lolly**.

sweet corn *noun* the yellow kernels or seeds of the corn cob, which you can eat as a vegetable.

sweetheart *noun* someone loved by a person.

NOTE This is often used as a way of addressing someone.

sweet potato *noun* (*plural* **sweet potatoes**) a tropical plant with a tube-like root which can be eaten as a vegetable.

swell *verb* (**swells**, **swelling**, **swelled**, **has swollen** *or* **has swelled**)
1. If part of your body **swells** or **swells up**, it becomes larger, usually because of an injury or illness: *My finger swelled to twice its size when I hit it with a hammer.* **2.** If numbers or quantities **swell**, they increase: *The city's population has swelled to over a million.* **3.** If something **swells** or **swells up**, it fills with air or liquid and becomes larger and rounder.
–*noun* **4.** an increase in size, amount or force. **5.** the movement of the waves of the sea: *There is a big swell today.*
☐ **swelling**, *noun* –**swollen**, *adjective*

swelter *verb* If you **swelter**, you feel very hot: *Instead of sweltering here, why don't we go to the beach?*
☐ **sweltering**, *adjective*

swerve *verb* To **swerve** is to turn aside suddenly: *She swerved at the last minute and lost control of the car.*
☐ **swerve**, *noun*

swift *adjective* fast or quick: *Don't be too swift to criticise*; *She gave a swift response.*
☐ **swiftly**, *adjective* –**swiftness**, *noun*

swill *noun*
1. any liquid or partly liquid food for animals, especially pigs.
–*verb* **2.** If you **swill** a drink, you drink it down greedily.

swim *verb* (**swims**, **swimming**, **swam**, **has swum**)
1. To **swim** is to move through water by movements of the arms, legs, fins or tail. **2.** If you **swim** a stretch of water, you move across or along it by swimming: *He can swim the length of the pool in just over a minute.* **3.** If your head **swims**, you feel as if your head is spinning and you may lose consciousness.
☐ **swim**, *noun* –**swimmer**, *noun* –**swimming**, *noun*

swimsuit *noun* a piece of clothing to wear when you are swimming.

swindle *verb* To **swindle** someone is to cheat them out of money.
☐ **swindle**, *noun* –**swindler**, *noun*

swine *noun* (*plural* **swine**)
1. a pig. **2.** *Informal* someone you think is unpleasant or rude.

swing[1] *verb* (**swings**, **swinging**, **swung**, **has swung**)
1. If you **swing**, you move yourself or you make something move to and fro: *I was swinging too high and then I fell off*; *She was swinging her arms in time with the song.* **2.** If someone or something **swings**, it moves or makes something move in a curve: *The bus swung around the sharp bend*; *The cat swung open the cat door.*
–*noun* **3.** a swinging movement. **4.** a change, especially in the number of votes for a political party in an election: *They are predicting a swing to the government in that electorate.* **5.** a seat hung from above, on which you sit and swing to and fro for fun.

swing[2] *noun* a kind of jazz music, popular in the 1940s, usually played by big bands.

swipe *noun*
1. a blow with a sweep of the arm: *He took a swipe at his opponent.*
–*verb* **2.** *Informal* If you **swipe** something, you take or steal it quickly: *I think somebody has swiped my eraser.* **3.** If you **swipe** a card with a magnetic strip, such as a credit card, you move it quickly through the slot of a machine that is able to read such cards: *The sales assistant told me to swipe my card and then key in my PIN.*
–*phrase* **4. swipe at**, If you **swipe at** something, you hit it by swinging something like a stick or club: *He swiped at the ball with the bat.*

swirl *verb* To **swirl** is to move in a whirling way: *The skirts of the dancers swirled around in a brilliant blur of reds and purples.*
☐ **swirl**, *noun* –**swirly**, *adjective*

swish *verb* To **swish** is to make the sound that something makes when it moves quickly through the air: *Her long satin skirt swished as she moved through the room*; *The horse swished its tail at the flies.*
☐ **swish**, *noun*

switch *noun* (*plural* **switches**)
1. a button for turning an electric current on or off, directing an electric current, or making or breaking a circuit. **2.** a changing or turning: *a switch in their loyalties.* **3.** See **switchboard**.
–*verb* **4.** To **switch** things is to change them about: *They switched to another dentist*; *You'll have to switch directions – we're not getting any closer.*
–*phrase* **5. switch off**, to make an electrical appliance stop: *Switch off the television.* **6. switch on**, to make an electrical appliance start: *Could you switch on the light, please.*

switchboard *noun* a central telephone number where an operator connects calls to other numbers.

THE SHORT FORM of this is **switch**.

swivel /*say* **swiv**-uhl/ *verb* (**swivels**, **swivelling**, **swivelled**, **has swivelled**) To **swivel** is to turn about or swing around: *She swivelled in the chair to see what was going on.*

swoon *verb*
1. If you **swoon**, you become unconscious: *She swoons whenever she sees blood.*
–*phrase* **2. swoon over**, to have such a strong feeling for as to almost faint: *I swoon over him every time I see him!*

swoop *verb*
1. If something like a bird or aeroplane **swoops**, it suddenly moves downwards through the air: *The large bird swooped on its prey.* **2.** If someone **swoops** on a place, they make a sudden attack on it: *The police swooped in a dawn raid on the suspect's flat.*
☐ **swoop**, *noun*

sword /*say* sawd/ *noun* a weapon with a long pointed blade fixed in a handle.

☑ SPELLING TIP *Silent letter alert*: don't forget the silent *w* following the *s*.

swordfish *noun* (*plural* **swordfish** *or* **swordfishes**) a large sea fish with the upper jaw lengthened into a sword-like weapon.

syllable /*say* **sil**-uh-buhl/ *noun* a part of a word which must have a single vowel sound in it: *'Crocodile' has three syllables and 'alligator' has four.*

☑ SPELLING TIP *Letter 'y' alert*: this word begins with *sy* (not *si*). Also remember the double *l*.

syllabus /*say* **sil**-uh-buhs/ *noun* (*plural* **syllabuses** *or* **syllabi** /*say* **sil**-uh-buy/) a plan of what is to be taught in a course of lessons.

symbol *noun*
1. something that stands for or means something else: *A marriage ring is a symbol of love.* **2.** a letter, number or other mark used to stand for something: *The symbol for iron is Fe.*
☐ **symbolic**, *adjective* –**symbolise**, *verb*: *A crown symbolises royalty.* –**symbolism**, *noun*

ANOTHER SPELLING for **symbolise** is **symbolize**.
A SIMILAR WORD (for definition 1) is **emblem**.

symmetry /*say* **sim**-uh-tree/ *noun* the arrangement of the parts of something so that they are all balanced in size and shape: *We were amazed by the perfect symmetry of the butterfly's wings.*
☐ **symmetrical**, *adjective* –**symmetrically**, *adverb*

sympathise *verb* If you **sympathise** with someone, you **1.** share with them in a feeling of sorrow or trouble: *We all sympathised with Evan when his dog was run over.* **2.** understand and agree with them: *We sympathised with her wanting to hear the news as soon as possible.*
☐ **sympathiser**, *noun*

ANOTHER SPELLING is **sympathize**.
A SIMILAR WORD (for definition 1) is **commiserate**.

sympathy /*say* **sim**-puh-thee/ *noun*
1. a feeling shared with someone else, especially in sorrow or trouble: *They showed their sympathy by visiting and talking to her.* **2.** an agreement in ideas, likes or dislikes: *I am not in sympathy with any of their ridiculous ideas.*
☐ **sympathetic**, *adjective* –**sympathetically**, *adverb*

ANOTHER WORD (for definition 1) is **compassion**.

☑ SPELLING TIP *Letter 'y' alert*: the vowel in the first syllable is a *y* (not *i*). Like many words with a *y* spelling, **sympathy** comes from Greek. It is made up of the prefix *sym-* (a form of *syn-*, meaning 'association' or 'together') and *pathy* (from the Greek word for 'feeling').

symphony /*say* **sim**-fuh-nee/ *noun* (*plural* **symphonies**) a musical composition for a full orchestra, usually with four movements or parts.
☐ **symphonic**, *adjective*

☑ SPELLING TIP *Letter 'y' alert*: the vowel in the first syllable is a *y* (not *i*). Like many words with a *y* spelling, **symphony** comes from Greek. It is made up of the prefix *sym-* (a form of *syn-*, meaning 'association' or 'together') and *phony* (from the Greek word for 'sound'). Think of *phone* to remind yourself of the *ph* spelling.

symposium /*say* sim-**poh**-zee-uhm/ *noun* (*plural* **symposiums** *or* **symposia**) a meeting for discussion.

symptom /*say* **simp**-tuhm/ *noun*
1. something that shows that you have a disease or illness of some kind: *A high temperature is a symptom of the flu.* **2.** any sign that shows that something exists: *Her bad behaviour is a symptom of her problems at home.*
☐ **symptomatic**, *adjective*

synagogue /*say* **sin**-uh-gog/ *noun* a Jewish place of worship.

☑ SPELLING TIP *Silent letter alert*: don't forget the *ue* at the end which you do not hear when the word is pronounced. Also remember the *y* spelling in the first syllable in this word which comes from the Greek word for 'meeting' or 'assembly'.

synchronise /*say* **sing**-kruh-nuyz/ *verb* **1.** If you **synchronise** events, you make them happen at the same time: *We had to synchronise getting home with the beginning of our favourite TV show.* **2.** If you **synchronise** watches, you make them show the same time: *We had to synchronise our watches for the orienteering course.*

☐ **synchronisation**, *noun*

ANOTHER SPELLING is **synchronize**.

syncopate /*say* **sing**-kuh-payt/ *verb* To **syncopate** music is to change the rhythm of it by putting the beat in unexpected places.

☐ **syncopation**, *noun*

syndicate *noun* /*say* **sin**-duh-kuht/ **1.** a group of people or business companies who combine to carry out an expensive project: *The contract for the bridge has gone to a large syndicate.*

–*verb* /*say* **sin**-duh-kayt/ **2.** If a piece of writing, an image or a film is **syndicated**, it is published or provided for simultaneous publishing in a number of newspapers or magazines in different places.

☑ SPELLING TIP *Letter 'y' alert*: the vowel in the first syllable is a *y* (not *i*). Also remember the *ate* ending (which sounds like 'uht').

syndrome /*say* **sin**-drohm/ *noun* in medicine, a particular group of signs or a type of behaviour that shows that a disease or a condition exists: *Some syndromes are difficult to identify.*

synonym /*say* **sin**-uh-nim/ *noun* a word having the same or very similar meaning as another: *'Happy' and 'glad' are synonyms.*

☐ **synonymous** /*say* suh-**non**-uh-muhs/, *adjective*

THE OPPOSITE is **antonym**.
SEE the Grammar and Punctuation Guide appendix.

synopsis /*say* suh-**nop**-suhs/ *noun* (*plural* **synopses** /*say* suh-**nop**-seez/) a summary or outline, often a written summary of a longer piece of writing: *We have to give a synopsis of our presentation to the teacher.*

synoptic chart *noun* a chart or map showing the weather conditions over a large area at a particular time.

syntax *noun* the pattern for forming a sentence or a phrase in a particular language.

synthesis /*say* **sin**-thuh-suhs/ *noun* (*plural* **syntheses** /*say* **sin**-thuh-seez/) the mixing together of parts into a whole: *My dad said the synthesis of his beauty and my mother's brains made me what I am!*

☐ **synthesise**, *verb*

ANOTHER SPELLING for **synthesise** is **synthesize**.
COMPARE this with **analysis** (definition 2).

synthesiser *noun* a machine, usually a computer, which makes speech or music.

ANOTHER SPELLING is **synthesizer**.

synthetic /*say* sin-**thet**-ik/ *adjective* made from artificial substances, not natural ones: *Synthetic fibres don't let your body breathe.*

syphon /*say* **suy**-fuhn/ *noun* See **siphon**.

syringe /*say* suh-**rinj**/ *noun* **1.** a small tube that draws in and pushes out liquid, used to clean wounds or, when fitted to a needle, to inject liquid into or take it out of the body.

–*verb* **2.** When someone **syringes** an area, like your ear, they use a syringe to clean, wash or inject it.

☑ SPELLING TIP *Letter 'y' alert*: the first vowel sound is spelt with a *y*. **Syringe** comes from a Greek word meaning 'pipe' or 'channel'.

syrup *noun* a thick, sweet, sticky liquid: *strawberry syrup.*

☐ **syrupy**, *adjective*

☑ SPELLING TIP *Letter 'y' alert*: the vowel in the first syllable is a *y* (not *i*). Also remember that there is only one *r* and only one *p*. Rap it out as *sy + rup*.

system *noun* **1.** the way something is organised or arranged: *Our voting is based on a democratic system.* **2.** an organised way of doing something: *Once you've set up a system, things will be easier.* **3.** a set of connected parts: *the education system.*

☐ **systematic**, *adjective* –**systematically**, *adverb*

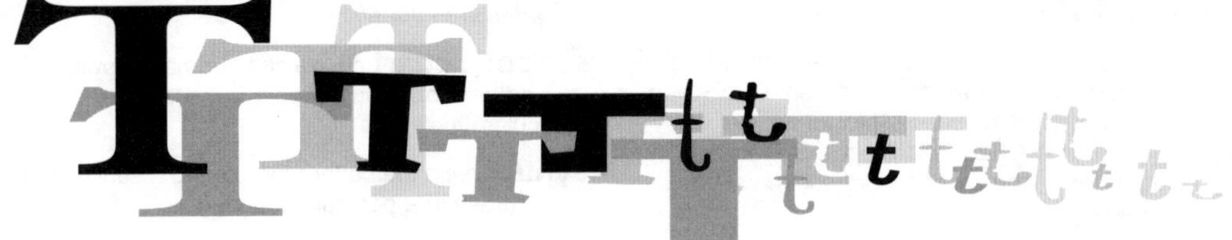

tab *noun* a small, flat, thin piece of some material attached to an item of clothing or something similar.

tabby *noun* (*plural* **tabbies**) a cat with a striped coat.
□ **tabby**, *adjective*

table *noun*
1. a piece of furniture which has a flat top resting on one or more legs. **2.** a plan or chart setting out items or numbers: *a table of contents*; *a multiplication table.*

tableau /*say* **tab**-loh/ *noun* (*plural* **tableaux** /*say* **tab**-lohz, **tab**-loh/ *or* **tableaus**) a group of people arranged to form a picture or scene: *It was a very formal tableau – the wife sitting prim on her seat in the foreground with her husband standing behind.*

☑ SPELLING TIP *Tricky vowel sound*: *eau* spelling for the 'oh' sound at the end. **Tableau** has this spelling because it comes from French (meaning 'table' or 'picture'). Another word like this is *bureau*.

tablespoon *noun* a large spoon used for measuring or serving, equal to about three teaspoons.

tablet *noun*
1. a small, flat, solid piece of medicine. **2.** a flat piece of some hard material that you can carve or write on: *The names of the winners were carved on a tablet of marble.* **3.** a small, flat, portable computer which has a virtual keyboard on the screen.
–*adjective* **4.** having to do with the format of a tablet (definition 3).

ANOTHER TERM (for definition 3) is **tablet computer**.

tablet computer *noun* See **tablet** (definition 3).

table tennis *noun* a game rather like tennis but played indoors on a table, using small bats and a very light, hollow, plastic ball.

ANOTHER TERM for this is **ping-pong**.

tabloid *noun* a newspaper with many pictures and short articles and with pages that are not too large to be easily held and read: *Many people read the tabloids in the train.*
□ **tabloid**, *adjective*: *a tabloid story.*

taboo /*say* tuh-**booh**/ *adjective* strictly forbidden because of custom or religion: *Swearing is taboo in front of my parents.*
□ **taboo**, *noun*: *a strict taboo on kicking and biting.*

tabouli /*say* tuh-**booh**-lee/ *noun* a salad of cracked wheat, chopped parsley, mint, tomato, oil and lemon juice, originating in Lebanese cooking.

OTHER SPELLINGS are **tabouleh** and **tabbouli**.

tack *noun*
1. a small nail, such as is used in making shoes or for putting up pictures. **2.** a zigzag movement or sharp turn, used when sailing into the wind.
–*verb* **3.** If a boat **tacks**, it sails diagonally first in one direction and then in the other in order to move forward against the wind. **4.** If you **tack** when you are sewing, you use large, loose stitches to hold pieces of cloth together before sewing them properly.
–*phrase* **5. tack on** (or **onto**), to join loosely or roughly to: *The last paragraph seems to have been tacked on without thought.*

tackle *noun*
1. equipment, especially for fishing or sailing. **2.** the ropes and blocks used for lifting, lowering or moving heavy weights.
–*verb* **3.** If you **tackle** a problem or piece of work, you deal with it: *It's time you tackled your homework.* **4.** In sports such as football and hockey, if you **tackle** your opponent, you try to get the ball from them.
□ **tackler**, *noun* –**tackling**, *noun*

tacky *adjective* (**tackier**, **tackiest**) slightly sticky: *Their fingers were tacky from eating toffee.*
□ **tackiness**, *noun*

taco /*say* **tah**-koh, **tak**-oh/ *noun* a flat piece of crisp corn bread folded around a spicy savoury filling, originating in Mexican cooking.

tact *noun* a sense of the right time to do or say something: *He had the tact to leave the room when he realised that they wanted to have a private talk.*
□ **tactful**, *adjective* –**tactless**, *adjective*

tactics /*say* **tak**-tiks/ *plural noun* a plan of action, especially for placing and moving soldiers and ships at war: *The general outwitted the opposing forces with superior tactics.*
□ **tactic**, *noun*: *an effective tactic.* –**tactical**, *adjective* –**tactician** /*say* tak-**tish**-uhn/, *noun*

tactile *adjective*
1. having to do with the sense of touch: *He has lost the tactile sensation in the injured part of his hand*; *We went on a tactile walk in the National Park to feel things like different leaves and seed pods.* **2.** inviting to the touch: *Velvet is a very tactile material.*
☐ **tactility**, *noun*

tadpole *noun* a young frog or toad in the earliest stage of its life during which it develops legs and becomes able to leave the water.

tag *noun*
1. a small piece of paper or material, fixed to something else, to give information about it: *The tag showed where the dress was made.* **2.** something, such as a binding of plastic, metal, and so on, at the end of a cord.
–*verb* (**tags**, **tagging**, **tagged**, **has tagged**) **3.** If you **tag** something, you fix a small sign to it: *to tag luggage.* **4.** To **tag** is to follow closely, especially without being invited: *My little brother tags along whenever we go outside to play.*

tai chi /*say* tuy **chee**/ *noun* a form of exercises based on Chinese martial arts.

WORD HISTORY from Chinese words meaning 'fist of the Great Absolute'

tail *noun*
1. the end of the backbone in some animals, especially when it forms a separate movable part of the body, as with cats, dogs, horses, and so on. **2.** the end or bottom of anything: *a shirt tail.* **3. tails**, **a.** a black formal suit for men with a long-tailed coat. **b.** the side of a coin opposite that with the picture of a head on it: *Heads or tails?* **4.** *Informal* a person who follows someone to watch where they go and what they do.
–*verb* **5.** *Informal* If you **tail** someone, you follow them to see where they go and what they do: *Police have been tailing the suspect all week.*

☑ SPELLING TIP Don't confuse the spelling of **tail** with **tale** which has the same sound. A **tale** is a story.

tailor *noun*
1. someone who makes or repairs clothes, especially for men.
–*verb* **2.** If you **tailor** something to suit someone, you change it to fulfil their exact needs, in the same way as a tailor makes clothes to fit each customer: *They tailored the show to appeal to a younger audience.*
☐ **tailor-made**, *adjective*

taint *verb* To **taint** is to spoil slightly: *The water is tainted*; *His reputation has been tainted.*
☐ **taint**, *noun*

taipan /*say* **tuy**-pan/ *noun* a venomous brown snake found in Australia and New Guinea.

WORD HISTORY from an Aboriginal language of Queensland called Wik-Mungkan

take *verb* (**takes**, **taking**, **took**, **has taken**)
1. If you **take** something, you hold it or grasp it in your hand: *He took the glass and lifted it to his lips*; *Could you take this parcel while I open the door?* **2.** If you **take** something, you accept it: *He refused to take any money for his trouble*; *I'm sorry, this seat is taken.* **3.** If you **take** something somewhere, you carry or transport it away from the place where you usually are: *Don't forget to take your keys with you.* **4.** If you **take** someone somewhere, you go with them and you are in charge in some way: *They took the children to the zoo.* **5.** If you **take** something from someone, you remove it without their permission: *Who's taken my pen?* **6.** If something **takes** a certain length of time, that is the amount of time that is needed for it: *The journey takes about two hours.* **7.** If a container **takes** a certain quantity of something, that is the amount that it is able to hold: *This hall can take up to 500 people.* **8.** If you **take** a means of transport, you use it to travel: *If you miss the bus you'll have to take a taxi.* **9.** If you **take** a road or route, you travel along it: *You can save time by taking a short cut.* **10.** If you **take** something in a particular manner, that is the attitude you have towards it: *She takes her work seriously.* **11.** In arithmetic, if you **take** one number from another, you subtract it: *What do you get when you take 5 from 13?* **12.** If you **take** medicine, you use it: *The doctor prescribed some tablets for me to take.* **13.** If you **take** a certain size in clothes or shoes, that is the size that fits you.
–*phrase* **14. take after**, to be or look like: *She takes after her aunt.* **15. take in**, **a.** to deceive or trick. **b.** to make smaller: *She had to take in the waist.* **16. take off**, **a.** to leave. **b.** to copy: *They take off his accent.* **17. take out**, **a.** to remove or extract: *to take out a tooth.* **b.** to treat to dinner, a film, and so on: *to take out a girl.*

takeaway *noun*
1. a meal that you buy already prepared in a shop. **2.** a shop where you buy those meals.
☐ **takeaway**, *adjective*: *a takeaway meal.*

ANOTHER WORD (for definition 1) is **takeout**.

take-off *noun* the moment when an aircraft leaves the ground and begins to fly.

takeover *noun* the gaining or taking of control, especially of another business or country.

talcum powder *noun* a fine, soft powder, used for putting on your body after a bath or shower.

tale *noun* a story about some real or imaginary event.

☑ SPELLING TIP Don't confuse the spelling of **tale** with **tail** which has the same sound. An animal's **tail** is the moving part at the end of its spine.

talent *noun* skill or ability: *His writing shows talent.*
☐ **talented**, *adjective*

talisman /*say* **tal**-uhz-muhn/ *noun* something considered to be lucky or magical: *The old grey cap was his talisman and he always took it when he travelled.*

talk *verb* To **talk** is to **1.** speak, or express in words: *I could hear them talking in the next room; It can help to talk about your problems with a friend.* **2.** give or reveal information: *The police tried to make them talk.* **3.** discuss: *They are talking sport.*
–*noun* **4.** an occasion for talking, such as a speech or conference. **5.** a conversation: *They had a long talk.* **6.** gossip or the person whom the gossip is about: *the talk of the town.*
–*phrase* **7. talk down to**, to speak to in a way that suggests that you are superior: *He talked down to the younger boys.* **8. talk into**, to persuade someone to do something they were not originally intending to do: *I have talked my friend into going swimming with me.*
☐ **talkative**, *adjective* –**talker**, *noun*

tall *adjective*
1. of more than average height: *a tall building*; *a tall woman.* **2.** having a particular height: *He is 1.9 metres tall.*

tally *noun* (*plural* **tallies**)
1. a record or account of an amount counted or owed: *We had to keep a tally of the tickets we had sold.*
–*verb* (**tallies**, **tallying**, **tallied**, **has tallied**) **2.** If you **tally** things, you add them together: *The judges tallied the final scores.* **3.** If two amounts or statements **tally**, they agree with each other: *His story doesn't tally with the facts.*

talon /*say* **tal**-uhn/ *noun* the claw, especially of a bird of prey, such as the eagle.

tambourine /*say* tam-buh-**reen**/ *noun* a small drum which has small, round pieces of metal set into a frame, and is played by hitting and shaking it.

> ☑ SPELLING TIP *Tricky 'uh' sound*: the middle vowel is spelt *ou*. Also remember the *ine* ending.

> WORD HISTORY from a French word meaning 'little drum'

tame *adjective*
1. If an animal or bird is **tame**, it is used to people and is not afraid of them: *The ducks in the park are so tame they'll eat out of your hand.* **2.** If something is **tame**, it isn't very exciting: *We stopped watching the thriller because it was too tame.*
–*verb* **3.** To **tame** an animal is to bring it under human control: *to tame a lion cub.*
☐ **tameness**, *noun* –**tamer**, *noun* –**tamely**, *adverb*

tamper *verb* If you **tamper** with something, you interfere so as to change or damage it in some way: *Someone's been tampering with the lock on the car door and it's broken.*

tampon *noun* a small cotton cylinder used to absorb the flow of blood from the vagina during menstruation.

tan *verb* (**tans**, **tanning**, **tanned**, **has tanned**)
1. When you **tan**, you become brown in the sun: *She tans her legs*; *His skin tans easily.* **2.** To **tan** an animal skin is to change it into leather by soaking and treating it: *to tan a hide.*
–*noun* **3.** a suntan. **4.** a yellowish-brown colour.
☐ **tan**, *adjective* –**tanner**, *noun*

tandem *adverb*
1. one behind another.
–*noun* **2.** a bicycle for two riders.
☐ **tandem**, *adjective*

tandoori /*say* tan-**dooh**-ree/ *adjective* having to do with food that is flavoured with spices and cooked in a very hot clay oven, originating in Indian cooking: *tandoori chicken.*

tang *noun* a strong, salty or sharp flavour or smell: *We could taste a lemony tang.*
☐ **tangy**, *adjective* (**tangier**, **tangiest**)

tangent /*say* **tan**-juhnt/ *noun*
1. a straight line which touches a curve. **2.** a sudden new direction: *The conversation went off at a tangent, so I didn't get around to asking how the house got its name.*
☐ **tangent**, *adjective*

tangerine /*say* tan-juh-**reen**/ *noun* a type of mandarin.

> WORD HISTORY named after the Moroccan seaport of *Tangier*

> ☑ SPELLING TIP *Tricky 'uh' sound*: the middle vowel is spelt *e*. Also remember the *ine* ending.

tangible /*say* **tan**-juh-buhl/ *adjective*
1. having a physical existence, so it can be touched and felt: *We enjoyed eating the tangible results of Dad's cooking classes.* **2.** real and certain, not imaginary: *Have you any tangible evidence for what you are saying?*

tangle *verb* To **tangle** something is to get it into a confused mess: *The cords to my computer are tangled.*
☐ **tangle**, *noun*

tango *noun* (*plural* **tangos**)
1. a dramatic dance of South American origin, danced by couples.
–*verb* (**tangoes**, **tangoing**, **tangoed**, **has tangoed**) **2.** To **tango** is to dance the tango.

tank *noun*
1. a container for liquid, such as petrol or water. **2.** a heavy fighting vehicle armed with cannons and machine guns.

tankard *noun* a beer mug, or other large cup, sometimes with a lid.

tanker *noun* a large vehicle or vessel for carrying oil or other liquids in large quantities.

tantalise *verb* If someone or something **tantalises** you, they cause you to think about something that you want but cannot have: *We were tantalised by the smell of hot chips but Mum said we didn't have time to stop and buy some.*
□ **tantalising**, *adjective*: *A tantalising smell came from the kitchen.*

ANOTHER SPELLING is **tantalize**.

tantrum *noun* a childish fit of temper or anger: *She throws a tantrum whenever she doesn't get her own way.*

Taoism /*say* **dow**-iz-uhm, **tow**-iz-uhm/ *noun* a Chinese philosophy which encourages people not to interfere with nature and to be sincere and honest.
□ **Taoist**, *noun* a follower of Taoism.

tap[1] *verb* (**taps**, **tapping**, **tapped**, **has tapped**) To **tap** is to hit lightly.
□ **tap**, *noun*

tap[2] *noun*
1. something used to control the flow of liquid: *The laundry tap is dripping.*
–*verb* (**taps**, **tapping**, **tapped**, **has tapped**) **2.** To **tap** something is to make use of some of it: *He was able to tap his reserves of energy.* **3.** If someone **taps** a telephone line, etc., they attach a special connection to it so that they can listen secretly to the calls: *She is afraid the spies have tapped her phone.*

tape *noun*
1. a long strip of cloth, paper or a similar material. **2.** a plastic strip coated with magnetic powder, used to record sound and pictures, and to store information from computers. **3.** a tape measure.
–*verb* **4.** If you **tape** something, you record it on tape: *I taped the CD she lent me.*

tape measure *noun* a long strip for measuring made of material, plastic or metal, marked with standard units such as millimetres and centimetres.

taper *verb*
1. If something **tapers**, it gradually narrows or becomes thin at one end: *Her jeans tapered in at the ankles*; *He tapered the stick to a point.*
–*noun* **2.** a very thin candle.
□ **tapering**, *adjective*

tape recorder *noun* a machine which records sounds on magnetic tape and can play them back.
□ **tape-record**, *verb* –**tape recording**, *noun*

tapestry *noun* (*plural* **tapestries**) a piece of cloth with a design which has been woven or embroidered, usually by hand.

tapeworm *noun* a flat or tape-like worm which lives in the intestine of people and animals.

taproot *noun* the big main root of a plant from which the other roots branch.

tar *noun*
1. a thick, black, sticky substance obtained from wood or coal, especially used for making roads.
–*verb* (**tars**, **tarring**, **tarred**, **has tarred**) **2.** To **tar** something, such as a road surface, is to cover it with tar.

tarantula /*say* tuh-**ran**-chuh-luh/ *noun*
1. a large, furry spider of mostly tropical areas. **2.** a venomous spider of Europe.

ANOTHER NAME (for definition 1) is **huntsman**.
WORD HISTORY named after the Italian seaport of *Taranto*, where the European spider is common

☑ SPELLING TIP Remember the second *t* in this word. With the *u* following, it has a 'ch' sound and you don't hear the *t*.

target *noun*
1. something which you aim at in order to hit or reach: *His dart hit the centre of the target*; *My target is to swim eight laps of the pool.* **2.** someone who is the focus of negative comment: *He is the target of much criticism.*
–*verb* (**targets**, **targeting**, **targeted**, **has targeted**) **3.** When you **target** something, you aim at that thing: *The special teaching program targets children who have difficulty learning to read.*

tariff *noun*
1. a charge for importing something into a country. **2.** the price charged for a room in a hotel.

☑ SPELLING TIP *Single/double letter alert*: only one *r*, but double *f* (which you could think of as standing for 'final fee' to remind you).

tarmac *noun*
1. a mixture of tar and small stones used to make the surface of roads. **2.** an airport runway.

WORD HISTORY formed by blending the words *tar* + *macadam* (a road surface of broken stones)

tarnish *verb*
1. If metal **tarnishes**, it loses shine and becomes stained: *The silver spoon had tarnished badly and needed polishing.* **2.** If something **tarnishes** someone's reputation, it makes them seem less honourable: *Suspicions that she had stolen the money tarnished her good name.*
□ **tarnish**, *noun* –**tarnished**, *adjective*

tarpaulin /*say* tah-**paw**-luhn/ *noun* a large canvas or other waterproof cover.

tarragon *noun* a strong-smelling herb used in cooking and salads.

☑ SPELLING TIP *Double letter alert*: double *r*. If you remember there are three words hiding in

tarragon – *tar*, *rag* and *on* – you will remember the double *r*.

tart[1] *adjective* sour or sharp: *Lemons have a tart taste*; *a tart reply.*
☐ **tartly**, *adverb* –**tartness**, *noun*

tart[2] *noun* a shallow pie with no top crust, filled with fruit or something sweet.

tartan *noun* the checked, woollen cloth in the colours of the different Scottish Highland clans, or any similar checked cloth.
☐ **tartan**, *adjective*

task *noun* a piece of work, or a duty.

Tasmanian devil *noun* a fierce, black-and-white, meat-eating marsupial, found in Tasmania.

tassel *noun* a bunch of silk, or other threads, to make something look pretty.

☑ SPELLING TIP *Double/single letter alert:* double *s*, but only one *l* at the end. Also remember that the ending is *el* (not *le*).

taste *noun*
1. the sense which experiences flavour. **2.** flavour: *Ice-cream has a sweet taste.* **3.** a liking or enjoyment: *Is this music to your taste?* **4.** a sense of what belongs or is attractive: *She has good taste in clothes.* **5.** a first experience: *She is looking forward to a taste of life at sea.*
–*verb* **6.** If you **taste** food or drink, you eat or drink a small amount of it in order to test its flavour: *Taste this and tell me if it needs salt.* **7.** If food or drink **tastes** of something, it has a certain flavour: *My meat tastes of garlic*; *This soup tastes horrible.*
☐ **tasteful**, *adjective* –**tasteless**, *adjective* –**taster**, *noun*

tasty *adjective* (**tastier**, **tastiest**) full of flavour: *Tomatoes grown in lots of sun are really tasty.*
☐ **tastiness**, *noun*

tatters *noun in the phrase* **in tatters**, very badly torn: *His shirt was in tatters.*

tattoo[1] *noun*
1. a signal on a trumpet or drum or any similar beating noise. **2.** an outdoor military display.

tattoo[2] *noun*
1. an ink picture permanently printed into someone's skin with needles.
–*verb* (**tattoos**, **tattooing**, **tattooed**, **has tattooed**) **2.** If someone **tattoos** your skin, they draw a design on it, prick small holes and fill them with dye.

taunt *verb* If someone **taunts** you, they tease you and say things they know will make you upset and angry.
☐ **taunt**, *noun* –**taunting**, *adjective*

taut /*say* tawt/ *adjective* stretched tight: *We pulled the rope taut.*
☐ **tautly**, *adverb* –**tautness**, *noun*

☑ SPELLING TIP Don't confuse the spelling of **taut** with **taught** which has the same sound. **Taught** is the past form of the verb **teach**: *She taught French at the local high school for many years.*

tavern *noun* a place where food and alcoholic drink can be bought.

tawdry *adjective* cheap and showy: *a shop full of tawdry junk.*

tawny *adjective* (**tawnier**, **tawniest**) yellowish-brown, like the colour of a lion's coat.

WORD HISTORY from a French word meaning 'tanned'

tax *noun*
1. money which people have to pay each year to the government, usually a part of the value of their income, property, goods bought, and so on.
–*verb* **2.** If a government **taxes** something, it charges a tax on it: *Luxury goods are usually heavily taxed.* **3.** If something **taxes** you, it takes away your energy: *The long, hot days taxed his strength.*
☐ **taxation**, *noun*: *the system of taxation.* –**taxing**, *adjective*: *a taxing job.* –**taxable**, *adjective*: *taxable income.*

taxi *noun* (*plural* **taxis**)
1. a car with a driver who will take you where you want to go for a sum of money which is worked out on the distance you travel.
–*verb* (**taxis**, **taxiing**, **taxied**, **has taxied**) **2.** If an aircraft **taxis** or is **taxied**, it moves along the runway before taking off, or after landing: *The pilot taxied the plane into its position for take-off.*

ANOTHER WORD (for definition 1) is **cab**. This is because **taxi** is a short form of **taxicab** which is another name still used but not so commonly as in the past.

☑ SPELLING TIP The spelling of this word is unusual but not difficult, if you remember the *x* and then the *i* at the end. It comes from *taxe*, the French word for 'charge'.

T-ball *noun* a type of softball for children in which the ball is not thrown to the batter, but is hit from a pole at waist height.

tea *noun*
1. a drink made by pouring boiling water onto the dried leaves of a shrub which is grown mainly in China, India and Sri Lanka. **2.** the dried leaves of this shrub. **3.** a late afternoon or evening meal: *The children had tea at six.*

WORD HISTORY from the Chinese word *ch'a*.

☑ SPELLING TIP Don't confuse the spelling of **tea** with **tee** which has the same sound but is spelt with a double *e*. A **tee** is a small support for the ball that you use in golf.

teach *verb* (**teaches**, **teaching**, **taught** /*say* tawt/, **has taught**) If you **teach** someone to do something, you show or tell them how to do it and help them until they are able to do it well: *My brother taught me to swim*; *She is teaching me how to use the computer.*
☐ **teacher**, *noun* –**teaching**, *noun*: *religious teachings.*

☑ SPELLING TIP Don't confuse the spelling of the past tense **taught** with **taut** which has the same sound. **Taut** describes something which is stretched tight.

teak *noun* a hard, long-lasting wood used for ship building and furniture.

team *noun*
1. a group of people who share an activity, such as sport or work: *A new player joined the team.* **2.** a number of animals strapped together to do work: *a team of horses.*
–*phrase* **3. team up with**, to work together with: *We teamed up with another class to raise money for the earthquake victims*.

☑ SPELLING TIP Don't confuse the spelling of **team** with **teem** which has the same sound but is spelt with a double *e*. To **teem** is to rain very hard, or to swarm with small animals.

tear[1] /*rhymes with* here/ *noun*
1. a drop of water that falls from the eyes, caused by sadness or pain.
–*phrase* **2. in tears**, crying: *We were in tears by the end of the sad film.*
☐ **tearful**, *adjective* –**tearfully**, *adverb*

☑ SPELLING TIP Don't confuse the spelling of **tear** with **tier** which has the same sound but is spelt with *ie*. A **tier** is one level in a series of levels.

tear[2] /*rhymes with* bear/ *verb* (**tears**, **tearing**, **tore**, **has torn**)
1. If something **tears** or if you **tear** it, it is pulled apart, or a piece is pulled off it: *She tore her skirt*; *Canvas doesn't tear easily.* **2.** If you **tear** something, you remove it or pull it away: *She tore the letter from his hands and stormed off*; *He couldn't tear himself from the TV.*
–*noun* **3.** a place where something has been pulled apart: *My shirt has a tear in it.*
–*phrase* **4. tear into**, to attack violently, either with the body or with words. **5. tear off**, to hurry away.

tease /*say* teez/ *verb*
1. If someone **teases** you, they make fun of you in a way which is not serious but can be embarrassing: *Blake's friends teased him for liking 1980s music.* **2.** To **tease** something is to separate it into threads: *to tease wool.*
☐ **tease**, *noun*: *He's a terrible tease.* –**teasing**, *adjective* –**teasingly**, *adverb*

teaspoon *noun* a small spoon which holds about five millilitres.

teat *noun*
1. the nipple of a female mammal. **2.** the rubber top on a baby's bottle which is shaped like a nipple.

tea-tree *noun* a shrub with small leaves and red, white or pink flowers, found in Australia and New Zealand.

ANOTHER SPELLING is **ti-tree**.

technical /*say* **tek**-nik-uhl/ *adjective*
1. having to do with practical science and machinery: *a technical education.* **2.** using words or covering topics that only an expert would understand: *technical language.*
☐ **technicality**, *noun* –**technically**, *adverb* –**technician**, *noun*

technique /*say* tek-**neek**/ *noun*
1. the way of doing or performing something: *Her swimming technique is influenced by her coach.* **2.** practical skill or knowledge: *His paintings show both talent and technique.*

☑ SPELLING TIP Remember that the end of **technique** is spelt *ique* (although it sounds like 'eek'). It might help if you think of other words which have the same spelling for this sound, such as *antique* and *boutique*. These are all spelt like this because they come from French. The beginning of **technique** can also be tricky. Remember the *ch* spelling for the 'k' sound (as in *technical* and other related words).

technology /*say* tek-**nol**-uh-jee/ *noun* (*plural* **technologies**)
1. the use of practical science in industry, and so on. **2.** the methods, practices, or equipment by which this is done: *a country with a developed technology.*
☐ **technological**, *adjective* –**technologically**, *adverb* –**technologist**, *noun*

tectonic *adjective* having to do with the structure and movement of the earth's crust.

☑ SPELLING TIP Notice that this word does not belong to the set of *technique*, *technology*, etc., where the 'k' sound is spelt by *ch*. In **tectonic** there is a *c* only for this sound. However, like the other words, **tectonic** comes from Greek (from the word for 'carpenter' or 'builder').

tedious /*say* **tee**-dee-uhs/ *adjective* long and boring: *a tedious afternoon*; *a tedious movie.*
☐ **tediously**, *adverb* –**tedium**, *noun*

tee *noun*
1. the starting place for each hole in golf. **2.** a plastic or wooden holder from which a player drives a golf ball.

–verb in the phrase (**tees**, **teeing**, **teed**, **has teed**) **3. tee off**, to hit the ball from a tee.

> ☑ SPELLING TIP Don't confuse the spelling of **tee** with **tea** which has the same sound but is spelt with *ea*. **Tea** is a drink made by pouring boiling water onto dry leaves.

teem[1] *verb in the phrase* **teem with**, to be full of something: *The park was teeming with people.*
☐ **teeming**, *adjective*

> ☑ SPELLING TIP Don't confuse the spelling of **teem** with **team** which has the same sound but is spelt with *ea*. A **team** is a group of people who share an activity, especially in sport.

teem[2] *verb* If it **teems**, it rains very hard.

> ☑ SPELLING TIP See **teem**[1].

teenager *noun* someone who is aged between 12 and 20.
☐ **teenage**, *adjective*

teepee */say* **tee**-pee/ *noun* a Native American tent made of skins.

> ANOTHER SPELLING is **tepee**.

teeter *verb* If someone or something **teeters**, they almost lose their balance.

teethe */say* teedh/ *verb* (**teethes**, **teething**, **teethed**, **has teethed**) To **teethe** is to grow teeth: *The baby has started to teethe.*

teetotal */say* **tee**-tohtl, tee-**tohtl**/ *adjective* If someone is **teetotal**, they do not drink alcohol at all or they are opposed to anyone drinking alcohol.
☐ **teetotalism**, *noun* –**teetotaller**, *noun*

telecast *noun* a television broadcast.

telecommunications *plural noun* the sending of messages by telephone, radio or satellite.

telegram *noun* a message sent by telegraph: *My grandfather was sent a telegram when he won the lottery years ago.*

telegraph *noun* a system or device for sending messages by electric signals along a wire.

telepathy */say* tuh-**lep**-uh-thee/ *noun* the sharing or passing on of information or thoughts between one person's mind and another without speaking, writing or using actions: *She often phones just as I'm about to call her – it must be telepathy.*
☐ **telepathic** */say* tel-uh-**path**-ik/, *adjective* –**telepathically**, *adverb*

telephone */say* **tel**-uh-fohn/ *noun*
1. a means of speaking to someone else over a long distance, usually powered by electricity: *I spoke to him by telephone last week.* **2.** the instrument used to do this: *Please answer the telephone.*
–verb **3.** When you **telephone** someone, you speak to or call them by telephone: *I telephoned her last night.*
☐ **telephonic** */say* tel-uh-**fon**-ik/, *adjective* –**telephonically**, *adverb* –**telephonist** */say* tuh-**lef**-uh-nuhst/, *noun*

> THE SHORT FORM of this is **phone**.

telescope *noun*
1. a tube-shaped instrument with powerful lenses which make distant objects seem closer.
–verb **2.** If something **telescopes**, its parts fold away into each other, similar to the way the sliding tubes of a jointed telescope fit together: *The first and second carriages telescoped with the impact of the train crash.*
☐ **telescopic**, *adjective*

television *noun*
1. the sending of pictures by radio waves which are picked up by the receiving sets of viewers. **2.** a television set or receiver.
☐ **televise**, *verb*: *The interview with the prime minister will be televised live.*

> THE ABBREVIATION is **TV**.
> ANOTHER SPELLING for **televise** is **televize**.

tell *verb* (**tells**, **telling**, **told**, **has told**)
1. If you **tell** someone something, you give them some information: *She told me that she was getting married soon*; *Can you tell me how much it will cost to repair this watch?* **2.** If you **tell** a lie, story or joke, you say it: *He's good at telling stories to children.* **3.** If you **tell** someone to do something, you order them to do it: *She told us not to run in the corridor.* **4.** If you can **tell** that something has happened, you can still see the signs of it: *I've corrected the mistake and you can't tell where it was.*
–phrase **5. tell off**, *Informal* to scold. **6. tell on**, to inform on.

teller *noun* someone who works behind a counter in a bank receiving and paying out the customers' money.

telltale *adjective*
1. revealing, especially what is not meant to be known: *There were some telltale signs that Mum had been reading the paper – coffee stains were all over it.*
–noun **2.** *Informal* someone who tells people about something bad that someone else has done.

temper *noun*
1. the particular state of mind or mood someone is in: *Despite the problems, she remained in a surprisingly good temper.* **2.** an angry or resentful mood: *a fit of temper*; *He can get into a temper very easily.*
–verb To **temper** is to **3.** strengthen by changes of temperature: *You have to temper steel correctly to make a good knife.* **4.** make less severe:

Her criticism was tempered with helpful suggestions.

temperament *noun* a type of personality particular to a person or the way they naturally are: *She has a good, even temperament.*
☐ **temperamental**, *adjective* moody: *She is always so temperamental you have to be careful what you say.* –**temperamentally**, *adverb*

temperance *noun*
1. moderation and self-control, especially in drinking alcohol. **2.** the complete avoidance of alcohol: *an early movement advocating temperance.*

temperate /*say* **tem**-puh-ruht/ *adjective* moderate and steady: *Please be more temperate in your use of language.*
☐ **temperately**, *adverb* –**temperateness**, *noun*

temperature /*say* **tem**-pruh-chuh/ *noun*
1. a measure of the degree of heat or cold of something or someone. **2.** an abnormally high amount of heat in the body: *If you have a temperature, you are probably ill.*

tempest *noun* a violent storm or a violent disturbance: *A huge tempest blew up in the night*; *He was overcome by a tempest of emotions.*

NOTE This word is used in literature rather than ordinary language.
WORD HISTORY from a Latin word meaning 'season'

tempestuous /*say* tem-**pes**-chooh-uhs/ *adjective* full of very strong feelings: *They have a tempestuous relationship but have stayed married.*
☐ **tempestuously**, *adverb*

temple[1] *noun* a large building where people worship.

temple[2] *noun* the flat part on either side of the forehead.

tempo *noun* speed, rhythm or pattern: *music with a fast tempo*; *the tempo of modern life.*

temporary /*say* **temp**-ree/ *adjective* lasting for a short time only: *a temporary solution.*
☐ **temporarily**, *adverb*

THE OPPOSITE is **permanent**.

☑ SPELLING TIP You need to remember that this word has four syllables, although you hear only two when you say it. Concentrate on the *orary* ending and rap it out as *tem+por+a+ry*.

tempt *verb* If someone or something **tempts** you, they encourage you to do something which possibly you really should not do, by making it seem very attractive: *These advertisements tempt people to spend more than they can afford*; *Can I tempt you to another helping?*
☐ **temptation**, *noun*: *He resisted the temptation to steal.* –**tempter**, *noun* –**tempting**, *adjective* –**temptingly**, *adverb*

NOTE A woman who tempts someone can be called a **temptress**.

tempura /*say* tem-**pooh**-ruh/ *noun* a food made from seafood or vegetables coated in a light batter and deep-fried in oil, originating in Japanese cooking.

ten *noun*
1. a cardinal number, nine plus one (9+1). **2.** the symbol for this number, as 10 or X.
☐ **ten**, *adjective* –**tenth**, *adjective*, *noun*

tenacious /*say* tuh-**nay**-shuhs/ *adjective*
1. If something is **tenacious**, it holds on firmly: *a tenacious tentacle.* **2.** If someone is **tenacious**, they stubbornly keep trying to do something: *She won the race because she was too tenacious to give up.*
☐ **tenaciously**, *adverb* –**tenacity** /*say* tuh-**nas**-uh-tee/, *noun*

tenant *noun* someone who pays rent for the use of a house, land or a flat.
☐ **tenancy**, *noun*

tend[1] *verb* If something **tends** to happen, it is likely to happen: *It tends to be cold at night*; *I tend to be cross when I'm tired.*
☐ **tendency**, *noun* (*plural* **tendencies**): *She has a tendency to get stomach aches.*

tend[2] *verb* If you **tend** someone or something, you watch or look after them: *The nurse is tending him*; *to tend a fire.*

tender[1] *adjective*
1. not tough or hard: *It was just a tender young shoot and didn't stand up to the heat.* **2.** warm and affectionate: *He regarded her with tender feelings.* **3.** gentle or delicate: *She gave them a tender hug.* **4.** painful to feel or discuss: *tender to the touch*; *Don't speak about his death – it's still too tender a subject.*
☐ **tenderly**, *adverb* –**tenderness**, *noun*

tender[2] *verb*
1. If you **tender** something, you offer it: *He tendered his hand and they shook on the deal.*
–*noun* **2.** an offer of a price to do a particular job: *The tenders for building the new bridge have to be in by Friday.*

tendon *noun* a cord of strong body substance joining a muscle to a bone.

ANOTHER WORD for this is **sinew**.

tendril *noun* a twisted, thread-like part, as of a climbing plant.

☑ SPELLING TIP *Single letter alert*: only one *l* at the end.

tenement /*say* **ten**-uh-muhnt/ *noun* a building divided into flats, especially one in the poorer, crowded parts of a large city.

tennis *noun* a game in which two players, or two pairs of players, use racquets to hit a ball over a central net.

tenor /*say* **ten**-uh/ *noun*
1. a man with a singing voice in the higher range. 2. the course of thought or meaning running through something spoken or written: *I didn't hear all the speech but I caught the tenor of it.*
☐ **tenor**, *adjective*: *a tenor voice.*

NOTE The range of a **tenor** is above that of a **baritone** or a **bass**, but below that of an **alto** or a **soprano**.
A SIMILAR WORD (for definition 2) is **drift**.

tenpin bowling *noun* a sport, played inside, in which a ball is bowled down a wooden alley at an arrangement of pins, the intention being to knock down as many as possible.

tense[1] *adjective*
1. If something is **tense**, it is stiff or stretched tight: *tense muscles.* 2. If someone is **tense**, they find it hard to relax: *He was too tense to sleep the night before the exam.*
–*verb* 3. If something **tenses**, it becomes tense: *The cat's muscles tensed*; *He tensed his body as he prepared to lift the weight.*
☐ **tensely**, *adverb* –**tension**, **tenseness**, *noun*

tense[2] *noun* the form of a verb which shows the time of an action.

SEE **present tense**, **past tense**, **future tense**. See also the Grammar and Punctuation Guide appendix.

tent *noun* a movable shelter made of canvas or nylon, held up by poles and ropes, or other support, used when camping, etc.

tentacle *noun* a thin, flexible, arm-like part on an animal such as an octopus, used for feeling and grasping.

tentative *adjective* unsure or cautious: *The puppy tried a few tentative steps into the waves.*
☐ **tentatively**, *adverb*

tenuous *adjective* weak or vague: *We have a tenuous connection in that our grandparents were related, but really we hardly know each other.*
☐ **tenuously**, *adverb*

tepid /*say* **tep**-uhd/ *adjective* lukewarm or slightly warm.
☐ **tepidly**, *adverb*

teppanyaki /*say* tep-uhn-**yah**-kee/ *noun* a food made from pieces of meat or fish roasted in oil on a hot plate, thus flavouring the oil in which vegetables are then cooked.

ANOTHER FORM is **teppan yaki**.

teriyaki /*say* te-ree-**ah**-kee/ *noun* a food made from meat, chicken or seafood, soaked in a mixture containing soy sauce and grilled, originating in Japanese cooking.

term *noun*
1. a division of the year in schools and colleges. 2. a period of time: *in the short term.* 3. a descriptive or naming word or group of words: *Her speech was full of technical terms.* 4. **terms**, conditions of agreement.
☐ **terminology**, *noun* special words or phrases belonging to a particular subject: *computer terminology.*

terminal *adjective*
1. If an illness is **terminal**, it cannot be cured and in the end causes the death of the patient: *The doctor says his condition is terminal.*
–*noun* 2. the end of a railway line or other travel route where passengers and goods arrive and leave: *an air terminal.* 3. a point where current enters or leaves in an electrical circuit. 4. See **computer terminal**.
☐ **terminally**, *adverb*: *terminally ill.*

terminate *verb*
1. To **terminate** something is to bring it to an end: *They terminated the show because it was losing money.* 2. If something **terminates**, it comes to an end or stops: *This flight terminates in Melbourne.*
☐ **termination**, *noun*

terminus /*say* **ter**-muhn-uhs/ *noun* (*plural* **terminuses** *or* **termini** /*say* **ter**-muh-nuy/) a station at the end of a railway line or bus route.

termite *noun* a pale-coloured insect which can destroy wooden buildings and furniture.

ANOTHER TERM for this is **white ant**, though it is not really an ant.

terrace *noun*
1. a narrow, flattened area on the side of a hill: *a rice terrace.* 2. a row of houses joined together, each one sharing a common wall. 3. **terrace house**, one of these houses: *We live in the end terrace house.*
☐ **terraced**, *adjective*

☑ SPELLING TIP *Double/single letter alert*: double *r*. Also remember the *ace* ending.

terracotta *noun*
1. a clay used for pipes, roof tiles and other similar things. 2. a brownish-red colour.
☐ **terracotta**, *adjective*

WORD HISTORY from an Italian word meaning 'baked earth'

terrain *noun* a part of the land surface, with its natural features in mind: *rough terrain.*

WORD HISTORY from a French word meaning 'earth'

terrestrial *adjective* living or growing on land, rather than the sea or sky: *Most mammals are terrestrial.*

terrible *adjective*
1. If something is **terrible**, it causes people to feel shock or great fear: *The story was about a terrible monster.* **2.** If you say something is **terrible**, you mean that it is very bad: *The traffic was terrible this morning.*
□ **terribly**, *adverb*

terrier *noun* a kind of small dog, originally used for hunting.

terrific *adjective Informal* **1.** very great: *It exploded with a terrific noise.* **2.** very good: *terrific fun.*
□ **terrifically**, *adverb*

terrify *verb* (**terrifies**, **terrifying**, **terrified**, **has terrified**) If something **terrifies** you, it frightens you very much: *Snakes terrify me.*
□ **terrified**, *adjective*: *a terrified look on her face.*
–**terrifying**, *adjective*: *a terrifying experience.*

> ☑ SPELLING TIP *Double letter alert*: double *r*. Also remember that the following letter is an *i*. If you realise you will *err if* you forget this, you should get **terrify** correct.

territory *noun* (*plural* **territories**)
1. any area of land, especially a region thought of as belonging to someone: *enemy territory.* **2.** the land and waters under the control of a particular government, ruler, and so on: *Australia has several overseas territories.*
□ **territorial**, *adjective*

> ☑ SPELLING TIP *Double letter alert*: double *r* (as in the Latin word *terra*, meaning 'land', on which this word is based). Also remember the *ory* ending.

terror *noun* a very strong fear.

terrorise *verb* If someone **terrorises** you, they keep you in fear, often with threats of violence: *Vandals were roaming the streets and terrorising the neighbourhood.*

> ANOTHER SPELLING is **terrorize**.

terrorist *noun* someone who commits violent actions, such as killing or threatening people, for political reasons, usually to try to make the government of a country do what he or she wants: *The prime minister described the bomb attack as the work of terrorists.*
□ **terrorism**, *noun*

terry towelling *noun* a cotton cloth with loops on both sides, used to make towels, dressing gowns, etc.

terse *adjective* A **terse** way of speaking is short and almost rude: *His terse answer made me think he was angry.*
□ **tersely**, *adverb* **terseness**, *noun*

tertiary /*say* **ter**-shuh-ree/ *adjective*
1. If something is **tertiary**, it is third in order or importance. **2. Tertiary** education is the third stage of schooling at a college or university, following secondary education.

test *noun*
1. a trial to decide something: *a test of strength.* **2.** a set of questions to answer, designed to show how much you know about something: *a history test.*
–*verb* **3.** To **test** something is to try to find if it is true or not, or if it exists or not, or how good it is: *I'll test the water to see if it's hot enough*; *These questions are to test the class's knowledge.*
□ **tester**, *noun*

testament *noun* a will.
□ **testamentary**, *adjective*

> NOTE This word is now mainly used in the phrase *last will and testament.*

testicle /*say* **tes**-tik-uhl/ *noun* one of the two round male sex glands in the scrotum.

> ANOTHER WORD for this is **testis**. This is a more formal, medical word.

testify *verb* (**testifies**, **testifying**, **testified**, **has testified**)
1. If you **testify** in a law court, you say what you know and swear that it is true: *She testified that she had seen the crime.* **2.** If something **testifies** to something else, it gives evidence that it is true: *Her red eyes testified to the fact that she had been crying.*

testimonial *noun*
1. a statement about someone or something giving an account of their good qualities. **2.** something given or done for someone as an expression of admiration or gratitude.
□ **testimonial**, *adjective*: *a testimonial dinner.*

testimony /*say* **tes**-tuh-muh-nee/ *noun* (*plural* **testimonies**)
1. a statement of what you know to be true, given in a law court: *He was called as a witness to give testimony about what he had seen.* **2.** evidence: *His good results are testimony to the hard work he has put in.*

test match *noun* one of a series of international sporting events, usually cricket or Rugby football.

tetanus /*say* **tet**-nuhs/ *noun* an infectious, often deadly disease, which causes extreme stiffness of the muscles of the jaw and other parts of the body.

> NOTE An old-fashioned word for this is **lockjaw**.
> WORD HISTORY from a Greek word meaning 'spasm' (of muscles)

> ☑ SPELLING TIP Remember the *a* in the middle of **tetanus**, which you don't hear when the word

is said. Also notice the *us* ending. Rap it out as *tet+a+nus*.

tether *noun*
1. a rope or chain for tying up an animal.
–verb **2.** If you **tether** an animal, you tie it up: *The white goats were tethered on the soft green grass.*
–phrase **3. at the end of your tether**, at the limit of your patience or resources: *I can't cope with his tantrums any more – I'm at the end of my tether.*

text *noun*
1. written words, as in a book, document, on a computer, and so on. **2.** a written, spoken or visual work, especially when regarded as being of a distinctive type because of special features of its subject matter, form or language. **3.** the main body of words in a book, not including the notes, index and other extra material. **4.** See **textbook**.
–verb **5.** To **text** someone is send them a text message.
□ **textual**, *adjective*

texta *noun* a thick pen, usually in a bright colour.

ANOTHER NAME for this is a **felt pen**.
WORD HISTORY trademark

textbook *noun* a book setting out the information for a course of study in a subject.

THE SHORT FORM of this is **text**.

textile *noun* any woven material used for clothing, curtains and so on.

text message *noun*
1. an SMS message sent to someone's mobile phone.
–verb **2.** To **text message** someone is to send them an SMS message.

THE SHORT FORM of this is **text**.

texture *noun* the roughness or smoothness of a material: *Silk has a smooth texture, while canvas is rough in texture.*

than *conjunction*
1. a word used after adjectives, adverbs, and certain other comparative words, such as *other*, *otherwise*, *else*, and so on, to introduce the second part of the comparison: *He is taller than I am.*
–preposition **2.** in comparison with: *He is taller than me.*

thank *verb*
1. If you **thank** someone, you tell them that you are grateful to them: *We thanked them for their kindness.*
–interjection **2. thanks** or **thank you**, words you use to say that you are grateful for something.
□ **thankful**, *adjective*: *We are thankful for your help.* –**thankless**, *adjective*: *a thankless task.*

that *pronoun* (*plural* **those**)
1. You use **that a.** to show a person, thing, or idea, and so on, which has been pointed out, mentioned, or suggested to you: *That is my brother.* **b.** to show one of two or more people, things, and so on, already mentioned, referring to the one that is further away: *That is riper than this.* **2.** as the subject or object of a clause giving extra information about someone or something already mentioned: *How old is the car that was stolen?*
–adjective **3. That** is used to show **a.** a person, thing, or idea: *That man is my grandfather.* **b.** the one of two or more people, things, and so on, that is further away: *It was that book I wanted, not this one.*
–adverb **4.** You use **that** with other adverbs and adjectives to show the exact degree and so on: *that much*; *that far.*
–conjunction **5. That** introduces a clause which stands for a noun: *That he will come is certain.*
–phrase **6. that is**, more exactly and precisely: *I see him often, that is, once a week.* **7. that's that**, that is the end of the matter: *I've lost it, so that's that.*

thatch *noun* material such as dried straw, grass or leaves used to cover a roof.
□ **thatched**, *adjective*: *a thatched hut.* –**thatching**, *noun*

thaw *verb* To **thaw** is to melt: *The sun is thawing the snow*; *The ice is beginning to thaw.*
□ **thaw**, *noun*

the *definite article* You use the definite article before nouns: **1.** when a particular thing or person is being referred to, made clear by the surrounding words or situation (opposed to *a* or *an*): *The book I've just finished reading was terrific*; *Pass me the milk please.* **2.** to mark a noun as being used to identify a class, type, etc.: *Our job is to help the poor*; *The dog is a quadruped.*

theatre /*say* **thear**-tuh/ *noun*
1. a building or hall for presenting plays or other shows. **2.** the activity of presenting, performing or writing plays: *She has always loved the theatre*; *He would like a career in theatre, possibly as a stage designer.* **3.** a cinema. **4.** a room in a hospital where operations are performed.

theatrical /*say* thee-**at**-rik-uhl/ *adjective*
1. in or belonging to a theatre: *My uncle loves the stage and works in theatrical production.* **2.** aiming to create an effect: *Her speech, manners and gestures are all quite theatrical.*
□ **theatrically**, *adverb*

theft *noun* the act or crime of stealing.

NOTE This comes from the word **thief**.

their *pronoun* a form of **they** that shows something belongs to them: *The crabs have gone back into their shells.*

☐ **theirs**, *pronoun*: *Don't take those cakes – they are theirs.*

☑ SPELLING TIP Don't confuse the spelling of **their** with **there** or **they're**, both of which sound the same. **There** means 'in that place': *Look at the kangaroos over there*. **They're** is a short form of *they are*.

them *pronoun* the form of **they** you use after a verb: *Give them back.*

theme *noun* the subject of a speech, book, or piece of music.

then *adverb*
1. at the time: *I was younger then.* **2.** immediately or soon afterwards: *He stopped, and then began again.* **3.** next in order of time, or of place: *He unlocked the door, then walked inside*; *Down the road there's a shop, then a park.* **4.** at another time: *I'm coming back tomorrow – I'll do it then.* **5.** in that case: *If it gets hot, then I'll wear a hat.*

theology *noun* (*plural* **theologies**)
1. the study of religion. **2.** a collection of beliefs held by a particular religion: *Christian theology.*
☐ **theologian**, *noun* –**theological**, *adjective*

theorem /*say* **thear**-ruhm/ *noun* a statement containing something to be proved in mathematics.

☑ SPELLING TIP *Tricky vowel sound*: *eo* spelling for the 'ear' sound, as in the related word *theory.*

theory /*say* **thear**-ree/ *noun* (*plural* **theories**)
1. an explanation based on reason and what you notice around you: *a theory of the universe.* **2.** a suggested explanation with little or no basis in fact: *I think I know why she's been so upset, but it's only a theory.* **3.** the part of a subject which deals with principles or ideas rather than practice: *As well as learning to play the piano, I have lessons in music theory.*
☐ **theoretical**, *adjective* –**theorise**, *verb*: *to theorise about the origins of the universe.*

ANOTHER SPELLING for **theorise** is **theorize**.

☑ SPELLING TIP *Tricky vowel sound*: *eo* spelling for the 'ear' sound. This comes from the Greek word *theoria*, meaning 'thinking' or 'idea'.

therapy /*say* **the**-ruh-pee/ *noun* healing treatment for a physical or mental problem: *speech therapy*; *psychological therapy.*
☐ **therapeutic** /*say* the-ruh-**pyooh**-tik/, *adjective* –**therapist**, *noun*

there *adverb*
1. in or at that place: *The book is there, on the top shelf.* **2.** at that particular point: *I've weeded up to there, so you can do the rest.* **3.** into or to that place: *Go in there.*
–*pronoun* **4.** that place: *He comes from there too.* **5.** used to begin a sentence or clause in which the verb comes before its subject: *There is no hope.*
–*interjection* **6.** an exclamation used to show satisfaction, and so on: *There! It's done!*

☑ SPELLING TIP Don't confuse the spelling of **there** with **their** or **they're**, both of which have the same sound. **Their** is a form of *they* that shows something belongs to them: *The boys are with their mother.* **They're** is a short form of *they are*.

therefore /*say* **dhair**-faw, dhair-**faw**/ *adverb* as a result: *That car uses less petrol and is therefore cheaper to run.*

☑ SPELLING TIP The trick with this word is to split it into its two parts and make sure you get the spelling of both right. The first part is the word *there*, meaning 'that place' (don't confuse it with *their*). The second part is *fore* (don't confuse it with the number *four*). In fact, *fore* in this word does not have the meaning 'to the front' but is a form of the word *for*. So the basic meaning of **therefore** is 'for there' in the sense of 'for that reason'.

thermal *adjective* having to do with heat: *thermal energy.*

thermometer /*say* thuh-**mom**-uh-tuh/ *noun* an instrument for measuring temperature.

☑ SPELLING TIP Although you say this word with the emphasis on the *mom* in the middle, the spelling will be easier if you see that it is made up of *thermo-* (a prefix meaning 'heat' or 'temperature') and *meter* (a measuring instrument).

thermos *noun* a special container used to keep liquid food or drink at a constant temperature.

ANOTHER TERM for this is **thermos flask**.
WORD HISTORY from a trademark, based on a Greek word meaning 'hot'

thermostat *noun* a device for keeping a temperature steady: *The thermostat was broken and the oven overheated.*

thesaurus /*say* thuh-**saw**-ruhs/ *noun* (*plural* **thesauruses** *or* **thesauri** /*say* thuh-**saw**-ruy/) a book of words arranged in groups which have a similar meaning.

☑ SPELLING TIP Remember the spelling of the ending: *saurus*. With this ending, you might think that **thesaurus** was the word for a kind of dinosaur, rather than a book of words. In fact, it comes from the Greek word for 'treasury' or 'storehouse'.

these *pronoun*, *adjective* See **this**.

thesis /*say* **thee**-suhs/ *noun* (*plural* **theses** /*say* **thee**-seez/)
1. an idea, argument or explanation, especially one to be discussed and proved. **2.** a book-length essay presented by a student for a higher university degree.

☑ SPELLING TIP *Tricky vowel sound*: a single *e* to spell the 'ee' sound.

they *pronoun* the plural of **he, she** and **it** that comes before a verb: *They stole away during the night.*

SEE ALSO **them**, **their** and **theirs**.

they'd a short form of *they had* or *they would*.

they'll a short form of *they will*.

they're a short form of *they are*.

☑ SPELLING TIP Don't confuse the spelling of **they're** with **their** or **there**, both of which have the same sound. **Their** is a form of *they* that shows something belongs to them: *The boys are riding their bikes*. **There** means 'in that place': *Look at the kangaroos over there!* To test which word you have, say it in full as *they are* and see if it makes sense. If it does, then **they're** is correct.

they've a short form of *they have*.

thick *adjective*
1. having a larger than normal distance from top to bottom or from one side to the other: *The letter was too thick to go under the door.* **2.** dense or packed closely together: *a thick forest*; *a thick fog.* **3.** not flowing or pouring easily: *This soup is too thick for my liking.* **4.** measuring as stated between two opposite surfaces: *The ice on the lake was ten centimetres thick.*
☐ **thickly**, *adverb* –**thicken**, *verb* –**thickness**, *noun*

THE OPPOSITE (of definitions 1–3) is **thin**.
A SIMILAR WORD (for definition 2) is **dense**.

thicket *noun* a thick growth of shrubs or small trees.

thief *noun* (*plural* **thieves**) someone who steals.

SIMILAR WORDS are **robber** and **burglar**. A **burglar** is someone who steals by breaking into a house or other building.

thieve /*say* theev/ *verb* If someone **thieves**, they steal.

thigh *noun*
1. in humans, the part of the leg above the knee. **2.** the upper part of the leg of a bird, such as a chicken, eaten as food.

thimble *noun* a protective cover for the top of the finger, usually metal, and worn to stop the needle pricking your finger when you are sewing.

thin *adjective*
1. having a smaller than normal distance from one side to the other: *You must be cold in that thin dress.* **2.** having parts that are packed loosely together: *We flew through some thin cloud.* **3.** flowing or pouring easily: *a thin soup*; *The paint was too thin and dripped everywhere.* **4.** not having much flesh on their body: *We found a thin, starving cat.* **5.** not convincing: *The evidence was very thin.*
–*verb* (**thins**, **thinning**, **thinned**, **has thinned**) **6.** If you **thin** something, or something **thins**, it becomes less crowded: *I thinned the seedlings so the strongest had room to grow*; *The crowd began to thin.* **7.** If you **thin** a liquid, you make it more runny or watery: *to thin paint.*
☐ **thinly**, *adverb* –**thinness**, *noun*

THE OPPOSITE (of definitions 1–3) is **thick**; the opposite (of definition 4) is **fat**.
SIMILAR WORDS (for definition 4) are **slim**, **slender**, **skinny**, **lean** and **slight**. **Slim** and **slender** are usually used to describe someone who is pleasantly thin, while **skinny** is used to describe someone who is too thin. Someone with a **lean** build is thin in a fit, strong way. A **slight** person is thin and small.

thing *noun*
1. a real object that is not alive. **2.** some object which is not or cannot be easily described: *What's that funny thing on your desk?* **3.** a matter or affair: *Things are going well for them.*

think *verb* (**thinks**, **thinking**, **thought**, **has thought**)
1. When you **think**, you form an idea in your mind: *I often think about my friends*; *I tried to think what to do next*; *Think carefully before you make a decision.* **2.** If you **think** that something is the case, that is your opinion but you are not completely certain or you do not have proof: *I think I'm getting a cold*; *When do you think it will be ready?* **3.** If you **think** of something, you remember it: *I often think of those happy times we spent together.* **4.** If you are **thinking** of doing something, you are considering doing it: *We're thinking of going to see a movie tonight.* **5.** If you **think** of someone or something, you take account of them: *He never thinks of anyone but himself.*
–*phrase* **6. think better of**, to decide against something that you had originally intended. **7. think little of**, to have a low opinion of. **8. think nothing of**, to not be worried or hesitant about: *'I'm sorry to have taken up so much of your time.' 'Think nothing of it.'*
☐ **thinker**, *noun*

third *adjective*
1. next in order after the second: *He was third in the queue after my friend and me*; *The third letter of the alphabet is 'C'.*
–*noun* **2.** one of the three equal parts of something: *Twenty minutes is a third of an hour.*

thirst *noun*
1. an uncomfortable feeling of dryness in the mouth and throat caused by the need for a drink. **2.** an eager desire: *a thirst for travel.*
–*verb* **3.** If you **thirst** for something, you want it very much: *to thirst for knowledge.*
☐ **thirsty**, *adjective* (**thirstier**, **thirstiest**)

thirteen *noun*
1. a cardinal number, ten plus three (10 + 3). **2.** a symbol for this number, as 13 or XIII.
□ **thirteen**, *adjective* –**thirteenth**, *adjective*, *noun*

thirty *noun* (*plural* **thirties**)
1. a cardinal number, ten times three (10 × 3). **2.** a symbol for this number, as 30 or XXX. **3. thirties**, the numbers from 30 to 39 of a series, especially with reference to the years of a person's age, or the years of a century.
□ **thirtieth**, *adjective*, *noun* –**thirty**, *adjective*

this *pronoun* (*plural* **these**)
1. You use **this** to show **a.** a person, thing, or idea pointed out, mentioned, and so on: *This is your seat.* **b.** the nearest of one or two people, things, and so: *This is a prettier hat than that.*
–*adjective* **2.** You use **this** to show **a.** a person, thing, or idea pointed out, mentioned, and so on: *This book is very boring.* **b.** the nearest of one or two people, things, and so on: *This way is quicker than that.*
–*adverb* **3. This** is used with adjectives and adverbs of amount to say exactly how much: *Do you like this much milk in your tea?*

thistle /*say* **this**-uhl/ *noun* a plant with prickly leaves and purple or white flowers.

☑ SPELLING TIP *Silent letter alert*: don't forget the *st* (not double *s*) spelling. The *t* is silent.

thong *noun*
1. a narrow strip of leather. **2.** a sandal, held loosely on the foot by two strips of leather, rubber, etc.

thorax /*say* **thaw**-raks/ *noun* (*plural* **thoraces** /*say* **thaw**-ruh-seez/ *or* **thoraxes**)
1. the chest in human beings or a similar part in other animals. **2.** the part of an insect's body between its head and abdomen.

WORD HISTORY from a Greek word meaning 'breastplate' or 'chest'

thorn *noun* a sharp-pointed prickle on the stem of a plant.
□ **thorny**, *adjective* (**thornier**, **thorniest**)

thorough /*say* **thu**-ruh/ *adjective*
1. If you are **thorough** in doing something, you do it very carefully so as not to miss anything: *He's a thorough worker.* **2.** If an action is **thorough**, it is done carefully and completely: *This room needs a thorough clean.*
□ **thoroughly**, *adverb* –**thoroughness**, *noun*

☑ SPELLING TIP *Tricky vowel sounds*: *o* (not *u* for the first vowel sound, and *ough* for the 'uh' ending. This word is related to *through* although the sound is different (a **thorough** examination of something goes carefully through it). Think of the spelling of *through* and remember to add the *o* between the *th* and the *r*.

thoroughfare *noun* a public road or way through a place.

☑ SPELLING TIP This word is made up of *thorough* and *fare*. See the spelling tip at **thorough**. Then remember the spelling of *fare*, as in the money you pay to go on transport (don't confuse it with *fair*). The word part *fare* here has its old meaning of a 'path' or 'way', which is where the modern meaning comes from.

those *pronoun*, *adjective* See **that**.

though /*say* dhoh/ *conjunction* in spite of the fact that: *Though we had no money to spend, we had a good time.*

☑ SPELLING TIP *Tricky vowel sound*: *ough* for the 'oh' sound. It can be confusing as other words with this spelling can sound quite different. It might help to think of another word with the same spelling and sound, such as *dough*.

thought /*say* thawt/ *verb*
1. the past tense and past participle of **think**.
–*noun* **2.** the forming of ideas in your mind. **3.** an idea: *I've just had a thought!* **4.** consideration or reflection: *Give it thought before you agree.*

☑ SPELLING TIP *Tricky vowel sound*: *ough* for the 'aw' sound. Other words like this are *bought* and *brought*.

thoughtful /*say* **thawt**-fuhl/ *adjective*
1. If someone is **thoughtful**, they are thinking hard about something: *Joe was quiet and thoughtful for several hours after receiving the news.* **2.** If someone is **thoughtful**, they are kind and think about other people: *It was very thoughtful of you to remember my birthday.*
□ **thoughtfully**, *adverb* –**thoughtfulness**, *noun*

thoughtless /*say* **thawt**-luhs/ *adjective* If what someone says or does is **thoughtless**, it shows that they do not think about being kind to other people: *It was very thoughtless of her to start talking about how well she had done in the exam when Jack was so upset about his results.*
□ **thoughtlessly**, *adverb* –**thoughtlessness**, *noun*

thousand *noun*
1. a cardinal number, ten times one hundred (10 × 100). **2.** a symbol for this number, as 1000 or M. **3.** a great number or amount: *a thousand pardons.*
□ **thousand**, *adjective* –**thousandth**, *adjective*, *noun*

thrash *verb*
1. If someone **thrashes** a person or animal, they hit them hard and repeatedly, usually as a punishment: *The cruel old woman used to thrash her dogs.* **2.** If you **thrash** someone in a match or contest, you defeat them decisively: *The home team was thrashed in the finals.*
□ **thrashing**, *noun*

thread /*rhymes with* red/ *noun*
1. a very thin cord of cotton, wool or other fibre spun out to a great length and used for sewing or weaving cloth. **2.** a thin line or length of anything: *the thread of a spider's web.* **3.** a continuing idea in a story: *I stopped listening because I lost the thread.* **4.** a raised spiral strip on a screw.
–*verb* **5.** If you **thread** a needle, you make a piece of thread go through its eye, so that you can use it to sew.

threadbare *adjective* worn and thin: *The towels in the old hotel were threadbare*; *His argument was threadbare and unconvincing.*

threat /*rhymes with* bet/ *noun*
1. a warning of an intention to hurt or rob someone: *Terrified by his threats, she handed over her handbag.* **2.** a possible danger: *a threat of flood.*
☐ **threaten**, *verb*: *to threaten to hurt someone.* –**threatening**, *adjective*

three *noun*
1. a cardinal number, two plus one (2 + 1). **2.** a symbol for this number, as 3 or III.
☐ **three**, *adjective*

three-dimensional *adjective* If something is **three-dimensional**, it has, or seems to have, length, breadth and height and therefore a solid look.

> THE ABBREVIATION is **3D**.

thresh *verb* If someone **threshes** rice, wheat or other such plants, they separate the grains from the rest of the plant by beating.

threshold /*say* **thresh**-hohld/ *noun*
1. the entrance to a house or building: *He crossed the threshold and closed the door behind him.* **2.** a beginning point: *the threshold of a career.*

> ☑ SPELLING TIP There are only two *h*'s in this word and they are not side by side. You have to remember this because the word sounds as if there are two *h*'s side by side in the middle of the word – one in the *sh* at the end of *thresh* and another at the start of *hold*.

thrift *noun* careful management of money and supplies.
☐ **thrifty**, *adjective* (**thriftier**, **thriftiest**)

thrill *verb*
1. If something **thrills** you, it makes you feel excited and happy: *She was thrilled at winning the prize.*
–*noun* **2.** a sudden wave of emotion, as great excitement, shock or fear: *the thrill of making a parachute jump.*
☐ **thrilling**, *adjective* –**thrilled**, *adjective*

thriller *noun* an exciting story, especially one about a crime.

thrive *verb* If people or things **thrive**, they grow or develop well: *These plants thrive in warm climates.*
☐ **thriving**, *adjective*: *a thriving family.*

throat *noun*
1. the front of the neck below the chin. **2.** the passage from the mouth to the stomach or lungs.

throb *verb* (**throbs**, **throbbing**, **throbbed**, **has throbbed**) To **throb** is to beat regularly and strongly: *His heart throbbed*; *The engine throbbed.*
☐ **throb**, *noun*: *We could hear the throb of a helicopter.*

throne *noun*
1. the special chair used by a king, queen or bishop on important occasions. **2.** the office or power of a king or queen: *to be loyal to the throne.*

> ☑ SPELLING TIP Don't confuse the spelling of **throne** with **thrown** which has the same sound. **Thrown** is the past participle of the verb **throw**.

throng *noun*
1. a crowd: *Throngs of teenagers had lined up from early morning for tickets.*
–*verb* **2.** If people **throng** somewhere, they crowd or press there: *People thronged at the department store door eager for the sales.*

throttle *verb*
1. To **throttle** someone is to choke or strangle them.
–*noun* **2.** a device in a vehicle such as a lever which controls the flow of petrol into the engine and therefore the vehicle's speed.

through /*say* throoh/ *preposition*
1. in at one end, side, and so on, and out at the other, of: *The bullet passed through his body.* **2.** between or among the parts of: *to swing through the trees.* **3.** during the whole period of: *to work through the night.*
–*adverb* **4.** completely: *wet through.*
–*adjective* **5.** going through the whole of a distance without stopping: *a through train.*
–*phrase* **6. go through**, to wear out: *to go through three pairs of shoes in less than a year.*

> ANOTHER SPELLING is **thru** but this is not suited to formal writing.

> ☑ SPELLING TIP *Tricky vowel sound*: *ough* for the 'ooh' sound. Don't confuse **through** with **threw** which sounds the same. **Threw** is the past tense of *throw*.

throughout *preposition*
1. at every part of, or at every time within: *There were celebrations throughout the country*; *There have been wars throughout history.*
–*adverb* **2.** in every part, or at every time: *In this building there are lifts throughout*; *She has been very courageous throughout.*

> ☑ SPELLING TIP If you remember the spelling of *through*, you will be all right with this word. Just add *out* at the end.

throw *verb* (**throws**, **throwing**, **threw**, **has thrown**)
1. If you **throw** something, you cause it to move through the air by a sudden movement of your arm: *They were throwing the ball to each other.* **2.** If you **throw** something somewhere, you put it there quickly or carelessly: *Throw your things on the bed and come and join the party.* **3.** If you **throw** a party, you arrange it and take charge of it: *My parents threw a party for my birthday.*
–*phrase* **4. throw out**, to get rid of: *to throw out your old clothes.* **5. throw up**, *Informal* to be sick or vomit.
□ **throw**, *noun*: *It's my throw*; *a throw of the ball.*

☑ SPELLING TIP Don't confuse the spelling of the past form **threw** with **through** which has the same sound. **Through** means 'from one side to another'. Also, don't confuse the spelling of the past participle **thrown** with **throne**, which has the same sound. A **throne** is the special chair a king or queen sits on.

thrust *verb* (**thrusts**, **thrusting**, **thrust**, **has thrust**) To **thrust** is to force or push hard: *She thrust a knife into the hard shell*; *I thrust my way to the front of the crowd.*
□ **thrust**, *noun*

thud *noun*
1. a heavy bumping sound: *My school bag fell to the floor with a thud.*
–*verb* (**thuds**, **thudding**, **thudded**, **has thudded**) **2.** When something **thuds**, it makes a heavy, bumping sound: *The kangaroo thudded through the bush.*

thug *noun* someone who is rough and violent.
□ **thuggish**, *adjective*

WORD HISTORY from the name of a group of robbers and murderers in India who strangled their victims

thumb /*rhymes with* sum/ *noun*
1. the inner finger that is much shorter and thicker than the others.
–*verb* **2.** To **thumb** something is to turn it over using your thumb: *I thumbed through the dictionary.*
–*phrase* **3. be all thumbs**, to be clumsy and awkward.

☑ SPELLING TIP *Silent letter alert*: don't forget the *b* at the end. Other words with a similar spelling are *dumb* and *crumb*.

thump *verb*
1. If you **thump** something, you hit it hard: *She thumped her fist on the table angrily.* **2.** If something **thumps**, it makes a soft, heavy sound: *The box thumped onto the floor*; *My heart was thumping with excitement.*
□ **thump**, *noun*: *My heart gave a great thump.*

thunder *noun*
1. the loud noise that follows a flash of lightning in a storm, caused by the violent disturbance of the air by electricity. **2.** any loud noise like this: *the thunder of applause.*
–*verb* **3.** To **thunder** is to give out thunder, or a noise as loud as thunder: *It thundered last night*; *The horses thundered down the track.*
□ **thunderous**, *adjective* –**thundery**, *adjective*: *thundery showers.*

thunderbolt *noun*
1. a flash of lightning and thunder. **2.** something that suddenly frightens or surprises you.

Thursday *noun* the fifth day of the week.

THE ABBREVIATION is **Thur** or **Thurs**.

thus *adverb* as a result: *We recycle paper and thus reduce waste.*

thwart /*rhymes with* short/ *verb* If someone **thwarts** someone or something, they oppose or stop them from succeeding: *The police thwarted their attempt to get away.*

☑ SPELLING TIP Think of **thwarting** a wart that is growing on your skin to remind yourself of the *wart* spelling after the *th* beginning.

thyme /*say* tuym/ *noun* a common garden herb that is used in cooking.

☑ SPELLING TIP *Silent letter alert*: don't forget the *h* following the *t* at the start. Also notice the *y* spelling of the vowel sound. Don't confuse *thyme* with *time* (the passing of hours, days and so on) which has the same sound.

tiara /*say* tee-**ah**-ruh/ *noun* a piece of jewellery that looks like a tiny crown.

tick[1] *noun*
1. the sound made by a clock. **2.** a small mark (✓) used to show that something has been done correctly. **3.** *Informal* a moment: *Can you wait just a tick?*
–*verb* **4.** To **tick** is to make ticking sounds. **5.** If you **tick** something, you mark it correct with a tick.

tick[2] *noun* a tiny blood-sucking creature whose poison can paralyse animals such as dogs and cats.

ticket *noun*
1. a small printed card which shows that you have paid for something: *a bus ticket.* **2.** a label or tag showing how much something costs.

tickle *verb*
1. If you **tickle** someone, you rub them lightly with the tips of your fingers on sensitive parts of their body to make them laugh: *She tickled the baby's feet and made him giggle.* **2.** If your nose or throat **tickles**, you have a feeling of itching there that makes you want to sneeze or cough.
□ **tickle**, *noun*

ticklish *adjective*
1. sensitive to being tickled: *Are you ticklish behind the knees?* 2. *Informal* difficult and needing to be handled carefully: *Making up the invitation list was a bit ticklish – trying to ask everyone we wanted and not the ones we didn't.*

tidal wave *noun* See **tsunami**.

tide *noun*
1. the rise and fall of the ocean, twice each day. 2. a movement which comes and goes like a tide: *the rising tide of crime.*
–*verb in the phrase* 3. **tide over**, to help through a difficult time: *Will an apple tide you over until lunch?*; *I lent her some money to tide her over until next week.*
☐ **tidal**, *adjective*

tidings *plural noun* news or information: *Messengers were sent with tidings of the rescue.*

tidy *adjective* (**tidier**, **tidiest**)
1. If something is **tidy**, everything is in its right place: *a tidy desk*; *a tidy room.* 2. A **tidy** person is in the habit of keeping everything in good order.
–*verb* (**tidies**, **tidying**, **tidied**, **has tidied**) 3. When you **tidy** something, you make it tidy or neat: *I must tidy my room.*
☐ **tidily**, *adverb*

tie *verb* (**ties**, **tying**, **tied**, **has tied**)
1. If you **tie** something, you hold it in place with string or rope: *We tied a name tag to the back of each chair*; *The parcel was neatly wrapped and tied.* 2. If you **tie** something, such as string or rope, you loop it into a knot or bow: *I stopped to tie my shoelaces.* 3. If you **tie** with someone in a competition, you come equal with them: *The teams tied with 38 points each.*
–*noun* 4. a string or tape used to tie things. 5. a strip of cloth worn around your neck and knotted under your collar.
–*phrase* 6. **tie in**, to relate to or fit in: *That doesn't tie in with the rest of his story.* 7. **tie up**, to fasten by tying: *to tie up a ship to a wharf.*

tier /*rhymes with* here/ *noun* a row or layer: *tiers of seats in a theatre.*

> ☑ SPELLING TIP Don't confuse the spelling of **tier** with **tear**. When **tear** is pronounced in the same way as **tier**, it refers to a drop of water that falls from your eye when you are crying.

tiger *noun* a large wild animal of the cat family which has yellow-brown fur with black stripes.

> NOTE The male is a **tiger**; the female is a **tigress**; the young is a **cub**.

tiger snake *noun* a very venomous Australian snake with striped markings.

tight *adjective*
1. firm and not easily moved or loosened: *I can't unscrew the lid – it's too tight*; *She kept a tight grasp on my arm.* 2. fitting very closely: *New shoes often feel tight at first.* 3. having no room or time to spare: *a tight squeeze*; *We just caught the plane, but it was pretty tight.* 4. *Rather informal* mean with money.
☐ **tight**, *adverb* –**tighten**, *verb*: *to tighten your grip.* –**tightly**, *adverb* –**tightness**, *noun*

tightrope *noun* a wire stretched tightly above the ground for acrobats to balance on.

tights *plural noun* 1. a close-fitting piece of clothing covering the body from the waist to the feet, worn especially when doing exercise, or by dancers and so on. 2. See **pantihose**.

tile *noun*
1. a thin, flat piece of baked clay, a number of which are used to cover roofs, floors, walls and other surfaces.
–*verb* 2. To **tile** something is to put tiles on it: *to tile a roof.* 3. In computers, if you **tile** different windows on a screen you arrange them so that you can see their content side by side.

till[1] *preposition*, *conjunction* until.

till[2] *verb* To **till** land is to dig and prepare it for planting crops: *to till the garden.*

> A SIMILAR WORD is **cultivate**.

tiller *noun* a handle joined to a boat's rudder, used for steering.

tilt *verb* To **tilt** is to lean or slope: *She tilted the bottle to pour out the last of the water*; *Tilt it to the right.*
☐ **tilt**, *noun*

timber *noun*
1. wood that has been cut ready for building.
–*adjective* 2. made of timber: *a timber house.*

timbre /*say* **tim**-buh, **tam**-buh/ *noun* the particular sound an instrument makes: *The flute and clarinet have different timbres.*

> WORD HISTORY from a Greek word meaning 'tambourine' or 'kettledrum'

> ☑ SPELLING TIP Notice the *re* ending in **timbre**. Don't confuse it with **timber** (*er* ending) which has the same sound as the first pronunciation. **Timber** is cut wood.

time *noun*
1. the passing of the hours, days, weeks, months and years. 2. a particular moment shown by a clock: *What is the time?* 3. a particular period or moment: *The 19th century was a time of scientific discovery*; *It is time to go home.* 4. an occasion: *Do you remember the first time we met?*; *However many times I do it, I can't get it right.* 5. the rhythm or tempo of a piece of music. 6. **times**, lots of, or multiplied by. In writing mathematical equations the **times sign** (×) is used to represent this word, as in $2 \times 5 = 10$: *I know that 5 times 4 is 20.*
–*verb* 7. If you **time** a race, etc., you measure or record its time or speed. 8. If you **time**

something, you choose the moment for it: *She timed her arrival perfectly.*
–*phrase* **9. for the time being**, temporarily, or just for the moment. **10. from time to time**, occasionally. **11. in time**, **a.** soon or early enough. **b.** after some time. **c.** following the correct rhythm or tempo. **12. on time**, at the right time; not late.
☐ **timer**, *noun* –**timeless**, *adjective* everlasting: *timeless beauty.*

time line *noun* a line with dates marked on it to show the order in which events have happened: *Our teacher drew a time line to show the main events in Australian history.*

ANOTHER FORM is **timeline**.

timely *adjective* (**timelier**, **timeliest**) happening at just the right time: *a timely phone call.*
☐ **timeliness**, *noun*

timepiece *noun* a clock or watch, especially an old-fashioned one.

timeshift *verb* To **timeshift** a radio or television program is to record it in order to listen to or view it at a more convenient time.
☐ **timeshifting**, *noun*

time signature *noun* a sign of two numbers written one above the other at the beginning of a piece of music indicating the rhythm.

COMPARE this with **key signature**.

timetable *noun*
1. a list of the times when buses, trains, ferries, and so on, arrive and leave. **2.** a list of the times when lessons, etc., begin.

timid *adjective* shy and easily frightened.
☐ **timidity**, *noun* –**timidly**, *adverb*

timing *noun* control of the best time for something to happen: *The timing of the news release was perfect.*

timorous /*say* **tim**-uh-ruhs/ *adjective* timid or fearful.
☐ **timorously**, *adverb*

timpani /*say* **tim**-puh-nee/ *plural noun* a set of kettledrums.

tin *noun*
1. a light, silver-coloured metal that cans and cooking containers are made of. **2.** a metal container, such as a can or a pan: *a tin of soup*; *a cake tin.*
–*verb* (**tins**, **tinning**, **tinned**, **has tinned**) **3.** To **tin** something is to seal it up and preserve it in a tin: *to tin pineapple.*
☐ **tinned**, *adjective*: *tinned fish.*

tinder *noun* dry paper or twigs that catch fire easily.

tinea /*say* **tin**-ee-uh/ *noun* a skin disease which makes the skin between the toes red and sore.

WORD HISTORY from a Latin word meaning 'gnawing worm'

☑ SPELLING TIP *Tricky vowel sound*: remember that the vowel before the final *a* is *e* (not *i*).

tingle *verb*
1. If part of your body **tingles**, you have a slightly uncomfortable feeling on the skin there: *My fingers tingled when I touched the wire.* **2.** If you **tingle** with something, you have a prickly feeling because of it: *to tingle with cold*; *to tingle with excitement.*
☐ **tingle**, *noun* –**tingling**, *adjective*

tinker *verb* If you **tinker** with something, you spend time making small changes to it, often trying to fix it: *He's always tinkering with his model aeroplanes.*

tinkle *verb* If something **tinkles**, it jingles or rings lightly: *We could hear spoons tinkling against glasses.*
☐ **tinkle**, *noun*

tinny *adjective* (**tinnier**, **tinniest**)
1. not made strongly and likely to fall apart: *It was such a tinny watch it fell apart within a week.*
2. having a hollow metallic sound.

tinsel *noun* cheap, shiny coloured strips which glitter and are made for decoration: *They decorated the tree with red and gold tinsel.*
☐ **tinselly**, *adjective*

tint *noun*
1. a colour, especially a delicate or pale colour.
2. a dye for the hair.
–*verb* **3.** To **tint** something is to dye or colour it slightly: *to tint your hair.*

tiny *adjective* (**tinier**, **tiniest**) very small or minute.

tip[1] *noun* the pointed part at the end: *the tips of my toes.*

tip[2] *verb* (**tips**, **tipping**, **tipped**, **has tipped**)
1. To **tip** something is to make it tilt over: *If you tip the bucket the sand will spill out.* **2.** If you **tip** something, you make it fall out of a tilted container: *I tipped cereal into my bowl.*
–*noun* **3.** a place where people can leave their rubbish.

tip[3] *noun*
1. money given in thanks to someone who has done something for you: *to leave a tip for the waiter.* **2.** a piece of useful information: *She gave me a tip on where to sit for the best view.*
–*verb* (**tips**, **tipping**, **tipped**, **has tipped**) **3.** When you **tip** someone, you give them money in thanks for something they have done for you: *We tipped the waiter for his good service.*
–*phrase* **4. tip off**, to warn of trouble or danger.

A SIMILAR WORD (for definition 2) is **hint**.

tipsy *adjective* slightly drunk: *From the way he was talking we thought he was tipsy.*
☐ **tipsily**, *adverb* –**tipsiness**, *noun*

tiptoe *verb* If you **tiptoe**, you walk softly and carefully on the tips of your toes.

tirade /*say* tuy-**rayd**/ *noun* a long, angry speech.

tire *verb* If something **tires** you, you want to rest or sleep because it makes you lose a lot of energy: *A day of walking around the zoo really tired us.*

☑ SPELLING TIP Don't confuse the spelling of **tire** with **tyre** which sounds the same. A **tyre** is the rubber part around the outside of the wheel of a car or bike.

tired *adjective*
1. feeling that you want to rest or sleep: *Let's put these tired children to bed.*
–*phrase* **2. tired of**, bored with: *I'm tired of hearing him talk about himself.*
☐ **tiredness**, *noun*

SIMILAR WORDS (for definition 1) are **sleepy**, **weary**, **exhausted** and **worn out**. If you are **exhausted** or **worn out**, you are very tired and completely without energy.

tissue /*say* **tish**-ooh/ *noun*
1. the substance of which living things are made: *muscle tissue.* **2.** soft, thin paper, especially a piece used as a paper handkerchief.

titanic /*say* tuy-**tan**-ik/ *adjective* of enormous size or strength.

titbit *noun*
1. a delicious morsel of food. **2.** an especially interesting piece of gossip or other information.

title *noun*
1. the name of a book, film or piece of music. **2.** a name showing someone's job or rank in society. **3.** the legal right to own property or a certificate stating this: *the title to a house.*
–*verb* **4.** If you **title** something, you give it a name: *to title a book.*
☐ **titled**, *adjective*

titter *verb* If someone **titters**, they giggle in a silly or nervous way.
☐ **titter**, *noun*

to *preposition* a word indicating **1.** movement or direction towards something: *from north to south.* **2.** a limit of degree, time, or amount: *to this day*; *full to the lid.* **3.** contact or attachment: *The paper stuck to the wall*; *He held to his opinions.* **4.** addition or amount: *adding two to ten.*
–*adverb* **5.** to a contact point or closed position: *Pull the door to.*
–*phrase* **6. to and fro**, to and from some place or thing: *I've been going to and fro all day trying to get everything organised for the party.*

☑ SPELLING TIP Don't confuse the spelling of **to** with **too** or **two**, both of which sound the same.

The most common meanings of **too** are 'also', 'in addition' and 'more than is required'; **two** is a number.

toad *noun* an animal similar to a frog, but bigger, which lives on land.

toadstool *noun* a plant like a mushroom, but usually poisonous.

toast[1] *noun*
1. sliced bread cooked until it is brown on both sides.
–*verb* **2.** When you **toast** a slice of bread, you cook it until it is brown on both sides.
☐ **toaster**, *noun*

toast[2] *noun*
1. someone or something you honour with a special drink: *The prime minister will be our next toast.* **2.** the act of drinking in this way: *a toast to the president.*
–*verb* **3.** When you **toast** someone, you drink a toast to them: *We toasted the winner.*

tobacco *noun*
1. a plant whose leaves are dried and used for smoking in cigarettes, cigars and pipes. **2.** the dried leaves themselves.

☑ SPELLING TIP *Single/double letter alert*: only one *b*, but double *c*.

toboggan *noun*
1. a light sledge used for sliding over snow or ice.
–*verb* (**toboggans**, **tobogganing**, **tobogganed**, **has tobogganed**) **2.** To **toboggan** is to slide along in a toboggan.

☑ SPELLING TIP *Single/double letter alert*: only one *b*, but double *g*. You could think of 'gliding gleefully' as you **toboggan** down that hill.

today *noun*
1. this present day: *Today is my birthday.* **2.** this present time or age: *The cars of today cause less pollution than they used to.*
☐ **today**, *adverb*: *Let's go there today.*

toddle *verb* If a very young child or an old person **toddles**, they walk in short, unsteady steps.
☐ **toddler**, *noun* a very young child.

toe *noun*
1. in humans and other animals, one of the end members or digits of the foot. **2.** a part of a sock, stocking or shoe, to cover the toes.
–*noun in the phrase* **3. on your toes**, wide awake or prepared to act. **4. tread on someone's toes**, to offend, especially by acting in another person's area of responsibility.
–*verb in the phrase* **5. toe the line**, to behave according to the rules.

☑ SPELLING TIP Don't confuse the spelling of **toe** with **tow** which sounds the same. To **tow** something is to drag or pull it.

toffee *noun* a sticky sweet made from sugar, water and sometimes butter.

tofu /*say* **toh**-fooh/ *noun* a white curd made from soy bean milk, used in cooking, especially in foods originating in Asian cooking.

ANOTHER NAME for this is **bean curd**.
WORD HISTORY from a Chinese word meaning 'fermented bean'

toga /*say* **toh**-guh/ *noun* a robe worn by people in ancient Rome.

together *adverb*
1. into or to one place, gathering, mass, and so on: *to call the people together.* **2.** so that separate parts are joined: *Staple the papers together*; *Multiply these numbers together.* **3.** into or in a relationship: *to bring strangers together.* **4.** taken or thought of together: *This one cost more than all the others together.* **5.** at the same time: *You cannot have both together.*
–*adjective* **6.** *Rather informal* calm and in control: *He is quite together these days.*
□ **togetherness**, *noun*

toggle *noun* a type of fastener, made of a small bar or pin which fits through a loop of rope or chain.

toil *verb* If you **toil**, you **1.** work hard for a long time. **2.** walk with great difficulty: *He toiled up the hill with the heavy bag.*
□ **toil**, *noun*

toilet *noun*
1. a bowl for getting rid of waste matter from the body, especially a bowl connected to a pipe in which the waste is removed with water. **2.** a room where people go to use a toilet.

OTHER WORDS for this are **lavatory** and **loo**. **Lavatory** is a more formal word, while **loo** is rather informal.
WORD HISTORY from a French word meaning 'cloth'

token *noun*
1. a ticket or disc used instead of money to pay for something. **2.** a sign or symbol of something: *This gift is a token of my love for you.*

tolerate *verb* If you **tolerate** something you do not like or agree with, you allow it to happen: *His parents tolerated his bad manners.*
□ **tolerable**, *adjective* –**tolerance**, *noun* –**tolerant**, *adjective*

toll[1] *verb* To **toll** a bell is to ring it loudly and slowly, especially when someone has died.

toll[2] *noun*
1. a fee paid for crossing a bridge or driving on an expressway. **2.** the price paid in terms of numbers of people dead: *The road toll always increases during holidays.*

tollway *noun* a road that you must pay money to travel on.

tom *noun* the male of various animals, especially a cat.

tomahawk *noun* a small axe, first used by the Native Americans.

WORD HISTORY from a Native American word meaning 'war club' or 'ceremonial object'

tomato *noun* (*plural* **tomatoes**) a juicy red fruit, eaten as a cooked vegetable or raw in salads.

tomb /*say* toohm/ *noun* a burial place, especially one made of stone.

☑ SPELLING TIP *Silent letter alert*: don't forget the silent *b* at the end. The letters *omb* make an 'oohm' sound in this word. Another word like this is *womb*.

tomboy *noun* a girl who acts in a way that some people think is more how a boy usually acts, such as taking part in adventurous activities, being noisy, etc.

tombstone *noun* a stone over someone's burial place, usually with their name and dates of birth and death cut into it.

OTHER WORDS for this are **gravestone** and **headstone**.

tomorrow *noun* the day after today.

tom-tom *noun* an African or Native American drum.

ton /*say* tun/ *noun*
1. a unit of mass in the imperial system, equal to approximately 1016 kilograms. **2.** *Informal* any heavy weight: *This bag weighs a ton.* **3. tons**, *Informal* very many or a good deal: *I've invited tons of people to my party.*

COMPARE definition 1 with **tonne**.

tone *noun*
1. a musical sound: *I could hear the rich tones of his guitar.* **2.** a musical interval equal to two semitones. **3.** the lightness or darkness of a colour: *a beige tone.* **4.** the style or quality of something: *His rude joke lowered the tone of the meeting.*
–*verb in the phrase* **5. tone down**, to soften or make less: *to tone down your efforts.* **6. tone in**, to match: *Those shoes will tone in with your new shorts.* **7. tone up**, to make strong and fit: *Exercise tones up your body.*

tongs *plural noun* a tool with two arms hinged together, used for picking up things.

tongue /*rhymes with* hung/ *noun*
1. the mass of muscle in the mouth that helps in eating food and shaping the sounds of human speech. **2.** a language or dialect: *a foreign tongue.* **3.** the loose, flat piece of leather under the laces of some shoes. **4.** the clapper, or piece

of metal, that hangs inside a bell and makes a sound when it hits the side.

> ☑ SPELLING TIP *Silent letter alert*: don't forget the silent *ue* at the end. Also remember the *o* spelling where you might expect a *u*.

tonic *noun*
1. something that makes you stronger, healthier and more cheerful. **2.** in music, the first note or degree of a scale.
□ **tonic**, *adjective*

tonight *noun* the night of this present day: *Tonight's concert will be in the hall.*
□ **tonight**, *adverb*: *Come over tonight.*

tonne /*rhymes with* on/ *noun* a measure of mass in the metric system equal to 1000 kilograms.

> THE SYMBOL for this is **t**.
> COMPARE this with **ton** (definition 1).

tonsil *noun* either of the two lumps inside and at the back of the throat.

> ☑ SPELLING TIP *Single letter alert*: only one *l* at the end, but remember that it is doubled in the word *tonsillitis*.

tonsillitis /*say* ton-suh-**luy**-tuhs/ *noun* an illness in which the tonsils become infected and painful.

> ☑ SPELLING TIP The spelling of **tonsillitis** will be easier if you see that it is made up of *tonsil* (with the final *l* doubled) and the suffix *-itis* (meaning 'inflamed condition'). Think of a similar word such as *appendicitis*. They both end with *-itis* (spelt with *is*, not *us*, at the end).

too *adverb*
1. also or in addition: *young, clever, and rich too.* **2.** more than is wanted, or than should be: *too long*; *too many pupils.*
–*phrase* **3. only too**, very: *I'm only too glad to help you.*

> ☑ SPELLING TIP Don't confuse the spelling of **too** with **to** or **two**, both of which have the same sound. The most common way **to** is used is to indicate movement in the direction of a place or person; **two** is a number.

tool *noun*
1. any instrument used for doing work, such as a hammer or knife. **2.** anything used like a tool to do work or to cause some result: *Education is a tool that opens many doors.*

toot *verb* If a horn or whistle **toots** or if someone **toots** it, it makes a noise in short blasts: *The car horn tooted loudly*; *The train driver tooted the whistle.*
□ **toot**, *noun*

tooth *noun* (*plural* **teeth**)
1. one of the hard bone-like parts or growths inside the mouths of humans and animals, used for eating. **2.** any tooth-like part of a comb, rake or saw.

top[1] *noun*
1. the highest point or surface of anything: *the top of the mountain.* **2.** a part thought of as higher: *the top of the paddock.* **3.** a covering or lid such as on a box or bottle. **4.** an outer piece of clothing for the upper part of the body.
–*adjective* **5.** highest or upper: *the top floor.* **6.** *Informal* best or excellent: *He's a top student.*
–*verb* (**tops**, **topping**, **topped**, **has topped**) **7.** If you **top** something, you give it a top or put a top on it: *She topped the cake with icing.* **8.** If you **top** a group, you come first in that group: *She tops the class in maths.*
–*phrase* **9. on top of**, **a.** upon: *Giuseppe fell on top of me.* **b.** in control of: *I think I'm on top of my homework now.* **10. top off with**, to complete by adding a finishing touch: *He topped off his dinner with a large ice-cream.* **11. top up**, **a.** to fill up a partly filled container. **b.** to make an additional deposit of money into an account: *I have to top up my travel card before catching the train next week.*

top[2] *noun* a cone-shaped toy which is made to spin on its pointed end.

topic *noun* the subject of a speech, discussion, conversation, or piece of writing.

topical *adjective* dealing with things that are happening now: *a topical newspaper article.*
□ **topically**, *adverb*

topple *verb* If something **topples** or is **toppled**, it becomes unsteady and falls down: *The pile of books toppled over because it was too high*; *She knocked the pile of books and toppled them.*

topsy-turvy *adverb* upside down, backwards, or back to front.
□ **topsy-turvy**, *adjective*

torch *noun* (*plural* **torches**)
1. a light designed to be carried around and run on batteries. **2.** something with a burning flame which can be carried around or set into a holder. **3.** a tool which produces a very hot flame used for burning off paint or melting metal.

torment *verb* /*say* taw-**ment**/ If someone or something **torments** a person or animal, **1.** they give them great pain. **2.** they worry or annoy them greatly: *He was tormented by thoughts that he should have helped more.*
–*noun* /*say* **taw**-ment/ **3.** great pain or agony. **4.** something that causes pain or is a source of worry or trouble: *Her headaches were a torment to her.*
□ **tormentor**, *noun*

> ANOTHER SPELLING for **tormentor** is **tormenter**.

tornado *noun* (*plural* **tornadoes** *or* **tornados**) a violent whirlwind.

WORD HISTORY from a Spanish word meaning 'thunderstorm'

torpedo *noun* (*plural* **torpedoes**)
1. a cigar-shaped missile containing explosives, which can travel by itself under water when fired by a submarine.
–*verb* **2.** To **torpedo** something is to attack or destroy it by torpedo or torpedoes: *The ship was torpedoed during the war.*

torrent *noun*
1. a stream of water flowing with great speed or violence, or a violent downpour of rain. **2.** a violent stream or flow of anything: *They heaped a torrent of abuse on their tormentors.*

torrent file *noun* a computer file created from smaller parts of a file shared across the internet, each part being shared by a different user, making the process faster.

torso *noun* (*plural* **torsos**) the trunk of the human body.

tortilla /*say* taw-**tee**-yuh/ *noun* a flat bread made from corn, originating in Mexican cooking.

☑ SPELLING TIP Remember the double *l* in this word, which gives a 'y' rather than an 'l' sound. This is because **tortilla** comes from Spanish where it means 'little cake'.

tortoise /*say* **taw**-tuhs/ *noun* any of various reptiles which have feet with toes and a hard shell covering their bodies, most of which live on land.

COMPARE this with **turtle**.

torture *noun*
1. an act or method of causing severe pain, especially so as to gain information.
–*verb* **2.** If someone **tortures** another person, they intentionally cause severe pain to that person in order to get information from them or to punish them: *They tortured the spies to find out what they knew.*

toss *verb*
1. If you **toss** something, you throw it lightly and carelessly: *He tossed his dirty clothes into the laundry basket.* **2.** If you **toss** your head, you move it back with a sudden movement: *She had a habit of tossing her head to get the hair out of her eyes.* **3.** If someone or something **tosses** or is **tossed**, they keep moving from side to side: *The sick child tossed in his sleep all night*; *The ship was tossed in the rough seas.* **4.** If you **toss** a coin, you throw it in the air and decide something by guessing which side will be facing upwards after it lands on the ground: *We tossed a coin to decide who should go first.*
□ **toss**, *noun*

tot[1] *noun* a small child: *the little tots.*

tot[2] *verb in the phrase* (**tots**, **totting**, **totted**, **has totted**) **tot up**, *Informal* to add up: *The waiter totted up the bill.*

total *adjective*
1. whole: *What is the total cost?* **2.** complete or absolute: *a total recovery.*
–*noun* **3.** the sum or whole amount.
–*verb* (**totals**, **totalling**, **totalled**, **has totalled**) **4.** If you **total** something, you find its total: *The judges totalled the scores, then announced the winner.*
□ **totality**, *noun* –**totally**, *adverb*: *totally ruined.*

totalitarian /*say* toh-tal-uh-**tair**-ree-uhn/ *adjective* having to do with a government which has complete control and does not allow any opposition.
□ **totalitarianism**, *noun*

totem *noun*
1. something, often an animal, used as the special sign of a family or group. **2.** a statue or drawing of such a sign.
□ **totem**, *adjective*: *a totem pole.*

totter *verb* If someone **totters**, they walk with weak, unsteady steps: *The old man tottered back to his bed.*

touch /*say* tuch/ *verb*
1. If you **touch** something, you feel it with your hand or finger: *Touch it and see if it is still cold.* **2.** If two things **touch**, they come into contact: *The car was so small that the driver's head was touching the roof.* **3.** If something **touches** you, or you are **touched** by something, you feel strongly about it: *He was touched by her sincerity*; *Her story touched us deeply.*
–*noun* (*plural* **touches**) **4.** the sense of feeling. **5.** the act of touching or being touched: *Be careful – the slightest touch will leave a mark.* **6.** a small amount or slight degree of something: *She has a touch of flu.*
–*phrase* **7. touch on**, to talk or write about briefly: *He spoke at length without even touching on the real problems.* **8. touch up**, to improve by making small changes: *to touch up a painting.*

touchy *adjective* (**touchier**, **touchiest**)
1. irritable or easily offended: *Ann was very touchy because her hair didn't look right.* **2.** likely to irritate or offend: *We didn't talk about school uniforms because we knew it was a touchy issue.*

tough /*say* tuf/ *adjective*
1. Something that is **tough** is not easily broken and will not wear out quickly: *This material is as tough as leather.* **2.** Meat that is **tough** is difficult to cut and eat. **3.** Someone or something that is **tough** is strong and able to handle bad conditions: *They were trained to be tough soldiers*; *Four-wheel drive vehicles are tough and built for rough roads.* **4.** A **tough** problem or job is a difficult one: *That was the toughest exam I have ever sat for.* **5.** Actions that are **tough** are strict and strong: *The principal insisted on tough discipline.*

☐ **toughness**, *noun* –**toughen**, *verb*: *Exercise helps you toughen up.*

THE OPPOSITE (of definition 2) is **tender**[1].

☑ SPELLING TIP Remember that there is no *f* in **tough** – the spelling *ough* gives the 'uf' sound, as it does in some other words like *enough* and *rough*.

tour /*say* too-uh/ *verb* To **tour** is to travel through a place or to travel from one place to another: *The show toured Australia*; *We spent a week in New Zealand, touring around.*
☐ **tour**, *noun*

tourist *noun* someone who travels or tours for pleasure.
☐ **tourism**, *noun*

tournament /*say* **taw**-nuh-muhnt/ *noun*
1. a meeting for contests in sports, cards, and other similar things: *a tennis tournament.* **2.** a contest in medieval times where two knights on horseback fought for a prize.

tourniquet /*say* **taw**-nuh-kay/ *noun* a tight bandage or band, twisted or wrapped around your arm or leg to stop bleeding.

☑ SPELLING TIP *Silent letter alert*: don't forget the silent *t* at the end – the *et* spelling makes an 'ay' sound. Other words with this ending are *ballet* and *beret*. They all come from French. Also remember the *qu* spelling for the 'k' sound in **tourniquet** and the *our* spelling for the first vowel sound (which is pronounced 'aw').

tow /*rhymes with* no/ *verb*
1. To **tow** something is to pull it using a rope or chain: *They towed the car to the repair place.*
–*phrase* **2. in tow**, **a.** in the condition of being towed. **b.** following someone around, because they are in charge of you or are taking you somewhere: *She had her little sister in tow.*
☐ **tow**, *noun*

☑ SPELLING TIP Don't confuse the spelling of **tow** with **toe** which sounds the same. Your **toes** are at the end of your feet.

towards *preposition*
1. in the direction of: *to walk towards the north.* **2.** with respect to, or as regards: *My attitude towards you is unchanged.* **3.** just before: *towards 2 o'clock.* **4.** as a help or contribution: *to give money towards a gift.*

ANOTHER FORM is **toward**.

towel *noun*
1. a piece of cloth used for wiping and drying something wet.
–*phrase* **2. throw in the towel**, to give up or admit defeat.

towelling *noun* a type of cloth used for making towels, clothes, and so on.

☑ SPELLING TIP *Double letter alert*: this word comes from *towel* but remember that the *l* has been doubled.

tower *noun*
1. a tall, narrow structure that is usually part of a building like a church, but sometimes stands alone.
–*verb* **2.** To **tower** is to rise and stretch far upwards: *He has grown very tall and now towers over his younger sisters.*

town *noun*
1. a large area of houses, shops and offices where many people live and work, smaller than a city. **2.** the main shopping and business centre or area of a city: *She works in an office in town.* **3.** the people of a town: *The new library will benefit the whole town.*

town hall *noun* a large public building belonging to a town, used for meetings and gatherings.

town house *noun* a house built as part of a block of similar houses, usually on two levels, with its own entrance at ground floor.

township *noun* a small town or settlement.

toxin *noun* a poison produced by some plants and animals which can cause sickness and sometimes death.
☐ **toxic**, *adjective*

toy *noun*
1. an object, often a small copy of some familiar thing, for children or others to play with.
–*verb in the phrase* **2. toy with**, **a.** to handle aimlessly or carelessly: *He sat there toying with his meal.* **b.** to think or act without plan or serious purpose: *to toy with an idea.*
☐ **toy**, *adjective*: *a toy train.*

trace *noun*
1. a mark that shows that someone or something has been present, often a footprint or a track: *The robbers left traces in the dirt.* **2.** a very small amount: *The cake tastes of chocolate with just a trace of ginger*; *A trace of a frown crossed his usually happy face.*
–*verb* **3.** If you **trace** a person or thing, you find them by following their tracks or course: *The robber was traced as far as the border*; *to trace the source of a problem.* **4.** If you **trace** the development of something, you describe its course or history: *She can trace her family history back to the 17th century.* **5.** If you **trace** a drawing, you copy it by placing transparent paper over it and then following the lines of the original: *Maps of countries are hard to draw – it's easier to trace them.*
☐ **tracing**, *noun*

trachea /*say* truh-**kee**-uh/ *noun* (*plural* **tracheas** *or* **tracheae** /*say* truh-**kee**-ee/) See **windpipe**.

☑ SPELLING TIP *Tricky vowel sound*: remember that the vowel before the final *a* is *e* (not *i*). Also notice the *ch* spelling for the 'k' sound. **Trachea** comes from a Greek word meaning 'rough'.

track *noun*
1. a rough path. **2.** a structure of metal bars and sleepers on which a train runs. **3.** a mark or series of marks like footprints, left by anything that has passed along. **4.** a path or course laid out for racing. **5.** one of the separate parts on a recording such as a compact disc, containing one song or piece of music. **6.** in computers, the band or path on a tape or disk along which data is stored.
–*verb* **7.** To **track** someone or something is to follow their tracks or footprints in order to find them: *The hunter tracked the wild animal.* **8.** To **track** something is to follow its course by electronic means, as radar or sonar: *Police tracked the movement of the stolen car.*
–*adjective* **9.** In sport, **track** events are athletic competitions held on a running track.
–*phrase* **10. in your tracks**, just where you are standing: *He was stopped in his tracks.* **11. keep track of**, to keep sight or knowledge of. **12. lose track of**, to fail to stay in touch with. **13. off the track**, away from what is being talked or written about.

tracksuit *noun* a loose two-piece set of clothing worn when exercising or as casual wear.

tract *noun*
1. a stretch of land or water. **2.** a system or series of connected parts in the body: *the digestive tract.*

traction *noun*
1. the act of drawing or pulling something, especially along a surface. **2.** the force that prevents a wheel slipping: *Cars lose traction on roads which are wet after a long dry spell.*

tractor *noun* a powerful motor vehicle used to pull farm machinery and so on.

trade *noun*
1. the buying, selling or exchanging of goods. **2.** a particular kind of work: *'What's his trade?' 'He's an electrician.'*
–*verb* **3.** To **trade** is to buy, sell or exchange goods or other desirable things: *They traded in gold*; *The girls traded places with each other.*
–*phrase* **4. trade in**, to give as a part payment in exchange for something new: *My mother traded in her old car for a new one.*
☐ **trade**, *adjective* –**trader**, *noun*

ANOTHER WORD (for definition 1) is **commerce**.

trademark *noun* a name, sign or mark used to show that goods have been made by a particular company.

trade union *noun* an organisation or association of workers set up to help its members with any work problems, such as pay, working conditions, and so on, and for dealing with employers.
☐ **trade unionist**, *noun*

THE SHORT FORM of this is **union**.

tradition *noun*
1. the handing down of beliefs, customs and stories from one age group to another. **2.** the beliefs or customs that are handed down.
☐ **traditional**, *adjective*: *The dancers were dressed in traditional costume.* –**traditionally**, *adverb*

traffic *noun*
1. the coming and going of people or vehicles along a road, railway line, river, etc. **2.** the people or vehicles that travel along such a route. **3.** the business, trade, or dealings carried out between countries or people, sometimes illegally: *traffic in drugs.*
–*verb* (**traffics**, **trafficking**, **trafficked**, **has trafficked**) **4.** Someone who **traffics** in drugs, arms or stolen goods, buys and sells them illegally: *Police suspect he's been trafficking in stolen paintings.*
☐ **trafficker**, *noun*

☑ SPELLING TIP Remember that this word ends in *ic* (not *ick*). However, when you add *-ed* or *-ing*, or make the word **trafficker**, the *k* is added.

tragedy /*say* **traj**-uh-dee/ *noun*
1. a sad or serious play with an unhappy ending: *Shakespeare's tragedy of 'Hamlet'.* **2.** any very sad happening.
☐ **tragic**, *adjective* –**tragically**, *adverb*

WORD HISTORY from a Greek word meaning 'goat song'

☑ SPELLING TIP Remember the *g* spelling (think of *g* for 'gloomy' for the 'j' sound) and the *edy* (not *idy*) ending. It might help if you realise the word *age* is hidden inside the word **tragedy**.

trail *verb*
1. If you **trail** something or it **trails**, it follows along behind: *The fisherman trailed a line behind the boat*; *Her long scarf trailed in the wind.* **2.** If you **trail** someone or something, you follow after them: *The little girl trailed after her sister.* **3.** If you are **trailing** in a competition or game, you are falling behind your competitor or have a lower score: *At half-time our team was trailing by three goals.*
–*noun* **4.** a path or track made across rough country. **5.** footprints or smell left by a hunted animal or person. **6.** a line of dust or smoke left behind something moving.

☑ DO NOT CONFUSE **trail** with **trial**. A **trial** is the testing of something, especially a case to find out if a person is guilty or not in a law court.

trailer *noun*
1. a vehicle, made to be towed by a car or truck, used to carry loads. **2.** an advertisement for a film

soon to be shown, usually made up of scenes from it.

train *noun*
1. a number of railway carriages joined together and pulled by an engine. **2.** a line of people, cars, or animals travelling together: *a camel train.* **3.** something that is drawn along: *the train on a wedding dress.* **4.** a series of connected ideas: *a train of thought.*
–*verb* **5.** If you **train** a person or animal to do something, you teach them how to do it: *Flight attendants are trained to handle emergencies*; *He trained his dog to walk behind him.* **6.** If you **train** for a sports event, you make yourself physically fit by exercise and diet.
☐ **training**, *noun* –**trained**, *adjective*: *He's a trained engineer.*

trainee *noun* someone who is being taught how to do a particular job: *a medical trainee.*
☐ **trainee**, *adjective*: *a trainee teacher.*

trainer *noun*
1. someone who prepares racehorses for racing. **2.** someone who trains athletes in a sport. **3.** a shoe which is suitable for use in exercise or sport.

trait /*say* trayt, tray/ *noun* a feature or quality, especially of someone's character: *One of her best traits is her thoughtfulness.*

☑ SPELLING TIP *Silent letter alert*: don't forget the silent *t* at the end of this word, if you say it as in the first pronunciation. Don't confuse it with **tray** which is something flat for carrying things on.

traitor *noun* someone who deceives a person or country by helping their enemy.

tram *noun* a passenger car running on tracks, usually powered by electricity from a wire running above it.

tramp *verb*
1. To **tramp** is to step or walk heavily or steadily: *The class tramped downstairs.* **2.** If you **tramp** on something, you step heavily on it: *The horse tramped on my toes.*
–*noun* **3.** the act of tramping: *a tramp through the country.* **4.** the sound of a firm, heavy step. **5.** someone who travels about from place to place on foot, with no fixed home.

A SIMILAR WORD (for definition 5) is **vagrant**.

trample *verb* To **trample** something is to damage it by stepping heavily on it: *The animals trampled the grass under the tree.*

trampoline *noun* a frame with tightly stretched material attached to it by springs, on which you can jump for pleasure or sport.
☐ **trampolining**, *noun*

WORD HISTORY from an Italian word meaning 'springboard'

trance *noun*
1. a state of being not fully conscious. **2.** the condition of being completely lost in thought.

tranquil /*say* **trang**-kwuhl/ *adjective* peaceful or quiet.
☐ **tranquilly**, *adverb* –**tranquillity**, *noun*

☑ SPELLING TIP *Single letter alert*: only one *l* at the end, but remember that it is doubled when other words, such as *tranquillity* and *tranquilliser* are formed.

tranquilliser /*say* **trang**-kwuh-luy-zuh/ *noun* a drug for making anxious people or animals feel calm.
☐ **tranquillise**, *verb*: *The horse was tranquillised by the injection the vet gave it.*

ANOTHER SPELLING is **tranquillizer**.

trans- *prefix* a word part meaning: **1.** across or beyond, as in *transcontinental*. **2.** into another place or condition, as in *transmission*, *translate*.

WORD HISTORY this prefix comes from Latin

transact *verb* To **transact** a business arrangement or deal is to carry it through to a successful conclusion: *They transacted to sell half of the timber off in wood chips.*

transaction *noun*
1. a piece of business: *The transaction was finalised in one morning.* **2.** the managing or carrying on of business: *Their transactions are fairly cordial.*

transfer *verb* /*say* trans-**fer**/ (**transfers**, **transferring**, **transferred**, **has transferred**)
1. If you **transfer** something, you move it from one place to another: *We transferred our luggage from the trolley to the car*; *Let's transfer our attention to more urgent matters.*
–*noun* /*say* **trans**-fer/ **2.** the act of transferring or the fact of being transferred: *The transfer of classes to the new building is complete.* **3.** a drawing or pattern which will stick onto another surface: *These tattoo transfers can be put onto your arm.*
☐ **transference**, *noun* –**transferral**, *noun*

transfix *verb*
1. If you **transfix** something, you pierce it through or fix it fast with something sharp or pointed: *The insects were transfixed by small pins.* **2.** If you are **transfixed**, you are unable to move because of amazement or terror: *They were transfixed with horror at the sight that met them.*

transform *verb* If something is **transformed**, it is completely changed, usually for the better: *The new uniform transformed him into a neat-looking person.*
☐ **transformation**, *noun*

transformer *noun* an electrical device used for changing one voltage to another.

transfuse *verb*
1. If something **transfuses** a person or thing, it pours into or spreads through them: *Their faces were transfused with happiness.* **2.** To **transfuse** blood is to take it from one person or animal and inject it into another.
□ **transfusion**, *noun*

transistor *noun*
1. a small electronic device used in computers, radios, and so on, for controlling the flow of current. **2.** a small radio equipped with these devices.

transit *noun*
1. passing across or through: *The aircraft lost power in one of its engines while in transit over the Pacific.* **2.** the state of being carried from one place to another: *The parcel must have been lost in transit.*
□ **transition**, *noun*

transitive verb *noun* a verb that needs an object for it to make sense, such as *bring*.

COMPARE this with **intransitive verb**. Also see the Grammar and Punctuation Guide appendix.

translate *verb* If you **translate** what someone has said or written, you say or write it in another language: *He translated the book from Japanese into English.*
□ **translation**, *noun* –**translator**, *noun*

translucent /*say* tranz-**looh**-suhnt/ *adjective* allowing some light to come through, so that you can see things, but not clearly.

COMPARE this with **opaque** and **transparent**.

☑ SPELLING TIP The spelling of this word will be easier if you see that it is made up of the prefix *trans-* (meaning 'across' or 'through') and *lucent* (from the Latin word *lucens*, meaning 'shining').

transmission *noun*
1. the broadcasting of a radio or television program. **2.** the part of a motor which transmits the power from the engine to the wheels.

transmit *verb* (**transmits**, **transmitting**, **transmitted**, **has transmitted**)
1. If a signal or message is **transmitted** to a place, it is sent there by means of electronic equipment: *The game will be transmitted live from the ground.* **2.** If something is **transmitted** to a person or place, it is passed on to that person or place: *Knowledge of how to do the dance has been transmitted from generation to generation.*
□ **transmitter**, *noun*

transmute *verb* To **transmute** is to change from one nature or form to another: *Her fear was transmuted into fierce anger towards the intruders.*
□ **transmutation**, *noun*

transparency *noun*
1. the quality of being transparent or able to be seen through. **2.** something which is transparent, especially a transparent photograph projected onto a screen or looked at by light shining through from behind: *It is better to copy from the transparency than from the print.*

transparent *adjective*
1. allowing light to pass through so you can see through it: *This material is too transparent to be used for a dress.* **2.** easily understood, so there can be no doubt about it: *His motive for visiting is transparent – he wants to see you again.*
□ **transparently**, *adverb*

COMPARE (definition 1) with **opaque** and **translucent**.

transplant *verb* /*say* trans-**plant**, trans-**plahnt**/
1. If you **transplant** something or someone, you remove it from one place to another: *to transplant seedlings*; *They transplanted their whole family from England to Australia.*
–*noun* /*say* **trans**-plant, **trans**-plahnt/ **2.** the act of transplanting, especially the medical operation of taking an organ from one person's body and putting it into another person: *She is waiting to have a kidney transplant.* **3.** an organ of the body that has been transplanted in this way.

transport *verb* /*say* trans-**pawt**, **trans**-pawt/
1. If you **transport** people or goods, you move them from one place to another: *How are you going to transport the chair to your house?*
–*noun* /*say* **trans**-pawt/ **2.** a system or method of transporting: *public transport.* **3.** a ship, aircraft, or truck, used to transport people or goods.

transpose *verb*
1. If you **transpose** the position or order of something, you change it: *This description of the scene would be better transposed to the beginning of the story.* **2.** If you **transpose** two things, you change their places: *The team decided to transpose the goal shooter and the centre.*
□ **transposition**, *noun*

transverse /*say* **tranz**-vers, tranz-**vers**/ *adjective* lying or cutting across: *a transverse wave motion.*

transvestite *noun* someone who dresses in the clothing of the opposite sex, especially a man who dresses as a woman.

trap *noun*
1. a device for catching animals. **2.** a trick or any other way of catching someone by surprise. **3.** *Old-fashioned* a two-wheeled carriage drawn by a horse.
–*verb* (**traps**, **trapping**, **trapped**, **has trapped**)
4. To **trap** animals is to catch them using traps. **5.** If you **trap** a person, you trick or deceive them into doing something they don't want to do: *They trapped the man into admitting what he had done.* **6.** If you **are trapped** in a place, you cannot move

or get out of it: *Firefighters tried to reach the people trapped inside the burning building.*

trapdoor *noun* a door cut into a floor, ceiling or roof.

trapdoor spider *noun* a type of spider with a painful bite that digs tunnels in the ground, sometimes fitted with a lid which it is able to open or keep tightly closed.

trapeze /*say* truh-**peez**/ *noun* a short bar joined to the ends of two hanging ropes, on which gymnasts and acrobats perform.

WORD HISTORY perhaps from the *trapezium* shape the ropes form

☑ SPELLING TIP It is definitely not easy to perform on the **trapeze**. Think of this to remind you that the ending is spelt *eze* (not *ease* or *ese*).

trapezium /*say* truh-**pee**-zee-uhm/ *noun* a four-sided figure, with only two sides parallel.

WORD HISTORY from a Latin word meaning 'small table'

trash *noun*
1. rubbish or anything worthless or useless. **2.** nonsense or silly ideas or talk. **3.** people thought of as worthless.
–*verb Informal* **4.** To **trash** a place is to do a lot of damage to it: *Some people had a party in our friends' place while they were away, and trashed it.* **5.** To **trash** something that is not wanted is to get rid of it.

trauma /*say* **traw**-muh/ *noun*
1. a cut or injury to the body. **2.** an emotional shock which has a lasting effect on the mind.
☐ **traumatic**, *adjective*

travel *verb* (**travels**, **travelling**, **travelled**, **has travelled**)
1. If you **travel**, you are on a journey: *My father travels to work by car*; *Last year we travelled around Thailand.* **2.** You can say that something **travels** if it moves or goes somewhere: *Can you make the ball travel in a straight line?* **3.** *Informal* To **travel** is to move with speed: *That car was really travelling!*
–*noun* **4.** the act of travelling: *Travel is his main interest in life.* **5.** **travels**, journeys.
☐ **traveller**, *noun*

traverse /*say* truh-**vers**, **trav**-ers/ *verb* To **traverse** something is to pass across, over or through it: *The bridge traversed the river at its widest point.*

trawl *noun*
1. a strong net which is dragged along the sea bottom to catch fish.
–*verb* **2.** To **trawl** is to drag a trawl to catch fish.
☐ **trawler**, *noun* a type of boat used in fishing with a trawl.

ANOTHER TERM (for definition 1) is **trawl net**.

tray *noun* a flat piece of wood, plastic or metal used for holding or carrying things: *She brought out our lunch on a tray.*

treacherous /*say* **trech**-uh-ruhs/ *adjective*
1. A **treacherous** person is one who helps your enemy: *a treacherous ally.* **2.** An area that is **treacherous** is dangerous or risky: *Slow down – this is a treacherous part of the road.*
☐ **treacherously**, *adverb* –**treachery**, *noun*

☑ SPELLING TIP *Tricky vowel sound*: *ea* for the 'e' sound in the first syllable. It might help if you notice the word *reach* is hidden inside **treacherous**.

treacle *noun* a dark, sticky liquid made from sugar.
☐ **treacly**, *adjective*

tread /*rhymes with* led/ *verb* (**treads**, **treading**, **trod**, **has trodden**)
1. If you **tread** on something, you step or stand on it: *Be careful not to tread on the broken glass*; *Her dancing partner kept treading on her toes.* **2.** If you **tread** something into the ground or into a carpet, you crush or press it down with your feet: *The children trod the crumbs into the carpet.* **3.** If you **tread** in a particular way, you walk along in that way: *Tread softly or you'll wake the baby.*
–*noun* **4.** a step, or the sound it makes: *You could hear his tread on the stairs.* **5.** the part, especially of a tyre, which touches the road or any other surface.
–*phrase* **6.** **tread water**, to keep your body in an upright position and your head above water by moving your arms and legs.

treason *noun* the crime of helping an enemy of your country.
☐ **treasonable**, *adjective*

NOTE A person who commits treason is a **traitor**.

treasure /*say* **trezh**-uh/ *noun*
1. something worth a lot of money, such as gold and jewels, or anything which is highly valued: *His CD collection is his greatest treasure.*
–*verb* **2.** If you **treasure** something, you think of it as being precious: *He treasures your friendship.*
☐ **treasured**, *adjective*

☑ SPELLING TIP *Tricky vowel sound*: *ea* for the 'e' sound in the first syllable. Also remember the *sure* ending which sounds like 'zhuh'. Think of other words with this spelling and sound, such as *measure* and *pleasure*.

treasurer /*say* **trezh**-uh-ruh/ *noun*
1. someone in charge of the money belonging to a company, club or city. **2.** the government minister responsible for managing the finances of a country or state.

ANOTHER FORM This word (as in definition 2) is spelt with a capital letter when you are referring to a particular person.

treasury /*say* **trezh**-uh-ree/ *noun*
1. a place where money or valuables are kept. **2. Treasury**, the government department which manages a country's finances.

☑ SPELLING TIP This word is made up of *treasure* (with the final *e* dropped) and the suffix *-y*. See the spelling tip at **treasure**.

treat *verb*
1. If you **treat** someone in a certain way, you behave towards them that way: *He always treats people with kindness and respect*; *We were shocked to see how badly the animals were being treated.* **2.** If you **treat** something in a certain way, you consider it in that way or you handle it in that way: *He treated his punishment as a bit of a joke.* **3.** When a doctor **treats** a patient for an injury or illness, they try to make a patient well by giving them medical care: *There's still no effective way to treat the common cold.* **4.** If you **treat** someone, you pay for some special pleasure for them: *My father treated us all to ice-creams.*
–*noun* **5.** the gift of a drink, dinner or entertainment: *It's my treat this time.*
☐ **treatment**, *noun*

treaty *noun* (*plural* **treaties**) an agreement: *Both countries signed the peace treaty.*

treble *adjective*
1. high-pitched: *a treble voice.* **2.** three times as much as: *It's worth treble the price.*
–*verb* **3.** To **treble** something is to multiply it by three: *to treble the amount you study.*

ANOTHER WORD (for definitions 2 and 3) is **triple**.
THE OPPOSITE (of definition 1) is **bass**.

tree *noun* a plant with a trunk and roots, leaves, and woody branches.

trek *verb* (**treks**, **trekking**, **trekked**, **has trekked**) To **trek** is to walk or travel, especially over a long distance or with much difficulty: *They trekked inland through the jungle, looking for a way over the river.*
☐ **trek**, *noun* –**trekker**, *noun*

WORD HISTORY from a Dutch word meaning 'draw' or 'travel'

☑ SPELLING TIP Note the *k* ending (not *ck*). Also remember that the *k* is doubled when you add *-ed* or *-ing*, or make the word **trekker**.

trellis *noun* a support made of crossing strips of wood or other material, such as for a vine or creeper to grow on.

A SIMILAR WORD is **lattice**.

☑ SPELLING TIP *Double letter alert*: double *l* (think of 'lacy lattice'). Also notice that the ending is *is* (not *us* or *ice*).

tremble *verb*
1. If your body, voice, or part of your body **trembles**, it shakes slightly, usually because you're cold, weak or afraid: *My hands were trembling with the cold*; *Her voice trembled as she spoke.* **2.** If something **trembles**, it shakes slightly: *The leaves trembled in the wind.*
☐ **tremble**, *noun* –**trembly**, *adjective*

A SIMILAR WORD is **quiver**.

tremendous *adjective*
1. very large or important: *a tremendous size*; *It's a tremendous opportunity.* **2.** extremely good: *We had a tremendous time.*
☐ **tremendously**, *adverb*

tremor *noun* a shaking movement: *He has a tremor in his hand*; *An earth tremor shook the town.*

☑ SPELLING TIP *Single letter alert*: only one *m*. Also note the *or* ending. This is not one of those words where there can be either an *our* or *or* ending. It is always spelt *or*.

tremulous /*say* **trem**-yuh-luhs/ *adjective* shaky or uncertain: *Her tremulous voice betrayed her nervousness.*
☐ **tremulously**, *adverb*

trench *noun* (*plural* **trenches**) a long, deep hole in the ground, especially one dug to protect soldiers from enemy fire.

trend *noun*
1. a tendency or movement in a certain direction. **2.** a style or fashion.
–*verb* **3.** If something **trends** on a social network, it appears frequently: *The election is trending on Twitter.*
☐ **trendy**, *adjective* (**trendier**, **trendiest**) fashionable.

trespass *verb* If you **trespass** on someone's land or property, you enter it without their permission: *The boys were caught trespassing on a building site.*
☐ **trespass**, *noun* –**trespasser**, *noun*

trestle /*say* **tres**-uhl/ *noun* a plank supported by legs at each end, used as a kind of table.

☑ SPELLING TIP *Silent letter alert*: don't forget the *st* (not double *s*) spelling. The *t* is silent.

triad /*say* **truy**-ad/ *noun*
1. a group of three closely connected things, such as musical notes in a chord. **2.** a Chinese criminal gang, especially in Hong Kong.
☐ **triadic**, *adjective*

triage /*say* **tree**-ahzh/ *noun*
1. the procedure of sorting sick or injured people according to how urgently they need to be given medical care.
–*adjective* **2.** having to do with triage.
–*verb* **3.** To **triage** a patient is to sort them according to how urgently they need to be given medical care.

WORD HISTORY from a French word meaning 'pick'.

trial *noun*
1. a hearing of the facts or a trying of someone's guilt or innocence in a law court: *His trial will be next month.* **2.** a test or contest: *a trial of strength.* **3.** an experiment: *The trial of the new timetable was fairly successful.* **4.** a cause of suffering: *His young cousin's behaviour was a trial to him.*
–*verb* (**trials**, **trialling**, **trialled**, **has trialled**) **5.** To **trial** something is to test it.
–*phrase* **6. on trial**, going through a test or trial, especially in a law court.

☑ DO NOT CONFUSE **trial** with **trail**. To **trail** something or someone is to follow along behind them. A **trail** is a path through rough country or bush.

triangle *noun*
1. a flat, three-sided shape, formed by three straight lines which meet so as to form three angles. **2.** a percussion instrument made of a piece of metal bent into the shape of a triangle, which is played by striking it with a small metal rod.
☐ **triangular**, *adjective*

tribe *noun*
1. a group of people who believe they have a common ancestor, have many of the same customs and who usually live in the same area. **2.** any large group with something in common: *A tribe of supporters followed the team from game to game.*
☐ **tribal**, *adjective* –**tribally**, *adverb*

tribunal /*say* truy-**byooh**-nuhl/ *noun* a court of justice, or a place where judgements are made.

tributary /*say* **trib**-yuh-tree/ *noun* (*plural* **tributaries**) a stream flowing into a larger river.
☐ **tributary**, *adjective*

tribute *noun* a gift or speech made to show respect or regard for someone.

triceps /*say* **truy**-seps/ *noun* a muscle with three attachments to the bone, especially the muscle at the back of the upper arm.

☑ SPELLING TIP Remember that the first part of **triceps** is spelt *tri* (although it sounds like 'truy'). The prefix *tri-* means 'three', as in *tricycle*. A *tricycle* has three wheels and the **triceps** muscle has three 'heads' (meaning that it is joined at three places).

trick *noun*
1. something done to deceive or amuse. **2.** a skilful or clever act: *For my next trick, I'd like to juggle.* **3.** something which deceives your senses: *There's no-one there, it's just a trick of the light.* **4.** a habit or mannerism: *He has that trick of nodding while you speak.*
–*verb* **5.** If someone **tricks** you, they deceive you, usually in order to make you do something.
–*phrase* **6. do the trick**, to bring about the desired result.
☐ **trickery**, *noun* –**trickster**, *noun*

SIMILAR WORDS (for definition 1) are **hoax**, **practical joke**, **prank** and **ruse**; (for definition 5) **bluff**, **con**, **delude**, **doublecross**, **fool** and **hoodwink**.

trickle *verb* To **trickle** is to flow in a very small or slow stream: *Drops of rain trickled down the window.*
☐ **trickle**, *noun*

tricky *adjective* (**trickier**, **trickiest**)
1. If something is **tricky**, it is difficult to handle or deal with: *a tricky question.* **2.** If someone is **tricky**, they are given to playing tricks, especially in order to cheat or deceive.
☐ **trickiness**, *noun*

tricycle /*say* **truy**-sik-uhl/ *noun* a cycle with three wheels, one at the front and two at the back.

trifle *noun*
1. a small or worthless amount or thing.
–*verb in the phrase* **2. trifle with**, to treat too lightly: *Don't trifle with my feelings.*
☐ **trifler**, *noun*

trigger *noun*
1. the lever on a gun which you press to fire the bullet.
–*verb* **2.** If you **trigger** something, you start it off: *to trigger a reaction.*

WORD HISTORY from a Dutch word meaning 'pull'

trigonometry /*say* trig-uh-**nom**-uh-tree/ *noun* the part of mathematics that studies the relations between the sides and angles of triangles, and the calculations, etc., based on these.
☐ **trigonometric**, *adjective*

trill *noun*
1. a vibrating sound, especially when made up of two notes being rapidly repeated one after the other.
–*verb* **2.** If a sound **trills**, it rings out in a trill giving a vibrating effect.

trillion *noun* a million times a million, or 10^{12}.
☐ **trillion**, *adjective* –**trillionth**, *adjective*, *noun*

NOTE **Trillion** is sometimes used to mean 'a million times a billion', but this meaning is not used very much these days.

trilogy /*say* **tril**-uh-jee/ *noun* a series of three related works, such as three novels or plays.

trim *verb* (**trims**, **trimming**, **trimmed**, **has trimmed**)
1. If you **trim** something, such as your hair or a shrub, you cut small amounts off the ends of it, usually to make it look tidier: *I've just had my hair trimmed.* **2.** If you **trim** a piece of clothing or fabric, you add something to the edge of it in order to decorate it: *She trimmed the blouse with matching lace.*
–*adjective* **3.** If someone is **trim**, they are a healthy size and weight.

trimaran /*say* **truy**-muh-ran/ *noun* a sailing boat with three hulls.

trinity *noun* a group of three.

trinket *noun* a cheap ornament.

trio /*say* **tree**-oh/ *noun*
1. a group of three. **2.** a group of three musicians. **3.** a musical piece for three voices or performers.

trip *noun*
1. a journey: *She is just back from a world trip*; *We took a trip on a train.*
–*verb* (**trips**, **tripping**, **tripped**, **has tripped**) **2.** If you **trip**, your foot gets caught on something while you are walking, and you fall over or nearly fall over: *The boy tripped and fell*; *I tripped over a mat at the entrance to the shop.* **3.** If you **trip** someone, you make them catch their foot on something so that they fall over or nearly fall over. **4.** To **trip** something is to it set off: *He trod on the wire which trips the alarm.*
–*phrase* **5. trip up**, to make or cause to make a mistake.

tripe *noun*
1. the stomach of cattle when it is cleaned and sold as food. **2.** *Informal* worthless rubbish.

triple *verb*
1. To **triple** something is to multiply it by three.
–*adjective* **2.** having three parts: *a triple program.* **3.** three times as great: *a triple quantity.*

ANOTHER WORD (for definitions 1 and 3) is **treble**.

triplet *noun*
1. one of three children born at the same time to the same mother. **2.** a verse of poetry three lines long.

tripod /*say* **truy**-pod/ *noun* a three-legged stool support, such as for a camera.

trite *adjective* A saying or opinion that is **trite** is repeated so often that it is no longer effective or interesting.

triumph /*say* **truy**-umf/ *noun*
1. a victory or success.
–*verb* **2.** If you **triumph**, you achieve victory or success: *At last he triumphed over his fear of heights*; *She triumphed in the end.*
☐ **triumphant**, *adjective* –**triumphantly**, *adverb*

☑ SPELLING TIP Remember the *ph* spelling for the 'f' sound at the end.

trivial *adjective* unimportant: *trivial details.*
☐ **trivia**, *noun* unimportant things. –**trivialise**, *verb* –**triviality**, *noun*

ANOTHER SPELLING for **trivialise** is **trivialize**.
SIMILAR WORDS are **petty** and **trifling**.

troll[1] *noun* someone who posts messages in an internet discussion forum, chat room, etc., that are designed to be upsetting.
☐ **troller**, *noun*

troll[2] *noun* an imaginary being in fairytales, either a dwarf or giant, who lives underground.

trolley *noun*
1. a cart on wheels, used for carrying goods in a shop. **2.** a small table on wheels for carrying such things as food or crockery. **3.** a cart with low sides which runs on tracks: *The miners filled the trolley with ore.*

☑ SPELLING TIP Remember the *ey* (not just *y*) ending.

trombone *noun* a brass wind instrument, on which the notes are changed by sliding a tube in and out.
☐ **trombonist**, *noun*

WORD HISTORY from an Italian word meaning 'trumpet'

troop *noun*
1. a group or band of people, animals, or things: *a circus troop*; *a troop of scouts.* **2. troops**, a large number of soldiers.
–*verb* **3.** If people **troop** somewhere, they walk there together in a large group: *The children all trooped down the stairs after their teacher.*
☐ **trooper**, *noun*

trophy /*say* **troh**-fee/ *noun* (*plural* **trophies**)
1. a prize won in a contest. **2.** a souvenir kept from a war or a hunt.

tropic *noun*
1. either of two lines of latitude $23\frac{1}{2}°$ north and south of the equator, known as the **Tropic of Cancer** and the **Tropic of Capricorn**. **2. the tropics**, the area of land lying between these bands.
☐ **tropical**, *adjective*

trot *verb* (**trots**, **trotting**, **trotted**, **has trotted**) hen an animal such as a horse **trots** it moves at a fast but steady speed, with a gait in which a front leg moves at the same time as the opposite back leg.
☐ **trot**, *noun*: *to go at a trot.*

troubadour /*say* **trooh**-buh-daw/ *noun* a minstrel or ballad singer.

☑ SPELLING TIP Remember that the ending is *our* (not *or*). This is because **troubadour** comes from French.

trouble /*rhymes with* bubble/ *verb*
1. If something **troubles** you, it makes you feel upset or worried: *His parents are very troubled by his lack of enthusiasm*; *What troubles me is that we may not finish on time.* **2.** You can use **trouble** when you want to ask someone to do something for you: *May I trouble you to post this letter for me?*
–*noun* **3.** a difficulty or an unhappy situation: *to make trouble*; *to be in trouble.* **4.** effort: *She went to a lot of trouble to find it.* **5.** any problem or disorder: *industrial trouble*; *heart trouble.*
□ **troubled**, *adjective*: *a troubled expression.* –**troublemaker**, *noun* –**troublesome**, *adjective* –**troubling**, *adjective*: *troubling news.*

NOTE This word (as in definition 2) is rather formal.

trough /*rhymes with* off/ *noun*
1. a long, low container for animal feed or water, or any similar hole in the ground. **2.** an area of low pressure on a weather map.

☑ SPELLING TIP Remember that there is no *f* in **trough** – the spelling *ough* gives the 'off' sound, as it does in *cough*.

trounce *verb* To **trounce** someone is to defeat them utterly: *We trounced the opposition in the finals.*

troupe /*say* troohp/ *noun* a band or group of entertainers: *A troupe of variety performers took the stage.*
□ **trouper**, *noun*

☑ SPELLING TIP Don't confuse the spelling of **troupe** with **troop** which has the same sound and a related meaning. A **troop** is a group of soldiers or a group of people in general. **Troupe** is the French word for 'troop'. It is used with this spelling in English only to refer to a group of entertainers.

trousers *plural noun* clothing for the lower half of the body from waist to ankle, divided into two parts for the legs.

trousseau /*say* **trooh**-soh/ *noun* (*plural* **trousseaux** /*say* **trooh**-soh, **trooh**-sohz/ *or* **trousseaus**) linen and clothes collected by a woman for her marriage.

☑ SPELLING TIP *Tricky vowel sound: eau* spelling for the 'oh' sound at the end. **Trousseau** has this spelling because it comes from French. Another word like this is *bureau*.

trout *noun* (*plural* **trout**) a freshwater fish related to the salmon.

trowel *noun*
1. a flat tool with a handle used for spreading cement or plaster. **2.** a small garden spade.

truant *noun* someone who stays away from school without permission.
□ **truancy**, *noun* –**truant**, *adjective*

truce *noun* an agreement to end fighting for a time: *Both sides agreed to call a truce during the religious festival.*

A SIMILAR WORD is **armistice**.

truck *noun*
1. a motor vehicle with a back part for carrying goods. **2.** a railway goods carriage.
–*verb* **3.** If goods are **trucked** somewhere, they are transported by truck.

trudge *verb* To **trudge** is to walk heavily or slowly: *He trudged upstairs in his boots.*

true *adjective*
1. A **true** statement is based on facts and on real events: *I didn't know whether to believe him but he assured me that the story was true.* **2.** If you describe something as **true**, you mean that it has all the features of a particular thing and is real: *You're a true hero*; *He always hides his true feelings.* **3.** If someone is **true**, they are loyal: *As long as you need me, I'll be true.*
–*adverb* **4.** truly, or in a true manner: *Tell me true.*
–*phrase* **5. come true**, of a prediction or wish, to actually happen: *Her wish came true when she won the overseas holiday.*
□ **truism**, *noun* –**truly**, *adverb*

trump *noun*
1. in some card games, a card of a specially chosen suit (**trumps**), all the cards of which rank higher than any card of the other suits for a particular round of the game.
–*verb* **2.** To **trump** someone in a card game is to beat their card by playing a trump.
–*phrase* **3. trump up**, to invent dishonestly: *As usual, Lenny trumped up a reason to explain the missing paintings.*

trumpet *noun*
1. a brass wind instrument with a flared end.
–*verb* (**trumpets**, **trumpeting**, **trumpeted**, **has trumpeted**) **2.** To **trumpet** is to sound a trumpet or make a similar loud noise: *The elephants trumpeted to each other.* **3.** If you **trumpet** news or information, you tell it far and wide: *She trumpeted the news all around the school.*
□ **trumpeter**, *noun*

truncheon /*say* **trun**-shuhn/ *noun* a short stick or club, as used by police to keep order or defend themselves.

WORD HISTORY from a Latin word meaning 'stump'

trundle *verb* To **trundle** is to roll along, or to move on wheels: *Coal trucks trundled along tunnels deep below.*

trunk *noun*
1. the main or central part: *the trunk of a tree.* **2.** the main part of the body without the head, legs or arms. **3.** a box or chest for storing or transporting possessions. **4.** the long nose of an elephant.

ANOTHER WORD (for definition 2) is **torso**.

truss *verb*
1. To **truss** a person or thing is to bind or secure them: *The men were found trussed and gagged; Dad stuffed the turkey and then trussed it.* **2.** To **truss** something like a bridge is to support it, for example with bars and beams.
☐ **truss**, *noun*

trust *noun*
1. belief or confidence: *I have trust in you.* **2.** the expectation that someone can or will pay: *Can I take it on trust and pay you tomorrow?* **3.** responsibility: *a position of trust.* **4.** money or property held and managed by one person for another or others.
–*verb* **5.** If you **trust** someone, you believe they are honest and that you can depend on them: *It's hard to trust people who keep breaking promises.* **6.** If you say that you **trust** something will happen, you mean that you hope or expect it to happen: *I trust you will be there.*

trustee *noun* someone who manages business or property for another.

trustworthy *adjective* deserving of trust or confidence: *a trustworthy friend.*
☐ **trustworthiness**, *noun*

truth *noun*
1. what has really happened: *We need to find out the truth about the accident.* **2.** honesty: *We doubted the truth of his story.* **3.** a generally accepted fact or principle: *a scientific truth.*
☐ **truthful**, *adjective* –**truthfully**, *adverb*

try *verb* (**tries**, **trying**, **tried**, **has tried**)
1. If you **try** to do something that you want to do, you make an effort to do it: *He tried to fix it but failed; Try and do it by yourself.* **2.** If you **try** something, you do it or use it to find out how good or useful it is: *He tried two phones before he found one that worked.* **3.** If you **try** a place or person, you go to that place or person because you think you could get something you want from them: *He tried the hardware store but they didn't have what he needed.* **4.** If someone is **tried**, they go to a court, and a judge and jury decides if they are guilty of a crime that they have been accused of: *His case will be tried next week.* **5.** If you **try** someone's patience, you make it hard for them to stay patient: *His constant complaining tries my patience.*
–*noun* (*plural* **tries**) **6.** an instance of trying to do something: *have another try.*

A SIMILAR WORD (for definitions 1 and 6) is **attempt**.

tsar /*say* zah/ *noun* the emperor of Russia in earlier times.

☑ SPELLING TIP Another spelling is **czar**. Notice that both the spellings begin with a silent letter, either a *t* or a *c*.

T-shirt *noun* a light shirt, usually short-sleeved and without a collar.

ANOTHER SPELLING is **tee-shirt**.

tsunami /*say* sooh-**nah**-mee, tsooh-**nah**-mee/ *noun* an extremely large, often destructive sea wave caused by an earthquake beneath the sea.

ANOTHER TERM for this is **tidal wave**.

☑ SPELLING TIP *Silent letter alert*: don't forget the *t* at the beginning of this word, which is often not heard in the pronunciation. Also remember the *i* at the end. The word **tsunami** has an unusual spelling because it comes from Japanese.

tuan *noun* a small marsupial that looks like a mouse with a hairy-tipped tail. It lives mainly in trees and is endangered.

ANOTHER NAME for this is **phascogale**.
WORD HISTORY from an Aboriginal language of Victoria called Wathawurung

tub *noun* a round, flat-bottomed container: *a laundry tub; a tub of ice-cream.*

tuba /*say* **tyooh**-buh/ *noun* a brass wind instrument with a very low pitch.

☑ SPELLING TIP Don't confuse the spelling of **tuba** with **tuber** which has the same sound but is spelt with *er* at the end. A **tuber** is an underground stem, such as a potato.

tubby *adjective* (**tubbier**, **tubbiest**) short and fat.
☐ **tubbiness**, *noun*

tube *noun*
1. a narrow, hollow pipe which liquid or gas can flow through. **2.** a soft, narrow container, sealed at one end, with a lid at the other: *a toothpaste tube; a tube of paint.*

tuber /*say* **tyooh**-buh/ *noun* an underground plant stem, such as a potato, from which new plants may grow.

WORD HISTORY from a Latin word meaning 'bump' or 'swelling'

☑ SPELLING TIP Don't confuse the spelling of **tuber** with **tuba** which has the same sound but is spelt with *a* at the end. A **tuba** is a large, brass wind instrument.

tuberculosis /*say* tuh-ber-kyuh-**loh**-suhs/ *noun* an infectious disease of the lungs in which small lumps or swellings are produced.
☐ **tubercular**, *adjective* –**tuberculous**, *adjective*

THE ABBREVIATION is **TB**.

tuck *verb*
1. If you **tuck** one thing such as cloth or paper into another, you push or fold the loose edges of it inside the other thing so that it looks tidy: *Tuck your shirt into your trousers.* **2.** If you **tuck** something somewhere, you press it into a place where it will be safe: *He tucked the coins into his pocket.*
–*noun* **3.** a narrow fold: *You'll need to sew a tuck in the waist.*
–*phrase* **4. tuck in, a.** to cover snugly with the bed clothes: *My mother tucks me in each night.* **b.** *Informal* to eat heartily.

tucker *noun Informal and rather old-fashioned* food: *I feel like some tucker.*

tuckshop *noun* a school canteen.

Tuesday *noun* the third day of the week.

THE ABBREVIATION is **Tue** or **Tues**.
WORD HISTORY from a Latin word meaning 'day of Mars'

tuft *noun* an upright bunch, such as of hair, grass or feathers.
☐ **tufted**, *adjective*

tug *verb* (**tugs**, **tugging**, **tugged**, **has tugged**)
1. If you **tug** something or at something, you pull it with quick, strong movements: *The boy kept tugging at his mother's sleeve to get her attention.* **2.** To **tug** something is to pull it along, as with a tugboat.
–*noun* **3.** a hard pull. **4.** See **tugboat**.

tugboat *noun* a small, powerful boat which is used to pull along other ships.

THE SHORT FORM of this is **tug**.

tuition /*say* tyooh-**ish**-uhn/ *noun* teaching: *He needs extra tuition in maths.*

☑ SPELLING TIP Remember that this word has two separate *t*'s – one at the beginning and one as part of the *tion* ending which, as in many other words, sounds like 'shuhn'.

tulip *noun* a cup-shaped flower of various colours, which grows from a bulb.

tumble *verb*
1. If you **tumble**, you fall with a circular or rolling movement: *He tumbled off his bicycle as he turned the corner.* **2.** If something **tumbles**, it falls or rolls along quickly: *The pile of books came tumbling down as I reached for it; The prices in the stock market tumbled.*
☐ **tumble**, *noun*

tumbler *noun* a drinking glass.

tummy *noun* (*plural* **tummies**) *Informal* the stomach, where food is partly digested.

tumour *noun* an abnormal swelling in someone's body, especially one made up of an unusual growth of cells.

ANOTHER SPELLING is **tumor**.

tumult /*say* **tyooh**-mult/ *noun*
1. a noisy disturbance or uproar. **2.** a mental or emotional disturbance: *Seeing her mother after so many years caused a tumult of emotions.*
☐ **tumultuous**, *adjective*

tuna *noun* (*plural* **tuna** *or* **tunas**) a large sea fish with pink flesh, used for food.

tundra *noun* a treeless Arctic plain with mosses, lichens and dwarfed plants.

WORD HISTORY from a Russian word meaning 'marshy plain'

tune *noun*
1. a number of musical notes, played or sung, one after the other, that form a pattern. **2.** correct pitch: *My guitar is out of tune.*
–*verb* **3.** To **tune** a musical instrument is to change it so that it has correct pitch. **4.** To **tune** an engine, television or radio is to change it so that it works properly: *If you tune the TV you'll get a better picture.*
–*phrase* **5. call the tune**, to be in a position to command or control. **6. change your tune**, to change your opinions.
☐ **tuneful**, *adjective* –**tuner**, *noun*

tunic *noun*
1. a coat worn as part of a military or other uniform. **2.** a sleeveless dress worn as part of a school uniform.

tunnel *noun*
1. an underground passage, especially a large one for trains or cars.
–*verb* (**tunnels**, **tunnelling**, **tunnelled**, **has tunnelled**) **2.** If someone or something **tunnels** somewhere, they make a tunnel: *The wombat tunnelled into the side of the river bank.*

☑ SPELLING TIP *Double/single letter alert*: double *n* in the middle and only one *l* at the end. However, when you add *-ed* or *-ing*, the *l* is doubled.

turban *noun* a head covering, usually worn by men in some religions, made of a long piece of cloth wound around the head.

turbine *noun* a turning motor in which a wheel with blades is driven by a liquid or gas passing through it.

turbulence *noun* violent disturbance or storminess in the air.
☐ **turbulent**, *adjective*

tureen /*say* tuh-**reen**, tyooh-**reen**/ *noun* a large, deep dish with a cover, for holding soup at the table.

turf *noun* (*plural* **turfs** *or* **turves**)
1. a grass surface including both the grass and the earth in which the roots are growing. 2. a piece of this.
–*verb in the phrase* 3. **turf out**, *Informal* to throw out something because you no longer need it.

turkey *noun* a large bird, originally from America, bred for eating.

NOTE The male is a **cock**; the female is a **hen**; the young is a **poult**.

turmoil *noun* wild disorder: *The school was in turmoil when the electricity failed.*

turn *verb*
1. If you **turn** something or if it **turns**, it moves around a particular point. It keeps moving around, or it stops and faces in a different direction: *The wheels of the car were turning quickly*; *He turned the page and saw the photo.* 2. If you **turn**, you change the position of your body so that you face in a different direction: *He turned to look at the clock.* 3. If you **turn** in a particular direction or turn a corner, you change the direction in which you are moving: *Turn right at the next street.* 4. If you **turn** a handle, key, and so on, you twist it with your hand in order to control or start something: *She turned the key to start the car.* 5. If something **turns** red, cold, violent, etc., it becomes red, cold, violent, etc.: *He turned nasty*; *Her face turned white.* 6. If you **turn** something into something else, you change it to be that thing: *She turned the bits of metal into a beautiful sculpture.*
–*noun* 7. a movement of rotation, whether complete or not: *a slight turn of the handle.* 8. a chance to do something or get something, coming in order to each of a number of people: *It's my turn to choose.* 9. a change of direction: *He made a turn to the right.*
–*phrase* 10. **take turns**, to do in order one after another. 11. **turn off**, a. to stop the flow of: *to turn off the tap.* b. to switch off: *to turn off the light.* c. to start a strong dislike in: *His bad manners turned me off.* d. to lose interest in: *to turn off basketball.* 12. **turn on**, a. to start the supply of: *Turn on the water.* b. to excite or interest: *That band really turns me on.* 13. **turn out**, a. to switch off: *Turn out the light.* b. to produce or make: *The factory turns out 300 packets an hour.* c. to become or develop: *She has turned out well.* d. to come along: *A large crowd turned out to hear her.* 14. **turn up**, a. to arrive: *He turned up unexpectedly.* b. to be found: *Have your keys turned up yet?* c. to increase the strength of: *Turn up the music.* d. to fold, especially so as to shorten: *She turned up the legs of the jeans.*

turnip *noun* a plant with a thick white or yellow root which is eaten as a vegetable.

turnstile *noun* a turning gate that allows one person to pass at a time.

turntable *noun* the turning surface on which a record in a gramophone rests.

turpentine *noun*
1. an oil used for dissolving paint; originally from a tree, now usually made from petroleum. 2. a very tall, rough-barked tree, commonly found in eastern Australia.

THE SHORT FORM (of definition 1) is **turps**.

turquoise /*say* **ter**-kwoyz/ *noun*
1. a greenish-blue stone used in jewellery. 2. a greenish-blue colour.
☐ **turquoise**, *adjective*

☑ SPELLING TIP **Turquoise** comes from a French word meaning 'Turkish'. This will help you to remember the *tur* spelling at the start. Also notice the *qu* spelling for the 'kw' sound.

turret *noun* a small tower at a corner of a building.

turtle *noun* any of various reptiles which have flippers and a hard shell covering their bodies, most of which live in the sea.

COMPARE this with **tortoise**.

tusk *noun* the very long tooth, usually one of a pair, that certain animals such as the elephant or walrus have.

tussle *verb* If people **tussle**, they struggle or fight roughly.
☐ **tussle**, *noun*

tussock *noun* a tuft or clump of grass.

tutor *noun* a teacher, especially either one who teaches privately or one in a university.

tutu *noun* a short ballet skirt, usually made out of layers of net-like material.

tuxedo /*say* tuk-**see**-doh/ *noun* a man's black jacket, worn on formal occasions.

WORD HISTORY named after a US country club at *Tuxedo* Park, in New York State

TV *noun* See **television**.

tweed *noun* a rough woollen cloth in a variety of weaves and colours, originally from Scotland.

tweet[1] *noun*
1. the weak chirp of a young or small bird.
–*verb* 2. When a bird **tweets**, it utters a tweet or tweets.

tweet[2] *verb*
1. To **tweet** is to post a message on the social network site Twitter.
–*noun* 2. such a message.

tweezers *plural noun* small pincers for pulling out hairs or picking up small objects.

twelve *noun*
1. a cardinal number, ten plus two (10+2). **2.** a symbol for this number, as 12 or XII.
☐ **twelfth**, *adjective*, *noun* –**twelve**, *adjective*

☑ SPELLING TIP Notice in particular the spelling of the adjective and noun form **twelfth**. When you add the *-th* ending, not only do you drop the final *e* of **twelve**, but the *v* changes to an *f*.

twenty *noun* (*plural* **twenties**)
1. a cardinal number, ten times two (10×2). **2.** a symbol for this number, as 20 or XX. **3. twenties**, the numbers from 20 to 29 of a series, especially with reference to the years of a person's age, or the years of a century, especially the 20th.
☐ **twentieth**, *adjective*, *noun* –**twenty**, *adjective*

twice *adverb*
1. two times: *Write twice a week*; *I've been to Brisbane twice.* **2.** doubly: *twice as much*; *twice as big.*

twiddle *verb* If you **twiddle** something, you turn it round and round, especially in a useless or irritating way: *to twiddle your thumbs*; *to twiddle the radio dial.*

twig *noun* a small, thin branch of a tree.

twilight *noun* the weak light from the sky after sunset.

☑ SPELLING TIP Notice that **twilight** contains the word *light* with its *ight* spelling.

twin *noun*
1. one of two children or animals born at the same birth. **2.** one of two things that match or look like each other.
☐ **twin**, *adjective*

twine *verb*
1. If you **twine** something, you twist or wind it: *She twined her fingers through her hair*; *She twined her hair into a knot.*
–*noun* **2.** string made of two or more threads twisted together.

twinge *noun* a pain that lasts only a moment: *a twinge of rheumatism*; *a twinge of regret.*

twinkle *verb* To **twinkle** is to shine with little flashes of light: *The stars twinkled in the sky*; *His eyes twinkled with amusement.*
☐ **twinkle**, *noun*: *the twinkle in your eye.*

twirl *verb* To **twirl** is to spin rapidly: *The dancers twirled around the room.*

twist *verb*
1. If you **twist** something or if it twists, one end of it moves or turns in one direction while the other end turns in the opposite direction or remains in the same position: *She twisted the end of the plastic bag and tied a knot in it*; *He twisted around to see who was sitting behind him.* **2.** If something **twists** or is **twisted**, it bends or moves out of its natural shape: *Her face was twisted in pain.* **3.** If you **twist** part of your body, such as your wrist or ankle, you injure it by turning it too far in an unusual direction: *He twisted his ankle when he jumped off the bus.* **4.** If you **twist** something, you turn it around in a circular direction: *Twist the knob to the left to open the door.* **5.** If a river or road **twists**, it has sharp turns or bends along it. **6.** If you **twist** what someone has said, you change the intended meaning of it: *She always manages to twist my words to make me look like a fool.*
☐ **twist**, *noun* –**twisted**, *adjective*

twitch *verb*
1. If you **twitch** something, you give it a short, sudden pull: *He twitched the rope out of her hands.* **2.** If something **twitches**, it gives a slight but sudden movement: *His mouth twitched with fear.*
☐ **twitch**, *noun* –**twitchy**, *adjective* (**twitchier**, **twitchiest**): *She was very twitchy as the exams approached.*

two *noun*
1. a cardinal number, one plus one (1+1). **2.** a symbol for this number, as 2 or II.
–*phrase* **3. put two and two together**, to draw an answer or judgement from certain facts, events, and so on.
☐ **two**, *adjective*

☑ SPELLING TIP Remember the *w* in **two**. Don't confuse it with **to** or **too**, both of which have the same sound. **To** indicates movement in the direction of a place or person; **too** means 'also', 'in addition', or 'more than is required'.

NOTE Something or someone that is number two, or comes next after the first, is the **second**.

two-up *noun* a game in which two coins are spun in the air and bets are laid on both falling either heads up or tails up.

tycoon *noun* a businessperson who is very rich and powerful.

type *noun*
1. a kind: *a type of vegetable.* **2.** metal letters used in the past for printing. **3.** printed letters: *a word in bold type.*
–*verb* **4.** To **type** is to write using a keyboard: *to type a letter.*
☐ **typist**, *noun*

typewriter *noun* a machine with a keyboard, which produces numbers and letters like those used in printing.

typhoid /*say* **tuy**-foyd/ *noun* a serious infectious disease that affects the intestines, causing fever and often death.

ANOTHER FORM The full name is **typhoid fever**.

typhoon /*say* tuy-**foohn**/ *noun* a violent storm like a cyclone or hurricane.

☑ SPELLING TIP *Letter 'y' alert*: don't forget the *ty* start to this word (from the Greek word *typhon* meaning 'violent wind'). Also remember the *ph* spelling for the 'f' sound (think of a 'powerful hurricane' to remind you).

typical /*say* **tip**-i-kuhl/ *adjective*
1. Something that is **typical** of a particular group or class of things has the main signs or the distinctive qualities of that group of things: *a typical summer's day*; *typical tropical plants.* **2.** If someone's behaviour is **typical** of them, it is their usual behaviour: *She spoke with typical honesty.*
☐ **typically**, *adverb*

tyranny /*say* **ti**-ruh-nee/ *noun*
1. complete or unchecked power. **2.** unfairly harsh government.
☐ **tyrannise**, *verb*

ANOTHER SPELLING for **tyrannise** is **tyrannize**.

☑ SPELLING TIP *Letter 'y' alert*: don't forget the *ty* start to this word. Also remember that there is one *r*, but a double *n*.

tyrant /*say* **tuy**-ruhnt/ *noun*
1. a ruler of a country who has unlimited power. **2.** anyone in a position of power who uses it cruelly and unjustly.

tyre *noun* a rubber tube fitted around the wheel of a vehicle.

☑ SPELLING TIP Don't confuse the spelling of **tyre** with **tire** which sounds the same. If something **tires** you, you want to have some sleep or rest. The spelling **tire** is also used in American English for the band around a wheel, but the spelling you should learn for this is **tyre**.

U u

udder *noun* the part of the body which produces milk in some female animals, such as cows and goats, usually hanging and bag-like and with more than one teat.

UFO /*say* yooh ef **oh**/ *noun* (*plural* **UFOs** *or* **UFO's**) an unknown object seen flying in the sky.

WORD HISTORY short for *unidentified flying object*

ugly *adjective* (**uglier**, **ugliest**) If something or someone is **ugly**, they are not pleasant to look at.
☐ **ugliness**, *noun*

ukulele /*say* yooh-kuh-**lay**-lee/ *noun* a musical instrument like a small guitar but with only four strings.

WORD HISTORY from a Hawaiian word meaning 'jumping flea'

ulcer *noun* a sore which is slow to heal, on the skin or on an inside part of the body like the lining of the stomach.
☐ **ulcerate**, *verb* –**ulcerous**, *adjective*

ultimate /*say* **ul**-tuh-muht/ *adjective* final or most important: *The ultimate objective is to get to the finals.*
☐ **ultimately**, *adverb*

☑ SPELLING TIP *Tricky 'uh' sound*: the middle vowel sound is spelt *i*. Also remember the *ate* ending (which sounds like 'uht'). Rap it out as *ul+ti+mate*.

ultimatum /*say* ul-tuh-**may**-tuhm/ *noun* (*plural* **ultimatums** *or* **ultimata**) a final statement of terms or conditions: *He issued an ultimatum that if we didn't come to training, we would not be in the team.*

ultra- *prefix* a word part meaning **1.** beyond, as in *ultraviolet*. **2.** excessively, as in *ultralight*.

WORD HISTORY this prefix comes from Latin

ultrasound *noun* sound waves often used instead of X-rays to make images of things inside the body.

ultraviolet *adjective* beyond the violet end of the light range: *The ultraviolet light rays from the sun can burn you.*

umbilical cord /*say* um-**bil**-uh-kuhl kawd, um-buh-**luy**-kuhl/ *noun* the tube which connects an unborn baby or animal to the lining of its mother's womb, and through which it receives food and oxygen.

umbrella *noun* a circular screen on a portable structure which is used for a shelter against rain or sun.

WORD HISTORY from an Italian word meaning 'shade'

umpire *noun*
1. someone who makes certain that a game is played according to the rules. **2.** someone asked to make a decision in an argument between two or more other people or parties.
–*verb* **3.** If someone **umpires** a game of sport, they act as an umpire in it.

ANOTHER WORD for this is **referee**.

un- *prefix* a word part meaning **1.** not, as in *uncertain*. **2.** the opposite, as in *undo*.

WORD HISTORY this prefix comes from Old English

unanimous /*say* yooh-**nan**-uh-muhs/ *adjective* If a decision is **unanimous**, everyone involved is in complete agreement: *There was a unanimous decision to add lamingtons to the canteen list.*
☐ **unanimity** /*say* yooh-nuh-**nim**-uh-tee/, *noun* –**unanimously**, *adverb*

☑ SPELLING TIP The first part of this word, *un*, comes from *unus* the Latin word for 'one', just as it does in *union*. This is why it makes a 'yoohn' sound. The other part of the word comes from *animus*, the Latin word for 'mind'. Note that the Latin *us* ending has been replaced with the English adjective suffix *-ous*. So when people are **unanimous**, they are 'of one mind'.

unassuming *adjective* modest or not making any special claims about yourself: *Her quiet unassuming manner won her many friends.*

unbending *adjective* firm or determined: *He had a cold, unbending personality.*

uncanny *adjective* weird or unnatural: *I had an uncanny sensation that somebody was watching me.*
☐ **uncannily**, *adverb* –**uncanniness**, *noun*

uncertain *adjective*
1. not sure: *I am uncertain what the cost is.* **2.** not to be depended on: *Her future prospects are uncertain.*
☐ **uncertainly**, *adverb* –**uncertainty**, *noun*

☑ SPELLING TIP See **certain**.

uncle *noun*
1. the brother of your father or mother. 2. your aunt's husband.

unconscious /*say* un-**kon**-shuhs/ *adjective*
1. If you are **unconscious**, you are not aware of what is going on around you, usually because you are sick or injured: *She was unconscious when her wisdom teeth were taken out.* 2. If you are **unconscious** of something, you are not aware of it: *She was absorbed in eating and unconscious of the fact that everyone else was waiting till the whole table was served.*
☐ **unconsciously**, *adverb* –**unconsciousness**, *noun*

☑ SPELLING TIP See **conscious**.

uncouth /*say* un-**koohth**/ *adjective* rough and bad-mannered.

under *preposition*
1. beneath: *under a table*; *under the sea*; *under a window.* 2. with the weight or burden of: *to sink under a load.* 3. less than: *under one kilo.* 4. subject to the power, direction, and so on, of: *under someone's influence*; *under supervision*; *born under a lucky star.* 5. in accordance with: *under the provisions of the law.* 6. in the process of: *under repair.*
–*adverb* 7. beneath the surface: *to go under.*
☐ **under**, *adjective*: *the under surface.*

underarm *adverb* in sporting movements, with the arm remaining below the shoulder: *Bowling underarm is discouraged in cricket.*
☐ **underarm**, *adjective*: *underarm deodorant.*

undercarriage *noun* the parts of an aeroplane under the body, which support it on the ground or when taking off and landing.

undercurrent *noun*
1. a current under the surface of the water. 2. a hidden condition or tendency: *There was an undercurrent of mutual suspicion which weakened the group.*

underestimate *verb* To **underestimate** something is to judge it at too low a rate, value or amount: *We underestimated how much money to put aside for the teacher's present and had to use some of the picnic money.*

undergo *verb* (**undergoes**, **undergoing**, **underwent**, **has undergone**) If you **undergo** something, you 1. experience or go through it: *Dad has to undergo a driving test to operate trucks.* 2. suffer: *You would not believe what people undergo in that country.*

undergraduate *noun* a university student who has not yet received a degree.

underground *adjective*
1. If something is **underground**, it is underneath the ground: *Many farmers depend on underground water sources.* 2. If a movement or group is described as **underground**, it is secret or illegal: *During the war she worked for an underground organisation fighting against the invaders.*
☐ **underground**, *adverb*: *The cables run underground.*

undergrowth *noun* shrubs and low plants growing beneath or among trees.

underhand *adjective* secret and sly: *We could tell that something underhand had gone on but we couldn't prove it.*

underline *verb*
1. If you **underline** writing, you draw a line underneath it. 2. If you **underline** a point you are making, you stress the importance of it.

underneath *preposition* under or beneath: *He proposed to her underneath the old gum tree.*

underpants *plural noun* an article of underwear covering the lower part of the body from the waist to the top of the legs.

underpass *noun* a road or pathway which goes under a railway or another road.

understand *verb* (**understands**, **understanding**, **understood**, **has understood**)
1. If you **understand** something, it is clear to you in your mind: *Do you understand the maths homework?* 2. If you **understand** someone, you see the meaning of what they are telling you: *She spoke so fast that I couldn't understand her.* 3. If you **understand** a word or a language, you know its meaning: *I understand Italian but I can't speak it very well.* 4. If you **understand** someone or something, you are aware of their nature and why they behave in a certain way: *I understand why you are angry.*
☐ **understandable**, *adjective*

understanding *noun*
1. ability to understand or grasp ideas. 2. knowledge: *His understanding in many areas of music is quite remarkable.* 3. a private agreement: *They had an understanding about who would use the bathroom first in the morning.*
–*adjective* 4. sympathetic: *He gave her an understanding look.*
–*phrase* 5. **on the understanding that**, on condition that: *He lent her the money on the understanding that it would be repaid within a month.*

understate *verb* If someone **understates** something, they describe it as being less than what it actually is: *The man had understated his income and had to pay a lot of money to the Tax Office.*
☐ **understatement**, *noun*

understudy *noun* (*plural* **understudies**) an actor or singer who stands by to replace someone who is unable to perform, usually because of illness.

undertake *verb* (**undertakes**, **undertaking**, **undertook**, **has undertaken**) If you **undertake** to do something, you promise to do it: *The school band undertook to play at the hospital fete.*

undertaker *noun* someone whose job is to prepare bodies for burial or cremation, and arrange funerals.

undertaking *noun*
1. a solemn promise to do something: *We made an undertaking to be there early.* **2.** a task: *It is not an easy undertaking looking after my little niece.*

underwear *noun* clothing such as singlets, and underpants and bras, worn under other clothes.

underworld *noun*
1. the world of criminals and criminal activities. **2.** according to ancient myth, a world beneath the earth which is inhabited by the spirits of all the people who have died.

undo *verb* (**undoes**, **undoing**, **undid**, **has undone**) If you **undo** something, you open, untie or release it: *Carefully, she undid the bandage.*

unearth *verb*
1. If you **unearth** something, you dig it up out of the ground: *The dog unearthed a bone.* **2.** If you **unearth** something, you find it after a lot of searching: *They finally unearthed the book under a pile of rubbish.*

uneasy *adjective* (**uneasier**, **uneasiest**) If you are **uneasy** about something, you feel anxious and worried about it: *I felt uneasy about lying to my mother.*
☐ **unease**, *noun* –**uneasily**, *adverb* –**uneasiness**, *noun*

unfeeling *adjective* not caring or sympathetic towards other people.

unfold *verb*
1. If you **unfold** something, you spread or open it out. **2.** If a story **unfolds**, it becomes known little by little.

unforeseen *adjective* not expected: *Unless something unforeseen crops up, we should get there by 4 o'clock.*

unfortunate *adjective* not lucky: *You were very unfortunate to miss out on a ticket to the concert*; *It was unfortunate that it rained on the day of the picnic.*
☐ **unfortunately**, *adverb*

ungainly *adjective* clumsy or awkward.
☐ **ungainliness**, *noun*

unicorn /*say* **yooh**-nuh-kawn/ *noun* an imaginary animal like a horse with a single, long horn growing in the middle of its forehead.

WORD HISTORY from a Latin word meaning 'having one horn'

uniform *noun* distinctive clothes, usually all the same, worn by people to show they have a particular job or go to a particular school.
☐ **uniform**, *adjective* the same everywhere or for everyone.: *The uniform reaction was one of surprise.* –**uniformity**, *noun* –**uniformly**, *adverb*

unify /*say* **yooh**-nuh-fuy/ *verb* (**unifies**, **unifying**, **unified**, **has unified**) If something **unifies** things or people, it makes them join together as a single unit: *Anger about the new building development has unified everyone in the neighbourhood.*
☐ **unification**, *noun*

A SIMILAR WORD is **unite**.

uninterested *adjective* If you are **uninterested** in something, you do not want to know about something. You lack interest in it: *Some people are completely uninterested in dogs.*
☐ **uninteresting**, *adjective*

☑ DO NOT CONFUSE this with **disinterested**. If you are **disinterested**, you are not involved in something and so are able to be fair in judging it.

union /*say* **yoohn**-yuhn/ *noun*
1. a number of things joined together as one. **2.** See **trade union**.

unique /*say* yooh-**neek**/ *adjective* To be **unique** is be different from all the others: *A person's DNA is unique to them.*
☐ **uniquely**, *adverb* –**uniqueness**, *noun*

☑ SPELLING TIP Remember the *ique* spelling of the 'eek' sound in this word which comes from French. The first part of this word, *un*, comes from *unus* the Latin word for 'one', just as it does in *union*. This is why it makes a 'yooh' sound.

unisex *adjective* suitable for both females and males: *a unisex hair salon.*

unison /*say* **yooh**-nuh-suhn/ *noun in the phrase* **in unison** singing or saying the same thing all together: *It is usually easier to sing in unison than to sing in parts.*

unit *noun*
1. a single person or thing or the whole of a group of people or things. **2.** an amount used in measurement: *A gram is the basic unit of weight.* **3.** one out of a number of separately owned homes in the same building.

OTHER WORDS (for definition 3) are **flat** and **apartment**. See the note at **flat**^{2}.

unite *verb* To **unite** is to join together as one: *Everybody united to vote out the unpopular leader.*
☐ **united**, *adjective*: *united opposition.*

unity /*say* **yooh**-nuh-tee/ *noun*
1. the state of being one or a united whole. **2.** a feeling of agreement in a group.

universal *adjective* including and affecting everyone, everything and every place.
☐ **universality**, *noun* –**universally**, *adverb*

universe *noun* the whole of space and everything that exists in it.

ANOTHER WORD for this is **cosmos**.

university *noun* (*plural* **universities**) a place where research is done and where you can study to earn a degree after secondary education.

THE SHORT FORM of this, used in rather informal language, is **uni**.

unleaded petrol /*say* un-**led**-uhd/ *noun* petrol that does not contain tiny bits of lead and is therefore not as harmful to people and the environment.

COMPARE this with **leaded petrol**.

unless *conjunction* except on condition that: *I am not going unless you go.*

unlike *preposition*
1. different from: *The new plant was unlike any they had seen before.* **2.** not in the nature of: *It is unlike her not to want to come.*

unlikely *adjective*
1. probably not true: *It seemed unlikely that they could have broken in.* **2.** probably not going to happen: *It is unlikely that we will arrive before lunchtime.* **3.** unusual or unexpected: *It was an unlikely place to see a fox.*
☐ **unlikelihood**, *noun*

unnerve *verb* To **unnerve** someone is to upset them or make them nervous: *Standing at the edge of a cliff always unnerves me.*
☐ **unnerving**, *adjective*

unravel *verb* (**unravels**, **unravelling**, **unravelled**, **has unravelled**)
1. If you **unravel** something or it **unravels**, you untie it or it becomes separated into threads: *She spent hours unravelling the twisted cords*; *His old woollen jumper had unravelled at the wrists.* **2.** If you **unravel** a complicated situation, you work out what the sense of it is: *It will take a very wise person to unravel the mess we have got ourselves into.*

unreal *adjective*
1. imaginary or not really existing: *He had to admit that his dreams of becoming the world's biggest soccer star were unreal.* **2.** *Informal* amazing or unbelievable: *To see my favourite group in the flesh was unreal!*
☐ **unreality**, *noun*

unrest *noun* an angry feeling of dissatisfaction: *More civil unrest has broken out.*

unruly *adjective* disobedient or uncontrollable: *The unruly students had to go to the principal's office.*

unscathed *adjective* not hurt or injured: *Considering the fall he had, it is amazing that he was unscathed.*

unseemly *adjective* not proper or decent: *Jason's unseemly language got him into trouble.*
☐ **unseemliness**, *noun*

unsightly *adjective* not pleasant to look at: *The doctor said that the unsightly marks on his face would soon fade.*

unthinkable *adjective* If something is **unthinkable**, it does not deserve to be considered or thought about: *It was unthinkable that Mum would have forgotten to write to us.*

until *conjunction*
1. up to the time that or when: *I will wait until you come.* **2.** before: *He did not arrive until the lesson was over.*
–*preposition* **3.** up to the time of: *He stayed until midnight.* **4.** before: *He did not go until midnight.*

NOTE This word (as in definitions 2 and 4) is always used in negative ('not') sentences.

☑ SPELLING TIP *Single letter alert*: only one *l* at the end. This can be confusing because the word on which **until** is based, *till*, has a double *l*.

unwieldy /*say* un-**weel**-dee/ *adjective* difficult to handle or manage: *The paintings are not heavy to carry – just unwieldy.*

☑ SPELLING TIP Remember that **unwieldy** is spelt with *ie* (to spell the 'ee' sound), as in the word *wield*. This follows the rule that *i* comes before *e* except after *c*. Think of similar words such as *field* and *shield*.

unwitting *adjective*
1. not meant or intended: *He apologised for his unwitting rudeness.* **2.** not knowing, or unaware: *Because they happened to be standing in the doorway, they became unwitting helpers in the capture of the thief.*
☐ **unwittingly**, *adverb*

unzip *verb* (**unzips**, **unzipping**, **unzipped**, **has unzipped**)
1. When you **unzip** a piece of clothing, you undo the zip on it. **2.** If you **unzip** computer data that has been put into a form that takes less storage, you put it back into its original form.

up *adverb*
1. to or in a higher place: *to climb up to the top of a ladder*; *the vase is up out of the way.* **2.** to or in an upright position: *Stand up.* **3.** to, near, or at a higher rank or condition: *to move up in the world.*
–*preposition* **4.** to or at a higher place on or in: *up the stairs.*
–*adjective* **5.** going upwards: *an up escalator.* **6.** out of bed: *He's up now.*

–*phrase* **7. up to, a.** If something is **up to** someone, it is their responsibility to do it: *It is up to you to report it to the police.* **b.** If someone is **up to** a task or a position, they are able to do or perform it: *Are you up to learning the piece by Friday?*

upbringing *noun* the care and education that is given by parents or similar people to someone during their childhood.

update *verb* /*say* up-**dayt**/
1. If you **update** something, you bring it up to date. You change it according to the way things are now: *The news database is updated every week with the latest events.*
–*noun* /*say* **up**-dayt/ **2.** a version of something, especially a piece of information or news, that has been brought up to date: *I'd like an update on the cricket score.*

upgrade *verb*
1. To **upgrade** someone or something is to promote them or make them more important: *They upgraded our teacher to deputy principal*; *All the library positions have been upgraded.* **2.** If you **upgrade** something, you improve it: *We upgraded our computer to a newer model.*

upheaval *noun* a complete change or great disturbance: *The builders were renovating the kitchen and the whole house was in upheaval.*

uphold *verb* (**upholds**, **upholding**, **upheld**, **has upheld**) To **uphold** something is to support it or keep it unchanged: *My father upholds all the rules my mother makes.*

upholster *verb* To **upholster** pieces of furniture, such as lounges, chairs and so on, is to provide them with coverings, stuffing and springs.
□ **upholsterer**, *noun* –**upholstery**, *noun*

upkeep *noun* the work or cost of looking after something or someone.

uplift *verb*
1. To **uplift** something is to lift it up. **2.** If someone or something **uplifts** you, it causes you to feel better, especially spiritually or mentally: *Waking up on the beach to the sound of the waves uplifted our spirits.*

upload *verb* To **upload** data is to transfer or copy it from a computer to a larger system, such as from a personal computer to a network.
□ **upload**, *noun*

COMPARE this with **download**.

upon *preposition* on: *upon the ground.*

upper *adjective*
1. higher or highest in place, position or rank: *There were scratches on her upper arm*; *Kids with names at the upper end of the alphabet always get chosen first.* **2.** facing upwards: *We only had to paint the upper side of the table.*

upper case *adjective* If letters are **upper case**, they are capital letters, such as *A, B, C* and so on.

COMPARE this with **lower case**.

upright *adjective*
1. If something is **upright**, it is positioned straight upwards or vertical: *The machine placed the bowling pins upright as soon as they were knocked down.* **2.** If someone is **upright**, they are honest and just: *He was an upright ruler and the whole country loved him.*
□ **upright**, *adverb*: *to sit upright.*

uprising *noun* a violent rebellion against a government or other authority by a large number of people.

A SIMILAR WORD is **revolt**.

uproar *noun* a noisy disturbance: *There was an uproar in the stadium as the goal was kicked.*

upset *verb* /*say* up-**set**/ (**upsets**, **upsetting**, **upset**, **has upset**)
1. If something **upsets** you, it causes you to feel unhappy or worried: *The news of the tragedy has upset everybody.* **2.** If something **upsets** your plans, it makes it hard for you to go ahead as you had intended: *The storm upset our plans to go to the beach.* **3.** If something such as food or drink **upsets** you, it makes you feel sick.
–*noun* /*say* **up**-set/ **4.** a slight illness, especially of the stomach. **5.** an emotional disturbance. **6.** an unexpected defeat.
□ **upset**, *adjective*: *an upset stomach.* –**upsetting**, *adjective*: *upsetting news.*

upstairs *adverb* /*say* up-**stairz**/
1. up the stairs.
–*noun* /*say* **up**-stairz/ **2.** an upper storey or storeys.

uptake *noun* the act of understanding or grasping facts: *She was quick on the uptake and was in control of the job by the second day.*

uptight *adjective Informal* nervous or worried: *Everyone gets uptight before a music exam.*

up-to-date *adjective*
1. including the most recent facts: *The most up-to-date report is that the yachts are just coming into the harbour.* **2.** modern: *Scilla makes a point of wearing only the most up-to-date clothes.*

upwards *adverb* towards a higher place, position, level, or degree.

ANOTHER FORM is **upward**.

uranium /*say* yooh-**ray**-nee-uhm/ *noun* a white radioactive metal which comes from a yellow substance in the ground and which can be used to produce nuclear weapons and energy.

urban *adjective* to do with a city or town: *Urban traffic is much heavier than rural traffic.*

urchin *noun Old-fashioned* a child who is poor and dressed in ragged, dirty clothes.

WORD HISTORY from the Latin word for 'hedgehog'

urge *verb*
1. If you **urge** someone to do something, you try hard to persuade them to do it.
–*noun* **2.** a strong natural desire: *She felt a sudden urge to get out of the musty hall into the fresh air.*
☐ **urging**, *noun*

urgent *adjective* Something **urgent** needs immediate action or attention: *an urgent message.*
☐ **urgency**, *noun* –**urgently**, *adverb*

urinal /*say* **yooh**-ruh-nuhl, yuh-**ruy**-nuhl/ *noun* a long trough or bowl with running water for men to urinate in while standing.

urine /*say* **yooh**-ruhn, **yooh**-ruyn/ *noun* liquid produced by the kidneys and passed from the body as a waste product.
☐ **urinary**, *adjective* –**urinate**, *verb* –**urination**, *noun*

URL *noun* the address of a web page on the internet.

WORD HISTORY short for *uniform resource locator*

urn *noun*
1. a kind of container, especially one for holding the ashes of someone who has been cremated. **2.** a container used for heating water.

☑ SPELLING TIP Don't confuse the spelling of **urn** with **earn** which sounds the same. To **earn** something is to receive it in return for working, or to deserve to get it.

us *pronoun* the form of **we** that comes after a verb: *Music surrounded us.*

usage *noun*
1. the way of using or treating: *The toy had worn out quickly because of rough usage from the two boys.* **2.** a custom or practice: *The government is urging increased usage of public transport.* **3.** the way in which a language is used: *'Bonzer' is a rather old-fashioned Australian usage.*

USB *noun* a computer port for connecting devices such as a USB drive, keyboard, printer, digital camera or scanner to a computer to allow the transfer of data.

WORD HISTORY short for *Universal Serial Bus*

USB drive *noun* a small portable information storage device that plugs into the USB port of a computer: *Adam downloaded his project onto the USB drive he kept on his key ring.*

OTHER TERMS for this are **memory stick** and **USB stick**.

use *verb* /*say* yoohz/
1. If you **use** something, you do something with it for a particular purpose: *My pen's run out – may I use yours?* **2.** If someone **uses** you, they take advantage of you. They get you to do things for them but they are not willing to do anything in return: *I hate the way she uses her friends to help her in projects – and then contributes nothing herself.*
–*noun* /*say* yoohs/ **3.** the act of using: *The program is designed to encourage the use of creativity; Her use of the car ended in disaster.* **4.** the state of being used: *Is the hall in use on Saturday?* **5.** a way of being used: *Wood has many different uses.* **6.** the ability to use something: *After her stroke, my grandmother lost the use of her left arm.* **7.** a need for using something: *Let's throw them out if you have no use for them any more.* **8.** the ability to be used in a helpful way: *Are these computer images of any use to you?*
☐ **useable**, *adjective* –**useful**, *adjective* –**useless**, *adjective* –**user**, *noun*

used[1] /*say* yoohzd/ *adjective* having been made use of: *They recycle used paper.*

used[2] /*say* yoohst/ *in the phrase* **used to**, If you are **used to** doing something, you are familiar with doing it: *We are used to working hard at school.*

usher *noun* someone who shows people to their seats at any public gathering or entertainment.

usherette *noun* a woman who shows people to their seats in a cinema or theatre.

usual *adjective* normal or customary: *It is usual to have three meals a day.*
☐ **usually**, *adverb*

utensil /*say* yooh-**ten**-suhl/ *noun* an instrument, tool, or container, especially one of those used for cooking or eating: *My aunt wants all her kitchen utensils to be matching.*

WORD HISTORY from a Latin word meaning 'useful'

uterus /*say* **yooh**-tuh-ruhs/ *noun* (*plural* **uteri** /*say* **yooh**-tuh-ruy/ *or* **uteruses**) the part of the body of a female in which a baby grows.

ANOTHER WORD for this is **womb**.

utilise *verb* To **utilise** something is to put it into use: *Our neighbours said we were welcome to utilise their trampoline at the party.*
☐ **utilisation**, *noun*

ANOTHER SPELLING is **utilize**.

utility *noun*
1. usefulness. **2.** a service run by the government, such as public transport, gas or electricity supply. **3.** a small truck.

ANOTHER WORD (for definition 3), used in informal language, is **ute**.

utmost *noun*
1. the greatest amount possible: *The festivities would strain the small town's resources to the utmost.* **2.** the best that you can do: *We tried our utmost to behave for the visitor.*
☐ **utmost**, *adjective*: *It is of utmost importance that you listen.*

ANOTHER FORM is **uttermost**.

utopia /*say* yooh-**toh**-pee-uh/ *noun* a completely perfect place or society.

WORD HISTORY from the name of an imaginary island described in a book by English statesman and writer Sir Thomas More (1516) as being perfect in law, politics, etc.

utter[1] *verb* To **utter** something is to say it: *He uttered only one word but that was enough.*
☐ **utterance**, *noun*

utter[2] *adjective* complete or total: *There was utter quiet in the empty hall.*
☐ **utterly**, *adverb*

U-turn *noun*
1. a turn made by a car or other vehicle so that it faces the way it has just come. **2.** any complete change of direction.

vacant /*say* **vay**-kuhnt/ *adjective*
1. If a place is **vacant**, it is not occupied or being used by anyone: *The room was vacant; The house next to ours is vacant – the owners are trying to let it.* **2.** If a job is **vacant**, no-one is doing it: *Mum heard that there is a vacant position at the local bank and is going to apply for it.* **3.** If you have a **vacant** look, you seem as if you have not understood something or are not concentrating: *She looked at the teacher with a vacant expression. Maybe she didn't hear the question.*
☐ **vacancy**, *noun* (*plural* **vacancies**) –**vacate**, *verb*: *to vacate a room.*

vacation *noun*
1. a holiday. **2.** the time of the year when a place such as a school or university is closed.

vaccine /*say* vak-**seen**, **vak**-seen/ *noun* a preparation made from the germs that give you a disease, which is administered to you to give you a mild form of that disease and stop you from being seriously ill with it later on.
☐ **vaccinate**, *verb* –**vaccination**, *noun*

WORD HISTORY from a Latin word meaning 'having to do with cows', because the first vaccines were made from the germs of a cow disease

☑ SPELLING TIP *Double letter alert*: there is a double *c* in **vaccine** but each *c* makes a different sound – the first has a 'k' sound and the second an 's' sound.

vacuum /*say* **vak**-yoohm/ *noun*
1. a space completely free of matter. **2.** an enclosed space from which air or other gas has been removed, such as by an air pump. **3.** See **vacuum cleaner**.

☑ SPELLING TIP *Single/double letter alert*: only one *c* but notice that the *u* is doubled.

vacuum cleaner *noun* a machine that sucks up dirt from floors.

THE SHORT FORM of this is **vacuum**.

vagina /*say* vuh-**juy**-nuh/ *noun* the passage in the body of a female that leads from the uterus to the outside of the body.

vagrant /*say* **vay**-gruhnt/ *noun* someone who travels from place to place instead of having a settled home.

A SIMILAR WORD is **tramp**.

vague /*say* vayg/ *adjective* If something is **vague**, it is not clear or certain: *I had a vague feeling that something was missing.*
☐ **vaguely**, *adverb* –**vagueness**, *noun*

☑ SPELLING TIP Don't forget the *ue* at the end. The spelling *ague* gives an 'ayg' sound in this word.

vain *adjective*
1. A person who is **vain** is proud, especially about the way they look. **2.** A **vain** attempt is one that is useless: *My dad made a vain attempt to catch the intruder.*
–*phrase* **3. in vain**, uselessly or without effect.
☐ **vanity**, *noun*

A SIMILAR WORD (for definition 1) is **conceited**.

☑ SPELLING TIP Remember the *ai* spelling. Don't confuse **vain** with **vein** or **vane**, both of which sound the same. A **vein** is a blood vessel taking the blood back to the heart. A **vane** is something designed to move with the wind, such as a *weathervane*.

valentine *noun*
1. a present or message of love or friendship sent to someone on St Valentine's Day, 14 February. **2.** the person you choose to send this message to.

valet /*say* **val**-ay, **val**-uht/ *noun* a male servant who looks after his employer's clothes and other personal things.

☑ SPELLING TIP *Silent letter alert*: if you say this word as in the first pronunciation, you will need to remember the silent *t* at the end. **Valet** is spelt like this because it comes from French.

valiant *adjective* brave or courageous: *The crowd made a valiant attempt to get the beached whales back to sea.*
☐ **valiantly**, *adverb*

valid *adjective*
1. If something such as a ticket is **valid**, it is officially in order. **2.** If something such as an argument or decision is **valid**, it is based on sound reasoning: *They have a valid objection to the proposal.*
☐ **validity**, *noun*

valley *noun* the low land between hills or mountains, usually with a river flowing through it.

valour *noun* braveness or courage.

ANOTHER SPELLING is **valor**.

valuable *adjective*
1. worth a lot of money: *The painting was extremely valuable and insured for millions.* 2. of great use or importance: *My maths coaching has been valuable in helping me at school.*
–*noun* 3. **valuables**, things that are valuable, such as jewellery: *It was crazy to leave valuables in the car!*

value *noun*
1. the amount of money something is worth: *A swimming pool adds great value to the price of a house.* 2. what makes something worthwhile or useful: *The extra coaching I had in maths was of great value.* 3. **values**, the beliefs and ideas about what is important, held by a person or community of people: *The offenders were warned that their values had to be in line with those of the larger community.*
–*verb* 4. If you **value** something, you think it is important or it is precious to you: *I always value advice from my grandmother*; *I value my bike more than all my other things.* 5. If someone **values** something, they work out how much it is worth: *Their house is valued at more than a million dollars.*
☐ **valuation**, *noun* –**valuer**, *noun*

valve *noun*
1. the part of a pipe or other passage that opens and shuts to control the flow of liquid or gas. 2. one of the two or more separable parts of the shell of a sea animal, such as a mussel.

vampire *noun* an imaginary, supernatural being, believed to be a dead person come back to life, who sucks blood from living people during the night.

WORD HISTORY from a Turkish word meaning 'witch'

van *noun* a covered vehicle, lighter and smaller than a truck, for carrying goods.

WORD HISTORY short for *caravan*

vandal *noun* someone who intentionally destroys or damages things.
☐ **vandalise**, *verb*: *to vandalise a train.* –**vandalism**, *noun*

ANOTHER SPELLING for **vandalise** is **vandalize**.

vane *noun*
1. a blade on a windmill. 2. a flat piece of metal or other material on a roof, which turns with the wind to show which direction it is blowing from.

ANOTHER WORD (for definition 2) is **weather-vane**.

☑ SPELLING TIP Don't confuse the spelling of **vane** with **vain** or **vein**, both of which have the same sound. If someone is **vain**, they are very proud of themselves. A **vein** is one of the small tubes that carries blood through your body.

vanguard *noun*
1. the front part of an army. 2. any leading position: *They were in the vanguard of the crowd surging towards the gates.*

vanilla *noun* a liquid made from a plant, used to flavour food.

☑ SPELLING TIP *Single/double letter alert*: only one *n* but a double *l*. Rap it out as *va+nil+la*.

vanish *verb* If something **vanishes**, it disappears. It can no longer be seen: *The ship vanished over the horizon.*

vanity *noun* (*plural* **vanities**)
1. extreme pride in yourself: *Her vanity will be her downfall.* 2. something that someone is vain about: *He was a genuinely simple person with no affectations and no vanities.*

vanquish *verb* To **vanquish** is to defeat: *He had vanquished his opponent through skill and cunning.*

NOTE This word is used in literature or formal writing rather than ordinary language.

vapour *noun* a cloud of a gas-like substance, such as fog, mist, or steam.
☐ **vaporise**, *verb* –**vaporisation**, *noun* –**vaporiser**, *noun* –**vaporous**, *adjective*

ANOTHER SPELLING is **vapor**. Another spelling for **vaporise** is **vaporize**.

variable *adjective*
1. likely to vary or change: *The venue had to be suitable for the variable weather that was forecast.* 2. able to be changed: *The menu is variable depending on how much you want to pay.*
☐ **variably**, *adverb*

variation *noun*
1. a change or alteration: *Dad asked the architect for a few variations to the original plan.* 2. a different form of something: *Naran told me a good variation to the basic hummus recipe.*

variegated /*say* **vair**-ree-uh-gay-tuhd/ *adjective* marked with different colours: *The valley was a variegated panorama of greens and browns.*

☑ SPELLING TIP *Tricky 'uh' sound*: the vowel sound before the *g* is spelt *e*. Think of the related word *variety* to remind you.

variety /*say* vuh-**ruy**-uh-tee/ *noun*
1. a change from what usually happens: *For a bit of variety, we tried the new ride at the show.* 2. a number of things of different kinds: *The early explorers found an amazing variety of marsupials.* 3. kind or type: *Apples and pears are varieties of fruit.*

various /*say* **vair**-ree-uhs/ *adjective* If things are described as **various**, there are several different ones. Often you use this word to refer to a number of things, without giving details: *There are various things that confuse me in maths.*
☐ **variously**, *adverb*

varnish *noun*
1. a liquid coating which, when dry, gives a hard, shiny look to a surface.
–*verb* **2.** If someone **varnishes** a surface, they apply varnish to it.

vary /*say* **vair**-ree/ *verb* (**varies**, **varying**, **varied**, **has varied**)
1. If something **varies**, it is different at different times: *The reception on the mobile varies according to where I am standing.* **2.** If you **vary** something, you change it: *We decided to vary our training time.*
☐ **variant**, *adjective* –**varying**, *adjective*

vase /*say* vahz/ *noun* a container for flowers.

☑ SPELLING TIP Remember that there is no *r* in this word. The *ase* spelling gives an 'ahz' sound.

vassal *noun* someone in feudal times who lived on land owned by nobility and had to fight and work for them in return.

vast *adjective* very great: *There are vast numbers of items on supermarket shelves.*
☐ **vastly**, *adverb* –**vastness**, *noun*

vat *noun* a very large container for liquids.

vaudeville /*say* **vaw**-duh-vil/ *noun* a light theatrical entertainment, mainly with musical and comedy acts.

☑ SPELLING TIP Remember the *ille* ending to this word, which comes from French.

vault[1] /*say* vawlt, volt/ *noun*
1. an underground room, especially one for storing valuable things or one where dead people are buried. **2.** an arched roof or something thought to be similar: *We looked up into the vault of the cathedral.*
☐ **vaulted**, *adjective*: *a vaulted ceiling.*

vault[2] /*say* vawlt, volt/ *verb*
1. If you **vault** over something like a fence or gate, you leap or jump over it with your hands supported on something: *He vaulted over the fence.* **2.** If you **vault** something, you jump over it in this way: *Can you vault the fence?*
☐ **vault**, *noun*

WORD HISTORY from a Latin word meaning 'roll'

VCR *noun* See **video cassette recorder**.

veal *noun* meat from a calf.

veer *verb* To **veer** is to change direction: *Where the road veers right, you will see a sign*; *Dad had to veer to avoid the cat.*

vegetable /*say* **vej**-tuh-buhl/ *noun* any plant of which the whole or a part is used as food: *The vegetables I don't like are spinach and brussels sprouts.*
☐ **vegetable**, *adjective*

☑ SPELLING TIP There are three separate *e*'s in **vegetable**. Don't forget the second *e* which you usually don't hear when people say the word. Rap it out as *ve+ge+ta+ble*.

vegetarian *noun* someone who does not eat meat or fish and lives mainly or totally on vegetable food.
☐ **vegetarian**, *adjective*

☑ SPELLING TIP Remember that this word comes from *vegetable* and so has the same *vege* beginning.

vegetation *noun* the whole plant life of a particular area: *Much of the vegetation was cleared for grazing animals.*

☑ SPELLING TIP Remember that this word has the same *vege* beginning as *vegetable*.

vehement /*say* **vee**-uh-muhnt/ *adjective* strong or passionate: *Her answer was swift and vehement.*
☐ **vehemence**, *noun* –**vehemently**, *adverb*

☑ SPELLING TIP *Silent letter alert*: don't forget the *h* in **vehement**. Also notice that there is a single *e* on either side of the *h*. Rap it out as *ve+he+ment*.

vehicle /*say* **vee**-ik-uhl/ *noun* a form of transport, such as a car or bicycle.
☐ **vehicular** /*say* vuh-**hik**-yuh-luh/, *adjective*

☑ SPELLING TIP *Silent letter alert*: don't forget the *h* in **vehicle**. Rap it out as *ve+hi+cle*.

veil /*rhymes with* pale/ *noun* a piece of material that women wear to cover their head and face.
☐ **veiled**, *adjective*

vein /*say* vayn/ *noun*
1. one of the small tubes that carries blood through the body back to the heart. **2.** a line on a leaf or insect's wing. **3.** a layer of coal, gold, etc., in the middle of rock.

☑ SPELLING TIP Remember the *ei* spelling for the 'ay' sound. Don't confuse **vein** with **vain** or **vane**, both of which sound the same. If someone is **vain**, they are very proud of themselves. A **vane** is something designed to move with the wind, such as a *weathervane*.

velcro *noun* a type of fastening tape made of two fabric strips, one with many tiny nylon hooks and the other with nylon loops, that stick firmly together when pressed.
☐ **velcro**, *adjective*

WORD HISTORY trademark

velocity /*say* vuh-**los**-uh-tee/ *noun* (*plural* **velocities**) rate of motion in a given direction: *The maximum velocity the vehicle will go is 150 kilometres an hour.*

velvet *noun* a kind of soft, thick material that feels rather like fur.
□ **velvet**, *adjective* –**velvety**, *adjective*

vendetta *noun* a feud in which the family of a murder victim tries to get revenge by killing the murderer or one of the murderer's family.

veneer /*say* vuh-**near**/ *noun*
1. a thin layer of wood, plastic, etc., used to cover the surface underneath. **2.** something which covers up something unpleasant: *Don't trust her – that smile is just a veneer!*

venerable *adjective* worthy of respect because of age or importance.
□ **venerate**, *verb* to respect.

vengeance /*say* **ven**-juhns/ *noun*
1. harm done to someone in return for harm they have done to you.
–*phrase* **2. with a vengeance**, very strongly or forcefully.

A SIMILAR WORD (for definition 1) is **revenge**.

☑ SPELLING TIP Don't forget the *e* before the *ance* ending. Think of the related word *revenge* – take off the *re* and add *ance*.

venison *noun* meat from a deer.

venom *noun* the poison that spiders and snakes use when they bite.
□ **venomous**, *adjective*

vent *noun*
1. an opening to let smoke or gases out.
–*verb* **2.** If you **vent** feelings, you express or show them: *He finally vented his frustration and absolutely exploded at a meeting.*

ventilate *verb* If you **ventilate** a room, you replace the air in it with fresh air: *We opened all the windows to try to ventilate the room.*
□ **ventilation**, *noun* –**ventilator**, *noun*

ventricle /*say* **ven**-trik-uhl/ *noun* either of the two main cavities of the heart from which blood is pumped out.

COMPARE this with **auricle**.

ventriloquism /*say* ven-**tril**-uh-kwiz-uhm/ *noun* a way of speaking without moving your lips so that your voice seems to come from somewhere else.
□ **ventriloquist**, *noun*

venture *noun*
1. something you set out to do, especially something which has risks attached: *It was an exciting venture even though it had potential problems.*
–*verb* **2.** If you **venture** to do something, you risk or dare to do it: *She ventured to say that things had been going badly for quite a while; Matt ventured an opinion that was immediately pounced on by the others.*
□ **venturesome**, *adjective* bold.

venue /*say* **ven**-yooh/ *noun* a place where an event is held: *The venue will be either the town hall or the sports complex.*

verandah *noun* a partly open part on the outside of a house, usually covered by the main roof.

ANOTHER SPELLING is **veranda**.
WORD HISTORY from a Portuguese word for 'railing', which came from a Latin word meaning 'rod'

verb *noun* a word in a sentence which tells you what someone or something does or feels, such as 'annoyed' and 'stop' in the sentence *If anyone annoyed my dog, I would stop them.*

SEE the Grammar and Punctuation Guide appendix.

verbal *adjective*
1. Verbal means relating to words or language: *The stroke affected parts of his verbal ability.* **2. Verbal** refers to spoken rather than written language: *She can read and write French but her verbal skills need improving.* **3.** In talking about language, **verbal** means relating to verbs: *The verbal equivalent of 'proposal' is 'propose'.*
□ **verbalise**, *verb*: *I sometimes find it difficult to verbalise my thoughts.* –**verbally**, *adverb*

ANOTHER SPELLING for **verbalise** is **verbalize**.

verbatim /*say* vuh-**bay**-tuhm/ *adverb* using exactly the same words: *The teacher wanted us to repeat verbatim the list of rivers on the east coast.*

verdict *noun* the judge's or jury's decision or answer in a law court.

verge *noun*
1. the very edge: *I was on the verge of saying 'yes' and then I thought again.* **2.** the strip of dirt or grass at the edge of a road.
–*verb in the phrase* **3. verge on**, to come close to: *The way he talks verges on rudeness.*

verger *noun* the caretaker of the interior of a church.

verify *verb* (**verifies**, **verifying**, **verified**, **has verified**) If you **verify** something, you prove it to be true or correct: *At the shop they always verify that your signature matches the one on your credit card.*
□ **verifiable**, *adjective* –**verification**, *noun*

vermin *plural noun* harmful, troublesome, or unpleasant animals collectively, such as rats, cockroaches, and fleas.

WORD HISTORY from a French word meaning 'worm'

versatile *adjective* To be **versatile** is to be able to do a variety of things: *She is versatile on the stage – everything from rap to ballet.*
☐ **versatility**, *noun*: *Such versatility is amazing!*

verse[1] *noun*
1. poetry: *We had to write about our life in verse.* **2.** a group of lines that go together in a song or poem.

verse[2] *verb Informal* To **verse** someone in a game or competition is to play against them: *Which team are we versing this week?*

WORD HISTORY from *versus*

version *noun*
1. someone's description of what happened compared with someone else's: *Everybody had different versions of who started the fight.* **2.** a particular form of something: *The film version left out a lot of detail that was in the book.*

versus /*say* **ver**-suhs/ *preposition* against: *It is us versus them.*

THE ABBREVIATION is **v** or **vs**.

vertebra /*say* **ver**-tuh-bruh/ *noun* (*plural* **vertebrae** /*say* **ver**-tuh-bree, **ver**-tuh-bray/) a bone of the spine.

vertebrate /*say* **ver**-tuh-bruht, **ver**-tuh-brayt/ *noun* an animal with a backbone: *Both humans and chooks are vertebrates.*
☐ **vertebrate**, *adjective*

COMPARE this with **invertebrate**.

☑ SPELLING TIP *Tricky 'uh' sound*: the middle vowel sound is spelt *e*. In fact, there are three *e*'s in **vertebrate**. You could think of them as making a backbone for the word to hold it together.

vertex /*say* **ver**-teks/ *noun* (*plural* **vertices** /*say* **ver**-tuh-seez/*or* **vertexes**)
1. the top or highest point of something: *We had to mark the vertex of the triangle 'A' and the other two points 'B' and 'C'.* **2.** the point where two sides of an angle or three or more sides of a solid meet: *We had to measure the angles at each of the vertices.*

vertical *adjective* If something is **vertical**, it stands straight up or at right angles to the horizon: *The vertical structure you see over there is a mobile phone tower.*
☐ **vertically**, *adverb*

COMPARE this with **horizontal**.

vertigo /*say* **ver**-tuh-goh/ *noun* a feeling of dizziness, often experienced when looking down from a high place.

verve *noun* lively enthusiasm: *She played with verve and confidence.*

very *adverb*
1. in a high degree: *We were very sorry for interrupting the violin performance.*
–*adjective* **2.** You can use **very** to add emphasis or to mean 'exact' or 'actual': *That is the very thing I was going to say!*; *She shuddered at the very suggestion.*

vessel *noun*
1. a ship or boat. **2.** a hollow container, such as a cup or bottle. **3.** a tube which carries watery substances inside the body, such as a blood vessel.

☑ SPELLING TIP *Double letter alert*: double *s*. Also remember the *el* (not *le*) ending.

vest *noun*
1. a piece of underwear which looks like a sleeveless T-shirt. **2.** a waistcoat.

vestibule /*say* **vest**-uh-byoohl/ *noun* an entrance hall.

vestige /*say* **vest**-ij/ *noun* the last trace of something that was once there.
☐ **vestigial** /*say* ves-**tij**-uhl/, *adjective*

vet *noun*
1. a doctor who treats animals.
–*verb* (**vets**, **vetting**, **vetted**, **has vetted**) **2.** If you **vet** someone or something for a particular purpose, you check very carefully to make certain they are suitable and acceptable.

NOTE This word (as in definition 1) is a short form of the formal term **veterinary surgeon**.

veteran *noun*
1. someone who has worked for a long time in a particular job or in any position. **2.** a returned soldier.
–*adjective* **3.** experienced: *a veteran actor.*

veterinary surgeon /*say* **vet**-ruhn-ree, **vet**-uh-ruhn-ree/ *noun* someone whose job is to treat sick animals.

ANOTHER NAME for this is **veterinarian**.
THE SHORT FORM of this is **vet**.

☑ SPELLING TIP It's no wonder that people use the short word **vet**, because **veterinary** is difficult to spell. You need to remember that it has five syllables, although you often hear only three or four when you say it. Concentrate on the *er* after the *t* and the *ary* ending, and rap it out as *vet+er+in+a+ry*.

veto /*say* **vee**-toh/ *noun* (*plural* **vetoes**)
1. the power or right to prevent something.
–*verb* (**vetoes**, **vetoing**, **vetoed**, **has vetoed**) **2.** If someone **vetoes** something like a proposal, a bill in parliament or something like that, they prevent it by using their power of veto.

vex *verb* If you **vex** someone, you annoy or worry them.
☐ **vexation**, *noun* –**vexatious**, *adjective* –**vexed**, *adjective*

viaduct /*say* **vuy**-uh-dukt/ *noun* a bridge with many arches, which carries a road or railway over a valley.

vibes[1] *plural noun Informal* See **vibraphone**.

vibes[2] *plural noun Informal* the feeling you get, good or bad, just from being in a place: *The vibes I was getting from the group were distinctly unfriendly.*

vibrant *adjective* bright, lively and exciting: *The vibrant colours in the fashion parade were a completely new look.*
☐ **vibrancy**, *noun* –**vibrantly**, *adverb*

vibraphone *noun* an electronic musical instrument like a xylophone, often used in jazz.

ANOTHER WORD for this is **vibes**.

vibrate *verb* If something **vibrates**, it shakes rapidly: *The washing machine was vibrating violently.*
☐ **vibration**, *noun*

vicar *noun* a priest, especially one in charge of some Anglican parishes.
☐ **vicarage**, *noun* a vicar's house.

vice[1] *noun*
1. behaviour which is morally bad: *The film was about vice and corruption in the New York underworld.* **2.** a fault or bad habit: *Her worst vice is talking too much.*

vice[2] *noun* a tool which closes around something and holds it tightly in place while you work on it.
☐ **vice-like**, *adjective*: *a vice-like grip.*

WORD HISTORY from a Latin word meaning 'vine'

vice-regal *adjective* having to do with someone appointed as a deputy by a king or queen, such as a governor-general or governor of a state.

vice versa /*say* vuy-suh **ver**-suh, vuys **ver**-suh/ *adverb* the other way round from what you have just said, as in the sentence *Allie helps me and vice versa*, which means *Allie helps me and I help Allie*.

vicinity *noun* (*plural* **vicinities**) a local area or place nearby: *There are three video shops in our vicinity.*

vicious /*say* **vish**-uhs/ *adjective* very cruel or harmful: *It was a vicious attack on her reputation.*
☐ **viciously**, *adverb* –**viciousness**, *noun*

victim *noun* someone who suffers harm or injury: *the murderer's victims*; *a victim of a car accident.*

victimise *verb* If someone **victimises** another person, they punish or harm them unfairly.
☐ **victimisation**, *noun*

ANOTHER SPELLING is **victimize**.

victory *noun* (*plural* **victories**) a win or success in a contest.
☐ **victor**, *noun* –**victorious**, *adjective*

video *noun* (*plural* **pianos**)
1. a film recorded on videotape: *Let's watch a video tonight*; *They made a video of the wedding.* **2.** a cassette holding a videotape: *We keep all the videos on that shelf.* **3.** a video cassette recorder: *Our video isn't working.*
–*verb* **4.** If you **video** something, you record it on a videotape.
☐ **video**, *adjective*: *video games.*

video cassette recorder *noun* a machine that records and plays back images and sounds recorded on a videotape.

THE ABBREVIATION is **VCR**.
THE SHORT FORMS are **video** and **video recorder**.

videotape *noun* magnetic tape used for recording film or television pictures and sound.

vie *verb* (**vies**, **vying**, **vied**, **has vied**) If you **vie** with someone, you compete against them or try to beat them in some activity.

view *noun*
1. whatever you can see from a particular place: *You get a good view of the game from the middle of the grandstand.* **2.** an idea or opinion: *We had to write about our views on pollution.*
–*verb* **3.** If you **view** something, you look at it or inspect it: *A big crowd came to view the exhibition.*
–*phrase* **4. in view of**, because of. **5. on view**, displayed for all to see.
☐ **viewer**, *noun*

vigil /*say* **vij**-uhl/ *noun* the act of keeping watch at night: *The protesters held a night-long vigil outside the parliament.*

vigilant /*say* **vij**-uh-luhnt/ *adjective* alert and watchful.
☐ **vigilance**, *noun* –**vigilantly**, *adverb*

vigour *noun* energy and strength.
☐ **vigorous**, *adjective*

ANOTHER SPELLING is **vigor**.

vile *adjective* If something is **vile**, it is very unpleasant or disgusting: *His vile language offended everybody.*
☐ **vilely**, *adverb* –**vileness**, *noun*

villa *noun*
1. a country house, usually a large or important one, especially in a Mediterranean country. **2.** a small house, often one of a set of connected dwellings.

village *noun* a small town in the country.
☐ **villager**, *noun*

villain /*say* **vil**-uhn/ *noun* a wicked person: *Everyone hissed when the villain came onto the stage.*

☐ **villainy**, *noun* wickedness. –**villainous**, *adjective*

☑ SPELLING TIP *Double letter alert*: double *l*. Also remember the *ain* ending (which sounds like 'uhn'). You could think of a **villain** in a *villa* to help you remember these parts of the spelling – and this is in fact the origin of the word. See the note at **villein**.

villein /*say* **vil**-uhn/ *noun* someone in feudal times, with a little more freedom than a serf.

☑ SPELLING TIP Don't confuse the spelling of **villein** with **villain** which sounds the same. A **villain** is a wicked person. In fact, these words are related. **Villain** comes from the earlier word **villein** which came into English from French, from the Latin word for 'a worker at a villa or country estate'.

vindicate /*say* **vin**-duh-kayt/ *verb* If something **vindicates** a person, it shows they are right or innocent when previously they were thought to be wrong or guilty: *The teacher's decision to get us to sing music from all over the world was vindicated by the fantastic audience response.*
☐ **vindication**, *noun*

vindictive *adjective* spiteful or full of revenge: *Scribbling all over my favourite books was a vindictive thing for my sister to do.*
☐ **vindictively**, *adverb*

vine *noun* a climbing plant.

vinegar /*say* **vin**-uh-guh, **vin**-i-guh/ *noun* a sour liquid made from wine or cider and used to flavour food.

☑ SPELLING TIP Remember that the middle vowel sound is spelt *e*. Think of it as being part of *vine*. The word part *vine* is actually related to the word *wine* (coming from *vin*, the French word for 'wine'), but you can remember it by thinking of a *vine* – after all, both wine and **vinegar** come from grapes which grow on a *vine*. Also remember the *ar* ending.

vineyard /*say* **vin**-yuhd/ *noun* a farm where grapes are grown for wine-making.

☑ SPELLING TIP **Vineyard** is made up of two words – *vine* and *yard*. Think of this to remind yourself of the spelling, especially the *e* at the end of the first part.

vintage *noun*
1. wine made in a certain year or from a particular crop.
–*adjective* **2.** A **vintage** car is an old car of a type that is not made any more, which people buy and work on to bring back to good condition, usually as a hobby.

vinyl /*say* **vuy**-nuhl/ *noun* a type of plastic.

☑ SPELLING TIP *Letter 'y' alert*: the second vowel sound is spelt with a *y*. The suffix *-yl* appears in the names of several materials and chemicals.

viola /*say* vee-**oh**-luh/ *noun* a stringed instrument played with a bow, like a violin but a little bigger.

NOTE The **viola** is lower in pitch than the **violin** and higher than the **cello** and **double bass**.

violate *verb*
1. If someone **violates** something like a law, rule, or agreement, they break it: *They violated the peace agreement.* **2.** If someone **violates** another person or a special place, they treat them brutally, showing no respect: *The frenzied crowd violated the temple.*
☐ **violation**, *noun*

violent *adjective*
1. If someone is **violent**, they are angry and use force to injure people or destroy things. **2.** If something such as a storm or an explosion is **violent**, it has great force and is very destructive.
☐ **violence**, *noun* –**violently**, *adverb*

violet *noun*
1. a small plant with purple, blue, yellow or white flowers. **2.** a bluish-purple colour.
☐ **violet**, *adjective*

violin *noun* a stringed instrument played with a bow and held between your shoulder and chin.
☐ **violinist**, *noun*

NOTE The **violin** is higher in pitch than the **viola**, **cello** and **double bass**.

violoncello /*say* vuy-uh-luhn-**chel**-oh/ *noun* See **cello**.

VIP *noun* someone who has an important position or is famous, and so receives special treatment: *The VIPs were all seated in the front row.*

WORD HISTORY an acronym made by joining the first letters of *very important person*

viper *noun* a type of very venomous snake.

virgin *noun*
1. someone, especially a female, who has never had sexual intercourse.
–*adjective* **2.** If something such as land or forest is described as **virgin**, it is in its original natural state. It has not been cultivated or spoiled by humans: *virgin forest.*
☐ **virginal**, *adjective* –**virginity**, *noun*

virile /*say* **vi**-ruyl/ *adjective* strong, forceful, and masculine.
☐ **virility**, *noun*

virtual /*say* **ver**-chooh-uhl/ *adjective*
1. as if it were really so: *She was a virtual prisoner in her own house.* **2.** in computers,

existing only as a representation, as opposed to physically: *a virtual bookshop.*
☐ **virtually**, *adverb*

☑ SPELLING TIP Remember the *t* in this word. With the *u* following, it has a 'ch' sound and you don't hear the *t*.

virtue /*say* **ver**-chooh/ *noun*
1. goodness or proper behaviour: *We all had a sense of virtue after we had visited the old people's home.* **2.** a good quality: *The debate was about whether cleanliness or honesty was the most important virtue.*
☐ **virtuous**, *adjective* –**virtuously**, *adverb*

☑ SPELLING TIP Remember the *t* in this word. With the *u* following, it has a 'ch' sound and you don't hear the *t*.

virtuoso /*say* ver-chooh-**oh**-soh/ *noun* (*plural* **virtuosos** *or* **virtuosi** /*say* ver-chooh-**oh**-see/) a highly skilled musician.
☐ **virtuosity**, *noun*

virulent /*say* **vi**-ruh-luhnt/ *adjective* A **virulent** disease or poison is very harmful and powerful.
☐ **virulence**, *noun* –**virulently**, *adverb*

virus *noun*
1. a very small living thing that causes disease. **2.** any disease caused by a virus. **3.** in computers, a hidden program which is especially written to cause annoyance or damage to information already on the computer.
☐ **viral**, *adjective*

☑ SPELLING TIP Remember that the ending is *us*, as in many words coming from Latin. The meaning of *virus* in Latin was 'a slimy liquid' or 'poison'.

visa /*say* **vee**-zuh/ *noun* a stamp or written notice put in your passport, giving you permission to enter a certain country.

WORD HISTORY from the Latin word meaning 'see'

viscount /*say* **vuy**-kownt/ *noun* a British nobleman ranking below an earl and above a baron.

☑ SPELLING TIP *Silent letter alert*: don't forget the silent *s* before the *c*. This is because the first part of the word is *vis*, which comes from the French word for *vice* in the sense of 'deputy'.

NOTE A woman with this rank is called a **viscountess**.

visible *adjective* able to be seen: *The lighthouse is visible from a long distance.*
☐ **visibility**, *noun* –**visibly**, *adverb*

vision *noun*
1. the power or sense of seeing: *My new glasses improved my vision.* **2.** the power of imagining: *The hall would never have been built without his vision.* **3.** a mental image: *I had visions of hot toast dripping with melted cheese.*
☐ **visionary**, *adjective*

ANOTHER WORD (for definition 1) is **sight**.

visit *verb* (**visits**, **visiting**, **visited**, **has visited**) If you **visit** a person or place, you go to see them, usually for a fairly short time.
☐ **visit**, *noun* –**visitor**, *noun*

visor /*say* **vuy**-zuh/ *noun* the movable part of a hard protective hat, which can be pulled down over your eyes.

visual *adjective* **Visual** means relating to seeing or sight: *visual aids*; *visual images.*
☐ **visually**, *adverb*

visual display unit *noun* a screen attached to a computer which displays data.

THE ABBREVIATION is **VDU**.

visualise *verb* If you **visualise** something, you form a mental picture of it: *We tried to visualise what she would look like now that she had been away for two years.*

ANOTHER SPELLING is **visualize**.

vital *adjective* If something is **vital**, it is necessary or very important: *It was vital to find a new drummer for the band.*
☐ **vitally**, *adverb*: *vitally important.*

vitality *noun* energy or vigour.

vitamin /*say* **vuy**-tuh-muhn, **vit**-uh-muhn/ *noun*
1. any of a number of substances present naturally in food, and necessary in small quantities for good health. **2.** a chemical preparation of such a substance.

vivacious /*say* vuh-**vay**-shuhs/ *adjective* lively or energetic: *The dance company put on a vivacious presentation.*
☐ **vivaciously**, *adverb* –**vivacity** /*say* vuh-**vas**-uh-tee/, *noun*

vivid /*say* **viv**-uhd/ *adjective*
1. If something such as a colour or a design is **vivid**, it is very bright and strong. **2.** If something such as a description is **vivid**, it is clear and full of life: *His story was full of vivid detail and we were mesmerised.*
☐ **vividly**, *adverb* –**vividness**, *noun*

vixen *noun* a female fox.

NOTE The male is a **dog**.

vocabulary /*say* voh-**kab**-yuh-luh-ree/ *noun* the total number of words used by someone or by a particular group of people: *She is trying to add to her vocabulary by learning one new word a day.*

vocal *adjective*
1. Something that is **vocal** has to do with the human voice: *The singer has a broad vocal*

range. **2.** If someone is **vocal**, they are continually making their views known: *The protesters were very vocal about their concerns.*
☐ **vocally**, *adverb*

vocal cords *plural noun* the folds in the lining of the throat which move as air from the lungs passes them, making distinctive sounds.

vocalist *noun* a singer.

vocation *noun* an occupation, business or profession, especially one which you seriously believe in: *He saw nursing as a vocation with lifelong satisfaction.*

vodka *noun* a strong alcoholic drink made from grain and potatoes, originating in Russia.

WORD HISTORY from a Russian word meaning 'little water'

vogue /*say* vohg/ *noun* fashion: *Things that were in vogue twenty years ago have come back in.*

☑ SPELLING TIP Don't forget the *ue* at the end. The spelling *ogue* gives an 'ohg' sound in this word.

voice *noun*
1. the sound or sounds you make with your mouth especially when you speak or sing. **2.** the quality or condition of the voice for singing: *A virus had affected his voice and he decided not to appear.* **3.** the right to express an opinion: *The committee said that parents should have more voice in school decisions.*
–*verb* **4.** If you **voice** something like an opinion, you state it: *She voiced her disapproval very openly.*

voicemail *noun*
1. a way of recording messages over the telephone so that you can listen to them later: *We used to have an answering machine but now we have voicemail.* **2.** a telephone message that you get in this way: *There were a lot of voicemails waiting for us when we got back from holidays.*

void *adjective* If something is **void** it is **1.** without legal force: *The contract was declared void because a major provision was breached.* **2.** empty: *The official's approach was entirely void of any humanitarian feeling.*
–*noun* **3.** an empty space: *Because of the thick fog, we felt we were in a void – we could see nothing.*

volatile /*say* **vol**-uh-tuyl/ *adjective*
1. turning to vapour quickly: *Pure alcohol is a volatile substance.* **2.** likely to change suddenly and quickly: *a volatile personality*; *a volatile situation which could lead to war.*

volcano *noun* (*plural* **volcanoes** *or* **volcanos**) a mountain with an opening in the top, through which molten rock, steam and ashes burst out when it is active.
☐ **volcanic**, *adjective*

WORD HISTORY named after *Vulcan*, the Roman god of fire

volition /*say* vuh-**lish**-uhn/ *noun* an act of will or purpose: *The actor said he had decided of his own volition to spend more time doing commercials.*

volley *noun*
1. the firing of a number of guns together. **2.** an outpouring at one time: *There was a volley of wild and hearty clapping.* **3.** the return of a ball before it bounces in games such as tennis, volleyball, and so on.
–*verb* **4.** If you **volley** in tennis. you return the ball before it bounces.

volleyball *noun* a team game in which a large ball is volleyed by hand or arm over a net.

volt *noun* a measurement of electric force.
☐ **voltage**, *noun*

THE SYMBOL for this is **V**.

voluble *adjective* marked by a ready and continuous flow of words: *a voluble talker*; *a overly voluble speech.*
☐ **volubility**, *noun* –**volubly**, *adverb*

volume *noun*
1. a book, especially one of a series. **2.** the space occupied by a body or substance, measured in cubic units. **3.** an amount, especially a large amount: *The volume of criticism the radio station received was worrying.* **4.** loudness: *The volume on the TV was too high.*

voluminous /*say* vuh-**loohm**-uh-nuhs/ *adjective*
1. forming enough to fill a book: *Her voluminous correspondence kept her busy.* **2.** large or full: *Voluminous black clouds filled the sky.*
☐ **voluminously**, *adverb*

voluntary /*say* **vol**-uhn-tree/ *adjective*
1. If a decision is **voluntary**, it is done or made by free will or choice: *David made a voluntary decision to share the chocolates.* **2.** If work is **voluntary** it is unpaid: *The hospital is advertising for voluntary helpers.*
☐ **voluntarily**, *adverb*

☑ SPELLING TIP Remember that **voluntary** ends with *ary*, although the *a* is usually not pronounced. Rap it out as *vol*+*un*+*ta*+*ry*.

volunteer *noun*
1. someone who offers to do something, such as to join the army, of their own free will.
–*verb* **2.** If you **volunteer** to do something, you offer to do it without being forced.

vomit *verb* (**vomits**, **vomiting**, **vomited**, **has vomited**) If you **vomit**, you throw up food from your stomach out through your mouth: *After eating chips, and then going on the roller-coaster, I couldn't stop vomiting.*
☐ **vomit**, *noun*

☑ SPELLING TIP *Single letter alert*: only one *m* and only one *t* at the end. Also notice that you do not double the final *t* when you add *-ed* or *-ing*, following the rule that the consonant remains single if the final syllable is not stressed.

vortex /*say* **vaw**-teks/ *noun* (*plural* **vortexes** *or* **vortices** /*say* **vaw**-tuh-seez/) a whirling movement of air, as in a whirlwind, or water, as in a whirlpool.

vote *noun*
1. a formal indication of the wishes of a group, shown by putting hands up or marking a piece of paper outlining choices.
–*verb* **2.** When you **vote**, you say what your choice is in some decision that is being made, often in an election: *Which candidate will you vote for?*

vouch *verb in the phrase* **vouch for someone**, to guarantee that someone will be appropriate in a particular situation or to make yourself responsible for them.

voucher *noun* a piece of paper that shows what you are entitled to receive: *Each club was given a $200 voucher to buy new sports equipment*; *We gave Mum a gift voucher for her birthday.*

vow *noun*
1. a serious promise that lasts for ever.
–*verb* **2.** If you **vow** to do something, you make a serious promise to do it: *He vowed to avenge his father's death.*

vowel *noun*
1. a speech sound made by allowing air to pass through the middle of your mouth without being blocked by your tongue or lips. **2.** a letter, *a*, *e*, *i*, *o*, *u*, or sometimes *y*, used to represent the sound of a vowel.

COMPARE this with **consonant**. See also the Grammar and Punctuation Guide appendix.

voyage *noun*
1. a journey by sea or air to somewhere quite far away.
–*verb* **2.** If you **voyage**, you travel a long distance by sea or air.
☐ **voyager**, *noun*

vulgar *adjective* rude or bad-mannered: *My mother thought the new people next door were noisy and vulgar.*
☐ **vulgarity**, *noun*

vulnerable /*say* **vuln**-ruh-buhl/ *adjective*
1. If someone is **vulnerable**, they are likely to suffer something unpleasant because they are in a weak position: *He hadn't been getting enough sleep and was vulnerable to sickness*. **2.** If a species of animal is **vulnerable**, it might soon become endangered unless action is taken to protect it.
☐ **vulnerability**, *noun*

☑ SPELLING TIP Don't forget the *l* in this word which some people don't pronounce when they say it. **Vulnerable** comes from the Latin word *vulnus*, meaning 'wound', so the basic meaning is 'able to be wounded'.

vulture *noun* a large bird, usually with a bald head, related to the eagles, hawks, and falcons, which feeds on the flesh of dead animals.

vulva *noun* the external female sexual organs.

wad /*say* wod/ *noun*
1. a small lump or pad of anything soft: *a wad of hair*; *a wad of cottonwool.* **2.** a roll or bundle: *She dropped a wad of newspapers into the recycling bin.*

waddle /*say* **wod**-uhl/ *verb* If someone **waddles**, they walk like a duck, taking short steps and rolling from side to side.
☐ **waddle**, *noun*

waddy /*rhymes with* body/ *noun* (*plural* **waddies**) a heavy, wooden war club traditionally used by Aboriginal people.

WORD HISTORY from an Aboriginal language of New South Wales called Dharug

wade *verb* If you **wade** through water, you walk through it although it impedes your movement.
☐ **wader**, *noun*

wafer *noun* a thin, crisp biscuit.

waffle[1] /*say* **wof**-uhl/ *noun* a crisp, batter cake with a pattern of squares left by the hinged appliance in which it is cooked.

waffle[2] /*say* **wof**-uhl/ *verb Informal* To **waffle** is to talk or write at great length with no real knowledge.

waft /*rhymes with* soft/ *verb* If something **wafts**, it blows lightly: *Curtains wafted in and out with the breeze*; *The scent of wattle wafted on the wind.*

wag *verb* (**wags**, **wagging**, **wagged**, **has wagged**)
1. To **wag** something is to make it move quickly from side to side: *The dog wagged its tail*; *He wagged his finger to show he didn't like what she was doing.* **2.** *Informal* To **wag** school is to not go there when you are meant to.

wage *noun*
1. money that is paid regularly to someone who works.
–*verb* **2.** To **wage** war is to start a war or fight and continue it: *The enemy countries waged war against each other for three years.*

NOTE This word (as in definition 1) is often used in the plural, as in *He does not earn very good wages.*

wager *noun*
1. a bet.
–*verb* **2.** If you **wager** something, you bet it: *He wagered his winnings on the last race.*

wagon *noun*
1. a four-wheeled, heavy cart. **2.** a railway truck.

ANOTHER SPELLING is **waggon**.

waif *noun* a child that has no home, or who looks pale and thin as if they are not looked after.

wail *noun*
1. a long, sad cry.
–*verb* **2.** If someone **wails**, they utter a long, sad cry: *The baby wailed loudly for her lost toy.*

☑ SPELLING TIP Don't confuse the spelling of **wail** with **whale** which sounds the same. A **whale** is a very large mammal that lives in the sea.

waist *noun* the part of the body between the ribs and hips.

☑ SPELLING TIP Don't confuse the spelling of **waist** with **waste** which sounds the same. To **waste** something is to use more of it than you need or you use it when you don't really need to.

waistcoat *noun* a close-fitting, sleeveless piece of clothing which reaches to the waist and buttons down the front, often worn under a jacket.

wait *verb*
1. If you **wait**, you remain somewhere until something happens. **2.** If you are **waiting**, you are expecting something to happen: *I'm still waiting for a reply to my letter.* **3.** If something is **waiting**, it is ready for you: *Your coffee is waiting.* **4.** If you say something cannot **wait**, you mean that it is urgent and must be dealt with immediately.
–*phrase* **5. wait on**, to serve food and drinks to: *to wait on someone.*
☐ **wait**, *noun*: *a long wait.*

☑ SPELLING TIP Don't confuse the spelling of **wait** with **weight** which sounds the same. Something's **weight** is how heavy it is.

waiter *noun* someone who serves food and drink to you at your table in a restaurant or hotel.

NOTE A woman with this job can be called a **waitress**. The term **waitperson** is often used these days for either a man or a woman.

waive /*say* wayv/ *verb* If you **waive** something, you **1.** decide not to insist on it: *The library agreed to waive the fine.* **2.** put it off for the moment: *The teacher waived the deadline for today's homework.*

☑ SPELLING TIP Notice the *ai* spelling in this word. Don't confuse it with **wave**, the movement in the sea, which has the same sound.

wake[1] *verb* (**wakes**, **waking**, **woke**, **has woken**) **1.** If you **wake** up, you stop sleeping: *I always wake up early.* **2.** If you **wake** someone up, you rouse them from sleep: *His mother always wakes him up at seven.*
□ **wakeful**, *adjective*

NOTE Although **wake** is usually followed by *up*, you can use it by itself, as in *Please wake me early in the morning.* However, this is more formal.

wake[2] *noun* the track left by a ship or other object moving the water.

walk *verb* To **walk** is to move along by putting one foot after the other.
□ **walk**, *noun* –**walker**, *noun* –**walking**, *noun*

walkie-talkie *noun* a light radio that you can carry, used by police, soldiers, and so on, to send and receive messages.

walkover *noun* an easy victory.

wall *noun* **1.** one of the sides of a building or room. **2.** a brick or stone structure acting as a boundary fence or barrier.

wallaby *noun* (*plural* **wallabies**) any of several types of kangaroo-like animals. Some species are endangered or vulnerable.

NOTE The wallaby belongs to a class of animals called **marsupials**.
WORD HISTORY from an Aboriginal language of New South Wales called Dharug

wallaroo *noun* a large kangaroo with shaggy, dark fur that lives in rocky or hilly land.

WORD HISTORY from an Aboriginal language of New South Wales called Dharug

wallet *noun* a small folding case for paper money and so on, which can be carried in your pocket or handbag.

wallop *verb Informal* To **wallop** something or someone is to beat them hard: *He walloped the snake with a big stick*; *She'll wallop you when she finds out she's been tricked.*
□ **wallop**, *noun*

wallow *verb* If you **wallow** in something, you lie or roll about in it: *The dog wallowed in the muddy puddle*; *We wallowed about in the shallow lagoon.*

walnut /*say* **wawl**-nut/ *noun* **1.** a type of nut which you can eat, grown on a tree which first grew in Europe. **2.** the wood of this tree, used for making furniture.

☑ SPELLING TIP *Single letter alert*: only one *l*. The first part of this word has nothing to do with a wall, but comes from an old German word meaning 'foreign'.

walrus /*say* **wawl**-ruhs, **wol**-ruhs/ *noun* a large, warm-blooded sea animal with flippers and large tusks.

waltz /*say* wawls, wols/ *noun* **1.** a type of dance in which you and your partner move in circles to music with a 1-2-3 beat. **2.** a piece of music for this dance.
–*verb* **3.** When you **waltz**, you dance a waltz: *They waltzed around the room.*

wan /*say* won/ *adjective* **1.** pale or lacking in colour: *a wan complexion*; *a wan light.* **2.** sickly: *a wan smile.*

wand /*rhymes with* bond/ *noun* a thin stick or rod, especially one used by a magician or fairy that is said to work magic.

wander /*rhymes with* yonder/ *verb* **1.** If you **wander**, you go around from place to place. **2.** If your mind **wanders**, you do not think about what you should be doing and you start thinking about other things.
□ **wander**, *noun* –**wanderer**, *noun*

☑ SPELLING TIP *Tricky vowel sound*: remember the *a* spelling for the 'o' sound in the first syllable. Don't confuse this word with **wonder** (rhymes with *under*). To **wonder** is to think about something with curiosity or surprise.

wane *verb* If something **wanes** it grows, or seems to grow, smaller or less: *Support for the government has waned.*

THE OPPOSITE is **wax**[2].

wangle *verb Informal* If you **wangle** something, you get it by cunning or by being very persuasive: *She wangled a free ticket to the concert.*
□ **wangle**, *noun*

want *verb* To **want** is to **1.** feel a need or desire for: *to want your dinner*; *always wanting something new.* **2.** wish or desire: *I want to see you.* **3.** have none or little of: *He wants common sense.* **4.** have a need for: *The house wants cleaning.* **5.** wish or feel likely to: *They can go out if they want.* **6.** be poor or needy.
–*noun* **7.** something wanted or needed: *to see to someone's wants.* **8.** an absence or lack of something necessary: *plants dying for want of rain.* **9.** poverty: *to live in want.*

wanton /*say* **won**-tuhn/ *adjective* **1.** done or behaving without thought or sense, often with bad results: *She is very concerned about the wanton destruction of rainforests*; *wanton vandalism.* **2.** not controlled in sexual behaviour.
□ **wantonly**, *adverb* –**wantonness**, *noun*

war *noun*
1. fighting with weapons between countries, or between groups within a nation. **2.** a particular example of such fighting: *the war in Iraq.* **3.** any other fighting: *a war against poverty*; *a war of words.*
–*verb* (**wars**, **warring**, **warred**, **has warred**) **4.** If two countries or groups **war** with each other, they fight each other: *They have been warring with the council for years.*
□ **warfare**, *noun* –**warlike**, *adjective*

☑ SPELLING TIP Don't confuse the spelling of **war** with **wore** which sounds the same. **Wore** is the past tense of **wear**, to carry or have on your body.

waratah /*say* wo-ruh-**tah**, **wo**-ruh-tah/ *noun* an Australian shrub with large red flowers.

WORD HISTORY from an Aboriginal language of New South Wales called Dharug

☑ SPELLING TIP *Single letter alert*: only one *r*. Also remember the *h* at the end, and the fact that each of the three vowels in this word is an *a* though they each have a different sound. (After all, it is an Australian plant.)

warble *verb* To **warble** is to sing with trills, like a bird.

ward *noun*
1. a room or division in a hospital. **2.** a young person who has been legally placed under the care or control of a court of law or department of government.
–*verb in the phrase* **3. ward off**, to turn aside: *We put a scarecrow in the vegetable garden to ward off birds.*

warden *noun* someone who is given the care or responsibility of something.

warder *noun* a prison officer.

wardrobe *noun*
1. a cupboard for keeping clothes in. **2.** someone's clothes, or the costumes used by actors.

ware *noun*
1. wares, articles for sale: *The market stalls sold wares ranging from homemade jam to antique jewellery.* **2.** a particular kind of article produced for sale: *glassware*; *silverware.*

NOTE This word (as in definition 2) is now chiefly used in combination with some other word, as in the examples.

☑ SPELLING TIP Don't confuse the spelling of **ware** with **wear** or **where**, both of which have the same sound. When you **wear** clothes, you have them on; **where** asks the question 'at what place?'.

warehouse *noun* a large building for storing goods.

warfare *noun* fighting between armies.

warhead *noun* the part of a rocket, bomb, or torpedo containing the explosive.

warlock *noun* a man who is thought to have the power of magic, especially one in a story who uses magic to do evil.

SIMILAR WORDS are **sorcerer** and **wizard**.

warm *adjective*
1. If something is **warm**, it **a.** has some heat that can be felt: *warm water.* **b.** keeps heat in: *warm clothes*; *a warm house.* **2.** If someone is **warm**, they are kind and affectionate: *a warm welcome.*
–*verb* **3.** When you **warm** something, you make it warm: *to warm milk*; *Warm your feet by the fire.*
–*phrase* **4. warm to**, to grow affectionate or friendly towards: *I did not warm to her at first, but now we are close friends.*
□ **warmly**, *adverb*: *to smile warmly.* –**warmth**, *noun*

warm-blooded *adjective* A **warm-blooded** animal has a body temperature which stays more or less the same regardless of the surrounding temperature.

COMPARE this with **cold-blooded** (definition 2)

warn *verb* If you **warn** someone, you tell them about possible problems or dangers: *They warned us that high winds were expected*; *Flashing lights warn of a railway crossing ahead.*
□ **warning**, *noun*

☑ SPELLING TIP Don't confuse the spelling of **warn** with **worn** which sounds the same. Something is **worn** if it is shabby or damaged from frequent use; **worn** is also a past form of the verb **wear**.

warp *verb* If something **warps**, it loses its shape and becomes bent or curved: *Your tennis racquet will warp if you leave it outside.*
□ **warped**, *adjective* distorted: *a warped sense of humour.*

warrant /*say* **wo**-ruhnt/ *noun*
1. a paper issued by a magistrate allowing a police officer to make an arrest or to carry out a search of a building.
–*verb* **2.** If someone **warrants** something, they give a formal promise or guarantee about it: *The company has warranted to repair the television if it breaks down in the first twelve months.* **3.** If something **warrants** a particular action, it demands or requires it: *The crime warrants investigation.*

warranty /*say* **wo**-ruhn-tee/ *noun* (*plural* **warranties**) a formal promise or assurance that you can depend on the quality of what you have bought: *Do not buy a television without a warranty.*

warren *noun*
1. a series of connecting burrows where many rabbits live. 2. a building or area where many poor people live in overcrowded conditions.

warrigal /*say* **wo**-ruh-guhl/ *noun*
1. See **dingo**.
–*adjective* 2. wild or untamed.

WORD HISTORY from an Aboriginal language of New South Wales called Dharug

warrior /*say* **wo**-ree-uh/ *noun* a soldier or fighter.

☑ SPELLING TIP *Tricky vowel sound*: the first vowel sound is spelt with an *a*. You will remember this by thinking of the related word *war*. Double the *r* and add *ior* (not *ier*) and you have **warrior**. Rap it out as *war+ri+or*.

wart *noun* a small, hard lump on the skin, caused by a virus.

wary /*say* **wair**-ree/ *adjective* watchful or careful.

was *verb* the first and third person singular past tense indicative of the verb **be**.

NOTE For an explanation of *indicative*, see **mood**[2]. See also the Grammar and Punctuation Guide appendix.

wasabi /*say* wuh-**sah**-bee/ *noun* a green paste made from the roots of an Asian plant, used as a hot spice with Japanese food.

wash *verb*
1. When you **wash** something, you clean it with water. 2. When you **wash**, you wash your body. 3. If something is **washed** somewhere, it is carried there by water: *I washed the spider down the drain.*
–*noun* 4. an act of washing: *Give the clothes a good wash.* 5. waves made by a ship, boat, etc.: *The ferry's wash splashed against the jetty.*
–*phrase* 6. **wash out**, a. to remove by washing: *wash out a stain.* b. to cause to be stopped: *The rain washed out the football match.* 7. **wash up**, to wash the plates, cutlery, etc., after a meal: *Let's wash up before the movie starts.*
☐ **washable**, *adjective* –**washing**, *noun*

washer *noun*
1. a flat ring of rubber or metal used to make a joint or nut (definition 3) fit tightly. 2. See **face washer**.

washing machine *noun* a machine that washes clothes automatically.

wasn't a short form of *was not*.

wasp *noun* a four-winged insect that stings.

waste *verb*
1. If you **waste** something, you use more of it than you need or you use it when you do not really need to: *to waste food*; *Don't waste water by leaving the tap running.* 2. If you **waste** something, you don't take advantage of it: *to waste time.* 3. If you say something is **wasted** on someone, you mean that they don't understand it: *The joke was wasted on her, as she didn't know what he was talking about.*
–*noun* 4. something that is left over from a process and unwanted: *industrial waste*; *Waste is passed from the body as urine or faeces.* 5. useless spending or use without enough result: *a waste of material*; *a waste of money.*
–*adjective* 6. unwanted or left over from some process: *waste product*; *waste matter.*
–*phrase* 7. **go to waste**, to fail to be used. 8. **lay waste**, to destroy or ruin. 9. **waste away**, to grow thin: *She has been ill for so long that she seems to be just wasting away.*
☐ **wastage**, *noun* –**wasteful**, *adjective*

☑ SPELLING TIP Don't confuse the spelling of **waste** with **waist** which sounds the same. Your **waist** is the part of your body between your ribs and hips.

watch *verb*
1. If you **watch** something, you look at it attentively for some time: *We watched the parade go past*; *Watch how I fold the sheets.* 2. If you **watch** someone or something, you keep a careful eye on them: *Police watched the suspect for weeks before they arrested him.* 3. If you tell someone to **watch** what they do, you are warning them to be careful: *Watch how you handle that knife – it's very sharp.*
–*noun* (*plural* **watches**) 4. a guard: *The drovers kept watch over their animals at night.* 5. a small clock which you wear on your wrist.
–*phrase* 6. **watch out**, to be alert or be on your guard. 7. **watch out for**, a. to avoid, or to beware of: *Watch out for broken glass.* b. to look for: *I like to watch out for my father when he comes home.* 8. **watch over**, to guard or protect.
☐ **watcher**, *noun* –**watchful**, *adjective*

water *noun*
1. the colourless, transparent liquid which forms rain, rivers, lakes, and oceans.
–*verb* 2. When you **water** something, you pour water on it: *I watered the pot plants.*
–*phrase* 3. **in deep** (or **hot**) **water**, in trouble. 4. **water down**, a. to make a drink weaker by adding water. b. to weaken: *to water down an argument.*
☐ **watery**, *adjective*

watercolour *noun*
1. paint made from colour mixed with water rather than oil. 2. a painting done in watercolour.
☐ **watercolourist**, *noun*

ANOTHER SPELLING is **watercolor**.

watercress *noun* a leafy salad vegetable with a peppery taste.

waterfall *noun* a steep fall or flow of water, usually from a great height.

waterfront *noun*
1. land next to a body of water, such as the ocean or a lake. **2.** the wharves in a port.

waterhole *noun* a natural hole or hollow in which water collects, such as one where animals come to drink, or one in the dried-up course of a river, etc.

waterlily *noun* (*plural* **waterlilies**) a water plant with large flowers and flat leaves that float.

waterlogged *adjective* Ground that is **waterlogged** is completely soaked with water: *We couldn't play sport because the field was waterlogged.*

watermark *noun*
1. a line showing the greatest height that water has risen to. **2.** a mark, usually the maker's name or trademark, made in paper and able to be seen when held up to the light. **3.** a copyright notice or other mark which is inserted in digital audio, video or images.
□ **watermark**, *verb*

ANOTHER FORM of (definition 3) is **digital watermark**.

watermelon *noun* a large melon with green skin and dark pink flesh.

water polo *noun* a game played by two teams of seven swimmers each, in which the object is to pass a ball into the opposing team's goal.

waterproof *adjective* made of, or coated with, material which prevents water getting through.

water rights *plural noun* **1.** the right to control an area of water, especially the rights of the original inhabitants of a country to control an area of water where they have traditionally fished. **2.** the right to use water from a particular stream, lake, or canal that has been restricted from use by most people.

watershed *noun* the ridge line at the top of a range of hills dividing two drainage areas or river basins.

waterski *verb* (**waterskis**, **waterskiing**, **waterski'd** *or* **waterskied**, **has waterski'd** *or* **has waterskied**) To **waterski** is to travel on special skis over water, towed by a fast boat.

watertight *adjective*
1. completely sealed against water. **2.** having no fault or weakness: *a watertight agreement.*

watt /*say* wot/ *noun* a unit of electrical power.

THE SYMBOL for this is **W**.

☑ SPELLING TIP *Double letter alert*: double *t* at the end. Don't confuse this word with *what*, whatever you do!

wattle *noun*
1. a small tree that grows in warm areas of the world, and has small, ball-shaped, yellow flowers. **2.** a coloured fleshy part hanging from the throat of certain birds such as the turkey.

ANOTHER NAME (for definition 1) is **acacia**.

wave *noun*
1. a movement in the form of a long raised line on the surface of a liquid, especially the sea. **2.** a movement that travels through air or water and which we experience as light, sound, and so on: *a sound wave.* **3.** a sudden rush of feeling: *A wave of panic swept through the crowd.* **4.** an up-and-down or side-to-side movement of the hand used as a sign of greeting or farewell.
–*verb* **5.** When you **wave** to someone, you give them a wave with your hand: *He waved goodbye.* **6.** When you **wave** something, you move it up and down or from side to side: *I waved my flag.*
□ **wavy**, *adjective* (**wavier**, **waviest**)

wavelength *noun*
1. one full wave movement, such as from the top of one wave to the top of the next. **2.** a way of thinking: *They get on so well because they are on the same wavelength.*

waver *verb*
1. If something **wavers**, it sways to and fro, as in the breeze. **2.** If someone **wavers**, they hesitate, unable to make up their mind.

wax[1] *noun*
1. a fairly hard greasy substance that is easy to melt: *Wax dripped from the candle*; *She polished the table with furniture wax.*
–*verb* **2.** If you **wax** something, you rub or polish it with wax.

wax[2] *verb* To **wax** is to grow, or seem to grow, bigger: *The moon is waxing.*

THE OPPOSITE is **wane**.

way *noun*
1. manner or means: *This is the way I peel potatoes.* **2.** direction: *Go that way.* **3.** passage or progress: *She slowly made her way through the crowded room.* **4.** road, path, route, or passage: *a way through the forest.*
–*phrase* **5. give way, a.** to move away. **b.** to give in. **6. go out of your way**, to make a special effort. **7. out of the way, a.** so as not to block or keep back: *Get your feet out of the way.* **b.** dealt with: *I'm glad to have that essay out of the way.* **8. under way, a.** moving along: *Once the track is checked, the train will be under way.* **b.** in progress: *The conference is under way.*

wayfarer *noun* a traveller, especially on foot.

waylay *verb* (**waylays**, **waylaying**, **waylaid**, **has waylaid**) To **waylay** someone is to lie in wait for them, especially in order to attack them: *He was sneaking up to his room when his parents waylaid him with questions about why he was home so late.*

way-out *adjective Rather informal* quite different from the usual: *way-out ideas.*

wayward *adjective* acting in a way that people think is not right or proper: *a wayward teenager.*

we *pronoun* the plural form of **I**: *We are catching the midday train.*

SEE ALSO **us** and **our**.

weak *adjective*
1. likely to break or fall down: *a weak structure.* **2.** not healthy or strong. **3.** lacking in force or strength: *a weak government*; *a weak argument.*
☐ **weaken**, *verb* –**weakly**, *adverb* –**weakness**, *noun*

☑ SPELLING TIP Don't confuse the spelling of **weak** with **week** which sounds the same but is spelt with *ee*. A **week** is a period of seven days.

weakling *noun* a weak person or animal.

weal *noun* a mark or swelling on the skin made by a blow.

A SIMILAR WORD is **welt**.

wealth /*say* welth/ *noun*
1. a large store of money and property. **2.** a rich supply: *a wealth of ideas.*
☐ **wealthy**, *adjective* (**wealthier**, **wealthiest**)

☑ SPELLING TIP *Tricky vowel sound*: *ea* spelling for the 'e' sound. **Wealth** comes from an old word *weal*, meaning 'wellbeing', and has the same sound and spelling pattern as *health*.

wean *verb* To **wean** a baby is to start feeding it with food other than its mother's milk: *We are weaning the puppies.*

weapon /*say* **wep**-uhn/ *noun*
1. an instrument used in fighting, such as a gun, bomb, missile, and so on.
–*phrase* **2. weapon of mass destruction**, a weapon, such as a nuclear one, capable of killing a great number of people.

THE ABBREVIATION for **weapon of mass destruction** is **WMD**.

☑ SPELLING TIP *Tricky vowel sound*: *ea* spelling for the 'e' sound in the first syllable of **weapon**.

wear *verb* (**wears**, **wearing**, **wore**, **has worn**)
1. When you **wear** a piece of clothing, you have it on your body: *He was wearing a blue shirt.*
–*phrase* **2. wear away**, to get rid of bit by bit: *Erosion has worn away the soil.* **3. wear off**, to gradually reduce or get less: *The pain is beginning to wear off.* **4. wear out**, **a.** to wear or use until no longer fit for use: *to wear out shoes.* **b.** to make very tired: *Working two jobs is really wearing me out.* **c.** to cause to be used up: *You have worn out your welcome.*
☐ **wear**, *noun*: *beach wear.* –**wearable**, *adjective*

☑ SPELLING TIP Don't confuse the spelling of **wear** with **where** or **ware**, all of which have the same sound. **Where** asks the question 'at what place?'; a **ware** is particular kind of manufactured article that you can buy, such as *silverware* or *software*.

weary /*say* **wear**-ree/ *adjective* (**wearier**, **weariest**)
1. tired.
–*verb* (**wearies**, **wearying**, **wearied**, **has wearied**) **2.** When something **wearies** you, it makes you weary: *Age shall not weary them*; *Her endless questions weary me.*
☐ **weariness**, *noun*

weasel *noun* a small, fierce European animal that eats mice, rabbits and other small animals.

weather /*say* **wedh**-uh/ *noun*
1. the state of the atmosphere as far as heat and cold, wetness and dryness are concerned.
–*verb* **2.** If something **weathers**, it changes because of the effects of weather on it: *The rocks have weathered into curious shapes.* **3.** If you **weather** a change or difficulty, you manage to get through it safely: *to weather a crisis.*
☐ **weathered**, *adjective*

☑ SPELLING TIP Don't confuse the spelling of **weather** with **whether** or **wether**, both of which sound the same. **Whether** is a word which introduces the first of two alternatives: *I do not know whether it's going to be sunny or rainy.* A **wether** is a castrated ram.

weatherboard *adjective* having a covering of overlapping wooden boards: *a weatherboard house.*

weathervane *noun* a flat piece of metal fixed on a roof, which moves with the wind and shows its direction.

weave *verb* (**weaves**, **weaving**, **wove**, **has woven**)
1. When someone **weaves** cloth, they make it by crossing threads over and under each other on a machine called a loom. **2.** If you **weave** something, you wind it in and out: *She wove her hair into a plait*; *We could see him weaving through the crowd towards us.*
☐ **weave**, *noun*

web *noun*
1. the fine silk-like net made by spiders to catch insects. **2. the Web**, See **World Wide Web**.

webbed *adjective* If an animal has **webbed** feet, it has skin between the toes, usually to help with swimming.
☐ **webbing**, *noun*

NOTE An animal with webbed feet is described as **web-footed**.

webcam *noun Informal* a digital video camera linked to a computer so that images can be sent over the internet.

ANOTHER FORM is **web cam**.
WORD HISTORY short for *web camera*

web page *noun* a document with a unique address on the World Wide Web.

THE SHORT FORM of this is **page**.
ANOTHER FORM is **webpage**.

web portal *noun* a website which gives information and provides links to a number of other websites with related information.

THE SHORT FORM of this is **portal**.

website *noun* a place on the World Wide Web that you can access by the internet.

ANOTHER FORM is **web site**. This is often shortened to **site**.

wed *verb* (**weds**, **wedding**, **wed**, **has wed**) *Rather old-fashioned* To **wed** someone is to marry them: *They were wed at noon.*

WORD HISTORY from an Old English word meaning 'pledge'

we'd a short form of *we would* or *we had*.

wedding *noun* a marriage ceremony.
☐ **wedding**, *adjective*: *a wedding dress.*

wedge *noun*
1. a piece of wood or metal, thinner at one end than the other, which can be used to block up a narrow space.
–*verb* **2.** If you **wedge** something somewhere, you thrust, drive or fix it there: *He wedged himself into a corner*; *She wedged the door open.*

wedlock *noun Old-fashioned* the state of being married.

Wednesday /*say* **wenz**-day/ *noun* the fourth day of the week.

THE ABBREVIATION is **Wed**.

☑ SPELLING TIP *Silent letter alert*: don't forget the *d* before the *n* in this word. It is there because **Wednesday** comes from an Old English word meaning 'Woden's day' (Woden was the chief Anglo-Saxon god). Rap it out as *Wed+ nes+ day.*

wee[1] *adjective* very small.

NOTE This word is used mainly by Scottish people.

wee[2] *verb Informal* To **wee** is to urinate.
☐ **wee**, *noun*

weed *noun*
1. a useless plant growing where it is not wanted.
–*verb* **2.** When you **weed** a garden, you remove weeds from it.
–*phrase* **3. weed out**, to remove something or someone unwanted: *The coach is trying to weed out the weaker players.*

weedy *adjective* (**weedier**, **weediest**) thin and weak.

week *noun* a period of seven days.

☑ SPELLING TIP Don't confuse the spelling of **week** with **weak** which sounds the same but is spelt with *ea*. Something **weak** is likely to break or fall down.

weekday *noun* any day of the week except Saturday or Sunday.

weekend *noun* the time from Friday evening, or Saturday, to Monday morning, when most people do not have to work or go to school.

weekly *adverb*
1. once a week: *The bottles are collected weekly.*
–*noun* (*plural* **weeklies**) **2.** a paper or magazine that comes out once a week.
☐ **weekly**, *adjective*: *weekly news.*

weep *verb* (**weeps**, **weeping**, **wept**, **has wept**) To **weep** is to show sorrow or any other emotion by crying.

weevil *noun* a kind of beetle which destroys grain, nuts, fruit, and trees.

weigh /*sounds like* way/ *verb*
1. If you **weigh** something, you measure how heavy it is with a scale or balance. **2.** If something or someone **weighs** a particular amount, that is how heavy they are: *The boxer weighed 85 kilos.*
–*phrase* **3. weigh on**, to cause worry or problems to: *His words of warning weighed on my mind*; *The responsibilities of the new job have begun to weigh on her.*

☑ SPELLING TIP *Tricky vowel sound*: remember the *eigh* spelling for the 'ay' sound, as in some other words like *eight* and *weight*. Don't confuse **weigh** with **way** or **whey**, both of which sound the same. A **way** of doing something is the manner or fashion in which you do it; **whey** is the watery part of milk separated from the curd, formed in cheese-making.

weight /*say* wayt/ *noun*
1. an amount of heaviness. **2.** the force of gravity on something, which varies with its position on the earth. **3.** a heavy object.
–*phrase* **4. pull your weight**, to do your fair share of work. **5. throw your weight around** (or **about**), to use your authority, influence, and so on, when it is not necessary.
☐ **weightlessness**, *noun* –**weighty**, *adjective* (**weightier**, **weightiest**)

☑ SPELLING TIP *Tricky vowel sound*: *eigh* spelling for the 'ay' sound, as in *weigh* from which this word is formed. Don't confuse **weight** with **wait** which sounds the same. To **wait** is to stay or rest until something happens.

weir /*rhymes with* ear/ *noun* a small dam across a river.

☑ SPELLING TIP *Exception to rule*: remember that **weir** is spelt with *ei*, breaking the rule that *i* comes before *e*, except after *c*. This is because that rule only works when the sound is 'ee' as in *believe*. In **weir** the vowel sound is 'ear', not 'ee', and so the rule does not apply.

weird /*say* weard/ *adjective* very strange.
☐ **weirdly**, *adverb* –**weirdness**, *noun*

☑ SPELLING TIP *Exception to rule*: remember that **weird** is spelt with *ei*, breaking the rule that *i* comes before *e*, except after *c*. This is because the vowel sound is 'ear', not 'ee', and so the rule does not apply.

welcome *interjection* **1.** a quite formal way of greeting someone: *Welcome, ladies and gentlemen.*
–*noun* **2.** a kindly greeting: *a warm welcome.*
–*verb* **3.** When you **welcome** someone, you greet them: *She welcomed her guests.*
☐ **welcome**, *adjective*: *a welcome change.*

☑ SPELLING TIP *Single letter alert*: only one *l*. Though this word is formed from *well* and *come*, you have to remember that one of the *l*'s in *well* has been dropped.

welcome to country *noun* a ceremony at the start of a public event in Australia in which someone who is a representative of the traditional Indigenous custodians of the land on which the event is taking place welcomes those attending the event.

ANOTHER FORM This can also be spelt with capital letters.
SEE the Welcome to Country and Acknowledgement of Country appendix for more information.

weld *verb* If you **weld** two pieces of metal, you join them together by applying intense heat.
☐ **weld**, *noun* –**welder**, *noun*

welfare *noun* the state of being healthy and having a good way of life: *animal welfare*; *We are concerned about the welfare of the whole community.*

☑ SPELLING TIP *Single letter alert*: only one *l*. Though this word is formed from *well* and *fare* (in an old sense of 'go'), you have to remember that one of the *l*'s in *well* has been dropped.

well[1] *adverb* (**better**, **best**)
1. in a good way: *He cooks well.* **2.** thoroughly: *Mix the paint well.* **3.** clearly: *I can hear it quite well.*
–*interjection* **4.** This word is often used to **a.** show surprise: *Well! I would have never have guessed that.* **b.** begin talking after a pause or interruption: *Well, as I was saying, we can't afford it.*
–*adjective* (**better**, **best**) **5.** satisfactory or in good health: *Are you feeling well?*; *All is well.*
–*phrase* **6. as well**, in addition: *She is bringing a friend as well.* **7. as well as**, in addition to: *He was handsome as well as rich.*

well[2] *noun*
1. a hole made in the ground to obtain water, oil, or other substances.
–*verb in the phrase* **2. well up**, to come to the surface: *Tears welled up in his eyes.*

we'll the short form of *we will*.

wellbeing *noun* the state of being healthy and contented.

well-meaning *adjective* having good intentions.

well-off *adjective* wealthy.

ANOTHER TERM for this is **well-to-do**.

welt *noun* a raised mark on the skin, usually from a blow with a stick or whip.

A SIMILAR WORD is **weal**.

were *verb* the past tense indicative plural and subjunctive singular and plural of the verb **be**.

NOTE For an explanation of *indicative* and *subjunctive*, see **mood**[2]. See also the Grammar and Punctuation Guide appendix.

we're a short form of *we are*.

weren't a short form of *were not*.

werewolf /*say* **wair**-woolf/ *noun* (*plural* **werewolves**) in old-fashioned belief, a man who changes into a wolf when there is a full moon.

WORD HISTORY from the Old English word for 'man' added to *wolf*

west *noun* the direction in which the sun sets.
☐ **west**, *adjective*, *adverb* –**westerly**, *adjective*: *westerly winds.*

NOTE The opposite direction is **east**.

western *adjective*
1. lying in or towards the west: *western suburbs.*
–*noun* **2.** a story or film about life in the American west when people from Europe were first settling there during the 19th century.

wet *adjective* (**wetter**, **wettest**)
1. If something is **wet**, it is soaked or covered with water or some other liquid. **2.** When something such as paint or clay is **wet**, it has not dried out yet: *The paint's still wet.* **3.** When it is **wet**, it is raining: *It's been wet all day.*
–*noun* **4. the wet**, the rainy season in central and northern Australia, from December to March.

–*verb* (**wets**, **wetting**, **wet**, **has wet**) **5.** If you **wet** something, you make it wet: *Wet your hair thoroughly, then apply the shampoo.*
☐ **wetness**, *noun*

ANOTHER FORM This word (as in definition 4) is sometimes spelt with a capital letter: **the Wet**. SIMILAR WORDS (for definition 1) are **damp**, **moist**, **soaked**, **soaking**, **sodden** and **soggy**. Things that are **damp** or **moist** are slightly wet. The other words describe things that are extremely wet. **Soggy** usually describes something that has become unpleasantly soft because of being wet: *soggy ground*, *soggy toast*.

wet blanket *noun Informal* a person who has a discouraging or depressing effect: *Julie was a wet blanket because she wouldn't agree with any of our suggestions for having fun.*

wether *noun* a ram castrated when young.

☑ SPELLING TIP Don't confuse the spelling of **wether** with **weather** or **whether**, both of which sound the same. The **weather** is sunshine or rain. **Whether** is the word that introduces the first of two alternatives: *Do you know whether she is coming or not?*

wetland *noun* an area of land which is frequently or permanently covered by shallow water, such as a marsh or swamp, with plants and animals that are adapted to live in these conditions.

ANOTHER FORM This is often used in the plural form, **wetlands**.

wetsuit *noun* a tight rubber piece of clothing worn by divers and surfers to keep in body heat.

we've a short form of *we have*.

whack *Rather informal*
–*noun* **1.** a sharp blow.
–*verb* **2.** If you **whack** something, you strike it with a whack: *He whacked the ball over the fence.*

whale *noun* a very large sea mammal that used to be hunted for its valuable oil.
☐ **whaler**, *noun* –**whaling**, *noun*

NOTE The male is a **bull**; the female is a **cow**; the young is a **calf**.

☑ SPELLING TIP Don't confuse **whale** with **wail** which sounds the same. To **wail** is to give a long, sad cry.

wharf /*say* wawf/ *noun* (*plural* **wharves** *or* **wharfs**) a structure built along or out from the shore of a port, where ships can load and unload.

WORD HISTORY from an Old English word meaning 'dam'

☑ SPELLING TIP *Tricky vowel sound*: *ar* spelling for the 'aw' sound. Another word with this sound and spelling pattern is *dwarf*. Also remember the silent *h* following the *w*, as in many other words.

what *pronoun* **1.** asking for something to be named or stated: *What is your name?*; *What did he do?* **2.** asking about the nature, character, class, origin, and so on, of a thing or person: *What is that animal?* **3.** asking about the importance of something: *What is wealth without health?* **4.** the thing that: *This is what he says.* **5.** anything that: *Say what you please.*
–*adverb* **6.** how much?: *What does it matter?*

whatever *pronoun* **1. a.** anything that: *Do whatever you like.* **b.** no matter what: *Do it, whatever happens.* **2.** what ever? what?: *Whatever do you mean?*
–*adjective* **3.** any … that: *Whatever worth the work has is due to you.* **4.** no matter what: *Whatever blame he might receive, he'll still carry on.* **5.** what or who … it may be: *For whatever reason, he is unwilling*; *any person whatever.*

NOTE This word (as in definition 2) is used to give force to a question.

wheat *noun* the grain of a widely grown cereal plant, used for making flour.

wheedle /*say* **weed**-uhl/ *verb* If you **wheedle**, you try to get something by coaxing or persuasion: *He wheedled a free bus ride by saying he did not have enough money for the fare.*

wheel *noun*
1. a circular frame or solid disc turning on an axle, used in machinery and on vehicles.
–*verb* **2.** If you **wheel** something, you roll or push it on wheels: *to wheel a bicycle.* **3.** If you **wheel**, you turn around: *He wheeled about to have a look.*
☐ **wheeled**, *adjective*: *wheeled vehicles.*

wheelbarrow *noun* a small cart, usually with one wheel at the front and two legs, which you lift when you wheel it along.

wheelchair *noun* a chair on wheels, used by invalids and those unable to walk.

wheeze *verb* If you **wheeze**, you breathe with difficulty and with a whistling sound.
☐ **wheeze**, *noun* –**wheezy**, *adjective*

whelk /*say* welk/ *noun* a large shellfish with a spiral shell.

when *adverb*
1. at what time?: *When are you coming?*
–*conjunction* **2.** at what time: *Do you know when he is coming?* **3.** at the time that: *We'll ring you when we are ready to go.* **4.** at any time: *He gets impatient when he is kept waiting.*
–*pronoun* **5.** what time: *Since when have you known this?*

whenever *conjunction*
1. at any time when: *Come whenever you like.*
–*adverb* **2.** when?: *Whenever did he say that?*

NOTE This word (as in definition 2) is used to give emphasis to a question.

where *adverb*
1. in or at what place?: *Where is he?* **2.** in what position?: *Where do you want to stand?* **3.** to what place?: *Where are you going?* **4.** from what source?: *Where did you get this information?*
–*conjunction* **5.** in, at, or to what place, or point: *Find where the trouble is*; *Find out where he's gone.* **6.** in a position, or place in which: *There are cases where it is better not to know the truth*; *The book is where you left it.*
–*pronoun* **7.** what place: *Where have you come from?* **8.** the place in which: *This is where we live.*

☑ SPELLING TIP Don't confuse the spelling of **where** with **wear** or **ware**, all of which have the same sound. To **wear** clothes is to have them on; a **ware** is a particular kind of manufactured article that you can buy.

whereabouts *noun* the place where someone or something is: *We don't know his whereabouts.*

wherever *conjunction*
1. in, at, or to, whatever place.
–*adverb* **2.** where?: *Wherever did you find that?*

NOTE This word (as in definition 2) is used to give emphasis to a question.

☑ SPELLING TIP Remember that, although **wherever** is made up of *where* and *ever*, it has only one *e* in the middle, because the *e* at the end of *where* has been dropped when the words were joined. Also remember the silent *h* following the *w*, as in *where* and many other words.

whet /*sounds like* wet/ *verb* (**whets**, **whetting**, **whetted**, **has whetted**) To **whet** something is to sharpen it: *to whet a knife*; *The holiday brochures whetted our appetite for the real thing.*

☑ SPELLING TIP Remember that this word begins with *wh* for the 'w' sound. Don't confuse it with **wet** (meaning 'not dry'), which sounds the same.

whether /*say* **wedh**-uh/ *conjunction* a word introducing the first of two or more possible happenings, and sometimes repeated before the second one: *It matters little whether we go or whether we stay.*

☑ SPELLING TIP Remember the silent *h* following the *w* in **whether**, as in many other words. Don't confuse it with **weather** or **wether**, both of which sound the same. The **weather** is sunshine or rain; a **wether** is a castrated ram.

whey /*sounds like* way/ *noun* the watery part of milk separated from the curd, formed in cheese-making.

☑ SPELLING TIP Don't confuse the spelling of **whey** with **way** or **weigh**, both of which sound the same. A **way** of doing something is the manner or fashion in which you do it; to **weigh** something is to measure how heavy it is.

which *pronoun* **1.** of a certain number, what one?: *Which of these do you want?* **2.** what particular one: *She knows which she wants*; *Choose which one you like.*
–*adjective* **3.** what one (of a number of items): *Which book do you want?*

☑ SPELLING TIP Remember the silent *h* following the *w* in **which**, as in many other words. Don't confuse it with **witch**. A **witch** is a woman who can do magic.

whichever *pronoun* **1.** any one that: *Take whichever you prefer.* **2.** no matter which: *Hats really suit you, so whichever you buy will look great.*
–*adjective* **3.** no matter which: *Whichever film you want to see is fine with me.*

whiff *noun*
1. a slight smell: *a whiff of perfume.* **2.** a slight suggestion or sign: *a whiff of scandal.*

while *noun*
1. a space of time: *a long while.*
–*conjunction* **2.** during or in the time that: *Stay here while I'm out.*
–*phrase* **3. once in a while**, occasionally.

whim *noun* a sudden change of mind without an obvious reason.

whimper *verb* To **whimper** is to cry with low, plaintive sounds.
☐ **whimper**, *noun*

whimsical *adjective* odd in an amusing way.

whine *verb* To **whine** is to make a high, continuous noise, as a dog does when in pain.
☐ **whine**, *noun*

whinge /*say* winj/ *verb* If someone **whinges**, they complain constantly or about unimportant things.
☐ **whinger**, *noun*

whinny *verb* (**whinnies**, **whinnying**, **whinnied**, **has whinnied**) When a horse **whinnies**, it makes a neighing sound.
☐ **whinny**, *noun* (*plural* **whinnies**)

whip *noun*
1. a long piece of rope or leather attached to a handle, used to hit animals such as racehorses.
–*verb* (**whips**, **whipping**, **whipped**, **has whipped**) **2.** To **whip** someone or something is to hit them with a whip. **3.** If you **whip** a liquid food, such as cream, you beat it with light, quick strokes until it thickens.
–*phrase* **4. whip out**, to bring out with a sudden movement: *She whipped out a camera.* **5. whip up**, to rouse: *to whip up support.*

whirl *verb* If something **whirls**, it turns or spins around rapidly: *The blades of the helicopter whirled and then it lifted off the ground.*
☐ **whirl**, *noun*: *a whirl of dust.*

whirlpool *noun* a circular current, as in a river or sea, which draws things into its centre.

whirlwind *noun* a very strong wind that blows in a spiral.

whirr *verb* When something **whirrs**, it makes a low buzzing sound while moving or working: *I could hear the sewing machine whirring away in the room next door.*
☐ **whirr**, *noun*

whisk *noun*
1. a light, sweeping stroke: *The mare got rid of the flies with a whisk of her tail.* **2.** a kitchen tool used for beating eggs, cream and so on.
–*verb* **3.** If you **whisk** something, you move it lightly and rapidly: *She whisked off the blanket*; *He whisked me out of the room.*

whisker *noun*
1. one of the long bristles on the face of a cat or similar animal. **2. whiskers**, a man's beard and moustache.

whisky /*say* **wisk**-ee/ *noun* a strong alcoholic drink made from grain.

WORD HISTORY from a Gaelic word meaning 'water of life'

whisper *verb* If you **whisper**, you speak very softly with your breath rather than your voice.
☐ **whisper**, *noun*

whist /*say* wist/ *noun* a card game played by two pairs of people.

whistle /*say* **wis**-uhl/ *verb*
1. If you **whistle**, you make a high noise by pushing your breath through your lips when they are nearly closed: *What's that tune you're whistling?* **2.** If something **whistles**, it makes a high sound: *We could hear the wind whistling all night.*
–*noun* **3.** a small device which produces one or more notes when you blow through it, or when steam goes through it. **4.** the sound produced by a whistle or by whistling.

☑ SPELLING TIP *Silent letter alert*: don't forget the silent *t* after the single *s*.

white *adjective*
1. of the colour of milk. **2.** light or fairly light in colour: *white wine*; *white coffee*; *white meat.* **3.** having light skin like a European: *a white man.*
–*noun* **4.** a white colour. **5.** the clear part of an egg, which turns white when it is cooked.
☐ **whiten**, *verb* –**whiteness**, *noun*

ANOTHER FORM For definition 5, you can also say **eggwhite**.

white ant *noun* an insect which eats through wood.

NOTE Scientists classify it as a **termite**, not as an ant.

white blood cell *noun* a white or colourless corpuscle in the blood, which fights disease-producing micro-organisms.

whiteboard *noun* a large white plastic board used for writing or drawing on with a special felt pen.

white elephant *noun* something useless which can cost a lot of money to maintain: *The sporting complex has become a white elephant because nobody uses it.*

white flag *noun* an all-white flag, used as the symbol of surrender.

white heat *noun* heat great enough to cause metal to glow white.

white lie *noun* a lie told for reasons of kindness or politeness.

white-out *noun* a thin white paint that is used to cover written mistakes on paper.

ANOTHER TERM for this is **liquid paper**.

white shark *noun* a very large, aggressive shark of warm seas, which is bluish grey on top and white underneath.

OTHER NAMES are **great white shark** and **white pointer**.

whitewash *noun*
1. a white liquid that people use to whiten walls and ceilings. **2.** anything used to cover up faults and give a good appearance on the surface.

whiting *noun* fish that lives in the estuaries of rivers and in the sea around Australia, which is good to eat.

whittle *verb*
1. If you **whittle** something, you cut, trim or shape it by taking off bits with a knife. **2.** To **whittle** something is to make it less, a little at a time: *I'm whittling down my debts.*

whiz[1] *verb* (**whizzes**, **whizzing**, **whizzed**, **has whizzed**) When something **whizzes**, it moves with a humming or hissing sound: *An arrow whizzed through the air.*

whiz[2] *noun Rather informal* someone who is very good at something: *a whiz at computers.*

who *pronoun* **1.** what person?: *Who told you so?*; *Who is the man in uniform?* **2.** the person that: *I know who did it.*

whoever *pronoun* **1.** whatever person: *Whoever wants it may have it.* **2.** who ever?, or who?: *Whoever is that?*

NOTE This word (as in definition 2) is used to give emphasis to a question.

whole /*say* hohl/ *adjective*
1. If something is **whole**, it exists as one thing. It is not divided into separate parts: *Swallow the tablet whole.* **2. Whole** also refers to the total quantity of something: *I didn't see the whole movie.* **3.** You can use **whole** for emphasis: *a whole new outlook on life*; *You mean I have to wait a whole week for the results?*
–*noun* **4.** the total quantity, amount, or number.
–*phrase* **5. on the whole**, in general.
☐ **wholly**, *adverb*

☑ **SPELLING TIP** *Silent letter alert*: remember the silent *w* at the start of **whole**. Don't confuse it with **hole**. You can have a **hole** in your pocket or dig a **hole** in the ground.

wholemeal *noun* flour made from the whole grain of wheat.

whole number *noun* a number without fractions, such as 0, 1, 2, 3 and so on.

ANOTHER NAME for this is **integer**.

wholesale *noun*
1. the sale of goods, usually in large quantities, to shop owners rather than directly to the public.
–*verb* **2.** To **wholesale** goods is to sell them by wholesale: *That company wholesales computers.*
☐ **wholesale**, *adjective*: *wholesale prices.* –**wholesaler**, *noun*

COMPARE this with **retail**.

wholesome *adjective* healthy and good for you: *I bought a wholesome lunch of salad and fresh fruit juice.*
☐ **wholesomeness**, *noun*

☑ **SPELLING TIP** You will be able to spell this word if you see that it is made up of *whole* (with an old-fashioned sense of 'healthy') and the suffix *-some* (meaning 'tending towards' or 'involving').

who'll the short form of *who will*.

whom /*say* hoohm/ *pronoun* **Whom** is used instead of **who** when it is the object of a verb or preposition: *He is the man whom I saw yesterday.*

☑ **SPELLING TIP** Remember that **whom** is made up of *who* with just the letter *m* added.

whoop /*say* woohp/ *noun*
1. a loud cry or shout: *He gave a whoop of delight.*
–*verb* **2.** If you **whoop**, you make a loud excited cry or shout: *She whooped with glee.*

whooping cough /*say* **hooh**-ping/ *noun* an infectious disease of the air passages, caught mostly by children, which produces a cough followed by a loud, forceful taking in of breath.

☑ **SPELLING TIP** *Silent letter alert*: don't forget the silent *w* at the beginning of **whooping** in the name of this illness. This word has nothing to do with *hoop* (a toy in the shape of a ring) but is related to *whoop* (a call or cry) which used to be pronounced as 'hoohp'.

whore /*say* haw/ *noun Old-fashioned* a female prostitute.

☑ **SPELLING TIP** *Silent letter alert*: don't forget that this word starts with a silent *w*.

who's a short form of *who is* or *who has*.

whose *pronoun* belonging to whom: *Whose is this book?*

why *adverb*
1. for what cause, reason, or purpose?: *Why did you go?*
–*conjunction* **2.** for what cause or reason: *I know why he said that.* **3.** for which: *This is the reason why she refused.* **4.** the reason for which: *That is why I raised this question again.*

wick *noun* the twisted threads in a candle or light which draw up the melted wax or oil to be burnt.

wicked /*say* **wik**-uhd/ *adjective*
1. evil and harmful: *a story about a wicked witch.* **2.** very bad or wrong: *a wicked crime.* **3.** *Informal* extremely good or excellent: *a wicked movie.*
☐ **wickedly**, *adverb* –**wickedness**, *noun*

wickerwork *noun* things made of willow twigs plaited or woven together: *The room was furnished with three chairs and two small tables of white painted wickerwork.*

wicket *noun* the set of three pieces of wood with two bails on top at which the bowler aims the ball in cricket.

wide *adjective*
1. If something solid is **wide**, it measures a large amount from one side to the other: *The table's too wide to fit through the doorway.* **2.** If an opening is **wide**, there is a large amount of empty space: *The doorways are very wide in these old houses.* **3.** You use **wide** to describe how much something measures from one side to the other: *At this point in its course the river is only a few metres wide.*
–*adverb* **4.** fully: *Open wide!*; *He is wide awake.* **5.** far to the side: *The tennis shot went wide of the line.*
☐ **widely**, *adverb* –**widen**, *verb* –**widespread**, *adjective* –**width**, *noun*

widow *noun* a woman whose husband has died and who has not married again.

widower *noun* a man whose wife has died and who has not married again.

wield /*say* weeld/ *verb* If you **wield** something, you control and use it: *He wields his surgical knife with great skill*; *to wield influence.*

☑ SPELLING TIP Remember the *ie* spelling for the 'ee' sound. This follows the rule that *i* comes before *e* except after *c*.

wife *noun* (*plural* **wives**) the woman to whom a man is married.

wig *noun* an artificial covering of hair for the head.

wiggle *verb* When something or someone wiggles, they move with short motions from side to side: *The fish wiggled out of my hands and splashed back into the water*; *We wiggled through the narrow opening.*

wigwam /*say* **wig**-wom/ *noun* a Native American hut made of poles with bark, mats or skins laid over them.

WORD HISTORY from a Native American word meaning 'dwelling'

wild *adjective*
1. If an animal or plant is **wild**, it lives or grows in its natural state. It is not kept or cultivated by humans. **2.** If something is **wild**, it is uncontrolled and possibly violent: *There are wild storms here in the summer.*
–*noun* **3. wilds**, a wilderness: *in the wilds of Africa.*
–*phrase* **4. grow wild**, to occur in nature: *These fruits grow wild.* **5. in the wild**, in natural surroundings, usually a long way from civilisation or other people: *She is fond of camping in the wild.* **6. run wild, a.** to grow without care or control. **b.** to behave in an uncontrolled way.
☐ **wildly**, *adverb* –**wildness**, *noun*

wildcard *noun*
1. in some card games, a playing card to which the holder may choose to give the value of any other card. **2.** a character that is not a letter or number, used especially in computer searches to represent any character or set of characters.
–*adjective* **3.** having to do with a wildcard: *a wildcard search.*

wildebeest /*say* **wil**-duh-beest/ *noun* (*plural* **wildebeests**, **wildebeest**) a kind of African antelope with curved horns and a long tail.

ANOTHER WORD for this is **gnu**.

wilderness /*say* **wil**-duh-nuhs/ *noun* a natural area of country, such as forest, desert, and so on, without roads or houses.

wildlife *noun* animals, birds and insects living in their natural surroundings.

wilful *adjective*
1. A **wilful** action is done on purpose: *an act of wilful vandalism.* **2.** A **wilful** person is stubborn and hard to control: *a wilful child.*
☐ **wilfully**, *adverb*

☑ SPELLING TIP *Single letter alert*: the *l* is single both times it appears in this word. Though the first part comes from *will*, one of the *l*'s is dropped when **wilful** is formed. And, as usual, the suffix *-ful* (meaning 'full of') is spelt with one *l*.

will[1] *verb* **Will** is used to **1.** show that someone intends to do something or that something is going to happen in the future: *We will leave on the early train.* **2.** indicate willingness to do something: *I will gladly help if you need me.*

NOTE This is always used with another verb in the form **will** or **would**. See *modal verbs* in the Grammar and Punctuation Guide appendix.

will[2] *noun*
1. the power of choosing your own actions. **2.** wish or desire: *against his will*; *the will of the people.* **3.** purpose or strength: *the will to succeed*; *a battle of wills.* **4.** a legal document stating what a person wants done with their property after their death.
–*verb* **5.** If you **will** something to happen, you try to make it happen by the strength of your thoughts and wishes: *We were all willing her to win.*
–*phrase* **6. at will**, at someone's own choice: *to wander at will.*

willing *adjective* If you are **willing**, you are happy to do something: *She is always willing to help.*
☐ **willingly**, *adverb* –**willingness**, *noun*

willow *noun* a tree which has strong but easily bent branches which are used in the making of baskets, and so on.

willpower *noun*
1. control over your own desires and actions: *Sometimes it takes a lot of willpower to ignore TV ads.* **2.** strength of will: *He has great willpower.*

willy-willy *noun* (*plural* **willy-willies**) a sudden strong wind that moves around in tight circles, then disappears.

WORD HISTORY from an Aboriginal language of Western Australia called Yindjibarndi

wilt *verb* If a plant **wilts**, it becomes soft and lifeless: *The seedlings wilted in the sun.*
☐ **wilted**, *adjective*: *wilted flowers*

wily /*say* **wuy**-lee/ *adjective* (**wilier**, **wiliest**) A **wily** person is tricky or deceitful.
☐ **wiliness**, *noun*

wimp *noun Informal* a weak, cowardly person.

WORD HISTORY perhaps from *Wimpy* the timid character in the comic strip *Popeye*

win *verb* (**wins**, **winning**, **won**, **has won**)
1. If you **win** a match, competition or argument, you are successful. You beat the others: *She won the 800 metres.* **2.** If you **win** something, you gain it, especially in a competition: *I won second prize in the lottery.*

–phrase **3. win over**, to persuade, or gain the favour or support of: *She won him over with her sound arguments.*
□ **win**, *noun* –**winner**, *noun*

wince *verb* If you **wince**, you start or draw back because of pain or a blow.
□ **wince**, *noun*

winch *noun* (*plural* **winches**)
1. a device for pulling or lifting heavy objects, consisting of a wire rope wound round a drum turned by a crank or motor.
–verb **2.** To **winch** something is to lift or move it with a winch.

wind[1] */rhymes with* pinned/ *noun*
1. a current of moving air, especially as in a storm. **2.** breath: *I just need to get my wind back after walking up that hill.* **3.** gas coming from your stomach or bowel.
–verb **4.** If you **wind** someone, you take their breath away by hitting them in the chest or stomach.
□ **windy**, *adjective* (**windier**, **windiest**)

wind[2] */rhymes with* lined/ *verb* (**winds**, **winding**, **wound**, **has wound**)
1. To **wind** is to turn first one way and then another: *The path winds up the hill.* **2.** To **wind** something is to twist it or roll it into a ball: *to wind wool.*
–phrase **3. wind down**, **a.** to relax after a very active time. **b.** of a clock, to run down. **c.** to reduce the size or force of: *to wind down an operation.*

windbreak *noun* a protection from the wind such as a fence or row of trees.

windcheater *noun* a close-fitting jacket or jumper worn for protection against the wind.

windfall *noun* an unexpected piece of good fortune.

wind farm *noun* a group of turbines that are set up in a windy location and are used to turn the energy from wind into electricity.

wind instrument *noun* a musical instrument that you play by blowing.

windmill *noun* a mill for grinding or pumping which is set moving by the wind turning a set of arms or sails.

window *noun*
1. an opening in a wall for letting in light and air and usually having panes of glass. **2.** an area on a computer screen in which a particular program is run or data displayed.

windpipe *noun* the tube that carries air from the throat to the lungs.

NOTE The scientific word for this is **trachea**.

windscreen *noun* the sheet of glass which forms the front window of a car or other vehicle.

windward *adverb*
1. towards the wind: *to sail windward.*
–adjective **2.** facing the wind: *the windward side.*
□ **windward**, *noun*

THE OPPOSITE is **leeward**.

wine *noun* an alcoholic drink made, usually from grapes.

wing *noun*
1. the part of the body of a bird or insect that is used for flying. **2.** one of the long, flat parts that stick out from either side of an aeroplane. **3.** a part of a building which is joined to the main part: *A new wing was built on to the hospital.* **4.** a political group within a larger group: *the left wing.* **5.** one of the two side areas of play in games of football, hockey, soccer and similar sports. **6.** someone who plays in this place on the field.
–verb **7.** To **wing** is to fly using wings: *The swans were winging their way across the sky.*
–phrase **8. in the wings**, quietly ready to do something when needed.

wink *verb* If you **wink**, you shut one eye and then open it again, usually as a sign to someone: *She winked to tell me she was joking.*
□ **wink**, *noun*

winning *adjective*
1. being the winner: *the winning candidate.* **2.** charming: *a winning smile.*
–noun **3. winnings**, something won, especially money: *He used his winnings to buy us all an ice-cream.*

winter *noun* the coldest season of the year, following autumn.
□ **wintry**, *adjective*

wipe *verb*
1. If you **wipe** something, you clean or dry it by rubbing its surface, usually with something such as a cloth: *He wiped his glasses on his sleeve.* **2.** If you **wipe** something, or **wipe** it off or away, you remove it from a surface by rubbing something over it: *He wiped the sweat from his brow.*
–phrase **3. wipe out**, to destroy or defeat completely.
□ **wipe**, *noun* –**wiper**, *noun*

wire *noun*
1. a long piece of thin metal that can be bent: *a fence made of wire*; *an electric wire.*
–verb **2.** If you **wire** something to something else, you fasten them together using wire: *to wire the fence together*; *His broken jaw needed to be wired.* **3.** To **wire** a house is to provide it with electricity.
□ **wiring**, *noun*: *electrical wiring.*

wireless *noun*
1. *Old-fashioned* a radio.
–adjective **2.** not using telephone lines, cables, etc.: *wireless technology.*

wiry *adjective* (**wirier**, **wiriest**)
1. like wire in shape or stiffness: *wiry grass*; *wiry hair.* 2. thin and strong: *a wiry person.*

wisdom *noun*
1. the quality of being wise: *We had the wisdom to bring an umbrella.* 2. knowledge or learning: *Ancient wisdom has been passed down in folk stories.*

wise *adjective*
1. If you are **wise**, you are able to judge what is true or right: *a wise person.* 2. If a decision or action is **wise**, it is sensible: *She made the wise choice to stay on at school.*
□ **wisely**, *adverb*

wisecrack *noun Rather informal* a smart or amusing remark.
□ **wisecracker**, *noun*

wish *verb*
1. If you **wish** to do something, you want or desire to do it: *I wish to visit the pyramids.* 2. If you **wish**, you express your desire for something. You make a wish: *She wished she had a new bike.* 3. If you **wish** someone something, you say it to them: *She wished them a good trip.*
–*noun* 4. something you wish for: *Did you get your wish?* 5. the act of wishing: *I made a wish.*
–*phrase* 6. **wish for**, to want to get or receive: *She wished for a new bike as a present.*
□ **wishful**, *adjective*

wishbone *noun* a bone shaped like a Y in the chest of birds such as chickens.

WORD HISTORY this bone got its name from the belief that when two people pull it apart, the one getting the longer piece will have their wish come true

wishy-washy *adjective* without strength or force: *a wishy-washy speech.*

wisp *noun* someone or something that is small or thin: *a wisp of a girl*; *a wisp of hair*; *a wisp of mist.*
□ **wispy**, *adjective* (**wispier**, **wispiest**)

wistful *adjective* thoughtful in a sad way: *She gave us a wistful smile.*
□ **wistfully**, *adverb* –**wistfulness**, *noun*

wit *noun*
1. the ability to be amusing in a clever way. 2. someone with this ability. 3. **wits**, mental abilities or common sense: *Being the youngest in the family seemed to sharpen her wits*; *He usually keeps his wits about him.*
□ **quick-witted**, *adjective* –**witticism** /*say* **wit**-uh-siz-uhm/, *noun* –**witty**, *adjective* (**wittier**, **wittiest**)

witch *noun* (*plural* **witches**) a woman thought to have the power of magic, especially one in a story who uses magic to do evil.
□ **witchcraft**, *noun*

☑ SPELLING TIP Don't confuse the spelling of **witch** with **which**. **Which** is a word that introduces a question.

witchdoctor *noun* a man thought to have magical powers for healing or harming others.

witchetty grub *noun* a large white grub that can be eaten.

WORD HISTORY from an Aboriginal language of South Australia called Adnyamathanha

with *preposition*
1. in the company of: *I will go with you.* 2. in some particular relation to: *to mix water with milk.* 3. understanding the thinking of: *Are you with me?* 4. by the use or means of: *Cut it with a knife.* 5. in the care or keeping of: *Leave it with me.*
–*phrase* 6. **with it**, *Informal* a. aware of a situation: *Get with it. He's already got a girlfriend.* b. fashionable: *You have to have the right clothes if you want be with it.*

withdraw *verb* (**withdraws**, **withdrawing**, **withdrew**, **has withdrawn**)
1. To **withdraw** is to move back or away: *He withdrew to the shade of the verandah.* 2. If you **withdraw** something, you take it back: *I demand that you withdraw what you said about me.* 3. If you **withdraw** money from the bank, you take it out.
□ **withdrawal**, *noun*

A SIMILAR WORD (for definition 1) is **retreat**.

wither /*say* **widh**-uh/ *verb* To **wither** is to become dried up and shrunken: *Without water, the plants withered and died*; *The prime minister's popularity is withering away.*

withhold /*say* widh-**hohld**/ *verb* (**withholds**, **withholding**, **withheld**, **has withheld**) To **withhold** something is to hold it back: *to withhold payment*; *to withhold information.*

☑ SPELLING TIP *Double letter alert*: double *h*. This is because **withhold** is made up of *with* (in an old-fashioned sense of 'away') and *hold*, and so gets the *h* from both of these words.

within *preposition*
1. inside: *She placed the bookmark within the book.* 2. in or into the inside area of: *within a city.* 3. not outside: *within view.*

without *preposition*
1. lacking or not with: *without help.* 2. free from: *without pain.*
–*adverb* 3. lacking: *We must take this or go without.*

withstand *verb* (**withstands**, **withstanding**, **withstood**, **has withstood**) To **withstand** something is to stand or hold firm against it: *She withstood his requests for more money*; *This material will withstand heavy use.*

A SIMILAR WORD is **resist**.

witness *noun*
1. someone who sees or hears something by being present: *I was a witness to their argument.* **2.** someone who states what they know, especially in a court of law, because they were where something happened.
–*verb* **3.** If you **witness** something, you are a witness to it: *We witnessed the accident.* **4.** If you **witness** a document, you sign it to say that you have seen someone else sign it.

wizard *noun*
1. a man thought to have the power of magic, especially one in a story. **2.** someone who is very good at something: *a wizard at computers.*
☐ **wizardry**, *noun*

wizened /*say* **wiz**-uhnd/ *adjective* dried up and shrunken: *a brown and wizened old man.*

wobbegong /*say* **wob**-ee-gong/ *noun* a kind of Australian shark.

WORD HISTORY possibly from an Aboriginal language of New South Wales

wobble *verb* To **wobble** is to move unsteadily or make something move unsteadily from side to side: *The chair wobbles because one leg is broken*; *He wobbled his loose tooth.*
☐ **wobble**, *noun* –**wobbly**, *adjective*

woe *noun* great sadness.
☐ **woeful**, *adjective*

NOTE This word is used in literature rather than ordinary language.

wog[1] *noun Informal* someone from another country, especially someone from southern Europe.

NOTE This word will offend people.

wog[2] *noun Informal* a germ that causes a sickness: *I think I've picked up a stomach wog.*

wok *noun* a large, round-bottomed, metal bowl used for cooking, especially for food originating in Asian cooking.

wolf *noun* (*plural* **wolves**)
1. a large, wild, flesh-eating, dog-like animal of Europe, Asia, and North America.
–*verb* **2.** If you **wolf** your food, you eat it quickly and hungrily: *They wolfed down their lunch.*
–*phrase* **3. cry wolf**, to pretend there is danger when there really is not.

Wollemi pine /*say* **wol**-uh-muy/ *noun* a kind of pine tree, dating from prehistoric times, with lime-green leaves shaped like those of a fern.

WORD HISTORY named after *Wollemi* National Park in NSW in which it was discovered in 1994

woman /*say* **woom**-uhn/ *noun* (*plural* **women** /*say* **wim**-uhn/) an adult female human being.
☐ **womanhood**, *noun* –**womanish**, *adjective* –**womanly**, *adjective*

womb /*rhymes with* room/ *noun* the uterus.

☑ SPELLING TIP *Silent letter alert*: don't forget the silent *b* at the end. The letters *omb* make the 'oohm' sound in this word. Another word like this is *tomb*.

wombat *noun* a short-legged, heavy marsupial that burrows holes. Some species are endangered.

WORD HISTORY from an Aboriginal language of New South Wales called Dharug

wonder /*rhymes with* under/ *verb*
1. If you **wonder** about something, you think about it with curiosity: *I wonder what I will get for my birthday.* **2.** Sometimes you use 'I **wonder**' or 'I was **wondering**' to introduce a remark indirectly: *I was wondering if you'd mind swapping places with me?*
–*noun* **3.** something strange and surprising: *It is a wonder that you didn't see him at the party.* **4.** the feeling caused by something strange and surprising: *We listened with wonder to the story of his miraculous escape.*

☑ SPELLING TIP *Tricky vowel sound*: remember the *o* spelling for the 'u' sound in the first syllable. Also, don't confuse **wonder** with **wander**. To **wander** (rhymes with *yonder*) is to go about with no definite aim or fixed course.

wonderful *adjective* extremely good or excellent.
☐ **wonderfully**, *adverb*

SIMILAR WORDS are **fabulous**, **magnificent**, **marvellous** and **sensational**.

won't the short form of *will not*.

won ton /*say* **won** ton/ *noun* a small ball of spicy pork wrapped in thin dough, usually boiled and served in soup, originating in Chinese cooking.

woo *verb*
1. *Old-fashioned* To **woo** someone is to try to win their love, especially so as to marry them: *My grandfather says that he wooed my grandmother for two years before she agreed to marry him.* **2.** If an organisation **woos** someone, it seeks their approval: *The company wooed new investors.*
☐ **wooer**, *noun*

wood *noun*
1. the hard substance that makes up most of the trunk and branches of a tree. **2.** this substance cut up and used in various ways, such as building houses and making furniture. **3.** an area covered thickly with trees: *The little house stands on the edge of a wood.*
☐ **woody**, *adjective*: *a woody plant.*

ANOTHER WORD (for definition 2) is **timber** (definition 1).

NOTE This word (as in definition 3) is often plural: *Be careful not to get lost in the woods!*

☑ SPELLING TIP Don't confuse the spelling of **wood** with **would** which sounds the same. **Would** is always used with another verb: *Would you be able to help me?*

woodblock *noun*
1. a block of wood with a raised design on it for printing from. 2. a print made in this way.

ANOTHER WORD for this is **woodcut**.

wooden *adjective*
1. made of wood: *a wooden bench.* 2. stiff and clumsy: *a wooden way of walking.* 3. without interest or liveliness: *a wooden stare*; *a wooden performance.*

woodpecker *noun* a bird with a hard, strong beak for digging into wood after insects.

woodwind *noun* the group of musical wind instruments that includes the flutes, clarinets, saxophones, oboes and bassoons.

woodwork *noun*
1. things made of wood. 2. the making of wooden things: *He is good at woodwork.*

A SIMILAR WORD (for definition 2) is **carpentry**.

wool *noun*
1. the soft curly hair of sheep and some other animals. 2. thread or cloth made from sheep's wool: *a coat of wool.*
☐ **woollen**, *adjective*

woolly *adjective*
1. made of wool or something similar: *a woolly scarf.* 2. not clear or firm: *a woolly message.*

woomera *noun* a strong piece of wood with a notch at the end, traditionally used by Aboriginal people to help throw a spear.

WORD HISTORY from an Aboriginal language of New South Wales called Dharug

woozy /*say* **wooh**-zee/ *adjective Informal* dizzy and faint from sickness.
☐ **woozily**, *adverb* –**wooziness**, *noun*

word *noun*
1. a sound or group of sounds which stands for an idea, action, or object and which is a basic part of a language. 2. the group of letters you use to write down these sounds. 3. speech or talk: *She had a word with the class about bringing mobile phones to school.* 4. a remark: *I did not hear one kind word all day.* 5. a promise: *He gave his word.* 6. order or command: *Don't move until I give the word.* 7. news: *Word is just coming through of another attack.*
–*verb* 8. If you **word** a speech or piece of writing, you choose the right words to express your meaning: *She worded her letter very carefully.*
–*phrase* 9. **word for word**, of a repeated message, report, and so on, using exactly the same words as the original.

word cloud *noun* a digital design consisting of a selected group of words which appear in differing fonts, colours, etc., to form a pattern of text.

word processor *noun* a computer program used to store written material and change it when necessary.

wordy *adjective* using too many words: *a wordy explanation.*
☐ **wordily**, *adverb* –**wordiness**, *noun*

work *noun*
1. effort made by the body or mind to do something: *There's still some work to do before the job is finished.* 2. something that needs to be done by effort: *school work*; *Swimming can be hard work.* 3. something made by effort: *a work of art*; *a musical work.* 4. a job by which you earn money: *Her work is teaching.*
–*verb* 5. If you **work**, you make an effort: *You should work when you're in class.* 6. Someone who **works** has a job with which they earn money: *She works in a coffee shop.* 7. If something **works**, it acts or operates properly: *This light isn't working.* 8. If you learn how to **work** something, you can use or operate it properly: *Do you know how to work this machine?*
–*phrase* 9. **work out**, a. to solve, find out or calculate by thinking: *to work out an answer*; *to work out a sum.* b. to turn out: *I hope our plan works out all right.* c. to train or practise a sport or exercise: *He works out every morning.*

SIMILAR WORDS (for definitions 1 and 5) are **labour**, **slog** and **toil**. These all refer to very hard work; (for definition 4) **business**, **career**, **employment**, **occupation**, **position**, **profession** and **trade**.

workable *adjective* able to be put into operation: *They will test the system to see if it is workable*; *a workable idea.*

worker *noun*
1. someone or something that works. 2. someone who has a particular job: *an office worker.* 3. someone who is employed in a factory or does work with their hands: *The dispute between management and the workers has been settled.*

workman *noun* (*plural* **workmen**) a man who does physical, mechanical, or industrial work.

work-out *noun*
1. a performance for practice or training, or as a trial or test. 2. physical exercise: *Mum goes to the gym for a work-out most days.*

workplace *noun* a place of employment.

workshop *noun* a place where work is done, usually work on cars, appliances, and so on.

world *noun*
1. the earth and everyone who lives on it. **2.** a particular area of life or interest: *the insect world*; *the world of art.*
–*phrase* **3. out of this world**, *Informal* excellent or as good as you could imagine. **4. think the world of**, to think very highly of.

world-class *adjective* among the best in the world: *a world-class singer.*

worldly *adjective*
1. interested only in the things that concern us in our life on earth, rather than in any other life after death. **2.** used to the ways of the world.
□ **worldliness**, *noun*

world music *noun* folk music or the music of different cultures and nationalities from around the world.

World Wide Web *noun* a linked set of computers storing information, which it is possible to search through on the internet.

THE SHORT FORM of this is **the Web**. The abbreviation **www** or **WWW** is also used.

worm /*rhymes with* firm/ *noun*
1. a long, thin animal with a soft body and no legs that moves by sliding along. **2.** *Informal* someone you think is weak or dishonest.
–*verb in the phrase* **3. worm into**, to get by roundabout means: *to worm into a teacher's good books.* **4. worm out of**, **a.** to get by persistent, roundabout means: *to worm a secret out of a person.* **b.** to avoid: *to worm out of your responsibilities.*

worn *verb*
1. past participle of **wear**.
–*adjective* **2.** If something such as a piece of clothing or a floor covering is **worn** or **worn out**, it is thin or damaged because it has been used so much. **3.** If someone looks **worn** or **worn out**, they look tired and older than they really are, usually because they are busy, worried or sick.

☑ SPELLING TIP Don't confuse the spelling of **worn** with **warn** which sounds the same. To **warn** someone is to tell them of possible danger.

worry /*rhymes with* hurry/ *verb* (**worries**, **worrying**, **worried**, **has worried**)
1. If you **worry** about something, you feel anxious and concerned about what might happen or go wrong. **2.** If you tell someone not to **worry** about something, you mean that they should not take any trouble with it: *Don't worry about cleaning up.* **3.** If something **worries** you, it makes you anxious or concerned: *He wasn't worried by the outcome.* **4.** If something **worries** you, it troubles or disturbs you: *The noise of the fan began to worry me.* **5.** When one animal **worries** another, it bites it and shakes it repeatedly.
□ **worried**, *adjective* –**worrying**, *adjective*

worse *adjective*
1. Something that is **worse** is bad to a greater degree: *The weather is worse than it was yesterday.*
–*adverb* **2.** in a more unpleasant, evil, or severe way.
–*phrase* **3. the worse for wear**, looking old or in bad condition because of too much use: *That sofa is the worse for wear.* **4. worse off**, less lucky or having less money.

NOTE For other forms of the adjective see **bad**.

worship /*say* **wer**-shuhp/ *noun*
1. the showing of deep honour and respect for a god in a ceremony or prayer. **2.** great love, honour, and respect.
–*verb* (**worships**, **worshipping**, **worshipped**, **has worshipped**) **3.** If you **worship** a god, you show your honour and respect with prayer and ceremony. **4.** If you **worship** someone or something, you love and respect them very much: *He worships his grandmother.*
□ **worshipper**, *noun*

☑ SPELLING TIP *Tricky vowel sound*: *or* spelling for the 'er' sound in the first syllable.

worst *adjective* bad to the greatest degree: *This is worst bushfire season for years.*

NOTE For other forms see **bad**.

worth *noun*
1. value or importance: *a painting of great worth.*
2. quantity or amount: *five years worth of work.*
–*phrase* **3. be worth**, to be equal in value to: *It isn't worth much money.*
□ **worthless**, *adjective*

worthwhile *adjective* useful or good enough to spend time on: *a worthwhile visit.*

worthy /*say* **wer**-dhee/ *adjective* (**worthier**, **worthiest**)
1. deserving respect or admiration: *a worthy achievement.*
–*phrase* **2. worthy of**, good enough for: *a meal worthy of a sultan.*
□ **worthiness**, *noun*

would /*sounds like* wood/ *verb* You use **would**
1. to indicate actions that used to happen continually, in the past: *When he was little his mother would cut his hair.* **2.** to show that you want to do something: *I would love to come to the party.* **3.** to make questions more polite: *Would you like another drink?*

NOTE **Would** is the past tense of **will**[1]. It is always used with another verb. See *modal verbs* in the Grammar and Punctuation Guide appendix.

☑ SPELLING TIP Don't confuse the spelling of **would** with **wood** which sounds the same.

> **Wood** is the hard substance that makes up most of the trunk and branches of a tree.

would-be *adjective* wishing or planning to be: *a would-be comedian.*

wouldn't a short form of *would not*.

wound[1] /*say* woohnd/ *noun*
1. an injury such as a cut, burn, or bruise.
–*verb* **2.** To **wound** is to hurt or injure: *The explosion wounded many people*; *I was wounded by her nasty remark.*
☐ **wounded**, *adjective*: *wounded soldiers.*

> ☑ SPELLING TIP *Tricky vowel sound*: *ou* spelling for the 'ooh' sound.

wound[2] /*say* wownd/ *verb* the past tense and past participle of **wind**[2].

wrangle *verb* If two people **wrangle**, they argue or quarrel noisily: *They wrangled over how much Tim should pay for the damage he caused to the fence.*
☐ **wrangle**, *noun*

wrap *verb* (**wraps**, **wrapping**, **wrapped**, **has wrapped**)
1. If you **wrap** something, you fold paper or some other material around it so as to cover it completely: *James wrapped Lyn's present in green paper.* **2.** If you **wrap** yourself in something, you fold it around you so as to keep warm or covered: *She sat on the couch wrapped in a blanket.*
☐ **wrap**, *noun* –**wrapper**, *noun* –**wrapping**, *noun*

> ☑ SPELLING TIP Remember the silent *w* at the beginning of **wrap**. Don't confuse it with **rap** which sounds the same. To **rap** is to strike something with a quick, light blow.

wrath /*say* roth/ *noun Old-fashioned* anger.

> ☑ SPELLING TIP *Tricky vowel sound*: *a* spelling for the 'o' sound. You could remember this unusual spelling by thinking that there is a 'rat' in this word. Also remember the silent *w* at the start, as in other words beginning with *wr*.

wreak *verb* If something or someone **wreaks** havoc or destruction, they cause great damage: *The rain wreaked havoc with the gala cricket match.*

> ☑ SPELLING TIP Remember the silent *w* at the start of this word, and the *ea* spelling. Don't confuse it with **reek** which sounds the same. To **reek** is to give off a terrible smell.

wreath /*say* reeth/ *noun* flowers and leaves tied together to make a ring.

wreathe /*say* reedh/ *verb* If something **wreathes** something, it surrounds it: *Fog wreathed the city.*

wreck *verb*
1. If you **wreck** something, you ruin or destroy it.
–*noun* **2.** something, especially a ship, that has been wrecked.
☐ **wreckage**, *noun* –**wrecker**, *noun*

wren *noun* a very small bird with a long upright tail.

wrench *verb*
1. If you **wrench** something, you twist it roughly: *He wrenched the handle off the door*; *I fell and wrenched my ankle.*
–*noun* (*plural* **wrenches**) **2.** a sudden, sharp twist. **3.** a type of spanner.

wrest *verb* If you **wrest** something from someone, you pull or grab it roughly: *He wrested the ball from my grasp.*

wrestle /*say* **res**-uhl/ *verb*
1. To **wrestle** with someone is to fight with them and try to throw them to the ground without using any weapons. **2.** To **wrestle** with something is to make a great effort to deal with it successfully: *He wrestled with the problem for days.*
☐ **wrestler**, *noun* –**wrestling**, *noun*

> ☑ SPELLING TIP *Silent letter alert*: don't forget the *st* (not double *s*) spelling. The *t* is silent. Also remember the silent *w* at the start, as in other words beginning with *wr*.

wretch *noun* (*plural* **wretches**) someone who is very miserable and unfortunate.

wretched /*say* **rech**-uhd/ *adjective*
1. poor, miserable and pitiful: *a wretched, starving dog.* **2.** worthless or irritating: *The wretched car won't start.*
☐ **wretchedly**, *adverb* –**wretchedness**, *noun*

wriggle *verb*
1. To **wriggle** is to twist and turn like a snake or worm.
–*phrase* **2. wriggle out of**, to manage to avoid or escape: *He usually seems to wriggle his way out of trouble.*
☐ **wriggly**, *adjective* (**wrigglier**, **wriggliest**)

wring *verb* (**wrings**, **wringing**, **wrung**, **has wrung**) To **wring** something is to twist and squeeze it: *She wrung as much water as she could from the dripping clothes*; *He was wringing his hands in grief.*
☐ **wringer**, *noun*

> ☑ SPELLING TIP Remember the silent *w* at the start of this word. Don't confuse it with **ring**. You wear a **ring** on your finger. Bells **ring** when they give out a clear musical sound. When you **ring** someone, you telephone them.

wrinkle *noun*
1. a fold on something that is usually smooth.
–*verb* **2.** When something **wrinkles** or if someone or something **wrinkles** it, it gets a wrinkle or

wrinkles in it: *The paper had wrinkled around the edges*; *She wrinkled her nose.*
□ **wrinkled**, *adjective*: *a wrinkled shirt.*

wrist *noun* the joint where the hand meets the arm.

write *verb* (**writes**, **writing**, **wrote**, **has written**)
1. To **write** is to form letters, characters or words with a pen, pencil, or something similar: *He wrote on the blackboard.* **2.** If you **write** something, you create it using words: *She is writing a book.*
–*phrase* **3. write down**, to put down in writing. **4. write to**, to compose or make up a letter and send it to: *I wrote to my sister last week.*
□ **writer**, *noun* –**writing**, *noun* –**written**, *adjective*

SPELLING HINT Don't confuse the spelling of **write** with **right** or **rite** both of which have the same sound. Something is **right** if it is fair or good. A **rite** is a ceremony, often a religious one, as in *the holy rite of baptism*.

write-off *noun Rather informal* **1.** a car that has been so badly smashed that it can't be repaired. **2.** a period of time that is wasted because you do not get anything done: *The whole afternoon was a write-off – we couldn't play because of the rain.*

writhe /*say* ruydh/ *verb* To **writhe** is to twist and wriggle, as if in pain or embarrassment.

wrong *adjective*
1. bad or evil: *It is wrong to steal.* **2.** not correct: *I dialled the wrong number.*
–*verb* **3.** If you **wrong** someone, you hurt them or treat them unfairly.
–*noun in the phrase* **4. in the wrong**, **a.** guilty: *You should say sorry because you are in the wrong.* **b.** mistaken or not correct.
□ **wronged**, *adjective* –**wrongful**, *adjective* –**wrongly**, *adverb*

wry /*say* ruy/ *adjective* (**wrier** /*say* **ruy**-uh/, **wriest** /*say* **ruy**-uhst/)
1. using humour in a clever but unemotional way, often in relation to something unpleasant or upsetting: *She made a wry joke about living in a war zone.* **2.** showing displeasure or disgust: *He made a wry face at the filthy state of the kitchen.*
□ **wryly**, *adverb*

☑ SPELLING TIP Don't confuse the spelling of **wry** with **rye** which has the same sound. **Rye** is a kind of grain.

X-ray *noun*
1. a ray that can pass through something solid. **2.** a photograph of the inside of someone's body, used by doctors to help diagnose disease.
–*verb* **3.** To **X-ray** someone or something, is to take an X-ray of them: *My arm was X-rayed to see if it was broken*; *All the luggage was X-rayed before being loaded onto the plane.*

xylophone /*say* **zuy** -luh-fohn/ *noun* a musical instrument made of a row of wooden bars of different lengths which you hit with small wooden hammers.

☑ SPELLING TIP Concentrate on remembering the *xylo* start to this word (the *x* makes a 'z' sound). Think of *x* and *y* coming next to each other in the alphabet. The last part is *phone*, a word you know well. It is used here as a suffix, as in several other words relating to sound. Some other musical instruments that have this ending are *saxophone* and *vibraphone*.

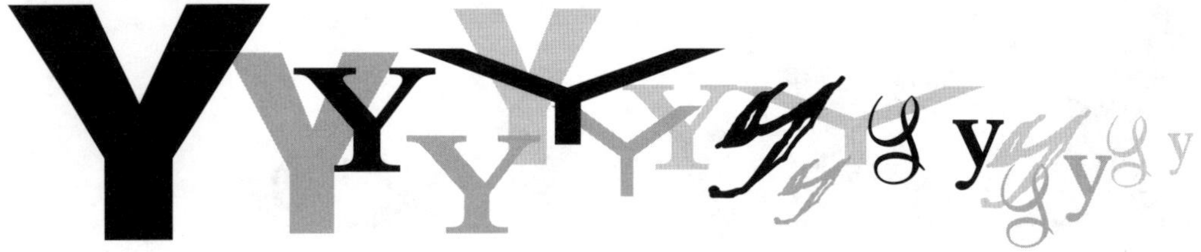

yabby *noun* (*plural* **yabbies**) a small Australian crayfish which lives in fresh water.

WORD HISTORY from an Aboriginal language of Victoria called Wembawemba

yacht /*rhymes with* cot/ *noun* a sailing boat used for sport or pleasure.
☐ **yachting**, *noun*

☑ SPELLING TIP *Silent letter alert*: don't forget the silent *ch* before the *t*. Also remember that the vowel sound is spelt with an *a* (although it sounds like 'o'). Rap it out as *ya+cht* (saying 'ya-chuht'!!) to remind yourself.

yak¹ *noun* a long-haired, wild ox found in the highlands of Tibet.

yak² *verb* (**yaks**, **yakking**, **yakked**, **has yakked**) *Informal* If someone **yaks**, they talk on and on without saying anything very important.
☐ **yak**, *noun*: *They had a bit of a yak.*

yakitori /*say* yak-uh-**taw**-ree/ *noun* a food made of small pieces of chicken soaked in soy sauce and cooked on a skewer, originating in Japanese cooking.

yakka *noun Informal* work: *The fete organisers thanked everyone for the hard yakka they had put in.*

WORD HISTORY from an Aboriginal language of Queensland called Yagara

yam *noun* a potato-like tropical plant used as food.

Yamatji /*say* **yam**-uh-jee/ *noun* an Aboriginal person from mid-western Western Australia.
☐ **Yamatji**, *adjective*: *Yamatji traditions.*

WORD HISTORY from the Watjari language of mid-western Western Australia

yank *verb* If you **yank** something, you pull it suddenly: *Our side yanked really hard on the rope and the others all fell over.*
☐ **yank**, *noun*

Yank *noun Informal* an American.

NOTE Some people find the use of this word offensive.

yap *verb* (**yaps**, **yapping**, **yapped**, **has yapped**) If an animal **yaps**, it barks with short, high sounds: *The terrier yapped and yapped until its master came out of the shops.*
☐ **yap**, *noun* –**yapping**, *noun*

yard¹ *noun* a unit of length in the imperial system, a little smaller than a metre.

yard² *noun*
1. the fenced ground around a house or other building. **2.** a fenced or walled area in which any work or business is carried on: *The second-hand car yard was littered with old wrecks.*

yarmulke /*say* **yah**-mool-kuh/ *noun* a skullcap traditionally worn by Jewish men and boys, especially in a synagogue.

ANOTHER SPELLING is **yarmulka**.

yarn *noun*
1. nylon, cotton or wool thread used for knitting and weaving. **2.** a long story, especially one about unlikely happenings.

yawn *verb* When you **yawn**, you open your mouth very wide and take a deep breath, usually because you are tired or bored: *He was so tired he kept yawning all through the talk.*
☐ **yawn**, *noun*

year *noun*
1. the period of twelve months in their regular order. Each year has 365 days, or 366 if it is a leap year. The **calendar year** goes from 1 January to 31 December; the **financial year** usually goes from 1 July to 30 June. **2. years**, a very long time: *It will be years before I get bored with chess.*
☐ **yearly**, *adjective*, *adverb*

yearn /*rhymes with* burn/ *verb* If you **yearn** to do something or **yearn** for something, you want to do it or want it very much: *Jane yearns to travel to remote parts of the world.*
☐ **yearning**, *noun*

yeast *noun* a substance which causes the dough to rise when you make bread.

yell *verb* If you **yell**, you call out loudly or shout: *Sam yelled a welcome*; *They yelled for help.*
☐ **yell**, *noun*

yellow *adjective* If something is **yellow**, it has a bright colour like that of an egg yolk, lemons, and so on.
☐ **yellow**, *noun* –**yellowish**, *adjective*

yellow box *noun* a large spreading type of gum tree which grows in eastern Australia.

NOTE Bees make excellent honey from the flowers of this tree.

yellowcake *noun* uranium in the form in which it is dug out of the ground.

yelp *verb* To **yelp** is to give a quick, sharp cry: *The boy yelped when he felt the bee sting him.*
☐ **yelp**, *noun*

yes *adverb*
1. a word used to express agreement, or to mark the addition of some thing emphasising a previous statement: *Yes, you may go*; *I know, yes, I know.*
–*noun* (*plural* **yeses**) **2.** an answer of 'yes'.

yesterday *noun* the day before today: *Yesterday was a bad day because it rained the whole time.*
☐ **yesterday**, *adverb*: *We finished our project yesterday.*

yet *adverb*
1. at the present time: *Don't go yet.* **2.** up to a particular time; thus far: *He had not yet come.*

yeti /*say* **yet**-ee/ *noun* (*plural* **yetis**) a human-like creature supposed to live in the mountains of Tibet.

ANOTHER TERM for this is the **abominable snowman**.

yield /*say* yeeld/ *verb* To **yield** is to **1.** produce: *The good rains this year have yielded monster crops.* **2.** stop fighting or resisting: *Dad eventually yielded and said we could get a video.*
–*noun* **3.** the quantity of something yielded: *The yield is more than a tonne a hectare.*

☑ SPELLING TIP Remember the *ie* spelling for the 'ee' sound. This follows the rule that *i* comes before *e* except after *c*.

yodel *verb* (**yodels**, **yodelling**, **yodelled**, **has yodelled**) If you **yodel**, you sing with rapid changes between your normal voice and a very high or falsetto voice, as Swiss mountaineers do: *Yodelling in the bathroom in the morning is not allowed in our house.*
☐ **yodel**, *noun*

yoga /*say* **yoh**-guh/ *noun*
1. in the Hindu religion, the coming together of the human soul with the universal spirit or god. **2.** a set of exercises which involve deep breathing and holding unusual body positions, in order to reach a calm, peaceful state of mind.

WORD HISTORY from a Sanskrit word meaning 'union'

yoghurt /*say* **yoh**-guht, **yog**-uht/ *noun* a food made by the controlled curdling of milk.

ANOTHER SPELLING is **yogurt**.

yogi /*say* **yoh**-gee/ *noun* (*plural* **yogis**) someone who is a master in yoga.

yoke *noun*
1. a device consisting of a piece of wood with curved ends fitting over the necks of two oxen pulling a load. **2.** a shaped piece in clothing, fitted about the neck, shoulders or hips, from which the rest of the clothing hangs.

yolk /*say* yohk/ *noun* the yellow part of an egg.

☑ SPELLING TIP Remember the *olk* spelling for the 'ohk' sound. You cannot hear the *l*. Don't confuse **yolk** with **yoke** which has the same sound. A **yoke** is a piece of wood fitting over the necks of two animals pulling a load.

Yolngu /*say* **yol**-ngooh/ *noun* an Aboriginal person from north-eastern Arnhem Land.
☐ **Yolngu**, *adjective*: *Yolngu traditions.*

WORD HISTORY from the Yolngu group of languages of Arnhem Land

yonder *adjective Rather old-fashioned* being in that place or over there: *Admire the view from yonder hill.*
☐ **yonder**, *adverb*: *That's north, over yonder.*

you *pronoun* the pronoun you use when you are talking to one person or to a group of people: *Would you like to play a game of chess?*

SEE ALSO **your** and **yours**.

you'd a short form of *you had* or *you would*.

you'll a short form of *you will*.

young /*say* yung/ *adjective*
1. If a person, animal or plant is **young**, they have not lived for very long: *You can tell how young my dog is from his teeth*; *We snapped off young branches to mark our track.*
–*plural noun* **2.** an animal's babies: *Tadpoles are the young of frogs.* **3.** young children: *Both old and young can enjoy our national parks.*

THE OPPOSITE (of definition 1) is **old**.

☑ SPELLING TIP *Tricky vowel sound*: *oung* for the 'ung' sound. Remember the *o*. You can do this by thinking that 'you are young' and the word *you* appears in **young** with the letters *ng* following.

youngster *noun* a child or young person.

your *pronoun* the form of **you** used before a noun to show that something belongs to or is done by you: *It's your move.*
☐ **yours**, *pronoun*: *Are these shoes yours?*; *Yours will turn up.*

☑ SPELLING TIP Don't confuse the spelling of **your** with **you're**. **You're** is short for *you are*.

you're a short form of *you are*.

> ☑ SPELLING TIP Don't confuse the spelling of **you're** with **your** which sounds the same. **Your** is the form of **you** used to show that something belongs to you. To test which word you have, say it in full as *you are* and see if it makes sense. If it does, then **you're** is correct.

youth *noun*
1. a young man: *He was only a youth when war was declared.* **2.** young people: *The youth of the island always left to get work and only old people remained.* **3.** the time when you are young: *My father says he remembers his youth well.*
□ **youthful**, *adjective*

you've a short form of *you have*.

yoyo *noun* (*plural* **yoyos**) a toy made of two round, flat-sided pieces of wood or plastic with a length of string wound between them by which you can make it spin up and down.

yucky *adjective Informal* Something **yucky** is disgusting or unpleasant.

> ANOTHER SPELLING is **yukky**.

yum cha /*say* yum **chah**/ *noun* a meal in which you choose small single serves of many different offerings of Chinese food displayed on trolleys.

yummy *adjective* (**yummier**, **yummiest**) *Informal* Something **yummy** is very good, especially to eat: *I'm sorry I ate your slice of cake, but it looked so yummy I simply couldn't help myself.*

zany /*say* **zay**-nee/ *adjective* (**zanier**, **zaniest**) funny in a silly or crazy way: *The cartoon was full of zany situations that made me laugh.*

zeal /*say* zeel/ *noun* eagerness or enthusiasm: *We had heaps of zeal at the beginning of the year – until about March.*
☐ **zealous** /*say* **zel**-uhs/, *adjective*: *My mum is a zealous campaigner for animal rights.*

zebra *noun* a wild, horse-like African animal covered with black and white stripes.

NOTE The male is a **stallion**; the female is a **mare**; the young is a **colt**.

Zen *noun* a Buddhist sect that is popular in Japan, which believes that you should meditate if you want to understand the universe.

WORD HISTORY from a Sanskrit word meaning 'religious meditation'

zero *noun* (*plural* **zeros** *or* **zeroes**)
1. the figure or symbol '0': *Put a zero on the list next to the classes where nobody is coming.* **2.** nothing: *The effectiveness of my gumboots was zero because the soles were all cracked.*

zest *noun* eager enjoyment: *We attacked the party table with zest*; *My grandfather says that his zest for life increases the older he gets.*
☐ **zestful**, *adjective*

zigzag *noun*
1. a line with sharp turns first to one side and then to the other.
–*verb* (**zigzags**, **zigzagging**, **zigzagged**, **has zigzagged**) **2.** To **zigzag** is to lie or move in a zigzag line: *The track zigzagged through the bush.*
☐ **zigzag**, *adjective*

zinc *noun* a bluish-white metallic element.

zip *noun*
1. a fastener consisting of two rows of metal or plastic teeth and a sliding piece which joins or separates them.
–*verb* (**zips**, **zipping**, **zipped**, **has zipped**) **2.** *Informal* If you **zip** somewhere, you move there quickly: *Mum asked me to zip down to the shop for some milk.* **3.** To **zip** computer data is to put it into a form that uses less storage.
–*phrase* **4. zip up**, to fasten with a zip: *Make sure you zip up your jacket – it's cold outside.*

OTHER WORDS (for definition 1) are **zipper** and **zip-fastener**.

zip file *noun* a computer file that is compressed into a smaller size so that it is easier to store or to send over the internet.

zipper *noun* See **zip**.

zither *noun* a musical instrument made of strings that you pluck, stretched over a box.

zodiac /*say* **zoh**-dee-ak/ *noun* a part of the sky forming an imaginary belt through which the sun, moon and planets appear to travel, and which contains twelve constellations which are named and used in astrology.

zombie *noun*
1. in the beliefs of some West Indian religions, a dead body brought back to life by supernatural means. **2.** *Informal* someone who looks like a zombie and whose brain seems not to be functioning.

WORD HISTORY from a West African word meaning 'good-luck charm'

zone *noun*
1. an area marked off and used for a special purpose: *an industrial zone.*
–*verb* **2.** To **zone** an area of land is to set it aside for a particular purpose: *Another two hundred hectares have been zoned for parks.*
☐ **zoning**, *noun*

zoo *noun* an area of land with enclosed areas or cages where live animals are kept for public viewing.

zoology /*say* zoh-**ol**-uh-jee/ *noun* the science or study of animal life.

☑ SPELLING TIP You can remember the spelling of the first part of this word by thinking of a zoo. Here *zoo-* is a prefix meaning 'having to do with animals'. The other part of the word is the suffix *-logy*, meaning 'the study of'.

zoom *verb* To **zoom** is to **1.** move quickly: *He zoomed by on his motorbike.* **2.** go up suddenly: *The rocket let off a 'whoosh' as it zoomed upwards.*

zucchini /*say* zuh-**kee**-nee, zooh-**kee**-nee/ *noun* (*plural* **zucchinis**) a small, green vegetable marrow, usually picked when very young.

☑ SPELLING TIP *Silent letter alert*: don't forget the silent *h* following the double (not single) *c*. Also remember the *ini* ending. **Zucchini** has this spelling because it comes from Italian.

GRAMMAR AND PUNCTUATION GUIDE

In this Guide, you will find many of the terms that are used to talk about the grammar of English. You will also find guidance on punctuation. The Guide is arranged like a dictionary, with terms appearing in alphabetical order.

You will occasionally find directions to look up other entries. This simply means that the information you are looking for is under the other headword, or that you will find more information there. Sometimes a slightly specialised word will appear in SMALL CAPITALS. If you don't know what the word means, you can look it up under its own heading in the Grammar and Punctuation Guide.

abbreviations

1. An **abbreviation** is a shortened form of a word which stands for the whole word.

Av *Avenue*

A **contraction** is a special kind of abbreviation which starts and ends with the same letters as the full word.

Ave *Avenue*

2. punctuation of abbreviations

Rules for punctuating abbreviations have varied over the years. Today there are a number of different but acceptable ways of abbreviating words. The most common pattern at present is as follows:

2.1. Abbreviations beginning with capitals do not have a full stop.

Mon (*Monday*)

PhD (*Doctor of Philosophy*)

Dr (*Doctor*)

ABC (*Australian Broadcasting Corporation*)

2.2. Abbreviations beginning with a lower-case letter do have a full stop, unless they are also contractions, in which case they do not.

cont. (*continued*)

k.p.h. (*kilometres per hour*)
(abbreviations)

vb (*verb*)
(contraction)

2.3. Certain groups of words are regarded as special cases:

Symbols for units of measurement and chemical elements do not have full stops.

km (*kilometre*)

ha (*hectare*)

Fe (*iron*)

Ca (*calcium*)

Acronyms do not have full stops.

UNICEF (*United Nations International Children's Emergency Fund*)

See **acronyms**.

2.4. The abbreviations *a.m.* and *p.m.* may also be written *am* and *pm*.

2.5. It is now customary not to use any punctuation marks in addresses on envelopes, parcels, etc.

abstract nouns

See **nouns** 2.1.

acronyms

1. An acronym is a word formed from the initial letters of other words, and pronounced in terms of the sound of these letters, for example **AIDS** (Acquired Immune Deficiency Syndrome).

A similar formation which is pronounced in terms of the names of the letters is not an acronym, for example **WA** (Western Australia).

2. Acronyms tend to start out with capital letters which are then reduced to lower-case letters as the acronym becomes accepted as a word in its own right and people cease to analyse it into all the bits that it stands for.

However, if there is the possibility of confusion with some other word that is spelt the same way, they do not become lower case. So *AIDS* keeps its capital letters, so as not to be confused with *aids*. Note that acronyms do not have full stops.

active

See **verbs** 6.

adjectives

1. An adjective is a word which describes or adds meaning to a noun or pronoun. It may appear in a sentence either before or after the noun or pronoun it modifies.

A long snake appeared.

The snake was long.

It was frightening to all.

Nevertheless there are some adjectives which are usually only found after their nouns.

bargains galore

president elect

There are other adjectives which usually follow a verb or are limited to particular contexts. You can say

The child was asleep.

or

Asleep, the child looked sweet.

but not

an asleep child

Instead you could say

a sleeping child

2. comparisons

Adjectives change form when they are used to show how two or more things compare with each other. Those with only one syllable usually add the suffixes *-er* (when only two things are involved) or *-est* (when more than two things are involved).

Helen is quick. She is quicker than Nick.

She is the quickest member of the team.

Adjectives with more than one syllable usually have *more* placed before them when only two things are involved or *most* placed before them when more than two things are involved.

beautiful

more beautiful

most beautiful

Exceptions to this are adjectives of two syllables ending in *-y*, *-le* and *-ow*.

happy	*happier*	*happiest*
simple	*simpler*	*simplest*
shallow	*shallower*	*shallowest*

Adjectives with *-er*, or *more*, like *quicker* and *more beautiful* are said to be in the **comparative degree**.

Adjectives with *-est* or *most*, like *quickest* and *most beautiful*, are said to be in the **superlative degree**.

adverbs

1. An adverb is a word which modifies, or tells us something extra about, a verb, an adjective, or another adverb. It may come before or after the word it modifies.

He ran quickly.
(The adverb modifies the verb ran.)

She was really pretty.
(The adverb modifies the adjective pretty.)

He'll come very soon.
(The adverb modifies the adverb soon.)

2. Many adverbs end in *-ly*, like *quickly* and *really* above. But some of the most common adverbs, like *soon*, do not. Adverbs like *soon* which are without the *-ly* suffix can be called **flat adverbs**.

Come quick!

She sang well.

Because they don't have the *-ly* ending, flat adverbs can look like adjectives. This can lead people to use an adjective when they should be using an adverb.

He hit him hard.
(Hard is a flat adverb.)

She was running very good.
(Good is an adjective incorrectly used instead of adverb.)

She was running very well.
(Well is a flat adverb.)

3. Adverbs can be named by the sort of extra meaning they bring to a sentence.

She plays the piano well.
(In this sentence well tells us how she plays – adverb of manner.)

She practises frequently.
(In this sentence frequently tells us when she practises – adverb of time.)

She plays locally.
(In this sentence locally tells us where she plays – adverb of place.)

4. Adverbs change form when used in comparing two or more things. Those with only one syllable usually add the suffix *-er* when two things are involved, or *-est* when more than two are involved.

Nick arrived sooner than Helen.

Among all the girls, she sang (the) loudest.

Those with two or more syllables usually have *more* placed before them when only two things are involved, or *most* when more than two things are involved.

Nick came up the stairs more quickly than Helen.

Among all the girls, she sang (the) most tunefully.

There are a few exceptions to this pattern. For example *early* becomes *earlier* and *earliest*, not *more early* and *most early*.

Adverbs with *-er* and *more* are said to be in the **comparative degree**.

Those with *-est* and *most* are said to be in the **superlative degree**.

antonyms

An antonym is a word which has an opposite meaning to another word:

Fast is an antonym of slow.

Some examples of antonyms are:

quick	*slow*
hot	*cold*
dead	*alive*
buy	*sell*

Although they mean the opposite, antonyms always have a common element shared between them such as:

speed	*quick/slow*
temperature	*hot/cold*
life	*dead/alive*
exchange of goods	*buy/sell*

Antonyms contrast with **synonyms**.

apostrophe

The apostrophe (') has two major functions – to show that something has been left out and to show possession.

1. omission

1.1. The apostrophe's original function in English was to show where part of a word had been omitted. It is still used in this way where two words run together into a contraction:

I've	*I have*
he'll	*he will*
we'd	*we would*
let's	*let us*
it's	*it is*

1.2. Apostrophes are also used by writers who want to show when a speaker pronounces words in a non-standard way, omitting one or more sounds.

'em	*them*
huntin'	*hunting*

2. possession

2.1. The apostrophe and a following *s* is the regular way of marking the POSSESSIVE CASE in English, for singular nouns and words called *indefinite pronouns*:

a dog's dinner *anyone's guess*

This is not so with personal pronouns:

hers *yours* *its*

2.2. Plural nouns which end in *s* add the apostrophe at the end to mark their possessive form:

citizens' rights *teachers' children*

Plural nouns which do not end in *s* are treated in the same way as singulars:

children's day *the mice's squeaking*

2.3. Personal names ending in *s* are these days usually given the regular treatment of the apostrophe followed by *s*, whatever their number of syllables or their sound:

Burns's poetry *Dickens's novels*

2.4. Apostrophes are no longer used in several kinds of expression where the idea of possession is weak:

Expressions of time

three years jail

Official names, titles and phrases

State Girls High School

Teachers Federation

Plumbers and Gasfitters Union

Visitors Book

Place names

Kings Cross

St Marys

3. plurals

3.1. The apostrophe with *s* should never be used to mark the plural form of a noun.

The plural of *tomato* is *tomatoes*, not *tomato's*.

The plural of *horse* is *horses*, not *horse's*.

3.2. An apostrophe is used for the plural forms of single letters or numbers:

p's and q's *1's and 2's*

However, groups of letters or numbers do not require the apostrophe:

MPs *747s* *1980s*

articles

See **definite article / indefinite articles**

aspect

See **verbs** 9.

auxiliary verbs

See **verbs** 2.2.

be

The verb be has more different parts than any other verb in English.

Present Tense	*Past Tense*
I am	*I was*
you are	*you were*
he/she/it is	*he/she/it was*
we are	*we were*
they are	*they were*

Present participle

being

Past participle

been

Many parts of this verb form contractions in the usual way with *not*:

is not	*isn't*	*are not*	*aren't*
were not	*weren't*	*was not*	*wasn't*

However *am* behaves differently. It is the verb and not the word *not* which is abbreviated when you say *I'm not* rather than *I amn't*, which is incorrect. To ask a question you may either say *am I not?* or, more commonly, *aren't I?*.

brackets

In any piece of writing, there may be a need to break into the main flow of words with a thought or an explanation which somehow relates to the point being made, but which is not grammatically part of the main flow of words. In conversation the rise and fall of the voice, pauses, even a change in tone of voice, may all clearly mark off the words which are added. In writing, this must be shown in some other way. In this example, dashes are used.

Helen – she was the one we met last week – said she couldn't stand him.

Sometimes even commas are enough. See **comma**; **dash**.

When a greater separation is needed, it may be best to use **brackets**. These are pairs of symbols which have been specially designed for the purpose. They include:

round brackets or parentheses (. . .)

square brackets [. . .]

curly brackets or braces {. . . }

angle brackets <. . . >

slash brackets /. . . /

Except in scientific or technical writing, it is rare for any of these to be used except round brackets, and occasionally square brackets. Square brackets can be used to enclose information relating to the text but separate from it, as in

[*solution on page 53*]

The prime minister said that he [*the leader of the opposition*] *was completely mistaken.*

Round brackets, or parentheses, are by far the most common.

For information on how these are used, see **parenthesis**.

capital letters

1. Each letter of the alphabet can be written in different ways depending on the form of handwriting used or the different typeface or font chosen. Nevertheless all the varieties can be seen as falling into just two major categories – the big letters (**capital letters**) and the small. These may also be called the **upper-case** and **lower-case** letters.

2. The titles of books, films, etc., can be in capital letters throughout, as can some usually shortish advertisements and headlines in newspapers, but texts of any kind which are of more significant length, are typically in lower-case letters with capitals reserved for the first letters only of the first word of each sentence and of particular words, usually names. The following names are usually capitalised.

people	*Alice Jackson*
institutions	*Commonwealth Bank*
titles	*Lady Veronica Hardcastle*
degrees	*Professor Jones PhD*
places	*Melbourne*
natural features	*Pacific Ocean*
nations	*France*
peoples	*Inuit*
languages	*French*
established religions	*Hinduism*
their followers	*Hindus*
significant periods	*Middle Ages*
events	*Olympic Games*
special days	*Christmas Day*

case

Nouns and pronouns can be said to have one variety or other of **case** depending on the type of relationship they have with other words in the sentence or phrase where they are found.

1. subjective case

A noun or pronoun which does the action which the related verb in the same sentence or clause describes, is said to be in the **subjective case**. That is, the noun or pronoun is the subject of the verb.

The water is falling.
(In this sentence *water* is the subject of *falling*.)

She was singing a song which we all liked.
(In this sentence *She* is the subject of *was singing* and *we* is the subject of *liked*.)

The subjective case is sometimes called the **nominative case**. See **subject**.

2. objective case

2.1. A noun or pronoun which 'receives' the action which the related verb in the same sentence or clause describes, is said to be in the **objective case**. That is, the noun or pronoun is the object of the verb.

The car hit the water.
(In this sentence *water* is the object of *hit*.)

The song pleased her.
(In this sentence *her* is the object of *pleased*.)

2.2. A noun or pronoun which follows a preposition to which it is linked, is also said to be in the **objective case**. That is, the noun or pronoun is the object of the preposition.

after the storm
(In this phrase *storm* is the object of the preposition *after*.)

He sang for her.
(In this sentence *her* is the object of the preposition *for*.)

The objective case is sometimes called the **accusative case**. See **object** 1; **prepositions**.

3. possessive case

A noun or pronoun which implies ownership, is said to be in the **possessive case**. It may be in a phrase, clause or sentence.

Her phone rang during the movie.

The possessive case is sometimes called the **genitive case**.

4. pronouns

English PERSONAL PRONOUNS often change form with case.

I like Helen.
(*I* is in the subjective case)

Helen likes me.
(*me* is in the objective case)

Helen likes my hat.
(*my* is in the possessive case)

Helen said 'The hat is mine.'
(*mine* is in the possessive case)

English nouns change their form with case only for the possessive.

The dog likes Helen.
(*dog* is in the subjective case)

Helen likes the dog.
(*dog* is in the objective case)

The dog's bone is small.
(*dog's* is in the possessive case)

clauses

A clause is a group of words containing a finite verb (see **verbs** 3.1). There are two main types:

1. principal clauses / main clauses

A principal clause can generally stand by itself as a complete sentence or message.

I enjoy my work.

The meeting was cancelled.

There may be two or more principal clauses joined together, in which case they are often called **coordinate clauses**. They must be joined by a conjunction, such as 'and', 'but', or 'or'.

The letters are typed and the files are in order.

I have finished the research but I have not written the report.

2. subordinate clauses / dependent clauses

A subordinate clause cannot stand alone as a sentence.

I arrived before the bank opened.

She told me that he needed an operation.

Before the bank opened is not a complete sentence. It needs something else (*I arrived*) to make it complete. In the second example, *that he needed an operation* is similarly incomplete needing *She told me* to make a sentence.

Subordinate clauses can be given names related to the sort of grammatical function they perform.

2.1. adverbial clauses

An adverbial clause is one which performs the function of an adverb and can be thought to answer questions like 'when?', 'where?', 'how?' and 'why?'.

I arrived before the bank opened.
(This answers the question *when?* and is an adverbial clause of time.)

Helen went where she wouldn't be disturbed.
(This answers the question *where?* and is an adverbial clause of place.)

As quickly as he could, Nick hid the biscuits.
(This answers the question *how?* and is an adverbial clause of manner.)

The car skidded because the road was covered with ice.
(This answers the question *why?* and is an adverbial clause of reason.)

2.2. noun clauses

A noun clause is one which performs the function of a noun acting as a subject or object. It may indicate what is said, felt, or thought. Often a noun clause begins with the conjunction 'that' (but this can often be omitted), or with some other conjunction like 'what', 'which', 'who', etc.

That he had had the operation was news to me.

She told me (that) he needed an operation.

I soon learnt what I should do.

Nick knew who was behind all the trouble.

2.3. adjectival clauses / relative clauses

An adjectival clause performs the function of an adjective. It adds meaning to a noun or pronoun which usually comes before it. Very often the adjectival clause begins with one of the relative pronouns, *who*, *whom*, *whose*, *which* or *that*.

The car (which) he had bought us was green.
(In this sentence the clause is adding meaning to *car*.)

The farmer, whose crop was wheat, went bankrupt.
(In this sentence the clause is adding meaning to *farmer*.)

The team that came last in the competition were not pleased.
(In this sentence the clause is adding meaning to *team*.)

collective nouns

See **nouns** 4.

colon

1. The colon (:) is often used to signal that a set of examples will follow.

The food must be simple: chicken, green salad and wine.

2. Colons are also used to show that what follows is to a rewording of what has just been said, or can give more details.

His career was cut short by illness: a great loss to the scientific community.

The evening was wonderful: dinner, a movie and a long walk along the beach.

3. The colon is also used to introduce speech.

3.1. A colon is often used to introduce a quotation.

The principal was heard to say: 'The students in our school are all trying hard.'

3.2. Colons are commonly used in setting out the dialogue of a play, or in transcripts of interviews used in court records, etc.:

Judge: *Were you drinking at the Landmark Hotel on Saturday night?*

Prisoner: *No, sir.*

comma

The comma (,) is a punctuation mark which is used to separate a word or group of words from others in the same written sentence. Its usual purpose is to help the reader understand the structure of the sentence and so arrive correctly at its intended meaning.

1.1. Where it is helpful to do so, commas may be used to mark off a whole phrase or clause from the rest.

Arriving at the station, they realised the train had just left.

(The comma in this sentence marks off a *phrase*.)

The two friends were going to the shops first, then to the swimming pool.

(The comma in this sentence marks off a *phrase*.)

The workers, when conditions in the factory became too bad, went on strike.

(The commas in this sentence mark off a *clause*.)

1.2. Sometimes commas, instead of dashes and brackets, are used to enclose a word, phrase, or clause which is added to a sentence, but which is not actually part of the sentence grammatically.

The end result, chaos, is what any half-intelligent person would expect.

(The commas in this sentence mark off a *word*.)

The dog, a great ugly brute, snarled fiercely.

(The commas in this sentence mark off a *phrase*.)

The workers went on strike, and they had every reason to, and soon conditions were improved.

(The commas in this sentence mark off a *clause*).

2.1. In a sentence containing a list, commas are used to separate the items listed.

Each bouquet was made of roses, tulips, lilies and lavender.

The use of *and* before the last item in such a list is usual. No comma comes before *and* if, as above, the last item is more or less the same sort of item as the others. If, however, it is of a different kind or different grammatical structure, a comma does come before *and*.

The bouquet was made of daisies, carnations, daffodils, and any other flower which the children found attractive.

2.2. A group of adjectives applied to the same noun is like a list and it used to be usual to separate each from the others by a comma, although no comma was used after the last adjective before the noun.

A huge, black, cheerful dog was approaching.

Nowadays many writers prefer not to use commas between adjectives coming before a noun.

A huge black cheerful dog was approaching.

commands

A command is an order to someone to do something.

Bring the car around the back.

Verbs used in commands are said to be in the IMPERATIVE MOOD. See **verbs** 10.2.

See **exclamation mark** 2.

common nouns

See **nouns** 1.

comparative

See **adjectives** 2 and **adverbs** 4.

compounds

A compound is a term made up of two or more parts. Compounds can be one solid word, hyphenated or open (written with a space).

childbirth surfboard paperback (solid)

newly-married son-in-law up-to-date (hyphenated)

square dance, lead pencil, red cedar (open)

See **hyphen** 1.

compound verbs

See **verbs** 2.

concrete nouns

See **nouns** 2.2.

conjunctions

A conjunction is a word which joins words, phrases, clauses, sentences, etc., together.

1. A **coordinating conjunction** joins similar forms.

invoices and receipts (two nouns)

Phone him or send a fax. (two principal clauses)
attractive but expensive (two adjectives)

2. A **subordinating conjunction** is used to relate dependent or subordinate parts (usually subordinate adverbial clauses) to the main part of a sentence.

Ask him when he arrives.

Because we were late, the meeting was delayed.

The results are conclusive, as this graph will indicate.

In these sentences *when*, *because* and *as* are the subordinating conjunctions beginning the subordinate clauses.

consonants

See **vowels/consonants.**

continuous aspect

See **verbs** 9.2.

contractions

1. There are two types of contractions. One type is an abbreviation of a single word which keeps the first and last letters of the original.

Mrs	*M(ist)r(es)s*
ne'er	*ne(v)er*

See **abbreviations**.

2. The other type of contraction reduces two words to a single one in which an apostrophe shows where a letter or letters have been removed.

we're	*we (a)re*
could've	*could (ha)ve*

In the rare cases of letters having been removed from two places, only a single apostrophe is usually used.

shan't	*sha(ll) n(o)t*

This second type of contraction is usual in conversation or in dialogue in plays and novels, but, unless a very informal tone is being sought in your writing, you would normally write out both words in full.

coordinate clauses

See **clauses** 1.

coordinating conjunctions

See **conjunctions** 1.

count nouns

See **nouns** 3.1.

dash

1.1. The dash (–) is often used to show where a sentence has been interrupted or broken off.

He was about to – Oh, I mustn't spoil the story for you.

1.2. A dash is often used in informal writing to separate parts of a sentence, instead of commas and other regular punctuation marks.

I'll come as fast as I can – once the speeches are over.

2. In pairs, dashes may be used to enclose a PARENTHESIS in mid-sentence.

He had crawled up to the road – heaven knows how – with two broken legs.

Note that the dashes here could be replaced by parentheses (round brackets).

definite article/indefinite articles

1. definite article

1.1. In English the word **the** is the only definite article.

You use it to refer to a specific instance of the class of things which is being talked about. Which particular instance being referred to is usually identified in the surrounding words.

The dog next door barked all night.

Here the following phrase 'next door' provides the identification.

Often the identification is provided by a previous mention in the text.

She was driving her new car. The car was not behaving very well.

Sometimes it is understood because there is only one instance existing in the current context.

the Prime Minister

the moon

1.2. The definite article is also used when the whole of a category is being referred to.

The tiger likes to hunt at night.

Here every tiger has been referred to.

2. indefinite articles

In English the indefinite articles are **a** and **an** and, according to some people, **some**.

2.1. The indefinite articles **a** and **an** are used before singular COUNT NOUNS, and most often refer to a person or thing that is not a particular one, or one that is known.

A woman suddenly turned the corner.

This implies that we do not know who this woman was and that she has not been mentioned before in the text.

Like the definite article, these two indefinite articles can be used also to refer to the whole of the category.

A tiger likes to hunt at night.

2.2. Whether to use **a** or **an** is decided by the pronunciation of the beginning of the following word.

A is used when the next word begins with a consonant *sound*. **An** is used when the next word begins with a vowel *sound*.

a dog

an awful dog

an hour

an apple

a red apple

a union

In the examples above, *union* looks like it starts with a vowel, but the sound is actually *y*, and *hour*, although it has an *h* in its spelling, starts with a vowel sound.

2.3. When a noun with an indefinite article is in the plural, it has no article at all.

a tiger
(singular)

tigers
(plural)

direct object

See **object** 1.

direct speech / direct quotation

Words which are written down exactly as someone has said them are referred to as **direct speech**.

'I have no further interest in you at all', she said coldly.

The term **direct quotation** applies to words which are written down exactly as someone else has written them down before.

The prime minister's comment in the paper, 'We must be ahead of the new technology', was a starting point for discussion.

Direct speech and direct quotations are both always written between quotation marks.

See **indirect speech / indirect quotation**; **quotation marks**.

exclamation mark

1. The exclamation mark (!) is used at the end of an EXCLAMATION.

You're a blast from the past!

Half your luck!

2. In commands, the exclamation mark is used for those which are emphatic.

Quick march!

Get out!

But it is not used with commands intended to guide or instruct the reader.

Place the meat on a well-greased baking dish.

exclamations

An exclamation is an utterance that is said or cried out suddenly.

How fantastic!

Oh, no!

See **exclamation mark**.

full stop

1. Full stops (.) are used to mark the end of sentences other than those which are direct questions or exclamations. Questions have QUESTION MARKS and exclamations have EXCLAMATION MARKS.

The meeting started at midday.

He asked what we were going to do.

Would you shut the door please.

The second sentence above has a full stop because the question in it is indirect.

The third sentence, though worded like a question, is actually a polite command.

2. Full stops are not usually used in headlines and headings, nor in the captions or labels on pictures, diagrams and tables.

Full stops are sometimes called **periods** or **full points**.

For the use of full stops with abbreviations, see **abbreviations** 2.

future tense

See **verbs** 8.

gender

In grammar, gender is a set of classes, such as masculine, feminine and neuter. In many languages, all nouns belong to a gender, but in English only the pronouns show gender. For example, *she* is feminine, *he* is masculine and *it* is neuter.

have

The verb **have** is one of the most commonly used in English. This is because, in addition to its common meaning of 'to own', and, in the compound verb **have to** (meaning 'must'), it functions as an AUXILIARY VERB.

I have six bikes.
(to own)

He has to see the manager.
(must)

They have come back early.
(auxiliary verb)

They had been corrected.
(auxiliary verb)

hyphen

1. hyphens in compounds

Hyphens (-) can serve to link the parts of a compound.

all-embracing

go-ahead

mother-in-law

owner-operator

passer-by

thirty-five

Some compounds are written as one word and some as two separate words. Your dictionary should guide you on how to write a compound.

2. hyphens to make meaning clear

2.1. In compounds and some words with prefixes, a hyphen is sometimes used to separate the two parts to prevent misreading. The hyphen in *under-age* prevents us from seeing the word *rage*. The hyphen in *re-educate* prevents us from seeing the word *reed*.

2.2. The separating hyphen distinguishes words such as *re-cover* and *re-mark* from *recover* and *remark*. In such cases quite a difference in meaning hangs on the hyphen.

Re-cover means to cover again, whereas *recover* means to bet better, and *re-mark* means to mark again and *remark* means to comment.

3. hyphens and numbers

3.1. Hyphens are generally used when writing two-word numbers under one hundred.

twenty-seven

twenty-seventh

3.2. Hyphens are used when fractions are written in words.

two-thirds

one-fifth

imperative mood

See **verbs** 10.2.

imperfect aspect

See **verbs** 9.2.

indefinite articles

See **definite article / indefinite articles**.

indicative mood

See **verbs** 10.1.

indirect object

See **object** 2.

indirect speech / indirect quotation

Indirect speech gives the general meaning of what someone has said or written, but unlike DIRECT SPEECH, does not reproduce the exact words used.

'I have no further interest in you at all', she told him coldly.

(direct speech)

She told him coldly that she had no further interest in him at all.

(indirect or reported speech)

See **direct speech / direct quotation**.

infinitives

See **verbs** 4.

inflections

An inflection is an ending which is attached to a base word to show NUMBER, TENSE, PERSON, ASPECT, etc.

The ending *-s* (or *-es*) on a noun to show that it is a plural is an inflection, as are the various verb endings which indicate person, tense, aspect, etc.

he stays *he stayed* *he was staying*

interjections

Interjections are words or expressions which are outside the grammatical structure of a sentence. Such words and expressions as *Ouch!* or *Oh my goodness!* are not part of the structure of the sentence but are utterances that stand on their own. Interjections are usually indicated with an EXCLAMATION MARK.

intransitive verbs

See **verbs** 7.

inverted commas

See **quotation marks**.

its/it's

Its is the form of the possessive case of the PERSONAL PRONOUN **it**. It never has an apostrophe.

The horse looks old. I don't like its chances.

It's is a shortened form of **it is** or **it has**. It always has an apostrophe.

The horse looks old. It's quite decrepit.

It's not going to rain I tell you!

main clauses

See **clauses** 1.

modal verbs

See **verbs** 2.4.

mood

See **verbs** 10.

nouns

A **noun** is the name for a person, thing, emotion, idea, group, etc.

1.1. A **common noun** refers to any member of a type or class:

river house car child

1.2. A **proper noun** is the name for one particular member of a class, and usually has a capital letter:

Perth Solar System

Lady Luck Ben Chifley

2.1. An **abstract noun** refers to something that our five senses (touch, sight, hearing, smell and taste) cannot pick up:

love nationalism luck character

2.2. A **concrete noun** refers to something that our senses can pick up:

paper sun light chair people

3.1. A **count noun** is a noun referring to objects which can be thought of as existing in numbers so that groups of the objects can be counted.

A banana is yellow.

Bananas are yellow.

3.2. A mass noun is a noun referring to an object which is thought of as existing in bulk, such as *butter* and *wheat*. It is not normally able to be counted as a set of individual items. Such nouns take a singular verb.

Butter is good on toast.

Other names for mass nouns are **uncount nouns** and **non-count nouns**.

4. A **collective noun** refers to a collection of similar things:

herd group jury fleet

Collective nouns may take singular verbs if you think of them as single units.

Our team was the best in the whole competition.

They may take plural verbs if you think of the things (or persons) within them as individuals.

The team were all elated by the win.

number

In grammar, a noun, pronoun or verb can refer to one or a number of persons or objects. If it refers to one, it is singular in **number**. If it refers to more than one, it is plural. See **plural/singular**.

object

1. direct object

The word referring to the person or thing affected by the action of a verb is said to be the **direct object**, or often just the **object**, of the verb.

The earthquake damaged the century-old temple.

Her car must have hit the newly-painted fence very hard.

The object can be singular as above, or plural as follows:

The earthquake damaged several buildings.

The object can be found by asking *who?* or *what?* after the verb. For instance, in the last sentence above, one would say 'The earthquake damaged what?'. The answer is 'several buildings'.

The nouns or pronouns in the object referring to whatever is directly affected by the action of the verb are in the OBJECTIVE (or ACCUSATIVE) CASE. In the examples above, the nouns *church*, *fence* and *buildings* are in the objective case.

2. indirect object

In some sentences whose verbs have a direct object, a second object may be found which refers to the person or thing affected by, or benefited by, the action of the verb.

Helen brought me this shirt from London.

Her car gave the newly-painted fence a tremendous blow.

This second object is called the **indirect object** and can usually be identified because *to* and *for* can be put in front of it when the sentence is slightly rearranged.

Helen brought this shirt from London for me.

Her car gave a tremendous blow to the newly-painted fence.

Indirect objects can also be singular or plural.

objective case

See **case** 2.

parenthesis

A parenthesis is either or both of two round brackets ( ) used with various functions.

1. Parentheses can enclose a whole sentence which has been inserted into another one.

Computer analysis of the novel The Dark Tower *by CS Lewis, published after his death, has shown it to be a forgery. (Many readers thought it too unpleasant to be the work of the master.) The computer compared its language with that of his other novels, and found marked differences in style.*

Such a sentence carries the normal full stop. When if appears within another sentence, however, the full stop is left off.

The details of the analysis (see below) have surprised many readers.

2. Parentheses often enclose a word which is offered to explain or add to a point.

She moved from Wellington (NZ) to Wellington (NSW).

3. Parentheses may be used around a letter which allows an alternative reading of the sentence.

The speaker's grasp of the issue(s) was less than strong.

4. When something is included in parentheses at the end of a sentence, the final full stop always goes outside.

The talk has been cancelled (the speaker is ill).

participles

See **verbs** 5.

part of speech

The part of speech is the grammatical category into which a word in a particular context may be placed. In traditional English grammar, we generally say that there are eight parts of speech: nouns, pronouns, adjectives, verbs, adverbs, prepositions, conjunctions, and interjections. Each of these is described in its alphabetical place in this guide, and extra information about the various types is given there.

passive

See **verbs** 6.

past participles

See **verbs** 5.4.

past tense

See **verbs** 8.

perfect aspect

See **verbs** 9. 1.

person

In grammar, person is a grouping applied to personal pronouns and to verbs. It has nothing to do with people. There are three kinds:

1. first person

First person applies to the person(s) speaking or writing. So **I** and **we**, together with their other forms like **me**, **our**, etc., are all in the first person. Also, any verbs which have **I** or **we** as their subjects are in the first person.

I usually take my dog for a walk in the mornings.

2. second person

Second person applies to the person(s) or thing(s) spoken to or written to. So **you**, together with its other forms like **your**, etc., are all in the second person. Also any verbs which has **you** as its subject is in the second person.

Do you want to bring your dog?

3. third person

Third person applies to the person(s) or thing(s) spoken about or written about. So **he**, **she**, **it** and **they**, together with their other forms like **him**, **hers**, **its** and **them**, etc., are all in the third person. Also any verbs which have **he**, **she**, **it**, **they**, or any thing being discussed as their subjects are in the third person.

She loves her new bike.

The horse now lives in its own stable.

In modern English the verb does not as a rule change in form with person or number. Nevertheless, the third person singular present tense does take a different ending in most verbs.

I swim

you swim

he swims

we all swim

they swim

personal pronouns

A personal pronoun stands for a person or thing. Examples are *I*, *we*, *you*, *he*, *she*, *it* and *they*, etc. See **pronouns** 1.

phrases

A phrase is a group of words which are felt to belong together but which do not have a finite verb (See **Verbs** 3).

Please reply by return email.

Phrases may be classified by the function they perform. The phrase above modifies the verb *reply*, saying when to reply. Since it does the work of an adverb, it is an adverbial phrase.

A bright but softly shining moon lit the scene.
(This tells us that a *moon* lit the scene – it is a *noun phrase*.)

plural/singular

Nouns, pronouns and verbs are said to be **plural**, **in the plural** or **plural in number** if they refer to more than one person or thing. They are said to be **singular**, **in the singular** or **singular in number** if they refer to only one person or thing.

1. nouns

1.1. Nouns which show their plurality in writing by just adding *-s* or *-es* are called regular. The choice is predictably determined by the nature of the preceding sound.

one dog	*two dogs*
one watch	*two watches*

1.2. However, other nouns form plurals in different ways for a variety of reasons. These plurals are called irregular.

goose	*geese*
ox	*oxen*
foot	*feet*
criterion	*criteria*

1.3. For the erroneous use of *'s* to mark plural forms, see **apostrophe** 3.1.

2. pronouns

The personal pronouns change with number. See **pronouns** 1.

3. verbs

In English, only one form of the verb regularly shows the difference between singular and plural – the third person present tense singular verb is marked by an ending spelt either *-s* or *-es* depending on the nature of the sound which comes before it. The plural does not change.

She sings./They sing.

Helen watches carefully./The two sisters watch carefully.

possessive adjectives

Possessive adjectives are words like *my*, *his*, *our*, etc. They are the possessive case of the PERSONAL PRONOUNS in the forms which come before their noun.

your pen

their car

Compare **possessive pronouns**.

See **pronouns** 1.

possessive case

See **case** 3.

possessive pronouns

Possessive pronouns are words like *mine*, *his*, *ours*, etc. They are the possessive case of the PERSONAL PRONOUNS in the forms which follow their noun.

The pen is yours.

The car is theirs.

Compare **possessive adjectives**.

See **pronouns** 1.

predicate

Sentences may be thought of as being in two parts – the SUBJECT, which is *who* or *what* is being discussed, and the **predicate**, which is what is being said about it. The subject may be identified by asking 'who?' or 'what?' before the main verb. The predicate is everything else in the sentence.

The cat in the corner would not eat her dinner because it was cold.

Who or what would not eat?

the cat in the corner

So 'the cat in the corner' must be the subject of this sentence, and everything else, 'would not eat her dinner because it was cold' must be the predicate.

As in this sentence, predicates very often follow their subjects. But cases where they come before them are not rare.

Without any warning and with her claws out, up jumped an angry cat.

Who or what jumped up?

an angry cat

So 'an angry cat' is the subject of the sentence, and everything else, 'Without any warning and with her claws out, up jumped' is the predicate. See **subject**.

prepositions

A preposition is a word which shows the relationship between a noun (or pronoun) and some other word(s) in the sentence.

That book is on the shelf above the desk, between the atlas and the dictionary.

He talked to me for a long time.

The noun or pronoun following a preposition is said to be its object. Nouns as objects of prepositions are not different in form from the same nouns as subjects but many pronouns are.

The library is near. (subject)

Come to the library. (object)

Library has the same form as a subject and as an object.

We are here. (subject)

Come to us. (object)

We is in the subjective and *us* is in the objective case.

See **case** 2.2.

present participles

See **verbs** 5.1.

present tense

See **verbs** 8.

principal clauses

See **clauses** 1.

pronouns

Pronouns are words which take the place of nouns. Using them avoids having to repeat those nouns.

Helen loves cars. They (cars) fascinate her (Helen).

There are several types of pronoun:

1. personal pronouns

Personal pronouns are those which replace nouns referring to persons or things.

Nick came in. He looked tired.
(In this sentence *He* refers to a person, *Nick*.)

The car stopped. It was very old.
(In this sentence *It* refers to a thing, *the car*.)

Personal pronouns often change form with change of case.

I play soccer. (*I* – subjective case)

She hit me. (*she* – objective case)

The ball is mine. (*mine* – possessive case)

She likes tennis. (*she* – subjective case)

Helen liked her. (*her* – objective case)

The book was hers. (*hers* – possessive case)

We can list all these changes in a table.

Possessive (1) forms are used in front of their nouns, possessive (2) forms after them.

This is my book.

This book is mine.

Whose book is this? Mine!

Possessive (1) forms may also be called **possessive adjectives**.

2. impersonal pronoun

It is sometimes called an impersonal pronoun when it does not replace any noun.

It seemed sad to me.

It was raining very hard.

3. indefinite pronouns

Indefinite pronouns are those which do not specify which person(s) or thing(s) are being referred to. They include words like *one*, *some*, *anyone*, *anybody*, *anything*, *someone*, *somebody*, *something*, *noone*, *nobody*, *nothing*, *each*, and, for some writers, the impersonal pronoun *it*, as in *It is raining*.

Anyone can see what to do.

Somebody has been here before us.

Also included are *they* and *you* when they refer to unspecified persons generally, in much the same way that *one*, *some*, etc., do.

One does not know which way to turn.

You would think he'd know better.

They say the river's rising.

There is sometimes a problem in sentences where reference is made back to an indefinite pronoun with singular number. Consider the following:

Each must make up his own mind.

or

Each must make up his or her own mind.

or

Each must make up their own mind.

In the past, a masculine pronoun like *his* was considered to include both males and females in sentences like this. Over the past few decades this convention has been found to be unacceptable to many people and the clear inclusion of females was preferred, as in *his or her*. Others thought this was too clumsy and preferred to use the plural form *their* even though it referred to a singular entity – *each person*.

This solution is the one being adopted more and more these days.

4. interrogative pronouns

Interrogative pronouns are those which play a part in making a sentence into a question. They are *who*, its objective case form *whom*, its possessive case form *whose*, along with *what* and *which*.

4.1. The *who* forms may be used only with reference to human beings.

Whose is that hat?

Who did that?

Whom seems to be used in interrogative situations only by rather formal speakers. So while '*Whom* did you see?' and 'For *whom* did you buy it?' are both strictly speaking grammatically correct, it is much more usual to say '*Who* did you see?' and '*Who* did you buy it for?'.

4.2. *What* can be used with reference to non-human living things, or non-living things.

What was that horse that won the race?
(what horse?)

Now what will I choose to eat first?
(what food?)

4.3. *Which* may be used with reference to all living and non-living things in situations which distinguish between alternatives.

Which is the taller? Helen or her sister?

Of these two tables, which is the cheaper?

5. relative pronouns

Relative pronouns are those which appear at, or very near, the beginning of ADJECTIVAL or RELATIVE CLAUSES. They are *who*, its objective case form *whom*, its possessive case form *whose*, along with *that* and *which*.

Singular Number			
CASE	1st person	2nd person	3rd person
subjective	*I*	*you*	*her, she, it*
objective	*me*	*you*	*him, her, it*
possessive (1)	*my*	*your*	*his, her, its*
possessive (2)	*mine*	*yours*	*his, hers, its*
Plural Number			
CASE	1st person	2nd person	3rd person
subjective	*we*	*you*	*they*
objective	*us*	*you*	*them*
possessive (1)	*our*	*your*	*their*
possessive (2)	*ours*	*yours*	*theirs*

5.1. The *who* forms are used only to human beings.

Where is the boy who just spoke?

5.2. *That* is used to refer to any living creatures or to things.

Where is the boy that just spoke?

The horse that won the race collapsed.

The house that he saw yesterday is the one he's buying.

5.3. *Which* is used to non-human living creatures or to things.

The germs which showed up in the test were lethal.

This is the hammer which was used by the murderer.

See **clauses** 2.3.

6. reflexive pronouns

The reflexive pronouns are *myself*, *yourself*, *himself*, *herself*, *itself*, *ourselves*, *yourselves* and *themselves*.

6.1. They are used when the object of a verb is the same person or persons as the subject referred to.

She hit herself on the finger.

proper nouns

See **nouns** 1.2.

question mark

The question mark (?) is used after any word or string of words which functions as a question.

Can you give me a lift to the station?

When?

You mean it?

These are all direct questions, even the last example which at first glance does not seem to be written in question form. In speech the rise of the voice would tell us this is a direct question and in writing only the question mark tells us that this is so. Indirect questions require no question mark.

I asked when she wanted a lift.

Sentences which are phrased like direct questions, but which function as polite commands, also have full stops rather than question marks.

Could you pass me the salt, please.

questions

1. Many questions can be thought of as having been made from sentences which are STATEMENTS. Statements can be converted into questions in many ways.

1.1. In speech, very often changing the way the voice rises and falls is enough. The following is a statement in which the voice falls on *now*.

He's going now.

The following is a statement in which the voice rises on *now*, which is more heavily stressed.

He's going now?

1.2. Sentences which have verbs in the simple present or simple past tense are converted with the help of the auxiliary *do*.

Nick plays golf. / Does Nick play golf?

Helen played golf. / Did Helen play golf?

1.3. Sentences with compound verbs often need to be rearranged so that one auxiliary comes first.

Nick had been playing golf. / Had Nick been playing golf?

Helen was doing the banking. / Was Helen doing the banking?

1.4. Very often statement sentences merely have added to them a so-called negative **tag question** (or tag-end question), like *won't you?* or *doesn't she?*

You'll enjoy that, won't you?

The train is late, isn't it?

Quite often the negative tag question is a question that the speaker doesn't really need to have answered. The purpose is often merely to encourage the other person in the conversation to speak back. It is a form of social behaviour, an attempt at bonding with the person addressed.

2. Some questions are not so easily thought of as being tied to matching statements. These are the ones which depend on one or more of a group of special question words.

Who made that noise?

Which door is broken?

Where is the key?

When did he do it, and why?

quotation marks

1. Quotation marks (' ' or " ") are used primarily to show that the words enclosed are the exact words of a speaker or writer.

'It's gone very quiet', she said.

Their use for the occasional quotation is also standard, as in

'To be or not to be' is Shakespeare's most famous speech opener.

In long block quotations which run to several paragraphs, the quotation marks may be placed at the start of each paragraph, and the end of the last paragraph only.

2. Quotation marks are also used from time to time to draw attention to a word which the writer feels differs in some way from the other words in the text. It might be just one colloquial word in a formal sentence.

A true 'petrolhead' tries to own as many cars as possible.

3. The titles of poems, songs and short stories are often placed in quotation marks:

'Advance Australia Fair' is the national anthem of Australia.

4. Quotation marks may be either single or double.
Whichever is chosen, the other will be needed for contrast when it comes to 'quotes within quotes'.

'Oh, I know more lines of "Waltzing Matilda" than most people,' she said.

5.1. When a quotation does not begin a sentence, it may have a comma or colon before it or there may be no punctuation mark at all.

Nick said, 'I don't feel well'.

As he sank to the ground, Nick said: 'I don't feel well'.

Nick said 'I don't feel well'.

5.2. The major punctuation marks belonging to a quotation go inside the quotation marks. This applies to exclamation marks, question marks and quotation marks.

'Will you drive the sports car – your "toy"?' he asked.

5.3. When a quotation is split, a comma is usually inserted. It can go outside or inside the quotation marks.

'It's over', she said, 'and done with'.

'It's over,' she said, 'and done with'.

Note that the quotation is resumed without a capital letter after *she said*.

6. Quotation marks are also called **inverted commas**, or given the shortened forms **quote marks** or **quotes**.

reflexive pronouns

See **pronouns** 6.

reflexive verbs

Reflexive verbs are verbs whose subject and object are the same. The object is a reflexive pronoun which agrees in number, person and gender with the subject.

She scratched herself.

They saw themselves in the mirror.

relative clauses

See **clauses** 2.3; **pronouns** 5.

relative pronouns

See **pronouns 5**.

semicolon

1. The semicolon (;) is sometimes used between main clauses which are placed next to each other in the same sentence. That is, it divides such a sentence into parts which could stand alone. The semicolon suggests that there is some connection between them, however fine that connection may be.

He had no further plans; he just wanted to leave.

2. The semicolon is used with the comma in dividing items in a series, when the items themselves contain commas:

My tour group included three Australians, young and friendly; two Japanese couples, polite but shy; five Americans; and a lone, middle-aged New Zealander.

Without the semicolons, commas would have had to have been used both within and between the items listed. The boundaries between them would have been less clear.

sentences

1. A sentence is a group of words, or even one word, which conveys a self-contained and complete meaning.

When written, a sentence always begins with a capital letter and ends with a full stop, a question mark or an exclamation mark.

He saw the car coming quickly down the road.

Oh yeah?

Come on!

2. It is usual for a sentence to have a finite verb (see **verbs** 3.1). But instances where this is not the case are quite common, especially in answer to questions.

When did Helen get home? Some time about one o'clock.

3. A **simple sentence** is made up of just one PRINCIPAL CLAUSE.

The late rains had been welcome.

4. A **compound sentence** has two or more principal clauses which are joined together by COORDINATING CONJUNCTIONS, that is, the words *and*, *but* and *or*. The clauses can be called COORDINATE CLAUSES.

The car was packed and we were ready to leave.

The late rains had been welcome but the farmers were still worried.

I will go to town or I will go to the university.

5. A **complex sentence** has at least one principal clause and one or more SUBORDINATE CLAUSES, each of which may be introduced by a SUBORDINATING CONJUNCTION.

I will go to town because I need to pick up my watch.

In this sentence *I will go to town* is the principal clause and *because I need to pick up my watch* is the subordinate clause introduced by the subordinating conjunction *because*.

See **clauses**.

simple past

See **verbs** 1 and 8.

simple present

See **verbs** 1 and 8.

simple verbs

See **verbs** 1.

singular

See **plural/singular**.

square brackets

Square brackets [ ] have various technical uses in particular subject areas, such as mathematics. In general use they occur to mark off a comment, explanation or correction by an editor, etc., in someone else's writing or a quotation of their speech.

'I will report to the Prime Minister as soon as I get there [Canberra]', the ambassador said.

statements

Statements are sentences of the type which offer information.

The ship is entering the harbour now.

The other sentence types are QUESTIONS, COMMANDS and EXCLAMATIONS.

When is the ship due? (question)

Signal the ship to enter the harbour now. (command)

What a wonderful sight! (exclamation)

subject

Sentences may be thought of as being in two parts – the **subject**, which is who or what is being discussed, and the **predicate**, which is what is being said about it. The subject may be identified by asking 'who?' or 'what?' before the main verb. The predicate is everything else in the sentence.

The director's fiery speech in the boardroom impressed Nick greatly.

What impressed Nick?

the director's fiery speech in the boardroom

So the subject of this sentence is *the director's fiery speech in the board-room* and its predicate is *impressed Nick greatly*.

See **object**; **predicate**.

subjective case

See **case** 1.

subjunctive mood

See **verbs** 10.3.

subordinate clauses

See **clauses** 2.

subordinating conjunctions

See **conjunctions** 2.

superlative

See **adjectives** 2 and **adverbs** 4.

syllable

A syllable is a segment of speech consisting of one vowel sound, with or without surrounding consonant sounds.

A syllable can form a whole word

owe far pike

or part of a word

wa-ter (two syllables)

pro-nun-ci-a-tion (five syllables)

synonyms

Synonyms are words which have roughly the same meaning, such as *joy*, *gladness*, *elation*.

However, it is rarely the case that words are perfectly interchangeable. They usually have slightly different meanings or are used in different situations. Compare **antonyms**.

tense

See **verbs** 8.

transitive verbs

See **verbs** 7.

uncount nouns

See **nouns** 3.2.

upper-case letters/lower-case letters

See **capital letters**.

verbs

A verb is a word which tells us what people or things do, or what is done to them.

I drive taxis.
(This tells us what *I* do)

Both cars are being towed into town.
(This tells us what is being done to *the cars*)

1. simple verbs

Simple verbs consist of one word only.

He drives here often.

2. compound verbs

2.1. Compound verbs consist of more than one word.

He has driven here often.

Frequently, a compound verb consists of a **main verb**, in one or other of its forms (in this case *driven*), together with one or more words which are called **auxiliaries** or **modals** (in this case *has*).

The main verb tells us what sort of action is being referred to while the auxiliary tells us something about the action – when it happens, perhaps.

She will sing tomorrow.

In this sentence, *sing* is the main verb and *will* is the auxiliary.

2.2. auxiliary verbs

These are verbs which are used with a main verb to show the TENSE, ASPECT and MOOD of the verb.

Have and *be* are commonly used as auxiliaries, as are the modals, such as *can*, *could*, *must*, *will*, *should*, etc.

He has gone to town.

In this sentence, *has gone* is a compound verb using the auxiliary *has*, and in the following *should drive* is the compound verb using the modal auxiliary *should*.

They should drive more carefully.

2.3. adverbial particles

These are words such as *up*, *down*, *in*, *out*, etc., which in other contexts are simply adverbs but are here part of the main verb itself.

Help me wash up.
(The verb is *wash up*.)

Turn out the light, please.
(The verb is *turn out*.)

Remember to bring in the clothes.
(The verb is *bring in*.)

In these examples the verb and adverbial particle together make a single unit of meaning. This type of compound verb is a **phrasal verb**.

2.4. modal verbs

Words like *can*, *must*, *ought* and *will* together with any other forms they may have like *could* and *would*, can combine with main verbs to play a part in establishing tense, aspect and mood (see 9, 10, 11 below).

You must have seen her.

It could have happened, I suppose.

Sometimes these verbs are called **modal verbs** or **modals**.

3. finite and non-finite verbs

3.1. Finite verbs have subjects and a sense of completeness. They may be simple or compound and are said to have NUMBER and PERSON, which they take from their SUBJECTS.

3.2. Non-finite verbs do not have subjects or a sense of completeness. Nor are they said to have number or person although, most of them, like finite verbs, do have tense. They cannot be used alone to form a clause, but can be used to make phrases.

Non-finite verbs include parts of compound finite verbs like auxiliaries and modals, and participles, as well as infinitives.

Having enjoyed the day they looked forward to the evening.

To fish is a great delight for many.

4. infinitives

In English the infinitive is often taken to be a verb form together with a preceding 'to'. Hence *to come*, *to sing* and *to go* are all infinitives.

The infinitive is actually the form of the verb that has not been changed because of its subject or tense. The forms of the verb which follow certain modal auxiliaries are just as much infinitives as the 'to' forms.

You need not come.	*You need to come.*
I will sing.	*I want to sing.*
We both must go.	*We both are required to go.*

5. participles

The verb has two types of participle:

5.1. present participles

Present participles are verb forms ending in *-ing*. When they immediately follow a form of the verb *to be* they help make the continuous tenses (those which refer to continuing actions) of verbs.

I am reading this book slowly.
(present continuous tense)

They were walking in the bush.
(past continuous tense)

5.2. Present participles are often used as adjectives.

a running river

5.3. They are also often used as nouns.

Flying is my main interest.
(In this sentence the present participle has a noun function and is the subject of *is*.)

5.4. past participles

Past participles are verb forms which can directly follow forms of the verb *to have* in compound verbs. (They can also follow forms of the verb *to be* as the present participles do, but can be distinguished from them by never ending in *-ing*.)

We had attacked the position the day before.

The position had been attacked quite often.

Regularly formed past participles end in *-ed*, but in fact, the most frequently used ones often are not regular.

I have done what you wanted.

I was quite overcome by the applause.

6. active and passive verbs

Verbs which have subjects which perform the actions which their verbs describe are said to be **active**.

The president closed the meeting.

Verbs which have subjects which receive the actions which their verbs describe are said to be **passive**.

The meeting was closed by the president.

All passive verbs are compound verbs and include some form of the verb *to be*.

7. transitive and intransitive verbs

Verbs which have DIRECT OBJECTS are said to be **transitive**.

The pilot flew the plane very recklessly.

(In this sentence *plane* is the direct object of *flew*.)

Verbs which have no direct objects are said to be **intransitive**.

She went to her room and thought very hard.

(Asking *who*? or *what*? after *went* and *thought* gives no answer. So neither has a direct object.)

Some verbs can be used as both transitive and intransitive verbs.

He spoke kind words.

(In this sentence *spoke* is transitive because *kind words* is the direct object.)

She stood and spoke.

(In this sentence *spoke* is intransitive because there is no direct object.)

8. tense

8.1. A verb usually indicates when the action it refers to takes place in relation to the time when the verb is spoken or written.

If the action is at the same time, the verb has **present tense**.

The boat is coming into the harbour now.

If the action was at a time before this, the verb has **past tense**.

The boat came into the harbour yesterday.

If the action will be at a time subsequent to this, the verb has **future tense**.

The boat will come into the harbour tomorrow.

8.2. Very often the tense of a verb is indicated by its form. Note how the forms of the verb *to come* used above show the tense.

A few verbs do not change form with certain tenses and so their tenses have to be deduced from the nearby 'time' words, or other verbs.

I set the dining-room table every day.

(The verb *set* is present tense because of *every day*.)

I set the table just before she got home.

(The verb *set* is past tense because of *got*.)

8.3. It is quite common to use present tense forms to indicate future action and to depend on 'time' words in the context to make the timing clear.

We are going overseas again next summer.

Such verbs may be described as present in form but future in tense.
The verb **go** is commonly used in the present continuous tense with the particle **to** to indicate future action.

We are all going to regret this.

9. aspect

The aspect of a verb is that part of its meaning which indicates whether the action it refers to is complete or not.

9.1. perfect aspect

Verbs with perfect aspect refer usually to actions which are complete. The perfect aspect uses forms of the auxiliary verb *have*.

I have finished my homework.

9.2. continuous, progressive or imperfect aspect

Verbs with continuous aspect refer to actions which are not completed but are still in progress. The continuous aspect uses forms of the auxiliary verb *be*.

I am still finishing my homework.

10. mood

The **mood** of a verb is that part of its meaning which reflects the attitude of the speaker or writer towards what is being conveyed.

10.1. indicative mood

Verbs in the indicative mood reflect no particular attitude on the part of the speaker or writer. They convey plain information or ask straightforward questions.

It rained all day yesterday.

Have you seen the scissors?

10.2. imperative mood

Verbs in the imperative mood are those which are used for commands, encouragements or simple requests.

Stop it!

Please pass the mustard.

Go home, now!

10.3. subjunctive mood

Verbs in the subjunctive mood reflect some uncertainty, doubt, improbability or wish.

If I were prime minister, I would soon fix things up.

The subjunctive mood also occurs in some indirect requests or orders.

We demand that he return the money at once.

The verbs in the two examples so far given all have forms which tell us they are subjunctive, not indicative, in mood. But English uses very few of these and the role of expressing wishes, doubt, etc., is often given over to compound verbs which have *may* or *might* in them.

May you live happily ever after.
(*May* here expresses a wish.)

Of course it might have happened that way I suppose.
(*Might* here expresses doubt.)

vowels/consonants

It is often said that the English alphabet has only five vowels, namely *a*, *e*, *i*, *o*, and *u*, and that all the other letters are consonants. Yet clearly *y* acts as a vowel in words like *chilly* and *ply* just as it acts as a consonant in words like *yacht* and *yawn*.

This approach through letters of the conventional alphabet is not very helpful, even if we allow six vowel letters instead of five.

A truer picture of things emerges if we concentrate on sounds rather than the letters we use to indicate them. A vowel sound might then be defined as any sound that can be found in the middle slot in a word frame like 'h-d', as in *heed*, *hid*, *head*, *had*, *hard*, *hod*, *hoard*, *hood*, etc.

At once we begin to see that there are many more than five or six vowel sounds in English. If we group with them the diphthongs (vowel-like sounds during which you must move your tongue), the number increases again. The diphthongs are the vowel-like sounds of *high*, *hay*, *hoy*, *how*, *hoe*, *here*, *hair*, and *tour*.

The consonant sounds of the language can be similarly identified, the large number of sounds of English identified in this way giving a better picture of the building blocks out of which our language is made than the twenty-six letters of the traditional alphabet.

who/whom

Whom is the objective form of **who**, so strictly speaking you would say

The man whom I saw yesterday gave me his card.

Whom did you see?

In fact, the use of **whom** can sound slightly formal in speech and it is very common to hear

The man who I saw yesterday gave me his card.

Who did you see?

COUNTRIES OF THE WORLD

COUNTRY	PEOPLE	OFFICIAL/MAIN LANGUAGE(S)	CAPITAL
Afghanistan	Afghan, Afghani	Pashto, Dari (Persian)	Kabul
Albania	Albanian	Albanian	Tirana
Algeria	Algerian, Algerine	Arabic	Algiers
Andorra	Andorran	Catalan, French, Spanish	Andorra la Vella
Angola	Angolan	Portuguese	Luanda
Antigua and Barbuda	Antiguan	English	St John's
Argentina	Argentine, Argentinian	Spanish	Buenos Aires
Armenia	Armenian	Armenian	Yerevan
Australia	Australian	English	Canberra
Austria	Austrian	German	Vienna
Azerbaijan	Azerbaijani	Azerbaijani	Baku
Bahamas, the	Bahamian	English	Nassau
Bahrain	Bahraini	Arabic	Manama
Bangladesh	Bangladeshi	Bengali	Dhaka
Barbados	Barbadian	English	Bridgetown
Belarus	Belarusian	Belarusian	Minsk
Belgium	Belgian	Dutch, French, German	Brussels
Belize	Belizean	English, Spanish, Carib, Maya	Belmopan
Benin	Beninese	French	Porto-Novo
Bhutan	Bhutanese	Dzongkha	Thimphu
Bolivia	Bolivian	Spanish, Quechua, Aymará	Sucre (judicial), La Paz (legislative)
Bosnia and Herzegovina	Bosnian	Bosnian	Sarajevo
Botswana	Botswanan	Tswana, English	Gaborone
Brazil	Brazilian	Portuguese	Brasília
Brunei	Bruneian	Malay, English	Bandar Seri Begawan
Bulgaria	Bulgarian	Bulgarian	Sofia
Burkina Faso	–	French, Mossi	Ouagadougou
Burma, see Myanmar			
Burundi	Burundian	French, Kirundi	Bujumbura
Cabo Verde	Cabo Verdean	Portuguese	Praia
Cambodia	Cambodian	Khmer, French	Phnom Penh
Cameroon	Cameroonian	French, English	Yaoundé
Canada	Canadian	English, French	Ottawa

COUNTRY	PEOPLE	OFFICIAL/MAIN LANGUAGE(S)	CAPITAL
Cape Verde, see Cabo Verde			
Central African Republic	–	French, Sango	Bangui
Chad	Chadian	French, Arabic	N'Djamena
Chile	Chilean	Spanish	Santiago
China	Chinese	Chinese (Mandarin)	Beijing
Colombia	Colombian	Spanish	Bogotá
Comoros	Comorian, Comoran	French, Arabic, Comorian	Moroni
Congo, Democratic Republic of	Congolese	French, English	Kinshasa
Congo, Republic of	Congolese	French	Brazzaville
Costa Rica	Costa Rican	Spanish	San José
Côte d'Ivoire (Ivory Coast)	Ivorian	French	Abidjan (former), Yamoussoukro (official)
Croatia	Croat, Croatian	Croatian	Zagreb
Cuba	Cuban	Spanish	Havana
Cyprus	Cypriot	Greek, Turkish	Nicosia
Czech Republic	Czech	Czech	Prague
Denmark	Dane	Danish	Copenhagen
Djibouti	Djibouti	Arabic, French	Djibouti
Dominica	Dominican	English	Roseau
Dominican Republic	Dominican	Spanish	Santo Domingo
East Timor, see Timor-Leste			
Ecuador	Ecuadorian	Spanish, Quechua	Quito
Egypt	Egyptian	Arabic	Cairo
El Salvador	Salvadoran	Spanish	San Salvador
Equatorial Guinea	Guinean	Spanish	Malabo
Eritrea	Eritrean	Tigrinya	Asmara
Estonia	Estonian	Estonian	Tallinn
Ethiopia	Ethiopian	Amharic	Addis Ababa
Fiji	Fijian	English, Fijian, Hindi	Suva
Finland	Finn, Finlander, Finnish	Finnish, Swedish	Helsinki
France	French	French	Paris
Gabon	Gabonese	French, Fang	Libreville
Gambia, The	Gambian	English	Banjul
Georgia	Georgian	Georgian	Tbilisi
Germany	German	German	Berlin
Ghana	Ghanian	English	Accra
Greece	Greek	Greek	Athens
Grenada	Grenadian	English	St George's
Guatemala	Guatemalan	Spanish	Guatemala City
Guinea	Guinean	French	Conakry

COUNTRY	PEOPLE	OFFICIAL/MAIN LANGUAGE(S)	CAPITAL
Guinea-Bissau	Guinean	Portuguese	Bissau
Guyana	Guyanan	English	Georgetown
Haiti	Haitian	French, Haitian Creole	Port-au-Prince
Holy See (Vatican City)	N/A	Italian	Vatican City
Honduras	Honduran	Spanish, English	Tegucigalpa
Hungary	Hungarian	Hungarian	Budapest
Iceland	Icelandic	Icelandic	Reykjavik
India	Indian	Hindi, English	New Delhi
Indonesia	Indonesian	Bahasa Indonesia	Jakarta
Iran	Iranian	Farsi (Persian)	Teheran
Iraq	Iraqi	Arabic, Kurdish	Baghdad
Ireland, Republic of	Irish	Irish (Gaelic), English	Dublin
Israel	Israeli	Hebrew, Arabic	Jerusalem
Italy	Italian	Italian	Rome
Jamaica	Jamaican	English	Kingston
Japan	Japanese	Japanese	Tokyo
Jordan	Jordanian	Arabic	Amman
Kazakhstan	Kazakh	Kazakh	Astana
Kenya	Kenyan	Swahili, English	Nairobi
Kiribati	I-Kiribati	Gilbertese, English	Tarawa
Korea, North	North Korean	Korean	Pyongyang
Korea, South	South Korean	Korean	Seoul
Kosovo	Kosovar, Kosovan	Albanian, Serbian	Priština
Kuwait	Kuwaiti	Arabic	Kuwait City
Kyrgyzstan	Kyrgyz	Kyrgyz, Russian	Biškek
Laos	Laotian	Lao	Vientiane
Latvia	Latvian	Latvian	Riga
Lebanon	Lebanese	Arabic	Beirut
Lesotho	–	English, Sesotho	Maseru
Liberia	Liberian	English	Monrovia
Libya	Libyan	Arabic	Tripoli
Liechtenstein	Liechtensteiner	German (Alemannic)	Vaduz
Lithuania	Lithuanian	Lithuanian	Vilnius
Luxembourg	Luxembourger	French, German	Luxembourg
Macedonia	Macedonian	Macedonian	Skopje
Madagascar	Madagascan	Malagasy, French	Antananarivo
Malawi	Malawian	English, Chichewa	Lilongwe
Malaysia	Malaysian	Malay, English	Kuala Lumpur
Maldives	Maldivian	Divehi	Malé
Mali	Malian	French	Bamako
Malta	Maltese	Maltese, English	Valletta

COUNTRY	PEOPLE	OFFICIAL/MAIN LANGUAGE(S)	CAPITAL
Marshall Islands	Marshallese	Marshallese, English	Majuro
Mauritania	Mauritanian	French, Arabic	Nouakchott
Mauritius	Mauritian	English, French Creole	Port Louis
Mexico	Mexican	Spanish	Mexico City
Micronesia, Federated States of	Micronesian	English	Palikir
Moldova	Moldovan	Romanian	Chişinău
Monaco	Monacan, Monegasque	French	Monaco-Ville
Mongolia	Mongolian	Khalkha Mongolian	Ulaanbaatar
Montenegro	Montenegrin	Montenegro Serbian	Cetinje (presidential seat), Podgorica (official)
Morocco	Moroccan	Arabic	Rabat
Mozambique	–	Portuguese	Maputo
Myanmar	Myanmar	Myanmar (Burmese)	Nay Pyi Taw
Namibia	Namibian	English	Windhoek
Nauru	Nauruan	Nauruan, English	Yaren (de facto)
Nepal	Nepalese, Nepali	Nepali	Kathmandu
Netherlands, the	Dutch	Dutch	Amsterdam
New Zealand	New Zealander	English, Maori	Wellington
Nicaragua	Nicaraguan	Spanish	Managua
Niger	Nigerien	French	Niamey
Nigeria	Nigerian	English	Abuja
Norway	Norwegian	Norwegian	Oslo
Oman	Omani	Arabic	Muscat
Pakistan	Pakistani	Urdu	Islamabad
Palau	Palauan	Palauan, English	Melekeok
Panama	Panamanian	Spanish	Panama City
Papua New Guinea	Papua New Guinean	Neo-Melanesian, Pidgin, Motu, English	Port Moresby
Paraguay	Paraguayan	Spanish, Guaraní	Asunción
Peru	Peruvian	Spanish, Quechua, Aymara	Lima
Philippines, the	Filipino	Pilipino, English	Manila
Poland	Pole, Polish	Polish	Warsaw
Portugal	Portuguese	Portuguese	Lisbon
Qatar	Qatari	Arabic	Doha
Romania	Romanian	Romanian	Bucharest
Russia	Russian	Russian	Moscow
Rwanda	Rwandan	French, Rwanda	Kigali
Samoa	Samoan	Samoan, English	Apia
San Marino	San Marinese	Italian	San Marino
São Tomé and Príncipe	–	Portuguese	São Tomé
Saudi Arabia	Saudi	Arabian, Saudi Arabic	Riyadh

COUNTRY	PEOPLE	OFFICIAL/MAIN LANGUAGE(S)	CAPITAL
Senegal	Senegalese	French	Dakar
Serbia	Serb, Serbian	Serbian	Belgrade
Seychelles	–	English, French, Creole	Victoria
Sierra Leone	Sierra Leonean	English	Freetown
Singapore	Singaporean	Malay, Chinese, English, Tamil	Singapore
Slovakia	Slovak, Slovakian	Slovak	Bratislava
Slovenia	Slovene, Slovenian	Slovene	Ljubljana
Solomon Islands	Solomon Islander	English, Neo-Melanesian, Pidgin	Honiara
Somalia	Somali, Somalian	Somali, Arabic, English, Italian	Mogadishu
South Africa	South African	English, Afrikaans, and 9 other official African languages	Pretoria (executive), Cape Town (legislative), and Bloemfontein (judicial)
South Sudan	South Sudanese	Arabic, English	Juba
Spain	Spaniard, Spanish	Spanish	Madrid
Sri Lanka	Sri Lankan, Sinhalese	Sinhalese, Tamil, English	Colombo (former), and Sri Jayawardenapura Kotte (official)
St Kitts and Nevis	–	English	Basseterre
St Lucia	St Lucian	English	Castries
St Vincent and the Grenadines	–	English	Kingstown
Sudan	Sudanese	Arabic	Khartoum
Suriname	Surinamese	Dutch, English	Paramaribo
Swaziland	Swazi	English, Swazi	Mbabane (administrative), Lobamba (royal and legislative)
Sweden	Swede, Swedish	Swedish	Stockholm
Switzerland	Swiss	German, French, Italian	Bern
Syria	Syrian	Arabic	Damascus
Tajikistan	Tajik	Tajik	Dushanbe
Tanzania	Tanzanian	Swahili, English	Dodoma
Thailand	Thai	Thai	Bangkok
Timor-Leste	East Timorese	Tetum, Portuguese	Dili
Togo	Togolese	French	Lomé
Tonga	Tongan	Tongan, English	Nuku'alofa
Trinidad and Tobago	Trinidadian	English	Port of Spain
Tunisia	Tunisian	Arabic, French	Tunis
Turkey	Turk, Turkish	Turkish	Ankara
Turkmenistan	Turkmen	Turkmen	Ashgabat
Tuvalu	Tuvaluan	Tuvaluan, English	Funafuti
Uganda	Ugandan	Swahili, English	Kampala
Ukraine	Ukrainian	Ukrainian	Kiev
United Arab Emirates	–	Arabic	Abu Dhabi
United Kingdom	Briton, British	English	London

COUNTRY	PEOPLE	OFFICIAL/MAIN LANGUAGE(S)	CAPITAL
United States of America	American	English	Washington
Uruguay	Uruguayan	Spanish	Montevideo
Uzbekistan	Uzbek	Uzbek	Tashkent
Vanuatu	Ni-Vanuatu, Vanuatuan	Bislama, French, English	Port Vila
Vatican City, see Holy See			
Venezuela	Venezuelan	Spanish	Caracas
Vietnam	Vietnamese	Vietnamese	Hanoi
Yemen	Yemeni	Arabic	Sana'a
Zambia	Zambian	English	Lusaka
Zimbabwe	Zimbabwean	English, and Bantu languages	Harare

MAJOR ANNUAL FESTIVALS AND CELEBRATIONS

IN AUSTRALIA

NAME OF FESTIVAL	DATES	CELEBRATING OR REMEMBERING
Anzac Day	25 April	The anniversary of the landing of Australian and New Zealand Army Corps forces at Gallipoli in Turkey in 1915 during World War I. It is observed as a public holiday, with the holding of dawn services and marches.
Australia Day	26 January	The anniversary of the landing of Governor Phillip and the First Fleet at Sydney Cove in 1788 which began British settlement in Australia; observed as a public holiday.
Boxing Day	26 December	The day after Christmas Day, observed as a public holiday (in the past, the day on which Christmas boxes or presents were given to employees).
Chinese New Year	January / February *varying dates*	A festival marked by two weeks of celebrations, starting with the new moon of the first day of the new year in the Chinese calendar and ending on the full moon 15 days later. The final day is known as the Festival of the Lanterns, celebrated at night with lantern displays and a parade.
Christmas Day	25 December	The Christian festival commemorating the birth of Jesus Christ, now generally observed as an occasion for gifts, greetings and family gatherings.
Diwali (Deepavali) (Festival of Lights)	October / November *varying dates*	A four-day Hindu festival, (Festival of Lights) celebrated with feasting and the lighting of lamps to mark the victory of good over evil. Customarily there is exchange of sweets or giving of gifts, and fireworks. Falls on the first day of the new moon.
Easter (Western Easter)	March / April *varying dates*	A Christian festival in commemoration of the crucifixion and resurrection of Jesus Christ, lasting for four days, from Good Friday to the following Monday (Easter Monday). Good Friday is observed as the anniversary of the crucifixion of Jesus. Easter Sunday is observed as the anniversary of the resurrection. The term Easter may refer to the whole period or to Easter Sunday alone. Easter Sunday is the Sunday following the first full moon on or after 21 March.
Eid-ul-Adha (Id-ul-Adha)	*varying dates*	An Islamic festival which commemorates the obedience of Abraham (Ibrahim) in sacrificing Isaac (Ishak). It begins on the 10th day of the month of Dhu'l-Hijja and lasts three to four days, marking the end of the Haj (pilgrimage) season. Traditionally, animals are sacrificed and their meat given to the poor.

NAME OF FESTIVAL	DATES	CELEBRATING OR REMEMBERING
Eid-ul-Fitr (Id-ul-Fitr)	*varying dates*	An Islamic festival marking the end of Ramadan and lasting for two days. Families reunite, new clothes are worn, homes are redecorated. An important custom is for people to ask forgiveness from those whom they have wronged.
Father's Day	First Sunday in September	A day set aside for the honouring of fathers, as by acts of affection or giving of presents.
Halloween	31 October	This is the eve (or evening) before All Saints' Day (a festival in the Christian calendar). It dates back to pre-Christian times when it was believed that witches and ghosts were all around on this evening. Traditionally, it was celebrated by dressing up and wearing masks. In some countries, including Australia in recent years, the evening is marked by children dressing up as witches, etc., and asking for treats.
Hanukkah (Chanukah) (Feast of Dedication)	November / December *varying dates*	A Jewish festival in commemoration of the victory of the Maccabees and the rededication of the temple in 165 BC. It begins on the 25th of the month of Kislev and lasts eight days.
Mother's Day	Second Sunday in May	A day set aside the honouring of mothers, as by acts of affection or the giving of presents.
New Year's Day	1 January	The first day of the calendar year, observed as a public holiday.
Orthodox Christmas	6 or 7 January	The Christian festival of Christmas, observed by some Orthodox or Eastern Rite Christian churches on these traditional dates, rather than 25 December.
Orthodox Easter	April / May *varying dates*	The festival of Easter as observed by the Orthodox and Eastern Rite churches. The date is determined in the Julian Calendar and usually occurs after the Western Easter but on some occasions on the same date.
Pesach (Passover) (Feast of Unleavened Bread)	March / April *varying dates*	A Jewish festival, commemorating the passing over or sparing of the Hebrews at the time when they were delivered from slavery in Egypt about 3500 years ago in the mass exodus from Egypt led by Moses. The festival starts on the 15th day of the month of Nissan and lasts eight days.
Purim	February / March *varying dates*	A Jewish festival, held on the 14th day of the month of Adar, commemorating the time when the Jews of Persia were saved by Queen Esther from a planned massacre.
Ramadan	*varying dates*	The ninth month in the Islamic calendar, during which a daily fast is observed, celebrating the time when God revealed the Koran (Qur`an) to Mohammed. During this month Muslims fast from dawn to sunset and eat small meals at night and visit friends and family. There are public prayers and reciting of the Koran.
Remembrance Day	11 November	The anniversary of the end of World War I on 11 November 1918, when the armistice was signed, marked by a two-minute silence at 11 a.m.

NAME OF FESTIVAL	DATES	CELEBRATING OR REMEMBERING
Rosh Hashana (Jewish New Year)	September / October *varying dates*	A two-day Jewish holiday celebrated at the start of the Jewish New Year (on the 1st and 2nd of the month of Tishri), marked by earnest reflection and prayers, and the blowing of the shophar (ram's horn) in the synagogue.
St Valentine's Day	14 February	A day when tokens of affection (valentines) are given.
Sukkoth (Feast of Tabernacles)	September / October *varying dates*	A Jewish harvest festival, beginning on the 15th day of the month of Tishri and lasting eight days, commemorating the time when the Israelites lived in temporary shelter in the wilderness.
Vesak (Wesak) (Buddha Day)	May / June *varying dates*	The major Buddhist festival, celebrating the life, enlightenment and death of Lord Buddha, held on the day of the first full moon of the fifth month (Vesak being the name of this month in the Pali language). Buddhist communities vary as to whether they follow the solar calendar, in which case this day falls in May, or the lunar calendar, in which case it may be in May or June.
Yom Kippur (Day of Atonement)	September / October *varying dates*	A Jewish fast day observed on the 10th day of the month of Tishri. It is the most sacred date in the Jewish year, with prayers of penitence offered at the synagogue throughout the day.

WELCOME TO COUNTRY

AND ACKNOWLEDGEMENT OF COUNTRY

When you are at a ceremony or meeting, such as a school assembly or another public event, you will often hear someone open the ceremony with a **Welcome to Country** or an **Acknowledgement of Country**. This is a very important way to show respect to the Indigenous people of Australia and their culture, and to recognise their special position as the first people to live in Australia.

A **Welcome to Country** is a welcome given by someone, such as an Aboriginal elder, who is a representative of the traditional Indigenous custodians of the land on which the event is taking place. The welcome may be a speech only or it may include a performance. This depends on the region where the welcome is taking place.

An **Acknowledgement of Country** is an official recognition of the Indigenous traditional custodians of a locality and can be performed by either a non-Indigenous or an Indigenous person.

The wording may be different in different places, but here are some examples of what is commonly said in an Acknowledgement of Country:

> *I would like to acknowledge and pay respect to the traditional custodians of the land on which this meeting takes place, and to pay respect to elders both past and present.*
>
> *I would like to acknowledge the _______ people who are the traditional custodians of this land. I would also like to pay respect to elders both past and present of the _______ nation and extend that respect to other Aboriginal people present.*
>
> *(The name of the people who are the traditional custodians would be filled in.)*